Frommer's®

W9-DEH-400

POSTCARDS FROM ITALY

To "ensure" your return to the Eternal City, come and throw a coin in Rome's most famous fountain, the Trevi, where a triumphant Neptune is flanked by Tritons. See chapter 4.

Of all ancient Rome's great buildings, only the Pantheon remains intact and is the burial place of Italian monarchs. At the center of its dome is an 18-foot oculus, letting in the only light. See chapter 4. © RAGA/The Stock Market.

When it came to buying a harlot or conducting other business, the Roman Forum was the place to go. What you'll find today are only bits of temples and arches—the Forum was used for years as a quarry. See chapter 4. © Dave Bartruff Photography.

Banded by white, pink, and green marble, Giotto's campanile and the Duomo, topped by Brunelleschi's red-tiled dome, rise in the heart of Florence. See chapter 5. © Kevin Galvin Photography.

Star of the Accademia in Florence, Michelangelo's David *stands beneath the rotunda of a room built especially for him. He may have become a cliché, but you can't deny his masculine perfection. See chapter 5. © A. B. Wadham/Tony Stone Images.*

Seen here through lush grapevines, the walled town of San Gimignano is known as the Manhattan of Tuscany because its 13 towers (remaining from the 72 original) lend it a skyscraper skyline. See chapter 6. © John Elk III Photography.

Tuscany and Umbria are famed for their vineyards, producing some of Italy's finest wines. The best known is Chianti Classico. See chapters 1 and 6 for details on how to visit the top wineries. © Joe Englander/The Viesti Collection, Inc.

Siena's fan-shaped Piazza del Campo is where the famous Palio horse race takes place twice each year. Its 335-foot Torre del Mangia provides stunning views of the countryside. See chapter 6. © Kevin Galvin Photography.

Often overlooked, the ancient university city of Bologna is a panorama of marbled sidewalks and porticos and sienna-colored buildings. See chapter 7. © Guido Alberto Rossi/The Image Bank.

Ravenna achieved its cultural peak as part of the Byzantine Empire and is famed for its astonishing mosaics. This example in the Archepiscopal Museum shows Christ as a warrior in partial armor. See chapter 7. © Scala/Art Resource.

Venice may be sinking $2^1/_2$ inches per decade, but its "streets filled with water," the bridges spanning them, and the gondolas plying them make the city unforgettable. See chapter 8.
© Gerard Pile/Tony Stone Images.

Venice's Carnevale is a resuscitation of an outlawed 18th-century bacchanalia. For the week-long party, revelers in papier-mâché masks and period costumes fill the city. See chapters 2 and 8. © F. Hidalgo/The Image Bank.

In northeast Italy, the limestone Dolomites boast some peaks soaring to 10,500 feet. The mountains are perfect for hiking in summer and skiing in winter. See chapter 9. © Ric Ergenbright Photography.

One of the loveliest sites in Verona is the 14th-century Giardino Giusti, with a "monster balcony" offering an incomparable view of Romeo and Juliet's city. See chapter 9. © Robert Essel/The Stock Market.

Milan's flamboyant Duomo is Italy's largest Gothic cathedral. It was begun in 1386 and has seen numerous changes—even Napoléon added to the facade. See chapter 10. © Jose Fuste Raga/The Stock Market.

Milan's shopping scene is famous: You can find everything from the funkiest art glass to the hottest leather goods to the trendiest couture. See chapter 10. © Mark Ferri/The Stock Market.

Lake Como, 30 miles north of Milan, is set beautifully amid the Italian Alps. Along its shore are resorts like the Villa d'Este and many private villas. See chapter 10. © Robert Everts/Tony Stone Images.

Genoa, dividing the Italian Riviera in two, is Italy's premier port. Its harbor makes for an interesting stroll, particularly where the old town borders the marina. See chapter 12.

The A.D. 79 eruption of Mt. Vesuvius buried Pompeii under volcanic ash. These frescoes are in the most magnificent of the villas excavated, the House of the Vettii. See chapter 13.

On Capri, where emperors like Tiberius went in search of "amusement," you can take the funicular up to the lofty heights for views of Vesuvius and the Bay of Naples. See chapter 13.
© Len Kaufman Photography.

Hewed out of Mt. Tauro, the Greek Theater is Taormina's top site. The Romans modified it, and the 2nd-century remains you see overlook Mt. Etna. See chapter 15. © James Marshall Photography.

Near Palermo is the fishing port of Cefalù, whose beaches, mix of architectural styles, and narrow streets were captured in the Oscar-winning Cinema Paradiso. *See chapter 15. © Simeone Huber/Tony Stone Images.*

Here's what the critics say about Frommer's:

"Amazingly easy to use. Very portable, very complete."

—*Booklist*

♦

"The only mainstream guide to list specific prices. The Walter Cronkite of guidebooks—with all that implies."

—*Travel & Leisure*

♦

"Complete, concise, and filled with useful information."

—*New York Daily News*

♦

"Hotel information is close to encyclopedic."

—*Des Moines Sunday Register*

♦

"Detailed, accurate and easy-to-read information for all price ranges."

—*Glamour Magazine*

Other Great Guides for Your Trip:

Frommer's Tuscany & Umbria

Frommer's Rome

Frommer's Italy from $70 a Day

Frommer's Portable Venice

Frommer's® 2001

Italy

by Darwin Porter & Danforth Prince

HUNGRY MINDS, INC.
New York, NY • Cleveland, OH • Indianapolis, IN
Chicago, IL • Foster City, CA • San Francisco, CA

About The Authors

A native of North Carolina, **Darwin Porter** was a bureau chief for the *Miami Herald* when he was 21 and later worked in television advertising. A veteran travel writer, he wrote Frommer's first-ever guide to Italy many years ago and has been a frequent traveler there ever since. He is joined by **Danforth Prince,** formerly of the Paris bureau of the *New York Times,* who has lived in Italy and traveled there extensively. As a team, they've written other best-selling Frommer guides, including *Frommer's Rome.*

Hungry Minds, Inc.

909 Third Avenue
New York, NY 10022
www.frommers.com

ISBN 0-7645-6136-7
ISSN 1044-2170

Editors: Kenneth Shields and Lisa Renaud/Dog-Eared Pages
Production Editor: M. Faunette Johnston
Photo Editor: Richard Fox
Design by Michele Laseau
Staff Cartographers: John Decamillis, Roberta Stockwell, Elizabeth Puhl
Front cover photo: Positano, on the Amalfi Coast
Production by Hungry Minds Indianapolis Production Department

Special Sales

For general information on Hungry Minds' products and services please contact our Consumer Care department; within the U.S. at 800-762-2974, outside the U.S. at 317-572-3993 or fax 317-572-4002. For sales inquiries and reseller information, including discounts, bulk sales, customized editions, and premium sales, please contact our Customer Care department at 800-434-3422.

Manufactured in the United States of America

5 4 3 2

Contents

List of Maps

AN INVITATION TO THE READER

In researching this book, we discovered many wonderful places—hotels, restaurants, shops, and more. We're sure you'll find others. Please tell us about them, so we can share the information with your fellow travelers in upcoming editions. If you were disappointed with a recommendation, we'd love to know that, too. Please write to:

Frommer's Italy 2001
Hungry Minds, Inc.
909 Third Avenue
New York, NY 10022

AN ADDITIONAL NOTE

Please be advised that travel information is subject to change at any time—and this is especially true of prices. We therefore suggest that you write or call ahead for confirmation when making your travel plans. The authors, editors, and publisher cannot be held responsible for the experiences of readers while traveling. Your safety is important to us, however, so we encourage you to stay alert and be aware of your surroundings. Keep a close eye on cameras, purses, and wallets, all favorite targets of thieves and pickpockets.

WHAT THE SYMBOLS MEAN

✪ Frommer's Favorites

Our favorite places and experiences—outstanding for quality, value, or both.

The following abbreviations are used for credit cards:

AE	American Express	MC	MasterCard
CB	Carte Blanche	DISC	Discover
DC	Diners Club	V	Visa

FIND FROMMER'S ONLINE

www.frommers.com offers up-to-the-minute listings on almost 200 cities around the globe—including the latest bargains and candid, personal articles updated daily by Arthur Frommer himself. No other Web site offers such comprehensive and timely coverage of the world of travel.

1

The Best of Italy

Italy is so packed with attractions that it's hard to know where to start. But that's where we come in. In this chapter is our personal, opinionated list of what we consider to be its top highlights. Our list will get you started and point you toward some of the possibilities for designing your own vacation. Whether this is your first trip or your 10th, you're bound to come away with your own favorites to add to the list.

1 The Best Travel Experiences

- **Visiting the Art Cities:** When Italy consisted of dozens of principalities, its art treasures were concentrated in many small capitals, each blessed with the patronage of a papal representative or ducal family. Consequently, these cities became treasure troves of exquisite paintings, statues, and frescoes displayed in churches, monasteries, and palaces, whose architects are now world acclaimed. Although Rome, Florence, and Venice are the best known, you'll find stunning collections in Assisi, Cremona, Genoa, Mantua, Padua, Parma, Palermo, Pisa, Siena, Taormina, Tivoli, Turin, Verona, and Vicenza.
- **Dining Italian Style:** One of the most cherished pastimes of the Italians is eating out. Regardless of how much pizza and lasagna you've had in your life, you'll never taste any that is better than the real thing in Italy. Each region has its own specialties, some handed down for centuries. If the weather is fine and you're dining outdoors with a view of, perhaps, a medieval church or piazza, you'll find your experience the closest thing to heaven in Italy. Buon appetito!
- **Attending Mass in St. Peter's Basilica:** With the exception of some sites in Jerusalem, St. Peter's in the Vatican is Christendom's most visible and important building. The huge size of the church is daunting. For many visitors, attending mass here is a spiritual highlight of their lives. Your fellow faithful are likely to come from every corner of the world. See chapter 4.
- **Attending a Papal Audience:** Many Catholic visitors to Rome eagerly await papal audiences every Wednesday morning, when the pope addresses the general public. If the day is fair, these audiences are sometimes held in St. Peter's Square. All are welcome. See chapter 4.

- **Riding Venice's Grand Canal:** The S-shaped Canal Grande, curving for 2 miles along historic buildings and under ornate bridges, is the most romantic waterway in the world. Most first-timers are stunned by the variety of Gothic and Renaissance buildings, the elaborate styles of which could fill a book on architecture. A ride on the canal will give you ever-changing glimpses of the city's poignant beauty. Your ride doesn't have to be on a gondola; any public *vaporetto* (ferry) sailing between Venice's rail station and Piazza San Marco will provide a heart-stopping view. See chapter 8.
- **Getting Lost in Venice:** The most obvious means of transport in Venice is by boat; an even more appealing method is on foot, traversing hundreds of canals, large and small, and crossing over the arches of medieval bridges. Getting from one point to another can be like walking through a maze—but you won't be hassled by traffic, and the sense of the city's beauty, timelessness, and slow decay is almost mystical. See chapter 8.
- **Spending a Night at the Opera:** More than 2,000 new operas were staged in Italy during the 18th century, and since then, Italian opera fans have earned a reputation as the most demanding in the world. Venice was the site of Italy's first opera house, the Teatro di San Cassiano (1637), but it eventually gave way to the fabled La Fenice, which burned down in 1996 and is being restored; in the meantime, opera is presented under a tent at Palafenice. Milan's La Scala is possibly the world's most prestigious opera house, especially for *bel canto.* There's also a wide assortment of outdoor settings, like Verona's Arena, one of the largest surviving amphitheaters. Suitable for up to 20,000 spectators and known for its fine acoustics, the Arena presents operas in July and August, when moonlight and the perfumed air of the Veneto add to the charm. See chapters 8, 9, and 10.
- **Shopping Milan:** Milan is one of Europe's hottest fashion capitals. You'll find a range of shoes, clothing, and accessories unequaled anywhere else, except perhaps Paris or London. Even if you weren't born to shop, stroll along the streets bordering Via Montenapoleone and check out the elegant offerings from Europe's most famous designers. See chapter 10.
- **Experiencing the Glories of the Empire:** Even after centuries of looting, much remains of the legendary Roman Empire. Of course, Rome boasts the greatest share (the popes didn't tear down *everything* to recycle into churches) — you'll find everything from the Roman Forum and the Pantheon to the Colosseum and the Baths of Caracalla. And on the outskirts, the long-buried city of Ostia Antica, the port of ancient Rome, has been unearthed and is remarkable. Other treasures are scattered throughout Italy, especially in Sicily. The hordes of sightseers descend on Pompeii also, the city buried by volcanic ash from Mt. Vesuvius in A.D. 79, and Herculaneum, buried by lava on that same day. Our favorite spot is Paestum, along Campania's coast; its ruins, especially the Temple of Neptune, are alone worth the trip to Italy. See chapters 4, 13, and 15.

2 The Most Romantic Getaways

- **Spoleto:** Spoleto is as ancient as the Roman Empire and as timeless as the music presented there every summer during its world-renowned arts festival. The architecture of this quintessential Umbrian hill town is centered around a core of religious buildings from the 13th century. It's even more romantic during the off-season, when the crowds are less dense. See chapter 6.
- **Portofino:** This is the world's most famous small port, largely because of the well-preserved buildings surrounding its small circular harbor. Located 22 miles

southeast of Genoa in the heart of the Italian Riviera, Portofino is charming, chic, and cosmopolitan. A cluster of top-notch hotels caters to the very rich and famous. See chapter 12.

- **Capri:** Floating amid azure seas south of Naples, Capri is called the "Island of Dreams"; everywhere you'll find the aroma of lemon trees in bloom. Roman emperors Augustus and Tiberius both went there for R&R, and since the late 1800s celebrities have flocked to Capri for an escape. A boat ride around the island's rugged coastline is one of our favorite things to do. See chapter 13.
- **Ravello:** It's small, sunny, and loaded with notable buildings (such as its 1086 cathedral). Despite its choice position on the Amalfi coast, Ravello manages to retain the aura of an old-fashioned village. Famous residents have included writer Gore Vidal. See chapter 13.
- **Taormina:** This resort, the loveliest place in Sicily, is brimming with regional charm, chiseled stonework, and a sense of the ages. Favored by wealthy Europeans and dedicated artists, especially in midwinter, when the climate is delightful, Taormina is a fertile oasis of olive groves, grapevines, and orchards. Visitors will relish the delights of the sun, the sea, and the medieval setting. See chapter 15.

3 The Best Museums

- **Musei Vaticani** (the Vatican, Rome): Rambling, disorganized, and poorly labeled they may be, but these buildings are packed to the rafters with treasures accumulated over the centuries by the popes. Among them are the incomparable Sistine Chapel, such sculptures as *Laocoön* and the *Belvedere Apollo,* buildings whose walls were almost completely executed by Raphael, and endless collections of art ranging from (very pagan) Greco-Roman antiquities to Christian art by famous European masters. See chapter 4.
- **Museo Nazionale di Villa Giulia** (Rome): Mysterious and for the most part undocumented, the Etruscans were the ancestors of the Romans. They left a legacy of bronze and marble sculpture, sarcophagi, jewelry, and representations of mythical heroes, some of which were excavated at Cerveteri, a stronghold north of Rome. Most startling about the artifacts is their sophisticated, almost mystical sense of design. The Etruscan collection is housed in a papal villa dating from the 1500s. See chapter 4.
- **Galleria degli Uffizi** (Florence): This 16th-century Renaissance palace was the administrative headquarters, or *uffizi* (offices), for the Duchy of Tuscany when the Medicis controlled Florence. It's estimated that up to 90% of Italy's artistic patrimony is stored in this building, the crown jewel of Italy's museums. (In 1993 the Uffizi was the target of a car bomb, which caused considerable damage, but the museum has staged an amazing recovery.) See chapter 5.
- **Museo Nazionale del Bargello** (Florence): The severely angular 13th-century exterior of Il Bargello, in the heart of Florence, is permeated with the raw power of the governing magistrate (*bargello*) who built it. Today its collection of sculpture and decorative accessories is without equal in Italy, including works by Michelangelo and Donatello. See chapter 5.
- **Palazzo Pitti** (Florence): The spheres of influence that dominated Florence during its most creative years revolved around the Medicis and the Pittis, who ruled the city from their respective banks of the Arno. The Pittis moved into this palazzo in 1560, after it was enlarged with two new wings. Today it houses seven museums containing everything from paintings by old masters (like Raphael and Titian) to works by modern artists and a collection of antique silver. See chapter 5.

- **Galleria Nazionale dell'Umbria** (Perugia): Italian Renaissance art has its roots in Tuscan and Umbrian painting from the 1200s. This collection, on the top floor of the Palazzo dei Priori (parts of which date from the 1400s), contains a world-class collection of paintings, most executed in Tuscany or Umbria between the 13th and the 18th centuries. Included are works by Fra Angelico, Piero della Francesco, Perugino, Duccio, and Gozzoli, among others. See chapter 6.
- **Galleria dell'Accademia** (Venice): It's one of the most richly stocked art museums in Italy, boasting hundreds of paintings, many of them Venetian, executed between 1300 and 1790. Among the highlights are works by Bellini, Carpaccio, Giorgione, Titian, and Tintoretto. See chapter 8.
- **Collezione Peggy Guggenheim** (Venice): One of the Western world's most comprehensive and brilliant modern-art collections is housed in an unfinished palazzo along the Grand Canal. The collection is like a cavalcade of 20th-century art, including works by Max Ernst (one of Ms. Guggenheim's former husbands), Picasso, Braque, Magritte, Giacometti, and Moore. See chapter 8.
- **Pinacoteca di Brera** (Milan): Milan is usually associated with wealth and corporate power, and those two things can buy a city its fair share of art and culture. The foremost place to see Milan's artistic treasures is the Brera Picture Gallery, whose collection—shown in a 17th-century palace—is especially rich in paintings from the schools of Lombardy and Venice. See chapter 10.
- **Museo Poldi-Pezzoli** (Milan): In 1881 this museum's wealthy benefactor donated his extensive art collection to his hometown, thereby creating the base for one of Italy's most influential museums. Included are Persian carpets, portraits by Cranach of Martin Luther and his wife, works by Botticelli and Bellini, and massive amounts of decorative art. See chapter 10.
- **Museo Archeologico Nazionale** (Naples): Naples and the region around it have yielded more sculptural treasures from the Roman Empire than anywhere else. Many of these riches have been accumulated in a rambling building designed as a barracks for the Neapolitan cavalry in the 1500s. Much of the loot excavated from Pompeii and Herculaneum, as well as the Renaissance collections of the Farnese family, is in this museum, which boasts a trove of Greco-Roman antiquities. See chapter 13.

4 The Best Cathedrals

- **Basilica di San Pietro** (the Vatican, Rome): Its roots began with the first Christian emperor, Constantine, in A.D. 324. By 1400 the Roman basilica was in danger of collapsing, prompting the Renaissance popes to commission plans for the largest, most impressive, most jaw-dropping cathedral the world had ever seen. Amid the rich decor of gilt, marble, and mosaics are countless artworks, including Michelangelo's *Pietà*. Other sights here are a small museum of Vatican treasures and the eerie underground grottoes containing the tombs of former popes. An elevator ride (or a rigorous climb) up the tower to Michelangelo's dome provides panoramic views of Rome. See chapter 4.
- **Il Duomo** (Santa Maria del Fiore, Florence): Begun in the late 1200s and consecrated 140 years later, the pink, green, and white marble Duomo was a symbol of Florence's prestige and wealth. It's loaded with world-class art and is one of Italy's largest and most distinctive religious buildings. A view of its red-tiled dome, erected over a 14-year period in what was at the time a radical new design by Brunelleschi, is worth the trip to Florence. Other elements of the Duomo are Giotto's *Campanile* (bell tower) and the octagonal Baptistery (a Romanesque building with renowned bronze doors). See chapter 5.

- **Basilica di San Francesco** (Assisi): St. Francis, protector of small animals and birds, was long dead when construction began on this double-tiered showcase of the Franciscan brotherhood. Interior decoration, in many cases by Cimabue and Giotto, reached a new kind of figurative realism in Italian art around 1300, long before the masters of the Renaissance carried the technique even further. Consecrated in 1253, the cathedral is one of the highlights of Umbria and the site of many religious pilgrimages. It took a direct hit from the 1997 earthquakes but has miraculously made a recovery. See chapter 6.
- **Il Duomo** (Orvieto): A well-designed transition between the Romanesque and Gothic styles, this cathedral was begun in 1290 and completed in 1600. It sheltered an Italian pope (Clement VII) when Rome was sacked by French soldiers in 1527. Part of the building's mystery derives from Orvieto's role as an Etruscan stronghold long before Italy's recorded history. See chapter 6.
- **Il Duomo** (Milan): Begun in 1386 and finally completed in 1809 on orders of Napoléon, Milan's Duomo is an ornate and unusual building. Gathered around a triangular gable bristling with 135 pointed and chiseled spires, it's both massive and airy. The interior is as severe as its exterior is ornate. See chapter 10.

5 The Best Ruins

- **Roman Forum** (Rome): Two thousand years ago, most of the known world was directly affected by decisions made in the Roman Forum. Today classicists and archaeologists wander among its ruins, conjuring up the glory that was Rome. What you'll see today is a pale, rubble-strewn version of the site's original majesty—it's now surrounded by modern boulevards packed with whizzing cars. See chapter 4.
- **Palatine Hill** (Rome): According to legend, the Palatine Hill was the site where Romulus and Remus (the orphaned infant twins who survived in the wild by being suckled by a she-wolf) eventually founded the city. Although Il Palatino is one of the seven hills of ancient Rome, you'll find it hard to distinguish it as such because of the urban congestion rising all around. The site is enhanced by the Farnese Gardens (*Orti Farnesiani*), laid out in the 1500s on the site of Tiberius's palace. See chapter 4.
- **The Colosseum** (Rome): Rome boasts only a handful of other ancient monuments that survive in such well-preserved condition. A massive amphitheater set incongruously amid a maze of modern traffic, the Colosseum was once the setting for gladiator combat, lion-feeding frenzies, and public entertainment whose cruelty was a noted characteristic of the Empire. All three of the ancient world's classical styles (Doric, Ionic, and Corinthian) are represented, superimposed in tiers one above the other. See chapter 4.
- **Villa Adriana** (near Tivoli): Hadrian's Villa slumbered in rural obscurity until the 1500s, when Renaissance popes ordered its excavation. Only then was the scale of this enormous and very beautiful villa from A.D. 134 appreciated. Its builder, Hadrian, who had visited almost every part of his empire, wanted to incorporate the widespread wonders of the world into one fantastic building site. And he succeeded. See chapter 4.
- **Ostia Antica** (near Rome): During the height of the Roman Empire, Ostia ("mouth" in Latin) was the harbor town set at the point where the Tiber flowed into the sea. As Rome declined, so did Ostia, and by the early Middle Ages, the town had almost disappeared, its population decimated by malaria. In the early 1900s, archaeologists excavated the ruins of hundreds of ancient buildings, many of which you can view. See chapter 4.

- **Herculaneum** (Campania): Legend says that Herculaneum was founded by Hercules. The historical facts tell us that it was buried under rivers of volcanic mud one fateful day in A.D. 79 after the eruption of Mt. Vesuvius. Seeping into the cracks of virtually every building in town, the scalding mud preserved the timbers of hundreds of structures that would otherwise have rotted during the normal course of time. Devote at least 2 hours to seeing some of the best-preserved houses from the ancient world. See chapter 13.
- **Pompeii** (Campania): Once it was an opulent resort filled with 25,000 wealthy Romans. In A.D. 79, the same eruption that devastated Herculaneum (above) buried Pompeii under at least 20 feet of boiling volcanic ash and pumice stone. Beginning around 1750, Charles of Bourbon ordered the systematic excavation of the ruins — the treasures hauled out of Pompeii sparked a wave of interest in the classical era throughout northern Europe. See chapter 13.
- **Paestum** (Campania): Paestum was discovered by accident around 1750 when local bureaucrats tried to build a road across the heart of what had been a thriving ancient city. Paestum originated as a Greek colony around 600 B.C., fell to the Romans in 273 B.C., and declined into obscurity in the final days of the empire. Today amateur archaeologists can follow a well-marked walking tour through the excavations. See chapter 13.
- **La Valle dei Templi** (Sicily): Although most of the Valley of the Temples in Agrigento lies in ruins, it is one of Europe's most beautiful classical sites, especially in February and March when the almond trees surrounding it burst into pink blossoms. One of the site's five temples dates from as early as 520 B.C.; another (though never completed) ranks as one of the largest temples in the ancient world. See chapter 15.
- **Segesta** (Sicily): Even its site is impressive: a rocky outcropping surrounded on most sides by a jagged ravine. Built around 430 B.C. by the Greeks, Segesta's Doric colonnade is one of the most graceful in the ancient world. The site is stark and mysterious and was believed to have been destroyed by the Saracens (Muslim raiders) in the 11th century. See chapter 15.
- **Selinunte** (Sicily): The massive columns of Selinunte lie scattered on the ground, as if an earthquake had punished its builders, yet this is one of our favorite ancient ruins in Italy. Around 600 B.C., immigrants from Syracuse built Selinunte into an important trading port. The city was a bitter rival of neighboring Segesta (above) and was destroyed around 400 B.C., then again in 250 B.C. by the Carthaginians. See chapter 15.

6 The Best Wine-Growing Regions

- **Latium** (Lazio): The region around Rome is known for predominantly white wines that include Marino, Est! Est!! Est!!!, Colli Albani, and the widely visible Frascati ("the wine of the popes and the people"). All these are derived almost exclusively from Malvasia and Trebbiano grapes or, in some cases, from combinations of the two. The region's most famous producers of Frascati are **Fontana Candida,** Via di Fontana Candida, 00040 Monte Porzio Catone, Roma (☎ **06/942-0066**), whose winery, 14 miles southwest of Rome, was built around 1900; and **Gotto D'Oro-Cantina Sociale di Marino,** Via del Divino Amore 115, 00040 Frattocchie, Roma (☎ **06/935-6931** and 06/935-6932). To arrange visits, contact the **Gruppo Italiano Vini,** Villa Belvedere, 37010 Calmasino, Verona (☎ **045/626-0600**).

- **Tuscany (Toscana) and Umbria:** Some of Italy's most scenic vineyards lie nestled among the verdant rolling hills of these two stately regions. In fact, the most famous kind of wine in Italy (Chianti) is indelibly associated with Tuscany, whereas the (usually white) Orivieto and the (usually red) Torgiano are closely associated with Umbria. One of Tuscany's largest vintners is **Villa Banfi,** Castello Banfi, Sant'Angelo Scalo, Montalcino, 53020 Siena (☎ **0577/840-111**). Near Siena are two other good choices: **Biondi-Santi,** Loc. Greppo, 53024 Montalcino (☎ **0577/847-121**), and **Casa Vinicola L. Cecchi,** Loc. Casina dei Ponti, 53011 Castellina in Chianti (☎ **0577/743-024**).
- **Emilia-Romagna:** Comprised of two distinct areas (Emilia, to the west of Bologna, around the upriver Po Valley; and Romagna, to the east, centered around the delta of the Po), the region is known to gastronomes as the producer of some of Italy's best food, with wines worthy of its legendary cuisine. Emilia's most famous wine is Lambrusco, 50 million bottles of which are produced every year near Modena and Reggio Emilia. Less well known but also highly rated are the Colli Piacentini wines, one of the rising stars for which is **Cantine Romagnoli,** Via Provinciale, Villo di Vigolzone 29020 (☎ **0523/870-129**). Wines from Romagna are produced from Sangiovese, Trebbiano, and Albana grapes and are almost universally well respected, cropping up on wine lists throughout the country.
- **The Veneto:** The humid flatlands of the eastern Po Valley have produced memorable reds and whites in great abundance since the days of the Venetian doges. Output includes massive quantities of everything from soft white Soaves and Pinot Grigios to red Valpolicellas and Merlots. Important vineyards in the region are **Azienda Vinicola Fratelli Fabiano,** Via Verona 6, 37060 Sona, near Verona (☎ **045/608-1111**), and **Fratelli Bolla,** Piazza Cittadella 3, 37122 Verona (☎ **045/809-0911**). Smaller, but well respected because of recent improvements to its vintages, is **Nino Franco** (known for its sparkling prosecco), in the hamlet of Valdobbiadene, Via Garibaldi 177, 31049 Treviso (☎ **0423/972-051**). For information on these and the dozens of other producers in the Veneto, contact the **Azienda di Promozione Turistica,** Via Leoncino 61, 37121 Verona (☎ **045/592-828**).
- **Trentino-Alto Adige:** The two most important wine-producing regions of northwestern Italy are the Alto Adige (also known as the Bolzano or Sudtirol region) and Trento. The loftier of the two, the Alto Adige, was once part of the Austro-Hungarian province of the South Tyrol. More Germanic than Italian, it clings to its Austrian traditions and folklore and grows an Italian version of the *gewürztraminers* (a fruity white) that would more often be found in Germany, Austria, and Alsace. Venerable wine growers include **Alois Lageder** (founded in 1855), Tenuta Loüwengang, Vicolo dei Conti, in the hamlet of Magré (☎ **0471/817-256**), and **Schloss Turmhof,** Entiklar, Kurtatsch, 39040 (☎ **0471/880-122**). The Trentino area, a short distance to the south, is one of the leading producers of Chardonnay and sparkling wines fermented using methods developed centuries ago. A winery worth a visit is **Cavit Cantina Viticoltori,** Via del Ponte 31, 38100 Trento (☎ **0461/922-055**).
- **Friuli–Venezia Giulia:** This region in the cool alpine foothills of northeastern Italy produces a light, fruity vintage that's especially appealing when young. One of the largest and best-respected wineries here is **Livio Felluga,** Via Risorgimento 1, Brazzano di Cormons, 34071 Gorizia (☎ **0481/60203**). Another worthy producer known for its high-quality wines is **Eugenio Collavini Vini &**

Spumanti, Via della Ribolla Gialla 33040, Corno di Rosazzo, Udine (☎ **0432/753-222**).

- **Lombardy** (Lombardia): The Po Valley has always been known for its flat vistas, midsummer humidity, fertile soil, and excellent wines. The region produces everything from dry still reds to sparkling whites with a champagnelike zest. **Guido Berlucchi,** Piazza Duranti 4, Borgonato di Cortefranca, 25040 Brescia (☎ **030/984-451**), one of Italy's largest wineries, is especially willing to receive visitors.
- **The Piedmont** (Piemonte): Reds with rich and complex flavors make up most of the wine output of this rugged high-altitude region near Italy's border with France. One of the most interesting vineyards is headquartered in a 15th-century abbey near the hamlet of Alba: **Antiche Cantine dell'Annunziata,** Abbazia dell'Annunziata, La Morra, 12064 Cuneo (☎ **0173/50-185**).
- **Campania:** The wines produced in the harsh, hot landscapes of Campania, around Naples in southern Italy, seem stronger, rougher, and in many cases more powerful than those grown in gentler climes. Among the most famous are the *Lacryma Christi* (Tears of Christ), a white that grows in the volcanic soil near Naples, Herculaneum, and Pompeii; Taurasi, a potent red; and Greco di Tufo, a pungent white laden with the odors of apricots and apples. One of the most frequently visited vineyards is **Mastroberardino,** 75-81 Via Manfredi, Atripalda, 83042 Avellino (☎ **0825/626-123**).
- **Sicily:** Because of its hot climate and volcanic soil, Sicily is home to countless vineyards, many of which just produce simple table wines. Of the better vintages, the best-known wine is Marsala, a sweet dessert wine produced in both amber and ruby tones. Its production was given a great boost by the British, whose fleet paid frequent calls in Sicily throughout England's Age of Empire. Lord Nelson himself was an avid connoisseur, encouraging its production and spurring local vintners to produce abundant quantities. One top producer is **Regaleali,** Contrada Regaleali, 93010 Vallelunga, Pratameno Caltanisetta (☎ **0921/542-522**), a historic enterprise near Palermo run by the Tasca d'Almerita family; this winery is also known for its sauvignon-based Nozze d'Oro and such full-bodied reds as Rosso del Conte (whose bouquet has been referred to by connoisseurs as "huge"). Two other names that evoke years of wine-making traditions, thanks to their skill at producing Cerasuolo di Vittoria and Moscato di Pantelleria, are **Cantine Torrevecchia di Favuzza Giuseppe,** Via Ariosto 10A, 90144 Palermo (☎ **0932/989-400**), and **Corvo Duca di Salaparuta,** a 19th-century winery in the hills above Palermo. For information, contact the **Casa Vinicola Duca di Salaparuta,** Via Nazionale, SS113, Casteldaccia, 90014 Palermo (☎ **091/953-988**).

7 The Best Luxury Hotels

- **Hotel de la Ville Inter-Continental Roma** (Rome; ☎ **800/327-0200** in the U.S.): Less stuffy than its neighbor, the Hassler, the Inter-Continental enjoys the same swank location at the top of the Spanish Steps (near an obelisk and a Renaissance church). If you want to splurge in Rome, this is the place to do it. The hotel was built in the 19th century on the site of the ancient gardens of Lucullus. The public rooms boast a 1930s elegance, and the smartly styled guest rooms reflect classic Roman styling. The view from the rooftop terrace is stunning. See chapter 3.

- **Villa San Michele** (Fiesole, near Florence; ☎ **800/237-1236** in the U.S.): This former 15th-century monastery is set behind a facade reputedly designed by Michelangelo. Brigitte Bardot once selected it for one of her honeymoons (no one remembers with which husband). Many visitors consider this hill-town hotel a worthy escape from Florence's often oppressive summer congestion. With a decor that no set designer could ever duplicate, it evokes the charm of an aristocratic private villa. See chapter 5.
- **Hotel Cipriani** (Venice; ☎ **800/992-5055** in the U.S.): This exclusive, elegant hotel is situated in a 3-acre garden on the Isola della Giudecca, one of the calmer islands that compose the ancient city of Venice. The grand hotel was built as a cloister in the 15th century and is centered around a large modern pool. See chapter 8.
- **Gritti Palace** (Venice; ☎ **800/325-3535** in the U.S.): The namesake of Andrea Gritti, a doge who ruled Venice with an iron hand until his death in 1538, this property is the gem of one of the world's most elegant hotel chains (CIGA). The exquisite interiors offer a taste of Venice's historic opulence. See chapter 8.
- **Miramonti Majestic Grand Hotel** (Cortina d'Ampezzo; ☎ **0436/4201**): Designed like a massive mountain fortress, this hotel is in the heart of Italy's most glamorous alpine resort. The clientele seems to relish the hotel's Italian panache amid the bracing air of the Dolomites. Despite the modern amenities, there's a 19th-century quality about this place. See chapter 9.
- **Grand Hotel Villa d'Este** (Cernobbio; ☎ **031/3481**): Built in 1568, this splendid palace in the Lake District is one of the world's most famous Renaissance-era hotels. Step inside and you're surrounded by frescoed ceilings, impeccable antiques, and many other exquisite details. Ten magnificently landscaped acres, parts of which have been nurtured since the 1500s, surround the hotel. Cool breezes are provided by nearby Lake Como and the proximity to the Swiss and Italian Alps. See chapter 10.
- **Albergo Splendido** (Portofino; ☎ **800/237-1236** in the U.S.): Built as a monastery in the 14th century and abandoned because of attacks by North African pirates, this monument was rescued during the 19th century by an Italian baron, who converted it into a summer home for his family. The posh hillside retreat on the Italian Riviera now accommodates a sophisticated crowd, including many film stars. The scent of mimosas fills the air, and the sea views are blissful. See chapter 12.
- **Grand Hotel Quisisana Capri** (Capri; ☎ **081/837-0788**): This hotel, on a part of the island sheltered from the sometimes annoying winds, was established as a health spa by an English doctor around 1850. It's large, supremely comfortable, and intricately linked to the allure that made Capri popular with the Roman emperors. See chapter 13.
- **Hotel di San Pietro** (near Positano; ☎ **089/875-455**): The only marker identifying this cliffside hotel in the Campania region is a 15th-century chapel set beside the winding road. The hotel doesn't advertise, protects the privacy of its guests, and offers frequent transportation into that hub of midsummer glamour, Positano, less than a mile away. Strands of bougainvillea twine around the dramatically terraced white exterior walls; the rooms resemble suites and offer views of the sea. See chapter 13.
- **Palazzo San Domenico** (Taormina, Sicily; ☎ **0942/23-701**): This is one of Europe's great stylish old hotels, a 500-year-old Dominican monastery whose severe lines and dignified bulk are softened with antique tapestries, fragrant

gardens, and a sense of the eternal that only Sicily can give. Since its transformation into a hotel in 1896, its guests have included movie legends Dietrich, Garbo, and Loren. See chapter 15.

8 The Best Moderately Priced Hotels

- **Hotel Venezia** (Rome; ☎ **06/445-7101**): Near Rome's main rail terminal, this hotel features Murano glass chandeliers in the guest rooms and public areas, which were recently renovated. Some units have balconies overlooking the street, and everything is well maintained. See chapter 3.
- **Hotel Bellettini** (Florence; ☎ **055/213-561**): If you're looking for a place with *A Room with a View* atmosphere, head for this Renaissance palazzo midway between the Duomo and the rail station. It's a family-run affair with an old-time atmosphere evoked by terra-cotta floors and stained-glass windows. The rooms are a bit plain but very comfortable. See chapter 5.
- **Hotel Palazzo Bocci** (Spello, near Assisi; ☎ **0742/301-021**): Built in the late 18th century and renovated and transformed into a hotel in 1992, this palace is posh, tasteful, and reasonably priced. Many of the public and private rooms have sweeping views of the valley below. See chapter 6.
- **Hotel Roma** (Modena; ☎ **059/222-218**): In the 1700s, this building was among the real-estate holdings of the duca d'Este. Today it's likely to be the temporary home of whatever opera star happens to be singing in Pavarotti's hometown. Flourishing as a hotel since the 1950s, the Roma, in the historic heart of town, is comfortable and uncomplicated. See chapter 7.
- **La Residenza** (Venice; ☎ **041/528-5315**): Many of this hotel's guests are art lovers who return to Venice year after year. Built in the 14th century, its interior walls have some of the most charming stucco work in Venice. On the medieval piazza outside, older citizens feed pigeons while younger ones play soccer. See chapter 8.
- **Hotel Menardi** (Cortina d'Ampezzo; ☎ **0436/2400**): Built a century ago, this alpine inn exudes Austrian *gemütlichkeit* (coziness), with blazing fireplaces and windows that overlook a view of alpine meadows and rugged crags. Best of all, it's a short uphill walk from one of Italy's most glamorous resorts. See chapter 9.
- **Hotel Florence** (Bellagio; ☎ **031/950-342**): A private villa in the 19th century, this hotel boasts a dignified facade, an arbor with tumbling wisteria, and stone-sided terraces overlooking a lake. A series of renovations in 1990 brought it tastefully up-to-date, and Saturday-night jazz concerts and an American-style bar have made it better than ever. See chapter 10.
- **Albergo Nazionale** (Portofino; ☎ **0185/269-575**): This excellent moderately priced choice is in the heart of Italy's most photographed harbor, in the most expensive pocket of posh on the Italian Riviera. Antique furnishings, coved ceilings, and hand-painted Venetian furniture add to the charm and luxury, but nothing equals the view of the harbor from some windows. See chapter 12.
- **Palazzo Murat** (Positano; ☎ **089/875-177**): Along the curvy Amalfi drive, the Murat is a reasonably priced retreat in a pricey resort that's big on charm and nostalgia. Jasmine and bougainvillea grow profusely in the garden, and the atmosphere is a bit baroque. This was the former retreat of Napoléon's brother-in-law, the king of Naples. The steep streets are tortuous to climb, but you're following in the footsteps of the rich and famous if you anchor here. See chapter 13.

9 The Best Restaurants

- **Relais Le Jardin** (Rome; ☎ **06/361-3041**): The restaurant of the dignified Lord Byron Hotel, in an upscale residential neighborhood a short drive from the center of Rome, the Relais is always on the short list of the country's best. There are places in Rome with better views, but not with such an elegant setting. The service is impeccable, and the menu varies according to what's in season. See chapter 3.
- **Don Chisciotte** (Florence; ☎ **055/475-430**): This Florentine palazzo near the rail station continues year after year to serve some of the most creative cuisine, with an emphasis on fresh seafood, though this is an inland city. Long before Michelin got around to discovering its allure, we've been dining here on such delights as a risotto of broccoli and baby squid or filet of turbot with radicchio sauce. See chapter 5.
- **San Domenico** (Imola, outside Bologna; ☎ **0542/29-000**): Convenient to either Bologna or Ravenna, Italy's undisputed best restaurant is in the unlikely town of Imola. Most deluxe restaurants aspire to, yet don't achieve, the perfection you'll taste here. The Italian menu declares its dedication to the culinary traditions of the noble families of Italy, offering the most luxurious food and the most elaborate preparations money can buy. The wine list is one of the country's finest. See chapter 7.
- **Harry's Bar** (Venice; ☎ **041/528-5777**): It's legendary, it's lighthearted, and it's fun. First made famous by writer Ernest Hemingway, Harry's Bar still serves sublime food in the formal dining room upstairs. The Bellini, peach juice with *prosecco* (Italian sparkling wine), was born here. See chapter 8.
- **Antico Martini** (Venice; ☎ **041/522-4121**): Founded in 1720 as a spot to enjoy the newly developed rage of coffee drinking, this restaurant is one of the very best in Venice. Replete with paneled walls and glittering chandeliers, the Martini specializes in Venetian cuisine. See chapter 8.
- **Ristorante il Desco** (Verona; ☎ **045/595-358**): Set in a former palazzo, this restaurant is the best in the Veneto region of northeastern Italy. Its culinary repertoire emphasizes a *nuova cucina* (nouvelle cuisine) that makes use of the freshest ingredients. The wine selections are excellent. See chapter 9.
- **Ristorante Tivoli** (Cortina d'Ampezzo; ☎ **0436/866-400**): At this charming and friendly restaurant, a cozy chalet on a hillside above the town, enjoy such flavorful dishes as stuffed rabbit in onion sauce, filet of veal with pine nuts and basil, and a delectable saffron-flavored salmon. See chapter 9.
- **Peck's Restaurant** (Milan; ☎ **02/876-774**): In the 19th century, an entrepreneur from Prague moved to Lombardy and founded the most upscale delicatessen (Peck) in Milan. The same management also runs this sumptuously elegant restaurant. You're likely to dine surrounded by the business moguls who run Italy. See chapter 10.
- **Ristorante da Vittorio** (Bergamo; ☎ **035/218-060**): On a busy commercial boulevard in a town known for its feudal fortifications, this restaurant stresses regional cuisine with an array of risottos, pastas, and game dishes. See chapter 10.
- **L'Aquila Nigra** (Mantua; ☎ **0376/327-180**): To reach this restaurant, which used to be a Renaissance palace, you'll have to meander through a labyrinth of narrow alleyways in the historic heart of Mantua. Inside, the high-ceilinged rooms offer elegant food, served with dignified panache. See chapter 10.

- **Gran Gotto** (Genoa; ☎ **010/583-644**): Despite its excellent cuisine, this place manages to remain lighthearted, irreverent, and richly connected to the seafaring life of this ancient Italian port. The *zuppa di pesce* (a Riviera version of a Marseillaise bouillabaisse) is worth the trip to Genoa. See chapter 12.
- **La Cantinella** (Naples; ☎ **081/764-8684**): The only Michelin-starred restaurant in Naples, La Cantinella serves some of the best and most refined seafood in Campania. Opening onto the bay of Santa Lucia, this will be the highlight of your culinary tour of the area. Time-tested Neapolitan classics are served here along with an array of more imaginative dishes. Grilled fish can be prepared as you like it, and chances are you'll like it a lot. See chapter 13.

10 The Best Buys

- **Ceramics:** The town of Faenza, in Emilia-Romagna, has been the center of pottery making, especially majolica, since the Renaissance. Majolica, also known as *faïence,* is a type of hand-painted, glazed, and heavily ornamented earthenware. Of course, you don't have to go to Faenza to buy it, as shops throughout the country carry it. Tuscany and Umbria are also known for their earthenware pottery, carried by many shops in Rome and Florence.
- **Fashion:** Italian fashion is world renowned. Pucci and Valentino led the parade, to be followed by Armani, Missoni, Gucci, Versace, and Ferre. Following World War II, Italian design began to compete seriously against the French fashion monopoly. Today Italian designers like Krizia are among the arbiters of the world fashion scene. Milan dominates with the largest selection of boutiques, followed by Rome and Florence. Ironically, a lot of "French" fashion is now designed and manufactured in Italy, in spite of what the label says.
- **Glass:** Venetian glass, ranging from the delicate to the grotesque, is famous the world over. In Venice you'll find literally hundreds of stores peddling Venetian glass in a wide range of prices. Here's the surprise: A great deal of Venetian glass today isn't manufactured on Murano (an island in the Venetian lagoon) but in the Czech Republic. That doesn't mean the glass is unworthy, though. Many factories outside Italy turn out high-quality glass products that are then shipped to Murano, where many so-called glass factories aren't factories at all but storefronts selling this imported "Venetian" glass.
- **Gold:** The tradition of shaping jewelry out of gold dates from the time of the Etruscans, and this ancient tradition is going strong in Italy today with artisans still toiling in tiny studios and workshops. Many of the designs they follow are based on ancient Roman originals. Of course, dozens of gold jewelers don't follow tradition at all but design original and often daring pieces. Many shops will even melt down your old gold jewelry and refashion it into something more modern.
- **Lace:** For centuries, Italy has been known for its exquisite and delicate lace, fashioned into everything from women's undergarments to heirloom tablecloths. Florence long ago distinguished itself for the *punto Firenze* (Florentine stitch) made by cloistered nuns, though this tradition has waned over the years. Venetian lace is even more famous, including some of the finest products in the world, especially *tombolo* (pillow lace), macramé, and an expensive form of lace known as chiacchierino. Of course, the market today is also flooded with cheap machine-made stuff, which a trained eye can quickly spot. Although some pieces, such as a bridal veil, might cost millions of lire, you'll often find reasonably priced collars, handkerchiefs, and doilies in Venice and Florence boutiques.

- **Leather:** The Italians (not just Gucci designers) are the finest leather craftspeople in the world. From boots to luggage, from leather clothing to purses (or wallets), Italian cities—especially Rome, Florence, Venice, and Milan—abound in leather shops selling quality goods. This is one of Italy's best values, in spite of the substandard work that's now appearing. If you shop carefully, you can still find lots of handcrafted Italian leather products.
- **Prints and Engravings:** Ever since the Renaissance, Italy has been a shopping mecca for engravings and prints, especially Rome and Florence. Wood engravings, woodcuts, mezzotints, copper engravings—you name it and you'll find it. Of course, you have to be a careful shopper. Some prints are genuine antiques and works of rare art, but others are rushed off the assembly line and into the shops. Since you can no longer go to Italy and take home Roman antiques or a crate of Raphaels, you'll have to content yourself with these relatively inexpensive prints and engravings—admittedly reproductions but collectors' items nonetheless.
- **Religious Objects and Vestments:** The religious objects industry in Italy is big and bustling, centered mostly in the Greater Vatican area in Rome. The biggest concentration of shops in Rome is near the ancient Church of Santa Maria sopra Minerva. These shops have it all, from cardinals' birettas and rosary beads to religious art and vestments.

2

Planning Your Trip: The Basics

This chapter is devoted to the where, when, and how of your trip—the advance planning required to get it together and take it on the road. Because you may not know exactly where in Italy you want to go or what surrounds the major city you want to see, we begin with a quick rundown on the various regions.

1 The Regions in Brief

Italy is about the size of the state of Arizona in the U.S., but the peninsula's shape gives you the impression of a much larger area; the ever-changing seacoast contributes to this feeling, as do the large islands of Sicily and Sardinia. Bordered on the northwest by France, on the north by Switzerland and Austria, and on the east by Slovenia (formerly part of Yugoslavia), Italy is still a land largely surrounded by the sea.

Italy was late in developing a national identity: Only in 1870 were its 20 regions united under a central government. It may be a late bloomer among European nations, but its culture has flourished since antiquity, and no other country boasts as many reminders of its heritage, ranging from Rome's Colosseum to Sicily's Greek ruins.

Two areas within Italy's boundaries aren't under the control of the Italian government: the **State of Vatican City** and the **Republic of San Marino.** Vatican City's 109 acres were established in 1929 by a concordat between Pope Pius XI and Benito Mussolini, acting as head of the Italian government; the agreement also gave Roman Catholicism special status in Italy. The pope is the sovereign of the State of Vatican City, which has its own legal system and post office. (The Republic of San Marino, with a capital of the same name, strides atop the slopes of Mt. Titano, 14 miles/23km from Rimini. It's small and completely surrounded by Italy, so it still exists only by the grace of Italy.)

Here's a brief rundown of the cities and regions covered in this guide:

ROME & LATIUM

The region of **Latium** is dominated by **Rome,** capital of the ancient empire and the modern nation of Italy, and **Vatican City,** the independent papal state. Containing vast lodes of the world's artistic treasures, Latium is a land of myth, legend, grandeur, and ironies. Much of the civilized world was once ruled from here, going back to

The Regions of Italy

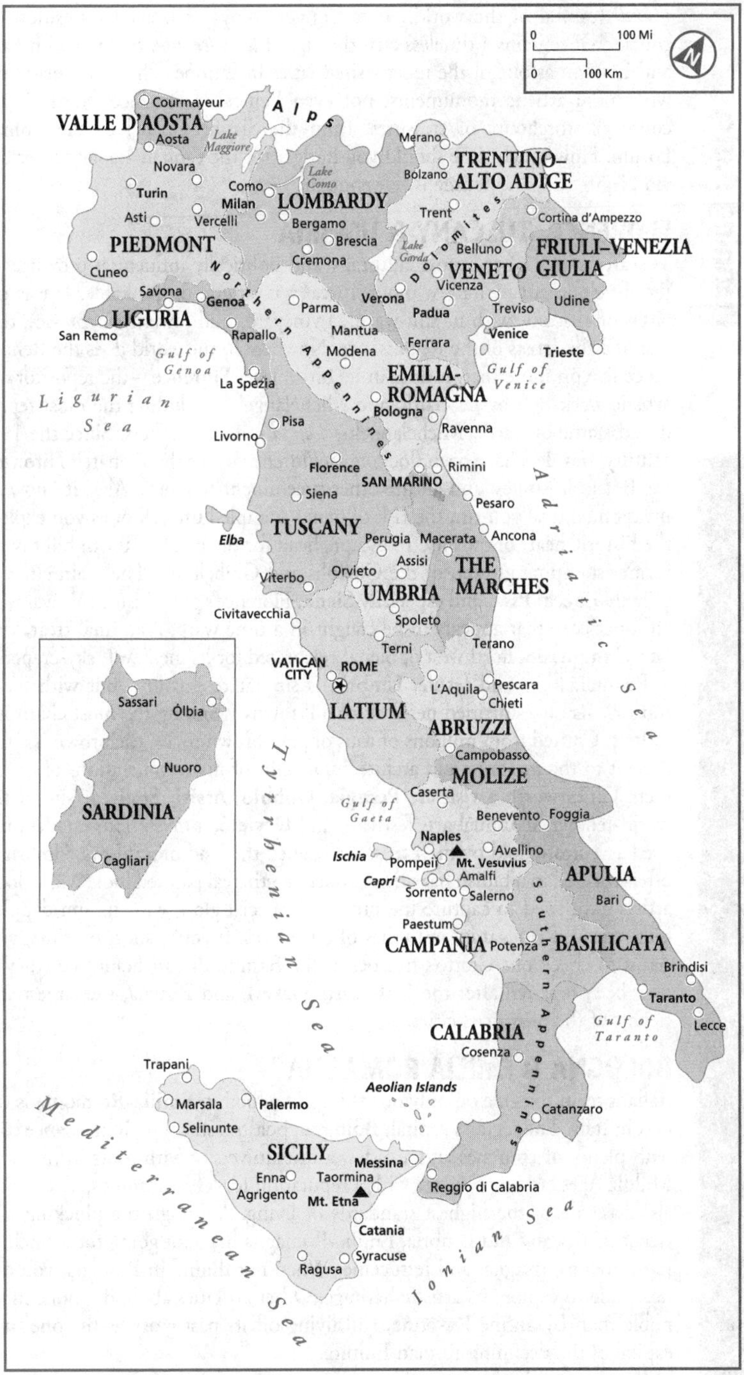

the days when Romulus and Remus are said to have founded Rome on April 21, 753 B.C. For generations, Rome was justifiably referred to as *caput mundi* (capital of the world). It no longer enjoys such a lofty position, of course, but remains a timeless city, the city of *la dolce vita,* ranking with Paris and London as one of the most visited cities in Europe. There's no place else with more artistic monuments, not even Venice or Florence. Rome is the country's storehouse of treasures, from the Sistine Chapel to the Roman Forum. How much time should you budget for the capital? Italian writer Silvio Negro said, "A lifetime is not enough."

FLORENCE, TUSCANY & UMBRIA

Tuscany is one of the most culturally and politically influential provinces—the development of Italy without Tuscany is simply unthinkable. It was the vistas of Tuscany, with its sun-warmed vineyards and towering cypresses, that inspired the artists of the Renaissance. Nowhere in the world does the Renaissance live on more than it does in its birthplace, **Florence**—the repository of artistic works left by Leonardo and Michelangelo (including the most reproduced statue on earth, Michelangelo's *David*), among others. Since the 19th century, travelers have been flocking to Florence to see the Donatello bronzes, the Botticelli smiles, and all the other preeminent treasures. Alas, it's now an invasion, and so you run the risk of being trampled underfoot as you explore the historic heart of the city. To escape, head for the nearby Tuscan hill towns, former stamping ground of the Guelphs and Ghibellines. The main cities to visit are **Lucca, Pisa,** and especially **Siena,** Florence's great historical rival with an inner core that appears to be caught in a time warp. As a final treat, visit **San Gimignano,** northwest of Siena, celebrated for its medieval "skyscrapers."

Pastoral, hilly, and fertile, **Umbria** is similar to Tuscany, but with fewer tourists. Its once-fortified network of hill towns is among the most charming in Italy. Crafted from millions of tons of gray-brown rocks, each town is a testament to the masonry and architectural skills of many generations of craftsmen. Cities worth a visit are **Perugia, Gubbio, Assisi, Spoleto** (site of the world-renowned annual arts festival), and **Orvieto,** a mysterious citadel once used as a stronghold by the Etruscans. Called the land of shadows, Umbria is often covered in a bluish haze that evokes an ethereal painted look. Many local artists have tried to capture the province's special glow, with its sun-dappled hills, terraced vineyards, and miles of olive trees. If you're short on time, visit Assisi to check out Giotto's frescoes at the Basilica di San Francesco (they've now been repaired after the 1997 earthquakes), and Perugia, the largest and richest of the province's cities.

BOLOGNA & EMILIA-ROMAGNA

Italians seem to agree on only one thing: The food in **Emilia-Romagna** is the best in Italy. The region's capital, **Bologna,** boasts a stunning Renaissance core with plenty of churches and arcades, a fine university with roots in the early Middle Ages, and a populace with a reputation for leftist leanings. The region also has one of the highest standards of living. Although the pluckings are richer in Tuscany and Umbria, Emilia-Romagna has a lot going for it, including tortellini, lasagna, and fettuccine. When not dining in Bologna, you can take time to explore its artistic heritage. Other art cities abound—none more noble than Byzantine **Ravenna,** still living off its past glory as the one-time capital of the declining Roman Empire.

If you can visit only one more city in the region, make it **Parma,** to see the city center with its Duomo and baptistery and to view its National Gallery.

This is the home of parmigiano reggiano cheese and prosciutto. Also noteworthy is the hometown of opera star Pavarotti, **Modena,** which is known for its cuisine, its cathedral, and its Este Gallery. The crowded Adriatic resort of **Rimini** and the medieval stronghold of **San Marino** are at the periphery of Emilia-Romagna.

VENICE, THE VENETO & THE DOLOMITES

Northeastern Italy is one of Europe's treasure troves, encompassing **Venice** (which is arguably the world's most beautiful city), the surrounding **Veneto** region, and the mighty **Dolomites** (including the **South Tyrol,** which Italy annexed from Austria after World War I). The Veneto, dotted with rich museums and some of the best architecture in Italy, sprawls across the verdant hills and flat plains between the Adriatic, the Dolomites, Verona, and the edges of Lake Garda. For many generations, the fortunes of the Veneto revolved around Venice, with its sumptuous palaces, romantic waterways, Palazzo Ducale, and Basilica di San Marco. Aging, decaying, and sinking into the sea, Venice is so alluring we almost want to say, visit it even if you have to skip Rome and Florence. As special as Venice and its islands in the lagoon are, we also recommend you tear yourself away and visit at least three fabled art cities in the "Venetian Arc": **Verona,** of Romeo and Juliet fame; **Vicenza,** to see the villas of Andrea Palladio where 16th-century aristocrats lived; and **Padua,** with its Giotto frescoes.

The region of **Trentino-Alto Adige** is far richer in culture, artistic treasures, and activities than the Valle d'Aosta (below), and its ski resort, **Cortina d'Ampezzo,** is far more fashionable than Courmayeur in the northwestern corridor. Its most interesting base (especially if you want to see the Austrian version of Italy) is **Trent (Trento),** the capital of Trentino. In the extreme northeastern corner of Italy, the region of **Friuli-Venezia Giulia** is, in its own way, one of the most cosmopolitan and culturally sophisticated in Italy. Its capital is the seaport of **Trieste.** The area is filled with art from the Roman, Byzantine, and Romanesque-Gothic eras; and many of the public buildings (especially in Trieste) might remind you more of Vienna.

MILAN, LOMBARDY & THE LAKE DISTRICT

Flat, fertile, prosperous, and politically conservative, **Lombardy** is dominated by **Milan** as Latium is dominated by Rome. Lombardy is one of the world's leading commercial and cultural centers, and it has been ever since Milan developed into Italy's gateway to northern German-speaking Europe in the early Middle Ages. Although some people belittle Milan as an industrial city with a snobbish contempt for the poorer regions to the south, its fans compare it to New York. Milan's cathedral is Europe's third largest, its La Scala opera house is world-renowned, and its museums and churches are a treasure trove, one containing Leonardo's *Last Supper.* However, Milan still doesn't have the sights and tourist interest of Rome, Florence, and Venice. Visit Milan if you have the time, though you'll find more charm in the neighboring art cities of **Bergamo, Brescia, Pavia, Cremona,** and **Mantua.** Also competing for your time will be the gorgeous lakes of **Como, Garda,** and **Maggiore,** which lie near Lombardy's eastern edge.

PIEDMONT & VALLE D'AOSTA

At Italy's extreme northwestern edge, sharing a set of alpine peaks with France (which in some ways it resembles), **Piedmont** was the district from which Italy's dreams of unification spread in 1861. Long under the domination of the Austro-Hungarian Empire, Piedmont enjoys a cuisine laced with alpine cheeses and dairy products. It's proud of its largest city, **Turin,** called the "Detroit of Italy" since it's the home of the Fiat empire, as well as the home of vermouth, Asti Spumante, and the Borsalino hat. Even though Turin is a great cosmopolitan center, it doesn't have the antique charm of Genoa or the sophistication, world-class dining, and chic shopping of Milan. Turin's most controversial sight is the *Sacra Sindone* (Holy Shroud), which many Catholics believe is the exact cloth in which Christ's body was wrapped when lowered from the cross.

Italy's window on Switzerland and France, the **Valle d'Aosta** (the smallest region) often serves as an introduction to the country, especially for those journeying from France through the Mont Blanc tunnel. The introduction is misleading, however, as Valle d'Aosta stands apart from the rest of Italy, a semiautonomous region of towering peaks and valleys in the northwestern corridor. It's more closely linked to France (especially the region of Savoy) than to Italy, and its residents speak an ancient French-derived dialect. The most important city in this scenic region is the old Roman city of **Aosta** which, except for some ruins, is rather dull. More intriguing are two of Italy's major ski resorts, **Courmayeur** and **Breuil-Cervinia,** which are topped only by Cortina d'Ampezzo in the Dolomites (above). Many of the region's villages are crafted from gray rocks culled from the mountains that rise on all sides. The best time to visit is in summer or the deep of winter. Late spring and fall get rather sleepy in this part of the world.

GENOA & THE ITALIAN RIVIERA

Comprising most of the **Italian Riviera,** the region of **Liguria** incorporates the steeply sloping capital city of **Genoa,** charming medieval ports (**Portofino, Ventimiglia,** and **San Remo**), a huge naval base (La Spezia), and five traditional coastal communities (**Cinque Terre**). There's also a series of beach resorts (**Rapallo** and **Santa Margherita Ligure**) that resemble the French Riviera. Although overbuilt and overrun, the Italian Riviera is still a land of great beauty. It's actually two Rivieras: the **Riviera di Ponente** to the west, running from the French border to Genoa; and the **Riviera di Levante** to the east. Faced with a choice, we always gravitate toward the more glamorous and cosmopolitan Riviera di Levante. Italy's largest port, Genoa, also merits a visit for its rich culture and history.

NAPLES, THE AMALFI COAST & CAPRI

More than any other region, **Campania** reverberates with the memories of the ancient Romans, who favored its strong sunlight, fertile soil, and bubbling sulfurous springs. It manages to incorporate the anarchy of **Naples** with the elegant beauty of **Capri** and the **Amalfi Coast.** The region also contains many sites specifically identified in ancient mythology (lakes defined as the entrance to the Kingdom of the Dead, for example) and some of the world's most prolific ancient ruins (including **Pompeii, Herculaneum,** and **Paestum**). Campania is overrun, overcrowded, and over everything, but it still lures visitors. Allow at least a day for Naples, which has amazing museums and the world's worst traffic outside Cairo. Pompeii, Herculaneum, and Paestum are for the ruin collectors, while those seeking fun in the sun head for Capri or Portofino. The leading resorts along the Amalfi Drive (even though they're not exactly undiscovered) are **Ravello** (not on the sea) and **Positano** (on the sea). **Amalfi** and **Sorrento** also have beautiful seaside settings. However, their more affordable hotels tend to make them that much more crowded.

APULIA

Sun-drenched and poor, **Apulia** (depending on the dialect, *Le Puglie* or *Puglia*) forms the heel of the Italian boot. It's the most frequently visited province of Italy's Deep South; part of its allure lies in its string of coastal resorts. The *trulli* houses of **Alberobello** are known for their unique cylindrical shapes and conical flagstone-sheathed roofs. Among the region's largest cities are **Bari** (the capital), **Foggia,** and **Brindisi** (gateway to nearby Greece, with which the town shares many characteristics). Each of these is a modern disaster, filled with tawdry buildings, heavy traffic, and rising crime rates (tourists are often the victims). Most visitors pass right through Bari (though it's a favorite with backpackers), and the only real reason to spend a night in Brindisi is to catch the ferry to Greece the next morning.

SICILY

The largest Mediterranean island, **Sicily** is a land of beauty, mystery, and world-class monuments. It's a bizarre mix of bloodlines and architecture from medieval Normandy, Aragonese Spain, Moorish North Africa, ancient Greece, Phoenicia, and Rome. Since the advent of modern times, part of the island's primitiveness has faded, as thousands of newly arrived cars clog the narrow lanes of its biggest city, **Palermo.** Poverty remains widespread, yet the age-old stranglehold of the Mafia seems less certain because of the increasingly vocal protests of an outraged Italian public. On the eastern edge of the island is Mt. Etna, the tallest active volcano in Europe. Many of Sicily's larger cities (**Trapani, Catania,** and **Messina**) are relatively unattractive, but areas of ravishing beauty and eerie historical interest include **Syracuse, Taormina, Agrigento,** and **Selinunte.** Sicily's ancient ruins are rivaled only by those of Rome itself. The Valley of the Temples, for example, is worth the trip here.

2 Visitor Information

For information before you go, contact the **Italian Government Tourist Board.**

In the United States: 630 Fifth Ave., Suite 1565, New York, NY 10111 (☎ **212/245-4822;** fax 212/586-9249); 500 N. Michigan Ave., Suite 2240, Chicago, IL 60611 (☎ **312/644-0990;** fax 312/644-3019); 12400 Wilshire Blvd., Suite 550, Los Angeles, CA 90025 (☎ **310/820-0098;** fax 310/820-6367).

In Canada: 1 place Ville-Marie, Suite 1914, Montréal, PQ H3B 2C3 (☎ **514/866-7667;** fax 514/392-1429).

In the United Kingdom: 1 Princes St., London W1R 8AY (☎ **020/7 408-1254;** fax 020/7493-6695).

You can also write directly (in English or Italian) to the provincial or local tourist boards of the areas you plan to visit. Provincial tourist boards (**Ente Provinciale per il Turismo**) operate in the principal towns of the provinces. Local tourist boards (**Azienda Autonoma di Soggiorno e Turismo**) operate in all places of tourist interest; you can get a list from the Italian National Tourist Office. If you are in Italy and need to get information, call the toll-free number (only within Italy, ☎ **800/11-77-00**). If you are calling from another country, dial ☎ **06/877-000-01.** The service is available daily from 8am to 11pm in five languages, dispensing information concerning transportation, health assistance, events, museums, safety, hotels, information points, and tourist assistance.

On the Web, the Italian National Tourist Board sponsors the site www.italiantourism.com or www.enit.it.

3 Entry Requirements & Customs

ENTRY REQUIREMENTS

U.S., Canadian, U.K., Irish, Australian, and New Zealand citizens with a **valid passport** don't need a visa to enter Italy if they don't expect to stay more than 90 days and don't expect to work there. If after entering Italy you find you want to stay more than 90 days, you can apply for a permit for an extra 90 days, which as a rule is granted immediately. Go to the nearest *questura* (police headquarters) or to your home country's consulate. If your passport is lost or stolen, head to your consulate as soon as possible for a replacement.

CUSTOMS

WHAT YOU CAN BRING INTO ITALY Foreign visitors can bring along most items for personal use duty-free, including fishing tackle, a pair of skis, two tennis racquets, a baby carriage, two hand cameras with 10 rolls of film, and 200 cigarettes or a quantity of cigars or pipe tobacco not exceeding 250 grams (0.05 oz.). There are strict limits on importing alcoholic beverages. However, for alcohol bought tax-paid, limits are much more liberal than in other countries of the European Union.

There are no restrictions on the amount of foreign currency you can bring into Italy, though you should declare the amount. Your declaration proves to the Italian Customs office that the currency came from outside the country, and therefore you can take out the same amount or less. Italian currency taken into or out of Italy may not exceed 200,000L in denominations of 50,000L or lower.

WHAT YOU CAN BRING HOME Check with your country's Customs or Foreign Affairs department for the latest guidelines—including information on items that you are not allowed to bring into your home country—just before you leave home, since regulations frequently change.

Returning **U.S. citizens** who've been away for 48 hours or more are allowed to bring back, once every 30 days, $400 worth of merchandise duty-free. You'll be charged a flat rate of 10% duty on the next $1,000 worth of purchases. Be sure to have your receipts handy. On gifts, the duty-free limit is $100. You can't bring fresh foodstuffs into the United States; tinned foods, however, are allowed. For more information, contact the **U.S. Customs Service,** 1301 Constitution Ave. (P.O. Box 7407), Washington, D.C. 20044 (☎ **202/927-6724;** www.customs.ustreas.gov/travel/travel.htm), and request the free pamphlet "Know Before You Go."

U.K. citizens should contact HM Customs & Excise Passenger Enquiries (☎ **0181/910-3744;** www.open.gov.uk).

For a clear summary of **Canadian** rules, visit the comprehensive Web site of the **Canada Customs and Revenue Agency** at www.ccra-adrc.gc.ca.

Citizens of **Australia** should request the helpful Australian Customs brochure *Know Before You Go,* available by calling ☎ **1-300/363-263** from within Australia, or 61-2/6275-6666 from abroad. For additional information, go online at www.dfat.gov.au and click on HINTS FOR AUSTRALIAN TRAVELLERS.

For New Zealand customs information, contact the **New Zealand Customs Service** at ☎ **09/359-6655,** or go online at www.customs.govt.nz.

4 Money

CURRENCY

The basic unit of Italian currency is the **lira** (plural: **lire**), which you'll see abbreviated as **L.** Coins are issued in denominations of 10L, 20L, 50L, 100L, 200L, 500L, and 1,000L, and bills come in denominations of 1,000L, 2,000L, 5,000L, 10,000L, 50,000L, 100,000L, and 500,000L. Coins for 50L and 100L come in two sizes each (the newer ones both around the size of a dime). The most common coins are the 200L and 500L ones, and the most common bills are the 1,000L, 5,000L, and 10,000L.

With the arrival of the euro, things will change considerably. Until then, interbank exchange rates are established daily and listed in most international newspapers. To get a transaction as close to this rate as possible, pay for as much as possible with credit cards. ATMs and bank cards offer close to the same rate, plus an added-on fee for cash transaction.

THE EURO

The **euro,** the new single European currency, became the official currency of Italy and 10 other participating countries on **January 1, 1999.** You may run into prices quoted in euros here and there, but it's not universally used yet.

Although the euro technically took effect in 1999—at which time the exchange rates of participating countries were locked in together and are now fluctuating against the dollar in sync—this change applies mostly to financial transactions between banks and businesses in Europe. The Italian lira remains the only currency in Italy for cash transactions. That is, until **December 21, 2001,** when more and more businesses will start posting their prices in euros alongside those in Italian lire, which will continue to exist (you'll already see some stores listing euro prices). Currently the euro can be used in noncash transactions, such as checks and credit cards.

On **January 1, 2002,** euro banknotes and coins will be introduced. Over a maximum 6-month transition period, Italian lire banknotes and coins will be withdrawn from circulation and the euro will become the official currency of Italy. The symbol of the euro is a stylized *E:* €. Its official abbreviation is "EUR."

For more details on the euro, check out www.europa.eu.int/euro.

Exchange rates are more favorable at the point of arrival. Nevertheless, it's often helpful to exchange at least some money before going abroad (standing in line at the ***cambio*** [exchange bureau] in the Milan or Rome airport may make you miss the next bus leaving for downtown). Check with any of your local American Express or Thomas Cook offices or major banks. Or order Italian lire in advance from the following: **American Express** (☎ **800/221-7282;** cardholders only), **Thomas Cook** (☎ **800/223-7373**), or **International Currency Express** (☎ **888/842-0880**).

It's best to exchange currency or traveler's checks at a bank, not a *cambio,* hotel, or shop. Currency and traveler's checks (for which you'll receive a better rate than cash) can be changed at all principal airports and at some travel agencies, such as American Express and Thomas Cook. Note the rates and ask about commission fees; it can sometimes pay to shop around and ask the right questions.

TRAVELER'S CHECKS

Traveler's checks once were the only sound alternative to traveling with dangerously large amounts of cash—they were as reliable as currency, unlike personal checks, but could be replaced if lost or stolen, unlike cash. But these

The Italian Lira, the U.S. Dollar, the U.K. Pound & the Euro

For American Readers: At this writing, $1 U.S. = approximately 1,800L (or 100L = 5¢), and this was the rate of exchange used to calculate the dollar values given throughout this book (amounts over $5 have been rounded to the nearest dollar). The rate fluctuates from day to day and might not be the same when you travel to Italy.

For British Readers: The ratio of the British pound to the lira fluctuates constantly. Currently, £1 = approximately 3,007L (or 100L = 0.03 pence).

Regarding the Euro: Even though the euro isn't yet in widespread use, it will become an increasingly important international currency during the lifetime of this edition. At press time, the euro was fixed at 1,936.27L, a rate that's likely to remain constant throughout the lifetime of this edition. As regards the U.S. dollar, however, the euro fluctuates from time to time. At press time, the euro equaled approximately U.S.$1.10 (or U.S.$1 = 91 eurocents). For up-to-date conversion ratios at the time of your trip, check with any international bank.

Lira	U.S.$	U.K.£	Euro€	Lira	U.S.$	U.K.£	Euro€
50	.03	0.02	0.03	10,000	5.50	3.33	5.20
100	0.05	0.03	0.05	20,000	11.00	6.65	10.40
300	0.16	0.10	0.16	25,000	13.75	8.31	13.00
500	0.27	0.17	0.26	30,000	16.50	9.98	15.60
700	0.38	0.23	0.36	35,000	19.25	11.65	18.20
1,000	0.55	0.33	0.52	40,000	22.00	13.30	20.80
1,500	0.82	0.50	0.78	45,000	24.75	15.00	23.40
2,000	1.10	0.67	1.04	50,000	27.50	16.63	26.00
3,000	1.65	1.00	1.56	100,000	55.00	33.25	52.00
4,000	2.20	1.33	2.08	150,000	82.50	49.90	78.00
5,000	2.75	1.66	2.60	200,000	110.00	66.50	104.00
7,500	4.10	2.50	3.90	500,000	275.00	66.30	260.00

days, traveler's checks seem less necessary because most larger cities have 24-hour ATMs, allowing you to withdraw small amounts of cash as needed. Many banks, however, impose a fee every time you use a card at an ATM in a different city or bank. If you plan to withdraw money every day, you might be better off with traveler's checks—provided you don't mind showing an ID every time you want to cash a check.

You can get traveler's checks at almost any bank. **American Express** offers checks in denominations of $10, $20, $50, $100, $500, and $1,000. You'll pay a service charge ranging from 1 to 4%. You can also get American Express traveler's checks over the phone by calling ☎ **800/221-7282** or 800/721-9768; you can also purchase checks online at www.americanexpress.com. AmEx gold or platinum cardholders can avoid paying the fee by ordering over the telephone; platinum cardholders can also purchase checks fee-free in person at AmEx Travel Service locations (check the Web site for the office nearest you). American Automobile Association members can obtain checks fee-free at most AAA offices.

Visa offers traveler's checks at Citibank branches and other financial institutions nationwide; call ☎ **800/227-6811** to locate the purchase location near you. **MasterCard** also offers traveler's checks through **Thomas Cook Currency Services**; call ☎ **800/223-9920** for a location near you.

If you carry traveler's checks, be sure to keep a record of their serial numbers (separately from the checks, of course), so that you're ensured a refund in case they're lost or stolen.

ATMS

ATMs are linked to a national network that most likely includes your bank at home. Both the **Cirrus** (☎ **800/424-7787;** www.mastercard.com/atm) and the **Plus** (☎ **800/843-7587;** www.visa.com) networks have automated ATM locators listing the banks in Italy that'll accept your card. Or just search out any machine with your network's symbol emblazoned on it.

You can also get a cash advance through Visa or MasterCard (contact the issuing bank to enable this feature and get a PIN), but note that the credit card company will begin charging you interest immediately and many have begun assessing a fee every time. American Express card cash advances are usually available only from AMEX offices.

Important note: Make sure the PINs on your bankcards and credit cards will work in Italy. You'll need a **four-digit code** (six digits won't work), so if you have a six-digit code you'll have to go into your bank and get a new PIN for your trip. If you're unsure about this, contact Cirrus or Plus (above). Be sure to check the daily withdrawal limit at the same time.

CREDIT CARDS

Credit cards are invaluable when traveling—a safe way to carry money and a convenient record of all your expenses. You can also withdraw cash advances from your cards at any bank (though you'll start paying hefty interest the moment you receive the cash and you won't receive frequent-flyer miles on an airline credit card). At most banks, you don't even need to go to a teller; you can get a cash advance at an ATM with your PIN.

Note, however, that many banks, including Chase and Citibank, have begun to charge a 2% service fee for transactions in a foreign currency (3% or a minimum of $5 on cash advances).

Almost every credit card company has an emergency toll-free number you can call if your wallet or purse is stolen. They may be able to wire you a cash advance off your credit card immediately, and in many places, they can deliver an emergency card in a day or two. The issuing bank's number is usually on the back of the credit card (which doesn't help you much if the card was stolen). A toll-free **information directory** at ☎ **800/555-1212** will provide the number for you. The U.S. emergency number for **Citicorp Visa** is ☎ **800/336-8472. American Express** cardholders and traveler's check holders should call ☎ **800/221-7282,** and **MasterCard** holders should call ☎ **800/307-7309.**

5 When to Go

April to June and **late September to October** are the best months for touring Italy—temperatures are usually mild and the crowds aren't quite so intense. Starting in mid-June, the summer rush really picks up, and from **July to mid-September** the country teems with visitors. **August** is the worst month: Not only does it get uncomfortably hot, muggy, and crowded, but the entire country goes on vacation at least from August 15 to the end of the month—and a good percentage of Italians take off the entire month. Many hotels, restaurants, and shops are closed (except at the spas, beaches, and islands, which are where 70% of the Italians head to). From **late October to Easter,** most attractions go on shorter winter hours or are closed for renovation. Many hotels and restaurants take a month or two off between **November and February,** spa and beach destinations become padlocked ghost towns, and it can get much colder than you'd expect (it may even snow).

High season on most airlines' routes to Rome usually stretches from June to the beginning of September. This is the most expensive and most crowded time to travel. **Shoulder season** is from April to May, early September to October, and December 15 to 24. **Low season** is November 1 to December 14 and December 25 to March 31.

WEATHER

It's warm all over Italy in summer; it can be very hot in the south, especially inland. The high temperatures (measured in Italy in degrees Celsius) begin in Rome in May, often lasting until sometime in October. Winters in the north of Italy are cold, with rain and snow, but in the south the weather is warm all year, averaging 50°F in winter.

For the most part, it's drier in Italy than in North America, so high temperatures don't seem as bad since the humidity is lower. In Rome, Naples, and the south, temperatures can stay in the 90s for days, but nights are most often comfortably cooler.

The average high temperatures in **Rome** are 82°F (27.8°C) in June, 87°F (30.5°C) in July, and 86°F (30°C) in August; the average lows are 63°F (17.2°C) in June and 67°F (19.4°C) in July and August. In **Venice,** the average high temperatures are 76°F (24.4°C) in June, 81°F (27.2°C) in July, and 80°F (26.6°C) in August; the average lows are 63°F (17.2°C) in June, 66°F (18.8°C) in July, and 65°F (18.3°C) in August.

HOLIDAYS

Offices and shops in Italy are closed on the following **national holidays:** January 1 (New Year's Day), Easter Monday, April 25 (Liberation Day), May 1 (Labor Day), August 15 (Assumption of the Virgin), November 1 (All Saints' Day), December 8 (Feast of the Immaculate Conception), December 25 (Christmas Day), and December 26 (Santo Stefano).

Closings are also observed in the following cities on **feast days** honoring their patron saints: Venice, April 25 (St. Mark); Florence, Genoa, and Turin, June 24 (St. John the Baptist); Rome, June 29 (Sts. Peter and Paul); Palermo, July 15 (St. Rosalia); Naples, September 19 (St. Gennaro); Bologna, October 4 (St. Petronio); Cagliari, October 30 (St. Saturnino); Trieste, November 3 (St. Giusto); Bari, December 6 (St. Nicola); and Milan, December 7 (St. Ambrose).

Italy Calendar of Events

For major events in which tickets should be procured well before arriving, check with **Edwards & Edwards** in the United States at ☎ **800/223-6108.**

January

- **Carnevale,** Piazza Navona, Rome. This festival marks the last day of the children's market and lasts until dawn of the following day. Usually January 4 to 5.

- **Epiphany celebrations,** nationwide. All cities, towns, and villages in Italy stage Roman Catholic Epiphany observances. One of the most festive celebrations is the Epiphany Fair at Rome's Piazza Navona. Usually January 5 to 6.
- **Festa di Sant'Agnese,** Sant'Agnese Fuori le Mura, Rome. During this ancient ceremony two lambs are blessed and shorn, and their wool is used later for palliums (Roman Catholic vestments). Usually January 17.
- **Festival della Canzone Italiana (Festival of Italian Popular Song),** San Remo, the Italian Riviera. At this 3-day festival, major artists perform the latest Italian song releases. Late January.
- **Foire de Saint Ours,** Aosta, Valle d'Aosta. Observing a tradition that has existed for 10 centuries, artisans from the mountain valleys display their wares—often made of wood, lace, wool, or wrought iron—created during the long winter. Late January.

February

- **Almond Blossom Festival,** Agrigento, Sicily. This folk festival includes song, dance, costumes, and fireworks. First half of February.
- ✪ **Carnevale,** Venice. At this riotous time, theatrical presentations and masked balls take place throughout Venice and on the islands in the lagoon. The balls are by invitation only (except the Doge's Ball), but the street events and fireworks are open to everyone. Contact the **Venice Tourist Office,** San Marco, Giardinetti Reali, Palazzo Selva, 30124 Venezia (☎ **041/522-6356**). The week before Ash Wednesday, the beginning of Lent.

March

- **Festa di Santa Francesca Romana,** Piazzale del Colosseo near Santa Francesco Romana in the Roman Forum. A blessing of cars is performed at this festival. Usually March 9.
- **Festa di San Giuseppe,** the Trionfale Quarter, north of the Vatican, Rome. The heavily decorated statue of the saint is brought out at a fair with food stalls, concerts, and sporting events. Usually March 19.

April

- **Holy Week observances,** nationwide. Processions and age-old ceremonies—some from pagan days, some from the Middle Ages—are staged. The most notable procession is led by the pope, passing the Colosseum and the Roman Forum up to Palatine Hill; a torchlit parade caps the observance. Sicily's observances are also noteworthy. Beginning 4 days before Easter Sunday; sometimes at the end of March but often in April.
- **Easter Sunday (Pasqua),** Piazza di San Pietro, Rome. In an event broadcast around the world, the pope gives his blessing from the balcony of St. Peter's.
- **Scoppio del Carro (Explosion of the Cart),** Florence. At this ancient observance, a cart laden with flowers and fireworks is drawn by three white oxen to the Duomo, where at the noon mass a mechanical dove detonates it from the altar. Easter Sunday.
- **Festa della Primavera,** Rome. The Spanish Steps are decked out with banks of azaleas and other flowers; later, orchestral and choral concerts are presented in Trinità dei Monti. Dates vary.

May

- ✪ **Maggio Musicale Fiorentino (Musical May Florentine),** Florence. Italy's oldest and most prestigious music festival emphasizes music from the 14th to the 20th century but also presents ballet and opera. Some concerts and ballets are presented free in Piazza della Signoria; ticketed events (concerts 35,000L to 110,000L/$17.50 to $55; operas 45,000L to 200,000L/$22.50 to $100; ballet 25,000L to 55,000L/$12.50 to $27.50) are held at the Teatro Comunale, Via Solferino 15, or the Teatro della Pergola, Via della Pergola 18. For schedules and tickets, contact the **Maggio Musicale Fiorentino/Teatro Comunale,** Corso Italia 15, 50123 Firenze (☎ **055/27-791** or 055/211-158). Late April to beginning of July.

- **Concorso Ippico Internazionale (International Horse Show),** Piazza di Siena in the Villa Borghese, Rome. Usually May 1 to 10, but the dates can vary.
- **Corso dei Ceri (Race of the Candles),** Gubbio, Umbria. In this centuries-old ceremony celebrating the feast day of St. Ubaldo, the town's patron saint, 1,000-pound 30-foot wooden "candles" (*ceri*) are raced through the streets of this perfectly preserved medieval hill town. May 15.

June

- **San Ranieri,** Pisa, Tuscany. The town honors its patron saint with candle-lit parades, followed the next day by eight rower teams competing in 16th-century costumes. June 16.
- **Festival di Ravenna,** Ravenna, Emilia-Romagna. This summer festival of international renown draws world-class classical performers. A wide range of performances are staged, including operas, ballets, theater presentations, symphonic music concerts, solo and chamber pieces, oratorios, and sacred music. Tickets start at 25,000L ($12.50), and reservations are needed for the most popular events. For details, call ☎ **0544/21-38-95** (fax 0544/21-58-40; e-mail: ra.festival@netgate.it). Mid-June to July.
- **Calcio in Costume (Ancient Football Match in Costume),** Florence. This is a revival of a raucous 16th-century football match, pitting four teams, in medieval costumes, against one another. There are four matches, usually culminating around June 24, feast day of San Giovanni.

✪ **Festival di Spoleto,** Spoleto, Umbria. Dating from 1958, this festival was the artistic creation of maestro and world-class composer Gian Carlo Menotti, who continues to be very visible and still presides over the event. International performers convene for 3 weeks of dance, drama, opera, concerts, and art exhibits in this Umbrian hill town north of Rome. The main focus is to highlight music composed from 1300 to 1799. For tickets and details, contact the **Spoleto Festival,** Piazza Duomo 8, 06049 Spoleto (☎ **0743/220-320** or 0743/45-028; fax 0743/220-321). For further information, call ☎ **167/565-600** (toll-free in Italy only) or 0743/44-700; www.spoletofestival.net. June 28 to July 14.

- **Gioco del Ponte,** Pisa, Tuscany. Teams in Renaissance costume take part in a much-contested tug-of-war on the Ponte di Mezzo, which spans the Arno River. Last Sunday in June.
- **Festa di San Pietro,** St. Peter's Basilica, Rome. This most significant Roman religious festival is observed with solemn rites. Usually around June 29.
- **Son et Lumière,** Rome. The Roman Forum and Tivoli areas are dramatically lit at night. Early June to end of September.
- **Shakespearean Festival,** Verona, the Veneto. Ballet, drama, and jazz performances are included in this festival of the Bard, with a few performances in English. June to September.

- **Biennale d'Arte (International Exposition of Modern Art),** Venice. One of the most famous art events in Europe takes place during alternate odd-numbered years. June to October.

July

- ✪ **Il Palio,** Piazza del Campo, Siena, Tuscany. Palio fever grips this Tuscan hill town for a wild and exciting horse race from the Middle Ages. Pageantry, costumes, and the celebrations of the victorious *contrada* (sort of a neighborhood social club) mark the spectacle. It's a "no rules" event: Even a horse without a rider can win the race. For details, contact the **Azienda di Promozione Turistica,** Piazza del Campo 56, 53100 Siena (☎ **0577/ 280-551**). July 2 and August 16.
- ✪ **World Pride,** Rome. If you're gay or lesbian, you should be interested to know that in 2001 Rome will host the first-ever **World Pride** gathering. A host of art exhibits, performances, and cultural and political events will take place, culminating in a mass demonstration in downtown Rome. For comprehensive information, call ☎ **06/541-3985** or visit www.mariomieli.it or www.interpride.org. July 1–9, 2001.
- **Arena di Verona (Arena Outdoor Opera Season),** Verona, the Veneto. Culture buffs flock to the 20,000-seat Roman amphitheater, one of the world's best preserved. Early July to mid-August.
- **Festa di Nolantri,** Rome. Trastevere, the most colorful quarter, becomes a gigantic outdoor restaurant, with tables lining the streets and merry-makers and musicians providing the entertainment. After reaching the quarter, find the first empty table and try to get a waiter—but keep a close eye on your valuables. For details, contact the **Ente Provinciale per il Turismo,** Via Parigi 11, 00185 Roma (☎ **06/4889-9253** or 06/4889-9255). Mid-July.
- **Umbria Jazz,** Perugia, Umbria. The Umbrian region hosts the country's (and one of Europe's) top jazz festivals, featuring world-class artists. Mid- to late July.
- **Festa del Redentore (Feast of the Redeemer),** Venice. This festival marks the lifting of the plague in July 1578, with fireworks, pilgrimages, and boating on the lagoon. Third Saturday and Sunday in July.
- **Festival Internazionale di Musica Antica,** Urbino, the Marches. A cultural extravaganza, as international performers converge on Raphael's birthplace. It's the most important Renaissance and baroque music festival in Italy. For details, contact the **Azienda di Promozione Turistica,** Piazza del Rinascinento 1, 61029 Urbino (☎ **0722/26-13**). Ten days in late July (usually July 18 to July 28).

August

- **Festa delle Catene,** San Pietro in Vincoli, Rome. The relics of St. Peter's captivity go on display in this church. August 1.
- **Torre del Lago Puccini,** near Lucca, Tuscany. Puccini operas are performed in this Tuscan lakeside town's open-air theater, near the celebrated composer's former summertime villa. Throughout August.
- **Rossini Opera Festival,** Pesaro, Italian Riviera. The world's top *bel canto* specialists perform Rossini's operas and choral works at this popular festival. Mid-August to late September.
- ✪ **Venice International Film Festival,** Venice. Ranking after Cannes, this festival brings together stars, directors, producers, and filmmakers from all over the world. Films are shown more or less constantly between 9am and 3am in various areas of the Palazzo del Cinema on the Lido.

Although many of the seats are reserved for international jury members, the public can attend virtually whenever they want, pending available seats. For information, contact the **Venice Film Festival,** c/o the La Biennale office, Ca' Giustinian, Calle del Ridotto 1364A, 30124 Venezia. Call ☎ **041/521-8838** for details on how to acquire tickets, or check out www.labiennale.com. August 30 to September 9.

September

- **Regata Storica,** the Grand Canal, Venice. Here's a maritime spectacular—many gondolas participate in the canal procession, though gondolas don't race in the regatta itself. First Sunday in September.
- **Giostra del Saraceno (Joust of the Saracen),** Arezzo, Tuscany. A colorful procession in full historical regalia precedes the tilting contest of the 13th century, with knights in armor in the town's main piazza. First Sunday in September.
- **Partita a Scacchi con Personnagi Viventi (Living Chess Game),** Marostica, the Veneto. This chess game is played in the town square by living chess pieces in period costume. The second Saturday/Sunday of September during even-numbered years.
- **Sagra dell'Uva,** Basilica of Maxentius, the Roman Forum, Rome. At this harvest festival, musicians in ancient costumes entertain and grapes are sold at reduced prices. Dates vary, usually early September.

October

- **Sagra del Tartufo,** Alba, Piedmont. This festival honors the expensive truffle in Alba, Italy's truffle capital, with contests, truffle-hound competitions, and tastings of this ugly but very expensive and delectable fungus. For details, contact the **Azienda di Promozione Turistica,** Piazza Medford 3, 12051 Alba (☎ **0173/35-833**). October 7 to 29.

December

- **La Scala Opera Season,** Teatro alla Scala, Milan. At the most famous opera house of them all, the season opens on December 7, the feast day of Milan's patron St. Ambrogio, and runs into July. Even though opening-night tickets are close to impossible to get, it's worth a try; call ☎ **02/80-70-41** for information or 02/80-91-26 for reservations.
- **Christmas Blessing of the Pope,** Piazza di San Pietro, Rome. Delivered at noon from the balcony of St. Peter's Basilica, the pope's words are broadcast around the world. December 25.
- **New Year's Eve 2000.** At press time, no official festivities for the *real* turn of the millennium have been announced, but you can be assured of major parties all over Italy, particularly in Rome. And of course, there'll be a special Mass at St. Peter's.

6 Health & Insurance

STAYING HEALTHY

If you worry about getting sick away from home, you may want to consider **medical travel insurance** (see "Travel Insurance," below). In most cases, however, your existing health plan will provide all the coverage you need. Be sure to carry your identification card in your wallet.

If you suffer from a chronic illness, consult your doctor before your departure. For conditions like epilepsy, diabetes, or heart problems, wear a **Medic Alert Identification Tag** (☎ **800/ID-ALERT;** www.medicalert.org), which will immediately alert doctors to your condition and give them access to your records through Medic Alert's 24-hour hot line.

Pack prescription medications in your carry-on luggage. Carry written prescriptions in generic, not brand-name form, and dispense all prescription medications from their original labeled vials. If you wear contact lenses, pack an extra pair in case you lose one.

Contact the **International Association for Medical Assistance to Travelers (IAMAT; ☎ 716/754-4883** or 416/652-0137; www.sentex.net/~iamat). This organization offers tips on travel and health concerns in the countries you'll be visiting, and lists many local English-speaking doctors. In Canada call **519/836-0102.**

INSURANCE

There are three kinds of travel insurance: trip-cancellation, medical, and lost-luggage coverage. **Trip-cancellation insurance** is a good idea if you have paid a large portion of your vacation expenses up front (say, by purchasing a package deal). Make sure you buy it from an outside vendor, though, not from your tour operator; you don't want to put all your eggs in one basket.

Rule number one: Check your existing policies before you buy any additional coverage you may not need.

Your existing health insurance should cover you if you get sick while on vacation—though if you belong to an HMO, you should check to see whether you are fully covered when away from home. For independent travel health-insurance providers, see below.

Your homeowner's or renter's insurance should cover stolen luggage. The airlines are responsible for only a very limited amount if they lose your luggage on an overseas flight, so if you plan to carry anything really valuable, keep it in your carry-on bag.

The differences between **travel assistance** and insurance are often blurred, but, in general, the former offers on-the-spot assistance and 24-hour hot lines (mostly oriented toward medical problems), whereas the latter reimburses you for travel problems (medical, travel, or otherwise) after you have filed the paperwork. The coverage you should consider will depend on how much protection is already contained in your existing health insurance or other policies. Some credit and charge card companies may insure you against travel accidents if you buy plane, train, or bus tickets with their cards. Before purchasing additional insurance, read your policies and agreements carefully. Call your insurers or credit-card companies if you have any questions.

If you do require additional insurance, try one of the companies listed below. But don't pay for more than you need. If you need only trip-cancellation insurance, don't purchase coverage for lost or stolen property, which should be covered by your homeowner's or renter's policy. Trip-cancellation insurance costs approximately 6 to 8% of the total value of your vacation.

Among the reputable issuers of travel insurance are **Access America** (**☎ 800/284-8300;** www.accessamerica.com) and **Travel Guard International** (**☎ 800/826-1300;** www.travel-guard.com). One company specializing in accident and medical care is **Travel Assistance International** (Worldwide Assistance Services; **☎ 800/821-2828** or 202/828-5894).

7 Tips for Travelers with Special Needs

FOR TRAVELERS WITH DISABILITIES

Laws in Italy have compelled rail stations, airports, hotels, and most restaurants to follow a stricter set of regulations about **wheelchair accessibility** to rest rooms, ticket counters, and the like. Even museums and other attractions have conformed to the regulations, which mimic many of those presently in effect in the United States. Always call ahead to check on the accessibility in hotels, restaurants, and sights you wish to visit.

With overcrowded streets, more than 400 bridges, and difficult-to-board *vaporetti,* Venice has never been accused of being too user-friendly for those with disabilities. Nevertheless, some improvements have been made. The Venice tourist office distributes a free map called *Veneziapertutti* ("Venice for All"), illustrating what parts of the city are accessible and listing accessible churches, monuments, gardens, public offices, hotels, and rest rooms. According to various announcements, Venice in the future will pay even more attention to this issue, possibly adding retractable ramps operated by magnetic cards.

Moss Rehab ResourceNet (www.mossresourcenet.org) is a great source for information, tips, and resources relating to accessible travel. You'll find links to a number of travel agents who specialize in planning trips for disabled travelers here and through **Access-Able Travel Source** (www.access-able.com), another excellent online source. You'll also find relay and voice numbers for hotels, airlines, and car-rental companies on Access-Able's user-friendly site, as well as links to accessible accommodations, attractions, transportation, tours, local medical resources and equipment repairers, and much more.

You can join the **Society for the Advancement of Travelers with Handicaps** (SATH), 347 Fifth Ave., Suite 610, New York, NY 10016 (☎ **212/447-7284;** fax 212/725-8253; www.sath.org), to gain access to their vast network of connections in the travel industry. They provide information sheets on destinations and referrals to tour operators who specialize in travelers with disabilities. Their quarterly magazine, *Open World,* is full of good information and resources.

A World of Options, a 658-page book of resources for disabled travelers, covers everything from biking trips to scuba outfitters. It costs $35 ($30 for members) and is available from **Mobility International USA** (☎ **541/343-1284,** voice and TDD; www.miusa.org). Annual membership for Mobility International is $35, which includes their quarterly newsletter, "Over the Rainbow."

You may also want to join a tour catering to travelers with disabilities. One of the best operators is **Flying Wheels Travel** (☎ **800/535-6790;** www.flyingwheels.com), offering various escorted tours and cruises, with an emphasis on sports, as well as private tours in minivans with lifts. Other reputable operators are **Accessible Journeys** (☎ **800/TINGLES** or 610/521-0339; www.disabilitytravel.com), for slow walkers and wheelchair travelers; **The Guided Tour** (☎ **215/782-1370**); and **Directions Unlimited** (☎ **800/533-5343**).

For British travelers, the **Royal Association for Disability and Rehabilitation (RADAR),** Unit 12, City Forum, 250 City Rd., London EC1V 8AF (☎ **020/7250-3222**), publishes three holiday "fact packs" for £2 each or £5 for all three. The first provides general info, including planning and booking a holiday, insurance, and finances; the second outlines transportation available when going abroad and equipment for rent; the third deals with specialized accommodations. Another good resource is the **Holiday Care Service,** Imperial Building, 2nd Floor, Victoria Road, Horley, Surrey RH6 7PZ (☎ **01293/774-535;** fax 01293/784-647), a national charity advising on accessible accommodations for the elderly and persons with disabilities. Annual membership is £30.

FOR GAYS & LESBIANS

Since 1861, Italy has had liberal legislation regarding homosexuality, but that doesn't mean it has always been looked on favorably in a Catholic country.

Homosexuality is much more accepted in the north than in the south, especially in Sicily, though Taormina has long been a gay mecca. However, all major towns and cities have an active gay life, especially Florence, Rome, and Milan, which considers itself the "gay capital" of Italy and is the headquarters of **ARCI Gay,** the country's leading gay organization with branches throughout Italy. Capri is the gay resort of Italy, rivaled only by the gay beaches of Venice.

As a companion to this guide, you may want to pick up ***Frommer's Gay & Lesbian Europe,*** with helpful chapters on Rome, Florence, Venice, and Milan.

If you want help planning your trip, the **International Gay & Lesbian Travel Association** (IGLTA; ☎ **800/448-8550** or 954/776-2626; www.iglta.org) can link you with the appropriate gay-friendly service organization or tour specialist. With around 1,200 members, it offers quarterly newsletters, marketing mailings, and a membership directory that's updated quarterly. Members are kept informed of gay and gay-friendly hoteliers, tour operators, and airline and cruise-line representatives.

Out and About (☎ **800/929-2268** or 212/645-6922; www.outandabout.com) has been hailed for its "straight" reporting about gay travel. It offers a monthly newsletter packed with good information on the global gay and lesbian scene, and its Web site features links to gay and lesbian tour operators and other gay-themed travel links. *Out and About's* guidebooks are available at most major bookstores and through **A Different Light Bookstore,** 151 W. 19th St. (☎ **800/343-4002** or 212/989-4850; www.adlbooks.com).

Other general-type U.S. gay and lesbian travel agencies include **Family Abroad** (☎ **800/999-5500** or 212/459-1800) and **Above and Beyond Tours** (☎ **800/397-2681**). In the United Kingdom, try **Alternative Holidays** (☎ **020/7701-7040**; fax 020/7708-5668; e-mail info@alternativeholidays.com).

FOR SENIORS

One of the benefits of age is that travel often costs less. Always bring an ID card, especially if you've kept your youthful glow. Also mention the fact that you're a senior when you first make your travel reservations, since many airlines and hotels offer discount programs for senior travelers.

Members of the **American Association of Retired Persons (AARP;** ☎ **800/424-3410;** www.aarp.org) get discounts on hotels, airfares, and car rentals. The AARP offers members a wide range of special benefits, including *Modern Maturity* magazine and a monthly newsletter. If you're not already a member, do yourself a favor and join.

SAGA International Holidays, 222 Berkeley St., Boston, MA 02116 (☎ **800/343-0273**), offers inclusive tours and cruises for those 50 and older. SAGA also sponsors the more substantial **"Road Scholar Tours"** (☎ **800/621-2151**), which are fun-oriented but with an educational bent.

If you want something more than the average vacation or guided tour, try **Elderhostel** (☎ **877/426-8056;** www.elderhostel.org) or the University of New Hampshire's **Interhostel** (☎ **800/733-9753**), both variations on the same theme: educational travel for senior citizens. On these escorted tours, the days are packed with seminars, lectures, and field trips; and the sightseeing is all led by academic experts. The courses in both programs are ungraded, involve no homework, and often focus on the liberal arts. They're not luxury vacations but are fun and fulfilling.

FOR STUDENTS

The best resource for students is the **Council on International Educational Exchange (CIEE).** It can set you up with an ID card (see below), and its travel branch, **Council Travel Service (CTS),** 205 E. 42nd St., New York, NY 10017 (☎ **800/226-8624** in the United States to find your local branch, or 212/822-2700; www.counciltravel.com), is the world's biggest student travel agency operation. It can get you discounts on plane tickets, rail passes, and the like. Ask them for a list of CTS offices in major cities, so you can keep the discounts flowing (and aid lines open) as you travel.

From CIEE you can obtain the $18 **International Student Identity Card (ISIC),** the only officially acceptable form of student ID, good for cut rates on rail passes, plane tickets, and other discounts. It also provides you with basic health and life insurance and a 24-hour help line. If you're no longer a student but are still under 26, you can get a **GO 25 card** from the same people; it'll get you the insurance and some of the discounts (but not student admission prices in museums). CTS also sells **Eurailpasses** and **YHA (Youth Hostel Association)** passes and can book hostel or hotel accommodations.

CTS's **U.K. office** is at 28A Poland St. (Oxford Circus), London WIV 3DB (☎ **020/7437-7767**); the **Italy office** is at Via Genova 16, 00184 Roma (☎ **06-46791**). In Canada, **Travel CUTS,** 200 Ronson St., Suite 320, Toronto, ONT M9W 5Z9 (☎ **800/667-2887** or 416/614-2887; www.travelcuts.com), offers similar services. **Usit Campus,** 52 Grosvenor Gardens, London SW1W 0AG (☎ **020/7730-3402;** www.campustravel.co.uk), opposite Victoria Station, is Britain's leading specialist in student and youth travel.

8 Getting There

BY PLANE

High season on most airlines' routes to Rome is usually June to the beginning of September. This is the most expensive and most crowded time to travel. **Shoulder season** is April to May, early September to October, and December 15 to 24. **Low season** is November 1 to December 14 and December 25 to March 31.

FROM NORTH AMERICA Fares to Italy are constantly changing, but you can expect to pay somewhere in the range of $400 to $800 for a direct round-trip ticket from New York to Rome in coach class.

Flying time to Rome from New York, Newark, and Boston is 8 hours, from Chicago 10 hours, and from Los Angeles 12½ hours. Flying time to Milan from New York, Newark, and Boston is 8 hours, from Chicago 9¼ hours, and from Los Angeles 11½ hours.

American Airlines (☎ **800/433-7300;** www.aa.com) offers daily nonstop flights to Rome from Chicago's O'Hare, with flights from all parts of American's vast network making connections into Chicago. **TWA** (☎ **800/ 892-4141;** www.twa.com) offers daily nonstop flights from New York's JFK to Rome, Milan, and Venice. **Delta** (☎ **800/241-4141;** www.delta-air.com) also flies from New York's JFK to both Milan and Rome; separate flights depart every evening for both destinations. **United** (☎ **800/538-2929;** www.ual.com) has service to Milan only from Dulles in Washington, D.C. **US Airways** (☎ **800/428-4322;** www.usairways.com) offers one flight daily to Rome out of Philadelphia (you can connect through Philly from most major U.S. cities). And **Continental** (☎ **800/525-0280;** www.flycontinental.com) flies twice daily to Rome from its hub in Newark.

Canadian Airlines International (☎ **800/426-7000;** www.cdnair.ca) flies daily from Toronto to Rome. Two of the flights are nonstop; the others touch down en route in Montréal, depending on the schedule.

British Airways (☎ **800/AIRWAYS;** www.british-airways.com), **Virgin Atlantic Airways** (☎ **800/862-8621;** www.fly.virgin.com), **Air France** (☎ **800/237-2747;** www.airfrance.com), **Northwest/KLM** (☎ **800/374-7747;** www.klm.nl), and **Lufthansa** (☎ **800/645-3880;** www.lufthansa-usa.com) offer some attractive deals for anyone interested in combining a trip to Italy with a stopover in, say, Britain, Paris, Amsterdam, or Germany.

Alitalia (☎ **800/223-5730** in the United States, 514/842-8241 in Canada; www.alitalia.it/english/index.html) is the Italian national airline, with nonstop flights to Rome from different North American cities, including New York (JFK), Newark, Boston, Chicago, and Miami. Nonstop flights into Milan are from New York (JFK), Newark, and Los Angeles. From Milan or Rome, Alitalia can easily book connecting domestic flights if your final destination is elsewhere in Italy. Alitalia participates in the frequent-flyer programs of other airlines, including Continental and US Airways.

FROM THE UNITED KINGDOM Operated by the European Travel Network, www.discount-tickets.com is a great online source for regular and discounted airfares to destinations around the world. You can also use this site to compare rates and book accommodations, car rentals, and tours. Click on "Special Offers" for the latest package deals. Students should also try **Campus Travel** (☎ **0171/730-2101;** www.usitcampus.co.uk).

British newspapers are always full of classified ads touting slashed fares to Italy. One good source is ***Time Out.*** London's ***Evening Standard*** has a daily travel section, and the Sunday editions of almost any newspaper will run many ads. Although competition is fierce, one well-recommended company that consolidates bulk ticket purchases and then passes the savings on to its consumers is **Trailfinders** (☎ **020/7937-5400** in London). It offers access to tickets on such carriers as SAS, British Airways, and KLM.

CEEFAX, a British TV information service included on many home and hotel TVs, runs details of package holidays and flights to Italy and beyond. Just switch to your CEEFAX channel and you'll find a menu of listings that includes travel information.

Both **British Airways** (☎ **0345/222-111** in the U.K.; www.british-airways.com) and **Alitalia** (☎ **020/7602-7111;** www.alitalia.it/english/index.html) have frequent flights from London's Heathrow to Rome, Milan, Venice, Pisa (the gateway to Florence), and Naples. Flying time from London to these cities is from 2 to 3 hours. British Airways also has one direct flight a day from Manchester to Rome. **Virgin Atlantic** doesn't serve Italy at all at press time.

Fly for Less: Tips for Getting the Best Airfares

- **Take advantage of APEX fares.** Advance-purchase booking, or APEX, fares are often the key to getting the lowest fare. You generally must be willing to make your plans and buy your tickets as far ahead as possible: The **21-day APEX** is seconded only by the **14-day APEX,** with a stay in Italy of 7 to 30 days. Since the number of seats allocated to APEX fares is sometimes less than 25% of plane capacity, the early bird gets the low-cost seat. There's often a surcharge for flying on a weekend, and cancellation and refund policies can be strict.
- **Watch for sales.** You'll almost never see sales during July and August or the Thanksgiving or Christmas seasons, but at other times you can get

great deals. In the last couple of years, there have been amazing deals on winter flights to Rome. If you already hold a ticket when a sale breaks, it may pay to exchange it, even if you incur a $50 to $75 penalty charge. Note, however, that the lowest-priced fares are often nonrefundable, require advance purchase of 1 to 3 weeks and a certain length of stay, and carry penalties for changing dates of travel. So, when you're quoted a fare, make sure you know exactly what the restrictions are before you commit.

- If your schedule is flexible, ask if you can secure a cheaper fare by **staying an extra day** or by **flying midweek.** (Many airlines won't volunteer this information.)
- **Consolidators,** also known as bucket shops, are a good place to find low fares, often below even the airlines' discounted rates. There's nothing shady about the reliable ones—basically, they're just big travel agents who get discounts for buying in bulk and pass some of the savings on to you. Before you pay, however, ask for a confirmation number from the consolidator and then call the airline itself to confirm your seat. Be prepared to book your ticket with a different consolidator—there are many to choose from—if the airline can't confirm your reservation. Also be aware that consolidator tickets are usually nonrefundable or come with stiff cancellation penalties.

  We've gotten great deals on many occasions from ✪ **Cheap Tickets** (☎ **800/377-1000**; www.cheaptickets.com). **Council Travel** (☎ **800/226-8624;** www.counciltravel.com) and **STA Travel** (☎ **800/781-4040;** www.sta.travel.com) cater especially to young travelers, but their bargain-basement prices are available to people of all ages. Other reliable consolidators include **Lowestfare.com** (☎ **888/278-8830;** www.lowestfare.com); **1-800/AIRFARE** (www.1800airfare.com); **Cheap Seats** (☎ **800/451-7200;** www.cheapseatstravel.com); and **1-800/FLY-CHEAP** (www.flycheap.com).
- Search the **Internet** for cheap fares—though it's still best to compare your findings with the research of a dedicated travel agent, if you're lucky enough to have one, especially when you're booking more than just a flight. A few of the better-respected virtual travel agents are **Travelocity** (www.travelocity.com) and **Microsoft Expedia** (www.expedia.com).

  Smarter Living (www.smarterliving.com) is a good source for great last-minute deals. Take a moment to register, and every week you'll get an e-mail summarizing the discount fares available from your departure city. The site also features concise lists of links to hotel, car rental, and other hot travel deals.

  See **"Planning Your Trip: An Online Directory,"** on p. 47 for further discussion on this topic and other recommended sites.

BY TRAIN

If you plan to travel heavily on the European rails, you'll do well to secure the latest copy of the ***Thomas Cook European Timetable of Railroads.*** This 500-plus-page timetable accurately documents all of Europe's mainline passenger rail services. It's available from **Forsyth Travel Library,** 226 Westchester Ave., White Plains, NY 10604 (☎ **800/367-7984;** www.forsyth.com), for $27.95 (plus $4.95 shipping in the U.S. and $5.95 in Canada), or at travel specialty stores like **Rand McNally,** 150 E. 52nd St., New York, NY 10022 (☎ **212/758-7488**).

New electric trains have made travel between France and Italy faster and more comfortable than ever before. **France's TGVs** travel at speeds of up to

185 miles per hour and have cut travel time between Paris and Turin from 7 to 5½ hours and between Paris and Milan from 7½ to 6¾ hours. **Italy's ETRs** travel at speeds of up to 145 miles per hour and currently run between Milan and Lyon (5 hours), with a stop in Turin.

EUROPE-WIDE RAIL PASSES

EURAILPASS Many travelers to Europe take advantage of one of the greatest travel bargains, the **Eurailpass,** which permits unlimited first-class rail travel in any country in western Europe (except the British Isles) and Hungary in eastern Europe. Oddly, it doesn't include travel on the rail lines of Sardinia, which are organized independently of the rail lines of the rest of Italy.

The advantages are tempting: There are no tickets; simply show the pass to the ticket collector and then settle back to enjoy the scenery. Seat reservations are required on some trains. Many of the trains have couchettes (sleeping cars), for which an extra fee is charged. Obviously, the 2- or 3-month traveler gets the greatest economic advantages. To obtain full advantage of a 15-day or 1-month pass, you'd have to spend a great deal of time on the train.

Eurailpass holders are entitled to considerable reductions on certain buses and ferries, as well. You'll get a 20% reduction on second-class accommodations from certain companies operating ferries between Naples and Palermo or for crossings to Sardinia and Malta.

A **Eurailpass** is $554 for 15 days, $718 for 21 days, $890 for 1 month, $1,260 for 2 months, and $1,558 for 3 months. Children 3 and under travel free providing they don't occupy a seat (otherwise they're charged half fare); children 4 to 11 are charged half fare. If you're under 26, you can buy **a Eurail Youthpass,** entitling you to unlimited second-class travel for $388 for 15 days, $499 for 21 days, $623 for 1 month, $882 for 2 months, and $1,089 for 3 months.

The **Eurail Saverpass,** valid all over Europe for first class only, offers discounted 15-day travel for groups of three or more people traveling together April to September or two people traveling together October to March. The price is $470 for 15 days, $610 for 21 days, $756 for 1 month, $1,072 for 2 months, and $1,324 for 3 months.

The **Eurail Flexipass** allows you to visit Europe with more flexibility. It's valid in first class and offers the same privileges as the Eurailpass. However, it provides a number of individual travel days you can use over a much longer period of consecutive days. That makes it possible to stay in one city and yet not lose a single day of travel. There are two passes: 10 days of travel in 2 months for $654 and 15 days of travel in 2 months for $862.

Having many of the same qualifications and restrictions as the previously described Flexipass is the **Eurail Youth Flexipass.** Sold only to travelers under 26, it allows 10 days of travel within 2 months for $458 and 15 days of travel within 2 months for $599.

EUROPASS The **Europass** is more limited than the Eurailpass but may offer better value for visitors traveling over a smaller area. It's good for 2 months and allows 5 days of rail travel within three to five European countries (Italy, France, Germany, Switzerland, and Spain) with contiguous borders. For individual travelers, 5 days of travel costs $348 in first class, $233 in second; 6 days of travel $368 in first class, $253 in second; 8 days of travel $448 in first class, $313 in second; 10 days of travel, $528 in first class, $363 in second; and 15 days of travel $728 in first class, $513 in second.

For travelers under 26, a **Europass Youth** is available. The fares are 35% to 55% off those quoted above, and the pass is good only for second-class travel. Unlike the adult Europass, there's no discount for a companion.

Where to Buy a Pass

In **North America,** you can buy these passes from travel agents or rail agents in major cities like New York, Montréal, and Los Angeles. Eurailpasses are also available from the North American offices of CIT Tours (see "Getting Around Italy," below) or through **Rail Europe** (☎ **800/438-7245;** www.raileurope.com). No matter what everyone tells you, you can buy Eurailpasses in Europe as well as in America (at the major train stations), but they're more expensive. Rail Europe can also give you information on the rail/drive versions of the passes.

For details on the rail passes available in the **United Kingdom,** stop in at or contact the **International Rail Centre,** Victoria Station, London SW1V 1JZ (☎ **0990/848-848**). The staff can help you find the best option for the trip you're planning. Some of the most popular are the **Inter-Rail** and **Under 26** passes, entitling you to unlimited second-class travel in 26 European countries.

Under 26 tickets are a worthwhile option for travelers under 26. They allow you to move leisurely from London to Rome, with as many stopovers en route as you want, using a different route southbound (through Belgium, Luxembourg, and Switzerland) from the return route northbound (exclusively through France). All travel must be completed within 1 month of the departure date. Under 26 tickets from London to Rome cost from £133 for the most direct route or from £209 for a roundabout route through the south of France.

Wasteels, adjacent to Platform 2 in Victoria Station, London SW1V 1JZ (☎ **020/7834-7066**), will sell a **Rail Europe Senior Pass** to U.K. residents for £5. With it, a British resident over 60 can buy discounted tickets on many of Europe's rail lines. To qualify, you must present a valid British Senior Citizen rail card, available for £16 at any BritRail office upon presentation of proof of age and British residency.

BY CAR

If you're already on the Continent, particularly in a neighboring country such as France or Austria, you may want to drive to Italy. However, you should make arrangements in advance with your car-rental company.

It's also possible to drive from London to Rome, a distance of 1,124 miles (1,810km), via Calais/Boulogne/Dunkirk, or 1,085 miles (1,747km) via Oostende/Zeebrugge, not counting channel crossings by Hovercraft, ferry, or the Chunnel. Milan is some 400 miles (644km) closer to Britain than is Rome. If you cross over from England and arrive at one of the continental ports, you still face a 24-hour drive. Most drivers play it safe and budget 3 days for the journey.

Most of the roads from western Europe leading into Italy are toll-free, with some notable exceptions. If you use the Swiss superhighway network, you'll have to buy a special tax sticker at the frontier. You'll also pay to go through the St. Gotthard Tunnel into Italy. Crossings from France can be through the Mont Blanc Tunnel, for which you'll pay, or you can leave the French Riviera at Menton and drive directly into Italy along the Italian Riviera toward San Remo.

If you don't want to drive such distances, ask a travel agent to book you on a Motorail arrangement where the train carries your car. This service, however, is good only to Milan, as there are no car and sleeper expresses running the 400 miles (644km) south to Rome.

9 Escorted Tours & Independent Package Tours

The biggest operator of escorted tours is **Perillo Tours** (☎ **800/431-1515** or 201/307-1234 in the United States; www.perillotours.com), family operated for three generations—perhaps you've seen the TV commercials featuring the "King of Italy," Mario Perillo, and his son. Since it was founded in 1945, it has sent more than a million travelers to Italy on guided tours. Perillo's tours cost much less than you'd spend if you arranged a comparable trip yourself. Accommodations are in first-class hotels, and guides tend to be well qualified and well informed.

Another contender is **Italiatour,** a company of the Alitalia Group (☎ **800/845-3365** or 212/765-2183; www.italiatour.com), offering a wide variety of tours through all parts of Italy. It specializes in packages for independent travelers (not tour groups) who ride from one destination to another by train or rental car. In most cases, the company sells pre-reserved accommodations, which are usually less expensive than if you had reserved them yourself. Because of the company's close link with Alitalia, the prices quoted for air passage are sometimes among the most reasonable on the retail market.

Trafalgar Tours (☎ **800/854-0103;** www.trafalgartours.com) is one of Europe's largest tour operators, offering affordable guided tours with lodgings in unpretentious hotels. Check with your travel agent for more information on these tours (Trafalgar takes calls only from agents).

One of Trafalgar's leading competitors is **Globus/Cosmos Tours** (☎ **800/221-0090;** www.globusandcosmos.com). Globus has first-class escorted coach tours of various regions lasting from 8 to 16 days. Cosmos, a budget branch of Globus, sells escorted tours of about the same length. Tours must be booked through a travel agent, but you can call the 800 number for brochures. Another competitor is **Insight Vacations** (☎ **800/582-8380**), which books superior first-class, fully escorted motor-coach tours lasting from 1 week to a 36-day grand tour.

Finally, **Abercrombie & Kent** (☎ **800/323-7308** in the U.S., or **020/7730-9600** in the U.K.) offers a variety of luxurious premium packages. Your overnight stays will be in meticulously restored castles and exquisite Italian villas, most of which are four- and five-star accommodations. Several trips are offered, including tours of the Lake Garda region and the southern territory of Calabria. The company's Web site is **www.abercrombiekent.com**.

The oldest travel agency in Britain, **Cox & Kings** (☎ **020/7873-5006**) specializes in unusual, if pricey, holidays. Their Italy offerings include organized tours through the country's gardens and sites of historic or aesthetic interest, opera tours, pilgrimage-style visits to sites of religious interest, and food- and wine-tasting tours. The staff is noted for their focus on tours of ecological and environmental interest.

10 Getting Around Italy

BY PLANE

Italy's domestic air network on **Alitalia** (☎ **800/223-5730** in the United States, or 020/7602-7111 in the U.K.; www.alitalia.it/english/index.html) is one of the largest and most complete in Europe. There are some 40 airports serviced regularly from Rome, and most flights are under an hour. Fares vary, but some discounts are available. Tickets are discounted 50% for passengers 2 to 11 years old; for passengers 12 to 22, there's a youth fare. And anyone can get a 30% reduction by taking domestic flights departing at night.

BY TRAIN

Trains provide a medium-priced means of transport, even if you don't buy the Eurailpass or one of the special Italian Railway tickets (below). As a rule of thumb, second-class travel usually costs about two-thirds the price of an equivalent first-class trip. A couchette (a private fold-down bed in a communal cabin) requires a supplement above the price of first-class travel. In a land where mamma and bambini are highly valued, children 4 to 11 receive a discount of 50% off the adult fare, and children 3 and under travel free with their parents.

An **Italian Railpass** (known in Italy as a **BTLC Pass**) allows non-Italian citizens to ride as much as they like on Italy's entire rail network. Buy the pass in the United States or at main train stations in Italy, have it validated the first time you use it at any rail station, and ride as frequently as you like within the time validity. An 8-day pass is $273 first class and $182 second, a 15-day pass $341 first class and $228 second, a 21-day pass $396 first class and $264 second, and a 30-day pass $478 first class and $318 second. All passes have a $15 issuing fee per class.

With the Italian Railpass and each of the other special passes, a supplement must be paid to ride on certain rapid trains, designated **ETR-450** or **Pendolino trains.** The rail systems of Sardinia are administered by a separate entity and aren't included in the Railpass or any of the other passes.

Another option is the **Italian Flexirail Card,** which entitles you to a predetermined number of days of travel on any rail line in a certain time period. It's ideal for passengers who plan in advance to spend several days sightseeing before boarding a train for another city. A pass giving 4 possible travel days out of a block of 1 month is $216 first class and $144 second, a pass for 8 travel days stretched over a 1-month period $302 first class and $202 second, and a pass for 12 travel days within 1 month $389 first class and $259 second.

You can buy these passes from any travel agent or by calling ☎ **800/248-7245.** You can also call ☎ **800/EURAIL** or **800/EUROSTAR.**

Travel Times Between the Major Cities

	Distance	Air Travel Time	Train Travel Time	Driving Time
Florence to Milan	298km/185 mi	55 min	2½ hrs	3½ hrs
Florence to Venice	281km/174 mi	2 hrs, 5 min	4 hrs	3 hrs, 15 min
Milan to Venice	267km/166 mi	50 min	3½hrs	3 hrs, 10 min
Rome to Florence	277km/172 mi	1 hr, 10 min	2½ hrs	3 hrs, 20 min
Rome to Milan	572km/355 mi	1 hr, 5 min	5 hrs	6 hrs, 30 min
Rome to Naples	219km/136 mi	50 min	2½ hrs	2½ hrs
Rome to Venice	528km/327 mi	1 hr, 5 min	5 hrs, 15 min	6 hrs
Rome to Genoa	501km/311 mi	1 hr	6 hrs	5 hrs, 45 min
Rome to Turin	669km/415 mi	1 hr, 5 min	9–11 hrs	7 hrs, 45 min

BY BUS

Italy has an extensive and intricate bus network, covering all regions. However, because rail travel is inexpensive, the bus isn't the preferred method of travel. Besides, drivers seem to go on strike every 2 weeks.

One of the leading bus operators is **SITA,** Viale del Cadorna 105, Florence (☎ **055/47821**). SITA buses serve most parts of the country, especially the central belt, including Tuscany, but not the far frontiers. Among the largest of the other companies, with special emphasis in the north and central tiers, is **Autostradale,** Piazzale Castello, Milan (☎ **02/801-161**). **Lazzi,** Via Mercadante 2, Florence (☎ **055/363-041**), goes through Tuscany, including Siena, and much of central Italy.

Where these nationwide services leave off, **local bus companies** operate in most regions, particularly in the hill sections and the alpine regions where rail travel isn't possible. For more information, see "Getting There" in the various city, town, and village sections.

BY CAR

U.S. and Canadian drivers don't need an **International Driver's License** to drive a rented car in Italy. However, if driving a private car, they need such a license.

You can apply for an International Driver's License at any **American Automobile Association (AAA)** branch. You must be at least 18 and have two 2-by-2-inch photos and a photocopy of your U.S. driver's license with your AAA application form. The actual fee for the license can vary, depending on where it's issued. To find the AAA office nearest you, check the local phone directory or contact **AAA's national headquarters** at (☎ **800/222-4357** or 407/444-4240; www.aaa.com). Remember that an International Driver's License is valid only if physically accompanied by your original driver's license and only if signed on the back. In Canada, you can get the address of the **Canadian Automobile Association** closest to you by calling ☎ **613/247-0117.**

The **Automobile Club d'Italia (ACI),** Via Marsala 8, 00185 Roma (☎ **06/4998-2389**), is open Monday to Friday 8am to 2pm. The ACI's 24-hour **Information and Assistance Center (CAT)** is at Via Magenta 5, 00185 Roma (☎ **06-4477**). Both offices are near the main rail station (Stazione Termini).

RENTALS Many of the most charming landscapes in Italy lie away from the main cities, far away from the train stations. For that, and for sheer convenience and freedom, renting a car is usually the best way to explore the country. But you have to be a pretty aggressive and alert driver who won't be fazed by super-high speeds on the autostrada or by narrow streets in the cities and towns. Italian drivers have truly earned their reputation as bad but daring.

However, the legalities and contractual obligations of renting a car in Italy (where accident and theft rates are very high) are a little complicated. To rent a car here, a driver must have nerves of steel, a sense of humor, a valid driver's license, and a valid passport and (in most cases) be over 25. Insurance on all vehicles is compulsory, though any reputable rental firm will arrange it in advance before you're even given the keys.

The three major rental companies in Italy are **Avis** (☎ **800/331-2112;** www.avis.com), **Budget** (☎ **800/527-0700;** www.budgetrentacar.com), and **Hertz** (☎ **800/654-3131;** www.hertz.com). U.S.-based companies specializing in European car rentals are **Auto Europe** (☎ **800/223-5555;** www.autoeurope.com), **Europe by Car** (☎ **800/223-1516,** 800/252-9401 in California, or 212/581-3040 in New York; www.europebycar.com), and **Kemwel** (☎ **800/678-0678;** www.kemwel.com).

In some cases, slight discounts are offered to members of the American Automobile Association (AAA) or the American Association of Retired Persons (AARP). Be sure to ask.

Each company offers a **collision-damage waiver (CDW)** at $15 to $25 per day (depending on the car's value). Some companies include CDWs in the prices they quote; others don't. This extra protection will cover all or part of the repair-related costs if you have an accident. (In some cases, even if you buy the CDW, you'll pay $200 to $300 per accident. Ask questions before you sign.) If you don't have CDW and have an accident, you'll usually pay for all damages, up to the car's replacement cost. Because most newcomers aren't familiar with local driving customs and conditions, we highly recommend you buy the CDW. (But first check your existing auto insurance and also see what's available through your credit cards. Note that credit cards may cover collision but will usually not cover liability.) In addition, because of Italy's rising theft rate, all three of the major U.S.-based companies offer theft and break-in protection policies (Avis and Budget require it). For pickups at most Italian airports, all three companies must impose a 10% government tax. To avoid that charge, consider picking up your car at an inner-city location. There's also an unavoidable 19% government tax, though more and more companies are including this in the rates they quote.

GASOLINE Gasoline (known as *benzina*) is expensive in Italy. Be prepared for sticker shock every time you fill up even a medium-sized car with *super benzina,* which has the octane rating appropriate for most of the cars you'll be able to rent. It's priced throughout the country at around 1,900L (95¢) per liter (about 7,000L/$3.50 per gallon). Gas stations on the autostrade are open 24 hours, but on regular roads gas stations are rarely open on Sunday, many close from noon to 3pm for lunch, and most shut down after 7pm. Make sure the pump registers zero before an attendant starts refilling your tank. A popular scam, particularly in the south, is to fill your tank before resetting the meter, so you pay not only your bill but the charges run up by the previous motorist.

DRIVING RULES The Italian Highway Code follows the Geneva Convention, and Italy uses international road signs. Driving is on the right, passing on the left. Violators of the highway code are fined; serious violations may also be punished by imprisonment. In cities and towns, the speed limit is 50 kilometers per hour (kmph), or 31 miles per hour (m.p.h.). For all cars and motor vehicles on main roads and local roads, the limit is 90 kmph, or 56 m.p.h. For the autostrade (national express highways), the limit is 130 kmph, or 81 m.p.h. Use the left lane only for passing. If a driver zooms up behind you on the autostrade with his or her lights on, that's your sign to get out of the way! Use of seat belts is compulsory.

ROAD MAPS The best touring maps are published by the **Automobile Club d'Italia (ACI)** and the **Italian Touring Club,** or you can buy the maps of the **Carta Automobilistica d'Italia,** covering Italy in two maps on a scale of 1:800,000 (1cm = 8km). These two maps should fulfill the needs of most motorists.

All maps mentioned above are sold at certain newsstands and at all major bookstores in Italy, especially those with travel departments. Many travel bookstores in the United States also carry them. If U.S. outlets don't have these maps, they often offer **Michelin's red map of Italy** (no. 988), on a scale of 1:1,000,000 (1cm = 10km).

BREAKDOWNS & ASSISTANCE In case of car breakdown or for any tourist information, foreign motorists can call ☎ **116** (nationwide telephone service). For road information, itineraries, and all sorts of travel assistance, call ☎ **06-4477** (ACI's information center located near the Automobile Club d'Italia). Both services operate 24 hours.

A Home Away from Home: Renting Your Own Apartment or Villa

If you're looking to rent a villa or an apartment, one of the best agencies to call is **Rentals in Italy** (☎ **800/726-6702** or 805/987-5278; www.rentvillas.com). It's the representative for the Cuendet properties, some of the best in Italy, and its agents are very helpful in tracking down the perfect place to suit your needs. Cuendet's representatives in the United Kingdom, and one of the best all-around agents in London, is **International Chapters** (☎ **020/7586-9451**). **Marjorie Shaw's Insider's Italy** (☎ **718/855-3878;** members.aol.com/italitin/mshaw/htm) is a small, upscale outfit run by a very personable agent who's thoroughly familiar with all her properties and with Italy in general.

For some of the top properties, call the local representative of the **Cottages to Castles** group. In the U.S., that's the **Parker Company, Ltd.** (☎ **800/280-2811** or 617/596-8282; www.theparkercompany.com). In the U.K., contact **Cottages to Castles** (☎ **1622/762-883**). One of the most reasonably priced agencies is **Villas and Apartments Abroad, Ltd.** (☎ **800/433-3020**). **Vacanze in Italia** (☎ **800/533-5405** or 413/528-6610; www.homeabroad.com) handles hundreds of rather upscale rentals. A popular but very pricey agency is **Villas International** (☎ **800/221-2260** or 415/281-0910; www.villasintl.com).

If you want to stay in a historic palazzo, contact **Abitare la Storia,** Località L'Amorosa, 53048 Sinalunga, Siena (☎ **0577-632-256;** fax 0577/632-160; www.arbitarelastoria.it). This nonprofit organization represents owner-managed hotels, residences, restaurants, and convention centers around Italy, in the city and the country.

11 Tips on Dining

For a quick bite, go to a ***bar.*** Although bars in Italy do serve alcohol, they function mainly as cafes. Prices have a split personality: *al banco* is standing at the bar, while *à tavola* means sitting at a table where you'll be waited on and charged two to four times as much. In bars you can find *panini* sandwiches on various rolls and *tramezzini* (giant triangles of white-bread sandwiches with the crusts cut off). These both run 2,000 to 6,000L ($1 to $3) and are traditionally put in a kind of tiny press to flatten and toast them so the crust is crispy and the filling hot and gooey; microwaves have unfortunately invaded and are everywhere, turning panini into something resembling a soggy hot tissue.

Pizza a taglio or ***pizza rustica*** indicates a place where you can order pizza by the slice—though Florence is infamous for serving some of Italy's worst pizza this way. Florentines fare somewhat better at ***pizzerie,*** casual sit-down restaurants that cook large, round pizzas with very thin crusts in wood-burning ovens. A ***tavola calda*** (literally "hot table") serves ready-made hot foods you can take away or eat at one of the few small tables often available. The food is usually very good, and you can get away with a full meal at a *tavola calda* for well under 25,000L ($12.50). A ***rosticceria*** is the same type of place, and you'll see chickens roasting on a spit in the window.

A full-fledged restaurant will go by the name ***osteria, trattoria,*** or ***ristorante.*** Once upon a time, these terms meant something—*osterie* were basic places where you could get a plate of spaghetti and a glass of wine; *trattorie* were casual places serving full meals of filling peasant fare; and *ristoranti* were fancier places, with waiters in bow ties, printed menus, wine lists, and hefty prices. Nowadays, fancy restaurants often go by the name of *trattoria* to cash in on the associated charm factor, trendy spots use *osteria* to show they're hip, and simple inexpensive places sometimes tack on *ristorante* to ennoble themselves.

The ***pane e coperto*** (bread and cover) is a 1,500 to 5,000L (75¢ to $2.50) cover charge that you must pay at most restaurants for the mere privilege of sitting at the table. Most Italians eat a leisurely full meal—appetizer and first and second courses—at lunch and dinner and will expect you to do the same, or at least a first and second course. To request the bill, ask *"Il conto, per favore"* (eel *con*-toh, pore fah-*vohr*-ay). A tip of 15% is usually included in the bill these days, but if you're unsure, ask *"È incluso il servizio?"* (ay een-*cloo*-soh eel sair-*vee*-tsoh?).

You'll find at many restaurants, especially larger ones and in cities, a ***menu turistico*** (tourist's menu), costing from 15,000 to 50,000L ($7.50 to $25), sometimes called ***menu del giorno*** (menu of the day). This set-price menu usually covers all meal incidentals—including table wine, cover charge, and 15% service charge—along with a first course (*primo*) and second course (*secondo*), but it almost always offers an abbreviated selection of pretty bland dishes: spaghetti in tomato sauce and slices of pork. Sometimes a better choice is a ***menu à prezzo fisso*** (fixed-price menu). It usually doesn't include wine but sometimes covers the service and *coperto* and often offers a wider selection of better dishes, occasionally house specialties and local foods. Ordering à la carte, however, offers you the best chance for a memorable meal. Even better, forego the menu entirely and put yourself in the capable hands of your waiter.

The ***enoteca*** wine bar is a growing, popular marriage of a wine bar and an *osteria,* where you can sit and order from a host of local and regional wines by the glass (usually 2,500L to 8,000L/$1.50 to $4.70) while snacking on finger foods (and usually a number of simple first course possibilities) that reflect the region's fare. Relaxed and full of ambience and good wine, these are great spots for light and inexpensive lunches—perfect to educate your palate and recharge your batteries.

Fast Facts: Italy

American Express Offices are found in Rome at Piazza di Spagna 38 (☎ **06/67-641**), in Florence on Via Dante Alighieri (☎ **055/50-981**), in Venice at San Marco 1471 (☎ **041/520-0844**), and in Milan at Via Brera 3 (☎ **02/7200-3693**). See individual city listings.

Business Hours Regular business hours are generally Monday to Friday 9am (sometimes 9:30am) to 1 and 3:30pm (sometimes 4) to 7 or 7:30pm. In July and August, **offices** may not open in the afternoon until 4:30 or 5pm. **Banks** are open Monday to Friday 8:30am to 1 or 1:30pm and 2 or 2:30 to 4pm and closed all day Saturday, Sunday, and national holidays. The *riposo* (midafternoon closing) is often observed in Rome, Naples, and most southern cities; however, in Milan and other northern and central cities the custom has been abolished by some merchants. Most shops are closed on Sunday, except for certain tourist-oriented stores that are now permitted to remain open on Sunday during the high season. If you're in Italy in summer and the heat is intense, we suggest that you, too, learn the custom of the *riposo.*

Drugstores At every drugstore *(farmacia)* there's a list of those that are open at night and on Sunday.

Electricity The electricity in Italy varies considerably. It's usually alternating current (AC), varying from 42 to 50 cycles. The voltage can be anywhere from 115 to 220. It's recommended that any visitor carrying electrical appliances obtain a transformer. Check the exact local current at the hotel where you're staying. Plugs have prongs that are round, not flat; therefore, an adapter plug is also needed.

Embassies/Consulates In case of an emergency, embassies have a 24-hour referral service.

The **U.S. Embassy** is in Rome at Via Vittorio Veneto 119A (☎ **06/46-741;** fax 06/488-2672). **U.S. consulates** are in Florence at Lungarno Amerigo Vespucci 38 (☎ **055/239-8276;** fax 055/284-088) and in Milan at Via Principe Amedeo 2–10 (☎ **02/29-03-51-41**). There's also a consulate in Naples on Piazza della Repubblica 1 (☎ **081/583-8111**). The consulate in Genoa is at Via Dante 2 (☎ **010/58-44-92**). For consulate hours, see individual city listings.

The **Canadian Consulate** and passport service is in Rome at Via Zara 30 (☎ **06/445-981**). The **Canadian Embassy** in Rome is at Via G. B. de Rossi 27 (☎ **06/445-981;** fax 06/445-98750).

The **U.K. Embassy** is in Rome at Via XX Settembre 80A (☎ **06/482-5441;** fax 06/487-3324). The **U.K. Consulate** in Florence is at Lungarno Corsini 2 (☎ **055/284-133;** fax 055/219-112). The **Consulate General** in Naples is at Via Francesco Crispi 122 (☎ **081/663-511;** fax 081/761-3720). In Milan, contact the office at Via San Paolo 7 (☎ **02/723-001**).

The **Australian Embassy** is in Rome at Via Alessandria 215 (☎ **06/852-721;** fax 06/852-723-00). The **Australian Consulate** is in Rome at Corso Trieste 25 (☎ **06/852-721**).

The **New Zealand Embassy** is in Rome at Via Zara 28 (☎ **06/441-7171;** fax 06/440-2984). The **Irish Embassy** in Rome is at Piazza di Campitelli 3 (☎ **06/697-912;** fax 06/679-2354). For consular queries, dial ☎ **06/697-91211.**

Emergencies Dial ☎ **113** for ambulance, police, or fire. In case of a breakdown on an Italian road, dial ☎ **116** at the nearest telephone box; the nearest Automobile Club of Italy (ACI) will be notified to come to your aid.

Legal Aid The consulate of your country is the place to turn for legal aid, though offices can't interfere in the Italian legal process. They can, however, inform you of your rights and provide a list of attorneys. You'll have to pay for the attorney out of your pocket—there's no free legal assistance. If you're arrested for a drug offense, about all the consulate will do is notify a lawyer about your case and perhaps inform your family.

Liquor Laws Wine with meals has been a normal part of family life for hundreds of years in Italy. Children are exposed to wine at an early age, and consumption of alcohol isn't anything out of the ordinary. There's no legal drinking age for buying or ordering alcohol. Alcohol is sold day and night throughout the year, since there's almost no restriction on the sale of wine or liquor in Italy.

Mail Mail delivery in Italy is notoriously bad. Your family and friends back home may receive your postcards in 1 week, or it might take 2 weeks (sometimes longer). Postcards, aerogrammes, and letters weighing up to 20 grams sent to the United States and Canada cost 1,300L (65¢), to the United Kingdom and Ireland 800L (40¢), and to Australia and New Zealand 1,400L (70¢). You can buy stamps at all post offices and at *tabacchi* (tobacco) stores.

Newspapers/Magazines In major cities, it's possible to find the *International Herald Tribune* or *USA Today* as well as other English-language newspapers and magazines, including *Time* and *Newsweek,* at hotels and news kiosks. The *Rome Daily American* is published in English.

Police Dial ☎ **113,** the all-purpose number for police emergency assistance in Italy.

Rest Rooms All airport and rail stations, of course, have rest rooms, often with attendants, who expect to be tipped. Bars, nightclubs, restaurants, cafes, gas stations, and all hotels have facilities as well. Public toilets are also found near many of the major sights. Usually they're designated as *WC* (water closet) or *donne* (women) or *uomini* (men). The most confusing designation is *signori* (gentlemen) and *signore* (ladies), so watch that final *i* and *e!* Many public toilets charge a small fee or employ an attendant who expects a tip, so always keep a few 200L and 500L coins on hand. It's also a good idea to carry some tissues in your pocket or purse—they often come in handy.

Safety The most common menace, especially in large cities, particularly Rome, is the plague of pickpockets and roving gangs of Gypsy children who virtually surround you, distract you in all the confusion, and steal your purse or wallet. Never leave valuables in a car and never travel with your car unlocked. A U.S. State Department travel advisory warns that every car (whether parked, stopped at a traffic light, or even moving) can be a potential target for armed robbery.

Taxes As a member of the European Union, Italy imposes a **value-added tax** (called **IVA** in Italy) on most goods and services. The tax that most affects visitors is the one imposed on hotel rates, which ranges from 9% in first- and second-class hotels to 19% in deluxe hotels.

Non-EU (European Union) citizens are entitled to a **refund of the IVA** if they spend more than 300,000L ($150) at any one store, before tax. To claim your refund, request an invoice from the cashier at the store and take it to the Customs office (*dogana*) at the airport to have it stamped before you leave. *Note:* If you're going to another EU country before flying home, have it stamped at the airport Customs office of the last EU country you'll be in (for example, if you're flying home via Britain, have your Italian invoices stamped in London). Once back home, mail the stamped invoice (keep a photocopy for your records) back to the original vendor within 90 days of the purchase. The vendor will, sooner or later, send you a refund of the tax you paid at the time of your original purchase. Reputable stores view this as a matter of ordinary paperwork and are businesslike about it. Less-honorable stores might lose your dossier. It pays to deal with established vendors on large purchases. You can also request that the refund be credited to the credit card with which you made the purchase; this is usually a faster procedure.

Calling Italy

To call Italy from the United States, dial the **international prefix, 011;** then Italy's **country code, 39;** then the city code (for example, **06** for Rome and **055** for Florence), which is now built into every number; then the actual **phone number.**

Note that numbers in Italy range from four to eight digits in length. Even when you're calling within the same city, you must dial that city's area code—including the zero. A Roman calling another Rome number must dial 06 before the local number.

Many shops are now part of the **"Tax Free for Tourists"** network (look for the sticker in the window). Stores participating in this network issue a check along with your invoice at the time of purchase. After you have the invoice stamped at Customs, you can redeem the check for cash directly at the Tax Free booth in the airport (in Rome, it's past Customs; in Milan's airports the booth is inside the Duty Free shop) or mail it back in the envelope provided within 60 days.

Telephone A **local phone call** in Italy costs around 220L (10¢). **Public phones** accept coins, precharged phone cards (*scheda* or *carta telefonica*), or both. You can buy a *carta telefonica* at any *tabacchi* (tobacconists; most display a sign with a white *T* on a brown background) in increments of 5,000L ($2.50), 10,000L ($5), and 15,000L ($7.50). To make a call, pick up the receiver and insert 200L or your card (break off the corner first). Most phones have a digital display that'll tell you how much money you've inserted (or how much is left on the card). Dial the number, and don't forget to take the card with you after you hang up.

To **call from one city code to another,** dial the city code, complete with initial zero, then the number. To **dial direct internationally,** dial **00,** then the country code, the area code, and the number. **Country codes** are as follows: the United States and Canada 1, the United Kingdom 44, Ireland 353, Australia 61, New Zealand 64. Make international calls from a public phone if possible, because hotels almost invariably charge ridiculously inflated rates for direct dial, but bring plenty of *schede* to feed the phone. Calls dialed directly are billed on the basis of the call's duration only. A reduced rate is applied 11pm to 8am on Monday to Saturday and all day Sunday. Direct-dial calls from the United States to Italy are much cheaper, so arrange for whomever to call you at your hotel.

Italy has recently introduced a series of **international phone cards** *(scheda telefonica internazionale)* for calling overseas. They come in increments of 50 (12,500L/$6.25), 100 (25,000L/$12.50), 200 (50,000L/$25), and 400 (100,000L/$50) *unita* (units), and they're usually available at tabacchi and bars. Each *unita* is worth 250L (15¢) of phone time; it costs 5 *unita* (1,250L/65¢) per minute to call within Europe or to the United States or Canada and 12 *unita* (3,000L/$1.50) per minute to call Australia or New Zealand. You don't insert this card into the phone; merely dial ☎ **1740,** then * 2 (star 2), for instructions in English when prompted.

To ring the free **national telephone information** (in Italian) in Italy, dial ☎ **12. International information** is available at ☎ **176** but costs 1,200L (60¢) a shot.

To make **collect or calling card calls,** drop in 200L (10¢) or insert your card, dial one of the numbers below, and an American operator will shortly come on to assist you (as Italy has yet to discover the joys of the Touch-Tone phone, you'll have to wait for the operator to come on). The following calling-card numbers work all over Italy: **AT&T** ☎ 172-1011, **MCI** ☎ 172-1022, **Sprint** ☎ 172-1877. To make collect calls to a country besides the United States, dial ☎ **170** (free), and practice your Italian counting in order to relay the number to the Italian operator. Tell him or her you want it *a carico del destinatario.*

Don't count on all Italian phones having Touch-Tone service! You may not be able to access your voice mail or answering machine if you call home from Italy.

Time In terms of standard time zones, Italy is 6 hours ahead of eastern standard time in the United States. Daylight saving time goes into effect in Italy each year from the end of March to the end of September.

Tipping This custom is practiced with flair in Italy—many people depend on tips for their livelihoods. In **hotels,** the service charge of 15% to 19% is already added to a bill. In addition, it's customary to tip the chambermaid 1,000L (50¢) per day; the doorman (for calling a cab) 1,000L (50¢); and the bellhop or porter 3,000 to 5,000L ($1.50 to $2.50) for carrying your bags to your room. A concierge expects about 15% of his or her bill, as well as tips for extra services performed, which could include help with long-distance calls. In expensive hotels these lire amounts are often doubled.

In **restaurants and cafes,** 15% is usually added to your bill to cover most charges. If you're not sure whether this has been done, ask *"È incluso il servizio?"* (ay een-*cloo*-soh eel sair-*vee*-tsoh?). An additional tip isn't expected, but it's nice to leave the equivalent of an extra couple of dollars if you've been pleased with the service. Checkroom attendants expect 1,500L (75¢), and washroom attendants should get 500 to 700L (25¢ to 35¢). Restaurants are required by law to give customers official receipts.

Taxi drivers expect at least 15% of the fare.

Water Most Italians take mineral water with their meals; however, tap water is safe everywhere, as are public drinking fountains. Unsafe sources will be marked ACQUA NON POTABILE. If tap water comes out cloudy, it's only the calcium or other minerals inherent in a water supply that often comes untreated from fresh springs.

Planning Your Trip: An Online Directory

Frommer's Online Directory will help you take better advantage of the travel-planning information available online. Part 1 lists general Internet resources that can make any trip easier, such as sites for obtaining the best possible prices on airline tickets. In Part 2 you'll find some top sites specifically for Italy.

This is not a comprehensive list, but a discriminating selection to get you started. Recognition is given to sites based on their content value and ease of use. Inclusion here is not paid for—unlike some Web-site rankings, which are based on payment. Finally, remember that this is a press-time snapshot of leading Web sites; some undoubtedly will have evolved, changed, or moved by the time you read this.

1 The Top Travel-Planning Web Sites

By Lynne Bairstow

Lynne Bairstow is the co-author of *Frommer's Mexico*, and the editorial director of *e-com* magazine.

WHY BOOK ONLINE?

Online agencies have come a long way over the past few years, now providing tips for finding the best fare and giving you suggested travel dates or times that will yield the lowest price if your plans are at all flexible. Other sites even allow you to establish the price you're willing to pay, and then they check the airlines' willingness to accept it. However, in some cases, these sites may not always yield the best price. Unlike a travel agent, for example, they may not have access to charter flights offered by wholesalers.

Online booking sites aren't the only places to reserve airline tickets—all major airlines have their own Web sites and often offer incentives (bonus frequent flyer miles or net-only discounts, for example) when you buy online or buy an e-ticket.

The new trend is toward conglomerated booking sites. By mid-2000, a consortium of U.S. and European-based airlines is planning to launch an as-yet unnamed Web site that will offer fares lower than those available through travel agents. United, Delta, Northwest, and Continental have initiated this effort, based on their success at selling airline seats on their own sites.

Check Out Frommer's Site

We highly recommend **Arthur Frommer's Budget Travel Online (www.frommers.com)** as an excellent travel-planning resource. Of course, we're a little biased, but you'll find indispensable travel tips, reviews, monthly vacation giveaways, and online booking. Among the most popular features of this site are the regular "Ask the Expert" bulletin boards, which feature Frommer's authors answering your questions via online postings.

Subscribe to Arthur Frommer's Daily Newsletter **(www.frommers.com/newsletters)** to receive the latest travel bargains and inside travel secrets in your e-mailbox every day. You'll read daily headlines and articles from the dean of travel himself, highlighting last-minute deals on airfares, accommodations, cruises, and package vacations.

Search our Destinations archive **(www.frommers.com/ destinations)** of more than 200 domestic and international destinations for great places to stay and dine, and tips on sightseeing. Once you've researched your trip, the online reservation system **(www.frommers.com/booktravelnow)** takes you to Frommer's favorite sites for booking your vacation at affordable prices.

The best of the travel planning sites are now highly personalized; they store your seating preferences, meal preferences, tentative itineraries, and credit-card information, allowing you to quickly plan trips or check agendas.

In many cases, booking your trip online can be better than working with a travel agent. It gives you the widest variety of choices, control, and the 24-hour convenience of planning your trip when you choose. All you need is some time—and often a little patience—and you're likely to find the fun of online travel research will greatly enhance your trip.

WHO SHOULD BOOK ONLINE?

Online booking is best for travelers who want to know as much as possible about their travel options, for those who have flexibility in their travel dates, and for bargain hunters.

One of the biggest successes in online travel for both passengers and airlines is the offer of last-minute specials, such as American Airlines' weekend deals or other Internet-only fares that must be purchased online. Another advantage is that you can cash in on incentives for booking online, such as rebates or bonus frequent-flyer miles.

Business and other frequent travelers also have found numerous benefits in online booking as advances in mobile technology provide travelers with the ability to check flight status, change plans, or get specific directions from handheld computing devices, mobile phones, and pagers. Some sites will even e-mail or page a passenger if his or her flight is delayed.

Online booking is increasingly able to accommodate complex itineraries, even for international travel. The pace of evolution on the Net is rapid, so you'll probably find additional features and advancements by the time you visit these sites. The future holds ever-increasing personalization and customization for online travelers.

TRAVEL-PLANNING & BOOKING SITES

Below are listings for sites for planning and booking travel. The following sites offer domestic and international flight, hotel, and rental-car bookings, plus news, destination information, and deals on cruises and vacation packages. Free (one-time) registration is required for booking.

Travelocity (incorporates Preview Travel). www.travelocity.com; www.previewtravel.com; www.frommers.travelocity.com

Travelocity is Frommer's online travel-planning and booking partner. Travelocity uses the SABRE system to offer reservations and tickets for more than 400 airlines, plus reservations and purchase capabilities for more than 45,000 hotels and 50 car-rental companies. An exclusive feature of the SABRE system is its **Low Fare Search Engine,** which automatically searches for the three lowest-priced itineraries based on a traveler's criteria. Last-minute deals and consolidator fares are included in the search. If you book with Travelocity, you can select specific seats for your flights with online seat maps, and also view diagrams of the most popular commercial aircraft. Its hotel finder provides street-level location maps and photos of selected hotels. With the **Fare Watcher** e-mail feature, you can select up to five routes and receive e-mail notices when the fare changes by $25 or more.

Travelocity's **Destination Guide** includes updated information on some 260 destinations worldwide—supplied by Frommer's.

Note to AOL Users: You can book flights, hotels, rental cars, and cruises on AOL at keyword: Travel. The booking software is provided by Travelocity/Preview Travel and is similar to the Internet site. Use the AOL "Travelers Advantage" program to earn a 5% rebate on flights, hotel rooms, and car rentals.

Expedia. expedia.com

Expedia is Travelocity's major competitor. It offers several ways of obtaining the best possible fares: **Flight Price Matcher** service allows your preferred airline to match an available fare with a competitor; a comprehensive **Fare Compare** area shows the differences in fare categories and airlines; and **Fare Calendar** helps you plan your trip around the best possible fares. Its main limitation is that like many online databases, Expedia focuses on the major airlines and hotel chains, so don't expect to find too many budget airlines or one-of-a-kind B&Bs here.

TRIP.com. www.trip.com

TRIP.com began as a site geared toward business travelers, but its innovative features and highly personalized approach have broadened its appeal to leisure travelers as well. It is the leading travel site for those using mobile devices to access Internet travel information.

TRIP.com includes a trip-planning function that provides the average and lowest fare for the route requested, in addition to the current available fare. An on-site "newsstand" features breaking news on airfare sales and other travel specials. Among its most popular features are Flight TRACKER and intelliTRIP. **Flight TRACKER** allows users to track any commercial flight en route to its destination anywhere in the U.S., while accessing real-time FAA-based flight monitoring data. **intelliTRIP** is a travel search tool that allows users to identify the best airline, hotel, and rental-car rates in less than 90 seconds.

In addition, the site offers e-mail notification of flight delays, plus city resource guides, currency converters, and a weekly e-mail newsletter of fare updates, travel tips, and traveler forums.

Yahoo Travel. www.travel.yahoo.com
Yahoo is currently the most popular of the Internet information portals, and its travel site is a comprehensive mix of online booking, daily travel news, and destination information. The **Best Fares** area offers what it promises, plus provides feedback on refining your search if you have flexibility in travel dates or times. There is also an active section of Message Boards for discussions on travel in general and specific destinations.

LAST-MINUTE DEALS & OTHER ONLINE BARGAINS

There's nothing airlines hate more than flying with lots of empty seats. The Net has enabled airlines to offer last-minute bargains to entice travelers to fill those seats. Most of these are announced on Tuesday or Wednesday and are valid for travel the following weekend, but some can be booked weeks or months in advance. You can sign up for weekly e-mail alerts at the airlines' own sites or check sites that compile lists of these bargains, such as **Smarter Living** or **WebFlyer** (see below). To make it easier, visit a site that will round up all the deals and send them in one convenient weekly e-mail.

Important Note: See "Getting There," in chapter 2 for the Web addresses of airlines serving Italy. These sites offer schedules and flight booking, and most have pages where you can sign up for e-mail alerts for weekend deals and other late-breaking bargains.

Cheap Tickets. www.cheaptickets.com
Cheap Tickets has exclusive deals that aren't available through more-mainstream channels. One caveat about the Cheap Tickets site is that it will offer fare quotes for a route, and later show this fare as not valid for your dates of travel—most other Web sites, such as Expedia, consider your dates of travel before showing what fares are available. Despite its problems, Cheap Tickets can be worth the effort because its fares can be lower than those offered by its competitors.

✪ 1travel.com. www.1travel.com
Here you'll find deals on domestic and international flights and hotels. 1travel.com's **Saving Alert** compiles last-minute air deals so you don't have to scroll through multiple e-mail alerts. A feature called "Drive a little using low-fare airlines" helps map out strategies for using alternative airports to find lower fares. And **Farebeater** searches a database that includes published fares, consolidator bargains, and special deals exclusive to 1travel.com. *Note:* The travel agencies listed by 1travel.com have paid for placement.

Bid for Travel. www.bidfortravel.com
Bid for Travel is another of the travel auction sites, similar to Priceline (see below), which are growing in popularity. In addition to airfares, Internet users can place a bid for vacation packages and hotels.

LastMinuteTravel.com. www.lastminutetravel.com
Suppliers with excess inventory come to this online agency to distribute unsold airline seats, hotel rooms, cruises, and vacation packages. The site has great deals but an excess of advertisements and slow-loading graphics.

Moment's Notice. www.moments-notice.com
As the name suggests, Moment's Notice specializes in last-minute vacation deals. You can browse for free, but if you want to purchase a trip you have to join Moment's Notice, which costs $25.

✪ Priceline.com. travel.priceline.com
Priceline lets you "name your price" for domestic and international airline tickets and hotel rooms. You select a route and dates, guarantee with a credit

card, and make a bid for what you're willing to pay. If one of the airlines in Priceline's database has a fare lower than your bid, your credit card will automatically be charged for a ticket.

Be aware that Priceline has some restrictions. You can't say when you want to fly—you have to accept any flight leaving between 6am and 10pm on the dates you selected, and you may have to make a stopover. No frequent-flyer miles are awarded, and tickets are nonrefundable and can't be exchanged for another flight. So if your plans change, you're out of luck. However, Priceline can be good for travelers who have to take off on short notice (and who are thus unable to qualify for advance purchase discounts). Just be sure to shop around first, because if you overbid you'll be required to purchase the ticket—and Priceline will pocket the difference between what it paid for the ticket and what you bid.

Priceline says that over 35% of all reasonable offers for domestic flights are being filled on the first try, with much higher fill rates on popular routes (New York to San Francisco, for example). They define "reasonable" as not more than 30% below the lowest generally available advance-purchase fare for the same route.

Smarter Living. www.smarterliving.com
Best known for its e-mail dispatch of weekend deals on 20 airlines, Smarter Living also keeps you posted about last-minute bargains.

SkyAuction.com. www.skyauction.com
An auction site with categories for airfare, travel deals, hotels, and much more.

Travelzoo.com. www.travelzoo.com
At this Internet portal, more than 150 travel companies post special deals. It features a Top 20 list of the best deals on the site, selected by its editorial staff each Wednesday night. This list is also available via an e-mailing list, free to those who sign up.

WebFlyer. www.webflyer.com
WebFlyer is a comprehensive online resource for frequent flyers and also has an excellent listing of last-minute air deals. Click on "Deal Watch" for a roundup of weekend deals on flights, hotels, and rental cars from domestic and international suppliers.

ONLINE TRAVELER'S TOOLBOX

Exchange Rates. www.x-rates.com
See what your dollar or pound is worth in Italian lire.

✪ **Foreign Languages for Travelers. www.travlang.com**
Learn basic terms in more than 70 languages, and click on any underlined phrase to hear what it sounds like. (*Note:* speakers and free audio software are required.) This site also offers hotel and airline finders with excellent prices and a simple system to get the listings you are looking for.

InnSite. www.innsite.com
Listings for inns and B&Bs around the globe. Find an inn at your destination, have a look at images of the rooms, check prices and availability, and then send e-mail to the innkeeper if you have further questions. This is an extensive directory of bed and breakfast inns, but it only includes listings if the proprietor submitted one (*note:* it's free to get an inn listed). The descriptions are written by the innkeepers, and many link to the inns' own Web sites.

Check Your E-mail While You're on the Road

You don't have to be out of touch just because you don't carry a laptop while you travel. Web browser–based free e-mail programs make it much easier to stay in e-touch.

Just open a freemail account at a browser-based provider, such as **MSN Hotmail (hotmail.com)** or **Yahoo! Mail (mail.yahoo.com).** AOL users should check out **AOL Netmail,** and **USA.NET (www.usa.net)** comes highly recommended for functionality and security. You can find hints, tips, and a mile-long list of freemail providers at **www.emailaddresses.com.**

Be sure to give your freemail address to the family members, friends, and colleagues with whom you'd like to stay in touch while you're in Italy. All you'll need to check your freemail account while you're away from home is a Web connection, easily available at Internet cafes, copy shops, and cash- and credit-card Internet-access machines (often available in hotel lobbies or business centers). After logging on, just point the browser to **www.hotmail.com, www.yahoo.com,** or the address of any other service you're using. Enter your user name and password, and you'll have access to your mail, both for receiving and sending messages to friends and family back home, for just a few dollars an hour.

The Net Café Guide **(www.netcafeguide.com/mapindex.htm)** will help you locate Internet cafes at hundreds of locations around the globe. This guide has also listed specific locations of cybercafes in Rome and Florence. Cybercafes come and go, and are becoming more widespread, so you're likely to find them in more and more cities across Italy by the time you travel.

U.S. Customs Service Traveler Information. **www.customs.ustreas.gov/travel/index.htm**

HM Customs & Excise Passenger Enquiries. **www.open.gov.uk.**

Canada Customs and Revenue Agency. **www.ccra-adrc.gc.ca.**

Australian Customs. **www.dfat.gov.au**

New Zealand Customs Service. **www.customs.govt.nz.**
Planning a shopping spree and wondering what you're allowed to bring home? Check the latest regulations at these thorough sites.

Visa ATM Locator. **www.visa.com/pd/atm/**

MasterCard ATM Locator. **www.mastercard.com/atm**
Find ATMs in hundreds of cities around the world. Both sites include maps for some locations, and both list airport ATM locations, some with maps.

The Weather Channel. **www.weather.com**
Weather forecasts for cities around the world.

2 The Top Web Sites for Italy

Updated by Matthew Garcia

Many of the following sites give users the option of using English or Italian. Although some will initially come up in Italian, you can follow the icons for English versions. If the location of the English version isn't evident at first, scroll down to find an American or British flag.

The major problem with Web sites that cover Italy (and, I'm sure, many other destinations) is updating—or rather, the lack thereof. Many people think that Web sites must be more up-to-date than guidebooks, but so far that's definitely not true. One way to check on how stale the information might be is to use a search engine that tells you when each site was updated—I like AltaVista for this, but there are others. If you run across a description or listing of an establishment or event that you know will make or break your trip, *always* double-check that information; call ahead before you block out time for an activity or destination that might turn out to be closed.

COUNTRY GUIDES

Dolce Vita. www.dolcevita.com
The self-proclaimed "insider's guide to Italy" is all about style—as it pertains to fashion, cuisine, design, and travel. A scrolling bulletin at the site shares factoids, survey results, and other bits of Italian news, and the events section brims with major performing arts, music, and museum happenings. While clearly driven by consumers and advertisers, Dolce Vita is a good place to stay current on trends in modern Italian culture.

✪ **In Italy Online. www.initaly.com**
This extensive site helps you find all sorts of accommodations (including country villas, historic homes, and gay-friendly hotels) and includes tips on shopping, dining, driving, and viewing works of art. In Italy Online has an information-packed section dedicated to each region of Italy, plus a section on books and movies to help enjoy the Italian experience at home. Join the mailing list for monthly updates.

Italian Tourist Web Guide. www.itwg.com
Need help planning your travel schedule? Be sure to check out the Italian Tourist Web Guide, which each month recommends new itineraries for art lovers, nature buffs, wine enthusiasts, and other Italiophiles. The site features a searchable directory of accommodations, transportation tips, and city-specific lists of restaurants and attractions.

Italy Hotel Reservation. www.italyhotel.com
With close to 10,000 listings solely for Italy, this functional site is an ideal place to research and reserve lodgings.

Italy in a Flash. www.italyflash.com
This site offers hotel information, railway and airline schedules, the latest exchange rates, weather, and current news.

ItalyTour.com. www.italytour.com
Search ItalyTour.com for all things Italian. This vast directory covers arts, culture, business, tours, entertainment, restaurants, lodging, real estate, news and media, shopping, sports, transportation, and major Italian cities. It's not the most excitingly designed site, but it does include photo collections and videos in the Panorama section.

Travel Europe: Italy. www.traveleurope.it
Take a look at the travel packages highlighted in this guide, or do some travel planning of your own by clicking on one of the many cities and regions on the map of Italy at the top. Although there's some discussion of art and history, most of the site is taken up by hotel information. You can also book online if you wish.

Travel.org: Italy. www.travel.org/italy.html
Stroll region-by-region through Italy with help from this directory, or cut to the chase by getting a rundown on food, lodging, nightlife, currency, and language. This site links to countless Italy resources, both in English and in Italian.

✪ **Wandering Italy. www.wandering.com**
Amid lyrical travel stories of language mishaps and cobblestone streets, penned by an international brood of tourists, Wandering Italy takes you on virtual reality tours of spots such as the village of Marciana Marina and the Piazza San Marco. This site's slide shows reveal views of stunning scenery and artwork from more than 25 of Italy's cities.

AROUND ITALY

THE AMALFI COAST & CAPRI

Amalfi and the Amalfi Coast. www.starnet.it/italy/incostam.htm
While promoting the lemon liqueur and stained glass produced on the Amalfi Coast, this site provides a map and a photo-illustrated historical overview of each of the region's little cities and villages. Hotel and restaurant links lead to simple ads. If you're inclined to learn something on your vacation, check out the cooking school.

✪ **Capri Online. www.caprionline.com or www.capri.it.**
This site glistens with enticing photographs of beaches and beautiful scenery, and descriptions of seafood dishes and luxury lodgings. A profile showcases a local artist and his miniature ceramic replica of Capri. On the practical side, you can look through the directory of hotels, ranked by stars, or download free travel brochures and maps.

APULIA

Welcome to Apulia. www.inmedia.it/Puglia/eng
Make reservations online to stay in a three- to five-star hotel in the heel of Italy's boot. Take a virtual tour through the castles of the Adriatic Valley, the Trulli district, or view the nature and archeology of the Upper Murgia.

BOLOGNA

Gambero Rosso: Bologna. www.gamberorosso.it/e/bologna/bologna.asp
Get the inside scoop on Bolognan cuisine from Gambero Rosso's decidedly particular critics, who steer you away from the tourist traps and toward eateries that capture Bologna's culinary history. The site's writers are equally selective in their hotel recommendations.

Information About Bologna. archiginnasio.dsnet.it/engl_bologna.html
Although this site doesn't score a lot of points for design, it does provide the travel staples: hotel and restaurant reviews, museum hours and prices, bookstore and theater directories, and, whenever possible, links. A bonus: essays and poems by an American student smitten with Bologna. A drawback: lack of recent updates make it unreliable for current event planning.

FLORENCE

Firenze by Net (**www.mega.it/florence**) and Firenze Net (**english.firenze.net**) are both Italy-based Web sites with English translations and good general information on Florence. **Informacittà (www.informacitta.net)** is an excellent little guide to this month's events, exhibits, concerts, and theater; the English-language version was still pending as of this writing, however.

See also "Tuscany," below.

Florence Information. www.firenze.turismo.toscana.it.
This is the official tourist office site for Florence, but as of this writing, it's only in Italian (though an English version is coming). If you're fluent in Italian, or if you find the promised English version up and running, you'll find a wealth of up-to-date information (events, museums, practical details) on Florence and Tuscany, including a searchable "hotels" form that allows you to specify amenities, categories, and the like; the site responds by spitting out a list of where you can get contact info and see current room rates.

Florence Online. www.fionline.it/wel_eng.html
Use the tourism section of this Florence site to book a hotel room, consult a map, or plan a day of sightseeing followed by a night on the town.

Florence and The Divine Comedy. english.firenze.net/dante
See Florence through the eyes of Dante. While a narrator reads passages written by the famous author, you can see photos of key Florence spots mentioned in *The Divine Comedy* and learn about the history of each place. You can also find a helpful directory of Florentine museums, monuments, and tour guides.

Florence by Net. www.florence.ala.it
Most of the attractions listed within this site are ranked—hotels by luxury, restaurants by price, and museums by importance. You'll also find links to Florence's concert listings, weather reports, business information, and Internet facilities.

Your Way to Florence. www.arca.net/florence.htm
If you're going to Florence to see the magnificent works of art housed there, first take a peek at this site, a combined tour guide and Florence art history lesson that includes a glossary of art terms such as "altar frontal" (no, this doesn't refer to Michelangelo's *David*). The site provides hotel reviews and city news as well.

The Italian Riviera

Liguria. www.emmeti.it/welcome/liguria/index.uk.html
This guide to the scythe-shaped region known as the Italian Riviera encompasses Genova, Savona, Imperia, and La Spezia. The hotel sections include information on room rates, amenities, and locations and offer online booking.

Milan

Milan International Home Page. www.milanoin.it/index_eng.asp
After taking an online tour through the museums, monuments, parks, libraries, exhibits, shops, and fairs of Italy's fashion capital, search for a restaurant by ethnicity or for a hotel by neighborhood. Although this site's seemingly random mix of Italian and English is a bit confusing, and can make navigating difficult, the sheer volume of information, combined with helpful icons, makes it a worthwhile stop.

Milan City Center Map and Guide.
www.citylightsnews.com/ztmimp1.htm
A big map shows the location of each of Milan's highlights as well as hotels by Brera (a sponsor). Click on the name of an attraction for a description and photo. Visit the links page for guides to arts, entertainment, government, schools, sports, business, news, and, of course, shopping.

Milan Malpensa Airport. www.airwise.com/airports/europe/MXP/
It would be hard to get lost in the airport in Milan after visiting this site, which provides an extensive overview of the terminal along with information

on airlines, ground transportation to and from Malpensa, car rentals, parking, and airport hotels.

Naples

Naples in Virtual Reality. ww2.webcomp.com/virtuale/us/napoli/movie.htm
This site will give you a good idea of what you can see in Napoli. The virtual reality tour shows the Piazza del Plebiscito, Il Maschio Angioino, the Galleria Umberto, and other great artifacts. It's almost like being there.

Pompeii

Pompeii Forum Project. pompeii.virginia.edu
The University of Virginia and the National Endowment for the Humanities explore urban history and design in an unearthed Pompeii. Their site is full of cool photos, educational information, and even some virtual reality segments and video clips.

Rome

Nerone: The Insider's Guide. www.nerone.cc
Get tips on everything from museums to Roman public toilets. Check the site's events menu to see which arts and entertainment highlights will coincide with your visit to the Eternal City. Sort through archives of the Nerone newspaper as well.

Roma Online. www.romaonline.net/eng
This online tourist guide has pictures, QuickTime video, and virtual renderings of Roman monuments and sights around the city. There is also information on getting around, enjoying the city's parks, sports, and shopping.

Rome Guide. www.romeguide.it
Click on the British flag for the English version of this site, which is so chock-full of information you'll need a pickax to excavate it. Each click of the mouse reveals multiple new layers of tourist information, extending beyond the typical hotel/restaurant listings and into ecotourism opportunities, walking tours, nightclubs, airfares, and other specifics. One unique feature is the ability to search for upcoming cultural events by venue.

Time Out Rome. www.timeout.co.uk
Download the latest issue of *Time Out Rome,* which offers a great up-to-date listing of events and exhibits.

✪ Traveling with Ed and Julie. www.twenj.com/romevisit.htm
Seasoned travelers advise first-timers on what to do when in Rome. Musing romantically about the ancient city, the pair will guide you to hotels, restaurants, excursions, quiet spots, tips on seeing Rome with kids, and, of course, attractions such as the Vatican and the Colosseum.

Vatican: The Holy See. www.vatican.va
The official site of the Vatican offers audio and video programs in multiple languages to accompany profiles of all the popes, the Vatican museum, the Roman Curia, and the Vatican library.

Sicily

Sicily For Tourists. www.sicily.infcom.it
Follow this site's ready-made itineraries to see the many treasures lurking in Palermo in the form of parks, cathedrals, great works of art, and nightlife. This site also has information about Sicilian culture, events, transportation,

lodging, public services, and businesses. Note that the events calendar does not seem to be regularly updated.

Etna Decade Volcano. www.geo.mtu.edu/~boris/ETNA.html
Learn everything you ever wanted to know about Mt. Etna, one of the world's most active volcanoes, which has been erupting in Sicily since about 1500 B.C. The site offers spectacular (and alarmingly recent) photographs, facts and figures, maps, weather forecasts, and a geology lesson or two.

TURIN

Tourism in Turin. www.comune.torino.it/turismo
Thumb through this vast Italian-language guide for the history of Turin and its symbols, cuisine, monuments, leisure activities, and academic centers. For a sample of the city's visual pleasures, check out the online photo gallery or virtual postcard rack.

TUSCANY

See also "Florence," above.

Chianti Doc Marketplace. www.chianti-doc.com
Taste a bit of Chianti's flavor at this site before traveling to the famous wine region. Take a quick online course in grape producing and Chianti Classico wines. You can also peek at Alitalia flight schedules and get information on booking vacation rentals in Chianti or Sienna.

Farm Holidays in Tuscany. www.toscana.agriturismo.net
Book your accommodations at this site if you'd like to stay on a Tuscan farm or at a rural bed-and-breakfast after traipsing through Tuscany countryside wineries. To help win you over, the site presents a photo-filled virtual tour of the province's cities, villages, and lovely landscapes.

Florence Bike Pages. www.abeline.it/fbp.htm
If you want to bike around Tuscany on your own, head for this helpful site. You'll find bike maps of Florence and Tuscany, instructions on how to bike solo, and information on bike supplements for the trains (many trains have a cargo car for bikes; on train schedules look for a bike icon that designates these trains).

The Heart of Tuscany. www.nautilus-mp.com/tuscany/indexing.htm
For each of five major art towns in Tuscany, this site provides a historical overview, photographs, maps, and a shopping guide. You'll find information on a range of accommodations, including historic residences, farmhouses, vacation rentals, and hotels, some of which take reservations online. More useful for its overview of the area than for updated information.

✪ Know it All: Know Tuscany. www.knowital.com
As the name suggests, this travel guide does seem to know it all about lodging, dining, and Tuscan wines. Set up everything from an agri-tourism stay at a Lucca vineyard estate to a romp through the tourist sites of Pisa. You'll even get some useful facts about weather, mosquitoes, and computer modems.

Pisa Online. www.pisaonline.it/e-default.htm
Once you've seen the tower, stick around to check out Pisa's art galleries, restaurants, shops, pubs, discos, golf courses, and hotels—with guidance from this site.

✪ Tourism in Tuscany. www.turismo.toscana.it
This is the official site for Tuscany, with an English-language version available. There are suggested itineraries, plus information on accommodations, dining,

spas, festivals, and the artistic heritage of the region. You'll also find links to every provincial tourist office site.

THE VENETO & THE DOLOMITES

Dolomiti Web. **www.dolomiti.it/eng**
This site is organized seasonally so that you can check out winter sports, spring fairs, and fall harvesting. Look through electronic postcards of the mountainous terrain. Make hotel reservations online.

Verona: City of Art and History. **www.intesys.it/tour/eng/verona.html**
Don't let the Montagues and Capulets bog you down; there's a lot more to do in Verona than reenact the scene at Juliet's balcony. For suggestions, peruse some itineraries here, where tours are based on historic themes such as Roman Verona, Verona as a city state, Austrian Verona, and the city's churches and monasteries. And if you must see the balcony, there's a Shakespeare tour as well.

VENICE

Baby Boomer's Venice. **www.writing.org/venice.htm**
For the post-backpacker/pre-senior tour set, this guide hits the spot. Navigate Venice's canals and gelato stands with help from a fellow baby boomer, who can tell you where to stay—and where *not* to stay—and point you to online reservation sites.

Carnival of Venice. **www.carnivalofvenice.com/uk**
Experience the carnival celebration of the city of gondolas (although the 2000 party has long been over, there is still no updated 2001 information in its place at press time—I assume this site will be updated as 2001 information becomes available). Or explore past carnivals, dating back to the year 1268, in the mask-filled historic section of this online guide to one of Italy's most grand annual events. Travelers also can find information about transportation, city services, and other Venice basics.

Venice, Italy Index. **www.iuav.unive.it/~juli/venindx.html**
A hodgepodge of information as varied and colorful as the city itself, this site can tell you about everything from the history of Venetian glass to how to learn Italian. If you're concerned about the murky sludge that passes for water in Venice, check the environment section for lagoon facts and figures.

Venice World. **www.veniceworld.com**
Modeled after a standard American Web directory, this site lists links to Venice's accommodations, centers for the arts, nightclubs, restaurants, sporting events, travel agencies, Internet service providers, transportation, schools, newspapers, and so forth.

Venezia Net. **www.doge.it**
Learn about the history of one of Europe's most heavily trodden tourist spots. Take virtual tours of the Doges' Palace and the Piazza San Marco. Skim through directories of hotels and travel agencies. Find out when you can catch the Carnival celebration or the Venice Film Festival.

GETTING AROUND

Autostrade S.P.A. **www.autostrade.it**
This site is a valuable resource for anyone brave enough to drive in Italy. The interactive Motorway Map helps you plan your route and prepare for the toll booths you'll encounter along the way. The site also offers traffic forecasts, safety tips, and lists of service stations.

CIT Tours. www.cittours.com
This tour company specializes in trips to Italy. Even if you're not interested in one of their group tours, you can buy all kinds of European rail passes online on this site, from Eurailpasses to passes that are specifically for the Italian railway system. The Italian Flexirail Card, in particular, entitles holders to a predetermined number of days on any rail line of Italy within a certain period. It must be purchased before you arrive in Italy, making CIT Tours a valuable contact.

Rail Europe. www.raileurope.com
Rail Europe lets you buy Eurail, Europass, and Brit Rail railroad passes online, as well as rail and drive packages and point-to-point travel in 35 European countries. Even if you don't want a rail pass, the site offers invaluable first- and second-class fare and schedule information for the most popular European rail routes.

Rail Pass Express. www.eurail.com
A good source for Eurail pass information, purchasing, and deals.

✪ **Subway Navigator. http://metro.ratp.fr:10001/bin/cities/english**
An amazing site with detailed subway route maps for Milan and Palermo and dozens of other cities around the world. Select a city and enter your departure and arrival points. Subway Navigator maps out your route and tells you how long the trip should take. It will even show your route on a subway map.

3 Settling into Rome

Rome is a city of images and sounds, all vivid and all unforgettable. You can see one of the most striking images at dawn—ideally from Janiculum Hill—when the Roman skyline, with its bell towers and cupolas, gradually comes into focus. As the sun rises, the full Roman symphony begins. First come the peals of church bells calling the faithful to Mass. Then the streets fill with cars, taxis, tour buses, and Vespas, the drivers gunning their engines and blaring their horns. Next the sidewalks become overrun with office workers, chattering as they rush off to their desks, but not before ducking into a cafe for their first cappuccino. Added to the mix are shop owners loudly throwing up the metal grilles protecting their stores and the fruit-and-vegetable stands being overrun with Romans out to buy the day's supply of fresh produce, haggling over prices and caviling over quality.

Around 10am the visitors—you included, Frommer's guidebook in hand—take to the streets, battling the crowds and traffic as they wend from Renaissance palaces and baroque buildings to ancient ruins like the Colosseum and the Forum. After you've spent a long day in the sun, marveling at the sights you've seen millions of times in photos and movies and in your dreams, you can pause to experience the charm of Rome at dusk. Find a cafe at summer twilight, and watch the shades of pink and rose turn to gold and copper as night falls. That's when a new Rome awakens. The cafes and restaurants grow more animated, especially if you've found one in an ancient piazza or along a narrow alley deep in Trastevere. After dinner, you can stroll by the lighted fountains and monuments (the Trevi Fountain and the Colosseum look magical at night) or through Piazza Navona and have a gelato—and the night is yours.

Most journalists are giving Rome an "A" for the way it's pulled off the Jubilee celebrations. Most foreign visitors who've been interviewed have told the press that it's like visiting "one of the world's great open-air museums." As of this writing, the huge crowds that were predicted had not reached the highest numbers that optimistic city officials had expected—perhaps thousands were afraid to visit because of all the advance warning about the hordes descending on the capital for the celebration. But perhaps due to this lighter crowd, the Jubilee has been running fairly smoothly.

In this chapter you'll find all the details to help you settle into Rome: how to get there and how to get around, where to find a comfortable hotel room, and where to enjoy great meals. In the next chapter we'll show you Rome's historic sites and magnificent museums, its varied shopping scene, its cultural highlights, and its nightlife.

1 Essentials

ARRIVING

BY PLANE Chances are you'll arrive at Rome's **Leonardo da Vinci International Airport** (☎ **06-65-951** or 06-6595-3640), popularly known as **Fiumicino,** $18^1/_2$ miles (30km) from the city center. (If you're flying by charter, you might wing into Ciampino Airport; see below.)

After you leave Passport Control, you'll see two **information desks** (one for Rome, one for Italy; ☎ **06-65-95-6074**). At the Rome desk you can pick up a general map and some pamphlets from Monday to Saturday 8:30am to 7pm; the staff can also help you find a hotel room if you haven't reserved ahead. A ***cambio*** (money exchange) operates daily 7:30am to 11pm, offering surprisingly good rates. **Luggage storage** is available 24 hours daily in the main arrivals building, costing 5,000L ($2.50) per bag.

There's a **train station** in the airport. To get into the city, follow the signs marked *treni* for the 30-minute shuttle to Rome's main station, **Stazione Termini** (arriving on Track 22). The shuttle runs 7:30am to 10pm for 16,000L ($8) one way. On the way you'll pass a machine dispensing tickets, or you can buy them in person near the tracks if you don't have small bills on you. When you arrive at Termini, get out of the train quickly and grab a baggage cart. It's a long schlep from the track to the exit or to the other train connections, and baggage carts can be scarce.

A **taxi** from Da Vinci to the city costs 75,000L ($37.50) and up for the 1-hour trip, depending on traffic. The expense may be worth it if you have a lot of luggage or just don't want to be bothered with the train trip. Call ☎ **06-6645,** 06-3570, or 06-4994 for information.

If you arrive on a charter flight at **Ciampino Airport** (☎ **06-794-941**), you can take a COTRAL bus, departing every 30 minutes or so for the Anagnina stop of *Metropolitana* (subway) Line A. Take Line A to Stazione Termini, where you can make your final connections. Trip time is about 45 minutes, costing 1,500L (75¢). A **taxi** from this airport to Rome costs the same as the one from the Da Vinci airport (above), but the trip is shorter (about 40 minutes).

BY TRAIN OR BUS Trains and buses (including trains from the airport) arrive in the center of old Rome at the silver **Stazione Termini,** Piazza dei Cinquecento (☎ **1478/880-88**); this is the train, bus, and subway transportation hub for all Rome and is surrounded by many hotels (especially cheaper ones).

If you're taking the **Metropolitana** (subway), follow the illuminated red-and-white M signs. To catch a **bus,** go straight through the outer hall and enter the sprawling bus lot of Piazza dei Cinquecento. You'll also find **taxis** there.

The station is filled with services. At a branch of the **Banca San Paolo di Torino** (between Tracks 8 to 11 and Tracks 12 to 15), you can exchange money. **Informazioni Ferroviarie** (in the outer hall) dispenses information on rail travel to other parts of Italy. There's also a **tourist information booth** here, along with baggage services, newsstands, and snack bars.

BY CAR From the north, the main access route is the **Autostrada del Sole (A1),** cutting through Milan and Florence, or you can take the coastal route, **SSI Aurelia,** from Genoa. If you're driving north from Naples, you take the southern lap of the **Autostrada del Sole (A2).** All the autostrade join with the **Grande Raccordo Anulare,** a ring road encircling Rome, channeling traffic into the congested city. Long

A Few Train Station Warnings

In Stazione Termini, you'll almost certainly be approached by touts claiming to work for a tourist organization. They really work for individual hotels (not always the most recommendable) and will say almost anything to sell you a room. Unless you know something about Rome's layout and are savvy, it's best to ignore them.

Be aware of all your belongings at all times, and keep your wallet and purse away from professionally experienced fingers. Never ever leave your bags unattended for even a second, and while making phone calls or waiting in line, make sure your attention doesn't wander from any bags you've set by your side or on the ground. Be aware if someone asks *you* for directions or information—it's likely meant to distract you and easily will.

Ignore the taxi drivers soliciting passengers right outside the terminal; they can charge as much as triple the normal amount. Instead, line up in the official taxi stand in Piazza dei Cinquecento.

---

before you reach this road, you should study a map carefully to see what part of Rome you plan to enter and mark your route accordingly. Route markings along the ring road tend to be confusing.

Warning: Return your rental car immediately, or at least get yourself to a hotel, park your car, and leave it there until you leave Rome. Don't even try to drive in Rome—the traffic is just too nightmarish.

VISITOR INFORMATION

Information is available at three locations maintained by the Azienda Provinciale di Turismo (APT). They are a kiosk at **Leonardo da Vinci International Airport** (☎ **06-6595-6074**); a kiosk in **Stazione Termini** (☎ **06-487-1270**); and a kiosk and **administrative headquarters** at Via Parigi 5 (☎ **06-4889-9253**). The headquarters are open Monday to Friday 8:15am to 7:15pm (Saturday to 2pm). The office at the airport and the one at the Stazione Termini are open daily 8:15am to 7:15pm. However, don't expect much help from these offices.

More helpful, and stocking maps and brochures, are the offices maintained by the **Comune di Roma** at various sites around the city, with red-and-orange or yellow-and-black signs saying COMUNE DI ROMA—PUNTI DI INFORMAZIONE TURISTICA. They're staffed daily 9am to 6pm, except the one at Termini (daily 8am to 9pm). Here are the addresses and phone numbers: in Stazione Termini (☎ **06-4890-6300**); in Piazza dei Cinquecento, outside Termini (☎ **06-4782-5194**); in Piazza Pia, near the Castel Sant'Angelo (☎ **06-6880-9707**); in Piazza San Giovanni in Laterano (☎ **06-7720-3598**); along Largo Carlo Goldoni (☎ **06-6813-6061**), near the intersection of Via del Corso and Via Condotti; on Via Nazionale, near the Palazzo delle Esposizioni (☎ **06-4782-4525**); on Largo Corrado Ricci, near the Colosseum (☎ **06-6992-4307**); on Piazza Sonnino in Trastevere (☎ **06-5833-3457**); on Piazza Cinque Lune, near Piazza Navona (☎ **06-6880-9240**); and on Piazza Santa Maria Maggiore (☎ **06-4788-0294**).

Enjoy Rome, Via Varese 39, near the train station (☎ **06-445-1843;** fax 06-445-0734; www.enjoyrome.com; e-mail: info@enjoyrome.com), was begun by a wonderful young English-speaking couple, Fulvia and Pierluigi. They dispense info about almost everything in Rome and are far more pleasant and organized than the Board of Tourism. They'll also help you find a hotel room, with no service charge (in anything from a hostel to a three-star hotel). Summer hours are Monday to Friday

8:30am to 7pm and Saturday 8:30am to 1:30pm; winter hours are Monday to Friday 8:30am to 1:30pm and 3:30 to 6pm.

CITY LAYOUT

Arm yourself with a detailed street map, not the general overview handed out free at tourist offices. Most hotels hand out a pretty good version at their front desks.

The bulk of ancient, Renaissance, and baroque Rome (as well as the train station) lies on the east side of the **Tiber River (Fiume Tevere),** which meanders through town. However, several important landmarks are on the other side: **St. Peter's Basilica** and the **Vatican,** the **Castel Sant'Angelo,** and the colorful **Trastevere** neighborhood.

The city's various quarters are linked by large boulevards (large at least in some places) that have mostly been laid out since the late 19th century. Starting from the **Vittorio Emanuele Monument,** a controversial pile of snow-white Brescian marble that's often compared to a wedding cake, there's a street running practically due north to **Piazza del Popolo** and the city wall. This is **Via del Corso,** one of the main streets of Rome—noisy, congested, always crowded with buses and shoppers, called simply "Il Corso." To its left (west) lie the Pantheon, Piazza Navona, Campo de' Fiori, and the Tiber. To its right (east) you'll find the Spanish Steps, the Trevi Fountain, the Borghese Gardens, and Via Veneto.

Back at the Vittorio Emanuele Monument, the major artery going west (and ultimately across the Tiber to St. Peter's) is **Corso Vittorio Emanuele.** Behind you to your right, heading toward the Colosseum, is **Via del Fori Imperiali,** laid out in the 1930s by Mussolini to show off the ruins of the imperial forums he had excavated, which line it on either side. Yet another central conduit is **Via Nazionale,** running from **Piazza Venezia** (just in front of the Vittorio Emanuele Monument) east to **Piazza della Repubblica** (near Stazione Termini). The final lap of Via Nazionale is called **Via Quattro Novembre.**

Neighborhoods in Brief

This section will give you some idea of where you may want to stay and where the major attractions are located. It may be hard to find a specific address, though, because of the narrow streets of old Rome and the little, sometimes hidden, *piazze* (squares). Numbers usually run consecutively, with odd numbers on one side of the street and evens on the other. However, in the old districts the numbers will sometimes run up one side to the end, then run back in the opposite direction on the other side. Therefore, no. 50 could be opposite no. 308.

Near Stazione Termini The main train station, **Stazione Termini,** adjoins **Piazza della Repubblica,** and most likely this will be your introduction to Rome. Much of the area is seedy and filled with gas fumes from all the buses and cars, but it has been improving. If you stay here, you may not get a lot of atmosphere, but you'll have a lot of affordable options and a very convenient location, near the transportation hub of the city and not too far from ancient Rome. There's a lot to see here, like the **Basilica di Santa Maria Maggiore** and the **Baths of Diocletian.** Some high-class hotels are sprinkled in the area, including the **Grand,** but many are long past their heyday.

Recently, the neighborhoods on either side of Stazione Termini have improved greatly, and some streets are now attractive. The best-looking area is ahead and to your right as you exit the station on the Via Marsala side. Most budget hotels here occupy a floor or more of a palazzo, and the entries are often drab, though upstairs they're often charming or at least clean and livable. In the area to the left of the station as you exit, the streets are wider, the traffic is heavier, and the noise level is higher. This area off Via Giolitti is being redeveloped, and now most streets are in good condition. A few still need improvement, and caution at night is a given.

Via Veneto & Piazza Barberini In the 1950s and early 1960s, **Via Veneto** was the haunt of the *dolce vita* set, as the likes of King Farouk and Swedish actress Anita Ekberg paraded up and down the boulevard to the delight of the paparazzi. The street is still here and is still the site of luxury hotels and elegant cafes and restaurants, though it's no longer the happening place to be. It's lined with restaurants catering to those tourists who've heard of this famous boulevard from decades past, but the restaurants are mostly overpriced and overcrowded. Rome city authorities would like to restore this legendary street to some of its former glory by banning vehicular traffic on the top half. It makes for a pleasant stroll in any case.

To the south, Via Veneto comes to an end at **Piazza Barberini,** dominated by the 1642 **Triton Fountain (Fontana del Tritone),** a baroque celebration with four dolphins holding up an open scallop shell in which sits a triton blowing into a conch. Overlooking the square is the **Palazzo Barberini.** In 1623, when Cardinal Maffeo Barberini became Pope Urban VIII, he ordered Carlo Maderno to build a palace here; it was later completed by Bernini and Borromini.

Ancient Rome Most visitors explore this area first, taking in the **Colosseum, Palatine Hill, Roman Forum, Imperial Forums,** and **Circus Maximus.** The area forms part of the *centro storico* (historic district)—along with **Campo de' Fiori** and **Piazza Navona** and the **Pantheon,** which are described below (we've considered them separately for the purposes of helping you locate hotels and restaurants). Because of its narrow streets, airy piazzas, antique atmosphere, and great location, this is a good place to stay. If you base yourself here, you can walk to the monuments and avoid the hassle of Rome's inadequate public transportation.

Campo de' Fiori & the Jewish Ghetto South of Corso Vittorio Emanuele and centered around **Piazza Farnese** and the market square of **Campo de' Fiori,** many buildings in this area were constructed in Renaissance times as private homes. Stroll along **Via Giulia**—Rome's most fashionable street in the 16th century—with its antiques stores, interesting hotels, and modern art galleries.

West of Via Arenula lies one of the city's most intriguing districts, the old **Jewish Ghetto,** where the dining options far outnumber the hotel options. In 1556 Pope Paul IV ordered the Jews, about 8,000 at the time, to move into this area. The walls weren't torn down until 1849. Although we think that ancient and medieval Rome has a lot more atmosphere, this area is close to many attractions and makes a great place to stay. Nevertheless, hoteliers will sock it to you on prices.

Piazza Navona & the Pantheon One of the most desirable areas of Rome, this district is a maze of narrow streets and alleys dating from the Middle Ages and is filled with churches and palaces built during the Renaissance and baroque eras, often with rare marble and other materials stripped from ancient Rome. The only way to explore it is on foot. Its heart is **Piazza Navona,** built over Emperor Domitian's stadium and bustling with sidewalk cafes, palazzi, street artists, musicians, and pickpockets. There are several hotels in the area and plenty of *trattorie.* Rivaling it—in general activity, the cafe scene, and nightlife—is the area around the **Pantheon,** which remains from ancient Roman times and is surrounded by a district built much later (this "pagan" temple was turned into a church and rescued, but the buildings that once surrounded it are long gone). If you'd like to stay in medieval Rome, you face the same 30 to 50% increase in hotel prices as you do for ancient Rome.

Piazza del Popolo & the Spanish Steps **Piazza del Popolo** was laid out by Giuseppe Valadier and is one of Rome's largest squares. It's characterized by an obelisk brought from Heliopolis in lower Egypt during the reign of Augustus. At the end of the square is the **Porta del Popolo,** the gateway in the 3rd-century Aurelian wall. In the mid-16th century, this was one of the major gateways into the old city. If you enter the piazza along Via del Corso from the south, you'll see twin churches, **Santa Maria del Miracoli** and **Santa Maria di Montesanto,** flanking the street. But the square's major church is **Santa Maria del Popolo** (1442–47), one of the best examples of a Renaissance church in Rome.

Ever since the 17th century, the **Spanish Steps** (the former site of the Spanish ambassador's residence) have been a meeting place for visitors. Keats lived in a house opening onto the steps, and some of Rome's most upscale shopping streets fan out from it, including **Via Condotti.** The elegant **Hassler,** one of Rome's grandest hotels, lies at the top of the steps. If you want to stay in this part of town, you must be willing to part with a lot of extra lire. This area charges some of the city's highest prices, not only for hotels but also for restaurants, designer silk suits, and leather loafers.

Around Vatican City Across the Tiber, **Vatican City** is a small city-state, but its influence extends around the world. The **Vatican Museums, St. Peter's,** and the **Vatican Gardens** take up most of the land area, and the popes have lived here for 6 centuries. The neighborhood contains some good hotels (and several bad ones), but it's somewhat removed from the more happening scene of ancient and Renaissance Rome, and getting to and from it can be time consuming. And the area is rather dull at night and contains few, if any, of Rome's finest restaurants. Vatican City and its surrounding area are best for exploring during the day.

Trastevere Rome's most authentic district, **Trastevere** is a place where you can see how real people live away from the touristy areas. It lies across the Tiber; and its people are of mixed ancestry, including Jewish, Roman, and Greek, and they speak their own dialect. The area centers around the ancient churches of **Santa Cecilia** and **Santa Maria in Trastevere.** Home to many young expatriates, the district became a gathering place for hedonists and bohemians after World War II. There are those who speak of it as a "city within a city"—or at least a village within a city. It's said that the language is rougher and the cuisine spicier, and though Trastevere doesn't have the glamorous hotels of central Rome, it does have some of the last remaining authentic Roman dining. This used to be a great hunting ground for budget travelers, but foreigners from virtually everywhere have been buying real estate en masse here, so change is in the air.

Testaccio In A.D. 55, Nero ordered that Rome's thousands of broken amphoras and terra-cotta roof tiles be stacked in a carefully designated pile to the east of the Tiber, just west of Pyramide and today's Ostia Railway Station. Over the centuries, the mound grew to a height of around 200 feet and then was compacted to form the centerpiece for one of the city's most unusual neighborhoods, **Testaccio.** Eventually,

Handy Tip

Rome has *four* daily rush hours: to work, to home for lunch *(riposo),* back to work, to home in the evening.

houses were built on the terra-cotta mound and caves dug into its mass to store wine and foodstuffs. Bordered by the Protestant cemetery, Testaccio is home to restaurants with very Roman cuisine. However, don't wander around here alone at night; the area still has a way to go before regentrification.

The Appian Way **Via Appia Antica** is a 2,300-year-old road that has witnessed much of the history of the ancient world. By 190 B.C. it extended from Rome to Brindisi on the southeast coast, and its most famous sight today is the **catacombs,** the graveyards of patrician families (despite what it says in *Quo Vadis?,* they weren't used as a place for Christians to hide out while fleeing persecution). This is one of the most historically rich areas of Rome to explore, but not a viable place to stay.

Prati The little-known **Prati** district is a middle-class suburb north of the Vatican. It's been discovered by budget travelers because of its affordable *pensioni,* though it's not conveniently located for much of the sightseeing you'll want to do. The **Trionfale flower-and-food market** itself is worth the trip. The area also abounds in shopping streets less expensive than those found in central Rome, and street crime isn't much of a problem.

Parioli Rome's most elegant residential section, **Parioli** is framed by the green spaces of the **Villa Borghese** to the south and the **Villa Glori** and **Villa Ada** to the north. It's a setting for some of the city's finest restaurants, hotels, and nightclubs. It's not exactly central, however, and can be a hassle if you're dependent on public transportation. Parioli lies adjacent to Prati, but across the Tiber to the east, and, like Prati, is one of the safer districts.

Monte Mario On the northwestern precincts of Rome, **Monte Mario** is the site of the deluxe **Cavalieri Hilton,** an excellent stop to take in a drink and the panorama of Rome. If you plan to spend a lot of time shopping and sightseeing in the heart of Rome, it's a difficult and often expensive commute. The area lies north of Prati, away from the hustle and bustle of central Rome. Bus no. 913 runs from Piazza Augusto Imperator near Piazza del Popolo to Monte Mario.

2 Getting Around

Rome is excellent for walking, with sites of interest often clustered together. Much of the inner core is traffic-free, so you'll need to walk whether you like it or not. However, in many parts of the city it's hazardous and uncomfortable because of the crowds, heavy traffic, and narrow sidewalks. Sometimes sidewalks don't exist at all, and it becomes a sort of free-for-all with pedestrians competing for space against vehicular traffic (the traffic always seems to win). Always be on your guard. The hectic crush of urban Rome is considerably less during August, when many Romans leave town for vacation.

BY SUBWAY

The **Metropolitana,** or **Metro** for short, is the fastest means of transportation, operating daily 5:30am to 11:30pm. It has two underground lines: **Line A** goes between Via Ottaviano (near St. Peter's) and Anagnina, stopping at Piazzale Flaminio (near Piazza del Popolo), Piazza di Spagna, Piazza Vittorio Emanuele, and Piazza San Giovanni in Laterano. **Line B** connects the Rebibbia District with Via Laurentina, stopping at Via Cavour, Stazione Termini, the Colosseum, the Circus Maximus, the Pyramid, St. Paul's Outside the Walls, and E.U.R. (A section of Rome about 3.6 miles south of the historic center of the city, E.U.R. is an urban development dating from

Rome Metropolitana

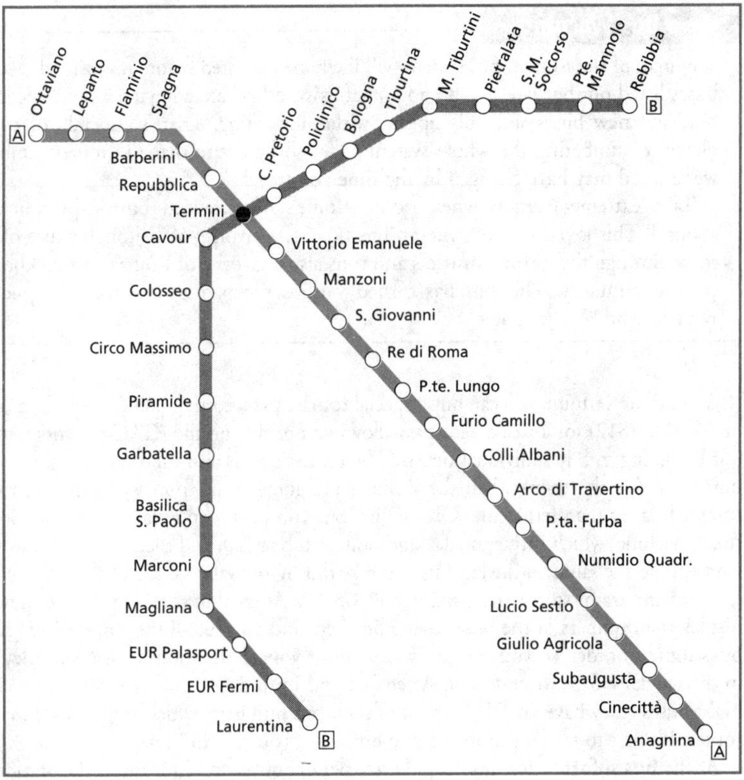

the Mussolini era; its fascist architecture is full of showy marble and granite.) A big red "M" indicates the entrance to the subway.

Tickets are 1,500L (75¢) and are available from *tabacchi* (tobacco shops), many newsstands, and vending machines at all stations. These machines accept 50L, 100L, and 200L coins, and some will take 1,000L notes. Some stations have managers, but they won't make change. Booklets of tickets are available at tabacchi and in some terminals. You can also buy a **tourist pass** on either a daily or a weekly basis (see below).

Building a subway system for Rome hasn't been easy, since every time workers start digging they discover an old temple or other archaeological treasure, and heavy earthmoving has to cease for a while.

BY BUS & TRAM

Roman buses and trams are operated by an organization known as **ATAC (Azienda Tramvie e Autobus del Comune di Roma)**, Via Volturno 65 (☎ **06-46-951** for information).

For 1,500L (75¢) you can ride to most parts of Rome, though it can be slow-going in all that traffic and the buses are often very crowded. Your ticket is valid for 75 minutes, and you can get on many buses and trams during that time by using the same ticket. Ask where to buy bus tickets, or buy them in tabacchi or bus terminals. You must have your ticket before boarding, as there are no ticket-issuing machines on the vehicles.

Two Bus Warnings

Any map of the Roman bus system will likely be outdated before it's printed. Many buses listed on the "latest" map no longer exist; others are enjoying a much-needed rest, and new buses suddenly appear without warning. There's also talk of completely renumbering the whole system soon, so be aware that the route numbers we've listed may have changed by the time you travel.

Take extreme caution when riding Rome's overcrowded buses—pickpockets abound! This is particularly true on bus no. 64, a favorite of visitors because of its route through the historic districts and thus also a favorite of Rome's vast pickpocketing community. This bus has earned various nicknames, like the "Pickpocket Express" and "Wallet Eater."

At Stazione Termini, you can buy a special **tourist pass,** costing 6,000L ($3) for a day or 24,000L ($12) for a week. This pass allows you to ride on the ATAC network without bothering to buy individual tickets. The tourist pass is also valid on the subway—but never ride the trains when the Romans are going to or from work, or you'll be smashed flatter than fettuccine. On the first bus you board, you place your ticket in a small machine, which prints the day and hour you boarded, and then you withdraw it. And you do the same on the last bus you take during the valid period of the ticket.

Buses and trams stop at areas marked FERMATA. At most of these, a yellow sign will display the numbers of the buses that stop there and a list of all the stops along each bus's route in order, so you can easily search out your destination. In general, they're in service daily 6am to midnight. After that and until dawn, you can ride on special night buses (they have an "N" in front of their bus number), which run only on main routes. It's best to take a taxi in the wee hours—if you can find one.

At the **bus information booth** at Piazza dei Cinquecento, in front of the Stazione Termini, you can purchase a directory complete with maps summarizing the routes.

Although routes change often, a few old reliable routes have remained valid for years, such as **no. 27** from Stazione Termini to the Colosseum, **nos. 75** and **170** from Stazione Termini to Trastevere, and **no. 492** from Stazione Termini to the Vatican. But if you're going somewhere and are dependent on the bus, be sure to carefully check where the bus stop is and exactly which bus goes there—don't assume it'll be the same bus the next day.

BY TAXI

If you're accustomed to hopping a cab in New York or London, then do so in Rome. If not, take less-expensive means of transport, or walk. Avoid paying your fare with large bills—invariably, taxi drivers claim they don't have change, hoping for a bigger tip (stick to your guns and give only about 10%). Don't count on hailing a taxi on the street or even getting one at a stand. If you're going out, have your hotel call one. At a restaurant, ask the waiter or cashier to dial for you. If you want to phone for yourself, try one of these numbers: ☎ **06-6645,** 06-3570, or 06-4994.

The meter begins at 4,500L ($2.25) for the first 3 kilometers and then rises 1,300L (65¢) per kilometer. Every suitcase is 2,000L ($1), and on Sunday a 2,000L ($1) supplement is assessed. There's another 5,000L ($2.50) supplement 10pm to 7am.

BY CAR

All roads may lead to Rome, but you don't want to drive once you get here. Since the reception desks of most Roman hotels have at least one English-speaking person, call ahead to find out the best route into Rome from wherever you're starting out. You're usually allowed to park in front of the hotel long enough to unload your luggage. You'll want to get rid of your rental car as soon as possible or park in a garage.

To the neophyte, Roman driving will appear like the chariot race in *Ben-Hur.* When the light turns green, go forth with caution. Many Roman drivers in the other part of the intersection will still be going through the light even though it has turned red. Roman drivers in gridlocked traffic move bravely on, fighting for every inch of the road until they can free themselves from the tangled mess. To complicate matters, many zones, such as that around Piazza di Spagna, are traffic-free.

You may want to rent a car to explore the countryside around Rome or drive on to another city. You'll save the most money if you reserve before leaving home. But if you want to book a car here, know that **Hertz** is at Via Vittorio Veneto 156, near the parking lot of the Villa Borghese (☎ **06-321-6831;** Metro: Barberini); **Italy by Car** at Via Ludovisi 60 (☎ **06-482-0966;** Bus: 95 or 116); and **Avis** at Stazione Termini (☎ **06-428-24-728;** Metro: Termini). **Maggiore,** an Italian company, has an office at Via di Tor Cervara 225 (☎ **06-229-351**). There are also branches of the major rental agencies at the airport.

Fast Facts: Rome

American Express The Rome offices are at Piazza di Spagna 38 (☎ **06-67-641;** Metro: Spagna). The travel service is open Monday to Friday 9am to 5:30pm and Saturday 9am to 12:30pm. Hours for the financial and mail services are Monday to Friday 9am to 5pm. The tour desk is open during the same hours as those for travel services and also Saturday 2 to 2:30pm (May to October).

Baby-Sitters Most hotel desks in Rome will help you secure a baby-sitter. Inquire as far in advance as possible and request an English-speaking sitter. You won't always get one, but it pays to ask. A good choice is **Angels Baby Sitting Services** at Via delle Quattro Fontane (☎ **06-420-13-080** or 06-329-56-95), which offers British, American, or Australian baby- sitters, available for a few hours or even for one or more days. Rates range from 12,000 to 25,000L ($6 to$12.50) per hour.

Banks In general, banks are open Monday to Friday 8:30am to 1:30pm and 3 to 4pm. Some banks keep afternoon hours from 2:45 to 3:45pm. There's a branch of **Citibank** at Via Abruzzi 2 (☎ **06-478-171;** Metro: Barberini). The bank office is open Monday to Friday 8:30am to 1:30pm.

Currency Exchange There are exchange offices throughout the city, and they're also at all major rail and air terminals, including Stazione Termini, where the *cambio* (exchange booth) beside the rail information booth is open daily 8am to 8pm. At some *cambi,* you'll have to pay commissions, often 1.5%. Banks, likewise, often charge commissions.

Dentists To find a dentist who speaks English, call the **U.S. Embassy** in Rome at ☎ **06-46-741.** You may have to call around in order to get an appointment. There's also the 24-hour **G. Eastman Dental Hospital,** Viale Regina Elena 287 (☎ **06-844-831;** Metro: Policlinico).

Doctors For a doctor, call the U.S. Embassy (see "Fast Facts: Italy" in chapter 2), which will provide a list of doctors who speak English. All big hospitals have a 24-hour first-aid service (go to the emergency room—*Pronto Soccorso*). You'll find English-speaking doctors at the privately run **Salvator Mundi International**

Hospital, Viale delle Mura Gianicolensi 67 (☎ **06-588-961;** Bus: 41). For medical assistance, the **International Medical Center** is on 24-hour duty at Via Giovanni Amendola 7 (☎ **06-488-2371;** Metro: Termini). You could also contact the **Rome American Hospital,** Via Emilio Longoni 69 (☎ **06-22-551**), with English-speaking doctors on duty 24 hours. A more personalized service is provided 24 hours by **MEDI-CALL,** Studio Medico, Via Salaria 300, Palazzina C, interno 5 (☎ **06-884-0113;** Bus: 3, 4, or 57). It can arrange for qualified doctors to make a house call at your hotel or anywhere in Rome. In most cases, the doctor will be a GP who can refer you to a specialist if needed. Fees begin at around $100 per visit and can go higher if a specialist or specialized treatments are necessary.

Drugstores A reliable pharmacy is **Farmacia Internazionale,** Piazza Barberini 49 (☎ **06-487-1195;** Metro: Barberini), open day and night. Most pharmacies are open 8:30am to 1pm and 4 to 7:30pm. In general, pharmacies follow a rotation system, so several are always open on Sunday.

Embassies/Consulates See "Fast Facts: Italy," in chapter 2.

Emergencies Dial **113** for an ambulance or to call the police; to report a fire, call **115**.

Internet Access You can log onto the Web in central Rome at **Thenetgate,** Piazza Firenze 25 (☎ **06-689-3445;** Bus: 116). Summer hours are Monday to Saturday 10:30am to 12:30pm and 3:30 to 10:30pm and winter hours daily 10:40am to 8:30pm. A 20-minute visit costs 5,000L ($2.50), with 1 hour (including mailbox) for 10,000L ($5). Access is free on Saturdays 10:30 to 11am and 2 to 2:30pm. You can kill two birds with one stone just north of Stazione Termini at **Splash,** Via Varese 33 (☎ **06-4938-2073;** Metro: Termini), a do-it-yourself Laundromat (13,000L/$6.50 per load, including soap) with a satellite TV and four computers hooked up to the Net (5,000L/$2.50 per half hour).

Mail It's easiest just to buy stamps and mail letters and postcards at your hotel's front desk. Stamps *(francobolli)* can also be bought at *tabacchi* (tobacco shops/newsstands). You can buy special stamps at the **Vatican City Post Office,** adjacent to the information office in St. Peter's Square; it's open Monday to Friday 8:30am to 7pm and Saturday 8:30am to 6pm. Letters mailed at Vatican City reach North America far more quickly than mail sent from within Rome for the same cost.

Newspapers/Magazines You can get the *International Herald Tribune, USA Today, The New York Times,* and *Time* and *Newsweek* magazines at most newsstands. The expatriate magazine (in English) *Wanted in Rome* comes out monthly and lists current events and shows. If you want to try your hand at reading Italian, the Thursday edition of the newspaper *La Repubblica* contains "Trova Roma," a magazine supplement full of cultural and entertainment listings, and *Time Out* now has a Rome edition.

Police See "Emergencies," above.

Rest Rooms Facilities are found near many of the major sights and often have attendants, as do those at bars, clubs, restaurants, cafes, and hotels, plus the airports and the rail station. (There are public rest rooms near the Spanish Steps, or you can stop at the McDonald's there—one of the nicest branches of the Golden Arches you'll ever see!) You're expected to leave 200 to 500L (10¢ to 25¢) for the attendant. It's not a bad idea to carry some tissues in your pocket when you're out and about.

Safety Pickpocketing is the most common problem. Men should keep their wallets in their front pocket or inside jacket pocket. Purse snatching is also commonplace, with young men on Vespas who'll ride past you and grab your purse. To avoid trouble, stay away from the curb and keep your purse on the wall side of your body and the strap across your chest. Don't lay anything valuable on tables or chairs where it can be grabbed up. Gypsy children have long been a particular menace, though the problem isn't as severe as in years past. If they completely surround you, you'll often virtually have to fight them off. They may approach you with pieces of cardboard hiding their stealing hands. Just keep repeating a firm *no!*

Telephone The **country code** for Italy is **39.** The **city code** for Rome is **06;** use this code when calling from *anywhere* outside or inside Italy—you must add it even within Rome itself (and you must now include the zero every time, even when calling from abroad). See the Fast Facts at the end of chapter 2 (or the back cover of this book) for complete details on how to call Italy, how to place calls within Italy, and how to call home once you're in Italy.

3 Accommodations

You'll find Rome's hotels better than ever, many newly renovated or spruced up to greet the hordes of visitors who arrived during Jubilee Year. If you like to gamble and arrive without a reservation, head quickly to the **airport information desk** or, once you get into town, to the offices of **Enjoy Rome** (see "Visitor Information," above)—their staff can help you reserve a room, if any are available.

See the "The Neighborhoods in Brief," section earlier in this chapter to get an idea of where you may want to base yourself.

All the hotels listed serve breakfast (often a buffet with coffee, fruit, rolls, and cheese), but it's not always included in the room rate, so check the listing carefully.

Nearly all hotels are heated in the cooler months, but not all are air-conditioned in summer, which can be vitally important during a stifling July or August. The deluxe and first-class ones are, but after that, it's a toss-up. Be sure to check the listing carefully before you book a stay in the dog days of summer!

NEAR STAZIONE TERMINI

VERY EXPENSIVE

Hotel Artemide. Via Nazionale 22, 00184 Roma. ☎ **06-489-911.** Fax 06-4899-1700. www.travel.it/roma/artemide/artemide.html. E-mail: hotel.artemide@tiscalinet.it. 79 units. A/C MINIBAR TV TEL. 490,000–540,000L ($245–$270) double; 630,000L ($315) suite. Rates include breakfast. AE, MC, DC, V. Parking 30,000L ($15). Metro: Piazza Repubblica.

The Artemide was transformed from a 19th-century palazzetto into a four-star hotel. Near the train station, it combines stylish simplicity with modern comforts against a backdrop of art nouveau motifs. The original stained-glass skylight dome was retained in the lobby. The guest rooms are furnished in natural colors and have good furnishings, including elegantly comfortable beds, and such extras as safes and spacious marble bathrooms with hair dryers. Nonsmoking units are available.

Dining/Diversions: Caffè Caffeteria Nazionale serves a Mediterranean cuisine, along with light buffets, for both dinner and lunch, afternoon tea, and mid-afternoon snacks. An American bar is open daily from 7am to midnight.

Amenities: Concierge, room service, laundry/dry cleaning.

Rome Accommodations

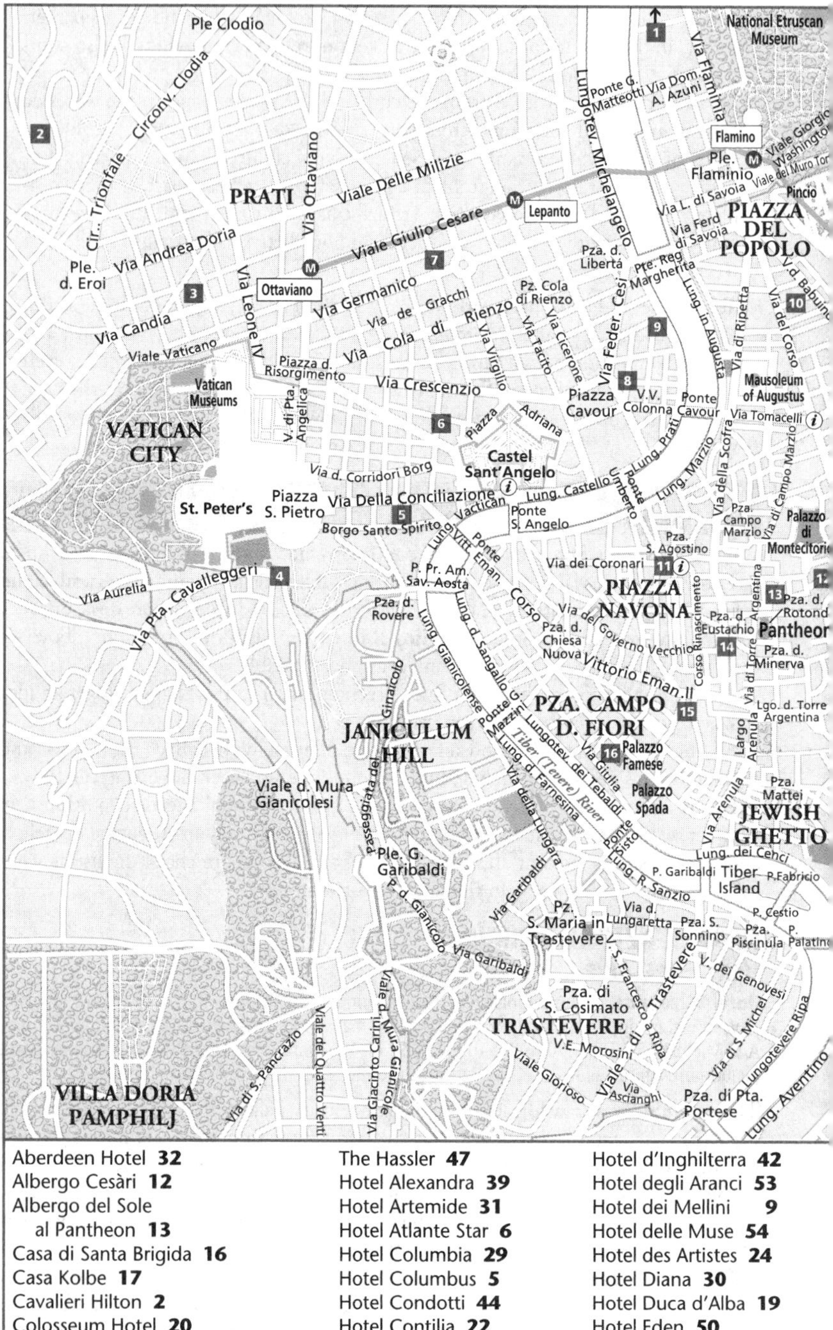

Aberdeen Hotel **32**	The Hassler **47**	Hotel d'Inghilterra **42**
Albergo Cesàri **12**	Hotel Alexandra **39**	Hotel degli Aranci **53**
Albergo del Sole al Pantheon **13**	Hotel Artemide **31**	Hotel dei Mellini **9**
Casa di Santa Brigida **16**	Hotel Atlante Star **6**	Hotel delle Muse **54**
Casa Kolbe **17**	Hotel Columbia **29**	Hotel des Artistes **24**
Cavalieri Hilton **2**	Hotel Columbus **5**	Hotel Diana **30**
Colosseum Hotel **20**	Hotel Condotti **44**	Hotel Duca d'Alba **19**
The Excelsior **52**	Hotel Contilia **22**	Hotel Eden **50**
	Hotel Corot **26**	Hotel Emmaus **4**

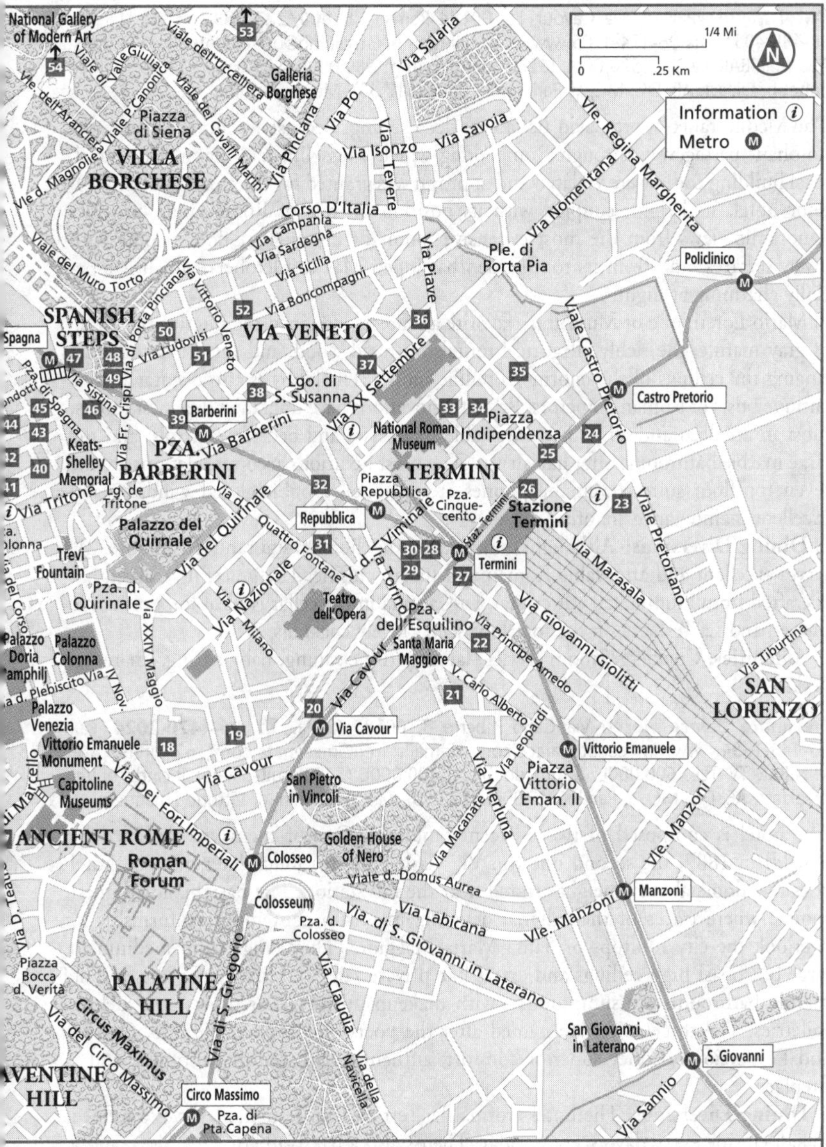

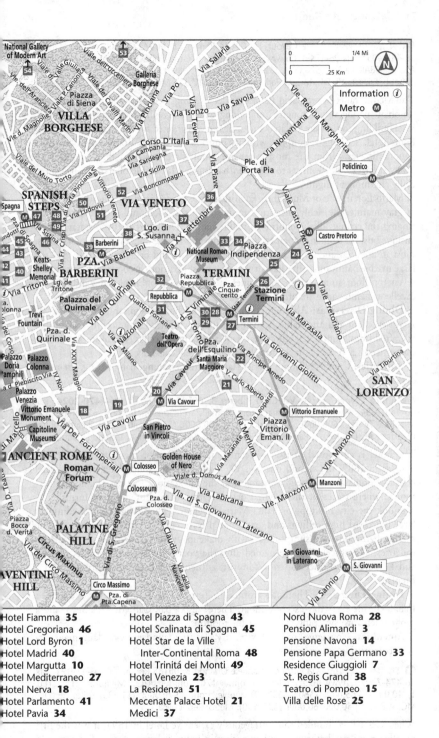

Hotel Fiamma **35**
Hotel Gregoriana **46**
Hotel Lord Byron **1**
Hotel Madrid **40**
Hotel Margutta **10**
Hotel Mediterraneo **27**
Hotel Nerva **18**
Hotel Parlamento **41**
Hotel Pavia **34**
Hotel Piazza di Spagna **43**
Hotel Scalinata di Spagna **45**
Hotel Star de la Ville Inter-Continental Roma **48**
Hotel Trinitá dei Monti **49**
Hotel Venezia **23**
La Residenza **51**
Mecenate Palace Hotel **21**
Medici **37**
Nord Nuova Roma **28**
Pension Alimandi **3**
Pensione Navona **14**
Pensione Papa Germano **33**
Residence Giuggioli **7**
St. Regis Grand **38**
Teatro di Pompeo **15**
Villa delle Rose **25**

Hotel Mediterraneo. Via Cavour 15, 00184 Roma. ☎ **800/223-9832** in the U.S., or 06-488-4051. Fax 06-474-4105. www.bettojahotels.it. E-mail: hb@bettojahotels.it. 274 units. A/C MINIBAR TV TEL. 520,000L ($260) double; from 580,000L ($290) suite. Rates include buffet breakfast. AE, DC, MC, V. Parking 35,000L ($17.50). Metro: Termini.

The Mediterraneo sports vivid Italian art deco styling. Because it's located on the triumphant passageway through Rome along which Mussolini had planned to travel, local building codes were violated and approval was granted for the creation of this 10-floor hotel. Its height, coupled with its position on one of Rome's hills, provides panoramic views from the most expensive rooms on the highest floors (some with lovely terraces) and from its roof garden/bar (open May to October), which is especially charming at night.

Mario Loreti, one of Mussolini's favorite architects, designed the interior sheathing of gray marble, the richly allegorical murals of inlaid wood, and the art deco friezes ringing the ceilings of the enormous public rooms. The lobby is also decorated with antique busts of Roman emperors. Recent renovations have upgraded the guest rooms, most in art deco and all with comfortable mattresses and bedside controls, and the large marble bathrooms offer hair dryers. The most luxurious accommodations are the seven top-floor suites (even the phones are antique). Double-glazed windows and excellent maintenance are other pluses.

Dining/Diversions: Although unheralded, the hotel restaurant, Ristorante 21, serves excellent and affordable Roman and Italian cuisine. The gracefully curved bar is crafted from illuminated cut crystal. La Cantina in the cellar is ideal for a romantic dinner, and La Terrazza on the top floor serves lovely cocktails.

Amenities: Concierge, room service, laundry/dry cleaning, baby-sitting, car-rental desk.

Mecenate Palace Hotel. Via Carlo Alberto 3, 00185 Roma. ☎ **06-4470-2024.** Fax 06-446-1354. www.mecenatepalace.com. E-mail: info@mecenate.com. 62 units. A/C MINIBAR TV TEL. 600,000L ($300) double; 1,400,000L ($700) suite. Rates include buffet breakfast. AE, DC, MC, V. Parking 45,000L ($22.50). Metro: Termini or Vittorio Emanuele.

The hotel is composed of two adjacent buildings. One of them was designed by Rinaldi in 1887, the second one (on Via Carlo Alberto) much later on. The hotel rises five floors above a neighborhood near the rail station. The pastel-colored guest rooms, where traces of the original detailing mix with contemporary furnishings, overlook the city rooftops or Santa Maria Maggiore. They range from medium to large but boast high ceilings and extras like private safes and luxury mattresses. The marble bathrooms are sumptuous—with makeup mirrors, hair dryers, and deluxe toiletries. The three suites are named after the poets/philosophers Virgilio, Orazio, and Properzio and offer superior comfort, authentic 19th-century antiques, and a fireplace.

Dining/Diversions: The hotel's formal La Terraza Papi restaurant serves a refined Italian cuisine every day except Sunday. There's also a bar, Caffè di Papa Sisto, and a roof garden with sweeping views over the rooftops.

Amenities: Concierge, room service, dry cleaning/laundry, twice-daily maid service, baby-sitting, secretarial services.

✪ **St. Regis Grand.** Via Vittorio Emanuele Orlando 3, 00185 Roma. ☎ **06-47-091.** Fax 06-474-7307. www.luxurycollection.com. 170 units. A/C MINIBAR TV TEL. 1,210,000–1,265,000L ($605–$632.50) double; from 2,970,000L ($1,485) suite. AE, DC, MC, V. Parking 50,000–60,000L ($25–$30). Metro: Repubblica.

When César Ritz founded this outrageously expensive hotel in 1894, it was the first to offer a private bathroom and two electric lights in every room. Today, a $35

Accommodations Near Stazione Termini & Via Veneto

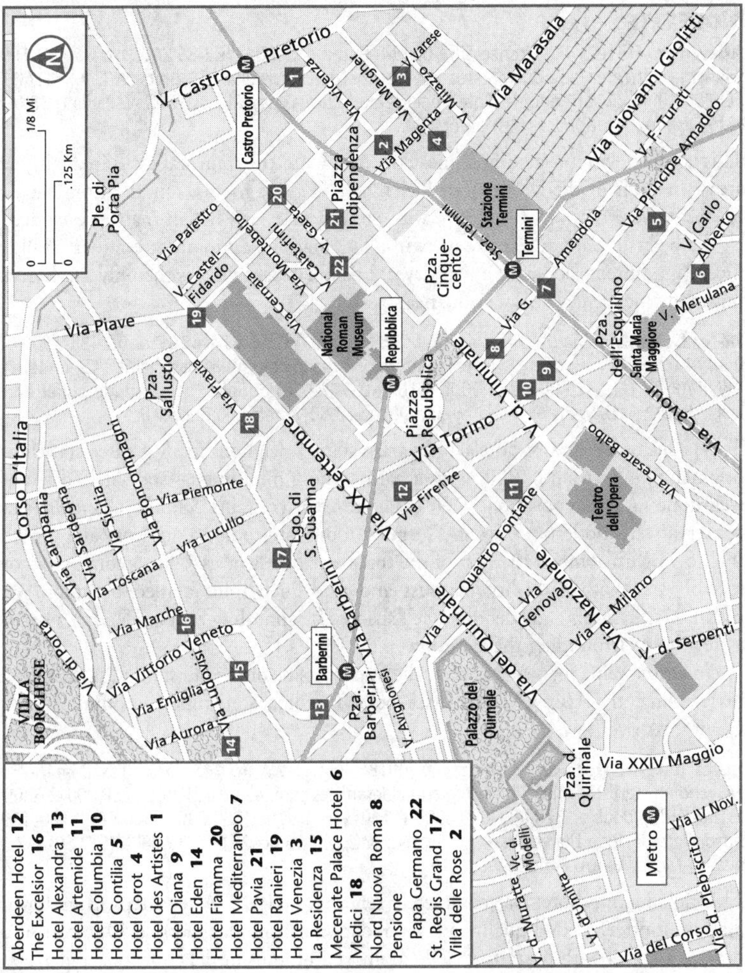

million restoration has vastly improved it. Restored to its former glory, it is a magnificent Roman palazzo in the heart of the city, combining Italian and French styles in decoration and furnishings. The lobby is decked out with Murano chandeliers, columns, and marble busts and cherubs. Guest rooms, most of which are exceedingly spacious, are luxuriously furnished with everything from sumptuous mattresses to Murano chandeliers. Hand-painted frescoes are installed above each headboard, and the bathrooms are done in fabulous marble.

Dining/Diversions: The formal restaurant, Vivendo, is one of the most elegant hotel dining rooms in Rome, serving a refined international and Italian cuisine, with superior food and deluxe service. There is also the less-formal Grand Hall Café, plus Rome's most elegant hotel bar, the aptly named Le Grand Bar.

Amenities: 24-hour butler service, fitness center, massage rooms, laundry/valet, baby-sitting.

MODERATE

Aberdeen Hotel. Via Firenze 48, 00184 Roma. ☎ **06-482-3920.** Fax 06-482-1092. www.travel.it/roma/aberdeen. E-mail: hotel.aberdeen@travel.it. 26 units. A/C MINIBAR TV TEL. 300,000L ($150) double. Rates include buffet breakfast. AE, DC, MC, V. Parking 38,000L ($19). Metro: Repubblica. Bus: 64 or 170.

This completely renovated hotel near the opera and the train station is in a fairly safe area—in front of the Ministry of Defense. The guest rooms, ranging from small to medium, were renovated in 1998, with comfortable new Italian mattresses added to all the beds, usually queen size or twins. The marble bathrooms are rather small but nicely appointed, each with a hair dryer. The breakfast buffet is the only meal served, but many inexpensive trattorie lie nearby.

Hotel Columbia. Via del Viminale 15, 00184 Roma. ☎ **06-474-4289** or 06-488-3509. Fax 06-474-0209. www.venere.it/roma/columbia. E-mail: columbia@flashnet.it. 45 units. A/C MINIBAR TV TEL. 325,000–345,000L ($162.50–$172.50) double. Rates include buffet breakfast. AE, DC, MC, V. Parking nearby 35,000L ($17.50). Metro: Repubblica.

This is one of the newest hotels in the train station neighborhood. A three-star choice, originally built around 1900, with a hardworking multilingual staff, it underwent a well-done radical renovation (1997). The interior contains Murano chandeliers and conservatively modern furniture. The guest rooms are compact and cozy and can hold their own with some of the best of the three-star hotels nearby. Each contains a comfortable bed with a quality mattress and fine linen, plus a tiled bathroom with medium-size towels and adequate shelf space. The appealing roof garden has a bar and a view over surrounding the rooftops.

Under the same management, on the opposite side of the rail station, is the Columbia's sibling, the **Hotel Venezia** (see below), which sometimes accommodates the Columbia's overflow.

Hotel des Artistes. Via Villafranca 20, 00185 Roma. ☎ **06-445-4365.** Fax 06-446-2368. www.hoteldesartistes.com. E-mail: info@hoteldesartistes.com. 45 units. TV TEL. 260,000–270,000L ($130–$135) double; 320,000–330,000L ($160–$165) triple; 380,000–390,000L ($190–$195) quad. Rates include buffet breakfast. AE, DC, MC, V. Parking 25,000–35,000L ($12.50–$17.50) nearby. Metro: Castro Pretorio. Bus: 310.

This no-smoking hotel was completely renewed in 1997. A few steps from Termini Station, it offers a good-quality accommodation at a moderate price. One part of the hotel is a hostel with dormitory-style rooms, bathrooms in the corridors, and a TV in each room; rates for those accommodations range from 170,000L ($85) for a triple to 220,000L ($110) for a quad. Regular rooms range from small to medium in size, some of them decorated with oriental rugs. The furniture is simple but classic, and the maid service is excellent. The hotel's rooms have private bathrooms, small but neat and just renovated, offering hair dryers and small shower stalls. Breakfast is the only meal served, but an intimate bar is open daily from 7am to 2am. The roof garden, open 24 hours, is an ideal place to socialize with other visitors or local people, as well. Amenities include a concierge, baby-sitting, tour desk, and rentals for cars, scooters, and bicycles.

Hotel Diana. Via Principe Amedeo 4, 00185 Roma. ☎ **06-482-7541.** Fax 06-486-998. www.hoteldianaroma.com. E-mail: diana@venere.it. 186 units. A/C MINIBAR TV TEL. 330,000L ($165) double; 450,000L ($225) suite. Rates include breakfast. AE, DC, MC, V. Parking 35,000L ($17.50).

In the heart of 19th-century Rome, the Diana has been totally renovated in an inviting art deco style, recapturing its early 1900s heyday. It offers an elegant yet comfortable atmosphere, as evoked by the spacious lobby and welcoming lounges. The guest rooms are tastefully furnished in floral fabrics, the walls covered in English-style striped tapestry in soft greens and creamy tones. The beds boast luxury mattresses and first-rate linens. The bathrooms are tiled with attractive ceramics, offering hair dryers and heated towel racks. Nonsmoking units are available. Amenities include concierge, room service, and laundry/dry cleaning.

The hotel's restaurant offers a menu of classic Italian dishes and daily seasonal specialties. The American Bar in summer moves to the rooftop terrace, where lunch and dinner can be served; shaded by tents and surrounded by plants, you'll have sweeping views over the ancient roofs.

Hotel Ranieri. Via XX Settembre 43, 00187 Roma. ☎ **06-420-145-31.** Fax 06-420-145-43. www.hotelranieri.com. E-mail: hotel.ranieri@italyhotel.com. 47 units. A/C MINIBAR TV TEL. 230,000–350,000L ($115–$175) double. Rates include breakfast. AE, DC, MC, V. Parking 30,000–45,000L ($15–$22.50). Metro: Repubblica.

The Ranieri is a winning three-star hotel in a restored old building. The guest rooms received a substantial renovation in 1995, when new furniture, carpets, wall coverings, and even new bathrooms were added. They're a bit small but reasonably comfortable for two persons, with mattresses that are still firm. The bathrooms aren't very big but are well equipped with hair dryers. The public rooms, the lounge, and the dining room are attractively decorated, in part with contemporary art. You can arrange for a home-cooked meal in the dining room, which offers five different fixed-price menus ranging from 30,000 to 50,000L ($15 to $25) per person.

✪ **Hotel Venezia.** Via Varese 18 (near Via Marghera), 00185 Roma. ☎ **06-445-7101.** Fax 06-495-7687. www.hotelvenezia.com. E-mail: info@hotelvenezia.com. 61 units. A/C MINIBAR TV TEL. 325,000–345,000L ($162.50–$172.50) double; 465,000L ($232.50) triple. Rates include buffet breakfast. AE, DC, MC, V. Parking 35,000L ($17.50). Metro: Termini.

Just when you've decided the whole city was full of overpriced hotels, the cheerful Venezia will restore your faith in affordable rooms. The location is good—3 blocks from the rail station, in a relatively quiet business/residential area with a few old villas. Its public rooms are charming. Some guest rooms are furnished in 17th-century style, though a few are beginning to look worn (the last renovation was in 1991); the rest are in modern style. All units are spacious, boasting Murano chandeliers, first-rate beds and mattresses, and bathrooms with hair dryers; some have balconies for surveying the street action. The management really cares, and the helpful staff speaks English.

Medici. Via Flavia 96, 00187 Roma. ☎ **06-482-7319.** Fax 06-474-0767. www.hotelmedici.com. 69 units. MINIBAR TV TEL. 260,000–330,000L ($130–$165) double. Rates include breakfast. AE, DC, MC, V. Parking 35,000–40,000 L ($17.50–$20). Metro: Piazza della Repubblica.

The Medici, built in 1906, is near the rail station and the shops along Via XX Settembre. Many of its better guest rooms overlook an inner patio garden with Roman columns and benches. All rooms were renovated in 1997 in classic Roman style, with a generous use of antiques and first-class Italian mattresses. The cheapest are a good buy, for they're only slightly smaller than the others (but they have older furnishings and no air-conditioning). The bathrooms are small but well organized, and hair dryers are available upon request. Breakfast is the only meal served.

Nord Nuova Roma. Via Giovanni Amendola 3, 00185 Roma. ☎ **800/223-9832** in the U.S., or 06-488-5441. Fax 06-481-7163. www.bettojahotels.it. 158 units. A/C MINIBAR TV TEL. 320,000L ($160) double. Rates include breakfast. AE, DC, MC, V. Parking 35,000–45,000L ($17.50–$22.50). Metro: Termini or Repubblica.

Although rather plain, this hotel is the best bargain in the Bettoja chain and a good choice for families. It was built in 1935; it's in a convenient position near Stazione Termini and the Dioclezione Bath. Rooms are quite spacious and bright. The standard rooms range from small to spacious and are well furnished, though the pieces are often aging. Nonetheless, the beds are comfortable, most often twins or doubles. Each bathroom is fairly roomy. You can arrange a savory lunch or dinner at the nearby Massimo d'Azeglio Restaurant, and there's an intimate bar.

Villa delle Rose. Via Vicenza 5, 00185 Roma. ☎ **06-445-1788.** Fax 06-445-1639. www.venere.it/roma/villadellerose. E-mail: villadellerose@flashnet.it. 37 units. TV TEL. 180,000–300,000L ($90–$150) double. Rates include continental breakfast. AE, DC, MC, V. Free parking (only 4 cars). Metro: Termini or Castro Pretorio.

Located less than 2 blocks north of the rail station, this hotel began in the late 1800s as a villa with a dignified cut-stone facade inspired by the Renaissance. Despite many renovations, the ornate trappings of the original are still visible, such as the lobby's Corinthian-capped marble columns and the flagstone-covered terrace that is part of the verdant back garden. Much of the interior has been recently redecorated and upgraded with traditional wall coverings, new carpets, new mattresses, and tiled bathrooms. Breakfasts in the garden do a lot to add country flavor to an otherwise very urban and noisy location. The English-speaking staff is helpful and tactful.

INEXPENSIVE

Hotel Contilia. Via Principe Amadeo 79d–81, 00185 Roma. ☎ **06-446-6942.** Fax 06-446-6904. E-mail: contilia@tin.it. 40 units. A/C TV TEL. 150,000–300,000L ($75–$150) double. Rates include breakfast. AE, DC, MC, V. Parking 30,000L ($15); free on street. Metro: Termini.

As the automatic doors part to reveal a stylish marble lobby with Persian rugs and antiques, you might step back to double-check the address. The popular old-fashioned Pensione Tony Contilia of yesteryear has taken over this building's other small hotels and upgraded itself into one of the best choices in the neighborhood. The guest rooms have been redone in modern midscale comfort, with perfectly firm beds and built-in units. The double-glazed windows keep out traffic noise, and the rooms overlooking the cobblestone courtyard are even more quiet. Oddly, the smallish contemporary bathrooms lack shower curtains.

Hotel Corot. Via Marghera 15–17, 00185 Roma. ☎ **06-4470-0900.** Fax 06-4470-0905. www.hotelcorot.it. E-mail: hotel.corot@mclink.it. 28 units. A/C MINIBAR TV TEL. 180,000–240,000L ($90–$120) double; 220,000–280,000L ($110–$140) triple; 250,000–320,000L ($125–$160) quad. Rates include breakfast. AE, DC, MC, V. Parking 30,000L ($15) for 1st night, 19,000L ($9.50) for the 2nd. Metro: Termini.

This modernized hotel (renovated in 1997) occupies the second and third floors of an early 1900s building that contains a handful of apartments and another, somewhat inferior hotel. The Corot is a safe, if not thrilling, bet north of the train station. You register in a small paneled street-level area and then take an elevator to your high-ceilinged guest room. Each room has simple but traditional furniture, including a good bed, and a modern bathroom with a hair dryer. There's a bar near a sunny window in one of the public rooms.

Hotel Fiamma. Via Gaeta 61, 00185 Roma. ☎ **06-481-8436.** Fax 06-488-3511. www.travel.it/roma/ianr. E-mail: fiamma.travel@travel.it. 78 units. A/C MINIBAR TV TEL. 300,000–320,000L ($150–$160) double. Rates include breakfast. AE, DC, MC, V. Parking 35,000L ($17.50) nearby. Metro: Termini.

On the far side of the Baths of Diocletian, the Fiamma is in a renovated building, with five floors of shuttered windows and a ground floor faced with marble and plate-glass windows. The hotel is an enduring favorite, if a bit past its prime. The lobby is long and bright, filled with a varied collection of furnishings, like overstuffed chairs and blue enamel railings. On the same floor is an austere marble breakfast room. Some of the comfortably furnished guest rooms, ranging from small to medium-size, are air-conditioned. The mattresses are a bit worn but still comfortable, and the small bathrooms are tiled, with adequate shelf space.

Hotel Pavia. Via Gaeta 83, 00185 Roma. ☎ **06-483-801.** Fax 06-481-9090. www.travel.it/roma/hotelpavia. E-mail: hotelpavia@hotmail.com. 25 units. A/C MINIBAR TV TEL. 250,000L ($125) double. Rates include breakfast. AE, DC, MC, V. Parking 25,000L ($12.50). Metro: Termini.

The Pavia, in a much-renovated 100-year-old villa, is a popular choice on this quiet street near the gardens of the Baths of Diocletian. You take a wisteria-covered passage to reach the recently modernized reception area and tasteful public rooms, where the staff is friendly. The front guest rooms tend to be noisy, but that's the curse of all Termini hotels. All the rooms are comfortable and fairly attractive, with mattresses that have just been replaced. The maids keep everything beautifully maintained, including the medium-sized bathrooms with new plumbing and hair dryers. You don't get grand style, but the quality of the rooms makes this an exceptional bargain.

Pensione Papà Germano. Via Calatafimi 14A, 00185 Roma. ☎ **06-486-919.** Fax 06-478-2520. www.hotelpapagermano.it. E-mail: info@hotelpapagermano.it. 17 units, 7 with private bathroom. TV TEL. 90,000L ($45) double without bathroom, 110,000L ($55) double with bathroom; 100,000L ($50) triple without bathroom; 160,000L ($80) triple with bathroom. AE, DC, MC, V. Metro: Termini.

Papà Germano is about as basic as anything in this book, but it's clean and decent. This 1892 building, on a block-long street immediately east of the Baths of Diocletian, has undergone some recent renovations yet retains its modest ambience. The pensione offers clean accommodations with plain furniture, good mattresses, hair dryers, well-maintained showers, and you'll find a high-turnover crowd of European and North American students. The energetic English-speaking owner, Gino Germano, offers advice on sightseeing. No breakfast is served, but dozens of cafes nearby open early.

NEAR VIA VENETO & PIAZZA BARBERINI

VERY EXPENSIVE

The Excelsior. Via Vittorio Veneto 125, 00187 Roma. ☎ **800/325-3589** in the U.S., or 06-47-081. Fax 06-482-6205. www.luxurycollection.com. 321 units. A/C MINIBAR TV TEL. 700,000–800,000L ($350–$400) double; 1,350,000–2,400,000L ($675–$1,200) suite. AE, DC, DISC, MC, V. Parking 70,000L ($35). Metro: Piazza Barberini.

If money is no object, here's a good place to spend it. The baroque corner tower of this limestone palace, overlooking the U.S. Embassy, is a landmark in Rome. You enter a string of cavernous reception rooms with thick rugs, marble floors, gilded garlands decorating the walls, and Empire furniture. Everything looks just a tad dowdy today, but the Excelsior endures, seemingly as eternal as Rome itself, in no small part because of the exceedingly hospitable staff.

The guest rooms come in two varieties: new (the result of a major renovation) and traditional. The old ones are a bit worn, while the newer ones have more imaginative color schemes and plush carpeting. All are spacious and elegantly furnished, always with deluxe mattresses and often with antiques and silk curtains. Most rooms are unique; many have sumptuous Hollywood-style marble bathrooms with hair dryers and bidets.

Dining/Diversions: The Excelsior Bar (daily 10:30am to 1am) is the most famous on Via Vittorio Veneto, and La Cupola is known for its national and regional cuisine, with spa cuisine and kosher food prepared on request. The Gran Caffè Doney, with sidewalk tables, is a perfect place for excellent drinks, appetizers, and Sunday brunch.

Amenities: Room service, laundry/valet, baby-sitting, beauty salon, barbershop.

Hotel Eden. Via Ludovisi 49, 00187 Roma. ☎ **800/225-5843** in the U.S., or 06-478-121. Fax 06-482-1584. www.hotel-eden.it. E-mail: reservations@hotel-eden.it. 119 units. A/C MINIBAR TV TEL. 940,000–1,150,000L ($470–$575) double; from 2,460,000L ($1,230) suite. AE, CB, DC, DISC, MC, V. Parking 45,000L ($22.50). Metro: Piazza Barberini.

For several generations after its 1889 opening, this hotel near the top of the Spanish Steps reigned over one of the world's most stylish shopping neighborhoods. Hemingway, Callas, Ingrid Bergman, Fellini—all checked in during its heyday. It was bought by Trusthouse Forte in 1989 and reopened in 1994 after 2 years (and $20 million) of renovations that enhanced its grandeur and added the amenities its five–star status calls for. The Eden's hilltop position guarantees a panoramic city view from most guest rooms, and its rates ensure that all those rooms are elegantly appointed and spacious, with a decor harking back to the late 19th century, plus marble-sheathed bathrooms with deluxe toiletries and makeup mirrors. Amenities include fax machines, dual-line phones with data ports, safes, TVs with VCRs, and ample closet space. Some of the front rooms open onto balconies with views of Rome.

Dining/Diversions: There is a piano bar and a glamorous restaurant, La Terrazza (see "Dining," later in this chapter).

Amenities: Concierge, 24-hour room service, dry cleaning/laundry, newspaper delivery on request, secretarial service (prior notification), gym and health club.

EXPENSIVE

Hotel Alexandra. Via Vittorio Veneto 18, 00187 Roma. ☎ **06-488-1943.** Fax 06-487-1804. www.venere.it/roma/alexandra. E-mail: alexandra@venere.it. 64 units. A/C MINIBAR TV TEL. 390,000L ($195) double; 600,000L ($300) suite. Rates include buffet breakfast. AE, DC, MC, V. Parking 30,000L ($15). Metro: Piazza Barberini.

This is one of your few chances to stay on Via Veneto without going broke (though it's not exactly cheap). Set behind the dignified stone facade of what was a 19th-century mansion, the Alexandra offers immaculate guest rooms. Those facing the front are exposed to roaring traffic and street life; those in back are quieter but with less of a view. The rooms range from rather cramped to medium-sized, but each has been recently redecorated, filled with antiques or tasteful contemporary pieces. They have extras like swing-mirror vanities and brass or wood bedsteads with frequently renewed mattresses. The bathrooms are small to medium. Breakfast is the only meal served, though a staff member can carry drinks to you in the reception area. The breakfast room is especially appealing: Inspired by an Italian garden, it was designed by noted architect Paolo Portoghesi.

MODERATE

La Residenza. Via Emilia 22–24, 00187 Roma. ☎ **06-488-0789.** Fax 06-485-721. www.italyhotel.com/roma/la_residenza. E-mail: hotel.la.residenza@italyhotel.com. 29 units. A/C MINIBAR TV TEL. 310,000–350,000L ($155–$175) double; 350,000–410,000L ($175–$205) suite. Rates include buffet breakfast. AE, MC, V. Parking (limited) 10,000L ($5). Metro: Piazza Barberini.

La Residenza, in a superb but noisy location, successfully combines the intimacy of a town house with the elegance of a four-star hotel. It's a bit old-fashioned and homelike but still a favorite of international travelers. The converted villa has an ivy-covered courtyard and a series of upholstered public rooms with Empire divans, oil portraits, and rattan chairs. Terraces are scattered throughout. The guest rooms are generally spacious, containing bentwood chairs and built-in furniture, including beds with quality mattresses. The dozen or so junior suites boast balconies. The bathrooms have hair dryers, robes, even ice machines.

NEAR ANCIENT ROME

MODERATE

Colosseum Hotel. Via Sforza 10, 00184 Roma. ☎ **06-482-7228.** Fax 06-482-7285. www.italyhotel.com/roma/colosseum. E-mail: colosseum@venere.it. 47 units. TV TEL. 239,000–245,000L ($119.50–$122.50) double. Rates include breakfast. AE, DC, MC, V. Parking 35,000L ($17.50). Metro: Cavour.

Two short blocks southwest of Santa Maria Maggiore, this hotel offers affordable and comfortable (yet small) rooms. Someone with flair and lots of lire designed the public areas and upper halls, which hint at baronial grandeur. The drawing room, with its long refectory table, white walls, red tiles, and provincial armchairs, invites lingering. The guest rooms are furnished with well-chosen antique reproductions (beds of heavy carved wood, dark-paneled wardrobes, leatherwood chairs); all have stark white walls and some have old-fashioned plumbing in the bathrooms. Most rooms have air-conditioning.

Hotel Duca d'Alba. Via Leonina 14, 00184 Roma. ☎ **06-484-471.** Fax 06-488-4840. www.italyhotel.com/roma/duca_dalba. E-mail: duca_dalba@venere.it. 27 units. A/C MINIBAR TV TEL. 200,000–370,000L ($100–$185) double; 300,000–400,000L ($150–$200) suite. Rates include breakfast. AE, DC, MC, V. Parking 40,000–50,00 L ($20–$25). Metro: Cavour.

A bargain near the Roman Forum and the Colosseum, this hotel lies in the Suburra neighborhood, which was once pretty seedy but is being gentrified. Completely renovated, the Duca d'Alba yet retains an old-fashioned air (it was built in the 19th century). The guest rooms have elegant Roman styling, with soothing colors, light wood pieces, luxurious beds and bedding, safes, and bathrooms with hair dryers. The most desirable rooms are the four with private balconies.

Hotel Nerva. Via Tor di Conti 3, 00184 Roma. ☎ **06-678-1835.** Fax 06-699-22204. 19 units. A/C MINIBAR TV TEL. 230,000–360,000L ($115–$180) double. Rates include breakfast. AE, MC, V. Metro: Colosseo.

Some of the Nerva's walls and foundations date from the 1500s, others from a century later, but the modern amenities date only from 1997. The site, above and a few steps from the Roman Forum, will appeal to any student of archaeology and literature, and the warm welcome from the Cirulli brothers will appeal to all. The decor is accented with wood panels and terra-cotta tiles; some guest rooms even retain the original ceiling beams. The furniture is contemporary and comfortable, with excellent beds and mattresses. The tiled bathrooms have adequate shelf space.

INEXPENSIVE

Casa Kolbe. Via San Teodoro 44, 00186 Roma. ☎ **06-679-4974.** Fax 06-699-41550. 65 units. TEL. 140,000L ($70) double. AE, MC, V. Metro: Circo Massimo.

Occupying an 1800s building, the Casa Kolbe (often full of bus tour groups from North America and Germany) has a great position between the Palatine and the Campidoglio. The guest rooms, painted in old-fashioned tones of deep red and brown, are simple and well kept, even if some are a bit battered from use. The mattresses may be thin but still have comfort in them, and the bathrooms are small. Many rooms overlook a small garden. The hotel dining room, open only to guests, serves affordable set menus.

NEAR CAMPO DE' FIORI

MODERATE

Casa di Santa Brigida. Via Monserato 54 (off Piazza Farnese). Postal address: Piazza Farnese 96, 00186 Roma. ☎ **06-6889-2596.** Fax 06-6889-1573. www.brigidine.org. E-mail: brigida@mclink.it. 20 units. TEL. 250,000L ($125) double. Rates include breakfast. DC, MC, V. Bus: 46, 62, or 64.

Across from the Michelangelo-designed Palazzo Farnese on a quiet square a block from Campo de' Fiori, Rome's best (and poshest) convent hotel is run by the friendly sisters of St. Bridget in the house where that Swedish saint died in 1373. Rooms where Santa Brigida lived and died are on the first floor. The library is quite large. This convent hotel accepts people of every age and creed. The rates are justified by the comfy and roomy old-world guest rooms with antiques or reproductions on parquet (lower level) or carpeted (upstairs) floors. The bathrooms are a little old but at least have shower curtains, and the beds are heavenly firm. There's a roof terrace, library, and church.

Teatro di Pompeo. Largo del Pallaro 8, 00186 Roma. ☎ **06-6830-0170.** Fax 06-6880-5531. 13 units. A/C TV TEL. 350,000L ($175) double. Rates include breakfast. AE, DC, MC, V. Bus: 64.

Built atop the ruins of the Theater of Pompey, from about 55 B.C., this small charmer lies near the spot where Julius Caesar met his end on the Ides of March. Intimate and refined, it's on a quiet piazzetta near the Palazzo Farnese and Campo de' Fiori. The rooms are decorated in an old-fashioned Italian style with hand-painted tiles, and the beamed ceilings date from the days of Michelangelo. The guest rooms range from small to medium, each with a good mattress and a tidy but cramped tiled bathroom.

NEAR PIAZZA NAVONA & THE PANTHEON

VERY EXPENSIVE

Albergo del Sole al Pantheon. Piazza della Rotonda 63, 00186 Roma. ☎ **06-678-0441.** Fax 06-6994-0689. www.italyhotel.com/roma/solealpantheon. E-mail: hotsole@flashnet.it. 25 units. A/C MINIBAR TV TEL. 570,000L ($285) double; 750,000L ($375) junior suite. Rates include buffet breakfast. AE, DC, MC, V. Bus: 64.

You're obviously paying for the million-dollar view, but you may find it's worth it to be across from the Pantheon, one of antiquity's great relics. (Okay, so you're above a McDonald's, but one look at the Pantheon at sunrise and you won't think about Big Macs.) This building was constructed in 1450 as a home, and the first records of it as a hostelry appeared in 1467, making it one of the world's oldest hotels. The layout is amazingly eccentric and on various levels—prepare to walk up and down a lot of three- or four-step staircases. The guest rooms vary greatly in decor, none award-winning and much of it hit or miss, with compact tiled bathrooms. The windows are double-glazed, but the rooms opening onto the piazza still tend to be noisy at all hours. The quieter rooms overlook the courtyard but are sans the view.

Dining: Breakfast is the only meal served, but there are dozens of trattorie in the neighborhood.

Amenities: Room service, laundry/dry cleaning, baby-sitting (not always available), twice-daily maid service.

Family-Friendly Hotels

Cavalieri Hilton *(see p. 91)* This hotel is like a resort, with a pool, gardens, and plenty of grounds for children to run and play. It's only 15 minutes from the center of Rome, which you can reach via the hotel shuttle bus.

Hotel Nord Nuova Roma *(see p. 77)* For the family on a budget who wants to be near the rail station, this is a good choice because many of the rooms are quite spacious and extra beds can be added. It's also near a family-friendly restaurant run by the same people.

Hotel Ranieri *(see p. 77)* This hotel offers a family-style atmosphere, with some rooms large enough to comfortably house families of three or four. Baby cots are on hand as well.

Hotel Venezia *(see p. 77)* At this good moderately priced family hotel near Stazione Termini, the rooms have been renovated and most are large enough to hold extra beds for children.

Hotel Raphael. Largo Febo 2, 00186 Roma. ☎ **06-682-831.** Fax 06-687-8993. www.raphaelhotel.com. E-mail: info@raphaelhotel.com. 72 units. A/C MINIBAR TV TEL. 500,000–600,000L ($250–$300) double; 700,000–800,000L ($350–$400) suite. Breakfast 35,000L ($17.50). AE, DC, MC, V. Parking 45,000L ($22.50). Bus: 70, 81, 87, or 115.

Adjacent to Piazza Navona, the Raphael is within easy walking distance of many sites. The ivy-covered facade invites you to enter the lobby, decorated with antiques that rival the cache in local museums (even a Picasso ceramics collection). The guest rooms (some quite small) were recently refurbished with a Florentine touch and contain quality mattresses on double or twin beds. Some of the suites have private terraces.

Dining: The elegant restaurant/bar, Café Picasso, serves a French/Italian cuisine. From the hotel's rooftop garden terrace, Bramante, you can enjoy a panoramic view over the ancient city while you dine in the summer.

Amenities: Room service, fitness room, baby-sitting, laundry, currency exchange.

MODERATE

Albergo Cesàri. Via di Pietra 89A, 00186 Roma. ☎ **06-679-2386.** Fax 06-679-0882. www.venere.it/roma/cesari/cesari.html. E-mail: cesari@venere.it. 48 units. A/C MINIBAR TV TEL. 300,000–340,000L ($150–$170) double; 400,000L ($200) triple; 450,000L ($225) quad. Rates include buffet breakfast. AE, DC, MC, V. Parking 50,000L ($25). Bus: 492 from Stazione Termini.

The Cesàri, on an ancient street, has occupied its desirable location between the Trevi Fountain and the Pantheon since 1787. Its well-preserved exterior harmonizes with the Temple of Neptune and many little antiques shops nearby. The guest rooms (some suitable for the disabled) have mostly functional modern pieces, but there are a few traditional trappings to maintain character; the mattresses are fine and firm. In 1998, all the accommodations and the breakfast room were completely renovated.

INEXPENSIVE

Pensione Navona. Via dei Sediari 8, 00186 Roma. ☎ **06-686-4203.** Fax 06-6880-3802. 35 units, 30 with bathroom. 130,000L ($65) double without bathroom, 180,000–220,000L ($90–$110) double with bathroom; 230,000L ($115) triple with bathroom. Rates include breakfast. No credit cards. Bus: 70, 81, 87, or 115.

This pensione is on a small street radiating from Piazza Navona's southeastern tip. The rooms aren't as glamorous as the exterior, but the Navona offers decent accommodations, many of which have been renovated and some of which open to views of the central courtyard. Run by an Australian-born family of Italian descent, it boasts ceilings high enough to help relieve the midsummer heat and an array of architectural oddities (the legacy of the continual construction this palace has undergone since 1360). The beds, most often twins or doubles, have fine linens and good mattresses. You can get an air-conditioned room by request for 40,000L ($20) per night (only in the doubles with bathroom).

NEAR PIAZZA DEL POPOLO & THE SPANISH STEPS

VERY EXPENSIVE

The Hassler. Piazza Trinità dei Monti 6, 00187 Roma. ☎ **800/223-6800** in the U.S., or 06-699-340. Fax 06-678-9991. www.hotelhasslerroma.com. E-mail: info@hasslerroma@inclink.net. 100 units. A/C MINIBAR TV TEL. 790,000–950,000L ($395–$475) double; from 2,600,000L ($1,300) suite. AE, CB, DC, MC, V. Parking 50,000L ($25). Metro: Piazza di Spagna.

The Hassler, rebuilt in 1944 to replace the 1885 original, uses the Spanish Steps as its grand entrance. Its crown has become a bit tarnished, but it possesses such a mystique from tradition and the one-of-kind location that it can get away with charging astronomical rates. The lounges and the guest rooms, with their "Italian Park Avenue" trappings, all strike a faded if still glamorous 1930s note.

The guest rooms range from small singles to some of the most spacious suites in town. High ceilings make them appear larger than they are, and many of them open onto private balconies or terraces. The mattresses are deluxe and the beds suitable for a president or king (you'll likely see one or two of each). Only medium in size, the bathrooms are classy, complete with hair dryers and a range of deluxe body and hair products. The front rooms, though dramatically overlooking the Spanish Steps, are often noisy at night, but the views are worth it. For panoramas of the Roman rooftops, ask for a room on the top floor.

Dining/Diversions: The Hassler Roof Restaurant is a favorite with visitors and Romans alike for its fine cuisine and view. Its Sunday brunch is a popular rendezvous time. The Hassler Bar is ideal, if a little formal, for cocktails; in the evening it has piano music.

Amenities: Room service, laundry, limousine, in-room massages, nearby fitness center, tennis court (summer), free bicycles.

Hotel d'Inghilterra. Via Bocca di Leone 14, 00187 Roma. ☎ **06-69-981.** Fax 06-679-8601. www.charminghotels.it/inghilterra. E-mail: hir@charminghotel.it. 106 units. A/C MINIBAR TV TEL. 540,000L ($270) double; from 1,050,000L ($525) suite. Breakfast 34,000L ($17). AE, DC, MC, V. Parking 40,000L ($20). Metro: Piazza di Spagna.

The Inghilterra holds onto its traditions and heritage, even though it has been renovated. Situated between Via Condotti and Via Borgogna, this hotel in the 17th century was the guest house of the Torlonia princes. If you're willing to spend a king's ransom, Rome's most fashionable small hotel is comparable to the Hassler and Inter-Continental. The rooms have mostly old pieces (gilt and lots of marble, mahogany chests, and glittery mirrors), complemented by modern conveniences. Some, however, are just too cramped, though all boast quality mattresses and fine linen. The preferred rooms are higher up, opening onto a tile terrace, with a balustrade and a railing covered with flowering vines and plants. The bathrooms have been refurbished and offer deluxe toiletries and hair dryers.

Dining/Diversions: The Roman Garden serves excellent Roman dishes. The English-style bar with its paneled walls, tip-top tables, and old lamps is a favorite gathering spot in the evening. The Roman Garden Lounge offers light lunches and snacks.

Accommodations Near the Spanish Steps

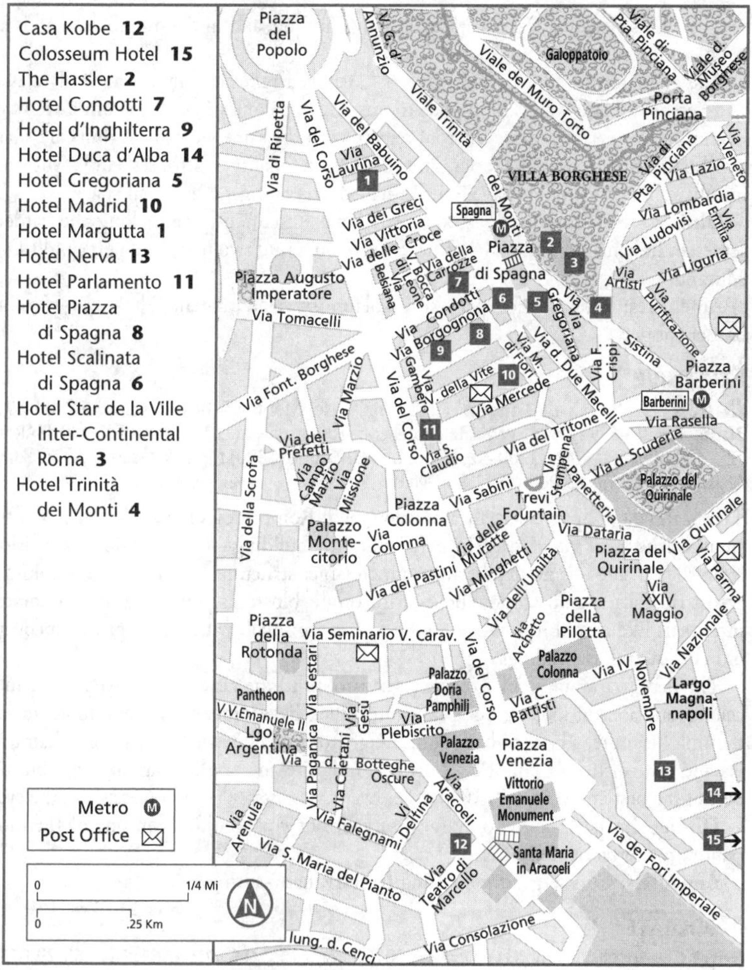

Amenities: Concierge, room service, dry cleaning/laundry, baby-sitting, car-rental desk, secretarial services, gym.

✪ **Hotel de la Ville Inter-Continental Roma.** Via Sistina 67–69, 00187 Roma. ☎ **800/327-0200** in the U.S. and Canada, or 06-67-331. Fax 06-678-4213. www.interconti.com. E-mail: rome@interconti.com. 192 units. A/C MINIBAR TV TEL. 700,000–810,000L ($350–$405) double; from 1,110,000L ($555) suite. Rates include continental breakfast. AE, DC, MC, V. Parking 45,000L ($22.50). Metro: Piazza di Spagna or Barberini.

We prefer this place, designed in 1924 by Hungarian architect Jozef Vago, to the overpriced glory of the Hassler next door. The hotel looks deluxe (it's officially rated first class) from the minute you walk through the revolving door, where a smartly uniformed doorman greets you. Once inside this palace, built in the 19th century on the site of the ancient Gardens of Lucullus, you'll find Oriental rugs, marble tables, brocade furniture, and an English-speaking staff. There are endless corridors leading to what at first seems a maze of ornamental lounges. Some of the public rooms have a sort of 1930s elegance and others are strictly baroque, and in the middle of it all is an open courtyard.

The guest rooms and the public areas have been renovated in a beautifully classic and yet up-to-date way. The higher rooms with balconies have panoramic views of Rome, and you're free to use the roof terrace with the same view. Most units are small but boast chintz-covered fabrics, fine beds with quality mattresses, and concealed minibars. The bathrooms have built-in hair dryers and generous shelf space.

Dining/Diversions: La Piazzetta de la Ville Restaurant, overlooking the garden, serves an Italian/international cuisine. Inside you'll find two bars, La Saletta and I Due Murano.

Amenities: Room service, baby-sitting, laundry/valet, car-rental desk, beauty salon, barber shop.

EXPENSIVE

✪ **Hotel Scalinata di Spagna.** Piazza Trinità dei Monti 17, 00187 Roma. ☎ **06-679-3006.** Fax 06-6994-0598. www.italyhotel.com/roma/scalinata. 16 units. A/C MINIBAR TV TEL. 400,000–500,000L ($200–$250) double; 600,000L ($300) triple. Rates include breakfast. AE, MC, V. Parking 45,000L ($22.50). Metro: Spagna.

The Scalinata di Spagna has always been one of Rome's best choices, at the top of the steps, across from the Hassler. Its delightful little building—only two floors are visible from the outside—is nestled between much larger structures, with four relief columns across the facade and window boxes with bright blossoms. The recently redecorated interior is like an old inn's—the public rooms are small, with bright print slipcovers, old clocks, and low ceilings.

The decor varies radically from one guest room to the next. Some have low beamed ceilings and ancient-looking wood furniture; others have loftier ceilings and more run-of-the-mill furniture. The tiled bathrooms range from small to medium but offer hair dryers and state-of-the-art plumbing. The best units are any overlooking the steps, but the best of the best are room nos. 10 and 12. Everything is spotless and pleasing to the eye.

Dining: Breakfast is the only meal served, but you'll enjoy it on one of the most panoramic terraces in all Rome.

Amenities: Concierge, dry cleaning/laundry, baby-sitting.

MODERATE

Hotel Condotti. Via Mario de' Fiori 37, 00187 Roma. ☎ **06-679-4661.** Fax 06-679-0457. www.venere.it/roma/condotti. 16 units. A/C MINIBAR TV TEL. 310,000–490,000L ($155–$245) double; 350,000–520,000L ($175–$260) minisuite. Rates include buffet breakfast. AE, DC, MC, V. Metro: Piazza di Spagna.

The Condotti is small, choice, and terrific for shoppers intent on being near the tony boutiques. The staff, nearly all of whom speak English, is cooperative and hardworking. The mostly blue-and-white modern rooms may not have much historic charm, but they're comfortable and soothing. Renovated in 1991, each is decorated with traditional furnishings, including excellent beds—usually twins. Room 414 is often requested because it has a geranium-filled terrace. There's no bar or restaurant, but dry cleaning/laundry, a car rental, and a tour desk are extras.

Hotel Gregoriana. Via Gregoriana 18, 00187 Roma. ☎ **06-679-4269.** Fax 06-678-4258. 20 units. A/C TV TEL. 380,000L ($190) double. Rates include breakfast. AE, DC, V. Parking 30,000–40,000L ($15–$20). Metro: Spagna.

The intimate Gregoriana has many fans, including guests from the Italian fashion industry. The matriarch of an aristocratic family left the building to an order of nuns in the 19th century, but they eventually retreated to other quarters. (There might be an elevated spirituality in Room C, as it used to be a chapel.) The elevator cage is a black-and-gold art deco fantasy. The smallish guest rooms provide comfort and fine Italian design, and the door to each bears a reproduction of an Erté print whose fanciful characters indicate the letter designating that room. Each has a queen or double bed, with a firm mattress. The bathrooms are a bit small but always spotless, with hair dryers.

Hotel Madrid. Via Mario de' Fiori 93–95, 00187 Roma. ☎ **06-699-1511.** Fax 06-679-1653. www.hotel-madrid.net. 26 units. A/C MINIBAR TV TEL. 350,000L ($175) double; 500,000L ($250) suite. Rates include breakfast. AE, DC, MC, V. Parking 40,000–45,000L ($20–$22.50) nearby. Metro: Piazza di Spagna.

Despite modern touches in the comfortable, if minimalist, guest rooms, the interior of the Madrid manages to evoke fin-de-siècle Roma. Guests often take their breakfast amid ivy and blossoming plants on the roof terrace with a panoramic view of rooftops and the distant dome of St. Peter's. Some of the doubles are large, with scatter rugs, veneer armoires, and shuttered windows, but others are quite small; so make sure you know what you're getting before you check in. Each bed (usually double or twin) is fitted with a good mattress. The bathrooms were renovated in 1998.

Hotel Piazza di Spagna. Via Mario de' Fiori 61, 00187 Roma. ☎ **06-679-6412.** Fax 06-679-0654. 17 units. A/C MINIBAR TV TEL. 310,000–400,000L ($155–$200) double. Rates include breakfast. AE, MC, V. Parking 25,000L ($12.50) nearby. Metro: Piazza di Spagna. Bus: 590.

About a block from the downhill side of the Spanish Steps, this hotel was just a run-down pensione until new owners took it over in the 1990s and substantially upgraded it. It's small but classic, with an inviting atmosphere. The guest rooms (some very small) boast a functional streamlined decor; some even have Jacuzzis in the tiled bathrooms. Dry cleaning, laundry, and room service (7am to 6pm) are available.

Hotel Trinità dei Monti. Via Sistina 91, 00187 Roma. ☎ **06-679-7206.** Fax 06-699-0111. 25 units. A/C MINIBAR TV TEL. 290,000–340,000L ($145–$170) double. Rates include breakfast. AE, DC, MC, V. Metro: Barberini or Piazza di Spagna.

Between two of the most-visited piazzas in Rome (Barberini and Spagna), this is a well-maintained friendly place. The hotel occupies the second and third floors of an antique building, and its guest rooms come with herringbone-patterned parquet floors and big windows and are comfortable if not flashy. Each has a good mattress and a tidy tiled bathroom. The hotel's social center is a simple coffee bar near the reception desk. Don't expect anything terribly fancy, but the welcome is warm and the location ultraconvenient.

INEXPENSIVE

Hotel Margutta. Via Laurina 34, 00187 Roma. ☎ **06-322-3674.** Fax 06-320-0395. 24 units. 190,000–260,000L ($95–$130) double; 250,000L ($125) triple. Rates include breakfast. AE, DC, MC, V. Metro: Flaminio.

The Margutta, on a cobblestone street near Piazza del Popolo, offers attractively decorated guest rooms, a helpful staff, and a simple breakfast room. The best rooms are the three on the top floor, offering a great view. Two of these three (nos. 50 and 51) share a terrace, and the larger room has a private terrace. (There's usually a 20 to 35% supplement for these.) Drawbacks? No air-conditioning, no room phones. However, each room comes with a comfortable bed containing a good mattress, plus a small but tidy bathroom.

✪ **Hotel Parlamento.** Via delle Convertite 5 (at the intersection with Via del Cor.), 00187 Roma. ☎ **06-679-2082.** Fax 06-6992-1000. 23 units. TV TEL. 200,000L ($100) double. Rates include breakfast. AE, DC, MC, V. Parking 28,000–30,000L ($14–$15). Metro: Spagna.

The Parlamento has four-star class at two-star prices with a friendly pensione-style reception. The street traffic is so heavy that the management installed an effective *double set* of double-glazed windows. The furnishings are antiques or reproduction, and the firm beds are backed by carved wood or wrought-iron headboards. Fifteen rooms are air-conditioned, and the bathrooms were recently redone with hair dryers, heated towel racks, phones, and (in a few) even marble sinks. *Note:* It's a three-story hotel with a recently added elevator. Rooms are different in style, the most desirable are no. 82 with its original 1800s furniture, and nos. 104, 106, and 107 because they open onto the roof garden. You can enjoy the chandeliered and tromp l'oeil breakfast room or carry your cappuccino up to the small roof terrace with its view of San Silvestro's bell tower.

NEAR VATICAN CITY

VERY EXPENSIVE

✪ **Hotel Atlante Star.** Via Vitelleschi 34, 00193 Roma. ☎ **06-687-3233.** Fax 06-687-2300. www.atlantehotels.com. E-mail: atlante.star@atlantehotels.com. 90 units. A/C MINIBAR TV TEL. 580,000L ($290) double; from 750,000L ($375) suite. Rates include buffet breakfast. AE, DC, MC, V. Parking 40,000L ($20). Metro: Ottaviano. Bus: 23, 64, or 492.

The Atlante Star is a first-class hotel with striking views of St. Peter's. The tastefully renovated lobby is covered with dark marble, chrome trim, and exposed wood; the upper floors will make you feel as if you're on a luxury ocean liner (no icebergs in sight). This stems partly from the lavish use of curved and lacquered surfaces, walls upholstered in printed fabrics, and wall-to-wall carpeting. Even the door handles are deco. The guest rooms are small but posh, with all the modern comforts, like elegant beds with quality mattresses and modern bathrooms with hair dryers. The royal suite has a Jacuzzi. If there's no room here, the owner will try to accommodate you in his less-expensive **Atlante Garden** nearby.

Dining: Les Etoiles is an elegant roof-garden choice at night, with a 360° view of Rome and an illuminated St. Peter's in the background. The flavorful cuisine is inspired in part by Venice. There is also a less-formal restaurant, Terrazza Paradiso, serving international cuisine.

Amenities: 24-hour room service, laundry/valet, baby-sitting, express checkout, foreign-currency exchange, secretarial services in English, translation services.

Hotel Columbus. Via della Conciliazione 33, 00193 Roma. ☎ **06-686-5435.** Fax 06-686-4874. 92 units. A/C MINIBAR TV TEL. 570,000L ($285) double; 660,000L ($330) suite. Rates include buffet breakfast. AE, CB, DC, MC, V. The hotel has a few free parking spaces. Bus: 62 or 64.

An impressive 15th-century palace, the Columbus was once the home of the cardinal who became Pope Julius II and tormented Michelangelo into painting the Sistine Chapel. The building looks much as it must have centuries ago: a severe time-stained facade, small windows, and heavy wooden doors leading from the street to the colonnades and arches of the inner courtyard. The cobbled entranceway leads to a reception hall and a series of baronial public rooms. Note the main salon with its walk-in fireplace, oil portraits, battle scenes, and Oriental rugs.

The guest rooms are considerably simpler than the salons, furnished with comfortable modern pieces. All are spacious, but a few are enormous and still have such original details as decorated wood ceilings and frescoed walls. The best and quietest rooms front the garden. The bathrooms are medium in size and offer all the standards, like up-to-date plumbing, hair dryers and toiletries.

Dining: Many guests like La Veranda so much they prefer to dine here at night instead of roaming the streets looking for a trattoria. Standard Italian cuisine is served: time-tested recipes made with fresh ingredients rather than anything too innovative.

Amenities: Concierge, room service, dry cleaning/laundry, car-rental desk.

EXPENSIVE

Hotel dei Mellini. Via Muzio Clementi 81, 00193 Roma. ☎ **06-324-771.** Fax 06-3247-7801. www.hotelmellini.com. E-mail: info@hotelmellini.com. 80 units. A/C MINIBAR TV TEL. 500,000L ($250) double; 780,000L ($390) suite. Rates include breakfast. AE, DC, MC, V. Parking 40,000L ($20). Metro: Lepanto or Flaminio.

Built as a neoclassical-style home in the early 1900s, this town house in a quiet neighborhood without a lot of traffic was abandoned in 1970 and stood as an empty shell for years. Then it got a radical transformation and opened in 1995 as a four-star hotel. It consists of two interconnected buildings, one with four floors and one with six; the top is graced with a terrace overlooking the baroque cupolas of at least three churches. A small staff, headed by the highly capable Roberto Altezza, maintains the lovely guest rooms, whose decor includes art deco touches, Italian marble, mahogany furniture, and beds with fine linen and quality mattresses. The tiled bathrooms have adequate shelf space. Nonsmoking rooms are available.

Dining/Diversions: Other than a simple platter of food the staff might rustle up on short notice, breakfast is the only meal served. The breakfast room is extremely pleasant, adjoining a small green courtyard. There's also a hospitable American bar.

Amenities: Concierge, room service, dry cleaning/laundry, courtesy car, car-rental desk, nearby gym.

INEXPENSIVE

Hotel Emmaus. Via delle Fornaci 23, 00165 Roma. ☎ **06-638-0370.** Fax 06-635-658. 29 units. MINIBAR TV TEL. 200,000L ($100) double. Rates include breakfast. AE, DC, MC, V. Parking 25,000–30,000L ($12.50–$15) nearby. Metro: Ottaviano. Bus: 65.

Because of its relatively low prices and location near the Vatican, you might share this hotel with Catholic pilgrims from all over the world. Occupying an older building last renovated and upgraded in 1992, it offers unpretentious and basic but comfortable accommodations. The guest rooms have recently been renovated but are still quite small, fitted with good mattresses on twin or double beds. Each comes with a small but efficiently organized bathroom. There's a breakfast area.

Hotel Sant'Angelo. Via Mariana Dionigi 16, 00193 Roma. ☎ **06-322-0758.** Fax 06-320-4451. www.novaera.it/hsa. E-mail: has@novaera.it. 31 units. TV TEL. 160,000–270,000L ($80–$135) double; 180,000–300,000L ($90–$150) triple. Rates include breakfast. MC, V. Parking 35,000L ($17.50). Metro: Lepanto.

This hotel, right off Piazza Cavour (northeast of the Castel Sant'Angelo) and a 10-minute walk from St. Peter's, is in a relatively untouristy area. Maintained and operated by several members of the Torre family, it occupies the second and third floors of an imposing 200-year-old building whose other floors house offices and private apartments. The rooms are simple, modern, and clean, with wooden furniture and views of either the street or a rather bleak but quiet courtyard. Rooms are quite small but not cramped, all painted in a different shade of blue. Each has a good mattress resting on a comfortable bed, plus a small tiled bathroom.

Pension Alimandi. Via Tunisi 8, 00192 Roma. ☎ **06-3972-3948.** Fax 06-3972-3943. 30 units. A/C TV TEL. 220,000L ($110) double. AE, MC, V. Parking 30,000L ($15). Metro: Ottaviano.

Named after the three brothers who run it (Luigi, Enrico, and Paolo), this friendly guest house was built as an apartment house in 1908 in a bland residential neighborhood. The guest rooms are comfortable, albeit a bit small, with unremarkable contemporary furniture and cramped but modern-looking bathrooms. All have been upgraded and fitted with fine mattresses on the beds, most often doubles. Each of the three upper floors is serviced by two elevators leading down to a simple lobby. The social center and most appealing spot is the roof garden, with potted plants, a bar, and views of St. Peter's dome.

Residence Giuggioli. Via Germanico 198, 00192 Roma. ☎ **06-324-2113.** 5 units, 2 with bathroom. 130,000L ($65) double without bathroom, 150,000L ($75) double with bathroom. No credit cards. Parking 25,000–40,000L ($12.50–$20) in nearby garage. Metro: Ottaviano.

The force behind this place is Sra. Gasparina Giuggioli, whose family founded this guest house in the 1940s. It occupies most of the second floor of a five-story 1870s apartment house, with high-ceilinged rooms that were originally much grander but whose noble proportions are still obvious. Three of the five rooms have balconies overlooking the street; the one with the private bathroom is no. 6. The Giuggioli is always crowded, partly because the owner is so convivial and partly because the rooms are larger than expected and have a scattering of antiques and reproductions (though the mattresses could use replacing). There's no breakfast or other meal service, but there are cafes nearby.

If this place is full, walk a few flights to the similar **Pensione Lady** (☎ **06-324-2112**), where up to seven rooms might be available at about the same rates.

IN PARIOLI

VERY EXPENSIVE

✪ **Hotel Lord Byron.** Via G. de Notaris 5, 00197 Roma. ☎ **06-322-0404.** Fax 06-322-0405. www.lordbyronhotel.com. E-mail: info@lordbyronhotel.com. 37 units. A/C MINIBAR TV TEL. 500,000–750,000L ($250–$375) double; from 1,200,000L ($600) suite. Rates include breakfast. AE, DC, MC, V. Parking 45,000L ($22.50). Metro: Flaminio. Bus: 52.

Lots of sophisticated travelers with hefty wallets are forgetting about the old landmarks (the Grand and Excelsior) and choosing this chic boutique hotel. The Lord Byron exemplifies modern Rome—an art deco villa set on a residential hilltop in Parioli, an area of embassies and exclusive town houses at the edge of the Villa Borghese. From the curving entrance steps off the staffed parking lot in front, you'll notice striking design touches. Flowers are everywhere, the lighting is discreet, and everything is on an intimate scale. Each guest room is unique, but most have lots of mirrors, upholstered walls, sumptuous beds, spacious bathrooms with gray marble accessories, hair dryers, and big dressing room/closets. Ask for room no. 503, 602, or 603 for great views.

Dining/Diversions: Relais Le Jardin is one of Rome's best restaurants (see "Dining," later in this chapter). The hotel has a sophisticated bar, Il Salotto, a good place for afternoon tea, drinks, or piano music in the evening.

Amenities: Concierge, room service, laundry/valet, currency exchange.

MODERATE

Hotel degli Aranci. Via Barnaba Oriani 11, 00197 Roma. ☎ **06-808-5250.** Fax 06-807-0202. 55 units. A/C MINIBAR TV TEL. 380,000L ($190) double; from 500,000L ($250) suite. Rates include breakfast. AE, DC, MC, V. Free parking. Bus: 3 or 53.

This former villa is on a tree-lined street, surrounded by similar villas now often used as consulates and diplomats' homes. Most of the accommodations have tall windows opening onto city views and are filled with provincial furnishings or English-style reproductions, including good beds fitted with fine mattresses and linen and tiled bathrooms with adequate shelf space. Scattered about the public rooms are memorabilia of ancient Rome, such as medallions of soldiers in profile, old engravings of ruins, and classical vases. A marble-topped bar in an alcove off the sitting room adds a relaxed touch. From the glass-walled breakfast room at the rear, you can see the tops of orange trees.

INEXPENSIVE

Hotel delle Muse. Via Tommaso Salvini 18, 00197 Roma. ☎ **06-808-8333.** Fax 06-808-5749. www.venere.it/roma/muse. E-mail: hmuse@flashnet.it. 61 units. TV TEL. 160,000–240,000L ($80–$120) double; 200,000–290,000L ($100–$145) triple. Rates include buffet breakfast. AE, CB, DC, MC, V. Parking 30,000L ($15). Bus: 360.

This three-star hotel, half a mile north of the Villa Borghese, is a winning but undiscovered choice run by the efficient English-speaking Giorgio Lazar. Most rooms have been renovated but remain rather minimalist. Nonetheless, there's reasonable comfort here, with good mattresses and tidy bathrooms. In summer, Sr. Lazar operates a restaurant in the garden. A bar is open 24 hours in case you get thirsty at 5am. There's also a TV room, a writing room, and a dining room.

IN MONTE MARIO

VERY EXPENSIVE

Cavalieri Hilton. Via Cadlolo 101, 00136 Roma. ☎ **800/445-8667** in the U.S. and Canada, or 06-35091. Fax 06-3509-2241. www.cavalieri-hilton.it. E-mail: info@cavalieri-hilton.it. 376 units. A/C MINIBAR TV TEL. 700,000–900,000L ($350–$450) double; from 1,400,000L ($700) suite. AE, CB, DC, DISC, MC, V. Parking 40,000L ($20). Free shuttle bus to/from city center.

A 15-minute drive from the center of Rome, the Cavalieri Hilton has all the amenities of a resort hotel. Overlooking Rome and the Alban Hills from atop Monte Mario, it's set among 15 acres of trees, flowering shrubs, and stonework. Its facilities are amazingly complete.

The entrance leads into a lavish red-and-gold lobby, whose sculpture and winding staircases are usually flooded with sun from the massive windows. The guest rooms and suites, many with panoramic views, are contemporary and stylish. Soft furnishings in pastels are paired with Italian furniture in warm-toned woods, including beds with deluxe mattresses and linen. Each unit has a keyless electronic lock, individually controlled heating and air-conditioning, a color TV with in-house movies, a radio, bedside controls for all the gadgets, and a spacious balcony. The bathrooms, sheathed in Italian marble, come with large mirrors, hair dryers, international electric sockets, vanity mirrors, piped-in music, and phones. There are facilities for travelers with disabilities.

Dining: The stellar La Pergola restaurant boasts one of the best views in Rome; its light Mediterranean menu emphasizes seafood like tagliolini with tiger prawns in pesto. In summer, Il Giardino dell'Uliveto, with a pool veranda, is an ideal choice.

Amenities: Concierge, room service, laundry/valet, tennis courts, jogging paths, indoor shop arcade, outdoor pool. The hotel's health and fitness center could be the setting for a film on late Empire decadence, with its triple-arched Turkish bath, marble, and mosaics; there's a 55-foot indoor pool and a state-of-the-art weight room.

4 Dining

Rome remains one of the world's great capitals for dining, with even more diversity today than ever before. Most of its trattorie haven't changed their menus in a quarter of a century (except to raise the prices, of course), but there's an increasing number of chic upscale spots with chefs willing to experiment, as well as a growing handful of

Rome Dining

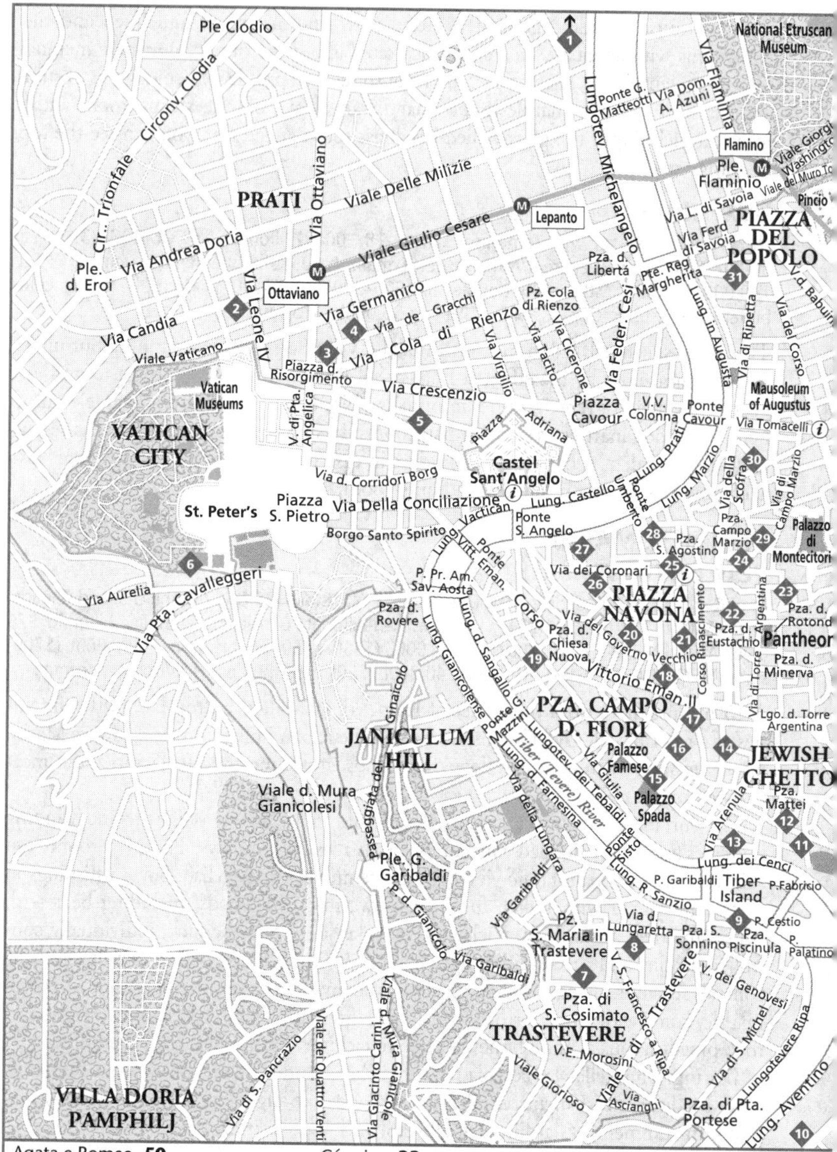

Agata e Romeo **50**
Al Ceppo **32**
Alberto Ciarla **7**
Alvaro al Circo Massimo **47**
Antica Hostaria l'Archeologia **48**
Arancia Blu **51**
Aurora 10 da Pino il Sommelier **36**
Babington's Tea Rooms **38**
Bramante **25**
Césarina **33**
Checchino dal 1887 **10**
Colline Emiliane **41**
Da Giggetto **12**
Dal Bolognese **31**
El Toulà **30**
Girarrosto Toscano **34**
Hostaria dei Bastioni **2**
Hostaria Nerone **46**
Il Bacaro **29**
Il Dito e La Luna **52**
Il Drappo **19**
Il Miraggio **43**
Il Quadrifoglio **44**
Il Ristorante 34 **40**
Insalata Ricca **16**
Insalata Ricca 2 **18**
Insalata Ricca 6 **3**
L'Eau Vive **22**
La Cisterna **9**

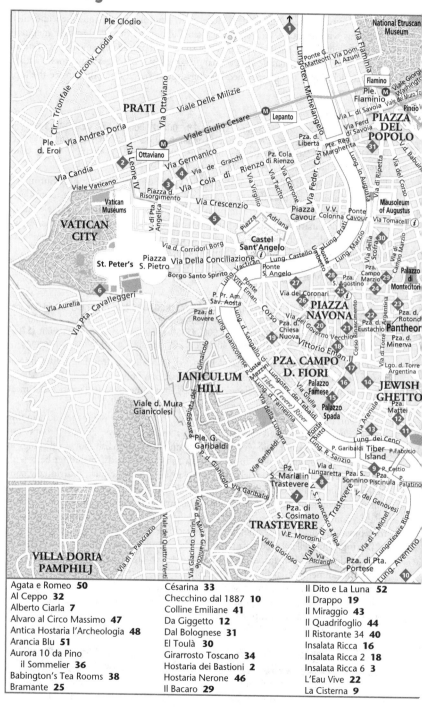

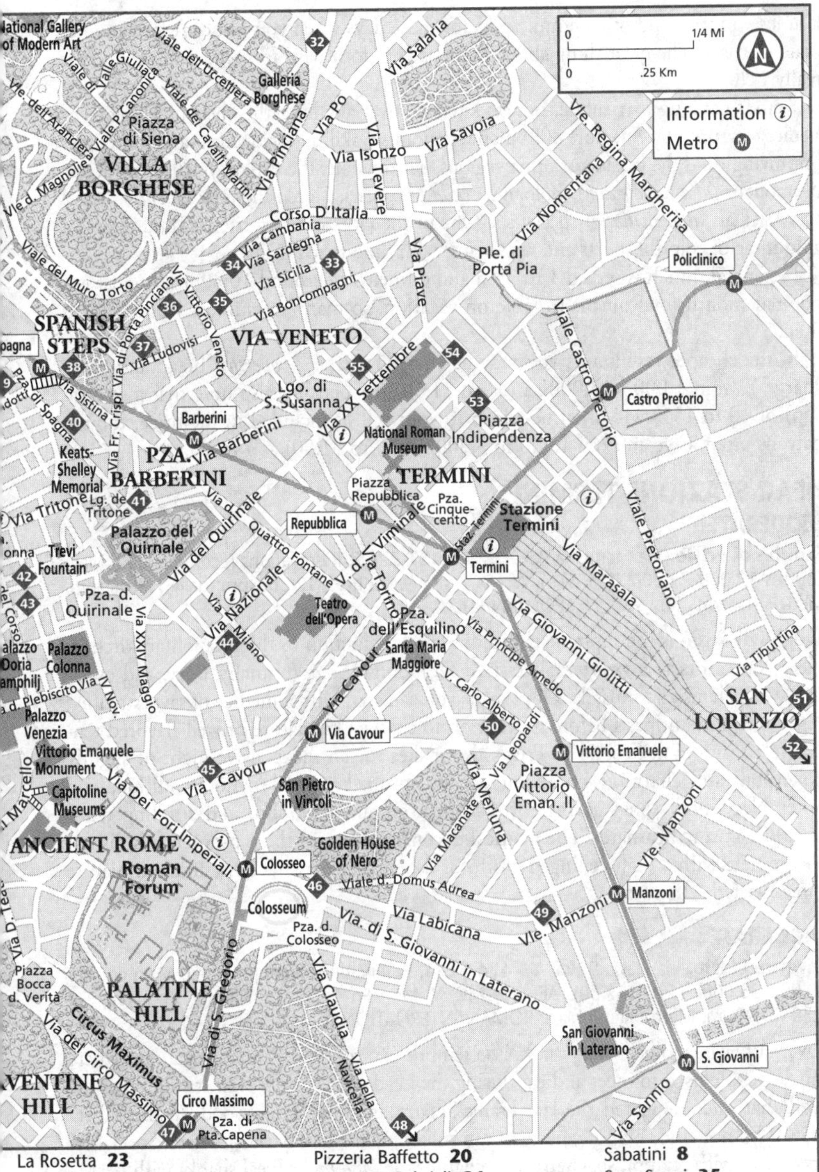

La Rosetta **23**
La Terrazza **37**
Le Maschere **14**
Les Etoiles **5**
Monte Arci **53**
Montevecchio **26**
Osteria dell'Antiquario **27**
Otello alla Concordia **39**
Piperno **13**
Pizzeria Baffetto **20**
Quinzi & Gabrieli **24**
Quirino **42**
Relais Le Jardin **1**
Ristorante al Cardello **45**
Ristorante da Pancrazio **15**
Ristorante del Pallaro **17**
Ristorante Giardinaccio **6**
Ristorante Il Matriciano **4**
Sabatini **8**
Sans Souci **35**
Scoglio di Frisio **49**
Taverna Flavia **55**
Tre Scalini **21**
Trimani Wine Bar **54**
Troiani **28**
Vecchia Roma **11**

Chinese, Indian, and other ethnic spots for those days when you just can't face another plate of pasta. The great thing about Rome is you don't have to spend a fortune to eat really well.

Rome's cooking isn't subtle, but its kitchens rival anything the chefs of Florence or Venice can turn out. A feature of Roman restaurants is skill at borrowing—and sometimes improving on—the cuisine of other regions. Throughout the capital you'll come across Neapolitan *(alla napoletana)*, Bolognese *(alla bolognese)*, Florentine *(alla fiorentina)*, and even Sicilian *(alla siciliana)* specialties. One of the city's oldest sections, Trastevere, is a gold mine of colorful streets and restaurants with time-tested recipes.

In general, lunch is served 1 to 3pm and dinner 8 to around 10:30pm. August is a popular month for Romans to leave on vacation, so many restaurants will be closed then.

In the cheaper restaurants you may be charged a *pane e coperto* ("bread and cover charge"), from 1,000 to 3,000L (50¢ to $1.50) per person. Also note that a *servizio* (tip) of 10 to 15% will often be added to your bill or included in the price, though patrons often leave an extra 1,000 to 3,000L (50¢ to $1.50) as a token.

NEAR STAZIONE TERMINI

MODERATE

Scoglio di Frisio. Via Merulana 256. ☎ **06-487-2765.** Reservations recommended. Main courses 12,000–32,000L ($6–$16). AE, DC, MC, V. Mon–Fri 12:30–3pm; daily 7:30–11pm. Metro: Manzoni. Bus: 714. NEAPOLITAN/PIZZA.

Scoglio di Frisio is the supreme choice for an introduction to the Neapolitan kitchen. Here you can taste a *genuine* plate-sized Neapolitan pizza (crunchy, oozy, and excellent) with clams and mussels. Or perhaps you can start with a medley of savory stuffed vegetables and antipasti before moving on to chicken cacciatore or well-flavored tender veal scaloppini. Scoglio di Frisio also makes for an inexpensive night of slightly hokey but still charming entertainment, as cornball "O Sole Mio" renditions and other Neapolitan songs spring forth from a guitar, mandolin, and strolling tenor (Mario Lanza reincarnate). The nautical decor (in honor of the top-notch fish dishes) is complete with a high-ceilinged grotto of fishers' nets, crustaceans, and a miniature three-masted schooner.

MODERATE

Taverna Flavia. Via Flavia 9. ☎ **06-474-5214.** Reservations recommended. Main courses 20,000–35,000L ($10–$17.50). AE, DC, MC, V. Mon–Fri 12:30–3pm and 7:30–11pm, Sat 7:30–11:30pm. Metro: Repubblica. ROMAN/INTERNATIONAL.

Taverna Flavia, a block from Via XX Settembre, is a robustly Roman restaurant where movie people used to meet and eat during the heyday of *la dolce vita.* It still serves the food that once delighted the late Frank Sinatra and the "Hollywood on the Tiber" crowd. It's not chic anymore, but you can still enjoy the hearty classics here. Specialties are risotto with scampi, spaghetti with champagne, *osso bucco* (veal shank) with peas, a delectable seafood salad, and a to-die-for fondue with truffles. There's a daily regional dish (it might be Roman-style tripe prepared in such a savory manner that it tastes far better than you might expect). A chef always prepares our favorite salad in Rome: Veruska, made with five kinds of lettuce and mushrooms, including fresh truffles.

INEXPENSIVE

Monte Arci. Via Castelfirdardo 33. ☎ **06-494-1220.** Reservations recommended. Main courses 15,000–20,000L ($7.50–$10); fixed-price menu 50,000L ($25). AE, DC, V. Mon–Fri 12:30–3pm and 7–11:30pm; Sat 7–11:30pm. Closed Aug. Metro: Stazione Termini. ROMAN/SARDINIAN.

Dining Near Stazione Termini & Via Veneto

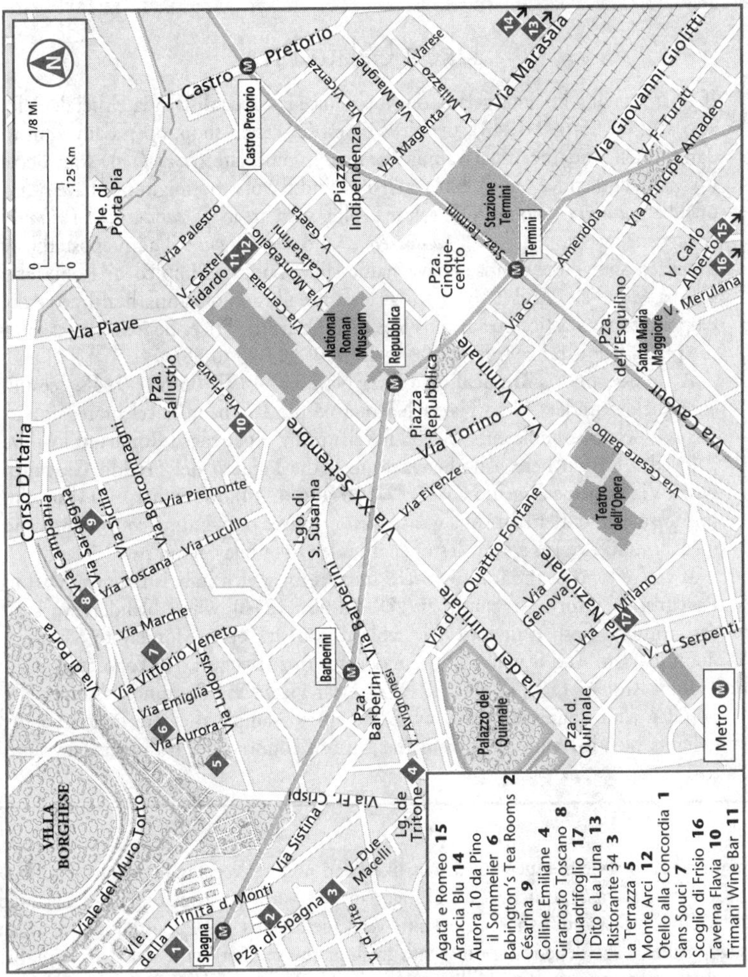

Monte Arci, on a cobblestone street near Piazza Indipendenza, is set behind a sienna-colored facade. It features low-cost Roman and Sardinian specialties (you'll spend even less for pizza) like *nialoreddus* (a regional form of gnocchetti); pasta with clams, lobster, or the musky-earthy notes of porcini mushrooms; green and white spaghetti with bacon, spinach, cream, and cheese; and delicious lamb sausage flavored with herbs and pecorino cheese. Much of the food is just like mamma would make, with the strengths and weaknesses that implies.

Trimani Wine Bar. Via Cernaia 37B. ☎ **06-446-9630.** Reservations recommended. Main courses 12,000–26,000L ($6–$13); glass of wine (depending on vintage) 3,500–20,000L ($1.75–$10). AE, DC, MC, V. Mon–Sat 11:30am–3:30pm and 6pm–12:30am (in Dec open also on Sun). Closed 2 weeks in Aug. Metro: Repubblica or Castro Pretorio. CONTINENTAL.

Opened as a tasting center for French and Italian wines, spumantis, and liqueurs, this elegant wine bar has a lovely decor (stylish but informal) and comfortable seating. More than 30 wines are available by the glass, and to accompany them you can choose

Take a Gelato Break

If you're craving luscious gelato, our top choice is ✪ **Giolitti,** Via Uffici del Vicario 40 (☎ **06-699-1243**), the city's oldest ice-cream shop, open daily 7am to 2am. You'll find the usual vanilla (*vaniglia*), chocolate (*cioccolato*), strawberry (*fragola*), and coffee (*caffè*), but you'll also find flavors you might not have heard of, like *gianduia* (chocolate hazelnut), plus such treats as *cassata alla siciliana, zabaglione* (see appendix B), *mascarpone,* and *maron glacé.* The preposterously oversized showpiece sundaes have names like Coppa Olimpico di Roma and Coppa Mondiale. And if you want at least the illusion of eating healthy, try the Coppa Primanata (ice cream plus lots of fresh fruit). Prices here and at each of the places below range from 2,500 to 16,000L ($1.25 to $8).

A close second is **Tre Scalini,** Piazza Navona 30 (☎ **06-687-9148;** see full entry below under "Near Piazza Navona & the Pantheon"), celebrated for its *tartufo.* Gelato connoisseurs say you haven't really experienced Rome until you've enjoyed a tartufo here. Another favorite is the **Palazzo del Freddo Giovanni Fassi,** Via Principe Eugenio 65–67 (☎ **06-446-4740**). More than 100 years old, this ice-cream outlet (part of a gelato factory) turns out yummy concoctions and specializes in rice ice cream. It's open Tuesday to Sunday, noon to 12:30am.

If you're fond of the frothy *frullati* frappes for which Italy is famous, head to **Pascucci,** Via Torre Argentina 20 (☎ **06-686-4816**), where blenders work all day grinding fresh fruit into delectable drinks. It's open Monday to Saturday, noon to 1am. And if you're in the mood for frozen yogurt, try **Yogofruit,** P. G. Travani Arquati 118 (☎ **06-587-972**), near Piazza San Sonnino. It's especially popular with young Romans, who line up to sample the tart frozen yogurt delights blended with fruit from the Latium countryside. It's open daily 6am to 11pm.

from a bistro-style menu, with dishes like salad niçoise, vegetarian pastas, herb-laden bean soups (*fagiole*), quiche, and Hungarian goulash. Also available is a wider menu including meat and fish courses like veal medallions with roasted potatoes and sage, grilled fish (depending on what's fresh at the market) with steamed vegetables, or shell of scampi au gratin filled with salmon. The specialty is the large choice of little "bruschette" with cheese and prosciutto, since the chef orders every kind of prosciutti and cheese, from all over Italy. The dishes are matched with the appropriate wines. Among the desserts, the specialty deservedly wins many friends: chestnut mousse served with a sauce of white wine (*Verduzzo di Ronco di Viere*), covered by whipped cream and meringue.

Trimani maintains a well-stocked shop about 40 yards from its wine bar, at V. Goito 20 (☎ **06-446-9661**), where an astonishing array of Italian wines is for sale.

IN SAN LORENZO

INEXPENSIVE

✪ **Arancia Blu.** Via dei Latini 55–65 (at Via Arunci). ☎ **06-445-4105.** Reservations highly recommended. Main courses 12,000–16,000L ($6–$8). AE, V. Daily 8pm–midnight. Bus: 71. INVENTIVE VEGETARIAN ITALIAN.

Fabio Bassan and Enrico Bartolucci offer Rome's best vegetarian cuisine. Under soft lighting and wood ceilings, surrounded by wine racks and university intellectuals, the friendly waiters will help you compile a menu to fit any dietary need. The dishes at this trendy spot are inspired by peasant cuisines from across Italy and beyond. The appetizers range from hummus and tabbouleh to zucchini-and-saffron quiche or salad with apples, gorgonzola, and balsamic vinegar. The main courses change seasonally and may be lasagna with red onions, mushrooms, zucchini, and ginger; *couscous con verdure* (vegetable couscous); or *ravioli ripieni di patate e menta* (ravioli stuffed with potatoes and mint served under fresh tomatoes and Sardinian sheep's cheese). They offer 250 wines and inventive desserts like pears cooked in wine and juniper, served with orange-honey *semifreddo* or dark chocolate cake with warm orange sauce.

Il Dito e La Luna. Via dei Sabelli 49–51, San Lorenzo. ☎ **06-494-0726.** Reservations recommended. Main courses 19,000–24,000L ($9.50–$12). No credit cards. Mon–Sat 8pm–midnight. Metro: Piazza Vittorio. SICILIAN/ITALIAN.

This charming, unpretentious bistro has counters and service areas accented with the fruits of a bountiful harvest. The menu—divided between traditional Sicilian and creative up-to-date recipes prepared with flair—includes orange-infused anchovies served on orange segments, a creamy flan of mild onions and mountain cheese, and seafood couscous loaded with shellfish. The pastas are excellent, particularly the square-cut spaghetti *(tonnarelli)* with mussels, bacon, tomatoes, and exotic mushrooms. Even those not particularly enamored with fish might like the *baccaal[ag] mantecato* (baked and pulverized salt cod) with lentils. The specialty of the house is *caponata di melanzane*, chopped eggplant stewed in tomato sauce with onions and potatoes.

NEAR VIA VENETO & PIAZZA BARBERINI

VERY EXPENSIVE

✪ **La Terrazza.** In the Hotel Eden, Via Ludovisi 49. ☎ **06-478-121.** Reservations recommended. Main courses 42,000–78,000L ($21–$39); fixed-price menu 130,000L ($65). AE, DC, MC, V. Daily 12:30–2:30pm and 7:30–10:30pm. Metro: Barberini. ITALIAN/INTERNATIONAL.

La Terrazza and Relais Le Jardin (under "In Parioli," later in this chapter) serve the city's finest cuisine; at La Terrazza, you also get a sweeping view over St. Peter's. The service manages to be formal and flawless yet not intimidating. Chef Enrico Derfligher, the wizard behind about a dozen top-notch Italian restaurants around Europe, prepares a seasonally changing menu that's among the most polished in Rome. You might start with zucchini blossoms stuffed with ricotta and black olives or lobster medallions with apple purée and black truffles. Main courses may include red tortelli (whose coloring comes from tomato mousse) stuffed with mascarpone cheese and drizzled with lemon, sea bass baked in a crust of black olives and salt with oregano and potatoes, or grilled tagliata of beef with radicchio salad and aniseed sauce. On our last visit, we shared a superb "symphony" of seafood: a platter of perfectly seasoned Mediterranean sea bass, turbot, gilthead, and prawns for two. There's even a macrobiotic fixed-price menu, plus an authentic Roman menu. A sweet wine accompanies all the desserts—try the strawberry mousse with mango sauce or the ricotta cheesecake with raisins, rum, and chocolate sauce.

✪ **Sans Souci.** Via Sicilia 20. ☎ **06-482-1814.** Reservations recommended. Main courses 40,000–70,000L ($20–$35). AE, CB, DC, DISC, MC, V. Tues–Sun 8pm–1am. Closed Aug 10–30. Metro: Barberini. FRENCH/ITALIAN.

Not long ago, Sans Souci was getting a little tired, but now it's bounced back, and Michelin has restored its coveted star. As you step into the dimly lit lounge, the maître d' will present you with the menu, which you can peruse while sipping a drink amid tapestries and glittering mirrors. The menu is ever changing, though the classics never disappear. A great beginning is the goose-liver terrine with truffles, one of the chef's signatures. The fish soup is, according to one Rome restaurant critic, "a legend to experience." The soufflés are popular (such as artichoke, asparagus, and spinach), as are the succulent truffle-filled ravioli, homemade foie gras, and tender Normandy lamb. Save room for a special dessert soufflé (prepared for two), such as chocolate and Grand Marnier.

MODERATE

Aurora 10 da Pino il Sommelier. Via Aurora 10. ☎ **06-474-2779.** Reservations recommended. Main courses 22,000–35,000L ($11–$17.50). AE, DC, MC, V. Tues–Sun noon–3pm and 7–11pm. Metro: Barberini. ITALIAN.

Skip the tourist traps along Via Veneto and walk another block or two for the much better food and lovely service here. The wait staff is welcoming to foreigners, though you'll also dine with regulars from the chic neighborhood. The place is noted for its array of more than 250 wines, representing every province. The linguine with chunky lobster and the *rigatoni alla siciliana* with eggplant, black olives, and tomato sauce are better than your mamma made (if your mamma was Livia Soprano). The fish is fresh every day, and the chefs grill it to perfection. The exquisite meat dishes include grilled strips of fillet with seasonal vegetables. Among the more delectable desserts are crème brûlée and Neapolitan babba, filled with liqueur.

Césarina. Via Piemonte 109. ☎ **06-488-0828.** Reservations recommended. Main courses 18,000–30,000L ($9–$15). AE, DC, MC, V. Mon–Sat 12:30–3pm and 7:30–11pm. Metro: Barberini. Bus: 52, 53, 63, or 80. EMILIANA-ROMAGNOLA/ROMAN.

Specializing in the cuisines of Rome and the region around Bologna, this place has grown considerably since matriarch Césarina Masi opened it around 1960 (many Rome veterans fondly remember her strict supervision of the kitchen and how she'd lecture regulars who didn't finish their tagliatelle). Although Césarina passed away in the mid-1980s, her traditions are kept going. The polite staff roll a trolley from table to table laden with an excellent *bollito misto* (an array of well-seasoned boiled meats) and often follow with misto Césarina—four kinds of creamy handmade pasta, each with a different sauce. Equally appealing are the *saltimbocca* (veal with ham) and the *cotoletta alla bolognese* (tender veal cutlet baked with ham and cheese). A dessert specialty is *semifreddo* Césarina with hot chocolate, so meltingly good it's worth the 5 pounds you'll gain.

Colline Emiliane. Via Avignonesi 22 (off Piazza Barberini). ☎ **06-481-7538.** Reservations highly recommended. Main courses 35,000–60,000L ($17.50–$30). MC, V. Sat–Thurs 12:45–2:45pm and 7:45–10:45pm. Closed Aug. Metro: Barberini. EMILIANA-ROMAGNOLA.

Serving the *classica cucina bolognese,* Colline Emiliane is a small family-run place—the owner is the cook and his wife makes the pasta (about the best you'll find in Rome). The house specialty is an inspired *tortellini alla panna* (with cream sauce and truffles), but the less-expensive pastas are excellent too, like *maccheroni al funghetto* and *tagliatelle alla bolognese.* As an opener, we suggest *culatello di Zibello,* a delicacy from a small town near Parma known for having the world's finest prosciutto. Main courses include *braciola di maiale* (boneless rolled pork cutlets stuffed with ham and cheese, breaded, and sautéed) and an impressive *giambonnetto* (roast veal Emilian style with roast potatoes).

Girarrosto Toscano. Via Campania 29. ☎ **06-482-3835.** Reservations required. Main courses 25,000–40,000L ($12.50–$20). AE, CB, DC, MC, V. Thurs–Tues 12:30–2:30pm and 7:30–11pm. Bus: 95 or 116. Metro: Barberini. TUSCAN.

Girarrosto Toscano, facing the walls of the Borghese Gardens, draws large crowds, so you may have to wait. Under a vaulted cellar ceiling, it serves some of Rome's finest Tuscan fare. Begin by trying the enormous selection of fresh antipasti, from little meatballs and melon with savory prosciutto to *frittate* (omelettes) and delectable Tuscan salami. You're then given a choice of pasta, like creamy fettuccine. Although expensive, the delicately flavored *bistecca alla fiorentina* (grilled steak seasoned with oil, salt, and pepper) is worth every lira if you're in the mood to splurge. Fresh fish from the Adriatic is served daily. Order with care if you're on a budget; both meat and fish are priced according to weight and can run considerably higher than the prices above.

NEAR ANCIENT ROME

VERY EXPENSIVE

Agata e Romeo. Via Carlo Alberto 45. ☎ **06-446-6115.** Reservations recommended. Main courses 40,000–50,000L ($20–$25). AE, DC, MC, V. Mon–Sat 1–3pm and 8–11:30pm. Metro: Vittorio Emanuele. NEW ROMAN.

One of the most charming places near the Vittorio Emanuele Monument is this striking duplex restaurant in turn-of-the-century Liberty style. You'll enjoy the creative cuisine of Romeo Caraccio (who manages the dining room) and his wife, Agata Parisella (who prepares her own version of sophisticated Roman food). Look for pasta garnished with broccoli and cauliflower and served in skate broth, as well as a crisp *sformato* loaded with eggplant, parmigiano, mozzarella, and fresh Italian herbs. Sweet-tasting swordfish might be served thinly sliced as roulade and loaded with capers and olives; beans will probably be studded with savory mussels, clams, and pasta. For dessert, consider Agata's *millefoglie,* puff pastry stuffed with almonds and sweetened cream. In 1998 they added a charming wine cellar offering a wide choice of international and domestic wines.

EXPENSIVE

Alvaro al Circo Massimo. Via dei Cerchi 53. ☎ **06-678-6112.** Reservations required. Main courses 20,000–35,000L ($10–$17.50). AE, MC, V. Tues–Sun 12:30–3:30pm and 7:30–11pm. Closed Aug. Metro: Circo Massimo. ITALIAN.

Alvaro, at the edge of the Circus Maximus, is the closest thing you'll find in Rome to a genuine provincial inn, right down to the hanging corncobs and rolls of fat sausages. The antipasti and pastas are fine, the meat courses are even better, and the fresh fish is never overcooked. Other specialties are tagliolini with mushrooms and truffles and briny-flavored roasted turbot with potatoes. The larder is especially well stocked with exotic seasonal mushrooms, including black truffles rivaling the ones you'd find in Spoleto. A basket of fresh fruit rounds out the meal. The atmosphere is comfortable and mellow.

MODERATE

Il Quadrifoglio. Via del Boschetto 19. ☎ **06-482-6096.** Reservations recommended. Main courses 20,000–30,000L ($10–$15). AE, DC, MC, V. Mon–Sat 7pm–midnight. Closed Aug. Metro: Cavour. NEAPOLITAN.

In a grandiose palace, this well-managed restaurant lets you sample the flavors and herbs of Naples and southern Italy. You'll find a tempting selection of antipasti, like anchovies, peppers, capers, onions, and breaded and fried eggplant, all garnished with fresh herbs and virgin olive oil. The pastas are made daily, usually with tomato- or oil-based sauces and always with herbs and aged cheeses. Try a zesty rice dish (one of the best is *sartù di riso,* studded with vegetables, herbs, and meats), followed by a hard-to-resist grilled octopus or a simple but savory *granatine* (meatballs, usually of veal,

Quick Bites

At **Dar Filettaro a Santa Barbara,** just off the southeast corner of Campo de' Fiori at Largo dei Librari 88 (☎ **06-686-4018**), you can join the line of people threading their way to the back of the bare room to order a filet of *baccalà* (salt cod) fried golden brown *da portar via* (wrapped in paper to eat as you take a *passeggiata,* or stroll). It costs 5,000 to 18,000L ($2.50 to $9); they're closed Sunday.

Lunchtime offers you the perfect opportunity to savor Roman fast food: ***pizza rustica,*** by the slice (often called *pizza à taglio),* half-wrapped in waxed paper for easy carrying. Just point to the bubbling, steaming sheet with your preferred toppings behind the counter and hand over a few thousand lire; 4,000L ($2) buys a healthy portion of "plain" tomato sauce: basil-and-cheese *pizza margherita. Pizza rossa* (just sauce) and *pizza con patate* (with cheese and potatoes) cost even less, as does the exquisitely simple *pizza bianca* (plain dough brushed with olive oil and sprinkled with salt and sometimes rosemary).

A ***rosticceria*** is a *pizza à taglio* with spits of chickens roasting in the window and a few pasta dishes kept warm in long trays. You can also sit down for a quick pasta or prepared meat dish steaming behind the glass counters at a ***tavola calda*** (literally "hot table") for about half the price of a *trattoria.* A Roman ***bar,*** though it does indeed serve liquor, is more what we'd call a cafe, a place to grab a cheap *panino* (flat roll stuffed with meat, cheese, and/or vegetables) or *tramezzino* (large, triangular sandwiches on white bread with the crusts cut off—like giant tea sandwiches).

bound together with mozzarella). Dessert anyone? A longtime favorite is *torta caprese,* with hazelnuts and chocolate.

INEXPENSIVE

Hostaria Nerone. Via Terme di Tito 96. ☎ **06-474-5207.** Reservations recommended. Main courses 15,000–20,000L ($7.50–$10). AE, DC, V. Mon–Sat noon–3pm and 7–11pm. Metro: Colosseo. Bus: 85, 87, 75, 175, or 117. ROMAN/ITALIAN.

Built atop the ruins of the Golden House of Nero, this trattoria is run by the energetic De Santis family, who cook, serve, and handle the large crowds of hungry locals and visitors. Opened in 1929 at the edge of the Colle Oppio Park, it contains two compact dining rooms, plus a terrace lined with flowering shrubs that offers a view over the Colosseum and the Bath of Trajan. The copious antipasti buffet represents the bounty of Italy's fields and seas. The pastas include savory spaghetti with clams and, our favorite, *pasta fagioli* (with beans). There's also grilled crayfish and swordfish and Italian sausages with polenta. Roman-style tripe is a local favorite, but you may want to skip it for the *osso bucco* (braised veal shanks) with mashed potatoes and seasonal mushrooms. The wide list of some of the best of Italian wines is priced reasonably.

Ristorante al Cardello. Via del Cardello 1 (at the corner of Via Cavour). ☎ **06-474-5259.** Reservations recommended. Main courses 14,000–20,000L ($7–$10). AE, DC, MC, V. Mon–Sat noon–3pm and 7–11pm. Closed Aug. Metro: Cavour or Colosseo. ROMAN/ABRUZZI.

Conveniently close to the Colosseum, this restaurant has thrived since the 1920s, when it opened in the semicellar of an 18th-century building. We always love the antipasti buffet, where the flavorful marinated vegetables reveal the bounty of the

Italian harvest; at 10,000L ($5) per person for a good serving, it's a great deal. You might follow with *bucatini* (thick spaghetti) *all'amatriciana;* tender roast lamb with potatoes, garlic, and mountain herbs; or a thick hearty stew. A Roman food critic, dining with us, claimed he always comes here when he wants to eat like a peasant (and that's a compliment).

NEAR CAMPO DE' FIORI & THE JEWISH GHETTO

Vegetarians looking for monstrous salads (or anyone who just wants a break from all those heavy meals) can find great food at **Insalata Ricca,** Largo dei Chiavari 85 (☎ **06-6880-3656**). See the review under "Near Piazza Navona," later in this section.

EXPENSIVE

Il Drappo. Vicolo del Malpasso 9. ☎ **06-687-7365.** Reservations required. Main courses 20,000–45,000L ($10–$22.50); fixed-price menus (including Sardinian wine) 65,000–70,000L ($32.50–$35). AE, DC, MC, V. Mon–Sat 7pm–midnight. Closed Aug 15–31. Bus: 46, 62, or 64. SARDINIAN.

Il Drappo, a favorite of the local artsy crowd, is on a narrow street near the Tiber and is run by a woman known to her regulars only as "Valentina." You have your choice of two tastefully decorated dining rooms festooned with patterned cotton draped from the ceiling. Flowers and candles are everywhere. Fixed-price dinners reflecting diverse choices may begin with wafer-thin *carte di musica* (sheet-music paper) topped with tomatoes, green peppers, parsley, and olive oil, then followed with fresh spring lamb in season, fish stew made with tuna caviar, or one of the strong-flavored regional specialties. For dessert, try the *seadas* (cheese-stuffed fried cake in special dark honey). Valentina's cuisine is a marvelous change of pace from the typical Roman diet, showing an inventiveness that keeps us coming back again and again.

Piperno. Via Monte de' Cenci 9. ☎ **06-6880-6629.** Reservations recommended. Main courses 30,000–40,000L ($15–$20). AE, DC, MC, V. Tues–Sat noon–2:30pm and 8–10:30pm; Sun noon–2:30pm. Bus: 23. ROMAN/JEWISH.

This longtime favorite, opened in 1856 and now run by the Mazzarella and Boni families, celebrates the Jerusalem artichoke, incorporating it into a number of recipes. You'll be served by a uniformed crew of hardworking waiters, whose advice and suggestions are worth considering. You might begin with aromatic *fritto misto vegetariano* (artichokes, cheese-and-rice croquettes, mozzarella, and stuffed squash blossoms) before moving on to a fish fillet, veal, succulent beans, or a pasta creation. Many of the foods are fried or deep-fried and benefit from a technique that leaves them flaky and dry, not at all greasy. (The deep-fried artichokes, when submerged in hot oil, open their leaves until they resemble a lotus—but are infinitely more delicious.)

MODERATE

Da Giggetto. Via del Portico d'Ottavia 21/A. ☎ **06-686-1105.** Reservations recommended. Main courses 18,000–30,000L ($9–$15). AE, DC, MC, V. Tues–Sun 12:30–3pm and 7:30–11pm. Closed Aug 1–15. Bus: 62, 64, 75, 90, or 170. ROMAN/JEWISH.

Da Giggetto is right next to the Theater of Marcellus, and old Roman columns extend practically to its doorway. Romans flock to this bustling trattoria for its special traditional dishes. None is more typical than *carciofi alla giudia,* baby-tender fried artichokes—a true delicacy. The cheese concoction called *mozzarella in carrozza* is another delight, as are the zucchini flowers stuffed with mozzarella and anchovies, our personal favorite. You could also sample shrimp sautéed in garlic and olive oil or one of Rome's best versions of *saltimbocca* (veal with ham).

Ristorante da Pancrazio. Piazza del Biscione 92. ☎ **06-686-1246.** Reservations recommended. Main courses 18,000–35,000L ($9–$17.50); fixed-price menu 50,000L ($25). AE, DC, MC, V. Thurs–Tues noon–3pm and 7:30–11:15pm. Closed 2 weeks in Aug (dates vary). Bus: 46, 62, or 64. ROMAN.

This place is popular as much for its archaeological interest as for its food. One of its two dining rooms is gracefully decorated in the style of an 18th-century tavern; the other occupies the premises of Pompey's ancient theater and is lined with carved capitals and bas-reliefs. In this historic setting, you can enjoy time-tested Roman food that's among the finest in the area. Once a simple fishermen's dish, flavorful *risotto alla pescatora* (with seafood) enjoys a certain chic today, and the scampi is grilled to perfection. Pancrazio is another restaurant that prepares two classics with great skill: saltimbocca (veal with ham) and tender roast lamb with potatoes. For a superb pasta, opt for the ravioli stuffed with artichoke hearts.

Ristorante del Pallaro. Largo del Pallaro 15. ☎ **06-6880-1488.** Reservations recommended. Fixed-price menu 32,000L ($16). No credit cards. Tues–Sun 1–3pm and 7:30pm–1am. Bus: 46, 62, or 64. ROMAN.

The cheerful woman in white who emerges with clouds of steam from the bustling kitchen is owner Paola Fazi, running two simple dining rooms where value-conscious Romans go for good food at bargain prices. (She also claims—though others dispute it—that Julius Caesar was assassinated on this very site.) The fixed-price menu is the only choice and has made the place famous. Ms. Fazi prepares everything with love, as if she were feeding her extended family. As you sit down, your antipasto, the first of eight courses, appears. Then comes the pasta of the day, followed by roast veal, white meatballs or (Friday only) dried cod, along with potatoes and eggplant. For your final courses, you're served mozzarella, cake with custard, and fruit in season. The meal also includes bread, mineral water, and half a liter of the house wine.

Vecchia Roma. Via della Tribuna di Campitelli 18. ☎ **06-686-4604.** Reservations recommended. Main courses 24,000–40,000L ($12–$20). AE, DC. Thurs–Tues 1–3pm and 8–11pm. Closed 10 days in Aug. Bus: 64, 90, 90b, 97, or 774. ROMAN/ITALIAN.

Family-Friendly Restaurants

Césarina *(see p. 98)* A longtime family favorite, this restaurant offers the most kid-pleasing pastas in town, each handmade and presented with a different sauce. You can request a selection of three kinds of pasta on one plate so finicky young diners can try a little taste of each.

Otello alla Concordia *(see p. 108)* This place is as good as any to introduce your child to hearty Roman cuisine. If your child doesn't like the spaghetti with clams, then maybe the eggplant parmigiana will do. Families can dine in an arbor-covered courtyard.

Tre Scalini *(see p. 107)* All families visit Piazza Navona at some point, and this is the best choice if you'd like a dining table overlooking the square. Perhaps a juggler or a fire eater will come by to entertain the crowds. The cookery is Roman and the menu wide enough to accommodate most palates—including children's. The *tartufo* (ice cream with a coating of bittersweet chocolate, cherries, and whipped cream) at the end of the meal is a classic bound to please.

Dining Near Campo de' Fiori & Piazza Navona

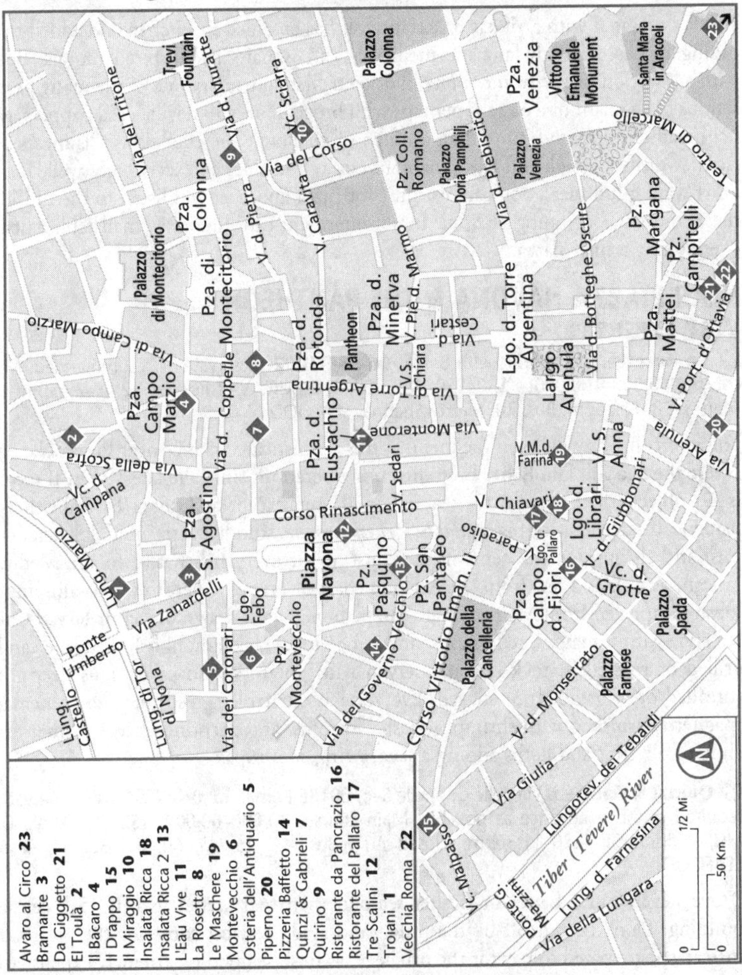

Vecchia Roma is a charming, moderately priced trattoria in the heart of the Ghetto. Movie stars have frequented the place, sitting at the crowded tables in one of the four small dining rooms (the back room is the most popular). The owners are known for their *frutti de mare* (fruits of the sea), a selection of briny fresh seafood. The minestrone is made with fresh vegetables, and an interesting selection of antipasti, including salmon or vegetables, is always available. The pastas and risottos are savory, like *linguine alla marinara* with calamari—the "green" risotto with porcini mushrooms is reliably good. The chef's specialties are lamb and *spigola* (a type of white fish).

INEXPENSIVE

Le Maschere. Via Monte della Farina 29 (near Largo Argentina). ☎ **06-687-9444.** Reservations recommended. Main courses 14,000–22,000L ($7–$11). AE, DC, MC, V. Tues–Sun 7:30–11pm. Closed Aug. Bus: 46, 62, or 64. CALABRESE.

Le Maschere specializes in the fragrant, often-fiery cooking of Calabria's Costa Viola, with lots of fresh garlic and wake-up-your-mouth red peppers. In a cellar from the

1600s decorated with artifacts of Calabria, it has enlarged its kitchen and added three dining rooms, all with fantastic medieval- and Renaissance-inspired murals. Begin with a selection of *antipasti calabresi.* For your first course, try one of the many preparations of eggplant or a pasta—perhaps with broccoli or with devilish red peppers, garlic, bread crumbs, and more than a touch of anchovy. The chef also grills meats and fresh swordfish caught off the Calabrian coast, and does so exceedingly well. If you don't want a full meal, you can visit just for pizza and beer and listen to the music at the piano bar, beginning at 8pm. In summer, you can dine at a small table outside overlooking a tiny piazza.

NEAR PIAZZA NAVONA & THE PANTHEON

VERY EXPENSIVE

✪ **La Rosetta.** Via della Rosetta 8. ☎ **06-686-1002.** Reservations recommended. Main courses 60,000–100,000L ($30–$50). AE, CB, DC, MC, V. Thurs–Fri 12:45–2:45pm and Mon–Sat 8–11:30pm. Bus: 70. Metro: Spagna. SEAFOOD.

You won't find any meat on the menu at this sophisticated choice near Piazza Navona, where the Riccioli family has been directing operations since the late 1960s. If money is no object, there's no better seafood in Rome, except at Quinzi & Gabrieli (see below). An excellent start is *insalata di frutti di mare,* studded with squid, lobster, octopus, and shrimp. Menu items include just about every fish native to the Mediterranean, as well as a few from the Atlantic coast of France. There's even a sampling of lobster imported from Maine, which can be boiled with drawn butter or served Catalan style with tomatoes, red onions, and wine sauce. Hake, monkfish, and sole can be grilled or roasted in rock salt and served with potatoes, and calamari is deep-fried (breaded or unbreaded) or stewed. Everyone at our table agreed that the homemade spaghetti garnished with shrimp, squash blossoms, and pecorino cheese, with a drizzling of olive oil and herbs adding a savory zing, was tops.

✪ **Quinzi & Gabrieli.** Via delle Coppelle 5–6, 00185 Roma. ☎ **06-687-9389.** Reservation required as far in advance as possible. Main courses 40,000–60,000L ($20–$30). AE, DC, MC, V. Mon–Sat 7:30–11:30pm. Closed Aug. Bus: 44, 46, 55, 60, 61, 62, 64, or 65. SEAFOOD.

We've never found better or fresher seafood than that served in this 15th-century building. Don't be put off by the rough-and-ready service; come for the great taste instead. Be prepared to pay for the privilege, as fresh seafood is extremely expensive in Rome. Alberto Quinzi and Enrico Gabrieli have earned their reputation on their simply cooked and presented *fresh* fish (heavy sauces aren't used to disguise old fish), like sea urchins, octopus, sole, and red mullet. In fact, the restaurant is known for its raw seafood, like a delicate carpaccio of swordfish, sea bass, and deep-sea shrimp. The house specialty is spaghetti with lobster. Sometimes the headwaiters will prepare wriggling crab or scampi on the grill right before you. In summer, French doors lead to a small dining terrace.

EXPENSIVE

✪ **L'Eau Vive.** Via Monterone 85. ☎ **06-6880-1095.** Reservations recommended. Main courses 22,000–40,000L ($11–$20); fixed-price menus 15,000L ($7.50), 30,000L ($15), and 50,000L ($25). AE, MC, V. Mon–Sat 12:30–2:30pm and 8–10:30pm. Closed Aug 1–20. Bus: 64, 70, 81, 87, or 115. FRENCH/INTERNATIONAL.

Here you'll find an elegant dining experience, with unique food and atmosphere. Fine French cuisine and a daily exotic dish are prepared and served by a lay sisterhood of missionary Christians from five continents who dress in traditional costumes. Nonsmokers can skip the plain stuccoed vaulting downstairs and head to the *piano nobile* of the 16th-century Palazzo Lantante della Rovere, where the high ceilings are gorgeously frescoed. Pope John Paul II dined here when he was archbishop of Krakow, and today some jet-setters have adopted it as their favorite spot. You'll never know until you arrive what the dishes for the evening will be. On previous occasions we've enjoyed beef fillet flambé with cognac, toasted goat cheese coated with mustard and almond slivers, and duck fillet in Grand Marnier sauce with puff-fried potatoes. The homemade pâtés are always flavorful. At 10pm, the recorded classical music is interrupted so the sisters can sing the "Ave Maria of Lourdes," and some evenings they interpret a short Bible story in ballet.

Troiani. Via dei Soldati 28. ☎ **06-6880-5950.** Reservations recommended. All main courses 43,000L ($21.50). AE, DC, MC, V. Tues–Sat 1–2:30pm and Tues–Sun 8–10:30pm. Bus: 70, 87, or 90. ITALIAN.

In a new location that's a great improvement over the former cramped setting, Chef Angelo Troiani still is on the A-list of Roman chefs, even though he now has a lot more diners to feed. Seasonal Italian cooking and creative culinary innovation make for solid good taste. Since 1989 Angelo, along with his two brothers, has excited the discriminating palates of Rome. Start off with a warm seafood salad made with clams, mussels, white fish, and a giant prawn with al dente vegetables and a "mayonnaise of the sea," a fragrant lemony sauce. Even the ravioli is stuffed creatively, with ingredients and inspiration that change with the seasons. Worthy main courses, all of which cost the same, include saddle of rabbit that might be stuffed with porcini mushrooms and served with an onion marmalade, or a boned rack of lamb cooked in an herb and vegetable crust. For dessert consider a slice of almond and bitter chocolate cake accented with fresh currants.

MODERATE

Bramante. Via della Pace 25. ☎ **06-6880-3916.** Reservations recommended. Main courses 20,000–30,000L ($10–$15). AE, DC, MC, V. Mon–Sat 5pm–1am, Sun noon–1am. Closed Dec 24. Bus: 44, 46, 55, 60, 61, 62, 64, 65. ROMAN.

In an exquisite 18th-century structure on a cobblestone street in back of the Piazza Navona, this cafe-restaurant opens onto a delightful small square of vine-draped taverns. The establishment is named for the 16th-century church on the square which was designed by the architect Bramante. Behind the ivy-covered facade the interior is completely hand painted; white candles illuminate the marble bar, making for a cozy, inviting atmosphere. The owner, Mr. Giuseppe, tries to make visitors appreciate Italian food and traditions, and succeeds admirably. Almost all his dishes are handmade, and the cooks use only the freshest ingredients such as parmigiano, fresh vegetables, and extra virgin olive oil. Recipes are simple but rich in Mediterranean flavor. No fish is served, but you can taste wonderful pastas made with fresh tomato sauce, garlic, and pasta, or else try something heavier such as braised beef or tender grilled steak flavored with herbs and served with potatoes.

Insalata Ricca 2. Piazza Pasquino 72 (southwest of Piazza Navona). ☎ **06-6830-7881.** Reservations recommended. Main courses 8,000–25,000L ($4–$12.50); salads 7,000–14,000L ($3.50–$7). AE, MC, V. Daily 12:15–3:15pm and 7pm–12:30am. Bus: 46, 62, or 64. ITALIAN/ SALADS.

A need for more vegetarian restaurants and lighter low-fat fare in Rome helped a single little trattoria, hawking entree-size salads, grow into a small chain. Most people call ahead for an outdoor table, though on summer days you may prefer the smoke-free air-conditioning inside. The more popular of the oversized salads are the *baires* (lettuce, rughetta, celery, walnuts, apples, Gorgonzola) and *siciliana* (lettuce, rughetta, sun-dried tomatoes, green olives, corn, hard salted ricotta). Also on the menu are dishes like *gnocchi verdi al gorgonzola* (spinach gnocchi with Gorgonzola sauce) and *pasta integrale* (whole-wheat pasta in tomato-and-basil sauce). The branches near Campo de' Fiori and near the Vatican (mentioned under their respective neighborhoods) offer the same basic menu.

Montevecchio. Piazza Montevecchio 22A. ☎ **06-686-1319.** Reservations required. Main courses 24,000–32,000L ($12–$16). AE, MC, V. Tues–Sun 7:30pm–midnight. Closed Aug 10–25 and Dec 26–Jan 9. Bus: 60 or 64. Metro: Spagna. ROMAN/ITALIAN.

To visit, you must negotiate the winding streets of one of Rome's most confusing neighborhoods, near Piazza Navona. The heavily curtained restaurant on this Renaissance piazza is where both Raphael and Bramante had studios and where Lucrezia Borgia spun many of her intrigues. The entrance opens onto a high-ceilinged room filled with rural mementos and bottles of wine. Your meal might begin with a strudel of porcini mushrooms followed by the invariably good pasta of the day, perhaps a *bombolotti* succulently stuffed with prosciutto and spinach. Then you might choose roebuck with polenta, roast Sardinian goat, or veal with salmon mousse. Each of these dishes is prepared with flair and technique, and the food takes advantage of the region's bounty.

Osteria dell'Antiquario. Piazzetta di S. Simeone 26/27, Via dei Coronari. ☎ **06-6879694.** Reservations recommended. Main courses 28,000–40,000L ($14–$20). AE, DC, MC, V. Tues–Sat 12:30–2:30pm and 8–11pm; Mon 8–11pm. Closed 15 days in mid-Aug, Christmas, Jan 1–15. Bus: 70, 87, or 90. INTERNATIONAL/ROMAN.

This virtually undiscovered osteria has a good location, a few blocks down the Via dei Coronari as you leave the Piazza Navona and head toward St. Peter's. In a stone-built stable from the 1500s, this restaurant has three dining rooms used in winter, although in fair weather diners prefer to retreat outdoors to a table on the terrace. Shaded by umbrellas, tables face a view of the Palazzo Lancillotti. We like to begin with a delectable appetizer of sautéed shellfish (usually mussels and clams), but you might opt for the risotto with porcini mushrooms. For a main course, you can go experimental with the fillet of ostrich covered by a slice of ham and grated Parmesan, or else opt for shellfish flavored with saffron. The fish soup with fried bread is excellent, as is an array of freshly made soups and pastas. Veal rolls made Roman style and turbot flavored with fresh tomatoes and basil are other excellent choices. This is dining in the classic Roman style.

Pizzeria Baffetto. Via del Governo Vecchio 114. ☎ **06-686-1617.** Reservations not accepted. Pizza 6,000–10,000L ($3–$5). No credit cards. Daily 6:30pm–1am. Closed Aug. Bus: 46, 62, or 64. PIZZA.

Our Roman friends always take out-of-towners here when they request the best pizza in Rome. Arguably, Pizzaria Baffetto fills the bill and has done so admirably for the past 80 years. Pizzas are sold as *piccolo,* small; *media,* medium; or *grande,* large. Most pizza aficionados order the margherita, which is the simplest version with mozzarella and a delectable tomato sauce, but a wide range of toppings is served. The chef is proud of his pizza Baffetto, the house specialty. It comes with a topping of tomato sauce, mozzarella, mushrooms, onions, sausages, roasted peppers, and eggs. The pizza crusts are delightfully thin, and the pies are served piping hot from the intense heat of the ancient ovens.

Quirino. Via delle Muratte 84. ☎ **06-679-4108.** Reservations recommended. Main courses 20,000–35,000L ($10–$17.50); fish dishes 25,000–30,000L ($12.50–$15). AE, MC, V. Mon–Sat 12:30–3:30pm and 7–11pm. Closed 3 weeks in Aug. Metro: Barberini or Spagna. ROMAN/ITALIAN/SICILIAN.

Quirino is a good place to dine after you've tossed your coin into the Trevi. The atmosphere is typical Italian, with hanging Chianti bottles, a beamed ceiling, and muraled walls. We're fond of the mixed fry of tiny shrimp and squid rings, and the vegetarian pastas are prepared only with the freshest ingredients. The regular pasta dishes are fabulous, especially our favorite: homemade pasta with baby clams and porcini mushrooms. The *pasta alla Norma* with tomatoes and eggplant has won the approval of many a demanding Italian opera star. A variety of fresh and tasty fish is always available and always grilled to perfection. For dessert, try the yummy chestnut ice cream with hot chocolate sauce or the homemade cannoli.

Tre Scalini. Piazza Navona 30. ☎ **06-687-9148.** Reservations recommended. Main courses 24,000–32,000L ($12–$16). AE, DC, MC, V. Thurs–Tues noon–3pm and 7–11pm. Closed Dec–Feb. Bus: 70, 87, or 90. ROMAN/ITALIAN.

Opened in 1882, this is the most famous restaurant on Piazza Navona—a landmark for ice cream as well as for more substantial meals. Yes, it's crawling with tourists, but its waiters are a lot friendlier and more helpful than those at the nearby Passetto, and the setting can't be beat. The cozy bar on the upper floor offers a view over the piazza, but most visitors opt for the ground-floor cafe or restaurant. During warm weather, try to snag a table on the piazza, where the people-watching is extraordinary.

The Lombard specialty of risotto with porcini mushrooms is worthy of the finest restaurants in Milan, the carpaccio of sea bass is worthy of a three-star restaurant in Paris, and the roast duck with prosciutto wins many a devoted fan. One cook confided to us, "I cook dishes to make people love me." If that's the case, try his *saltimbocca* (veal with ham) and roast lamb Roman style—and you'll fall in love. No one will object if you order just a pasta and salad. Their famous tartufo (ice cream coated with bittersweet chocolate, cherries, and whipped cream) makes a fantastic dessert.

NEAR PIAZZA DEL POPOLO & THE SPANISH STEPS

VERY EXPENSIVE

✪ **El Toulà.** Via della Lupa 29B. ☎ **06-687-3498.** Reservations required for dinner. Main courses 40,000–46,000L ($20–$23); 5-course menu degustazione 120,000L ($60); 4-course menu *veneto* 100,000L ($50). AE, DC, MC, V. Tues–Fri noon–3pm and 7:30–11pm; Mon and Sat 7:30–11pm. Closed Aug. Bus: 81, 90, 90b, 628, or 913. ROMAN/VENETIAN.

El Toulà, offering sophisticated haute cuisine, is the glamorous flagship of an upscale chain that's now gone international. The setting is elegant, with vaulted ceilings, large archways, and a charming bar. The impressive, always-changing menu has one section devoted to Venetian specialties, in honor of the restaurant's origins. Items include tender *fegato* (liver) *alla veneziana,* vegetable-stuffed calamari, a robust *baccala* (codfish mousse with polenta), and *broetto,* a fish soup made with monkfish and clams. Save room for the seasonal selection of sorbets and sherbets (the cantaloupe and fresh strawberry are celestial)—you can request a mixed plate if you'd like to sample several. El Toulà usually isn't crowded at lunchtime. The wine list is extensive and varied, but hardly a bargain.

MODERATE

Babington's Tea Rooms. Piazza di Spagna 23. ☎ **06-678-6027.** Main courses 35,000–55,000L ($17.50–$27.50); brunch 48,000L ($24). AE, CB, DC, DISC, MC, V. Daily 9am–8:30pm. Metro: Spagna. ENGLISH/MEDITERRANEAN.

When Victoria was on the throne in 1893, an Englishwoman named Anne Mary Babington arrived in Rome and couldn't find a place for "a good cuppa." With stubborn determination, she opened her own tearooms near the foot of the Spanish Steps, and the rooms are still going strong, though the prices are terribly inflated because of its fabulous location. You can order everything from Scottish scones and Ceylon tea to a club sandwich and American coffee. Brunch is served at all hours. Pastries cost 4,000 to 13,000L ($2 to $6.50); a pot of tea (dozens of varieties available) goes for 12,000L ($6).

Dal Bolognese. Piazza del Popolo 1–2. ☎ **06-361-1426.** Reservations required. Main courses 18,000–30,000L ($9–$15). AE, DC, MC, V. Tues–Sun 12:30–3pm and 8:15pm–1am. Closed 20 days in Aug. Metro: Flaminio. BOLOGNESE.

This is one of those rare dining spots that's chic but actually lives up to the hype with truly noteworthy food. Young actors, shapely models, artists from nearby Via Margutta, and even corporate types on expense accounts show up, trying to land one of the few sidewalk tables. To begin, we suggest *misto di pasta:* four pastas, each with a different sauce, arranged on the same plate. A worthy substitute would be thin slices of savory Parma ham or the delectable prosciutto and vine-ripened melon. For your main course, specialties that win hearts year after year are *lasagne verde* and *tagliatelle alla bolognese.* The chefs also turn out the town's most recommendable veal cutlets bolognese topped with cheese. They're not inventive, but they're simply superb.

You may want to cap your evening by dropping into the **Rosati** cafe next door (or its competitor, the **Canova,** across the street), to enjoy one of the tempting pastries.

Il Bacaro. Via degli Spagnoli 27, near Piazza delle Coppelle. ☎ **06-686-4110.** Reservations recommended. Main courses 18,000–30,000L ($11–$18). MC, V. Mon–Sat 8pm–midnight. Metro: Spagna. ITALIAN.

Unpretentious and very accommodating to foreigners, this restaurant contains only about a half dozen tables and operates from an ivy-edged hideaway alley near Piazza di Spagna. The restaurant is well known for its fresh and tasty cheese. This was a palazzo in the 1600s, and some vestiges of the building's former grandeur remain, despite an impossibly cramped kitchen where the efforts of the staff to keep the show moving are nothing short of heroic. The offerings are time-tested and flavorful: homemade ravioli stuffed with mushrooms and parmigiano (in season), grilled beef fillet with roasted potatoes, and an unusual version of warm carpaccio of beef. What dish do we prefer year after year? Admittedly it's an acquired taste, but it's radicchio stuffed with Gorgonzola.

Inexpensive

Il Ristorante 34 (Al 34). Via Mario de' Fiori 34. ☎ **06-679-5091.** Reservations required. Main courses 17,000–30,000L ($8.50–$15); fixed-price menu 55,000L ($27.50). AE, DC, MC, V. Tues–Sun 12:30–3pm and 7:30–10:30pm. Closed 1 week at Easter and 3 weeks in Aug. Metro: Spagna. ROMAN/ITALIAN.

Il Ristorante 34, very good and increasingly popular, is close to Rome's most famous shopping district. Its long, narrow interior is sheathed in scarlet wallpaper, ringed with modern paintings, and capped with a vaulted ceiling. In the rear, stop to admire a display of *dolce* proudly exhibited near the entrance to the bustling kitchen. The chef might whip caviar and salmon into the noodles to enliven a dish or add generous chunks of lobster into the risotto. He also believes in rib-sticking fare like pasta lentil soup or meatballs in a sauce with "fat" mushrooms. One of his most interesting pastas comes with a pumpkin-flavored cream sauce, and his spaghetti with clams is among the best in Rome.

Otello alla Concordia. Via della Croce 81. ☎ **06-679-1178.** Reservations recommended. Main courses 14,000–30,000L ($7–$15); fixed-price menu 40,000L ($20). AE, DC, MC, V. Mon–Sat 12:30–3pm and 7:30–11pm. Closed 2 weeks in Feb. Metro: Piazza di Spagna. ROMAN.

On a side street amid the glamorous boutiques near the northern edge of the Spanish Steps, this is one of Rome's most consistently reliable restaurants. A stone corridor from the street leads into the dignified Palazzo Povero. Choose a table in the arbor-covered courtyard or the cramped but convivial dining rooms. Displays of Italian bounty decorate the interior, where you're likely to rub elbows with many of the shopkeepers from the fashion district. The *spaghetti alle vongole veraci* (with clams) is excellent, as are Roman-style *saltimbocca* (veal with ham), *abbacchio arrosto* (roast baby lamb), eggplant parmigiana, a selection of grilled or sautéed fish dishes (including swordfish), and several preparations of veal.

NEAR VATICAN CITY

The no. 6 branch of **Insalata Ricca,** the popular chain of salad-and-light-meals restaurants, is across from the Vatican walls at Piazza del Risorgimento 5 (☎ **06-3973-0387**). See the review under "Near Piazza Navona," earlier in this section.

VERY EXPENSIVE

✪ **Les Etoiles.** In the Hotel Atlante Star, Via dei Bastioni 1. ☎ **06-689-9494.** Reservations required. Main courses 60,000–120,000L ($30–$60). AE, DC, MC, V. Daily 12:30–2:30pm and 7:30–10:30pm. Metro: Ottaviano. MEDITERRANEAN.

Les Etoiles ("The Stars") deserves all the stars it receives. At this garden in the sky, you'll have an open window over Rome's rooftops—a 360° view of landmarks, especially the floodlit dome of St. Peter's. A flower terrace contains a trio of little towers named Michelangelo, Campidoglio, and Ottavo Colle. In summer everyone wants a table outside, but in winter almost the same view is available near the picture windows. Savor the textures and aromas of sophisticated Mediterranean cuisine with perfectly balanced flavors, perhaps choosing quail in a casserole with mushrooms and herbs, delectable artichokes stuffed with ricotta and pecorino cheeses, Venetian-style risotto with squid ink, and roast suckling lamb perfumed with mint. The creative chef is justifiably proud of his many regional dishes, and the service is refined, with an exciting French and Italian wine list.

MODERATE

Ristorante Il Matriciano. Via dei Gracchi 55. ☎ **06-321-2327.** Reservations required. Main courses 14,000–28,000L ($7–$14). DC, MC, V. Daily 12:30–3pm and 8pm–midnight. Closed Aug 5–25. Metro: Ottaviano. ROMAN.

Il Matriciano is a family restaurant with a devoted following and a convenient location near St. Peter's. The food is good but mostly country fare. In summer, try to get one of the sidewalk tables behind a green hedge and under a shady canopy. For openers, you might enjoy a bracing *zuppa di verdura* (vegetable soup) or creamy *ravioli di ricotta*. From many dishes, we recommend *scaloppa alla valdostana* or *abbacchio* (suckling lamb) *al forno*, each evocative of the region's bounty. The specialty, and our personal favorite, is *bucatini matriciana,* a variation on the favorite sauce in the Roman repertoire, *amatriciana,* richly flavored with bacon, tomatoes, and basil. Dining at the convivial tables, you're likely to see an array of Romans, including prelates and cardinals ducking out of the nearby Vatican for a meal.

INEXPENSIVE

Hostaria dei Bastioni. Via Leone IV 29. ☎ **06-397-230-34.** Reservations recommended Fri–Sat. Main courses 12,000–20,000L ($6–$10). AE, DC, MC, V. Mon–Sat noon–3pm and 7–11:30pm. Closed July 15–Aug 1. Metro: Ottaviano. ROMAN.

This simple but well-managed restaurant is about a minute's walk from the entrance to the Vatican Museums and has been open since the 1960s. Although a warm-weather terrace doubles the place's size during summer, many diners prefer the inside room as an escape from the roaring traffic. In a dining room suitable for only 50, you can order from the staples of Rome's culinary repertoire, like *fisher's risotto* (a broth-simmered rice dish studded with fresh fish, usually shellfish), a vegetarian *fettuccine alla bastione* with orange-flavored creamy tomato sauce, an array of grilled fresh fish, and *saltimboca* (veal with ham). The food is first rate, particularly at the prices charged.

Ristorante Giardinaccio. Via Aurelia 53. ☎ **06-631-367.** Reservations recommended, especially on weekends. Main courses 15,000–40,000L ($7.50–$20); fixed-price menus 15,000–60,000L ($7.50–$30). AE, DC, MC, V. Daily 12:15–3:15pm and 7:15–11:15pm. Bus: 46, 62, or 98. ITALIAN/MOLISIAN/ROMAN.

This popular restaurant, operated by Nicolino Mancini, is only a stone's throw from St. Peter's. Unusual for Rome, it offers Molisian specialties from southeastern Italy. It's rustically decorated in the country-tavern style with dark wood and exposed stone. Flaming grills provide succulent versions of perfectly done quail, goat, and other dishes, but perhaps the mutton goulash would be more adventurous. You can order many pastas, including homemade *taconelle* with lamb sauce. Vegetarians will like the large self-service selection of antipasti made from market-fresh ingredients. This is robust peasant fare, a perfect introduction to the cuisine of an area rarely visited by Americans.

IN TRASTEVERE

EXPENSIVE

Alberto Ciarla. Piazza San Cosimato 40. ☎ **06-581-8668.** Reservations required. Main courses 20,000–48,000L ($10–$24); fixed-price menus 80,000–120,000L ($40–$60). AE, DC, MC, V. Mon–Sat 8:30pm–12:30am. Closed 1 week in Jan and 1 week in Aug. Bus: 44, 75, 170, 280, or 718. SEAFOOD.

The Ciarla, in an 1890 building set in an obscure corner of an enormous square, is Trastevere's best restaurant and one of its most expensive. You'll be greeted with a cordial reception and a lavish display of seafood on ice. A dramatically modern decor plays light against shadow for a Renaissance chiaroscuro effect. The specialties include a handful of ancient recipes subtly improved by Signor Ciarla (an example is the soup of pasta and beans with seafood). Original dishes include a delectable fish in orange sauce, savory spaghetti with clams, and a full array of delicious shellfish. The sea bass fillet is prepared in at least three ways, including an award-winning version with almonds.

Sabatini. Piazza Santa Maria in Trastevere 13. ☎ **06-581-2026.** Reservations recommended. Main courses 20,000–60,000L ($10–$30); fixed-price menu 110,000L ($55). AE, DC, MC, V. Daily noon–3pm and 8pm–midnight. Closed 2 weeks in Aug (dates vary). Bus: 45, 65, 170, 181, or 280. ROMAN/SEAFOOD.

This is a real neighborhood spot in a lively location. (You may have to wait for a table even if you have a reservation.) In summer, tables are placed on the charming piazza and you can look across at the church's floodlit golden frescoes. The dining room sports beamed ceilings, stenciled walls, lots of paneling, and framed oil paintings. The spaghetti with seafood is excellent, and the fresh fish and shellfish, especially grilled scampi, may tempt you as well. For a savory treat, try *pollo con peperoni,* chicken with red and green peppers. The large antipasti table is one of the delights of this district, and the delicious pastas, the superb chicken and veal dishes, and the white Frascati wine or the house Chianti continue to delight year after year. (Order carefully, though; your bill can skyrocket if you choose grilled fish or the Florentine steaks.)

MODERATE

La Cisterna. Via della Cisterna 13. ☎ **06-581-2543.** Reservations recommended. Main courses 20,000–32,000L ($10–$16). AE, DC, MC, V. Mon–Sat 7pm–1:30am. Bus: 44, 75, 170, 280, or 710. ROMAN.

If you like traditional home cooking based on the best regional ingredients, head here. La Cisterna, named for an ancient well from imperial times discovered in the cellar, lies deep in the heart of Trastevere. For more than 75 years it has been run by the wonderful Simmi family. In good weather you can dine at sidewalk tables. If it's rainy or cold, you'll be in rooms decorated with murals. In summer you can inspect the antipasti out on the street before going in. From the ovens emerge Roman-style suckling lamb that's amazingly tender and seasoned with fresh herbs and virgin olive oil. The fiery hot *rigatoni all'amatriciana* is served with red-hot peppers, or you may decide on another delectable pasta dish, *papalini romana,* wide noodles flavored with prosciutto, cheese, and eggs. The shrimp is grilled to perfection, and you can rely on the chef selecting an array of fresh fish for dishes like flaky sea bass baked with fresh herbs.

IN TESTACCIO

MODERATE

Checchino dal 1887. Via di Monte Testaccio 30. ☎ **06-574-3816.** Reservations recommended. Main courses 20,000–35,000L ($10–$17.50). AE, DC, MC, V. Tues–Sat 12:30–3pm and 8–11pm; Sun 12:30–3pm; June–Sept closed on Sun. Bus: 75 from Termini Station. ROMAN.

During the 1800s, a wine shop flourished here, selling drinks to the butchers working in the nearby slaughterhouses. In 1887 the ancestors of the restaurant's present owners began serving food, too. Slaughterhouse workers in those days were paid part of their meager salaries with the *quinto quarto* (fifth quarter) of each day's slaughter (the tail, feet, intestines, and other parts not for the squeamish). Following centuries of Roman traditions, Ferminia, the wine shop's cook, somehow transformed these products into the tripe and oxtail dishes that form an integral part of the menu. Many Italian diners come here to relish the *rigatoni con pajata* (pasta with small intestines), *coda alla vaccinara* (oxtail stew), *fagioli e cotiche* (beans with intestinal fat), and other examples of *la cucina povera* (food of the poor). In winter a succulent wild boar with dried prunes and red wine is served. Safer and possibly more appetizing is the array of salads, soups, pastas, steaks, cutlets, grills, and ice creams. The English-speaking staff is helpful, tactfully proposing alternatives if you're not ready for Roman soul food.

ON THE APPIAN WAY

MODERATE

Antica Hostaria l'Archeologia. Via Appia Antica 139. ☎ **06-788-0494.** Reservations recommended Sat–Sun. Main courses 20,000–30,000L ($10–$15); fixed-price menu from 28,000L ($14). AE, DC, MC, V. Fri–Wed 12:30–3:30pm and 7:30–11pm. Bus 218 from San Giovanni or 660 from colli Albani. ROMAN/GREEK.

A short walk from the catacombs of St. Sebastian, the family-run Hostaria l'Archeologia is like an 18th-century village tavern with lots of atmosphere, strings of garlic and corn, oddments of copper hanging from the ceiling, earth-brown beams, and sienna-washed walls. In summer you can dine in the garden out back under the wisteria. From the kitchen emerges an array of first-rate dishes, like gnocchi with wild boar sauce and a special favorite of ours—*veal alla massenzio* (with artichokes, olives, and mushrooms). An eternal favorite is braised beef, tender chunks cooked in a Barolo wine sauce. Many Roman families visit on the weekend. Of special interest is the wine cellar, excavated in an ancient Roman tomb, with bottles dating from 1800. (You go through an iron gate, down some stairs, and into the underground cavern. Along the way, you can still see the holes once occupied by funeral urns.)

IN PARIOLI

VERY EXPENSIVE

✪ Relais Le Jardin. In the Hotel Lord Byron, Via G. de Notaris 5. ☎ **06-361-3041.** Reservations required. Main courses 28,000–60,000L ($14–$30). AE, DC, MC, V. Mon–Sat 1–3pm and 8–10:30pm. Closed Aug. Bus: 52. ITALIAN/TRADITIONAL.

Relais Le Jardin is one of the best places to go for both traditional and creative cuisine, and a chichi crowd with demanding palates packs it nightly. There are places in Rome with better views, but not with such an elegant setting, inside one of the capital's most exclusive small hotels. The lighthearted decor combines white lattice work with bold colors and flowers. The service is impeccable.

The pastas and soups are among the finest in town. We were particularly taken by the tonnarelli pasta with asparagus and the smoked ham with concassé tomatoes. The chef can take a dish once served only to the plebes in ancient times, such as bean soup with clams, and make it something elegant. For your main course, you can choose from a delectable roast loin of lamb with artichoke romana or the tender grilled beef sirloin with hot chicory and sautéed potatoes. The chef also creates a fabulous risotto with pheasant sauce, asparagus, black truffle flakes, and a hint of fresh thyme—it gets our vote as the best risotto around.

MODERATE

Al Ceppo. Via Panama 2. ☎ **06-841-9696.** Reservations recommended. Main courses 20,000–32,000L ($10–$16). AE, DC, MC, V. Tues–Sun 12:30–3pm and 8–11pm. Closed last 2 weeks of Aug. Bus: 4, 52, or 53. ROMAN.

Because the place is somewhat hidden (though only 2 blocks from the Villa Borghese, near Piazza Ungheria), you're likely to rub elbows with more Romans than tourists. It's a longtime favorite, and the cuisine is as good as it ever was. "The Log" features an open wood-stoked fireplace on which the chef roasts lamb chops, liver, and bacon to perfection. The beefsteak, which hails from Tuscany, is succulent. Other dishes we continue to delight in are *linguine monteconero* (with clams and fresh tomatoes); savory spaghetti with peppers, fresh basil, and pecorino cheese; swordfish fillet filled with grapefruit, parmigiano, pine nuts, and dry grapes; and a fish *carpaccio* (raw sea bass) with a green salad, onions, and green pepper. Save room for dessert, especially the apple cobbler, pear-and-almond tart, or chocolate meringue hazelnut cake.

INEXPENSIVE

Il Miraggio. Vicolo Sciarra 59. ☎ **06-678-0226.** Reservations recommended. Main courses 13,000–20,000L ($6.50–$10). AE, MC, V. Thurs–Tues 12:30–3:30pm and 7:30–11pm. Closed 15 days in Feb. Metro: Barberini. Bus: 56, 60, 62, 81, 85, 95, 160, 175, 492, or 628. ROMAN/SARDINIAN/SEAFOOD.

You may want to escape the roar of traffic along Via del Corso by ducking into this informal spot on a crooked side street (about midway between Piazza Venezia and Piazza Colonna). It's a cozy neighborhood setting with rich and savory flavor in every dish. The risotto with scampi or the fettuccine with porcini mushrooms will have you begging for more. Some dishes are classic, like roast lamb with potatoes, but others are more inventive, like sliced stew beef with arugula. The grilled scampi always is done to perfection, or you may prefer a steaming kettle of mussels flavored with olive oil, lemon juice, and fresh parsley. We're especially fond of the house specialty, *spaghetti alla bottarga* with roe sauce, especially if it's followed by *spigola alla vernaccia* (sea bass sautéed in butter and vernaccia wine from Tuscany). For dessert, try the typical Sardinian *seadas,* thin-rolled pastry filled with fresh cheese, fried, and served with honey.

Exploring Rome

4

For the Jubilee, decades' worth of grime from car exhaust and other pollution was scrubbed from the city's facades, revealing the original glory of the Eternal City (though Rome could still stand even more work on this front), and ancient treasures like the Colosseum were shored up. Many of the most popular areas (such as the Trevi Fountain and Piazza Navona) are sparkling and inviting again. Without a doubt, the *Frommer's* cleanup prize goes to the "artists" who transformed dingy Piazza di Sant'Ignazio into the rococo gem it was always meant to be. Even the churches along Via del Corso, including that jewel of the baroque era, San Marcello, shine again.

Before the Jubilee year began, it looked as if many of the projects were never going to be completed in time. After a dismal beginning with slow progress, Romans rallied and managed to remove most of the scaffolding for the Jubilee. Some projects were finished with only minutes to spare, but the city is up and running to receive visitors to its newly restored historic district. During Easter celebration in 2000, the streets of the capital were almost deserted, as thousands of visitors crammed historic squares, monuments, and museums. St. Peter's Square alone was filled with some 129,000 people who came for the Pope's celebration of Easter Mass. At some of the more popular attractions, waits of two hours or more were not unheard of, but at most attractions we found the crowds moving along well during the early months of 2000. (The wait at the Colosseum has been particularly long, but visitors have been coming and going from the Roman Forum without delays.)

Whether the city's ancient monuments are still time-blackened or newly gleaming, they are a constant reminder that Rome was one of the greatest centers of Western civilization. In the heyday of the Empire, all roads led to Rome, with good reason. It was one of the first cosmopolitan cities, importing slaves, gladiators, great art—even citizens—from the far corners of the world. Despite its carnage and corruption, Rome left a legacy of law; a heritage of great art, architecture, and engineering; and an uncanny lesson in how to conquer enemies by absorbing their cultures.

But ancient Rome is only part of the spectacle. The Vatican has had a tremendous influence on making the city a tourism center. Although in the past Vatican architects stripped down much of the city's glory, looting ancient ruins for their precious marble, they created great

Rome Attractions

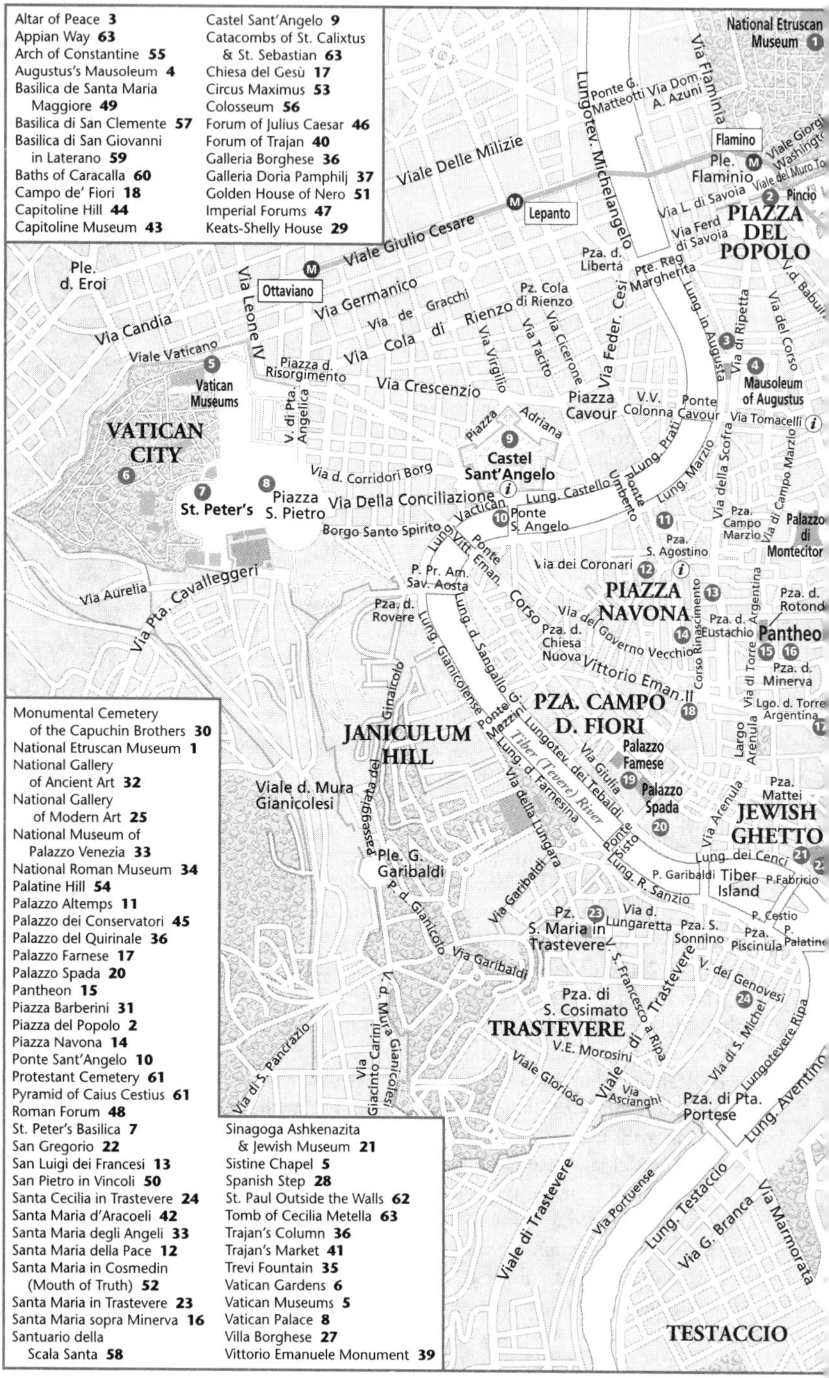

0
1/4 Mi
0
.25 Km
N
Information
Metro
National Gallery of Modern Art
25
Viale di Valle Giulia
Viale dell'Uccelliera
Galleria Borghese
26
Vle. dell'Aranciera
Viale P. Canonica
Piazza di Siena
Viale del Cavalli Marini
Vle d. Magnolie
VILLA BORGHESE
27
Via Pinciana
Via Po
Via Salaria
Via Isonzo
Via Savoia
Via Tevere
Vle. Regina Margherita
Via Nomentana
Corso D'Italia
Via Campania
Via Sardegna
Via Sicilia
Via Boncompagni
Via Piave
Ple. di Porta Pia
Policlinico
Viale del Muro Torto
Via di Porta Pinciana
Via Vittorio Veneto
SPANISH STEPS
Spagna
VIA VENETO
Via Ludovisi
Viale Castro Pretorio
Castro Pretorio
Pza. di Spagna
28
Via Sistina
29
Via Fr. Crispi
Barberini
30
Lgo. di S. Susanna
Via XX Settembre
Piazza Indipendenza
National Roman Museum
34
33
Keats-Shelley Memorial
PZA. BARBERINI
Via Barberini
31
32
TERMINI
Piazza Repubblica
Pza. Cinquecento
Stazione Termini
Viale Pretoriano
Via Tritone
Lg. de Tritone
Repubblica
Staz. Termini
Termini
Palazzo del Quirinale
Via d. Quattro Fontane
V. d. Viminale
Via Marsala
35
Trevi Fountain
36
Via del Quirinale
Via Nazionale
Via Torino
Teatro dell'Opera
Via Giovanni Giolitti
Pza. d. Quirinale
Via Milano
Pza. dell'Esquilino
49
Via Principe Amedeo
Via Tiburtina
Palazzo Doria Pamphilj
Palazzo Colonna
Via XXIV Maggio
Santa Maria Maggiore
V. Carlo Alberto
SAN LORENZO
37
Via d. Plebiscito
Via IV Nov.
Via Cavour
Palazzo Venezia
40
41
38
Via Cavour
Via Leopardi
Vittorio Emanuele
39
Vittorio Emanuele Monument
50
San Pietro in Vincoli
Via Merulana
Piazza Vittorio Eman. II
46
47
Via Cavour
Marcello
42
43
Capitoline Museums
44
45
Via Dei Fori Imperiali
48
51
Vle. Manzoni
Via Macanate
ANCIENT ROME
Golden House of Nero
Colosseo
Roman Forum
Viale d. Domus Aurea
Manzoni
Vle. Manzoni
Colosseum
Via Labicana
55
56
Pza. d. Colosseo
Via di S. Giovanni in Laterano
57
52
Piazza Bocca d. Verità
54
PALATINE HILL
Via di S. Gregorio
Via Claudia
53
Circus Maximus
Via del Circo Massimo
San Giovanni in Laterano
58
S. Giovanni
59
Via della Navicella
AVENTINE HILL
Circo Massimo
Pza. di Pta.Capena
Via Sannio
Pza. di Pla. Metronia
Viale Aventino
Piazza Albania
Via Druso
Via Gallia
Pza. Tuscolo
Re di Roma
Via Antonina
60
Baths of Caracalla
d. S. Anselmo
Piramide
61
62
63

Renaissance treasures and even occasionally incorporated the old into the new—as Michelangelo did when turning the Baths of Diocletian into a church. And in the years that followed, Bernini adorned the city with the wonders of the baroque, especially his glorious fountains.

1 St. Peter's & the Vatican

If you want to know more about the Vatican, check out its Web site at www.vatican.va.

IN VATICAN CITY

In 1929 the Lateran Treaty between Pope Pius XI and the Italian government created the **Vatican,** the world's second-smallest sovereign independent state. It has only a few hundred citizens and is protected (theoretically) by its own militia, the curiously uniformed (some say by Michelangelo) Swiss guards.

The only entrance to the Vatican for the casual visitor is through one of the glories of the Western world: Bernini's **St. Peter's Square (Piazza San Pietro).** As you stand in the huge piazza, you'll be in the arms of an ellipse partly enclosed by a majestic **Doric-pillared colonnade.** Atop it stands a gesticulating crowd of some 140 saints. Straight ahead is the facade of **St. Peter's Basilica** (Sts. Peter and Paul are represented by statues in front, Peter carrying the keys to the kingdom), and to the right, above the colonnade, are the dark brown buildings of the **papal apartments** and the **Vatican Museums.** In the center of the square is an **Egyptian obelisk,** brought from the ancient city of Heliopolis on the Nile delta. Flanking the obelisk are two 17th-century **fountains.** The one on the right (facing the basilica) by Carlo Maderno, who designed the facade of St. Peter's, was placed here by Bernini himself; the other is by Carlo Fontana.

On the left side of Piazza San Pietro is the **Vatican Tourist Office** (☎ **06-6988-4466** or 06-6988-4866), open Monday to Saturday 8:30am to 7pm. It sells maps and guides that'll help you make more sense of the riches you'll be seeing in the museums. It also accepts reservations for tours of the Vatican Gardens and tries to answer questions.

From in front of this office, a **shuttle bus** leaves for the entrance to the Vatican Museums; the shuttle runs daily every 30 minutes from when the museums open to an hour before they close and costs 2,000L ($1). Take it! It's a long and generally uninteresting walk from the piazza to the museum entrance, and on the bus's route you'll pass through some of the Vatican's lovely gardens.

✪ **Basilica di San Pietro (St. Peter's Basilica).** Piazza San Pietro. ☎ **06-6988-4466** or 96/688-4466 (for information on celebrations). Basilica (including grottoes) free. Guided tour of excavations around St. Peter's tomb 15,000L ($7.50); children younger than 15 are not admitted. Stairs to the dome 7,000L ($3.50); elevator to the dome 8,000L ($4); Sacristy (with Historical Museum) 9,000L ($4.50). Basilica (including the sacristy and treasury) Oct–Mar daily 7am–6pm; Apr–Sept daily 7am–7pm. Grottoes daily 8am–5pm. Dome Oct–Mar daily 8am–5pm; Apr–Sept 8am–6pm. Bus: 46. Metro: Ottaviano/San Pietro, then a long stroll.

In ancient times, the Circus of Nero, where St. Peter is said to have been crucified, was slightly to the left of where the basilica is now located. Peter was buried here in A.D. 64 near the site of his execution, and in 324 Constantine commissioned a basilica to be built over Peter's tomb. That structure stood for more than 1,000 years, until it verged on collapse. The present basilica, mostly completed in the 1500s and 1600s, is predominantly High Renaissance and baroque. Inside, the massive scale is almost too much to absorb, showcasing some of Italy's greatest artists: Bramante, Raphael, Michelangelo, and Maderno. In a church of such grandeur—overwhelming in its detail of gilt, marble, and mosaic—you can't expect much subtlety. It's meant to be overpowering.

The Vatican

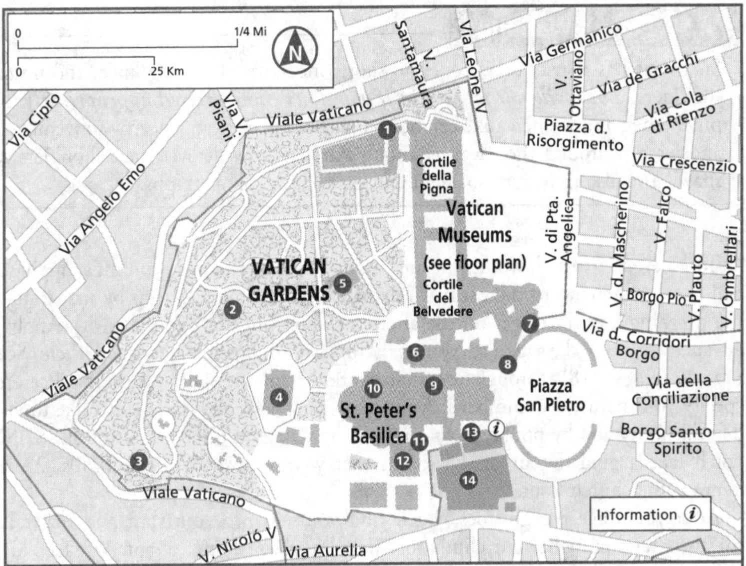

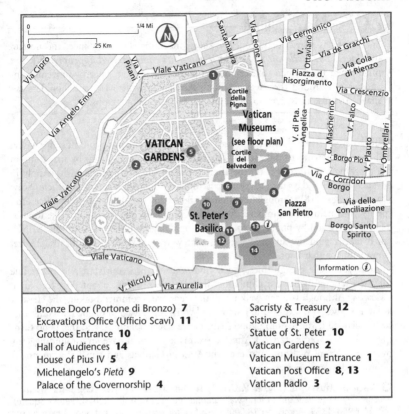

Bronze Door (Portone di Bronzo) **7**
Excavations Office (Ufficio Scavi) **11**
Grottoes Entrance **10**
Hall of Audiences **14**
House of Pius IV **5**
Michelangelo's *Pietà* **9**
Palace of the Governorship **4**
Sacristy & Treasury **12**
Sistine Chapel **6**
Statue of St. Peter **10**
Vatican Gardens **2**
Vatican Museum Entrance **1**
Vatican Post Office **8, 13**
Vatican Radio **3**

In the nave on the right (the first chapel) stands one of the Vatican's greatest treasures: Michelangelo's exquisite ***Pietà,*** created while the master was still in his early 20s but clearly showing his genius for capturing the human form. (The sculpture has been kept behind reinforced glass since a madman's act of vandalism in the 1970s.) Note the incredibly lifelike folds of Mary's robes and her youthful features (although she would've been middle-aged at the time of the Crucifixion, Michelangelo portrayed her as a young woman to convey her purity).

Much farther on, in the right wing of the transept near the Chapel of St. Michael, rests Canova's neoclassic **sculpture of Pope Clement XIII.** The truly devout stop to kiss the feet of the 13th-century **bronze of St. Peter,** attributed to Arnolfo di Cambio (at the far reaches of the nave, against a corner pillar on the right). Under Michelangelo's dome is the celebrated twisty-columned **baldacchino** (1524) by Bernini, resting over the papal altar. The 96-foot-high ultrafancy canopy was created in part, so it's said, from bronze stripped from the Pantheon, though that's up for debate.

In addition, you can visit the **treasury,** filled with jewel-studded chalices, reliquaries, and copes. One robe worn by Pius XII strikes a simple note in these halls of elegance. The sacristy now contains a **Historical Museum (Museo Storico)** displaying Vatican treasures, including the large 1400s bronze tomb of Pope Sixtus V by Antonio Pollaiuolo and several antique chalices.

You can also head downstairs to the **Vatican grottoes,** with their tombs of the popes, both ancient and modern (Pope John XXIII gets the most adulation). Behind a wall of glass is what's assumed to be the tomb of St. Peter himself.

A St. Peter's Warning

St. Peter's has a strict dress code: no shorts, no skirts above the knee, and no bare shoulders. ***They will not let you in if you don't come dressed appropriately.*** In a pinch, men and women alike can buy a big cheap scarf from a nearby souvenir stand and wrap it around their legs as a long skirt or throw it over their shoulders as a shawl. You also must remain silent and cannot take photographs.

To go even farther down, to the area around St. Peter's tomb, you must apply several days beforehand to the **excavations office** (you could also stop by first thing in the morning and try to get on the afternoon tour, but don't count on it). Apply in advance (4 or 5 days before you plan to visit, if possible) at the Ufficio Scavi (☎ 06-6988-5318), through the arch to the left of the stairs up the basilica. You specify your name, the number in your party, language, and dates you'd like to visit. They'll notify you by phone of your admission date and time. For 15,000L ($7.50), you'll take a guided tour of the tombs that were excavated in the 1940s, 23 feet beneath the church floor.

After you leave the grottoes, you'll find yourself in a courtyard and ticket line for the grandest sight: the climb to **Michelangelo's dome,** about 375 feet high. (*Warning:* Although you can walk up all the steps, we recommend taking the elevator as far as it goes. It'll save you 171 steps, and you'll *still* have 320 to go. The climb isn't recommended if you're not in good shape or are claustrophobic—and there's no turning back once you've started.) After you've made it, you'll have an astounding view over the rooftops of Rome and even the Vatican Gardens and papal apartments. A photo op if ever there was one.

✪ **Vatican Museums (Musei Vaticani) & the Sistine Chapel (Cappella Sistina).** Vatican City, Viale Vaticano (a long walk around the Vatican walls from St. Peter's Square). ☎ **06-6988-3333.** Admission 18,000L ($9); free for everyone the last Sun of each month (be ready for a crowd). Mid-Mar to late Oct, Mon–Fri 8:45am–3:45pm, Sat and last Sun of the month 8:45am–12:45pm. Off-season, Mon–Sat and last Sun of the month 8:45–12:45pm. Closed all national and religious holidays (except Easter week) and Aug 15–16. Metro: Ottaviano/San Pietro.

The Vatican Museums boast one of the world's greatest art collections. It's a gigantic repository of treasures from antiquity and the Renaissance, all housed in a labyrinthine series of lavishly adorned palaces, apartments, and galleries leading you to the real gem: the Sistine Chapel. The Vatican Museums occupy a part of the papal palaces built from the 1200s onward. From the former papal private apartments, the museums were created over a period of time to display the vast treasure trove of art acquired by the Vatican.

You'll climb a magnificent spiral ramp to get to the ticket windows. After you're admitted, you can choose your route through the museum from **four color-coded itineraries** (A, B, C, D) according to the time you have (from 1½ to 5 hours) and your interests. You determine your choice by consulting large-size panels on the wall and then following the letter/color of your choice. All four itineraries culminate in the Sistine Chapel. Obviously, 1, 2, or even 20 trips will not be enough to see the wealth of the Vatican, much less to digest it. With that in mind, we've previewed only a representative sampling of the masterpieces on display (in alphabetical order).

Borgia Apartments: Frescoed with biblical scenes by Pinturicchio of Umbria and his assistants, these rooms were designed for Pope Alexander VI (the infamous Borgia

Will you have enough stories to tell your grandchildren?
©2000 Yahoo! Inc.
Yahoo! Travel
Do You Yahoo!?

The Vatican Museums

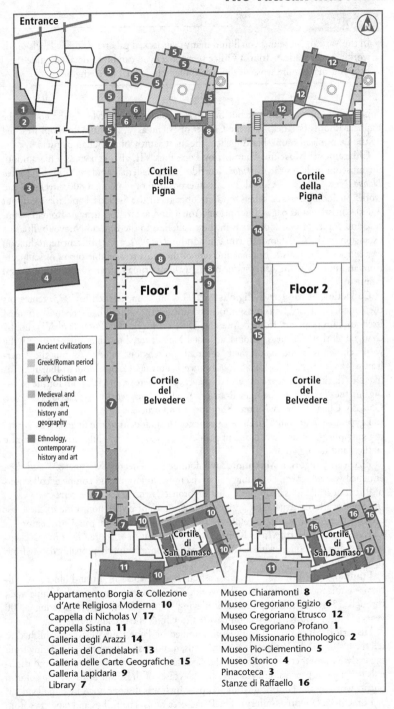

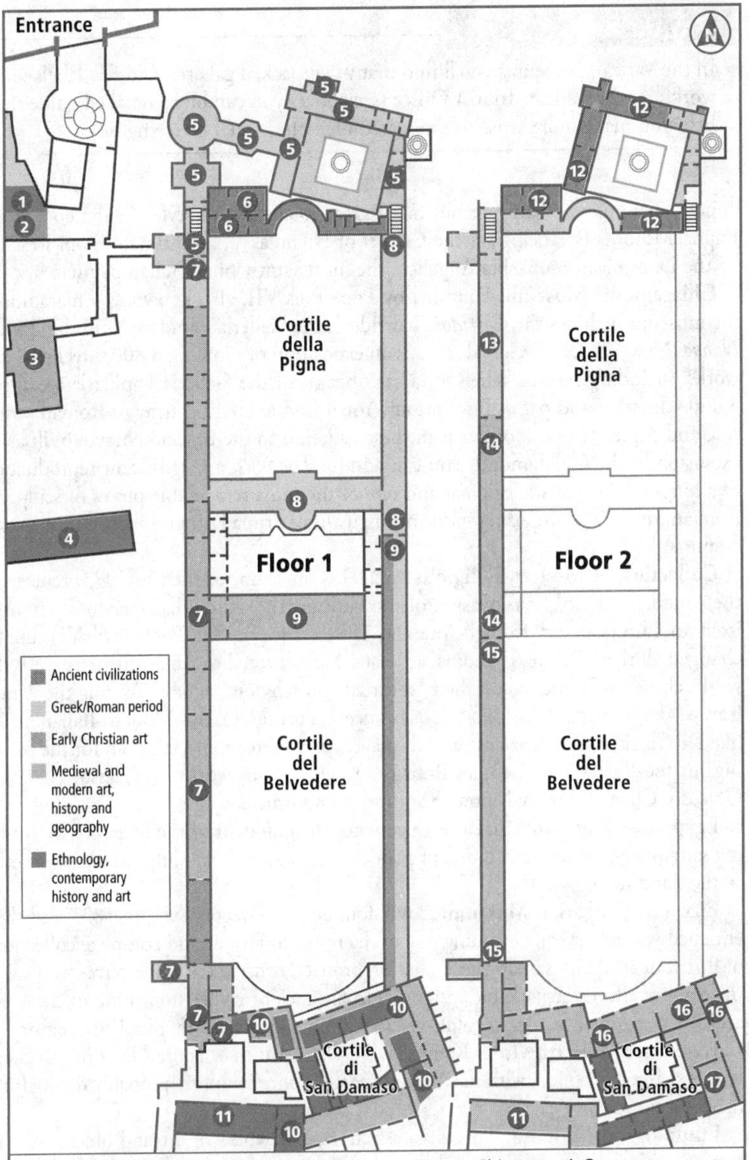

Appartamento Borgia & Collezione d'Arte Religiosa Moderna **10**
Cappella di Nicholas V **17**
Cappella Sistina **11**
Galleria degli Arazzi **14**
Galleria del Candelabri **13**
Galleria delle Carte Geografiche **15**
Galleria Lapidaria **9**
Library **7**
Museo Chiaramonti **8**
Museo Gregoriano Egizio **6**
Museo Gregoriano Etrusco **12**
Museo Gregoriano Profano **1**
Museo Missionario Ethnologico **2**
Museo Pio-Clementino **5**
Museo Storico **4**
Pinacoteca **3**
Stanze di Raffaello **16**

Buy the Book

In the Vatican Museums you'll find many overpacked galleries and few labels on the works. At the Vatican Tourist Office (see above) you can buy a detailed guide that'll help you make more sense of the incredible riches you'll be seeing here.

pope). They may be badly lit but boast great splendor and style. At the end of the Raphael Rooms (see below) is the Chapel of Nicholas V, an intimate room frescoed by the Dominican monk Fra Angelico, the most saintly of all Italian painters.

Chiaramonti Museum: Founded by Pope Pius VII, also known as Chiaramonti, the museum includes the *Corridoio* (corridor), the Galleria Lapidaria, and the *Braccio Nuovo* (New Side). The Corridor hosts an exposition of more than 800 Greek-Roman works, including statues, reliefs, and sarcophagi. In the Galleria Lapidaria are about 5,000 Christian and pagan inscriptions. You'll find a dazzling array of Roman sculpture and copies of Greek originals in these galleries. In the Braccio Nuovo, built as an extension of the Chiaramonti, you can admire *The Nile,* a magnificent reproduction of a long-lost Hellenistic original and one of the most remarkable pieces of sculpture from antiquity. The imposing statue of Augustus of Prima Porta presents him as a regal commander.

Collection of Modern Religious Art: This museum, opened in 1973, represents the American artists' first invasion of the Vatican (the church had previously limited itself to European art from before the 18th century). But Pope Paul VI's hobby changed all that. Of the 55 rooms, at least 12 are devoted to American artists. All the works chosen were judged on their "spiritual and religious values." Among the American works is Leonard Baskin's 5-foot bronze sculpture of *Isaac.* Modern Italian artists like De Chirico and Manzù are also displayed, and there's a special room for the paintings of the Frenchman Georges Rouault. You'll also see works by Picasso, Gauguin, Gottuso, Chagall, Henry Moore, Kandinsky, and others.

Egyptian-Gregorian Museum: Experience the grandeur of the pharaohs by studying sarcophagi, mummies, statues of goddesses, vases, jewelry, sculptured pink-granite statues, and hieroglyphics.

Etruscan-Gregorian Museum: It was founded by Gregory XIV in 1837 and then enriched year after year, becoming one of the most important and complete collections of Etruscan art. With sarcophagi, a chariot, bronzes, urns, jewelry, and terra-cotta vases, this gallery affords remarkable insights into an ancient civilization. One of the most acclaimed exhibits is the Regolini-Galassi tomb, unearthed in the 19th century at Cerveteri (see "Side Trips from Rome: Tivoli, Ostia Antica & More," later in this chapter). It shares top honors with the *Mars of Todi,* a bronze sculpture probably dating from the 5th century B.C.

Ethnological Museum: This is an assemblage of works of art and objects of cultural significance from all over the world. The principal route is a half-mile walk through 25 geographical sections, displaying thousands of objects covering 3,000 years of world history. The section devoted to China is especially interesting.

Historical Museum: This museum, founded by Pope Paul VI, was established to tell the history of the Vatican. It exhibits arms, uniforms, and armor, some dating from the early Renaissance. The carriages displayed are those used by the popes and cardinals in religious processions. Among the showcases of dress uniforms are the colorful outfits worn by the Pontifical Army Corps, which was discontinued by Pope Paul VI.

Pinacoteca (Picture Gallery): The Pinacoteca houses paintings and tapestries from the 11th to the 19th century. As you pass through room 1, note the oldest picture at the Vatican, a keyhole-shaped wood panel of the *Last Judgment* from the 11th century. In room 2 is one of the finest pieces—the *Stefaneschi Triptych* (six panels) by Giotto and his assistants. Bernardo Daddi's masterpiece of early Italian Renaissance art, *Madonna del Magnificat,* is also here. And you'll see works by Fra Angelico, the 15th-century Dominican monk who distinguished himself as a miniaturist (his *Virgin with Child* is justly praised—check out the Madonna's microscopic eyes).

In the Raphael salon (room 8), you can view three paintings by the Renaissance giant himself: the *Coronation of the Virgin, the Virgin of Foligno,* and the massive *Transfiguration* (completed shortly before his death). There are also eight tapestries made by Flemish weavers from cartoons by Raphael. In room 9, seek out Leonardo da Vinci's masterful but uncompleted *St. Jerome with the Lion,* as well as Giovanni Bellini's *Pietà* and one of Titian's greatest works, the *Virgin of Frari.* Finally, in room 10, feast your eyes on one of the masterpieces of the baroque, Caravaggio's *Deposition from the Cross.*

Pio Clementino Museum: Here you'll find Greek and Roman sculptures, many of which are immediately recognizable. The rippling muscles of the *Belvedere Torso,* a partially preserved Greek statue (1st century B.C.) much admired by the artists of the Renaissance, especially Michelangelo, reveal an intricate knowledge of the human body. In the rotunda is a large gilded bronze of *Hercules* from the late 2nd century B.C. Other major sculptures are under porticoes opening onto the Belvedere courtyard. From the 1st century B.C., one sculpture shows Laocoön and his two sons locked in an eternal struggle with the serpents. The incomparable *Apollo Belvedere* (a late Roman reproduction of an authentic Greek work from the 4th century B.C.) has become the symbol of classic male beauty, rivaling Michelangelo's *David.*

Raphael Rooms: While still a young man, Raphael was given one of the greatest assignments of his short life: the decoration of a series of rooms in the apartments of Pope Julius II. The decoration was carried out by Raphael and his workshop from 1508 to 1524. In these works, Raphael achieves the Renaissance aim of blending classic beauty with realism. In the first chamber, the Stanza dell'Incendio, you'll see much of the work of Raphael's pupils but little of the master—except in the fresco across from the window. The figure of the partially draped Aeneas rescuing his father (to the left of the fresco) is sometimes attributed to Raphael, as is the surprised woman with a jug balanced on her head to the right.

Raphael reigns supreme in the next and most important salon, the Stanza della Segnatura, the first room decorated by the artist, where you'll find the majestic *School of Athens,* one of his best-known works, depicting such philosophers from the ages as Aristotle, Plato, and Socrates. Many of the figures are actually portraits of some of the greatest artists of the Renaissance, including Bramante (on the right as Euclid, bent over and balding as he draws on a chalkboard), Leonardo da Vinci (as Plato, the bearded man in the center pointing heavenward), and even Raphael himself (looking out at you from the lower-right corner). While he was painting this masterpiece, Raphael stopped work to walk down the hall for the unveiling of Michelangelo's newly finished Sistine Chapel ceiling. He was so impressed that he returned to his *School of Athens* and added to his design a sulking Michelangelo sitting on the steps. Another well-known masterpiece here is the *Disputa del Sacramento.*

The *Stanza d'Eliodoro,* also by the master, manages to flatter Raphael's papal patrons (Julius II and Leo X) without compromising his art (though one rather fanciful fresco depicts the pope driving Attila from Rome). Finally, there's the *Sala di Constantino,* which was completed by his students after Raphael's death. The loggia, frescoed with more than 50 scenes from the Bible, was designed by Raphael, but the actual work was done by his loyal students.

✪ **Sistine Chapel:** Michelangelo considered himself a sculptor, not a painter. While in his 30s, he was commanded by Julius II to stop work on the pope's own tomb and to devote his considerable talents to painting ceiling frescoes (an art form of which the Florentine master was contemptuous). Michelangelo labored for 4 years (1508-12) over this epic project, which was so physically taxing it permanently damaged his eyesight. All during the task he had to contend with the pope's incessant urgings to hurry up; at one point Julius threatened to topple Michelangelo from the scaffolding—or so Vasari relates in his *Lives of the Artists.*

It's ironic that a project undertaken against the artist's wishes would form his most enduring legend. Glorifying the human body as only a sculptor could, Michelangelo painted nine panels, taken from the pages of Genesis, and surrounded them with prophets and sibyls. The most notable panels detail the expulsion of Adam and Eve from the Garden of Eden and the creation of man; you'll recognize the image of God's outstretched hand as it imbues Adam with spirit. (You may want to bring along binoculars so you can see the details better.)

The Florentine master was in his 60s when he began the masterly *Last Judgment* on the altar wall. Again working against his wishes, Michelangelo presented a more jaundiced view of people and their fate; God sits in judgment and sinners are plunged into the mouth of hell.

A master of ceremonies under Paul III, Monsignor Biagio da Cesena, protested to the pope about the "shameless nudes" painted by Michelangelo. Michelangelo showed he wasn't above petty revenge by painting the prude with the ears of a jackass in hell. When Biagio complained to the pope, Paul III maintained he had no jurisdiction in hell. However, Daniele de Volterra was summoned to drape clothing over some of the bare figures—thus earning for himself a dubious distinction as a haberdasher.

On the side walls are frescoes by other Renaissance masters, like Botticelli, Perugino, Signorelli, Pinturicchio, Roselli, and Ghirlandaio. If these paintings had been displayed by themselves in other chapels, they would be the object of special pilgrimages. But since they have to compete unfairly with the artistry of Michelangelo, they're virtually ignored by most visitors.

The restoration of the Sistine Chapel in the 1990s touched off a worldwide debate among art historians. The chapel was on the verge of collapse, from both its age and the weather, and restoration has taken years, as restorers used advanced computer analyses in their painstaking and controversial work. They reattached the fresco and repaired the ceiling, ridding the frescoes of their dark and shadowy look. Critics claim that in addition to removing centuries of dirt and grime—and several of the added "modesty" drapes—the restorers removed a vital second layer of paint as well. Purists argue that many of the restored figures seem flat compared with the originals, which had more shadow and detail. Others have hailed the project for saving Michelangelo's masterpiece for future generations to appreciate and for revealing the vibrancy of his color palette.

Vatican Library: The library is richly decorated, with frescos created by a team of Mannerist painters commissioned by Sixtus V.

Vatican Gardens. North and west of the Vatican. See below for tour information.

Separating the Vatican from the secular world on the north and west are 58 acres of lush gardens filled with winding paths, brilliantly colored flowers, groves of massive oaks, and ancient fountains and pools. In the midst of this pastoral setting is a small summer house, Villa Pia, built for Pope Pius IV in 1560 by Pirro Ligorio. The gardens contain medieval fortifications from the 9th century to the present. Water spouts profusely from a variety of fountains.

Papal Audiences

When the pope is in Rome, he gives a public audience every Wednesday beginning at 10:30am (sometimes at 10am in summer). It takes place in the Paul VI Hall of Audiences, though sometimes St. Peter's Basilica and St. Peter's Square are used to accommodate a large attendance. Anyone is welcome, but you must first obtain a **free ticket** from the office of the Prefecture of the Papal Household, accessible from St. Peter's Square by the Bronze Door, where the right-hand colonnade (as you face the basilica) begins. The office is open Monday to Saturday 9am to 1pm. Tickets are readily available on Monday and Tuesday; sometimes you won't be able to get into the office on Wednesday morning. Occasionally, if there's enough room, you can attend without a ticket.

You can also write ahead to the **Prefecture of the Papal Household,** 00120 Città del Vaticano (☎ **06-698-83114**), indicating your language, the dates of your visit, the number of people in your party, and (if possible) the hotel in Rome to which the cards should be sent the afternoon before the audience. American Catholics, armed with a letter of introduction from their parish priest, should apply to the **North American College,** Via dell'Umiltà 30, 00187 Roma (☎ **06-690-011**).

At noon on Sunday, the pope speaks briefly from his study window and gives his blessing to the visitors and pilgrims gathered in St. Peter's Square. From about mid-July to mid-September, the Angelus and blessing take place at the summer residence at Castelgandolfo, some 16 miles (26km) out of Rome and accessible by metro and bus.

To make a reservation to visit the Vatican Gardens, send a fax to **06-698-851-00.** Once the reservation is accepted, you have to go to the Vatican information office (at Piazza San Pietro, on the left side looking at the facade of St. Peter's) and pick up the tickets two or three days before your visit at the gardens. Tours of the gardens are Monday, Tuesday, Thursday, Friday, and Saturday at 10am; they last for 2 hours and the first half hour is by bus. The cost of the tour is 20,000L ($10). For further information, contact the **Vatican Tourism Office** (☎ **06-698-844-66,** or 06-698-848-66).

NEAR VATICAN CITY

Castel Sant'Angelo. Lungotevere Castello 50. ☎ **06-681-9111.** Admission 10,000L ($5) Tues–Sun 9am–8pm. Closed second and last Wed of the month. Bus: 23, 46, 49, 62, 87, 98, 280, or 910. Metro: Ottaviano, then a long stroll.

This overpowering castle on the Tiber was built in the 2nd century as a tomb for Emperor Hadrian; it continued as an imperial mausoleum until the time of Caracalla. If it looks like a fortress, it should—that was its function in the Middle Ages. It was built over the Roman walls and linked to the Vatican by an underground passage that was much used by the fleeing papacy, who escaped from unwanted visitors like Charles V during his 1527 sack of the city. In the 14th century, it became a papal residence, enjoying various connections with Boniface IX, Nicholas V, and Julius II, patron of Michelangelo and Raphael. But its legend rests largely on its link with Pope Alexander VI, whose mistress bore him two children (those darlings of debauchery, Cesare and Lucrezia Borgia).

The highlight here is a trip through the Renaissance apartments with their coffered ceilings and lush decoration. Their walls have witnessed some of the most diabolical plots and intrigues of the High Renaissance. Later, you can go through the dank cells that once echoed with the screams of Cesare's victims of torture. The most famous figure imprisoned here was Benvenuto Cellini, the eminent sculptor/goldsmith, remembered chiefly for his candid *Autobiography.* Now an art museum, the castle halls display the history of the Roman mausoleum, along with a wide-ranging selection of ancient arms and armor. You can climb to the top terrace for another one of those dazzling views of the Eternal City.

2 The Colosseum, the Roman Forum & Highlights of Ancient Rome

THE TOP SIGHTS IN ANCIENT ROME

✪ **The Colosseum (Colosseo).** Piazzale del Colosseo, Via dei Fori Imperiali. ☎ **06-700-4261.** Admission 10,000L ($5) all levels. Oct–Jan 15 daily 9am–3pm; Jan 16–Feb 15 daily 9am–4pm; Feb 16–Mar 17 daily 9am–4:30pm; Mar 18–Apr 16 daily 9am–5pm; Apr 17–Sept daily 9am–7pm. Guided tours in English with an archaeologist 3 times per morning on Sun and holidays 6,000L ($3). Tickets to Palatine Hill also sold at box office for 12,000L ($6).

Now a mere shell, the Colosseum still remains the greatest architectural legacy from ancient Rome. Vespasian ordered the construction of the elliptical bowl, called the Amphitheatrum Flavium, in A.D. 72; it was inaugurated by Titus in A.D. 80 with a bloody combat, lasting many long weeks, between gladiators and wild beasts. At its peak, under the cruel Domitian, the Colosseum could seat 50,000. The Vestal Virgins from the temple screamed for blood, as more and more exotic animals were shipped in from the far corners of the Empire to satisfy jaded tastes (lion versus bear, two humans vs. hippopotamus, or whatever). Not-so-mock naval battles were staged (the canopied Colosseum could be flooded), and the defeated combatants might have their lives spared if they put up a good fight. Many historians now believe that one of the most enduring legends about the Colosseum (that Christians were fed to the lions) is unfounded.

Long after the Colosseum ceased to be an arena to amuse sadistic Romans, it was struck by an earthquake. Centuries later it was used as a quarry, its rich marble facing stripped away to build palaces and churches. On one side, part of the original four tiers remains; the first three levels were constructed in Doric, Ionic, and Corinthian styles, respectively, to lend variety. Inside, the seats are gone, as is the wooden floor.

Efforts are currently underway to restore and shore up the Colosseum, but they seem to be dragging. As of this writing, scaffolding still covers one section, but that should be gone by the time you arrive. The Colosseum has become the turnstile for Rome's largest traffic circle, around which thousands of cars whip daily, spewing exhaust over this venerable monument. In addition to reinforcing the structure, workers are attempting to clean off a layer of grime. Ambitious plans are also underway to allow visitors to explore the interior more fully by 2002. For now, you can explore on your own or rent an audio guide for 7,000L ($3.50).

The **Arch of Constantine,** the highly photogenic memorial next to the Colosseum, was erected by the Senate in A.D. 315 to honor Constantine's defeat of the pagan Maxentius (306). Many of the reliefs have nothing whatever to do with Constantine or his works but tell of the victories of earlier Antonine rulers (they were apparently lifted from other, long-forgotten memorials).

Historically, the arch marks a period of great change in the history of Rome and thus the history of the world. Converted to Christianity by a vision on the battlefield, Constantine ended the centuries-long persecution of the Christians (during which

Ancient Rome & Attractions Nearby

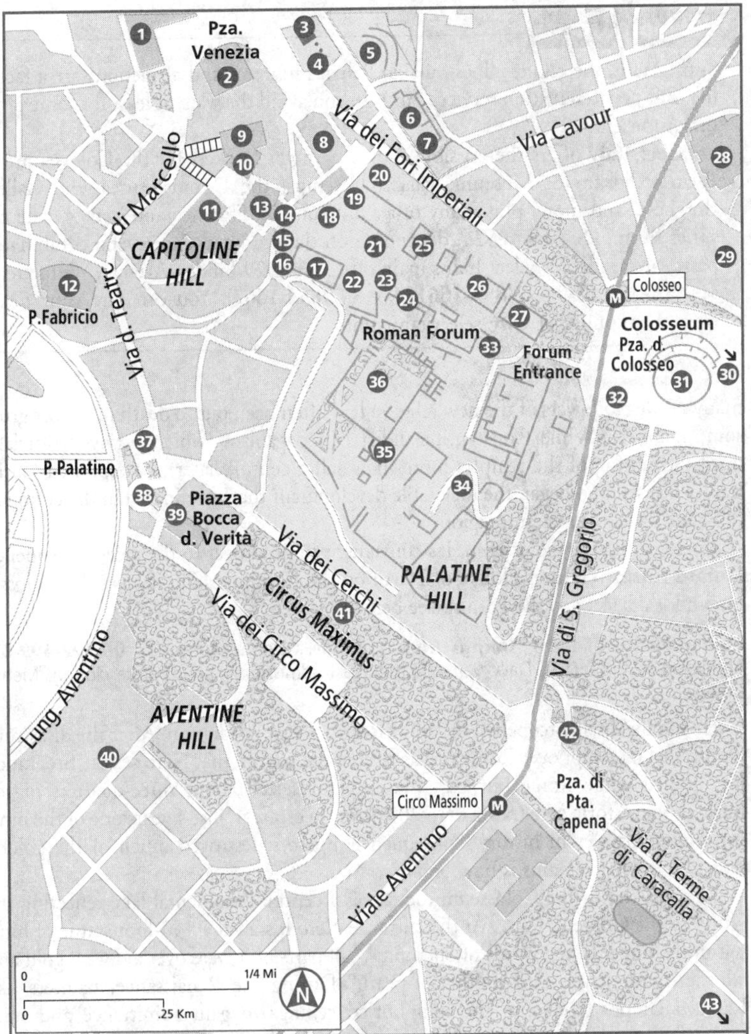

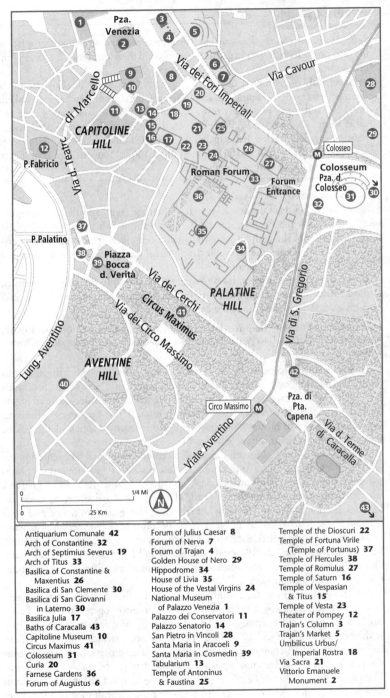

Antiquarium Comunale **42**
Arch of Constantine **32**
Arch of Septimius Severus **19**
Arch of Titus **33**
Basilica of Constantine & Maxentius **26**
Basilica di San Clemente **30**
Basilica di San Giovanni in Laterno **30**
Basilica Julia **17**
Baths of Caracalla **43**
Capitoline Museum **10**
Circus Maximus **41**
Colosseum **31**
Curia **20**
Farnese Gardens **36**
Forum of Augustus **6**
Forum of Julius Caesar **8**
Forum of Nerva **7**
Forum of Trajan **4**
Golden House of Nero **29**
Hippodrome **34**
House of Livia **35**
House of the Vestal Virgins **24**
National Museum of Palazzo Venezia **1**
Palazzo dei Conservatori **11**
Palazzo Senatorio **14**
San Pietro in Vincoli **28**
Santa Maria in Aracoeli **9**
Santa Maria in Cosmedin **39**
Tabularium **13**
Temple of Antoninus & Faustina **25**
Temple of the Dioscuri **22**
Temple of Fortuna Virile (Temple of Portunus) **37**
Temple of Hercules **38**
Temple of Romulus **27**
Temple of Saturn **16**
Temple of Vespasian & Titus **15**
Temple of Vesta **23**
Theater of Pompey **12**
Trajan's Column **3**
Trajan's Market **5**
Umbilicus Urbus/ Imperial Rostra **18**
Via Sacra **21**
Vittorio Emanuele Monument **2**

No More Lines

Sun or rain, the endless lines outside Italian museums and attractions are a fact of life. But new reservation services can help you avoid the wait, at least for some of the major museums.

Select Italy offers the possibility to reserve your tickets for the Colosseum, the Palatine Forum & Museum, Palazzo Altemps, the Domus Aurea, the Galleria Borghese, and more, plus many other museums in Florence and Venice. The cost varies from U.S. $15 to $24, depending on the museum, and several combination passes are available. Select Italy's main office is at 329 Linden Avenue, Wilmette, IL 60091-2788 (☎ **847/853-1661;** fax 847/853-1667). You can buy your tickets from them online at www.selectitaly.com.

---

many devout followers of the new religion had often been put to death in a most gruesome manner). While Constantine didn't ban paganism (which survived officially until the closing of the temples more than half a century later), he espoused Christianity himself and began the inevitable development that culminated in the conquest of Rome by the Christian religion.

After visiting the Colosseum, it's convenient to head over to the recently reopened **Domus Aurea (Golden House of Nero)** on the Esquiline Hill; it faces the Colosseum and is adjacent to the Forum (see below).

Golden House of Nero (Domus Aurea). Via della Domus Aurea. ☎ **06-397-499-07.** Admission 12,000L ($6). Daily 9am–7:45pm. Last admission 1 hour before closing. Metro: Colosseo.

"Nero's Folly" finally reopened in 1999 after a 15-year restoration. After the disastrous fire of A.D. 64 swept over Rome (it has never been proven that Nero set the fire, much less fiddled while Rome burned), the emperor seized about three-quarters of the burned-out historic core (more than 200 acres) to create in just 4 years one of the most sumptuous palaces in history. Subsequent emperors destroyed much of the golden palace, but what remains is now on view.

The area that is the Colosseum today was a central ornamental lake reflecting the glitter of the Golden House. At the entrance Nero installed a 150-foot statue of himself in the nude. In the words of Suetonius, "all parts of it were overlaid with gold and adorned with jewels and mother-of-pearl." During the Renaissance, painters like Raphael chopped holes in the long-buried ceilings to gain admittance and were inspired by the frescoes and small "grotesques" of cornucopia and cherubs. The word *grotto* comes from this palace, as the palace is believed to have been built underground. Remnants of these almost-2,000-year-old frescoes and fragments of mosaics remain. Out of the original 250 rooms, 30 are now open to the public. Some of the sculptures that survived are also on view.

Practical matters: To visit the Domus Aurea, you must make a reservation at Centro Servizi per l'Archeologia, Via Amendola 2 (Metro: Colosseo; open Monday to Saturday 9am to 1pm and 2 to 5pm. But it's easier to book your visit by calling Select Italy at the number above or call ☎ **06-397-499-07,** where a recorded message both in Italian and English will guide you through the reservation process. Be aware that usually you have to call at least one week ahead of the date you've scheduled your visit. The guided tours, both with a guide or with audio-guides, last about one hour from 9am to 7pm. Visitors enter in groups of no more than 25, with gaps of 15 minutes between one group and the other.

Of particular interest are the Hall of Hector and Andromache (*Sala di Ettore e Andromaca*), once illustrated with scenes from Homer's *Iliad;* the Hall of Achilles (*Sala di Achille*), with a gigantic shell decoration; the Hall of Ninfeo (*Sala di Ninfeo*), which once had a waterfall; and the Hall of the Gilded Vault (*Sala della Volta Dorata*), depicting satyrs raping nymphs, plus Cupid driving a chariot pulled by panthers. You'll be amazed by the beauty of the floral frescoes along the *cryptoportici* (long corridors); the longest is about 200 feet. The most spectacular sight is the Octagonal Hall, Nero's banqueting hall, where the menu included casseroles of flamingo tongues and other rare dishes.

When Nero moved in, he shouted, "At last I can start living like a human being!"

✪ **Roman Forum (Foro Romano), Palatine Hill (Palatino), and Palatine Museum (Museo Palatino).** Via dei Fori Imperiali. ☎ **06-699-0110.** Forum free admission; Palatine Hill 12,000L ($6). Apr–Sept daily 9am–8pm; Oct–Mar daily 9am–sunset. Last admission 1 hour before closing. Closed holidays. Metro: Colosseo. Bus: 27, 81, 85, 87, or 186.

When it came to cremating Caesar, purchasing a harlot for the night, sacrificing a naked victim, or just discussing the day's events, the Roman Forum was the place to be. Traversed by the **Via Sacra (Sacred Way),** the Broadway of ancient Rome, the Forum was built in the marshy land between the Palatine and Capitoline hills and flourished as the center of Roman life in the days of the Republic, before it gradually lost prestige to the Imperial Forums.

You'll see only ruins and fragments, an arch or two, and lots of overturned boulders, but with some imagination you can feel the rush of history here. That any semblance of the Forum remains today is miraculous, since it was used for years (like the Colosseum) as a quarry. Eventually it reverted to what the Italians call a *campo vaccino* (cow pasture). But excavations in the 19th century began to bring to light one of the world's most historic spots.

By day, the columns of now-vanished temples and the stones from which long-forgotten orators spoke are mere shells. Bits of grass and weed grow where a triumphant Caesar was once lionized. But at night, when the Forum is silent in the moonlight (you can get a dramatic view of the floodlit ruins from the Campidoglio), it isn't difficult to imagine vestal virgins still guarding the sacred temple fire. (The maidens were assigned to keep the temple's sacred fire burning, but to keep their own passions under control. Failure to do the latter sent them to an early grave—alive!)

You can spend at least a morning wandering alone through the ruins of the Forum. If you're content with just looking at the ruins, you can do so at your leisure. But if you want the stones to have some meaning, buy a detailed plan at the gate (the temples are hard to locate otherwise).

Turn right at the bottom of the entrance slope to walk west along the old Via Sacra toward the arch. Just before it on your right is the large brick **Curia** built by Julius Caesar, the main seat of the Roman Senate (pop inside to see the 3rd-century marble inlay floor).

The triumphal **Arch of Septimius Severus** (A.D. 203) displays time-bitten reliefs of the emperor's victories in what are today Iran and Iraq. During the Middle Ages, Rome became a provincial backwater, and frequent flooding of the nearby river helped to rapidly bury most of the Forum. This former center of the empire became a cow pasture. Some bits did still stick out above ground, including the top half of this arch, which was used to shelter a barbershop! It wasn't until the 19th century that people really became interested in excavating these ancient ruins to see what Rome in its glory must have been like.

Just to the left of the arch, you can make out the remains of a cylindrical lump of rock with some marble steps curving off it. That round stone was the **Umbilicus**

Urbus, considered the center of Rome and of the entire Roman empire; and the curving steps are those of the **Imperial Rostra,** where great orators and legislators stood to speak and the people gathered to listen. Nearby, the much-photographed trio of fluted columns with Corinthian capitals supporting a bit of architrave form the corner of the **Temple of Vespasian and Titus** (emperors were routinely turned into gods upon dying).

Start heading to your left toward the eight Ionic columns marking the front of the **Temple of Saturn** (rebuilt 42 B.C.), which housed the first treasury of Republican Rome. It was also the site of one of the Roman year's biggest annual blowout festivals, the December 17 feast of *Saturnalia,* which, after a bit of tweaking, we now celebrate as Christmas. Now turn left to start heading back east, past the worn steps and stumps of brick pillars outlining the enormous **Basilica Julia,** built by Julius Caesar. Past it are the three Corinthian columns of the **Temple of the Dioscuri,** dedicated to the Gemini twins, Castor and Pollux.

Beyond the bit of curving wall that marks the site of the little round **Temple of Vesta** (rebuilt several times after fires started by the sacred flame housed within), you'll find the partially reconstructed **House of the Vestal Virgins** (A.D. 3rd–4th century) against the south side of the grounds. This was the home of the consecrated young women who tended the sacred flame in the Temple of Vesta. Vestals were young girls chosen from patrician families to serve a 30-year-long priesthood. During their tenure, they were among Rome's most venerated citizens, with unique powers like the ability to pardon condemned criminals. The cult was quite serious about the "virgin" part of the job description—if any of Vesta's earthly servants were found to have "misplaced" their virginity, the miscreant Vestal was summarily buried alive. (Her amorous accomplice was merely flogged to death.) The overgrown rectangle of their gardens has lilied goldfish ponds and is lined with broken, heavily worn statues of senior Vestals on pedestals (and, at any given time when the guards aren't looking, two to six tourists are posing as Vestal Virgins on the empty pedestals).

The path dovetails back to join Via Sacra at the entrance. Turn right and then left to enter the massive brick remains and coffered ceilings of the 4th-century **Basilica of Constantine and Maxentius.** These were Rome's public law courts, and their architectural style was adopted by early Christians for their houses of worship (the reason so many ancient churches are called "basilicas").

Return to the path and continue toward the Colosseum, veering right to the second great surviving triumphal arch, the **Arch of Titus** (A.D. 81), on which one relief depicts the carrying off of treasures from Jerusalem's temple—look closely and you'll see a menorah among the booty. The war that this arch glorifies ended with the expulsion of Jews from the colonized Judea, signaling the beginning of the Jewish Diaspora throughout Europe. From here you can enter and climb the only part of the Forum's archaeological zone that still charges admission, the **Palatine Hill** (with the same hours as the Forum).

The Palatine, tradition tells us, was the spot on which the first settlers built their huts, under the direction of Romulus. In later years, the hill became a patrician residential district that attracted such citizens as Cicero. In time, however, the area was gobbled up by imperial palaces and drew a famous and infamous roster of tenants, like Livia (some of the frescoes in the House of Livia are in miraculous condition), Tiberius, Caligula (he was murdered here by members of his Praetorian Guard), Nero, and Domitian.

Only the ruins of its former grandeur remain today, and you really need to be an archaeologist to make sense of them, as they're more difficult to understand than those in the Forum. But even if you're not interested in the past, it's worth the climb for the panoramic view of both the Roman and the Imperial Forums, as well as the Capitoline Hill and the Colosseum.

In 1998 the **Palatine Museum (Museo Palatino)** here finally reopened, displaying a good collection of Roman sculpture from the ongoing digs in the Palatine villas. In summer you can take guided tours in English Monday to Sunday at noon for 6,000L ($3); call in winter to see if they're still available. If you ask the museum's custodian, he may take you to one of the nearby locked villas and let you in for a peek at surviving frescoes and stuccoes. The entire Palatine is slated for renewed excavations, so be on the lookout for many areas to be roped off at first, but soon even more than before will be open to the public.

Imperial Forums (Fori Imperiali). Via de Fori Imperiali. Free admission. Metro: Colosseo. Keep to the right side of the street.

It was Mussolini who issued the controversial orders to cut through centuries of debris and junky buildings to carve out Via dei Fori Imperiali, thereby linking the Colosseum to the grand 19th-century monuments of Piazza Venezia. Excavations under his fascist regime began at once, and many archaeological treasures were revealed.

Begun by Julius Caesar as an answer to the overcrowding of Rome's older forums, the Imperial Forums were at the time of their construction flashier, bolder, and more impressive than the buildings in the Roman Forum. This site conveyed the unquestioned authority of the emperors at the height of their absolute power. On the street's north side, you'll come to a large outdoor restaurant, where Via Cavour joins the boulevard. Just beyond the small park across Via Cavour are the remains of the **Forum of Nerva,** built by the emperor whose 2-year reign (A.D. 96-98) followed that of the paranoid Domitian. You'll be struck by just how much the ground level has risen in 19 centuries. The only really recognizable remnant is a wall of the Temple of Minerva with two fine Corinthian columns. This forum was once flanked by that of Vespasian, which is now gone. It's possible to enter the Forum of Nerva from the other side, but you can see it just as well from the railing.

The next forum you approach is the **Forum of Augustus,** built before the birth of Christ to commemorate the emperor's victory over the assassins Cassius and Brutus in the Battle of Philippi (42 B.C.). Like the Forum of Nerva, you can enter this forum from the other side (cut across the wee footbridge).

Continuing along the railing, you'll see the vast semicircle of **Trajan's Market,** Via Quattro Novembre 94 (☎ **06-679-0048**), whose teeming arcades stocked with merchandise from the far corners of the Roman world collapsed long ago, leaving only a few cats to watch after things. The shops once covered a multitude of levels, and you can still wander around many of them. In front of the perfectly proportioned facade (designed by Apollodorus of Damascus at the beginning of the 2nd century) are the remains of a great library, and fragments of delicately colored marble floors still shine in the sun between stretches of rubble and tall grass. Trajan's Market is worth the descent below street level. To get there, follow the service road you're on until you reach the monumental Trajan's Column on your left, where you turn right and go up the steep flight of stairs leading to Via Nazionale. At the top, about half a block farther on the right, you'll see the entrance. It's open Tuesday to Sunday 9am to 4:30pm. Admission is 4,000L ($2).

Before you head down through the labyrinthine passages, you might like to climb the **Tower of the Milizie,** a 12th-century structure that was part of the medieval headquarters of the Knights of Rhodes. The view from the top (if it's open) is well worth the climb.

You can enter the **Forum of Trajan** on Via Quattro Novembre near the steps of Via Magnanapoli. Once through the tunnel, you'll emerge into the newest and most beautiful of the Imperial Forums, built between A.D. 107 and 113 and designed by Greek architect Apollodorus of Damascus (who laid out the adjoining market). There are many statue fragments and pedestals bearing still-legible inscriptions, but more interesting is the great Basilica Ulpia, whose gray marble columns rise roofless into the sky. This forum was once regarded as one of the architectural wonders of the world.

Beyond the Basilica Ulpia is **Trajan's Column,** in magnificent condition, with intricate bas-relief sculpture depicting Trajan's victorious campaign (though from your vantage point, you'll be able to see only the earliest stages). The next stop is the **Forum of Julius Caesar,** the first of the Imperial Forums. It lies on the opposite side of Via dei Fori Imperiali. This was the site of the Roman stock exchange, as well as of the Temple of Venus.

After you've seen the wonders of ancient Rome, you might continue up Via dei Fori Imperiali to Piazza Venezia, where the white Brescian marble **Vittorio Emanuele Monument** dominates the scene. (You can't miss it.) Italy's most flamboyant landmark, it was built in the late 1800s to honor the first king of Italy. It has been compared to everything from a frosty wedding cake to a Victorian typewriter and has been ridiculed because of its harsh white color in a city of honey-gold tones. An eternal flame burns at the Tomb of the Unknown Soldier. The interior of the monument has been closed for many years, but you'll come to use it as a landmark as you figure your way around the city.

Circus Maximus (Circo Massimo). Between Via dei Cerchi and Via del Circo Massimo. Metro: Circo Massimo.

The Circus Maximus, with its elongated oval proportions and ruined tiers of benches, will remind you of the setting for *Ben-Hur.* Today a formless ruin, the once-grand circus was pilfered repeatedly by medieval and Renaissance builders in search of marble and stone. At one time, 250,000 Romans could assemble on the marble seats while the emperor observed the games from his box high on the Palatine Hill.

The circus lies in a valley formed by the Palatine on the left and the Aventine on the right. Next to the Colosseum, it was the most impressive structure in ancient Rome, located certainly in one of the most exclusive neighborhoods. For centuries, the pomp and ceremony of imperial chariot races filled this valley with the cheers of thousands.

When the dark days of the 5th and 6th centuries fell, the Circus Maximus seemed a symbol of the complete ruination of Rome. The last games were held in A.D. 549 on the orders of Totilla the Goth, who had seized Rome in 547 and established himself as emperor. He lived in the still-glittering ruins on the Palatine and apparently thought the chariot races in the Circus Maximus would lend credibility to his charade of an Empire. It must've been a pretty miserable show, since the decimated population numbered something like 500 when Totilla recaptured the city. The Romans of these times were caught between Belisarius, the imperial general from Constantinople, and Totilla the Goth, both of whom fought bloodily for control of Rome. After the travesty of 549, the Circus Maximus was never used again, and the demand for building materials reduced it, like so much of Rome, to a great dusty field.

✪ **Capitoline Museum (Museo Capitolino) and Palazzo dei Conservatori.** Piazza del Campidoglio. ☎ **06-6710-2071.** Admission (to both) 10,000L ($5). Free on last Sun of each month. Tues–Sun 9am–7pm. Bus: 44, 89, 92, 94, or 716.

Of Rome's seven hills, the **Capitoline (Campidoglio)** is the most sacred—its origins stretch way back into antiquity (an Etruscan temple to Jupiter once stood on this

A Tip to a View

Standing on Piazza del Campidoglio, walk around the right side of the Palazzo Senatorio to a terrace overlooking the city's best panorama of the Roman Forum, with the Palatine Hill and the Colosseum as a backdrop. It's great day or night—at night the Forum is dramatically floodlit.

spot). The approach is dramatic as you climb the long sloping steps by Michelangelo. At the top is a perfectly proportioned square, **Piazza del Campidoglio,** also laid out by the Florentine artist. Michelangelo positioned the bronze equestrian statue of Marcus Aurelius in the center, but it has now been moved inside for protection from pollution (a copy was placed on the pedestal in 1997). The other steps adjoining Michelangelo's approach will take you to Santa Maria d'Aracoeli (see below).

One side of the piazza is open; the others are bounded by the **Senatorium (Town Council),** the statuary-filled **Palace of the Conservatori (Curators),** and the **Capitoline Museum.** These museums house some of the greatest pieces of classical sculpture in the world.

The **Capitoline Museum,** built in the 17th century, was based on an architectural sketch by Michelangelo. In the first room is *The Dying Gaul,* a work of majestic skill that's a copy of a Greek original dating from the 3rd century B.C. In a special gallery all her own is the *Capitoline Venus,* who demurely covers herself. This statue was the symbol of feminine beauty and charm down through the centuries (also a Roman copy of a 3rd-century B.C. Greek original). *Amore* (Cupid) and *Psyche* are up to their old tricks near the window.

The famous equestrian statue of Marcus Aurelius, whose years in the piazza made it a victim of pollution, has recently been restored and is now kept in the museum for protection. This is the only bronze equestrian statue to have survived from ancient Rome, mainly because it was thought for centuries that the statue was that of Constantine the Great, and papal Rome respected the memory of the first Christian emperor. It's beautiful, though the perspective is rather odd. The statue is housed in a glassed-in room on the street level, the Cortile di Marforio; it's a kind of Renaissance greenhouse, surrounded by windows.

Palace of the Conservatori, across the way, was also based on a Michelangelo architectural plan and is rich in classical sculpture and paintings. One of the most notable bronzes, a Greek work of incomparable beauty dating from the 1st century B.C., is *Lo Spinario* (a little boy picking a thorn from his foot). In addition, you'll find *Lupa Capitolina* (the *Capitoline Wolf*), a rare Etruscan bronze that may date from the 5th century B.C. (Romulus and Remus, the legendary twins who were suckled by the wolf, were added at a later date). The palace also contains a *Pinacoteca* (Picture Gallery)—mostly works from the 16th and 17th centuries. Notable canvases are Caravaggio's *Fortune-Teller* and his curious *John the Baptist, The Holy Family* by Dosso Dossi, *Romulus and Remus* by Rubens, and Titian's *Baptism of Christ.* The entrance courtyard is lined with the remains (head, hands, foot, and a kneecap) of an ancient colossal statue of Constantine the Great.

Baths of Caracalla (Terme di Caracalla). Via delle Terme di Caracalla 52. ☎ **06-575-8626.** Admission 8,000L ($4). Oct–Jan daily 9am–4pm; Jan 16–Feb 15 daily 9am–4:30pm; Feb 16–Mar 15 daily 9am–5pm; Mar 16–31 daily 9am–5:30pm; Apr–Sept daily 9am–7pm. Last admission 1 hour before closing. Closed holidays. Bus: 628.

Named for the emperor Caracalla, the baths were completed in the early 3rd century. The richness of decoration has faded, and the lushness can be judged only from the shell of brick ruins that remain. In their heyday, they sprawled across 27 acres and could handle 1,600 bathers at one time. A circular room, the ruined caldarium for very hot baths, had been the traditional setting for operatic performances in Rome, until it was discovered that the ancient structure was being severely damaged.

OTHER ATTRACTIONS NEAR ANCIENT ROME

Santa Maria d'Aracoeli. Piazza d'Aracoeli. ☎ **06-679-8155.** Free admission. Daily 6:30am–5pm. Bus 44, 46, or 75.

On the Capitoline Hill, this landmark church was built for the Franciscans in the 13th century. According to legend, Augustus once ordered a temple erected on this spot, where a sibyl, with her gift of prophecy, forecast the coming of Christ. In the interior are a coffered Renaissance ceiling and a mosaic of the Virgin over the altar in the Byzantine style. If you're enough of a sleuth, you'll find a tombstone carved by the great Renaissance sculptor Donatello. The church is known for its **Bufalini Chapel,** a masterpiece by Pinturicchio, who frescoed it with scenes illustrating the life and death of St. Bernardino of Siena. He also depicted St. Francis receiving the stigmata. These frescoes are a high point in early Renaissance Roman painting. You have to climb a long flight of steep steps to reach the church, unless you're already on neighboring Piazza del Campidoglio, in which case you can cross the piazza and climb the steps on the far side of the Museo Capitolino (see above).

National Museum of Palazzo Venezia (Museo Nazionale di Palazzo di Venezia). Via del Plebiscito 118. ☎ **06-679-8865.** Admission 8,000L ($4). Tues–Sun 9am–2pm. Bus: 57, 65, 70, or 75.

The Palazzo Venezia, in the geographic heart of Rome near Piazza Venezia, served as the seat of the Austrian Embassy until the end of World War I. During the Fascist regime (1928–43), it was the seat of the Italian government. The balcony from which Mussolini used to speak to the people was built in the 15th century. You can now visit the rooms and halls containing oil paintings, porcelain, tapestries, ivories, and ceramics. No one particular exhibit stands out—it's the sum total that adds up to a major attraction. The State Rooms occasionally open to host temporary exhibits.

Santa Maria in Cosmedin. Piazza della Bocca della Verità 18. ☎ **06-678-1419.** Free admission. Summer daily 9am–1pm and 2:30–6pm; winter daily 10am–1pm and 3–5pm. Metro: Circo Massimo.

This little church was begun in the 6th century but was subsequently rebuilt, and a Romanesque campanile was added at the end of the 11th century, though its origins go back to the 3rd century. The church was destroyed several times by earthquakes or by foreign invasions, but it has always been rebuilt.

People come not for great art treasures but to see the **"Mouth of Truth,"** a large disk under the portico. As Gregory Peck demonstrated to Audrey Hepburn in the film *Roman Holiday,* the mouth is supposed to chomp down on the hands of liars who insert their paws. (According to local legend, a former priest used to keep a scorpion in back to bite the fingers of anyone he felt was lying.)

The purpose of this disk (which is not of particular artistic interest) is unclear. One hypothesis says that it was used to collect the faithful's donations to God, which were introduced through the open mouth.

Basilica di San Clemente. Via San Giovanni in Laterano at Piazza San Clemente, Via Labicana 95. ☎ **06-7045-1018.** Basilica free; excavations 4,000L ($2). Mon–Sat 9am–12:30pm and 3–6pm; Sun 10am–12:30pm and 3–6pm. Metro: Colosseo.

Seeing the Sights at Night

Some of Rome's most popular monuments, archaeological sites, and museums have not only begun staying open until 8 or 10pm during summer but also engaging in **Art and Monuments Under the Stars.** For these special summer schedules, they reopen one or more nights from around 8:30 to 11:30pm. The offering includes guided tours (often in English), concerts, or simply general admission to sights for night owls, with tours of some ancient sites usually closed to the public, like the Tomb of Augustus and the Stadium of Domitian (under Piazza Navona). This is a developing phenomenon, so we can't give you many specifics, but keep your eyes peeled to the events guides from mid-June to September.

From the Colosseum, head up Via San Giovanni in Laterano to this basilica. It isn't just another Roman church—far from it. In this church-upon-a-church, centuries of history peel away. In the 4th century A.D., a church was built over a secular house from the 1st century, beside which stood a pagan temple dedicated to Mithras (god of the sun). Down in the eerie grottoes (which you can explore on your own), you'll discover well-preserved frescoes from the 9th to the 11th century. The Normans destroyed the lower church, and a new one was built in the 12th century. Its chief attraction is the bronze-orange mosaic (from that period) adorning the apse, as well as a chapel honoring St. Catherine of Alexandria with frescoes by Masolino.

Basilica di San Giovanni in Laterano. Piazza San Giovanni in Laterano 4. ☎ **06-6988-6433.** Basilica free; cloisters 4,000L ($2). Summer daily 7am–6:45pm (off-season to 6pm). Metro: San Giovanni. Bus: 4, 16, 30, 85, 87, or 174.

This church (not St. Peter's) is the cathedral of the diocese of Rome, where the pope comes to celebrate mass on certain holidays. Built in A.D. 314 by Constantine, it has suffered the vicissitudes of Rome, forcing it to be rebuilt many times. Only fragmented parts of the baptistry remain from the original.

The present building is characterized by its 18th-century facade by Alessandro Galilei (statues of Christ and the Apostles ring the top). A 1993 terrorist bomb caused severe damage, especially to the facade. Borromini gets the credit (some say blame) for the interior, built for Innocent X. It's said that, in the misguided attempt to redecorate, frescoes by Giotto were destroyed (remains believed to have been painted by Giotto were discovered in 1952 and are now on display against a column near the entrance on the right inner pier). In addition, look for the unusual ceiling and the sumptuous transept and explore the 13th-century cloisters with twisted double columns. The popes used to live next door at the **Palazzo Laterano** before the move to Avignon in the 14th century.

Across the street is the **Santuario della Scala Santa (Palace of the Holy Steps),** Piazza San Giovanni in Laterano (☎ **06-7049-4619**). It's alleged that the 28 marble steps here (now covered with wood for preservation) were originally at Pontius Pilate's villa in Jerusalem and that Christ climbed them the day he was brought before Pilate. According to a medieval tradition, the steps were brought from Jerusalem to Rome by Constantine's mother, Helen, in 326, and they've been in this location since 1589. Today pilgrims from all over the world come here to climb the steps on their knees. This is one of the holiest sites in Christendom, though some historians say the stairs may date only to the 4th century.

✪ **San Pietro in Vincoli (St. Peter in Chains).** Piazza San Pietro in Vincoli 4A (off Via degli Annibaldi). ☎ **06-488-2865.** Free admission. Spring/summer daily 7am–12:30pm and 3:30–7pm (autumn/winter to 6pm). Metro: V. Cavour, then cross the boulevard and walk up the flight of stairs. Turn right and you'll head into the piazza; the church will be on your left.

This recently renovated church was founded in the 5th century to house the chains that bound St. Peter in Palestine (they're preserved under glass). But the drawing card is the tomb of Pope Julius II, with one of the world's most famous sculptures: **Michelangelo's *Moses.*** As readers of Irving Stone's *The Agony and the Ecstasy* know, Michelangelo was to have carved 44 magnificent figures for the tomb. That didn't happen, of course, but the pope was given a great consolation prize—a figure intended to be "minor" that's now numbered among Michelangelo's masterpieces. In the *Lives of the Artists,* Vasari wrote about the stern father symbol of Michelangelo's *Moses:* "No modern work will ever equal it in beauty, no, nor ancient either." *Moses* is badly lit, so bring 500L coins to turn on the light box.

3 The Pantheon & Attractions near Piazza Navona & Campo de' Fiori

THE PANTHEON & NEARBY ATTRACTIONS

The Pantheon stands on **Piazza della Rotonda,** a lively square with cafes, vendors, and great people-watching.

✪ **The Pantheon.** Piazza della Rotonda. ☎ **06-6830-0230.** Free admission. Mon–Sat 9am–6pm, Sun 9am–1pm. Bus: 46, 62, 64,170, or 492 to Largo di Torre.

Of all ancient Rome's great buildings, only the Pantheon ("All the Gods") remains intact. It was built in 27 B.C. by Marcus Agrippa and reconstructed by Hadrian in the early 2nd century A.D. This remarkable building, 142 feet wide and 142 feet high (a perfect sphere resting in a cylinder) and once ringed with white marble statues of Roman gods in its niches, is among the architectural wonders of the world because of its dome and its concept of space. Animals were sacrificed and burned in the center, and the smoke escaped through the only means of light, the oculus, an opening at the top 18 feet in diameter. Michelangelo came here to study the dome before designing the cupola of St. Peter's (whose dome is 2 feet smaller than the Pantheon's). The walls are 25 feet thick, and the bronze doors leading into the building weigh 20 tons each. About 125 years ago, Raphael's tomb was discovered here (fans still bring him flowers). Vittorio Emanuele II, king of Italy, and his successor, Umberto I, are interred here as well.

Galleria Doria Pamphilj. Piazza del Collegio Romano 2 (off Via del Corso). ☎ **06-679-7323.** Gallery 13,000L ($6.50) adults, 10,000L ($5) students/seniors; apartments 5,000L ($2.50). Gallery Fri–Wed 10am–5pm. Apartments Fri–Wed 10:30am–12:30pm. Private visits can be arranged. Metro: Colosseo or Cavour, then a long stroll.

This museum offers a look at what it was like to live in an 18th-century palace. It's been restored to its former splendor and expanded to include four rooms long closed to the public. It's partly leased to tenants (on the upper levels), and there are shops on the street level—but you'll overlook all this after entering the grand apartments of the Doria Pamphilj family, which traces its lineage to before the great 15th-century Genoese admiral Andrea Doria. The apartments surround the central court and gallery. The **ballroom, drawing rooms, dining rooms,** and **family chapel** are full of gilded furniture, crystal chandeliers, Renaissance tapestries, and family portraits. The **Green Room** is especially rich, with a 15th-century Tournay tapestry, paintings by Memling and Filippo Lippi, and a seminude portrait of Andrea Doria by Sebastiano del Piombo. The **Andrea Doria**

The Pantheon & Attractions Nearby

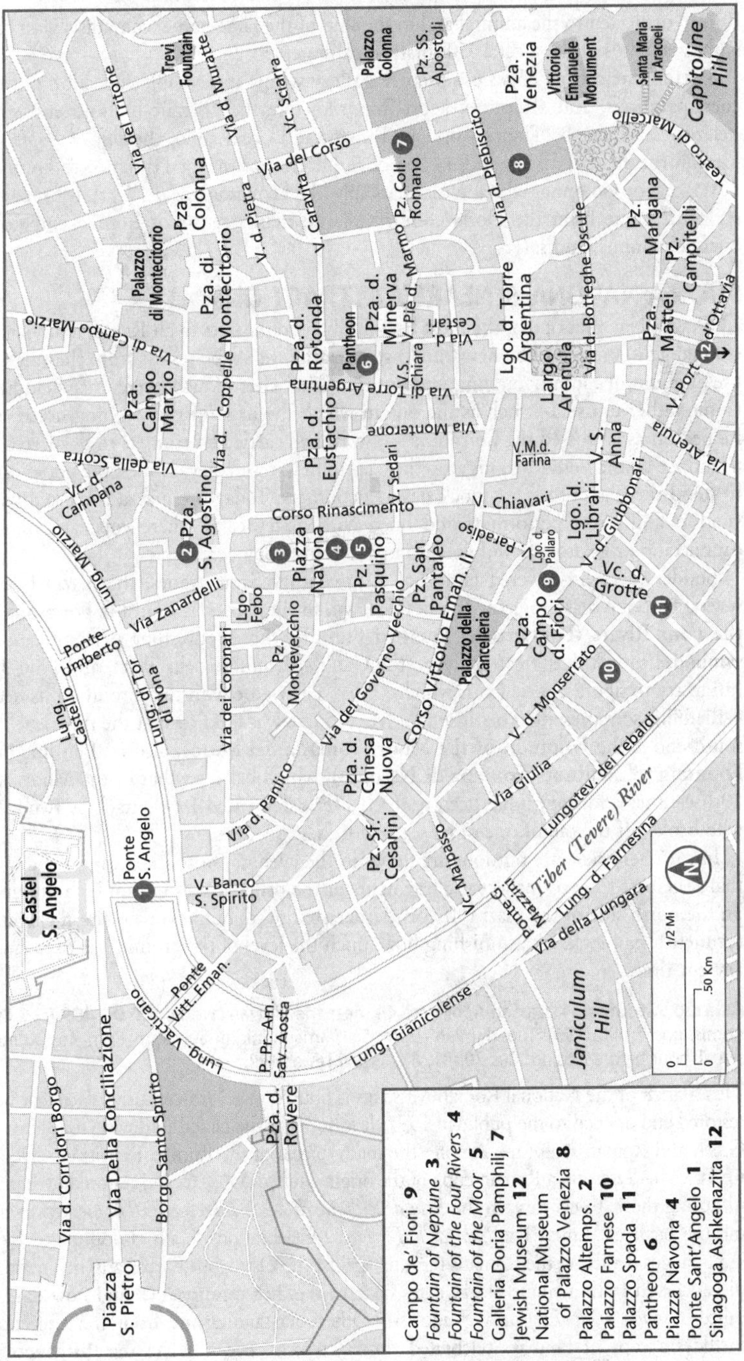

Room, dedicated to the admiral and to the ship of the same name, contains a glass case with mementos of the great 1950s maritime disaster.

Skirting the central court is a **picture gallery** with a memorable collection of frescoes, paintings, and sculpture. Most important are the portrait of Innocent X by Velázquez, *Salome* by Titian, works by Rubens and Caravaggio, the *Bay of Naples* by Pieter Brueghel the Elder, and a copy of Raphael's portrait of Principessa Giovanna d'Aragona de Colonna (who looks remarkably like Leonardo's *Mona Lisa*). Most of the sculpture came from the Doria country estates: marble busts of Roman emperors, bucolic nymphs, and satyrs.

PIAZZA NAVONA & NEARBY ATTRACTIONS

✪ **Piazza Navona,** one of the most beautifully baroque sites in all Rome, is an ocher-colored gem, unspoiled by new buildings or traffic. Its shape results from the ruins of the Stadium of Domitian, lying underneath. Great chariot races were once held here (some rather unusual—such as the one in which the head of the winning horse was lopped off as it crossed the finish line and was then carried by runners to be offered as a sacrifice by the Vestal Virgins atop the Capitoline). In medieval times, the popes used to flood the piazza to stage mock naval encounters. Today the piazza is packed with vendors and street performers and lined with pricey cafes where you can enjoy a cappuccino or gelato and indulge in unparalleled people-watching.

Besides the twin-towered facade of 17th-century Santa Agnes, the piazza boasts several baroque masterpieces. The best known, in the center, is Bernini's **Fountain of the Four Rivers (Fontana dei Quattro Fiumi),** whose four stone personifications symbolize the world's greatest rivers: the Ganges, Danube, della Plata, and Nile. It's fun to try to figure out which is which. (*Hint:* The figure with the shroud on its head is the Nile, so represented because the river's source was unknown at the time.) At the south end is the **Fountain of the Moor (Fontana del Moro),** also by Bernini. The **Fountain of Neptune (Fontana di Nettuno),** which balances that of the Moor, is a 19th-century addition; it has been restored after a demented 1997 attack by two men who broke off the tail of one of its sea creatures.

In summer, there are outdoor art shows in the evening, but visit during the day—that's the best time to inspect the fragments of the original stadium under a building on the north side of the piazza. If you're interested, walk out at the northern exit and turn left for a block. It's astonishing how much the level of the ground has risen since ancient times.

Palazzo Altemps. Piazza San Apollinare 44, near the Piazza Navona. ☎ **06-489-035-00.** Admission 12,000L ($6). Tues–Fri 9am–9pm; Sat 9am–midnight; Sun 9am–8pm. Last admission 1 hour before closing. Bus 70, 81, 87, 115, 116, or 492.

This branch of the National Roman Museum is housed in a 15th-century palace that was restored and opened to the public in 1997. It is home to the fabled Ludovisi Collection of Greek and Roman sculpture. Among the masterpieces of the Roman Renaissance, you'll find the *Ares Ludovisi*, a Roman copy of the original dated 330 B.C. and restored by Bernini during the 17th century. In the *Sala delle Storie di Mosè* is *Ludovisi's Throne,* representing the birth of Venus. The *Sala delle Feste* (the Celebrations' Hall) is dominated by a sarcophagus depicting the Romans fighting against the Ostrogoth Barbarians; this masterpiece, carved from a single block, dates back to the 2nd century A.D. and nowadays is called *Grande Ludovisi* (Great Ludovisi). Other outstanding art from the collection includes a copy of Phidias's celebrated *Athena,* which once stood in the Parthenon in Athens. (The Roman copy here is from the 1st century B.C., since the original *Athena* is lost to history.) The huge *Dionysus with Satyr* is from the 2nd century A.D.

CAMPO DE' FIORI & THE JEWISH GHETTO

During the 1500s, **Campo de' Fiori** was the geographic and cultural center of secular Rome, site of dozens of inns that would almost certainly have been reviewed by this guide. From its center rises a statue of the severe-looking monk Giordano Bruno, whose presence is a reminder that religious heretics were occasionally burned at the stake here. Today, circled by venerable houses, the campo is the site of an **open-air food market** held Monday to Saturday from early in the morning until around noon (or whenever the food runs out).

Built from 1514 to 1589, the **Palazzo Farnese,** on Piazza Farnese, was designed by Sangallo and Michelangelo, among others, and was an astronomically expensive project for the time. Its famous residents have included a 16th-century member of the Farnese family, plus Pope Paul III, Cardinal Richelieu, and the former Queen Christina of Sweden, who moved to Rome after abdicating. During the 1630s, when the heirs couldn't afford to maintain the palazzo, it became the site of the French Embassy, as it still is (it's closed to the public). For the best view of it, cut west from Via Giulia along any of the narrow streets (we recommend Via Mascherone or Via dei Farnesi).

Palazzo Spada, Capo di Ferro 3 (**☎ 06-686-1158**), built around 1550 for Cardinal Gerolamo Capo di Ferro and later inhabited by the descendants of several other cardinals, was sold to the Italian government in the 1920s. Its richly ornate facade, covered in high-relief stucco decorations in the Mannerist style, is the finest of any building from 16th-century Rome. The State Rooms are closed, but the richly decorated courtyard and a handful of galleries of paintings are open. Admission is 4,000L ($2) on Tuesday to Saturday 9am to 7pm and Sunday 9am to 1pm. Bus: 44, 56, 60, 65, 75, 170, or 710.

Also in this neighborhood stands the **Sinagoga Ashkenazita** (**☎ 06-6840-061**), open only for services. Trying to avoid all resemblance to a Christian church, the building (1874–1904) evokes Babylonian and Persian details. The synagogue was attacked by terrorists in 1982 and since then has been heavily guarded by *carabinieri* (a division of the Italian army) armed with machine guns. It houses the **Jewish Museum** (**☎ 06-6840-061**), open Monday to Thursday 9am to 5pm, Friday 9am to 2pm, and Sunday 9am to 12:30pm. Admission is 10,000L ($5). Many rare and even priceless treasures are here, including a Moroccan prayer book from the early 14th century and ceremonial objects from the 17th-century Jewish Ghetto.

4 The Spanish Steps, the Trevi Fountain & Attractions Nearby

ON OR AROUND PIAZZA DI SPAGNA

✪ **The Spanish Steps** (Scalinata di Spagna; Metro: Spagna) are filled in spring with azaleas and other flowers, flower vendors, jewelry dealers, and photographers snapping pictures of visitors. The steps and the square (Piazza di Spagna) take their names from the Spanish Embassy, which used to be headquartered here. Designed by Italian architect Francesco de Sanctis and built from 1723 to 1725, they were funded almost entirely by the French as a preface to Trinità dei Monti at the top.

The steps and the piazza below are always packed with a crowd: strolling, reading in the sun, browsing the vendors' carts, and people-watching. Near the steps, you'll also find an American Express office, public rest rooms (near the Metro stop), and the most sumptuous McDonald's we've ever seen (cause for uproar among the Romans when it first opened).

Keats-Shelley House. Piazza di Spagna 26. ☎ **06-678-4235.** Admission 5,000L ($2.50). May–Sept Mon–Fri 9am–1pm and 3–6pm; Sat 11am–2pm and 3–6pm. Guided tours by appointment. Metro: Spagna.

At the foot of the Spanish Steps is this 18th-century house where John Keats died of consumption on February 23, 1821, at age 25. Since 1909, when it was bought by well-intentioned English and American literary types, it has been a working library established in honor of Keats and poet Percy Bysshe Shelley, who drowned off the coast of Viareggio with a copy of Keats in his pocket. Mementos range from the kitsch to the immortal and are laden with nostalgia. The apartment where Keats spent his last months, carefully tended by his close friend Joseph Severn, shelters a strange death mask of Keats as well as the "deadly sweat" drawing by Severn.

✪ **Trevi Fountain (Fontana dei Trevi).** Piazza di Trevi. Metro: Barberini.

As you elbow your way through the summertime crowds around the Trevi Fountain, you'll find it hard to believe that this little piazza was nearly always deserted before the film *Three Coins in the Fountain* brought the stampede of tour buses. Today this newly restored gem is a must on everybody's itinerary.

Supplied by water from the Acqua Vergine aqueduct and a triumph of the baroque style, it was based on the design of Nicolo Salvi (who's said to have died of illness contracted during his supervision of the project) and was completed in 1762. The design centers around the triumphant figure of Neptunus Rex, standing on a shell chariot drawn by winged steeds and led by a pair of tritons. Two allegorical figures in the side niches represent good health and fertility.

On the southwestern corner of the piazza is a somber, not particularly spectacular-looking church, **SS. Vincenzo e Anastasio,** with a strange claim to fame. Within it survive the hearts and intestines of several centuries of popes. According to legend, the church was built on the site of a spring that burst from the earth after the beheading of St. Paul; the spring is one of the *three* sites where his head is said to have bounced off the ground.

Palazzo del Quirinale. Piazza del Quirinale. Free admission (but a passport or similar ID is required for entrance). Sun 9am–1pm. Metro: Barberini.

Until the end of World War II, this palace was the home of the king of Italy, and before that, it was the residence of the pope. Despite its Renaissance origins (nearly every important architect in Italy worked on some aspect of its sprawling premises), it's rich in associations with ancient emperors and deities. The colossal statues of the dioscuri Castor and Pollux, which now form part of the fountain in the piazza, were found in the nearby great Baths of Constantine; and in 1793 Pius VI had the ancient Egyptian obelisk moved here from the Mausoleum of Augustus. The sweeping view of Rome from the piazza, which crowns the highest of the seven ancient hills of Rome, is itself worth the trip.

AROUND VIA VENETO & PIAZZA BARBERINI

Piazza Barberini lies at the foot of several Roman streets, among them Via Barberini, Via Sistina, and Via Vittorio Veneto. It would be a far more pleasant spot were it not for the heavy traffic swarming around its principal feature, Bernini's **Fountain of the Triton (Fontana del Tritone).** For more than 3 centuries, the strange figure sitting in a vast open clam has been blowing water from his triton. Off to one side of the piazza is the aristocratic side facade of the **Palazzo Barberini,** named for one of Rome's powerful families; inside is the **Galleria Nazionale d'Arte Antica** (see below).

The Renaissance Barberini reached their peak when a son was elected pope as Urban VIII; he encouraged Bernini and gave him great patronage.

As you go up Via Vittorio Veneto, look for the small fountain on the right corner of Piazza Barberini—it's another Bernini, the small **Fountain of the Bees (Fontana delle Api).** At first they look more like flies, but they're the bees of the Barberini, the crest of that powerful family complete with the crossed keys of St. Peter above them (the keys were always added to a family crest when a son was elected pope).

National Gallery of Ancient Art (Galleria Nazionale d'Arte Antica). Via Quattro Fontane 13. ☎ **06-481-4430.** Admission 10,000L ($5). Mon–Fri 10am–2pm; Sat 9am–7pm; Sun and holidays 9am–1pm. Metro: Barberini.

Palazzo Barberini, right off Piazza Barberini, is one of the most magnificent baroque palaces in Rome. It was begun by Carlo Maderno in 1627 and completed in 1633 by Bernini, whose lavishly decorated rococo apartments, the **Gallery of Decorative Art (Galleria d'Arte Decorativa),** are on view. This gallery is part of the **National Gallery of Ancient Art.**

The bedroom of Princess Cornelia Costanza Barberini and Prince Giulio Cesare Colonna di Sciarra stands just as it was on their wedding night, and many household objects are displayed in the decorative art gallery. In the chambers, which boast frescoes and hand-painted silk linings, you can see porcelain from Japan and Bavaria, canopied beds, and a wooden baby carriage.

On the first floor is a splendid array of paintings from the 13th to the 16th century, most notably *Mother and Child* by Simone Martini and works by Filippo Lippi, Andrea Solario, and Francesco Francia. Il Sodoma has some brilliant pictures here, like *The Rape of the Sabines* and *The Marriage of St. Catherine.* One of the best-known paintings is Raphael's beloved *La Fornarina,* the baker's daughter who was his mistress and who posed for his Madonna portraits. Titian is represented by his *Venus and Adonis.* Also here are Tintorettos and El Grecos. Many visitors come just to see the magnificent Caravaggios, including *Narcissus.*

Monumental Cemetery of the Capuchin Brothers (Cimitero Monumentale dei Padri Cappuccini). Beside the Church of the Immaculate Conception, Via Vittorio Veneto 27. ☎ **06-487-1185.** Donation required. Fri–Wed 9am–noon and 3–6pm. Metro: Barberini.

One of the most horrifying sights in all Christendom, this is a series of chapels with hundreds of skulls and crossbones woven into mosaic "works of art." To make this allegorical dance of death, the bones of more than 4,000 Capuchin brothers were used. Some of the skeletons are intact, draped with Franciscan habits. The creator of this chamber of horrors? The tradition of the friars is that it was the work of a French Capuchin. Their literature suggests you should visit the cemetery while keeping in mind the historical moment of its origins, when Christians had a rich and creative cult for their dead and great spiritual masters meditated and preached with a skull in hand. Those who've lived through the days of crematoriums and other such massacres may view the graveyard differently, but to many who pause to think, this sight has a message. It's not for the squeamish, however. The entrance is halfway up the first staircase on the right of the church.

NEAR PIAZZA DEL POPOLO

The newly restored ✪ **Piazza del Popolo** is haunted with memories. According to legend, the ashes of Nero were enshrined here, until 11th-century residents began complaining to the pope about his imperial ghost. The **Egyptian obelisk** dates from the 13th century B.C., removed from Heliopolis to Rome during Augustus's reign (it stood at the Circus Maximus). The piazza was designed in the early 19th century by Valadier, Napoléon's architect. The lovely **Santa Maria del Popolo** (with two Caravaggios) is at its northern curve, and opposite are almost-twin baroque churches, overseeing the never-ending traffic.

Altar of Peace (Ara Pacis). Lungotevere Augusta ☎ **06-3600-3471.** Admission 3,750L ($1.90). Tues–Sat 9am–7pm; Sun 9am–1pm. Bus: 70,81,186, or 628.

In an airy glass-and-concrete building beside the eastern banks of the Tiber rests a reconstructed treasure from the reign of Augustus. It was built by the Senate as a tribute to that emperor and the peace he had brought to the Roman world. On the marble wall, you can see portraits of the imperial family—Augustus, Livia (his second wife), Tiberius (Livia's son from her first marriage and Augustus's successor), even Julia (Augustus's unfortunate daughter, who divorced her first husband to marry Tiberius and then was exiled by her father for her sexual excesses). The altar was reconstructed from literally hundreds of fragments scattered in museums for centuries. A major portion came from the foundations of a Renaissance palace on the Corso. The reconstruction (quite an archaeological adventure story in itself) took place during the 1930s.

Augustus's Mausoleum (Mausoleo Augusteo). Piazza Augusto Imperatore. Bus: 81, 115, or 590. Metro: Spagna.

This seemingly indestructible pile of bricks has been here for 2,000 years and will probably remain for another 2,000. Like the larger tomb of Hadrian across the river, this was once a circular marble-covered affair with tall cypresses, symmetrical groupings of Egyptian obelisks, and some of Europe's most spectacular ornamentation. Many of the 1st-century emperors had their ashes deposited in golden urns inside, and it was probably because of this crowding that Hadrian decided to construct an entirely new tomb (the Castel Sant'Angelo) for himself in another part of Rome. The imperial remains stayed intact here until the 5th century, when invading barbarians smashed the bronze gates and stole the golden urns, emptying the ashes on the ground outside. After periods when it functioned as a Renaissance fortress, a bullfighting ring, and a private garden, the tomb was restored in the 1930s by Mussolini, who might have envisioned it as a burial place for himself. You can't enter, but you can walk along the four streets encircling it.

5 In the Villa Borghese

Villa Borghese, in the heart of Rome, is 3½ miles (6km) in circumference. One of Europe's most elegant parks, it was created by Cardinal Scipione Borghese in the 1600s. Umberto I, king of Italy, acquired it in 1902 and presented it to the city of Rome. With lovely landscaped vistas, the greenbelt is crisscrossed by roads, but you can escape from the traffic and seek a shaded area under a pine or oak tree to enjoy a picnic or simply relax. On a sunny weekend afternoon, it's a pleasure to stroll here and see Romans at play, relaxing or in-line skating. There are a few casual cafes and some food vendors throughout; you can also rent bikes here. In the northeast of the park is a small zoo; the park is also home to a few outstanding museums.

✪ **Galleria Borghese.** Piazza Scipione Borghese 5 (off Via Pinciano). ☎ **06-841-7645** for information. Admission 12,000L ($6). Nov–Apr, Tues–Sun 9am–7pm; May–Oct, Tues–Sun 9am–7pm. Bus: 56 or 910.

This legendary art gallery shut its doors in 1984 and appeared to have closed forever. However, in early 1997, after a complete restoration, it returned in all its fabulous glory.

This treasure trove includes such masterpieces as Bernini's *Apollo and Daphne,* Titian's *Sacred and Profane Love,* Raphael's *Deposition,* and Caravaggio's *Jerome.* The collection began with the gallery's founder, Scipione Borghese, who by the time of his death in 1633 had accumulated some of the greatest art of all time, even managing to acquire Bernini's early sculptures. Some paintings were spirited out of Vatican museums and even confiscated when their rightful owners were hauled off to prison until they became "reasonable" about turning over their art. The great collection suffered at the hands of Napoléon's notorious sister, Pauline, who married Prince Camillo Borghese in 1807 and sold most of the ancient collection (many works are now in the Louvre in Paris). One of the most popular pieces of sculpture in today's gallery, ironically, is Canova's life-size sculpture of Pauline in the pose of *Venus Victorious.* (When Pauline was asked whether she felt uncomfortable posing in the nude, she replied, "Why should I? The studio was heated.")

Important Tip: No more than 300 visitors at a time are allowed on the ground floor, and no more than 90 on the upper floor. Reservations are essential, so call ☎ **06-328-101** (Mon–Fri 9am–6pm). However, the number always seems to be busy. If you'll be in Rome for a few days, try stopping by in person on your first day to reserve tickets for a later day. Before you leave home, you can also contact **Select Italy** to reserve tickets for this museum, and other major museums in Florence and Venice, cutting down on your time spent waiting in line. The cost varies from 39,000 to 79,000L ($19.50 to $39.50), depending on the museum, and several combination passes are available. Select Italy's main office is at 329 Linden Avenue, Wilmette, IL 60091-2788 (☎ **847/853-1661**; fax 847/853-1667; www.selectitaly.com).

✪ **National Etruscan Museum (Museo Nazionale di Villa Giulia).** Piazzale di Villa Giulia 9. ☎ **06-320-1951.** Admission 8,000L ($4). Tues–Sat 9am–7pm; Sun 9am–2pm. Metro: Flaminio.

This 16th-century papal palace shelters a priceless collection of art and artifacts from the mysterious Etruscans, who predated the Romans. Known for their sophisticated art and design, they left a legacy of sarcophagi, bronze sculptures, terra-cotta vases, and jewelry, among other items. If you have time for only the masterpieces, head for room seven, with a remarkable 6th-century B.C. *Apollo from Veio* (clothed, for a change). The other two widely acclaimed statues here are *Dea con Bambino* (*Goddess with a Baby*) and a greatly mutilated but still powerful *Hercules* with a stag. In room eight, you'll see the lions' sarcophagus from the mid–6th century B.C., which was excavated at Cerveteri, north of Rome.

Finally, one of the world's most important Etruscan art treasures is the bride and bridegroom coffin from the 6th century B.C., also dug out of the tombs of Cerveteri (in room nine). Near the end of your tour, another masterpiece of Etruscan art awaits you in room 33: the Cista Ficoroni, a bronze urn with paw feet, mounted by three figures, dating from the 4th century B.C.

National Gallery of Modern Art (Galleria Nazionale d'Arte Moderna). Viale delle Belle Arti 131. ☎ **06-322-4151.** Admission 12,000L ($6). Tues–Sat 9am–7pm; Sun 9am–1pm. Bus: 56 or 910.

This gallery of modern art is a short walk from the Etruscan Museum (see above). With its neoclassic and Romantic paintings and sculpture, it makes a dramatic change from the glories of the Renaissance and ancient Rome. Its 75 rooms also house the largest collection in Italy of 19th- and 20th-century works by Balla, Boccioni, De Chirico, Morandi, Manzù, Burri, Capogrossi, and Fontana. Look for Modigliani's *La Signora dal Collaretto* and large *Nudo.* There are also many works of Italian optical and pop art and a good representation of foreign artists, including Degas, Cézanne,

Monet, and van Gogh. Surrealism and expressionism are well represented by Klee, Ernst, Braque, Mirò, Kandinsky, Mondrian, and Pollock. You'll also find sculpture by Rodin. Several other important sculptures, including one by Canova, are on display in the museum's gardens. You can see the collection of graphics, the storage rooms, and the Department of Restoration by appointment Tuesday to Friday.

6 The Appian Way & the Catacombs

Of all the roads that led to Rome, **Via Appia Antica** (built in 312 B.C.) was the most famous. It eventually stretched all the way from Rome to the seaport of Brindisi, through which trade with the colonies in Greece and the East was funneled. (According to Christian tradition, it was along the Appian Way that an escaping Peter encountered the vision of Christ, causing him to go back into the city to face subsequent martyrdom.) The road's initial stretch in Rome is lined with the great monuments and ancient tombs of patrician Roman families—burials were forbidden within the city walls as early as the 5th century B.C.—and, beneath the surface, miles of tunnels hewn out of the soft tufa stone.

These tunnels, or **catacombs,** were where early Christians buried their dead and, during the worst times of persecution, held church services discreetly out of the public eye. A few of them are open to the public, so you can wander through mile after mile of musty-smelling tunnels whose soft walls are gouged out with tens of thousands of burial niches (long shelves made for two to three bodies each). In some dank, dark grottoes (never stray too far from your party or one of the exposed lightbulbs), you can still discover the remains of early Christian art. The requisite guided tours, hosted by priests and monks, feature a smidgen of extremely biased history and a large helping of sermonizing.

The Appia Antica has been a popular Sunday lunch picnic site for Roman families (following the half-forgotten pagan tradition of dining in the presence of one's ancestors on holy days). This practice was rapidly dying out in the face of the traffic fumes that for the past few decades have choked the venerable road, but a 1990s initiative has closed the Via Appia Antica to cars on Sundays, bringing back the picnickers and bicyclists—along with in-line skaters and a new Sunday-only bus route to get out here.

You can take bus 218 from the San Giovanni Metro stop, which follows the Appia Antica for a bit, then veers right on Via Ardeatina at Domine Quo Vadis? Church. After another long block, the 218 stops at the square Largo M.F. Via d. Sette Chiese to the San Domitilla catacombs; or walk left down Via d. Sette Chiese to the San Sebastiano catacombs.

An alternative is to ride the Metro to the Colli Albani stop and catch bus 660, which wraps up the Appia Antica from the south, veering off it at the San Sebastiano catacombs (if you're visiting all three, you can take the 218 to the first two, walk to San Sebastiano, then catch the 660 back to the Metro). On Sundays the road is closed to traffic, but bus 760 trundles from the Circo Massimo Metro stop down the Via Appia Antica, turning around after it passes the Tomb of Cecila Metella.

Of the monuments on the Appian Way, the most impressive is the **Tomb of Cecilia Metella,** within walking distance of the catacombs. The cylindrical tomb honors the wife of one of Julius Caesar's military commanders from the Republican era. Why such an elaborate tomb for such an unimportant person in history? Cecilia Metella happened to be singled out for enduring fame because her tomb has remained and the others have decayed.

Catacombs of St. Callixtus (Catacombe di San Callisto). Via Appia Antica 170. ☎ **06-513-6725.** Admission 8,000L ($4) adults, 4,000L ($2) children 6–15; children 5 and under free. Apr–Oct Thurs–Tues 8:30am–noon and 2:30–5:30pm (to 5pm Nov–Mar). Bus: 218 from Piazza San Giovanni in Laterano to Fosse Ardeatine; ask driver to let you off at Catacombe di San Callisto.

"The most venerable and most renowned of Rome," said Pope John XXIII of these funerary tunnels. The founder of Christian archaeology, Giovanni Battista de Rossi (1822–94), called them "catacombs par excellence." These catacombs are often packed with tour-bus groups, and they have perhaps the most cheesy tour, but the tunnels are simply phenomenal. They're the first cemetery of the Christian community of Rome, burial place of 16 popes in the 3rd century. They bear the name of St. Callixtus, the deacon whom Pope St. Zephyrinus put in charge of them and who was later elected pope (A.D. 217–22) in his own right. The complex is a network of galleries stretching for nearly 12 miles (19km), structured in five levels and reaching a depth of about 65 feet. There are many sepulchral chambers and almost half a million tombs of early Christians. Paintings, sculptures, and epigraphs (with such symbols as the fish, anchor, and dove) provide invaluable material for the study of the life and customs of the ancient Christians and the story of their persecutions.

Entering the catacombs, you see at once the most important crypt, that of the nine popes. Some of the original marble tablets of their tombs are still preserved. The next crypt is that of St. Cecilia, the patron of sacred music. This early Christian martyr received three ax strokes on her neck, the maximum allowed by Roman law, which failed to kill her outright. Farther on, you'll find the famous Cubicula of the Sacraments with its 3rd-century frescoes.

Catacombs of St. Sebastian (Catacombe di San Sebastiano). Via Appia Antica 136. ☎ **06-785-0350.** Admission 8,000L ($4) adults, 4,000L ($2) children 6–15; children 5 and under free. Mon–Sat 8:30am–noon and 2:30–5pm. Closed Nov.

Today the tomb of St. Sebastian is in the basilica, but his original tomb was in the catacombs under it. From the reign of Valerian to the reign of Constantine, the bodies of St. Peter and St. Paul were hidden in the catacombs, which were dug from tufa, a soft volcanic rock. The big church was built in the 4th century. The tunnels here, if stretched out, would reach a length of 7 miles (11km). In the tunnels and mausoleums are mosaics and graffiti, along with many other pagan and Christian objects from centuries even before the time of Constantine. The tour here is one of the shortest and least satisfying of all the catacomb visits.

✪ **Catacombs of St. Domitilla (Catacombe di San Domitilla).** Via d. Sette Chiese 283. ☎ **06-511-0342.** Admission 8,000L ($4) adults; 4,000L ($2) children 6–14. Wed–Mon 8:30am–noon and 2:30–5pm. Closed Jan.

This oldest of the catacombs is also the hands-down winner for most enjoyable catacomb experience. Groups are small, most guides are genuinely entertaining and personable, and, depending on the mood of the group and your guide, the visit may last anywhere from 20 minutes to over an hour. You enter through a sunken 4th-century church. There are fewer "sights" than in the other catacombs—although the 2nd-century fresco of the Last Supper is impressive—but some of the guides actually hand you a few bones out of a tomb niche. (Incidentally, this is the only catacomb where you'll still see bones; the rest have emptied their tombs to rebury the remains in ossuaries on the inaccessible lower levels.)

Beneath It All: Touring Roma Sotteranea

Talk about the "underground" and a growing legion of Romans will excitedly take up the story, offering tidbits about where to go, who to talk to, what's been seen, and what's allegedly awaiting discovery around the next bend in the sewer. The sewer? That's right. **Roma Sotteranea (Subterranean Rome)** is neither subway nor trendy arts movement but the vast historic ruins of a city that has been occupied for nearly 3,000 years, the first 2 millenniums of which are now largely buried by natural sediment and artificial landfills. Archaeologists estimate these processes have left the streets of ancient Rome as much as 20 yards beneath the surface.

A little too deep for you? Consider this: Each year, an inch of dust in the form of pollen, leaves, pollution, sand, and silt from disintegrating ruins settles over Rome. That silt has really taken a toll in its own right. Archaeologists estimate the ruins of a one-story Roman house will produce debris 6 feet deep over its entire floor plan. When you multiply that by more than 40,000 apartment buildings, 1,800 palaces, and numerous giant public buildings, a real picture of the burial of the ancient city presents itself. You should also take note of the centuries-old Roman tradition of burying old buildings in landfills, which can raise the level of the earth up to several yards all at once. In fact, past builders have often filled up massive stone ruins with dirt or dug down through previous landfills to the columns and vaults of underlying structures and then laid a foundation for a new layer of Roman architecture.

As a result, many buildings on the streets today actually provide direct access to Rome's inner world. Doorways lead down to hidden crypts and shrines—the existence of which are closely guarded secrets. Nondescript locked doors in churches and other public buildings often open on whole blocks of the ancient city, streets still intact. For example, take **San Clemente,** the 12th-century basilica east of the Colosseum, where a staircase in the sacristy leads down to the original 4th-century church. Not only that, but a staircase near the apse goes down

7 More Attractions

AROUND STAZIONE TERMINI

Basilica di Santa Maria Maggiore. Piazza di Santa Maria Maggiore. ☎ **06-488-1094.** Free admission. Daily 7am–7pm. Metro: Termini.

This great church, one of Rome's four major basilicas, was built by Pope Liberius in A.D. 358 and rebuilt by Pope Sixtus III from 432 to 440. Its 14th-century **campanile** is the city's loftiest. Much doctored in the 18th century, the church's facade isn't an accurate reflection of the treasures inside. Restoration of the 1,600-year-old church is scheduled for completion in 2000. The basilica is especially noted for the 5th-century Roman mosaics in its nave, as well as for its coffered ceiling, said to have been gilded with gold brought from the New World. In the 16th century, Domenico Fontana built a now-restored "Sistine Chapel." In the following century, Flaminio Ponzo designed the **Pauline (Borghese) Chapel** in the baroque style. The church also contains the tomb of Bernini, Italy's most important baroque sculptor/architect. Ironically, the man who changed the face of Rome with his elaborate fountains is buried in a tomb so simple it takes a sleuth to track it down (to the right near the altar).

to an earlier Roman apartment building and temple, which in turn leads down to a giant public building dating back to the Great Fire (A.D. 64). Another interesting doorway to the past is in the south exterior wall of **St. Peter's,** leading down to an intact necropolis. That crumbling brick entry in the gardens on the east side of Esquiline Hill carries you into the vast **Domus Aurea (Golden House),** Nero's residence, built on the ruins left by the Great Fire (see the entry for the Colosseum).

Don't expect a coherent road map of this subterranean world; it's a meandering labyrinth beneath the streets. A guided tour can be useful, especially those focusing on Roman excavations and anything to do with church crypts. Several tour companies now offer selected subterranean views, lasting 90 to 120 minutes and costing 25,000 to 50,000L ($12.50 to $25). The best are provided by **Itinera** (☎ **06-275-7323**) and **LUPA** (☎ **06-574-1974**), both run by trained archaeologists. **Città Nascosta** (☎ **06-321-6059**) offers offbeat tours to less-visited churches and monuments and advertises the week's schedule via a recorded phone announcement that changes every week.

For those who want still more access to this world, the Italian monthly magazine ***Forma Urbis*** features the photos of Carlo Pavia, who (armed with lights, camera, hip boots, and oxygen mask) slogs through ancient sewage and hordes of jumping spiders, giant rats, and albino insects to record part of the ancient city that has never been seen before. Pavia's most bizarre discovery was a series of plants from North Africa and the Arab world growing in rooms beneath the Colosseum. The theory is they grew from seeds that fell from the coats of exotic animals sent into the arena to battle gladiators.

It's probably true that much of the underground will remain inaccessible to the general public. However, influential citizens, like Emanuele Gattis, a retired government archaeologist who oversaw more than 30 years' worth of construction projects in Rome, are urging government leaders to direct money into opening up more of the city's buried past.

MUSEO NAZIONALE ROMANO

Originally, this museum occupied only the Diocletian Baths. Today it is divided into four different sections: Palazzo Massimo alle Terme; *Terme di Diocleziano* (Diocletian Baths), with the annex Octagonal Hall; and Palazzo Altemps (which is near Piazza Navona; see section 3 of this chapter for a complete listing).

Palazzo Massimo alle Terme. Largo di Villa Peretti 67. ☎ **06-489-035-00.** Admission 12,000L ($6); the same ticket will admit you to the Diocletian Baths. Tues–Sun 9am–8pm. Last admission 1 hour before closing. Metro: Termini.

If you'd like to go wandering in a virtual garden of classical statues, head for this palazzo, built from 1883 to 1887 and opened as a museum in 1998. Much of the art here, including the frescoes, stuccoes, and mosaics, was discovered in excavations in the 1800s but has never been put on display before.

If you ever wanted to know what all those emperors from your history books looked like, this museum will make them live again, togas and all. In the central hall are works representing the political and social life of Rome at the time of Augustus Caesar. Note the statue of the emperor with a toga covering his head, symbolizing his role as the head priest of state. Other works include an altar from Ostia Antica, the ancient port of Rome, plus a statue of a wounded Niobid from 440 B.C. that is a masterwork of expression and character. Upstairs, stand in awe at all the traditional art from the 1st century B.C. to the Imperial Age. The most celebrated mosaic is of the *Four Charioteers.* In the basement is a rare numismatic collection and an extensive collection of Roman jewelry.

Gterme di Diocleziano (Diocletian Bath) and the Aula Ottagona (Octagonal Hall). Viale E. di Nicola 79. ☎ **06-489-035-00.** Admission to the Baths 12,000L ($6), Octagonal Hall free. The same ticket will admit you to Palazzo Massimo alle Terme. Tues–Fri 9am–2pm; Sat–Sun 9am–1pm. Last admission 1 hour before closing. Metro: Termini.

Near Piazza dei Cinquecento, which fronts the rail station, this museum occupies part of the 3rd-century A.D. Baths of Diocletian and part of a convent that may have been designed by Michelangelo. The Diocletian Baths were the biggest thermal baths in the world. Nowadays they host a marvelous collection of funereal art works, such as sarcophagi, and decorations dating back to the Aurelian period. The Baths also have a section reserved for temporary exhibitions.

The Octagonal Hall occupies the southwest corner of the central building of the Diocletian Baths. Here you can see the *Lyceum Apollo*, a copy of the 2nd-century A.D. work inspired by the Prassitele. Also worthy of a note is the *Aphrodite of Cyrene*, a copy dating back to the second half of the 2nd century A.D. and discovered in Cyrene, Libya.

IN THE TESTACCIO AREA & SOUTH

Protestant Cemetery. Via Caio Cestio 6. ☎ **06-574-1900.** Free admission, but a 1,500 to 2,000L (75¢–$1) offering is customary. Apr–Sept Tues–Sun 9am–6pm (Oct–Mar to 4:30pm). Metro: Piramide. Bus: 23 or 27.

Near Porta San Paola, in the midst of cypress trees, lies the old cemetery where John Keats is buried. In a grave nearby, Joseph Severn, his "deathbed" companion, was interred beside him 6 decades later. Dejected and feeling his reputation as a poet diminished by the rising vehemence of his critics, Keats asked that the following epitaph be written on his tombstone: "Here lies one whose name was writ in water." A great romantic poet Keats certainly was, but a prophet, thankfully not. Percy Bysshe Shelley, author of *Prometheus Unbound,* drowned off the Italian Riviera in 1822, before his 30th birthday, and his ashes rest beside those of Edward John Trelawny, fellow romantic and man of the sea.

Pyramid of Caius Cestius. Piazzale Ostiense. Metro: Piramide.

From the 1st century B.C., the Pyramid of Caius Cestius, about 120 feet high, looks as if it belongs to the Egyptian landscape. It was constructed during the "Cleopatra craze" in architecture that swept across Rome. You can't enter the pyramid, but it's a great photo op. And who was Caius Cestius? He was a rich magistrate in imperial Rome whose tomb is more impressive than his achievements. You can visit at any time.

St. Paul Outside the Walls (Basilica di San Paolo Fuori le Mura). Via Ostiense 184. ☎ **06-541-0341.** Free admission. Basilica daily 7am–6:30pm; cloisters daily 9am–1pm and 3–6pm. Metro: San Paolo Basilica.

The Basilica of St. Paul, whose origins go back to the time of Constantine, is Rome's fourth great patriarchal church; it's believed to have been erected over the tomb of St. Paul. The basilica fell victim to fire in 1823 and was subsequently rebuilt. It is the second-largest church in Rome after St. Peter's. From the inside, its windows may appear to be stained glass, but they're actually translucent alabaster. With its forest of single-file columns and mosaic medallions (portraits of the various popes), this is one of the most streamlined and elegantly decorated churches in Rome. Its most important treasure is a 12th-century candelabra by Vassalletto, who's also responsible for the remarkable cloisters, containing twisted pairs of columns enclosing a rose garden. Of particular interest is the *baldachino* (rich embroidered fabric of silk and gold, usually fixed or carried over an important person or sacred object) of Arnolf di Cambio dated 1285 that miraculously wasn't damaged in the fire. The Benedictine monks and students sell a fine collection of souvenirs, rosaries, and bottles of Benedictine every day except Sunday and religious holidays.

IN TRASTEVERE

From many vantage points in the Eternal City, the views are panoramic, but one of the best spots for a memorable vista is the ✪ **Janiculum Hill (Gianicolo),** across the Tiber, not one of the "Seven Hills" but certainly one of the most visited (and a stop on many bus tours). The view is at its best at sundown or at dawn, when the skies are often fringed with mauve. The Janiculum was the site of a battle between Giuseppe Garibaldi and the forces of Pope Pius IX in 1870—an event commemorated with statuary. Take bus no. 41 from Ponte Sant'Angelo.

Santa Cecilia in Trastevere. Piazza Santa Cecilia 2. ☎ **06-589-9289.** Church free; Cavallini frescoes 3,000L ($1.50); excavations 3,000L ($1.50). Main church and excavations daily 8am–noon and 3–7pm; frescoes Tues and Thurs 10–11:30am, Sun 11:30am–noon. Bus: 44, 75, 170, or 181.

A cloistered and still-functioning convent with a fine garden, Santa Cecilia contains a difficult-to-visit fresco by Cavallini in its inner sanctums and a late 13th-century *baldachino* (rich embroidered fabric of silk and gold, usually fixed or carried over an important person or sacred object) by Arnolfo di Cambio over the altar. The church is built on the reputed site of Cecilia's long-ago palace, and for a small fee you can descend under the church to inspect the ruins of some Roman houses as well as peer through a gate at the stuccoed grotto beneath the altar.

Santa Maria in Trastevere. Piazza Santa Maria in Trastevere. ☎ **06-581-4802.** Free admission. Daily 7am–7pm. Bus: 44, 75, 170, or 181.

This Romanesque church at the colorful center of Trastevere was built around A.D. 350 and is one of the oldest in Rome. The body was added around 1100 and the portico in the early 1700s. The restored mosaics on the apse date from around 1140, and below them are the 1293 mosaic scenes depicting the life of Mary done by Pietro Cavallini. The faded mosaics on the facade are 12th or 13th century, and the octagonal fountain in the piazza is an ancient Roman original that was restored and added to in the 17th century by Carlo Fontana.

8 Organized Tours

Because of the sheer number of sights to see, some first-time visitors like to start out with an organized tour. While few things can really be covered in any depth on these overview tours, they're sometimes useful for getting your bearings.

One of the leading tour operators is **American Express,** Piazza di Spagna 38 (☎ **06-67641;** Metro: Spagna). One popular tour is a 4-hour orientation of Rome and the Vatican, which departs most mornings at 9:30am and costs 70,000L ($35) per person. Another 4-hour tour, which focuses on the Rome of antiquity (including visits to the Colosseum, the Roman Forum, the ruins of the Imperial Palace, and San Pietro in Vincoli), costs 60,000L ($30). April to October, a popular excursion outside

Rome is a 5-hour bus tour to Tivoli, where tours are conducted of the Villa d'Este and its spectacular gardens and the ruins of the Villa Adriana, all for 70,000L ($35) per person.

The agency **Enjoy Rome,** Via Varese 39 (☎ **06-445-18-43;** fax 06-445-07-34; www.enjoyrome.com), makes the 1-day sprint from Rome to Pompeii as inexpensive and painless as possible with an 8:30am-to-5:30pm round-trip daily tour by air-conditioned minivan (fitting eight passengers), costing 65,000L ($32.50). The trip is 3 hours one-way, with an English-speaking driver. You're on your own once you reach the archaeological site and there's no imposed restaurant lunch: That's what keeps their prices the lowest around.

Another option is **Scala Reale,** Via Varese 52 (☎ **888/467-1986** in the U.S., or 06-4470-0898), a cultural association founded by American architect Tom Rankin. He offers small-group tours and excursions focusing on the architectural and artistic significance of Rome. Tours include visits to monuments, museums, and piazzas as well as to neighborhood trattorie. In addition, custom-designed tours are available. Tours begin at 60,000L ($30). Children 12 and under are admitted free to walking tours. Tour discounts are available for a group of four.

9 Shopping

Rome offers temptations of every kind. You might find hidden oases of charm and value in lesser-known neighborhoods, but in our limited space below we've summarized certain streets known throughout Italy for their shops. The monthly rent on these famous streets is very high, and those costs are passed on to you. Nonetheless, a stroll down some of these streets presents a cross section of the most desirable wares in Italy.

Although Rome has many wonderful boutiques, you'll find better shopping in Florence and Venice. If you're continuing on to either of these cities, hold off a bit.

Shopping hours are generally Monday 3:30 to 7:30pm and Tuesday to Saturday 9:30 or 10am to 1pm and 3:30 to 7 or 7:30pm. Some shops are open on Monday mornings, however, and some don't close for the afternoon break.

THE TOP SHOPPING STREETS

VIA BORGOGNONA This street begins near Piazza di Spagna, and both the rents and the merchandise are chic and ultraexpensive. Like its neighbor, Via Condotti, Via Borgognona is a mecca for wealthy well-dressed women and men from around the world. Its storefronts have retained their baroque or neoclassical facades.

VIA COLA DI RIENZO Bordering the Vatican, this long, straight street runs from the Tiber to Piazza Risorgimento. Since the street is wide and clogged with traffic, it's best to walk down one side and then up the other. Via Cola di Rienzi is known for stores selling a wide variety of merchandise at reasonable prices—from jewelry to fashionable clothes and shoes.

VIA CONDOTTI Easy to find because it begins at the base of the Spanish Steps, this is Rome's poshest and most visible upper-bracket shopping street. Even the recent incursion of some less elegant stores hasn't diminished the allure of Via Condotti as a consumer's playground for the rich and super rich. For us mere mortals, it's a great place for window-shopping and people-watching.

VIA DEL CORSO Not attempting the stratospheric image or prices of Via Condotti or Via Borgognona, Via del Corso boasts styles aimed at younger consumers. There are, however, some gems scattered amid the shops selling jeans and sporting equipment. The most interesting stores are nearest the fashionable cafes of Piazza del Popolo.

VIA FRANCESCO CRISPI Most shoppers reach this street by following Via Sistina (see below) one long block from the top of the Spanish Steps. Near the intersection of these streets are several shops well suited for unusual and less expensive gifts.

VIA FRATTINA Running parallel to Via Condotti, it begins, like its more famous sibling, at Piazza di Spagna. Part of its length is closed to traffic. Here the concentration of shops is denser, though some aficionados claim that its image is slightly less chic and prices are slightly lower than at its counterparts on Via Condotti. It's usually thronged with shoppers who appreciate the lack of motor traffic.

VIA NAZIONALE The layout recalls 19th-century grandeur, but the traffic is horrendous; crossing Via Nazionale requires a good sense of timing and a strong understanding of Italian driving patterns. It begins at Piazza della Repubblica and runs down almost to the 19th-century monuments of Piazza Venezia. You'll find an abundance of leather stores (more reasonable in price than those in many other parts of Rome) and a welcome handful of stylish boutiques.

VIA SISTINA Beginning at the top of the Spanish Steps, Via Sistina runs to Piazza Barberini. The shops are small, stylish, and based on the tastes of their owners. The pedestrian traffic is less dense than on other major streets.

VIA VITTORIO VENETO Via Veneto is filled these days with expensive hotels and cafes and an array of relatively expensive stores selling shoes, gloves, and leather goods.

SHOPPING A TO Z

ANTIQUES Some visitors to Italy consider the treasure trove of antiques for sale the country's greatest treasure. But prices have risen to alarming levels as wealthy Europeans increasingly outbid one another in a frenzy. Any antiques dealer who risks the high rents of central Rome is acutely aware of valuations. So you might find gorgeous pieces, but you're not likely to find any bargains.

Beware of fakes; remember to insure anything you have shipped home; and for larger purchases—anything more than 300,000L ($174) at any one store—keep your paperwork in order to obtain your tax refund (see "Fast Facts: Italy," in chapter 2).

Via dei Coronari, buried in a colorful section of the Campus Martius, is lined with stores offering magnificent vases, urns, chandeliers, chaises, refectory tables, and candelabra. To find the street's entrance, turn left out of the north end of Piazza Navona and pass the excavated ruins of Domitian's Stadium—it will be just ahead. There are more than 40 antiques stores in the next 4 blocks. Bring your pocket calculator, and keep in mind that stores are frequently closed between 1 and 4pm.

Italian furniture from the days of Caesar through the 19th century is for sale at **Ad Antiqua Domus,** Via Paola 25–27 (☎ **06-686-1530;** Bus: 41, 46B, or 98). It's as much a museum of Italian furniture design through the ages as it is a shop. A second location is at Via dei Coronari 41 (☎ **06-686-1186;** Bus: 70, 81, or 87).

A mecca for the antiques hound, **ArtImport,** Via del Babuino 150 at the corner with Via dei Greci (☎ **06-322-13-30;** Metro: Spagna), always has something for sale that's intriguing and tasteful. There's an emphasis on silver, including goblets, elegant bowls, candlesticks, and candelabra.

BOOKSTORES Catering to the English-speaking communities of Rome and staffed by Brits, Australians, and Americans, the **Economy Book and Video Center,** Via Torino 136 (☎ **06-474-6877;** Metro: Repubblica; Bus: 64, 70, or 170), sells only English-language books (new and used, paperback and hardcover), greeting cards, and videos.

The **Lion Bookshop,** Via dei Greci 33 (☎ **06-3265-4007;** Metro: Spagna; Bus: 117), is the oldest English-language bookshop in town, specializing in literature, both American and English. It also sells children's books and photographic volumes on both Rome and Italy. A vast choice of English-language videos is for sale or rent. It's closed in August.

DEPARTMENT STORES In Piazza Colonna, **La Rinascente,** Via del Corso 189 (☎ **06-679-7691;** Bus: 117), is an upscale store offering clothing, hosiery, perfume, cosmetics, housewares, and furniture. It also has its own line of clothing (Ellerre) for men, women, and children. This is the largest of the Italian department-store chains, with another branch at Piazza Fiume.

A DISCOUNTER **Discount System,** Via del Viminale 35 (☎ **06-482-3917;** Metro: Repubblica), sells menswear and women's wear by many of the big names (Armani, Valentino, Cerruti, Fendi, and Krizia). Even if an item isn't from a famous designer, it often came from a factory that produces some of the best quality of Italian fashion. If you find something you like, know that it'll be priced at around 50% of its original price, and it just might be a cut-rate gem well worth your effort.

FASHION The exclusive **Angelo,** Via Bissolati 34 (☎ **06-474-1796;** Metro: Barberini), is a custom tailor for discerning men and has been featured in *Esquire* and *GQ*. Angelo employs the best cutters and craftspeople, and his taste is impeccable. Custom shirts, dinner jackets, and even casual wear can be made on short notice. If you don't have time to wait, he'll ship anywhere. The outlet also sells ready-made items like cardigans, cashmere pullovers, evening shirts, suits, and overcoats.

Battistoni, Via Condotti 61A (☎ **06-678-6241;** Metro: Spagna), is known for the world's finest men's shirts. As Marlene Dietrich once noted, "With that said, you don't need to sell the shop anymore." It also hawks a cologne, *Marte* (Mars), for the "man who likes to conquer."

✪ **Emporio Armani,** Via del Babuino 140 (☎ **06-3600-2197;** Metro: Spagna), stocks relatively affordable menswear crafted by the designer who has dressed perhaps more stage and screen stars than any other in Italy. If these prices aren't high enough for you, try the more expensive line a short walk away at **Giorgio Armani,** Via Condotti 77 (☎ **06-699-1460;** Metro: Spagna). The merchandise here is sold at sometimes staggering prices that are still often 30% less than what you'd pay in the States.

Dating to 1870, **Schostal,** Via del Corso 158 (☎ **06-679-1240;** Bus: 117), is for men who like their garments (from underwear to cashmere overcoats) conservative and well crafted. The prices are more reasonable than you might think, and the staff is courteous and attentive. Behind all the chrome mirrors is swank **Valentino,** Via Mario de' Fiori 22 (☎ **06-678-3656;** Metro: Spagna), where you can become the most fashionable man in town—if you can afford to be. Valentino's women's haute couture is sold around the corner at Via Bocca di Leone 15 (☎ **06-679-5862;** Metro: Spagna).

The prices at **Benetton,** Via Condotti 18 (☎ **06-679-7982;** Metro: Spagna), are a little more down to earth. Famous for sweaters, tennis wear, blazers, and sportswear, this company has suffered (like every other clothier) from inexpensive Asian copies of its designs. The original, however, is still the greatest.

At **Gianfranco Ferré,** Via Borgognona 6 (☎ **06-679-7445;** Metro: Spagna), you can find the women's line of this famous designer whose clothes have been called "adventurous." There is also clothing for men.

Givenchy, Via Borgognona 21 (☎ **06-678-4058;** Metro: Spagna), is the Roman headquarters of one of the great designer names of France. Here you'll find ready-to-wear

garments for stylish women with warm Italian weather in mind. It also features tasteful shirts and pullovers for men.

Max Mara, Via Frattina 28 at Largo Goldoni (☎ **06-679-3638;** Metro: Spagna), is one of the best outlets in Rome for women's wear if you like to look chic. The fabrics are appealing and the alterations free.

Rapidly approaching the stratospheric upper levels of Italian fashion is ✪ **Renato Balestra,** Via Sistina 67 (☎ **06-679-5424;** Metro: Spagna or Barberini), whose women's clothing attains standards of lighthearted elegance at its best. This branch carries a complete line of the latest ready-to-wear.

Baby House, Via Cola di Rienzo 117 (☎ **06-321-4291;** Metro: Spagna), offers stylish clothing for the under-15 set. This shop is for the budding young fashion plate, with threads by Valentino, Bussardi, and Biagiotti.

A FLEA MARKET On Sundays 7am to 1pm, every peddler from Trastevere and the surrounding Castelli Romani sets up a temporary shop at the sprawling **Porta Portese open-air flea market,** near the end of Viale Trastevere (catch bus no. 75 to Porta Portese, then take a short walk to Via Portuense). The vendors are likely to sell merchandise ranging from secondhand paintings of Madonnas and termite-eaten Il Duce wooden medallions, to pseudo-Etruscan hairpins, bushels of rosaries, 1947 TVs, and books printed in 1835. Serious shoppers can often ferret out a good buy. If you've ever been impressed with the bargaining power of the Spaniard, you haven't seen anything till you've bartered with an Italian. By 10:30am the market is full of people. As at any street market, beware of pickpockets.

FOOD & FOOD MARKETS At old-fashioned ✪ **Castroni,** Via Cola di Rienzo 196 (☎ **06-687-4383;** Bus: 32 or 81), you'll find an amazing array of unusual foodstuffs from around the Mediterranean. If you want herbs from Apulia, pepperoncino oil, cheese from the Valle d'Aosta, or that strange brand of balsamic vinegar whose name you can never remember, Castroni will have it. Filled to the rafters with the abundance of agrarian Italy, it also carries foods that are exotic in Italy but commonplace in North America, like taco shells, corn curls, and peanut butter.

Near Santa Maria Maggiore, Rome's largest market takes place Monday to Saturday 7am to noon at **Piazza Vittorio Emanuele** (Metro: Vittorio Emanuele). Most of the vendors at the gigantic market sell fresh fruit, vegetables, and other foodstuff, though some stalls are devoted to cutlery, clothing, and the like. There's probably little to tempt the serious shopper, but the insight into Roman life is invaluable.

A market of even greater charm is held Monday to Saturday 6am to noon at **Campo de' Fiori** (Bus: 46, 62, or 64). This is Rome's most picturesque food market—but it's also the priciest.

GIFTS **Grispigni,** Via Francesco Crispi 59 at Via Sistina (☎ **06-679-0290;** Metro: Spagna or Barberini), sells a large assortment of leather-covered boxes, women's purses, compacts, desk sets, and cigarette cases. There's also a constantly changing array of gifts if you're searching for some "small item" to take back.

Anatriello Argenteria Antica e Moderna Roma, Via Frattina 123 (☎ **06-678-9601;** Metro: Spagna), is known for stocking new and antique silver, some of it among the most unusual in Italy. All the new items are made by Italian silversmiths, in designs ranging from the whimsical to the dignified. Also displayed are antique pieces of silver from England, Germany, and Switzerland.

HOUSEWARES **Spazio Sette,** hidden at Via d. Barberi off Largo di Torre Argentina (☎ **06-686-9747**), is far and away Rome's best housewares emporium, a design boutique of department store proportions. It goes way beyond the Alessi tea kettles to fill three huge floors with the greatest names, and latest word, in Italian and international design.

Another good bet is **Bagagli,** Via Cam. Marzio 42 (☎ **06-687-1406**), offering a good selection of Alessi, Rose and Tulipani, and Villeroy & Boch china in a pleasantly kitschy old Rome setting that comes complete with cobblestone floors.

Bargain hunters should head to one of **Stock Market's** two branches, at Via d. Banchi Vecchi 51–52 (☎ **06-686-4238**) or near the Vatican at via Tacito 60 (☎ **06-3600-2343**). You'll find mouthwatering prices on last year's models, overstock, slight irregulars, and artistic misadventures in design that the pricier boutiques haven't been able to move. Most is moderately funky household stuff, but you never know when you'll find a gem of design hidden on the shelves.

If the big names don't do it for you, you may prefer **c.u.c.i.n.a.,** Via di Babuino 118A (no phone), a stainless steel shrine to everything you need for a proper Italian kitchen, sporting designs that are as beautiful in their simplicity as they are utilitarian.

JEWELRY Rome's most prestigious jeweler for more than a century, ✪ **Bulgari,** Via Condotti 10 (☎ **06-679-3876;** Metro: Spagna), boasts a shop window that's a visual attraction in its own right. Bulgari designs combine classical Greek aesthetics with Italian taste, changing in style with the years yet clinging to tradition. Prices range from "affordable" to "the sky's the limit."

At **E. Fiore,** Via Ludovisi 31 (☎ **06-481-9296;** Bus: 95 or 115), you can choose a jewel and have it set to your specifications. Or you can make your selection from a rich assortment of charms, bracelets, necklaces, rings, brooches, corals, pearls, and cameos. Also featured are elegant watches, silverware, and gold ware.

One of the city's best gold- and silversmiths, **Federico Buccellati,** Via Condotti 31 (☎ **06-679-0329;** Metro: Spagna), specializes in neo-Renaissance creations. The designs of the handmade jewelry and hollowware recall those of Renaissance gold master Benvenuto Cellini.

Siragusa, Via delle Carrozze 64 (☎ **06-679-7085;** Metro: Spagna), is more like a museum than a shop, specializing in unusual jewelry based on ancient carved stones or archaeological pieces. Handmade chains, for example, often hold coins and beads from the 3rd and 4th centuries B.C. discovered in Asia Minor.

LEATHER Italian leather is among the very best in the world; it can attain butter-soft textures more pliable than cloth. You'll find hundreds of leather stores in Rome, many of them excellent.

At **Alfieri,** Via del Corso 1–2 (☎ **06-361-1976;** Bus: 117), you'll find virtually any garment you can think of (except for the blatantly erotic) fashioned in leather. Opened in the 1960s with a funky counterculture slant, it prides itself on leather jackets, boots, bags, belts, shirts, hats, pants for men and women, short shorts, and skirts that come in at least 10 (sometimes neon) colors. Although everything is made in Italy, be alert that the virtue of this place is the reasonable prices rather than the ultrahigh quality (check the stitching and operability of zippers, or whatever, before you invest).

Despite the postmodern sleekness of its shop, **Campanile,** Via Condotti 58 (☎ **06-678-3041;** Metro: Spagna), bears a pedigree going back to the 1870s and an impressive inventory of well-crafted leather jackets, belts, shoes, bags, and suitcases. The quality is high.

If famous names in leather wear appeal to you, you'll find most of the biggies at **Casagrande,** Via Cola di Rienzo 206 (☎ **06-687-4610;** Bus: 32 or 81), like Fendi and its youth-conscious offspring, Fendissime, plus Cerruti, Mosquino, and Valentino. This well-managed store has developed an impressive reputation for quality and authenticity since the 1930s. The prices are more reasonable than those for equivalent merchandise in some other parts of town.

Fendi, Via Borgognona 36–40 (☎ **06-679-7641;** Metro: Spagna), is mainly known for its avant-garde leather goods, but it also has furs, stylish purses, ready-to-wear clothing, and a new line of men's clothing and accessories. Fendi also carries gift items, home furnishings, and sports accessories.

Of course, **Gucci,** Via Condotti 8 (☎ **06-679-0405** Metro: Spagna), has been a legend since 1900. Its merchandise consists of high-class leather goods, like suitcases, handbags, wallets, shoes, and desk accessories. It also has elegant menswear and women's wear, including beautiful shirts, blouses, and dresses, as well as ties and neck scarves. *La bella figura* is alive and well here, and the prices have never been higher.

Saddlers Union, Via Condotti 26 (☎ **06-679-8050;** Metro: Spagna), is a great place to look for well-crafted leather accessories. The wide selection of bags might lure you here, but there's plenty more—belts, wallets, shoes, briefcases, and other finely crafted items.

LINGERIE **Tomassini di Luisa Romagnoli,** Via Sistina 119 (☎ **06-488-1909;** Metro: Spagna or Barberini), offers delicately beautiful lingerie and negligees, all original designs of Luisa Romagnoli. Most of the merchandise is of shimmery Italian silk; other items, to a lesser degree, are of fluffy cotton or frothy nylon.

Vanità, Via Frattina 70 (☎ **06-679-1743;** Metro: Spagna), features lingerie in *all* colors—no rainbow can match the selection. Yes, you can get black or white, but take the time to browse and you'll discover hues you've never dreamed of.

MARKETS The mother lode of Roman bazaars is Porta Portese, a flea market off Piazza Ippolito Nievo that is one of Europe's premier permanent garage sales. You'll find everything from antique credenzas and bootleg CDs to old clothes and birds that squawk "ciao," all in a carnival atmosphere of haggling and jostling. Brace yourself for crowds and a few beggars, and keep your eyes out for pickpockets. The market runs every Sunday from dawn to lunchtime.

Campo de' Fiori, once the site of medieval executions, is today one of Rome's most lively squares—a cobblestoned expanse that starts bustling in the predawn as the florists arrange bouquets, and fruit and vegetable vendors set up their stalls. It all winds down after lunch, but the square comes alive again later in the evening as Romans and tourists gather in this area for dining and nightlife.

MOSAICS Mosaics are an art form as old as the Roman Empire. And many of the objects displayed at **Savelli,** Via Paolo VI 27 (☎ **06-830-7017;** Metro: San Paola), were inspired by ancient originals discovered in thousands of excavations, including those at Pompeii and Ostia. Others, especially the floral designs, depend on the whim and creativity of the artist. Objects include tabletops, boxes, and vases. The cheapest mosaic objects begin at around $125 and are unsigned products crafted by students at an art school partially funded by the Vatican. Objects made in the Savelli workshops that are signed by the individual artists (they tend to be larger and more elaborate) range from $500 to $25,000. The outlet also contains a collection of small souvenir items like key chains and carved statues.

PORCELAIN One of the most prestigious retail outlets for porcelain in the city, **Richard Ginori,** Piazza Trinità dei Monti 18B (☎ **06-679-3836;** Metro: Spagna), contains a roster of the impeccably crafted porcelain of Richard Ginori. Anything you buy can be shipped.

PRINTS & ENGRAVINGS At ✪ **Alberto di Castro,** Via del Babuino 71 (☎ **06-361-3752;** Metro: Spagna), you'll find Rome's largest collection of antique prints and engravings. In rack after rack are depictions of everything from the Colosseum to the Pantheon, each evocative of the best architecture in the Mediterranean world, priced from $25 to $1,000 depending on the age and rarity of the engraving.

Alinari, Via Alibert 16A (☎ **06-679-2923;** Metro: Spagna), takes its name from the famed 19th-century Florentine photographer. Original prints and photos of Alinari are almost as prized as paintings in national galleries, and you can pick up your own here.

Giovanni B. Panatta Fine Art Shop, Via Francesco Crispi 117 (☎ **06-679-5948;** Metro: Spagna or Barberini), sells excellent color and black-and-white prints covering a variety of subjects, from 18th-century Roman street scenes to astrological charts. There's also a selection of reproductions of medieval and Renaissance art that's attractive and reasonably priced.

Fava, Via del Babuino 180 (☎ **06-361-0807;** Metro: Spagna), recaptures the era when Neapolitans sold 17th- and 18th-century pictures of the eruptions of Vesuvius, once highly sought after by collectors. Many of these "volcanic paintings" of yesteryear can still cause a conflagration today. This is really unusual art from the attics of the days of yore.

RELIGIOUS OBJECTS In a neighborhood loaded with purveyors of religious art and icons, **Anna Maria Gaudenzi,** Piazza della Minerva 69A (☎ **06-790-0431;** Bus: 116), claims to be the oldest of its type in Rome. If you collect depictions of the Madonna, paintings of the saints, exotic rosaries, chalices, small statues, or medals, you can feel secure in knowing that thousands of pilgrims have spent their money here before you. Whether you view its merchandise as a devotional aid or as bizarre kitsch, this shop has it all.

SHOES At **Dominici,** Via del Corso 14 (☎ **06-361-0591;** Bus: 117), a few steps from Piazza del Popolo, you'll find an amusing collection of men's and women's shoes in a pleasing variety of vivid colors. The style is aggressively young and the quality good.

Ferragamo, Via Condotti 66–73 (☎ **06-679-8402;** Metro: Spagna), sells elegant footwear, plus women's clothing and accessories and ties, in an atmosphere full of Italian style. There are always many customers waiting to enter the shop; management allows them to enter in small groups. Figure on a 30-minute wait.

Fragiacomo, Via Condotti 35 (☎ **06-679-8780;** Metro: Spagnaq), sells shoes for men and women in a champagne-colored showroom with gilt-painted chairs and big display cases.

Lily of Florence, Via Lombardia 38A off Via Vittorio Veneto (☎ **06-474-0262;** Bus: 116), has a shop in Rome, with the same merchandise that made the outlet so well known in the Tuscan capital. The colors come in a wide range, the designs are stylish, and the leather texture is of good quality. Lily sells shoes for both men and women and features American sizes with prices 30 to 40% less than in the States.

WINE & LIQUOR At the historic **Buccone,** Via Ripetta 19 (☎ **06-361-2154;** Bus: 698 or 926), the selection of wines and gastronomic specialties is among the finest in Rome.

Opened in 1821, **Trimani,** Via Goito 20 (☎ **06-446-9661;** Metro: Castel Pretorio; Bus: 3, 4, or 36), sells wines and spirits from Italy, among other offerings. Purchases can be shipped to your home.

Ai Monasteri, Piazza delle Cinque Lune 76 (☎ **06-6880-2783;** Bus: 70, 81, or 87), is a treasure trove of liquors (including liqueurs and wines), honey, and herbal teas made in Italian monasteries and convents. You can buy excellent chocolates and other candies as well. You make your selections in a quiet atmosphere reminiscent of a monastery, just 2 blocks from Bernini's Fountain of the Four Rivers in Piazza Navona. The shop will ship some items home for you.

10 Rome After Dark

When the sun goes down, Rome's palaces, ruins, fountains, and monuments are bathed in a theatrical white light. Few evening occupations are quite as pleasurable as a stroll past the solemn pillars of old temples or the cascading torrents of Renaissance fountains glowing under the blue-black sky.

The Fountain of the Naiads (*Fontana delle Naiadi*) on Piazza della Repubblica, the Fountain of the Tortoises (*Fontana della Tartarughe*) on Piazza Mattei, and the Trevi Fountain (*Fontana dei Trevi*) are particularly beautiful at night (see the photo insert at the beginning of this guide). The Capitoline Hill is magnificently lit after dark, with its measured Renaissance facades glowing like jewel boxes. Behind the Senatorial Palace is a fine view of the illuminated Roman Forum. If you're across the Tiber, Piazza San Pietro (in front of St. Peter's) is impressive at night without the tour buses and crowds. And a combination of illuminated architecture, Renaissance fountains, and sidewalk shows and art expos enliven Piazza Navona. If you're ambitious and have a good sense of direction, try exploring the streets to the west of the piazza, which look like a stage set when lit at night.

Even if you don't speak Italian, you can generally follow the listings of special events and evening entertainment featured in ***La Repubblica,*** a leading Italian newspaper. ***Trova Roma,*** a special weekly entertainment supplement (good for the coming week) is published in this paper on Thursday. The minimagazines ***Metropolitan*** and ***Wanted in Rome*** have listings of jazz, rock, and such and give an interesting look at expatriate Rome. The daily ***Il Messaggero*** lists current cultural news, especially in its Thursday magazine supplement, ***Metro.*** And ***Un Ospite a Roma,*** available free from the concierge desks of top hotels, is full of details on what's happening.

During the peak of summer, usually in August, all nightclub proprietors seem to lock their doors and head for the seashore, where they operate alternate clubs. Some close at different times each year, so it's hard to keep up-to-date. Always have your hotel check to see if a club is operating before you make a trek to it. (Dance clubs in particular open and close with freewheeling abandon.)

Be aware that there are no inexpensive nightclubs in Rome. Many of the legitimate nightclubs, besides being expensive, are highlighted by hookers plying their trade.

THE PERFORMING ARTS

CLASSICAL MUSIC Concerts given by the orchestra of the **Academy of St. Cecilia,** Via della Conciliazione 4 (☎ **06-688-01044;** Bus: 62 or 982), usually take place at Piazza Villa Giulia, site of the Etruscan Museum, from late June to late July; in winter they're held in the academy's concert hall on Via della Conciliazione. Sometimes other addresses are used for the concerts, including a handful of historic churches. Performance nights are Saturday, Sunday, Monday, or Tuesday; Fridays feature chamber music. Tickets run 25,000 to 80,000L ($12.50 to $40).

The **Teatro Olimpico,** Piazza Gentile da Fabriano (☎ **06-323-4890;** Metro: Flaminio), hosts a widely divergent collection of singers, both classical and pop, who perform according to a schedule that sometimes changes at the last minute. Occasionally the space is devoted to chamber orchestras or visiting foreign orchestras. Tickets run 20,000 to 80,000L ($10 to $40).

Check the daily papers for **free church concerts** given around town, especially near Easter and Christmas.

OPERA If you're in the capital for the opera season, usually late December to June, you may want to attend the historic **Teatro dell'Opera,** Piazza Beniamino Gigli 1, off Via Nazionale (☎ **06-481-601;** Metro: Repubblica). Nothing is presented in August; in summer, the venue usually switches elsewhere. Call ahead or ask your concierge before you go. Tickets are 25,000 to 300,000L ($12.50 to $150).

DANCE Performances of the Rome Opera Ballet are given at the **Teatro dell'Opera** (above). The regular repertoire of classical ballet is supplemented by performances of internationally acclaimed guest artists, and Rome is on the major agenda for troupes from around the world, including the Alvin Ailey dancers. Watch for announcements in the weekly entertainment guides about other venues, including the Teatro Olimpico, or even open-air ballet performances.

A MEAL & A SONG

Da Ciceruacchio, Piazza dei Mercanti at Via del Porto 1, in Trastevere (☎ **06-580-6046;** Bus: 23), was once a sunken jail (the vine-covered walls date from the 18th century). Folkloric groups appear throughout the evening, especially singers of Neapolitan songs, accompanied by guitars and harmonicas—a rich repertoire of old-time favorites, some with bawdy lyrics. Charcoal-broiled steaks and chops are served along with lots of local wine, and bean soup is a specialty. You can dine Tuesday to Sunday 7pm to midnight for 40,000 to 60,000L ($20 to $30). You can also go here after 11pm and have a dessert and a glass of champagne, enjoying the music, all for 15,000L ($7.50).

Da Meo Patacca, Piazza dei Mercanti 30, in Trastevere (☎ **06-5833-1086;** Bus: 23), serves bountiful "Roman country" meals. The atmosphere is one of extravaganza, primitive and colorful in a carnival sense—it's touristy, but good fun if you're in the mood. Downstairs is a vast cellar with strolling musicians and singers. Many menu offerings are as adventurous as the decor (wild boar, wild hare, quail), but you'll also find corn on the cob, pork and beans, thick-cut sirloins, and chicken on a spit. Expect to spend 55,000L ($27.50) and up for a meal. In summer you can dine at outdoor tables. It's open daily 8 to 11:30pm.

Roman rusticity is combined with theatrical flair at **Fantasie di Trastevere,** Via di Santa Dorotea 6, in Trastevere (☎ **06-588-1671;** Bus: 23, 65, or 280), where the famous actor Petrolini made his debut. In the 16th century, this restaurant was an old theater built for Queen Cristina of Sweden and her court. The cuisine isn't subtle but is bountiful. Such dishes as the classic *saltimbocca* (ham with veal) are preceded by tasty pasta, and everything is aided by Castelli Romani wines. Accompanying the main dishes is a big basket of warm country herb bread. Expect to pay 80,000 to 120,000L ($40 to $60) for a full meal. If you visit for a drink, the first one will be 35,000L ($17.50). Some two dozen folk singers and musicians in regional costumes perform, making it a festive affair. Meals begin daily at 8pm, with piano bar music 8:30 to 9:30pm, followed by the show, lasting till 10:30pm.

BARS & CAFES

Unless you're dead set on making the Roman nightclub circuit, try what might be a far livelier and less expensive scene—sitting late at night on **Via Veneto, Piazza della Rotonda, Piazza del Popolo,** or one of Rome's other piazzas, all for the cost of an espresso, a cappuccino, or a Campari.

If you're looking for some scrumptious **ice cream,** see café Rosati and Giolitti below as well as the box "Take a Gelato Break," in chapter 3.

ON VIA VENETO Back in the 1950s (a decade that *Time* magazine gave to Rome, in the same way it conceded the 1960s and later the 1990s to London), **Via Vittorio**

Veneto rose in fame as the choicest street in Rome, crowded with aspiring and actual movie stars, their directors, and a fast-rising group of card-carrying members of the jet set. Today the beautiful people wouldn't be caught dead on Via Veneto—it's become touristy. Nevertheless, you may want to check it out for old times' sake.

Sophisticated **Harry's Bar,** Via Vittorio Veneto 150 (☎ **06-484-643;** Metro: Barberini), is a perennial favorite. Every major Italian city (like Florence and Venice) seems to have one, and Rome is no exception, though this one has no connection with the others. In summer, tables are placed outside. For those who wish to dine outdoors but want to avoid the scorching sun, there's an air-conditioned sidewalk cafe open May to November. Meals inside cost about double what you'd pay outside. In back is a small dining room serving some of the finest (and priciest) food in central Rome. The restaurant inside is open Monday to Saturday 12:30 to 3pm and 7:30pm to 1am. Outside you can eat from noon to midnight. The bar is open Monday to Saturday 11am to 2am (closed August 1 to 10), and the piano bar is open nightly from 9:30pm, with live music starting at 11pm.

Caffè de Paris, Via Vittorio Veneto 90 (☎ **06-488-5284;** Metro: Barberini), is popular in summer, when the tables spill right out onto the sidewalk and the passing crowd walks through the maze. It's open Wednesday to Monday from 8am to 1:30am and Tuesday to midnight.

ON PIAZZA DEL POPOLO At the center of **Piazza del Popolo** is a 13th-century B.C. Egyptian obelisk, and around it are Santa Maria del Popolo and almost-twin baroque churches.

Café Rosati, Piazza del Popolo 5A (☎ **06-322-5859;** Bus: 117), has been around since 1923 and attracts a crowd of all persuasions who drive up in Maseratis and Porsches. It's really a sidewalk cafe/ice-cream parlor/candy store/confectionery/ristorante that has been swept up in the fickle world of fashion. The later you go, the more interesting the action will be. It serves lunch and dinner daily noon to 11pm.

The management of **Canova Café,** Piazza del Popolo 16 (☎ **06-361-2231;** Bus: 117), has filled this place with boutiques selling expensive gift items, like luggage and cigarette lighters, yet many Romans still consider the Canova to be *the* place on the piazza. It has a sidewalk terrace for people-watching, plus a snack bar, a restaurant, and a wine shop. In summer you'll have access to a courtyard whose walls are covered with ivy and where flowers grow in terra-cotta planters. A buffet meal is 25,000L ($12.50) and up. Food is served daily noon to 3:30pm and 7 to 11pm, but the bar is open 8am to midnight or 1am depending on the crowd.

Night & Day, Via Dell'Oca 50 (☎ **06-320-2300;** Bus: 116), is a popular Irish pub near Piazza del Popolo. Open daily 5pm to 5am, it doesn't really get hot until 2am, when many dance clubs close for the evening. American music is played as you down your Harps and Guinness. Amazingly, foreigners are issued drink cards, making all their drinks 6,000L ($3) instead of the 8,000L ($4) usually charged. There's never a cover.

NEAR THE PANTHEON The **Piazza della Rotonda,** across from the Pantheon, is the hopping place to be after dark, especially in summer.

Di Rienzo, Piazza della Rotonda 8–9 (☎ **06-686-9097;** Bus: 116), the top cafe on this piazza, is open daily 7am to 1 or 2am. In fair weather, you can sit at one of the sidewalk tables (if you can find one free). In cooler weather, you can retreat inside, where the walls are inlaid with the type of marble found on the Pantheon's floor. Many types of pastas appear on the menu, as does *risotto alla pescatora* (fisherman's rice) and several meat courses. You can also order pizzas.

Tazza d'Oro, Piazza della Rotonda, Via degli Orfani 84 (☎ **06-678-2792;** Bus: 116), is known for serving its own brand of espresso. Another specialty, ideal on a hot summer night, is *granità di caffè* (coffee that has been frozen, crushed into a velvety slushlike ice, and placed in a glass between layers of whipped cream). It's open daily 7:30am to 1am.

Strongly brewed coffee is liquid fuel to Italians, and many Romans will walk blocks and blocks for what they consider a superior brew. **Caffè Sant'Eustachio,** Piazza Sant'Eustachio 82 (☎ **06-686-1309;** Bus: 116), is one of Rome's most celebrated espresso shops, where the water supply is funneled into the city by an aqueduct built in 19 B.C. Rome's most experienced espresso judges claim the water plays an important part in the coffee's flavor, though steam forced through ground Brazilian coffee roasted on the premises has a significant effect as well. Buy a ticket from the cashier for as many cups as you want; then leave a small tip (about 900 to 1,000L/45¢ to 50¢) for the counter-person when you present your receipt. It's open Tuesday to Friday and Sunday 8:30am to 1am and Saturday 8:30am to 1:30am.

NEAR THE SPANISH STEPS Since 1760 the ✪ **Antico Caffè Greco,** Via Condotti 84 (☎ **06-679-1700;** Metro: Spagna), has been Rome's poshest coffee bar. Stendhal, Goethe, Keats, and D'Annunzio have sipped coffee here before you. Today you're more likely to see ladies who lunch on a shopping binge and American tourists, but there's plenty of atmosphere. In front is a wooden bar and beyond a series of small salons. You sit at marble-topped tables of Napoleonic design, against a backdrop of gold or red damask, romantic paintings, and antique mirrors. The house specialty is *paradisi,* made with lemon and orange. It's open Monday to Saturday 8am to 9pm (closed for 10 days in August).

One of the best places to taste Italian wines, brandies, and grappa is at **Enoteca Fratelli Roffi Isabelli,** Via della Croce 76B (☎ **06-679-0896;** Metro: Spagna). A stand-up drink in its darkly antique confines is the perfect ending to a visit to the nearby Spanish Steps. You can opt for a postage-stamp table in back or stay at the bar.

NEAR PIAZZA COLONNA For devotees of gelato, **Giolitti,** Via Uffici del Vicario 40 (☎ **06-699-1243;** Bus: 116), is one of the city's most popular nighttime gathering spots and the oldest ice-cream shop. Some of the sundaes look like Vesuvius about to erupt. Many people take gelato out to eat on the streets; others enjoy it in the post-Empire splendor of the salon inside. You can have your "coppa" daily 7am to 2am (closed at 1am in winter). There are many excellent, smaller gelaterie throughout Rome, wherever you see the cool concoction advertised as *produzione propria* (homemade). See the box "Take a Gelato Break," in chapter 3.

IN TRASTEVERE Several cafes in **Trastevere,** across the Tiber, are attracting crowds. Fans who saw *Fellini's Roma* know what **Piazza Santa Maria in Trastevere** looks like at night. The square, filled with milling throngs in summer, is graced with an octagonal fountain and a 12th-century church. Children run and play on the piazza, and occasional spontaneous guitar fests break out when the weather is good.

The **Café-Bar di Marzio,** Piazza Santa Maria in Trastevere 15 (☎ **06-581-6095;** Bus: 44, 75, or 170), is a warmly inviting place. It's strictly a cafe (not a restaurant), offering both indoor and outdoor tables at the edge of the square with the best view of its fountain. Marzio is open daily 7am to 2am (closed Monday in February).

LIVE-MUSIC CLUBS

At **Alexanderplatz,** Via Ostia 9 (☎ **06-3974-2171;** Bus: 23), you can hear jazz (not rock) Monday to Saturday 9pm to 2am, with live music beginning at 10:30pm. The good restaurant here serves everything from *gnocchi alla romana* to Japanese. There's no cover, but a 3-month membership is 12,000L ($6).

Big Mama, Vicolo San Francesco a Ripa 18 (☎ **06-581-2551;** Bus: 44, 75, or 170), is a hangout for jazz and blues musicians where you're likely to meet the up-and-coming stars of tomorrow and sometimes even the big names. It's open Monday to Saturday 9pm to 1:30am (closed June to September). For big acts, the cover is 20,000 to 30,000L ($10 to $15), plus 20,000L ($10) for a seasonal membership fee.

Fonclea, Via Crescenzio 82A (☎ **06-689-6302;** Bus: 32 or 39), offers live music every night: Dixieland, rock, and R&B. This is basically a cellar jazz place and crowded pub that attracts folks from all walks of Roman life. The music starts at 9:30pm and usually lasts until 12:30am. The club is open nightly 7pm to 2am (Friday and Saturday to 3:30am). There's also a restaurant featuring grilled meats, salads, and crêpes. A meal starts at 35,000L ($17.50), but if you want dinner it's best to reserve a table.

Saint Louis Music City, Via del Cardello 13A (☎ **06-4745076**) is another leading jazz venue. In large, contemporary surroundings, it features young and sometimes very talented newcomers rather than the big, better established names in jazz, and even puts on the occasional soul and funk act. At a restaurant on the premises, you can enjoy meals for 35,000L ($17.50) and up. The cover (including club membership) is 9,000L ($4.50). Saint Louis is open from Tuesday to Sunday from 9am to 2am.

Arciliuto, Piazza Monte Vecchio 5 (☎ **06-687-9419;** Bus: 42, 62, or 64), is a romantic candlelit spot that was reputedly once the studio of Raphael. Monday to Saturday 10pm to 2am, you can enjoy a music salon ambience, with a pianist, guitarist, and violinist. The presentation also includes live Neapolitan songs and new Italian madrigals, even current hits from Broadway or London's West End. This place is hard to find, but it's within walking distance of Piazza Navona. The cover is 35,000L ($17.50), including the first drink; it's closed July 20 to September 16.

NIGHTCLUBS & DANCE CLUBS

In a setting of high-tech futuristic rows of exposed pipes and ventilation ducts, **Alien,** Via Velletri 13–19 (☎ **06-841-2212;** Bus 3, 4, or 57), provides a bizarre space-age dance floor, bathed in strobe lights and rocking to the sounds of house/techno music. It's open Tuesday to Saturday 11pm to 5am, with a 30,000 to 35,000L ($15 to $17.50) cover that includes the first drink.

Gilda, Via Mario dei Fiori 97 (☎ **06-678-4838;** Metro: Spagna), is an adventurous nightclub/disco/restaurant. In the past it has hosted Diana Ross and splashy Paris-type revues. The artistic direction ensures first-class shows, a well-run restaurant, and disco music played between the live acts. The restaurant and pizzeria open at 9:30pm and occasionally present shows. An international cuisine is featured, with meals beginning at 45,000L ($22.50). The disco (midnight to 4am) presents music of the 1960s as well as modern recordings. The attractive piano bar, Swing, features Italian and Latin music. The cover is 40,000L ($20) and includes the first drink.

One of Rome's largest and most energetic nightclubs, **Alpheus,** Via del Commercio 36 (☎ **06-574-7826;** Bus: 713), contains three sprawling rooms, each with a

A Nightlife Note

A neighborhood with an edge, **Testaccio** is radical chic—don't wander around alone at night. The area still has a way to go before regentrification. However, Testaccio is the place to ask about what's hot in Rome when you arrive, as crowds are fickle.

different musical sound and an ample number of bars. You'll find areas devoted to Latin music, other areas playing rock, and an area devoted to jazz. Live bands come and go, and there's enough cultural variety in the crowd to keep everyone amused throughout the evening. It's open Tuesday to Sunday 10pm to 4am and charges 10,000 to 20,000L ($5 to $10) cover.

If you're looking for a little counterculture edge, where you might find the latest indie music from the U.K., head for **Black Out,** Via Saturnia 18 (☎ **06-7049-6791**), which occupies an industrial-looking site open only Thursday, Friday, and Saturday 10:30pm to 4am. Whenever it can manage, a live band is presented on Thursday—very late. The recorded music includes punk, retro, R&B, grunge, and whatever else happens to be in fashion. There's always one room (with an independent sound system) set aside as a lounge. The 10,000L ($5) cover on Thursday and the 15,000L ($7.50) cover on Saturday and Sunday include the first drink.

Everything about **Club Picasso,** Via Monte di Testaccio 63 (☎ **06-574-2975;** Bus: 95), seems straight out of L.A. R&B, rock, and funk blare out across a crowd that loves to dance. The door bouncer is extra-vigilant about screening out any troublemakers. Club Picasso is open Tuesday to Sunday 8pm to 4am. You can get affordable pizza and other fare to stave off the munchies. If you go there just to dance, the cover is 15,000L ($7.50) on Friday and 20,000L ($10) on Saturday, including the first drink.

Close to the American Embassy and Via Veneto, **Jackie O,** Via Boncompagni 11 (☎ **06-4288-5457;** Bus: 52, 53, 56, or 58), is a glittery club that draws an affluent, over-30 crowd. If you opt to go dancing here (it's not as frenzied as some might like), you might begin your evening with a drink at the piano bar and then perhaps end it in the restaurant, where meals average 80,000L ($40), without wine. It's open Tuesday to Sunday 8:30pm to 4am, and the 40,000L ($20) cover includes the first drink.

Radio Londra, Via Monte Testaccio 67 (no phone; Bus: 95), aims for London-style hip. Everyone tries to look and act as freaky as possible. Since Radio Londra is near the popular gay L'Alibi (see below), the downstairs club attracts many brethren, though the crowd is mixed. Upstairs is a pub/pizzeria where bands often appear; you can even order a veggie burger with a Bud. The club is open Wednesday to Monday 11:30am to 4am, and the pub/pizzeria serves Sunday, Monday, and Wednesday to Friday 9pm to 3am (to 4am on Saturday). The cover is 20,000L ($10), including the first drink.

GAY & LESBIAN CLUBS

Having survived since 1984, the **Hangar,** Via in Selci 69 (☎ **06-488-1397;** Metro: Cavour), is a landmark on the gay nightlife scene. It's on one of Rome's oldest streets, adjacent to the Forum, on the site of the palace once inhabited by Claudius's deranged wife Messalina. Each of the Hangar's two bars has an independent sound system. Women are welcome any night except Monday, when the club features videos and entertainment for men. The busiest nights are Saturday, Sunday, and Monday, when as many as 500 people cram inside. It's open Wednesday to Monday 10:30pm to 2:30am (closed for 3 weeks in August). There's no cover, but a membership card of 3,000L ($1.50) is needed.

L'Alibi, Via Monte Testaccio 44 (☎ **06-574-3448;** Bus: 95), in Testaccio, is a year-round venue on many a gay man's agenda. The crowd, however, tends to be mixed, both Roman and international, straight and gay, male and female. One room is devoted to dancing. It's open Tuesday to Sunday 11pm to 4am, and the cover is 25,000L ($12.50).

Angelo Azzuro, Via Cardinal Merry del Val 13 (☎ **06-580-0472;** Bus: 44, 75, or 170), is a gay hot spot deep in the heart of Trastevere, open Friday, Saturday, and Sunday 11pm to 4am. There's no food—men dance with men to recorded music. Women are also invited, and Friday is for women only. Cover, including one drink, is 20,000L ($10).

A fixture on the lesbian nighttime scene, **Joli Coeur,** Via Sirte 5 (☎ **06-8621-6240;** Bus: 52 or 56), attracts women from around Europe during its very limited hours (only Saturday and Sunday 11pm to 5am). Saturday is reserved for women only, though on Sunday the crowd can be mixed. The cover is 20,000L ($10) and includes the first drink.

11 Side Trips from Rome: Tivoli, Ostia Antica & More

Just a few miles from Rome, you can go back to the dawn of Italian history and explore the dank tombs the Etruscans left as their legacy or drink the golden wine of the towns in the Alban Hills (Castelli Romani). You can wander the ruins of Hadrian's Villa, the "queen of villas of the ancient world," or be lulled by the music of the baroque fountains in the Villa d'Este. You can turn yourself bronze on the beaches of Ostia di Lido or explore the remarkable ruins of Ostia Antica, Rome's ancient seaport.

Unless you're rushed beyond reason, allow at least 3 days to take a look at the attractions in the environs. We've highlighted the best of the lot below.

TIVOLI & THE VILLAS

Tivoli, known as Tibur to the ancient Romans, is 20 miles (32km) east of Rome on Via Tiburtina, about an hour's drive with traffic. If you don't have a car, take Metro Line B to the end of the line, the Rebibbia station. After exiting the station, board an Acotral bus for the trip the rest of the way to Tivoli. Generally, buses depart about every 20 minutes during the day. For information about the town, check with **Azienda Autonoma di Turismo,** Largo Garibaldi (☎ **0774/334-522**), Tivoli. Opening hours are Monday to Saturday 9am to 2:30pm and Tuesday to Friday 9am to 2pm and 3 to 6pm.

EXPLORING THE VILLAS

✪ **Villa d'Este.** Piazza Trento, Viale delle Centro Fontane. ☎ **0774/312-070.** Admission 10,000L ($5). The bus from Rome stops right near the entrance.

Like Hadrian centuries before, Cardinal Ippolito d'Este of Ferrara believed in heaven on earth, and in the mid–16th century he ordered this villa built on a hillside. The dank Renaissance structure, with its second-rate paintings, is hardly worth the trek from Rome, but the gardens below (designed by Pirro Ligorio) dim the luster of those at Versailles.

You descend the cypress-studded slope to the bottom and on the way are rewarded with everything from lilies to gargoyles spouting water, torrential streams, and waterfalls. The loveliest fountain is the **Ovato Fountain (Fontana dell Ovato)** by Ligorio. But nearby is the most spectacular achievement: the **Fountain of the Hydraulic Organ (Fontana dell'Organo Idraulico),** dazzling with its water jets in front of a baroque chapel, with four maidens who look tipsy. The work represents the genius of Frenchman Claude Veanard. The moss-covered **Fountain of the Dragons (Fontana dei Draghi),** also by Ligorio, and the so-called **Fountain of Glass (Fontana di Vetro)** by Bernini are the most intriguing. The best walk is along the promenade, with 100 spraying fountains. The garden is worth hours of exploration, but you'll need frequent rests after those steep climbs.

Villa Gregoriana. Largo Sant'Angelo. ☎ **0774/334-522.** Admission 3,500L ($1.75). May–Aug daily 10am–7:30pm; Sept daily 9:30am–6:30pm; Oct–Mar daily 9:30am–4:30pm; Apr daily 9:30am–6pm. The bus from Rome stops near the entrance.

The Villa d'Este dazzles with artificial glamour, but the Villa Gregoriana relies more on nature. The gardens were built by Pope Gregory XVI in the 19th century. At one point on the circuitous walk carved along a slope, you can stand and look out onto the most panoramic waterfall (Aniene) at Tivoli. The trek to the bottom on the banks of the Anio is studded with grottoes and balconies that open onto the chasm. The only problem is that if you do make the full descent, you may need a helicopter to pull you up again (the climb back up is fierce). From one of the belvederes, there's a panoramic view of the Temple of Vesta on the hill.

✪ **Hadrian's Villa (Villa Adriana).** Via di Villa Adriana. ☎ **0774/530-203.** Admission 8,000L ($4). Daily 9am–sunset (about 6:30pm in summer, 4pm Nov–Mar). Closed New Year's Day, May Day, and Christmas. Bus: 2 or 4 from Tivoli.

In the 2nd century A.D., the globe-trotting Hadrian spent the last 3 years of his life in the grandest style. Less than 4 miles (6km) from Tivoli, he built one of the greatest estates ever erected in the world and filled acre after acre with some of the architectural wonders he'd seen on his many travels. Perhaps as a preview of what he envisioned in store for himself, the emperor even created a representation of hell centuries before Dante got around to recording its horrors. Hadrian was a patron of the arts, a lover of beauty, and even something of an architect; and he directed the staggering feat of building much more than a villa: It was a self-contained world for a vast royal entourage and the hundreds of servants and guards they required to protect them, feed them, bathe them, and satisfy their libidos.

Hadrian erected theaters, baths, temples, fountains, gardens, and canals bordered with statuary throughout his estate. He filled the palaces and temples with sculpture, some of which now rest in the museums of Rome. In later centuries, barbarians, popes, and cardinals, as well as anyone who needed a slab of marble, carted off much that made the villa so spectacular. But enough of the fragmented ruins remain for us to piece together the story.

For a glimpse of what the villa used to be, see the plastic reconstruction at the entrance. Then, following the arrows around, look in particular for the **Marine Theater** (ruins of the round structure with Ionic pillars); the **Great Baths,** with some intact mosaics; and the **Canopus,** with a group of caryatids whose images are reflected in the pond, as well as a statue of Mars. For a closer look at some of the items excavated, you can visit the museum on the premises and a museum and visitor center near the villa parking area.

DINING

Albergo Ristorante Adriano. Via di Villa Adriana 194. ☎ **0774/535-028.** Reservations recommended. Main courses 24,000–32,000L ($12–$16). AE, DC, MC, V. Mon–Sat 12:30–2:30pm and 8–10pm; Sun 12:30–2:30pm. Bus: 2 or 4 from Tivoli. ITALIAN.

In a stucco-sided villa a few steps from the ticket office sits an idyllic stop for either before or after you visit Hadrian's Villa. It offers terrace dining under plane trees or indoor dining in a high-ceilinged room with terra-cotta walls, neoclassical moldings, and white Corinthian pilasters. The cooking is home-style, and the menu includes roast lamb, *saltimbocca* (veal cooked with ham), a variety of veal dishes, deviled chicken, salads and cheeses, and simple desserts. They're especially proud of their homemade pastas.

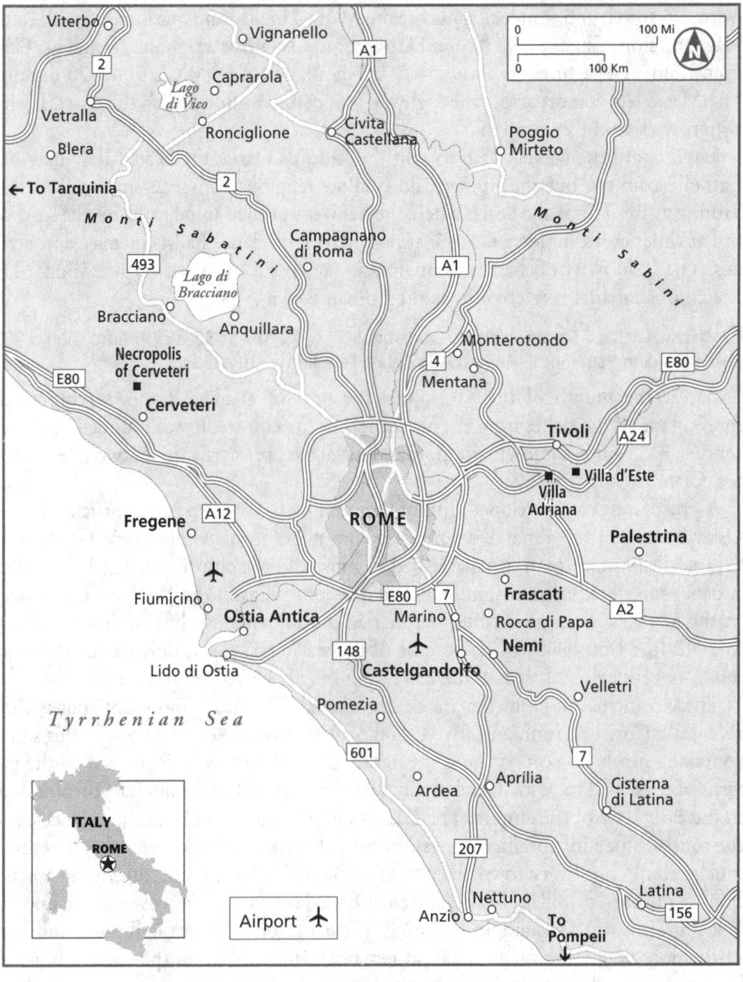

Le Cinque Statue. Via Quintillio Varo 8. ☎ **0774/335-366.** Reservations recommended. Main courses 14,000–26,000L ($7–$13). AE, DC, MC, V. Mon and Thurs–Sat 12:30–3pm and 7–11pm; Sun 12:30–3pm. Closed Aug 16–25. The Acotral bus from Rome stops nearby. ROMAN.

This restaurant takes its name from the quintet of old carved statues (like Apollo Belvedere and gladiators) decorating the place. Today this comfortable place is maintained by a hardworking Italian family that prepares an honest, unpretentious cuisine. Everything is accompanied by the wines of the hill towns of Rome. Begin with a pastiche of mushrooms or make a selection from the excellent antipasti. Try the rigatoni with fresh herbs, tripe fried Roman style, or mixed fry of brains and vegetables. All the pasta is freshly made. They also have a wide array of ice creams and fruits.

OSTIA ANTICA: ROME'S ANCIENT SEAPORT

Ostia Antica is one of the area's major attractions, particularly interesting to those who can't make it to Pompeii. If you want to see both ancient and modern Rome, grab your swimsuit, towel, and sunblock and take the Metro Line B from Stazione Termini to the Magliana stop. Change here for the Lido train to Ostia Antica, about 16 miles (26km) from Rome. Departures are about every half hour, and the trip takes only 20 minutes. The Metro lets you off across the highway that connects Rome with the coast. It's just a short walk to the excavations.

Later, board the Metro again to visit the **Lido di Ostia,** the beach. Italy may be a Catholic country, but the Romans don't allow religious conservatism to affect their bathing attire. This is the beach where the denizens of the capital frolic on the seashore and at times create a merry carnival atmosphere, with dance halls, cinemas, and pizzerias. The Lido is set off best at Castelfusano, against a backdrop of pinewoods. This stretch of shoreline is referred to as the Roman Riviera.

✪ **Ostia Antica's Ruins.** Viale dei Romagnoli 717. ☎ **06-5635-8099.** Admission 8,000L ($4). Tues–Sun 9am–6pm. Metro: Ostia Antica Line Roma-Ostia-Lido.

Ostia, at the mouth of the Tiber, was the port of ancient Rome, serving as the gateway for all the riches from the far corners of the empire. It was founded in the 4th century B.C. and became a major port and naval base primarily under two later emperors, Claudius and Trajan.

A prosperous city developed, full of temples, baths, theaters, and patrician homes. Ostia flourished for about 8 centuries before it began to wither away. Gradually it became little more than a malaria bed, a buried ghost city that faded into history. A papal-sponsored commission launched a series of digs in the 19th century; however, the major work of unearthing was carried out under Mussolini's orders from 1938 to 1942 (the work had to stop because of the war). The city is only partially dug out today, but it's believed that all the chief monuments have been uncovered.

These principal monuments are clearly labeled. The most important spot is **Piazzale delle Corporazioni,** an early version of Wall Street. Near the theater, this square contained nearly 75 corporations, the nature of their businesses identified by the patterns of preserved mosaics. Greek dramas were performed at the **ancient theater,** built in the early days of the empire. The classics are still aired here in summer (check with the tourist office for specific listings), but the theater as it looks today is the result of much rebuilding. Every town the size of Ostia had a forum, and during the excavations a number of pillars of the ancient **Ostia Forum** were uncovered. At one end is a 2nd-century B.C. temple honoring a trio of gods, Minerva, Jupiter, and Juno (little more than the basic foundation remains). In addition, in the enclave is a well-lit **museum** displaying Roman statuary along with some Pompeii-like frescoes. There are perfect picnic spots beside fallen columns or near old temple walls.

THE CASTELLI ROMANI

For the Roman emperor and the wealthy cardinal in the heyday of the Renaissance, the **Castelli Romani (Roman Castles)** exerted a powerful lure, and they still do. The Castelli aren't castles but hill towns—many of them with an ancient history and several producing wines that are well-regarded.

The ideal way to explore the hill towns is by car. But you can get a limited review by taking one of the buses that leaves every 20 minutes from Rome's Subaugusta stop on Metro Line A.

NEMI

The Romans flock to **Nemi** in droves, particularly from April to June, for the succulent **strawberries** grown there, acclaimed by some gourmets as Europe's finest. In May, there's a strawberry festival.

Nemi was also known to the ancients. A temple to the huntress Diana was erected on **Lake Nemi,** which was said to be her "looking glass." In A.D. 37, Caligula built luxurious barges to float on the lake. Mussolini drained Nemi to find the barges, but it was a dangerous time to excavate them from the bottom. They were senselessly destroyed by the Nazis during the infamous retreat.

At the **Roman Ship Museum (Museo delle Navi),** Via di Diana 15 (☎ **06-939-8040**), you can see two scale models of the ships destroyed by the Nazis. The major artifacts on display are mainly copies, as the originals now rest in world-class museums. The museum is open daily: October to March 9am to noon, April and May to 5:30pm, and June to September 9am to 7pm. Admission is 4,000L ($2). To reach the museum, head from the center of Nemi toward the lake.

The 15th-century **Palazzo Ruspoli,** a private baronial estate, is the focal point of Nemi, but the town itself invites exploration—particularly the alleyways the locals call streets and the houses with balconies jutting out over the slopes.

Dining

✪ **Ristorante Il Castagnone.** In the Diana Park Hotel, Via Nemorense 44. ☎ **06-936-4041.** Reservations recommended. Main courses 20,000–40,000L ($10–$20). AE, DC, MC, V. Tues–Sun noon–3pm and 8–10pm. Closed Nov. ROMAN/SEAFOOD.

This well-managed dining room of the town's best hotel takes a definite pride in a Roman-based cuisine emphasizing seafood above meat. The attentive formal service is usually delivered with a kind of gentle humor. Amid neoclassical accessories and marble, you can order delectable veal, chicken, beef, and fish dishes like fried calamari, spaghetti with shellfish in garlicky tomato-based sauce, and roasted lamb with potatoes and Mediterranean herbs. As you dine, expect a sweeping lake view from the restaurant's windows.

FRASCATI

About 13 miles (21km) from Rome on Via Tuscolana and some 1,073 feet above sea level, **Frascati** is one of the most beautiful of the hill towns. It's known for the wine to which it lends its name as well as for its villas, which luckily bounced back from the severe destruction caused by World War II bombers. To get there, take one of the Cotral buses leaving from the Anagina stop of Metro Line A. From there take the blue Cotral bus to Frascati. Again, the transportation situation in Italy is constantly in a state of flux, so check your route at the station.

Although Frascati wine is exported, and served in many of Rome's restaurants and trattorie, tradition holds that it's best near the vineyards from which it came. Romans drive up on Sunday just to drink it. To sample some of the golden white wine, head for **Cantina Comandini,** Via E. Filiberto 1 (☎ **06-942-0915**), right off Piazza

Reserving Winery Tours

While exploring the Castelli Romani, the hill towns around Rome, you might want to visit some of the better-known wineries. The region's most famous producers of Frascati are **Fontana Candida,** Via di Fontana Candida, 00040 Monte Porzio Catone, Roma (☎ **06-942-0066**), whose winery, 14 miles southwest of Rome, was built around 1900; and **Gotto D'Oro–Cantina Sociale di Marino,** Via del Divino Amore 115, 00040 Frattocchie, Roma (☎ **06-935-6931** and 06-935-6932). To arrange visits, contact the **Gruppo Italiano Vini,** Villa Belvedere, 37010 Calmasino, Verona (☎ **045/626-0600**).

Roma. The Comandini family welcomes you to the wine cellar, a regional tavern in which they sell Frascati from their own vineyards. You can drink the wine on the spot for 6,000L ($3) per liter or 2,000L ($1) per glass and can buy sandwiches to go with your vino. The tavern is open Monday to Saturday 4 to 8pm. Reservations are required.

Stand in the heart of Frascati, at Piazza Marconi, to see the most important of the estates: **Villa Aldobrandini,** Via Massala. The finishing touches to this 16th-century villa were added by Maderno, who designed the facade of St. Peter's in Rome, but you can visit only the gardens. Still, with its grottoes, yew hedges, statuary, and splashing fountains, it makes for an exciting outing. The gardens are open Monday to Friday 9am to 1pm and 3 to 5pm (to 6pm in summer), though you must go to the **Azienda di Soggiorno e Turismo,** Piazza Marconi 1 (☎ **06-942-0331**), to ask for a free pass. The office is open Monday to Saturday 8am to 2pm and also Tuesday to Friday 3:30 to 6:30pm in winter and 4 to 7pm in summer.

You may also want to visit the bombed-out **Villa Torlonia,** adjacent to Piazza Marconi. Its grounds have been converted into a public park whose chief treasure is the Theater of the Fountains, designed by Maderno.

If you have a car, you can continue about 3 miles (5km) past the Villa Aldobrandini to **Tuscolo,** an ancient spot with the ruins of an amphitheater dating from about the 1st century B.C. It offers what may be one of Italy's most panoramic views.

Dining

Cacciani Restaurant. Via Armando Diaz 13. ☎ **06-942-0378.** Reservations required on weekends. Main courses 20,000–35,000L ($12–$21). AE, DC, MC, V. Tues–Sun 12:30–3pm and 7:30–10:30pm. Closed Jan 7–19 and Aug 18–27. ROMAN.

Cacciani is the top restaurant in Frascati, where the competition has always been tough. It boasts a terrace commanding a view of the valley, and the kitchen is exposed to the public. To start, we recommend the pasta specialties, such as pasta cacio e pepe (pasta with caciocavallo cheese and black pepper) or the original spaghetti with seafood and lentils. For a main course, the baby lamb with a sauce of white wine and vinegar is always fine. There is, of course, a large choice of wine. If you call ahead, the Cacciani family will arrange a visit to several of Frascati's wine-producing villas, along with a memorable meal at their restaurant.

FREGENE

The fame of **Fregene**—a coastal city north of the Tiber and 24 miles (39km) from Rome—dates from the 1600s, when the land belonged to the Rospigliosi, a powerful Roman family. Pope Clement IX, a member of that family, planted a forest of pines that extends along the shoreline for 2½ miles (4km) and stands half a mile deep to protect the land from the strong winds of the Mediterranean. Today the pines make a dramatic backdrop for the resort's golden sands and luxurious villas. You can take a Civitavecchia-bound train from Rome's Stazione Termini to Fregene, the first stop. Or you can take the bus, which leaves from the Lepanto Metro stop and carries you to the center of Fregene.

Accommodations & Dining

La Conchiglia. Lungomare di Ponente 4, Fregene, 00050 Roma. ☎ **06-668-5385.** Fax 06-665-63185. E-mail:conhotel@ats.it. 42 units. A/C MINIBAR TV TEL. 200,000L ($100) double. Rates include breakfast. AE, DC, MC, V. Free parking.

La Conchiglia means "The Shell," and it's an appropriate name for this hotel and restaurant right on the beach with views of the water and the pines. It features a circular lounge with built-in curving wall banquettes facing a cylindrical fireplace. The bar in the cocktail lounge, which faces the terrace, is also circular. The guest rooms are comfortable and well furnished, ranging from medium to spacious, each with a fine mattress and quality linen.

It's also possible to stop by just for a good meal. Try, for example, spaghetti with lobster and grilled fish or one of many excellent meat dishes. Meals start at 50,000L ($25). The restaurant is open daily 1 to 3pm and 8 to 10pm.

ETRUSCAN HISTORICAL SIGHTS

CERVETERI (CAERE)

As you walk through Rome's Etruscan Museum (Villa Giulia), you'll often see *Caere* written under a figure vase or sarcophagus. This is a reference to the nearby town known today as **Cerveteri,** one of Italy's great Etruscan cities, whose origins may date from as far back as the 9th century B.C.

Of course, the Etruscan town has long since faded, but not the **Necropolis of Cerveteri** (☎ **06-994-0001**). The effect is eerie; Cerveteri is often called a "city of the dead." When you go beneath some of the mounds, you'll discover the most striking feature: The tombs are like rooms in Etruscan homes. The main burial ground is the Necropolis of Banditacca. Of the graves thus far uncovered, none is finer than the **Tomba Bella** (or the Reliefs' Tomb), the burial ground of the Matuna family. Articles like utensils and even house pets were painted in stucco relief. Presumably these paintings were representations of items the dead family would need in the world beyond. The necropolis is open Tuesday to Sunday 9am to 1 hour before sunset. Admission is 8,000L ($4).

Relics from the necropolis are displayed at the **Museo Nazionale Cerite,** Piazza Santa Maria Maggiore (☎ **06-994-1354**). The museum, housed within the ancient walls and crenellations of Ruspoldi Castle, is open Tuesday to Sunday 9am to 7pm. Admission is free.

You can reach Cerveteri by bus or car. If you're driving, head out Via Aurelia, northwest of Rome, for 28 miles (45km). By public transport, take Metro Line A in Rome to the Lepanto stop; from Via Lepanto you can catch a Cotral bus (☎ **06-324-4724**) to Cerveteri; the trip takes about an hour and costs 5,000L ($2.50). Once you're at Cerveteri, it's a 1¼-mile walk to the necropolis; follow the signs pointing the way.

TARQUINIA

If you wish to see tombs even more striking and more recently excavated than those at Cerveteri, go to **Tarquinia.** The medieval turrets and fortifications atop the rocky cliffs overlooking the sea seem to contradict the Etruscan name of Tarquinia. Actually, Tarquinia is the adopted name of the old medieval community of Corneto, in honor of the major Etruscan city that once stood nearby.

The main attraction in the town is the **Tarquinia National Museum,** Piazza Cavour (☎ **0776/856-036**), devoted to Etruscan exhibits and sarcophagi excavated from the necropolis a few miles away. The museum is housed in the Palazzo Vitelleschi, a Gothic palace from the mid–15th century. Among the exhibits are gold jewelry, black vases with carved and painted bucolic scenes, and sarcophagi decorated with carvings of animals and relief figures of priests and military leaders. But the biggest attraction is in itself worth the ride from Rome—the almost life-size pair of winged horses from the pediment of a Tarquinian temple. The finish is worn here and there and the terra-cotta color shows through, but the relief stands as one of the greatest Etruscan masterpieces ever discovered. The museum is open Tuesday to Sunday 9am to 7pm and charges 8,000L ($4) admission.

An 8,000L ($4) admission admits you to the ✪ **Etruscan Necropolis** (☎ **0766/856-308**), covering more than 4.5km (2½ miles) of rough terrain near where the ancient Etruscan city once stood. Thousands of tombs have been discovered, some of which haven't been explored even today. Others, of course, were discovered by looters, but many treasures remain even though countless pieces were removed to museums and private collections. The paintings on the walls of the tombs have helped historians reconstruct the life of the Etruscans—a heretofore impossible feat without a written history. The paintings depict feasting couples in vivid colors mixed from iron oxide, lapis lazuli dust, and charcoal. One of the oldest tombs (from the 6th century B.C.) depicts young men fishing while dolphins play and colorful birds fly high above. Many of the paintings convey an earthy, vigorous, sex-oriented life among the wealthy Etruscans. The tombs are generally open Tuesday to Sunday 9am to 5pm. You can reach the grave sites by taking a bus from the Barriera San Giusto to the Cimitero stop. Or try the 20-minute walk from the museum. Inquire at the museum for directions.

To reach Tarquinia by car, take Via Aurelia outside Rome and continue on the autostrada toward Civitavecchia. Bypass Civitavecchia and continue another 13 miles (21km) north until you see the exit signs for Tarquinia. As for public transport, going by train is preferred: A diretto train from Roma Ostiense station takes 50 minutes. Eight buses a day leave from the Via Lepanto stop in Rome for the 2-hour trip to the town of Barriera San Giusto, 1½ miles (2km) from Tarquinia. Bus schedules are available at the **tourist office** in Barriera San Giusto (☎ **0766/856-384**), open Monday to Saturday 8am to 2pm.

Florence

5

Except for Venice, no other European city lives off its past the way Florence (Firenze) does. After all, it was the birthplace of the Renaissance, an amazing outburst of activity from the 14th to the 16th century that completely changed the Tuscan town and the world. Under the benevolent eye (and purse) of the Medicis, Florence blossomed into an unrivaled repository of art and architectural treasures by geniuses like Botticelli, Brunelleschi, Cellini, Donatello, Fra Angelico, Ghiberti, Giotto, Leonardo, Michelangelo, and Raphael. Since the 19th century, it has been visited by millions wanting to see Michelangelo's *David,* Botticelli's *Birth of Venus,* Brunelleschi's dome on the Duomo, and Giotto's campanile.

At first glance, Florence may seem a bit foreboding. Architecturally, it's not the Gothic fantasy of lace that Venice is. Many of its palazzi look like severe fortresses, a characteristic of the Medici style. They were built, after all, to keep foreign enemies at bay. These facades, though, however uninviting, mask treasures within, as the thousands of visitors who overrun the narrow streets know. The locals bemoan this crush and at the same time welcome it, because it puts food on the table. "It's the price we pay for fame," laments a local merchant. "The visitors have crowded our city and strained our facilities, but they make it possible for me to own a villa in Fiesole and take my children on vacation to San Remo every year."

The city officials have been wise to keep the inner Renaissance core relatively free of modern architecture and polluting industry. Florence has industry, but it has been relegated to the suburbs. The city is relatively clean and safe as Italian cities go, with far less crime than Rome and certainly far less than Naples. You can generally walk the narrow cobblestone streets at night safely, though caution is always advised.

May and September are the ideal times to visit. The worst times are the week before and including Easter and June until the first week of September—Florence is literally overrun during these times, and the streets weren't designed for mass tourism. Temperatures in July and August hover in the 70s and 80s, dropping to a low of 45°F in December and January.

1 Essentials

ARRIVING

BY PLANE If you're flying from North America, the best air connection is Rome, where you can board a domestic flight to the **Galileo**

Galilei Airport at Pisa (☎ **050/500-707**), 58 miles west of Florence. If you're flying Air Europe (☎ **888/999-9090** in the U.S.; www.aireurope.it) from New York's JFK, there are six flights a week to Pisa. There's a **shuttle train** every hour or two (7am to 7pm) between the airport and Florence's Santa Maria Novella station; the trip takes a little over an hour and costs 8,000L ($4) one way.

Florence's small airport, **Amerigo Vespucci** (☎ **055/30-615**), is about 3 miles (5km) northwest of the city on Via del Termine, near A11. Many of the European airlines serve this airport, and it receives domestic flights from cities like Rome and Milan and international flights from cities like Brussels, Frankfurt, London, Munich, Nice, and Paris. ATAF **bus no. 62** runs between the airport and the Santa Maria Novella rail station every 20 minutes, costing 1,500L (75¢). The 15-minute **taxi ride** from the airport to the city should cost about 40,000L ($20).

Domestic air service is provided by **Alitalia,** Lungarno degli Acciaiuoli 1012 in Florence (☎ **055/27-881**).

BY TRAIN To get here from Rome, you can take the Pendolino (4 daily, 1¾ hours; make sure it's going to Santa Maria Novello station, not Rifredi; you must reserve tickets ahead), an EC or IC train (24 daily, just under 2 hours), or an *interregionale* (7 daily, about 3 hours). There are also about 16 trains daily from Milan (3 hours) through Bologna (1 hour). Venice is about 4 hours away.

Stazione Santa Maria Novella (S.M.N.), on Piazza della Stazione (☎ **055/2351** for rail information), which adjoins Piazza Santa Maria Novella. There's a **tourist-information office** opposite Track 16 (open daily from 8:30am to 9pm); it offers free maps and will reserve a hotel room for you for a small fee. You'll also find a currency-exchange office here (open Monday to Saturday 8:30am to 6:30pm). From the station, most of the major hotels are within easy reach, either on foot or by taxi or bus (exit out to the left coming off the tracks, and you'll find many bus lines as well as stairs down to the pedestrian underpass that leads directly to Piazza dell'Unità Italiana and saves you from the crazy traffic of the station's piazza).

Some trains into Florence stop at the **Stazione Campo di Marte,** on the eastern side of Florence—however, it's worth avoiding. A 24-hour bus service (no. 91) runs between the two terminals.

BY BUS It's a much better idea to take the train, but two long-distance bus lines service Florence: **SITA,** Viale Cadorna 103105 (☎ **055/483-651**), and **Lazzi Eurolines,** Piazza della Stazione 46 (☎ **055/215-155**). SITA connects Florence with such Tuscan hill towns as Siena, Arezzo, Pisa, and San Gimignano, and Lazzi Eurolines provides service from such cities as Rome and Naples.

BY CAR Florence, because of its central location, enjoys good autostrada connections with the rest of Italy, especially Rome and Bologna. A1 connects Florence with both the north and the south. Florence lies 172 miles (277km) north of Rome, 65 miles (105km) west of Bologna, and 185 miles (298km) south of Milan. Bologna is about an hour away by car, and Rome is 3 hours away. The Tyrrhenian coast is only an hour from Florence on A11 heading west.

Use a car only to get to Florence. Don't even think about trying to drive within the city, as most of central Florence is closed to all vehicles except those of locals. If your hotel doesn't have parking, head for one of the city-run garages. Although there's a garage under the train station, a better deal is the **Parterre** parking lot under Piazza Libertà, north of Fortezza del Basso. If you're staying at least one night in a hotel, you can park here, are welcome to use a free bike, and (on presentation of your hotel receipt as you leave or the hotel's stamp on your parking receipt), you'll pay only 15,000L ($7.50) per night.

VISITOR INFORMATION

Contact the **Azienda Promozione Turistica,** which has several branches: Via A. Manzoni 16 (☎ **055/233-20;** fax 055/234-6286), open Monday to Saturday 8:30am to 1:30pm; Via Cavour 1R (☎ **055/290-832;** fax 055/276-0383), open March to November Monday to Saturday 8:15am to 7:15pm and Sunday 8:15am to 1:45pm, and December to February Monday to Saturday 8:15am to 1:45pm; and just south of Piazza Santa Croce at Borgo Santa Croce 29R (☎ **055/23-40-444**), open same hours as the one at Via Cavour. There's also a small **Uffizio Informazioni Turistiche** inside the main train terminal.

CITY LAYOUT

Florence is a city designed for walking, with all the major sights in a concentrated area. The only problem is that the sidewalks in summer are almost unbearably crowded.

The ***centro storico*** (historic center) is split by the **Arno River,** which usually is serene but can at times turn ferocious with floodwaters. The major part of Florence, certainly its historic core with most of the monuments, lies on the north ("right") side of the river. But the "left" side isn't devoid of attractions, including some wonderful trattorie and some great shopping finds, not to mention the Pitti Palace and the Giardini di Boboli, a series of impressive formal gardens. In addition, you'll want to cross over to check out the panoramic views of the city from Piazzale Michelangiolo—especially breathtaking at sunset.

The Arno is spanned by eight bridges, of which the **Ponte Vecchio (Old Bridge),** lined with overhanging jewelry stores, is the most celebrated and most central. Many of these bridges were ancient structures until the Nazis, in a hopeless last-ditch effort, senselessly destroyed them in their "defense" of Florence in 1944. With tenacity, Florence rebuilt its bridges, using pieces from the destroyed structures whenever possible. The **Ponte Santa Trínita** is the second-most important bridge. It leads to **Via dei Tornabuoni,** the right bank's most important shopping street (don't look for bargains, however). At the Ponte Vecchio you can walk, again on the right bank of the Arno, along **Via per Santa Maria,** which becomes **Via Calimala.** This leads you into **Piazza della Repubblica,** a commercial district known for its cafes.

From here, you can take **Via Roma,** which leads directly into **Piazza di San Giovanni,** where you'll find the baptistry and its neighboring sibling, the larger **Piazza del Duomo,** with the world-famous cathedral and Giotto bell tower. From the far western edge of Piazza del Duomo you can take **Via del Proconsolo** south to **Piazza della Signoria,** to see the landmark Palazzo Vecchio and its sculpture-filled Loggia della Signoria.

High in the olive-planted hills overlooking Florence is the ancient town of **Fiesole,** with Etruscan and Roman ruins and a splendid cathedral.

The Red & the Black

Florence has two street-numbering systems—red (*rosso*) numbers or black (*nero*) numbers. Red numbers identify commercial enterprises, like shops and restaurants. Black numbers identify office buildings, private homes, apartment houses, or hotels. Renumbering without the color system is on the horizon, though no one seems exactly certain when it will be implemented. In this chapter, red-numbered addresses are indicated by an "R" following the building number, as in "39R."

Since street numbers are chaotic, it's better to get a cross street or some landmark if you're looking for an address along a long boulevard.

At the very least, arm yourself with a map from the tourist office (see "Visitor Information," above). Ask for the one *con un stradario* (with a street index), which shows all the roads and is better for navigation than their more generalized orientation version. But if you'd like to see Florence in any depth—particularly those little side streets—buy a **Falk map,** available at all bookstores and at most newsstands.

Neighborhoods In Brief

Florence isn't divided into neighborhoods the way many cities are. Most locals refer to either the left bank or the right bank of the Arno and that's about it, unless they head out of town for the immediate environs, such as Fiesole. The following selection of "neighborhoods"—most grouped around a palace, church, or square—is therefore rather arbitrary.

This section will give you some idea of where you may want to stay and where the major attractions are.

Centro Called simply that by Florentines, **Centro** could include all the historic heart of Florence, but mostly the term is used to describe the area southwest of the Duomo. This district isn't as important as it used to be, as Piazza della Signoria (see below) now attracts more visitors. Centro's heyday was in the 1800s, when it was filled with narrow medieval streets that were torn down to make a grander city center. Lost forever were great homes of the Medicis and the Sacchettis, among others. **Piazza della Repubblica,** though faded, is still lively day and night with its celebrated cafes, like **Giubbe Rosse** (1888) and **Caffè Gilli** (1733). Centro's **Via dei Tournabuoni** is the city's most elegant shopping street. Pause on this street at no. 83, **La Giacosa,** for a *battistero* (pastry) before continuing to survey the palazzi and the high-quality but high-priced merchandise.

Piazza del Duomo In the heart of Florence, **Piazza del Duomo** and its surrounding area are dominated by the tricolored **Duomo,** site of the former local grain and hay markets. It's one of the largest buildings in the Christian world, and you come on it unexpectedly because the surrounding buildings weren't torn down to give it breathing room. Capped by Brunelleschi's dome, the structure now dominates the skyline. Every visitor flocks here to see not only the Duomo but also the neighboring **campanile** (bell tower), one of Italy's most beautiful, and the **baptistry** across the way. Now consecrated to St. John the Baptist, the baptistry was originally a pagan temple honoring Mars. Its doors are among the jewels of Renaissance sculpture. Also in this neighborhood is the **Museo dell'Opera del Duomo,** a sculpture haven that includes some of the most important works of Donatello. The Duomo is a central location that's naturally loaded with hotels in all price categories. The streets to the north of the Duomo are long and often traffic-ridden, but those to the south make up a wonderful medieval tangle of alleys and tiny squares heading toward Piazza della Signoria.

Piazza della Signoria The core of pre-Renaissance Florence, this area has been the site of many dramatic moments, including Savonarola's "bonfire of the vanities," in which Florentines burned precious items like jewelry and paintings to purify themselves. The surrounding narrow streets from the Middle Ages were the former stamping ground of Dante and other legendary Florentines. Today, this heavily visited square is home to the **Loggia dei Lanzi,** with Cellini's *Perseus* holding up a beheaded Medusa, Florence's most photographed statue (the original was removed for restoration, and this is a copy), as well as Michelangelo's *David* (also a copy, the original having been moved inside to protect it from the elements). To the south are the **Galleria**

degli Uffizi and the **Palazzo Vecchio.** This is the city's civic heart and perhaps the best bet for museum hounds. It's a well-polished part of the tourist zone yet still retains the narrow medieval streets where Dante grew up—back alleys where tour-bus crowds rarely set foot. The few blocks just north of the Ponte Vecchio have good shopping, but unappealing modern buildings were planted here to replace the district that was destroyed in World War II. The whole neighborhood can be stiflingly crowded in summer, but in those moments when you catch it empty of tour groups, it remains the most romantic part of Florence.

Piazza Santa Maria Novella & the Train Station On the northwestern edge of central Florence is the large Piazza Santa Maria Novella, with its church of the same name. This area isn't all art and culture, however. Northwest of Santa Maria Novella is the city's busiest section, centered at **Piazza della Stazione,** where the **Stazione di Santa Maria Novella** is located. Like all rail stations in Italy, it's surrounded by budget hotels, some of dubious quality. Leading off of **Piazza dell'Unitá Italiana,** Via del Melarancio goes a short distance east to **San Lorenzo,** the first cathedral of Florence. Beyond San Lorenzo is **Piazza Madonna degli Aldobrandini,** one of the more forgettable squares were it not the entrance to the **Medici Chapels.** Because it is, thousands can be seen flocking here to see Michelangelo's tombs, whose allegorical figures of *Day* and *Night* are among the most famous sculptures of all time. Southwest of Piazza Santa Maria Novella, toward the Arno, is **Piazza Ognissanti,** a fashionable (albeit congested) Renaissance square opening onto the river. On this square are two of the city's most legendary hotels: the **Grand** and the **Excelsior.**

Piazza San Marco Although **Piazza San Marco** has none of the grandeur of the square of the same name in Venice, the piazza and its surroundings on the northern fringe of Centro are nevertheless one of the most important in Florence—centered around its church, now the **Museo di San Marco.** Located in a former Dominican monastery, the museum houses a collection of the greatest works of Fra Angelico, who decorated the walls of the monks' cells with edifying scenes. This area is also overrun by visitors, most rushing to the **Galleria dell'Accademia** on Via Ricasoli to see the monumental figure of *David* (1501–04) by Michelangelo. Other area highlights are **Piazza della Santissima Annunziata,** Florence's most beautiful, graced by an equestrian statue of Ferdinand I de' Medici by Bologna. The square is also the setting for **Santissima Annunziata,** the church of the Servite Order, built by Michelozzo in the 15th century.

Piazza Santa Croce This section and its **Piazza Santa Croce** is in the southeastern part of the old town, near the Arno, and is dominated by the Gothic church of **Santa Croce** (Holy Cross), completed in 1442. Once the scene of jousts and festivals, even *calcio* (a local game of football), the piazza in time became the headquarters of the Franciscans, who established a firm base there in 1218. The area is always full of visitors but isn't as congested as the areas above. The church contains the tombs of Michelangelo and Machiavelli, among others. A little distance to the north of Santa Croce is the **Casa Buonarroti,** on Via Ghibellina, which Michelangelo acquired for his nephew. Today it's a museum with a collection of Michelangelo works, mainly drawings, gathered by his nephew. From here you can follow Via Buonarroti to **Piazza dei Ciompi,** a lively square that's off the beaten track, filled with stalls peddling secondhand goods. Look for old coins, books, and even antique Italian uniforms.

Ponte Vecchio Southwest of Piazza della Signoria is the **Ponte Vecchio (Old Bridge)** area. The oldest of Florence's bridges, it's flanked by jewelry stores and will carry you to the Oltrarno. This has always been a strategic crossing place, even when it was a stone bridge. In the Middle Ages it was the center for leather craftspeople, fishmongers, and butchers, but over the years jewelers' shops have moved in. The **Vasari Corridor (Corridoio Vasariano)** runs the length of the bridge above the shops—built by Vasari in just 5 months. Actually, the Ponte Vecchio was almost destroyed on the night of August 4, 1944, when the Nazi hierarchy gave orders to blow up all the bridges along the Arno. Even though mined, the Ponte Vecchio was miraculously spared. One of the most congested parts of Florence, this area is on every visitor's itinerary.

Across the Arno The "left bank" of the Arno River, known as the **Oltrarno,** is home to the **Palazzo Pitti,** with its picture gallery and **Giardini di Boboli;** Massacio's frescoes in the church of **Santa Maria del Carmine;** artisans' workshops; some good restaurants; and the postcard panorama of Florence and its dome from **Piazzale Michelangiolo.** At the top of the gardens is an elegant fortress known as the **Forte Belvedere** (1590–95). It affords one of the most panoramic views of Florence and is well worth the climb. The center of this district is **Piazza Santo Spirito,** a lovely square shaded by trees.

2 Getting Around

Because Florence is so compact, walking is the ideal way to get around—and at times the only way, because of numerous pedestrian zones. In theory at least, pedestrians have the right of way at uncontrolled zebra crossings, but don't count on that should you encounter a speeding Vespa.

BY BUS

If you plan to use public buses, you must buy your ticket before boarding, but for 1,500L (75¢) you can ride on any public bus for a total of 60 minutes. A 3-hour pass is 2,500L ($1.25) and a 4-hour ticket costs 5,800L ($2.90). You can buy bus tickets at *tabacchi* (tobacconists) and newsstands. Once on board, you must validate your ticket in the box near the rear door or you stand to be fined 80,000L ($40), no excuses accepted. The local **bus station** (which serves as the terminal for ATAF city buses) is at Piazza della Stazione (☎ **055-56501**), behind the train station.

Bus routes are posted at bus stops, but the numbers of routes can change overnight, because of sudden repair work going on at one of the ancient streets—perhaps a water main broke overnight and caused flooding. We recently found that a bus route map printed only 1 week prior was already out of date. Therefore, if you're dependent on bus transport, you'll need to inquire that day for the exact number of the vehicle you wish to board.

BY TAXI

You can find taxis at stands at nearly all the major squares. Rates are a bit expensive: The charge is 1,500L (75¢) per kilometer, with a 6,500L ($3.25) minimum. If you need a **radio taxi,** call ☎ **055-4390** or 055-4798.

A Walking Warning

Be aware that some of the sidewalks are less than 3 feet wide, summer brings dense crowds, and traffic is hazardous. Although the general public can't drive in Florence, taxis, locals with parking permits, and endless numbers of motor scooters can and do. Also be sure to wear strong, sturdy shoes before facing the cobbled or flagstone streets.

BY BICYCLE & MOTOR SCOOTER

Bicycles and motor scooters, if you avoid the whizzing traffic, are two other practical ways of getting around. **Alinari,** near the rail station at Via Guelfa 85R (☎ **055/280-500**), rents bikes for 4,000 to 5,000L ($2 to $2.50) per hour or 20,000 to 30,000L ($10 to $15) per day, depending on the model. Also available are small-engined, rather loud motor scooters renting for 15,000L ($7.50) per hour, 50,000L ($25) per 5 hours, or 80,000L ($40) per day. Renters must be 18 or over and must leave a passport, driver's license, and the number of a valid credit card. Alinari is open Monday to Saturday 9:30am to 1pm and 3 to 7:30pm, Sunday (April to October) 10am to 1pm and 3 to 7pm.

BY CAR

Just forget it. Driving in Florence is hopeless—not only because of the snarled traffic and the maze of one-way streets but also because much of what you've come to see is in a pedestrian zone. If you arrive by car, look for prominently posted blue signs with the letter **P** that will lead you to the nearest garage. If your hotel doesn't have its own, someone on the staff will direct you to the nearest one or will arrange valet parking. Garage fees average 35,000 to 50,000L ($17.50 to $25), though vans or large luxury cars may cost as much as 60,000L ($30).

The most centrally located garages are the **International Garage,** Via Palazzuolo 29 (☎ **055/282-386**); **Garage La Stazione,** Via Alamanni (☎ **055/284-768**); **Autoparking SLL,** Via Fiesolana 19 (☎ **055/247-7871**); and **Garage Anglo-Americano,** Via dei Barbadori 5 (☎ **055/214-418**). If these are full, you can almost always find a space at the **Garage Porte Nuove,** Via delle Portenuove 21 (☎ **055/333-355**).

You will, however, need a car to explore the surrounding countryside of Tuscany in any depth. Car-rental agencies include **Avis,** Borgo Ognissanti 128R (☎ **800/831-8000** in North America or 055/213-629 locally; www.avis.com); **Italy by Car,** Vorgo Ognissanti 134R (☎ **055/287-161**); and **Hertz,** Via del Termine (☎ **800/654-3131** in North America or 055/307-370 locally; www.hertz.com).

Fast Facts: Florence

American Express The office is at Via Dante Alighieri 22R (☎ **055/50-981**); it's open Monday to Friday 9am to 5:30pm and Saturday 9am to 12:30pm.

Consulates The **U.S. Consulate** is at Lungarno Amerigo Vespucci 38 (☎ **055/239-8276**), open Monday to Friday 9am to 12:30pm and 2 to 3:30pm. The **U.K. Consulate** is at Lungarno Corsini 2 (☎ **055/284-133**), near Piazza Santa Trinità, open Monday to Friday 9:30am to 12:30pm and 2:30 to 4:30pm. Citizens of other English-speaking countries, including **Canada, Australia,** and **New Zealand,** should contact their diplomatic representatives in Rome (see chapter 3).

Currency Exchange Local banks have the best rates, and most are open Monday to Friday 8:30am to 1:30pm and 2:45 to 3:45pm. The tourist office (see "Visitor Information," earlier in this chapter) exchanges money at official rates when banks are closed and on holidays, but a commission is often charged. You can also go to the Ufficio Informazione booth at the rail station, open daily 7:30am to 7:40pm. American Express (above) also exchanges money. One of the best places to exchange currency is the post office (below).

Dentists/Doctors For a list of English-speaking doctors or dentists, consult your consulate or contact **Tourist Medical Service,** Via Lorenzo il Magnifico 59

(☎ **055/475-411**). Visits without an appointment are possible only Monday to Friday 11am to noon and 5 to 6pm. After hours, an answering service gives names and phone numbers of dentists and doctors who are on duty.

Emergencies For fire, call ☎ **115;** for an ambulance, call ☎ **118;** for the police, ☎ **113;** and for road service, ☎ **116.**

Hospitals Call the **General Hospital** of Santa Maria Nuova, Piazza Santa Maria Nuova 1 (☎ **055/27-581**).

Internet Access You can check your messages or send e-mail at **Internet Train,** Via dell'Orivolo 40R (☎ **055/234-5322;** e-mail: info@fionline.it; www.fionline.it).

Pharmacies The **Farmacia Molteni,** Via Calzaiuoli 7R (☎ **055/215-472**), is open 24 hours.

Police Dial ☎ **113** in an emergency. English-speaking foreigners who want to see and talk to the police should go to the **Ufficio Stranieri station,** Via Zara 2 (☎ **055/49-771**), where English-speaking personnel are available daily 9am to 2pm.

Post Office The **Central Post Office** is at Via Pellicceria 3, off Piazza della Repubblica (☎ **055/277-4322** for English-speaking operators), open Monday to Saturday 8:15am to 7pm. You can buy stamps and telephone cards at Windows 21 and 22. If you want your mail sent to Italy general delivery (*fermo posta*), have it sent in care of this post office (use the 50100 Firenze postal code). A foreign exchange office is open Monday to Friday 8:15am to 6pm; you can also exchange money (notes only) at ATMs on the ground floor daily 8:15am to 7pm. If you want to send packages of up to 20kg, go to the rear of the building and enter at Piazza Davantati 4.

Rest Rooms Public toilets are found in most galleries, museums, bars and cafes, and restaurants, as well as bus, train, and air terminals. Usually they're designated as *WC* (water closet) or *donne* (women) or *uomini* (men). The most confusing designation is *signori* (gentlemen) and *signore* (ladies), so watch that final *i* and *e!*

Safety Violent crimes are rare in Florence; most crime consists mainly of pickpockets who frequent crowded tourist centers, such as corridors of the Uffizi Galleries. Members of group tours who cluster together are often singled out as victims. Car thefts are relatively common: Don't leave your luggage in an unguarded car, even if it's locked in the trunk. Women should be especially careful in avoiding purse snatchers, some of whom grab a purse while whizzing by on a Vespa, often knocking the woman down. Documents like passports and extra money are better stored in safes at your hotel if available.

Telephone The **country code** for Italy is **39.** The **city code** for Florence is **055;** use this code when calling from *anywhere* outside or inside Italy—even within Florence itself (and you must now include the zero every time, even when calling from abroad). See the Fast Facts at the end of chapter 2 (or the back cover of this book) for complete details on how to call Italy, how to place calls within Italy, and how to call home once you're in Italy.

Public pay phones accept either coins (100L, 200L, or 500L coins) or a phone card (sometimes only one or the other). The latter, a *carta telefonica* (or *scheda telefonica*), is available at tabacchi and bars in 5,000L ($2.50), 10,000L ($5), and 15,000L ($7.50) denominations and can be used for local or international calls.

Break off the perforated corner of the card before using it. Local phone calls cost 280L (15¢), enough to put you in contact with AT&T, MCI, or Sprint's direct-dialing international operators (below). To make a call, lift the receiver, insert a coin or card, and dial.

You can place **long-distance and international calls** at the Telecom office north of the Duomo at Via Cavour 21R (open daily 8am to 9:45pm).

3 Accommodations

For sheer charm and luxury, Florence's accommodations are among the finest in Europe, and many of the grand old villas and palaces have been converted into hotels. There aren't too many cities where you can find a 15th- or 16th-century palace—tastefully decorated and most comfortable—rated a second-class *pensione.* Florence is equipped with hotels in all price ranges and with widely varying standards, comfort, service, and efficiency.

However, during summer there simply aren't enough rooms to meet the demand, so it's best to reserve well in advance. If you arrive without a reservation and don't want to wander around town on your own looking for a room, go in person (instead of calling) to the **Consorzio ITA office** (☎ **055/282-893**) in the rail terminal at Piazza della Stazione, open daily 8:45am to 8pm. The Consorizio ITA charges 4,500 to 15,000L ($2.25 to $7.50) for the service and collects the first night's room charge.

The most desirable, and often most expensive, place to stay in terms of shopping, nightlife, sightseeing, and restaurants is the historic heart on the Arno's right bank, especially in Centro and around the Duomo and Piazza della Signoria. Yes, this area is touristy, but staying here is a lot better than staying on the outskirts—inadequate public transport makes commuting difficult. Driving into the center is impossible, because of the heavy traffic and because major districts are pedestrian-only zones.

Opened in 1896, the legendary **Savoy Hotel,** Piazza della Repubblica 7, 50123 Firenze (☎ **055/283-313;** fax 055/284-840; www.rfhotels.com/savoy; e-mail: reservations@hotelsavoy.it), closed for renovations in 1999. When it reopens for the summer of 2000, it seems likely to be at the top of Florence's grand hotels. Ferragamo (of shoe fame) bought the landmark building, but it'll be operated by the Forte chain and will offer 101 rooms decorated sumptuously in a turn-of-the-century style just a few steps from some of the great treasures of the Renaissance. The hotel is also preparing to launch an international restaurant here, with both foreign and Italian regional specialties, many from Tuscany. Of course, the rates (not set at press time) will be astronomical. (Ferragamo is also behind the new Gallery Art Hotel, an elegant boutique hotel near the Uffizi.)

The cheapest lodgings in Centro are around the rail station; these are also the least desirable—with a few notable exceptions. The area directly around the Termini and Santa Maria Novella, though generally safe during the day, is the center of major drug dealing late at night and should be avoided then. This area isn't all budget lodgings, however; also here is Piazza Ognissanti (south of Piazza Santa Maria Novella toward the Arno), one of Florence's most fashionable squares and the home of the city's two most famous hotels. Also in the historic center, but less tourist trodden and a bit more tranquil, is the area around Piazza San Marco and the University quarter.

Once you cross the Arno, lodgings are much scarcer, though there are places to stay, including some *pensioni.* In general, prices are lower across the Arno, and you'll be near one of the major attractions, the Pitti Palace. Many luxury hotels exist on the outskirts of Florence, as do cheaper boardinghouses. Again, these are acceptable alternatives if

Florence Accommodations

Albergo Losanna **36**
Augustus Gallery Hotel Art **20**
Grand Hotel **10**
Grand Hotel Cavour **41**
Grand Hotel Villa Medici **8**
Hermitage Hotel **23**
Hotel Albani Firenze **4**
Hotel Ariele **9**
Hotel Astoria Palazzo Gaddi **14**
Hotel Augustus **22**
Hotel Bellettini **15**
Hotel Berkleys **3**
Hotel Calzaiuoli **42**
Hotel Casci **32**
Hotel Cellai **28**
Hotel Cimabue **29**
Hotel Continental **21**
Hotel Elite **7**
Hotel Europa **33**
Hotel Excelsior **11**
Hotel Helvetia & Bristol **16**
Hotel J and J **39**
Hotel La Due Fontane **35**
Hotel Le Vigne **12**
Hotel Malaspina **27**
Hotel Mario's **1**
Hotel Monna Lisa **40**
Hotel Morandi alla Crocetta **36**
Hotel Nuova Italia **5**
Hotel Regency **37**
Hotel Splendor **31**
Hotel Tornabuoni Beacci **17**
Hotel Torre Guelfa **19**
Hotel Vasari **2**
Hotel Villa Carlotta **25**
Loggiato dei Serviti **34**
Pensione Annalena **26**
Pensione Bretagna **18**
Pensione Burchianti **13**
Piccolo Hotel **30**
Plaza Hotel Lucchesi **44**
Savoy Hotel **43**
Torre di Bellosguardo **24**
Villa Azalée **6**
Villa La Massa **45**
Villa Montartino **46**

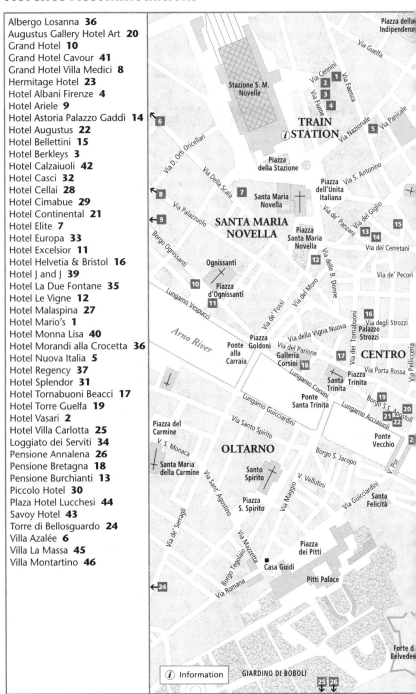

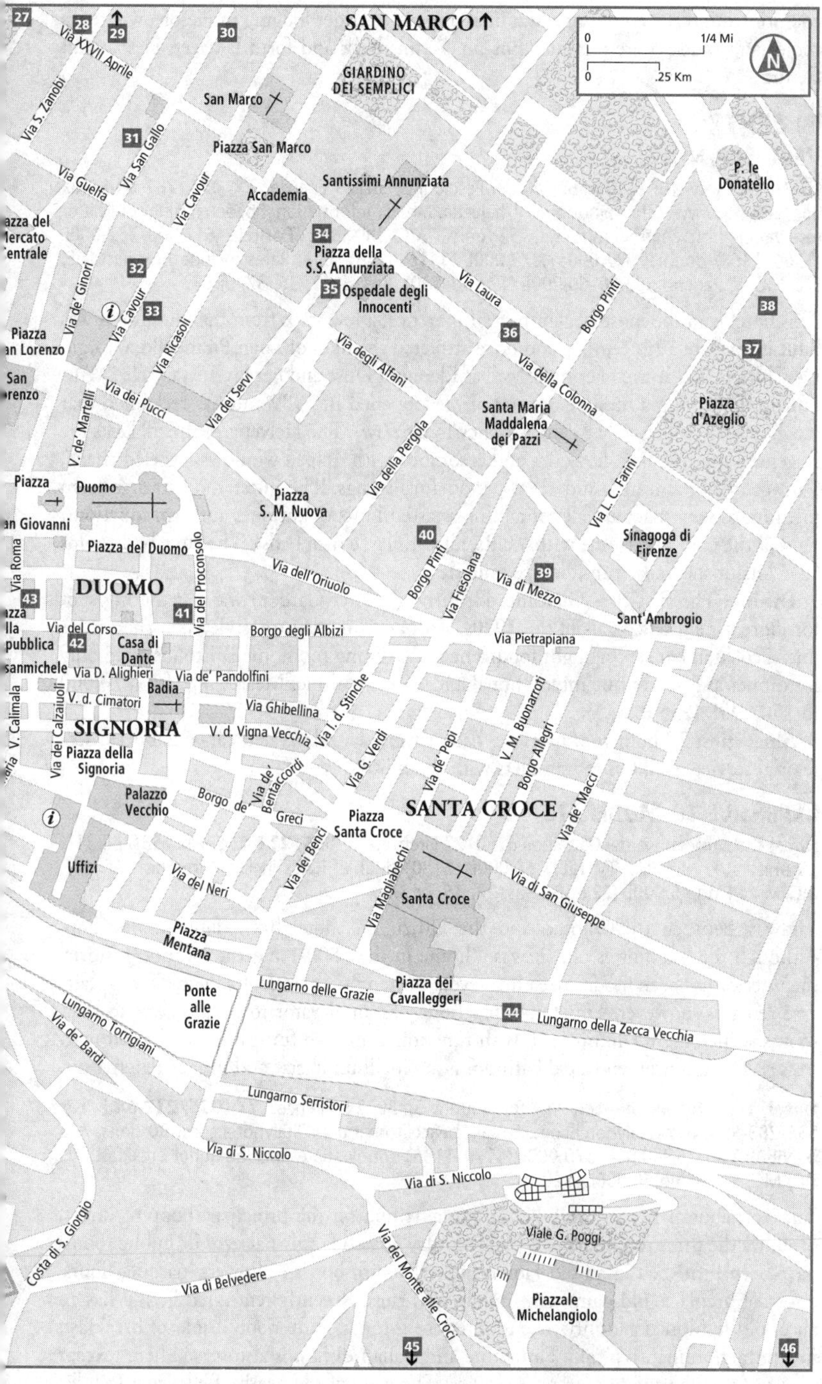
SAN MARCO
0 1/4 Mi
0 .25 Km
N
GIARDINO DEI SEMPLICI
San Marco
Piazza San Marco
Santissimi Annunziata
Accademia
Piazza della S.S. Annunziata
Ospedale degli Innocenti
P. le Donatello
Via XXVII Aprile
Via S. Zanobi
Via San Gallo
Via Guelfa
Via Cavour
Via de' Ginori
Via Ricasoli
Via dei Servi
Via dei Pucci
V. de' Martelli
Via Laura
Borgo Pinti
Via degli Alfani
Via della Colonna
Santa Maria Maddalena dei Pazzi
Piazza d'Azeglio
Via della Pergola
Via L. C. Farini
Piazza S. M. Nuova
Sinagoga di Firenze
Piazza San Lorenzo
Duomo
Piazza del Duomo
Via del Proconsolo
Via dell'Oriuolo
Borgo Pinti
Via Fiesolana
Via di Mezzo
Sant'Ambrogio
DUOMO
Via Roma
Via del Corso
Borgo degli Albizi
Via Pietrapiana
Casa di Dante
Via D. Alighieri
Via de' Pandolfini
Badia
V. d. Cimatori
Via Ghibellina
SIGNORIA
V. d. Vigna Vecchia
Via I. d. Stinche
Via G. Verdi
Via de' Pepi
V. M. Buonarroti
Borgo Allegri
Via de' Calzaiuoli
V. Calimala
Piazza della Signoria
Palazzo Vecchio
Borgo de' Greci
Via de' Bentaccordi
Piazza Santa Croce
SANTA CROCE
Via de' Macci
Uffizi
Via del Neri
Via dei Benci
Via Magliabechi
Santa Croce
Via di San Giuseppe
Piazza Mentana
Ponte alle Grazie
Lungarno delle Grazie
Piazza dei Cavalleggeri
Lungarno della Zecca Vecchia
Lungarno Torrigiani
Via de' Bardi
Lungarno Serristori
Via di S. Niccolo
Via di S. Niccolo
Viale G. Poggi
Costa di S. Giorgio
Via di Belvedere
Via del Monte alle Croci
Piazzale Michelangiolo
27 28 29 30 31 32 33 34 35 36 37 38 39 40 41 42 43 44 45 46

you don't mind the commute. As a final option, consider lodging in Fiesole, where it's cooler and much more tranquil. Bus no. 7 runs back and forth between Fiesole and Centro.

IN CENTRO

VERY EXPENSIVE

✪ **Hotel Helvetia & Bristol.** Via dei Pescioni 2, 50123 Firenze. ☎ **055/287-814.** Fax 055/288-353. www.charminghotels.it/helvetia. E-mail: information_hbf@charminghotels.it or reservation_hbf@charminghotels.it. 52 units. A/C MINIBAR TV TEL. 612,000–732,000L ($306–$366) double; 832,000–1,872,000L ($416–$936) suite. Rates include breakfast. AE, DC, MC, V. Parking 55,000–60,000L ($27.50–$30). Bus: 6, 11, 36, 37, or 68.

This hotel is in the most elegant part of Florence, a few steps from the Duomo. It was built in the late 19th century and once attracted the likes of Luigi Pirandello, Giorgio De Chirico, and Enrico Fermi, as well as Eleonora Duse and her lover, Gabriele D'Annunzio. Following a massive restoration, it reopened in 1989 and has reclaimed that old glory; it's rivaled only by the Regency (see below). The Helvetia & Bristol lacks the Regency's modern flair, however, and is somber, with draped windows, tasseled chairs, 15th-century paintings, and regal period furnishings. The guest rooms range from medium to very spacious, all containing a tasteful mix of antiques and reproductions, plus all the comforts (some with VCRs, all with large firm beds). The large bathrooms have lots of shelf space and deluxe toiletries.

Dining: The first-class Giardino d'Inverno (Winter Garden) was a gathering spot for Florentine intellectuals in the 1920s, with an 18th century–style open gallery. It's now a cocktail bar serving light food. The main dining room, the Bristol, is open only for dinner and serves fine international and Tuscan cuisine. Meals range from 70,000 to 150,000L ($35 to $75).

Amenities: 24-hour room service, baby-sitting, laundry/valet, car-rental desk, secretarial service, facilities for travelers with disabilities.

EXPENSIVE TO MODERATE

Hotel Calzaiuoli. Via dei Calzaiuoli 6, 50122 Firenze. ☎ **055/212-456.** Fax 055/268-310. 45 units. A/C MINIBAR TV TEL. 360,000L ($180) double. Rates include breakfast. AE, DC, MC, V. Parking 45,000L ($22.50). Bus: 22, 36, or 37.

Midway between the Duomo and the Uffizi, this hotel has a fabulous location. Although the building is old (it was a home in the 1800s) and the location historic, the interior has been modernized in a severe contemporary style. Its Pietra Serena staircase remains, however. This four-story hotel has an elevator to bring guests to their rooms, which are medium-sized, with functional modern furnishings and good mattresses. The recently renovated bathrooms are medium in size and immaculately kept.

Hotel Tornabuoni Beacci. Via Tornabuoni 3, 50123 Firenze. ☎ **055/212-645.** Fax 055/283-594. www.italyhotel.com. E-mail: beacci.tornabuoni@italyhotel.com. 30 units. A/C MINIBAR TV TEL. 340,000–370,000L ($170–$185) double. Rates include buffet breakfast. AE, DC, MC, V. Parking 40,000L ($20).

The Tornabuoni Beacci, near Piazza Santa Trinita on the principal shopping street, occupies the three top floors of a 16th-century Strozzi family palazzo. Its public rooms have been furnished in an old Florentine style, with bowls of flowers, parquet floors, a formal fireplace, old paintings, murals, and rugs. Recently renovated, it still has an air of old-fashioned gentility. The roof terrace is for late-afternoon drinks or breakfast; in summer, dinner, typically Florentine and Italian dishes, is also served here (except in August, when the restaurant is closed). The view of the nearby Bellosguardo hills,

Family-Friendly Hotels

Hotel Casci *(see p. 188)* This inexpensive gem has a great location in the historic district, and many of its rooms are rented as triples and quads, ideal for families.

Hotel Berkleys *(see p. 185)* The family on a budget gravitates to this modest hotel east of the rail station, occupying the top floor of an old apartment building. The hotel rents triples and quads suitable for families—all at a good price though a bit crowded.

Hotel Nuova Italia *(see p. 186)* Families get special discounts at this 17th-century building near the rail station, and the hotel offers some very spacious rooms suitable for large broods.

churches, towers, and rooftops is wonderful. The guest rooms are moderately well furnished but worn, and top-floor rooms, though a bit cramped, open onto views of the rooftops. The mattresses still have a lot of comfort in them. The loveliest part of the whole place is a cozy reading room with a 1600s tapestry.

INEXPENSIVE

Pensione Bretagna. Lungarno Corsini 6, 50123 Firenze. ☎ **055/289-618.** Fax 055/289-619. www.agora.stm.it/market/bretagna. E-mail: hotelpens.bretagna@agora.stm.it. 18 units, 9 with bathroom. TV TEL. 165,000L ($82.50) double without bathroom, 185,000L ($92.50) double with bathroom; 240,000L ($120) triple with bathroom. Rates include breakfast. AE, DC, MC, V. Parking 35,000L ($17.50). Bus: B, C, 37, or 11.

The Bretagna is in an early Renaissance palace that was the residence of Louis Napoléon in the 1820s, though it's rather simply furnished today. It's a good inexpensive choice, renovated in 1998, and run by a helpful staff, most of whom speak English. The public rooms are impressive, with gilded stucco work, painted ceilings, fireplaces, and a balcony overlooking the Arno. The guest rooms are small but cozy and well kept, with firm mattresses; the private bathrooms are small as well, and the hall bathrooms are always clean. Usually some hair dryers are available on request.

NEAR PIAZZA DEL DUOMO

EXPENSIVE

✪ **Hotel J and J.** Via di Mezzo 20, 50121 Firenze. ☎ **055/263-121.** Fax 055/240-282. www.jandjhotel.com. E-mail: jandj@dada.it. 19 units. A/C MINIBAR TV TEL. 450,000–500,000L ($225–$250) double; 550,000L ($275) junior suite; from 630,000L ($315) suite. Rates include breakfast. AE, DC, MC, V. Parking 35,000–45,000L ($17.50–$22.50). Bus: A.

A 5-minute walk from Santa Croce, this charming hotel was built in the 16th century as a monastery and underwent a massive restoration in 1990. You'll find many sitting areas throughout, including a flagstone-covered courtyard with stone columns and a salon with vaulted ceilings and preserved ceiling frescoes. The guest rooms combine an unusual mix of modern furniture with the original beamed ceilings. The suites usually contain sleeping lofts and, in some cases, rooftop balconies overlooking Florence's historic core. Most of the rooms are surprisingly spacious, and each comes with a luxury mattress and good linen. The bathrooms contain robes and hair dryers; some even have whirlpool tubs.

Dining: Breakfast, the only meal offered, is served in a room filled with cane chairs. Tables here overlook a lovely courtyard.

Amenities: Concierge, laundry/dry cleaning, room service at breakfast.

MODERATE

Grand Hotel Cavour. Via del Proconsolo 3, 50122 Firenze. ☎ **055/282-461.** Fax 055/218-955. www.hotelcavour.com. E-mail: info@hotelcavour.com. 91 units. A/C MINIBAR TV TEL. 320,000L ($160) double. Rates include buffet breakfast. AE, CB, DC, MC, V. Parking 40,000–45,000L ($20–$22.50). Bus: 14, 23, or 71.

Opposite the Bargello, this 13th-century palace stands on one of Florence's noisiest streets (even double-glazed windows can't quite blot out the sounds). Check out the coved main lounge, with its frescoed ceiling and crystal chandelier, and the chapel now used as a dining room (the altar and confessional are still there). The guest rooms are traditional and comfortable but a little too claustrophobic; the beds are old, but the mattresses are still comfortable. The bathrooms have enough shelf space and hair dryers. On every floor is a bathroom specially fitted for travelers with disabilities.

At the front desk the professional English-speaking staff will offer you car-rental service and organize city tours on request. The roof terrace, "Michelangelo," offers a panoramic sweep over the Duomo, Palazzo Vecchio, and more. A refined Tuscan cuisine is served in the rather staid restaurant honoring Beatrice in its name. Besides the restaurant, tastefully decorated with frescoes by Galileo Chini, the hotel offers the charming atmosphere of the wine cellar "Cantina degli Angeli," featuring regional and national wines. Laundry and baby-sitting are available, as are facilities for the disabled.

NEAR PIAZZA SANTA MARIA NOVELLA & THE TRAIN STATION

VERY EXPENSIVE

Grand Hotel. Piazza Ognissanti 1, 50123 Firenze. ☎ **800/325-3589** in the U.S. and Canada, or 055/288781. Fax 055/217400. www.firenzealbergo.it/home/grandhotel. E-mail: info@theluxurycollection.firenze.net. 107 units. A/C MINIBAR TV TEL. 750,000–950,000L ($375–$475) double; from 1,600,000L ($800) suite. AE, DC, MC, V. Parking from 60,000L ($30). Bus: 6 or 17.

The Grand is a bastion of luxury across from the even more luxurious Excelsior (see below), but neither is as exclusive as the Regency (below). After a long slumber, the hotel was restored to some of its former glory when ITT Sheraton bought the CIGA chain, and its belle époque lounges are truly grand. The guest rooms and suites have a refined elegance meant to evoke 15th-century Florence, with silks, brocades, and real or reproduction antiques, and the most desirable overlook the Arno. The custom-made Italian mattresses are among the finest in town. The large bathrooms, adorned in two types of Italian marble, are filled with amenities, like shower caps, plush bathrobes, separate phone lines, hair dryers, cantilevered toilets, and designer bidets.

Dining/Diversions: A highlight is the restored Winter Garden, an enclosed court lined with arches where regional and seasonal specialties, along with an array of international dishes, are served. Guests gather at night in the Fiorino Bar to listen to piano music.

Amenities: Room service, baby-sitting, laundry/valet, currency exchange, facilities for travelers with disabilities.

Grand Hotel Villa Medici. Via il Prato 42, 50123 Firenze. ☎ **055/238-1331.** Fax 055/238-1336. www.venere.it/firenze/villa_medici. E-mail: villa.medici@italyhotel.com. 103 units. A/C MINIBAR TV TEL. 786,000L ($393) double; from 1,375,000L ($687.50) suite. AE, CB, DC, MC, V. Parking 45,000–60,000L ($22.50–$30). Bus: 9, 13, 16, 17, or 26.

This old-time favorite occupies an 18th-century Medici palace 2 blocks southwest of the train station. It generally appeals more to Europeans than to Americans, who may want more up-to-date facilities, though it was renovated in 1998 (when the guest rooms were spruced up and given new mattresses and electronic safes). The most peaceful rooms front the garden; however, during the day there's noise from the convent school next door. The Carrara-marble bathrooms are spacious and contain robes and hair dryers. We prefer the sixth-floor accommodations, as they open onto terraces. The staff is one of the best trained in Florence. Out back is a private garden (not Florence's finest) and a modest pool.

Dining/Diversions: The Lorenzo de' Medici and the Grill Lorenzino serve both international and Florentine cuisine. The restaurant is graced with marble pilasters and illuminated by Murano chandeliers, but the cuisine is only standard. A bar is open daily 8am to 1am, offering piano music after dinner.

Amenities: Room service, baby-sitting, laundry/valet, cleaning/pressing facilities, pool, fitness center.

Hotel Astoria Palazzo Gaddi. Via del Giglio 9, 50123 Firenze. ☎ **055/239-8095.** Fax 055/214-632. 106 units. A/C MINIBAR TV TEL. 550,000L ($275) double; from 720,000L ($360) suite. Rates include buffet breakfast. AE, DC, MC, V. Parking 40,000L ($20) nearby. Bus: 4.

Despite its location amid cheap hotels, this is an impressive Renaissance palace, and in the 17th century John Milton wrote parts of *Paradise Lost* in one of the rooms. It has been renovated and turned into a serviceable choice, with a helpful staff and experienced management. From the guest rooms on the upper floors, you'll have a view over the terra-cotta rooftops. All rooms have stylish traditional furnishings, with quality mattresses and fine linen, though some are decorated in a more sterile modern manner. The front rooms, overlooking a busy street, are noisiest. The bathrooms are first rate, with hair dryers.

Dining: The garden-style Palazzo Gaddi restaurant serves Tuscan cuisine. In summer, drinks and snacks are available on the recently opened roof garden.

Amenities: Room service, laundry, baby-sitting, car-rental desk, shopping boutique, currency exchange.

✪ **Hotel Excelsior.** Piazza Ognissanti 3, 50123 Firenze. ☎ **800/325-3535** in the U.S. and Canada, or 055/264-201. Fax 055/210-278. www.firenzealbergo.it/home/excelsior. E-mail: info@theluxurycollection.firenze.net. 191 units. A/C MINIBAR TV TEL. 680,000–770,000L ($340–$385) double; from 1,100,000L ($550) junior suite. AE, DC, MC, V. Parking 60,000L ($30). Bus: 6 or 17.

The sophisticated Excelsior is Florence's prime luxury address. The sumptuousness will bowl you over if the high prices don't first. This glamorous hotel boasts the best-trained staff in town. If you like glamour and glitz, check in here. Part of the hotel was once owned by Carolina Bonaparte, Napoléon's sister; the old palazzi were unified in 1927 and decorated with a liberal use of colored marbles, walnut furniture, oriental rugs, and neoclassical frescoes. The opulent guest rooms have 19th-century Florentine antiques, sumptuous fabrics, comfortable chairs, and great mattresses. The bathrooms boast heated towel racks, deluxe toiletries, and high ceilings. In these old palaces, expect accommodations to come in a variety of configurations. The rooms on the top floor have balconies overlooking the Arno and the Ponte Vecchio.

Dining/Diversions: Il Cestello serves an elegantly prepared international cuisine. The Donatello Bar is reviewed in "Florence After Dark," later in this chapter.

Amenities: Room service, baby-sitting, laundry/valet, express checkout, translation services, currency exchange, facilities for travelers with disabilities.

EXPENSIVE

Hotel Albani Firenze. Via Fiume 12, 50123 Firenze. ☎ **055/26-030.** Fax 055/211-045. www.hotelalbani.it. E-mail: info@hotelalbani.it. 90 units. A/C MINIBAR TV TEL. 380,000–530,000L ($190–$265) double; from 900,000L ($450) suite. Rates include breakfast. AE, DC, MC, V. Valet parking 35,000L ($17.50). Bus: 10, 12, 25, 31, or 32.

In 1993 a respected nationwide chain transformed a run-down pensione, a 10-minute walk from the Duomo, into one of Florence's most appealing four-star luxury hotels, set in a structure that was built around 1900 as a villa. Today, you'll find up-to-date comforts, artwork, and architectural embellishments. The high-ceilinged interiors sometimes verge on the theatrical but are never forbidding. The guest rooms, ranging from medium to spacious, possess style and grace, with mahogany beds and luxury mattresses, plus marble bathrooms with hair dryers.

Dining/Diversions: A restaurant serves traditional Italian and international food at lunch and dinner every day except Sunday. Adjacent is the hotel's bar, open daily 11am to 11pm; it serves wine by the glass and the usual array of American-style spirits and European brandies, cognacs, and liqueurs.

Amenities: Concierge, 24-hour room service, laundry/dry cleaning, newspaper delivery.

MODERATE

Hotel Malaspina. Piazza dell'Indipendenza 24, 50129 Firenze. ☎ **055/489-869.** Fax 055/474-809. E-mail: htmalsp@tin.it. 31 units. A/C MINIBAR TV TEL. 320,000L ($160) double. Rates include breakfast. AE, DC, MC, V. Bus: 10, 12, 25, 31, 32, or 91.

A 10-minute walk north of the Duomo, this three-story hotel opened in 1993, occupying a 19th-century structure (before that, it was a dorm for students at a nearby dentistry school). The interior has been carefully renovated and filled with traditional furniture that fits gracefully into the high-ceilinged public rooms and guest rooms. The windows are big, and the floors tend to be covered in glazed or terra-cotta tiles. The rooms are medium-sized, each with standard comforts, like a quality mattress and a bathroom with a hair dryer. Breakfast is the only meal served.

Hotel Mario's. Via Faenza 89, 50123 Firenze. ☎ **055/216-801.** Fax 055/212-039. www.webitaly.com/hotel.marios. E-mail: hotel.marios@webitaly.com. 16 units. A/C TV TEL. 170,000–290,000L ($85–$145) double; 220,000–360,000L ($110–$180) triple. Rates include breakfast. AE, CB, DC, MC, V. Parking 35,000L ($17.50). Bus: 10, 12, 25, 31, 32, or 91.

Two blocks from the rail station, this winning choice on the first floor of an old Florentine building has been a hotel since 1872, when the *Room with a View* crowd started arriving in search of the glory of the Renaissance. The spotless place has been completely restored and furnished in Florentine style. Mario Noce is a gracious host, and he and his staff speak English. Although you'll find cheaper inns in Florence, the service and hospitality make Mario's worth your lire. The guest rooms aren't very large but are furnished with taste; wrought-iron headboards frame firm mattresses. Several rooms open onto a small garden. The bathrooms are neat, with hair dryers and adequate shelf space. Breakfast is the only meal served; fresh flowers and fresh fruit are put out daily.

Hotel Vasari. Via B. Cennini 9–11, 50123 Firenze. ☎ **055/212-753.** Fax 055/294-246. 27 units. A/C MINIBAR TV TEL. 260,000L ($130) double. Rates include breakfast. AE, DC, MC, V. Parking 20,000L ($10). Bus 4, 7, 8, 10, or 13.

The Vasari has a rather literary history; for several years, it was the home of 19th-century French poet Alphonse de La Martine. Built in the 1840s as a home, it was a run-down two-star hotel until 1993, when its owners poured money into its renovation and upgraded it to one of the most reasonably priced three-star hotels in town. Its three stories are connected by elevator, and the rooms are comfortable, albeit somewhat spartan. Nonetheless, the beds are firm and the linen crisp. The tiled bathrooms, with hair dryers, are small but kept immaculate. Some of the public areas retain their elaborate vaulting.

Villa Azalée. Viale Fratelli Rosselli 44, 50123 Firenze. ☎ **055/214-242.** Fax 055/268-264. E-mail: villaazalee@fi.flashnet.it. 25 units. A/C MINIBAR TV TEL. 306,000L ($153) double; 412,000L ($206) triple. Rates include buffet breakfast. AE, DC, MC, V. Parking from 35,000L ($17.50) nearby. Bus: 1, 2, 9, 13, 16, 17, 26, 27, 29, 30, or 35.

The handsome Villa Azalée, with a big garden, is a remake of an 1870s home. The owners' personal touch is reflected in the atmosphere and the tasteful decor, featuring tall white-paneled doors with brass fittings, parquet floors, crystal chandeliers, and antiques mixed with good reproductions. We prefer the guest rooms in the villa instead of those in the more modern annex. They range from small to medium and boast an intimate elegant style; the second-floor rooms are better furnished and command greater views. Our favorite is no. 24 because it's larger and has a huge ceiling fresco from the 19th century. In the 19th century, the annex was the *scuderia* (stables), and the rooms here have been given a fake British style in their attempt to create a cozy Cotswold cottage look; the finest rooms are on the ground floor, as they're larger and more romantic, with heavy beamed ceilings. All the tiled bathrooms are small but well kept; they come with robes and hair dryers are available on request.

INEXPENSIVE

Hotel Ariele. Via Magenta 11, 50123 Firenze. ☎ **055/211-509.** Fax 055/268-521. 39 units. A/C TV TEL. 240,000L ($120) double; 300,000L ($150) triple. Rates include breakfast. AE, CB, DC, DISC, MC, V. Parking 25,000L ($12.50). Bus: A, B, or D.

A block from the Arno, the Ariele, a corner villa that has been converted into a roomy pensione, bills itself as "Your Home in Florence." The building is architecturally impressive, with large salons and lofty ceilings. The furnishings, however, combine antique with functional. The guest rooms are a grab bag of comfort; you can still get a good night's sleep even if the beds are a bit old (they're still firm). The bathrooms are cramped cubicles. Room service and baby-sitting are provided. Although breakfast is the only meal served, the staff will provide you with the names of some restaurants nearby, where the hotel's guests will receive discounts.

✪ **Hotel Bellettini.** Via di Conti 7, 50123 Firenze. ☎ **055/213-561.** Fax 055/283-551. www.firenze.net/hotelbelletini. E-mail: hotel.belletini@dada.it. 27 units, 23 with bathroom. A/C TV TEL. 170,000L ($85) double without bathroom, 200,000L ($100) double with bathroom. Rates include buffet breakfast. AE, DC, MC, V. Parking 35,000L ($17.50). Bus: 36 or 37.

For the kind of historic ambience you'll find here (not to mention the location midway between the Duomo and the rail station), this hotel charges refreshingly reasonable rates. The palazzo was built in the 1300s, with a history of innkeeping at least 300 years old, and is maintained by Tuscany-born sisters Marzia and Gina and their helpful staff. This place is so traditional—with terra-cotta floors, beamed ceilings, and touches of stained glass—you expect Henry James or Elizabeth Barrett Browning to check in at any minute. The rooms are plain (occasionally somewhat ascetic) but comfortable. About half have TVs, and many have sweeping views of Florence that could turn you into E. M. Forster. Even if this hotel isn't five star, it offers a comfortable ambience with queen or double beds, each with an aging but still firm mattress. The private bathrooms have adequate shelf space. Only two rooms per floor use the corridor bathrooms, so you'll rarely have to wait in line.

Hotel Berkleys. Via Fiume 11, 50123 Firenze. ☎ **055/238-2147.** Fax 055/212-302. 9 units. TV TEL. 170,000L ($85) double; 210,000L ($105) triple. Rates include breakfast. MC, V. Bus: 10, 12, 25, 31, or 91.

The pleasant but modest Berkleys, about a block east of the rail station, occupies the top floor of a 19th-century apartment building whose lower floors contain a pair of less desirable two-star hotels. The owners, the Andreoli family, are polite and friendly. The simple lobby leads into a breakfast nook and a bar area, where drinks are served on request. The guest rooms are a bit small but comfortable enough, with firm mattresses, and the baths are tiny though neat. Some rooms open onto balconies with views of Florence. Only two bedrooms have air conditioning. Amenities include room service and laundry service.

Hotel Elite. Via della Scala 12, 50123 Firenze. ☎ **055/215-395.** 8 units, 5 with private bathroom (3 with shower only). TV. 120,000L ($60) double with shower, 140,000L ($70) double with bathroom. No credit cards. Parking 30,000L ($15) nearby. Bus: 1, 2, 12, or 16.

The Elite is an attractive little pensione, located two floors above street level in a 19th-century apartment building about 2 blocks from the rail station. It's also convenient for exploring most of the major sights. Owner Maurizio Maccarini speaks English and is a welcoming host. The small hotel rents light and airy but small guest rooms, divided equally between singles and doubles. The corridor bathrooms are kept clean and usually you don't have to wait to use them.

Hotel Le Vigne. Piazza Santa Maria Novella 24, 50123 Firenze. ☎ **055/294-449.** Fax 055/230-2263. E-mail: hotel.levigne@dada.it. 26 units, 22 with private bathroom. A/C TV TEL. 160,000–200,000L ($80–$100) double with bathroom; 240,000L ($120) triple with bathroom; 280,000L ($140) quad. Rates include buffet breakfast. AE, DC, MC, V. Parking 35,000L ($17.50). Bus: 1, 2, 12, 16, 17, 22, 29.

Le Vigne offers comfortably furnished guest rooms and enjoys a prime location on one of the most central squares (the sitting room overlooks the square). An Italian family took over this 15th-century building and restored it in the early 1990s, preserving the old features, including frescoes, whenever possible. The small hotel is on the first floor (second floor if you're American) of this old-fashioned building. A few singles don't have bathrooms. The private bathrooms have adequate shelf space, and the hall bathrooms are fresh and neat, and usually there isn't a line to use them. The generous buffet breakfast is the only meal served.

Hotel Nuova Italia. Via Faenza 26, 50123 Firenze. ☎ **055/287-508.** Fax 055/210-941. www.nuovaitaliaflorence.it. E-mail: hotel.nuova.italia@dada.it. 20 units. A/C TV TEL. 198,000L ($99) double; 248,000L ($124) triple; 320,000L ($160) quad. Rates include breakfast. AE, MC, V. Parking 30,000L ($15) nearby. Bus: 10, 12, 25, 31, 32, or 91.

This little hotel, in a renovated 17th-century building a block from the rail station, has been welcoming *Frommer's* readers since 1958, when the first ones showed up with copies of *Europe on $5 a Day.* A Canadian guest, Eileen, met and fell in love with Luciano Viti, then a bellboy. Today they own the hotel and are grandparents with a new generation of Vitis waiting to take over one day. The guest rooms are pleasantly furnished and decorated with paintings and posters. Some large rooms are suitable for families, to whom the management grants special discounts. The furnishings, including the mattresses, were renewed in early 1999, and TVs were added. The bathrooms are small. The Vitis, who serve a fantastic cappuccino, will help you figure out how to get around Florence and offer tips on where to shop and what to do.

✪ **Pensione Burchianti.** Via del Giglio 6 (off Via Panzani), 50123 Firenze. ☎ and fax **055/21-27-96.** 11 units, 5 with shower only, 6 with bathroom. 120,000L ($60) double with shower, 160,000L ($80) double with bathroom. Rates include continental breakfast. No credit cards. Nearby parking 50,000L ($25). Bus: 4.

Opened in the late 19th century by the Burchianti sisters (the last of whom died in 1973) in the noble 16th-century Salimbeni palazzo, this once renowned pensione gets a star for sheer theatricality. It has hosted royals and VIPs (you may get Benito

Mussolini's room), and though much of that grandeur is now faded around the edges, you can still feel it. Leaded and stained-glass windows and doors, frescoed walls and ceilings, hand-painted coffered ceilings, and remnants of antique furniture fill the high-ceilinged guest rooms and public areas. Imaginative plumbing results in the eyesore addition of prefabricated shower stalls stuck in corners and sinks bolted onto precious 19th-century frescoed walls. Yet, the sunny salon and handsome breakfast room seem right out of a Merchant/Ivory film.

NEAR PIAZZA SAN MARCO

EXPENSIVE

Loggiato dei Serviti. Piazza SS. Annunziata 3, 50122 Firenze. ☎ **055/289-592.** Fax 055/289-595. www.venere.it/firenze/loggiato_serviti. E-mail: loggiato_serviti@italyhotel.com. 30 units. A/C MINIBAR TV TEL. 330,000L ($165) double; 365,000–900,000L ($182.50–$450) suite. Rates include buffet breakfast. AE, DC, MC, V. Parking 35,000–45,000L ($17.50–$22.50). Bus: 6, 31, or 32.

The amazing thing about this hotel is that it accepts paying guests at all—you'd think it could house a museum. But here you can wander through the premises of what was built in 1527 as a monastery (a symmetrical foil for the Ospedale degli Innocenti across the square); it's been a hotel since the early 1900s. In 1997 it was transformed from a run-down student place into a carefully restored three-star hotel. The guest rooms are artfully designed to emphasize the building's antique origins, usually with beamed or vaulted ceilings and terra-cotta floors. In 1998 and 1999 the canopies, tapestries, curtains, and mattresses were replaced, and some antiques added as well. The bathrooms, with hair dryers, are small to medium. There's a bar on the premises, but breakfast is the only meal served.

MODERATE

Hotel Cellai. Via 27 Aprile 14, 50129 Firenze. ☎ **055/489-291.** Fax 055/470-387. www.hotelcellai.it. E-mail: info@hotelcellai.it. 45 units. A/C MINIBAR TV TEL. 200,000–320,000L ($100–$160) double. Rates include breakfast. AE, DC, MC, V. Bus: 6, 31, or 32.

In the 1930s, the Cellai family began renting a handful of rooms. Eventually the enterprise grew into this large-scale place. Two blocks east of landmark Piazza della Indipendenza, it boasts dignified public rooms with terra-cotta floors and architectural details. The guest rooms are individually decorated, some with appealing contemporary paintings. Try to get one with a varnished wooden ceiling supported by very old beams; these rooms seem more appealing and a bit warmer. The beds are comfortable and the mattresses firm, and the bathrooms are tiny but well organized. Breakfast is the only meal served.

Hotel La Due Fontane. Piazza SS. Annunziata 14, 50122 Firenze. ☎ **055/210-185.** Fax 055/294-461. 57 units. A/C MINIBAR TV TEL. 300,000L ($150) double; 400,000L ($200) suite. Rates include breakfast. AE, CB, DC, DISC, MC, V. Parking 35,000–40,000L ($17.50–$20). Bus: 6, 31, or 32.

This hotel is a small 14th-century palace on Florence's best-known Renaissance square, right in the heart of all the sights. The hotel has been completely renovated and modernized and offers simply but tastefully furnished guest rooms that are well kept, if a bit uninspired. The upper-floor rooms offer the most tranquil night's sleep. Each room is unique, but all have firm mattresses and fine linen. The bathrooms are a decent size, some with hair dryers. Extras include a concierge, laundry service, personal hotel-bus service, car-rental facilities, boutiques, a business center, baby-sitting, and a bar.

INEXPENSIVE

Hotel Casci. Via Cavour 13, 50129 Firenze. ☎ **055/211-686.** Fax 055/239-6461. www.emmeti.it/casci.html. E-mail: casci@italyhotel.com. 25 units. A/C TV TEL. 150,000–220,000L ($75–$110) double; 190,000–290,000L ($95–$145) triple; 220,000–360,000L ($110–$180) quad. Rates include buffet breakfast. AE, DC, MC, V. Parking 35,000–40,000L ($17.50–$20). Bus: 11 or 17 from the Station.

The Casci is a well-run little hotel 200 yards from the rail station and 100 yards from Piazza del Duomo. As one reader wrote, "For location, location, location, there's nothing better in Florence." It dates from the 15th century, and some of the public rooms (like the breakfast room) feature the original frescoes. Giacchino Rossini, the famous composer of *The Barber of Seville* and *William Tell,* lived here from 1851 to 1855. The hotel is both traditional and modern, and the English-speaking reception staff looks after you very well. The guest rooms are comfortably furnished, each with a hair dryer and firm mattress. Every year, four or five units are upgraded and renovated. The few units overlooking the street are soundproof.

Hotel Cimabue. Via B. Lupi 7, 50129 Firenze. ☎ **055/471-989.** Fax 055/475-601. 16 units. TV TEL. 200,000–230,000L ($100–$115) double. Rates include buffet breakfast. AE, DC, MC, V. Parking 25,000L ($12.50). Bus: 17.

This hotel was built in 1904 as a Tuscan-style palazzo, and the most charming guest rooms are the six with original frescoed ceilings. Four of these are one floor above street level and the other on the ground floor. Each room has a comfortable bed with a quality mattress. They range from small to medium in size. The bathrooms are hardly spacious but do come with hair dryers. The hotel was recently renovated and has turn-of-the-century antiques that correspond to the building's age. Its Belgian-Italian management extends a warm multicultural welcome.

Hotel Europa. Via Cavour 14, 50129 Firenze. ☎ and fax **055/210-361.** 13 units. A/C TV TEL. 190,000L ($95) double; 240,000L ($120) triple. Rates include buffet breakfast. AE, MC, V. Parking 30,000–40,000L ($15–$20) nearby.

Two long blocks north of the Duomo, this 16th-century building has been a family-run hotel since 1925. Despite the antique appearance of the simple exterior, much of the interior has been modernized, though it contains plenty of homey touches. All but four of the guest rooms overlook the back, usually opening onto a view of Giotto's campanile and Brunelleschi's dome; those facing the street are noisier but benefit from double glazing. The rooms are small but decently furnished, with comfortable mattresses, plus a tiny but well-organized tile bathroom. Breakfast is the only meal served.

Hotel Morandi alla Crocetta. Via Laura 50, 50121 Firenze. ☎ **055/234-4747.** Fax 055/248-0954. www.hotelmorandi.it. E-mail: welcome@hotelmorandi.it. 10 units. A/C MINIBAR TV TEL. 240,000–290,000L ($120–$145) double; 310,000–390,000L ($155–$195) triple. Breakfast 20,000L ($10). AE, CB, DC, MC, V. Parking 30,000L ($15). Bus: 6, 7, 10, 17, 31, or 32.

This charming small hotel two blocks from the Accademia is run by one of Florence's most experienced hoteliers, the sprightly octogenarian Katherine Doyle, who came here from Ireland when she was 12. Although built in 1511 as a convent, it contains everything needed for a pensione and is on a back street near a university building. The rooms (small to medium) have been tastefully restored, filled with framed 19th-century needlework, beamed ceilings, antiques, firm mattresses, safes, fax machines, and radios. In the best Tuscan tradition, the tall windows are sheltered from the sun with heavy draperies. The bathrooms are of decent size, with adequate shelf space. You register in an austere salon filled with Persian carpets.

Hotel Splendor. Via S. Gallo 30, 50129 Firenze. ☎ **055/483-427.** Fax 055/461-276. 31 units, 25 with private bathroom. TV TEL. 200,000L ($100) double without bathroom, 270,000L ($135) double with bathroom; 340,000L ($170) triple with bathroom. Rates include buffet breakfast. AE, MC, V. Parking 35,000L ($17.50). Bus: 1, 6, 7, 10, 11, 17, 25, 33, 67, or 68.

The Splendor is within a 10-minute walk of the Duomo, yet the residential neighborhood it occupies is a world away from the crush in the tourist district. The hotel occupies three high-ceilinged floors of a 19th-century apartment building, and its elegantly faded public rooms evoke the kind of family-run pensione you'd expect in a Merchant/Ivory film. This is the domain of the Masoero family, whose homey rooms contain nice Florentine decorative touches and an eclectic array of semiantique furniture, with quality mattresses. Some of the units are also air-conditioned, and each comes with a safe. The tiny tiled bathrooms have hair dryers. Breakfast is the only meal served, but room service is available.

Piccolo Hotel. Via S. Gallo 51, 50129 Firenze. ☎ **055/475-519.** Fax 055/474-515. www.paginegialle.it/piccolofir. 10 units. TV TEL. 190,000L ($95) double. Rates include buffet breakfast. DC, MC, V. Parking 35,000–40,000L ($17.50–$20) nearby.

Situated in a very convenient position, close to the railway station and to all the principal monuments, this town-house hotel offers an intimate atmosphere. You'll feel at home, thanks to the wise advice of Ms. Angeloni, the English-speaking manager, who will guide you through Florence's secret beauties. Rooms are medium in size, some of them with a balcony, with simple, tasteful furniture and flowered bed linens. Bathrooms are a little small but well organized and neat, offering hair dryers and adequate shelf space. The only meal served is the generous buffet breakfast, but the hotel is surrounded by good restaurants. Besides the other standard services, there are some free bicycles available for guests.

ON OR NEAR PIAZZA MASSIMO D'AZEGLIO

Piazza Massimo d'Azeglio is a 12-minute walk northeast of the historic core.

VERY EXPENSIVE

✪ **Hotel Regency.** Piazza Massimo d'Azeglio 3, 50121 Firenze. ☎ **055/245-247.** Fax 055/234-6735. www.regency_hotel.com. E-mail: info@regency-hotel.com. 34 units. A/C MINIBAR TV TEL. 620,000–720,000L ($310–$360) double; from 970,000L ($485) suite. Rates include breakfast. AE, DC, MC, V. Parking 50,000L ($25). Bus: 6, 31, or 32.

The Regency is a villa of taste and exclusivity, a member of the leading hotels of the world. It lies a bit apart from the shopping-and-sightseeing center (great for tranquillity seekers) but is only a 15-minute stroll from the cathedral and quickly reached by taxi or bus. This hideaway, filled with stained glass, paneled walls, and reproduction antiques, offers exquisite accommodations, including some special rooms on the top floor with terraces. They boast numerous extras, like custom-made mattresses, double glazing, thick wool carpeting, coffered or beamed ceilings, expensive fabrics, thermostats, and safes. The large bathrooms are the town's most luxurious, with a wide range of deluxe toiletries, dual basins, hair dryers, bidets, and phones.

Dining: The attractive Relais Le Jardin is renowned for its *alta cucina.* You can also take your meals in the well-lit winter garden or on an inner courtyard in summer.

Amenities: Concierge, room service, baby-sitting, laundry/valet, nightly turndown, shoeshine, wake-up service, currency exchange.

Expensive

✪ **Hotel Monna Lisa.** Borgo Pinti 27, 50121 Firenze. ☎ **055/247-9751.** Fax 055/247-9755. www.monnalisa.it. E-mail: monnalis@ats.it. 30 units. A/C MINIBAR TV TEL. 350,000–500,000L ($175–$250) double; 430,000–620,000L ($215–$310) triple. Rates include breakfast. AE, DC, MC, V. Parking 20,000L ($10).

This hotel (yes, it's Monna with two *n*'s) once appeared in *Frommer's Europe on $5 a Day,* but its prices have skyrocketed and it can't be included even in the current *Europe from $60 a Day.* However, for old-world elegance in the setting of a 14th-century Tuscan palazzo, it's virtually unbeatable. The palazzo once belonged to the Neri family, whose most famous member, St. Philip Neri, was born in room no. 19. The facade is forbiddingly severe, in keeping with the architectural style of its heyday, but when you enter the reception rooms, you'll find an inviting atmosphere. Most of the great old guest rooms overlook an inner patio or a rear garden. They vary greatly in style and decor—some are quite spacious, others a bit cramped. Each is handsomely furnished with fine antiques and oil paintings, including Giambologna's original competition piece for the *Rape of the Sabines.* There are other works by neoclassical sculptor Giovanni Dupré (1817–82)—the hotel is still owned by a member of his family. Painted wood and coffered ceilings are found in many rooms. The bathrooms have recently been renovated; some have Jacuzzis.

Dining/Diversions: Breakfast is the only meal served, but there's an American-style bar. **Amenities:** Concierge, baby-sitting, laundry.

Inexpensive

Albergo Losanna. Via Vittorio Alfieri 9, 50121 Firenze. ☎ and fax **055/245-840.** 8 units, 3 with bathroom. TEL. 100,000L ($50) double without bathroom, 130,000L ($65) double with bathroom. Rates include breakfast. AE, MC, V. Parking 35,000–40,000L ($17.50–$20). Bus: 6.

The Losanna, a family-run place off Viale Antonio Gramsci, offers utter simplicity and cleanliness as well as insight into a typical Florentine atmosphere—the hotel seemingly belongs in the 1800s. The rooms are homey and well kept, though the mattresses could use replacing. The private bathrooms are cramped, without enough shelf space; the hall bathrooms are large and quite adequate; you rarely have to wait in line.

NEAR PIAZZA SANTA CROCE

Expensive

Plaza Hotel Lucchesi. Lungarno della Zecca Vecchia 38, 50122 Firenze. ☎ **055/26-236.** Fax 055/248-0921. www.plazalucchesi.it. E-mail: phl@plazalucchesi.it. 97 units. A/C MINIBAR TV TEL. 300,000–650,000L ($150–$325) double; 650,000–670,000L ($325–$335) suite. Rates include buffet breakfast. AE, DC, DISC, MC, V. Parking 28,000–40,000L ($14–$20). Bus: B, 13, 14, or 23.

This hotel (often a favorite with tour groups) was built in 1860 but has been renovated many times since. It lies along the Arno, a 10-minute walk from the Duomo and a few paces from Santa Croce. Its interior decor includes lots of glossy mahogany, acres of marble, and masses of fresh flowers. The guest rooms, ranging from medium to spacious, have recently been renewed, with new mattresses added. Every accommodation comes with a private safe, and 20 of them open onto balconies with views. Some no-smoking units are available. The bathrooms are a good size, with robes and hair dryers.

Dining/Diversions: A large breakfast buffet and dinner are served in the sunny La Serra. The food is only average, however; you'll do better at one of the restaurants nearby. The cocktail bar, The Café, is open daily from 10pm to midnight. Besides enjoying a drink here, you can also relax with the piano bar music. Every day from 4:30 to 7pm the bar serves a traditional English afternoon tea.

Amenities: Concierge, room service (7am to midnight), baby-sitting, laundry/valet, car-rental desk.

NEAR THE PONTE VECCHIO

EXPENSIVE

✪ **Augustus Gallery Hotel Art.** Vicolo dell'Oro 5, 50123 Firenze. ☎ **055/27-263.** Fax 055/268-557. 62 units. A/C TV TEL. 480,000–550,000L ($240–$275) double; from 800,000L ($400) suite. AE, DC, MC, V. Bus: 23 or 71.

The Ferragamo family is a style setter in Florence. Founding father, Salvatore, was known as shoemaker to the stars, having shod such Hollywood royalty as Greta Garbo. The Ferragamos continue to live in Florence and to set styles, most recently with this unique boutique hotel near the Ponte Vecchio. They have combined antique with modern more successfully than any other place in town. As befits its name, its art theme stretches from the public areas to the pin-striped guest rooms. Whimsical touches include the insect watercolors of Alberto Reggianini. The rectilinear armchairs are in suede and pigskin, and the books in the library were hand selected (often first editions of English classics). The bedrooms are of good size and among the most delightfully contemporary in Florence.

Dining/Diversions: Breakfast is the only meal served.

Amenities: Room service, concierge, baby-sitting.

Hotel Augustus. Vicolo dell'Oro 5, 50123 Firenze. ☎ **055/272-63.** Fax 055/268-557. www.lungarnohotels.it. E-mail: bookings@lungarnohotels.com. 62 units. A/C TV TEL. 520,000L ($260) double; 670,000L ($335) suite. Rates include buffet breakfast. AE, CB, DC, MC, V. Parking 30,000–40,000L ($15–$20). Bus: 23 or 71.

The Augustus is for those who require modern comforts while enjoying a historic setting. The exterior is rather pillbox modern, but the interior is light, bright, and comfortable. Some of the guest rooms open onto private balconies with garden furniture, though views of the Arno are often blocked by neighboring buildings. The decor consists of provincial pieces, and the overall effect is rather lackluster but well maintained. When the hotel was renovated in 1999, mattresses were replaced and new furnishings added. Each bathroom has a hair dryer.

Dining/Diversions: The expansive lounge and drinking area is like an illuminated cave, with a curving ceiling and built-in conversation areas. Snacks are served 8am to 11:30pm. Even though there's no restaurant, dozens are literally at your doorstep.

Amenities: Concierge, room service, laundry/dry cleaning, car-rental desk.

Hotel Continental. Lungarno Acciaiuoli 2, 50123 Firenze. ☎ **055/272-62.** Fax 055/283-139. www.lungarnohotels.it. E-mail: bookings@lungarnohotels.com. 48 units. A/C MINIBAR TV TEL. 480,000L ($240) double; from 625,000L ($312.50) suite. Rates include buffet breakfast. AE, CB, DC, MC, V. Valet parking 35,000–45,000L ($17.50–$22.50).

At the Ponte Vecchio's entrance, the Continental occupies some select real estate and is a better choice than the Augustus (see above). Through the lounge windows and from some of the rooms you can see the little jewelry and leather shops flanking the bridge. The hotel was created in the 1960s, so its style is utilitarian, with functional furniture softened by decorative accessories. You reach your room by the elevator or a wrought-iron staircase (parts of the old stone structure have been retained). The guest rooms range from medium to large and offer all the standard comforts, like quality mattresses. Some have balconies opening onto panoramic views. The bathrooms are well kept, with hair dryers. The roof terrace is a perfect place for viewing Piazzale Michelangiolo, the Pitti Palace, the Duomo and campanile, and Fiesole. Artists fight to get the penthouse suite up in the Torre Guelfa dei Consorti (tower).

Dining/Diversions: There's a small bar but no restaurant.

Amenities: Concierge (7am to midnight), room service, laundry/dry cleaning, in-room massage, baby-sitting.

MODERATE

Hermitage Hotel. Vicolo Marzio 1, Piazza del Pesce 1, 50122 Firenze. ☎ **055/287-216.** Fax 055/212-208. www.venere.it/firenze/hermitage/hermitage_it.html. E-mail: florence@hermitagehotel.com. 29 units. A/C TV TEL. 300,000–370,000L ($150–$185) double; 410,000L ($205) triple; 500,000L ($250) family room. Rates include breakfast. MC, V. Parking 35,000–40,000L ($17.50–$20).

On the Arno, the offbeat Hermitage is a charming place that has been recently renovated. It boasts a rooftop sun terrace offering a view of much of Florence, including the nearby Uffizi and the Duomo. You can take your breakfast under a leafy arbor surrounded by potted roses and geraniums. The success of this hotel has much to do with its English-speaking owner, Vincenzo Scarcelli, who has made it an extension of his home, furnishing it in part with antiques and well-chosen reproductions. Best of all is his warmth toward guests, many of whom keep coming back. The extremely small guest rooms are pleasantly furnished, many with 17th- to 19th-century Tuscan antiques, rich brocades, and good beds, plus double-glazed windows. The tiled bathrooms are superb, with hair dryers, deluxe little shampoos, and shower soaps. Breakfast is served in a dignified beam-ceilinged room. On the premises is a lounge bar tastefully decorated with antiques.

Hotel Torre Guelfa. Borgo SS. Apostoli 8 (between Via dei Tornabuoni and Via Per Santa Maria), 50123 Firenze. ☎ **055/239-6338.** Fax 055/239-8577. www.firenzealbergo.it. E-mail: torre.guelfa@flashnet.it. 16 units. A/C MINIBAR TV TEL. 300,000L ($150) double. Rates include breakfast. AE, MC, V. Bus: 6, 11, 36, 37, or 68.

One reason to stay here is to drink in the breathtaking 360° view from the hotel's 13th-century tower, the tallest privately owned tower in Florence's centro storico. Though you're just two steps from the Ponte Vecchio (and equidistant from the Duomo), you'll want to put sightseeing on hold and linger in your canopied iron bed with its good mattress, your room made even more inviting by warm-colored walls and paisley carpeting (for a view similar to the medieval tower's, ask for room no. 15 with its huge private terrace). In 1998 all the bathrooms were renovated, with more shelf space and hair dryers added.

The Torre Guelfa's young owners have created the **Relais Uffizi** (☎ **055/265-7909;** fax 055/267-0028), a sibling hotel a few cobbled lanes away. Similar in spirit, decor, price, and size (11 units), it isn't blessed with a tower but is housed in a handsome 14th-century palazzo. Or ask them about their new Tuscan hideaway, the **Villa Rosa** in Panzano, a 22-mile drive from Florence in the heart of Chianti; the 15 doubles with bathroom cost 200,000L ($100) (see chapter 6).

ACROSS THE ARNO

EXPENSIVE

Hotel Villa Carlotta. Via Michele di Lando 3, 50125 Firenze. ☎ **055/220-530.** Fax 055/233-6147. 32 units. A/C MINIBAR TV TEL. 290,000–460,000L ($145–$230) double. Rates include buffet breakfast. AE, DC, MC, V. Free parking. Bus: 11, 36, or 37.

This hotel was built during the Edwardian age as a villa and bought in the 1950s by Carlotta Schulmann. Her lavish renovations have transformed it into one of Florence's most charming smaller hotels. The aura is still very much like that of a private home, and it's located in a residential section. Rooms have silk wallpaper and bedspreads, firm mattresses, reproduction antiques, safe-deposit boxes, and crystal chandeliers;

each has a view of the garden. The bathrooms are exceedingly well maintained, with toiletries and hair dryers. The hotel is only a 10-minute walk from the Ponte Vecchio; by taxi, it's a 5-minute ride.

Dining: Il Bobolino serves meals ranging from fresh salads to full culinary regalias.

Amenities: Room service, baby-sitting, laundry/valet, car-rental desk.

MODERATE

Pensione Annalena. Via Romana 34, 50125 Firenze. ☎ **055/222-402.** Fax 055/222-403. www.hotelannalena.it. E-mail: annalena@hotelannalena.it. 20 units. TV TEL. 250,000–310,000L ($125–$155) double. Rates include breakfast. AE, DC, MC, V. Parking 25,000L ($12.50). Bus: C, 11, 36, or 37.

Built in the 15th century, the Annalena has had many owners, including the Medicis. In the past three-quarters of a century, it has been a haven for artists and writers (Mary McCarthy once wrote of its importance as a cultural center). During most of that time, it was the domain of the late sculptor Olinto Calastri, but now it's owned by Claudio Salvestrini. Most of the simply furnished rooms overlook a secret garden; five face an open-air galleria on the loggia, evoking an idyllic landscape that might've been painted by Gozzoli. Don't be put off by the lack of air-conditioning; the high ceilings and thick masonry walls almost guarantee a relatively comfortable temperature in summer. The bathrooms are small but have adequate shelf space. During World War II, the Annalena was the center of the underground, and many Jews and rebel Italians found safety hidden away in an underground room behind a secret door. The pensione is about a 5-minute walk from the Pitti and 10 minutes from the Ponte Vecchio.

ON THE OUTSKIRTS

VERY EXPENSIVE

✪ **Torre di Bellosguardo.** Via Roti Michelozzi 2, 50124 Firenze. ☎ **055/229-8145.** Fax 055/229-008. E-mail: torredibellosguardo@dada.it. 16 units. TEL. 480,000L ($240) double; 580,000L ($290) suite. Breakfast 35,000L ($17.50). AE, MC, V. Free parking. Bus: 12 or 13 to Pz. Tasso, where a taxi will take you up the hill.

On a breezy hilltop near the Arno's south bank, less than 2 miles (3km) southwest of the Duomo, this hotel occupies the premises of what in the 1300s was a private villa. A medieval aura lingers in its long halls and alfresco loggias. Framed by an avenue of timeless cypresses, the mansion was built by Guido Cavalcanti, a nobleman and friend of Dante. You register under the frescoed ceiling of a former ballroom, and the high-ceilinged guest rooms have hints of old-fashioned grandeur. If you can afford it, try for the romantic tower suite with its sweeping view. Air-conditioning is available in five rooms, but because of the hotel's location, it isn't always necessary. A pool is set in a sprawling park and garden.

Dining: Breakfast is the only meal served, but the sunny veranda or cool dining room seems to make up for this lack. The veranda is a tempting place to linger.

Amenities: Concierge, 24-hour room service.

✪ **Villa La Massa.** Via della Massa 24, 50012 Candeli, Firenze. ☎ **055/626-11.** Fax 055/633-102. www.villalamassa.com E-mail: villamssa@galactica.it 34 units. A/C MINIBAR TV TEL. 550,000–750,000L ($275–$375) double; from 900,000L ($450) suite. Rates include breakfast. AE, DC, MC, V. Free parking. Free shuttle bus to/from villa and Ponte Vecchio in Florence during the day.

The Villa d'Este on Lake Como, one of the most legendary hotels in Italy (see chapter 10), has opened this palace of charm and grace 5 miles southeast of Florence. (Ask about packages combining stays at both hotels.) On the banks of the Arno, in a secluded spot near the edge of the Chianti region, this 16th-century Medicean villa was built by the powerful Giraldi family, who owned it until the 19th century. It became a luxury hotel in 1948, and has been extensively restored and refurbished by the Villa d'Este. The guest rooms are spacious and opulently furnished, often with antiques, all with luxury mattresses and quality linen. The marble bathrooms are medium in size but state of the art, with hair dryers and deluxe toiletries. Eleven rooms are in an annex; try to get a room in the main house, with a view of the Arno.

Dining/Diversions: The magnificent Medici Hall is an ideal place to meet and socialize, as are the panoramic terraces. The restaurant, open to nonguests as well, serves Tuscan classics and offers a fine wine list.

Amenities: Concierge, room service, laundry/dry cleaning, tennis club, horseback riding, golf club nearby. By next year, there should be a new pool, spa, and sporting club.

Villa Montartino. Via Suor Maria Celeste 19/21 (corner with Via G. Silvani), 50125 Arcetri, Firenze. ☎ **055/223-520.** Fax 055/223-495. www.montartino.com. E-mail: info@montartino.com. 7 units, 4 apts. A/C MINIBAR TV TEL. 550,000–650,000L ($275–$325) double; 750,000–850,000L ($375–$425) suite; 2,500,000L ($1,250) apt per week. Rates include buffet breakfast. AE, DC, MC, V. Free parking. From Porta Romana, follow signs for Poggio Imperiale, turn right on Via San Felice; you'll see the villa on your left.

In the Florentine hills, always a source of inspiration for Tuscan poets, Villa Montartino is an oasis less than a mile from the Ponte Vecchio. A strategic tower during the 11th century, and then a patrician villa from 1500, the villa still retains the charm of the past after recent renovations. Rooms range from medium to spacious, each with its own character thanks to the wise choice of antiques matched with pieces of Florentine craftsmanship. Bathrooms are medium in size with mosaic tiles, modern and efficient accessories, and hair dryers. You can opt for a more independent accommodation in the apartments, which offer all the modern comforts integrated with the hotel services.

Dining/Diversions: During the summer, breakfast is served under the loggia surrounded by olive groves and vineyards, whose products are enjoyed in the cellar, Cantina della Torre. Even though a real restaurant doesn't exist, homemade meals can be arranged on request by the efficient owners.

Amenities: Twice-daily maid service, baby-sitting, hiking trails, outdoor heated pool, swimming lessons, water-gym courses, car service to and from the city center.

4 Dining

The Florentine table has always been set with the abundance of the Tuscan countryside. That means the region's best olive oil and wine, like Chianti; wonderful fruits and vegetables; fresh fish from the coast; and game in season. Meat lovers all over Italy sing the praise of *bistecca alla fiorentina,* an inch-thick juicy steak on the bone, often served with white Tuscan beans. Tuscan cuisine (except for some of its hair-raising specialties) should please most North Americans, since it's simply flavored, without rich spices, and based on the hearty produce from the hills. Florentine restaurants aren't generally as acclaimed by gourmets as those of Rome, though good, moderately priced places abound.

IN CENTRO

MODERATE

Al Lume di Candela. Via delle Terme 23R. ☎ **055/294-566.** Reservations required. Main courses 25,000–40,000L ($12.50–$20). AE. Tues–Sat noon–2:30pm and 7:30–11pm; Mon 7:30–11pm. Closed 1 week in Aug. Bus: C. TUSCAN/INTERNATIONAL.

Al Lume di Candela occupies a 13th-century tower that was partially leveled when its patrician family fell from grace (the prestige of Tuscan families was once reflected in how high their family towers soared). It serves typical Florentine cuisine in an elegant candlelit decor of English-style furnishings and De Chirico paintings. The food is precise, combining rich tastes and unusual flavors, but stick to the Tuscan dishes (avoid the bland international fare). Menu choices include *taglioni* with sage and porcini mushrooms, a light house-smoked salmon, veal chops stuffed with white beans *(cannellini)* and arugula, *maccheroncini* with thyme, and calamari seared in sherry with pecorino cheese. Tuscan rabbit appears in white grape sauce, based on a recipe from 1500. The desserts are made daily—the sponge cake covered in fresh raspberry cream is a summer delight. From the cellar emerge at least 200 wines, with Chianti Classico the wine of choice. One old-timer still remembers when Bing Crosby (then one of the world's richest entertainers) arrived here carrying a dog-eared copy of *Frommer's Europe on $5 a Day.* Bing is long gone and so are those cheap prices.

✪ **Cantinetta Antinori.** Piazza Antinori 3. ☎ **055/292-234.** Reservations recommended. Main courses 22,000–35,000L ($11–$17.50). AE, DC, MC, V. Mon–Fri 12:30–2:30pm and 7–10:30pm. Closed Aug and Dec 24–Jan 6. Bus: 6, 11, 36, 37, or 68. FLORENTINE/TUSCAN.

Behind the severe stone facade of the 15th-century Palazzo Antinori is one of Florence's most popular restaurants and one of the city's few top-notch wine bars. It's no wonder the cellars are so well stocked, since this is a showplace for the vintages of the oldest (600 years) and most distinguished wine company in Tuscany, Umbria, and Piedmont. You can sample these wines by the glass at the stand-up bar or by the bottle as an accompaniment to the meals served at wooden tables in the dining room, decorated with floor-to-ceiling racks of aged and dusty wine bottles. You can eat a full meal or just snacks. The food is standard but satisfying, and many of the ingredients come directly from the Antinori farms. Especially good are the sausages with white haricot beans, fresh Tuscan ewe's cheese, tripe Florentine style (for the traditionalist), fettuccine in duck sauce, thick oven-roasted Chiana beef (a bit pricey but worth it), and *stracotto al vino Peppole* (beef braised in strong Italian red wine).

Oliviero. Via delle Terme 51R. ☎ **055/287-643** or 055/212-421. Reservations required. Main courses 24,000–32,000L ($12–$16). AE, DC, MC, V. Mon–Sat 7:30pm–midnight. Closed Aug. Bus: 14, 23, or 71. TUSCAN.

This small but smart and luxurious dining room maintains the finest traditions of Tuscan cookery; highly select fresh ingredients are used in the seasonal menu. We've come across such appetizers as octopus salad with basil, string beans, and tomatoes; fried mussels and squash blossoms; and Tuscan ham with figs and bread coated with virgin olive oil. We recently enjoyed *pici* pasta with savory tomato sauce, fresh garlic, and spicy red peppers, followed by a grilled Tuscan sirloin steak, flavored with sage and rosemary and covered in a perfect Chianti sauce. Other main courses usually include fresh fish; grilled boned rabbit and young cock with shell beans; or ravioli stuffed with chopped liver and served with a delicate white onion sauce. For dessert, try the green-fig mousse with almonds and chocolate.

NEAR PIAZZA DEL DUOMO

INEXPENSIVE

Le Mossacce. Via del Proconsolo 55R. ☎ **055/294-361.** Reservations recommended. Main courses 12,000–25,000L ($6–$12.50). AE, DC, MC, V. Mon–Fri noon–2:30pm and 7–9:30pm. Closed Aug. Bus: 14. TUSCAN/FLORENTINE.

The 35-seat Le Mossacce is midway between the Bargello and the Duomo. It opened in the early 1900s, and within its 300-year-old walls hardworking waiters serve a wide

Florence Dining

Alle Murate **34**
Al Lume di Candela **16**
Buca dell'Orafo **39**
Buca Lapi **10**
Buca Mario **9**
Cafaggi **32**
Caffè Italiano **29**
Cantinetta Antinori **11**
Cantinetta del Verrazzano **27**
Cibreo **38**
Da Ganino **28**
Da Pennello **25**
Don Chisciotte **2**
Gelateria Vivoli **36**
Harry's Bar **15**
Il Cavallino **30**
Il Latini **12**
I Quattro Amici **1**
I' Toscano **31**
La Baruciola **23**
La Capannina di Sante **40**
La Carabaccia **8**
La Nandina **18**
Le Fonticine **3**
Le Mossacce **24**
Mamma Gina **21**
Oliviero **17**
Osteria del Caffè Italiano **36**
Osteria Numero Uno **14**
Paoli **26**
Pierot **19**
Ristorante Dino **37**
Ristorante Otello **4**
Sabatini **6**
Sostanza **7**
Trattoria Angiolino **20**
Trattoria Antellesi **5**
Trattoria Camillo **22**
Trattoria Garga **13**
Trattoria Pallottino **35**
Vecchia Firenze **33**

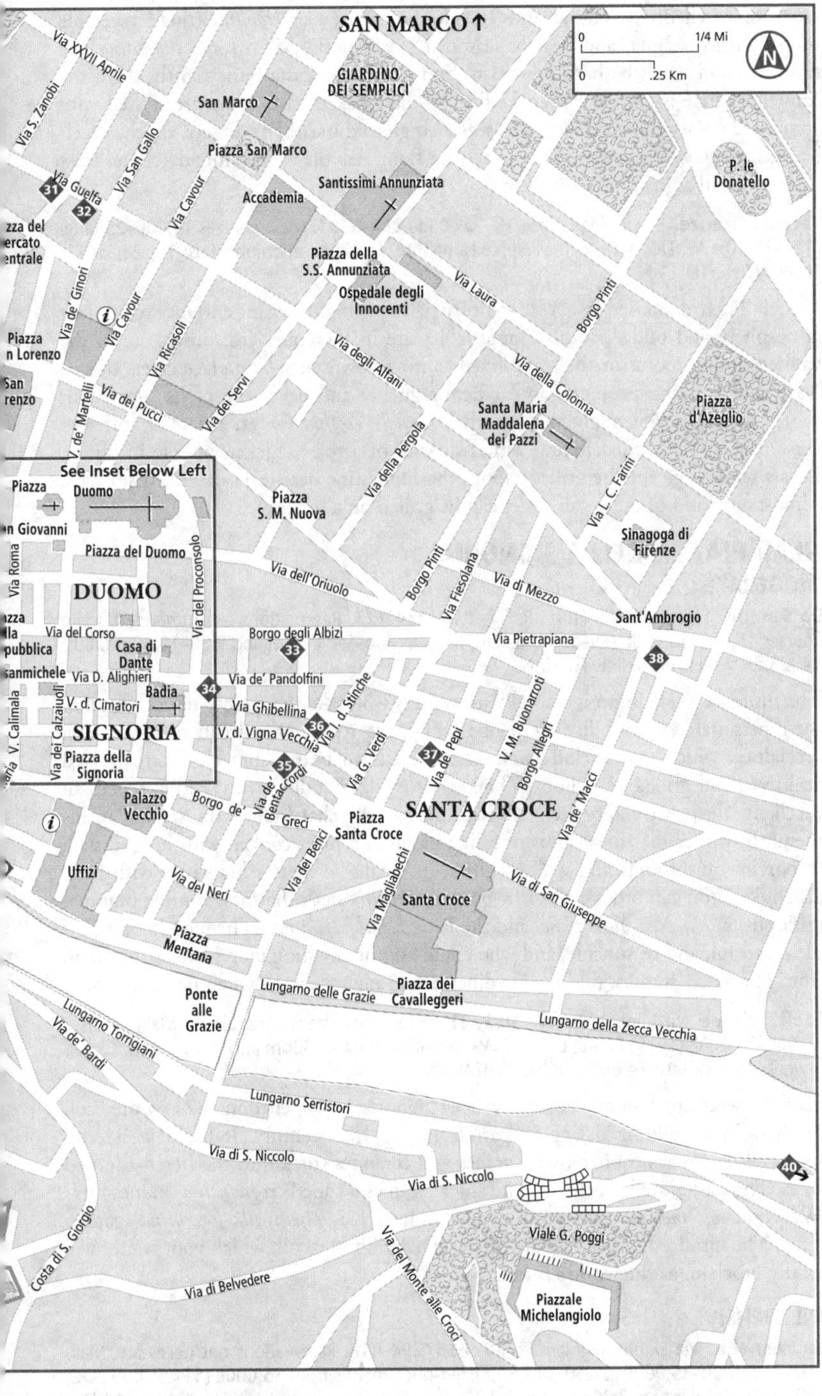
SAN MARCO
0
1/4 Mi
0
.25 Km
N
GIARDINO DEI SEMPLICI
San Marco
Piazza San Marco
Santissimi Annunziata
Accademia
Piazza della S.S. Annunziata
Ospedale degli Innocenti
Via XXVII Aprile
Via S. Zanobi
Via San Gallo
Via Guelfa
Via Cavour
Via de' Ginori
Via Ricasoli
Via dei Servi
Via dei Pucci
V. de' Martelli
Via Laura
Borgo Pinti
Via degli Alfani
Via della Colonna
Via della Pergola
P. le Donatello
Piazza d'Azeglio
Santa Maria Maddalena dei Pazzi
Via L. C. Farini
Sinagoga di Firenze
See Inset Below Left
Piazza
Duomo
Piazza del Duomo
DUOMO
Via Roma
Via del Corso
Casa di Dante
Via D. Alighieri
V. d. Cimatori
Badia
SIGNORIA
Piazza della Signoria
Via Calimala
Via dei Calzaiuoli
Via del Proconsolo
Piazza S. M. Nuova
Via dell'Oriuolo
Borgo Pinti
Via Fiesolana
Via di Mezzo
Sant'Ambrogio
Via Pietrapiana
Borgo degli Albizi
Via de' Pandolfini
Via Ghibellina
V. d. Vigna Vecchia
Via I. d. Stinche
Via G. Verdi
Via de' Pepi
V. M. Buonarroti
Borgo Allegri
Via de' Macci
Via de' Bentaccordi
Borgo de' Greci
Palazzo Vecchio
Piazza Santa Croce
SANTA CROCE
Uffizi
Via dei Benci
Via del Neri
Via Magliabechi
Santa Croce
Via di San Giuseppe
Piazza Mentana
Piazza dei Cavalleggeri
Lungarno delle Grazie
Ponte alle Grazie
Lungarno della Zecca Vecchia
Lungarno Torrigiani
Via de' Bardi
Lungarno Serristori
Via di S. Niccolo
Via di S. Niccolo
Viale G. Poggi
Via del Monte alle Croci
Costa di S. Giorgio
Via di Belvedere
Piazzale Michelangiolo
31
32
33
34
35
36
37
38
40

range of excellent Florentine and Tuscan specialties, like *ribollita* (thick vegetable soup), baked lasagna, and heavily seasoned baked pork. *Bistecca alla fiorentina* is a favorite—and you'll be hard-pressed to find it for less. Pasta buffs rightly claim the cannelloni here is among Florence's finest—these baked pasta tubes are stuffed with spinach, a savory tomato sauce, and seasoned ground meat. For dessert, try the excellent *castagnaccio,* a cake baked with chestnut flour. Ask the waiters for advice and trust them; we had a great meal this way.

Vecchia Firenze. Borgo degli Albizi 18. ☎ **055/234-0361.** Main courses 14,000–25,000L ($7–$12.50). AE, DC, MC, V. Tues–Sun 11am–3pm and 7pm–midnight. Bus: 14, 23, or 71. FLORENTINE/TUSCAN.

Vecchia Firenze, housed in a 14th-century palace with an elegant entrance, combines atmosphere and budget meals. Some tables are in the courtyard; others are in the vaulted dining rooms or the stone-lined cantina downstairs. The place caters to students and working people, who eat here regularly and never tire of its simple but hearty offerings. You might begin with *tagliatelle Vecchia Firenze* (there's a different version every day), then follow with a quarter of a roast chicken or sole in butter. Locals tend to go for the grilled rabbit, the Florentine beefsteak, or grilled sea bass. Almost any kind of meat you select can be grilled on a barbecue.

NEAR PIAZZA DELLA SIGNORIA

MODERATE

Da Ganino. Piazza dei Cimatori 4R. ☎ **055/214-125.** Reservations recommended. Main courses 18,000–30,000L ($9–$15). AE, DC, MC, V. Mon–Sat 1–3pm and 7:30–10:30pm. Bus: 14, 23, or 71. FLORENTINE/TUSCAN.

The intimate Da Ganino is staffed with waiters who take the quality of your meal as their personal responsibility. Someone will recite to you the frequently changing specialties, which may include well-seasoned Tuscan beans, spinach risotto, grilled veal liver, and grilled veal chops. The *tagliatelle* (flat noodles) with truffles makes an excellent if expensive appetizer. We like the way the chef follows the seasons in his menu. In winter that means lots of filling pastas and meat cooked with funghi, such as porcini mushrooms and white truffles; in spring he dresses his pastas with fresh artichokes. You can order a classic T-bone Fiorentina steak that has won the praise of critics from *The New York Times* and the Paris *Herald Tribune*. "The food here is simple, flavorful, and reasonable, and who could ask for anything more?" an art historian from Lawrence, Kansas, told us. He dines here 3 nights a week when he's in town.

Paoli. Via dei Tavolini 12R. ☎ **055/216-215.** Reservations required. Main courses 18,000–34,000L ($9–$17). AE, DC, MC, V. Wed–Mon noon–2:30pm and 7–10:30pm. Closed 3 weeks in Aug. Bus: 14 or 23. TUSCAN/ITALIAN.

Paoli, between the Duomo and Piazza della Signoria, was opened in 1824 by the Paoli brothers in a building dating in part from the 13th century. It has a wonderful medieval-tavern atmosphere, with arches and ceramics stuck into the fresco-adorned walls. The pastas are homemade, and the chef does a superb *rognoncino* (kidney) *trifolato* and *sole meunière*. A recommended side dish is *piselli alla fiorentina* (garden peas). The ultrafresh vegetables are often served with olive oil, which your waiter will loudly proclaim as the world's finest.

INEXPENSIVE

Da Pennello. Via Dante Alighieri 4R. ☎ **055/294-848.** Reservations not necessary. Main courses 15,000–35,000L ($7.50–$17.50); fixed-price menus from 35,000L ($17.50). AE, DC, MC, V. Tues–Sat noon–2:30pm and 7–10:30pm; Sun noon–2:30pm. Closed Aug and Dec 24–Jan 2. Bus: 14, 22, or 23. FLORENTINE/ITALIAN.

Focaccia & Chianti on the Run

Owned by the Castello di Verrazzano, one of Chianti's best-known wine-producing estates, the ✪ **Cantinetta del Verrazzano,** Via dei Tavolini 18–20R (☎ **055/268-590**), helped spawn a revival of stylish wine bars as convenient spots for fast-food breaks. It promises a delicious self-service lunch or snack of focaccia, plain or studded with peas, rosemary, onions, or olives; buy it hot by the slice or ask for *farcite* (sandwiches filled with prosciutto, arugula, cheese, or tuna). A glass of full-bodied Chianti makes this the perfect respite. Summer hours are Monday to Saturday 8am to 3:30pm and 5:30 to 9pm; winter hours are Monday to Saturday 8am to 9pm.

This informal trattoria offers many Florentine specialties on its à la carte menu and is known for its wide selection of antipasti; you can make a meal out of these delectable hors d'oeuvres. The ravioli is homemade, and one pasta specialty (loved by locals) is *spaghetti carrettiera,* with tomatoes and pepperoni. To follow that, you can have deviled roast chicken. The chef posts his daily specials, and sometimes it's best to order one of these, since the food offered was bought fresh that day at the market. A Florentine cake, *zuccotto,* rounds out the meal. Da Penello is on a narrow street near Dante's house, about a 5-minute walk from the Duomo.

Il Cavallino. Via della Farine 6R. ☎ **055/215-818.** Reservations recommended. Main courses 14,000–28,000L ($7–$14); fixed-price menus 35,000L ($17.50). AE, DC, MC, V. Mar–Oct, daily noon–3pm and 7–10:30pm; off-season, Thurs–Tues noon–3pm and Thurs–Mon 7–10:30pm. Bus: B. TUSCAN/ITALIAN.

A local favorite since the 1930s, Il Cavallino is on a tiny street (which probably won't even be on your map) leading off Piazza della Signoria at its northern end. There's usually a gracious reception at the door, especially if you called for a reservation. Two of the three dining rooms have vaulted ceilings and peach-colored marble floors; the main room looks out over the piazza. Menu items are typical hearty Tuscan fare, including an assortment of boiled meats in green herb sauce, grilled fillet of steak, chicken breast Medici style, and the inevitable Florentine spinach. The portions are large. Most diners prefer the house wine, but a limited selection of bottled wines is also available. "Every drop is a pleasure," the waiter assured us as he placed our carafe on the well-set table.

NEAR PIAZZA SANTA MARIA NOVELLA & THE TRAIN STATION

EXPENSIVE

Buca Mario. Piazza Ottaviani 16R. ☎ **055/214-179.** Reservations recommended. Main courses 30,000–50,000L ($15–$25). AE, DC, MC, V. Fri–Tues 12:15–2:30pm and 7:15–10:30pm. Closed Aug. Bus: 6, 9, 11, 36, 37, or 68. FLORENTINE.

Buca Mario, in business for a century, is one of Florence's most famous cellar restaurants, located in the 1886 Palazzo Niccolini. While diners sit at tables beneath the vaulted ceilings, the waiters (some of whom have worked in the States) will suggest an array of fine-textured homemade pastas, grilled T-bone, Dover sole, or beef carpaccio, followed by a tempting selection of desserts, like "grandmother cake," a lemon-and-almond cake. We always like to begin with a medley of cured pork specialties called *affettati toscani*—the tastiest selection of "cold cuts" you're likely to encounter in Florence. There's a wonderful exuberance about the place, but in the enigmatic words of one longtime patron, "It's not for the fainthearted."

✪ **Don Chisciotte.** Via Ridolfi 4R. ☎ **055/475-430.** Reservations recommended. Main courses 28,000–35,000L ($14–$17.50); fixed-price menu 90,000L ($45). AE, DC, MC, V. Tues–Sat 1–2:30pm; Mon–Sat 8–10:30pm. Bus: 20. ITALIAN/SEAFOOD.

One floor above street level in a Florentine palazzo, this restaurant is known for its creative cuisine and changing array of fresh fish. The soft pink dining room reflects the colors of the menu items, which are produced with a flourish from the kitchens. The cuisine is creative, based on flavors that are often enhanced by an unusual assortment of fresh herbs, vegetables, and fish stocks. Choose from risotto of broccoli and baby squid; red *taglioni* with clams, pesto, and cheese; black ravioli colored with squid ink and stuffed with a purée of shrimp and crayfish; and fillet of turbot with radicchio sauce.

I Quattro Amici. Via degli Orti Oricellari 29. ☎ **055/215-413.** Reservations recommended. Main courses 30,000–60,000L ($15–$30). AE, DC, MC, V. Daily noon–2:30pm and 7–10:30pm. Bus: D, 26, 27, or 35. SEAFOOD.

Run by four Tuscan entrepreneurs who have known one another since childhood, this restaurant occupies the street level of a modern building near the rail station and has a vaguely neoclassical decor. Specialties include pasta with shrimp and grappa, fish soup, fried shrimp, squid Livorno style, and grilled, stewed, or baked versions of all the bounty of the Mediterranean. The roast sea bass and roast snapper, flavored with Mediterranean herbs, are among the finest dishes. The vegetables are fresh and flavorful. Every Thursday, Friday, and Saturday evening, diners are treated to live music.

Osteria Numero Uno. Via del Moro 18/20R. ☎ **055/284-897.** Reservations recommended. Main courses 28,000–35,000L ($14–$17.50). AE, DC, MC, V. Mon 7pm–12:30am; Tues–Sat 11am–3pm and 6pm–midnight. Closed 2 weeks in Aug. Bus: C, 6, 9, 11, 36, 37, or 68. INTERNATIONAL/FLORENTINE.

This restaurant was once located at no. 1 (hence the name) on a street nearby and in 1985 moved to this 15th-century palazzo, a 3-minute walk from the rail station. The cuisine is a well-prepared, well-presented blend of international and Italian dishes. Many patrons (often lawyers, civil servants, and reporters) prefer the main dining room, with its vaulted ceiling and oversized fireplace, over the two adjacent rooms. Menu choices include taglioni with mushrooms (with or without truffles); ravioli stuffed with ricotta and basil or fresh artichokes; risotto with asparagus or sweet peppers; carpaccio of beef or salmon; chicken with marsala or parmigiano reggiano; turbot baked with artichokes, herbs, and potatoes; and Florentine beefsteak, usually for two. The atmosphere is often rushed, with harried waiters darting about.

Sabatini. Via de' Panzani 9A. ☎ **055/211-559.** Reservations recommended. Main courses 35,000–60,000L ($17.50–$30). AE, DC, MC, V. Tues–Sun 12:30–2:30pm and 7:30–10:30pm. Bus: 1, 6, 14, 17, or 22. FLORENTINE.

Despite its location near the rail station, Florentines and visitors alike have long extolled Sabatini as the finest of the restaurants characteristic of the city. To celebrate our annual return here, we order the same main course we had on our first visit (boiled Valdarno chicken with a savory green sauce). Back then we complained to the waiter that the chicken was tough. He replied, "But, of course!" Florentines like chicken with muscle, not the hothouse variety so favored by Americans. Having eaten a lot of Valdarno chicken since then, we're more appreciative of Sabatini's dish. But on subsequent visits we've found some of the other main courses more delectable, like the veal scaloppine with artichokes, sole meunière, classic beefsteak Florentine, and spaghetti *Sabatini* (a cousin of spaghetti carbonara but enhanced with fresh tomatoes). American-style coffee is served, following the Florentine cake called *zuccotto.*

✪ **Trattoria Garga.** Via del Moro 48R. ☎ **055/239-8898.** Reservations required. Main courses 30,000–50,000L ($15–$25). AE, DC, MC, V. Tues–Sat 7:30pm–midnight. Bus: 6, 9, 11, 36, 37, or 68. TUSCAN/FLORENTINE.

Some of the most creative cuisine in Florence is served here, between the Ponte Vecchio and Santa Maria Novella. The thick Renaissance walls contain paintings by both Florentine and American artists, including those painted by owners Giuliano Gargani and his Canadian wife, Sharon, along with their son, Andrea. Both operatic arias and heavenly odors emerge from a postage stamp-sized kitchen. Many of the Tuscan menu items are so unusual that Sharon's bilingual skills are put to good use: octopus with peppers and garlic, boar with juniper berries, grilled marinated quail, and "whatever strikes the mood" of Giuliano. One dish has earned a lot of publicity: *taglioni magnifico,* made with angel-hair pasta, orange and lemon rind, mint-flavored cream, and parmigiano reggiano. One of the most delectable pastas is spaghetti with raw artichokes and red pepper served with extra virgin olive oil. The chef prepares a cheesecake so well known in Florence that even New Yorkers give it a thumbs-up.

MODERATE

Buca Lapi. Via del Trebbio 1R. ☎ **055/213-768.** Reservations required for dinner. Main courses 22,000–38,000L ($11–$19). AE, DC, MC, V. Mon–Fri 12:30–2:30pm, Wed–Fri 7:30–10:30pm. Closed 2 weeks in Aug. Bus: 6, 11, 36, or 37. TUSCAN.

This cellar restaurant (under the Palazzo Antinori) opened in 1880 and is big on glamour, good food, and fun. The vaulted ceilings are covered with travel posters from all over the world. The cooks know how to turn out the classic dishes of the Tuscan kitchen with finesse, and there's a long table of interesting fruits, desserts, and vegetables. Skip the international fare. Specialties include *scampi giganti alla griglia* (supersized shrimp) and *bistecca alla fiorentina* (local beefsteak). In season, the *fagioli toscani all'olio* (Tuscan beans in native olive oil) are a delicacy. For dessert, try crepes Suzette or the local choice, *zuccotto,* a dome-shaped ice-cream cake studded with almonds and rich in chocolate. The wine list is full of reasonably priced Tuscan and Chianti wines.

Harry's Bar. Lungarno Vespucci 22R. ☎ **055/239-6700.** Reservations required. Main courses 20,000–38,000L ($10–$19). AE, MC, V. Mon–Sat noon–3pm and 7–11pm. Closed 1 week in Aug and Dec 18–Jan 8. Bus B. INTERNATIONAL/ITALIAN.

Take a Gelato Break

Opened in the 1930s and today run by the third generation of the Vivoli family, the ✪ **Gelateria Vivoli,** Via Isola delle Stinche 7R (☎ **055/292-334**), on a backstreet near Santa Croce, produces some of Italy's finest ice cream and provides the gelati for many of Florence's restaurants.

Buy a ticket first and then select your flavor. Choose from blueberry (*mirtillo*), fig (*fico*), melon (*melone*), and other fruits in season, as well as chocolate mousse (*mousse al cioccolato*) or coffee ice cream flavored with espresso. A special ice cream is made from rice (*gelato di riso*). You can also choose from a number of flavors of *semifreddi*—an Italian ice cream with a cream, instead of milk, base. The most popular flavors are almond (*mandorla*), *marengo* (a type of meringue), and *zabaglione* (eggnog). Others are *limoncini alla crema* (candied lemon peels with vanilla ice cream) and *aranciotti al cioccolate* (candied orange peels with chocolate ice cream). Prices range from 3,500 to 18,000L ($1.75 to $9), and it's open Tuesday to Sunday 8am to 1am (closed 3 weeks in August; dates vary).

Harry's Bar, in an 18th-century building in a prime position on the Arno, has been hosting expatriates and well-heeled visiting Yankees since 1953. It's not as full of chic celebs as it was in the '50s and '60s, but it's still the only place in Florence to get a perfect martini. The international menu is select and beautifully prepared, including risotto or *tagliatelle* (flat noodles) with ham, onions, and cheese and a tempting *gamberetti* (crayfish) cocktail. Harry has created his own tortellini, but his hamburger and his club sandwich are the most popular items. The chef also prepares about a dozen specialties daily: breast of chicken "our way," grilled giant-sized scampi, and lean broiled sirloin. An apple tart with cream nicely finishes off a meal. From March to the end of October, outside tables are available.

INEXPENSIVE

La Carabaccia. Via Palazzuolo 190R. ☎ **055/214-782.** Reservations recommended. Main courses 15,000–35,000L ($7.50–$17.50). AE, MC, V. Tues–Sat noon–2:30pm; Mon–Sat 7–11pm. Closed 15 days in Aug. Bus: 6, 9, 11, 36, 37, or 68. FLORENTINE.

Two hundred years ago, a *carabaccia* was a workaday boat, shaped like a hollowed-out half onion and used on the Arno to dredge silt and sand from the bottom. This restaurant still features the Medicis' favorite *zuppa carabaccia,* a creamy white onion soup with croutons (not in the French style, the chef rushes to tell you). You can, of course, eat more than onions here, and the menu changes daily. "It's always a delight," said one regular, "to come by every day to see what inspired the chef at the market." You can choose the soup of the day, followed by one of four or five pastas, such as a *crespelle* (crêpe) of fresh vegetables like asparagus or artichokes. Our savory swordfish baked in parchment with essence of fresh tomato was perfect, especially when served with the house wine, a white Galestro. You'll find the homemade breads irresistible (especially the onion variety).

Le Fonticine. Via Nazionale 79R. ☎ **055/282-106.** Reservations recommended for dinner. Main courses 18,000–30,000L ($9–$15). AE, DC, MC, V. Tues–Sat noon–2:30pm and 7–10pm. Closed Dec 24–Jan 5 and Aug. Bus: 11, 12, or 32. TUSCAN/BOLOGNESE.

Le Fonticine was part of a convent until owner Silvano Bruci converted both it and its garden into this hospitable restaurant. Today the richly decorated interior contains all the abundance of an Italian harvest, as well as the second passion of Signor Bruci's life, his collection of original modern paintings. The first passion, as a meal here reveals, is the cuisine he and his wife produce from recipes she collected from her childhood in Bologna. Proceed to the larger of the two dining areas; along the way you can admire dozens of portions of fresh pasta decorating the table of an exposed grill. At the far end of the room, a wrought-iron gate shelters the extensive wine collection. The food, served in copious portions, is both traditional and delectable. Begin with a platter of fresh antipasti or with samplings of three of the most excellent pasta dishes of the day. Then follow with *fegatini di pollo* (chicken liver), veal scaloppine, or one of the other main dishes.

Ristorante Otello. Via degli Orti Oricellari 36R. ☎ **055/216-517.** Reservations recommended. Main courses 14,000–32,000L ($7–$16). AE, DC, MC, V. Daily noon–3pm and 7:30–11pm. Bus: 1, 16, 17, 22, 23, 33, or 71. FLORENTINE/TUSCAN.

Located next to the train station, the Otello serves an animated crowd in comfortably renovated surroundings. Its antipasto Toscano is one of the best in town, an array of appetizing hors d'oeuvres that's practically a meal in itself. The waiter urges you to *"Mangi, mangi, mangi!"* and that's what diners do. You might want to try one of the wonderful pasta dishes, such as spaghetti with baby clams or *pappardelle* with garlic sauce. The meat and poultry dishes are equally delectable, including sole meunière and veal pizzaiola with lots of garlic.

✪ **Sostanza.** Via del Porcellana 25R. ☎ **055/212-691.** Reservations recommended. Main courses 16,000–32,000L ($8–$16). No credit cards. Mon–Fri noon–2:10pm and 7:30–9:30pm. Closed Aug and 2 weeks at Christmas. Bus: 6, 11, 12, or 36. FLORENTINE.

Sostanza, the city's oldest (opened 1869) and most revered trattoria, is where working people go for excellent moderately priced food. In recent years, however, it has also begun attracting a more sophisticated set, despite its somewhat funky atmosphere. (Florentines call the place "Troia," a word which means the trough but also suggests a woman of easy virtue.) The small dining room has crowded family tables, but when you taste what comes out of the kitchen, you'll know that fancy decor would be superfluous. Specialties include breaded chicken breast, a succulent T-bone, and tripe Florentine style (cut into strips, then baked in a casserole with tomatoes, onions, and parmigiano).

Trattoria Antellesi. Via Faenza 9R. ☎ **055/216-990.** Reservations recommended. Main courses 16,000–30,000L ($8–$15). AE, DC, MC, V. Daily noon–3pm and 7–10:30pm. Bus: 1, 6, 7, 11, 17, 33, 67, or 68. TUSCAN.

Occupying a 15th-century historic monument, steps from the Medici Chapels, this place is devoted almost exclusively to well-prepared versions of time-tested Tuscan recipes. Owned by Enrico Verrecchia and his Arizona-born wife, Janice, the restaurant prepares at least seven *piatti del giorno* (daily specials) that change according to the market's ingredients. Dishes may include *tagliatelle* (flat noodles) with porcinis or braised arugula, *crespelle alla fiorentina* (cheesy spinach crepe), *pappardelle* with wild boar, fresh fish (generally on Friday), Valdostana chicken, and superb *bistecca alla fiorentina* (local beefsteak). The array of quality Italian wines (with an emphasis on Tuscany) has for the most part been selected by Janice herself.

NEAR PIAZZA SAN MARCO

INEXPENSIVE

Cafaggi. Via Guelfa 35R. ☎ **055/294-989.** Reservations recommended. Main courses 14,000–30,000L ($7–$15). AE, MC, V. Mon–Sat noon–3pm and 7–10pm. Bus: 1, 6, 7, 11, 17, 33, 67, or 68. TUSCAN/SEAFOOD.

Atmospheric and charming, this 100-seat trattoria has flourished in this modestly proportioned palazzo since 1922. The tables are scattered throughout two old-fashioned dining rooms. The menu features Tuscan dishes, including Florentine beefsteak, steaming bowls of vegetarian soup, and very fresh salads and vegetables. Some of the newer menu items celebrate the robust quality of the Tuscan cuisine, notably a savory *risotto alla vedova* (widow's risotto) prepared with cuttlefish. *Caciucco* is a fish soup with shellfish, and once you've tasted spaghetti with sardines, pine nuts, and raisins, it might become addictive. You can also order various fish grilled to perfection, like scampi and swordfish. Forget the calories and try the *millefoglie alle creme* for dessert; it positively overflows with cream.

I' Toscano. Via Guelfa 70R. ☎ **055/215-475.** Reservations recommended at dinner. Main courses 15,000–30,000L ($7.50–$15). AE, DC, MC, V. Wed–Mon 12:30–3pm and 7–11pm. Closed 1 week in Aug. Bus: 6, 11, or 14. TUSCAN.

Bouquets of flowers liven up this restaurant's plain interior, but despite the understated setting, the place is a magnet for foodies who appreciate its Tuscan specialties. Menu items change with the seasons but are often at their best in late autumn and winter, when mixed platters with slices of wild boar, venison, partridge, and (when available) pheasant are a worthy substitute for the antipasti that tempt visitors the rest of the year. Always popular are the spinach-stuffed ravioli and the several forms of gnocchi or *tagliatelle* (flat noodles). Fish (usually sea bass or monkfish, panfried or grilled) is most prominent on Friday, but veal, turkey, pork, and Florentine beefsteaks are also offered.

NEAR PIAZZA SANTA CROCE

EXPENSIVE

✪ **Alle Murate.** Via Ghibellina 52R. ☎ **055/240-618.** Reservations recommended. Main courses 30,000–35,000L ($15–$17.50). AE, DC, MC, V. Tues–Sun 7:30–11:30pm. Closed 15 days at Christmas. Bus: 14. TUSCAN/SOUTHERN ITALIAN.

Young Umberto Montano owns the sophisticated Alle Murate, with a softly lit dining room, and he serves up some of the most creative Tuscan dishes in town. Yet the restaurant also offers classics of the south, like *orecchiette* sauced with broccoli, fish poached *acqua pazza* (with tomatoes, garlic, and parsley), and five-bean puree with cooked chicory. The chefs make a truly memorable lasagna, with mozzarella and fresh tomatoes. Several soufflés are prepared with seasonal vegetables (leeks or artichokes), and handmade *tortelli* (a kind of ravioli) is stuffed with small eggplants and served with butter-and-thyme sauce. There's nothing finer here than the *brasato di chianina* (veal braised with Brunello di Montalcino red wine) or baked sea bream with crunchy potatoes. The wine selection is prodigious (ask and you might get to see the ancient wine cellar). In an adjacent smaller room, the Vineria, the menu is different, the service not as good, but the food slightly cheaper.

You may also want to check out Montano's **Osteria del Caffè Italiano** and **Caffè Italiano** (see below).

Cibreo. Via Verrocchio 8R. ☎ **055/234-1100.** Reservations recommended in the restaurant, not accepted in the trattoria. Main courses 50,000L ($25) in the restaurant, 20,000L ($10) in the trattoria. AE, DC, MC, V (restaurant only). Tues–Sat 12:50–3pm and 7:30–11pm. Closed late July–early Sept. Bus: B or 14. MEDITERRANEAN.

The brainchild of the inventive Fabio Picchi and Benedetta Vitali, Cibreo consists of a restaurant, a less formal trattoria, and a cafe/bar across the street. The impossibly old-fashioned small kitchen doesn't have a grill and doesn't turn out pastas. Menu items include *sformato* (a soufflé made from potatoes and ricotta, served with parmigiano and tomato sauce), *inzimmino* (Tuscan-style squid stewed with spinach), and a flan of parmigiano, veal tongue, and artichokes. The *cicina* is garlicy and spicy. Some of the staff are expatriate New Yorkers who excel at explaining the menu. The restaurant takes its name from (and serves) an old Tuscan dish combining the organs, meat, and crest (or comb) of a chicken with tons of garlic, rosemary, sage, and wine. (Allegedly, it was so delectable it nearly killed Catherine de' Medici, for she consumed so much she was overcome with near-fatal indigestion.) It's prepared only on request, usually for specially catered meals ordered in advance. Chocoholics can finish off with the flourless chocolate cake, so sinfully good it should be outlawed.

INEXPENSIVE

✪ **Osteria del Caffè Italiano.** Via Isola delle Stinche 11–13R (2 blocks west of Piazza Santa Croce). ☎ **055/28-93-68.** Reservations for restaurant (not wine bar) suggested. Wine bar: Primi 8,000L ($4); secondi 14,000L ($7). Restaurant: Main courses 20,000–25,000L ($10–$12.50). DC, MC, V. Tues–Sun noon–1am. Bus: A or 14. WINE BAR/TUSCAN.

Housed in the 13th-century Palazzo Salviati, this new wine bar/trattoria is the brainchild of Umberto Montano (see Alle Murate, above, and Caffè Italiano, below). The front room is warmed by burnished wood paneling and made even more welcoming when you see the prices. Beneath a wrought-iron chandelier hanging from the vaulted 20-foot ceiling, you can sample delicious choices from the short menu. Look for the fresh *mozzarella di bufala* specially couriered from a private supplier in Naples every Thursday, Friday, and Saturday (not available June to August). Stop by any time they're not serving meals for a by-the-glass introduction to Montano's renowned wine cellar and an assortment of Tuscan *salumi.* Or come back in the evening to dine in the elegant restaurant in the back room and splurge with excellently prepared entrees from the grill and a more serious sampling of wine.

Don't miss Montano's handsome **Caffè Italiano,** Via Condotta 56R, off Via dei Calzaiuoli (☎ **055/29-1082;** Bus: 14, 23, or 71), which offers a delicious lunch and dinner to standing-room-only crowds (come early). It's open daily 12:30 to 3pm and 8 to 10pm. Umberto's restaurants were a big hit with Anne Bancroft and Mel Brooks while they were in town recently making a film.

✪ **Ristorante Dino.** Via Ghibellina 51R. ☎ **055/241-452.** Reservations recommended. Main courses 18,000–25,000L ($9–$12.50). AE, DC, MC, V. Tues–Sat noon–3pm and 7:30–10:30pm; Sun noon–2:30pm. Bus: 14. TUSCAN.

Located in a 14th-century building near the Casa Buonarroti, this animated restaurant has vaulted ceilings and a cuisine inspired by the Casini family. They enjoy studying old Florentine recipes, especially those of the Medici era, and trying to re-create them as faithfully as possible. Some examples are *carabaccia* (sliced onions and vegetables in their own broth), *stracotto del granduca* (the best beef cooked slowly in Chianti with raisins, pine nuts, mint, and cinnamon), *garetto Ghibellino* (pork shanks with celery and sage), and *pappa con il pomodoro* (bread, fresh tomatoes, fresh basil, and onions). More-modern dishes include *risotto della renza* (with a combination of fresh aromatic herbs gathered in the Florentine countryside), *coscia di vitella al mirto* (lean veal roasted with myrtle, celery, and leeks), and *peposo dei fornacini* (peppery beef stew served over bread).

Trattoria Pallottino. Isola delle Stinche 1R. ☎ **055/289-573.** Reservations recommended at dinner. Main courses 15,000–30,000L ($7.50–$15). AE, CB, DC, MC, V. Tues–Sun 12:30–2:30pm and 7:30–10:30pm. Bus: 14, 23, or 71. TUSCAN/FLORENTINE.

Less than a block from Piazza Santa Croce, on a narrow street, this distinctive restaurant contains two sometimes-cramped dining rooms. Flickering candles illuminate a timeless Italian scene where the staff works hard, usually with humor and style. Menu specialties are succulent antipasti, *taglioni* with cream and herbs, ravioli with spinach or pine nuts and cream sauce, *peposa* (a slab of beef marinated for at least 4 hours in a rich broth of ground black pepper, olive oil, and tomatoes), and *spaghetti fiacchiraia* (with spicy red chilies, olive oil, and tomatoes). Dessert might be vanilla custard drizzled with a compote of fresh fruit.

NEAR THE PONTE VECCHIO

MODERATE

La Nandina. Borgo SS. Apostoli 64R. ☎ **055/213-024.** Reservations recommended. Main courses 25,000–40,000L ($12.50–$20). AE, DC, MC, V. Mon 7–10:30pm; Tues–Sat noon–3pm and 7–10:30pm. Closed 2 weeks in Aug. Bus: 23 or 71. TUSCAN/INTERNATIONAL.

Opened in 1924, this family-run restaurant is just off the Arno, about a 4-minute walk from the Uffizi, and is an old favorite with both Florentines and visitors. You can have a cocktail in the plush lounge and dine in the 14th-century cellar. The cuisine consists of dishes from the provinces as well as from Rome and Venice and might include ravioli with flap mushrooms, spinach crepes, curried breast of capon, veal piccatina, several kinds of beefsteak, and a changing array of daily specials. All the food is high quality but not fussy.

Inexpensive

Buca dell'Orafo. Via Volta dei Girolami 28R. ☎ **055/213-619.** Main courses 14,000–30,000L ($7–$15). No credit cards. Tues–Sat 12:30–2:30pm and 7:30–10:30pm. Closed Aug and 2 weeks in Dec. Bus: B. FLORENTINE.

This is an authentic neighborhood restaurant whose cuisine is firmly rooted in Tuscan traditions and inspired by whatever happens to be in season. Accessible via an alley beneath a vaulted arcade adjacent to Piazza del Pesce, it's named after the *orafo* (goldsmith shop) that occupied its premises during the Renaissance. The place is usually stuffed with regulars, who appreciate that the chef has made almost no concessions to international palates. Your pasta (usually *taglioni*) will probably be garnished with a seasonal vegetable, like asparagus, broccoli rabe, mushrooms, peas, or asparagus. Florentine tripe and beefsteak are enduring favorites, as is *stracotto e fagioli* (beef braised in chopped vegetables and red wine), served with beans in tomato sauce.

Near Piazza Trinita

Inexpensive

✪ **Il Latini.** Via del Palchetti 6R (off Via Vigna Nuova). ☎ **055/210-916.** Reservations recommended. Main courses 15,000–28,000L ($7.50–$14). AE, DC, MC, V. Tues–Sun 12:30–2:30pm and 7:30–10:30pm. Closed 15 days in Aug and Dec 20–Jan 6. Bus: C, 6, 11, 36, or 37. TUSCAN/FLORENTINE.

Il Latini is loud and claustrophobic and the service borders on hysterical, but this is an enduringly popular place, with long lines. Diners pack the place for the enormous portions. A waiter will arrive to recite a list of items corresponding to antipasti, pasta, main course, and dessert. If you insist on seeing a printed menu, someone will probably find one, but it's more fun just to go with the flow. You can enjoy heaping portions of pastas like penne with meat and cream sauce, deep-fried zucchini flowers or artichokes, and grilled meats that include veal, chicken, beef, and pork. Don't expect decorative subtleties: The paintings are garish, and nobody is shy about displaying each and every framed award the place has ever earned.

Note that the Latini brothers have recently split and the cooks and wait staff have gone with Giovanni Latini to a new restaurant at Via dei Platani, Locandà La Steccaia, in nearby San Gimignano (☎ **0577/945-019**).

Across the Arno

Expensive

La Capannina di Sante. Piazza Ravenna, adjacent to the Ponte Giovanni da Verrazzano. ☎ **055/688-345.** Reservations recommended. Main courses 25,000–40,000L ($12.50–$20); fixed-price menu 110,000L ($55). AE, DC, MC, V. Mon–Sat 7:30pm–1am. Closed 1 week in Aug. Bus: 3, 31, or 32. SEAFOOD.

This unpretentious restaurant, featuring a river-view terrace, has functioned in more or less the same way on and off since 1935. It serves only the best and freshest seafood, prepared in a healthy manner, usually with olive oil or butter and Mediterranean seasonings. Examples are fillet of sea bass or turbot, mixed seafood grill, and an occasional portion of veal or steak. For an appetizer, we recommend the sampler of hot seafood—there's none finer in Florence. The wines are simple and straightforward, and the greeting is warm and friendly.

Moderate

Mamma Gina. Borgo San Jacopo 37R. ☎ **055/239-6009.** Reservations required for dinner. Main courses 25,000–38,000L ($12.50–$19). AE, DC, MC, V. Mon–Sat noon–2:30pm and 7–10:30pm. Closed 15 days in Aug. Bus: D. TUSCAN.

Mamma Gina is a rustic restaurant that prepares fine foods in the traditional manner. Although run by a corporation that operates other restaurants around Tuscany, this place is named after its founding matriarch, whose legend has continued despite her death in the 1980s. A few of the savory menu items are cannelloni Mamma Gina (stuffed with a puree of meats, spices, and vegetables), taglioni with artichoke hearts or mushrooms and whatever else is in season, and chicken breast Mamma Gina (baked northern Italian style with prosciutto and Emmenthaler cheese). This is an ideal spot for lunch after visiting the Pitti Palace.

Trattoria Cammillo. Borgo San Jacopo 57R (between the Ponte Vecchio and Ponte Santa Trinita). ☎ **055/212-427.** Reservations required. Main courses 22,000–50,000L ($11–$25). AE, DC, MC, V. Thurs–Tues noon–2:30pm and 7:30–10:30pm. Closed mid-Dec to Jan and Aug 1–21. Bus: C, 6, 11, 36, 37, or 68. TUSCAN.

On the ground floor of a former Medici palace, the Cammillo is one of the most popular (and perhaps the finest) of the Oltrarno dining spots. Its most serious rival is Mamma Gina (above). Snobbish boutique owners cross the Arno regularly to feast here; they know they'll get specialties like *tagliatelle* (flat noodles) flavored with fresh peas and truffles (it sounds like such a simple dish, but when prepared right it's a real treat). You'll also find excellent assortments of fried or grilled vegetables, fresh scampi and sole, fried deboned pigeon with artichokes, and chicken breast with truffles and parmigiano. Because of increased business, you're likely to be rushed through a meal.

INEXPENSIVE

La Baruciola. Via Maggio 61R. ☎ **055/218-906.** Reservations recommended. Main courses 12,000–18,000L ($6–$9). AE, DC, MC, V. Daily 12:30–2:30pm and 7–10:30pm. Bus: B or C. TUSCAN.

In a 16th-century building adjacent to the Pitti Palace, this restaurant celebrates the art of *cucina casalinga* (home cooking) and draws a busy crowd of Tuscans. In a pair of white dining rooms whose decor is understated, you can enjoy pastas such as homemade ravioli stuffed with dry mushrooms and penne with mushrooms and cream, or try *ribollita,* the heady vegetable soup of Tuscany, and a mixed platter of fish or smoked meat. The chef will even prepare a vegetarian lasagna. The place appeals to those who like simple well-prepared dishes, brimming with flavor but low in price.

Pierot. Piazza Tadeo Gaddi 25R. ☎ **055/702-100.** Reservations recommended. Main courses 18,000–30,000L ($9–$15). AE, DC, MC, V. Mon–Sat noon–3pm and 7–11pm. Closed July 10–31. Bus: 9, 11, or 36. SEAFOOD/TUSCAN.

Pierot is housed in a building constructed during the reign of Vittorio Emanuele. It specializes in seafood, which is a bit of an oddity in Florence, though a few other places feature seafood also. The seasonal menu varies with the availability of ingredients but may include linguine with *frutti di mare* (fruits of the sea), pasta with lobster sauce, and a choice of traditional Tuscan steaks, soups, and vegetables. Seafood risotto is deservedly a favorite. The wine list features some 120 choices.

Trattoria Angiolino. Via San Spirito 36R. ☎ **055/239-8976.** Reservations recommended. Main courses 16,000–25,000L ($8–$12.50). AE, DC, MC, V. Tues–Sun noon–2:30pm and 7–10:30pm. Bus: C, 6, 11, 36, 37, or 68. ITALIAN/TUSCAN.

This restaurant has thrived in this 14th-century building since the 1920s and has fed a friend or relative of virtually everyone in Florence. The decor is old-timey and warm, with a potbellied stove and brick floors, and the menu includes Tuscan and Italian dishes that many visitors remember from their childhood. Choose from an array of antipasti, steaming bowls of *pasta e fagioli* (beans), a roster of homemade pastas like ravioli and taglioni, veal and chicken cutlets prepared either Milanese or parmigiana style, and rich homemade cakes and pastries.

5 Seeing the Sights

Florence was the fountainhead of the Renaissance, the city of Dante and Boccaccio. For 3 centuries, the city was dominated by the Medici family, patrons of the arts and masters of assassination. But it's chiefly through Florence's incomparable artists that we know of the apogee of the Renaissance: Ghiberti, Fra Angelico, Donatello, Brunelleschi, Botticelli, Leonardo da Vinci, and Michelangelo.

In Florence we can trace the transition from medievalism to the age of "rebirth." For example, all modern painters owe a debt to an ugly, unkempt man named Masaccio (Vasari's "Slipshod Tom") who died at 27. Modern painting began with his frescoes in the Brancacci Chapel in Santa Maria del Carmine, which you can see today. Years later, Michelangelo painted a more celebrated Adam and Eve in the Sistine Chapel, but even this great artist never realized the raw humanity of Masaccio's Adam and Eve fleeing from the Garden of Eden.

Group tourism has so overwhelmed this city that in 1996 officials demanded that organized tour groups book their visits in advance and pay an admission fee. No more than 150 tour buses are allowed into the center at one time (considering how small Florence is, even that's a lot). Today there are more than seven tourists for each native Florentine. And that isn't counting the day-trippers, who rush off to Venice in the late afternoon. But despite all its traffic and inconveniences, Florence is still one of the world's greatest art cities.

If you have a limited amount of time or want to get an overall view before exploring on your own, many companies run guided bus tours of the main sights. The two virtually indistinguishable big names are **American Express** (☎ **055/50-981**) and **SitaSightseeing** (☎ **055/294-955**). They run morning tours of the major sights and separate afternoon tours of the top secondary sights; the cost is 60,000L ($30) per person for each half-day tour, museum admissions included. Both companies also run afternoon tours to Pisa (60,000L/$30) and the Chianti (55,000L/$27.50) and an all-day trip combining Siena and San Gimignano (100,000L/$50). To arrange any other kind of guided tour, visit the **Ufficio Guide Turistiche** at Via Roma 4 (☎ **055/2302-283**).

There's a daily walking tour called **Enjoy Florence** (☎ **167/274-819** toll free from anywhere in Italy; www.enjoyflorence.it). It departs daily at 10am (with a second tour on Monday, Wednesday, and Friday at 5pm) from the Thomas Cook exchange office just west of the Ponte Vecchio on the Duomo side of the river; it lasts 3 hours and costs 30,000L ($15) for those over 26 and 25,000L ($12.50) for those under 26.

THE TOP MUSEUMS

✪ **Uffizi Gallery (Galleria degli Uffizi).** Piazzale degli Uffizi 6. ☎ **055/238-85.** www.uffizi.firenze.it. Admission 12,000L ($6). Mon–Fri 8:30am–9pm; Sat 8:30am–midnight; Sun 8:30am–8pm (last entrance 45 min. before closing). Bus: 23 or 71.

When Anna Maria Ludovica, the last Medici grand duchess, died in 1737, she bequeathed to the people of Tuscany a wealth of Renaissance and even classical art. The paintings and sculptures had been accumulated by the powerful grand dukes during 3 centuries of rule that witnessed the height of the Renaissance. All this is housed in an impressive palazzo commissioned by Duke Cosimo de' Medici in 1560 and

A Note About Museum & Church Hours

Most stores close for long lunch breaks, and many of the museums close for the day at 2pm or earlier (the last entrance is at least 30 minutes before closing) and are closed on Mondays. The Uffizi, the Accademia, the Palazzo Vecchio, the Duomo and the Duomo Museum, the Campanile di Giotto, Santa Croce, the Pitti Palace, and the Boboli Gardens are among the attractions that remain open during *il riposo.* The first thing you should do is stop by the tourist office for an up-to-date listing of museum hours and possible extended hours (in 1998, some museums stayed open, and empty, until 11:30pm!).

Churches and markets are good alternatives for spending your afternoons, since they usually remain open till 7pm (however, churches, too, close for the long lunch break). The open-air Mercato San Lorenzo gets the lunch crowd; the stalls never close.

initiated by Giorgio Vasari to house the Duchy of Tuscany's administrative offices (*uffizi* means offices).

After several renovations following a terrorist bomb in 1993, the Uffizi now has a new look. A lobby has been added so that visitors don't have to wait in line outside; the galleries at the upper two floors are three times their previous size; the trompe l'oeil painting in the Loggiato sull'Arno has been restored to its original beauty; and walking down this hall, looking through the high windows, you'll have enchanting views of Florence. There's also a new bookstore on the premises.

You can buy tickets in advance online at www.selectitaly.com, or join a small tour that avoids the lines by logging onto www.arca.net, which has a full catalog of the museum's works on the Web.

The Uffizi is nicely grouped into periods or schools to show the development and progress of Italian and European art.

Room 2: Here you'll meet up with those rebels from Byzantium, Cimabue and his pupil Giotto, with their Madonnas and bambini. Since the Virgin and Child seem to be the overriding theme of the earlier Uffizi artists, it's enlightening just to follow the different styles over the centuries, from the ugly, almost midget-faced babies of the post-Byzantine works to the red-cheeked chubby cherubs that glorified the baroque. One of the great works in the center of the salon is Giotto's masterful *Ognissanti Maestà* (1310).

Room 3: Look for Simone Martini's *Annunciation,* full of grace; the halo around the head of the Virgin doesn't conceal her pouty mouth. Fra Angelico of Fiesole, a 15th-century painter lost in a world peopled with saints and angels, makes his Uffizi debut with (naturally) *Madonna and Bambino.* A special treasure is the *Santa Trinita Madonna* by Masaccio, who died at an early age but is credited as the father of modern painting: In his Madonnas and bambini, we see the beginnings of the use of perspective in painting. Fra Angelico's *Coronation of the Virgin* is also in this salon.

Room 8: Here you'll find Friar Filippo Lippi's superior *Coronation of the Virgin,* as well as a galaxy of charming Madonnas. He was a rebel among the brethren.

Rooms 10 to 14: These are the Botticelli rooms, with his finest works. Botticelli ("little barrels") was the nickname of the great master of women in flowing gowns, Sandro Filipepi. Many come to contemplate his *"Venus on the Half Shell":* This supreme conception of life (the *Birth of Venus*) really packs 'em in. Also check out *Minerva Subduing the Centaur,* which brought about renewed interest in mythological subjects. Botticelli's *Allegory of Spring* or *Primavera* is a gem; it depicts Venus in a

Florence Attractions

Academy Gallery **10**
Archaeology Museum **13**
Baptistry **25**
Bargello Museum **23**
Basilica di San Lorenzo **7**
Basilica di Santa Croce **16**
Basilica di Santa Maria Novella **3**
Buonarotti's House **15**
Duomo Museum **28**
Giardini di Boboli **1**
Giotto's Bell Tower **26**
Hospital of the Innocents **12**
Il Duomo (Cathedral of Santa Maria del Fiore) **27**
La Sinagoga di Firenze **14**
Loggia della Signoria **19**
Medici Chapels **4**
Mercato Centrale **5**
Orsanmichele **24**
Palazzo Medici-Riccardi **8**
Palazzo Pitti **1**
Palazzo Vecchio **21**
Piazza della Santissima Annunziata **11**
Piazza della Signoria **22**
Piazza San Lorenzo **6**
Piazza Santa Croce **17**
Piazzale Michelangiolo **18**
Ponte Vecchio **2**
St. Mark's Museum **9**
Uffizi Gallery **20**

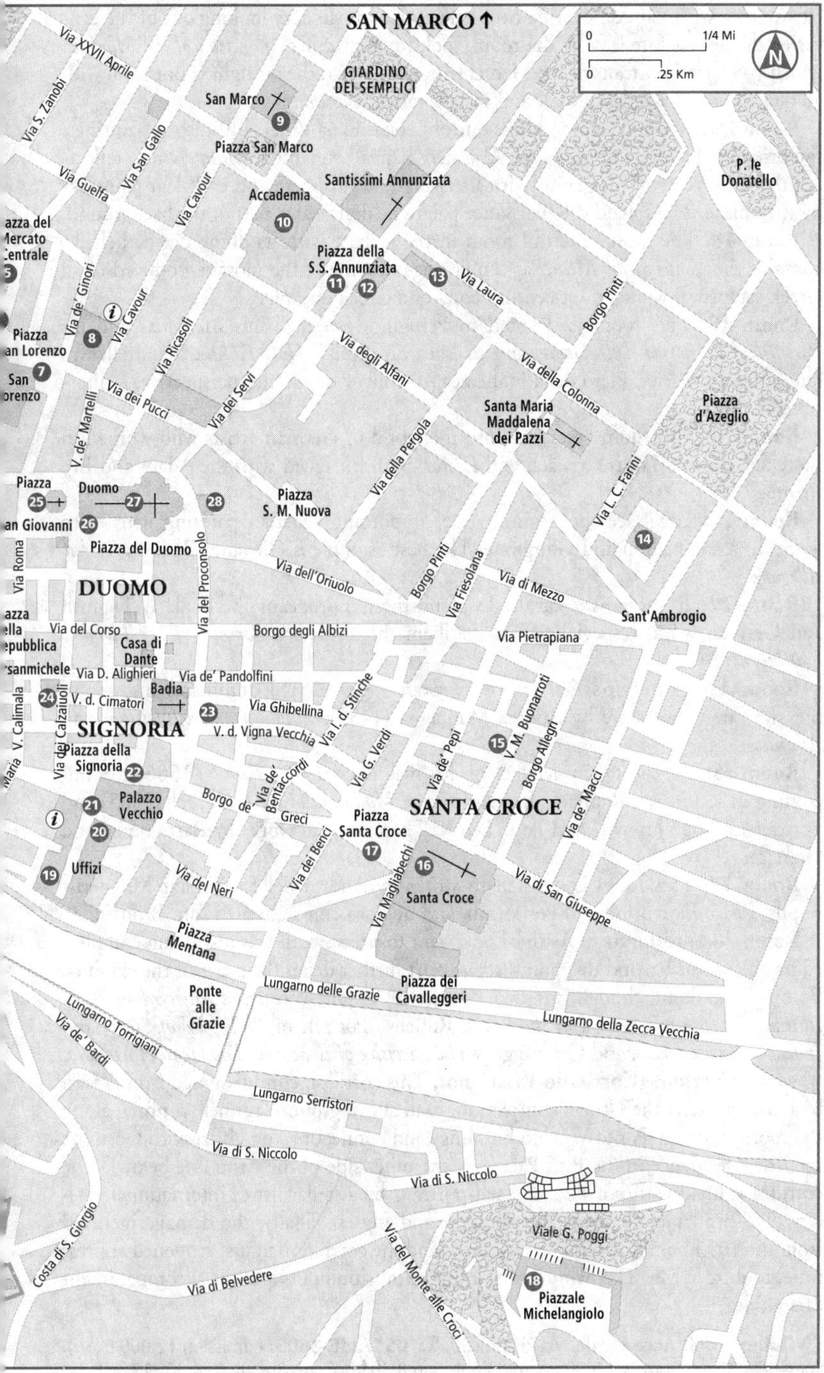
SAN MARCO ↑
0 1/4 Mi
0 .25 Km
N
GIARDINO DEI SEMPLICI
San Marco
Piazza San Marco
Santissimi Annunziata
Accademia
Piazza della S.S. Annunziata
P. le Donatello
Via XXVII Aprile
Via S. Zanobi
Via San Gallo
Via Guelfa
Via Cavour
Via de' Ginori
Via Laura
Borgo Pinti
Via degli Alfani
Via della Colonna
Via Ricasoli
Via dei Servi
Via dei Pucci
V. de' Martelli
Santa Maria Maddalena dei Pazzi
Piazza d'Azeglio
Via della Pergola
Via L. C. Farini
Piazza del Mercato Centrale
Piazza San Lorenzo
San Lorenzo
Piazza San Giovanni
Duomo
Piazza S. M. Nuova
Piazza del Duomo
DUOMO
Via Roma
Via del Proconsolo
Via dell'Oriuolo
Borgo Pinti
Via Fiesolana
Via di Mezzo
Sant'Ambrogio
Piazza della Repubblica
Via del Corso
Borgo degli Albizi
Via Pietrapiana
Orsanmichele
Casa di Dante
Via D. Alighieri
Via de' Pandolfini
Badia
V. d. Cimatori
Via Ghibellina
Via I. d. Stinche
SIGNORIA
V. d. Vigna Vecchia
Via G. Verdi
Via de' Pepi
V. M. Buonarroti
Borgo Allegri
Via Calimala
V. dei Calzaiuoli
Piazza della Signoria
Via de' Bentaccordi
Borgo de' Greci
Palazzo Vecchio
Piazza Santa Croce
SANTA CROCE
Via de' Macci
Uffizi
Via dei Benci
Via Magliabechi
Santa Croce
Via di San Giuseppe
Via del Neri
Piazza Mentana
Ponte alle Grazie
Lungarno delle Grazie
Piazza dei Cavalleggeri
Lungarno della Zecca Vecchia
Lungarno Torrigiani
Via de' Bardi
Lungarno Serristori
Via di S. Niccolo
Via di S. Niccolo
Costa di S. Giorgio
Via del Monte alle Croci
Viale G. Poggi
Via di Belvedere
Piazzale Michelangiolo

citrus grove with Cupid hovering over her head, and Mercury looking out of the canvas to the left. Before leaving the room, look for Botticelli's *Adoration of the Magi,* in which you'll find portraits of the Medici (the vain man at the far right is Botticelli with golden curls and a yellow robe), and his allegorical *Calumny.*

Room 15: Here you'll come across one of Leonardo da Vinci's unfinished paintings, the brilliant *Adoration of the Magi.* Also here hangs Leonardo's *Annunciation,* reflecting the early years of his genius with its twilight atmosphere and each leaf painstakingly in place. The splendid Renaissance palace he designed is part of the background.

Room 18: The most beautiful room in the gallery, with its dome of pearl shells, contains the *Venus of the Medici* at center stage; it's one of the most reproduced of all Greek sculptural works, a 1st-century copy of a Greek original.

Room 19: This room is devoted to Perugino, especially his *Madonna* and his *Portrait of Francesco delle Opere,* and to Luca Signorelli's *Holy Family.* Signorelli was taught by his master, Piero della Francesca, to convey depth and perspective, as illustrated by this work.

Room 20: This room takes you into the world of German artists who worked in Florence, notably Lucas Cranach and Dürer, both intrigued with the Adam and Eve theme.

Room 21: You'll see the beginnings of important Venetian painting here, with works by Giambellino and Giorgione. The best example is Giovanni Bellini's *Sacred Allegory.*

Room 22: It contains a cavalcade of northern Europeans, particularly Flemish and German works, especially Hans Holbein the Younger's *Portrait of Sir Richard Southwell.*

Room 23: Correggio's *Rest on the Flight to Egypt* (1515) dominates this room, but the finest pieces are by Andrea Mantagna (1489): *Epiphany, Circumcision,* and *Ascension.*

Room 25: The star here is Michelangelo's magnificent *Holy Family* (1506–08), but coming in second are Raphael's Leonardoesque *Madonna of the Goldfinch* (1505) and portraits of Pope Julius II and Pope Leo X. There are also works by Bartolomeo and Granacci.

Room 27: This room is devoted to works by Andrea del Sarto's star Mannerist pupils, Rosso Fiorentino and Pontormo, and by Portormo's adopted son, Bronzino.

Room 28 and the Rest: As this book went to press, work was just being completed on the rooms beyond this point, so we can't further detail the order of the exhibits. Be on the lookout, though, for two Venuses by Titian, Veronese's *Martyrdom of St. Justina,* Tintoretto's *Leda and the Swan,* Rubens's Portrait of *Philip IV of Spain* and *Judith and Holofernes,* and Caravaggio's *The Sacrifice of Isaac* and *The Head of Medusa.*

Vasari Corridor (Corridoio Vasariano): This corridor, commissioned from Vasari by Cosimo I after the Uffizi's completion, is an above-ground "tunnel" running along the rooftops of the Ponte Vecchio buildings and connecting the Uffizi with Cosimo's then-new residence in the Pitti Palace on the other side of the Arno (see below). The corridor is lined with portraits and self-portraits by a stellar list of international masters, like Bronzino, Reubens, Rembrandt, and Ingres. Finally, the damage incurred from the 1993 bombing has been repaired, and the corridor had just reopened at press time. Inquire at the ticket window regarding admission hours and the accompaniment of a guide.

✪ **Galleria dell'Accademia.** Via Ricasoll 60. ☎ **055/238-8609.** Admission 12,000 L ($6). Tues–Fri 8:30am–9pm; Sat 8:30am–midnight; Sun 8:30am–8pm. Bus: 1, 6, 7, 11, 17, 20, 25, 31, 32, or 33.

No More Lines

Sun or rain, the endless lines outside the Italian museums are a fact of life. But new reservation services can help you to avoid waiting, at least for some of the major museums.

Select Italy offers the possibility to reserve your tickets for The Uffizi, Boboli Gardens, Galleria dell'Accademia, and many other museums in Florence, Rome, and Venice. The cost varies from U.S. $11 to $24, depending on the museum, and several combination passes are available. Select Italy's main office is at 329 Linden Avenue, Wilmette, IL 60091-2788 (☎ **847/853-1661;** fax 847/853-1667). You can buy your tickets from them online at www.selectitaly.com.

If you're already in Florence and don't want to waste a half-day waiting to enter the Galleria degli Uffizi, Galleria dell'Accademia, Boboli Gardens, Pitti Palace, and many others, call **Firenze Musei** (☎ **055/282-828;** www.firenzemusei.it). The service is operating Monday to Friday from 8:30am to 6:30pm, and Saturday to 12:30pm. Requests must be made a minimum of 5 days in advance, and then you'll pick up the tickets at the museum booth on the day your visit has been approved. Cost is 2,000L ($1) plus, of course, the regular price of the museum admission.

You can also join a small tour that avoids the Uffizi lines on the Web at www.arca.net.

This museum boasts many paintings and sculptures, but they're completely overshadowed by one work: Michelangelo's colossal ✪ ***David,*** unveiled in 1504 and now the world's most fabled sculpture. It first stood in Piazza della Signoria but was moved to the Accademia in 1873 (a copy was substituted) and placed beneath the rotunda of a room built exclusively for its display. When he began work, Michelangelo was just 29. One of the most sensitive accounts we've ever read of how Michelangelo turned the 17-foot "Duccio marble" into *Il Gigante* (the Giant) is related in Irving Stone's *The Agony and the Ecstasy.* Stone describes a Michelangelo "burning with marble fever" who set out to create a *David* who "would be Apollo, but considerably more; Hercules, but considerably more; Adam, but considerably more; the most fully realized man the world had yet seen, functioning in a rational and humane world."

David is so overpowering in his majesty that many visitors head here just to see him and leave immediately after. (The wait to get in to see *David* can be up to an hour. Try getting there before the museum opens in the morning or an hour or two before closing time.) However, the hall leading up to him is lined with other Michelangelos, notably his quartet of celebrated *Prisoners* or *Slaves.* The statues are presumably unfinished, though art historians have found them more dramatic in their current state as they depict the struggles of figures to free themselves from stone. Michelangelo worked on these statues, originally intended for the tomb of Pope Julius II, for 40 years because he was never pleased with them. The gallery also displays Michelangelo's statue of St. Matthew, which he began carving in 1504.

The Accademia also owns a gallery of paintings, usually considered to be of minor importance (works by Santi di Tito, Granacci, and Albertinelli, for example). Yet there are masterpieces as well, notably Lo Scheggia's 1440s *Cassone Adimari,* a panel from a wedding chest.

✪ **Palazzo Pitti and the Giardini di Boboli (Boboli Gardens).** Piazza de' Pitti, across the Arno. ☎ **055/238-85.** Palatina 12,000L ($6); Modern Art Gallery 8,000L ($4); Argenti 4,000L ($2); Boboli Gardens 4,000L ($2). Galleria Palatina and Appartamenti Reali Tues–Fri

8am–9pm; Sat 8am–midnight; and Sun 8am–8pm. Museo degli Argenti and Modern Art Gallery daily 8:30am–1:30pm; closed the 1st, 3rd, and 5th Mon and the 2nd and 4th Sun of each month. Boboli Gardens June–Sept, daily 8:30am–7:45pm; Apr–May and Oct, daily 8:30am–6:45pm; Nov–Mar, daily 9am–5:45pm; closed the 1st and the last Mon of each month. Ticket office closes 1 hour before the gardens. Bus: B or C.

The massive bulk of the **Palazzo Pitti** is one of Europe's greatest artistic treasure troves, with the city's most extensive coterie of museums embracing a painting gallery second only to the Uffizi. It's a virtual cavalcade of the works of Titian, Rubens, Raphael, and Andrea del Sarto. Built in the mid–century (Brunelleschi was probably the original architect), this was once the residence of the powerful Medici family. It's located across the Arno (a 5-minute walk from the Ponte Vecchio).

Of the several museums in this complex, the most important is the first-floor **Palatine Gallery (Galleria Palatina),** housing one of Europe's great art collections, with masterpieces hung one on top of the other as in the days of the Enlightenment. If for no other reason, you should come for its Raphaels. After passing through the main door, proceed to the Sala di Venere (Venus), where you'll find Titian's *La Bella,* of rich and illuminating color (entrance wall), and his portrait of Pietro Aretino, one of his most distinguished works. On the opposite wall are Titian's *Concert of Music,* often attributed to Giorgione, and his portrait of Julius II.

In the Sala di Apollo (on the opposite side of the entrance door) are Titian's *Man with Gray Eyes*—an aristocratic, handsome romanticist—and his luminously gold *Mary Magdalene,* covered only with her long hair. On the opposite wall are van Dyck portraits of Charles I of England and Henrietta of France. This salon also contains some of the grandest works of Andrea del Sarto, notably his *Holy Family* and his *Deposition.*

In the Sala di Marte (entrance wall) is an important *Madonna and Child* by Murillo of Spain and the Pitti's best-known work by Rubens, *The Four Philosophers.* Rubens obviously had so much fun with this rather lighthearted work that he painted himself in on the far left (that's his brother, Filippo, seated). On the left wall is one of Ruben's most tragic and moving works, *Consequences of War*—an early *Guernica,* painted in his declining years.

In the Sala di Giove (entrance wall) are Andrea del Sarto's idealized *John the Baptist* in his youth and Fra Bartolomeo's *Descent from the Cross.* On the third wall (opposite the entrance wall) is the Pitti's second famous Raphael, *La Velata,* the woman under the veil, known as La Fornarina, his bakery-girl mistress.

In the following gallery, the Sala di Saturno, look to the left on the entrance wall to see Raphael's *Madonna of the Canopy.* On the third wall near the doorway is the greatest Pitti prize, Raphael's ***Madonna of the Chair,*** his best-known interpretation of the Virgin and what's probably one of the six most celebrated paintings in all Europe. In the Sala dell'Iliade (to your left on the entrance wall) is a work of delicate beauty, Raphael's rendition of a pregnant woman. On the left wall is Titian's *Portrait of a Gentleman,* which he was indeed. (Titian is the second big star in the gallery.) Other masterpieces are in the smaller rooms that follow, notably the Sala dell'Educazione di Giove, home to the 1608 *Sleeping Cupid* that "the divine" Caravaggio painted in Rome while escaping charges of murder in Malta.

The **Royal Apartments (Appartamenti Reali)** boast lavish reminders of when the Pitti was a private residence. This was once the home of the Kings of Savoy, when they presided over a unified Italy. Reopened in 1993 after a restoration, these apartments in all their baroque sumptuousness, including a flamboyant decor and works of art by del Sarto and Caravaggio, can be viewed only on a guided tour, usually Tuesday and Saturday (also on an occasional Thurs) 9 to 11am and 3 to 5pm. Tours leave every hour. Reservations are needed, so call ☎ **051/238-8614.**

The **Modern Art Gallery (Galeria d'Arte Moderna; ☎ 055/2388-616)** is hardly the world's finest, and you can skip it if you're exhausted after all those Titians. Nevertheless, it contains an important collection of 19th-century proto-Impressionist works of the Macchiaioli school, embracing many romantic and neoclassic pieces. Even if you don't like the art, the panoramic view from the top floor is worth the visit. The **Gallery of Costume (Galleria del Costume),** housed in the Palazzina della Meridiana wing of the Modern Art gallery, traces the history of dress over 2 centuries, from the tight corsets and wide panniers of the 18th century to the beginning of the loose flapper dresses in the 1920s. Some of the costumes are even older than this.

The ground-floor **Museum of Silver (Museo degli Argenti)** displays the household wares of the Medicis, everything from precious ivory, silver, and rare gems to Lorenzo the Magnificent's celebrated collection of vases. These precious stone vases spawned a vogue for *pietra dura* (precious stonework) in the 19th century (the English called it Florentine mosaic). One writer called the entire collection here "a camp glorification of the Medici." Many of the exhibits are in dubious taste. The Museo degli Argenti has a separate number to call for information (**☎ 055/2388-709**).

Behind the Pitti Palace are the **Boboli Gardens (Giardini di Boboli),** Piazza dei Pitti 1 (**☎ 055/265-171**), through which the Medicis romped. These Renaissance gardens were laid out by Triboli, a great landscape artist, in the 16th century. Although plans were drawn up for them in 1549, they weren't completed until 1656 and weren't open to the public until 1766. The Boboli is ever-popular for a stroll or an idyllic interlude in a pleasant setting. You can climb to the top of the Fortezza di Belvedere for a dazzling view of the city. The gardens are filled with fountains and statuary, such as *Venus* by Giambologna in the "Grotto" of Buontalenti. Our favorite? An absurd Mannerist piece depicting Cosimo I's court jester posing as a chubby Bacchus riding a turtle, next to the **Vasari Corridor** (see the entry for the Uffizi, above).

✪ **Bargello Museum (Museo Nazionale del Bargello).** Via del Proconsolo 4. **☎ 055/238-8606.** Admission 8,000L ($4). Tues–Sat 8:30am–1:50pm; 2nd and 4th Sun of the month 8:30am–1:50pm; 1st and 3rd Mon of the month 8:30am–1:50pm. Closed Jan 1, May 1, and Christmas. Bus: A, 14, or 23.

A short walk from Piazza della Signoria, this is a 1255 fortress palace whose dark underground chambers resounded with the cries of the tortured when it served as the city's jail and town hall during the Renaissance. Today the Bargello is a vast repository of some of the most important Renaissance sculpture, including works by Michelangelo and Donatello.

Here you'll see another Michelangelo *David* (referred to in the past as *Apollo*), chiseled perhaps 25 to 30 years after the statuesque figure in the Accademia. The Bargello *David* is totally different, effete when compared to its stronger brother. The armory here displays Michelangelo's grape-capped and drunk *Bacchus* (one of his earlier works, carved when he was 22), who's tempted by a satyr. Among the more significant sculptures is Giambologna's *Winged Mercury* (ca. 1564), a Mannerist masterpiece looking as if it's ready to take flight.

The Bargello displays two versions of Donatello's *John the Baptist,* one emaciated, the other a younger and much kinder man. Donatello was one of the outstanding and original talents of the early Renaissance, and in this gallery you'll learn why. His *St. George* is a work of heroic magnitude. According to an oft-repeated story, Michelangelo, upon seeing it for the first time, commanded it to "March!" Donatello's bronze *David* in this salon is truly remarkable; it was the first freestanding nude since the Romans stopped chiseling. As depicted, David is narcissistic (a stunning contrast to Michelangelo's later-day virile interpretation). For the last word, however, we'll have to call back our lady of the barbs, Mary McCarthy, who wrote: "His *David* . . . wearing nothing but a pair of fancy polished boots and a girlish bonnet, is a transvestite's and fetishist's dream of alluring ambiguity."

Look for at least one more work, another *David,* this one by Andrea del Verrocchio, one of the finest of the 15th-century sculptors. The Bargello also contains a large number of terra-cottas by the della Robbia clan.

St. Mark's Museum (Museo di San Marco). Piazza San Marco 1. ☎ **055/238-8608.** Admission 8,000L ($4). Daily 8:30am–1:50pm. Ticket office closes 30 min. before the museum. Closed 1st, 3rd, and 5th Sun of the month; 2nd and 4th Mon of the month; Jan 1, May 1, and Christmas. Bus: 1, 6, 7, 10, 11, 17, or 20.

This state museum is a handsome Renaissance palace whose cell walls are decorated with frescoes by the mystical Fra Angelico, one of Europe's greatest 15th-century painters. In the days of Cosimo de' Medici, San Marco was built by Michelozzo as a Dominican convent. It contained bleak, bare cells, which Angelico and his students brightened considerably with some of the most important works by this pious artist of Fiesole, who portrayed recognizable landscapes in vivid colors.

After buying a ticket, you enter the **Cloister of St. Anthony (Chiostro di Sant'Antonio),** designed by Michelozzo. Turn right in the cloister to enter the **Ospizio dei Pellegrini,** virtually a Fra Angelico gallery filled with painted panels and altarpieces. Here you'll see one of his better-known paintings, *The Last Judgment* (1431), depicting people with angels on the left dancing in a circle and lordly saints towering overhead. Hell, as it's depicted on the right, is infested with demons, reptiles, and sinners boiling in a stew. Much of hell was created by Angelico's students; his brush was inspired only by the Crucifixion, Madonnas, and bambini, or landscapes, of course. Henry James claimed that Angelico "never received an intelligible impression of evil; and his conception of human life was a perpetual sense of sacredly loving and being loved." Here also are his *Deposition* (ca. 1440), an altarpiece removed from Santa Trinita, and his *Madonna dei Linaiuoli,* commissioned by the flax workers' guild. Other works to look for are Angelico's panels from the life of Christ.

Now you can enter the courtyard, where a sign points the way to the **Chapter House (Capitolaire),** to the right of a large convent bell. Here you can see a large *Crucifixion and Saints* painted in 1442 by Fra Angelico. Returning to the courtyard, follow the sign into the **Refectory (Refettorio)** to see a *Last Supper* by Domenico Ghirlandaio, who taught Michelangelo how to fresco. This work is rather realistic, the tragic faces of the saints evoking a feeling of impending doom.

From the courtyard, you can go up to the second floor to view the highlight of the museum: Fra Angelico's ***The Annunciation.*** The rest of the floor is taken up with dorm cells, 44 small cells once used by the Dominicans (nos. 12 to 14 were once occupied by Savonarola and contain portraits of the reformer by Bartolomeo, who was plunged into acute melancholy by the jailing and torturing of his beloved teacher). Most of the cells were frescoed by Angelico and his students from 1439 to 1445 and depict scenes from the Crucifixion.

THE DUOMO, CAMPANILE & BAPTISTRY

In the heart of Florence, at **Piazza del Duomo** and **Piazza San Giovanni** (named after John the Baptist), is a complex of ecclesiastical buildings that form a triumvirate of top sights.

✪ **Il Duomo (Cattedrale di Santa Maria del Fiore).** Piazza del Duomo. ☎ **055/230-2885.** Cathedral free; excavations 5,000L ($2.50); cupola 10,000L ($5). Mar–Oct, Mon–Sat 8:30am–6:30pm. Off-season, Mon–Sat 8:30am–5:30pm. Bus: B, 14, 23, 36, 37, or 71.

The Duomo, graced by Filippo Brunelleschi's red-tiled dome, is the crowning glory of Florence and the star of the skyline. Before entering, take time to view the exterior with its geometrically patterned bands of white, pink, and green marble; this tricolor mosaic is an interesting contrast to the sienna-colored fortresslike palazzi around the city. The Duomo is one of the world's largest churches and represents the flowering of the "Florentine Gothic" style. Construction stretched over centuries: Begun in 1296, it was finally consecrated in 1436, though finishing touches on the facade were applied as late as the 19th century.

Volunteers offer free tours of the cathedral every day except Sunday 10am to 12:30pm and 3 to 5pm. Most of them speak English; if there are many of you and you want to confirm their availability, call ☎ **055/271-0757** (Tuesday to Friday, mornings only). Looking rather professorial and kindly, they can be found sitting at a table along the right (south) wall as you enter the Duomo. They expect no payment, but a nominal donation to the church is always appreciated. They also organize tours of Santa Croce and Santa Maria Novella.

Brunelleschi's efforts to build the **dome** (1420–36) could be the subject of a Hollywood script. At one time before his plans were accepted, the architect was tossed out on his derriere and denounced as an idiot. He eventually won the commission by a clever "egg trick," as related in Giorgio Vasari's *Lives of the Painters,* written in the 16th century: The architect challenged his competitors to make an egg stand on a flat piece of marble. Each artist tried to make the egg stand, but each failed. When it was Brunelleschi's turn, he took the egg and cracked its bottom slightly on the marble and thus made it stand upright. Each of the other artists said he could've done the same thing, if he'd known he could crack the egg. Brunelleschi retorted that they also would've known how to vault the cupola if they had seen his model or plans.

His dome, a "monument for posterity," was erected without supports. When Michelangelo began to construct a dome over St. Peter's, he paid tribute to Brunelleschi's earlier cupola in Florence: "I am going to make its sister larger, yes, but not lovelier."

Inside, the overall effect of the cathedral is bleak, since much of the decoration has been moved to the Duomo Museum (see below). However, note the recently restored frescoes covering the inside of the cupola; begun by Giorgio Vasari and completed by Federico Zuccari, they depict the Last Judgment. The three stained-glass windows by Ghiberti on the entrance wall are next to Uccello's giant clock using the heads of the four prophets. Some of the stained-glass windows in the dome were based on designs by Donatello (Brunelleschi's friend) and Ghiberti (Brunelleschi's rival). You can climb 463 spiraling steps to the ribbed dome for a view that's well worth the trek (however, you can climb only 414 steps and get the same view from Giotto's campanile, below).

Also in the cathedral are some terra-cottas by Luca della Robbia. In 1432 Ghiberti, taking time out from his "Gates to Paradise" for the Baptistry (see below), designed the tomb of St. Zenobius. Excavations in the depths of the cathedral have brought to light the remains of the ancient Cathedral of Santa Reparata (tombs, columns, and floors), which was probably founded in the 5th century and transformed in the following centuries until it was demolished to make way for the present cathedral. The entrance to the excavations is via a stairway near the front of this cathedral, to the right as you enter (look for the sign SCAVI DELLA CRIPTA DI SANTA REPARATA).

Incidentally, during some 1972 excavations, Brunelleschi's tomb was discovered, and new discoveries indicate the existence of a second tomb nearby. Giotto's tomb, which has never been found, may be in the right nave, beneath the campanile bearing his name.

✪ Giotto's Bell Tower (Campanile di Giotto). Piazza del Duomo. ☎ **055/230-2885.** Admission 10,000L ($5). Daily 8am–7pm. Closed Jan 1, Easter, Sept 8, and Christmas. Bus: B, 14, 23, 36, 37, or 71.

If we can believe the accounts of his contemporaries, Giotto was the ugliest man ever to walk the streets of Florence. It's ironic, then, that he left to posterity Europe's most beautiful *campanile* (bell tower), rhythmic in line and form. That Giotto was given the position of *capomastro* and grand architect (and pensioned for 100 gold florins for his service) is remarkable in itself, since he's famous for freeing painting from the confinements of Byzantium. He designed the campanile in the last 2 or 3 years of his life and died before its completion.

The final work was admirably carried out by Andrea Pisano, one of Italy's greatest Gothic sculptors (see his bronze doors on the baptistry). The "Tuscanized" Gothic tower, with bands of the same colored marble as the Duomo, stands 274 feet; and you can climb 414 steps to the top for a panorama of the sienna-colored city. After Giotto's death, Pisano and Luca della Robbia did some fine bas-relief and sculptural work, now in the Duomo Museum (see below).

If you can make the tough climb up (and up and up) the cramped stairs, the view from the top of Giotto's bell tower is unforgettable, sweeping over the city, the surrounding hills, and Medici villas.

✪ Baptistry (Battistero San Giovanni). Piazza San Giovanni. ☎ **055/230-2885.** Admission 5,000L ($2.50). Mon–Sat noon–6:30pm; Sun 9am–1pm. Bus: B, 14, 23, 36, 37, or 71.

Named after the city's patron saint, Giovanni (John the Baptist), the octagonal baptistry dates from the 11th and 12th centuries. It's the oldest structure in Florence and is a highly original interpretation of the Romanesque style, with bands of pink, white, and green marble to match the Duomo and campanile.

Visitors from all over the world come to gape at its three sets of **bronze doors.** In his work on two sets of the doors (the east and the north), Lorenzo Ghiberti reached the pinnacle of his artistry in quattrocento Florence. To win his first commission on the north doors, the 23-year-old sculptor had to compete against formidable opposition like Donatello, Brunelleschi (architect of the Duomo's dome), and Siena-born Jacopo della Quercia. Upon seeing Ghiberti's work, Donatello and Brunelleschi conceded defeat. By the time he'd completed the work on the north doors, Ghiberti was around 44. The gilt-covered panels (representing scenes from the New Testament, including the Annunciation, the Adoration, and Christ debating the elders in the temple) make up a flowing, rhythmic narration in bronze. To protect them from the elements, the originals were removed to the Duomo Museum (see below), but the copies are works of art unto themselves.

After his long labor, the Florentines gratefully gave Ghiberti the task of sculpting the east doors (directly opposite the Duomo entrance). Given carte blanche, he designed his masterpiece, choosing as his subject familiar scenes from the Old Testament, such as Adam and Eve at the creation. This time Ghiberti labored over the rectangular panels from 1425 to 1452 (he died in 1455). Upon seeing the finished work, Michelangelo is said to have exclaimed, "These doors are fit to stand at the gates of Paradise," and so they've been nicknamed the "Gates of Paradise" ever since. Ghiberti apparently agreed: He claimed he personally planned and designed the Renaissance—all on his own.

Shuttled off to adorn the south entrance and to make way for Ghiberti's "Gates of Paradise" were the baptistry's oldest doors, by Andrea Pisano, mentioned earlier for his work on Giotto's bell tower. For his subject, the Gothic sculptor represented the

"Virtues" as well as scenes from the life of John the Baptist, whom the baptistry honors. The door was completed in 1336. On the interior (just walk through Pisano's door—no charge— the dome is adorned with 13th-century mosaics, dominated by a figure of Christ. Mornings are reserved for worship.

Duomo Museum (Museo dell'Opera del Duomo). Piazza del Duomo 9. ☎ **055/230-2885.** Admission 10,000L ($5). Apr–Oct Mon–Sat 9am–6:50pm (to 5:20pm Nov–Mar). Bus: B, 14, 23, 36, 37, or 71.

This museum, across from the Duomo but facing the apse of Santa Maria del Fiore, is beloved by connoisseurs of Renaissance sculpture. It houses the sculpture that was removed from the campanile and the Duomo, in order to protect the pieces from the weather—and from visitors who want samples. A major attraction is an unfinished *Pietà* by Michelangelo, in the middle of the stairs. It was carved between 1548 and 1555, when the artist was in his 70s. In this vintage work, a figure representing Nicodemus (but said to have Michelangelo's face) is holding Christ. The great Florentine intended it for his own tomb, but he's believed to have grown disenchanted with it and to have attempted to destroy it. The museum has a Brunelleschi bust, as well as della Robbia terra-cottas. The premier attraction is the restored panels of Ghiberti's **"Gates of Paradise,"** which were removed from the baptistry. In gilded bronze, each is a masterpiece of Renaissance sculpture, perhaps the finest low-relief perspective in all Italian art.

You'll see bits and pieces from what was the old Gothic-Romanesque fronting of the cathedral, with ornamental statues, as conceived by the original architect, Arnolfo di Cambio. One of Donatello's early works, *St. John the Evangelist,* is here—not his finest hour, but anything by Donatello is worth looking at. One of his most celebrated works, the *Magdalene,* is in the room with the *cantorie* (see below). This wooden statue once stood in the baptistry and had to be restored after the 1966 flood. Dating from 1454 to 1455, it's stark and penitent.

A good reason for coming here is to see the **marble choirs (cantorie)** of Donatello and Luca della Robbia (the works face each other and are in the first room you enter after climbing the stairs). The della Robbia choir is more restrained, but it still "praises the Lord" in marble, with clashing cymbals and sounding brass that constitute a reaffirmation of life. In contrast, the dancing cherubs of Donatello's choir are a romp of chubby bambini. Of all Donatello's works, this one is the most lighthearted. But, in total contrast, lavish your attention on Donatello's *Zuccone,* one of his masterpieces, created for Giotto's bell tower.

ON OR NEAR PIAZZA DELLA SIGNORIA

The L-shaped ✪ **Piazza della Signoria,** though never completed, is one of Italy's most beautiful squares; it was the center of secular life in the days of the Medici and is today a virtual sculpture gallery. Through it pranced church robbers, connoisseurs of entrails, hired assassins seeking employment, chicken farmers from Valdarno, book burners, and many great men (including Machiavelli, on a secret mission to the Palazzo Vecchio, and Leonardo da Vinci, trailed by his entourage).

On the square is the controversial **Fountain of Neptune (Fontana di Neptuno;** 1560–75), with the sea god surrounded by creatures from the deep, as well as frisky satyrs and nymphs. It was designed by Ammannati, who later repented for chiseling Neptune in the nude. But Michelangelo, to whom Ammannati owed a great debt, judged the fountain inferior. Florentines used to mock it as *Il Biancone* ("big whitey"). Actually, the Mannerist bronzes around the basin aren't at all bad; many may have been designed by a young Giambologna.

Near the fountain is a **small disk in the ground,** marking the spot where Savonarola was executed. This zealous monk was a fire-and-brimstone reformer who rivaled Dante in conjuring up the punishment that hell would inflict on sinners. His chief targets were Lorenzo the Magnificent and the Borgia pope, Alexander VI, who excommunicated him. Savonarola whipped the Florentine faithful into an orgy of religious fanaticism but eventually fell from favor. Along with two other friars, he was hanged in the square in 1498. Afterward, as the crowds threw stones, a pyre underneath the men consumed their bodies. It's said the reformer's heart was found whole and grabbed up by souvenir collectors. His ashes were tossed into the Arno.

For centuries, Michelangelo's ***David*** stood in this square, but it was moved to the Accademia in the 19th century. The work you see on the square today is an inferior copy, commonly assumed by many first-timers to be Michelangelo's original. Near the towering statue stands Baccio Bandinelli's ***Heracles*** (1534). Bandinelli, however, was no Michelangelo, and his statue has been denounced through the centuries; Cellini dismissed it as a "sack of melons."

The 14th-century ✪ **Loggia della Signoria** (or **Loggia dei Lanzi**) houses a gallery of sculpture often depicting violent scenes. The most famous piece is a rare work by Benvenuto Cellini, the goldsmith and tell-all autobiographer. Critics have claimed his exquisite but ungentlemanly ***Perseus,*** holding up the severed head of Medusa, is the most significant Florentine sculpture since Michelangelo's *Night* and *Day.* However, what you see today is actually a copy; the original Perseus stood here from 1545 to 1996, when he was removed for restoration (the future of the original remains uncertain). Three other well-known pieces are Giambologna's bronze statue of **Duke Cosimo de' Medici** on horseback, celebrating the man who subjugated all Tuscany under his military rule; his ***Rape of the Sabines,*** an essay in three-dimensional Mannerism; and his ***Hercules with Nessus the Centaur,*** a chorus line of half a dozen Roman Vestal wallflowers.

Palazzo Vecchio. Piazza della Signoria. ☎ **055/276-8325.** Admission 10,000L ($5). Mon–Wed and Fri–Sat 9am–7pm; Thurs and Sun 9am–2pm; July 15–Sept 15, Mon and Fri 9am–11pm. Ticket office closes 1 hour before palace. Bus: 23 or 71.

The secular "Old Palace" is Florence's most famous and imposing palazzo. Gothic master builder Arnolfo di Cambio constructed it from 1299 to 1302, though it wasn't until 1540 that Cosimo I and the Medicis called it home. It's most remarkable architectural feature is the 308-foot tower, an engineering feat that required supreme skill at the time. Today the palazzo is occupied by city employees, but much is open to the public.

The 16th-century **Hall of the 500 (Salone dei Cinquecento),** the most outstanding part of the palace, is filled with Vasari and company frescoes as well as sculpture. A tragic loss to Renaissance art, the frescoes originally done by Leonardo da Vinci in 1503 melted when braziers were brought in to speed up the drying process. The ever-inventive Leonardo had used wax in his pigments, and of course the frescoes melted under the heat. As you enter the hall, look for Michelangelo's *Victory,* depicting an insipid-looking young man treading on a bearded older man (it has been suggested that Michelangelo put his own face on that of the trampled man). This 1533–34 statue was originally intended for the tomb of Pope Julius but was later acquired by the Medicis.

Later you can stroll through the rest of the palace, examining its apartments and main halls. You can also visit the private apartments of Eleanor of Toledo, the Spanish wife of Cosimo I, and a chapel that was begun in 1540 and frescoed by

Bronzino. The palace displays the original of Verrocchio's bronze putto (1476) from the courtyard fountain, called both *Winged Cherub Clutching a Fish* and *Boy with a Dolphin.* You'll also find a 16th-century portrait of Machiavelli that's attributed to Santi di Tito. Donatello's famous bronze group, *Judith Slaying Holofernes* (1455), once stood on Piazza della Signoria but was brought inside. The salons, such as a fleur-de-lis apartment, have their own richness and beauty.

Following his arrest, Savonarola was taken to the Palazzo Vecchio for more than a dozen torture sessions, including "twists" on the rack. The torturer pronounced Savonarola his "best" customer.

Orsanmichele. Via de' Calzaiuoli at Via Arte della Lana (north of Piazza della Signoria). ☎ **055/284-944.** Free admission. Daily 9am–noon and 4–6pm. Closed the 1st and last Mon of every month. Bus: 22, 36, or 37.

This 14th-century church is the last remnant of Florence's ornate Gothic architecture and was first built as a covered market with an upstairs granary, hence its appearance as a converted warehouse. The downstairs was eventually converted to an oratory, the open archways were bricked up, and the outside's tabernacles were decorated with donations from the city's powerful *arti* (guilds): the tanners, bankers, silk weavers, furriers, and goldsmiths, whose patron saints fill the 14 niches surrounding the exterior. Masters like Ghiberti, Donatello, and Giambologna were commissioned to cast the saints' images, which virtually compose a history of Florentine sculpture from the 14th to the 16th century (almost all have been relocated to the indoor museum and slowly replaced with copies).

In the candlelit interior, among the vaulted Gothic arches, stained-glass windows, and 500-year-old frescoes, is the encrusted 14th-century tabernacle by Andrea Orcagna, supporting and protecting the 1348 *Madonna and Child* painted by Giotto's student Bernardo Daddi. The entrance to the church's small museum (open daily 9am to 1:30pm, with free admission, though this may change soon) is on the building's west side in what once housed the powerful Wool Guild. Upstairs, in the old granary rooms, are eight of the original statues from the church's niches. (By the way, the name "Orsanmichele" is a corruption of "Church of St. Michael's of the Garden," the name of the church that occupied this site from the 8th to the 13th century, well before the granary was built.)

The Ponte Vecchio

Spared by the Nazis in their bitter retreat from the Allied advance in 1944, the "Old Bridge" at Via Por Santa Maria and Via Guicciardini is the last remaining medieval *ponte* spanning the Arno (the Germans blew up the rest). It was again threatened in the 1966 flood, when the waters of the Arno swept over it and washed away a fortune in jewelry from the goldsmiths' shops flanking the bridge.

The Ponte Vecchio was built in 1220, probably on the Roman site of a bridge for the Via Cassia, the ancient road running through Florence on its way to Rome. Vasari claims that Taddeo Gaddi reconstructed it in 1354, and Vasari himself designed the corridor running over it (see the Uffizi entry, above). Once home to butchers, it was cleared of this stench by Ferdinand de' Medici, who allowed these "vile arts" to give way to goldsmiths and jewelers, who have remained ever since.

Today the restored Ponte Vecchio is closed to vehicular traffic. The little shops continue to sell everything from the most expensive of Florentine gold to something simple—say, a Lucrezia Borgia poison ring.

NEAR PIAZZA SAN LORENZO

Piazza San Lorenzo and its satellite, **Piazza Madonna degli Aldobrandini,** are lively and colorful. A huge market, the **Mercato Centrale,** forms around the church of San Lorenzo, continuing all the way to the area of San Marco. For details, see "Shopping," later in this chapter.

✪ Medici Chapels (Cappelle Medicee). Piazza Madonna degli Aldobrandini 6. ☎ **055/ 238-85.** Admission 13,000L ($6.50). Tues–Sat 8:30am–4:15pm; Sun 8:30am–1:50pm. Closed 2nd and 4th Sun, and 1st, 3rd, and 5th Mon of each month. Bus: 1, 6, 7, 11, 17, 33, 67, or 68.

The Medici tombs are adjacent to the Basilica of San Lorenzo (see below). You enter the tombs, housing the "blue-blooded" Medici, in back of the church by going around to Piazza Madonna degli Aldobrandini. First you'll pass through the baroque **Chapel of the Princes (Cappella dei Principi),** that octagon of death often denounced for its "trashy opulence." In back of the altar is a collection of Italian reliquaries.

Hidden Gem: Discovered in a sepulchral chamber beneath the Medici Chapels with access via a trap door and a winding staircase was Michelangelo's only group of mural sketches. Apparently, he had used the walls as a giant doodling sheet. The drawings include a sketch of the legs of Duke Giuliano, Christ risen, and the *Laocoön,* the Hellenistic figure group. Fifty drawings, done in charcoal on plaster walls, were found. You can ask for a free ticket to view the sketches at the ticket office for the chapels.

The real reason you come here is to see the **New Sacristy (Nuova Sacrestia),** designed by Michelangelo as a gloomy mausoleum. "Do not wake me; speak softly here," Michelangelo wrote in a bitter verse. Working from 1521 to 1534, he created the Medici tombs in a style that foreshadowed the baroque. Lorenzo the Magnificent— a rulerwho seemed to embody the qualities of the Renaissance itself, and one of the greatest names in the history of the Medici family—was buried near Michelangelo's uncompleted *Madonna and Child* group, a simple monument evoking a promise unfulfilled.

Ironically, the finest groups of sculpture were reserved for two Medici "clan" members, who (in the words of Mary McCarthy) "would better have been forgotten." Both are represented by Michelangelo as armored, idealized princes of the Renaissance. In fact, Lorenzo II, duke of Urbino, depicted as "the thinker," was a deranged young man (just out of his teens before he died). Clearly, Michelangelo wasn't working to glorify these two Medici dukes. Rather, he was chiseling for posterity. The other two figures on Lorenzo's tomb are most often called ***Dawn*** and ***Dusk,*** with morning represented as a woman and evening as a man.

The two best-known figures, showing Michelangelo at his most powerful, are ***Night*** and ***Day*** at the feet of Giuliano, the duke of Nemours. *Night* is chiseled as a woman in troubled sleep and *Day* as a man of strength awakening to a foreboding world. These figures weren't the works of Michelangelo's innocence.

Basilica di San Lorenzo. Piazza San Lorenzo. ☎ **055/214-443.** Free admission, or 5,000 to 15,000L ($2.50 to $7.50) for special exhibitions. Library Mon–Sat 7:30–11:45am and 3:30–5:30pm; study room Mon–Sat 8am–2pm. Bus: 1, 6, 7, 11, 17, 33, 67, or 68.

This is Brunelleschi's 1426 Renaissance church, where the Medicis used to attend services from their nearby palace on Via Larga, now Via Camillo Cavour. Critic Walter Pater found it "great rather by what it designed or aspired to do, than by what it actually achieved." Most visitors flock to see Michelangelo's **New Sacristy** with his *Night* and *Day* (see the Medici Chapels, above), but Brunelleschi's handiwork deserves some time too.

Built in the style of a Latin cross, the church is distinguished by harmonious grays and rows of Corinthian columns. The **Old Sacristy (Vecchia Sacrestia;** walk up the nave, then turn left) was designed by Brunelleschi and decorated in part by Donatello (view his terra-cotta bust of St. Lawrence). The Old Sacristy is often cited as the first and finest work of the early Renaissance. Even more intriguing are the two bronze 1460 pulpits of Donatello, among his last works, a project carried out by students following his death in 1466. Scenes depict Christ's passion and resurrection.

After exploring the Old Sacristy, go through the first door (unmarked) on your right and you'll emerge outside. A sign will point to the entrance of the **Medici Laurentian Library (Biblioteca Medicea Laurenziana; ☎ 055/210-760)**, which you enter at Piazza San Lorenzo 9. Designed by Michelangelo to shelter the expanding collection of the Medicis, the library is a brilliant example of Mannerist architecture, its chief attraction a *pietra serna* flight of curving stairs. Michelangelo worked on it in 1524, but the finishing touches were completed in 1578 by Vasari and Ammannati. Michelangelo, however, designed the reading benches. The library is filled with some of Italy's greatest manuscripts, many of which are handsomely illustrated. In the rare book collection are autographs by Petrarch, Machiavelli, Poliziano, and Napoléon. You're kept at a distance by protective glass, but it's well worth the visit.

Palazzo Medici-Riccardi. Via Camillo Cavour 1. **☎ 055/276-0340.** Admission 6,000L ($3). Mon–Tues and Thurs–Sat 9am–12:30pm and 3–5pm; Sun 9am–noon. Bus: 1, 6, 7, 11, 17, 33, 67, or 68.

This palace, a short walk from the Duomo, was the home of Cosimo de' Medici before he took his household to the Palazzo Vecchio. At the apogee of the Medici power, it was adorned with some of the world's greatest masterpieces, such as Donatello's *David*. Built by Michelozzo in the mid–15th century, the brown stone building was also the scene, at times, of the court of Lorenzo the Magnificent. Art lovers visit today chiefly to see the mid-15th-century frescoes by Benozzo Gozzoli in the **Medici Chapel** (not to be confused with the Medici Chapels, above). Gozzoli's frescoes, depicting the journey of the Magi, form his masterpiece—they're a hallmark in Renaissance painting. Although taking a religious theme as his subject, the artist turned it into a gay romp, a pageant of royals, knights, and pages, with fun mascots like greyhounds and even a giraffe. It's a fairy-tale world come alive, with faces of the Medicis, along with local celebrities who were as famous as Madonna in their day but are known only to scholars today.

Another gallery, which you enter via a separate stairway, was frescoed by Luca Giordano in the 18th century, but his work seems merely decorative. The apartments, where the prefect lodges, aren't open to the public. The gallery, incidentally, may also be viewed free.

ON OR NEAR PIAZZA DELLA SANTISSIMA ANNUNZIATA

Lovely **Piazza della Santissima Annunziata** is surrounded on three sides by arcades. In the center is an equestrian statue of Grand Duke Ferdinand I by Giambologna. The **Hospital of the Innocents** stands on the eastern side. Once Brunelleschi wanted to create a perfectly symmetrical square here, but he died before his plans could be realized. The piazza is a popular student hangout.

Hospital of the Innocents (Ospedale degli Innocenti). Piazza della Santissima Annunziata 12. No phone. Admission 5,000L ($2.50). Thurs–Tues 8:30am–2pm; Sun 8:30am–1pm. Bus: 6, 31, or 32.

Opened in 1445, this was the world's first hospital for foundlings, though the Medici and Florentine bankers weren't known for welfare benefits. The building and the loggia with its Corinthian columns were conceived by Brunelleschi and marked the first architectural bloom of the Renaissance in Florence. On the facade are terra-cotta medallions done in blues and opaque whites by Andrea della Robbia, depicting babes in swaddling clothes.

Still used as an orphanage, the building no longer has its "lazy Susan," where Florentines used to deposit unwanted bambini, ring the bell, and then flee. It does contain an art gallery, and notable among its treasures is a terra-cotta *Madonna and Child* by Luca della Robbia, plus works by Sandro Botticelli. One of its most important paintings is *Adoration of the Magi* by Domenico Ghirlandaio (the chubby bambino looks a bit pompously at the Wise Man kissing his foot).

Archaeology Museum (Museo Archeologico). Via della Colonna 38. ☎ **055/235-75.** Admission 8,000L ($4). Nov–Aug Tues–Sat 9am–2pm; Sept also Sat 9pm–midnight; Oct also Sun 9am–8pm.

This museum, a short walk from Piazza della Santissima Annunziata, houses one of Europe's most outstanding Egyptian and Etruscan collections in a palace built for Grand Duchess Maria Maddalena of Austria. The Etruscan-loving Medicis began that collection, though the Egyptian loot was first acquired by Leopold II in the 1830s. Its Egyptian mummies and sarcophagi are on the first floor, along with some of the better-known Etruscan works. Pause to look at the lid to the coffin of a fat Etruscan (unlike the blank faces staring back from many of these tombs, this man's countenance is quite expressive).

One room is graced with three bronze Etruscan masterpieces, among the rarest objets d'art of these relatively unknown people. They include the *Chimera,* a lion with a goat sticking out of its back. This was an Etruscan work of the 5th century B.C., found near Arezzo in 1555. The lion's tail—in the form of a venomous reptile—lunges at the trapped beast. The others are *Minerva* and an *Orator,* ranging from the 5th to the 1st century B.C. Another rare find is a Roman bronze of a young man, the so-called *Idolino,* fished from the sea at Pesaro. The statue has always been shrouded in mystery; it may have been a Roman statue sculpted around the time of Christ. The François vase on the ground floor, from 570 B.C., is celebrated. A prize in the Egyptian department is a wood-and-bone chariot, beautifully preserved, that astonishingly dates back to a tomb in Thebes from the 14th century B.C.

ON PIAZZA SANTA MARIA NOVELLA

Hardly the most beautiful or tranquil square, **Piazza Santa Maria Novella** overflows with traffic from the rail station. Vendors, backpackers, beggars, and buses and taxis vie for precious space. Visitors will want to tolerate this furor for only one reason: to see the basilica.

Basilica di Santa Maria Novella. Piazza Santa Maria Novella. ☎ **055/282-187.** Church free; Spanish Chapel and cloisters 5,000L ($2.50). Church Mon–Fri 7am–noon and 3–6pm. Spanish Chapel and cloisters Sat–Thurs 8am–2pm. Bus: 6, 9, 11, 36, 37, or 68.

Near the rail station is one of Florence's most distinguished churches, begun in 1278 for the Dominicans. Its geometric facade, with bands of white and green marble, was designed in the late 15th century by Leon Battista Alberti, an aristocrat and true Renaissance man (philosopher, painter, architect, poet). The church borrows from, and harmonizes, the Romanesque, Gothic, and Renaissance styles.

In the left nave as you enter, the third large painting is the great Masaccio's *Trinità,* a curious work that has the architectural form of a Renaissance stage setting but whose figures (in perfect perspective) are like actors in a Greek tragedy. If you view the church at dusk, you'll see the stained-glass windows in the fading light cast kaleidoscope fantasies on the opposite wall.

Catching the View from Piazzale Michelangiolo

For a view of the wonders of Florence below and Fiesole above, climb aboard bus no. 12 or 13 at the Ponte alla Grazie (the first bridge east of the Ponte Vecchio) for a 15-minute ride to ✪ **Piazzale Michelangiolo,** an 1865 belvedere overlooking a view seen in many a Renaissance painting and on many a modern-day postcard. It's reached along Viale Michelangiolo. It's best at dusk, when the purple-fringed Tuscan hills form a frame for Giotto's bell tower, Brunelleschi's dome, and the towering hunk of stones that stick up from the Palazzo Vecchio. Another copy of Michelangelo's *David* dominates the square and gives the *piazzale* (wide piazza) its name (but note the spelling difference). Crown your trip with a gelato at the **Gelateria Michelangiolo** (☎ **055/234-2705**), open Wednesday to Sunday 7am to 2am.

Warning: At certain times during the day, the square is overrun with tour buses and peddlers selling trinkets and cheap souvenirs. If you go at these times, often midday in summer, you'll find the view of Florence is still intact—but you may be struck down by a Vespa or crushed in a crowd if you try to enjoy it.

Head straight up the left nave to the **Gondi Chapel (Cappella Gondi)** for a look at Brunelleschi's wooden *Christ on the Cross,* said to have been carved to compete with Donatello's same subject in Santa Croce (see below). According to Vasari in *Lives of the Artists,* when Donatello saw Brunelleschi's completed Crucifix, he dropped his apron full of eggs intended for their lunch. "You have symbolized the Christ," Donatello is alleged to have said. "Mine is an ordinary man." (Some art historians reject this story.)

In 1485 Ghirlandaio contracted with a Tornabuoni banker to adorn the sanctuary behind the main altar with frescoes illustrating scenes from the lives of Mary and John the Baptist. Michelangelo, a teenager at the time, is known to have studied under Ghirlandaio (perhaps he even worked on this cycle).

In the north transept, a staircase leads to the remarkable **Strozzi Chapel (Cappella Strozzi),** honoring St. Thomas Aquinas. Decorated between 1350 and 1357 by Nardo di Cione and Andrea Orcagna, it depicts Dante's *Purgatorio* and *Inferno.* On the left wall is *Paradiso.*

If time remains, you may want to visit the **cloisters,** going first to the Green Cloister and then to the splendid Spanish Chapel frescoed by Andrea di Bonaiuto in the 14th century (one panel depicts the Dominicans in triumph over heretical wolves).

ON OR NEAR PIAZZA SANTA CROCE

Every street leading to the famed **Piazza Santa Croce** thrives on tourism, usually packed with shops selling leather goods. The square has been an integral part of Florentine life for centuries, beginning when Franciscan friars used to preach here. The piazza used to be the playing field for *calcio* (a kind of football that's no longer played), and a marble disk in the center marks the center line of pitch. Today it's still devoted to popular gatherings, like games, events, and jousts.

Basilica di Santa Croce. Piazza Santa Croce 16. ☎ **055/244-619.** Church free; cloisters and church museum 8,000L ($4). Church Mon–Sat 8am–6:30pm; Sun 3–6:30pm. Museum and cloisters Thurs–Tues 10am–7pm. Bus: B, 13, 23, or 71.

Think of this as Tuscany's Westminster Abbey. This church shelters the tombs of everyone from Michelangelo to Machiavelli, from Dante (he was actually buried at Ravenna) to Galileo, who at the hands of the Inquisition "recanted" his concept that the Earth revolves around the sun. Just as Santa Maria Novella was the church of the Dominicans, Santa Croce, said to have been designed by Arnolfo di Cambio, was the church of the Franciscans.

In the right nave (first tomb) is the Vasari-executed monument to Michelangelo, whose 89-year-old body was smuggled back to his native Florence from its original burial place in Rome, where the pope wanted the corpse to remain. Along with a bust of the artist are three allegorical figures representing the arts. In the next memorial, a prune-faced Dante, a poet honored belatedly in the city that exiled him, looks down. Farther on, still on the right, is the tomb of Niccoló Machiavelli, whose *The Prince* (about Cesare Borgia) became a virtual textbook in the art of wielding power. Nearby is Donatello's lyrical bas-relief *The Annunciation.*

The Trecento frescoes are reason enough for visiting Santa Croce—especially those by Giotto to the right of the main chapel. Once whitewashed, the Bardi and Peruzzi chapels were "uncovered" in the mid–19th century in such a clumsy fashion they had to be drastically restored. Although badly preserved, the frescoes in the **Bardi Chapel (Cappella Bardi)** are most memorable, especially the deathbed scene of St. Francis. The cycles in the **Peruzzi Chapel (Cappella Peruzzi)** are of John the Baptist and St. John. In the left transept is Donatello's once-controversial wooden Crucifix—too gruesome for some Renaissance tastes, including that of Brunelleschi, who is claimed to have said: "You [Donatello] have put a rustic upon the cross." (Brunelleschi's "answer" to the Donatello version here can be seen in Santa Maria Novella.) Incidentally, the **Pazzi Chapel (Cappella Pazzi),** entered through the cloisters, was designed by Brunelleschi, with terra-cottas by Luca della Robbia.

Inside the monastery of this church, the Franciscan fathers established the **Leather School (Scuola del Cuoio)** at the end of World War II. The purpose of the school was to prepare young boys technically to specialize in Florentine leatherwork. The school has flourished and produced many fine artisans who continue their careers here. Stop in and see the work when you visit the church.

Buonarroti's House (Casa Buonarroti). Via Ghibellina 70. ☎ **055/241-752.** Admission 12,000L ($6). Wed–Mon 9:30am–1:30pm. Bus: 14.

Only a short walk from Santa Croce is the house Michelangelo managed to buy for his nephew, Lionardo. But it was Lionardo's son, named after Michelangelo, who turned the house into a virtual museum to his great uncle, hiring artists and painters to adorn it with frescoes. Turned into a museum by his descendants, the house was restored in 1964. It contains some fledgling work by the magnificent artist, as well as some models by him. Here you can see his *Madonna of the Stairs,* which he did when he was 16 (maybe younger), as well as a bas-relief he did later, the *Battle of the Centaurs.* The casa is enriched by many of Michelangelo's drawings and models, shown to the public in periodic exhibits. A curiosity among them is the wooden model for the San Lorenzo facade that Michelangelo designed but never constructed.

A SYNAGOGUE

La Sinagoga di Firenze. Via Farini 4. ☎ **055/234-6654.** Admission 6,000L ($3). Apr–Sept, Sun–Thurs 10am–1pm and 2–5pm, Fri 10am–1pm; Oct–Mar Mon–Thurs 11am–1pm and 2–5pm, Fri and Sun 10am–1pm. Closed Jewish holidays. Bus: 6, 31, or 32.

The synagogue is in the Moorish style, inspired by Constantine's Byzantine church of Hagia Sophia. Completed in 1882, it was badly damaged by the Nazis in 1944 but has been restored to its original splendor. A museum is upstairs, exhibiting, among other displays, a photographic record of the history of the ghetto that remained in Florence until 1859.

6 Shopping

THE SHOPPING SCENE

Skilled craftsmanship and traditional design unchanged since the days of the Medicis have made this a serious shopping destination. Florence is noted for its hand-tooled **leather goods** and various **straw merchandise,** as well as superbly crafted **gold jewelry.**

The whole city strikes many visitors as a gigantic department store. Entire neighbor hoods on both sides of the Arno offer good shops, though those along the medieval Ponte Vecchio (with some exceptions) are generally too touristy.

Florence isn't a city for bargain shopping, however. Most visitors interested in gold or silver jewelry head for the **Ponte Vecchio** and its tiny shops. It's difficult to tell one from another, but you really don't need to, since the merchandise is similar. If you're looking for a charm or souvenir, these shops are fine. But the heyday of finding gold jewelry bargains on the Ponte Vecchio is long gone.

The street for antiques is **Via Maggio;** some of the furnishings and objets d'art here are from the 16th century. Another major area for antiques shopping is **Borgo Ognissanti.** Florence's Fifth Avenue is **Via dei Tornabuoni,** the place to head for the best-quality leather goods, for the best clothing boutiques, and for stylish but costly shoes. Here you'll find everyone from Armani to Ferragamo.

The better shops are for the most part along Tornabuoni, but there are many on **Via Vigna Nuova, Via Porta Rossa,** and **Via degli Strozzi.** You might also stroll on the lungarno along the Arno. For some of the best buys in leather, check out **Via del Parione,** a short narrow street off of Tornabuoni.

Shopping hours are generally Monday 4 to 7:30pm and Tuesday to Saturday 9 or 10am to 1pm and 3:30 or 4pm to 7:30pm. During summer, some shops are open Monday morning. However, don't be surprised if shops are closed for several weeks in August or for the entire month.

SHOPPING A TO Z

ANTIQUES There are many outlets for antiques in Florence, many clustered along Via Maggio (but ouch! those high prices!). If you're in the market for such expensive purchases or if you just like to browse, try the following.

Chic **Adriana Chelini,** Via Maggio 28 (☎ **055/213-471**), specializes in 16th- and 17th-century furniture, from small to large pieces. It also carries some paintings and porcelain and glass items from later periods. The **Bottega San Felice,** Via Maggio 39R (☎ **055/215-479**), offers many intriguing items from the 19th century, sometimes in the style known as Charles X. The shop also sells more modern pieces, such as many art deco items and Biedermeier pieces.

Gallori Turchi, Via Maggio 14R (☎ **055/282-279**), is one of Florence's best antiques stores for the serious well-heeled collector. Some of its rare items date from the 16th century, ranging from polychrome figures to gilded Tuscan pieces, from Majolica to ceramics, from swords to pistols. The shop is closed 2 weeks in August. The Bartolozzis have been doing business at **Guido Bartolozzi,** Via Maggio 18R (☎ **055/215-602**), since 1887, when they were here to greet those on the Grand Tour. Their specialty is European antiques from the 16th to the 19th century. Furniture, tapestries, china, glassware, and many other items are on display. The eclectic **Paolo Romano,** Borgo Ognissanti 20R (☎ **055/293-294**), carries furniture, accessories, and objets d'art from the 16th to the 19th century. Many pieces are small and demure; others are more suitable to the place you'll move to when you become the next Bill Gates.

ART Opened in 1870 and thus Florence's oldest art gallery, **Galleria Masini,** Piazza Goldoni 6R (☎ **055/294-000**), is a few minutes' walk from the Excelsior and other leading hotels. The selection of modern and contemporary paintings by top artists is extensive, representing more than 500 Italian painters.

BOOKSTORES The oldest English bookstore in Florence devoted to American and British books and one of the finest bookstores in Europe, the **BM Bookshop,** Borgo Ognissanti 4R (☎ **055/294-575**), carries an excellent selection of paperbacks, travel guides, art and architecture books, history, Italian interest, fashion, design, and children's books, plus the city's largest collection of Italian cookbooks in English. The **Libreria il Viaggio,** Borgo Albizi 41R (☎ **055/240-489**), is a specialty bookstore selling maps and guidebooks from all over the world, in a wide variety of languages, including English.

CERAMICS & POTTERY Tiny **La Botteghina,** Via Guelfa 5R (☎ **055/287-367**), is a wonderful and reasonably priced outlet for true artisan ceramics, with gorgeous handpainted pieces from traditional ceramics centers in the nearby Tuscan hill towns.

The wide inventory at **Menegatti,** Piazza del Pesce, Ponte Vecchio 2R (☎ **055/215-202**), includes pottery from Florence, Faenza, and Deruta. There are also della Robbia reproductions made in red clay like the originals. Items can be shipped home for you.

FABRICS & EMBROIDERY In business for more than half a century, ✪ **Casa di Tessuti,** Via de' Pecori 20–24R (☎ **055/215-961**), is for fabric connoisseurs, with some of the nation's largest and highest-quality selections of linen, silk, wool, and cotton. The Romoli family are the longtime proprietors.

Although Florentine embroidery was once considered a dying art, **Cirri,** Via per Santa Maria 38–40R, near the Ponte Vecchio (☎ **055/239-6593**), keeps it alive, with hundreds of beautiful designs in linen, cotton, and silk.

FASHION Italian clothing from lesser-known designers like Caractere is available at **Glamour,** Borgo San Jacopo 49R (☎ **055/210-334**). The style is first rate, and the prices are more affordable than at most fashion houses in Florence. You'll find good-quality sweaters as well as blouses and skirts in various fabrics.

At **Loretta Caponi,** Piazza Antinori 4 (☎ **055/213-668**), the arched ceiling and gold-and-turquoise trim create a perfect atmosphere in which to browse through a wonderful selection of slip dresses, robes, linens, and children's wear in luxurious silks, velvets, and cottons.

Mariposa, Lungarno Corsini 2 (☎ **055/284-259**), offers women's and men's fashions from such famous designers as Krizia, Fendi, Rocco Barocco, Missoni, and Mimmina. Foreign customers are often granted a 20% discount on tax-free items.

Max Mara, Via del Pecori 23R (☎ **055/239-6590**), features high-quality women's clothes, with classic elegance and even a touch of flamboyance. The selection covers everything from hats and coats to suits and slacks.

In the center of town near the Duomo is **Romano,** Piazza della Repubblica (☎ **055/239-6890**), a glamorous clothing store for both women and men. The owners commissioned a curving stairwell to be constructed under the high ornate ceiling. But even more exciting are the leather and suede goods, along with an assortment of stylish dresses, shoes, and handbags. The prices are high, but so is the quality.

GLASS The small **Cose del '900,** Borgo Sant' Jacopo 45 (☎ **055/283-491**), is full of glass items of every description from 1900 to 1950: shot glasses, drinking glasses, centerpieces, and many art deco pieces.

Dating back to the era of the grand dukes, the art of grinding and engraving glass is still carried out at ✪ **Paola Locchi,** Via Burchiello 10 (☎ **055/229-8371**), with exquisite skill and craftsmanship. Seemingly every kind of engraved object is sold, some of it of stupendous size. You can even find engraved goblets that decorated the banqueting tables of the ancients.

HERBALISTS The **Antica Farmacia del Cinghiale,** Piazza del Mercato Nuovo 4R (☎ **055/282-128**), in business for some 3 centuries, is an *erboristeria,* dispensing herbal teas and fragrances, along with herbal potpourris. A pharmacy is also here.

The ✪ **Officina Profumo Farmaceutica di Santa Maria Novella,** Via della Scala 16N (☎ **055/216-276**), is the most fascinating pharmacy in Italy. Northwest of Santa Maria Novella, it opened in 1612, offering a selection of herbal remedies that were created by friars of the Dominican order. Those closely guarded secrets have been retained, and many of the same elixirs are still sold today. A wide selection of perfumes, scented soaps, shampoos, and potpourris, along with creams and lotions, is also sold. The shop is closed Saturday afternoon in July and August.

HOUSEWARES **Viceversa,** Via Ricasoli 53R (☎ **055/239-8281**), offers the latest kitchen gadgets: Robert Graves–designed teakettles, Alessi creations, Pavoni espresso machines, and much more, all produced with cutting-edge and whimsical design.

JEWELRY Buying jewelry is almost an art in itself, so proceed with caution. You'll find some stunning antique pieces, and, if you know how to buy, some good values.

Befani e Tai, Via Vacchereccia 13R (☎ **055/287-825**), is one of the most unusual jewelry stores in Florence; some of its pieces date from the 19th century. The store was opened after World War II by expert goldsmiths who were childhood friends. Some of their clients even design their own jewelry for special orders.

Faraone-Settepassi, Via dei Tornabuoni 25R (☎ **055/215-506**), one of the most distinguished jewelers of the Renaissance city, draws a well-heeled patronage.

Located away from the Ponte Vecchio, **Mario Buccellati,** Via dei Tornabuoni 6971R (☎ **055/239-6579**), a branch of the Milan store that opened in 1919, specializes in exquisite handcrafted jewelry and silver. A large selection of intriguing pieces at high prices is offered, though you can find moderately priced items as well.

Modern 18K gold jewelry is the specialty at **Elisabetta Fallaci,** Ponte Vecchio 22 (☎ **055/213-192**), all made in Florence. Look also for the beautiful enameled 18K gold boxes from the 1800s.

LEATHER Universally acclaimed, Florentine leather is still the fine product it always was—smooth, well shaped, and often in vivid colors.

The well-known Beltrami leather goods are sold at **Beltrami,** Via del Tornabuoni 48 (☎ **055/287-779**), as well as expensive evening clothes, heavyweight silk scarves, and fashions of the best quality. This is one of several Beltrami shops in the area. High fashion, high prices, and high quality are what you'll find here, but prices are significantly lower than what you'll pay for Beltrami in the States. The **Beltrami Spa,** Via del Panzani 1 (☎ **055/212-661**), offers last season's fashions at discounts of 20% to 50%. There are further discounts for multiple purchases, and since the original prices are still on the items, you can tell how much you're saving.

Sergio Bojola, Via dei Rondinelli 25R (☎ **055/211-155**), a leading name in leather, has distinguished himself in Florence by the variety of his selections, in both synthetic materials and beautiful leathers.

You'll find first-class quality and craftsmanship at ✪ **Cellerini,** Via del Sole 37 (☎ **055/282-533**), one of the city's master leathersmiths. Silvano Cellerini has been called a genius in leather. Original purses, shoulder bags, suitcases, accessories, wallets, and even a limited number of shoes (for both women and men) are sold.

The branch of **Gucci** at Via Tornabuoni 73R (☎ **055/264-011**) is the mother of all Gucci shops. Much imitated around the world, this Gucci product is nevertheless real. In general, prices are a bit cheaper here than in Milan and a lot less expensive than in the States. You'll find every Gucci item imaginable, from belts to shoes to shawls to the chic Gucci scarf.

Leonardo Leather Works, Borgo dei Greci 16A (☎ **055/292-202**), concentrates on two of the oldest major crafts of Florence: leather and jewelry. Leather goods include wallets, bags, shoes, boots, briefcases, clothing, travel bags, belts, and gift items, with products by famous designers. The jewelry department has a large assortment of gold chains, bracelets, rings, earrings, and charms.

Pollini, Via Calimala 12R near the Ponte Vecchio (☎ **055/214-738**), offers a wide array of stylized merchandise, like shoes, suitcases, clothing, and belts.

You can also watch the artisans at work at the **Leather School of Santa Croce** (enter through the right transept of Santa Croce church, ☎ **055/244-533**), and ask the embossers to stamp your initials or a Florentine lily onto a wallet or other item.

MARKETS Intrepid shoppers head for the **Mercato Nuovo (Straw Market** or **New Market**), two blocks south of Piazza della Repubblica. (It's called Il Porcellino by the Italians because of the bronze statue of a reclining wild boar—a copy of the one in the Uffizi.) Tourists pet its snout (which is well worn) for good luck. The market stands in the monumental heart of Florence, an easy stroll from the Palazzo Vecchio. It sells not only straw items but also leather goods (not the best quality), along with typical Florentine merchandise: frames, trays, hand-embroidery, table linens, and hand-sprayed and -painted boxes in traditional designs. The market is open Monday to Saturday 9am to 7pm.

However, even better bargains await those who make their way through the push-carts to the stalls of the open-air **Mercato Centrale** (**Mercato San Lorenzo**), in and around Borgo San Lorenzo, near the rail station. If you don't mind bargaining, which is imperative, you'll find an array of merchandise such as raffia bags, Florentine leather purses, sweaters, gloves, salt-and-pepper shakers, straw handbags, and art reproductions. It's open Monday to Saturday 9am to 7pm.

MOSAICS Florentine mosaics are universally recognized. Bruno Lastrucci, the director of **Arte Musiva,** Largo Bargellini 2 (☎ **055/241-647**), is one of the most renowned exponents of this art form. In the workshop you can see artisans—including some of Italy's major mosaicists—plying their craft, creating both traditional Florentine and modern designs. A selection of the most significant works is permanently displayed in the gallery.

There's also **Pitti Mosaici,** Piazza Pitti 16R and 23–24R (☎ **055/282-127**), where the artistry reflects generations of family tradition.

PAPER & STATIONERY **Giulio Giannini & Figlio,** Piazza Pitti 37R (☎ **055/212-621**), has been a family business for more than 140 years and is Florence's leading stationery store. Foreigners often snap up the exquisite merchandise for gift-giving later in the year.

The specialty at **Il Papiro,** Via Cavour 55R (☎ **055/215-262**), is parti-colored marbleized paper that's skillfully incorporated into objects ranging from bookmarks to photo albums. (Have a favorite relative who's getting married soon? These make great wedding albums.) More unusual are the marbleized wood (like music boxes) and leather items (couture-style purses and bags), as well as the marbleized fabric. The staff is charming, and the prices are reasonable, considering the high quality. There are branches at Piazza del Duomo 24R and Lugarno Acciaiuoli 42R (☎ **055/215-262** for both branches).

Opened in 1774 and maintained today by descendants of the original founders, **J Pineider,** Piazza della Signoria 13R (☎ **055/284-655**), is the oldest store in Florence specializing in printing and engraving. The most aristocratic-looking greeting cards, business cards, stationery, and formal invitations come from this outfit. Because most orders take between 2 and 3 weeks to fill, many clients place their orders here and then arrange to have the final product shipped home. The store also stocks a wide range of gifts, like beautifully crafted diaries, stationery, the kinds of desk sets you'd present to your favorite CEO, portfolios, address books, photo albums, and etchings of vistas unique to Florence.

Scriptorium, Via dei Servi 5R (☎ **055/211-804**), offers wonderful handsewn notebooks, journals, and photo albums made of thick paper and bound with soft leather covers.

PRINTS & ENGRAVINGS **Ducci,** Lungarno Corsini 24R (☎ **055/214-550**), hawks the best selection of historical prints and engravings covering the history of Florence from the 13th century. Also available are marble fruit, wooden items, and Florentine boxes covered with gold leaf.

Giovanni Baccani, Via della Vigna Nuova 75R (☎ **055/214-467**), has long been a specialist in this field. Everything it sells is old. "The Blue Shop," as it's called, offers a huge array of prints and engravings, often of Florentine scenes. Tuscan paper goods are also sold.

SHOES **Casadei,** Via del Tornabuoni 33R (☎ **055/287-240**), is an interesting shop that is painted white; its pillars make the room look like a small colonnade. This shop is one of four Casadei shops in Italy (others are in Rome and Ferrara and near Bologna). Locally produced women's shoes, boots, and handbags are sold, with prices beginning at 300,000L ($150).

Lily of Florence, Via Guicciardini 2R (☎ **055/294-748**), offers both men's and women's shoes in American sizes. For women, Lily distributes both her own creations and those of other well-known designers.

Salvatore Ferragamo, Via dei Tornabuoni 14R (☎ **055/292-123**), has long been one of the most famous names in shoes. The headquarters of this famed manufacturer were installed here in the Palazzo Ferroni, on the most fashionable shopping street of Florence, before World War II broke out. Ferragamo sells shoes for men and women, along with elegant boutique items, like men's and women's clothing, scarves, handbags, ties, and luggage.

SILVER **Pampaloni,** Borgo Santi Apostoli 47R (☎ **055/289-094**), is headed by Gianfranco Pampaloni, a third-generation silversmith. He often bases designs on past achievements (for example, a 1604 goblet by Roman artist Giovanni Maggi). The business was launched in 1902, and some of the classic designs turned out back then are still being made.

A fabled name among serious shoppers, **Brandimartre,** Via Bartolini 18R (☎ **055/239-381**), is Florence's best-stocked workshop and silver showcase. This semiprecious metal is exquisitely handcrafted into a number of dazzling items, including signature goblets. They even do frivolous designs for the man or women who has everything (a silver cheese grater, for example).

WINES **Il Cantinone,** Via Santo Spirito 6 (☎ **055/218-898**), describes itself as presenting a typical Florentine menu, but the emphasis is on Tuscan wines, such as Black Label, Santo Cristo, and Villa Antinori. Purchase your choice by the glass or by the bottle to take with you. And don't forget to try the vin santo, a Tuscan dessert wine, with almond cookies. If you want a little more sustenance, their fixed-price menus are 15,000 to 40,000L ($7.50 to $20).

The **Enoteca Gambi Romano,** Borgo SS. Apostoli 21–23R (☎ **055/292-646**), is a centrally located outlet for olive oil, vin santo, grappa, and (upstairs) lots of wine, including well-priced Tuscan labels.

7 Florence After Dark

Evening entertainment in Florence isn't an exciting prospect, unless you simply like to walk through the narrow streets or head toward Fiesole for a truly spectacular view of the city at night. The typical Florentine begins an evening early at one of the cafes listed below.

For theatrical and concert listings, pick up a free copy of ***Welcome to Florence,*** available at the tourist office. This handy publication contains information on recitals, concerts, theater productions, and other cultural offerings.

From May to July, the city welcomes classical musicians for its ✪ **Maggio Musicale** festival of cantatas, madrigals, concertos, operas, and ballets, many of which are presented in Renaissance buildings. Schedule and ticket information is available from **Maggio Musicale Fiorentino/Teatro Comunale,** Corso Italia 16, 50123 Firenze (☎ **055/27-791**). Tickets cost 40,000 to 200,000L ($20 to $100). For further information, visit the theater's Web site at www.maggiofiorentino.com.

THE PERFORMING ARTS

The ✪ **Teatro Comunale di Firenze/Maggio Musicale Fiorentino,** Corso Italia 16 (☎ **055/211-158**), is Florence's main theater, with opera and ballet seasons presented September to December and a concert season January to April. This theater is also the venue for the Maggio Musicale (see above), Italy's oldest and most prestigious festival that takes place late April to July and offers opera, ballet, concerts, recitals, cinema, and meetings. The box office is open Tuesday to Friday 10am to 4:30pm, Saturday 9am to 1pm, and 1 hour before the curtain.

The **Teatro della Pergola,** Via della Pergola 18 (☎ **055/247-9651**), is Florence's major legitimate theater, but you'll have to understand Italian to appreciate most of its plays. Plays are performed year-round except during the Maggio Musicale, when the theater becomes the setting for many of the festival events. Performances are Tuesday to Saturday at 8:45pm, and Sunday at 3:45pm. The box office is open until 1 hour before the start of performances.

The **Teatro Verdi,** Via Ghibellina 99 (☎ **055/212-320**), is a venue for prestigious dance and classical music events. Major operatic and ballet performances are often presented here as well, including big-name performers. Even a leading pop star has been known to dominate the stage.

Many cultural presentations are performed in churches. These might include open-air concerts in the cloisters of the **Badia Fiesolana** in Fiesole or at the **Ospedale degli Innocenti,** on summer evenings only. Orchestral offerings, performed by the Regional Tuscan Orchestra, are often presented at **Santo Stefano al Ponte Vecchio.**

LIVE-MUSIC CLUBS

In Dante's former neighborhood, **Chiodo Fisso,** Via Dante Alighieri 16R (☎ **055/238-1290**), is the best venue for Italian folk music. The owners refer to it as a "guitar club," and acoustic guitar sets are a regular feature. Drinks are a bit pricey: You can order a bottle of Chianti (hardly the best) for 25,000L ($12.50). Except for 2 weeks in August, the club is open daily 9pm to 3am, and the cover is 15,000L ($7.50).

In the cellar of an antique building in the historic heart of town, **Full-Up,** Via della Vigna Vecchia 2325R (☎ **055/293-006**), attracts college students who appreciate the club's two-in-one format. One section contains a smallish dance floor and recorded dance music; the other is a somewhat more restrained piano bar. The place can be fun, and even an older crowd feels at ease. It's open Wednesday to Monday 9pm to 3am, with a 15,000 to 25,000L ($7.50 to $12.50) cover that includes the first drink.

The **Red Garter,** Via de' Benci 33R (☎ **055/234-4904**), right off Piazza Santa Croce, has an American Prohibition-era theme and features everything from rock to bluegrass. The club is open Monday to Thursday 8:30pm to 1am and Friday to Sunday 9pm to 2am. There's no cover.

Within a 10-minute bus ride from Piazza del Duomo (take bus no. 29 or 30 to a point near Florence's airport), **Tenax,** Via Pratese 46A (☎ **055/308-160**), is Florence's premier venue for everything from live rock to hip-hop and rap. The bands come from throughout Italy and the rest of Europe. This place used to be a garage and is appropriately battered and grungy. Shows begin nightly except Monday at 10pm and continue to around 3am. The cover is 20,000 to 35,000L ($10 to $17.50), including the first drink.

CAFES

Café Rivoire, Piazza della Signoria 4R (☎ **055/214-412**), offers a classy and amusing old-world ambience with a direct view of the statues of one of our favorite squares in the world. You can sit at one of the metal tables on the flagstones outside or at one of the wooden tables in a choice of inner rooms filled with marble detailing and unusual oil renderings of the piazza outside. If you don't want to sit at all, try the bar, where many colorful characters talk, flirt, or gossip. There's a selection of small sandwiches, omelets, and ice creams, and the cafe is noted for its hot chocolate.

Giacosa, Via dei Tornabuoni 83R (☎ **055/239-6226**), is a deceptively simple-looking cafe with a stand-up bar and a handful of tables. Behind three Tuscan arches on a fashionable shopping street in the center of the old city, it has a warmly paneled interior, a lavish display of pastries and sandwiches, and a reputation as the birthplace of the *Negroni* (gin, Campari, and red vermouth). You can also wet your whistle with Italian and American coffee, and a range of cocktails. Light meals are served, and the cafe is famous for its ice cream.

The oldest and most beautiful cafe in Florence, **Gilli,** Piazza della Repubblica 39R, Via Roma 1 (☎ **055/213-896**), is a few minutes' walk from the Duomo. It was founded in 1789, when Piazza della Repubblica had a different name. You can sit at a brightly lit table near the bar or retreat to an intricately paneled pair of rooms to the side and enjoy the flattering light from the Venetian-glass chandeliers. Daily specials, sandwiches, toasts, and hard drinks are sold, along with an array of "tropical" libations.

The waiters at ✪ **Giubbe Rosse,** Piazza della Repubblica 1314R (☎ **055/212-280**), still wear the Garibaldi red coats as they did when this place was founded in 1888. It has always been known as a literary cafe, where intellectuals and writers met to discuss Italian politics and literature. It survived the Mussolini era and continues to attract an artsy crowd. You can enjoy coffee, drinks, and also salads and sandwiches surrounded by turn-of-the-century chandeliers and polished granite floors. Light lunches and full American breakfasts are specialties.

BARS & PUBS

The **Donatello Bar,** in the Hotel Excelsior, Piazza Ognissanti 3 (☎ **055/264-201**), is the city's most elegant watering hole. This bar and its adjoining restaurant, Il Cestello, attract well-heeled international visitors along with the Florentine cultural and business elite. The ambience is enlivened by a marble fountain and works of art, and piano music is featured daily 7pm to 1am.

If you ask whether the **Dublin Pub,** Via Faenza 27R (☎ **055/293-049**), is an Italian pub, the all-Italian staff will respond rather grandly that such a concept doesn't exist and pubs are by definition Irish. And once you get beyond the fact that virtually no one on the staff has ever been outside Tuscany and there's very little to do here except drink and perhaps practice your Italian, you might settle down and have a rollicking old (very Latin) time. Beers, at least, are appropriately Celtic and include Harp, Guinness, Kilkenny, and Strong's on tap. You'll find this pub near the Santa Maria Novella rail station.

After an initial success in Rome, **Fiddler's Elbow,** Piazza Santa Maria Novella 7R, near the rail station (☎ **055/215-056**), an Irish pub, has now invaded this city and has quickly become one of the most popular watering holes. An authentic pint of Guinness is the most asked-for item.

DANCE CLUBS

Meccanò, Viale degli Olmi 1 (☎ **055/331-371**), is Florence's best, biggest, and most international disco. Within a 20-minute bus ride from Piazza del Duomo, near the Parco della Cascine, it's one of the few discos in Italy to offer an indoor/outdoor setting that includes century-old trees, a terrace, and three dance floors. The music includes everything from punk to rock to funk to garage. Gays mix with the mostly straight crowd with ease, and the average age is 18 to 35. There's no real dress code, but if you opt to dine at the restaurant, you'll find that the crowd there is better dressed. Set menus are 35,000L ($17.50) and served beginning at 9pm. Don't be surprised if someone decides to dance on your table after you've finished eating. Dancing reigns supreme every night except Sunday, Monday, and Wednesday, 11:30pm to 4am. The cover is 25,000L ($12.50), including the first drink.

Space Electronic, Via Palazzuolo 37 (☎ **055/293-082**), is the only club with karaoke. The decor consists of gigantic carnival heads, wall-to-wall mirrors, and an imitation space capsule that goes back and forth across the dance floor. If karaoke doesn't thrill you, head to the new ground-floor pub, which stocks an ample supply of imported beers. On the upper level is a large dance floor with a wide choice of music and the best sound-and-light show in town. This place attracts a lot of foreign women who want to hook up with Florentine men on the prowl. The disco opens nightly at 11pm and usually goes until 4am. The 30,000L ($15) cover includes the first drink.

Yab, Via Sassetti 5R (☎ **055/215-161**), is right in the historic core of the city. Owned and operated by the same management as the larger and more raucous Meccanò (see above), it offers much the same kind of music, albeit in a smaller and more cramped setting. Partly because its interior is less well air-conditioned, it closes between May and October. Otherwise, hours are Wednesday to Saturday 9pm to 3am. The cover runs 20,000 to 30,000L ($10 to $15) and includes the first drink.

GAY & LESBIAN CLUBS

Arci-Gay/Arci-Lesbica Firenze, Via Leone 5/11R (☎ **055/398-772**), offers a new community center that's a good place to get all sorts of information, open Monday to Saturday 4 to 8pm.

Florence's leading gay bar, **Crisco,** Via San Egidio 43R (☎ **055/248-0580**), caters only to men and is in an 18th-century building containing a bar and a dance floor. Classified as a *club privato,* it's open on Wednesday, Thursday, Sunday, and Monday 10:30pm to 3:30am and Friday and Saturday 10:30pm to 5 or 6am. The cover is 15,000 to 20,000L ($7.50 to $10), depending on the night of the week.

Many of Tuscany's gay and lesbian community consider the **Santanassa Bar,** Via Pandolfini 26R (☎ **055/243-356**), a Saturday-night staple. In summer the crowd gets international. There's a bar on the street level, sometimes with live piano music, where many of the patrons seem to have known one another for years. On Friday and Saturday the cellar is transformed into a disco. It's open Tuesday to Sunday 10pm to 4am. The bar and disco are open year-round. The cover, including the first drink, is 15,000L ($7.50) Sunday to Thursday and 25,000L ($12.50) Friday and Saturday.

8 A Side Trip to Fiesole

For more extensive day trips, you can refer to the next chapter. But **Fiesole** is a virtual suburb of Florence.

When the sun shines too hot on Piazza della Signoria and the tourist crowd is dense, Florentines are likely to head for the hills, usually to Fiesole. But they'll encounter more tourists, since this town (once an Etruscan settlement) is the most popular outing from the city. Bus no. 7, leaving from Piazza San Marco, will take you here in 25 minutes and give you a panoramic view along the way. You'll pass fountains, statuary, and gardens strung out over the hills like a scrambled jigsaw puzzle.

EXPLORING THE TOWN

In Fiesole you won't find anything as dazzling as the Renaissance treasures of Florence; the town's charms are more subtle. Fortunately, all major sights branch out within walking distance of the main square, **Piazza Mino da Fiesole,** beginning with the **Cattedrale di San Romolo (Duomo).** At first this cathedral may seem austere, with its concrete-gray Corinthian columns and Romanesque arches. But it has its own beauty. Dating from A.D. 1000, it was much altered during the Renaissance, and in the Salutati Chapel are important sculptural works by Mino da Fiesole. It's open daily 7:30am to noon and 4 to 7pm.

Bandini Museum (Museo Bandini). Via Dupre 1. ☎ **055/59-477.** Admission (includes admission to Roman Theater and Civic Museum, below) 10,000L ($5). Mar–Sept daily 9:30am–6:30pm; Oct daily 9:30am–5:30pm; Nov–Feb daily 9:30am–4:30pm. Closed 1st Tues of each month.

This ecclesiastical museum, around to the side of the Duomo, belongs to the Fiesole Cathedral Chapter, established in 1913. On the ground floor are della Robbia terra-cotta works, as well as art by Michelangelo and Pisano. On the top floors are paintings by the best Giotto students, reflecting ecclesiastical and worldly themes, most of them the work of Tuscan artists of the 14th century.

Roman Theater and Civic Museum (Teatro Romano e Museo Civico). Via Portigiani 1. ☎ **055/59-477.** Admission (includes admission to Bandini Museum, above) 10,000L ($5). For hours, see the Bandini Museum above. Bus: 7.

On this site is the major surviving evidence that Fiesole was an Etruscan city 6 centuries before Christ and later a Roman town. In the 1st century B.C., a theater was built, the restored remains of which you can see today. Near the theater are the skeletonlike ruins of the bathrooms, which may have been built at the same time. Try to visit the Etruscan-Roman museum, with its many interesting finds that date from the days when Fiesole, not Florence, was supreme (a guide is on hand to show you through).

Museum of the Franciscan Missionaries (Museo Missionario Francescano Fiesole). Via San Francesco 13. ☎ **055/59-175.** Free admission (but a donation is expected). Church daily 8am–noon and 3–6pm. Museum Mon–Sat 9:30am–12:30pm and 3–6pm (to 7pm in summer). Bus: 7.

The hardest task you'll have in Fiesole is to take the steep goat-climb up to the Convent of San Francesco. You can visit the Gothic-style Franciscan church, built in the first years of the 1400s and consecrated in 1516. Inside are many paintings by well-known Florentine artists. In the basement of the church is the ethnological museum. Begun in 1906, the collection has a large section of Chinese artifacts, including ancient bronzes. An Etruscan-Roman section contains some 330 archaeological pieces, and an Egyptian section also has numerous objects.

ACCOMMODATIONS

Hotel Villa Aurora. Piazza Mino da Fiesole 39, Fiesole, 50014 Firenze. ☎ **055/59-100.** Fax 055/59-587. www.villaaurora.com. E-mail: h.aurora@fi.flashnet.it. 27 units. A/C MINIBAR TV TEL. 335,000–375,000L ($167.50–$187.50) double; 700,000L ($350) suite. Rates include continental breakfast. AE, DC, MC, V. Free parking. Bus: 7.

On Fiesole's main square, behind a facade of green shutters and ocher-colored stucco, the Aurora occupies what in the 18th century was a private home. In 1890 it became a hotel that catered almost exclusively to arts-conscious Brits making their Grand Tour. The hotel continues to rent rooms, which have been modernized and simplified and even include Jacuzzis. Views over faraway Florence are visible from the back rooms, which cost more than those overlooking the piazza. The rooms range from small to medium, each with comfortable beds fitted with fine mattresses and linens. Connecting doors can be opened between some rooms to create suites. On the premises are a back terrace with hanging vines and a pergola.

Pensione Bencista. Via Benedetto da Maiano 4, Fiesole, 50014 Firenze. ☎ and fax **055/59-163.** 44 units, 32 with private bathroom. TEL. 130,000L ($65) per person without bathroom, 150,000L ($75) per person with bathroom. Rates include half-board. No credit cards. Free parking. Bus: 7.

The Bencista has been the villa of the Simoni family for years. It was built around 1300, with additions made about every 100 years after that. In 1925 Paolo Simoni opened the villa to paying guests, and today it's run by his son, Simone Simoni. Its position, high up on the road to Fiesole, is commanding, with an unmarred view of the city and the hillside villas. The spread-out villa has many lofty old rooms furnished with family antiques and comfortable mattresses. They vary in size and interest; many are without private bathrooms and have hot and cold running water only. In chilly weather, guests meet one another in the evening in front of a huge fireplace. It's a 10-minute bus ride from the heart of Florence.

✪ **Villa San Michele.** Via Doccia 4, Fiesole, 50014 Firenze. ☎ **800/237-1236** in the U.S., or 055/59-451 or 055/567-8200. Fax 055/598-734. www.orient-expresshotels.com. E-mail: villasanmichele@firenze.net. 41 units. A/C MINIBAR TV TEL. 1,350,000–1,750,000L ($675–$875) double; 2,300,000–2,900,000L ($1,150–$1,450) suite. Rates include half-board. AE, DC, MC, V. Closed mid-Nov to mid-Mar. Bus: 7.

The San Michele is an ancient monastery of unsurpassed beauty in a memorable setting on a hill below Fiesole, a 15-minute walk south of the center. It was built in the 15th century, damaged in World War II, then carefully restored. The facade and loggia were reportedly designed by Michelangelo. A curving driveway, lined with blossoming trees and flowers, leads to the entrance, and a 10-arch covered loggia continues around the view side of the building to the Italian gardens at the rear.

Most of the guest rooms open onto the view; the others face the inner courtyard. Each is unique, some with iron or wooden canopy beds (with luxury mattresses), antique chests, Savonarola chairs, formal draperies, old ecclesiastical paintings, candelabra, and statues. In the old friars' cells, the units are rather austerely decorated in the spirit of their former role. The most elaborate room is no. 10, its gilded four-poster bearing a 1600s Virgin painted on the headboard. The Michelangelo Suite is the grand choice, a spacious room with a marble fireplace and a large whirlpool. All the rooms come with deluxe bathrooms, with robes and hair dryers.

Dining: Chairs and tables are set out on the loggia for moonlit dinners, at which a refined Tuscan cuisine is served.

Amenities: Concierge, room service, secretarial services, baby-sitting, shuttle bus to town, heated outdoor pool, solarium, facilities for the disabled.

DINING

You might also want to dine at the fine restaurant of the **Villa San Michele** (above).

Trattoria le Cave di Maiano. Via delle Cave 16. ☎ **055/59-133.** Reservations required. Main courses 20,000–35,000L ($10–$17.50); fixed-price lunch 70,000L ($35). AE, DC, MC, V. Tues–Sun 12:30–2:30pm; daily 7:30–10:30pm. Closed Aug 10–20. TUSCAN.

This former farmhouse is at Maiano, a 15-minute ride east from the heart of Florence and just a short distance south of Fiesole. It's a family-run place. The rustically decorated trattoria is a garden restaurant, with stone tables and large sheltering trees. We highly recommend the antipasto and homemade green tortellini. For a main course, there's golden grilled chicken or savory herb-flavored roast lamb. For side dishes, we suggest fried polenta, Tuscan beans, and fried potatoes. As a final treat, the waiter will bring you homemade ice cream with fresh raspberries.

6 Tuscany & Umbria

Rome may rule Italy's body, but Tuscany (Toscana) presides over its heart. The Tuscan landscapes look just like Renaissance paintings, with rolling plains of grass, cypress trees, and olive groves, ancient walled hill towns, and those fabled Chianti vineyards.

Tuscany was where the Etruscans first appeared in Italy. The Romans followed, absorbing and conquering them, and by the 11th century the region had evolved into a collection of independent city-states, such as Florence and Siena, each trying to dominate the others. Many of the cities we'll visit reached the apogee of their economic and political power in the 13th century. The Renaissance reached its apex in Florence, but it was slow to come to Siena, which remains a gem of Gothic glory.

The Renaissance brought with it new titans of art: Giotto, Michelangelo, and Leonardo. Ever since these geniuses "invented" the Renaissance, the world has flocked to Tuscany to see not just the land but also some of the world's greatest art. Critics claim, without much exaggeration, that Western civilization was "rediscovered" in Tuscany. Art flourished under the tutelage of the powerful Medicis, and the legacy remains of Masaccio, della Francesca, Signorelli, Raphael, Donatello, Botticelli, and countless others, plus the engineering feats of architects like Brunelleschi. Tuscany also became known for its men of letters, like Dante, Petrarch, and Boccaccio (who put the seal of approval on the Tuscan dialect by writing in the vernacular rather than in Latin).

Tuscany may be known for its Renaissance artists, but the small region of **Umbria,** at the heart of the Italian peninsula, is associated mainly with saints. Christendom's most beloved saints were born here, foremost of whom was St. Francis of Assisi, founder of the Franciscans. Also born here were St. Valentine, a 3rd-century bishop of Terni, and St. Clare, founder of the Order of Poor Clares.

However, Umbrian painters also contributed to the glory of the Renaissance. Il Perugino, whose lyrical works you can see in the National Gallery of Umbria in Perugia, is one such example.

Umbria's countryside, also the subject of countless paintings, remains as lovely as ever today: You'll pass through a hilly terrain dotted with chestnut trees, interspersed with fertile plains of olive groves and vineyards.

Tuscan Tours: Biking, Horseback Riding & More

Florence-based ✪ **I Bike Italy** (☎ **055-234-2371;** www.ibikeitaly.com; E-mail: I_bike_italy@compuserve.com) offers guided single-day rides in the Tuscan countryside, past olive groves, vineyards, castles, and vine-covered estates. Tours begin daily in Florence at 9am from the north end of Ponte alle Grazie. The company provides a shuttle service to carry you in/out of the city and 21-speed bicycles, helmets, water bottles, and a bilingual guide to show you the way, fix flats, and so on. Tours cover 15 to 30 scenic miles (24km to 48km), at an average speed of 3.2 miles per hour, and return to Florence around 5pm. The cost is 120,000 to 140,000L ($60 to $70) per person, lunch included.

Ciclismo Classico (☎ **800/866-7314** in the U.S.; www.ciclismoclassico.com) is one of the best biking outfitters and has more than a decade of experience leading biking and walking tours in Italy. From April to November, the outfit runs several guided tours through Tuscany, always van-supported, or they will help you arrange a do-it-yourself bike trip. Six- to 15-day trips usually include Italian and cooking lessons, along with wine tasting and cultural itineraries. Groups average 10 to 18 people, with all ages and ability levels welcome.

If you value a tour guide whose focus is customized to your interests, consider the offerings of **Custom Tours in Tuscany,** 206 Ivy Lane, Highland Park, IL 60035 (☎ **847-432-1814;** fax 847-432-1889), with up to 10 bilingual staff members familiar with Tuscany's art and culture. You tell the company what you want to see and do, and it tailors a day-long guided tour. Its staff can help you visit Florence's monuments, guide you through its "secret" alleyways, and show you where to buy antiques, gold, leather, extra-virgin olive oil, or linens at unbeatable prices. Its Tuscan day tours include visits to Lucca, Siena, San Gimignano, and Pietrasanta. They begin/end in Florence, where you should plan to do a lot of walking; outside Florence, the guide accompanies you in your own rented car or arranges for a car and driver. Fees are $375 per day for Florence tours or $475 for tours in the countryside (6 to 7 hours) for up to two. Extra persons are $30 each. Transport, meals, highway tolls, museum admissions, and gratuities aren't included.

At the heart of Chianti in Barberino Val d'Elsa is one of Tuscany's top horse-riding clubs, **Il Paretaio** (☎ **055-8050-050-9218;** fax 055-805-9231; E-mail: ilparetaio@dada.it). Besides lessons, you can opt for half- and full-day outings (English-style) around the countryside on any of the 20 horses and can stay in one of the six guest rooms (private bathrooms) in an early 18th-century stone farmhouse with a view—even the pool is beautifully sited. Dressage lessons are 50,000L ($25) per hour; full-day trail riding with a picnic is 130,000L ($65), room/board not included; and 1-week inclusive packages with 6 half days of trail riding and half board are 1,200,000L ($600) per person, double occupancy.

Only 12 1/2 miles (20km) from Florence in Pontassieve is the **Vallebona Ranch** (☎ **055-839-7246;** fax 055-839-8518; www.cavallowed.it/viagcavi.htm; E-mail: vallebona@iol.it). English riding is available, but Western is the tradition here. You can choose from lessons, full-day treks returning daily to the six guest rooms (shared bathrooms) at the centuries-old farmhouse (1-week package with full board 850,000L/$425 per person, double occupancy), or week-long inn-to-inn treks that begin/end at Vallebona (1,100,000L/$550) per person, double occupancy).

Tuscany & Umbria

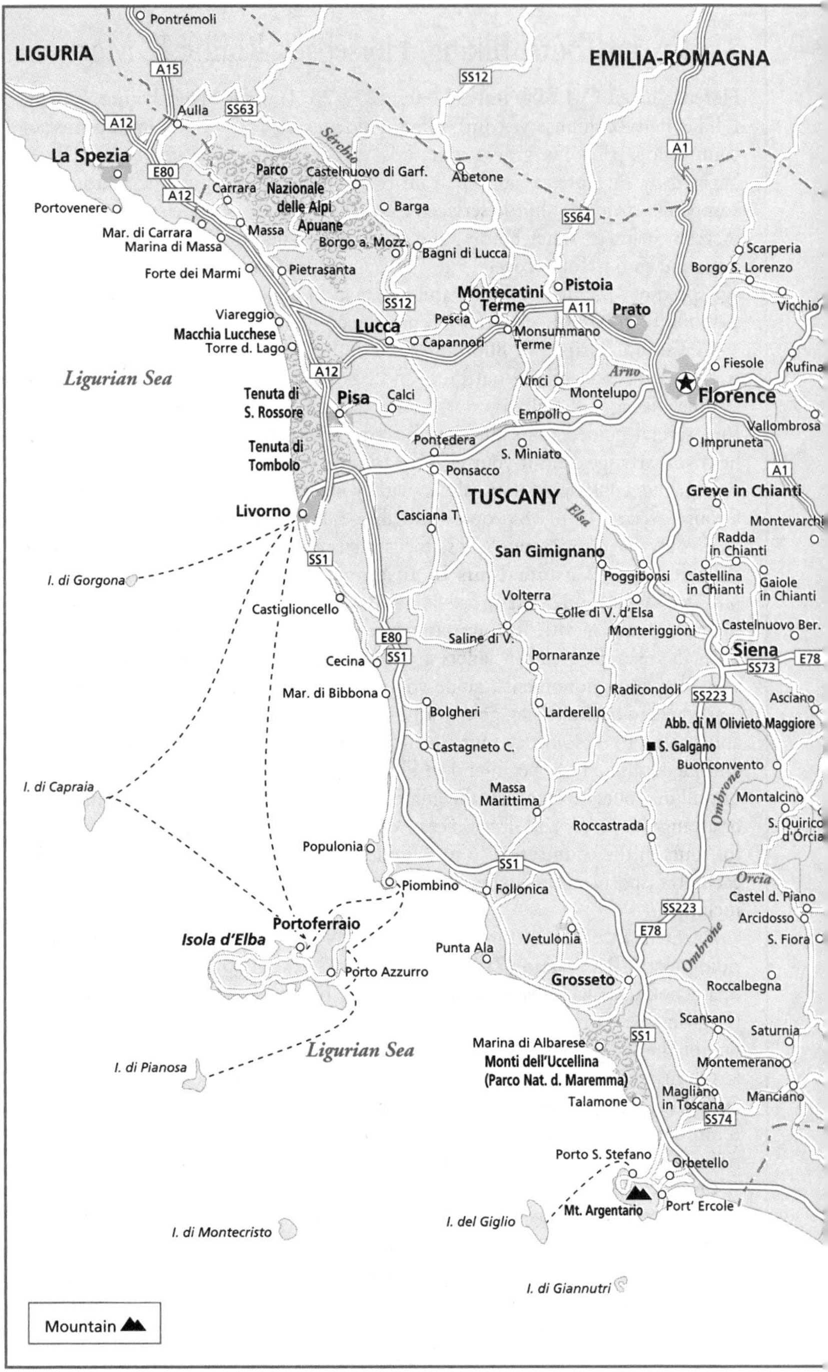

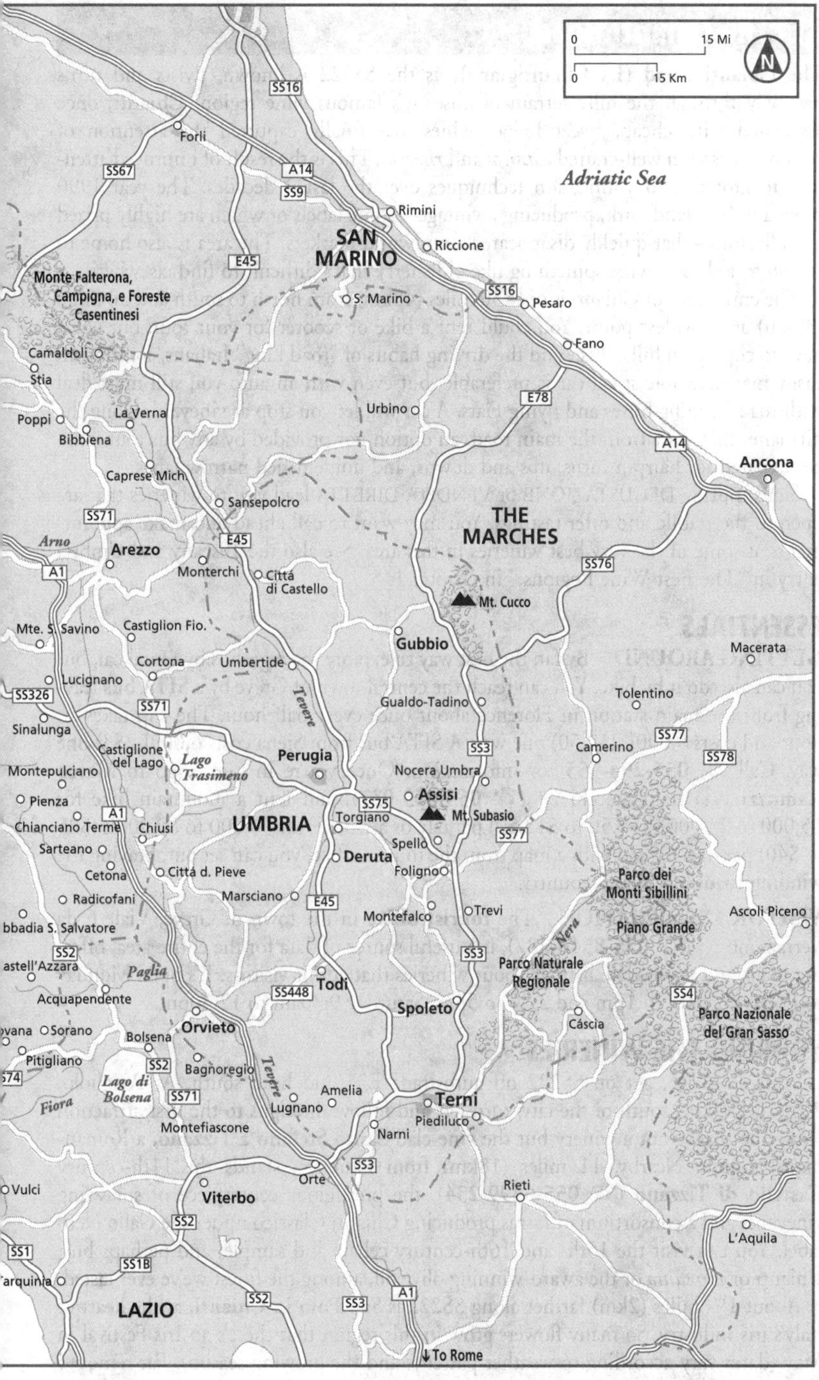

0
15 Mi
0
15 Km
N
Adriatic Sea
SS16
Forlì
SS67
A14
SS9
Rimini
SAN MARINO
Riccione
E45
Monte Falterona, Campigna, e Foreste Casentinesi
S. Marino
SS16
Pesaro
Fano
Camaldoli
Stia
Poppi
La Verna
Bibbiena
Urbino
E78
A14
Ancona
Caprese Mich.
Sansepolcro
THE MARCHES
SS71
Arno
E45
Arezzo
A1
Monterchi
Città di Castello
SS76
Mt. Cucco
Mte. S. Savino
Castiglion Fio.
Gubbio
Macerata
Cortona
Umbertide
Lucignano
SS326
Tevere
Gualdo-Tadino
Tolentino
SS71
Sinalunga
SS77
SS3
Camerino
SS78
Castiglione del Lago
Lago Trasimeno
Perugia
Montepulciano
Nocera Umbra
Pienza
Assisi
SS75
Mt. Subasio
A1
UMBRIA
Chianciano Terme
Chiusi
Torgiano
SS77
Sarteano
Spello
Deruta
Foligno
Parco dei Monti Sibillini
Cetona
Città d. Pieve
Radicofani
Marsciano
E45
Montefalco
Trevi
Ascoli Piceno
Abbadia S. Salvatore
Nera
Piano Grande
SS2
SS3
Castell'Azzara
Paglia
Parco Naturale Regionale
Todi
Acquapendente
SS448
SS4
Spoleto
Parco Nazionale del Gran Sasso
Sovana
Sorano
Orvieto
Bolsena
Cáscia
Pitigliano
SS2
Bagnoregio
SS74
Lago di Bolsena
SS71
Tevere
Amelia
Fiora
Lugnano
Terni
Piediluco
Montefiascone
Narni
SS3
Orte
Vulci
Viterbo
Rieti
SS2
L'Aquila
SS1
SS1B
Tarquinia
SS2
SS3
A1
LAZIO
To Rome

1 The Chianti Road

The Chianti Road (La Chiantigiana), as the SS222 is known, twists and turns narrowly through the hilly terrain of Tuscany's famous wine region. **Chianti,** once associated with cheap, sweet Italian wines, has finally captured the attention of connoisseurs with well-crafted *classicos* and *riservas.* This is the result of improved attention to growth and vinification techniques over the last 2 decades. The year 1990 proved to be a landmark, producing a vintage—some labels of which are highly prized by collectors—that quickly disappeared from world markets. The area is also home to *vin santo,* a dessert wine something like old sherry that's difficult to find elsewhere.

The entire area of Chianti is only 30 miles (48km) from north to south and 20 miles (32km) at its widest point. You could rent a bike or scooter for your tour, but you'd have to cope with hills, dust, and the driving habits of "road king" Italians. Renting an easily maneuverable small car is preferable, but even with an auto you still must deal with road-hogging buses and flying Fiats. A car will let you stop at vineyards along the dirt lanes that stray from the main road, an option not provided by any bus tour. Still, be prepared for hairpin turns, ups and downs, and unidentified narrow lanes.

Signs touting DEGUSTAZIONE or VENDITA DIRETTA lead you to wineries that are open to the public and offer tastings. You may want to call ahead and make appointments at some of the very best wineries in this area. See also the Tuscany and Umbria entry in "The Best Wine Regions," in chapter 1.

ESSENTIALS

GETTING AROUND By far, the best way to explore the region is by rental car, but you can also do it by bike. You can reach the central town of Greve by a **SITA bus** leaving from the main station in Florence about once every half hour. The trip takes an hour and costs 5,000L ($2.50) one way. A SITA bus from Siena costs 6,000L ($3) one way. Call ☎ **055-294-955** for information. Once you're in Greve, go to **Marco Ramuzzi,** Via Italo Stecchi 23 (☎ **055-853-037**), and rent a mountain bike for 15,000 to 25,000L ($7.50 to $12.50) per day or a scooter for 50,000 to 80,000L ($25 to $40) per day. Armed with a map from the tourist office, you can set out, braving the winding roads of Chianti country.

VISITOR INFORMATION The **tourist office** in the town of Greve, Viale 6 da Verrazzano 33 (☎ **055-8546-287**), is a useful source of data for the entire area, offering maps and up-to-date listings about wineries that admit visitors. It's open Monday to Friday 9:30am to 1pm and 2:30 to 5pm, Saturday 9:30am to 12:30pm.

TOURING THE WINERIES

Leaving Florence, get on SS222 off autostrada E35 and head south. At Petigliolo, 2½ miles (4km) south of the city, turn left and follow the signs to the first attraction along the road—not a winery but the vine-clad **Santo Stefano a Tizzano,** a Romanesque church. Nearby, 11 miles (18km) from Florence, stands the 11th-century **Castello di Tizzano** (☎ **055-6499-234**), the prestigious centerpiece of sprawling vineyards and a consortium of farms producing Chianti Classico under the Gallo Nero label. You can visit the 15th- and 16th-century cellars and sample, and perhaps buy, Chianti or *vin santo* or the award-winning olive oil, among the finest we've ever tasted.

About 1¼ miles (2km) farther along SS222 is **San Polo in Chianti,** at the heart of Italy's iris industry. So many flowers grow in this region that there's an Iris Festival in May (dates vary according to weather patterns and the growing season). Far removed

The Chianti Region

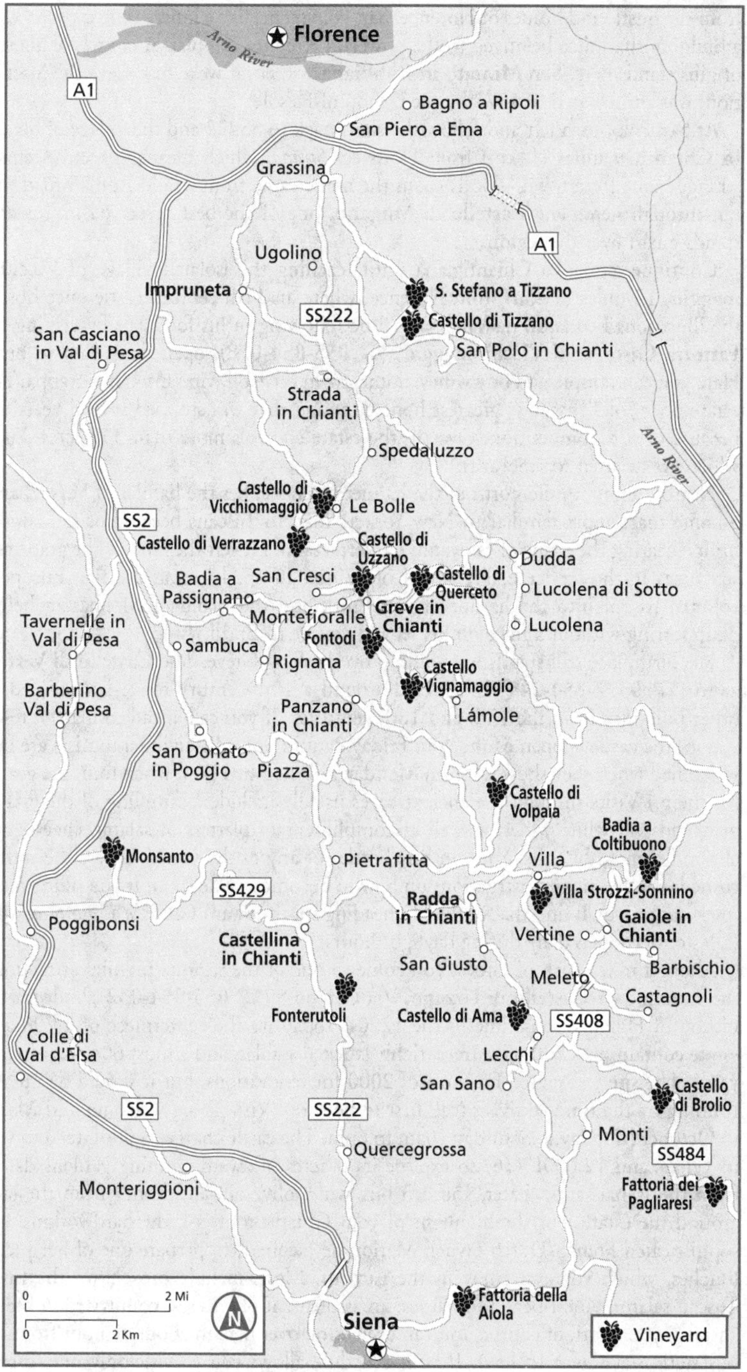
Florence
Arno River
A1
Bagno a Ripoli
San Piero a Ema
Grassina
A1
Ugolino
Impruneta
S. Stefano a Tizzano
SS222
Castello di Tizzano
San Casciano in Val di Pesa
San Polo in Chianti
Strada in Chianti
Spedaluzzo
Arno River
Castello di Vicchiomaggio
Le Bolle
SS2
Castello di Verrazzano
Castello di Uzzano
Dudda
Badia a Passignano
San Cresci
Castello di Querceto
Lucolena di Sotto
Greve in Chianti
Montefioralle
Lucolena
Tavernelle in Val di Pesa
Fontodi
Sambuca
Rignana
Castello Vignamaggio
Barberino Val di Pesa
Panzano in Chianti
Lámole
San Donato in Poggio
Piazza
Castello di Volpaia
Badia a Coltibuono
Monsanto
Pietrafitta
Villa
Villa Strozzi-Sonnino
SS429
Radda in Chianti
Gaiole in Chianti
Poggibonsi
Vertine
Castellina in Chianti
Barbischio
San Giusto
Meleto
Castagnoli
Fonterutoli
Castello di Ama
SS408
Colle di Val d'Elsa
Lecchi
San Sano
Castello di Brolio
SS2
SS222
Monti
Quercegrossa
SS484
Monteriggioni
Fattoria dei Pagliaresi
0
2 Mi
0
2 Km
N
Fattoria della Aiola
Siena
Vineyard

from the bustle and hordes of Florence, San Polo seems like a lonely time capsule, with a building that once belonged to the powerful Knights Templar. A church of ancient origins stands here, **San Miniato in Robbiana,** which, if we're to believe the inscription, was consecrated in 1077 by the bishop of Fiesole.

At San Polo, turn left and follow the signs back to SS222 and the village of **Strada in Chianti,** 9 miles (14km) from Florence. *Strada,* which means "street," seems a strange name for a town—locals claim the name came from an old Roman road that ran through here. The **Castello di Mugano,** one of the best preserved in Tuscany, stands guard over the region.

Continue along La Chiantigiana until reaching the isolated village of **Vicchiomaggio,** 12 miles (19km) from Florence, where an 11th-century castle once hosted the illustrious Leonardo da Vinci. You'll be following in his footsteps by visiting the **Fattoria Castello di Vicchiomaggio** (☎ **055-854-078**), open daily 8am to 8pm. Here you can sample and buy wines, homegrown olive oil, vin santo, and grappa. The estate once sold Tuscany's greatest honey, though that was stopped several years ago because of stiff competition. Overall, the estate controls more than 300 acres, 70 of which are devoted to vineyards.

Nearby, about a mile north of the hamlet of Greve, lies the hamlet of **Verrazzano,** a name that's more familiar to New Yorkers than to Tuscans because of the famous bridge bearing the name of Giovanni da Verrazzano. He left the land of the grape and set to sea in the service of François I of France. In 1524 he was the first European colonial to sail into the harbor of New York and the island of Manhattan before disappearing without a trace on his second voyage to Brazil.

His birthplace still stands on a hilltop overlooking Greve. The **Castello di Verrazzano** (☎ **0577-854-243**) is centered around a 10th-century tower surrounded by other buildings from the 15th and 16th centuries. If you call ahead to make a reservation, the castle is open Monday to Friday 8am to 5pm. (Individual tourists are best welcomed when they show up from Monday to Friday at 11am, when tours are geared for them.) Visits through the ancient caves usually include a sampling of the estate's great red and white wines, as well as complimentary platters of salami, cheese, and almond-scented biscuits. You can buy bottles of any of the wines. Unless the staff is rushed, you might get instructions on how to become a wine snob. If you didn't make reservations, you'll find that on SS222 heading south toward Greve is a *punto vendita* (sales outlet) open daily during daylight hours.

About a mile north of Greve, you come to one of the region's premier attractions, the stunning ✪ **Castello di Uzzano,** Via Uzzano 5 (☎ **055-854-032**), built for the bishop of Florence sometime in the 1200s. Today it's the centerpiece of a 700-acre estate containing 5,500 olive trees, richly stocked stables, and almost 60 acres of vineyards. The site was closed for most of 2000 for renovations, but it should be up and running by the time you visit (call first to be sure). Visitors are welcome mid-March to October Monday to Saturday 10am to 6pm. The castle charges 8,000L ($4) to visit its cellars and 12,000L ($6) to explore its 6 acres of award-winning gardens dating from the Renaissance. Later, you can buy wine, olive oil, and honey from the land around the estate. For the highlight of your Chianti tour, ask the hardworking and sophisticated French/Dutch owner, Marion de Jacobert, to prepare one of her picnic lunches, which you can enjoy in the gardens. Meals include prosciutto, the finest Tuscan salami, vine-ripened tomatoes, an assortment of cheeses, country fresh bread, and fruity Chianti, of course. You can even stroll over here in about an hour from the bus station at Greve (below). If your schedule allows you to visit only one Tuscan winery, make it this one, especially if you're dependent on public transportation.

On the premises are six apartments, with a kitchen, a TV, a phone, a minibar, an air-conditioner, and a stereo, priced at 300,000L ($150) double, without breakfast. Since the owner is an interior decorator, they're stylishly furnished, with such antiques as Empire beds resting under wooden ceilings. The kitchens are marvelously equipped with such luxuries as Richard Ginori china. Riding lessons from the stables can be arranged.

The road continues to **Greve in Chianti,** the region's unofficial capital, on the banks of the Greve River. Tuscany's grandest **wine fair** takes place here every September. Its central square is the funnel-shaped **Piazza del Mercatale,** with a statue honoring Giovanni da Verrazzano. Greve's castle long ago burned to the ground, but on Piazzetta Santa Croce you can visit the parish church**, Santa Croce,** containing a Bicci di Lorenzo triptych depicting the Annunciation. Greve is filled with wine shops (*enoteche*), yet we find it far more adventurous to buy from the wineries themselves.

Four miles (6km) from Greve, along the road signposted Figline Val d'Arno, you'll find a tranquil estate, the **Castello di Querceto,** Via Dudda 61 (☎ **055-859-21**). It boasts more than 125 acres of vineyards producing several grades of red Chianti and La Corte (made from the same Sangiovese grapes) and at least two whites (especially Le Giuncaie de Vernaccia). It's centered around a verdant park with an 11th-century castle that can be viewed only from the outside, the interior is not open to visitors. The staff is proud to show off the winery and cellars and will sell you wine, olive oil, and regional produce. Reservations are required.

Six miles south of Greve is **Fontodi,** Via San Leonino (☎ **055-852-005**; www.fontodi.com/benvenuti.htm), accessible via SS222, near the village of Panzano, half a mile southeast of Sant'Eufrosino. Here you'll find 155 acres of vineyards radiating from a stone villa built between the 18th and 19th centuries, plus wine tastings and sales of several grades of Chianti and a reputable table wine known as Flaccianello della Pieve. Reservations are required, and you should send a fax to ☎ **055-852-537.** Visits are possible Monday to Friday 8am to noon and 1:30 to 5:30pm.

South of Greve on SS222 is another highlight: ✪ **Vignamaggio,** Via Petriolo 5 (☎ **055-854-661**; www.vignamaggio.com), boasting a beautiful Renaissance villa that was once the residence of La Gioconda (Lisa Gherardini). With her enigmatic smile, she sat for the most famous portrait of all time, Leonardo da Vinci's *Mona Lisa,* now in Paris's Louvre. You can tour the gardens (some of the most beautiful in Tuscany) Monday to Friday if you call in advance for a reservation. If the classical statues and towering hedges seem familiar, it means you saw Kenneth Branagh's 1993 *Much Ado About Nothing,* which was shot here. After a tour of the gardens, you can enjoy a wine tasting in the front office. In 1404 the wine of this estate became the first red to be referred to as "Chianti." This is a private villa, and you can come here for a tasting of the wine, served along with snacks, costing 25,000 to 50,000L ($12.50 to $25) depending on your selection.

From Greve, continue 3½ miles (6km) south along the winding Chiantigiana to one of the most enchanting spots in the Chianti, the little agricultural village of **Panzano.** It's worth a walk around the grounds, and parts of its medieval castle, which once witnessed battles between Florence and Siena, remain. The village women make the finest embroidery around, and you may want to acquire some from the locals. If you're so charmed by Panzano you want to spend the night, contact the owners of the Torre Guelfa in Florence (☎ **055-239-6338;** fax 055-239-8577) and ask about their **Villa Rosa di Boscorotondo**, Via San Leolino 59, Panzana (☎ **055-852-577**; fax 055-856-0835; E-mail: villarosa@italyhotel.com). See chapter 5.

Farther south is the delightful hill town of **Castellina in Chianti,** with a population of only 3,000. Once a fortified Florentine outpost against the Sienese, it fell to Sienese-Aragonese forces in 1478. But when Siena collapsed in 1555 to Florentine forces, sleepy little Castellina was left to slumber for centuries. That's why the town has preserved its *quattrocento* look, with its once fortified walls virtually intact. Little houses were constructed into the walls and also nested on top of them. The covered walkway, Via della Volte, is the most historic in town. Although bottegas here sell Chianti and olive oils, you're better off delaying your purchases until later, because you're on the doorstep of some of the finest wineries in Italy.

After Castellina, detour from SS222 and head east along a tortuous winding road to **Radda in Chianti,** with a population of 1,700. Radda is surrounded by the rugged region of Monti del Chianti and was the ancient capital of Lega del Chianti. The streets of the village still follow their original plan from the Middle Ages. The main square with its somber **Palazzo Comunale,** bearing a fresco from the 1400s, will make you feel as if you've traveled back in a time capsule.

Another winery is in the hamlet of Rentennano, near the village of Monti. Here the **Fattoria San Giusto** (☎ **0577-747-121**) is the site of a 12th-century cellar that sits beneath a 15th-century villa. The centerpiece of 430 acres of farmland, 76 of which are devoted to vineyards, it produces two grades of Chianti as well as a simple table wine (Percarlo), which connoisseurs find surprisingly flavorful. Tastings are possible but only with a reservation and only for a minimum of three to four persons. Hours are Monday 8:30am to noon and 2 to 6pm and Saturday 8:30am to noon.

From Radda, continue along the winding road, signposted "Gaiole in Chianti." Along the way you'll come upon ✪ **Ristorante Badia a Coltibuono** (☎ **0577-749-498**), a wine estate/restaurant (see "Dining" below). Try to time your arrival for lunch, as the Tuscan food is excellent. Called "the abbey of the good harvest," this place was founded by Vallombrosian monks in 770, and they were the first vine growers of Chianti. For about 150 years, the Stucchi Prinetti family has been linked to the property. You should call for a reservation to visit. From Monday to Saturday there are guided tours 10:30am to 1pm, including a wine tasting for 6,000L ($3). A shop on site sells the wines of the region, Coltibuono olive oil, wine vinegars aged in casks, balsamic vinegar, and exquisite acacia, chestnut, heather, and manna honey.

After a meal, continue 6 miles (10km) east to the market town of **Gaiole in Chianti,** with a population of 5,000. You'll come to a local cooperative, the **Agricoltori Chianti Geografico,** Via Mulinaccio 10 (☎ **0577-749-489**; www.chiantinet.it/geografico), a branch of one of the region's largest associations of wine growers (more than 200). About 1¼ miles (2km) north of Gaiole in Chianti, it contains a modern wine-pressing facility with a prodigious output of (red) Chianti Classico and (white) Valdarbia. The local *vin santo* is made of trebbiano and malvasia grapes left to dry before pressing and then fermented in small oak barrels for about 4 years. The cooperative sells wine by the glass or bottle, as well as olive oil, the Chianti Colli Senesi, and the (white) Gallestro wines produced on its lands near Siena.

Many other wineries in the area are easily reached by car from Gaiole. One of the best is the towering ✪ **Castello di Brolio** (☎ **0577-73-01**), 6 miles (10km) south along SS484. This is the home of the Barone Ricasoli Wine House, famous since the 19th century for Ricasoli's experiments aimed at improving the quality of Chianti. Known as the Iron Baron, he inherited the property in 1829; in time he became one of the creators of a unified Italy and was elected its second prime minister. The property's history dates from 1141, when Florentine monks came here to live at a site whose vineyards go back to 1005. Caught up many times in the bombardments between the warring forces of Florence and Siena, the castle was later torn down, but then authorities in Florence ordered that it be reconstructed. Visiting hours are Monday to Friday 9am to noon and 2:30 to 5:30pm; admission is 10,000L ($5), and a tasting costs 15,000 L ($7.50). A cantina sells the award-winning wines.

Another interesting stop is **Fattoria dei Pagliaresi,** in the village of Castelnuovo in Berardenga (☎ **0577-359-070**), about 7½ miles (12km) southeast of Gaiole on SS484. In the mid-1990s, the charming English-speaking owner, Chiara Sanguineti, sold the cellars and vineyards to other growers, but the 300-year-old farmhouse she maintains sits amid vineyards, near ancient olive groves. You can tour the farm; taste or buy wine, grappa, honey, and olive oil; visit lovely gardens; and (if you reserve in advance) enjoy a well-prepared Tuscan farmhouse lunch for 30,000 to 40,000L ($15 to $20).

If you backtrack, taking SS408 to Siena, you can follow the signposts about 6 miles (10km) north to the **Fattoria della Aiola** (☎ **0577-322-615;** fax 0577-322-509), near the hamlet of Vagliagli, 12½ miles (20km) southwest of Gaiole. Site of a ruined medieval castle (only a wall and moat remain) and a 19th-century villa (not open to the public), it features 90 acres of vineyards that produce Chianti, Sangiovese, grappa, and Spumante "Aioli Brut" (a sparkling wine similar to champagne). The winery even produces olive oil and vinegar. This place receives a lot of visitors (including tour buses), so advance reservations or at least a phone call before arriving is a good idea.

ACCOMMODATIONS ALONG THE CHIANTI ROAD

The atmospheric Tuscan inns along the Chianti road are wonderful, and it's a good idea to break up a visit between Florence and Siena with a night at one of them. The best centers for overnighting are Greve, Radda, Gaiole, and Castellina (our favorite). Many of these inns are also noted for their good food and wine. Even if you're not a guest, you might visit for a meal.

There are also wonderful apartments for rent at Villa Vignamaggio (see "Touring the Wineries," above) and at **Castello di Uzzano,** just 1.2 miles (2km) north of Greve (☎ **055/055/854-032;** fax 055/055/854-375; faxes are preferred). Here, six apartments lie in medieval houses ringing the front courtyard of a beautiful villa located on a historic wine estate that has lovely views and formal gardens. The refined, rustic rooms are furnished with antiques, and the kitchens are fully equipped.

Albergo del Chianti. Piazza Matteotti 86, 50022 Greve in Chianti. ☎ and fax **055-85-37-63.** www.albergodelchianti.it. E-mail: info@albergodelchianti.it. 16 units. A/C MINIBAR TV TEL. 180,000L ($90) double. Rate includes buffet breakfast. Half-board 45,000L ($22.50) per person. MC, V.

At the edge of Greve's main square, with a facade and foundation as old (more than 1,000 years) as the square itself, is this charming small inn whose accommodations look out over a microcosm of rural Italy. Each cozy guest room is painted a different color; each room evokes old Tuscany and has a wrought-iron bedstead with a firm mattress. The small bathrooms are well kept. Aside from breakfast, dinner is the only meal served (only to hotel guests); it's always accompanied by a selection of regional wines. The Bussotti family takes good care of you in their restaurant; in warm weather, the food is served in a beautiful Mediterranean garden near the pool.

✪ **Borgo Argenina.** Localiatà Argenina (near San Marcellino Monti), 53013 Gaiole in Chianti. ☎ and fax **0577-747-117.** www.chiantinet.it/argenina. 7 units. MINIBAR TEL. 220,000L ($110) double; 280,000L ($140) apt. Rates include country breakfast. Ask about off-season discounts. No credit cards. Ask for directions when reserving.

From the flagstoned terrace of Elena Nappa's new hilltop B&B (she bought the whole medieval hamlet), you can see the farmhouse where Bertolucci filmed his gorgeous

Stealing Beauty in 1996. Against remarkable odds (she'll regale you with the anecdotes), she has created the rural retreat of her dreams—and yours, too. Elena's design talents (she was a fashion stylist in Milan) are amazing, and the guest rooms boast antique wrought-iron beds, deluxe mattresses, handmade quilts, hand-stitched lace curtains, and time-worn terra-cotta tiles. The bathrooms are made to look old-fashioned, though the plumbing is modern. Since the place isn't easy to find, English-speaking Elena will fax you directions when you reserve.

Castello di Spaltenna. Pieve di Spaltenna, 53013 Gaiole in Chianti. ☎ **0577-749-483.** Fax 0577-749-269. www.castellodispaltenna.it/html. E-mail: castellospaltenna@chiantinet.it. 30 units. MINIBAR TV TEL. 370,000–480,000L ($185–$240) double; 580,000–690,000L ($290–$345) suite. Rates include buffet breakfast. AE, DC, MC, V. Closed mid-Jan to Feb.

One of the region's most unique hotels is on a hill above Gaiole. Opened during the Middle Ages as a monastery, it retains some medieval flair, despite several enlargements and modifications. In the compound are a small medieval chapel, two soaring towers, and several stone-sided annexes, one housing some of the junior suites. The guest rooms are cozy and traditionally furnished, with all the modern conveniences. Look for wrought-iron or wooden headboards and terra-cotta floors whose tiles may be as much as 1,000 years old. Some rooms have fireplaces, and all enjoy views. The restaurant serves lunch and dinner daily noon to 2pm and 7:30 to 9:30pm, with main courses at 30,000 to 36,000L ($15 to $18). Tuscan specialties include Florentine beefsteak, homemade pastas, and fresh vegetables. There's also a pool.

Hotel Salivolpi. Via Fiorentina 89, 53011 Castellina in Chianti. ☎ **0577-740-484.** Fax 0577-740-998. www.hotelsalivolpi.com. E-mail: info@hotelsalivolpi.com. 19 units. TEL. 165,000L ($82.50) double. Rates include buffet breakfast. AE, DC, MC, V.

The good living continues at this farm setting against a backdrop that looks like a Renaissance painting. Salivolpi has been visited by some of the world's most discriminating travelers, who are drawn to its setting and ambience. The guest rooms are spread across three buildings, each beautifully maintained and decorated with Tuscan antiques. Only nine have TVs. The bathrooms are spotless. There's a pool and garden but no restaurant (some good ones are a short drive away).

✪ **Hotel Tenuta di Ricavo.** Località Ricavo 4, 53011 Castellina in Chianti (2 miles/3km north of town). ☎ **0577-740-221.** Fax 0577-741-014. www.romantikhotels.com/castellina. E-mail: ricavo@chiantinet.it. 23 units. MINIBAR TV TEL. 330,000–425,000L ($165–$212.50) double; 460,000L ($230) suite. Rates include breakfast. MC, V. Closed late Nov to early Apr.

Our favorite choice in the region, this place is a fantasy of what a Tuscan inn should look like. In fact, it's like a medieval village of stone houses, complete with a pool. On nippy nights, guests gather in the public lounge with its fireplace. The innkeepers rent beautifully furnished and maintained guest rooms, each with a comfortable mattress and a well-maintained bathroom. The restaurant, La Pecora Nera, run by Alessandro Lobrano, serves an excellent Tuscan cuisine, accompanied by the delectable wines of Chianti. Surrounding the compound are 445 acres of woodlands, with paths that are ideal for long walks or riding a mountain bike.

La Villa Miranda. Località Villa, 53107 Radda in Chianti. ☎ **0577-738-021.** Fax 0577-738-668. www.italyintour.com. 49 units. TV TEL. 110,000–240,000L ($55–$120) double; 250,000L ($125) suite. Breakfast 15,000L ($7.50). MC, V.

The Miranda was built on the site of a posthouse and became a small inn in 1842. The reigning duenna is Donna Miranda herself, somewhat of a local legend. Most of the antique-filled guest rooms in the outbuildings have amenities like minibars, air-conditioning, TVs, and phones, while those in the main structure are rather basic.

They're all intimate, with very comfortable mattresses. The restaurant is one of the finest in the area, specializing in regional fare like wild boar cooked in white wine. Mamma Miranda claims her *ribollita* is the best vegetable soup in Tuscany, and no one disagrees! Her homemade ravioli and tender Florentine beefsteak are equally delectable. If you've always resisted ordering mutton, try Mamma Miranda's. There are two pools and a tennis court.

Villa Casalecchi. Casalecchi 18, 53001 Castellina in Chianti. ☎ **0577-740-240.** Fax 0577-741-111. www.chiantinet.it/casalecchi. E-mail: casalecchi@chiantinet.it. 25 units. TV TEL. 330,000–390,000L ($165–$195) double. Rates include buffet breakfast. AE, DC, MC, V. Closed Nov to 1 week before Easter.

Almost as elegant as the Tenuta di Ricavo (see above), this four-star hotel is built against a hill. You arrive on the hilltop and enter into what's the top floor. The hotel is composed of a trio of buildings, with the main structure an elegant villa whose 16 units are spread across two floors. The guest rooms throughout range from small to medium, each furnished in part with 18th-century reproductions and often with canopied beds. The bathrooms are small but contain hair dryers. The restaurant serves a perfect Tuscan cuisine, with extremely fresh ingredients. In summer it's possible to dine in the evergreen garden. You can swim in a lovely pool or play tennis on the court (there's even a bocce alley). From here, you can visit wineries on a bike or on horseback (there are various stables in the area).

DINING ALONG THE CHIANTI ROAD

Some of the best food in Italy is served in Chianti, and all dishes are accompanied by the wine of the region.

Antica Trattoria La Torre. Piazza del Comune 13, Castellina in Chianti. ☎ **0577-740-236.** Reservations required in summer and weekends. Main courses 15,000–35,000L ($7.50–$17.50). AE, CB, DC, DISC, MC, V. Sat–Thurs noon–2:30pm and 7:30–9:30pm. Closed Sept 1–15. TUSCAN.

This old family-run dining room is on the principal square in an 18th-century building next to a medieval tower built around 1400. It depends on the harvest from the field, stream, and air to keep its good cooks busy. The Tuscan game, the fowl (like pigeon and guinea), and the local beef are the finest in the area. The Florentine beefsteak alone is worth the trip. Other typical dishes are delicious *ribolitta* (thick vegetable soup), pasta with game sauce, and meat grilled over charcoal with mushrooms. The best dessert is the homemade pine nut cake.

Borgo Antico. Via Case Sparse 115, Lucolena (10 miles/16km northeast of Greve). ☎ **055-851-024.** Reservations recommended. Main courses 18,000–25,000L ($9–$12.50). AE, MC, V. Apr–Oct Wed–Mon noon–3pm and 7–9:30pm; Nov–Dec and Feb–Mar Fri 7–9:30pm, Sat–Sun noon–3pm and 7–9:30pm. TUSCAN.

Opened more than 30 years ago in a 200-year-old compound of farmhouses and barns, this country inn is more upscale than you might think, thanks to the hardworking Marunti family, who haul in fresh produce from nearby farms every morning. The pastas are made fresh on the premises, and the desserts, especially such relatively simple concoctions as crema cotta and tiramisu, are wonderful. The Florentine-style beefsteaks are among the best in the region, tender and loaded with Mediterranean herbs and olive oil. The turkey fillet grilled with olive oil and the veal scallops with lemon juice or wine are worth the drive. As you dine, you'll enjoy views of the nearby slopes of Monte San Michele.

The Maruntis rent three simple guest rooms. None have a TV or phone, but the solid stone walls and old-time setting more than compensate. Each has a private bathroom, though in one case it's outside the bedroom. Doubles are 80,000 to 90,000L ($40 to $45). Because the owners spend their mornings out buying supplies, no breakfast is served.

✪ **Bottega del Moro.** Piazza Trieste 14R, Greve in Chianti. ☎ **055-853-753.** Reservations required. Main courses 19,000–30,000L ($9.50–$15). AE, CB, MC, V. Thurs–Tues 12:15–2:30pm and 7:15–9:30pm. Closed Nov and 1st week of June. TUSCAN.

Our favorite restaurant in Greve center occupies an early 20th-century stone-sided building that was a blacksmith's shop for many years. (Locals referred to the blacksmith as "The Moor" because of the charcoal that blackened his face, and ever since the nickname "Lair of the Moor" has been associated with this restaurant.) Run by English-speaking Elizabeth Tassi and her husband, Sergio, who oversees the kitchen, this restaurant specializes in a light, less oily version of Tuscan cuisine. Menu items include homemade ravioli with butter and sage; Florentine-style tripe, beefsteaks, and roasted rabbit from nearby fields; and skewered meat grilled to perfection. The unusual modern paintings in the two dining rooms are by a well-known local artist, Alvaro Baralie, a friend of the owners. A flowering terrace provides limited extra seating on the square during clement weather.

Il Vignale. Via XX Settembre 23, Radda in Chianti. ☎ **0577-738-094.** Reservations recommended. Main courses 35,000–45,000L ($17.50–$22.50). AE, DC, MC, V. Fri–Wed 12:30–3pm and 7:30–9:30pm. Closed Jan–Mar. TUSCAN.

This rustic yet elegant place is the area's best family-run dining room, turning out homestyle Tuscan cuisine that's flavorful and prepared with fresh ingredients. Every day something new appears, and the cuisine is quite creative. You can start with a typical crostini as an appetizer (similar to a small bruschette, with different kinds of prosciutto on top). Among the main courses are homemade soups and pastas, like *tagliatelle* (flat noodles) with wild boar sauce. In autumn some of the region's finest game dishes are offered, and you can order roast lamb stuffed with artichokes and aromatic herbs.

La Cantinetta. Via Mugnana 93, Spedaluzzo (1½ miles/2km north of Greve). ☎ **055-857-2000.** Reservations recommended. Main courses 12,000–30,000L ($6–$15). AE, DC, MC, V. Tues–Sun 12:30–2:30pm and 7:30–10:30pm (daily July–Aug). TUSCAN.

To experience rural Tuscany, consider a meal in the garden of this stone-sided restaurant built around 1800 as a farmhouse. It's been serving generous portions of pastas, risottos, and *peposo* (chunks of beef stewed in red wine with tomatoes and peppers) since the 1970s, usually to residents of the region. Tagliata with truffles or porcinis is a sure winner, as is chicken cooked with Tuscan vegetables. Adventurous palates sometimes enjoy the stuffed rabbit or stuffed pigeon. The setting, surrounded by the agrarian bounty of Tuscany, seems to enhance the food.

Montagliari. Via di Montagliari 29, Panzano (between Montagliari and Greve, ½ mile north of Panzano). ☎ **055-852-184.** Reservations recommended. Main courses 24,000–30,000L ($12–$15). DC, MC, V. Tues–Sun 1–3pm and 7:30–9pm. TUSCAN.

Associated with a local vineyard, Montagliari is a representative of agrarian Tuscan charm and culinary authenticity. Tables are set out in a garden, and the place is decorated like an old Tuscan farmhouse. The specialty here is wild boar cacciatore, which deserves a star. You can also order roasted lamb or rabbit with potatoes, penne with raw chopped tomatoes and homegrown basil, tortellini stuffed with minced meat, or roasted lamb in the age-old style of the Tuscan hills.

Ristorante Badia a Coltibuono. From Radda, continue along the winding road, signposted "GAIOLE IN CHIANTI." ☎ **0577-749-031.** Reservations required. Main courses 24,000–28,000L ($12–$14); fixed-price menu 80,000L ($40). MC, V. Apr–Oct daily 12:30–3pm and 7–9pm. TUSCAN.

This restaurant occupies a medieval building adjacent to the winery recommended above. It's very much a family affair, with owner Paolo Stucchi Prinetti the host in the dining room and the chef preparing food from recipes given a touch of originality by the mistress of the domain, Lorenza de' Medici (a cookbook author who also runs a cooking school next to the restaurant). The dishes are based on simple seasonal ingredients whose flavors are accented by fresh herbs and greens. Fresh pasta is made daily, and regional meat specialties include rabbit, lamb, and the extraordinary Chianina beef of Tuscany. Local goat and sheep milk cheese are served, and homemade desserts conclude the meals. The wine list highlights the vintages of Coltibuono.

2 Montecatini Terme: Italy's Top Spa

19 miles (31km) NE of Florence, 26 miles (42km) NE of Pisa

The best known of all Italian spas, Montecatini Terme has long drawn crowds who come for its curative waters and scenic location. It's a peaceful Tuscan town set among green hills in the valley called "Valdinievole." By 1890 it was a regular stop for some of the titled aristocrats of Europe. In the 20th century, it drew such luminaries as Gary Cooper, Rose Kennedy, and Gabriel D'Annunzio and was further immortalized in Fellini's *8½*.

ESSENTIALS

GETTING THERE From Florence, a **train** leaves for Montecatini every hour throughout the day. Trip time is 50 minutes, and a one-way passage is 8,500L ($4.25). Montecatini is home to two rail stations, about a mile apart. The larger and closer to Florence is **Montecatini Terme Monsummano,** Piazza Italia. More central to most of the hotels of the town center is **Montecatini Centro**, which might save a bit of transit time for passengers headed to the resort's center. For more details, call ☎ **1478-880-88** in Italy only.

Lazzi buses (☎ **0583-584-877** or 166-845-010 in Italy only) from Florence run frequently to Montecatini in less than an hour. If you have a **car,** take All from Florence or Pistoia, exiting at the signposted turnoffs to the spa.

VISITOR INFORMATION The **tourist office** is at Viale Verdi 66-68 (☎ **0572-772-244**), open Monday to Saturday 9am to 12:30pm and 3 to 6pm (Apr to Oct, also Sun 9am to 12:30pm).

SEEING THE SPA & TAKING THE CURE

Many visitors are just regular tourists who enjoy a restful stop in a spa town; others come to lose weight, to take the mud baths, and to visit the sauna-cum-grotto. The mineral waters are said to be the finest in Europe, and the most serious visitors go to the 19th-century **Tettuccio spa,** with its beautiful gardens, to fill their cups from the curative waters.

Modern thermal centers, **Stabilimenti Termali,** await you at virtually every turn. The focus of the long grand promenade is the **Parco dei Termi,** with its neoclassical temples. The park lies above a series of underground hot springs, the most ancient of which appears in documents as far back as 1370. It's customary to come here every day to drink a healthful tonic from the fountains set up on marble counters. Spa treatments at the thermal centers cost 8,000 to 20,000L ($4 to $10) for half a day (with tonics to drink) and 50,000 to 75,000L ($25 to $37.50) for mud baths and other more elaborate treatments. Full information and tickets are available from the **Società delle Terme,** Viale Verdi 41 (☎ **0572-77-81;** www.termemontecatini.it). Most thermal houses are open May to October.

Montecatini is filled with dozens of hotels and pensiones, mostly art nouveau buildings from the beginning of the 20th century, and many would-be visitors to Florence, unable to find a room in that overcrowded city, journey east to Montecatini instead. The spa has a season lasting from April to October, and the town really shuts down in the off-season.

When you tire of all that rest, you can take a funicular from Viale Diaz up to **Montecatini Alto** to enjoy its panoramic view. This town was important in the Middle Ages, containing about two dozen towers that were demolished in 1554 on orders of Cosimo de' Medici. You can walk along narrow streets to the ruins of a fortress, paying a short visit to St. Peter's Church. You'll invariably come across the main square, named for poet Giuseppe Giusti. From the hillside town, you can see Florence on a clear day.

Today Montecatini attracts some of the world's most fashionable people on the see-and-be-seen circuit, especially during the horse-racing season from April to October. It's filled with some of Europe's most expensive boutiques, so don't bother looking for bargains.

ACCOMMODATIONS

Grand Hotel Croce di Malta. Viale IV Novembre 18, 51016 Montecatini Terme. ☎ **0572-92-01.** Fax 0572-767-516 or 0572-772-184. www.crocedimalta.com. E-mail: crocedimalta@italway.it. 144 units. A/C MINIBAR TV TEL. 290,000L ($145) double; 460,000L ($230) suite. Rates include buffet breakfast. Half-board 40,000L ($20) per person. AE, DC, MC, V. Parking 20,000L ($10).

Built in 1911 in a residential neighborhood near the spa, this hotel has an imposing facade that rises from behind a screen of shrubbery and a terrace. It's the most accommodating of the upper-middle-bracket hotels, with touches of polished marble around the guest rooms and public areas. A helpful staff and affordable prices make it a perennial favorite. In 1997 the hotel added a four-story wing (where rooms have Jacuzzis). All accommodations are similarly furnished, with the same amenities and marble bathrooms with hair dryers, though not all units have safes. On site are an outdoor heated pool, a fitness club, a cocktail bar, and a good restaurant serving Tuscan and international dishes.

✪ **Grand Hotel & La Pace.** Via della Toretta 1, 51016 Montecatini Terme. ☎ **0572-75-801.** Fax 0572-78-451. www.lnv.com. E-mail: htlapace@tin.it. 150 units. A/C MINIBAR TV TEL. 590,000–640,000L ($295–$320) double; 750,000–850,000L ($375–$425) suite. AE, DC, MC, V. Closed Nov–Apr 1. Free parking.

The Grand has maintained its white-glove formality since 1869. It boasts frescoes, elaborate ceilings, flowered sun terraces, soaring columns, lots of gilt, and all the ornate detailing you'd expect. The guest rooms are less lavish than the public areas but are discreetly comfortable, each bed with a sumptuous mattress and fine linen. Most are quite spacious, with high ceilings. The bathrooms are decked out in Italian tiles or marble, with deluxe toiletries, hair dryers, and robes. If you want full access to Montecatini's health and beauty treatments, you must go into the nearby park. However, the hotel offers a limited array of supervised spa facilities on site.

Dining/Diversions: The Michelangelo is an elegant venue for Tuscan meals. An informal pool restaurant is also available, plus two bars, one with piano music. Musical presentations and cuisine theme nights are highlights of the summer season.

Amenities: Concierge, room service, health club with Jacuzzi and sauna, outdoor pool, tennis courts, laundry/dry cleaning, baby-sitting, secretarial services, business center, children's center, various shops and salons nearby.

Grand Hotel Vittoria. Viale della Libertà 2A, 51056 Montecatini Terme. ☎ **0572-79-271.** Fax 0572-910-520. www.hotelvittoria.it. E-mail: vittoria@hotelvittoria.it. 84 units. A/C MINIBAR TV TEL. 200,000–250,000L ($100–$125) double. Rates include breakfast. Half-board 30,000L ($15) per person. AE, MC, V. Parking 15,000L ($7.50).

This affordable hotel has a pleasantly old-fashioned air. Verdi stayed here shortly after the hotel opened, before it went through other transitions, including a brief stint as a monastery and as headquarters for the Nazis and then for the Americans during World War II. Away from the town center amid dignified homes, it's one of the best reasonably priced hotels in the area. Semiantique touches abound, like a double travertine stairway flanked by masses of flowers. The guest rooms are medium-sized and furnished in a refined but simple style, with all the standard comforts, such as good mattresses and fine linen. The bathrooms are a bit small but well organized, with hair dryers. On the premises are a small indoor pool, an outdoor pool, a tranquil garden, a tennis court, and a covered terrace. There's now a large-scale convention center as well as a "beauty farm" for spa-related rejuvenation.

Hotel Manzoni. Viale Manzoni 28, 51016 Montecatini Terme. ☎ **0572-70-175.** Fax 0572-911-012. www.italway.it/alberghi/manzoni. E-mail: manzoni@italway.it. 75 units. A/C MINIBAR TV TEL. 240,000–300,000L ($120–$150) double. Rates include half-board. AE, DC, MC, V. Free parking.

In a building more than 600 years old, the Simoncini-Greco family has run this hotel since 1921. They offer the best of both worlds, with 17th- to 19th-century furnishings and modern amenities, plus a landscaped garden, pool, lounge, recreation room, bar, and formal dining room. Most guest rooms are quite large and furnished with elegant Tuscan styling, with fine mattresses and linens. The tiled bathrooms are well maintained and frequently renovated. Free 18-speed touring bikes allow you to enjoy the surrounding parks and olive-covered hills. The restaurant's fine Mediterranean cuisine is rich in local seafood, meats, poultry, and homemade pastas, along with a delectable selection of fresh vegetables and desserts.

Hotel Villa Ida. Viale G. Marconi 55, 51016 Montecatini Terme. ☎ **0572-78-201.** Fax 0572-772-008. 21 units. A/C MINIBAR TV TEL. 110,000L ($55) double with breakfast, 170,000L ($85) double with half-board. AE, DC, MC, V. Free parking (25 spaces).

Bargain-hunting spa-goers gravitate to this 19th-century building that was radically upgraded in the late 1980s. It offers simple comforts, but everything is cozy and refined. A modern decor now graces the place, and the guest rooms are small but immaculately maintained. The bathrooms are also small but well organized. The hotel offers such extras as a library, TV lounge, and tavern for wine tasting, as well as two terraces ideal for an alfresco breakfast or dinner. The food is well prepared, though not necessarily aimed at the diet-conscious.

DINING

Gourmet. Via Amendola 6. ☎ **0572-771-012.** Reservations recommended. Main courses 30,000–45,000L ($15–$22.50). AE, DC, MC, V. Wed–Mon noon–2pm and 8–11pm. Closed Jan 7–20 and Aug 1–20. ITALIAN.

Located in a 19th-century building with a Liberty-style (the Italian term for art nouveau) interior, this is the best nonhotel restaurant in town. It prides itself on formal service and a cuisine that's more unusual than the run-of-the-mill pastas of lesser competitors. Menu items change seasonally and with the availability of ingredients, but you'll often find a spectacular array of antipasti ("antipasti fantasia") with seafood and fresh vegetables, ravioli stuffed with pulverized sea bass and herbs, risotto with scampi, and a medley of fruit garnishes (melon slices with lobster and honey-vinegar sauce, for example). Most items are delicious and beautifully presented. The desserts are made fresh daily and might include a Grand Marnier soufflé.

Ristorante Pietre Cavate. Via Pietre Cavate 11. ☎ **0572-95-42-58.** Reservations recommended. Main courses 32,000–60,000L ($16–$30). AE, DC, MC, V. Daily 7:30pm–midnight (closed Wed Nov–Mar). TUSCAN.

The Bertini and Menchi families are the creative force behind this warmly hospitable farmhouse less than a mile north of the town center, where there are three rustic-looking dining rooms. The cuisine is a celebration of Tuscany, with special emphasis on macaroni with tomato and parmigiano sauce, *pappardelle* with chunks of rabbit, stuffed onions, savory stews, and chunky cuts of veal, pork, and beef. Come here with an appetite and enjoy the view over the rooftops of Montecatini.

3 Lucca

45 miles (72km) W of Florence, 13 miles (21km) E of Pisa, 209 miles (336km) N of Rome

In 56 B.C., Caesar, Crassus, and Pompey met in Lucca and agreed to rule Rome as a triumvirate. By the time of the Roman Empire's collapse, Lucca was virtually the capital of Tuscany. Periodically in its valiant, ever-bloody history, this town was an independent principality, similar to Genoa. This autonomy attests to the fame and prestige it enjoyed. Now, however, Lucca is largely bypassed by time and travelers, rewarding the discriminating few.

By the late 1600s, Lucca had gained its third and final set of city walls. This girdle of ramparts is largely intact and is one of the major reasons to visit the town, where the architecture ranges from Roman to Liberty (the Italian term for art nouveau). Lucca was the birthplace of Giacomo Puccini, whose favorite watering hole, the Antico Caffè di Simo (see "Lucca After Dark," below), still stands.

Today, Lucca is best known for its *olio d'oliva lucchese,* the quality olive oil produced in the region outside the town's walls, and shoppers will be delighted to find a number of upscale boutiques here, testimony to an affluence not dependent on tourism. Thriving, cosmopolitan, and perfectly preserved, Lucca is a sort of Switzerland of the south: The banks have latticed Gothic windows, the shops look like well-stocked linen cupboards, children play in landscaped gardens, and geraniums bloom from the roofs of medieval tower houses.

ESSENTIALS

GETTING THERE At least 20 **trains** travel daily between Florence and Lucca. The trip takes 1¼ hours and costs 7,000L ($3.50) each way. The rail station is about a quarter-mile south of Lucca's historic core, a short walk from the city's ramparts. For rail information, call ☎ **1478-880-80.** If you don't have a lot of luggage, you can walk into the center; otherwise, most of the city's buses (notably nos. 3 and 6) and lots of taxis stand ready to take you there.

The **Lazzi bus** company (☎ **0583-584-877**) operates buses traveling between Florence and Lucca. They take less time than the train (50 minutes to an hour), and unlike the train, they carry passengers to a point within the city walls. Bus transit between Florence and Lucca, however, costs a bit more than the train: 9,000L ($4.50) each way. Buses pick up passengers in front of the rail station in Florence and drop them off in Lucca at both the rail station and the historic core at Piazzale Verdi, near the tourist office.

Lucca

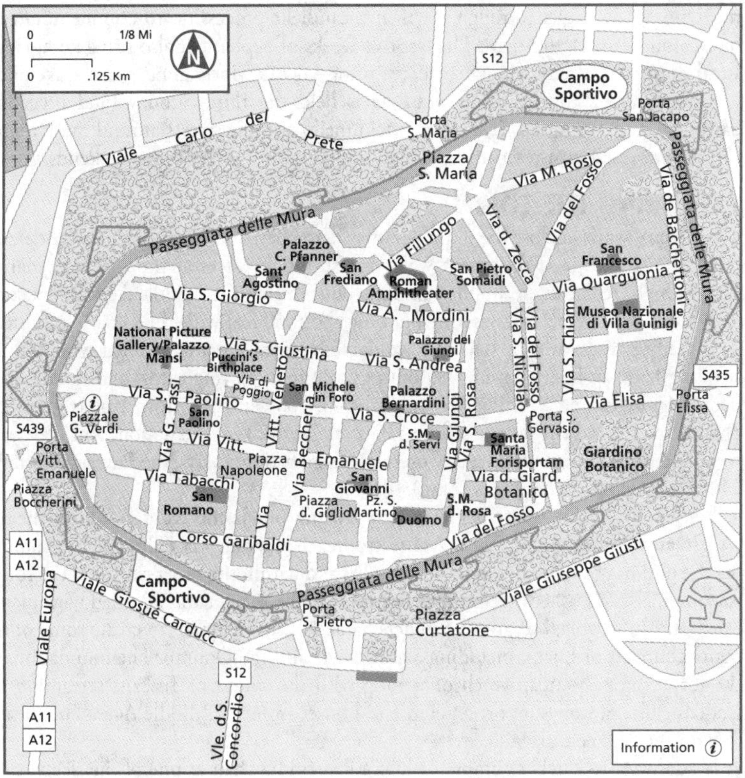

If you have a **car,** leave Florence and take All through Prato, Pistoia, and Montecatini (see above) before reaching the outskirts of Lucca. If you're in Pisa, take SS12.

VISITOR INFORMATION The Lucca **tourist office** is on Piazzale Verdi (☎ **0583-419-689**), open daily 9:30am to 6:30pm April to October (off-season to 3:30pm).

GETTING AROUND Lucca is a great place to rent a bike, especially since you can ride along the ancient city walls. Try the **city-sponsored** stand near the visitor's center on Piazzale Verdi (☎ **0583-442-937**), open from mid-March to October. **Antonio Poli,** Piazza Santa Maria 42 (☎ **0583-493-787**), is open daily from 8:30am to 7:30pm, except for Sundays in winter and Monday mornings year-round. Expect to pay about 4,000L ($2) per hour, or 20,000L ($10) for a whole day, to rent a good mountain bike.

SPECIAL EVENTS Sleepy Lucca comes to life during July and August at the time of the classical music festival the **Estate Musicale Lucchese.** Venues spring up everywhere, and the tourist office keeps a list. The town also comes alive on July 12, when residents don medieval costumes and parade through the city, the revelry continuing late into the night.

In Puccini's hometown you'll find a devotion to opera, and in October and November his work is showcased at the **Teatro Comunale del Giglio,** Piazza di Giglio (☎ **0583-467-521**). More classical music performances fill the town in September during the **Settembre Lucchese Festival,** highlighted by Volto Santo feast day on September 13. The crucifix bearing the "face" of Christ (normally housed in a chapel in the Duomo) is hauled through town in a candlelit procession to commemorate its miraculous journey to Lucca. The last two weeks of September also bring an **agricultural market** to Piazza San Michele, featuring Lucca's wines, honeys, and olive oils.

One of Italy's top **antiques markets** is held the third Sunday (and preceding Saturday) of every month in Piazza Antelminello and the streets around the Duomo. (Hotel and restaurant reservations are always harder to get on these weekends.)

EXPLORING THE TOWN

The ✪ **city walls** enclose the old town; they're the best-preserved Renaissance defense ramparts in Europe. The present walls, measuring 115 feet at the base and soaring 40 feet high, replaced crumbling ramparts built during the Middle Ages. They comprise a city park over 2.6 miles long but only about 60 feet wide, filled with leafy trees. The shady paved paths of Lucca's formidable bastions are always filled with couples strolling hand-in-hand, families on outings, old men playing cards, and hundreds of people on bikes (see "Getting Around," above). You can enter from 1 of 10 bastions; try the one behind the tourist office at **Piazzale Verdi.** For orientation, you may want to walk completely around the city on the tree-shaded ramparts, the **Passeggiata delle Mura,** a distance of 2½ miles (4km).

Besides the major sights below, worth seeking out is the **Roman Amphitheater (Anfiteatro Romano),** at Piazza Anfiteatro, reached along Via Fillungo. You can still see the outlines of its arches in its outer walls, and within the inner ring only the rough form remains to evoke what must've been. Once the theater was adorned with many-hued Tuscan marble, but greedy builders hauled off its materials to create some of the many churches of Lucca, including San Michele and the Duomo. The foundations of the former grandstands, which once rang with the sound of Tuscans screaming for gladiator blood, now support an ellipse of houses from the Middle Ages. The theater is from the 2nd century A.D.

If you want to catch a glimpse of Lucca life, find a chair at one of the sleepy cafes and pass the day away. In July and August, you can come to the **Piazza Guidiccioni** nearby and see a screening of the latest Italian and U.S. hits in the open air.

Cattedrale di San Martino (Duomo). Piazza San Martino. ☎ **0583-957-068.** Admission to cathedral free; sacristy and inner sanctum 3,000L ($1.50). Apr–Oct, daily 9:30am–8pm; Nov–Mar, daily 9:30am–5pm.

The Duomo is the town's main monument, dating back to 1060, though the present structure was mainly rebuilt during the following centuries. The facade is exceptional, evoking the Pisan-Romanesque style but with enough originality and idiosyncrasies to distinguish it from the Duomo at Pisa. Designed mostly by Guidetto da Como in the early 13th century, the west front contains three wide ground-level arches, surmounted by three scalloped galleries with taffylike twisting columns tapering in size.

The main relic inside (in some ways the religious symbol of Lucca itself) is the **Volto Santo,** a crucifix carved by Nicodemus (so tradition has it) from the Cedar of Lebanon. The face of Christ was supposedly chiseled onto the statuary.

The main art treasure lies in the sacristy: the **tomb of Ilaria del Carretto Guinigi,** sculpted by Jacopo della Quercia. Ilaria was a local aristocrat and the wife of Paolo Guinigi; she died in 1405 while still young. Her marble effigy, in regal robes and guarded by chubby bambini, rests atop the sarcophagus; the diffused mauve afternoon light casts a ghostly glow on her face. (Long-term plans include moving the tomb to the Duomo Museum described below.) Also in the sacristy is the superb Domenico Ghirlandaio *Madonna and Saints* altarpiece (1494).

Adjacent to the Duomo is the **Duomo Museum (Museo della Cattedrale;** ☎ **0583-490-530**). Admission is 5,000L ($2.50); open daily. Here you'll find some

Travel Tip

One mistake many people make when hopping from hill town to hill town is getting up early in the mornings to travel to the next destination. Since many of Tuscany and Umbria's sights are open only in the morning and almost all close for *riposo* from noonish to 3 or 4pm, this wastes valuable sightseeing time. Try to do your traveling just after noon, when everything is closing up. There's often a last train before *riposo* to wherever you're going; if you're driving, you can enjoy great countryside vistas under the noonday sun.

rather dusty-looking memorabilia and mostly minor artworks, except Matteo Civitali's late-15th-century choir screen (removed from the cathedral in 1987) and Jacopo della Quercia's majestic early 15th-century *St. John the Evangelist,* a sculpture.

San Frediano. Piazza San Frediano. ☎ **0583-493-627.** Free admission. Mon–Sat 9am–noon and 3–6pm; Sun 3–5pm.

Romanesque in style, this is one of Lucca's most important churches, built in the 12th and 13th centuries when the town enjoyed its greatest glory. The severe white facade is relieved by a 13th-century mosaic of Christ ascending, and the campanile rises majestically. The interior is dark, and visitors often speak in whispers. But the bas-reliefs on the Romanesque font add a note of comic relief: Supposedly depicting the story of Moses, among other themes, they show Egyptians in medieval armor chasing after the Israelites. Two tombs in the basilica (in the fourth chapel on the left) were the work of celebrated Sienese sculptor Jacopo della Quercia.

San Michele in Foro. Piazza San Michele. ☎ **0583-48-459.** Free admission. Daily 7:30am–12:30pm and 3–6pm.

This church often surprises first-timers, who mistake it for the Duomo. Begun in 1143, it's the most memorable example of the style and flair that the Lucchese brought to the Pisan-Romanesque school of architecture. The exquisite west front, employing the scalloped effect, is spanned by seven ground-level arches, then surmounted by four tiers of galleries, utilizing imaginatively designed columns. Dragon-slaying St. Michael, wings outstretched, rests on the friezelike peak of the final tier. Inside, seek out a Filippo Lippi painting, *Saints Sebastian, Jerome, Helen, and Roch,* on the far wall of the right transept. If you're here in September, the piazza outside, which was the old Roman forum, holds a daily colorful open market selling everything from olive oil to souvenirs of Tuscany.

National Picture Gallery and Palazzo Mansi Museum (Pinacoteca Nazionale e Museo di Palazzo Mansi). Via Galli Tassi 43. ☎ **0583-55-570**. Admission 8,000L ($4). Tues–Sat 9am–6:30pm; Sun 9am–2pm.

This palace was built for the powerful Mansi family, whose descendants are still some of the movers and shakers in town. Although Tuscany has far greater art collections, there are some treasures, notably a portrait of Princess Elisa by Marie Benoist. Elisa Bonaparte (1777–1820), who married into a local wealthy family, the Bacceocchis, was "given" the town by her brother Napoléon in 1805 when he made her princess of Lucca and Piombino. Unlike her profligate sister, Pauline Borghese in Rome, Elisa was a strong woman with a remarkable aptitude for public affairs (she laid out Piazza Napoleone, among other accomplishments). The collection is enriched by works from Lanfranco, Luca Giordano, and Tintoretto, among others, though not their greatest works. There's a damaged Veronese, but Tintoretto's *Miracle of St. Mark Freeing the Slave* is amusing—the patron saint of Venice literally dive-bombs from heaven to save the day.

Puccini's Birthplace (Casa Natale di Puccini). Via di Poggio 9. ☎ **0583-58-40-28.** Admission 5,000L ($2.50). Jan–Feb Tues–Fri 10am–1pm, Sat–Sun 3–6pm; Mar–May Tues–Sun 10am–1pm and 3–6pm; June–Sept daily 10am–6pm; Oct–Dec Tues–Sun 10am–1pm and 3–6pm.

This unpretentious house was the birthplace of one of Italy's greatest operatic composers, Giacomo Puccini (1858–1924). More than any other Italian town (except Milan, where opera is viewed with passion), Lucca celebrates the memory and achievements of Puccini, whose operas are enthusiastically performed every September during the Festival of Santa Croce. His house, near Piazza San Michele, contains the piano at which he composed *Turandot* and has several of his librettos, letters, objets d'art, and mementos.

SHOPPING

The sunny, scenic hills around Lucca have been famous since the days of the Romans for producing fabulous amber-colored olive oil. You won't have to look far to find it—every supermarket, butcher shop, and delicatessen in Lucca sells a baffling variety, in glass or metal containers. But if you want to travel into the surrounding hills to check out the production of this heart-healthy product, two of the best-known companies sell their products on premises evoking early 20th-century Tuscan farmhouse life: **Maionchi,** in the hamlet of Tofori (☎ **0583-978-194**), 11 miles (18km) northeast of Lucca; and **Camigliano,** V. per Sant'Andrea 49 (☎ **0583-490-420**), 6 miles (10km) northeast of Lucca.

A promenade along the town's best shopping streets, **Via Fillungo** and **Via del Battistero**, can satisfy most materialistic cravings. The best gift/souvenir shops are **Insieme,** Via Vittorio Emanuele 70 (☎ **0583-419-649**), and **Incontro,** Via Buia 9 (☎ **0583-491-225**), which places a special emphasis on Lucca's rustically appealing porcelain, pottery, tiles, and crystal.

The best wine shop in town is the **Enoteca Vanni,** Piazza Salvatore 7 (☎ **0583-491-902**; www.enotecavanni.com), with hundreds of bottles of local and Tuscan vintages.

If you're in town on the right weekend, check out the wonderful **antiques market.** (See "Special Events," at the beginning of this section.)

ACCOMMODATIONS

Hotel Villa La Principessa. Via Nuova Per Pisa 1616, 55050 Massa Pisana (Lucca). ☎ **0583-370-037.** Fax 0583-379-136. www.lunet.it/aziende/villaprincipessa. E-mail: principessa@lunet.it. 40 units. A/C MINIBAR TV TEL. 375,000–440,000L ($187.50–$220) double; 650,000L ($325) suite. Rates include breakfast. AE, DC, MC, V. Closed Nov–Mar. Free parking. Bus: 2.

Across from the Locanda l'Elisa (see below), this four-star hotel is less luxurious than its neighbor, but also less expensive. It's 2 miles (3km) south of the city walls, beside a meandering highway with sharp turns and limited visibility. The hotel is sheltered with hedges and flowering trees. It was built in 1320 as the home of one of the dukes of Lucca, Castruccio Castracani, who was later depicted by Machiavelli as the "Ideal Prince." Later, when the hills around Lucca were dotted with the homes of members of the Napoleonic court, the house was rebuilt in dignified 18th-century style. The guest rooms were renovated in 1997, and you'll find quality mattresses and luxurious linen. The bathrooms have plenty of shelf space and hair dryers.

Dining: The refined continental breakfast is the only meal offered.

Amenities: Concierge, room service, outdoor pool, nearby health club, jogging track and nature trails nearby, business center, laundry, in-room massage, baby-sitting.

Locanda L'Elisa. Via Nuova per Pisa, 1952, 55050 Massa Pisana (Lucca). ☎ **0583-379-737.** Fax 0583-379-019. www.lunet.it/azienda/locandaelisa. E-mail: locanda.elisa@lunet.it. 10 units. A/C MINIBAR TV TEL. 500,000L ($250) double; 600,000L ($300) junior suite. AE, DC, MC, V. Free parking. Bus: 2.

This Relais & Châteaux member is the region's most elegant hotel, 2 miles (3km) south of the city walls. In the mid–19th century, it was the home of an army officer who was the intimate companion of Napoléon's sister Elisa, who lived across the road. Today, both lovers' villas are upscale hotels (Elisa's is now the Hotel Villa La Principessa, above). Behind a dignified neoclassical facade, Locanda l'Elisa offers verdant gardens, a worthy collection of antiques, discreet service, and guest rooms larger and more plushly decorated than those of its sibling (all are junior suites). The bathrooms are spacious, with luxurious toiletries, sewing kits, hair dryers, and state-of-the-art plumbing.

Dining: Il Gazebo is recommended under "Dining," below.

Amenities: Room service, large pool, baby-sitting, laundry/dry cleaning.

Piccolo Hotel Puccini. Via di Poggio 9, 55100 Lucca. ☎ **0583-55-421.** Fax 0583-53-487. www.hotelpuccini.com. E-mail: info@hotelpuccini.com. 14 units. TV TEL. 135,000L ($67.50) double. AE, DC, MC, V. Free parking nearby.

Your best bet within the walls is this palace built in the 1400s, across from the house where Puccini was born (Puccini music often plays in the lobby). Right off Piazza San Michele and one of the most enchanting spots in Lucca, this little hotel is better than ever now that an energetic couple, Raffaella and Paolo, has taken over. Intimate and comfortable, the rooms are beautifully maintained, with freshly starched curtains, good beds, crisp linens, and tasteful furnishings. Some windows open onto the small square in front with a bronze statue of the great Puccini. The bathrooms are small but come with hair dryers and soft towels.

DINING

Don't forget to drop in at the **Antico Caffè di Simo,** Via Fillungo 58 (no phone), where Puccini used to come to eat and drink and perhaps dream about his next opera. At this historic cafe you can order the best gelato in town while taking in the old-time aura of faded mirrors, brass, and marble. The cafe is open Tuesday to Sunday 8am to 8pm.

✪ **Buca di Sant'Antonio.** Via della Cervia 1/5. ☎ **0583-55-881.** Reservations recommended. Main courses 25,000–35,000L ($12.50–$17.50). AE, DC, MC, V. Tues–Sun noon–3pm; Tues–Sat 7:30–11pm. Closed 3 weeks in July. TUSCAN.

On a difficult-to-find alley near Piazza San Michele, this is Lucca's finest restaurant. The 1782 building was constructed on the site of a chapel (Buca di Sant'Antonio) believed to be favorable for invoking the protective powers of St. Anthony. The cuisine is refined and inspired, respecting the traditional but also daring to be innovative. Menu items include homemade ravioli stuffed with ricotta and pulverized zucchini, pork ragout, codfish, and roast Tuscan goat with roast potatoes and braised greens. Try the house special dessert, *semifreddo Buccellato* (partially melted ice cream with local red berries).

Da Giulio in Pelleria. Via della Conce 45. ☎ **0583-55-948.** Reservations recommended. Main courses 15,000–30,000L ($7.50–$15). AE, DC, MC, V. Tues–Sat and 3rd Sun of the month noon–2:30pm and 7:15–10:15pm. Closed Christmas and Aug. LUCCHESE.

This restaurant holds fast to local traditions and time-honored recipes, with dishes like great minestrones, pastas, veal, hearty soups, and chicken dishes served in robust portions. Some regional dishes might be a little too adventurous for most North American tastes, such as *cioncia* (veal snout and herbs). New food items include a Lucchese specialty, *farinata,* a soup with a base of minestrone and white flour; cuttlefish with beets; sausages with beans; and a fabulous almond torte for dessert.

Giglio. Piazza del Giglio 2. ☎ **0583-494-058.** Reservations recommended. Main courses 20,000–35,000L ($10–$17.50). AE, DC, MC, V. Thurs–Tues noon–3pm; Thurs–Mon 7–10pm. Closed Jan 15–Feb 9. REGIONAL/TUSCAN.

In regional appeal and popularity, this place is rivaled only by the Buca di Sant'Antonio (see above). The secret to its appeal may be its rustic decor (including 16th-century architectural detailing), its attentive staff, and its fine interpretations of time-honored recipes. Menu items usually include steaming bowls of *minestra di farro,* homemade tortellini with meat sauce, dried codfish with chickpeas, stewed rabbit with olives, and *tortes* made from carrots or other vegetables or with a base of cream and chocolate.

Il Gazebo. In the Locanda l'Elisa, Via Nuova per Pisa 1952. ☎ **0583-379-737.** Reservations recommended. Main courses 25,000–32,000L ($12.50–$16); fixed-price menu 80,000–100,000L ($40–$50). AE, DC, MC, V. Mon–Sat 12:30–2:30pm and 7:30–10:30pm. Bus: 2. ITALIAN/TUSCAN.

Set in one of Tuscany's most elegant hotels, 2 miles (3km) south of Lucca's center, the restaurant is a re-creation of an English conservatory. The wraparound windows in the almost circular room offer garden views. The service, as you'd expect in a Relais & Châteaux, is impeccable. Menu items include upscale versions of Luccan recipes, like *farro Lucchese,* a red-bean soup with locally grown greens. Other dishes are steamed scampi with tomato sauce, smoked swordfish with grilled eggplant, and ravioli stuffed with herbed eggplant and served with prawn sauce. Each is prepared with refinement and skill. The chefs also serve vegetarian and low-cholesterol dishes.

Trattoria da Leo. Via Tegrimi 1. ☎ **0583-49-22-36.** Reservations recommended. Main courses 18,000–25,000L ($9–$12.50). No credit cards. Mon–Sat noon–2:30pm and 7:30–10:30pm. Daily Dec 8–31 and Aug 6–31. TUSCAN.

Known for its unpretentious approach to Tuscan cuisine and its family administration (almost no one speaks English, but there's a menu in English), this is a pleasant trattoria in a 16th-century building close to Piazza San Michele. The decor of the dining rooms (one large, one very small) is vaguely 1930s. The savory menu items include an array of pastas, most made fresh; *ministra di Farro;* fried chicken with fresh seasonal greens; steamed chicken with polenta; at least three versions of codfish; and liver with wild fennel.

4 Pisa

47 miles (76km) W of Florence, 207 miles (333km) NW of Rome

Few buildings in the world have captured imaginations as much as the **Leaning Tower of Pisa,** the single most instantly recognizable building in all the Western world (except perhaps for the Eiffel Tower). Perhaps visitors are drawn to it as a symbol of the fragility of people—or at least the fragility of their work. The Leaning Tower is a powerful landmark.

There's more to Pisa than meets the usual visitor's eye, however. There are other historic sights. And there's also the present: Go into the busy streets surrounding the university and the market, and you'll find a town resounding with the exuberance of its student population and its residents as they make the purchases of everyday life.

ESSENTIALS

GETTING THERE Both domestic and international **flights** arrive at Pisa's **Galileo Galilei Airport** (☎ **050-500-707;** www.pisa-airport.com). From the airport, trains

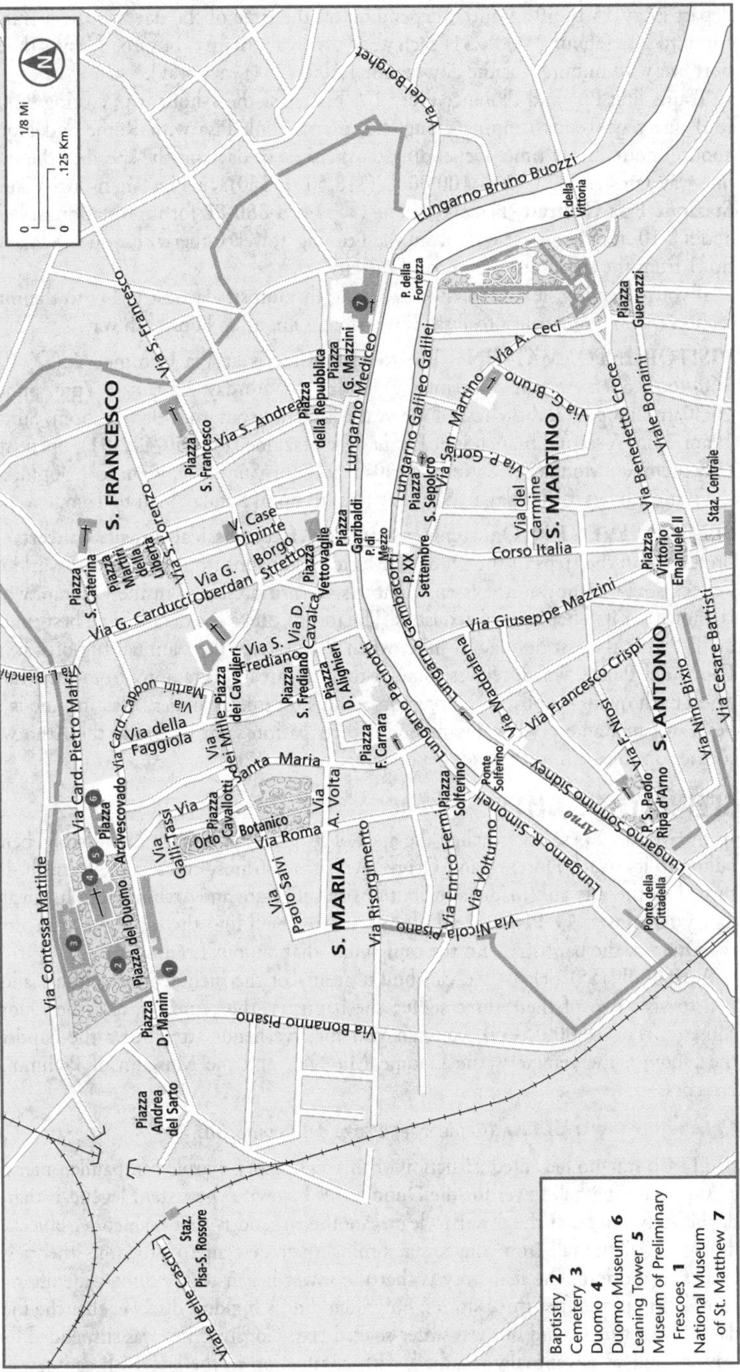
Baptistry 2
Cemetery 3
Duomo 4
Duomo Museum 6
Leaning Tower 5
Museum of Preliminary Frescoes 1
National Museum of St. Matthew 7
S. FRANCESCO
S. MARIA
S. MARTINO
S. ANTONIO
Arno
Via Contessa Matilde
Piazza del Duomo
Piazza Arcivescovado
Via Card. Pietro Maffi
Piazza D. Manin
Piazza Andrea del Sarto
Via Bonanno Pisano
Via Nicola Pisano
Via Risorgimento
Via Paolo Salvi
Via Roma
Orto Botanico
Via Santa Maria
Via G. Carducci
Via S. Lorenzo
Via S. Francesco
Via S. Andrea
Piazza S. Francesco
Piazza S. Caterina
Piazza Martiri della Libertà
Via G. Oberdan
Borgo Stretto
Piazza Vettovaglie
Piazza Garibaldi
Piazza della Repubblica
Piazza G. Mazzini
Lungarno Mediceo
Lungarno Pacinotti
Lungarno Gambacorti
Lungarno Galileo Galilei
Lungarno Bruno Buozzi
Lungarno Sonnino Sidney
Lungarno R. Simonelli
Via del Borghetto
Corso Italia
Via San Martino
Via Giuseppe Mazzini
Via Francesco Crispi
Via Benedetto Croce
Viale Bonaini
Via Nino Bixio
Via Cesare Battisti
Piazza Vittorio Emanuele II
Piazza Guerrazzi
Staz. Centrale
Staz. Pisa-S. Rossore
Viale delle Cascine
Ponte Solferino
Piazza Solferino
Ponte della Cittadella
P. della Fortezza
P. della Vittoria
P. di Mezzo
P. XX Settembre
P. S. Paolo Ripa d'Arno
Piazza dei Cavalieri
Piazza S. Frediano
Piazza D. Alighieri
Piazza F. Carrara
Via Enrico Fermi
Via Volturno
1/8 Mi
.125 Km

depart every 15 to 30 minutes, depending on the time of the day, for the 5-minute trip into Pisa (about 2,000L/$1) each way). As an alternative, bus no. 3 leaves the airport every 40 minutes for the city (about 1,500L/75¢) each way).

Trains link Pisa and Florence every 1½ hours for the 1-hour trip, costing 8,000L ($4) one-way. Trains running along the seacoast link Pisa with Rome and require about 3 hours travel time. Depending on the time of day and the speed of the train, one-way fares are 37,000 to 100,000L ($18.50 to $50). In Pisa, trains arrive at the **Stazione Pisa Centrale,** Piazza Stazione (☎ **1478-880-88** for information in Italy), about a 10- to 15-minute walk from the Leaning Tower. Otherwise, you can take bus no. 1 from the station to the heart of the city.

If you're **driving,** leave Florence by taking the autostrada west (A11) to the intersection (A12) going south to Pisa. Travel time is about an hour each way.

VISITOR INFORMATION The **tourist office** is at Via Cammeo 2 (☎ **050-560-464**), open April to September, Monday to Saturday 9:30am to 7pm, Sunday 10:30am-2:30pm, and the rest of the year Monday to Saturday 9am to 5pm, Sunday 10am-2pm. A second branch is at Piazza della Stazione (☎ **050-422-91**), open April to September, Monday to Saturday 9:30am to 7pm, Sunday 9:30am to 1:30pm, and the rest of the year Monday to Saturday 9am to 5pm, Sunday 9am to 1pm.

SPECIAL EVENTS On summer evenings, **free classical music concerts** are presented on the steps of the Duomo. Music aficionados from all over the world can be seen sprawled out on the lawn. Concerts are also presented in the Duomo, which is known for its phenomenal acoustics. The tourist office has details. The best time to be in Pisa is the last Sunday in June, when Pisans stage their annual tug-of-war, the **Gioco del Ponte,** which revives some of their pomp and ceremony from the Middle Ages. Each quadrant of the city presents richly costumed parades. Also in June is the Festa di San Ranieri, when Pisans honor their patron saint by lining the Arno with torches on the 16th, then staging a boat race on the 17th.

SEEING THE SIGHTS

In the Middle Ages, Pisa reached the apex of its power as a maritime republic before falling to its rivals, Florence and Genoa. As is true of most cities at their zenith, Pisa turned to the arts and made contributions in sculpture and architecture. Its greatest legacy remains at ✪ **Piazza del Duomo,** where you'll find the top three attractions: the Duomo, the baptistry, and the campanile (that famous Leaning Tower).

A 10,000L ($5) ticket (you can buy it at any of the included attractions) allows you to visit two of these three sights: the baptistry, the cemetery, and the Duomo Museum. For 18,000L ($9), you can visit the five major attractions: the baptistry, the Duomo, the cemetery, the Duomo Museum, and the Museum of Preliminary Frescoes.

✪ **Leaning Tower of Pisa** (Campanile). Piazza del Duomo. Bus: 1.

In 1174 Bonnano began construction of this eight-story marble campanile, intended as a freestanding bell tower for the Duomo (see below). A persistent legend is that he deliberately intended the tower to lean. Another legend is that Galileo let objects of different weights fall from the tower, timing their descent to prove his theories of bodies in motion. The real story is that the tower began to list some time after the completion of the first three stories; only then did its builders discover that the foundation wasn't rock solid but was water-soaked clay. Construction was suspended for a century and was eventually resumed, with completion in the late 14th century. The tower currently leans at least 14 feet from perpendicular. If it stood straight, it would measure about 180 feet tall.

New in 2000

By the time you arrive in Pisa, one of Tuscany's most important museums in years will have opened. The **Arsenale Medici,** on Lungarno Simonelli (along the Arno River), was built in the 12th century as a storehouse for the weapons and merchandise of the Medici family. It's a long, low-slung building beside the Arno, accessible via bus A from Pisa's main rail station. The high point of the collection is a series of 12 Roman wooden ships, one of which dates back to the 1st century B.C. (others are from the reigns of such emperors as the mighty Augustus).

The wooden ships, including an intact wooden warship, were discovered by construction workers digging to extend the San Rossore rail terminal in 1998. The find was hearalded around the world, some journalists calling it "a nautical Pompeii."

In the 10th and 11th centuries, Pisa was a major port city until its waters were buried by silt in the 12th century. The shore now is some 5 miles to the west. Archaeologists believe the ships were sunk in a flash flood. Much of the contents of the ships has been preserved, including clay vases—even wine some 20 centuries old. The contents of these rare fines, including personal paraphernalia and clothing of the sailors, is on display along with the ships.

Prices, hours, and even a phone number had not been established as of this writing, but inquire at the tourist office when you arrive, or, for more information, call the Archaeological Museum in Florence (☎ **055-52-15-446**).

The tower is slated to reopen to visitors sometime in 2001. Visitors haven't been allowed to climb it since 1990, when it was closed to the public because of dangerous conditions. Since that time, work has proceeded every year in an attempt to stabilize its tilt. Tons of soil were removed from under the foundation, and lead counterweights were placed at the monument's base. The last stages of the work were slated to be carried out in late 2000. Check with the tourist office when you arrive in Pisa to find out if the tower's open; if it is, they'll have the hours and admission charges.

Il Duomo. Piazza del Duomo 17. ☎ **050-560-547.** Admission 3,000L ($1.50). Mon–Sat 10am–7:30pm. Sightseeing visits are discouraged during masses and religious rites. Bus: 1.

This cathedral was designed by Buschetto in 1063, though in the 13th century Rainaldo erected the unusual facade with its four layers of open-air arches diminishing in size as they ascend. It's marked by three bronze doors, rhythmic in line, that replaced those destroyed in a disastrous 1595 fire. The most artistic is the original south Door of St. Ranieri, the only one to survive the fire; it was cast by Bonnano Pisano in 1180.

In the restored interior, the chief treasure is the polygonal pulpit by Giovanni Pisano, finished in 1310. It was damaged in the fire and finally rebuilt (with bits of the original) in 1926. It's held up by porphyry pillars and column statues symbolizing the Virtues, and the relief panels depict biblical scenes. The pulpit is similar to an earlier one by Giovanni's father, Nicola Pisano, in the baptistry across the way.

There are other treasures, too, like Galileo's lamp (which, according to unreliable tradition, the Pisa-born astronomer used to formulate his laws of the pendulum). At the entrance to the choir pier is a painting that appears to be the work of Leonardo but is in fact *St. Agnes and Lamb,* in the High Renaissance style by the great Andrea del Sarto. In the apse you can view a 13th-century mosaic, *Christ Pancrator,* finished in 1302 by Cimabue (it survived the great fire).

✪ **Baptistry (Battistero).** Piazza del Duomo. ☎ **050-560-547.** Admission (including entry to the Duomo Museum or the cemetery) 10,000L ($5). Apr–Sept daily 8am–7:30pm; Oct–Mar daily 9am–5pm. Closed Dec 31–Jan 1. Bus: 1.

Begun in 1153, the baptistry is like a Romanesque crown. Its most beautiful feature is the exterior, with its arches and columns, but you should visit the interior to see the hexagonal pulpit (1255–60) by Nicola Pisano. Supported by pillars resting on the backs of three marble lions, the pulpit contains bas-reliefs of the Crucifixion, the Adoration of the Magi, the presentation of the Christ Child at the temple, and the Last Judgment (many angels have lost their heads over the years). Column statues represent the Virtues. At the baptismal font is a contemporary John the Baptist by a local sculptor. The echo inside the baptistry shell has enthralled visitors for years.

Duomo Museum (Museo dell'Opera del Duomo). Piazza Arcivescovado. ☎ **050-560-547.** Admission (including entry to the baptistry or the cemetery) 10,000L ($5). Apr–Sept daily 8am–7:30pm; Oct–Mar daily 9am–5pm. Bus: 1.

This museum exhibits works of art removed from the monumental buildings on the piazza. The heart of the collection, on the ground floor, consists of sculptures spanning the 11th to the 13th century. A notable treasure is an Islamic griffin from the 11th century, a bronze brought back from the Crusades as booty. For decades it adorned the cupola of the cathedral before being brought here for safekeeping. The most famous exhibit is the *Madonna and the Crucifix* by Giovanni Pisano, carved from an ivory tusk in 1299. Also exhibited is the work of French goldsmiths, presented by Maria de' Medici to Archbishop Bonciani in 1616.

Upstairs are paintings from the 15th to the 18th century. Some of the textiles and embroideries date from the 15th century; another section of the museum is devoted to Egyptian, Etruscan, and Roman works. In the 19th century, Carlo Lasinio restored the Camposanto frescoes (see below) and made a series of etchings of each. These etchings were widely published, influencing the pre-Raphaelite artists of the time. When the Camposanto was bombed in 1944, the etchings were destroyed, but Lasinio's legacy provided an enduring record of what they were like.

Cemetery (Camposanto). Piazza del Duomo. ☎ **050-560-547.** Admission (including admission to the baptistry or the Duomo Museum) 10,000L ($5). Nov–Feb daily 9am–4:40pm; Mar and Oct daily 9am–5:40pm; Apr–Sept daily 8am–7:40pm. Bus: 1.

This cemetery was designed by Giovanni di Simone in 1278, but a bomb hit it in 1944 and destroyed most of the famous frescoes that had covered the inside (the fresco sketches are displayed at the Museo delle Sinopie, below). Recently it has been partially restored. It's said that the crusaders shipped earth from Calvary here on Pisan ships (the city was a great port before the water receded). The cemetery is of interest because of its sarcophagi, statuary, and frescoes. One room contains three of the frescoes from the 14th century that were salvaged from the bombing: *The Triumph of Death, The Last Judgment,* and *The Inferno,* with the usual assortment of monsters, reptiles, and boiling caldrons. *The Triumph of Death* is the most interesting, with its flying angels and devils. In addition, you'll find lots of white-marble bas-reliefs, including Roman funerary sculpture.

Museum of Preliminary Frescoes (Museo delle Sinopie). Piazza del Duomo. ☎ **050-560-547.** Admission 10,000L ($5). Apr–Sept daily 8am–7:30pm; Oct–Mar daily 9am–5pm. Closed Dec 31–Jan 1. Bus: 1.

Next to the baptistry, this is a showcase for the *sinopie* (preliminary sketches or frescoes) that were discovered under the charred remnants of the badly damaged frescoes at the cemetery (see above). Before World War II, the finished frescoes were one of the major attractions of Tuscany, but they were mainly destroyed in a 1944 air raid. From the wreckage, Pisans discovered the preparatory sketches the artists had created, which had been covered for centuries by the originals. The museum here also displays remnants of the finished frescoes, all rescued from the bomb site.

The museum is housed in medieval rooms of the New Hospital of Mercy (*Ospedale Nuovo della Misericordia*). The most interesting sketches are by Veneziano, Gaddi, and Traini, all from the 14th century. Displays also reveal how the fresco artists went about their work. In the 19th century, Carlo Lasinio made engravings of what the finished frescoes looked like, and these have been placed before the preliminary sketches to give you an idea of how the artists changed their conceptions along the way.

National Museum of St. Matthew (Museo Nazionale di San Matteo). Piazzetta San Matteo 1 (near Piazza Mazzini). ☎ **050-541-865.** Admission 8,000L ($4). Tues–Sat 9am–7pm; Sun 9am–1:30pm. Bus: 1.

This well-planned museum contains a good assortment of paintings and sculptures, many from the 13th to the 16th century. You'll find statues by Giovanni Pisano; Simone Martini's *Madonna and Child with Saints,* a polyptych; Nino Pisano's *Madonna del Látte* (Madonna of the Milk), a marble sculpture; Masaccio's *St. Paul,* painted in 1426; Domenico Ghirlandaio's two *Madonna and Saints* depictions; and works by Strozzi and Alessandro Magnasco.

SHOPPING

On the second weekend of every month, an **antiques fair** fills the Ponte di Mezzo. Virtually everything from the Tuscan hills is for sale, from fresh virgin olive oil to what one dealer told us was the "original" *Mona Lisa* (not the one hanging in the Louvre).

If you're not in town for the antiques fair, head for **Piazza Vettovaglie,** just off Via Borgo Stretto, which has a market daily 7am to 1:30pm. You'll find everything from old clothing to fresh Tuscan food products. The market sprawls outside its boundaries, spilling onto Via Domenio Cavalca. You can skip the restaurants for lunch and eat here; an array of little trattorie will fill you up at an affordable price. You can also pick up the makings for a picnic to enjoy later in the Tuscan hillsides.

Intriguing stores line **Via Borgo Stretto,** an arcaded street where mimes and street performers often entertain the shoppers.

ACCOMMODATIONS

Hotel d'Azeglio. Piazza Vittorio Emanuele II 18B, 56125 Pisa. ☎ **050-500-310.** Fax 050-28-017. 29 units. A/C MINIBAR TV TEL. 240,000L ($120) double. Rates include breakfast. AE, DC, MC, V. Parking 15,000L ($7.50).

A good safe nest for the night but not a lot more, this is an unremarkable first-class hotel near the rail station and the air terminal. It's viewed as the best in town, at least by Michelin, but don't expect too much; competition in innkeeping isn't too keen in Pisa. There's an American bar and a roof garden with a panoramic city view. The standard guest rooms are well maintained and comfortable, each with a good mattress. The bathrooms are small but have hair dryers.

Jolly Hotel Cavalieri. Piazza della Stazione 2, 56125 Pisa. ☎ **800/221-2636** in the U.S., or 050-43-290. Fax 050-502-242. www.jollyhotels.it. E-mail: pisa@jollyhotels.it. 100 units. A/C MINIBAR TV TEL. 295,000–390,000L ($147.50–$195) double. Rates include breakfast. AE, DC, MC, V. Parking 35,000–40,000L ($17.50–$20).

A bland chain-run property that hosts lots of business travelers, this seven-story hotel opens onto a view of the train station and its piazza. The guest rooms are filled with time-worn furniture, fine mattresses, paneling, and lots of glass. The best ones are on the fifth floor because they have balconies with good views. The bathrooms have hair dryers and adequate shelf space. The Restaurant Cavalieri, with an adjacent piano bar, serves lunch and dinner daily. Parking is often possible in the square in front of the station or in a nearby garage.

✪ **Royal Victoria.** Lungarno Pacinotti 12, 56126 Pisa. ☎ **050-940-111.** Fax 050-940-180. www.royalvictoria.it. 48 units, 40 with private bathroom. TV TEL. 115,000L ($57.50) double without bathroom, 175,000L ($87.50) double with bathroom; 189,000L ($94.50) triple with bathroom; 210,000L ($105) quad with bathroom. Rates include breakfast. AE, CB, DC, MC, V. Parking 30,000L ($15). Bus: 3, 4, or 7.

This isn't Pisa's most luxurious hotel, but it's our favorite, thanks to its sense of history (it occupies several medieval towers and houses, and is Pisa's only inn of real character). Adjacent to the Arno and within walking distance of most of the jewels in Pisa's crown, it was opened in 1839 by ancestors (five generations ago) of the genteel manager, Nicola Piegaja, who runs the place with his brother, overseeing the most helpful staff in town. The guest rooms are old fashioned, but the mattresses are fairly new and firm; the best accommodations are the three with balconies. The private bathrooms are medium-sized, and the hall bathrooms are small but perfectly kept (you usually don't have to wait in line). The bar is open 24 hours.

DINING

✪ **Al Ristoro dei Vecchi Macelli.** Via Volturno 49. ☎ **050-20-424.** Reservations required. Main courses 18,000–36,000L ($9–$18); fixed-price menus 55,000–100,000L ($27.50–$50). AE, DC. Mon–Tues and Thurs–Sat noon–3pm and 8–10:30pm. Closed 2 weeks in Aug. Bus: 1. INTERNATIONAL/PISAN.

This is Pisa's best and most formal restaurant, in a comfortably rustic 1930s building near Piazzetta di Vecchi Macelli. Locals claim the cuisine is prepared with something akin to love, and they prove their devotion by returning frequently. After selecting from a choice of two dozen seafood antipasti, you can enjoy homemade pasta with scallops and zucchini, fish-stuffed ravioli in shrimp sauce, gnocchi with pesto and shrimp, or roast veal with velvety truffle-flavored cream sauce.

Antica Trattoria Da Bruno. Via Luigi Bianchi 12. ☎ **050-560-818.** Reservations recommended for dinner. Main courses 20,000–35,000L ($10–$17.50). AE, DC, MC, V. Mon noon–2:30pm; Wed–Sun noon–3pm and 7–10:30pm. Bus: 2, 3, or 4. PISAN.

For around half a century, Da Bruno has flourished in this spot, 400 yards from the Leaning Tower. It's one of Pisa's finest restaurants, though it charges moderate tabs. Many in-the-know diners prefer the old-fashioned but market-fresh dishes of the Pisan kitchen, including hare with pappardelle, *zuppa alla paesana* (thick vegetable soup), and *baccalà con porri* (codfish with leeks and tomatoes). Some new specialties have appeared on the menu, such as *zuppa pisana* (minestrone with black cabbage) and wild boar with olives and polenta.

Emilio. Via Cammeo 44. ☎ **050-562-141.** Reservations recommended. Main courses 20,000–35,000L ($10–$17.50); fixed-price menu 16,000–26,000L ($8–$13). AE, DC, MC, V. Sat–Thurs noon–3:30pm and 7–10:30pm. Bus: 1. PISAN/ITALIAN.

Because of its well-prepared food and its proximity to Piazza del Duomo, this place is always packed. Inside, a large high window, similar to what you'd find in a church, filters light down upon the brick-walled interior. The menu features a fresh assortment of antipasti, spaghetti with clams, risotto with mushrooms, fish dishes like *branzini à l'Isolana* (oven-baked with tomatoes and vegetables), and Florentine beefsteaks. In season, try one of the game dishes with polenta. Grilled fish is always perfectly prepared. The chef's dessert specialty is *crema limoncello,* a mousse prepared with limoncello liqueur. "You come a stranger, but you leave a friend," the waiter said as we were leaving, forgetting he'd used that same line only a year ago.

5 San Gimignano: The Manhattan of Tuscany

26 miles (42km) NW of Siena, 34 miles (52km) SW of Florence

This golden lily of the Middle Ages is called the Manhattan of Tuscany since it preserves 13 of its noble towers, giving it a skyscraper skyline. The approach to the walled town is dramatic today, but once it must have been fantastic, for in the heyday of the Guelph and Ghibelline conflict **San Gimignano** (aka San Gimignano delle Belle Torri/San Gimignano of the Beautiful Towers) had as many as 72 towers. Its fortresslike severity is softened by the subtlety of its harmonious squares, and many of its palaces and churches are enhanced by Renaissance frescoes because San Gimignano could afford to patronize major painters.

But despite its beauty and authenticity, the town is just packed with tourists during the day. Stay overnight if you can, so you can enjoy the late afternoon or early evening and get a sense of the town without so many distractions. Go to one of the tasting room for a sample of the famous Vernaccia, the light white wine bottled inthe region.

ESSENTIALS

GETTING THERE The **rail station** nearest to San Gimignano is at Poggibonsi, serviced by regular trains from Florence and Siena. At Poggibonsi, buses depart from the front of the rail station at frequent intervals, charging 3,000L ($1.50) each way to the center of San Gimignano. For information, call ☎ **0577-933-646.**

Buses operated by TRA-IN (☎ **0577-204-111**) service San Gimignano from Florence with a change at Poggibonsi (trip time: 75 minutes); the one-way fare is 10,000L ($5). The same company also operates service from Siena, with a change at Poggibonsi (trip time: 50 minutes); the one-way fare is 9,000L ($4.50). In San Gimignano, buses stop at Piazzale Montemaggio, outside the Porta San Giovanni, the southern gate. You'll have to walk into the center, since vehicles aren't allowed in most of the town's core.

If you have a **car,** leave Florence (1½ hours) or Siena (1 hour and 10 minutes) by the Firenze-Siena autostrada and drive to Poggibonsi, where you'll need to cut west along a secondary route (S324) to San Gimignano. There are parking lots outside the city walls.

VISITOR INFORMATION The **Associazione Pro Loco,** Piazza del Duomo 1 (☎ **0577-940-008**), is open daily: November to February 9am to 1pm and 2 to 6pm and March to October 9am to 1pm and 3 to 7pm.

EXPLORING THE TOWN

In the town center is the **Piazza della Cisterna,** so named because of the 13th-century cistern in its heart. Connected with the irregularly shaped square is its satellite, **Piazza del Duomo,** whose medieval architecture of towers and palaces is almost unchanged. It's the most beautiful spot in town. On the square, the **Palazzo del Popolo** was designed in the 13th century, and its **Torre Grossa,** built a few years later, is believed to have been the tallest "skyscraper" (about 178 feet high) in town (see the entry for the Civic Museum below for how to climb this tower).

One **combination ticket,** available at any of the sites below, allows admission to all of them for 16,000L ($8) adults and 12,000L ($6) for children and students under 18.

Duomo Collegiata o Basilica di Santa Maria Assunta. Piazza del Duomo. ☎ **0577-940-316.** Church free; chapel 6,000L ($3) adults, children 5 and under free. Mar–Oct Mon–Fri 9:30am–7:30pm, Sat 9:30am–5pm, Sun 1–5pm; Nov–Feb Mon–Sat 9:30am–5pm and Sun 1–5pm.

Residents of San Gimignano still call this a Duomo (cathedral), even though it was demoted to a "Collegiata" after the town lost its bishop. Don't judge this book by its cover, though: It may be plain and austere on the outside, dating from the 12th century, but it is richly decorated inside. Actually, the facade for some reason was never finished.

Escaping from the burning Tuscan sun, retreat inside to a world of tiger-striped arches and a galaxy of gold stars. Head for the north aisle, where in the 1360s Bartolo di Fredi depicted scenes from the Old Testament. Two memorable ones are *The Trials of Job* and *Noah with the Animals.* Other outstanding works by this artist are in the lunettes off the north aisle, including a medieval view of the cosmography of the Creation. In the right aisle, panels trace scenes from the life of Christ: the kiss of Judas, the Last Supper, the Flagellation, and the Crucifixion. Seek out Bartolo's horrendous *Last Judgment,* one of the most perverse paintings in Italy. Abandoning briefly his rosy-cheeked Sienese madonnas, he depicted distorted and suffering nudes, shocking at the time.

The chief attraction here is the **Chapel of Santa Fina (Cappella Santa Fina),** designed by Giuliano and Benedetto da Maiano. Michelangelo's fresco teacher, Domenico Ghirlandaio, frescoed it with scenes from the life of a local girl, Fina, who became the town's patron saint. Her deathbed scene is memorable. According to accounts of the day, the little girl went to the well for water and accepted an orange from a young swain. When her mother scolded her for her wicked ways, she was so mortified that she prayed for the next 5 years, until St. Anthony called her to heaven.

Spend a few minutes in the small **Sacred Art Museum/Etruscan Museum (Museo d'Arte Sacra/Museo Etrusco)** to the left of the Duomo (enter from Piazza Pecori and an arch to the left of the Duomo's entrance). Its medieval tombstones, wooden sculptures, and Etruscan artifacts prove that the city's roots run deeper than the Middle Ages. It's open April to October, daily from 9:30am to 7:30pm; November to March, Tuesday to Sunday from 9:30am to 5pm. Admission is 7,000L ($3.50).

Civic Museum (Museo Civico). In the Palazzo del Popolo, Piazza del Duomo 1. ☎ **0577-990-312.** Admission 7,000L ($3.50). Mar–Oct daily 9:30am–7:30pm; Nov–Feb Tues–Sun 9:30am–12:30pm and 2:30–4:30pm.

This museum is installed upstairs in the *Palazzo del Popolo* (town hall). Most notable is the **Dante Salon (Sala di Dante),** where the poet supporter of the White Guelph spoke out for his cause in 1300. Look for one of the masterpieces of San Gimignano: *La **Maestà*** (a Madonna enthroned) by Lippo Memmi (later touched up by Gozzoli). The first large room upstairs contains the other masterpiece: a ***Madonna in Glory,*** with Sts. Gregory and Benedict, painted by Pinturicchio. On the other side of it are two depictions of the *Annunciation* by Filippino Lippi. On the opposite wall, note the magnificent Byzantine Crucifix by Coppo di Marcovaldo.

A Great View: Passing through the Museo Civico, you can scale the **Torre Grossa** and be rewarded with a bird's-eye view of this most remarkable town. The tower, the only one you can climb, is open during the same hours as the museum. Admission is 8,000L ($4) adults and 6,000L ($3) students under 18 and children.

Museum of Medieval Criminology (Museo di Criminologia Medioevale). Via del Castello 1. ☎ **0577-942-243.** Admission 15,000L ($7.50). Apr–Oct daily 10am–8pm; off-season daily 10am–6pm.

San Gimignano

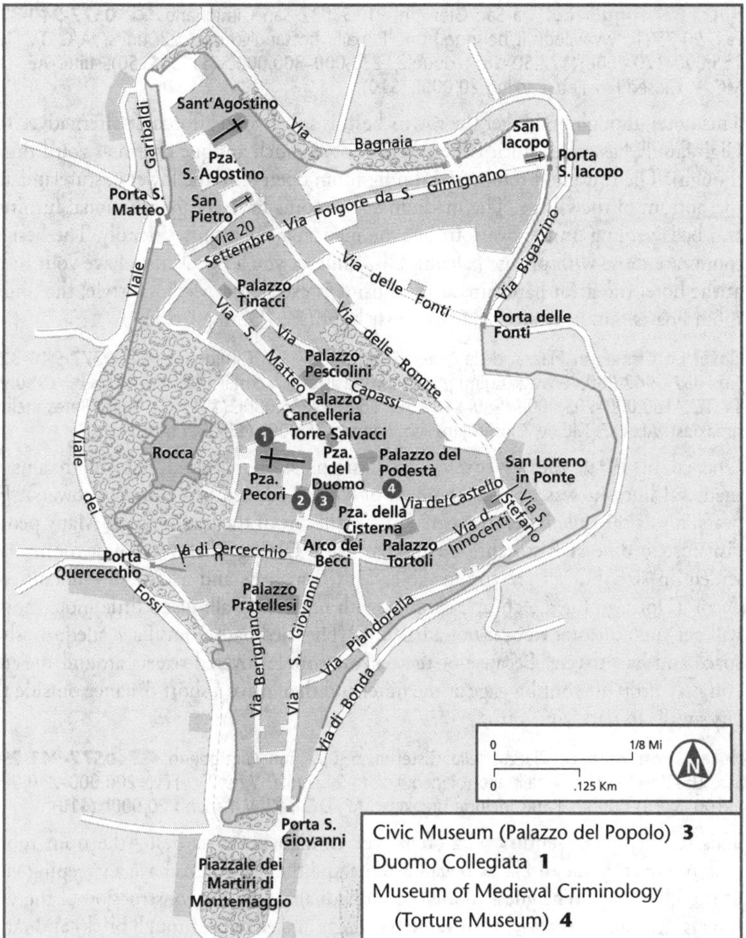

The Marquis de Sade would've taken delight in this bizarre place, also known as the Torture Museum. In this Tuscan chamber of horrors, some of the most horrendous instruments of torture are on display. In case you don't know just how the devices worked, descriptions are provided in English. The museum has a definite political agenda (including some pointed commentary on the continued use of capital punishment in the United States). The exhibits, such as cast-iron chastity belts, reveal some of the sexism inherently involved in torture devices, with the revelation that many have been updated for use around the world today, from Africa to South America. These include the garrote, that horror of the Inquisition trials of the 1400s. Fittingly enough, this chilling sight is housed in what locals call the *Torre del Diavolo* (Devil's Tower).

ACCOMMODATIONS

You can learn about additional choices, and see pictures of all the hotels, by pointing your Web browser to www.sangimignano.com.

Hotel Bel Soggiorno. Via San Giovanni 91, 53037 San Gimignano. ☎ **0577-940-375.** Fax 90-7521. www.logis.it/belsogg.htm. E-mail: hotsangi@tin.it. 22 units. A/C TV TEL. 155,000–170,000L ($77.50–$85) double; 230,000–300,000L ($115–$150) suite. AE, DC, MC, V. Closed Jan–Feb. Parking 20,000L ($10).

This hotel, though no longer the town's best, is still a good affordable alternative. The Gigli family has run it since 1886 (there's not as much antique charm as you'd think, though). The rear guest rooms and dining room open onto the lower pastureland and the bottom of the village. The medium-sized rooms have cheap, functional furniture and beds verging on the oversoft, but the management is quite friendly. The best 10 rooms are those with private balconies. In summer you'll be asked to have your meals at the hotel (no great hardship, as the cuisine is excellent). Medieval style, the dining room boasts murals depicting a wild boar hunt (see "Dining," below).

Hotel La Cisterna. Piazza. della Cisterna 24, 53037 San Gimignano. ☎ **0577-940-328.** Fax 0577-942-080. www.sangimignano.com/lacisterna. E-mail: lacisterna@iol.it. 49 units. TV TEL. 160,000–205,000L ($80–$102.50) double; 235,000L ($117.50) suite. Rates include breakfast. AE, DC, MC, V. Closed Jan–Feb. Parking 25,000L ($12.50) nearby.

Opened in 1919, the ivy-covered La Cisterna is modernized but still retains its medieval lines (it was built at the base of some 14th-century patrician towers). For years, it was the only hotel in town, and it's still one of the leading inns. Many people visit just to dine at Ristorante Le Terrazze (see "Dining," below). Guest rooms vary widely in size, but all are comfortable, with firm beds and a tastefully uncluttered decor. (Don't go for the cheapest rooms with no view at all; just a little more money will get you at least a view, if not a balcony.) The tiled bathrooms have adequate shelf space and hair dryers. Because of the narrow cobble-covered streets around the inn, you may drop off your luggage at the hotel and then drive a short distance outside the city's walls to park your car.

Hotel Leon Bianco. Piazza della Cisterna, 53037 San Gimignano. ☎ **0577-941-294.** Fax 0577-942-123. E-mail: leonbianco@iol.it. 21 units. A/C TV TEL. 200,000–230,000L ($100–$115) double. Rates include breakfast. AE, DC, MC, V. Parking 20,000L ($10).

This restored 11th-century villa offers San Gimignano at its best—the front rooms look out over medieval Piazza della Cisterna and the rear rooms have a sweeping view of the Elsa Valley. The guest rooms are individualized by the construction of the villa (one is rustically romantic, with vaulted ceilings and alcoves of rough brick) and range from small to medium; all have quality mattresses and fine linen. The bathrooms are well kept, with fluffy towels and hair dryers. The sunny roof terrace is a good place to order breakfast or a drink or to just lounge and relax. There's no restaurant on the premises, but several are a short stroll away.

Hotel Pescille. Località Pescille, 53037 San Gimignano. ☎ **0577-940-186.** Fax 0577-943-165. www.sangiminiano.com. E-mail: pescille@iol.it. 50 units. TV TEL. 180,000–340,000L ($90–$170) double. Rates include breakfast. AE, DC, MC, V. Closed Nov to mid-Mar. Head 2 miles north of San Giminiano, following the signs to Castel S. Giminiano and Volterra.

Few other hotels in the region convey as strong a sense of sleepy rural Tuscany, and though the blasé staff sometimes draws complaints, you might appreciate the tranquillity. About 2 miles from town, it's surrounded by vineyards and olive trees. The guest rooms are outfitted in an old-time style, often with countryside views. All are comfortable and charming (with first-rate mattresses), but the most striking is the Tower Room, overlooking San Gimignano's towers. Only 12 rooms are air-conditioned, 25 come with minibars, and 16 have balconies. Four are suited for travelers with disabilities. The bathrooms are small but neatly organized; only 12 rooms have hair dryers, but such equipment is available at the front desk. The bar serves coffee and drinks. Amenities include a swimming pool, solarium, and tennis court.

✪ **L'Antico Pozzo.** Via San Matteo 87, 53037 San Gimignano (near Porta San Matteo). ☎ **0577-942-014.** Fax 0577-942-177. www.anticopozzo.com. 18 units. A/C MINIBAR TV TEL. 200,000–220,000L ($100–$110) double; 250,000L ($125) junior suite. Rates include breakfast. AE, DC, MC, V. Closed Feb. Parking 25,000L ($10) in nearby garage or lot.

This is the top inn within the historic walls, a 15th-century palazzo converted to a hotel in 1990. It has a medieval atmosphere and lovely antique touches yet provides all the modern comforts (you'll even have Internet access here). Accommodations vary in size and decor, but none is small. Throughout, the furnishings are simple 19th-century wooden pieces, and the firm beds have cast-iron frames. "Superior" doubles have 17th-century ceiling frescoes, the smaller "standard" rooms on the third floor have wood floors and a view of the Rocca and a few towers, and the other rooms overlook the street or the rear terrace, where breakfast is served in summer.

✪ **Relais Santa Chiara.** Via Matteotti 15, 53037 San Gimignano. ☎ **0577-940-701.** Fax 0577-942-096. www.rsc.it. E-mail: rsc@rsc.it. 41 units. A/C MINIBAR TV TEL. 260,000–340,000L ($130–$170) double; 380,000–480,000L ($190–$240) suite. Rates include buffet breakfast. AE, DC, MC, V. Free parking.

This comfortable, upscale hotel lies in a residential neighborhood about a 10-minute walk south of the medieval ramparts. It's surrounded by elegant gardens and a pool, and its spacious public rooms contain Florentine terra-cotta floors and mosaics. The guest rooms are furnished in precious briarwood and walnut and include Jacuzzis and excellent mattresses (all have safes as well). Some enjoy views of the countryside; others overlook the hotel's garden. The bathrooms are medium in size, with hair dryers. There's no restaurant, but the hotel serves a buffet breakfast and lunchtime snacks in summer.

DINING

Ristorante Bel Soggiorno. In the Hotel Bel Soggiorno, Via San Giovanni 91. ☎ **0577-940-375.** Reservations recommended. Main courses 20,000–35,000L ($10–$17.50); fixed-price menu 50,000L ($25). AE, DC, MC, V. Thurs–Tues 12:30–2:30pm and 7:30–10pm. TUSCAN.

Thanks to windows overlooking the countryside and a devoted use of fresh ingredients from nearby farms, this restaurant gives you a strong sense of Tuscany's agrarian bounty. Two of the most appealing specialties (available only late summer to late winter) are roasted wild boar with red wine and mixed vegetables and *pappardelle* pasta garnished with a savory ragout of pheasant. Other pastas are pappardelle with roasted hare and risotto with herbs and seasonal vegetables. The main courses stress vegetable garnishes and thin-sliced meats that are simply but flavorfully grilled over charcoal.

Ristorante Le Terrazze. In La Cisterna, Piazza della Cisterna 24. ☎ **0577-940-328.** Reservations required. Main courses 20,000–37,000L ($10–$18.50). AE, DC, MC, V. Wed 7:30–10pm; Thurs–Mon 12:30–2:30pm and 7:30–9:30pm. Closed Jan–Feb. TUSCAN.

One of this restaurant's two dining rooms boasts stones laid in the 1300s, and the other has lots of rustic accessories and large windows overlooking the old town and the Val d'Elsa. The food features an assortment of produce from nearby farms. The soups and pastas make fine beginnings, and specialties of the house include delectable items like sliced fillet of wild boar with polenta and Chianti, goose breast with walnut sauce, *zuppa San Gimignanese* (a hearty minestrone), *vitello alla Cisterna* (veal) with buttered beans, Florentine-style steaks, and *risotto con funghi porcini*. A superb dessert is a local sweet wine, vin santo, accompanied by an almond biscuit called a *cantucci*.

SAMPLING THE VINO

San Gimignano produces its own white wine, **Vernaccia,** one of Italy's relatively esoteric (at least to foreigners) vintages. You'll find one of the widest selections in town, as well as samplings of Chianti from throughout Tuscany, at **Da Gustavo,** Via San Matteo 29 (☎ **0577-940-057**), which is run by the Beccuci family and has been thriving here since 1946. There's an informal stand-up bar where you can order by the glass. If you don't see what you're looking for on the shelves, ask—someone will probably haul it out from a storeroom the moment you mention its name.

EN ROUTE TO SIENA

Traveling from San Gimignano to Siena, you can take S324 east to Poggibonsi, then turn south on S2, following the path of the ancient Roman highway **Via Cassia,** now a little-traveled byway into Siena. Not only will you avoid the heavily trafficked autostrada, but also you'll absorb more of the history, architecture, and geography of the region, taking in the sight of its hillside vineyards, ancient walled villages, and historic tales of struggle. On SS323, 9 miles (16 km) north of Siena, is the town of **Monteriggioni,** built as a Sienese lookout fortress to guard against attack by the Florentines in 1213. The original walls are still intact and contain the 14 towers that once gave it an imposing skyline, looming up out of the wild, a symbol of Sienese might. A stop here will take you back in time, wandering the streets of a village little changed after more than 700 years of civilization.

6 Siena

21 miles (34km) S of Florence, 143 miles (230km) NW of Rome

After visiting Florence, it's altogether fitting, and certainly bipartisan, to call on the city that in the past has been labeled its natural enemy. In Rome you see classicism and the baroque and in Florence the Renaissance, but in the walled city of **Siena** you stand solidly planted back in the Middle Ages (see the photo insert at the beginning of this guide). Spread over three sienna-colored hills in Tuscany's center, Sena Vetus lies in Chianti country. Perhaps preserving its original character more markedly than any other city in Italy, it's even today a showplace of the Italian Gothic.

Regrettably, Siena is too often visited on a quick day trip. But those who tarry find that it is a city of contemplation and profound exploration, characterized by Gothic palaces, almond-eyed Madonnas, aristocratic mansions, letter-writing St. Catherine (patron saint of Italy), narrow streets, and medieval gates, walls, and towers.

We're almost grateful that Siena lost its battle with Florence, though such a point of view may be heretical. Had it continued to expand and change after reaching the zenith of its power in the 14th century, it would be markedly different today, influenced by the rising tides of the Renaissance and the baroque (which are represented here only in a small degree). But Siena retained its uniqueness; in fact, certain Sienese painters were still showing the influence of Byzantium in the late 15th century.

The university (founded 1240) is still a major force in the town, and the conversation you'll overhear between locals in the streets is the purest Italian dialect in the country. However, you may have to wait until evening, since most residents retreat into the seclusion of their homes during the days full of tour buses. They emerge to reclaim the cafes and squares at night, when most visitors have gone. In a nod to its reputation as a commercial leader during the Middle Ages, you can convert your dollars to lire at the **Monte dei Paschi,** the oldest bank in the world.

The Palio: A Spectacle of the Middle Ages

Each year on July 2 and again on August 16, Siena comes alive in the intense, colorful ✪ **Palio delle Contrade,** part historical pageant and part horse race. Each bareback-riding jockey represents a *contrada* (one of the 17 wards into which the city is divided), and each is identified by its characteristic colors. The race, which requires tremendous skill, takes place on Piazza del Campo in the historic heart of the city. Before the race, much pageantry parades by, with colorfully costumed men and banners evoking the 15th-century. The flag-throwing ceremony takes place at this time. And just as enticing is the victory celebration. All the pomp and ritual of the Middle Ages live again.

Three days before the big race, trial races are held, the final trial on the morning of the event. There may be 17 *contrade,* but because Piazza del Campo holds only 10, the wards are chosen by lot. Young partisans, flaunting the colors of their contrada, race through the medieval streets in packs. Food and wine are bountiful on the streets of each contrada on the eve of the race.

The event could easily be considered all in good fun, but locals take it deathly seriously. There have been kidnappings of the most skilled jockeys, and bribery is commonplace. Jockeys have been known to unseat the competition, though a riderless horse is allowed to win. The event has been cited for its cruelty because horses are sometimes impaled by guardrails along the track and jockeys have been caught on camera kicking the horses. In theory, riders are supposed to alternate whip strokes between their mounts and their competitors.

One Sienese who has attended 30 Palios has said, "Winning, not sportsmanship, is the only thing that's important. There are rules, but we Italians never bother to worry about rules. Instead of a horse race, you might call the event a rat race."

Don't buy expensive tickets for the day of the Palio. It's free to stand in the middle of the square, and a lot more fun. Just get to Piazza del Campo *very early* and bring a book and some refreshments, because you'll be trapped there for hours. The square will soon become impossibly crowded, and the temperature can range from rainy and cold to blistering hot. If it's a sunny day, it's a good idea to bring some sort of head covering, since most of the viewing area isn't shaded. For a memorable dinner and a lot of fun, join one of the 17 contrade holding a *cena* (supper) outdoors the night before the race. (You're likely to be invited by the first local you befriend. But while visitors are welcome, this is an event that's truly for the Sienese.)

ESSENTIALS

GETTING THERE The **rail** link between Siena and Florence is sometimes inconvenient, since you often have to change and wait at other stations, like Empoli. But trains run every hour from Florence, costing 8,500L ($4.25) one way. You arrive at the **station** at Piazza Fratelli Rosselli (☎ **0577-280-115**). This is an awkward half-hour climb uphill to the monumental heart; however, bus no. 2, 4, 6, or 10 will take you to Piazza Gramsci near the center.

TRA-IN, Piazza San Domenico 1 (☎ **0577-204-245**), offers bus service from all Tuscany in air-conditioned coaches. The one-way fare between Florence and Siena is

12,000L ($6). The trip takes 1 1/4 hours (actually faster than taking the train, and you'll be let off in the city center).

If you have a **car,** head south from Florence along the Firenze-Siena autostrada, a superhighway linking the two cities, going through Poggibonsi. (It has no route number; just follow the green autostrada signs for Siena).

Trying to drive into the one-way and pedestrian-zoned labyrinth that is the city center just isn't worth the headache. Siena's parking (☎ **0577-22-871**) is now coordinated, and all the lots charge 2,500L ($1.25) per hour or 40,000L ($20) per day (though almost every hotel has a discount deal with the nearest lot for anywhere from 40% to 100% off). Lots are well-signposted, just inside several of the city gates.

VISITOR INFORMATION The **tourist office** is at Piazza del Campo 56 (☎ **0577-280-551**). March to November, it's open Monday to Saturday 9am to 1pm and 3 to 7pm; December to February, hours are Monday to Friday 9am to 1pm and 3 to 7pm and Saturday 8am to 1pm. They'll give you a good free map.

EXPLORING THE MEDIEVAL CITY

There's much to see here. We'll start in the heart of Siena, the shell-shaped ✪ **Piazza del Campo,** described by Montaigne as "the finest of any city in the world." Pause to enjoy the **Fonte Gaia,** which locals sometimes call the fountain of joy, because it was inaugurated to great jubilation throughout the city, with embellishments by Jacopo della Quercia (the present sculptured works are reproductions; the badly beaten up original ones are found in the town hall). The square is truly stunning, designed like a sloping scallop shell; you'll want to linger in one of the cafes along its edge.

Civic Museum (Museo Civico) & Torre del Mangia. In the Palazzo Pubblico, Piazza del Campo. ☎ **0577-292-263.** Admission 10,000L ($5). Mid-Mar to Oct daily 10am–7pm; Nov to mid-Mar daily 10am-6:30pm. Bus: A, B, or N.

The Palazzo Pubblico (1288–1309) is filled with important artworks by some of the leaders in the Sienese school of painting and sculpture. This collection here resides in the Museo Civico.

In the **Globe Room (Sala del Mappomondo)** is Simone Martini's earliest-known work (ca. 1315), *La Maesta,* the Madonna enthroned with her child, surrounded by angels and saints. The other remarkable Martini fresco (on the opposite wall) is the equestrian portrait of Guidoriccio da Fogliano, general of the Sienese Republic, in ceremonial dress.

The next room is the **Peace Room (Sala della Pace),** frescoed from 1337 to 1339 by Ambrogio Lorenzetti; the allegorical frescoes show the idealized effects of good government and bad government. In this depiction, the most notable figure of the Virtues surrounding the king is *La Pace* (Peace). To the right of the king and the Virtues is a representation of Siena in peaceful times. On the left, Lorenzetti showed his opinion of "ward heelers," but some of the sting has inadvertently been taken out of the frescoes because the evil-government scene is badly damaged. (Actually, these were propaganda frescoes in their day, commissioned by the party in power, but they're now viewed as among the most important of all secular frescoes to come down from the Middle Ages.)

Accessible from the courtyard of the Palazzo Pubblico is the **Torre del Mangia,** the most prominent architectural landmark on the skyline of Siena. Dating from the 14th century, it soars to a height of 335 feet. The tower takes its name from a former bell-ringer, a sleepy fellow called *mangiagaudagni* ("eat the profits"). Surprisingly, it has no subterranean foundations. If you climb this needlelike tower (more than 500 steps!), you'll be rewarded with a drop-dead gorgeous view of the red-tile roofs of the city and

Central Siena

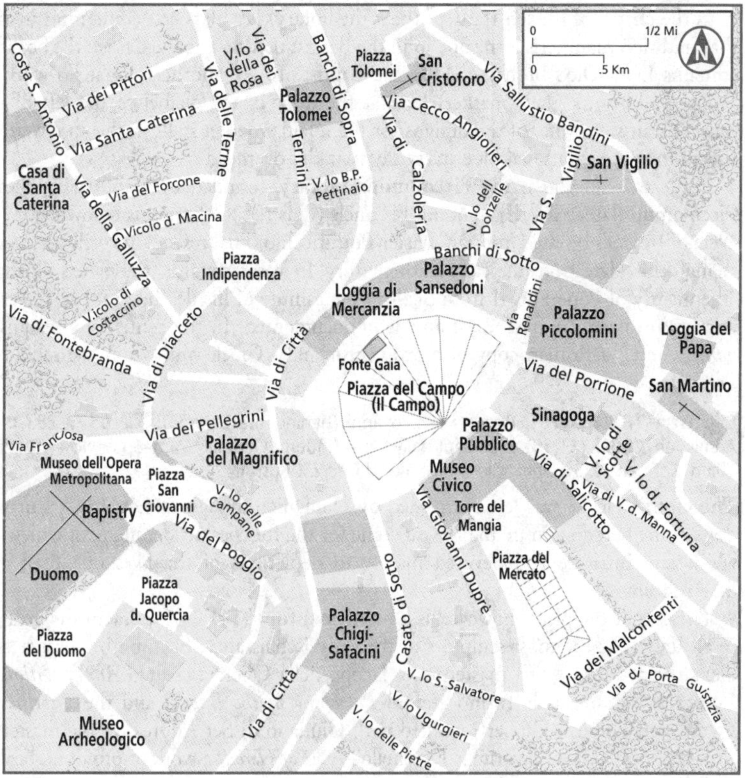

the surrounding Tuscan landscape. In the Middle Ages, this was Italy's second-tallest tower (Cremona has Siena beat). The tower is open the same hours as the Civic Museum, charging 7,000L ($3.50) for you to climb it.

✪ **Il Duomo & Piccolimini Library (Libreria Piccolomini).** Piazza del Duomo. ☎ **0577-283-048.** Duomo free; library 2,000L ($1). Duomo Nov–Mar 15 daily 8am–1pm and 2:30–5pm (Mar 16–Oct to 7:30pm). Library Mar 15–Oct daily 9am–7:30pm; Nov–Mar 16 daily 10am–1pm and 2:30–5pm. Closed Jan 1 and Dec 25. Bus: A.

At Piazza del Duomo, southwest of Piazza del Campo, stands an architectural fantasy. With its colored bands of marble, the Sienese **Duomo** is an original and exciting building, erected in the Romanesque and Italian Gothic styles in the 12th century. The dramatic facade, designed in part by Giovanni Pisano, dates from the 13th century, as does the Romanesque *campanile* (bell tower).

The zebralike interior of black-and-white stripes is equally stunning. The floor consists of various inlaid works of art depicting both biblical and mythological subjects (many are roped off to preserve the richness in design). Numerous artists worked on the floor, notably Domenico Beccafumi. The octagonal 13th-century pulpit is by Nicola Pisano (Giovanni's father), one of the most significant Italian sculptors before the dawn of the Renaissance. The Siena pulpit is his masterpiece; it reveals in relief such scenes as the slaughter of the innocents and the Crucifixion. The elder Pisano finished the pulpit in 1268, aided by his son and others. Its pillars are supported by four marble lions, again reminiscent of the Pisano pulpit at Pisa.

In the chapel of the left transept (near the library) is a glass box containing an arm that tradition maintains is the one John the Baptist used to baptize Christ; the box also contains Donatello's bronze of John the Baptist. To see another Donatello work in bronze (a bishop's grave marker) look at the floor in the chapel to the left of the pulpit's stairway. Some of the designs for the inlaid wooden stalls in the apse were by Riccio. A representational blue starry sky twinkles overhead.

Inside the Duomo is the **Piccolomini Library,** founded by Cardinal Francesco Piccolomini (later Pius III) to honor his uncle (Pius II); the library is renowned for its cycle of frescoes by the Umbrian master Pinturicchio. His frescoes are well preserved, though they date from the early 16th century. In Vasari's words, the panels illustrate "the history of Pope Pius II from birth to the minute of his death." Raphael's alleged connection with the frescoes, if any, is undocumented. In the center is an exquisite *Three Graces,* a Roman copy of a 3rd-century B.C. Greek work from the school of Praxiteles.

Baptistry (Battistero). Piazza San Giovanni (behind the Duomo). ☎ **0577-283-048.** Admission 3,000L ($1.50). Mar–Sept daily 9am–7:30pm; Oct daily 9am–6pm; Nov–Mar daily 10am–1pm and 2:30–5pm. Closed Jan 1 and Dec 25. Bus: A.

The Gothic facade was left unfinished by Domenico di Agostino in 1355. But you don't come here to admire that—you come for the frescoes inside, many of which are lavish and intricate and devoted mainly to depictions of the lives of Christ and St. Anthony.

The star of the place, however, is a **baptismal font** (1417–30), one of the greatest in all Italy. The foremost sculptors of the early Renaissance, from both Florence and Siena, helped create this masterpiece. Jacopo della Quercia created *Annunciation to Zacharias,* Giovanni di Turino crafted *Preaching of the Baptist* and the *Baptism of Christ,* and Lorenzo Ghiberti worked with Giuliano di Ser Andrea on the masterful *Arrest of St. John.* Our favorite is Donatello's *Feast of Herod,* a work of profound beauty and perspective.

Duomo Museum (Museo dell'Opera Metropolitana). Piazza del Duomo 8. ☎ **0577-42309.** Admission 6,000L ($3). Mar 16–Sept daily 9am–7:30pm; Oct daily 9am–6pm; Nov–Mar daily 9am–1:30pm. Closed Dec 25–Jan 1. Bus: A.

This museum houses paintings and sculptures created for the Duomo. On the ground floor is much interesting sculpture, including works by Giovanni Pisano and his assistants. But the real draw hangs on the next floor in the **Duccio Salon (Sala di Duccio):** his fragmented *La Maestà* (1308–11), a Madonna enthroned, one of Europe's greatest late-medieval paintings. The majestic panel was an altarpiece by Duccio di Buoninsegna for the cathedral, filled with dramatic moments illustrating the story of Christ and the Madonna. A student of Cimabue, Duccio was the first great name in the school of Sienese painting. Upstairs are the collections of the treasury, and on the top floor is a display of paintings from the early Sienese school.

✪ **National Picture Gallery (Pinacoteca Nazionale).** In the Palazzo Buonsignori, Via San Pietro 29. ☎ **0577-281-161.** Admission 8,000L ($4). Mon 8:30am–1:30pm; Tues–Sat 9am–7pm; Sun 8am–1pm. Bus: A.

Housed in a 14th-century palazzo near Piazza del Campo is the National Gallery's collection of the Sienese school of painting, which once rivaled that of Florence. Displayed are some of the giants of the pre-Renaissance, with most of the paintings covering the period from the late 12th century to the mid–16th century.

The principal treasures are on the second floor, where you'll contemplate the artistry of Duccio in **rooms 3 and 4.** Duccio was the first great Sienese master. **Rooms**

5 to 8 are rich in the art of the 14th-century Lorenzetti brothers, Ambrogio and Pietro. Ambrogio is represented by an *Annunciation* and a *Crucifix,* but one of his most celebrated works, carried out with consummate skill, is an almond-eyed *Madonna and Bambino* surrounded by saints and angels. Pietro's most important entry is an altarpiece, *Madonna of the Carmine,* made for a Siena church in 1329. Simone Martini's *Madonna and Child* (1321) is damaged but one of the best-known paintings here.

In the salons to follow are works by Giovanni di Paolo (*Presentation at the Temple*), Sano di Pietro, and Giovanni Antonio Bazzi (called Il Sodoma, allegedly because of his sexual interests). Of exceptional interest are the cartoons of Mannerist master Beccafumi, from which many of the panels in the cathedral floor were created.

St. Catherine's Sanctuary (Santuario e Casa di Santa Caterina). Costa di San Antonio. ☎ **0577-441-77.** Free admission (an offering is expected). Daily and holidays 8am–12:30pm and 2:30–6pm. Bus: A.

Of all the personalities associated with Siena, the most enduring legend surrounds St. Catherine, acknowledged by Pius XII in 1939 as Italy's patron saint. Born in 1347 to a dyer, the mystic was instrumental in persuading the papacy to return to Rome from Avignon. The house where she lived, between Piazza del Campo and San Domenico, has now been turned into a sanctuary; it's really a church and an oratory, with many artworks, located where her father had his dyeworks. On the hill above is the 13th-century **Basilica di San Domenico,** where a chapel dedicated to St. Catherine was frescoed by Il Sodoma.

Permanent Italian Library of Wine (Enoteca Italica Permanente). Fortezza Medicea. ☎ **0577-288-497.** Free admission. Mon noon–8pm; Tues–Sat noon–1am. Bus: C.

Owned/operated by the Italian government, this showcase for the finest wines of Italy would whet the palate of even the most demanding wine lover. An unusual architectural setting is designed to show bottles to their best advantage. The place lies just outside the entrance to an old fortress, at the bottom of an inclined ramp, behind a massive arched doorway. Marble bas-reliefs and wrought-iron sconces, along with regional ceramics, are set into the high brick walls of the labyrinthine corridors, the vaults of which were built for Cosimo de' Medici in 1560. There are several sunny terraces for outdoor wine tasting, an indoor stand-up bar, and voluminous lists of available vintages, for sale by the glass or the bottle. Special wine tastings for groups may be booked for 16,000L ($8) for two wines or 18,000L ($9) for three. Count yourself lucky if the bartender will agree to open an iron gate for access to the subterranean wine exposition; in the lowest part of the fortress, illuminated display racks contain bottles of recent vintages.

SHOPPING

Though Siena's shopping scene can't compete with that in Florence, you'll still find a good selection of stores and boutiques. The best of the lot is **Arcaico,** Via di Citta 81 (☎ **0577-281-144**), the centerpiece of three almost-adjacent shops stocking Siena's richest trove of ceramics and souvenirs (cachepots, religious figurines, decorative tiles, dinnerware painted in pleasing floral patterns, and wine and water jugs).

A worthy competitor is **Martini Marisa,** Via del Capitano 5 and 11 (☎ **0577-288-177**), purveyor of gift items, local stoneware, and porcelain. Also try the nearby **Zina Proveddi,** Via di Città 96 (☎ **0577-286-078**), smaller than either of its competitors but with a cozier feel and an emphasis on rustic and affordable handmade pottery and painted tiles set into wood. **Ceramiche Santa Caterina,** Via di Città 74-76 (☎ **0577-283-098**), offers sculpture, dishes, and tiles among the items for sale; custom orders are available on request (the owners say they can make anything you can describe in their Siena-based factories).

Specializing in older jewelry, **Antichità Saena Vetus,** Via di Città 53 (☎ **0577-42-395**), also handles furniture and paintings from the 1700s and 1800s and always has smaller pieces reasonably priced for the bargain hunter. There's also a small assortment of oil paintings, art objects, and small-scale furniture. If you're looking for old or old-fashioned engravings, out-of-print books, and art objects, head for **La Balzana,** Piazza del Campo 55 (☎ **0577-285-380**), an appealingly dusty venue that also includes an assortment of local pottery and souvenirs.

Utilizing the colors and designs of Renaissance Siena, **Siena Ricama,** Via di Città 61 (☎ **0577-288-339**), is the place to order custom-made hand-embroidered table and bed linens.

More contemporary is the intricately crafted knitwear at **Il Telaio,** Chiasso del Bargello 2 (☎ **0577-47-065**). Most of the stock includes artfully tailored women's jackets, scarves, and jumpers, though there's a small collection of pullovers for men. Focusing on smaller leather goods, **Mercatissimo della Calzatura e Pelletteria,** Viale Curtatone 1 (☎ **0577-2813-05**), is the largest store of its type in Siena. You'll find discounted prices on upscale Italian-made leather goods (handbags, suitcases, briefcases, and men's and women's shoes), and there's an inventory of tennis and basketball sneakers imported from Asia.

Siena merchants also sell some of Tuscany's finest wines. Virtually every street corner has an outlet for local Chianti (sold in individual bottles and sometimes four-packs and six-packs). Many of the finer bottles are wrapped in the distinctive straw sheathing. For the largest selection, head to the **Enoteca Italica Permanente** (see above). A Tuscan gourmet's delight, the **Enoteca San Domenico,** Via del Paradiso 56 (☎ **0577-271-181**), sells regional wines and grappa by the bottle, plus pasta, virgin olive oils, sauces, jams, and assorted sweets.

ACCOMMODATIONS

You'll definitely need hotel reservations if you're here for the Palio. Make them far in advance and secure your room with a deposit. If it looks as if Siena is full, you might want to check out some of the nearby accommodations in the Chianti region, north of Siena (see the beginning of this chapter). The **Siena Hotels Promotion** booth on Piazza San Domenico (☎ **0577-288-084;** shpnet@novamedia.it) will help you find a room for a small fee.

VERY EXPENSIVE

Certosa di Maggiano. Strada di Certosa 82, 53100 Siena. ☎ **0577-288-180.** Fax 0577-288-189. www.relaischateaux.fr/certosa. E-mail: certosa@relaischateaux.it. 17 units. A/C MINIBAR TV TEL. 700,000–800,000L ($350–$400) double; 1,000,000–1,100,000L ($500–$550) suite. Rates include buffet breakfast. AE, MC, V. Parking 60,000L ($30).

This early 13th-century Certosinian monastery lay in dusty disrepair until 1975, when Anna Grossi Recordati renovated it and began attracting a celebrity crowd. It lacks the facilities and formal service of the Park Hotel Siena (see below), but many guests prefer the intimacy of this retreat. The stylish public rooms fill the spaces between what used to be the ambulatory of the central courtyard, and the complex's medieval church still holds mass on Sunday. Most guest rooms are spacious, with antiques, art objects, sumptuous beds, and safes; one has a private walled garden. The bathrooms are medium in size, with hair dryers. The hotel isn't easy to find; there are some signs, but you may want to phone ahead for directions.

Dining: The small vaulted dining room contains a marble fireplace and entire walls of modern ceramics. It's open to nonguests who make a reservation. The cuisine is excellent.

Amenities: Concierge, room service, laundry/dry cleaning, secretarial services, baby-sitting, tennis court, outdoor heated pool, jogging track, tour desk.

EXPENSIVE

Jolly Hotel Excelsior. Piazza La Lizza, 53100 Siena. ☎ **800/221-2626** in the U.S., or 0577-288-448. Fax 0577-41-272. www.tradetours.com/italia/siena/joexce.htm. 126 units. A/C MINIBAR TV TEL. 300,000–410,000L ($150–$205) double; 360,000–610,000L ($180–$305) suite. Rates include breakfast. AE, CB, DC, MC, V. Parking 40,000–45,000L ($20–$22.50). Bus: C.

In the commercial center of Siena's newer section, this hotel is a distinguished member of a nationwide chain, though it lacks the ambience and beauty of the Certosa di Maggiano or the Park Hotel Siena. It was built as the Excelsior in the 1880s and completely renovated about a century later. The high-ceilinged lobby is stylishly Italian, with terra-cotta accents and white columns. The guest rooms offer modern but uninspired furniture (including soft mattresses) and many conveniences. The bathrooms have plenty of toiletries, with hair dryers.

Dining: The hotel's restaurant features both Tuscan and international dishes.

Amenities: Concierge, room service, laundry/dry cleaning, baby-sitting.

Park Hotel Siena. Via di Marciano 18, 53100 Siena. ☎ **0577-44-803.** Fax 0577-49-020. www.charminghotels.it/parkhotel. E-mail: reservation_phs@charminghotels.it. 70 units. A/C MINIBAR TV TEL. 400,000–600,000L ($200–$300) double; 750,000–1,200,000L ($375–$600) suite. AE, DC, MC, V. Closed Dec 3–Feb. Free parking. About a 12-min. drive 1 1/2 miles (2km) north of the city center.

This building was commissioned in 1530 by one of Siena's most famous Renaissance architects, was transformed into a luxury hotel around the turn of the century, and has remained the leading hotel in Siena ever since. It doesn't have the antique charm of the Certosa di Maggiano (above) but is more professionally run. A difficult access road leads around a series of hairpin turns (watch the signs carefully) to a villa with a view over green trees and suburban homes. The landscaped pool, double-glazed windows, upholstered walls, and plush carpeting have set new standards around here. The guest rooms are comfortably furnished, with firm mattresses on the twin or double beds. The bathrooms have adequate shelf space and good state-of-the-art plumbing. Several famous golf courses are nearby; golf packages are offered through the hotel, which has its own six-hole course, Villa Gori Golf Club.

Dining: Meals in the hotel restaurant L'Olivo may include wild mushroom salad with black truffles, tortellini with spinach and ricotta, and a regularly featured series of dishes from Tuscany, Umbria, or Emilia-Romagna.

Amenities: Room service, laundry/valet, pool, two tennis courts, six-hole golf course.

Villa Scacciapensieri. Via di Scacciapensieri 10, 53100 Siena. ☎ **0577-41-441.** Fax 0577-270-854. www.knowital.com/towns/sienandsan/htm/scacciapensieri.html. E-mail: villasca@tin.it. 31 units. A/C MINIBAR TV TEL. 300,000–390,000L ($150–$195) double; 500,000L ($250) suite. Rates include breakfast. AE, DC, MC, V. Closed Jan–Feb. Free parking. About 2 miles (3km) from Siena. Bus: 8 or 3.

This is one of Tuscany's lovely old villas, where you can stay in a personal, if timeworn, atmosphere. Standing on the crest of a hill, the villa is approached by a private driveway under shade trees. Although it's not as state-of-the-art as it once was, it's still preferred

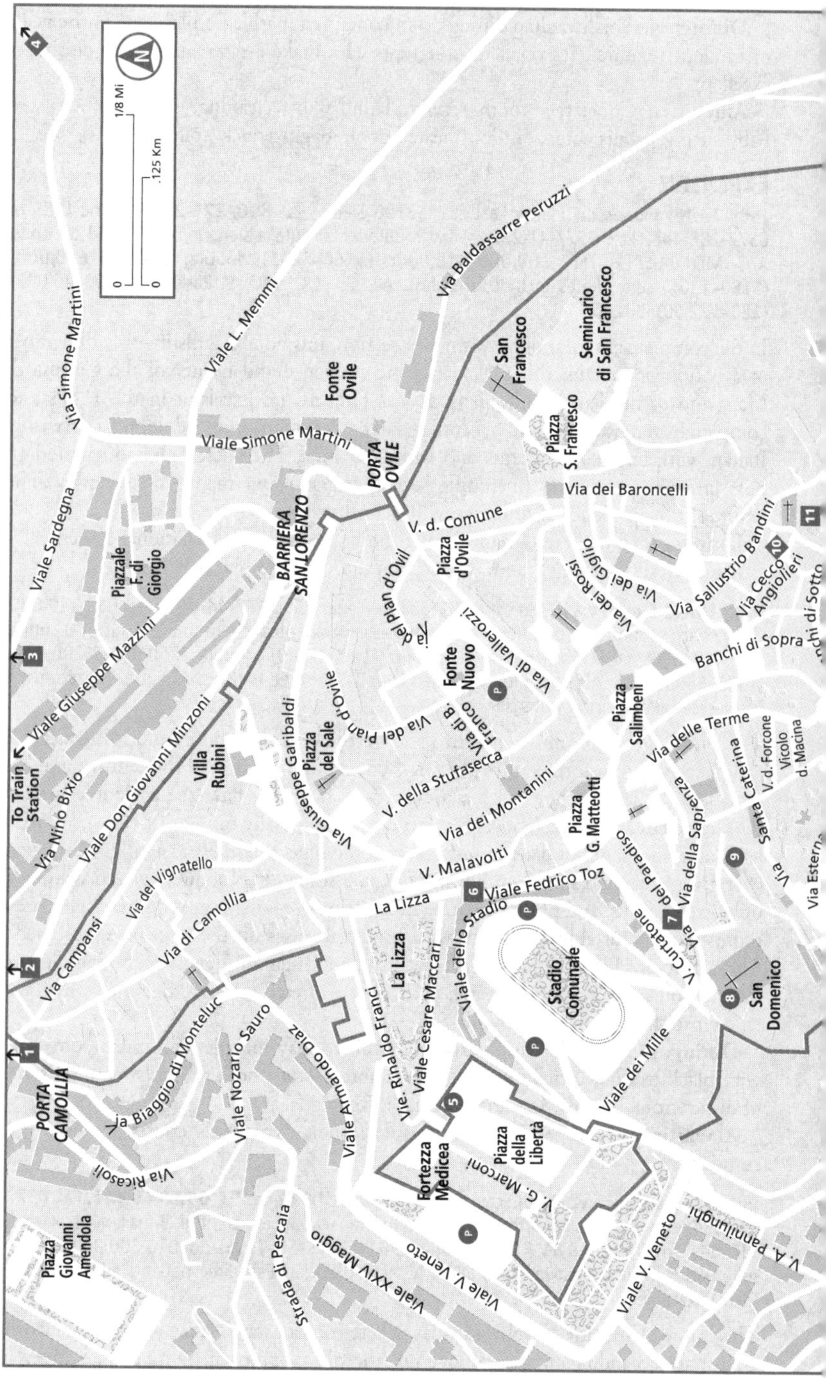
1/8 Mi
.125 Km
0
0
Via Simone Martini
Viale L. Memmi
Via Baldassarre Peruzzi
Fonte Ovile
San Francesco
Seminario di San Francesco
Piazza S. Francesco
Viale Simone Martini
PORTA OVILE
Via dei Baroncelli
Viale Sardegna
Piazzale F. di Giorgio
BARRIERA SAN LORENZO
V. d. Comune
Piazza d'Ovile
Via del Plan d'Ovile
Via del Giglio
Via dei Rossi
Via Sallustrio Bandini
Via Cecco Angiolieri
Banchi di Sopra
Viale Giuseppe Mazzini
Via di Vallerozzi
Fonte Nuovo
Via di B. Franco
Via del Pian d'Ovile
Piazza del Sale
Via Giuseppe Garibaldi
Viale Don Giovanni Minzoni
Villa Rubini
To Train Station
Via Nino Bixio
V. della Stufasecca
Via dei Montanini
Piazza Salimbeni
Via delle Terme
Santa Caterina
V. d. Forcone
Vicolo d. Macina
Via della Sapienza
Piazza G. Matteotti
Via del Paradiso
V. Malavolti
Via del Vignatello
Via Campansi
Via di Camollia
La Lizza
Viale Fedrico Toz
Viale dello Stadio
Stadio Comunale
V. Curtatone
San Domenico
Via Esterna
PORTA CAMOLLIA
Via Biaggio di Monteluc
Viale Nozario Sauro
Viale Armando Diaz
Vie. Rinaldo Franci
Viale Cesare Maccari
Viale dei Mille
Fortezza Medicea
Piazza della Libertà
V. G. Marconi
Via Ricasoli
Piazza Giovanni Amendola
Strada di Pescaia
Viale XXIV Maggio
Viale V. Veneto
V. A. Pannilunghi
1
2
3
4
5
6
7
8
9
10
11
P

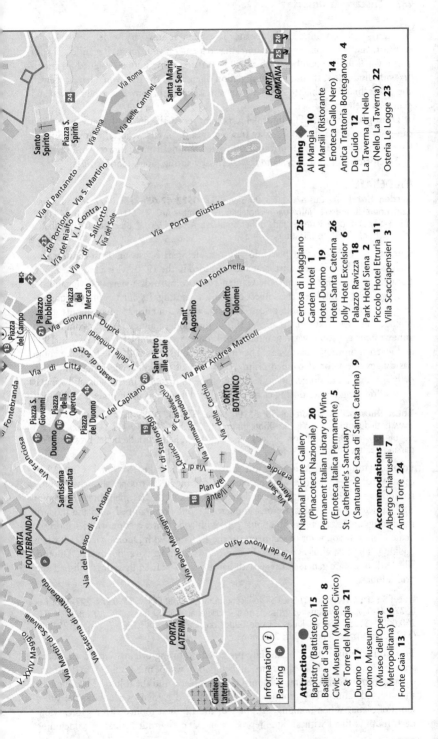

Attractions
Baptistry (Battistero) **15**
Basilica di San Domenico **8**
Civic Museum (Museo Civico) & Torre del Mangia **21**
Duomo **17**
Duomo Museum (Museo dell'Opera Metropolitana) **16**
Fonte Gaia **13**
National Picture Gallery (Pinacoteca Nazionale) **20**
Permanent Italian Library of Wine (Enoteca Italica Permanente) **5**
St. Catherine's Sanctuary (Santuario e Casa di Santa Caterina) **9**

Accommodations
Albergo Chiaruselli **7**
Antica Torre **24**
Certosa di Maggiano **25**
Garden Hotel **1**
Hotel Duomo **19**
Hotel Santa Caterina **26**
Jolly Hotel Excelsior **6**
Palazzo Ravizza **18**
Park Hotel Siena **2**
Piccolo Hotel Etruria **11**
Villa Scacciapensieri **3**

Dining
Al Mangia **10**
Al Marsili (Ristorante Enoteca Gallo Nero) **14**
Antica Trattoria Botteganova **4**
Da Guido **12**
La Taverna di Nello (Nello La Taverna) **22**
Osteria Le Logge **23**

by many tradition-minded Europeans. The guest rooms vary widely in style and comfort, and your opinion of this hotel may depend on your room. Regardless of your room, you'll find a good bed with a quality mattress. One suite is designed for travelers with disabilities. If your accommodation opens onto the rear, you'll have a view of the sweet hills of Chianti. Each newly renovated bathroom has a hair dryer and generous shelf space.

Dining/Diversions: The informal restaurant serves Tuscan and Italian cuisine. You can dine here Thursday to Tuesday (reserve ahead). In fair weather, you can dine or have a drink in the garden surrounded by Mediterranean trees, flowers, and shrubs.

Amenities: Room service, laundry/valet, baby-sitting, pool, tennis courts.

MODERATE

Garden Hotel. Via Custoza 2, 53100 Siena. ☎ **0577-47-056.** Fax 0577-46-050. www.gardenhotel.it. E-mail: info@gardenhotel.it. 122 units. A/C TV TEL. 210,000–340,000L ($105–$170) double. Rates include buffet breakfast. AE, DC, MC, V. Bus: 6 or 10. Less than a mile north of Siena's fortifications.

One of the really pleasant places to stay outside Siena boasts an 18th-century core built as a villa by a Sienese aristocrat and expanded in the 1970s with a modern annex. Located on the ledge of a hill, the Garden Hotel commands a view of Siena and the countryside that has been the subject of many a painting. Its outstanding features are its garden and its reasonable prices. The villa itself contains 25 guest rooms, high-ceilinged but less luxurious than the 100 in the modern annex. The air-conditioned annex rooms are conservatively modern. All rooms were completely renewed in 1998 and given sumptuous mattresses. The tiled bathrooms are small. The breakfast room has a flagstone floor, decorated ceiling, and view of the hills. The restaurant, open daily for lunch and dinner, includes some of the showrooms in the villa and sprawls onto a flowering terrace during clement weather. The pool is open June to September.

Hotel Duomo. Via Stalloreggi 38, 53100 Siena. ☎ **0577-289-088.** Fax 0577-43-043. www.hotelduomo.it. E-mail: info@hotelduomo.it. 23 units. A/C TV TEL. 250,000L ($125) double. 20%–40% less in slow periods. AE, DC, MC, V. Rates include buffet breakfast. Free parking nearby. Bus: A.

Located within the historic walls just south of its namesake, this hotel is in a 12th-century palazzo that once was the barracks for medieval troops, though the only reminders are the central staircase and the brickwork in the basement breakfast room. The carpeted guest rooms are of a modest size but not cramped, and the modern furnishings are as tasteful as functional gets, with good mattresses on wood-slat orthopedic frames. If you want to secure one of the 13 rooms with Duomo views, ask when booking. The best choices are nos. 61 and 62, with terraces overlooking the Duomo. The bathrooms are generally small, with hair dryers. The friendly staff is polished and professional.

Hotel Santa Caterina. Via Enea Silvio Piccolomini 7, 53100 Siena. ☎ **0577-221-105.** Fax 0577-271-087. www.sienanet.it/hsc. E-mail: hsc@sienanet.it. 19 units. A/C MINIBAR TV TEL. 250,000L ($125) double. Rates include buffet breakfast. AE, DC, MC, V. Parking 25,000L ($12.50) nearby (6 spaces). Bus: 2, A, or N.

This 18th-century villa is beautifully preserved, featuring original terra-cotta floors, sculpted marble fireplaces and stairs, arched entryways, beamed ceilings, and antique wooden furniture. Ms. Stefania Minuti runs this place, and she thinks of her guests as an extended family. The grounds include a terraced garden overlooking the valley south of Siena. When booking, ask for 1 of the 12 guest rooms with a garden view. Each room is filled with antique reproductions and chestnut furnishings, including fine mattresses. The bathrooms are small but beautifully kept, each with a hair dryer. There's no restaurant, but you'll find a bar and a breakfast veranda.

✪ **Palazzo Ravizza.** Pian dei Mantellini 34, 53100 Siena. ☎ **0577-280-462.** Fax 0577-221-597. www.palazzoravizza.it. E-mail: bureau@palazzoravizza.it. 38 units. TEL. 256,000–330,000L ($128–$165) double; 350,000–410,000L ($175–$205) suite. Rates include half-board. AE, DC, MC, V. Free parking. Bus: San Domenico.

This is an elegant small hotel, housed in a converted building from the 19th century. Every guest room has a few antiques along with ceiling frescoes. Some rooms also open onto a view of the garden. Each comes with a supremely comfortable bed and mattress, along with a small but tidily kept bathroom. The hotel lies within a short walk of Piazza del Campo. The on-site restaurant serves very good Tuscan food; almost every item is homemade, including the pasta and desserts. The free parking comes as a real plus in overcrowded Siena.

INEXPENSIVE

Albergo Chiaruselli. Viale Curtatone 9, 53100 Siena. ☎ **0577-280-562.** Fax 0577-271-177. E-mail: chiaruse@tin.it. 49 units. A/C TV TEL. 185,000L ($92.50) double; 250,000L ($125) triple. Rates include breakfast. AE, MC, V. Free parking (10 spaces). Bus: C.

Near Piazza San Domenico, the three-star Chiusarelli is in an ocher-colored 1870 building with Ionic columns and Roman caryatids supporting a second-floor loggia. The interior has been almost completely renovated, and each functional guest room contains a modern bathroom with a hair dryer. Ask for a room in back to escape the street noise. The hotel is just at the edge of the old city and is convenient to the parking areas at the sports stadium, a 5-minute walk away. The basement-level Ristorante Chiusarelli serves standard full meals (often to tour groups).

Antica Torre. Via di Fieravecchia 7, 53100 Siena. ☎ and fax **0577-222-255.** 8 units. TEL. 190,000L ($95) double. AE, DC, MC, V. Parking on street nearby.

The Landolfo family extends a warm welcome to international visitors in its restored 17th-century tower within the city walls in the southeastern sector of town, a 10-minute walk from Piazza del Campo. Small and graceful, the tower sits on top of a centuries-old potters' workshop that's now the breakfast room. Take a stone staircase to the somewhat cramped but comfortable guest rooms, each with some Tuscan antiques, iron filigree headboards, good mattresses, and marble floors. Try for one of the accommodations on top if you'd like a panoramic view of the medieval city and the rolling Tuscan hills. The bathrooms are small but tidily kept.

Piccolo Hotel Etruria. Via Donzelle 3, 53100 Siena. ☎ **0577-288-088.** Fax 0577-288-461. E-mail: hetruria@tin.it. 13 units. TV TEL. 125,000L ($62.50) double. AE, DC, MC, V. Closed around Dec 10–27. Bus: A, B, or N.

This small family-run hotel could thumb its nose at the big corporate chains because it offers equally comfortable modern amenities with twice the character and at a fourth the price. In both the main building and the annex across the street, the guest rooms have tiled floors, wood-toned built-in furnishings with stone-topped desks and end tables, leather strap chairs, and quite decent beds. The rooms aren't very spacious but at least medium-sized. The bathrooms have hair dryers and adequate shelf space. The only real drawback is the 12:30am curfew.

NEARBY ACCOMMODATIONS

✪ **Locanda dell'Amorosa.** Località Amorosa, 53048 Sinalunga. ☎ **0577-679-497.** Fax 0577-632-001. www.amorosa.it. E-mail: locanda@amorosa.it. 19 units. A/C MINIBAR TV TEL. 390,000–460,000L ($195–$230) double; 590,000L ($295) suite. Rates include breakfast.

AE, DC, MC, V. Closed Jan 6–Mar 5. Free parking. From Siena, drive southeast for 28 miles (45km) along SS326, following the signs first for Arezzo and then for Perugia.

Until the 1960s, this compound of agrarian buildings was a working farm, with its own school, a priest (who conducted masses in the chapel), and rich traditions of wine making and olive-oil production. In the 1980s, the compound was transformed into a hotel resembling a small Tuscan village, with 14th-century stonework. Today, thanks to substantial investments by local entrepreneur Carlo Citterio, few other hotels in the region evoke rural Tuscany with as much historic charm or finesse. There are still about 200 acres of farmland associated with the hotel, about 20 of which are devoted to wine making for the robust table wines (Sangioveto de Borgo) that continue to be produced here. What used to be the granary is now a convention center, favored for a weekend rendezvous by some of the region's corporations.

The guest rooms are formal, with spacious bathrooms (hair dryers included) and tasteful furnishings that go well with the rich tapestry of Tuscan life unfolding around the hotel. Some open onto panoramic countryside views, others onto the hotel's gardens.

Dining: Open for lunch and dinner daily except Sunday and lunch on Monday, the upscale restaurant serves main courses for about 30,000L ($15); the food is superb. Less formal meals are served in an area that used to be a storage cellar but has been charmingly renovated into a wine bar.

Villa Belvedere. Via Senese Belvedere, 53034 Colle di Val d'Elsa Siena. ☎ **0577-920-966.** Fax 0577-924-128. www.villabelvedere.com. E-mail: email@villabelvedere.com. 15 units. TV TEL. 265,000L ($132.50) double. Rates include buffet breakfast. AE, DC, MC, V. Exit the autostrada from Florence at Colle di Val d'Elsa Sud and follow the signs.

The Villa Belvedere, about 7½ miles (12km) from Siena and halfway to San Gimignano, occupies a 1795 building. In 1820 it was the residence of Ferdinand III, archduke of Austria and grand duke of Tuscany, and in 1845 Grand Duke Leopold II lived there. Surrounded by a large park with a pool, the hotel offers bar service, a garden with a panoramic view, and elegant dining rooms where typical Tuscan and classic Italian dishes are served. The warmly old-fashioned guest rooms, furnished partly with antiques, overlook the park. The tiled bathrooms are small but neatly organized. There's also a tennis court and an outside pool.

DINING

MODERATE

Al Mangia. Piazza del Campo 42. ☎ **0577-281-121.** Reservations recommended. Main courses 30,000–50,000L ($15–$25). AE, DC, MC, V. Tues–Sun noon–3:30pm and 7–10pm. Closed Wed Nov–Feb. Bus: A. TUSCAN/INTERNATIONAL.

Al Mangia, one of the center's most appealing restaurants, has outside tables overlooking the town hall. It was constructed more or less continuously between 1100 and the late 1600s. The food is artfully cooked and presented by a relatively formal well-trained staff, with excellent menu items changing with the seasons. Look for *pici alla Sienese* (thick noodles made only with flour and water) with a sauce of fresh tomatoes, tarragon, and cheese; spicy spaghetti with baby spring onions and sausages; *filetto alla terra di Siena* (grilled steak with a Chianti-and-tarragon sauce); osso buco with artichokes; and roasted boar *cacciatore* (hunter's style, with mushrooms and onions, available only in season). The homemade desserts include *panforte*, a cake enriched with almonds and candied fruits.

✪ **Antica Trattoria Botteganova.** Strada Chiantigiana 29 (reached via Porta Ovile, 1 mile north of the center of Siena). ☎ **0577-284-230.** Reservations recommended. Main courses 28,000–38,000L ($14–$19). AE, DC, MC, V. Tues–Sun 12:30–2:30pm and 8–10:30pm. Closed 10 days in Jan. Bus: 8 or 12. TUSCAN.

On the road leading north of the Siena to Chianti, just outside the city walls, this restaurant serves the finest meals in the city. Chef Michele Sonentino's cuisine pleases discerning locals as well as visitors. In his presentation and in his choice of first-class fresh ingredients, he tantalizes the palate based on the best of the season's offerings. Standard Italian dishes are given a modern touch; he serves old-time favorites along with more inventive platters. Try his tortelli, a kind of dumpling, stuffed with pecorino cheese and served with a hot parmigiano cheese sauce and truffled cream. Every day he offers perfectly baked or grilled fish along with the finest seasonal vegetables. Save room for *tortino di mele,* a little Sienese apple pie served warm. In the cellar is a choice of 400 wines, mainly Tuscan.

Osteria Le Logge. Via del Porrione 33. ☎ **0577-48-013.** Reservations recommended. Main courses 28,000–32,000L ($14–$16). AE, DC, MC, V. Mon–Sat noon–2:45pm and 7–10:30pm. Closed Nov 15–Dec 5. SIENESE/TUSCAN.

At the end of the 19th century, this place was a pharmacy, dispensing creams and medicines to cure the ill. Today it's been transformed into a bastion of superb cuisine in a refined and old-fashioned atmosphere. The menu, changed daily, overflows with freshness and flavor. Try the wild boar stew with spicy tomato sauce or the delectable baked duck stuffed with fennel or grapes. In autumn, devotees come here to sample pappardelle, a wide noodle dish with game sauce. The tender veal steaks are among the best in town, and you can also order taglierini pasta with black truffle sauce. Save room for one of the desserts, which are made fresh each morning.

INEXPENSIVE

Al Marsili (Ristorante Enoteca Gallo Nero). Via del Castoro 3. ☎ **0577-47-154.** Reservations recommended. Main courses 20,000–32,000L ($10–$16). AE, DC, MC, V. Tues–Sun 12:30–2:30pm and 7:30–10:30pm. Bus: A. SIENESE/ITALIAN.

This beautiful restaurant stands between the Duomo and Via di Città. You dine beneath crisscrossed ceiling vaults whose russet-colored brickwork was designed centuries ago. The antipasti offer some unusual treats, like polenta with chicken liver sauce; a medley of the best of Siena's cold cuts; and smoked venison, wild boar, and goose blended into a pâté. The wide selection of pastas ranges from the typical vegetable soup of Siena (*ribollita alla senese*) to a risotto with four cheeses. For your main course, you might opt for wild boar with tomato sauce. The *panna cotta* is a cream pudding with fresh berries and the *dolce Marsili* a soft cake flavored with coffee and mascarpone cream.

Da Guido. Vicolo Pier Pettinaio 7. ☎ **0577-280-042.** Reservations required. Main courses 16,000–23,000L ($8–$11.50). AE, DC, MC, V. Daily 12:30–3pm and 7:30–10pm. Bus: A. SIENESE/INTERNATIONAL.

Da Guido is a medieval Tuscan restaurant about 100 feet off the promenade near Piazza del Campo. It's decked out with crusty old beams, aged brick walls, arched ceilings, and iron chandeliers. Our approval is backed up by the testimony of more than 300 prominent people who've left autographed photos to adorn the walls of the three dining rooms. Meals seem to taste best when begun with selections from the antipasti table. Pastas that appeal to anyone who loves the taste of spring vegetables include *rustici alla Guido* (spaghetti laced with mushrooms, truffles, and fresh asparagus). Some of the best meat dishes are grilled over the kitchen's charcoal grill and include spicy chicken breast with rosemary, sage, garlic, and Tabasco sauce and *bistecca alla Guido,* grilled simply with a sauce of olive oil and rosemary.

La Taverna di Nello (Nello La Taverna). Via del Porrione 2830. ☎ **0577-289-043.** Reservations required. Main courses 18,000–30,000L ($9–$15). AE, DC, MC, V. Mar–Nov daily noon–3pm and 7–11pm; Dec and Feb Tues–Sat noon–3pm and 7–10pm. Closed Jan. Bus: A, B, or N. TUSCAN/VEGETARIAN.

On a narrow stone-covered street half a block from Piazza del Campo, the 1930s restaurant offers a tavern decor with brick walls, lanterns, racks of wine bottles, and sheaves of corn hanging from the ceiling. Best of all, you can view the forgelike kitchen with its crew of uniformed cooks busily preparing your dinner from behind a row of hanging copper utensils. Specialties include a salad of fresh radicchio, green lasagna ragout style, and lamb cacciatore with beans. Freshly made pasta is served every day. Your waiter will gladly suggest a local vintage. In 1998 the restaurant opened a wine bar offering more than 150 vintages from the south of Tuscany.

SIDE TRIPS FROM SIENA

MONTALCINO

Twenty-seven miles (43km) south of Siena, Montalcino is the home of the robust DOCG Brunello wine and its lighter-weight cousin, Rosso di Montalcino. Sleepy and small, Montalcino is still a well-to-do town that has remained unchanged since the 16th century, with lovely vistas. From Siena, a dozen or so TRA-IN buses make the 60- to 90-minute trip, costing 6,000L ($3) one way. The tourist office is on Via Costa del Municipio 8 (☎ and fax **0577-849-321**).

You'll find the best views from the 14th-century ✪ **Fortezza,** which also moonlights as the town's *enoteca.* Wines by the glass begin at 3,000L ($1.50), but spend a little more to sample the region's famous Brunello at 7,000L ($3.50); pair it with a savory plate of the local cheeses or salami at 8,000L ($4) for a perfect lunch. The other great place in town for wine tasting is in the Piazza del Popolo, at the **Caffè/ Fiaschetteria Italiana,** no. 6 (☎ **0577-849-043**), open Friday to Wednesday 7:30am to midnight. In the 19th-century ambience of the dining room, or at a few choice tables outside, you can revel in a self-styled Brunello tasting, with three or four varieties to choose from by the glass at 8,000 to 15,000L ($7.50). Brunello's most revered producer, Biondi-Santi, had two stellar years in 1993 and 1990. You can buy a bottle at the Fiaschetteria to bring home with you, if you want to part with 100,000L ($50).

In 1997 Montalcino's small **Civic Museum (Museo Civico)** moved its collection of Sienese paintings, which range from the 1400s to the Renaissance, to a new home, the handsomely restored former St. Augustine monastery on Via Ricasoli 31 (☎ **0577-846-014**). Admission is 8,000L ($4). It's open Tuesday to Sunday from 10am to 1pm and 2 to 5:40pm.

Outside the town walls, the 12th-century Cistercian **Abbazia di Sant'Antimo** (☎ **0577-835-659**) rests in its own pocket-sized vale amid olive trees and cypresses 6.3 miles (10km) south of Montalcino. One of Tuscany's most perfectly intact Romanesque churches, the abbey is especially worth visiting during the Gregorian chants performed daily by a handful of monks who still live there. Check the Montalcino tourist office for hours. While at Sant'Antimo, follow the signs for the nearby **Fattoria dei Barbi** (☎ **0577-848-277;** fax 0577-849-356), which has been in the same family since the 16th century and is one of the area's most respected producers of the full-bodied Brunello. Wine tastings are available Monday to Saturday, but so are excellent country meals (closed Wednesday) with most products direct from the estate's farm. Rustic accommodations at the inn will tempt you to stay on indefinitely.

PIENZA

This jewel of a Renaissance town 15 miles (24km) from Montalcino and 33 miles (53km) from Siena is easy to reach from Montalcino (to the west) by bus. (A rental car will make your life easier.)

When looking for a place to film *Romeo and Juliet* in 1968, director Franco Zefferelli found the perfect backdrop awaiting him in Pienza, so he bypassed "fair Verona" as the obvious choice. Pienza was also used in the Oscar-winning epic *The English Patient.* Despite its theatrical set depicting a medieval town, Pienza is more noteworthy as testament to the ambitions and ego of a quintessential Renaissance man. Pope Pius II (of Siena's illustrious Piccolomini family) was born here in 1405 when the town was called Corsignano, and in 1459 (a year after he was elected pope) he commissioned Florentine architect Bernardo Rossellino to level the medieval core of the town and create the first stage of what would be the model High Renaissance city. He renamed it Pienza, in his own honor.

The grand scheme didn't get very far (the pope died in 1464), but what has remained is perfectly preserved and has become a UNESCO-protected site. The graceful ✪ **Piazza Pio II** is the star of the town. Visit its **Palazzo Piccolomini** (the pope's residence, lived in by descendents of the Piccolomini family until 1968) and the **Duomo;** then walk behind the Duomo for **sweeping views** of the dormant Mt. Amiata and the wide Val d'Orcia. The piazza is also the location for the **tourist office**, Corso Rossellino 59 (☎ and fax **0578/749-071**). Ask about free guided tours of the town during summer.

You can see most of the town in half a day. It'll take only 5 minutes to cover Pienza's main drag, **Corso Rossellino,** whose food stores specialize in the gourmet products from this bountiful corner of Tuscany, namely wines, honey, and pecorino cheese (also known as *cacio*). Cheese tasting is more popular than wine tasting here, and stores offer their varieties of *fresco* (fresh), *semistagionato* (partially aged), *pepperocinato* (dusted with hot peppers), or *tartufi* (truffles). Taste as much cheese as you will, but by all means save room for lunch at the reasonably priced **Dal Falco,** Piazza Dante Alighieri 7 (☎ **0578/48551**), closed Friday. A meal of homemade *pici* pasta and a delicious grilled meat will cost around 30,000L ($15). Upstairs are six simple doubles with bathroom for 95,000L ($47.50).

7 Arezzo

50 miles (81km) SE of Florence

The most landlocked of all the towns of Tuscany, **Arezzo** was originally an Etruscan settlement and later a Roman center. The city flourished in the Middle Ages before its capitulation to Florence.

The walled town grew up on a hill, but large parts of the ancient city, including native son Petrarch's house, were bombed during World War II before the area fell to the Allied advance in the summer of 1944. Apart from Petrarch, famous sons of Arezzo have included Vasari, the painter/architect remembered chiefly for his history of the Renaissance artists, and Guido of Arezzo (sometimes known as Guido Monaco), who gave the world the modern musical scale before his death in the mid–11th century.

Today, Arezzo looks a little rustic, as if the glory of the Renaissance had long passed it by. But this isn't surprising when you consider that it lost its prosperity when Florence annexed it in 1348. Arezzo might look a bit down at the heels, but it really isn't. The city today has one of the biggest jewelry industries in western Europe. Little firms on the outskirts turn out an array of rings and chains, and bank vaults are overflowing with gold ingots. However, the inner core, which most visitors want to explore, didn't share in this gold and looks as if it needs a rehab.

If Arezzo looks familiar to you, then you might've seen Roberto Benigni's wonderful *La Vita è Bella (Life Is Beautiful),* which was partially filmed here.

ESSENTIALS

GETTING THERE A **train** comes from Florence at intervals of 20 to 60 minutes throughout the day. The trip takes between 40 and 60 minutes, costing 8,000 to 13,000L ($4 to $6.50) one way, depending on its speed. In Arezzo, trains depart and arrive at the **Stazione Centrale,** Piazza della Repubblica (☎ **1478-88-088**). Because there are no direct trains from Siena to Arezzo, rail passengers from Siena are required to make hot, prolonged, and tiresome rail transfers in the junction of Chiusi. Therefore, unless it happens to be Sunday (see below), it's better to opt for travel by bus if your point of origin is Siena.

Because of complicated transfers required en route and travel time of as much as 2½ hours each way, trips by **bus** from Florence to Arezzo aren't a good idea. Bus routes from Siena to Arezzo, however, are easier than the train transfers. Monday to Saturday, five buses per day travel from Siena directly to Arezzo. On Sunday, however, you'll have to take the train. For information on bus routes, call **ATAM Point** at ☎ **0575-38-2651** in Arrezo.

If you have a **car** and are in Rome, head north on A1; from Florence, head south on A1. In both directions, the turn-off for Arezzo is clearly marked.

VISITOR INFORMATION The **tourist office** is at Piazza della Repubblica 28 (☎ **0575-377-678**). April to September, it's open Monday to Saturday 9am to 1:15pm and 3 to 7pm and Sunday 9am to 1pm; October to May, hours are Monday to Saturday 9am to 1:15pm and 3 to 7pm and every first Sunday of the month 9am to 1pm.

SPECIAL EVENTS The biggest event on the Arezzo calendar is the **Giostra del Saraceno,** staged the third Sunday of June and the first Sunday of September on Piazza Grande. In a tradition unbroken since the 13th century, horsemen in medieval costumes reenact the lance-charging joust ritual, with balled whips cracking in the air.

EXPLORING THE TOWN

Stop by **Piazza Grande** to see the medieval and Renaissance palaces and towers that flank it, including the 16th-century loggia by Vasari.

✪ **Basilica di San Francesco.** Piazza San Francesco. ☎ **0575-20-630.** Free admission. Daily 8:30am–noon and 2–6:30pm. Guided 30-minute visits to the frescoes 10,000L ($5) on Mon–Sat 9:30–11:30am and 3–5pm; Sun 3–5pm; reserve at the number above.

This Gothic church was finished in the 14th century for the Franciscans. Inside is a Piero della Francesca masterpiece, a restored fresco cycle called ***Legend of the True Cross.*** His frescoes are remarkable for their grace, clearness, dramatic light effects, well-chosen colors, and ascetic severity. Vasari credited della Francesca as a master of the laws of geometry and perspective, and Sir Kenneth Clark called Piero's frescoes "the most perfect morning light in all Renaissance painting." The frescoes depict the burial of Adam, Solomon receiving the queen of Sheba at the court (the most memorable scene), the dream of Constantine with the descent of an angel, and the triumph of the Holy Cross with Heraclius, among other subjects.

Santa Maria della Pieve. Corso Italia. ☎ **0575-22-629.** Free admission. Mon–Sat 8am–1pm and 3–7pm; Sun 8am–1pm and 3–6:30pm.

This Romanesque church boasts a front of three open-air loggias (each pillar designed uniquely). The 14th-century bell tower is known as "the hundred holes" because it's riddled with windows. Inside, the church is bleak and austere, but there's a notable polyptych, *The Virgin with Saints,* by one of the Sienese Lorenzetti brothers (Pietro), painted in 1320.

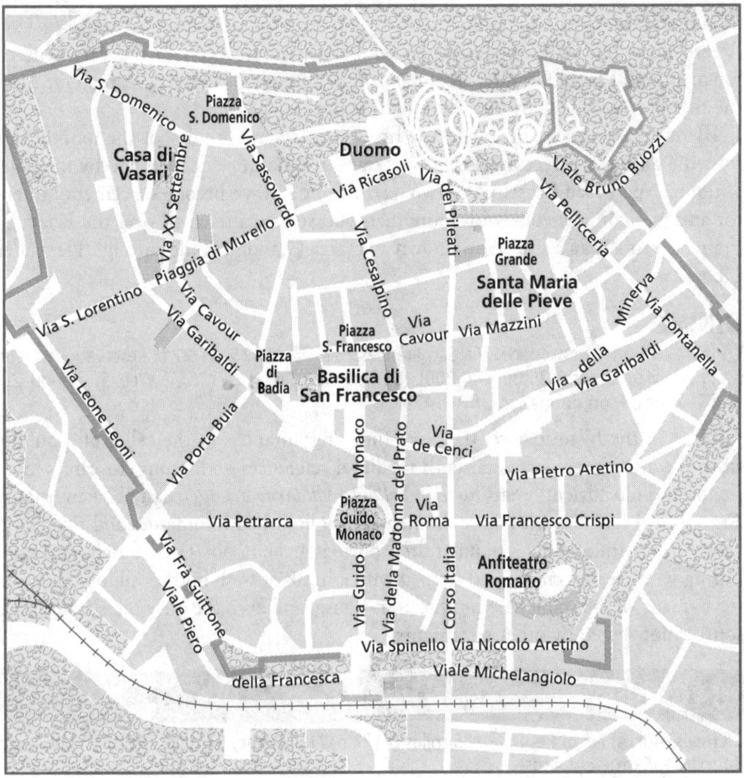

Petrarch's House (Casa di Petrarca). Via dell'Orto 28A. ☎ **0575-24-700.** Free admission (ring the bell to enter). Mon–Fri 10am–noon and 3–5pm; Sat 10am–noon. Closed Aug 1–25.

A short walk away from Santa Maria della Pieve, this house was rebuilt after war damage. Born at Arezzo in 1304, Petrarch was a great Italian lyrical poet and humanist who immortalized his love, Laura, in his sonnets. Actual mementos are few, but the house displays books, engravings, sketches, and even some furnishings from Petrarch's time.

House of Vasari (Casa Vasari). Via XX Settembre 55. ☎ **0575-300-301.** Free admission. Tues–Sat 9am–6:30pm; Sun 9am–noon.

This house was purchased by the artist (and the first art-history writer) in 1540. There are works by Vasari himself, but it's apparent that his fame rests on his *Lives of the Artists* more than it does on his actual artwork. His best works are *Virtue, Envy, and Fortune* and *Deposition.* Other works displayed are by Santi di Tito, Alessandro Allori, and Il Poppi.

Il Duomo. Piazza del Duomo. ☎ **0575-23-991.** Free admission. Daily 7am–12:30pm and 3–6pm.

The Duomo was built in the pure Gothic style, rare for Tuscany. It was begun in the 13th century, but the final touches (the facade) weren't applied until the outbreak of World War I. Its art treasures include stained-glass windows (1519–23) by Guillaume de Marcillat and a main altar in the Gothic style. Its main treasure, though, is ***Mary Magdalene,*** a Piero della Francesca masterpiece.

SHOPPING

Arezzo hosts one of Europe's biggest gold-jewelry industries. In the very center of town, around **Piazza Grande,** are dozens of antiques shops that have earned for Arezzo the title of "Ye Olde Curiosity Shop of Tuscany."

If you happen to be in Arezzo the first Saturday and Sunday of the month, don't miss the **antiques street market.** It was started some three decades ago by the Italian antiques expert Ivan Bruschi. For two days this little town becomes a center of interest for antiques connoisseurs, with more than 500 stalls scattered all over the Piazza San Francesco to Piazza Vasari (also known as Piazza Grande), going through Piazza della Libertá.

DINING

✪ **Buca di San Francesco.** Via San Francesco 1. ☎ **0575-23-271.** Reservations recommended. Main courses 25,000–40,000L ($12.50–$20). AE, DC, MC, V. Wed–Sun noon–2pm and 7–11pm; Mon noon–2pm. ITALIAN.

Located in the historic core, the city's finest restaurant is in the cellar of a building from the 1300s; it's decorated with medieval references and strong Tuscan colors of sienna and blue. Menu items include *pollo del Valdarno arrosto* (roast chicken from the Arno valley) flavored with anise, homemade tagliolini with tomatoes and ricotta, and calves' liver with onions. A popular first course is green noodles with a rich meat sauce, oozing with creamy cheese and topped with a hunk of fresh butter. All ingredients are fresh, many of the staples are produced in-house, and even the olive oil is from private sources not shared by other restaurants.

8 Gubbio

25 miles (40km) NE of Perugia, 135 miles (217km) N of Rome, 57 miles (92km) SE of Arezzo, 34 miles (55km) N of Assisi

Gubbio is one of the best-preserved medieval towns in Italy. It has modern apartments and stores on its outskirts, but once you press through that, you're firmly back in the Middle Ages. The best-known streets of its medieval core are **Via XX Settembre, Via dei Consoli, Via Galeotti,** and **Via Baldassini.** All these are in the old town (*Città Vecchia*), set against the steep slopes of Monte Ingino.

Since Gubbio is off the beaten track, it remains a fairly sleepy backwater today except for the intrepid shoppers who drive here to shop for ceramics (see below). Gubbio is almost as well known for ceramics as is Deruta. The last time Gubbio entered the history books was in 1944, when 40 hostages were murdered by the Nazis. Today, the central **Piazza dei Quaranta Martiri** is named for, and honors, those victims.

ESSENTIALS

GETTING THERE Gubbio doesn't have a rail station, so **train** passengers headed for Gubbio from other parts of Italy get off at the station of Fossato di Vico, 12 miles away, then transfer to one of the frequent buses that make the short trip on to Gubbio. One-way bus transfers to Gubbio from Fossato di Vico cost 4,000L ($2).

There are about eight **buses** a day into Gubbio from Perugia (see below). Trip time takes about 65 minutes, and a one-way ticket is 8,000L ($4). Buses arrive and depart from Piazza 40 Martiri (☎ **075-922-0066**) in the heart of town.

If you have a **car** and are coming from Rome, follow A1 to Orte and then take SS3 north 88 miles to its intersection with SS298 at Schéggia. Go southwest on SS298 for 8 miles to Gubbio. From Florence, take A1 south to Orte and then follow the directions above. From Perugia, this turnoff is 25 miles northeast on the SS298.

VISITOR INFORMATION The **tourist office,** at Piazza Oderisi 6 (☎ **075-922-0693**), is open October to February, Monday to Friday 8am to 2pm and 3 to 6pm, Saturday 9am to 1pm and 3 to 6pm; March to September, Monday to Friday 8am to 2pm and 3:30 to 6:30pm, Saturday 9am to 1pm and 3:30 to 6:30pm; Sunday year-round 9:30am to 12:30pm.

SPECIAL EVENTS The biggest annual bash is the ✪ **Corso dei Ceri** on May 15, one of Italy's top traditional festivals. It starts out with solemn ceremonies in the Piazza Grande in the morning and then turns into a wild free-for-all, as teams compete in races with giant candles, ringing bells, and vases hurled into the crowds to shatter, all culminating in a giant seafood banquet and a religious procession.

The last Sunday in May brings the **Palio della Balestra,** a traditional crossbow competition accompanied by an evening procession through the streets with lots of colorful medieval costumes.

The **Gubbio Festival** brings acclaimed international performers to town for 3 weeks of performances in late July; the town also stages free classical concerts in the ruins of the Roman theater.

EXPLORING THE OLD TOWN

If the weather is right, you can take a cable car up to **Monte Ingino,** at a height of 2,690 feet, for a panoramic view of the area. Service is daily: June to August 8:30am to 8pm (to 7:30pm April, May, and September to March). A round-trip ticket is 7,000L ($3.50).

In Gubbio, you can set about exploring a town that knew its golden age in the 1300s. Begin at **Piazza Grande,** the most important square. Here you can visit the Gothic **Palazzo dei Consoli** (☎ **075-927-4298**), housing the famed bronze *tavole eugubine,* a series of tablets as old as Christianity, discovered in the 15th century. The tablets contain writing in the mysterious Umbrian language. The museum has a display of antiques from the Middle Ages and a collection of not-very-worthwhile paintings. It's open daily: April to September, 10am to 1pm and 3 to 6pm; October to March, 10am to 1pm and 2 to 5pm. Admission is 7,000L ($3.50) .

The other major sight is the **Ducal Palace (Palazzo Ducale),** Via Ducale (☎ **075-927-5872**), built for Federico of Montefeltro. It's open Monday to Saturday 9am to 6:30pm and Sunday 9am to 1:30pm; admission is 4,000L ($2). Closed first Monday of the month.

After visiting the palace, you can go inside **Il Duomo,** Via Ducale (☎ **075-927-3980**), across the way. The cathedral is a relatively unadorned pink Gothic building with some stained-glass windows from the 12th century. It has a single nave. Inside, several arches support the ceiling. Of particular interest is the wood cross above the altar, an exquisite example of the Umbrian school of the 13th century. It's open daily 9am to 12:30pm and 3:30 to 8:30pm, and admission is free.

SHOPPING

Shopping is the major reason many visitors flock here. Gubbio's fame as a ceramics center had its beginnings in the 14th century. In the 1500s, the industry rose to the height of its fame. Sometime during this period, Mastro Giorgio pioneered a particularly intense, iridescent ruby red that awed his competitors. Today, pottery workshops are found all over town, the beautiful flowery plates lining the walls of shop doorways. You can't miss them.

Two of the best outlets are in the town center: **Ceramica Rampini,** at Via Leonardo da Vinci 94 (☎ **075-927-2963**) where you can visit the workshop, and the Rampini store at Via dei Consoli 52 (same phone). Its largest competitor, **La Mastro Giorgio,**

Piazza Grande 3 (☎ **075-927-1574**), will open its factory at Via Tifernate 10 (☎ **075-927-3616**), about half a mile from the center, to visitors who phone in advance for a convenient hour.

Gubbio is known for more than pots and vases: Its replicas of medieval crossbows (*balestre*) are prized as children's toys and macho decorative ornaments by aficionados of such things. If you want to add a touch of medieval authenticity to your den or office, head for **Medioevo,** Ponte d'Assi (☎ **075-927-2596**), or **Rafael & Giuliani Morelli,** Ponte d'Assi (☎ **075-927-1065**). Your souvenir will cost from 25,000L ($12.50) for a cheap version to as much as 150,000L ($75) for something much more substantial.

ACCOMMODATIONS

✪ **Hotel Relais Ducale.** Via Ducale 2 (overlooking Piazza Grande). ☎ **075-922-0157.** Fax 075-922-0159. www.mencarelligroup.com. E-mail: mencarelli@mencarelligroup.com. 32 units. MINIBAR TV TEL. 280,000–320,000L ($140–$160) double; 360,000L ($180) suite. Rates include breakfast. AE, MC, V.

This new hotel occupies the guest quarters of the dukes of Urbino, between their Palazzo Ducale and Piazza Grande. Hanging gardens shaded by palms and scented by jasmine offer views over the city's main square, its palazzi, and a breathtaking panorama. The elegant guest rooms boast parquet floors, damask bedspreads and curtains, and the occasional historical touch (stone vaulted ceilings) or modern luxury (Jacuzzis). Even if you're not staying here, stop by the hotel's Caffè Ducale, the most refined of the city's watering holes.

Hotel San Marco. Via Perugino 5, 06024 Gubbio. ☎ **075-922-0234.** Fax 075-927-3716. www.umbrars.com/sanmarco. E-mail: sanmarco@umbrars.com. 63 units. A/C TV TEL. 120,000–160,000L ($60–$80) double. Rates include breakfast. AE, DC, MC, V. Parking 20,000L ($10) in nearby garage.

Its unpromising location on the busiest corner in town is the San Marco's only drawback. Otherwise, this is a worthwhile hotel near a municipal parking lot. Built in stone-sided stages between 1300 and the 1700s, it contains an arbor-covered terrace and traditionally furnished guest rooms that are comfortable and well maintained, with firm mattresses. The bathrooms are small. The Restaurant San Marco serves Italian food beneath russet-colored brick vaulting.

Palace Hotel Bosone. Via XX Settembre 22, 06024 Gubbio. ☎ **075-922-0698.** Fax 075-22-0552. www.mencarelligroup.com/bosonepalace. E-mail: mencarelli@mencarelligroup.com. 32 units. MINIBAR TV TEL. 140,000–190,000L ($70–$95) double; 280,000–350,000L ($140–$175) suite. Rates include breakfast. AE, DC, MC, V. Closed 3 weeks in Feb. Free self-parking nearby.

This hotel once housed Dante Alighieri when it was owned by a patrician Gubbian family, the Bosone clan. Set at the meeting point of a flight of stone steps and a narrow street in the upper regions of town, it was built in the 1300s, enlarged during the Renaissance, and converted from a private home into a hotel in 1974. Ever since, it has been welcoming guests into its generally spacious stone-trimmed rooms, especially the Renaissance suites with stucco ceilings and 17th-century frescoes. The bathrooms come in a range of sizes, but all have hair dryers. Breakfast is the only meal served; for other meals, the staff directs guests to the Taverna del Lupo (see below).

✪ **Villa Montegranelli.** 2 miles (3km) SW of Gubbio. ☎ **075-922-0185.** Fax 075-927-3372. E-mail: montegra@tin.it. 21 units. TV TEL. 220,000–300,000L ($110–$150) double. Rates include breakfast. AE, DC, MC, V. Free parking.

The area's most tranquil retreat isn't in Gubbio but in this restored 18th-century manor house with a distant view of the town. The guest rooms are beautifully furnished, often with antiques and always with firm mattresses, and the bathrooms are modern and come with hair dryers. The public rooms have been restored in keeping with their original architecture of wood ceilings and stone walls. The staff is among the most helpful and efficient in the area, providing such thoughtful extras as a basket of fresh fruit in your room every day.

Even if you can't stay here, consider calling ahead and visiting for an excellent meal. Full dinners start at 50,000L ($25) and begin with market-fresh antipasti, followed by one of the superb homemade pastas, especially those with fresh asparagus. Veal in beet sauce is a classic dish.

DINING

You can also dine at the Hotel Relais Ducale's refined **Caffè Ducale** or at the restaurant of the **Villa Montegranelli** (see above).

Ristorante Federico de Montefeltro. Via della Repubblica 35. ☎ **075-927-3949.** Reservations recommended. Main courses 18,000–25,000L ($9–$12.50); fixed-price menu 25,000L ($12.50). AE, DC, MC, V. Fri–Wed noon–3pm and 7–11pm. ITALIAN/UMBRIAN.

Named after the feudal lord who built the ducal palace, this restaurant stands beside steeply inclined flagstones in the oldest part of the city. Inside is a pair of tavern-style dining rooms ringed with exposed stone and pinewood planking. Many of the specialties are based on ancient regional recipes, though the selection of tasty antipasti covers the traditions of most of the Italian peninsula. Menu items include platters garnished with truffles, roast suckling pig, several types of polenta, and spaghetti with mushrooms and tomato. Fresh fish is available on Friday. You'll also be served a local version of unleavened bread fried in oil as part of the meal.

Taverna del Lupo. Via Giovanni Ansidei 21. ☎ **075-927-4368.** Reservations recommended. Main courses 16,000–32,000L ($8–$16). AE, CB, DC, MC, V. Tues–Sun noon–3pm and 7–midnight. Closed Jan. ITALIAN/UMBRIAN.

This is the most authentically medieval of the many competing restaurants in Gubbio. Built in the 1200s, with unusual rows of tiles, it contains ceilings supported by barrel vaults and ribbing of solid stone, from which hang iron chandeliers. For such a relatively modest place, the menu is sophisticated and filled with the rich bounty from this part of Italy, each dish deftly prepared by a talented staff. Choose from a terrine of duck studded with truffles, supreme of pheasant, rich minestrones, or many of the pork, veal, and beef dishes that are distinctly Tuscan.

9 Perugia

50 miles (81km) SE of Arezzo, 117 miles (188km) N of Rome, 96 miles (155km) SE of Florence

Perugia was one of a dozen major cities in the mysterious Etruscan galaxy, and here you can peel away the epochs. For example, one of the town gates is called the **Arco di Augusto (Arch of Augustus).** The loggia spanning the arch dates from the Renaissance, but the central part is Roman. Builders from both periods used the reliable Etruscan foundation, which was the work of architects who laid stones to last.

Today the city, home to luscious Perugina chocolate, is the capital of Umbria; it has retained much of its Gothic and Renaissance charm, though it has been plagued with wars and swept up in disastrous events. The city is home to universities and art academies, attracting a young, vibrant crowd—some of whom can be seen in one of the zillions of local bars, pizzerias, music shops, or cafes enjoying the famous chocolate *baci* (kisses). To capture the essence of the Umbrian city, you must head for **Piazza IV Novembre** in the heart of Perugia. During the day, the square is overrun, so try to go late at night when the old town is sleeping. That's when the ghosts come out to play.

ESSENTIALS

GETTING THERE Perugia has **rail** links with Rome and Florence, but connections can be awkward. Usually, 2 trains per day from Rome connect in Foligno, where, if you miss a train, there can be a wait up to an hour or more. If possible, try to get one of the infrequent direct trains that take only 3 hours or even an IC train that cuts the trip down to 2½ hours. A one-way ticket from Rome is 20,000 to 30,000L ($10 to $15). Most trains from Florence connect in Terontola, though there are 5 daily direct trains as well. A one-way fare is 14,500L ($7.25), but direct trains impose a supplement of about 9,900L ($4.95). For information and schedules, call ☎ **075-500-7467.** The train station is well away from the main historic center of town, at Piazza Vittorio Veneto. Bus nos. 6, 7, 9, 11, and 12 run to Piazza Italia, which is as close as you can get to the center.

A daily **bus** arrives in Perugia, pulling into Piazza Partigiani, a short walk from the city's historic core. One-way fares from Rome are 25,000L ($12.50) for a transit that takes 2½ hours. The several buses that pull into Perugia from Florence charge 19,000L ($9.50) each way, for a trip that takes 2 hours. For information and schedules, call ☎ **075-500-9641.** Buses that operate exclusively in Perugia use Piazza Italia as their central base, departing and arriving there.

If you have a **car** and are coming from either Rome or Florence, Autostrada del Sole (A1) takes you to the cutoff east to Perugia. Just follow the signs. From Siena, SS73 winds its way to Perugia and connects with the autostrada. If you arrive by car, you can drive to your hotel to unload your baggage; after that, you'll be directed to a parking lot on the outskirts.

VISITOR INFORMATION The **tourist office** is at Piazza IV Novembre 3 (☎ **075-573-6458**), open Monday to Saturday 9am to 1pm and 4 to 6pm, Sunday and holidays 10am to 1pm (closed January 1 and December 25 and 26).

SPECIAL EVENTS The hottest time to visit Perugia is during Italy's foremost jazz festival, ✪ **Umbria Jazz,** mid-July 2001. Jazz heavies like Sonny Rollins and Keith Jarrett have shown up here to perform. For ticket sales and schedules, call ☎ **075-573-2432** (www.umbriajazz.com). Tickets are 25,000 to 80,000L ($12.50 to $40).

The weeklong **Eurochocolate Festival** is held annually from mid- to late October in Perugia. You can witness a chocolate-carving contest, when the scraps from the massive blocks are yours for the sampling, and entire multiple-course menus are created around the chocolate theme. Half-day lessons from visiting chefs are also available. For details, contact the Eurochocolate Organization (☎ **075-573-2670;** www.chocolate.perugia.it; E-mail: cpc@chocolate.perugia.it).

EXPLORING THE CITY

The central ✪ **Piazza IV Novembre** is one of the most beautiful squares in Italy. In the heart of the piazza is the **Grand Fountain (Fontana Maggiore),** built sometime in the late 1270s by a local architect, a monk named Bevignate. The fountain's artistic triumph stems from the sculptural work by Nicola Pisano and his son, Giovanni. Along the lower basin is statuary symbolizing the arts and sciences, Aesop's fables, the months of the year, the signs of the zodiac, and scenes from the Old Testament and Roman history. On the upper basin (mostly the work of Giovanni) is allegorical sculpture, such as a figure who represents Perugia, as well as sculptures of saints, biblical characters, and even 13th-century local officials. The fountain emerged spectacularly from a major restoration in 1999, gleaming white as new.

Most of the other major attractions either open onto Piazza IV Novembre or lie only a short distance away (see below).

Perugia

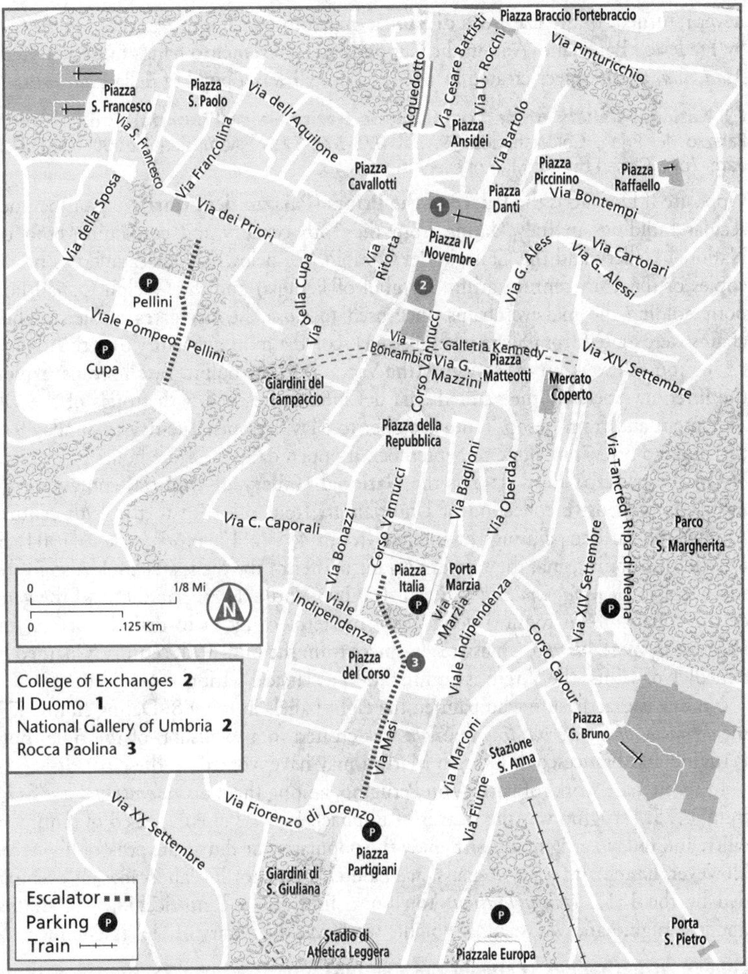

An escalator will take you from the older part of Perugia at the top of the hill and the upper slopes to the lower city. During construction, the old **Rocca Paolina** fortress, Via Marzia, was rediscovered, along with buried streets. The fortress had been covered over to make the gardens and viewing area at the end of Corso Vannucci in the last century. The old streets and street names have been cleaned up, and the area is well lighted, with an old wall exposed and modern sculpture added. The fortress was built in the 1500s by Sangallo. The Etruscan gate, **Porta Marzia,** is buried in the old city walls and can be viewed from Via Baglioni Sotterranea. This street lies in the fortress and is lined with houses, some from the 1400s. The escalator to the Rocca operates daily 6am to 1am; the Rocca is open daily 8am to 7pm.

Il Duomo (Cathedral of San Lorenzo). Piazza IV Novembre. ☎ **075-572-3832.** Free admission. Church daily 7am–12:30pm and 3:30–6:45pm. Cappelle open Mon–Sat 9–9:30am, 10:30–11am, 11:45am–12:45pm, 3:30–5:15pm; Sun 6–6:45pm.

The basilica was built in the Gothic style and dates from the 14th and 15th centuries. Its exterior is rather raw-looking, as if the builders had suddenly been called away and never returned. In the **Cappella di San Bernardino,** you'll find *Descent from the Cross* by Frederico Barocchio. And in the **Cappella del Sacremento** hangs Luca Signorelli's *Madonna,* an altarpiece created in 1484. Signorelli was a pupil of della Francesca.

✪ **National Gallery of Umbria (Galleria Nazionale dell'Umbria).** 3rd floor of the Palazzo dei Priori, Cor. Vannucci 19. ☎ **075-574-1257.** Admission 12,000L ($6). Daily 9am–7pm. Closed the 1st Mon of every month.

Opposite Il Duomo is the **Palace of the Priors (Palazzo dei Priori),** one of the finest secular buildings in Italy, dating from the 13th century and containing both the National Gallery and the Collegio del Cambio (see below). The facade holds bronze copies of the 13th-century griffin (symbol of Perugia) and the Guelph (papal) lion, both holding the massive chains once used to close the city gates of Siena. These chains were looted from Siena when Perugia scored a military victory over the town in 1358. You can walk up the stairway (the Vaccara) to the pulpit. By all means, explore the interior, especially the vaulted Sala dei Notari, frescoed with stories of the Old Testament and from Aesop. From October to May, it's open Tuesday to Sunday 9am to 1pm and 3 to 7pm (June to September, it's open daily the same hours).

On the palazzo's third floor is the **National Gallery of Umbria,** containing the most comprehensive collection of Umbrian art from the 13th to the 19th century. Among the earliest paintings of interest (room 4) is a *Virgin and Child* (1304) by Duccio di Buoninsegna, the first important master of the Sienese school. Also in this room is a small *Madonna and Child* (1405) by Gentile da Fabriano, one of the gems of the collection. In room 5 you'll see a masterpiece by Piero della Francesca, the *Polyptych of Sant'Antonio,* a massive altarpiece from the mid–15th century. Guarded by a medley of saints, the Virgin is enthroned in a classical setting.

No one is exactly sure who painted the eight panels in room 8. Dating from 1473, the *Miracles of St. Bernardino of Siena* was created in a workshop of the time. Both Perugino and Francesco di Giorgio Martini may have worked on these panels.

In room 9 are works of native-son Perugino, among them his *Adoration of the Magi* from 1475. Perugino was the master of Raphael. He was often accused of sentimentality, and today Perugino doesn't enjoy the popularity he did at the peak of his career. However, he remains a key Renaissance painter, noted for his landscapes, as exemplified by the 1517 *Transfiguration.* You'll also find art by Pinturicchio, who studied under Perugino and whose most notable work was the library of Siena's Duomo.

College of Exchanges (Collegio del Cambio). Corso Vannucci 25, street level of the Palazzo dei Priori (above). ☎ **075-572-8599.** Admission 5,000L ($2.50). Mar–Oct Mon–Sat 9am–12:30pm and 2:30–5:30pm, Sun and holidays 9am–12:30pm; Nov–Feb Tues–Sat 8am–2pm, Sun and holidays 9am–12:30pm. Closed New Year's Day, May Day, and Christmas.

During the Middle Ages, this section of the sprawling Palazzo dei Priori was conceived as a precursor of today's commodities exchanges, where grains, cloth, foodstuffs, gold, silver, and currencies were exchanged by the savvy merchants of Perugia. Today, its artistic and architectural appeal is for the most part centered around the **Hall of the Audience (Sala dell'Udienza),** a meeting room whose frescoes were painted by Perugino and his assistants, one of whom was a 17-year-old Raphael.

On the ceiling, Perugino represented the planets allegorically. The Renaissance master peopled his frescoes with the Virtues, sybils, and such biblical figures as Solomon. But his masterpiece is his own countenance. It seems rather ironic that (at least for once) Perugino could be realistic, even depicting a chubby face and double chins resting under a red cap. Another room of interest is the **Chapel of S. J. Battista (Cappella di S. J. Bastista),** which contains many frescoes painted by a pupil of Perugino, G. Nicola di Paolo.

SHOPPING

The most famous foodstuff in town comes from one of Italy's best-loved manufacturers of chocolates and bonbons, **Perugina.** Don't expect a high-glam outlet: Displays of the foil-wrapped chocolates crop up at tobacco shops, supermarkets, newspaper kiosks, and sometimes gas stations around the city. The selection includes *cioccolato al latte* (milk chocolate) and its darker counterpart, *cioccolato fondente*, both sold in everything from mouth-sized morsels (*baci*) to romance-sized decorative boxes. One always-reliable place to buy is the **Bar Ferrari,** Corso Vannucci 43 (☎ **075-575-6197**), which stockpiles Perugina products prominently amid the workaday bustle of one of the most popular bars/cafes in town.

Chocoholics who want even stronger doses of the stuff sometimes opt to visit the factory itself, which offers tours to those who phone in advance: The **Fabbrica Perugina** (☎ **075-52-761**), 3 miles (5km) west of Perugia's historic core, forms the centerpiece of the hamlet of San Sisto. It's open Monday to Friday 9am to 12:30 and 2:30 to 5pm (Saturday and Sunday by arrangement). Admission is free. Call to book your visit.

Looking for ceramics and souvenirs that'll last longer than chocolate? Head for Perugia's most interesting shops, **La Bottega dei Bassai,** Via Baglioni (☎ **075-572-3108**), and **Ceccucci,** Corso Vannucci 38 (☎ **075-573-5143**).

If you're searching for fashion, particularly the cashmere garments that are tailored and often designed in Perugia, consider a jaunt 4 miles (6km) south to the village of Ponta San Giovanni, where one of the largest inventories of cashmere garments (coats, suits, dresses, and sweaters) for men and women is stockpiled at **Big Bertha,** Ponte San Giovanni (☎ **075-599-7572**).

ACCOMMODATIONS

✪ **Hotel Brufani.** Piazza Italia 12, 06100 Perugia. ☎ **075-573-2541.** Fax 075-572-0210. www.italyhotels.com/sina/. E-mail: brufani@tin.it. 93 units. A/C MINIBAR TV TEL. 539,000L ($269.50) double; 880,000L ($440) suite. AE, CB, MC, V. Parking 40,000L ($20).

Situated at the top of the city, part of this five-star hotel was built by Giacomo Brufani in 1884 on the ruins of the ancient Rocca Paolina, a site known to the ancient Romans that later served as a papal address. At press time, the Brufani was joining forces with the much larger Palace Hotel Bellavista (they shared the same location) to become one of the leading five-star hotels in Umbria. The Bellavista was built in the late 1800s as a home for a prominent English family, the Collinses, who eventually married into the aristocratic Brufanis. Now there's a wedding again. Many of the medium-sized to spacious guest rooms open onto views of the countryside. Some of the grander rooms have antiques and frescoed ceilings, but all are elegant and filled with modern amenities like hair dryers.

Dining: The cafe/restaurant, Collins, is named for the great-grandfather of Mr. Bottelli, who succeeded the original owner, Mr. Brufani, nearly a century ago. It's the most formal dining room in Perugia, serving an array of international and Umbrian specialties.

Hotel Fortuna Perugia. Via Bonazzi 19, 06123 Perugia. ☎ **075-572-2845.** Fax 075-573-5040. www.umbriahotels.com. 33 units. A/C MINIBAR TV TEL. 180,000–214,000L ($90–$107) double. Rates include breakfast. AE, DC, MC, V. Parking 25,000L ($12.50) nearby.

Here's a chance to stay at a four-star hotel that in 1996 deliberately "downgraded" itself to three-star status and lowered its prices. In the heart of town, it dates from the 14th century but has been extensively reconstructed over the years. Today, arched leaded-glass doors lead to an interior of hardwood floors and tasteful art. The guest rooms boast sleek contemporary styling (often blond woods and flamboyant fabrics) and are filled with modern amenities, like deluxe mattresses. Even better than the rooms are the views, some of which might have inspired Perugino himself. The bathrooms are medium in size, with hair dryers. The hotel has a reading room, a cozy bar, and a rooftop terrace opening onto the tile roofs of the town and the Umbrian landscape. When the weather is right, guests take their cappuccinos and croissants here. There's no restaurant, but many trattorie are almost literally outside the door.

Hotel La Rosetta. Piazza Italia 19, 06121 Perugia. ☎ and fax **075-572-0841.** 96 units. MINIBAR TV TEL. 210,000–250,000L ($105–$125) double; 295,000L ($147.50) suite. Rates include breakfast. AE, DC, MC, V. Parking 30,000L ($15).

Since this Perugian landmark opened in 1927, it has expanded from a seven-room pensione to a labyrinthine complex (it's the big hangout for the musicians in town for the jazz festival). With its frescoed ceiling, Suite 55 has been declared a national treasure. (The bullet holes that papal mercenaries shot into the ceiling in 1848 have been artfully preserved.) The less grandiose guest rooms include decors ranging from slickly contemporary to Victorian to 1960s style. Each unit is peaceful, clean, and comfortable, with a firm mattress. The bathrooms range from small to medium, with hair dryers. The restaurant is recommended under "Dining," below.

Locanda della Posta. Corso Vannucci 97, 06121 Perugia. ☎ **075-572-8925.** E-mail: novelber@tin.it. 40 units. A/C MINIBAR TV TEL. 300,000L ($150) double; 360,000L ($180) suite. Rates include buffet breakfast. AE, DC, MC, V. Parking 25,000L ($12.50) in nearby garage.

Goethe and Hans Christian Andersen slept here—in fact, this used to be the only hotel in Perugia. It sits on the main street of the oldest part of town, behind an impressive ornate facade sculpted in the 1700s. The della Posta's views may not be as grand, but it's more nostalgic and inviting. The guest rooms are generally spacious, with fabric-covered walls, art nouveau floral prints, and sturdy wood furnishings, including firm beds. Each bathroom is well appointed.

Sangallo Palace Hotel. Via Masi 9, 06100 Perugia. ☎ **075-573-0202.** Fax 075-573-0068. www.sangallo.it. E-mail: hotel@sangallo.it. 93 units. A/C MINIBAR TV TEL. 210,000–314,000L ($105–$157) double; from 395,000L ($197.50) suite. Rates include breakfast. AE, DC, MC, V.

Ranking just under the Brufani, this palace in the historic zone is modern and elegant, so up-to-date with audiovisual facilities and such that it's the preferred choice for conferences held in Perugia. A roomy interior and a lobby of marble columns and fine furnishings are immediately welcoming. The halls are lined with reproductions of the works of Perugino, and over each bed is a framed reproduction of a Perugino or Pinturicchio. The medium-sized to spacious guest rooms boast many amenities, like private safes and wide beds with firm mattresses. Many open onto panoramic views of the countryside. Many of the tiled bathrooms have Jacuzzis.

Dining: Il Sangallo restaurant is justifiably praised for its Umbrian and national cuisine. Much of the produce comes from the Umbrian countryside, and the cellar is well stocked in regional wines. In summer, meals are served on the terrace.

Amenities: Room service, concierge, laundry/dry cleaning, indoor pool, gym.

DINING

Il Falchetto. Via Bartolo 20. ☎ **075-573-1775.** Reservations recommended. Main courses 30,000–60,000L ($15–$30). AE, CB, DISC, MC, V. Tues–Sun noon–2:30pm and 7:30–10:30pm. Closed Jan 15–31. UMBRIAN/ITALIAN.

This restaurant, a short walk from Piazza Piccinino (where you'll be able to park), has flourished in this 19th-century building since 1941. The dining room in the rear has the most medieval ambience, its stone walls dating from the 1300s. In summer you might like a table outside. Many of the dishes adhere to traditional themes and have a certain zest. Menu items include *tagliatelle* (flat noodles) with truffles, grilled trout from the Nera River, prosciutto several ways, pasta with chickpeas, grilled goat filet, and filet steak with truffles. One special dish is *falchetti* (gnocchi with ricotta and spinach). Some of the best Umbrian wines are served.

La Rosetta. In the Hotel La Rosetta, Piazza Italia 19. ☎ **075-572-0841.** Reservations recommended, especially in summer. Main courses 16,000–40,000L ($8–$20). AE, DC, MC, V. Tues–Sun 12:30–3pm and 7:30–10pm. UMBRIAN.

La Rosetta has gained more fame than the hotel containing it. Every politician from the area uses the restaurant, and during the Perugia jazz festival it's overrun with musicians. You'll find three dining areas: an intimate wood-paneled salon, a main dining area divided by Roman arches and lit by brass chandeliers, and a courtyard enclosed by the hotel's walls. Under shady palms, you can have a leisurely meal that's both simple and reliable. The choice is vast, but a few specialties stand out: To begin, the finest dishes are *spaghetti alla Norcina* (with truffle sauce) and *vol-au-vent di tortellini Rosetta.* Among the main dishes are grilled swordfish with truffle-stuffed tortellini and *scallopine Rosetta* (fillet of veal drenched in a sauce with rochefort cheese)—a regional specialty you either love or hate.

La Taverna. Via delle Streghe 8. ☎ **075-572-4128.** Reservations recommended. Main courses 20,000–30,000L ($10–$15). AE, DC, MC, V. Tues–Sun 12:30–2:30pm and 7:30–11pm. UMBRIAN.

One of Umbria's most innovative restaurants, La Taverna occupies a medieval house. Its entrance is at the bottom of one of the narrowest alleys in town, in the heart of the historic center. (Prominent signs indicate its position off Corso Vannucci.) Three dining rooms, filled with exposed masonry, oil paintings, and a polite staff, radiate from the high-ceilinged vestibule. The cuisine is inspired by Claudio Brugalossi, an Umbrian chef who spent part of his career in Tampa, Florida, working for the Hyatt chain. Menu choices include truffle-stuffed ravioli, tagliata with arugula, veal slices with raisins and pine nuts, and grilled red snapper.

✪ **Osteria del Bartolo.** Via Bartolo 30. ☎ **075-573-1561.** Reservations recommended. Main courses 25,000–40,000L ($12.50–$20); fixed-price tasting menu 125,000L ($62.50). AE, DC, MC, V. Mon–Sat 1–2:45pm and 8–10:30pm. Closed Jan. UMBRIAN.

In a palazzo with 14th-century foundations, this family-run restaurant is known for its fresh ingredients, culinary flair, and elegant presentations. Straight from the cookbooks of the 1600s, *botaccio* is farmer's bread stuffed with sausage, vegetables, and a sharp pecorino cheese and then baked in the oven. Also tempting are fresh tortelli with porcini mushrooms, ricotta, steamed tomatoes, and olive oil. The restaurant makes its own butter twice a day, its own bread once a day, and its own pasta with every order. The chef also makes his own desserts. There's enough distance between tables to allow discreet conversations.

Trattoria Ricciotto. Piazza Dante 19. ☎ **075-572-1956.** Reservations recommended. Main courses 18,000–30,000L ($9–$15); fixed-price menus 30,000–55,000L ($15–$27.50). AE, DC, V. Mon–Sat 12:30–3pm and 7:30–10pm. UMBRIAN.

Since 1888, this rustically elegant restaurant has been owned and operated by members of the Betti family, who cook, serve, and uncork the wine. In a building dating in part from the 14th century, it offers well-prepared dishes like fettuccine with truffles, *macaroni arrabbiata* (pasta with tomatoes and red and green peppers), spring lamb chasseur, and *fagotti Monte Bianco* (turkey with parmigiano, ham, and cream sauce).

One of the most satisfying meals is a platter with two cuts of veal, served with spinach soufflé and roasted potatoes. What's a good preface? Consider *tagliatelle* (flat noodles) with green olives, or macaroni with mushrooms and cream sauce.

PERUGIA AFTER DARK

Begin your evening by joining Italy's liveliest *passeggiata* (a promenade at dusk) along **Corso Vannucci,** a pedestrian strip running north to south. Everyone, especially the students of Perugia, seems to stroll here. Many drop into one of the little cafes or *enoteche* for a drink. If you cafe hop or wine-bar crawl, you can sample as many as 150 wines from 60 Umbrian vineyards—providing you can stay on your feet.

Two cafes outshine the rest: The better is chandelier-lit **Sandri Pasticceria,** Corso Vannucci 32 (☎ **075-572-4112**), offering drinks, cakes, pastries, and sandwiches. You can also order full meals, including eggplant parmigiana and veal cutlet Milanese. It's another outlet for the city's famous chocolates. Sandri's main competitor is **Caffè del Cambio,** Corso Vannucci 29 (☎ **075-572-4165**), a favorite of university students. The first room, with its vaulted ceiling, is most impressive; it contains racks of pastries, cones of ice cream, a long stand-up bar, and a handful of tiny tables. The low-ceilinged room in back is smoky, more crowded, and much livelier.

In the **Australian Pub,** Via del Verzaro 39 (☎ **075-572-0206**), the ambience is more southern hemisphere than southern Mediterranean. The **Hostaria del Lupo Mannaro,** Via Guardabassi 4, near Piazza Morlacchi (☎ **075-573-6827**), is an affordable Umbrian restaurant until about 10pm, when it transforms itself into a wine bar for a few hours. It's a funky, loud spot where, later in the evening, recorded music reverberates off the old stones of the very old vaulting.

A SIDE TRIP TO SHOP FOR CERAMICS IN DERUTA

One of the highlights of a trip to this part of Italy is shopping for a product that has been associated with Umbria since the days of the Renaissance painters. The manufacturing town of **Deruta,** 12½ miles (20km) south of Perugia off Via Flaminia (beside E45 in the direction of Rome), has more than 300 manufacturers lining both sides of the town's main street. If you're not driving, you can catch one of six daily buses marked "Perugia-Deruta" at Perugia's Piazza Partigiana.

By the way, don't even think of saying the word *porcelain* within earshot of anyone in town. (*Stoneware* or, even better, *glazed terra-cotta* is preferred.) Terra-cotta clay is formed into sturdy bowls, umbrella stands, plates, cups, and art objects; they're fired and then glazed with distinctive arabesques and bright colors before being fired again. Especially popular is a design associated with the region since the Renaissance (when Raphael commissioned some of the ceramic ware here): a motif of dragons cavorting amid flowers and vines.

The largest manufacturer, with some of the most reliable shipping services and the biggest sampling of wares, is **Ubaldo Grazie,** Via Tiberina 181 (☎ **075-971-0201**). It's a sophisticated place, selling fine copies of antique designs plus sleeker, more contemporary pieces. Many pieces of their colorfully painted stoneware are featured in Tiffany's, Bergdorf Goodman, and upscale mail-order catalogs like Williams-Sonoma. Their specialties include cachepots, vases, and dinnerware. Anything you buy on site can be shipped via UPS to any destination in the world. The factory outlet is open Monday to Friday 9am to 1pm and 2:30 to 6:30pm, Saturday 9am to 1pm. Free factory tours, lasting about half an hour, are sometimes offered to those who phone and reserve in advance.

A less comprehensive nearby competitor is **Antonio Margaritelli,** Via Tiberina 214 (☎ **075-971-1572**). Founded in 1975, this factory outlet stocks material that's roughly equivalent to that at the Ubaldo Grazie factories but with a less diverse selection.

Before you buy, you can get a fast education in the town's ceramic traditions from the **Museo della Ceramica Umbra,** Palazzo del Comune, Piazza dei Consoli (☎ **075-971-1143**). It's open Tuesday to Sunday 10am to 1pm and 3 to 6pm, charging 5,000L ($2.50) for a view of ceramics produced in the region between the 1500s and today. The museum was enlarged and expanded in 1997, almost as a gesture of civic pride.

10 Assisi

110 miles (177km) N of Rome, 15 miles (24km) SE of Perugia

Ideally placed on the rise to Mt. Subasio, watched over by the medieval Rocco Maggiore, the purple-fringed Umbrian hill town of **Assisi** retains a mystical air. The site of many a pilgrimage, Assisi is forever linked in legend with its native son, St. Francis. The gentle saint founded the Franciscan order and shares honors with St. Catherine of Siena as the patron saint of Italy. But he's remembered by many, even non-Christians, as a lover of nature (his preaching to an audience of birds is one of the legends of his life). Dante compared him to John the Baptist.

St. Francis put Assisi on the map, and making a pilgrimage here is one of the highlights of a visit to Umbria. Today, Italy's Catholic youth flock here for religious conferences, festivals, and reflection. But even without St. Francis, the hill town merits a visit for its interesting sights and architecture. Sightseers and pilgrims simply pack the town in summer, and at Easter or Christmas you're likely to be trampled underfoot. We've found it best and less crowded in spring or fall.

Assisi was hit by the devastating twin earthquakes that shook Umbria in 1997, but the recovery and restoration have been remarkable, although much remains yet to be done. Massive damage was caused to a great many historical sights, but the major attraction, the Basilica di San Francesco, reopened late in 1999 in time to greet visitors at the Jubilee.

ESSENTIALS

GETTING THERE Although there's no **rail station** in Assisi, the city lies within a 30-minute bus or taxi ride from the rail station in nearby Santa Maria degli Angeli. From Santa Maria degli Angeli, buses depart at 30-minute intervals for Piazza Matteotti, in the heart of Assisi. One-way fares are 2,500L ($1.25). If you're coming to Assisi from Perugia by train, expect to pay around 3,500L ($1.75) one way. If you're coming from Rome, expect to pay around 25,500L ($12.75) each way. From either of those points, expect a transfer en route in Foligno. Rail fares between Florence and Assisi are about 24,000L ($12) each way and usually require a transfer in the junction of Terontola.

Frequent **buses** connect Perugia (see above) with Assisi, the trip taking 1 hour and costing 6,500L ($3.25) one way. One bus a day arrives from Rome. Requiring about 3 hours, it costs 30,000L ($15) one way. Two buses pull in from Florence, taking 2 1/2 hours and costing 25,000L ($12.50) one way.

If you have a **car,** in 30 minutes from Perugia you can be in Assisi by taking S3 southwest. At the junction of Route 147, just follow the signs toward Assisi. But you'll have to park outside the town's core, as those neighborhoods are usually closed to traffic. (*Note:* The police officer guarding the entrance to the old town will usually let motorists drop off luggage at a hotel in the historic zone, with the understanding that you'll eventually park in a lot on the outskirts of town. Likewise, delivery vehicles are allowed to drop off supplies in the town's pedestrian zones daily 10am to noon and 4 to 6pm.)

VISITOR INFORMATION The **tourist office** is at Piazza del Comune 12 (☎ **075-812-534**), open Monday to Friday 8am to 2pm and 3:30 to 6:30pm, Saturday 9am to 1pm and 3:30 to 6:30pm, and Sunday 9am to 1pm.

SPECIAL EVENTS The first weekend after May 1 brings the **Calendimaggio** spring festival, with processions, medieval contests of strength and skill, late-night partying in 14th-century costumes, and singing duels on the main piazza.

EXPLORING THE TOWN

Piazza del Comune, in the heart of Assisi, is a dream for lovers of architecture from the 12th to the 14th century. On the square is a pagan structure, with six Corinthian columns, called the **Temple of Minerva (Tempio di Minerva),** from the 1st century B.C. With Minerva-like wisdom, the people of Assisi turned the interior into a baroque church so as not to offend the devout. Adjoining the temple is the 13th-century **Tower (Torre),** built by Ghibelline supporters. The site is open daily 7am to noon and 2:30pm to dusk.

✪ **Basilica di San Francesco.** Piazza San Francesco. ☎ **075-819-001.** Free admission. Daily 8:30am–5:30pm.

This important basilica, with both an upper (1230–53) and a lower church (1228–30), houses some of the most important **cycles of frescoes** in Italy, including works by such pre-Renaissance giants as Cimabue and Giotto. The basilica and its paintings form the most significant monument to St. Francis, a focal point of both high art and intense spirituality. After a major restoration effort involving some of Europe's greatest craftspeople, the basilica reopened to the public late in 1999 after having been closed in the aftermath of the 1997 earthquake, though some work is still going on as of this writing.

On the entrance wall, you can enjoy ✪ **Giotto's celebrated frescoes of St. Francis** preaching to the birds. In the nave is the cycle of 27 additional frescoes, some by Giotto, though the authorship of the entire cycle is uncertain. Many of these are almost surrealistic (in architectural frameworks), like a stage set that strips away the walls and allows you to see the actors inside. In the cycle, you can see pictorial evidence of the rise of humanism that led to Giotto's and Italy's split away from the rigidity of Byzantium.

The upper church also contains a damaged Cimabue masterpiece, his *Crucifixion.* Time and quakes have robbed the fresco of its former radiance, but its power and ghostlike drama remain at least on video. The cycle of badly damaged frescoes in the transept and apse are other works by Cimabue and his helpers.

The **lower church** was speedily reopened after the quakes, its damages only marginal. Reached by the entrance in Piazza Inferiore on the south side of the basilica, it's dark and mystical (if you're lucky enough to find a moment of calm between the arrival of fender-to-fender tour buses) and almost entirely covered with frescoes by the greatest pre-Renaissance painters of the 13th and 14th centuries. Look for Cimabue's faded but masterly *Virgin and Child* with four angels and St. Francis looking on from the far right; it's often reproduced in detail as one of Cimabue's greatest works. On the other side is the *Deposition from the Cross,* a masterpiece by Sienese artist Pietro Lorenzetti, plus a *Madonna and Child* with St. John and St. Francis (stigmata showing). In a chapel honoring St. Martin of Tours, Simone Martini of Siena painted a cycle of frescoes, with great skill and imagination, depicting the life and times of that saint. Finally, under the lower church is the **crypt of St. Francis,** with some relics of the saint. In the past, only scholars and clergymen were allowed access to the vaults containing these highly cherished articles, but now anyone can visit. Some of the items

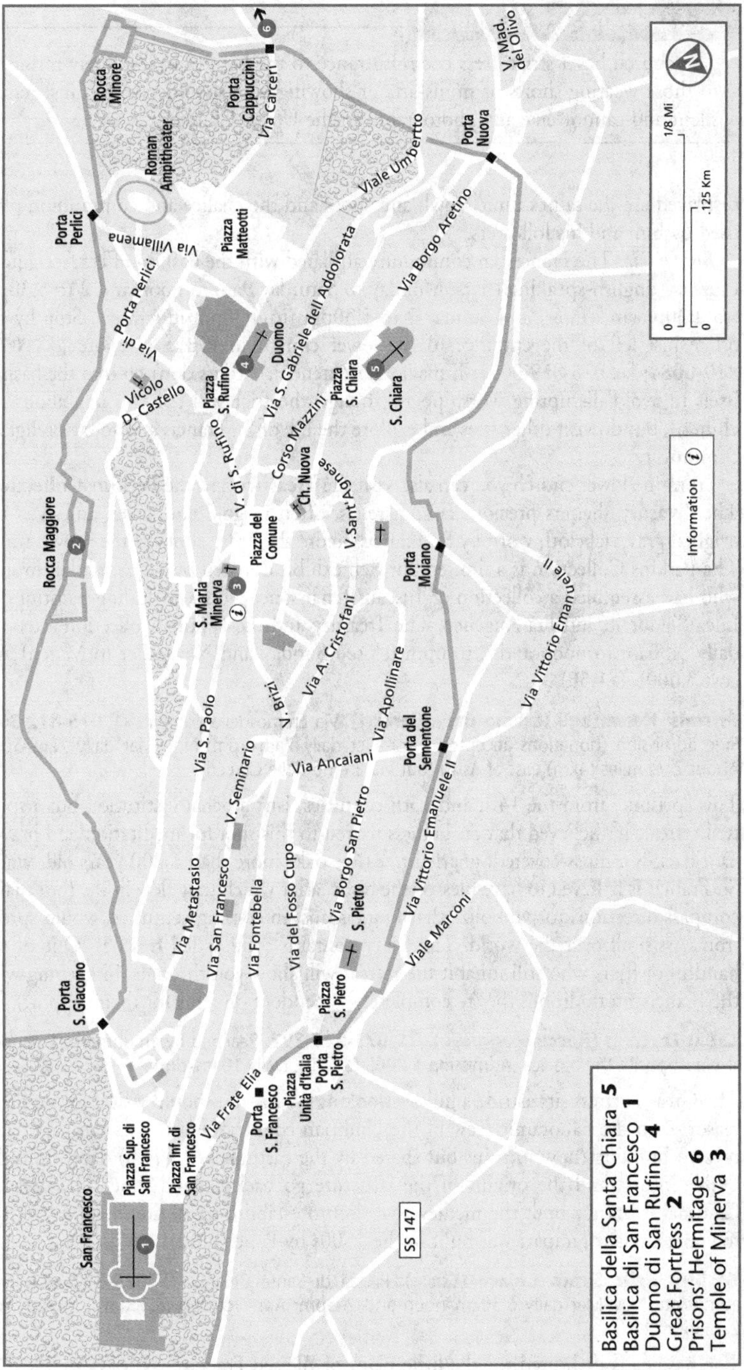
Basilica della Santa Chiara 5
Basilica di San Francesco 1
Duomo di San Rufino 4
Great Fortress 2
Prisons' Hermitage 6
Temple of Minerva 3
San Francesco
Piazza Sup. di San Francesco
Piazza Inf. di San Francesco
Via Frate Elia
Porta S. Francesco
Piazza Unità d'Italia
Porta S. Pietro
Piazza S. Pietro
S. Pietro
Porta S. Giacomo
Via Metastasio
Via San Francesco
Via Fontebella
Via del Fosso Cupo
Via Borgo San Pietro
Via Vittorio Emanuele II
Viale Marconi
SS 147
V. Seminario
Via S. Paolo
Via Ancaiani
Porta del Sementone
Via Apollinare
V. Brizi
Via A. Cristofani
Via Vittorio Emanuele II
Rocca Maggiore
S. Maria Minerva
Piazza del Comune
Porta Moiano
V. Sant'Agnese
Ch. Nuova
V. di S. Rufino
Corso Mazzini
Vicolo D. Castello
Piazza S. Rufino
Duomo
Via S. Gabriele dell'Addolorata
Piazza S. Chiara
S. Chiara
Via Borgo Aretino
Via di Porta Perlici
Via Villamena
Porta Perlici
Piazza Matteotti
Roman Ampitheater
Rocca Minore
Porta Cappuccini
Via Carceri
Viale Umbertto
Porta Nuova
V. Mad. del Olivo
Information
0
.125 Km
0
1/8 Mi

A San Francesco Warning

The church has a strict dress code: Entrance to the basilica is absolutely forbidden to those wearing shorts or miniskirts or showing bare shoulders. You must remain silent and cannot take any photographs in the Upper Church.

displayed are the saint's tunic, cowl, and shoes and the chalice and communion plate used by him and his followers.

Insider Tip: The Franciscan community affiliated with the basilica offers free guided tours by English-speaking friars: Monday to Saturday 9am to noon and 2 to 5:30pm (to 4:30pm in winter) and Sunday 2 to 5:30pm (to 4:30pm in winter). Stop by the office just left of the entrance to the lower church in Piazza Inferiore (☎ **075-819-0084;** fax 075-819-0035; E-mail: chiu@krenet.it). Tours don't go into the basilica itself to avoid disrupting worshippers (though the friar will tell you lots about the church), but do visit other sites and explore the life of St. Francis and today's religious community.

From the lower church you can also visit the **Treasury** and the **Perkins Collection.** The Treasury shelters precious church relics, often in gold and silver, and even the original gray sackcloth worn by St. Francis before the order adopted the brown tunic. The Perkins Collection is a limited but rich exhibit donated by a U.S. philanthropist who had assembled a collection of Tuscan/Renaissance works, including paintings by Luca Signorelli and Fra Angelico. The Treasury and the Perkins Collection are open daily 9:30am to noon and 2 to 6pm (closed Sunday and November to March) and cost 3,000L ($1.50) .

Prisons' Hermitage (Eremo delle Carceri). Via Eremo delle Carceri. ☎ **075-812-301.** Free admission (donations accepted). Apr–Oct daily 7am–7pm; Nov–Mar daily 7am–5pm. About 2$^{1}/_{2}$ miles (4km) east of Assisi (out Via Eremo delle Carceri).

This "prison," from the 14th and 15th centuries, isn't a penal institution but a spiritual retreat. It's believed that St. Francis retired to this spot for meditation and prayer. Out back is a moss-covered, gnarled *ilex* (live oak) more than 1,000 years old, where St. Francis is believed to have blessed the birds, after which they flew in the four major compass directions to symbolize that Franciscans, in coming centuries, would spread from Assisi all over the world. The friary contains some faded frescoes. One of the handful of friars who still inhabit the retreat will show you through (in keeping with the Franciscan tradition, they're completely dependent on alms for their support).

Great Fortress (Rocca Maggiore). ☎ **075-815-292.** Reached by an unmarked stepped street opposite the basilica. Admission 5,000L ($2.50). Daily 10am–dusk.

The Great Fortress sits astride a hill overlooking Assisi. You should visit if for no other reason than the panoramic view of the Umbrian countryside from its ramparts. The present building (now in ruins but spared by the earthquakes' wrath) dates from the 14th century, and the origins of the structure go back beyond time. The dreaded Cardinal Albornoz built the medieval version to establish papal domination over the town. A circular rampart was built in the 1500s by Pope Paul III.

Basilica della Santa Chiara (Clare). Piazza di Santa Chiara. ☎ **075-812-282.** Free admission. Nov–Mar daily 6:30am–noon and 2–5pm; Apr–Oct daily 6:30am–12:05pm and 2–6:55pm.

The basilica is dedicated to "the little plant of Blessed Francis," as St. Clare liked to describe herself. Born in 1193 into one of the noblest families of Assisi, Clare gave all her wealth to the poor and founded, together with St. Francis, the Order of the Poor Clares. She was canonized by Pope Alexander IV in 1255.

Though many of the frescoes that once adorned the basilica have been completely or partially destroyed (not as a result of the quakes), much remains that's worthy of note. Upon entering, your attention will be caught by the striking *Crucifix* behind the main altar, a painting on wood dating from the time of the church itself (ca. 1260). The work is by "the Master of St. Clare," who's also responsible for the beautiful icons on either side of the transept. In the left transept is an oft-reproduced fresco of the Nativity from the 14th century. The basilica houses the remains of St. Clare as well as the crucifix under which St. Francis received his command from above.

The closest bus stop is near Porta Nuova, the eastern gate to the city at the beginning of Viale Umberto I. The bus doesn't have a number; it departs from the depot in Piazza Matteotti for its first run to the train station at 5:35am and concludes its final run at 11:59pm. Buses arrive at half-hour intervals.

Beware: The custodian turns away visitors in shorts, miniskirts, plunging necklines, and backless or sleeveless attire.

Duomo di San Rufino. Piazza San Rufino. ☎ **075-812-285.** Church free; crypt and museum 3,000L ($1.50) . May–Oct daily 10am–noon and 2:30–6pm (weekends only Nov–Apr).

Built in the mid 12th century, the Duomo is graced with a Romanesque facade, greatly enhanced by rose windows. This is one of the finest churches in the hill towns, as important as the one at Spoleto. Adjoining it is a bell tower (*campanile*). Inside, the church has been baroqued, an unfortunate decision that destroyed the purity that the front suggests. St. Francis and St. Clare were both baptized here. The church was spared any damage during the quakes.

ACCOMMODATIONS

Space in Assisi tends to be tight, so reservations are vital. For such a small town, however, it has a good number of accommodations.

Albergo Ristorante del Viaggiatore. Via San Antonio 14, 06081 Assisi. ☎ **075-816-297** or 075-812-424. Fax 075-813-051. 16 units. TV TEL. 115,000L ($57.50) double. Half-board 80,000L ($40) per person. Rates include breakfast. DC, MC, V.

This budget choice offers a great value. The ancient town house has been totally renovated, though the stone walls and arched entryways of the lobby hint at its age. The high-ceilinged guest rooms are spacious and contemporary, with mattresses that are a bit thin but still offer comfort. The bathrooms, however, are cramped. The restaurant has been operated by the same family for years and offers excellent local and regional fare and wines.

Hotel dei Priori. Corso Mazzini 15, 06081 Assisi. ☎ **075-812-237.** Fax 075-816-804. www.assind.perugia.it/hotel/dpriori. E-mail: hpriori@assind.edisons.it. 34 units. 140,000–239,000L ($70–$119.50) double; 248,000–300,000L ($124–$150) suite. Rates include breakfast. AE, DC, MC, V. Parking 20,000L ($10) nearby.

Opened in 1923, this hotel occupies one of the town's most historic buildings, dating back to the 16th century, when it was known as the Palazzo Nepis. A homelike, somewhat old-fashioned Umbrian atmosphere prevails. Marble staircases and floors, terracotta, vaulted ceilings, and stone-arched doors remain from its heyday. Antiques and tasteful prints in both the guest rooms and the public areas add grace notes, along with a collection of Oriental rugs. Many of the rooms are a bit small, however, each with a comfortable bed and a tidy bath. The hotel also has a bar and serves Umbrian specialties only to hotel guests and only from April to October.

Hotel Giotto. Via Fontebella 41, 06082 Assisi. ☎ **075-812-209.** Fax 075-816-479. 72 units. TV TEL. 200,000–240,000L ($100–$120) double; 350,000L ($175) suite. Rates include breakfast. AE, DC, MC, V. Closed Nov–Mar. Free parking.

The Giotto is up-to-date and well run, built at the edge of town on several levels and opening onto panoramic views. Some of the foundations are 500 years old, but because of frequent modernizations it's hard to tell. Though targeted by tour groups, this is the best hotel in Assisi (the Subasio, its major competitor, is disappointing). It offers spacious modern public rooms and comfortable guest rooms; bright colors predominate, though many rooms look tatty. The small bathrooms still manage to have adequate shelf space. There are small formal gardens and terraces for meals or sunbathing.

Hotel Sole. Corso Mazzini 35, 06081 Assisi. ☎ **075-812-373** or 075-812-922. Fax 075-813-706. www.umbria.org/hotel/sole. E-mail: sole@techonet.it. 36 units. TV TEL. 120,000L ($60) double; 150,000L ($75) triple. Rates include breakfast. Half-board (Apr–Nov) 85,000L ($42.50) per person. AE, CB, DC, MC, V.

For Umbrian hospitality and a general down-home feeling, the Sole is a winner. The severe beauty of rough stone walls and ceilings, terra-cotta floors, and marble staircases pay homage to the past, balanced by big-cushioned chairs in the TV lounge and contemporary wrought-iron beds with comfortable mattresses and well-worn furnishings in the guest rooms. Some rooms are across the street in an annex. The hotel shows some wear and tear, but the price is right and the location is central. The family owners also offer one of the town's best cuisines under the 15th-century vaults of their restaurant open April to November. The food is so savory you might want to take the meal plan here—the restaurant is a good choice even if you aren't a guest.

✪ **Hotel Umbra.** Via dei Archi 6 (just off the west end of Piazza dei Commune), 06081 Assisi ☎ **075-812-240.** Fax 075-813-653. www.caribusiness.it/carifo/az/hotelumbra. 25 units. A/C MINIBAR TV TEL. 160,000–215,000L ($80–$108) double. Rates include breakfast. AE, DC, MC, V. Closed Jan–Easter. Parking 18,000L ($7.25).

Only the odd pointed-stone Gothic arch and a few other architectural elements remain from the collection of 13th-century houses from which the Umbra was converted. The large whitewashed rooms contain agreeable old antique dressers, desks, and armoires. Many rooms have views over the valley and rooftops; some have balconies. The new bathrooms are sheathed in marble or feature brass fixtures. The restaurant is well-regarded and offers outdoor dining on a terrace in summer.

St. Anthony's Guest House. Via Galeazzo Alessi 10, 06081 Assisi. ☎ **075-12-542.** Fax 075-813-723. 20 units. 80,000L ($40) double. Rates include breakfast. No credit cards. Closed Nov–Jan. Parking 5,000L ($2.50).

This isn't a traditional hotel, but a religious guesthouse. This special place provides economical comfortable rooms in a medieval villa turned guest house operated by the Franciscan Sisters of the Atonement (an order that originated in Graymoor, New York) and located on the upper ledges of Assisi. The guest rooms are small and rather basic (so are the bathrooms) and the mattresses a bit thin, but everything was renovated after the earthquake. For an extra 20,000L ($10), lunch is served at 1pm in a restored 12th-century dining room.

NEARBY ACCOMMODATIONS

✪ **Hotel Palazzo Bocci.** Via Cavour 17, 06038 Spello. ☎ **0742/301-021.** Fax 0742-301-464. www.emmeti.it/Pbocci.it.html. E-mail: bocci@bcsnet.it. 23 units. A/C MINIBAR TV TEL. 200,000–240,000L ($100–$120) double; 280,000–350,000L ($140–$175) suite. Rates include buffet breakfast. AE, CB, DC, DISC, MC, V. Head 6 1/2 miles (10km) southeast of Assisi along S147.

Located in the historic center of nearby Spello, this palace dates from the late 18th century. The owner bought it in 1989, renovated it, and opened it as a hotel in 1992. Inside is a courtyard with a view of the valley, a beautiful fountain, and two age-old palms. Taste and restraint went into designing the public rooms and guest rooms, some of which open onto panoramic views. Each soundproof room has hydromassage, a safe, a firm mattress, a writing desk with two chairs, and a hair dryer. There's a nice bar and a lush garden where drinks are served. A well-known restaurant, Il Molino, is in front of the hotel. The village has a pool (7,500L/$3.75 per hour) and tennis courts (20,000L/$10 per hour) within a 5-minute walk.

DINING

You may also want to try the wonderful restaurants at the **Hotel Sole** and the **Albergo Ristorante del Viaggiatore** (see above).

✪ **Il Medioevo.** Via Arco dei Priori 4B. ☎ **075-813-068.** Reservations recommended. Main courses 18,000–28,000L ($9–$14). AE, DC, MC, V. Thurs–Tues noon–2:30pm and 7:30–10pm. Closed Jan 7–Feb 7 and July 1–20. UMBRIAN/INTERNATIONAL.

Assisi's best restaurant is one of the architectural oddities in the town's historic center, with foundations at least 1,000 years old. It's an authentic medieval gem. Alberto Falsinotti and his family prepare superb versions of Umbrian recipes whose origins are as old as Assisi itself. Specialties are tortellini stuffed with minced turkey, veal, and beef and served with butter and parmigiano; roasted rabbit with red-wine sauce and truffles; and roast lamb with rosemary, potatoes, and herbs.

✪ **La Fortezza.** Via della Fortezza 2B. ☎ **075-81-2418.** Fax 075-819-8035. Reservations recommended. Main courses 11,000–22,000L ($5.50–$11). AE, DC, MC, V. Mon–Wed and Fri–Sun 12:30–2:30pm and 7–10:30pm. Closed Feb. UMBRIAN.

Up a stepped alley from Piazza del Comune, this lovely restaurant has been family run for 40 years and is prized for its high quality and reasonable prices. An exposed ancient Roman wall to the right of the entrance immediately establishes the antiquity of this palazzo with brick-vaulted ceilings; the rest dates from the 13th century. The delicious homemade pastas are prepared with sauces that follow the season's fresh offerings, while the roster of meats skewered or roasted on the grill (*alla brace*) range from veal and lamb to duck. La Fortezza also rents seven rooms upstairs.

Ristorante Buca di San Francesco. Via Brizi 1. ☎ **075-812-204.** Reservations recommended. Main courses 28,000–40,000L ($14–$20). AE, DC, MC, V. Tues–Sun noon–2:30pm and 7–9:30pm. Closed July 1–15. UMBRIAN/ITALIAN.

Evocative of the Middle Ages, this restaurant occupies the premises of a cave near the foundation of a 12th-century palace. Menu items change often, based on the availability of ingredients, but what you're likely to find are *spaghetti alla buca,* with exotic mushrooms and meat sauce; *umbricelli* (big noodles) with asparagus sauce; *cannelloni* (crepes) with ricotta, spinach, and tomatoes; *carlacca* (baked crepes) stuffed with cheese, prosciutto, and roasted veal; and *piccione alla sisana* (roasted pigeon with olive oil, capers, and aromatic herbs). There are about a hundred seats in the dining room and another 60 in the garden, overlooking Assisi's historic center.

11 Spoleto

80 miles (129km) N of Rome, 30 miles (48km) SE of Assisi, 130 miles (209km) S of Florence, 40 miles (64km) SE of Perugia

Hannibal couldn't conquer it, but Gian-Carlo Menotti did—and how! Before Maestro Menotti put Spoleto on the tourist map in 1958, it was known mostly to art lovers, teachers, and students. Today huge crowds flood this Umbrian hill town to attend performances of the world-famous **Spoleto Festival** (formerly known as the **Festival dei Due Mondi/Festival of Two Worlds),** most often held in June and July. Menotti searched and traveled through many towns of Tuscany and Umbria before making a final choice. When he saw Spoleto, he fell in love with it. And quite understandably.

ESSENTIALS

GETTING THERE **Trains** arrive several times a day from Rome, the fastest of which are IC (Inter-City) trains, a bit more expensive than ordinary trains, some of which might require a transfer. The one-way fare from Rome to Spoleto is 16,000 to 23,000L ($8 to $11.50), depending on the train speed. The fastest will take about 90 minutes; those requiring connections can take 2½ hours. Trains also run several times a day between Perugia and Spoleto, the ride lasting about an hour and costing 6,000 to 12,000L ($3 to $6) each way. The **rail station** in Spoleto (☎ **0743-48-516**) is at Piazza Polvani, just outside the historic heart. Notice the gigantic statue in front by Philadelphia-born artist Alexander Calder. Circolare bus A, B, C, or D will take you from the station into Piazza della Libertà in the town center, for a one-way fee of 1,200L (60¢). Buy your ticket for the Circolare at the bar, perhaps along with an espresso, in the rail station.

If you have a **car** and are coming from either Assisi or Perugia (above), continue along S3, heading south to the junction of Foligno, where you can pick up Hwy. 75 for the rest of the route into Spoleto. Driving time from Assisi is about 30 minutes.

VISITOR INFORMATION The **tourist office** is at Piazza della Libertà 7 (☎ **0743-220-311**). April to October, it's open Monday to Friday 9am to 1pm and 4 to 7pm, Sunday 4 to 7pm; November to March, hours are Monday to Saturday 9am to 1pm and 3:30 to 6:30pm, Sunday 10am to 1pm.

SPECIAL EVENTS The ✪ **Spoleto Festival** is an internationally acclaimed event. It's held annually, most often in June and July, and attracts the elite of the operatic, ballet, and theatrical worlds from Europe and America. Tickets for most events are 25,000 to 90,000L ($45), plus a 15% handling charge. For tickets in advance, contact the **Spoleto Festival,** Piazza Duomo 8, 06049 Spoleto (☎ **0743-220-320** or 0743-45-028; fax 0743-220-321). For further information, call ☎ **800/565-600** or 0743-44-700, visit online at www.spoletofestival.net, or e-mail info@spoletofestival.net. Once in Spoleto, you can get tickets at the **Teatro Nuovo** (☎ **0743-45-028**). Make your hotel reservations well in advance!

SEEING THE TOWN

Long before Tennessee Williams arrived to premiere a new play, Thomas Schippers to conduct the opera *Macbeth,* or Shelley Winters to do three one-act plays by Saul Bellow, Spoleto was known to St. Francis and Lucrezia Borgia (she occupied the 14th-century castle towering over the town, the Rocca dell'Albornoz). The town is filled with palaces, medieval streets, and towers built for protection at the time when visitors weren't as friendly as they are today. There are churches, churches, and more churches—some of which, like San Gregorio Maggiore, were built in the Romanesque style in the 11th century.

The tourist center of town is **Piazza del Duomo,** with its **Duomo.** A walk along Via del Ponte will bring you to the ✪ **Ponte delle Torri,** with nine towering pylons separating stately arches. The bridge is 264 feet high and 760 feet long, spanning a gorge. It's believed to date from the 13th century and is one of the most photographed sights in Spoleto. Even Goethe praised it when he passed this way in 1786.

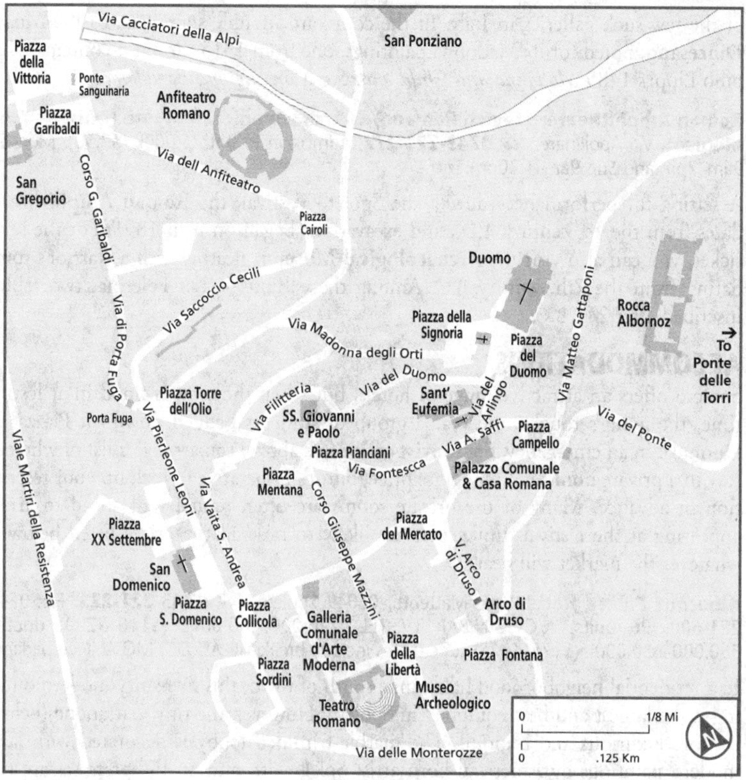

Motorists wanting a view can continue up the hill from Spoleto around a winding road (about 5 miles/8km) to **Monteluco,** an ancient spot 2,500 feet above sea level. Monteluco is peppered with summer villas. The monastery here was once frequented by St. Francis of Assisi.

Il Duomo. Piazza del Duomo. Free admission. Daily 8am–1pm and 3–6:30pm (to 5:30pm off-season).

The cathedral is a hodgepodge of Romanesque and medieval architecture, with a 12th-century campanile. Its facade is of exceptional beauty, renowned for its 1207 mosaic by Salsterno. You should visit the interior if for no other reason than to see the cycle of frescoes (1467–69) in the chancel by Filippo Lippi. His son, Filippino, designed the tomb for his father, but a mysterious grave robber hauled off the body one night about 2 centuries later. The keeper of the apse will be happy to unlock it for you. These frescoes, believed to have been carried out largely by students, were the elder Lippi's last work; he died in Spoleto in 1469. As friars went in those days, Lippi was a bit of a swinger; he ran off with a nun, Lucrezia Buti, who later posed as the Madonna in several of his paintings.

Sant'Eufemia & Diocese Museum (Museo Diocesano). Via Saffi, between Piazza del Duomo and Piazza del Mercanto. ☎ **0743-23-101** (museum). Admission to both 5,000L ($2.50). By reservation only, daily 10am–12:30pm and 3:30–7pm (to 6pm Nov–Feb).

The **Sant'Eufemia** church was built in the 11th century. Note the gallery above the nave, where women were required to sit, a holdover from the Eastern Church; it's one of the few such galleries in Italy. In the courtyard, double stairs lead to the **Museo Diocesano,** noted for its Madonna paintings, one from 1315. Room 5 contains Filippino Lippi's 1485 *Madonna and Child with Sts. Montano and Bartolomeo.*

Roman Amphitheater (Teatro Romano) & Archaeological Museum (Museo Archeologico). Via Apollinare. ☎ **0743-223-277.** Admission to both 5,000L ($2.50). Mon–Sat 9am–7pm and Sun 9am–1:30pm.

A setting for performances during the Spoleto Festival, the **Roman Amphitheater** dates from the 1st century A.D., and excavations began on it in 1891. For the same ticket, you can also visit the **Archaeological Museum** nearby, with a warrior's tomb dating from the 7th century B.C. Among the exhibits is Les Poletina, two tablets inscribed after 241 B.C.

ACCOMMODATIONS

Spoleto offers an attractive range of hotels, but when the crowds flood in at festival time, the going's rough (one year a group of students bedded down on Piazza del Duomo). In an emergency, the **tourist office** (see above) can arrange a list of where to stay in a private home at a moderate price, but it's imperative to lock up your reservation in advance. Many of the private rooms are often rented well ahead to artists appearing at the festival. Innkeepers are likely to raise all the prices listed below to whatever the market will bear.

Albornoz Palace Hotel. Viale Matteotti, 06049 Spoleto. ☎ **0743-221-221.** Fax 0743-221-600. 96 units. A/C MINIBAR TV TEL. 220,000–400,000L ($110–$200) double; 350,000–650,000L ($175–$325) suite. Rates include breakfast. AE, DC, MC, V. Free parking.

In a residential neighborhood half a mile south of town, this five-story modern building is the largest and best equipped in Spoleto. However, the tiny Gattapone (below) is more luxurious and tranquil. The marble-trimmed lobby is decorated with large modern paintings by American-born artist Sol Lewitt, and on the premises are two restaurants and a bar. The guest rooms are well appointed, with quality mattresses and fine linen, plus views over Spoleto, Monteluco, or the surrounding hills. The small bathrooms have hair dryers. A small garden in back contains a pool.

Hotel Charleston. Piazza Collicola 10, 06049 Spoleto. ☎ **0743-220-052.** Fax 0743-221-244. www.qsa.it/hotelcharleston. E-mail: hotelcharleston@krenet.it. 18 units. A/C MINIBAR TV TEL. 140,000–180,000L ($70–$90) double. Rates include breakfast. AE, DC, MC, V. Parking 15,000L ($7.50).

This tile-roofed, sienna-fronted building is from the 17th century and today serves as a pleasant hotel in the historic center. It's a solid and reliable choice, with wood-beamed ceilings, terra-cotta floors, and open fireplaces. Each of the large guest rooms has a ceiling accented with beams of honey-colored planking and comfortable mattresses. Many have been updated with new furnishings and bathrooms. The room TVs come with VCRs, and the front desk usually has a movie or two in English that you can rent. There's a sauna, as well as a bar, a library, and a sitting room with a writing table.

Hotel Clarici. Piazza della Vittoria 32, 06049 Spoleto. ☎ **0743-223-311.** Fax 0743-222-020. www.qsa.it/hotelclarici. E-mail: hotelclarici@krenet.it. 24 units. MINIBAR TV TEL. 160,000L ($80) double; 180,000L ($90) triple. Rates include breakfast. AE, DC, MC, V. Parking 10,000L ($5). Bus: A, B, C, or D.

The Clarici is rated only third class, but it's airy and modern, the best of the budget bets. The hotel doesn't emphasize style but rather the creature comforts: soft low beds, built-in wardrobes, steam heat, and an elevator. The bathrooms are well organized.

Twenty rooms are air-conditioned, and 14 open onto private balconies. There's a large terrace for sunbathing or sipping drinks.

Hotel dei Duchi. Viale Giacomo Matteotti 4, 06049 Spoleto. ☎ **0743-44-541.** Fax 0743-44-543. www.hoteldeiduchi.com. E-mail: hotel@hoteldeiduchi.com. 49 units. A/C MINIBAR TV TEL. 200,000L ($100) double; 400,000L ($200) suite. Rates include buffet breakfast. Half-board 120,000L ($60) per person. AE, DC, MC, V. Free parking.

This modern hotel is within walking distance of the major sights, yet it perches on a hillside with views and terraces. It lacks the style of the Gattapone and Albornoz Palace; its bland rooms seem geared to business travelers. Dei Duchi is graced with brick walls, open-to-the-view glass, and lounges with modern furnishings and original paintings. Some guest rooms have balconies, and all have bland bed coverings over good mattresses, wood-grained furniture, and built-in cupboards. The bathrooms are small but come with hair dryers. Half-board is required in high season. In summer you have a choice of two dining rooms, each airy and roomy.

✪ **Hotel Gattapone.** Via Del Ponte 6, 06049 Spoleto. ☎ **0743-223-447.** Fax 0743-223-448. www.caribusiness.it/gattapone. E-mail: gattapone@mail.caribusiness.it. 14 units. A/C TV TEL. 270,000L ($135) double; 390,000L ($195) suite. Breakfast 20,000L ($10); charge is added automatically unless you specify otherwise. AE, DC, MC, V. Free parking.

The stunning Gattapone is our first choice in town. It occupies two side-by-side stone 17th-century cottages among the clouds, clinging to the cliffs high on a twisting road leading to the ancient castle and the 13th-century Ponte delle Torri. It feels isolated and surrounded by nature, but it's only a couple of minutes' stroll to the Duomo. The interiors maximize views of the valley and the remarkable 14th-century arched bridge a few hundred feet away. The rooms are uniquely furnished, with comfortable beds, antiques, and plenty of space. All the bathrooms are well equipped, each with a hair dryer. Breakfast is the only meal served.

✪ **Hotel San Luca.** Via Interna della Mura 21, 06049 Spoleto. ☎ **0743-223-399.** Fax 0743-223-800. www.hotelsanluca.com. E-mail: hotelsanluca@email.caribusiness.it. 35 units. A/C MINIBAR TV TEL. 200,000–400,000L ($100–$200) double; from 420,000L ($210) suite. AE, DC, MC, V. Parking 25,000L ($12.50).

Occupying a restored building from the 19th century, this hotel is the most up-to-date in town, filled with ambience and style. Wherever you turn, there's a grace note of the past, like a roof garden and a spacious courtyard with a 1602 fountain. All the elegant guest rooms are spacious and furnished in a sober yet comforting style, with all the amenities. The bathrooms are particularly welcoming, with extras like hair dryers, phones, and towel warmers. Many rooms are also fitted with a massage bath. The public rooms respect the style of the building, with period furniture. A garden solarium and a good restaurant serving Umbrian specialties make this hotel even more alluring.

DINING

Il Tartufo. Piazza Garibaldi 24. ☎ **0743-40-236.** Reservations required. Main courses 30,000L ($15); fixed-price menus 30,000–65,000L ($15–$32.50). AE, DC, MC, V. Tues–Sat noon–3pm and 7:30–10:30pm; Sun noon–3pm. Closed July 15–31. UMBRIAN.

At Il Tartufo, near the amphitheater, you may be introduced to the Umbrian *tartufo* (truffle)—if you can afford it. It's served in the most expensive appetizers and main courses at Spoleto's oldest restaurant. This excellent tavern serves at least nine regional specialties using the black tartufo. A popular pasta dish (and a good introduction for neophyte palates) is *strengozzi al tartufo.* Or you may want to start with an omelet like *frittata al tartufo.* Main dishes of veal and beef are also excellently prepared. For such a small restaurant, the menu is large.

✪ **La Barcaccia.** Piazza Fratelli Bandiera. ☎ **0743-22-1171.** Reservations suggested. Main courses 15,000–28,000L ($7.50–$14); *menù turistico* 30,000L ($15). AE, DC, MC, V. Wed–Mon 12:30–2:30pm and 7:30–11:00pm. UMBRIAN.

This is one of Spoleto's finer restaurants, where you can have a modestly priced dinner if you resist its otherwise highly recommended truffle dishes. A safe way to dine is with the well-priced *menù turistico* that includes a choice of truffle-free pasta, a meat entree, a fresh vegetable, fruit, and service—everything except a glass of the local vino. A covered terrace extends the length of the restaurant in front, though the use of the small piazza as a parking lot does little to romanticize the view. An entree of mixed roast meats (*grigliata alla brace*) is the house's deservedly promoted specialty.

A SIDE TRIP TO TODI

For years, Todi lay slumbering in the Umbrian sun. Then the world moved in. Visa used it as a backdrop for a commercial, and the University of Kentucky keeps voting it "the most livable town in the world." This has brought a monied class from America rushing in to buy decaying castles and villas, hoping to convert them into holiday homes. And Todi has imitated Spoleto and now stages a **Festival di Todi,** attracting ballet, theatrical, and operatic stars during the first 10 days of each September.

Taking Route 418 out of Spoleto for 28 miles (45km) northwest will lead you to what the excitement is all about. At Acquasparta, get on Autostrada 3 northwest. Soon you'll come to this well-preserved medieval village, today a retreat for wealthy artists and diplomats. The setting with its Etruscan, Roman, and medieval past has been likened to a long-ago fairy tale.

On arriving, you'll enter the triangularly walled town through one of its three gates, named for the destinations of the roads leading away: **Rome** in the southwest wall, **Perugia** in the north, and **Orvieto** in the southeast. The remains of original Roman and Etruscan walls are also evident just inside the Rome gate. The central square, **Piazza del Popolo,** was built over a Roman forum and is as harmonious as any in Italy. It contains the 12th-century Romanesque-Gothic **cathedral** and three beautiful palaces: the **Palazzo del Popolo,** built in 1213; the **Palazzo del Capitano,** dating from 1292; and the 14th-century **Palazzo dei Priori,** with its trapezoidal tower. Each summer, all three (and the piazza) are filled with the wares of the **National Exhibit of Crafts (Mostra Nazionale dell'Artigianato).**

Also on view are **Santa Maria della Consolazione,** standing guard over Todi with its domes and exquisite stained glass, and the 13th-century **San Fortunato,** in the **Piazza della Repubblica,** burial site of the town's most famous citizen, the monk/medieval poet Jacopone. To the right of the church, a path leads uphill to the ruins of a 14th-century castle known as **La Rocca.** From here, a walk up the twisting Viale della Serpentina will reward you with a bird's-eye view of the surrounding valley. If the climb seems a bit much, check the view from **Piazza Garibaldi.**

Today, the artisans of Todi are particularly renowned for their woodwork. Examples of historical as well as contemporary craft are available for perusal or purchase, especially during the **National Exhibit of Crafts** along Piazza del Popolo.

While you're here, you might like to have lunch at **Umbria,** Via S. Bonaventure 13 (through the arch between the Palazzi del Popolo and Capitano; ☎ **075-894-2390**). Not only does it serve the best food in Todi, but it also has a terrific view from its vine-shaded terrace. Call ahead for reservations.

12 Orvieto

75 miles (121km) N of Rome, 47 miles (76km) SW of Perugia, 70 miles (113km) SW of Assisi

Built on a pedestal of volcanic rock above vineyards in a green valley, **Orvieto** is the Umbrian hill town closest to Rome and is often visited by those who don't have the time to explore other spots in Umbria. It lies on the Paglia, a tributary of the Tiber, and sits on an isolated rock some 1,035 feet above sea level. Crowning the town is its world-famed cathedral. A road runs from below up to Piazza del Duomo.

The most spectacularly sited hill town in Umbria (but not the most spectacular town), Orvieto was founded by the Etruscans, who were apparently drawn to it because of its good defensive possibilities. Likewise, long after its days as a Roman colony, it became a papal stronghold. It was a natural fortress, since its cliffs rise starkly from the valley below, even though Orvieto, when you finally reach it, is relatively flat. Although the tall, sheer cliffs on which the town stands saved it from the incursion of railroads and superhighways, time and traffic vibrations have caused the soft volcanic rock to disintegrate so that work is imminently necessary to shore up the town.

Orvieto is known for its white wine; the best place to enjoy it is at a wine cellar at Piazza del Duomo 2 as you contemplate the cathedral's facade.

ESSENTIALS

GETTING THERE Three **trains** a day arrive in Orvieto from Perugia. Because of frequent stops, the trip takes 1½ hours. A one-way ticket is 10,000L ($5). From Florence, the handful of trains making the trip require 2 hours, with a one-way ticket at 16,800L ($8.40). From Rome, the train takes 1½ hours and costs 12,300L ($6.15) each way. Orvieto's rail station (☎ **0763/300-434**) lies below the town in the valley; to get to the town center, take Bus A, departing at intervals of 40 minutes or less throughout the day and most of the night, or via a small funicular operating daily 7:15am and 8:30pm. One-way transit from the rail station to the town by either bus or funicular is 1,500L ($.75). For information, call the tourist office (see below).

If you have a **car** and are coming from Rome, drive for about 90 minutes (a distance of around 75 miles/121km north along A1) to Orvieto. From Perugia, head 26 miles (42km) south on SS3bis to Todi, then take SS448 for 15½ miles (25km) southwest to the intersection of SS205 and drive 5½ miles (9km) to Orvieto.

VISITOR INFORMATION The **tourist office,** at Piazza del Duomo 24 (☎ **0763-341-772**), is open Monday to Friday 8:15am to 1:50pm and 4 to 7pm, Saturday 10am to 1pm and 4 to 7pm, and Sunday 10am to noon and 4 to 7pm.

EXPLORING THE TOWN

✪ **Il Duomo.** Piazza del Duomo. ☎ **0763-341-167.** Church free; chapel 3,000L ($1.50). Apr–Sept daily 10am–1pm and 2:30–7:30pm; Oct–Mar daily 7:30am–1pm and 2:30–6:15pm.

Erected on the site of two older churches and dedicated to the Virgin, the Duomo was begun in 1288 (maybe even earlier) to commemorate the Miracle of Bolsena. This alleged miracle came out of the doubts of a priest who questioned the transubstantiation (the incarnation of Jesus Christ in the Host). However, so the story goes, at the moment of consecration, the Host started to drip blood. The priest doubted no more, and the Feast of Corpus Christi was launched.

The cathedral is known for its elaborately adorned facade, rich statuary, marble bas-reliefs, and mosaics. Pope John XXIII once proclaimed that on Judgment Day, God would send his angels down to earth to pick up this Duomo's facade and transport it back to heaven. The modern bronze portals are controversial, and many art historians journey from around the world to see them. Installed in 1970, they were the work of eminent sculptor Emilio Greco, who took as his theme the Misericordia, the seven acts of corporal charity. One panel depicts Pope John XXIII's famous visit to the prisoners of Rome's Queen of Heaven jail in 1960. Some critics have called the doors "outrageous"; others have praised them as "one of the most original works of modern sculpture." You decide.

The west facade, divided into three gables, boasts richly sculptured marble based on designs of Lorenzo Maitani of Siena. Four wall surfaces around the three doors are adorned with bas-reliefs, also based on Maitani designs. He worked on the facade until his death in 1330. The bas-reliefs depict scenes from the Bible, including the Last Judgment. After Maitani's death, Andrea Pisano took over, but the actual work carried on until the dawn of the 17th century.

Inside, the nave and aisles are constructed in alternating panels of black and of white stone. You'll want to seek out the **Cappella del Corporale,** with its mammoth silver shrine based on the design of the cathedral facade. This 1338 masterpiece, richly embellished with precious stones, was the work of Ugolino Vieri of Siena and designed to shelter the Holy Corporal from Bolsena (the cloth in which the bleeding Host was wrapped). The most celebrated chapel is the **Cappella di San Brizio,** which contains newly restored frescoes of the Last Judgment and the Apocalypse by Luca Signorelli, who was called in to complete them (they were begun by Fra Angelico). Michelangelo was said to have been inspired by the frescoes at the time he was contemplating the Sistine Chapel. The masterpiece was produced between 1499 and 1503 and cost $4.4 million to renovate. Only 25 persons per time are allowed to see the chapel.

Pozzo di San Patrizio (St. Patrick's Well). Viale Sangallo, off Piazza Cahen. ☎ **0763-343-768.** Admission 6,000L ($3). Apr–Oct daily 10am–7pm; Nov–Mar daily 10am–6pm.

St. Patrick's Well is an architectural curiosity, and in its day it was an engineering feat. Pope Clement VII ordered the well built when he feared Orvieto might come under siege and its water supply be cut off. The well was entrusted to the design of Antonio da Sangallo the Younger in 1527. It's some 200 feet deep and about 42 feet in diameter, cut into volcanic rock. Two spiral staircases, with about 250 steps, lead into the wells. These spiral ramps never meet.

Museum of Archaeology & Civic Museum (Musei Archeologici Faina e Civico). In the Palazzo Faina, Piazza del Duomo 29. ☎ **0763-341-511.** Admission 8,000L ($4). Mar 31–Sept 28 daily 10am–1pm and 3–7pm; Sept 29–Mar 30 Tues–Sun 10am–1pm and 2:30–5pm.

This museum across from the cathedral contains many Etruscan artifacts found in and around Orvieto. In addition to the stone sarcophagi, terra-cotta portraits, and vials of colored glass left by the Etruscans, it exhibits many beautiful Greek vases. Three of the most important objects are amphorae attributed to one of the finest of the Attic vase painters, Exekias (550-540 B.C.). They were found in a necropolis near Orvieto and are a gauge of the wealth of this former city-state.

Emilio Greco Museum (Museo Emilio Greco). In the Palazzo Soliano, Piazza del Duomo. ☎ **0763-344-605.** Admission 5,000L ($2.50). Apr–Sept Tues–Sat 10:30am–1pm and 2:30–6pm; Oct–Mar Tues–Sat 10:30am–1pm and 2:30–6pm.

This museum opened in 1991 to house an important art collection donated to the city by eminent sculptor Emilio Greco. A devoted advocate of civic pride and an internationally recognized sculptor best remembered in Orvieto for his sculpting of the

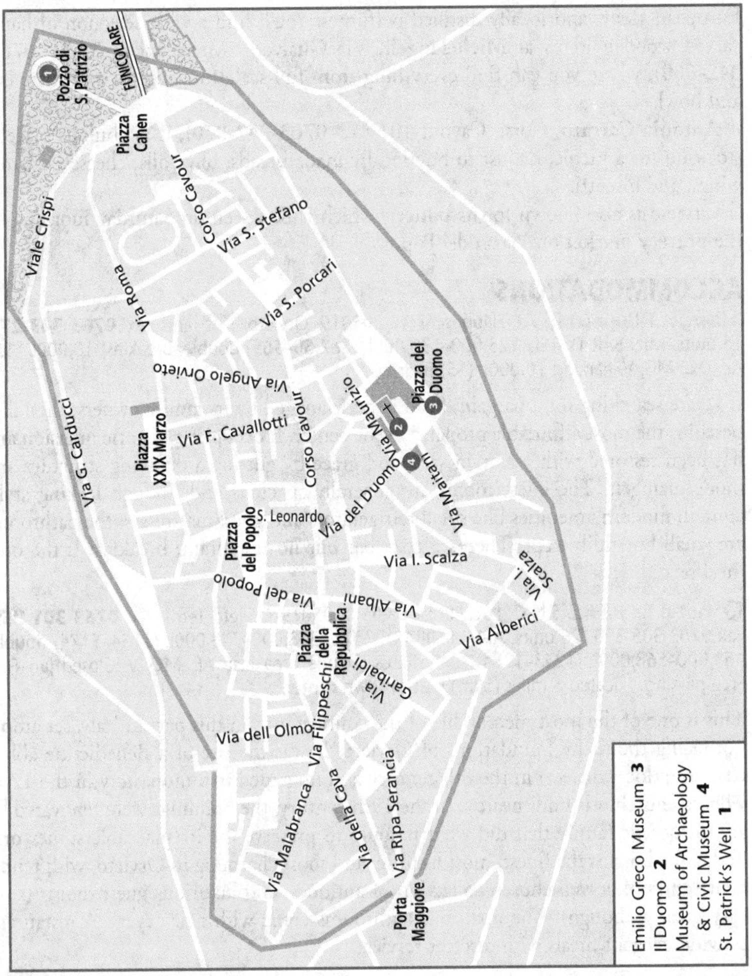

bronze doors in the front of the Duomo (see above), he died in 1996 in his mid-80s. You'll find 32 Greco sculptures and 60 graphic works (including lithographs, etchings, and drawings). The modern museum was designed by architect Giulio Savio on the ground floor of a 14th-century palazzo.

SHOPPING

Orvieto's local white wine, **Orvieto Classico,** is made from grapes that thrive in the local chalky soil and are sometimes fermented in caves around the countryside. You'll be able to buy glasses of the fruity wine ("liquid gold") at any bar or tavern in town, but if you want to haul a bottle or two back to your own digs, try the town's best wine shop, **Foresi,** Piazza del Duomo 2 (☎ **0763-341-611**).

You can also find lace and carved wooden objects here. For lace, go to **Duranti,** Via del Duomo 13 (☎ **0763-344-606**), which carries tablecloths, handkerchiefs, and frilly curtains, along with an occasional baptismal robe. You'll also find imported

European scents and locally distilled perfumes. You'll find a wide selection of hand-carved wooden items at **Michelangeli,** Via Gualverio Michelangeli 3 (☎ **0763-342-660**), where you can find everything from full-scale furniture to an ornate cup and bowl.

Antonia Carraro, Corso Cavour 101 (☎ **0763-342-870**), is a fabulous place to stock up for a picnic, or just to buy locally made breads, olive oils, cheeses, salamis, wines, and biscotti.

Orvieto is also known for its pottery, which is best seen on Saturday mornings at the **pottery market** on Piazza del Popolo.

ACCOMMODATIONS

Albergo Filippeschi. Via Filippeschi 19, 05019 Orvieto. ☎ and fax **0763-343-275.** 15 units. MINIBAR TV TEL. 125,000–130,000L ($62.50–$65) double. Breakfast 10,000L ($5). AE, DC, MC, V. Parking 10,000L ($5) nearby.

If you're searching for a bargain, head here. Managed by its family owners, the Filippeschi is the most affordable property in the center. It occupies a historic mansion and has been restored with a certain style and grace by gutting a decaying structure and modernizing it. The guest rooms are generally spacious and, though lacking style, contain modern amenities like small refrigerators and good mattresses; the bathrooms are small but tidily kept. There's a cozy bar but no restaurant; breakfast is the only meal served.

✪ **Hotel La Badia.** S.N.C. Località La Badia 8, 05019 Orvieto Terni. ☎ **0763-301-959.** Fax 0763-305-396. 26 units. A/C MINIBAR TV TEL. 308,000–348,000L ($154–$174) double; 468,000–568,000L ($243–$284) suite. Rates include breakfast. AE, MC, V. Closed Jan–Feb. Free parking. Located 3 miles (5km) east of town center.

This is one of the most memorable of the country inns in this part of Italy, set atop a hill facing the rocky foundations of Orvieto. It was the site of a Benedictine abbey (Badia, in local dialect) in the 8th century and upgraded to a monastery in the 12th, when a church was built nearby. In the 19th century, the buildings were renovated by an aristocratic family that did what it could to preserve the irreplaceable stonework. Today the hotel is the finest, most historic, and most charming in Orvieto, with tennis courts, a pool, a well-chosen collection of antiques, and luxurious guest rooms (sizes vary greatly, though). The luxurious bathrooms come with hair dryers. A restaurant provides elegant meals with discreet service.

Hotel Maitani. Via Maitani 5, 05018 Orvieto. ☎ and fax **0763-342-011.** 40 units. A/C TV TEL. 230,000L ($115) double; 270,000–310,000L ($135–$155) suite. AE, DC, V. Parking 20,000L ($10). Closed Jan 7–22.

The stone-sided building that houses this family-run hotel was built as a palazzo around 600 years ago. The guest rooms are mostly modern but do retain some reminders of their medieval origins. They're small but cozy and comfortable, with good beds. Breakfast is the only meal served, though several restaurants are nearby. If you have a car, it's best to try to check in early, as the hotel has parking space for only eight vehicles.

Hotel Palazzo Piccolomini. Piazza Ranieri 36, 05018 Orvieto. ☎ **0763-341-743.** Fax 0763-391-046. www.argoweb.it/hotel_piccolomini. E-mail: piccolomini.hotel@orvienet.it. 32 units. A/C MINIBAR TV TEL. 160,000–180,000L ($80–$90) double; 250,000L ($125) suite. Breakfast 15,000L ($7.50). AE, CB, DC, MC, V.

In 1998 this hotel opened in a converted Renaissance palazzo and began charging bargain prices. Looking very pretty in pink, this was the Orvieto home of the illustrious Tuscan family that gave us two popes. The building has emerged from a complete refurbishment that has kept the historical shell and its grand dimensions of vaulted ceilings and wide halls while creating a quasi-minimalist ambience with cool terra-cotta floors and white slipcovered furniture.

✪ **Villa Ciconia.** Via dei Tigli 69, 05019 Orvieto. ☎ **0763-305-582.** Fax 0763-302-077. 10 units. A/C MINIBAR TV TEL. 220,000–260,000L ($110–$130) double. Rates include breakfast. AE, DC, MC, V. Free parking. Bus: 3. The villa is 2½ miles (4km) from Orvieto.

This beautiful 16th-century villa (the best hotel in the environs) sits in an 8-acre park at the confluence of the Chain and Paglia rivers. It has the thick walls, terra-cotta floors, and beamed ceilings typical of its era. Huge chestnut beams run more than 13 yards along the ceiling of the lobby, and the main dining room features a great stone fireplace and a lacuna ceiling with ornate molding and frescoes around the walls. The spacious guest rooms have park views and period furnishings, including good beds with quality mattresses. The tiled bathrooms come with hair dryers. A room with air-conditioning is an extra 20,000L ($10) per night. You can use a nearby public sports center, which has an indoor Olympic-size pool, indoor and outdoor red-clay tennis courts, and horseback riding. The restaurant serves a wide variety of tasty regional dishes and a large selection of local and national wines. Truffles figure prominently on the menu.

DINING

Antica Trattoria dell'Orso. Via della Misericordia 18 (north of Piazza della Repubblica). ☎ **0763-341-642.** Reservations recommended. Main courses 12,000–18,000L ($6–$9). AE, DC, MC, V. Wed–Sun noon–2:30pm and 7:30–10pm; Mon noon–2:30pm only. Closed mid-Jan to mid-Feb. UMBRIAN.

The *umbrichelli* (Umbria's homemade spaghettilike specialty) is best served here *alla campagnola* ("country style" with zucchini, eggplant, and onions). Any of the fresh pastas, in fact, are must-trys at this unprepossessing trattoria full of locals, quasi-free of tourists because of its location one step too far off the beaten path (it's a 10-minute stroll from the Duomo). The ingredients of fresh market offerings and homegrown herbs help confirm the impression of a day in the country. Even the simplest dish (a frittata of asparagus or potatoes) is full of flavor and bears the masterful touch of chef Gabriele di Giandomenico.

La Grotta d. Funaro. Via Ripper Ceramic 41. ☎ **0763-343-276.** Reservations recommended. Main courses 14,000–25,000L ($7–$12.50). AE, DC, MC, V. Tues–Sun noon–3pm and 7pm–1am. UMBRIAN/PIZZA.

The cuisine is the type of fare Umbrian grandmothers have served for generations—fresh, flavorful, and nutritious, with no attempt to be creative. The setting, however, is a surprisingly dry cave below the city center that includes many eerie references to other days and other times. No one seems to have any idea how long the cave has been in everyday use (the staff believes it was part of the storerooms used by the ancient Etruscans). Menu items include an array of grilled meats (like lamb or pork with potatoes and vegetables), pastas flavored with local mushrooms and truffles, and very fresh vegetables. From a wood-burning oven emerge the most savory pizzas in town.

7 Bologna & Emilia-Romagna

In the northern reaches of central Italy, the region of Emilia-Romagna is known for its gastronomy and for its art cities, Modena and Parma. Here, such families as the Renaissance dukes of Ferrara rose in power and influence, creating courts that attracted painters and poets.

Bologna, the capital, stands at the crossroads between Venice and Florence and is linked by express highways to Milan and Tuscany. By basing yourself in this ancient university city, you can branch out in all directions: north for 32 miles (52km) to Ferrara; southeast for 31 miles (50km) to the ceramics-making town of Faenza; northwest for 25 miles (40km) to Modena with its Romanesque cathedral; or farther northwest for 34 miles (55km) to Parma, the legendary capital of the Farnese family duchy in the 16th century. Ravenna, famed for its mosaics, lies 46 miles (74km) east of Bologna on the Adriatic Sea.

Most of our stops in this region lie on the ancient Roman **Via Emilia,** which began in Rimini and stretched to Piacenza, a Roman colony that often attracted invading barbarians. This ancient land (known to the Romans as Æmilia, and to the Etruscans before them) is rich in architecture (Parma's cathedral and baptistry) and in scenic beauty (the green plains and the slopes of the Apennines). Emilia is one of Italy's most bountiful farming districts and sets a table highly praised in Europe, both for its wines and for its imaginatively prepared pasta dishes.

1 Bologna

32 miles (52km) S of Ferrara, 94 miles (151km) SW of Venice, 235 miles (378km) N of Rome

The manager of a hotel in Bologna once lamented: "The Americans! They spend a week in Florence, a week in Venice. Why not 6 days in Florence, 6 days in Venice, and 2 days in Bologna?" That's a good question.

Bologna is one of the most overlooked gems in Italy; we've found empty room after empty room here in summer, when the hotels in Venice and Florence were packed tight. Now it's true that Bologna boasts no Uffizi or Doge's Palace, but it does offer a beautiful city that's one of the most architecturally unified in Europe—a panorama of sienna-colored buildings, marbled sidewalks, and porticos. After fighting those crowds in Rome, Florence, and Venice, you might enjoy a few days away from the tourist crush.

Bologna's rise as a commercial power was almost assured by its strategic location at the geographic center between Florence and Venice. And its university, the oldest in Europe (founded 1088), has for years generated a lively interest in art and culture. It features the nation's best medical school as well as one of its top business schools. The bars, cafes, and squares fill up with students, and an eclectic mix of concerts, art exhibits, and avant-garde ballet and theater performances always marks the calendar.

Perhaps because the student population is so large, Bologna is a center of great tolerance, with the national gay alliance and several student organizations making their headquarters here. Politically, communism and socialism figure prominently in the voter profile, which may be why the region has been largely unscathed by the scandal and corruption of neighboring precincts, where blatant capitalism has led to Mafia-corrupted activity.

Bologna is also Italy's gastronomic capital. Gourmets flock here just to sample the cuisine: the pastas (tortellini, tagliatelle, lasagna verde), the meat and poultry specialties (zampone, veal cutlet bolognese, tender turkey breasts in sauce supreme), and the *mortadella,* Bologna's incomparable sausage, as distant a cousin to baloney as porterhouse is to the hot dog.

The city seems to take a vacation in August, becoming virtually dead. You'll notice signs proclaiming CHIUSO (closed) almost everywhere you look.

ESSENTIALS

GETTING THERE The international **Aeroporto Guglielmo Marconi** (☎ **051-647-9615**) is 4 miles (6km) north of the town center and serviced by such domestic carriers as Aermediterranea and ATI; all the main European airlines have connections through this airport. An **Aerobus** (no. 54) runs daily every 30 minutes (every 15 minutes during rush hours) from the airport to the air terminal at Bologna's rail station. A one-way ticket costs 7,000L ($3.50).

Bologna's **Stazione Centrale rail station** is at Piazza Medaglie d'Oro 2 (☎ **051-630-2111,** or 1478-88-088 toll-free in Italy only). Trains arrive hourly from Rome ($3^1/_2$ hours) and from Milan ($2^1/_2$ hours). Bus nos. 25 and 30 run between the station and the historic core of Bologna, Piazza Maggiore.

If you have a **car** and are coming from Florence, continue north along A1 until reaching the outskirts of Bologna, where signs direct you to the city center. Coming over the Apennines, A1 runs northwest to Milan just before the outskirts of Bologna. A13 cuts northeast to Ferrara and Venice, and A14 dashes east to Rimini, Ravenna, and the towns along the Adriatic.

VISITOR INFORMATION The **tourist office** is at Piazza Maggiore 6 (☎ **051-239-660**), open Monday to Saturday 9am to 7pm and Sunday 9am to 1pm. There are two other offices, one at the railway station, Piazza Medoglie d'Oro 2 (☎ **051-246-541**), and the other one at the airport, Via Tgriumvirato 84 (☎ **051-647-2036**). Both are open Monday to Saturday from 9am to 4pm.

GETTING AROUND Bologna is easy to cover on foot; most of the major sights are in and around Piazza Maggiore. However, if you don't want to walk, **city buses** leave for most points from Piazza Nettuno or Piazza Maggiore. Free maps are available at the storefront office of the **ATC (Azienda Trasporti Comunali)** at Piazza XX Settembre. You can buy tickets at one of many booths and tobacconists in Bologna. The ATC Customer Service Office is at Via IV Novembre 16A, open daily from 8am to 7:30pm. Tickets cost 1,800L (90¢) and last 60 minutes. A **citypass,** a booklet of 7 tickets each valid for 1 hour, costs 10,000L ($5). Once on board, you must have your ticket validated.

Taxis are on radio call at ☎ **051-72-727** or 051-534-141.

Emilia-Romagna

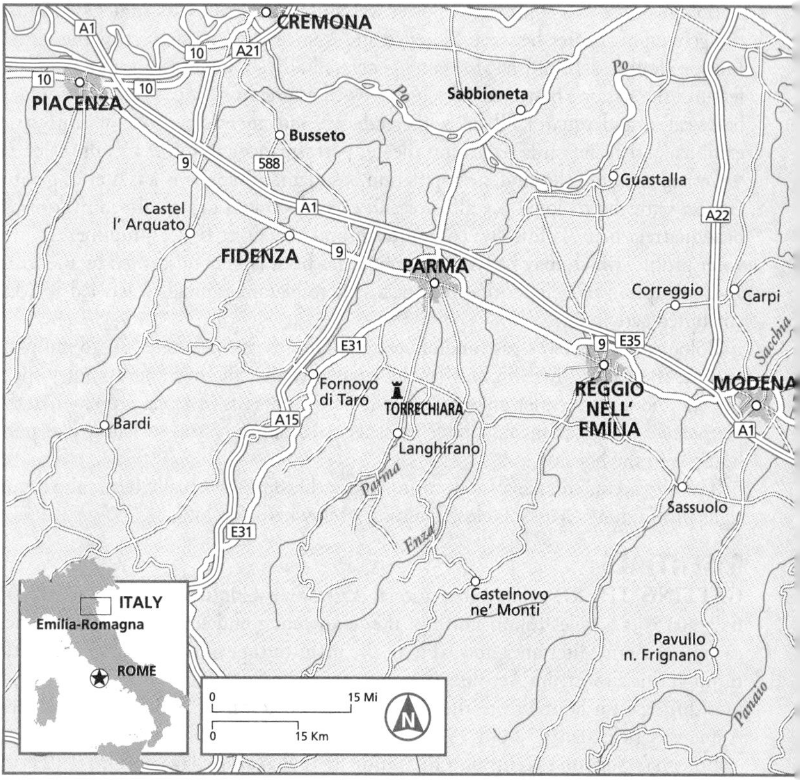

SEEING THE SIGHTS

On Piazza del Nettuno (adjacent to Piazza Maggiore) stands the ✪ **Neptune Fountain (Fontana di Nettuno),** which has gradually become a symbol of the city, though it was designed in 1566 by a Frenchman named Giambologna (the Italians altered his name). Viewed as irreverent by some, "indecent" by the Catholic Church, and magnificent by those with more liberal tastes, this 16th-century fountain depicts Neptune with rippling muscles, a trident in one arm, and a heavy foot on the head of a dolphin. The church forced Giambologna to manipulate Neptune's left arm to cover his monumental endowment. Giambologna's defenders denounced this as "artistic castration." Around his feet are four highly erotic cherubs, also with dolphins. At the base of the fountain, four very sensual sirens spout streams of water from their breasts.

Basilica di San Petronio. Piazza Maggiore. ☎ **051-22-5442.** Free admission. Apr–Sept daily 7:15am–1:30pm and 2:30–6:30pm; Oct–Mar daily 7:15am–1pm and 2–6pm.

Sadly, the facade of this enormous Gothic basilica honoring the patron saint of Bologna was never completed. Legend has it that the construction was greatly curtailed by papal decree when the Vatican learned that the Bologna city fathers had planned to erect a basilica larger than St. Peter's. Although the builders went to work in 1390, after 3 centuries the church was still not finished (nevertheless, Charles V was crowned emperor here in 1530). However, Jacopo della Quercia of Siena did grace the

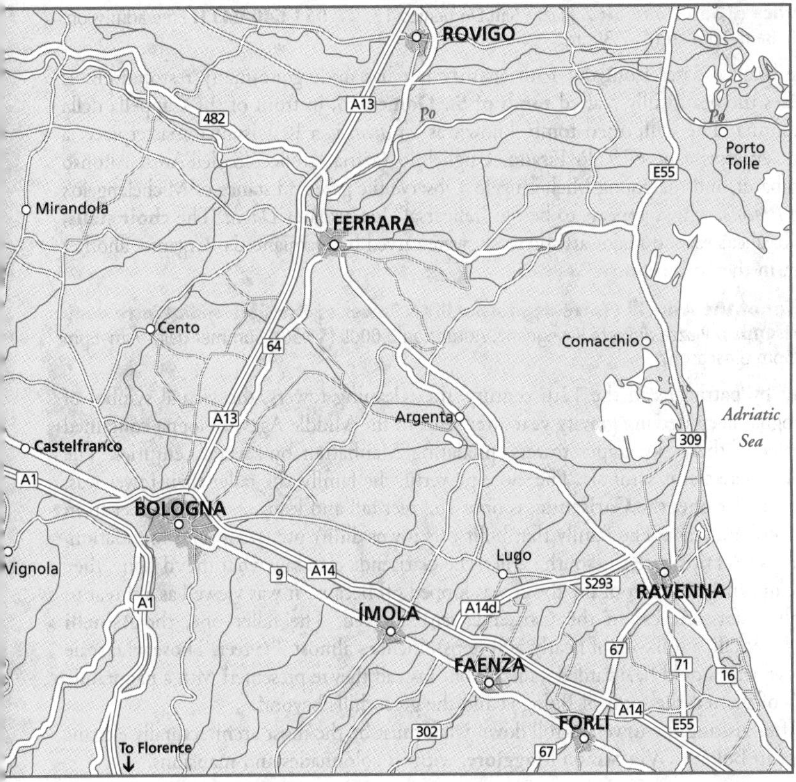

central door with a masterpiece Renaissance sculpture. Inside, the church could accommodate the traffic of New York's Grand Central Terminal. The central nave is separated from the aisles by pilasters shooting up to the flying ceiling arches. Of the 22 art-filled chapels, the most interesting is the **Bolognini Chapel (Cappella Bolognini),** the fourth on the left as you enter; it's embellished with frescoes representing heaven and hell. The purity and simplicity of line represent some of the best of the Gothic in Italy.

Palazzo Comunale. Piazza Maggiore 6. ☎ **051-03-526.** Each museum separately, 8,000L ($4); children 13 and under free. Tues–Sun 10am–6pm. Closed holidays. Bus: 11, 17, 25, 27, 30, or 37.

Built in the 14th century, this town hall has seen major restorations but happily retains its splendor. Enter through the courtyard; then proceed up the steps on the right to the **Communal Collection of Fine Arts (Collezioni Comunali d'Arte),** which includes many paintings from the 14th- to the 19th-century Emilian school. Another section, the **Museum of Giorgio Morandi (Museo di Giorgio Morandi),** is devoted to the works of this famed painter of Bologna (1890–1964). His subject matter (a vase of flowers or a box) might have been mundane, but he transformed these objects into works of art of startling intensity and perception. Some of his finest works are landscapes of Grizzana, a village where he spent many a lazy summer working and drawing. There's also a reconstruction of his studio.

Basilica di San Domenico. Piazza San Domenico 13. ☎ **051-640-0411.** Free admission. Daily 8am–1pm and 2–7:30pm.

The basilica dates from the 13th century but has undergone many restorations. It houses the beautifully crafted **tomb of St. Domenico,** in front of the Cappella della Madonna. The sculptured tomb, known as an *area,* is a Renaissance masterpiece, a joint enterprise of Niccolò Pisano, Guglielmo (a friar), Niccolò dell'Arca, Alfonso Lombardi, and the young Michelangelo. Observe the gaze and stance of Michelangelo's *San Procolo,* which appears to be the "rehearsal" for his later *David.* The **choir stalls,** the basilica's second major artistic work, were carved by Damiano da Bergamo, another friar, in the 16th century.

Tower of the Asinelli (Torre degli Asinelli) & Tower of the Garisenda (Torre degli Garisenda). Piazza di Porta Ravegnana. Admission 3,000L ($1.50). Summer daily 9am–6pm (to 5pm off-season).

Built by patricians in the 12th century, these leaning towers, the virtual symbol of Bologna, keep defying gravity year after year. In the Middle Ages, Bologna contained dozens of these skyscraper towers, predating Manhattan by several centuries. The towers were status symbols: The more powerful the family, the taller their tower was. The smaller one, the **Garisenda,** is only 162 feet tall and leans about 10½ feet from the perpendicular. The family that built this tower didn't prepare a solid foundation, and it sways tipsily to the south. When the Garisenda clan saw what they'd done, they gave up. In 1360, part of the tower was lopped off because it was viewed as a threat to public safety. Access to the Garisenda isn't allowed. The taller one, the **Asinelli** (334 feet tall, a walk-up of nearly 500 steps), inclines almost 7½ feet. Those who scale the Asinelli should be awarded a medal, but instead they're presented with a panoramic view of the red-tile roofs of Bologna and the green hills beyond.

After visiting the towers, stroll down what must be the most architecturally elegant street in Bologna, **Via Strada Maggiore,** with its colonnades and mansions.

Santo Stefano. Piazza Stefano 24. ☎ **051-223-256.** Free admission to church and museum. Mon–Sat 9am–1pm and 3:30–5:30pm; Sun and holidays 9am–12:45 and 3:30–6:30pm.

From the leaning towers (above), head up Via Santo Stefano to see four churches linked together. A church has stood on this site since the 5th century, which even then was a converted Temple of Isis. Charlemagne stopped here to worship on his way to France in the 8th century.

The first church you enter is the 11th-century **Church of the Crucifix (Chiesa di Crocifisso),** relatively simple with only one nave and a crypt. To the left is the entrance to **Santo Sepolcro,** a polygonal temple dating principally from the 12th century. Under the altar is the tomb of San Petronio (St. Petronius), modeled after the Holy Sepulchre in Jerusalem and adorned with bas-reliefs. Continuing left, you enter the churches of **Santi Vitale e Agricola.** The present building, graced with three apses, also dates from the 11th century. To reenter Santo Sepolcro, take the back entrance,

Reserving Winery Tours

Emilia's most famous wine is Lambrusco, 50 million bottles of which are produced every year near Modena and Reggio Emilia. Less well known but also highly rated are the Colli Piacentini wines, one of the rising stars for which is **Cantine Romagnoli,** Via Provinciale, Villo di Vigolzone 29020 (☎ **0523/870-129**). If you'd like to venture out into the countryside, you may want to call ahead and make an appointment for a tour and tasting, and get directions.

Bologna

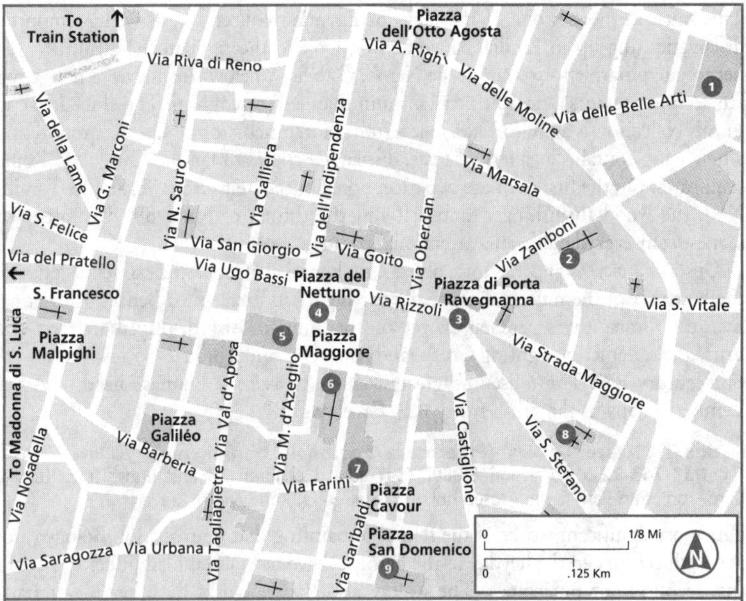

Archaeological Museum **7**
Basilica di San Domenico **9**
Basilica di San Petronio **6**
National Picture Gallery **1**
Neptune Fountain **4**
Palazzo Comunale **5**
San Giacomo Maggiore **2**
Santo Stefano **8**
Tower of the Asinelli & Tower of the Garisenda **3**

this time into the **Courtyard of Pilate (Piazza di Pilatus),** onto which several more chapels open. Legend has it that the basin in the courtyard was the one in which Pontius Pilate washed his hands after condemning Christ to death. (Actually, it's a Lombard bathtub from the 8th century.) Through the courtyard entrance to the right, proceed into the Romanesque **cloisters** from the 11th and 12th centuries. The names on the lapidary wall honor Bolognese war dead.

San Giacomo Maggiore (St. James). Piazza Rossini. ☎ **051-225-970.** Free admission. Daily 10am–1pm and 4–7:30pm.

This church was a Gothic structure in the 13th century but, like so many others, was altered and restored at the expense of its original design. Still, it's one of Bologna's most interesting churches, filled with art treasures. The **Bentivoglio Chapel (Cappella Bentivoglio)** is the most sacred haunt, though time has dimmed the luster of its frescoes. Near the altar, seek out a *Madonna and Child* enthroned, one of the most outstanding works of Francesco Erancia. The holy pair are surrounded by angels and saints, as well as by a half-naked Sebastian to the right. Nearby is a sepulchre of Antonio Bentivoglio, designed by Jacopo della Quercia, who labored so long over the doors to the Basilica of San Petronio. In the **Chapel of Santa Cecilia (Cappella di Santa Cecilia),** you'll discover important frescoes by Francia and Lorenzo Costa.

Archaeological Museum (Museo Civico Archeologico). Via dell'Archiginnasio 2. ☎ **051-233-849.** Admission 8,000L ($4). Tues–Fri 9am–2pm; Sat 9am–1pm and 3:30–7pm. Bus: 11, 17, 25, 30, or 37.

This museum houses one of Italy's major Egyptian collections, as well as important discoveries dug up in Emilia. As you enter, look to the right in the atrium to see a decapitated marble torso, said to be Nero's. One floor below street level, a new Egyptian section presents a notable array of mummies and sarcophagi. The chief attraction in this collection is a cycle of bas-reliefs from Horemheb's tomb. On the ground floor, a new wing contains a gallery of casts, displaying copies of famous Greek and Roman sculptures. On the first floor are two exceptional burial items from Verucchio (Rimini). Note the wood furnishings, footrests, and the throne of tomb 89, decorated with scenes from everyday life and ceremonial parades.

Upstairs are cases of prehistoric objects, tools, and artifacts. Etruscan relics constitute the best part of the museum, especially the highly stylized Askos Benacci, depicting a man on a horse that's perched on yet another animal. Also displayed are terra-cotta urns, a vase depicting fighting Greeks and Amazons, and a bronze Certosa jar from the 6th century B.C. The museum's greatest single treasure is Phidias's head of Athena Lemnia, a copy of the 5th-century B.C. Greek work.

National Picture Gallery (Pinacoteca Nazionale di Bologna). Via Belle Arti 56. ☎ **051-243-222.** Admission 8,000L ($4) adults; children 18 and under free. Tues–Sat 9am–2pm, Sun 9am–1pm. Closed holidays. Bus: 32,33, or 37.

The most significant works of the school of painting that flourished in Bologna from the 14th century to the heyday of the baroque have been assembled under one roof in this second-floor pinacoteca. The gallery also houses works by other major Italian artists, such as Raphael's *St. Cecilia in Estasi.* Guido Reni (1575–1642) of Bologna steals the scene with his *St. Sebastian* and his *Pietà,* along with his penetrating *St. Andrea Corsini, The Slaying of the Innocents,* and idealized *Samson the Victorious.* Other Reni works are *The Flagellation of Christ, The Crucifixion,* and his masterpiece, *Ritratto della Madre* (a revealing portrait of his mother that must surely have inspired Whistler). Then seek out Vitale de Bologna's (1330–61) rendition of St. George slaying the dragon—a theme in European art that parallels Moby Dick in America. Also displayed are works by Francesco Francia, and especially noteworthy is a polyptych attributed to Giotto.

SHOPPING

Collectors of art deco and art nouveau will find a variety of objets d'art at **Art Decorativi,** Via Santo Stefano 12A (☎ **051-222-758**). Obviously the stock changes, but expect to find items like Murano glass, dish sets, furniture, and lamps.

If you call puppeteer ✪ **Dimitrio Presini** (☎ **051-649-1837**), you might be able to set up an appointment to see his creations, but your chances are better if you show up at his workshop at Via Rizzoli 17 (no phone) between 1 and 6pm. Here you can tour the facilities and see how his puppets (including *burratini,* wooden puppets in handmade costumes) are made. You can't buy anything on the premises, but you can order a puppet that'll be made and shipped to you within 1 to 3 months. Presini specializes in local and regional characters but is capable of any custom work you may want.

The **Galleria Marescalchi,** Via Mascarela 116B (☎ **051-240-368**), features more traditional art, offering paintings and prints for view or sale by native son Morandi, Italian modern master De Chirico, and such foreigners as Chagall and Magritte.

Music lovers should head to **Bongiovanni,** Via Rizzoli 28E (☎ **051-225-722**), which stocks rare and popular recordings of operatic and classical scores on cassette, CD, and even vinyl.

An array of breads, pasta, and pastries makes **Atti,** Via Caprarie 7 (☎ **051-220-425**), tempting whether you're hungry or not. Among the pastries are the Bolognese specialty *certosino,* a heavy loaf resembling fruitcake, and an assortment of

The World's Greatest China Shop

Faenza, 36 miles (58km) southeast of Bologna, has lent its name to a form of ceramics called *faïence,* which originated on the island of Majorca, off Spain's coast. Faenza potters found inspiration in the work coming out of Majorca, and in the 12th century they began to produce their own designs, characterized by brilliant colors and floral decorations. The art reached its pinnacle in the 16th century, when the "hot-fire" process was perfected, during which ceramics were baked at a temperature of 1,742°F.

The legacy of this fabled industry is preserved today at the **International Museum of Ceramics (Museo Internazionale delle Ceramiche),** Via Campidori 2 (☎ **0546/21-240**), called "the world's greatest china shop." Housed here are works not only from the artisans of Faenza but also from around the world, including pre-Columbian pottery from Peru. Of exceptional interest are Etruscan and Egyptian ceramics and a wide-ranging collection from the Orient, even from the days of the Roman Empire.

Deserving special attention is the section devoted to modern ceramic art, including works by Matisse and Picasso. On display are Picasso vases and a platter with his dove of peace, a platter in rich colors by Chagall, a "surprise" from Matisse, and a framed ceramic plaque of the Crucifixion by Georges Rouault. Another excellent work, the inspiration of a lesser-known artist, is a ceramic woman by Dante Morozzi. Even the great Léger tried his hand at ceramics.

November to March, the museum is open Tuesday to Friday 9am to 1:30pm, Saturday 9am to 1:30pm and 3 to 6pm, and Sunday 9:30am to 1pm and 3 to 6pm. April to October, hours are Tuesday to Saturday 9am to 6pm and Sunday 9am to 7pm. Admission is 10,000L ($5). It's closed New Year's Day, May 1, August 15, and Christmas.

gastronomie (delectable heat-and-serve starters and main courses made fresh at the shop). If you want chocolate, head to **Majani,** Via Carbonesi 5 (☎ **051-234-302**), which claims to be Italy's oldest sweets shop, having made and sold confections since 1796. A wide assortment of chocolates awaits you, accompanied by several types of biscuits, and at Easter they also make chocolate eggs, rabbits, and lambs. At ✪ **Tamburini,** Via Caprarie 1 (☎ **051-234-726**), one of Italy's most lavish food shops, you can choose from an incredible array of gastronomie, including meats and fish, soups and salads, vegetables, and sweets, as well as fresh pasta to prepare at home. If you don't have anything to cook or serve your pasta in, **Schiavina,** Via Clavature 16 (☎ **051-223-438**), sells every kitchen utensil you might need, like cookware, silverware, glasses, dinnerware, and knives.

If you have hard-to-fit feet, walk to **Piero,** Via delle Lame 56 (☎ **051-558-680**), for attractive footwear for men and women in large sizes, ranging up to European size 53 for men (American size 20) and size 46 for women. Bruno Magli quickly made a name for himself after opening his first shoe factory in 1934. Today, **Bruno Magli** shops selling leather bags, jackets, and coats for men and women—in addition to shoes—are at Galleria Cavour 9 (☎ **051-266-915**) and Piazza della Mercanzia 2 (☎ **051-231-126**).

With styles ranging from elegant to casual, **Marisella,** Via Farini 4 (☎ **051-234-670**), offers women's wear by some of today's best Italian designers. A range of men's and women's clothes is available at **Paris, Texas,** Via Altabella 11

(☎ **051-225-741**), including (but not limited to) designer eveningwear; the location at Via dell'Indipendenza 67B (☎ **051-241-994**) focuses more on casuals like jeans and T-shirts. A third location is at Via Strada Maggiore (☎ **051-225-724**).

The Veronesi family has been closely tied to the jewelry trade for centuries. Now split up and competing among themselves, the various factions are represented by **Arrigo Veronesi,** Via dell'Archiginnasio 4F (☎ **051-230-811**), which sells modern jewelry and watches; **F. Veronesi & Figli,** Piazza Maggiore 4 (☎ **051-224-835**), which offers contemporary jewelry, watches, and silver using ancient designs; and **Giulio Veronesi,** with locations at Piazza di Re Enzo 1 (☎ **051-234-237**) and Galleria Cavour (☎ **051-234-196**), which sells modern jewelry and Rolex watches.

ACCOMMODATIONS

Bologna hosts four to six trade fairs a year, during which hotel room rates rise dramatically. Some hotels announce their prices in advance; others prefer to wait until bookings are actually being accepted, perhaps to see what the market will bear. At trade fair times (dates vary yearly; check with the tourist office), business clients from throughout Europe book the best rooms, and you'll be paying a lot of money to visit Bologna.

An important note on parking: Much of central Bologna is closed to cars without special permits from 7am to 8pm daily (including Sunday and holidays). When booking a room, be prepared to present your car registration number, which the hotel will then provide to the police to ensure you are not fined for driving in a restricted area. Also ask about parking facilities as well as the most efficient route to take to reach your hotel, since many streets in central Bologna are *permanently* closed to traffic. A permit is required to park in the center; hotel guests can purchase one through their hotel.

VERY EXPENSIVE

Grand Hotel Baglioni. Via dell'Indipendenza 8, 40121 Bologna. ☎ **051-225-445.** Fax 051-234-840. www.baglionihotel.com. E-mail: ghb@baghionihotels.com. 125 units. A/C MINIBAR TV TEL. 535,000–790,000L ($267.50–$395) double; 1,100,000–2,500,000L ($550–$1,250) suite. Rates include breakfast. AE, DC, MC, V. Parking 50,000L ($25).

The Baglioni boasts a location near Bologna's main square and is a wonderful atmospheric choice. Its four-story facade is crafted of the same reddish brick that distinguishes many of the city's older buildings, and the interior is noted for its wall and ceiling frescoes. Each soundproof guest room contains reproductions of antique furniture, beds with firm mattresses, and modern conveniences. They're generally spacious, the fourth-floor units being the largest. The marble bathrooms come with hair dryers, deluxe toiletries, and robes.

Dining: Fine Bolognese cooking is served in the elegant I Carracci (see "Dining," below).

Amenities: Room service, baby-sitting, laundry/valet, hairdresser.

EXPENSIVE

Hotel Corona d'Oro 1890. Via Oberdan 12, 40126 Bologna. ☎ **051-236-456.** Fax 051-262-679. www.cnc.it/bologna. E-mail:hotcoro@tin.it. 35 units. A/C MINIBAR TV TEL. 380,000–525,000L ($190–$262.50) double. Rates include buffet breakfast. AE, CB, DC, DISC, MC, V. Parking 35,000–40,000L ($17.50–$20).

This fine palazzo, home of the noble Azzoguidi family in the 15th century, preserves the architectural features of various periods, from the art nouveau in the hall to the medieval coffered ceiling in the meeting room to the frescoes (coats-of-arms and landscapes) in the rooms. The guest rooms are decorated according to various periods, yet they have fax and computer hookups and safes. Most are medium in size. The bathrooms are small but are equipped with hair dryers. The hotel is a short distance from Piazza Maggiore.

Hotel dei Commercianti. Via de' Pignattari 11, 40124 Bologna. ☎ **051-233-052.** Fax 051-224-733. www.cnc.it/bologna. E-mail: hotcom@tin.it. 35 units. A/C MINIBAR TV TEL. 335,000–525,000L ($167.50–$262.50) double; 735,000L ($367.50) suite. Rates include buffet breakfast. AE, CB, DC, DISC, MC, V. Parking 35,000–40,000L ($17.50–$20).

This hotel, located beside San Petronio in the pedestrian area of Piazza Maggiore, is near the site of the "Domus" (the first seat of the town hall) for the commune of Bologna in the 12th century. Recent restorations uncovered original wooden features, which you can see in the hall and the rooms in the old tower. Despite the centuries-old history, the atmosphere is bright and all modern amenities are offered. The guest rooms, most small or medium in size, are decorated with antique furniture and feature quality mattresses and safes. The bathrooms are decent-sized, with a hair dryer.

Hotel Orologio. Via IV Novembre 10, 40123 Bologna. ☎ **051-231-253.** Fax 051-260-552. www.cnc.it/bologna. E-mail:hotoro@tin.it. 35 units. A/C MINIBAR TV TEL. 315,000–525,000L ($157–$262.50) double. Rates include buffet breakfast. AE, CB, DC, DISC, MC, V. Parking 35,000–40,000L ($17.50–$20).

This charming small hotel faces the *orologio* (clock) on the civic center in the heart of medieval Bologna, with a view of Piazza Maggiore and the Podestà Palace. The guest rooms have modern furnishings and safes. Most are small but provide reasonable comfort, including firm mattresses and tidy bathrooms. This is the ideal place for those who wish to steep themselves in the past without forfeiting modern comforts.

Royal Hotel Carlton. Via Montebello 8, 40121 Bologna. ☎ **051-249-361.** Fax 051-249-724. www.monrifhotels.it. E-mail:carlton.res@monrifhotels.it. 251 units. A/C MINIBAR TV TEL. 475,000–630,000L ($237.50–$315) double; 850,000–1,500,000L ($425–$750) suite. Rates include buffet breakfast. AE, DC, MC, V. Parking from 30,000L ($15) in a garage, free outside.

Some claim that the Carlton, only a few minutes' walk from many of the national monuments, is the best hotel in Bologna, but we feel that the honor goes to the Baglioni (see above). The Hilton-style Carlton is a rather austere place with a triangular garden, catering mainly to business travelers. It's modern all the way, with a balcony and picture window for each room, though the views aren't particularly inspiring. The guest rooms range from medium to large, each with a comfortable bed, most often a twin or a double. The bathrooms are well equipped, with hair dryers and enough shelf space.

Dining: One of Bologna's most dramatic staircases sweeps from the second floor to a point near the comfortable American Bar, a grill restaurant serving decent regional and international food.

Amenities: Room service, baby-sitting, laundry/valet, newspaper delivery.

MODERATE

Albergo Al Cappello Rosso. Via dei Fusari 9, 40123 Bologna. ☎ **051-261-891.** Fax 051-227-179. www.italyhotel.com/capellorosso. E-mail: capellorosso@tin.it. 35 units. A/C MINIBAR TV TEL. 355,000L ($177.50) double. During trade fairs/congresses 480,000L ($240) double. Rates include breakfast. AE, DC, MC, V. Parking 35,000L ($17.50).

In the 14th century, the "Red Hat" in the hotel's name referred to the preferred headgear of the privileged tradesmen who stayed here. Now the hotel has been revamped into an ultramodern place with no hint of its past: If modern comfort is what you want or if you need a break from "rustic charm," this is for you. The guest rooms tend to be rather modular, small to medium in size, each with a good bed and firm mattress.

The bathrooms have hair dryers. A sleek brass-topped bar is in the hotel, but breakfast is the only meal served. The staff is gracious and willing to help.

Grand Hotel Elite. Via Aurelio Saffi 36, 40131 Bologna. ☎ **051-649-1432.** Fax 051-649-3539. www.hotelelite.it. E-mail: reservation@hotelelite.it. 175 units. A/C MINIBAR TV TEL. 230,000–300,000L ($115–$150) double; 330,000–580,000L ($165–$290) suite. Rates include breakfast. AE, DC, MC, V. Parking 30,000L ($15).

Located on the city's northwestern edge, a 12-minute walk from the center, this eight-story hotel was built in the 1970s as a combination of private apartments and hotel rooms. In 1993 the entire structure was transformed into a hotel. The guest rooms are unremarkable but comfortable (with firm mattresses); most are medium-sized, with functional furniture. The bathrooms are small but have adequate shelf space.

Even if you're not staying here, you may want to dine in the Cordon Bleu, which features international food and the classic cuisine of Emilia-Romagna (closed Sunday). Also popular is a bar, with comfortable banquettes and a good selection of whisky and regional wines. Additional amenities include concierge, room service, laundry/dry cleaning, a conference room, and baby-sitting.

Hotel Regina. Via dell'Indipendenza 51, 40121 Bologna. ☎ **051-248-878.** Fax 051-247-986. 61 units. A/C MINIBAR TV TEL. 280,000L ($140) double. Rates include breakfast. AE, DC, MC, V. Parking 35,000L ($17.50).

A good plain choice with moderate comfort, the Regina was built in the 1800s and modernized in the 1970s. The guest rooms range from small to medium but come with good mattresses on twins or doubles. The bathrooms are a bit cramped. The staff is helpful, and the maids keep everything spotless. There's a convivial bar and a sofa-filled lounge but no restaurant.

✪ **Hotel Roma.** Via Massimo d'Azeglio 9, 40123 Bologna. ☎ **051-226-322.** Fax 051-239-909. 86 units. A/C TV TEL. 260,000L ($130) double. Breakfast 20,000L ($10). AE, MC, V.

Near Piazza Maggiore, this is one of the best buys in Bologna, enjoying one of the most scenic locations despite the heavy traffic. Most of the guest rooms are roomy yet old-fashioned, with large closets, comfortable armchairs, and excellent beds with fine linen. The bathrooms are small but with adequate shelf space. The best rooms are on the top floor, where there's a terrace overlooking the city rooftops. On site is an excellent dining room serving both international and regional cuisine daily except on Sunday and in August.

Hotel Tre Vecchi. Via dell'Indipendenza 47, 40121 Bologna. ☎ **051-231-991.** Fax 051-224-143. E-mail: trevecchi@dada.it. 96 units. A/C MINIBAR TV TEL. 280,000–380,000L ($140–$190) double. Rates include buffet breakfast. AE, CB, DC, MC, V. Parking 30,000L ($15).

This hotel opened in the 1970s in a century-old building, a 5-minute walk from the train station. The guest rooms are clean, bright, and soundproofed. They're a bit cramped but still comfortable, with firm mattresses on the twin or double beds. The bathrooms are small but provide adequate shelf space. The best room is called Prestige—it's bigger than the others and boasts a Jacuzzi and a private terrace. The gentle humor in the name (Three Geriatrics) was the idea of the trio of aging entrepreneurs who founded the hotel. Breakfast is the only meal served.

DINING

EXPENSIVE

Ristorante al Pappagallo. Piazza della Mercanzia 3C. ☎ **051-232-807.** Reservations recommended. Main courses 35,000–40,000L ($17.50–$20). AE, DC, MC, V. Mon–Sat 12:30–2:30pm and 7:30–10:30pm. BOLOGNESE.

This restaurant has drawn a faithful following for decades; in past years, it has hosted Einstein, Hitchcock, and Toscanini. "The Parrot," still going strong, is on the ground floor of a Gothic mansion across from the 14th-century Merchants' Loggia (a short walk from the leaning towers). Start off with *lasagne verde al forno* (baked lasagna that gets its green color from minced spinach). For the main course, try the specialty: *filetti di tacchino,* superb turkey breasts baked with white wine, parmigiano, and truffles. The menu also features some low-calorie offerings. The restaurant boasts an impressive wine list and serves amber-colored Albana wine and sparkling red Lambrusco.

Moderate

Antica Osteria Romagnola. Via Rialto 13. ☎ **051-263-699.** Reservations recommended for dinner. Main courses 20,000–30,000L ($10–$15). AE, DC, MC, V. Tues 7:30–11pm; Wed–Sat 12:30–2:30pm and 7:30–11pm. Closed Jan 7–16 and Aug. ITALIAN.

In a building dating from 1600, the Romagnola offers cuisines from throughout Italy, including the distant south. You might begin with one of the well-flavored risottos or choose from a savory selection of antipasti. The variety of pastas is impressive, for example, ravioli with truffle essence, garganelli with zucchini, and pasta whipped with asparagus tips. You might also select a terrine of ricotta and arugula (the latter was considered an aphrodisiac by the ancient Romans). For your main course you might try a springtime specialty, *capretto* (roast goat) with artichokes and potatoes or filet mignon with aromatic basil.

Diana. Via dell'Indipendenza 24. ☎ **051-231-302.** Reservations recommended. Main courses 18,000–40,000L ($9–$20). AE, DC, MC, V. Tues–Sun noon–2:30pm and 7–10:30pm. Closed Jan 1–10 and Aug 1–28. REGIONAL/INTERNATIONAL.

Occupying a late medieval building in the heart of town, the Diana has been popular since 1920, offering three gracefully decorated dining rooms and a verdant terrace. It was named in honor of the goddess of the hunt because of the many game dishes it served when it first opened. In recent years, though game is still featured in season, the restaurant has opted for a staple of regional and international cuisine, all competently prepared. Begin with one of the city's most delicious appetizers: *spuma di mortadella,* a pâté made of mortadella sausage served with dainty white toast. You'll never eat baloney again.

Grassilli. Via del Luzzo 3. ☎ **051-237-938** or 051-222-961. Reservations required. Main courses 20,000–30,000L ($10–$15). AE, DC, MC, V. Thurs–Sat and Mon–Tues 12:30–2:30pm and 8–10:30pm; Sun 12:30–2:30pm. Closed July 15–Aug 10, Dec 24–Jan 6, and for dinner on holidays. BOLOGNESE/INTERNATIONAL.

Grassilli is a good bet for conservative regional cooking prepared with time-tested recipes. It's in a 1750s building on a narrow cobblestone alley, a short block from the leaning towers. There's also a street-side canopy for outdoor dining. At night the place can be festive, and your good time will be enhanced if you order a specialty like tortellini in mushroom cream sauce, the chef's special tournedos, tortellini *alla Bologna,* or grilled or roasted meat.

I Carracci. In the Grand Hotel Baglioni, Via dell'Indipendenza 8. ☎ **051-225-445.** Reservations required. Main courses 25,000–40,000L ($12.50–$20). AE, DC, MC, V. Mon–Sat 12:30–2:30pm and 7:30–10:30pm. Closed Aug 1–25. ITALIAN/INTERNATIONAL.

The chic Carracci is named after the family of artists who decorated the premises with frescoes. Its cuisine equals that of the Notai (see below), and the service is impeccable. The elegant dining room dates from the 16th century, with ceiling frescoes of the seasons painted in the 1700s by the Carracci brothers. The seasonally adjusted menu features the freshest produce and highest-quality meat, poultry, and fish. Dishes we've enjoyed are tortellini in brodo, *tagliatelle* (flat noodles) in ragout, veal scallop *alla bolognese,* wild boar cacciatore, and grilled salmon fillet. The wine list is among the region's finest.

Montegrappa da Nello. Via Montegrappa 2. ☎ **051-236-331.** Reservations recommended for dinner. Main courses 15,000–40,000L ($7.50–$20). AE, DC, MC, V. Tues–Sun noon–3pm and 7–11:30pm. Closed Sat–Mon July and Aug. BOLOGNESE/INTERNATIONAL.

Montegrappa da Nello, one of the few restaurants still doing classic Bolognese cuisine, serves wonderful pasta dishes. Franco and Ezio Bolini are the hosts, and they insist that all the produce be fresh. The menu offers *tortellina Montegrappa* (a pasta favorite served in cream-and-meat sauce) and *graminia* (a very fine white spaghetti presented with mushrooms, cream, and pepper). The restaurant is also known for its fresh white truffles and mushrooms. A heavenly salad is made with truffles, mushrooms, parmigiano, and artichokes. For a main course, *misto del cuoco* is a mixed platter of the chef's specialties, including *zampone, cotoletta alla bolognese,* and scaloppini with fresh mushrooms.

✪ **Nuovi Notai.** Via de' Pignattari 1. ☎ **051-228-694.** Reservations required. Main courses 18,000–30,000L ($9–$15); fixed-price menus 50,000–70,000L ($25–$35). AE, DC, MC, V. Mon–Sat noon–2:30pm and 7–11pm. ITALIAN/TUSCAN/UMBRIAN.

Behind a lattice- and ivy-covered facade next to the cathedral, within view of one of Italy's most beautiful squares, this sublime restaurant draws a loyal crowd. In summer, tables are placed outside. Music lovers and relaxing businesspeople appreciate the piano bar. The decor combines the belle epoque with Italian flair and includes artwork, hanging Victorian lamps, and clutches of flowers on each table. The fine cooking is based on the best local products, and menu items include a flan of cheese fondue, gratin of gnocchi with truffles, beef fillet cooked in a *cartoccio* (a paper bag) and garnished with porcini mushrooms, and deboned breast of wild goose.

Ristorante Luciano. Via Nazario Sauro 19. ☎ **051-231-249.** Reservations recommended. Main courses 18,000–55,000L ($9–$27.50). AE, DC, MC, V. Thurs–Tues noon–2pm and 7:30–10:30pm. Closed Aug. BOLOGNESE.

This restaurant, within walking distance of the city center, serves some of Bologna's best food at moderate prices. It has an art deco style and contains three large rooms with a real Bolognese atmosphere. We prefer the front room, opening onto the kitchen. As a novelty, on the street is a window looking directly into the kitchen. To begin your gargantuan repast, request the tortellini in rich cream sauce. Well-recommended main dishes are the *fritto misto all'Italiana* (mixed fry), *scaloppe con porcini* (veal with mushrooms), and *cotoletta alla bolognese,* veal layered with ham and parmigiano, then baked. A dramatic dessert is crêpes flambés.

INEXPENSIVE

The **Enoteca Italiana,** Via Marsala 2/B (☎ **051-235-989**), is an inviting and aromatic shop-cum-wine bar on a side street just north of Piazza Maggiore. You can stand at the bar and sip a local wine while enjoying a sandwich. For a moveable feast, you can stock up on ham, salami, and cheese at the deli counter, and enjoy a picnic at the nearby Neptune fountain.

On a stroll through the **Pescherie Vecchie,** the city's market area near the Due Torri, you can assemble a meal. Along the Via Drapperie and adjoining streets, salumerias, cheese shops, bakeries, and vegetable markets are heaped high with attractive displays. The stalls of Bologna's other food market, the **Mercato delle Erbe,** Via Ugo Bassi 2, are open Monday to Wednesday and Friday and Saturday from 7:15am to 1pm, and Monday to Wednesday again from 5 to 7pm.

The **Bar Roberto** at Via Orefici 9/A, near Bologna's central market, is probably the only smoke-free cafe in Italy. It turns out delicious homemade pastries that attract a loyal breakfast clientele.

Osteria del Moretto. Via di San Mamolo 5. ☎ **051-580-284.** Reservations recommended Fri–Sat. Main courses 18,000–24,000L ($9–$12). No credit cards. Mon–Sat 8pm–2:30am. BOLOGNESE.

This simple trattoria/bar has operated with few obvious changes on its simple menu since around 1900. Built as a convent in the 13th century, it lies near the Porto San Mamolo, in the historic core. Most of the stand-up patrons drink wine and often segue from drinks into a working-class meal. This might include selections from a platter of local cheese as an antipasto, *pasta e fagiole* (with beans), spaghetti bolognese, *salata Trentino* (a cold salad of meat and vegetables), eggplant parmigiana, and chicken—but no fish of any kind.

Osteria dell'Orsa. Via Mentana 1F. ☎ **051-231-576.** Reservations recommended. Main courses 14,000–18,000L ($7–$9). AE, MC, V. Daily noon–3pm and 7pm–1am. ITALIAN.

The restaurant, which offers some of the best *ragú alla bolognese* in town, occupies a 15th-century building near the university. Most diners opt for the high-ceilinged, medieval-looking main floor, though an informal cantina-like cellar room is open for additional seating. You won't go wrong if you preface a meal with any kind of pasta labeled *bolognese.* Other options are homemade tagliolini (with the ragout), veal cutlet *fiorentina* (with spinach), and tortelloni with cheese, ham, and mushroom sauce. If you feel adventurous, you can always try grilled donkey meat (*somarino*).

NEARBY DINING

✪ **San Domenico.** Via Gaspara Sacchi 1, Imola (21 miles/34km southeast of Bologna). ☎ **0542/29-000.** Reservations recommended. Main courses 50,000–60,000L ($25–$30); fixed-price lunch 65,000L ($32.50); fixed-price dinner 120,000L ($60). AE, DC, MC, V. Tues–Sun 12:30–2:30pm; Tues–Sat 8–10:30pm. Closed Jan 1–10 and 1 week in Aug. ITALIAN.

Foodies from all over Europe and America travel to the unlikely village of Imola to savor the offerings of what some food critics (ourselves included) consider the best restaurant in Italy. The restaurant can also be easily reached from Ravenna. The cuisine is sometimes compared to France's modern cuisine creations. However, owner Gian Luigi Morini claims his delectable offerings are nothing more than adaptations of festive regional dishes, except they're lighter, more subtle, and served in manageable portions.

A tuxedo-clad member of his talented young staff will escort you to a table near the tufted leather banquettes. Meals include heavenly concoctions made with the freshest ingredients. You might select goose-liver pâté studded with white truffles, fresh shrimp in creamy sweet bell-pepper sauce, roast rack of lamb with fresh rosemary, stuffed chicken supreme wrapped in lettuce leaves, or fresh handmade spaghetti with shellfish. Signor Morini has collected some of the best vintages in Europe for the past 30 years, with some bottles of cognac dating from the time of Napoléon.

BOLOGNA AFTER DARK

Since Bologna has a large population of students and graduate students, it has a vibrant, diverse nightlife scene, including lots of cafes that are packed with a young crowd. The Via del Pratello and, near the university, Via Zamboni and Via delle Belle Arte and their surrounding areas are the usual haunts of night owls. You can usually find a place for a drink, a shot of espresso, or a light meal as late as 2am.

One of the most central and popular spots is **Mocambo,** Via d'Azeglio 1E (☎ **051-229-516**), near the Duomo. Its major competitor, also facing the Duomo, is **Bar Giuseppe,** Piazza Maggiore 1 (☎ **051-264-444**), serving some of the best espresso and gelato in town. It stretches for at least a block beneath the arcades facing the Piazza Maggiore.

You'll want to retire at 10:30pm to the cellars of a 16th-century palazzo near the university at **Cantina Bentivoglio** at Via Mascarella 4B (☎ **051-265-416**). That's when you'll hear some of the best jazz in Bologna.

Cassero, Piazza Porta Saragozza 2 (☎ **051-644-6902**), is Bologna's most popular gay bar, with a noisy discolike atmosphere and floor shows. The biggest attraction here, though, is the setting—the club occupies one of Bologna's medieval gates, the top of which serves as a roof garden and open-air dance floor in good weather.

Osteria de Poeti, Via Poeti 1 (☎ **051-236-166**), is Bologna's oldest osteria and has been in operation since the 16th century. The brick-vaulted ceilings, stone walls, and ancient wine barrels provide just the sort of ambience you would expect to find in such a historic establishment. Stop in to enjoy the live jazz and folk music that's on tap most nights.

During July and August, the city authorities transform the **parks** along the town's northern tier into an Italian version of a German *biergarten,* complete with disco music under colored lights. Vendors sell beer and wine from indoor/outdoor bars set up on the lawns, and others hawk food and souvenirs. Events range from live jazz to classical concerts. Ask any hotelier or the tourist office for the schedule of midsummer events, or try your luck by taking either a taxi or (much less convenient) bus no. 25 or 91A from the main station to Arena Parco Nord.

The **Teatro Comunale,** Via Largo Respighi (☎ **051-529-999**), is the venue for major cultural presentations, including opera, ballet, and orchestral presentations. The **Circolo della Musica di Bologna,** Via Galliera 11 (☎ **051-227-032**), presents free classical music concerts in summer. For the rest of the year, there's always a cafe, bar, or pub nearby.

Another hot spot is the **Cantina Bentivoglio,** Via Mascarella 4B (☎ **051-265-416**), off Via delle Belle Arti, a fairly upmarket joint serving reasonably priced food and wine and staging great live jazz Tuesday to Sunday after 10:30pm, when there's less emphasis on food. The cover of 15,000L ($9) includes your first drink but is only for special concerts.

Bologna's most popular gay center is **Cassero,** Piazza Porta Saragozza 2 (☎ **051-644-6902**), in a medieval building that opens onto a third-floor terrace. This is the Bologna headquarters of Arcigay and Arcilesbiche, a gay and lesbian center organizing cultural meetings and entertainment. Thursday is set aside for women, on Friday theatrical performances of interest to the gay and lesbian community take place, and on Sunday disco fever takes over.

2 Ferrara

259 miles (417km) N of Rome, 32 miles (52km) N of Bologna, 62 miles (100km) SW of Venice

When Papa Borgia (Pope Alexander VI) was shopping for a third husband for the apple of his eye, darling Lucrezia, his gaze fell on the influential house of Este. From the 13th century, this great Italian family had dominated Ferrara, building up a powerful duchy and a reputation as patrons of the arts. Alfonse d'Este, son of the shrewd but villainous Ercole I, the ruling duke of Ferrara, was an attractively virile candidate for Lucrezia's much-used hand. (Her second husband was murdered, perhaps by her brother, Cesare, who was the apple of nobody's eye—with the possible exception of

Machiavelli. Her first marriage, a political alliance, was to Giovanni Sforza, but it was annulled in 1497.)

Although the Este family may have had reservations (after all, it was common gossip that the pope "knew" his daughter in the biblical sense), they finally consented to the marriage. As the duchess of Ferrara, a position she held until her death, Lucrezia bore seven children. But one of her grandchildren, Alfonso II, wasn't as prolific and left the family without a male heir. The greedy eye of Pope Clement VIII took quick action, gobbling up the city as his personal fiefdom in the waning months of the 16th century. The great house of Este went down in history, and Ferrara sadly declined under the papacy.

Incidentally, Alfonso II was a dubious patron of Torquato Tasso (1544–95), author of the epic *Jerusalem Delivered,* a work that was to make him the most celebrated poet of the Late Renaissance. The legend of Tasso (who's thought to have been insane, paranoid, or at least tormented) has steadily grown over the centuries. It didn't need any more boosting, but Goethe fanned the legend through the Teutonic lands with his late-18th-century drama *Torquato Tasso.* It's said that Alfonso II at one time made Tasso his prisoner.

Ferrara is still relatively undiscovered, especially by North Americans, but it's richly blessed, with much of its legacy intact—and you may bless the lack of crowds after fighting your way through some of Italy's most popular destinations. Among the historic treasures are a great cathedral and the Este Castle, along with enough ducal palaces to make for a fast-paced day of sightseeing. Its palaces, for the most part, have long been robbed of their lavish furnishings, but the faded frescoes, the paintings that weren't carted off, and the palatial rooms are reminders of the vicissitudes of power.

Modern Ferrara is one of the most health-conscious places in all Italy. Bicycles outnumber the automobiles on the road, and more than half the citizens get exercise by jogging. In fact, it's almost surreal: Enclosed in medieval walls under a bright sky, everywhere you look, you'll find the people of Ferrara engaged in all sorts of self-powered locomotion. Beware of octogenarian cyclists whizzing by you with shopping bags flapping in the wind.

ESSENTIALS

GETTING THERE Getting to Ferrara by **train** is fast and efficient, because it's on the main line between Bologna and Venice. A total of 33 trains a day originating in Bologna pass through. Trip time is 40 minutes, and the fare is 4,500L ($2.25) one way. Some 24 trains arrive from Venice ($1^1/_2$ hours); the one-way fare is 11,100L ($5.55). Ravenna is just an hour's trip away, with hourly departures all day long.

For information and schedules, call ☎ **0532-770-340** or 1478-88-088 (toll-free in Italy only).

From most destinations the train is best, but if you're in Modena (see below), you'll find 11 **bus** departures a day for Ferrara. Trip time is between $1^1/_2$ and 2 hours, and a one-way ticket is 8,500L ($4.25). In Ferrara, bus information for the surrounding area is available by calling ☎ **0532-240-679.**

If you have a **car** and are coming from Bologna, take A13 north. From Venice, take A4 southwest to Padua and continue on A13 south to Ferrara.

VISITOR INFORMATION The helpful **tourist office** is at Castello Estense, Piazza del Castello (☎ **0532-209-370**), open Monday to Saturday 9am to 1pm and 2 to 6pm, Sunday 9am to 1pm.

SPECIAL EVENTS Not quite as dramatic as its counterpart in Siena, Ferrara's **Palio di San Giorgio** is nevertheless a popular event held in the Piazza Ariostea the last Sunday of May. Two-legged creatures run first, in separate races for young men and young women. They are followed by donkeys and, finally, in the main event, horses ridden bareback by jockeys representing Ferrara's eight traditional districts.

During the summer, the streets of Ferrara seem like one great theater. Some excellent jazz and classical concerts are the main events of **Estate a Ferrara,** an outdoor festival that begins in early July and runs until late August, when the festivities are augmented by street musicians, mimes, and orators, who partake in the **Busker's Festival.**

EXPLORING THE TOWN

Ferrara's **medieval walls,** massive enough to be topped with trees and lawns, encircle the city with an aerie of greenery. The wide paths are ideal for biking, jogging, and strolling; they provide wonderful views of the city and surrounding farmland. Many hotels offer guests free use of bikes, or you can rent them from the lot outside the train station.

A cost-efficient way to tour Ferrara's many museums is to purchase a *biglietto cumulativo* for 20,000L ($10); it's valid for one week and is good for admission to most municipal museums. You can buy it at any of the participating museums.

Castello Estense. Largo Castello. ☎ **0532-299-233.** Admission 8,000L ($4) adults. Tues–Sun 9:30am–5pm. Bus: 1, 2, or 9.

A moated four-towered castle (lit at night), this proud fortress began as a bricklayer's dream near the end of the 14th century, though its face has been lifted and wrenched about for centuries. It was home to the powerful Estes, where the dukes went about their ho-hum daily chores: trysting with their own lovers, murdering their wives' lovers, beheading or imprisoning potential enemies, whatever. Today it's used for the provincial and prefectural administration offices, and you can view many of its once-lavish rooms—notably the **Salon of Games (Salone dei Giochi),** the **Salon of Dawn (Salone dell'Aurora),** and a **Lombardesque chapel** that once belonged to Renata di Francia, daughter of Louis XII. Parisina d'Este, wife of Duke Nicolò d'Este III, was murdered with her lover, Ugolino (the duke's illegitimate son), in the dank prison below the castle, creating the inspiration for Browning's "My Last Duchess."

Il Duomo & Duomo Museum (Museo del Duomo). Piazza Cattedrale. ☎ **0532-207-449.** Free admission, but donation appreciated. Tues–Sat 10am–noon and 3–5pm, Sun 10am–12:30pm and 3:30–5:30pm. Closed Jan 6–Mar 1. Bus: 1, 2, or 9.

A short stroll from the Este castle, the 12th-century **Duomo** weds the delicate Gothic with the more virile Romanesque. The offspring is an exciting pink marble facade. Behind the cathedral is a typically Renaissance **campanile (bell tower).** Inside, the massive structure is heavily baroqued, as the artisans of still another era festooned it with trompe l'oeil.

The entrance to the **Museo del Duomo** is to the left of the atrium as you enter. It's worth a visit just to see works by Ferrara's most outstanding 15th-century painter, Cosmé Tura. Aesthetically controversial, the big attraction here is Tura's St. George slaying the dragon to save a red-stockinged damsel in distress. Opposite is an outstanding Jacopo della Quercia work of a sweet, regal Madonna with a pomegranate in one hand and the Child in the other. Also from the Renaissance heyday of Ferrara are some bas-reliefs, notably a Giano *bifronte* (a mythological figure looking at the past and the future), along with some 16th-century *arazzi* (tapestries) woven by hand.

Civic Museum of Ancient Art (Museo Civico d'Arte Antica). In the Palazzo Schifanoia, Via Scandiana 23. ☎ **0532-64-178.** Admission 8,000L ($4). Daily 9am–7pm. Closed major holidays. Bus: 1, 2, or 9.

The Schifanoia Palace was built in 1385 for Albert V d'Este and enlarged by Borso d'Este (1450–71). The Ancient Art Museum was founded in 1758 and transferred to its present site in 1898. At first, only coins and medals were exhibited, but then the collection was enhanced by donations of archaeological finds, antique bronzes, small Renaissance plates and pottery, and other collections.

Art lovers are lured to the **Salon of the Months (Salone dei Mesi)** to see the astrological wall cycle, which represents the 12 months. Each month is subdivided into three horizontal bands: The lower band shows scenes from the daily life of courtiers and people, the middle the relative sign of the zodiac, and the upper the triumph of the classical divinity for that myth. Humanist Pellegrino Prisciani conceived the subjects of the cycle, though Cosmé Tura, the official court painter, was probably the organizer of the works. Tura was the founder of the Ferrarese School, to which belonged, among others, Ercole de' Roberti and Francesco del Cossa, who painted the March, April, and May scenes. The frescoes are complex, leading to varied interpretations as to their meaning.

Palazzo dei Diamanti. Corso Ercole d'Este 21. ☎ **0532-205-844** or 0532-209-988. Admission: Pinacoteca 8,000L ($4); Civic Gallery of Modern Art 12,000L ($6). Pinacoteca Tues–Sat 9am–2pm; Sun 9am–1pm. Civic Gallery of Modern Art daily 9am–7pm, when exhibits are staged.V. Bus: 3.

The Palazzo dei Diamanti, another jewel of Este splendor, is so named because of the 9,000 diamond-shaped stones on its facade. Of the handful of museums sheltered here, the **National Picture Gallery (Pinacoteca Nazionale)** is the most important. It houses the works of the Ferrarese artists—notably the trio of old masters, Tura, del Cossa, and Roberti. The collection covers the chief period of artistic expression in Ferrara from the 14th to the 18th century. Next in importance is the **Civic Gallery of Modern Art (Museo Civico d'Arte Moderne),** which sponsors the most important contemporary art exhibits in town. The other three museums in the palazzo aren't really worth your time.

Casa Romei. Via Savonarola 30. ☎ **0532-240-341.** Admission 4,000L ($2). Daily 8:30am–2pm. Bus: 3.

This 15th-century palace near the Este tomb was the property of John Romei, a friend and confidant of the fleshy Duke Borso d'Este, who made the Este realm a duchy. John (Giovanni) was later to marry one of the Este princesses, though we don't know if it was for love or power or both. In later years, Lucrezia and her gossipy coterie, riding in the ducal carriage drawn by handsome white horses, used to descend on the Romei house, perhaps to receive Borgia messengers from Rome. Its once-elegant furnishings have been carted off, but the chambers (many with terra-cotta fireplaces) remain, and the casa has been filled with frescoes and sculpture.

SHOPPING

Ferrara has a rich tradition of artisanship dating from the Renaissance. You can find some of the best, albeit expensive, products in the dozen or so antiques stores in the historic center. A particularly appealing dealer is **Antichita San Michele,** Via del Turco 22A (☎ **0532-211-055**).

You can also find beautifully designed, colorful ceramics at **Ceramica Artistica Ferrarese,** Via Baluardi 125 (☎ **0532-66-093**), and **La Marchesana,** Via Cortevecchia 38A (☎ **0532-240-535**).

More unusual is an outfit specializing in wrought iron: **Chierici,** Via Bartoli 17 (☎ **0532-67-057**), near the Ponte San Giorgio. Some of the smaller pieces, such as decorative brackets or fireplace tools, make good souvenirs.

The **Antica Salumeria Polesinati,** Via Mazzini 78 (☎ **0532-206-833**), and the **Enoteca Al Brindisi,** Via Adelardi 11 (☎ **0532-209-142**), stockpile the fruits of the Ferrarese harvest in historically evocative settings. And every month except August, on the first Saturday and first Sunday of the month, the **open-air antiques and handcraft markets** feature lots of junk amid the increasingly rare treasures. The markets are conducted 8am to 7pm in Piazza Municipale (mostly antiques and bric-a-brac) and Piazza Savonarola (mainly handcrafts and bric-a-brac).

ACCOMMODATIONS

✪ **Hotel Duchessa Isabella.** Via Palestro 68/70, 44100 Ferrara. ☎ **0532-202-121.** Fax 0532-202-638. www.relaischateaux.fr/isabella. E-mail: isabella@relaischateaux.fr. 27 units. A/C MINIBAR TV TEL. 490,000–540,000L ($245–$270) double; from 740,000L ($370) suite. Rates include breakfast. AE, DC, MC, V. Free parking. Closed Aug. Bus: 1, 2, 3, or 9.

Until the late 1980s, this was the home of the head of one of the region's most respected Jewish organizations. In 1990 it opened as a five-star hotel with a spectacular decor, named after the Este family's most famous ancestor, Isabella. Today it's a member of the illustrious Relais & Châteaux chain. The guest rooms are identified by the names of the flowers whose colors they most closely resemble. Each boasts a sense of history, is outfitted with all the modern amenities, and is very comfortable, with luxurious mattresses and fine linen. The plush bathrooms come with deluxe toiletries and hair dryers.

Dining: The elegant restaurant is set beneath lavishly gilded and painted ceilings. (In summer, dining moves out into the garden.) The cuisine is based on the traditional recipes of Emilia-Romagna, though a wide choice of less esoteric dishes is also available. The restaurant is closed on Sunday and Monday for dinner.

Amenities: Room service, laundry/valet, conference facilities, free use of bicycles. A horse-drawn landau takes guests on excursions around Ferrara's historic center.

Hotel Europa. Corso della Giovecca 49, 44100 Ferrara. ☎ **0532-205-456.** Fax 0532-212-120. E-mail: info@hoteleuropaferrara.com. 39 units. A/C MINIBAR TV TEL. 195,000L ($97.50) double; 250,000L ($125) suite. Rates include breakfast. AE, DC, MC, V. Parking 14,000L ($7). Bus: 1, 2, 3, or 9.

In the 1600s, this palace was built near the Castello d'Estense. In 1880 it was transformed into one of the most prestigious hotels in town, but during World War II portions of the rear were bombed and then repaired in a less grandiose style. The three-star place continues today, with a well-trained staff, reasonable prices, and guest rooms that are clean and comfortable, with antique furnishings and modern comforts like quality mattresses. A handful of rooms overlook the corso (they retain ceiling frescoes from the original construction). The bathrooms are small but equipped with fluffy towels and hair dryers. There's a bar but no restaurant; breakfast is the only meal served.

Ripagrande Hotel. Via Ripagrande 21, 44100 Ferrara. ☎ **0532-765-250.** Fax 0532-764-377. www.4net.com/business/ripa. E-mail: ripa@mbox.4net.it. 40 units. A/C MINIBAR TV TEL. 300,000–340,000L ($150–$170) double; 360,000–400,000L ($180–$200) junior suite. Rates include breakfast. AE, DC, MC, V. Parking free on street. Bus: 2, 3,6, 9, or 11.

The Ripagrande, one of the town's unusual hotels, occupies a Renaissance palace. Coffered ceilings, walls in Ferrarese brickwork, 16th-century columns, and a wide staircase with a floral cast-iron handrail characterize the entrance hall. Inside are two Renaissance courtyards decorated with columns and capitals. Half the guest rooms are junior suites with sleeping areas connected to an internal stairway. The rooms are spacious, with tasteful furnishings, often antique reproductions. Some are trilevel, with a garretlike bedroom above. The most desirable rooms are on the top floor, opening onto terraces overlooking the red-tile roofs. The bathrooms, though a bit small, have adequate shelf space and hair dryers. Laundry and room service are provided.

The hotel also has a well-known restaurant, Riparestaurant, which serves traditional dishes with a passion for genuine food. Examples of its recipes are *asticcio di macceroni,* a macaroni pie with fresh tomato sauce, several kinds of cheese, and basil; or *capellacci di zucca,* big dumplings stuffed with pumpkin. The atmosphere is romantic, and the restaurant has an excellent choice of wines.

DINING

You might like to put together a picnic to enjoy atop Ferrara's medieval walls. Buy what you need on the **Via Cortevecchia,** a narrow brick street near the cathedral where locals come to food-shop. It's lined with salumerias, cheese shops, and bakeries. The nearby **Mercato Communale,** at the corner of Via Santo Stefano and Via del Mercato, is crowded with food stalls and open till 1pm Monday through Saturday, and 3:30 to 7:30pm on Friday.

Grotta Azzurra. Piazza Sacrati 43. ☎ **0532-209-152.** Reservations recommended. Main courses 16,000–30,000L ($8–$15); fixed-price menus 35,000–60,000L ($17.50–$30). AE, MC, V. Mon–Tues and Thurs–Sun 12–2:30pm and 7–9:30pm. Closed July. Bus: 1, 2, 3, or 9. FERRARESE/SEAFOOD.

Behind a classic brick facade on a busy square, the Grotta Azzurra seems like a restaurant you might find on the sunny isle of Capri, not in Ferrara. However, the cuisine is firmly entrenched in the northern Italian kitchen. It's best to visit in autumn, when favorite dishes are wild boar and pheasant, usually served with polenta. Many sausages, served as antipasti, are made with game as well. More esoteric dishes include a boiled calf's head and tongue, while a local favorite is boiled stuffed pork leg. The chef is also an expert at grilled meats, especially pork, veal, and beef.

La Provvidenza. Corso Ercole d'Este 92. ☎ **0532-205-187.** Reservations required. Main courses 20,000–38,000L ($10–$19). AE, DC, MC, V. Tues–Sun noon–2:30pm and 8–10pm. Closed Aug 11–23. Bus: 1, 2, 3, or 9. FERRARESE/ITALIAN.

La Provvidenza, whose building is from around 1750, stands on the same street as the Palazzo dei Diamanti. It has a farm-style interior, with a little garden where you can dine in fair weather. The antipasti table is the finest we've seen (or sampled) in Ferrara. Hearty eaters should order a pasta, such as fettuccine with smoked salmon, before tackling the main course, perhaps perfectly grilled and seasoned veal chops. Other specialties are *pasticchio alla Ferrarese* (macaroni mixed with a mushroom-and-meat sauce laced with creamy white sauce) and *fritto misto di carne* (mixed grill). The dessert choice is wide and luscious.

FERRARA AFTER DARK

During July and August, concerts and temporary art exhibits are offered as part of the **Estate a Ferrara** program. The tourist office will provide a schedule of events and dates, which vary from year to year. During the rest of the year, you can rub elbows with fellow drinkers, and usually lots of students, at a refreshingly diverse collection of bars, pubs, and discos. The **Osteria Al Brindisi,** Via Adelardi 11 (☎ **0532-209-142**), claims, with some justification, to be the oldest wine bar in the world, with a tradition of uncorking bottles dating from the early 1400s. Wine begins at around 2,000L ($1) per glass and seems to taste best when accompanied by a few of the dozen *panini* (sandwiches).

North of the historic center, **Pelledoca,** Via Arianuova 21 (☎ **0532-248-952**), is another hot club, luring young locals as well as foreign visitors. Hours depend on the crowd.

3 Ravenna & Its Dazzling Mosaics

46 miles (74km) E of Bologna, 90 miles (145km) S of Venice, 81 miles (130km) NE of Florence, 227 miles (365km) N of Rome

Ravenna is one of the most unusual towns in Emilia-Romagna. Today, you'll find a sleepy town with memories of a great past, luring hordes of tourists to explore what remains. As the capital of the Western Roman Empire (from A.D. 402), the Visigoth Empire (from A.D. 473), and the Byzantine Empire under Emperor Justinian and Empress Theodora (A.D. 540–752), Ravenna became one of the greatest cities on the Mediterranean.

Ravenna achieved its cultural peak as part of the Byzantine Empire between the 6th and the 8th centuries and is known for the many well-preserved mosaics created during that time—the finest in all Western art and the most splendid outside Istanbul. Although it now looks much like any other Italian city, the low Byzantine domes of its churches still evoke its Eastern past.

ESSENTIALS

GETTING THERE With frequent **train** service and a short ride of only 1¼ hours by train from Bologna, Ravenna can be easily visited on a day trip; one-way fare is 7,500L ($3.75). There's also frequent service to Ferrara; one-way fare is 8,000L ($4). At Ferrara, you can make connections to Venice. The train station is a 10-minute walk from the center at Piazza Fernini (☎ **1478-88-088**). The tourist office (below) has rail schedules and more details; or you can call ☎ **0544-35-288** or 167/21-34-80 (toll-free in Italy only).

If you have a **car** and are coming from Bologna, head east along A14 or southeast of Ferrara on S309.

VISITOR INFORMATION The helpful **tourist office** is at Via Salara 8 (☎ **0544-35-404**). October to May, it's open Monday to Saturday 8:30am to 6pm and Sunday 10am to 4pm; June to September, hours are Monday to Saturday 8:30am to 7pm and Sunday 10am to 5pm. Stop in here first; they'll give you a good map and sell you a discount combination ticket to the city's attractions.

SPECIAL EVENTS If you're here in June and July, you can enjoy the **Ravenna Festival Internazionale.** Even Pavarotti and other greats might show up to perform. Tickets begin at 30,000L ($15) but go much higher. For information, call ☎ **0544-213-895;** for tickets, call ☎ **0544-325-77.** A **Dante Festival** takes place the second week in September, sponsored by the church of San Francesco. Call ☎ **0544-332-56** for details.

EXPLORING THE TOWN

You can see all the sights in one busy day. The center of Ravenna is **Piazza del Popolo,** which has a Venetian aura. To the south, off the colonnaded Piazza San Francesco, you can visit the **Tomba di Dante** on Via Dante Alighieri. After crossing Piazza dei Caduti and heading north along Via Guerrini, you reach the **Battistero Neoniano** at Piazza del Duomo. Directly southeast and opening onto Piazza Arcivescovado is the **Museo Arcivescovile** and the **Chapel of San Andrea.**

Ravenna

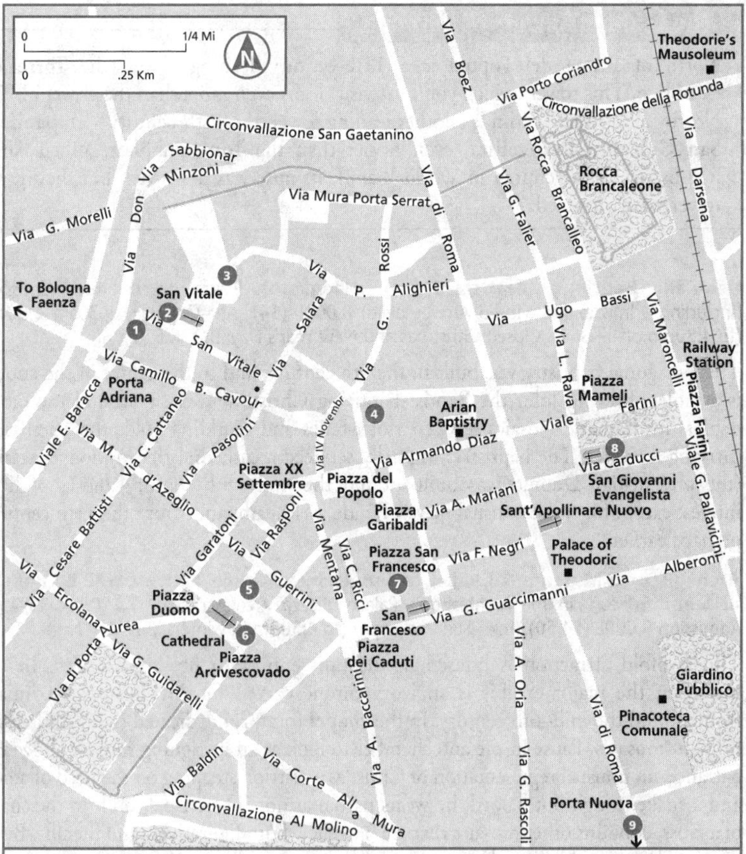

Archepiscopal Museum / Chapel of San Andrea **6**
Basilica of Sant'Apollinaire in Classe **9**
Campanile di San Giovanni Evangelista **8**
Dante's Tomb **7**
Mausoleom of Galla Placidia **3**
Museum & Basilica of San Vitale **2**
National Museum of Ravenna **1**
Neoniano Baptistry **5**
Torre del Pubblico **4**

Then you can head back to the tourist office, cutting west along Via San Vitale. This will take you to the **Basilica di San Vitale** and the **Mausoleum of Galla Placidia** behind the basilica. Nearby is the **Museo Nazionale di Ravenna** along Via Fiandrini (adjacent to Via San Vitale). To cap off your day, you can take bus no. 4 or 44 from the rail station or Piazza Caduti to visit the **Basilica of Sant'Appollinare in Classe,** reached along Via Romeo Sud.

If you're planning on seeing more than one sight, the most economical choice is to buy a **combination ticket** to visit these six monuments for 8,000L ($4): the Battistero della Neoniano, Archepiscopal Museum/Chapel of San Andrea, Church of San Vitale, Mausoleum of Galla Placidia, and Basilica of Sant'Apollinare. The ticket is available at the tourist office.

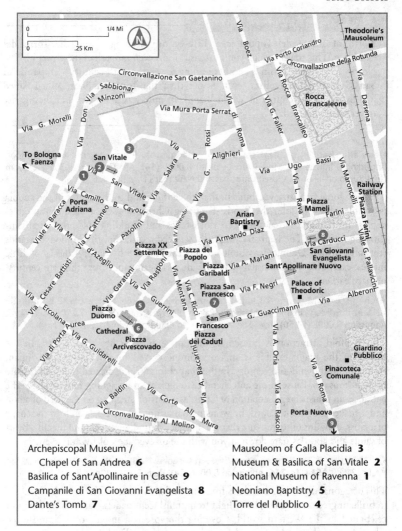

The Leaning Towers of Ravenna

North of Piazza del Popolo is a 12th-century leaning tower, the **Torre del Pubblico.** This tower (which you can't visit) leans even more than the Tower of Pisa. Nearby along Viale Farini is another leaning tower, the 12th-century **Campanile di San Giovanni Evangelista,** even tipsier than the Torre Pubblica. When Allied bombs struck the church in World War II, its apse was destroyed, but the mighty tower wasn't toppled.

Neoniano Baptistry (Battistero della Neoniano). Piazza del Duomo. Admission (including admission to Museo Arcivescovile) 8,000L ($4). Apr–Oct daily 9:30am–6:30pm (to 4:30pm off-season). Closed Christmas and New Year's Day. Bus: MB.

This octagonal baptistry was built in the 5th century, and in the center of the cupola is a tablet showing John the Baptist baptizing Christ. The circle around the tablet depicts in dramatic mosaics of deep violet-blues and sparkling golds the 12 crown-carrying Apostles. The baptistry originally serviced a cathedral that no longer stands (the present-day Duomo was built around the mid–18th century and is of little interest except for some unusual pews). Beside it is a campanile from the 11th century, perhaps earlier.

Archepiscopal Museum & Chapel of San Andrea (Museo Arcivescovile e Cappella di San Andrea). In the Archbishop's Palace, Piazza Arcivescovado. ☎ **0544-39-196.** Admission 9,000L ($4.50). Tues–Sun 9am–6pm (to 4:30pm in winter). Bus: 1, 11.

This twofold attraction is housed in the 6th-century Archbishop's Palace. In the **museum,** the major exhibit is an ivory throne carved for Archbishop Maximian, from around the mid–6th century. In the **chapel** (oratory) dedicated to St. Andrea are brilliant mosaics. Pause in the antechamber to look at an intriguing **mosaic** above the entrance, an unusual representation of Christ as a warrior, stepping on the head of a lion and a snake; tough but haloed, he wears partial armor. The chapel, built in the shape of a cross, contains other mosaics that are "angelic," both figuratively and literally. Busts of saints and apostles stare down at you with the ox-eyed look of Byzantine art.

✪ **Museum & Basilica of San Vitale (Museo e Basilica di San Vitale).** Via San Vitale 17. ☎ **0544-34-266.** Admission 8,000L ($4). Daily 9am–4:30pm. Bus: 1 or 11.

This octagonal domed church dates from the mid–6th century. The **mosaics** inside—in brilliant greens and golds, lit by light from translucent panels—are among the most celebrated in the Western world. Covering the apse is a mosaic of a clean-shaven Christ astride the world, flanked by saints and angels. To the right is a mosaic of Empress Theodora and her court, and to the left the man who married this courtesan/actress, Emperor Justinian, and his entourage.

✪ **Mausoleum of Galla Placidia.** Via San Vitale. ☎ **0544-34-266.** Admission 6,000L ($3). Apr–Sept, daily 9am–6pm (Oct–Mar to 4:30pm).

This 5th-century chapel is so unpretentious you'll think you're in the wrong place. But inside it contains some exceptional **mosaics** dating from antiquity, though they may not look it. Translucent panels bring the mosaics alive in all their grace and harmony, vivid with peacock blue, moss green, Roman gold, eggplant, and burnt orange. The mosaics in the cupola literally glitter with stars. Popular tradition claims that the cross-shaped structure houses the tomb of Galla Placidia, sister of Honorius, Rome's last emperor. Galla, who died in Rome in A.D. 450, is one of history's most powerful women. She became virtual ruler of the Western world after her husband, Ataulf, king of the Visigoths, died (only a virtual ruler because she became a regent for Valentinian III, who was only 6 at the time of his father's death).

National Museum of Ravenna (Museo Nazionale di Ravenna). Via Fiandrini (adjacent to Via San Vitale). ☎ **0544-34-424.** Admission 8,000L ($4). Tues–Sat 8:30am–6:30pm, Sun 8:30am–7:30pm. Bus: 1 or 11.

This museum contains archaeological objects from the early Christian and Byzantine periods: icons, fragments of tapestries, medieval armaments and armory, sarcophagi, ivories, ceramics, and bits of broken pieces from the stained-glass windows of San Vitale.

Basilica of Sant'Apollinare in Classe. Via Romeo Sud. ☎ **0544-527-004.** Admission 4,000L ($2). Daily 9am–5pm (to 6pm in summer). Bus: 4 or 44 from rail station (every 20 min.) or Piazza Caduti.

About 3½ miles (6km) south of the city (you can stop by on the way to Ravenna if you're heading north from Rimini), this church dates from the 6th century and was consecrated by Archbishop Maximian. Dedicated to St. Apollinare, the bishop of Ravenna, the early basilica stands side-by-side with a campanile, symbols of faded glory now resting in a lonely low-lying area. Inside is a central nave flanked by two aisles, the latter containing tombs of ecclesiastical figures in the Ravenna hierarchy. The floor (once carpeted with mosaics) has been rebuilt. Along the central nave are frescoed tablets. Two dozen marble columns line the approach to the apse, where you'll find the major reason for visiting the basilica: The **mosaics** here are exceptional, rich in gold and turquoise, set against a background of top-heavy birds nesting in shrubbery. St. Apollinare stands in the center, with a row of lambs on either side lined up as in a processional, the 12 lambs symbolizing the Apostles.

Dante's Tomb (Tomba di Dante). Via Dante Alighieri. Free admission. Daily 8am–7pm.

Right off Piazza Garibaldi, the final monument to Dante Alighieri, "the divine poet," isn't much to look at, graced with a marble bas-relief. But it's a far better place than he assigned to some of his fellow Florentines. The author of the *Divine Comedy,* in exile from his hometown, died in Ravenna on September 14, 1321. To the right of the small temple is a mound of earth in which Dante's urn went "underground" from March 1944 to December 1945 because it was feared his tomb might suffer from the bombings. Near the tomb is the 5th-century church of **San Francesco,** the site of the poet's funeral.

SHOPPING

One of the best places to admire (and buy) mosaics is the **Studio Acomena,** Via Ponte della Vecchia (☎ **0544-37-119**). Replicas of Christ, the Madonna, the saints, and penitent sinners appear in all their majesty amid more secular forms whose designs were inspired by Roman gladiators or floral and geometric motifs. Virtually anything

A Day at the Beach

By taking bus no. 70 from Ravenna, in just 20 minutes you can enjoy **white-sand beaches** set against a backdrop of pine forests. Lined with beach clubs, snack shops, and ice-cream stands, these beaches are extremely overcrowded during the sultry summer. The most beautiful beaches are found along a stretch called the **Punta Marina di Ravenna.** The Marina di Ravenna is also lively at night with pubs and discos open until the early hours.

can be shipped. **Scianna,** Via di Roma 30 (☎ **0544-37-556**), and **Luciana Notturni,** Via Arno 13 (☎ **0544-63-002**), are worthy competitors.

ACCOMMODATIONS

Hotel Bisanzio. Via Salara 30, 48100 Ravenna. ☎ **0544-217-111.** Fax 0544-32-539. www.bestwestern.com. 38 units. A/C MINIBAR TV TEL. 165,000–250,000L ($82.50–$125) double. Rates include buffet breakfast. AE, DC, MC, V. Parking 25,000L ($12.50).

A few minutes' walk from many of Ravenna's major sights, the Bisanzio is cheaper and has more personality than the Jolly Hotel (see below). The guest rooms at this pleasantly renovated modern hotel have attractive Italian styling, some with mottled batik wall coverings. They range from small to medium, each with a fine mattress and a bathroom that comes with a hair dryer. The uncluttered breakfast room has softly draped windows, and you have use of a garden.

Hotel Centrale Byron. Via IV Novembre 14, 48100 Ravenna. ☎ **0544-212-225.** Fax 0544-34-114. 54 units. A/C TV TEL. 180,000L ($90) double. Rates include breakfast. AE, DC, MC, V. Parking 25,000L ($12.50).

This art deco–inspired hotel is a few steps from Piazza del Popolo. The lobby is an elegant combination of white marble and brass detailing. The long, narrow public rooms, arranged "railroad style," include an alcove sitting room and a combination TV room, bar, and snack/breakfast room. The small guest rooms are simply but comfortably furnished, with decent mattresses. The bathrooms are a bit cramped as well.

Jolly Hotel. Piazza Mameli 1, 48100 Ravenna. ☎ **800/221-2626** in the U.S., or 0544-35-762. Fax 0544-216-055. 84 units. A/C MINIBAR TV TEL. 230,000–270,000L ($115–$135) double; from 370,000L ($185) suite. Rates include buffet breakfast. AE, DC, MC, V. Parking 30,000L ($15).

This hotel, built in 1950 in the postwar crackerbox style with a bunkerlike facade, contains a conservative decor of stone floors and lots of paneling. Ravenna doesn't have many first-class accommodations, so the Jolly has become a favorite of business travelers. Although the guest rooms are not style setters, they are however medium-sized and were last renovated in 1997, when new mattresses were added and furnishings upgraded. Five are suitable for travelers with disabilities. The tiled bathrooms come with hair dryers. La Matta restaurant serves standard local and international cuisine. Services include room service, baby-sitting, and laundry.

DINING

A walk through Ravenna's lively food market, the **Mercato Coperto,** will introduce you to the bounty of the land. It's near the center of town on Piazza Andrea Costa and is open Monday through Saturday from 7am to 2pm, and on Friday from 4:30 to 7:30pm.

The slick-looking **Sorbetteria Degli Esarchi,** Via IV Novembre 11 (☎ **0544-363-14**), off the Piazza del Popolo, is always packed with both tourists and locals. This place uses the freshest local ingredients and secret recipes to create delicious fruit-flavored sorbets and creamy gelatos, all made on the premises.

Bella Venezia. Via IV Novembre 16. ☎ **0544-212-746.** Reservations required. Main courses 16,000–24,000L ($8–$12). AE, DC, MC, V. Mon–Sat 12:15–2:30pm and 7–10pm. Closed Dec 23–Jan 15. ROMAGNOLA/ITALIAN.

The Bella Venezia is a few steps from Piazza del Popolo and next to the Byron (see above). Despite the name, the only Venetian dish prepared is delicious *fegato alla veneziana* (liver fried with onions). The repertoire is almost exclusively regional, with such dishes as risotto, *cappelletti alla romagnola* (cap-shaped pasta stuffed with ricotta, roasted pork loin, chicken breast, and nutmeg, served with meat sauce), and garganelli pasta served with whatever happens to be in season (baby asparagus, mushrooms, or peas). All pastas are made by hand, and the place is very family run and very old Italy.

Ristorante La Gardèla. Via Ponte Marino 3. ☎ **0544-217-147.** Reservations recommended. Main courses 16,000–26,000L ($8–$13). AE, DC, MC, V. Fri–Wed noon–2:30pm and 7–10pm. Closed Feb 10–20 and Aug 10–20. EMILIA-ROMAGNA/SEAFOOD.

La Gardèla, a few steps from one of Ravenna's startling leaning towers, is spread out over two levels, with paneled walls lined with racks of wine bottles. The waiters bring out an array of typical but savory dishes, like *tortelloni della casa* (made with ricotta, cream, spinach, tomatoes, and herbs) and *spezzatino alla contadina* (roast veal with potatoes, tomatoes, and herbs). Ravioli is stuffed with truffles, and one of their past best pasta dishes, *tagliatelle* (flat noodles), is offered with porcini mushrooms. The chefs prepare more fresh fish than ever before, most often from the Adriatic. Considering the quality of the food and the first-rate ingredients, this is Ravenna's best restaurant buy.

Ristorante Tre Spade. Via Faentina 136. ☎ **0544-500-522.** Reservations recommended. Main courses 18,000–35,000L ($9–$17.50). AE, DC, MC, V. Tues–Sat 12:30–2:30pm and 7:30–10:30pm. Sun 12:30–2:30pm. Closed first 3 weeks of Aug. INTERNATIONAL/EMILIAN/SEAFOOD.

This appealing spot keeps prices under control while magically combining solid technique and inventiveness. Specialties include an asparagus parfait accompanied by a zesty sauce of bits of green peppers and black olives and seafood that's creative and tasteful. This might be followed by taglioni with smoked-salmon sauce, veal cooked with sage, spaghetti with seafood (including clams in their shells), green gnocchi in Gorgonzola sauce, or roast game in season, plus a good collection of wines. The menu changes frequently, and daily specials are offered according to the market.

RAVENNA AFTER DARK

Beside the **Marina di Ravenna,** you'll find a handful of pubs and dance clubs. Our favorite of the bunch is the **Santa Fe,** Via delle Nazioni 180 (☎ **0544-530-239**).

Further entertainment is offered by the **Teatro di Ravenna**, Via di Roma 39 (☎ **0544-302-27**), which sponsors free summer concerts in the various squares and churches around town.

4 Modena

25 miles (40km) NW of Bologna, 250 miles (403km) NW of Rome, 81 miles (130km) N of Florence

After Ferrara fell to Pope Clement VIII, the Este family established a duchy at Modena in the closing years of the 16th century. This city in the Po Valley possesses many great art treasures evoking its more glorious past. On the food front, Modena's chefs enjoy an outstanding reputation in hard-to-please gastronomic circles. And traversed by the ancient Roman Via Emilia, Modena is a hot spot for European art connoisseurs.

Modena is an industrial zone blessed with Italy's highest per-capita income and can seem as sleek as the sports cars it produces. This is partially because of its 20th-century face-lift, the result of the city being largely rebuilt following the destructive World War II bombings. These factors create a stark contrast to both the antiquity and the poverty so noticeable in other regions. Modena is home to automobile and racing giants Ferrari, Maserati, and De Tomaso, and is known for producing Lambrusco wine and balsamic vinegar. Locals also proudly claim opera star Luciano Pavarotti as one of their greatest exports.

Many visitors who care little about antiquities come here to do business with the Ferrari or Maserati car plant (both off-limits to the general public). However, you can visit a showroom, the **Galleria Ferrari,** Via Dino Ferrari 43 in Maranello (☎ **0536-949-713**), a suburb of Modena. The showroom displays engines, trophies, and both antique and the latest Ferrari cars. It's open Tuesday to Sunday 9:30am to 12:30pm and 2:30 to 6pm, charging an admission of 15,000L ($9) adults or 5,000L ($3) ages 5 to 10. From the bus station on Via Bacchini in Modena, a bus marked MARANELLO departs hourly during the day. Ask at the tourist office (see below) for details and a map.

ESSENTIALS

GETTING THERE There are good **train** connections to/from Bologna (one train every 30 minutes); trip time is 20 minutes, and a one-way fare is 3,900L ($1.95). Trains arrive from Parma once per hour (trip time: 40 minutes); the one-way fare is 5,500L ($2.75). For information and schedules, call ☎ **1478-88-088** toll-free in Italy only.

If you have a **car** and are coming from Bologna, take A1 northeast until you see the turnoff for Modena.

VISITOR INFORMATION The **tourist office** is on Piazza Grande 17 (☎ **059-206-660**). It's open Monday, Tuesday, and Thursday to Saturday 8:30am to 1pm and 3 to 7pm, Wednesday 8:30am to 1pm, and Sunday 9:30am to 12:30pm.

SPECIAL EVENTS In July and August, Modena presents a series of theater, ballet, opera, and musical performances called **Sipario in Piazza.** You might even get to see Pavarotti perform. For details, contact the **Ufficio Sipario in Palazzo Comunale,** Piazza Grande (☎ **059-206-460**). Tickets are 20,000 to 55,000L ($10 to $27.50).

All of Modena seems to be a stage during one week each year at the end of June or beginning of July, when vendors, artists, mimes, and other performers take to the streets for the **Settimana Estense;** festivities culminate in a parade in which the town turns out in Renaissance attire.

SEEING THE SIGHTS

✪ **Il Duomo.** Piazza del Duomo. ☎ **059-216-078.** Free admission. Daily 10:30–11:50am and 3:30–7pm. Bus: 7, 12, or 14.

One of the glories of the Romanesque in northern Italy, Modena's cathedral was founded in the closing year of the 11th century and designed by an architect named Lanfranco. The cathedral, consecrated in 1184, was dedicated to St. Geminiano, the patron saint of Modena, a 4th-century Christian and defender of the faith. Towering from the rear is the **Ghirlandina,** a 12th- to 14th-century campanile, 285 feet tall. Leaning slightly, the bell tower guards the replica of the Secchia Rapita (stolen bucket), garnered as booty from the defeated Bolognese.

The facade of the Duomo features a 13th-century rose window by Anselmo da Campione. It also boasts Viligelmo's main entry, with pillars supported by lions, as well as Viligelmo bas-reliefs depicting scenes from Genesis. The south door, the so-called Princes' Door, was designed by Viligelmo in the 12th century and is framed by bas-reliefs illustrating scenes in the saga of the patron saint. You'll find an outside pulpit from the 15th century, with emblems of Matthew, Mark, Luke, and John.

Inside, there's a vaulted ceiling, and the overall effect is gravely impressive. The Modenese wisely restored the cathedral during the first part of the 20th century, so its present look resembles the original design. The gallery above the crypt is an outstanding piece of sculpture, supported by four lions. The pulpit is held up by two hunchbacks. And the crypt, where the body of the patron saint was finally taken, is a forest of columns; here you'll find Guido Mazzoni's *Holy Family* group in terra-cotta, completed in 1480.

✪ **Galleria Estense & Biblioteca Estense.** In the Palazzo del Musei, Piazza Sant'Agostino 48 (off Via Emilia). ☎ **059-222-145.** Gallery 8,000L ($4). Gallery Tues and Fri–Sat 9am–7pm; Wed–Thurs 9am–2pm; Sun 9am–1pm. Library Mon–Sat 9am–7pm. Bus: 7.

The **Galleria Estense** is noted for its paintings from the Emilian or Bolognese school from the 14th to the 18th century. The nucleus of the collection was created by the Este family in the heyday of their duchies in Ferrara and then Modena. Some of the finest work is by Spanish artists, including a miniature triptych by El Greco of Toledo and a portrait of Francesco I d'Este by Velázquez. Other works are Bernini's bust of Francesco I and paintings by Correggio, Veronese, Tintoretto, Carracci, Reni, and Guercino.

One of the greatest libraries in southern Europe, the **Biblioteca Estense** (☎ **059-222-248**) contains around 500,000 printed works and 13,000 manuscripts. An assortment of the most interesting volumes is kept under glass for visitors to inspect. Of these, the most celebrated is the 1,200-page *Bible of Borso d'Este,* bordered with stunning miniatures.

SHOPPING

If you want to go shopping, you can always cruise the car lots of the city (which has more Fiat factories than anywhere else in the world), looking for the best deal and hinting for invitations to one of the Agnelli family's cocktail parties. But if a car isn't in your budget, consider a bottle or two of the item that changed the face of salad making forever: balsamic vinegar. Right in the city center, **Fini,** Piazzale San Francesco (☎ **059-223-314**), sells bottles of Modena's aromatic variety, plus other fabulous food products. **Justi,** Via Farini 77 (☎ **059-441-203**), exports crates of the vinegar throughout Europe, as well as selling bottles on the premises.

ACCOMMODATIONS

Canalgrande Hotel. Corso Canalgrande 6, 41100 Modena. ☎ **059-217-160.** Fax 059-221-674. www.canalgrandehotel.it. E-mail: info@canalgrandehotel.it. 75 units. A/C MINIBAR TV TEL. 298,000L ($149) double; 450,000L ($225) suite. Rates include breakfast. AE, DC, MC, V. Parking 25,000L ($12.50). Bus: 7, 12, or 14.

Situated in the old town, the Canalgrande is housed in a 300-year-old stucco palace and has more atmosphere and charm than the more highly rated Fini. The Canalgrande boasts elaborate mosaic floors, Victorian-era furniture, elaborately carved and frescoed ceilings, and chandeliers. French doors open onto a beautiful garden with a central flowering tree that's always full of chirping birds (ask for a room facing it). The guest rooms are medium-sized, decorated in pastels and boasting fine mattresses; ongoing renovations are bringing them all up-to-date. Some of the best rooms open onto balconies, and the quieter ones are on the garden side. The new, marble-clad bathrooms have adequate shelf space. Under the basement's vaulted ceiling is a tavern, *La Secchia Rapita* (the Stolen Bucket), serving modest lunches and dinners Thursday to Tuesday.

Hotel Daunia. Via del Pozzo 158, 41100 Modena. ☎ **059-371-182.** Fax 059-374-807. 36 units. A/C MINIBAR TV TEL. 160,000L ($80) double. Rates include breakfast. AE, DC, MC, V. Free parking. Bus: 7, 12, or 14.

Away from the city center, the recently built Daunia boasts an exterior in a modified 18th-century design. Inside, it's modern Italian all the way, with gleaming brass, polished woods, eclectic contemporary furniture, and marble and tiled floors. The pleasant bar features a curved wood surface and sleek black wood and leather, but the breakfast room has a rather claustrophobic cafeteria feel. The guest rooms are comfortable but seem rather bare, with light-colored walls and neutral fabrics contrasting with the dark wood furnishings.

In an unusual arrangement, the hotel restaurant, Il Patriarca, is on the far side of the city center, and a free taxi shuttles you back and forth. It serves numerous variations of pizzas, antipasti, and Italian wines, along with traditional regional dishes.

Hotel Libertà. Via Blasia 10, 41100 Modena. ☎ **059-222-365.** Fax 059-222-502. www.tsc4.com/hotel-liberta. E-mail: hliberta@tsc4.com. 51 units. A/C MINIBAR TV TEL. 160,000L ($80) double; 280,000L ($140) suite. AE, CB, DC, DISC, MC, V. Parking 25,000L ($12.50). Bus: 4 or 7.

A modern hotel wrapped in an aged exterior, this lodge is mere steps from the cathedral and the Palazzo Ducale. Marble and terra-cotta floors run throughout, and the upscale bar features plush leather chairs and couches. The guest rooms favor floral wallpapers and blond-wood furniture; some top-floor rooms are made cozy by sloping ceilings with skylights. Each room provides a good night's sleep, since the mattresses are renewed as needed. The tiled bathrooms are compact. The hotel has a breakfast room, a TV lounge, a meeting room, and two garages (one on-site and the other nearby). Several restaurants are close by, and the staff particularly recommends Da Enzo (see below), 25 yards away.

Hotel Principe. Corso Vittorio Emanuele 94, 41100 Modena. ☎ **059-218-670.** Fax 059-237-693. 51 units. A/C MINIBAR TV TEL. 175,000L ($87.50) double. Rates include breakfast. AE, DC, MC, V. Free parking. Bus: 4 or 7.

Located close to the heart of the city, the appealingly priced Principe was mainly designed to attract commercial travelers to town, but it also offers the vacationing visitor comfort as well. Short on style, it's nonetheless a good choice, as its rooms are well appointed and come with fine linen and quality mattresses on its twin or double beds. The tiled bathrooms are small but have adequate shelf space. The impersonal look of the hotel is softened by the gracious reception of the staff.

DINING

To put together a wonderful picnic, pick your way through the food stalls of the outdoor market on **Via Albinelli,** open weekdays from 6:30am to 2pm and Saturday afternoons in summer from 5 to 7pm.

✪ **Fini.** Rua Frati Minori 54. ☎ **059-223-314.** Reservations recommended. Main courses 35,000–50,000L ($17.50–$25). AE, DC, MC, V. Wed–Sun 12:30–2:30pm and 8–10:30pm. Closed July 20–Aug 24 and Dec 22–Jan 3. Bus: 6 or 11. MODENESE/INTERNATIONAL.

A visit to this restaurant is well worth your making the trip to Modena. Fini is one of the best restaurants in Emilia-Romagna and is Pavarotti's favorite when he's in town. Its modernized art nouveau decor includes Picasso-esque murals and banquettes. For an appetizer, try the creamy green lasagna or the tortellini (prepared in six ways—for example, with truffles). For a main dish, the *gran bollito misto* reigns supreme. A king's feast of boiled meats, accompanied by a selection of four sauces, is wheeled to your table. After all this rich fare, you may settle for the fruit salad for dessert. Lambrusco is the superb local wine choice.

✪ **Osteria Giusti.** Vicolo Squallore 46. ☎ and fax **059-222-533.** Reservations essential at least a month in advance. Main courses 20,000–30,000L ($10–$15). AE, MC, V. Mon–Fri noon–3pm. Closed July 1–Sept 8 and Dec. Bus: 7 or 12. MODENESE.

We hesitate to list this five-table eatery only because it can be so hard to get a table—you must phone or fax for a reservation *far* in advance (see above)—but the experience of lunching here is well worth the effort. You enter through a shop fragrant with balsamic vinegars and parmigiano and put yourself in the hands of husband and wife Nano Morandi and Laura Galli. You might want to try the capon in two forms: a capon broth with tortellini (which, like all the pastas, is made on the premises) and a crunchy capon salad dribbled with aged balsamic vinegar. A *stinco* (roast joint) of veal or pork is the perfect dish with which to proceed, and do indulge in one of the delicious homemade cakes.

Ristorante Da Enzo. Via Coltellini 17 (off Piazza Mazzini). ☎ **059-225-177.** Reservations recommended. Main courses 16,000–30,000L ($8–$15); fixed-price menus 30,000–40,000L ($15–$20). AE, DC, MC, V. Tues–Sun noon–3pm and 7–10:30pm. Closed 3 weeks in Aug. Bus: 7, 12, or 14. MODENESE.

Well known in Modena, this restaurant is one floor above street level in an old building in the historic center's pedestrian zone. Specialties include all the classic dishes, like *zampone* (stuffed pigs' trotters), lasagna verde, *pappardelle* (wide noodles) with rabbit meat, several kinds of tortellini, and an array of grilled meats liberally seasoned with herbs and balsamic vinegar.

MODENA AFTER DARK

This bustling powerhouse of Italy's industrial machine offers enough evening diversion to amuse an entire assembly line of factory workers and enough culture to absorb an entire theater of Pavarotti fans.

Opera arrives in winter at the **Teatro Comunale,** Corso Canal Grande 85 (☎ **059-206-993** or 059-223-244 for reservations), and the summer brings a major opera festival.

Stroll through the neighborhood to the spot where everyone seems to gravitate on long hot evenings, the **Parco Amendola,** located to the south of Modena's historic core, filled with ice cream stands, cafes, and bars.

5 Parma

284 miles (457km) NW of Rome, 60 miles (97km) NW of Bologna, 75 miles (121km) SE of Milan

Parma, straddling Via Emilia, was the home of Correggio, Il Parmigianino, Bodoni (of typeface fame), and Toscanini and is also the home of *prosciutto* (Parma ham) and *parmigiano* (Parmesan) cheese. It rose in influence and power in the 16th century as the seat of the Farnese duchy, and even today is one of the most prosperous cities in Italy.

Upon the extinction of the male Farnese line, Parma came under the control of the French Bourbons. Its most beloved ruler, Marie-Louise, widow of Napoléon and niece of Marie Antoinette, arrived in 1815 after the Congress of Vienna awarded her this duchy. Marie-Louise became a great patron of the arts, and much of the collection she acquired is on display at the Galleria Nazionale (see below). Rising unrest in 1859 forced her abdication, and in 1860, following a plebiscite, Parma was incorporated into the kingdom of Italy.

The city has also been a mecca for opera lovers such as Verdi, the great Italian composer whose works include *Il Trovatore* and *Aïda.* He was born in the small village of Roncole, north of Parma, in 1813. In time, his operas echoed through the Teatro Regio, the opera house that was built under the orders of Marie-Louise. Because of Verdi, Parma became a center of music, and even today the opera house is jam-packed in season. It's said that the Teatro Regio is the most "critical Verdi house" in Italy.

ESSENTIALS

GETTING THERE Parma is conveniently served by the Milan–Bologna **rail** line, with 20 trains a day arriving from Milan (trip time: 80 minutes); the one-way fare is 11,700L ($5.85). From Bologna, 34 trains per day arrive in Parma (trip time: 1 hour); the one-way fare is 7,200L ($3.60). There are seven connections a day from Florence (trip time: 3 hours); a one-way fare is 16,000L ($8). For information and schedules, call ☎ **1478-88-088** toll-free in Italy only.

If you have a **car** and are in Bologna, head northwest along A1.

VISITOR INFORMATION The **tourist office** is at Via Melloni 1B (☎ **0521-218-889**), open Monday to Saturday 9am to 7pm and Sunday 9am to 1pm.

SPECIAL EVENTS Parma celebrates its musical traditions in July and August with **Concerti Nei Chiostri,** when classical concerts are staged in churches, cloisters, and piazzas around the city. Admission is 25,000L ($12.50) per event; the tourist office will provide a list of times and locations around the city, as will the festival office (☎ **0521-283-224**).

SEEING THE CITY

The gravel paths, wide lawns, and splashing fountains of the **Parco Ducale,** across the river from the Palazzo Pilotta, provide a nice retreat from Parma's more crowded areas.

✪ **Il Duomo.** Piazza del Duomo. ☎ **0521-235-886.** Free admission. Daily 9am–12:30pm and 3–7pm. Bus: 11.

Built in the Romanesque style in the 11th century, with 13th-century Lombard lions guarding its main porch, the dusty pink Duomo stands side-by-side with a **campanile (bell tower)** constructed in the Gothic-Romanesque style and completed in 1294. The facade of the cathedral is highlighted by three open-air loggias. Inside, two darkly elegant aisles flank the central nave. The octagonal cupola was frescoed by a master of light and color, Correggio (1494–1534), one of Italy's greatest painters of the High Renaissance. His fresco here, *Assumption of the Virgin,* foreshadows the baroque. The frescoes were painted from 1522 to 1534. In the transept to the right of the main altar is a somber Romanesque bas-relief, *The Deposition from the Cross,* by Benedetto Antelami, each face bathed in tragedy. Made in 1178, the bas-relief is the best-known work of the 12th-century artist, who was the most important sculptor of the Romanesque in northern Italy.

✪ **Baptistry (Battistero).** Piazza del Duomo 7. ☎ **0521-235-886.** Admission 5,000L ($2.50). Daily 9am–12:30pm and 3–7pm. Bus: 11.

Among the greatest Romanesque buildings in northern Italy, the baptistry was the work of Antelami. The project was begun in 1196, though the date it was actually completed is unclear. Made of salmon-colored marble, it's spanned by four open tiers (the fifth is closed off). Inside, the baptistry is richly frescoed with biblical scenes: a *Madonna Enthroned* and a *Crucifixion.* But it's the sculpture by Antelami that's the most worthy treasure and provides the basis for that artist's claim to enduring fame.

Abbey of St. John (San Giovanni Evangelista). Piazzale San Giovanni 1. ☎ **0521-235-592.** Free admission to church and cloisters; 4,000L ($2) for pharmacist's shop. Daily 6:30am–noon and 3–6pm; pharmacist's shop daily 9am–1:45pm. Bus: 11.

Behind the Duomo is this church of unusual interest. After admiring the baroque front, pass into the interior to see yet another cupola by Correggio. Working from 1520 to 1524, the High Renaissance master depicted the *Vision of San Giovanni.* Vasari liked it so much he became completely carried away in his praise, suggesting the "impossibility" of an artist conjuring up such a divine work and marveling that it could actually have been painted "with human hands." Correggio also painted a St. John with pen in hand, in the transept (over the door to the left of the main altar). Il Parmigianino, the second Parmesan master, did some frescoes in the chapel at the left of the entrance. You can visit the **abbey,** the **school,** the **cloister,** and a **pharmacist's shop** (☎ **0521-233-309**) where monks made potions for some 6 centuries, a practice that lasted until the closing years of the 19th century. Mortars and jars, some as old as the Middle Ages, line the shelves.

Arturo Toscanini Birthplace and Museum (Casa Natale e Museo di Arturo Toscanini). Via Rodolfo Tanzi 13. ☎ **0521-285-499.** Admission 3,000L ($1.50). Tues–Sat 10am–1pm and 3–6pm; Sun 10am–1pm. Bus: 11.

This is the house where the great musician/conductor was born in 1867. Toscanini was unquestionably the greatest orchestral conductor of the first half of the 20th century and one of the most astonishing musical interpreters of all time. He spent his childhood and youth in this house, which has been turned into a museum with interesting relics and a record library, containing all the recorded works he conducted.

No more than 25 persons per time are admitted inside.

✪ **National Gallery (Galleria Nazionale) & National Archaeological Museum (Museo Archeologico Nazionale).** In the Palazzo della Pilotta, Piazza della Pace, Via della Pilotta 5. ☎ **0521-233-309** (National Gallery) or 0521-233-718 (Archaeological Museum). National Gallery 12,000L ($6). Archaeological Museum 4,000L ($2). National Gallery daily 9am–1:30pm. Archaeological Museum Tues–Sun 9am–6:30pm. Bus: 11.

Palazzo della Pilotta once housed the Farnese family in Parma's heyday as a duchy in the 16th century. Badly damaged by bombs in World War II, it has been restored and turned into a palace of museums.

The **National Gallery** offers a limited but well-chosen selection of the works of Parma artists from the late 15th to the 19th century, notably paintings by Correggio and Parmigianino. In one room is an unfinished head of a young woman attributed to Leonardo. Correggio's *Madonna della Scala* (of the stairs), the remains of a fresco, is also displayed. But his masterpiece is *St. Jerome with the Madonna and Child.* Imbued with delicacy, it represents age, youth, love—a gentle ode to tenderness. In the next room is Correggio's *Madonna della Scodella* (with a bowl), with its agonized faces. You'll also see Correggio's *Coronation,* a golden fresco that's a work of great beauty, and his less successful *Annunciation.* One of Parmigianino's best-known paintings is *St. Catherine's Marriage,* with its rippling movement and subdued colors.

You can also view **St. Paul's Chamber (Camera di San Paolo),** which Correggio frescoed with mythological scenes, including one of Diana. The chamber faces onto Via Macedonio Melloni. On the same floor as the National Gallery is the **Farnese Theater (Teatro Farnese),** a virtual jewel box, evocative of Palladio's theater at Vicenza. Built in 1618, the structure was bombed in 1944 and has been restored. Admission to the theater is included in the admission to the gallery; however, should you wish to visit only the theater, there's a separate charge of 4,000L ($2).

Also in the palazzo is the **National Archaeological Museum.** It houses Egyptian sarcophagi, Etruscan vases, Roman- and Greek-inspired torsos, Bronze Age relics, and its best-known exhibit, the Tabula Alimentaria, a bronze-engraved tablet dating from the reign of Trajan and excavated at Velleia in Piacenza.

SHOPPING

Parma's most famous food product—*parmigiano* (Parmesan) cheese, the best being parmigiano reggiano—is savored all over the world. Virtually every corner market sells thick wedges of the stuff, but if you're looking to buy your cheese in a special setting, head for the **Salumería Garibaldi,** Via Garibaldi 42 (☎ **0521-235-606**). You might also take a walk through the city's **food market** at Piazza Ghiaia, near the Palazzo della Pilota; it's open Monday to Saturday from 8am to 1pm and 3 to 7pm.

Hoping to learn more about the region's famous hams and cheeses? There are well-funded bureaucracies in Parma whose sole functions are to encourage the world to use greater quantities of the city's tastiest products. They can arrange tours and visits to the region's most famous producers. For information about Parma cheeses, contact the **Consorzio del Parmigiano Reggiano,** Via Gramsci 26C (☎ **0521-292-700**). For insights into the dressing and curing of Parma hams, contact the **Consorzio del Prosciutto di Parma,** Via Marco dell' Arpa 8B (☎ **0521-243-987**).

The **Enoteca Fontana,** Via Farina 24A (☎ **0521-286-037**), sells bottles from virtually every vineyard in the region, and the staff is extremely knowledgeable.

ACCOMMODATIONS

Hotel Button. Strada San Vitale Borgo Salina 7 (off Piazza Garibaldi), 43100 Parma. ☎ **0521-208-09.** Fax 0521-238-783. 40 units. TV TEL. 180,000L ($90) double. Rates include continental breakfast. AE, DC, MC, V. Closed July 5–31. Free parking. Bus: 11.

The Button is a local favorite, one of the best bargains in the town center. This is a family-owned and -run hotel, and you're made to feel welcome. Perhaps you'll even join the locals gathered around the TV in the lounge to watch soccer games. The guest rooms are simple but comfortably furnished and generally spacious, though the decor is dull. Even so, the beds have quality mattresses and fine linen. The tiled bathrooms are a bit cramped but tidy. There's no restaurant, but the hotel bar is open 24 hours.

Hotel Farnese International. Via Reggio 51A, 43100 Parma. ☎ **0521-994-247.** Fax 0521-992-317. www.farnesehotel.it. E-mail: info@farnesehotel.it. 76 units. A/C MINIBAR TV TEL. 198,000–220,000L ($99–$110) double. Rates include breakfast. AE, DC, MC, V. Free parking outdoors, 15,000L ($7.50) indoors. Bus: 11.

This hotel is in a quiet area convenient to the town center, airport, and fairs. Parma specialties are served in the hotel restaurant, Il Farnese. The guest rooms, ranging from small to medium, are furnished in Italian marble and have good mattresses. The tiled bathrooms are kept tidy. Laundry and room service are provided.

✪ **Hotel Verdi.** Via Pasini 18, 43100 Parma. ☎ **0521-293-539.** Fax 0521-293-559. E-mail: hotelverdi@libero.it. 20 units. A/C MINIBAR TV TEL. 255,000–320,000L ($127.50–$160) double; 290,000–380,000L ($145–$190) suite. Breakfast 18,000L ($9). AE, CB, DC, DISC, MC, V. Free parking. Bus: 11.

Facing the Ducal Gardens (see below), this art nouveau hotel has preserved the elegance of its era while meeting the needs of today's visitors. In the public areas, sheer draperies warm the sunlight to a golden glow reflected off the black-and-gold marble floors. The guest rooms feature parquet floors, briarwood furnishings, fine linen, good mattresses, and safes. The marble-lined bathrooms include luxurious soaps, thick towels, and body oils as well as hair dryers. The adjacent Santa Croce restaurant offers a refined yet cordial atmosphere resplendent with period art, furnishings, and lighting in which to savor traditional cuisine and fine Italian wines. In summer a brick courtyard alive with greenery allows you to dine outdoors. To ensure vehicle safety, a guarded parking garage is at the rear of the hotel.

During the day you can walk through the **Ducal Gardens (Parco Ducale)**, landscaped by the French architect Petitot and decorated with statues by another Frenchman, Boudard. With its splashing fountains, wide expanses of greenery, and gravel paths, the gardens make a great place to relax. Admission is free.

Palace Hotel Maria Luigia. Viale Mentana 140, 43100 Parma. ☎ **0521-281-032.** Fax 0521-231-1126. www.italyhotel.com/sina. E-mail: maria.luigia@italyhotel.com. 107 units. A/C MINIBAR TV TEL. 400,000L ($200) double; 600,000L ($300) suite. Rates include buffet breakfast. AE, CB, DC, MC, V. Parking 25,000L ($12.50). Bus: 11.

This hotel, built of brick in 1974 near the station, was, and still is, a welcome addition to the Parma scene. It caters especially to business travelers, and we like it even more than the Stendhal (see below). Bold colors and molded-plastic built-ins set the up-to-date mood, and the comfortable modern rooms feature soundproof walls as well as other amenities, like deluxe mattresses. The bathrooms are medium in size, with hair dryers and luxury toiletries. There's an Italian-looking American bar on the premises. The hotel also has one of the best restaurants in Parma, Maxim's, which serves excellent Italian and international specialties daily. Room service is available 24 hours.

Park Hotel Stendhal. Via Bodini 3, 43100 Parma. ☎ **0521-208-057.** Fax 0521-285-655. www.rsadvnet.it/web/stendhal. E-mail: stendhal.htl@rsadvnet.it. 68 units. A/C MINIBAR TV TEL. 300,000–330,000L ($150–$165) double. Rates include breakfast. AE, DC, MC, V. Parking 25,000L ($12.50).

The Stendhal sits on a square near the opera house, a few minutes' walk from many of the important sights and 6 blocks south of the station. The guest rooms are well maintained and furnished with contemporary pieces that are reproductions of various styles, ranging from rococo to provincial. Try for one of the traditional-looking rooms where the furnishings are classic. The bathrooms come with hair dryers. For before- and after-dinner drinks, try the traditional American bar/lounge, with comfortable armchairs. La Pilotta restaurant serves a cuisine typical of Parma, with a medley of international dishes. Laundry and room service are provided.

DINING

The chefs of Parma are acclaimed throughout Italy. Of course, parmigiano reggiano has added just the right touch to millions of Italian meals, and the word *parmigiana* is quite familiar to American diners.

At the atmospheric **Enoteca Fontana,** Via Farina 24A (☎ **0521-286-037**), open daily 9am to noon and 3 to 9:45pm, you can stand at the ancient old bar or take a seat at one of the long communal tables and sample your choice of hundreds of wines from Emilia-Romagna, many of them from the immediate region. You may decide to order a light meal, too, from the short menu of panini, ham-and-cheese platters, and pastas.

The most popular pizzeria in Parma is open late (though it's closed Mondays) and is almost always crowded. You may have to wait at **Pizzeria La Duchesa,** Piazza Garibaldi 1 (☎ **0521-235-962**), especially if you want an outdoor table, but the pizzas are fabulous, especially when washed down with a carafe of Lambrusco.

Croce di Malta. Borgo Palmia 8. ☎ **0521-235-643.** Reservations recommended. Main courses 18,000–26,000L ($9–$13). AE, DC, MC, V. Mon–Sat 12:30–2:30pm and 7:30–11pm. PARMIGIANA.

Local legend has it that angry citizens plotted to assassinate the last duke of Parma while he was drowning in vino at this tavern. All the dishes for which Parma is famous are served, even some esoteric ones, like *cappelletti* (a pasta that turns magenta because it's made with beets) and *tortelli* (made a golden amber with the addition of pumpkin, though another version is made with potatoes). *Tagliatelle* (flat noodles) is served in almost any style. Other savory dishes are roast veal stuffed with cheese, and chicken flavored with wine and Gorgonzola.

✪ **La Greppia.** Via Garibaldi 39A. ☎ **0521-238-686.** Reservations required. Main courses 25,000–35,000L ($12.50–$17.50). AE, DC, MC, V. Wed–Sun 12:30–2:30pm and 7:30–10:30pm. Closed July. PARMIGIANA.

La Greppia has an unpretentious decor, yet it's near the top of every gourmet's list. The competition is keen in Parma, but its only serious rival is Parizzi (see below). Through a plate-glass window at one end of the dining room, you can see the all-woman staff at work in the kitchen. Leading the team is the co-owner, Paola Cavassini, and her good-natured husband, Maurizio Rossi, who presides over the dining room. The chefs adjust their menus depending on the season. Likely dishes are veal kidneys sautéed with fines herbes and a demi-glacé sauce, chicken breast with orange sauce, *pappardella alla Greppia* (with cream and dried porcinis), and roast rack of rabbit flavored with thyme. Many dishes are flavored with fresh thyme or mushrooms or even cherries. The chefs are known for preparing dishes based on recipes from 1500 to the second half of the 18th century. An example is *fegato ore due* (liver two o'clock), from the end of the 16th century: Veal liver is well seasoned and boiled for 2 hours with vegetables. Other antique recipes are *quadrucci,* a square-shaped pasta flavored with cabbage and ham, and *tagliatelle* (flat noodles) prepared using a chestnut flour and served with ricotta sauce. The fresh fruit tarts are succulent, but the kitchen is known for its compelling chocolate cake.

✪ **Parizzi.** Strada della Repubblica 71. ☎ **0521-285-952.** Reservations required. Main courses 20,000–35,000L ($10–$17.50). AE, DC, MC, V. Tues–Sat noon–2:30pm and 7–9:30pm. Closed Jan 7–14. PARMIGIANA.

In the historic center of town, the building that houses Parizzi dates to 1551, when it first opened as an inn; the current restaurant was opened in 1958 by the father of the present owner. Seated under the skylit patio, you'll enjoy rich cuisine. This restaurant is among the two best in Parma, comparable to La Greppia (see above). Both richly deserve the stars we've given them. After you're shown to a table in one of the good-sized rooms, a trolley cart filled with antipasti is wheeled before you, containing shellfish, stuffed vegetables, and marinated salmon. Then you might be tempted by *culatelo,* cured ham made from sliced haunch of wild boar; a pasta served with a sauce of herbs and parmigiano reggiano; a parmigiano soufflé with white truffles; roasted guinea fowl with Fonseca wine; or veal scaloppini layered with Fontina cheese and ham.

PARMA AFTER DARK

Life in Parma extends beyond munching on strips of salty ham and cheese. The **Teatro Regio,** Via Garibaldi, near Piazza della Pace (☎ **0521-218-678;** www.teatroregio.parma.it), is the site of concerts throughout the year, as well as the annual **Concerti Nei Chiostri** in June and July.

If you'd like to sample a glass or two of interesting wine, head for the bar section of a spot recommended in the shopping section, the **Enoteca Fontana,** Strada Farina 24A (☎ **0521-286-037**).

The city's most appealing American-style bar, with an admittedly heavy Italian accent, is **La Corriera Stravagante,** Via Prati 4 (☎ **0521-522-63**), where stiff drinks lubricate the conversation and the setting is accented by stonework and wooden tables. At **Bacco Verde,** Via Cavalloti (☎ **0521-230-487**), sandwiches, glasses of beer, and a wide selection of Italian wines are dispensed in a cramped but convivial setting ringed with antique masonry.

In the mood for dancing? Head for **Dadaumpa,** Via Emilio Este 48 (☎ **0521-483-802**), a stylish and light-hearted venue for European and New World dance tunes. More oriented toward students and the under-25 crowd is **Astrolabio,** Via Zarotta 86A (☎ **0521-460-538**).

8 Venice

One rainy morning as we were leaving our hotel (a converted palazzo), a decorative stone fell from the lunette, narrowly missing us. For a second it looked as if we were candidates for a gondola funeral cortege to the lagoon island of marble tombs, San Michele. In dismay, we looked back at the owner, who was leaning out from the doorway. Throwing up her hands, she sighed, "Venezia, Venezia," then went inside.

That woman had long ago made her peace with the decay that's eating away at this city. Venice (La Serenissima, or the Serene Republic) is a preposterous monument to both the folly and the obstinacy of humankind. It shouldn't exist, but it does, much to the delight of thousands of visitors, gondoliers, lace makers, hoteliers, restaurateurs, and glassblowers.

Centuries ago, in an effort to flee barbarians, Venetians left dry-dock and drifted out to a flotilla of "uninhabitable" islands in the lagoon. Survival was difficult enough, but no Venetian has ever settled for mere survival. The remote ancestors of the present inhabitants created the world's most beautiful city. To your children's children, however, Venice may be nothing more than a legend. It's sinking at a rate of about $2^1/_2$ inches per decade. Estimates are that if no action is taken soon, one-third of the city's art will deteriorate hopelessly within the next decade or so. Clearly, Venice is in peril. One headline proclaimed, "The Enemy's at the Gates."

But for however long it lasts, Venice, decaying or not, will be one of the highlights of your trip through Italy. It lacks the speeding cars and roaring Vespas of Rome; instead, you make your way through the city either by boat or on foot. It would be ideal if it weren't for the hordes of tourists that descend every year, overwhelming the squares and making the streets almost impossible to navigate. In the sultry summer heat of the Adriatic, the canals become a smelly stew. Steamy and overcrowded July and August are the worst times to visit; May, June, September, and October are much better.

Though Venice is one of the world's most enchanting cities, you do pay a price, literally and figuratively, for all this beauty. Venice is virtually selling its past to the world, even more so than Florence, and anybody who has been here leaves complaining about the outrageous prices, which can be double what they are elsewhere in the country. Since the 19th century, Venice has thrived on its visitors, but these high prices have forced out many locals. They've fled across the lagoon to dreary Mestre, an industrial complex launched to help boost the regional economy.

Today the city is trying belatedly to undo the damage its watery environs and tourist-based economy have wrought. In 1993, after a 30-year hiatus, the canals were again dredged in an attempt to reduce water loss and reduce the stench brought in with the low tides. In an effort to curb the other 30-year-old problem of residential migration to Mestre, state subsidies are now being offered to the citizens of Venice as an incentive to not only stay but also to renovate their crumbling properties.

Despite all its problems and relatively modest plans (so far) for saving itself, Venice still endures. But for how long? That is the question.

1 Essentials

ARRIVING

The arrival scene at unattractive **Piazzale Roma** is filled with nervous expectation; even the most veteran traveler can become confused. Whether arriving by train, bus, car, or airport limo, everyone walks to the nearby docks (less than a 5-minute walk) to select a method of transport to his or her hotel. The cheapest way is by *vaporetto* (public motorboat), the more expensive by gondola or motor launch (see "Getting Around," later in this chapter).

BY PLANE You can now fly from North America to Venice via Rome on Alitalia. You'll land at the **Aeroporto Marco Polo** (☎ **041-260-6111**) at Mestre, north of the city on the mainland. The **Cooperativa San Marco** (☎ **041-522-2303**) operates a *motoscafo* (shuttle boat) service departing from the airport and taking visitors to Piazza San Marco in about 30 minutes. The fare begins at 80,000L ($40) for up to six passengers (so if there are only two of you traveling together, talk to some of your fellow travelers and find a few others to share the ride and split the fare with you). If you've got some extra lire to spend, you can arrange for a **private water taxi** by calling ☎ **041-541-5084.** The cost of the ride to the heart of Venice is 130,000L ($65).

It's less expensive, however, to take a bus from the airport to the public hookup for transport into Venice. Run by the **Azienda Trasporti Veneto Orientale** (☎ **041-520-5530**), a shuttle bus links the airport with Piazzale Roma for 5,000L ($2.50). The trip takes about half an hour, and departures are about every 30 minutes daily 8:40am to 11:30pm. Even cheaper is a local bus company, **ACTV** (☎ **041-528-7886**), whose bus no. 5 makes the run for 1,400L (70¢). The ACTV buses depart every half hour and take about a half hour to reach Piazzale Roma. From Piazzale Roma, you get a vaporetto to take you to (or near) your hotel.

BY TRAIN Trains pull into the **Stazione di Santa Lucia,** at Piazzale Roma (☎ **1478/88-088** in Italy only). Travel time from Rome is about 5¼ hours, from Milan 3½, from Florence 4, and from Bologna 2 hours. The best and least expensive way to get from the station to the rest of town is taking a vaporetto that departs near the station's main entrance. There's also a **tourist office** at the station (☎ **041-529-8711**).

Anyone between the ages of 14 and 29 is eligible for a **Rolling Venice pass,** entitling you to discounts for museums, restaurants, stores, language courses, hotels, and bars. Valid for 1 year, it costs 5,000L ($2.50) and can be picked up at a special Rolling Venice office set up in the train station during summer.

BY CAR The autostrada links Venice with the rest of Italy, with direct routes from such cities as Trieste (driving time: 1½ hours), Milan (3 hours), and Bologna (2 hours). Bologna is 94 miles (151km) southwest of Venice, Milan 165 miles (266km) west, and Trieste 97 miles (156km) east. Rome is 327 miles southwest.

A Luggage Warning

If your hotel is near one of the public *vaporetto* stops, you can probably manage to haul your own luggage to its reception area. In any event, the one time-tested piece of advice for visitors to Venice is that excess baggage is bad news, unless you're willing to pay a public porter a small fortune to have him carry your bags to and from the docks. Porters can't accompany you and your baggage on the vaporetto, however. Just travel light!

If you arrive by car, there are several multitiered parking areas at the terminus where the roads end and the canals begin. One of the most prominent is the **Garage San Marco,** Piazzale Roma (☎ **041-523-5101**), near the vaporetto, gondola, and motor launch docks. You'll be charged 35,000 to 46,000L ($17.50 to $23) per day or maybe more, depending on the car size. From spring to fall, this municipal parking lot is nearly always filled. You can fax a reservation for a space however at ☎ **041-52-89969.** You're more likely to find parking on **Isola del Tronchetto** (☎ **041-520-7555**), costing 30,000L ($15) per day. From Tronchetto, take vaporetto no. 82 to Piazza San Marco. If you have heavy luggage, you'll need a water taxi. Parking is also available at Mestre.

VISITOR INFORMATION

Visitor information is available at the **Azienda di Promozione Turistica,** San Marco 71/F (☎ **041-52-98-711**). Summer hours are daily 9am to 5pm; off-season hours are daily 9:30am to 3:30pm. Posters around town with exhibit and concert schedules are more helpful. Ask for a schedule of the month's special events and an updated list of museum and church hours, since these can change erratically and often.

CITY LAYOUT

Venice lies 2½ miles (4km) from the Italian mainland (connected to Mestre by the Ponte della Libertà) and 1¼ miles (2km) from the open Adriatic. It's an archipelago of 118 islands. Most visitors, however, concern themselves only with **Piazza San Marco** and its vicinity. In fact, the entire city has only one piazza, which is San Marco (all the other squares are *campos*). Venice is divided into six quarters *(sestieri)*: **San Marco, Santa Croce, San Polo, Castello, Cannaregio,** and **Dorsoduro.**

Many of Venice's so-called streets are actually canals *(rios)*, somewhere around 150 in all, spanned by a total of 400 bridges. Venice's version of a main street is the **Grand Canal (Canal Grande),** which snakes through the city like an inverted S and is spanned by three bridges: the white marble **Ponte Rialto,** the wooden **Ponte Accademia,** and the stone **Ponte degli Scalzi.** The Grand Canal splits Venice into two unequal parts.

South of Dorsoduro, which is south of the Grand Canal, is the **Canele della Guidecca,** a major channel separating Dorsoduro from the large island of La Guidecca. At the point where Canale della Guidecca meets the **Canale di San Marco,** you'll spot the little **Isola di San Giorgio Maggiore,** with a church by Palladio. The most visited islands in the lagoon, aside from the **Lido,** are **Murano, Burano,** and **Torcello.**

If you really want to tour Venice and experience that hidden, romantic trattoria on a nearly forgotten street, don't even think about doing it unless you have a map that details every street and has an index on the back. The best of the lot is the **Falk map** of Venice, sold at many news kiosks and all bookstores.

Finding an Address

A maniac must've numbered Venice's buildings at least 6 centuries ago. Before you set out for a specific place, get detailed instructions and have someone mark the place on your map. Don't depend on street numbers; try to locate the nearest cross street. Since old signs and numbers have decayed over time, it's best to look for signs posted outside rather than for a number.

Every building has a street address and a mailing address. For example, a business at Calle delle Botteghe 3150 (3150 Botteghe St.) will have a mailing address of San Marco 3150, since it's in the San Marco sestiere and all buildings in each district are numbered continuously from 1 to 6,000. (To confuse things, several districts have streets of the same name, so it's important to know the sestiere.) In this chapter, we give the street name first, followed by the mailing address.

A broad street running along a canal is a *fondamenta,* a narrower street running along a canal is a *calle,* and a paved road is a *salizzada, ruga,* or *calle larga.* A *rio terra* is a filled canal channel now used as a walkway, and a *sottoportego* a passage beneath buildings. When you come to an open-air area, you'll often encounter the word *campo*—that's a reference to the fact that such a place was once grassy, and in days of yore cattle grazed there.

Neighborhoods in Brief

This section will give you some idea of where you may want to stay and where the major attractions are.

SAN MARCO Welcome to the center of Venice. Napoléon called it "the drawing room of Europe," and it's one crowded drawing room today. It has been the heart of Venetian life for more than a thousand years. **Piazza San Marco (St. Mark's Square)** is dominated by **St. Mark's Basilica**. Just outside the basilica is the **campanile (bell tower),** a reconstruction of the one that collapsed in 1902. Around the corner is the **Palazzo Ducale (Doge's Palace),** with its **Bridge of Sighs.** Piazza San Marco itself is lined with some of the world's most overpriced cafes, including **Florian's** (opened 1720) and **Quadri** (opened 1775). The most celebrated watering hole, however, is away from the square: **Harry's Bar,** founded by Giuseppe Cipriani but made famous by Hemingway. In and around the square are some of the most convenient hotels in Venice (though not necessarily the best) and an array of expensive tourist shops and trattorie.

CASTELLO The shape of Venice is often likened to that of a fish. If so, Castello is the tail. The largest and most varied of the six sestieri, Castello is home to many sights, such as the **Arsensale,** and some of the city's plushest hotels, such as the **Danieli.** One of the neighborhood's most notable attractions is the Gothic **Santa Giovanni e Paolo (Zanipolo),** the Pantheon of the doges. Cutting through the sestiere is **Campo Santa Maria Formosa,** one of Venice's largest open squares.

The most elegant street is **Riva degli Schiavoni,** which runs along the Grand Canal; it's lined with some of the finest hotels and restaurants and is one of the city's favorite promenades.

CANNAREGIO This is Venice's gateway, the first of the six sestieri. It lies away from the rail station at the northwest side of Venice and shelters about a third of the

Venice Orientation

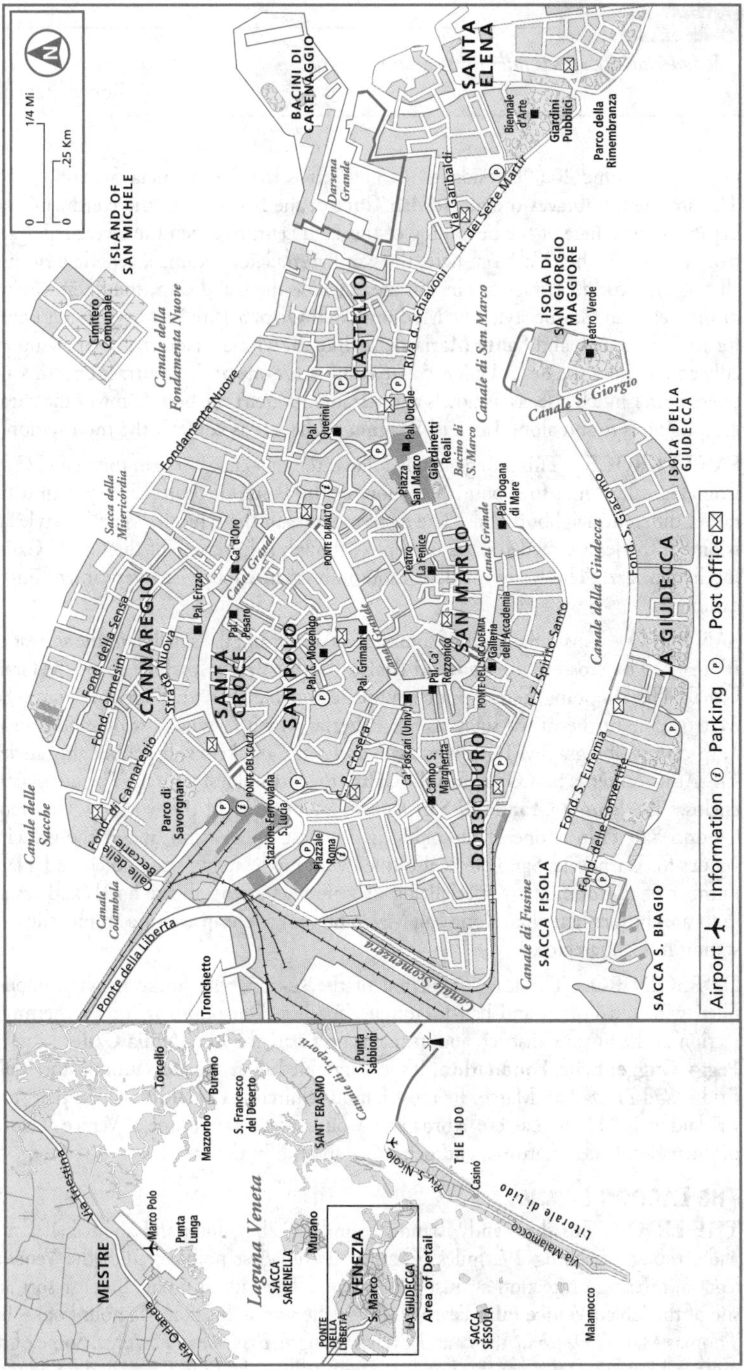

Impressions

Wonderful city, streets full of water, please advise.

—Robert Benchley

population, some 20,000 residents. At its heart is the **Santa Lucia Station** (1955). The area also embraces the old **Jewish Ghetto,** the first one on the continent. Jews began to move here at the beginning of the 16th century, when they were segregated from the rest of the city. From here, the word *ghetto* later became a generic term used all over the world. Attractions in this area include the **Ca' d'Oro,** the finest example of the Venetian Gothic style; the **Madonna dell'Orto,** a 15th-century church known for its Tintorettos; and **Santa Maria dei Miracoli,** with a Madonna portrait supposedly able to raise the dead. Unless you're coming for one of these attractions, this area doesn't offer much else, as its hotels and restaurants aren't the best. Some of the cheapest lodging is found along **Lista di Spagna,** to the left as you exit the train station.

SANTA CROCE This area generally follows the snakelike curve of the Grand Canal from Piazzale Roma to a point just short of the Ponte di Rialto. It's split into two rather different neighborhoods. The eastern part is in the typically Venetian style and is one of the least crowded parts of Venice, though it has some of the Grand Canal's loveliest palazzi. The western side is more industrialized and isn't very interesting to explore.

SAN POLO This is the heart of commercial Venice and the smallest of the six sestieri. It's reached by crossing the **Ponte di Rialto (Rialto Bridge),** which spans the Grand Canal. The shopping here is much more reasonable than that around Piazza San Marco. One of the major sights is the **Erberia,** which Casanova wrote about in his 18th-century biography. Both wholesale and retail markets still pepper this ancient site. At its center is **San Giacomo di Rialto,** the city's oldest church. The district also encloses the **Scuola Grande di San Rocco,** a repository of the works of Tintoretto. **Campo San Polo** is one of the oldest and widest squares and one of the principal venues for Carnevale. San Polo is also filled with moderately priced hotels and a large number of trattorie, many specializing in seafood. In general, the hotels and restaurants are cheaper here than along San Marco but not as cheap as those around the train station in Cannaregio.

DORSODURO The least populated of the sestieri, this funky neighborhood is filled with old homes and half-forgotten churches. Dorsoduro is the southernmost section of the historic district, and its major sights are the **Accademia Gallery** and the **Peggy Guggenheim Foundation.** It's less trampled than the areas around the Rialto Bridge and Piazza San Marco. Its most famous church is **La Salute,** whose first stone was laid in 1631. The **Zattere,** a broad quay built after 1516, is one of Venice's favorite promenades. Cafes, trattorie, and pensiones abound in the area.

THE LAGOON ISLANDS

THE LIDO This slim sandy island 7½ miles (12km) long and about half a mile wide, though reaching 2½ miles (4km) at its broadest point, cradles the Venetian lagoon, offering protection against the Adriatic. The Lido is a chic beach resort and site of the fabled **Venice Film Festival.** It was the setting for many famous books, like Thomas Mann's *Death in Venice* and Evelyn Waugh's *Brideshead Revisited.* Some of the most fashionable and expensive hotels are found along the Lido Promenade. The most famous are the **Grand Hotel Excelsior** and **Grand Hotel des Bains,** but there are cheaper places as well. The best way to get around is by bike or tandem, which you can rent at Via Zara and Gran Viale.

TORCELLO Lying 5½ miles (9km) northeast of Venice, Torcello is called "the mother of Venice," having been settled in the 9th century. It was once the most populous of the islands in the lagoon, but since the 18th century it has been nearly deserted. If you ever hope to find solitude in Venice, you'll find it here. It's visited today chiefly by those wishing to see its **Cattedrale di Torcello,** with its stunning Byzantine mosaics, and to lunch at the **Locanda Cipriani.**

BURANO Perched 5½ miles (9km) northeast of Venice, Burano is the most populous of the lagoon islands. In the 16th century, it produced the finest lace in Europe. Lace is still made here, but it's nothing like the product of centuries past. Inhabited since Roman times, Burano is different from either Torcello or Murano. Forget lavish palaces. The houses are often simple and small and painted in deep blues, strong reds, and striking yellows. The island is still peopled by fishers, and one of the reasons to visit is to dine at one of its trattorie, where, naturally, the specialty is fish.

MURANO This island, less than a mile (1km) northeast of Venice, has been famed for its glassmaking since 1291. Today Murano is the most visited island in the lagoon, as tons of guided tours visit the glassblowing shops. You can also visit a glass museum, the **Museo Vetrario di Murano** and see two of the island's notable churches, **San Pietro Martire** and **Santi Maria e Donato.** You'll likely be on the island for lunch, and there are a number of moderately priced trattorie.

2 Getting Around

Since you can't hail a taxi, at least not on land, get ready to walk and walk and walk. Of course, you can break up your walks with vaporetto or boat rides, which are great respites from dealing with the packed (and we mean *packed*) streets in summer.

However, note that in autumn, the high tide *(acqua alta)* is a real menace. The squares often flood, beginning with Piazza San Marco, one of the city's lowest points. Many visitors and locals wear knee-high boots to navigate their way. In fact, some hotels maintain a storage room full of boots in all sizes for their guests.

BY PUBLIC TRANSPORTATION

Much to the chagrin of the once-ubiquitous gondoliers, Venice's **motorboats (*vaporetti*)** provide inexpensive and frequent, if not always fast, transportation in this canal city. The service is operated by **ACTV (Azienda del Consorzio Trasporti Veneziano),** Calle Fisero, San Marco 1810 (☎ **041-528-7886**). An *accelerato* is a vessel that makes every stop and a *diretto* only express stops. The average fare is 6,000L ($3). Note that in summer the vaporetti are often fiercely crowded. Pick up a map of the system at the tourist office. They run daily, with frequent service 7am to midnight, then hourly midnight to 7am.

Visitors to Venice can buy a 10-ticket carnet costing 50,000L ($25), which must be validated before use and shown together with the matrix (the last ticket of the booklet).

The Grand Canal is long and snakelike and can be crossed via only three bridges, including the one at Rialto. If there's no bridge in sight, the trick in getting across is to use one of the ***traghetti* gondolas** strategically placed at key points. Look for them at the end of any passage called Calle del Traghetto. Under government control, the fare is only 1,000L (50¢).

BY MOTOR LAUNCH (WATER TAXI)

Motor launches ***(taxi acquei)*** cost more than public vaporettos, but you won't be hassled as much when you arrive with your luggage if you hire one of the many private ones. You may or may not have the cabin of one of these sleek vessels to yourself, since the captains fill their boats with as many passengers as the law allows before taking off. Your porter's uncanny radar will guide you to one of the inconspicuous piers where a water taxi waits.

The price of a transit by water taxi from Piazzale Roma (the road/rail terminus) to Piazza San Marco is 80,000L ($40) for up to four passengers and 100,000L ($50) for more than four. The captains adroitly deliver you, with luggage, to the canal-side entrance of your hotel or on one of the smaller waterways within a short walking distance of your destination. You can also call for a water taxi; try the **Cooperativa San Marco** at ☎ **041-522-2303.**

BY GONDOLA

You and your gondolier have two major agreements to reach: the price and the length of the ride. If you aren't careful, you're likely to be taken on both counts. It's a common sight to see a gondolier huffing and puffing to take his passengers on a "quickie," often reducing an hour to 15 minutes.

The "official" rate is 100,000L ($50) per hour, but we've never known anyone to honor it. The actual fare depends on how well you stand up to the gondolier, *beginning* at 150,000L ($75) for up to 50 minutes. Most gondoliers will ask at least double the "official" rate and reduce your trip to 30 to 40 minutes or even less. Prices go up after 8pm. In fairness to them, we must say their job is hard and has been overly romanticized: They row boatloads of tourists across hot, smelly canals with such endearments screamed at them as, "No sing! No pay!" And these fellows have to make plenty of lire while the sun shines, because their work ends when the first cold winds blow in from the Adriatic.

Two major stations where you can hire gondolas are **Piazza San Marco** (☎ **041-520-0685**) and **Ponte di Rialto** (☎ **041-522-4904**).

BY CAR

Obviously you won't need a car in Venice, but you might want one when you leave, to head off to nearby cities like Padua. Most of the car-rental agencies lie near the rail station in the traffic-clogged Piazzale Roma (meaning also that you can return a rental car here as you arrive in Venice). Of course, you'll save the most money if you reserve before leaving home.

Hertz is at Piazzale Roma 496E (☎ **800/654-3131** in the U.S., or 041-528-4091; www.hertz.com). November to March, it's open Monday to Friday 8am to 12:30pm and 3 to 5:30pm, Saturday 8am to 1pm; April hours are Monday to Friday 8am to 6pm, Saturday 8am to 1pm; May to October, hours are Monday to Friday 8am to 6pm, Saturday 8am to 1pm. **Europcar** (associated with National in the U.S.) is at Piazzale Roma 496H (☎ **800/328-4567** or 041-523-8616). May to October, it's open Monday to Friday 8:30am to 1pm and 2 to 6:30pm, Saturday to Sunday 8:30am to 12:30pm; November to April, hours are Monday to Friday 8:30am to noon and 2 to 6:30pm, Saturday 8:30am to noon. And **Avis** is at Piazzale Roma 496G (☎ **800/331-2112** in the U.S., or 041-522-5825; www.avis.com). November to March, it's open Monday to Friday 8:30am to 12:30pm and 2:30 to 6pm, Saturday and Sunday 8:30am to 12:30pm; April to October, hours are Monday to Friday 8am to 7pm, Saturday to Sunday 8:30am to 12:30pm.

Fast Facts: Venice

American Express The office is Salizzada San Moisè, San Marco 1471 (☎ **041-520-0844;** vaporetto: San Marco). The staff can arrange city tours and mail handling. May to October, hours are Monday to Saturday 8am to 8pm for currency exchange and 9am to 5:30pm for all other transactions; November to April, hours are Monday to Friday 9am to 5:30pm and Saturday 9am to 12:30pm.

Baby-Sitters In lieu of a central booking agency, arrangements have to be made individually at various hotels. Obviously, the more advance notice you give, the better your chances of getting an English-speaking sitter.

Consulates The **U.K. Consulate** is at Dorsoduro 1051, at the foot of the Accademia Bridge (☎ **041-522-7207;** vaporetto: Accademia), open Monday to Friday 10am to noon and 2 to 3pm. The **United States, Canada,** and **Australia** have consulates in Milan, about 3 hours away by train (see "Fast Facts: Milan" in chapter 10).

Currency Exchange There are many banks in Venice where you can exchange money. You might try the **Banca Commerciale Italiana,** Via XXII Marzo, San Marco 2188 (☎ **041-529-6811;** vaporetto: San Marco), or **Banco San Marco,** Calle Larga San Marco, San Marco 383 (☎ **041-529-3711;** vaporetto: San Marco).

Dentist/Doctor Your best bet is to have your hotel set up an appointment with an English-speaking dentist or doctor. The American Express office and the British Consulate also have lists. Also see "Hospitals," below.

Drugstores If you need a drugstore in the middle of the night, call ☎ **192** for information about which one is open (pharmacies take turns staying open late). A well-recommended central one is **International Pharmacy,** Via XXII Marzo, San Marco 2067 (☎ **041-522-2311;** vaporetto: San Marco).

Emergencies Call ☎ **113** for the police, ☎ **118** for an ambulance, or ☎ **115** to report a fire.

Hospitals Get in touch with the **Ospedale Civile Santi Giovanni e Paolo,** Campo Santi Giovanni e Paolo in Castello (☎ **041-94517;** vaporetto: San Toma), staffed with English-speaking doctors 24 hours a day.

Laundry/Dry Cleaning One of the most convenient coin-operated Laundromats and dry-cleaning enterprises is **Lavanderia Gabriella,** Calle Fiubera, San Marco 985 (☎ **041-522-1758;** vaporetto: San Marco), set behind Piazza San Marco. Its washing machines are available daily 8am to 7pm, and its dry-cleaning facilities Monday to Saturday 8am to 12:30pm and 3 to 7pm.

Police See "Emergencies," above.

Post Office The **main post office** is at Salizzada Fondaco dei Tedeschi, San Marco 5554 (☎ **041-271-7111;** vaporetto: Rialto), near the Rialto Bridge. It's open Monday to Saturday 8:15am to 5pm.

Rest Rooms These are available at Piazzale Roma and various other places but aren't as plentiful as they should be. A truly spotless one is at the foot of the Accademia Bridge (be sure to have some 500L coins). Often you'll have to rely on the rest rooms in cafes, though you should buy something, perhaps a light coffee, as in theory the toilets are for customers only. Most museums and galleries have public toilets. You can also use the public toilets at the Albergo Diurno, Via Ascensione, just behind Piazza San Marco. Remember, *signori* means men and *signore* women.

Safety The curse of Venice is the pickpocket. Violent crime is rare. But because of the overcrowding in vaporetti and even on the small narrow streets, it's easy to pick pockets. Purse snatchers are commonplace as well. They can dart out of nowhere, grab a purse, and disappear in seconds down some narrow dark alley. Keep valuables locked in a safe in your hotel, if one is provided.

Telephone See "Fast Facts: Italy," in chapter 2 for full details on how to call Venice from home and how to place international calls once you're here. The **city code** for Venice is **041;** use this code when calling from *anywhere* outside or inside Italy—even within Venice itself (and you must now include the zero every time, even when calling from abroad).

3 Accommodations

Venice has some of the most expensive hotels in the world, but we've also found some wonderful lesser-known moderately priced places, often on hard-to-find narrow streets. However, Venice has never been known as an inexpensive destination.

Because of their age and lack of uniformity, Venice's hotels offer widely varying rooms. For example, it's entirely possible to stay in a hotel generally considered "expensive" while paying only a "moderate" rate—if you'll settle for a less desirable room. Many "inexpensive" hotels and boarding houses have two or three rooms in the "expensive" category. Usually these are more spacious and open onto a view. Also, if an elevator is essential for you, always inquire in advance when booking a room, because they don't always exist in old buildings.

The cheapest way to visit Venice is to book into a *locanda* (small inn), which is rated below the *pensioni* (boarding house) in official Italian hotel lingo. Standards are highly variable in these places, many of which are dank, dusty, and dark. The rooms even in many second- or first-class hotels are often cramped, as space has always been a problem in Venice. It's estimated that in this "City of Light" at least half the rooms in any category are dark, so be duly warned. Those with lots of light and opening onto the Grand Canal carry a hefty price tag.

The most difficult times to find rooms are during the February Carnevale, around Easter, and from June to September. Because of the tight hotel situation, it's advisable to make reservations as far in advance as possible (months in advance for summer, and even a year in advance for Carnevale). After those peak times, you can virtually have your pick of rooms. Most hotels, if you ask at the reception desk, will grant you a 10% to 15% discount in winter (November to March 15). But getting this discount may require a little negotiation. A few hotels close in January if there's no prospect of business.

Should you arrive without a reservation, go to one of the **AVA (Hotel Association) reservation booths** throughout the area at the train station, the municipal parking garage at Piazzale Roma, the airport, and the information point on the mainland where the highway comes to an end. The main office is at Piazzale Roma (☎ **041-522-8640**). To get a room, you'll have to pay a deposit that's then rebated on your hotel bill. Depending on the hotel classification, deposits are 20,000 to 90,000L ($10 to $45) per person. All hotel booths are open daily 9am to 8 or 9pm.

See "The Neighborhoods in Brief" section to get an idea of where you might want to base yourself, whether it be in less touristy San Polo or Dorsoduro or amid the crowds in and around Piazza San Marco (where hotels tend to be expensive, but you're in the heart of the action).

NEAR PIAZZA SAN MARCO

VERY EXPENSIVE

✪ **Gritti Palace.** Campo Santa Maria del Giglio, San Marco 2467, 30124 Venezia. ☎ **800/325-3535** in the U.S., 416/947-4864 in Canada, or 041-794-611. Fax 041-520-0942. www.sheraton.com. 93 units. A/C MINIBAR TV TEL. 1,100,000–1,400,000L ($550–$700) double; from 2,400,000L ($1,200) suite. Rates include breakfast. AE, DC, MC, V. Vaporetto: Santa Maria del Giglio.

The Gritti, in a stately Grand Canal setting, is the renovated palazzo of 15th-century doge Andrea Gritti. Even after its takeover by ITT Sheraton, it's still a bit starchy and has a museum aura (some of the furnishings are roped off); but for sheer glamour and history, only the Cipriani (see below) tops it. For Hemingway it was his "home in Venice," and it has drawn some of the world's greatest theatrical, literary, political, and royal figures. The variety of guest rooms seems almost limitless, from elaborate suites to small singles. But throughout, the elegance is evident. The most spacious rooms face the campo, and we prefer the big corner doubles (second and third floors) with balconies overlooking the canal. Deluxe mattresses grace the antique beds, and thoughtful extras include private safes and thermostats. No-smoking rooms are available. Most of the bathrooms are sumptuous, sheathed in red Verona marble and amply stocked with robes and hair dryers. For a splurge, ask for Hemingway's old suite or the Doge Suite, once occupied by W. Somerset Maugham.

Dining: Ristorante Club del Doge is among the best in Venice but also flagrantly overpriced.

Amenities: 24-hour room service, baby-sitting, laundry/valet; use of the Hotel Excelsior's facilities on the Lido.

Hotel Bauer/Bauer Palace. Campo San Moisè, San Marco 1459, 30124 Venezia. ☎ **041-520-7022.** Fax 041-520-7557. www.bauervenezia.com. E-mail: bauer@bauervenezia.com. 210 units. A/C MINIBAR TV TEL. Hotel Bauer: 790,000–1,100,000L ($395–$550) double; from 1,200,000L ($600) suite. Bauer Palace: 1,050,000–1,180,000L ($525–$590) double; from 2,200,000L ($1,100) suite. AE, DC, MC, V. Vaporetto: San Marco.

This deluxe hotel, known since 1880 as the Grand Hotel d'Italie Bauer Grunwald but now as simply the Hotel Bauer, is better than ever. Long a favorite of prime ministers, royalty, and jet-setters, it's the combination of an ornate 13th-century palazzo facing the Grand Canal; a massive concrete wing that was "an architectural scandal" when it opened in the 1960s; and the new Bauer Palace, a VIP wing. The guest rooms are decorated in classic European style, with both French and Venetian pieces, as well as deluxe linen and mattresses and marble-clad bathrooms. The fabrics used throughout were specially designed for the Bauer.

Dining/Diversions: Fine Venetian and Mediterranean cuisine is served here, in either the main restaurant, The Bauer (with a view of the Grand Canal), or more informally in La Terrazza. The hotel bar is a chic place for a drink.

Amenities: Concierge, 24-hour room service, valet, fitness unit, hairdresser, baby-sitting, business center, golf, tennis, water sports, and riding arranged by staff.

EXPENSIVE

Hotel Casanova. Frezzeria, San Marco 1284, 30124 Venezia. ☎ **041-520-6855.** Fax 041-520-6413. www.side7.it/casanova/. E-mail: hotel.casanova.ve@iol.it. 49 units. A/C MINIBAR TV TEL. 450,000L ($225) double; 510,000L ($255) triple. Rates include breakfast. AE, DC, MC, V. Vaporetto: San Marco.

This former home is a few steps from Piazza San Marco. Although the name Casanova sounds romantic, the hotel doesn't have a lot of character; it does, however, contain a collection of church art and benches from old monasteries (sitting on flagstone floors

Venice Accommodations

Albergo Al Piave **22**
American Hotel **9**
Boston Hotel **17**
Danieli Royal Excelsior **27**
Doni Pensione **29**
Gritti Palace **10**
Hotel Abbazia **1**
Hotel ai do Mori **18**
Hotel Bauer/Bauer Palace **15**
Hotel Bisanzio **32**
Hotel Campiello **30**
Hotel Carpaccio **5**
Hotel Casanova **14**
Hotel Concordia **19**
Hotel do Pozzi **11**
Hotel Galleria **7**
Hotel Geremia **26**
Hotel Giorgione **24**
Hotel La Calcina **8**
Hotel La Fenice et des Artistes **13**
Hotel Marconi **3**
Hotel Montecarlo **20**
Hotel Rialto **23**
Hotel San Cassiano Ca' Favretto **2**
Hotel Saturnia International **12**
Hotel Savoia & Jolanda **28**
Hotel Scandinavia **21**
Hotel Violino d'Oro **16**
La Residenza **33**
Locanda ai Santi Apostoli **25**
Locanda Montin **8**
Locanda Sturion **4**
Londra Palace **31**
Pensione Accademia **6**

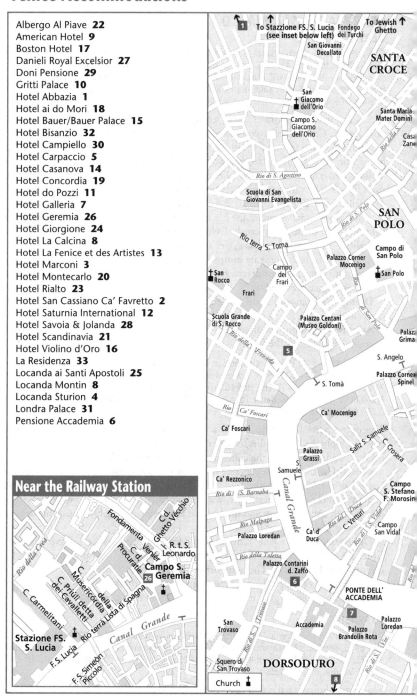

Near the Railway Station

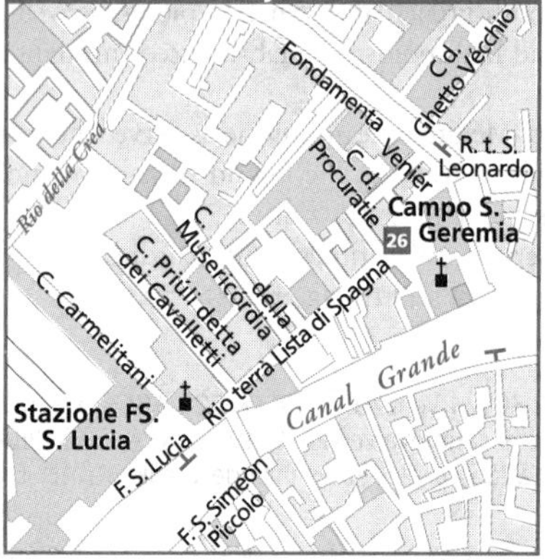

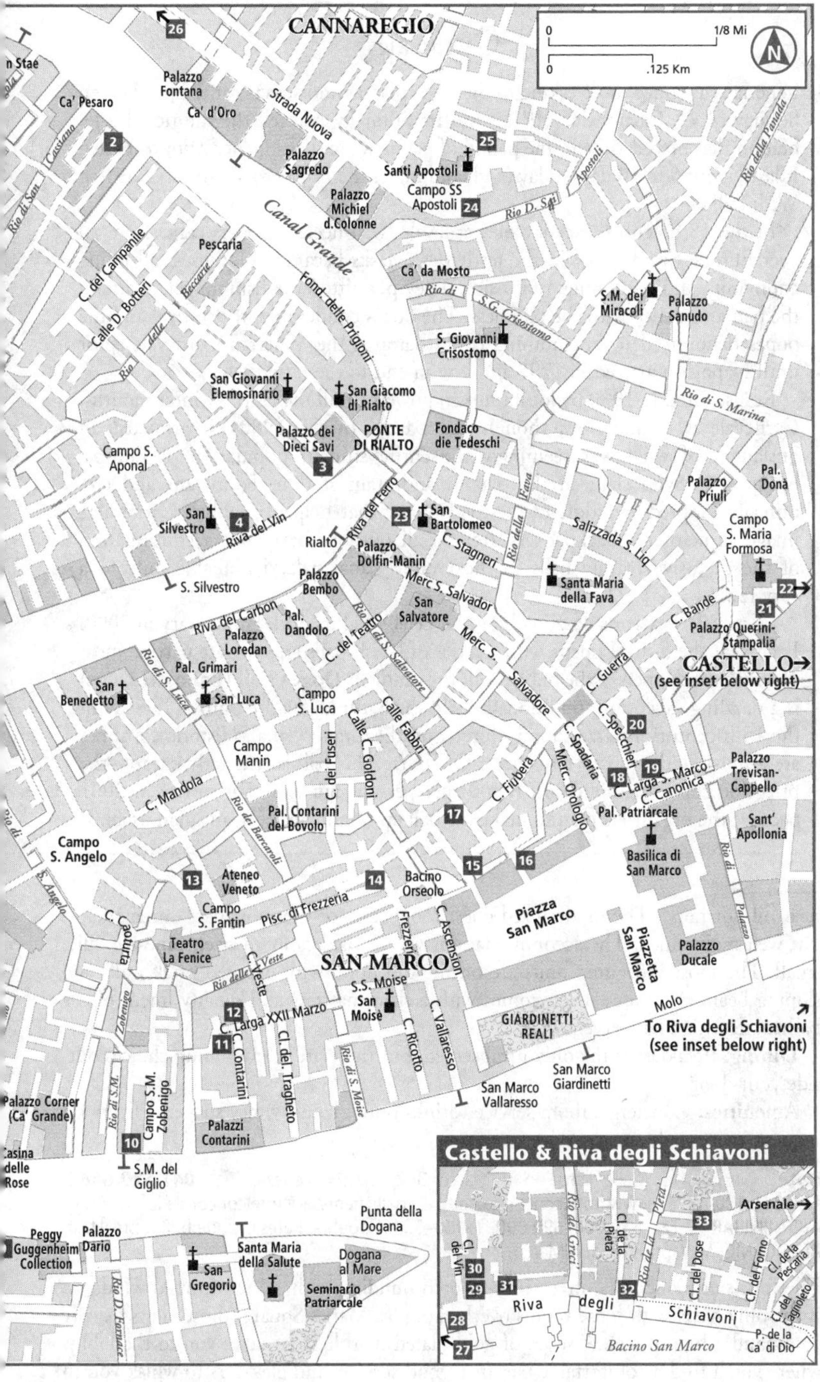
CANNAREGIO
0
1/8 Mi
0
.125 Km
N
Palazzo Fontana
Ca' d'Oro
Ca' Pesaro
Strada Nuova
Palazzo Sagredo
Santi Apostoli
Campo SS Apostoli
Palazzo Michiel d.Colonne
Canal Grande
Pescaria
C. del Campanile
Calle D. Botteri
Fond. delle Prigioni
Ca' da Mosto
S.M. dei Miracoli
Palazzo Sanudo
S. Giovanni Crisostomo
San Giovanni Elemosinario
San Giacomo di Rialto
Rio di S. Marina
Palazzo dei Dieci Savi
PONTE DI RIALTO
Fondaco die Tedeschi
Campo S. Aponal
San Silvestro
Riva del Vin
Riva del Ferro
San Bartolomeo
Rialto
Palazzo Dolfin-Manin
C. Stagneri
Salizzada S. Liq
Santa Maria della Fava
Palazzo Priuli
Pal. Donà
Campo S. Maria Formosa
S. Silvestro
Palazzo Bembo
Merc S. Salvador
Riva del Carbon
Pal. Dandolo
San Salvatore
Palazzo Loredan
C. del Teatro
Merc. S. Salvadore
C. Bande
Palazzo Querini-Stampalia
CASTELLO→
(see inset below right)
Pal. Grimari
San Benedetto
San Luca
Campo S. Luca
Calle Fabbri
C. Guerra
C. Specchieri
Campo Manin
C. Mandola
C. dei Fuseri
Calle C. Goldoni
C. Fiubera
Merc. Orologio
C. Spadaria
C. Larga S. Marco
C. Canonica
Palazzo Trevisan-Cappello
Pal. Contarini del Bovolo
Pal. Patriarcale
Sant' Apollonia
Campo S. Angelo
Basilica di San Marco
Ateneo Veneto
Bacino Orseolo
Campo S. Fantin
Pisc. di Frezzeria
Piazza San Marco
Piazzetta San Marco
Teatro La Fenice
C. Caotorta
Frezzeria
C. Ascensione
SAN MARCO
Palazzo Ducale
C. Veste
S.S. Moise
San Moisè
Molo
C. Larga XXII Marzo
GIARDINETTI REALI
To Riva degli Schiavoni (see inset below right)
C. Contarini
Cl. del Traghetto
C. Ricotto
C. Vallaresso
San Marco Giardinetti
San Marco Vallaresso
Palazzo Corner (Ca' Grande)
Campo S.M. Zobenigo
Palazzi Contarini
S.M. del Giglio
Punta della Dogana
Peggy Guggenheim Collection
Palazzo Dario
Santa Maria della Salute
Dogana al Mare
San Gregorio
Seminario Patriarcale
Castello & Riva degli Schiavoni
Arsenale→
Cl. del Vin
Cl. de la Pietà
Cl. del Dose
Cl. del Forno
Cl. de la Pescaria
Cl. del Cagnoleto
Riva degli Schiavoni
Bacino San Marco
P. de la Ca' di Dio
2 3 4 10 11 12 13 14 15 16 17 18 19 20 21 22 23 24 25 26 27 28 29 30 31 32 33

Carnevale

Venetians are once more taking to the open piazzas and streets for the pre-Lenten holiday of ✪ **Carnevale.** The festival traditionally marked the unbridled celebration that preceded Lent, the period of penitence and abstinence prior to Easter. It lasts about 5 to 10 days today (and culminates the Friday to Tuesday before Ash Wednesday).

In the 18th-century heyday of Carnevale, well-heeled revelers came from all over Europe to take part in the festivities. Masks became ubiquitous, affording anonymity and pardoning 1,000 sins. They permitted the fishmonger to attend the ball and dance with the baroness. The doges condemned the festival and the popes denounced it, but nothing could dampen the Venetian Carnevale spirit until Napoléon arrived in 1797 and put an end to the festivities.

Resuscitated in 1980 by local tourism powers to fill the empty winter months, Carnevale is calmer now, though just barely. In the 1980s, it attracted an onslaught of what was seemingly the entire student population of Europe, backpackers who slept in the piazzas and train station. Politicians and city officials adopted a middle-of-the-road policy that helped establish Carnevale's image as neither a backpackers' free-for-all outdoor party not a continuation of the exclusive private balls in the Grand Canal palazzi available only to a very few.

Carnevale was at its dazzling best as it celebrated its 20th anniversary in 2000. Each year the festival opens with a series of lavish balls and private parties, most of which aren't open to the public. But the candlelit **Doge's Ball (Ballo del Doge)** is a dazzling exception, traditionally held the Saturday before Shrove Tuesday in the 15th-century Palazzo Pisani Moretta on the Grand Canal. Historic costumes are a must, and you can rent them. Of course, this ball isn't exactly cheap—the price for 2000 was 600,000L ($300) per person, but expect it to rise in 2001 because the organizers plan to make the ball even more extravagant than usual. If

near oil portraits). The modernized guest rooms are for the most part unremarkable but well maintained. The accommodations vary considerably in size; some are quite small. The most intriguing units are on the top floor, with exposed brick walls and sloping beamed ceilings. Each comes with a firm mattress and quality linen, plus a bathroom with a hair dryer.

Dining: Breakfast is the only meal served, but there are many dining choices outside your door.

Amenities: Concierge, room service (drinks only), laundry, newspaper delivery on request, twice-daily maid service.

Hotel Concordia. Calle Larga, San Marco 367, 30124 Venezia. ☎ **041-520-6866.** Fax 041-520-6775. www.hotelconcordia.com. E-mail: venezia@hotelconcordia.it. 57 units. A/C MINIBAR TV TEL. 330,000–690,000L ($165–$345) double. Rates include buffet breakfast. AE, DC, MC, V. Vaporetto: San Marco.

The four-star Concordia, in a russet-colored building with stone-trimmed windows, is the only hotel with some rooms overlooking St. Mark's Square (those views usually command a high price). A series of gold-plated marble steps takes you to the lobby, where you'll find a comfortable bar area, good service, and elevators to whisk you to the labyrinthine halls. All of the (quite small) guest rooms are decorated in a Venetian you're interested in finding out more and arranging for a costume rental, contact Antonia Sautter at the Ballo del Doge at ☎ **041-523-3851** (fax 041-528-7543).

Even if you don't attend a ball, there's still plenty of fun in the streets. You'll find a patchwork of musical and cultural events, many of them free of charge, that appeal to all tastes, nationalities, ages, and budgets. At any given moment, musical events are staged in any of the city's dozens of piazzas—from reggae to zydeco to jazz to chamber music—and special art exhibits are mounted at numerous museums and galleries. The recent involvement of international corporate sponsors has met with a mixed reception, but it seems to be the wave of the future.

Carnevale is not for those who dislike crowds. The crowds are what it's all about. All of life becomes a stage, and everyone is on it. Whether you spend months creating an elaborate costume, or grab one from the countless stands set up around town, Carnevale is about giving in to the spontaneity of the magic and surprise around every corner, the mystery behind every mask. Masks and costumes are everywhere, with the emphasis on the historical, for Venice's Carnevale is a chance to relive the glory days of the 1700s, when Venetian life was at its most extravagant. Groups travel in coordinated getups that range from a contemporary passel of Fellini-esque clowns to the court of the Sun King in all its wigged-out glory. There are the Three Musketeers riding the vaporetto; your waiter appears dressed as a nun. The places to be seen in costume are the cafes lining Piazza San Marco. Don't expect to be seated at a full-view window seat unless your costume is straight off the stage of the local opera house. The merrymakers carry on until Shrove Tuesday, when the bells of San Francesco della Vigna toll at midnight. But before they do, the grand finale involves fireworks over the lagoon.

The city is the quintessential set, the perfect venue; Hollywood could not create a more evocative location. This is a celebration about history, art, theater, and drama. Venice and Carnevale were made for each other.

antique style, with small Murano chandeliers, coordinated fabrics, hand-painted furnishings, and firm mattresses, plus electronic safes. The marble bathrooms come with hair dryers.

Dining: Breakfast is the only meal served, but light meals and Italian snacks are available in the bar.

Amenities: 24-hour room service, baby-sitting, laundry/valet.

Hotel Saturnia International. Calle Larga XXII Marzo, San Marco 2399, 30124 Venezia. ☎ **041-520-8377.** Fax 041-520-7131. www.hotelsaturnia.it. E-mail: info@hotelsaturnia.it. 95 units. A/C MINIBAR TV TEL. 396,000–720,000L ($198–$360) double. Rates include breakfast. AE, DC, MC, V. Vaporetto: San Marco.

The Saturnia was created from a 14th-century palazzo. You're surrounded by richly embellished beauty: a grand hall with a wooden staircase, iron chandeliers, fine paintings, and beamed ceilings. The individually styled guest rooms are generally spacious and furnished with chandeliers, Venetian antiques, tapestry rugs, gilt mirrors, carved ceilings, and sumptuous mattresses. A few on the top floor have small balconies; others overlook the garden in back. The bathrooms are small to medium, each with a hair dryer.

Dining: La Caravella is recommended under "Dining," later in this chapter.

Amenities: Room service, baby-sitting, laundry/valet.

Family-Friendly Hotels

American Hotel *(see p. 374)* This secluded hotel is across the Grand Canal away from the tourist hordes. It's a solid moderately priced choice where many rooms are rented as triples.

Hotel Quattro Fontane *(see p. 377)* Long a Lido family favorite, this hotel guarantees fun in the sun. It's somewhat like staying in the big chalet of a Venetian family. There's a private beach too.

Pensione Accademia *(see p. 375)* The best of Venice's pensioni, this villa has a garden and large rooms. This former Russian Embassy was recently restored.

Hotel Scandinavia. Campo Santa Maria Formosa, Castello 5240, 30122 Venezia. ☎ **041-522-3507.** Fax 041-420-359. www.scandinaviahotel.com. E-mail: info@scandinaviahotel.com. 34 units. A/C MINIBAR TV TEL. 200,000–600,000L ($100–$300) double. Rates include breakfast. AE, DC, MC, V. Vaporetto: San Zaccaria or Rialto.

This hotel isn't actually in San Marco (it's in neighboring Castello, just off a colorful square), but it has a convenient location not far from Piazza San Marco. The public rooms are rococo, filled with copies of 18th-century Italian chairs and Venetian-glass chandeliers. The guest rooms are of a decent size and decorated in the Venetian style, but modern comforts have been added, such as firm mattresses. The bathrooms are a bit cramped but well organized; a hair dryer can be requested at the front desk. The lobby lounge overlooks the campo. Breakfast is the only meal served, but the hotel staff will direct you to several good dining spots within a short walk of the entrance.

Amenities: Baby-sitting, laundry, room service (breakfast only), concierge.

Hotel Violino d'Oro. Campiello Barozzi, San Marco 2091, 30124 Venezia. ☎ **041-277-0841.** Fax 041-277-1001. www.violinodoro.com. E-mail: violinodoro@violinodoro.com. 26 units. A/C MINIBAR TV TEL. 200,000–600,000L ($100–$300) double. Rates include breakfast. AE, DC, MC, V. Vaporetto: San Marco.

This three-floor nonsmoking hotel opened in 1999 in the restored 18th-century Palazzo Barozzi, near the Vivaldi church (hence the name). The midsize guest rooms are handsomely furnished, with luxury mattresses, two phones, and baths with hair dryers. Two rooms and the junior suite open onto private terraces, and two rooms are set up for persons with disabilities. Ms. Cristina and her family run the hotel with style and grace.

Dining/Diversions: Breakfast is the only meal served, offered in a bright Venetian room with crystal chandeliers. A bar is open 8am to midnight, and guests can also enjoy drinks in a third-floor solarium.

Amenities: Room service (8am to midnight), laundry service.

MODERATE

Boston Hotel. Ponte dei Dai, San Marco 848, 30124 Venezia. ☎ **041-528-7665.** Fax 041-522-6628. 42 units. A/C TEL. 260,000–320,000L ($130–$160) double. Rates include breakfast. AE, DC, MC, V. Closed Nov–Feb. Vaporetto: San Marco.

Built in 1962, the hotel was named after an uncle who left to seek his fortune in Boston and never returned. For the skinny guest, there's a tiny self-operated elevator and a postage stamp–sized street entrance. Most of the guest rooms, with parquet floors, have built-in features, plus chests and wardrobes. Some open onto tiny balconies overlooking the canal, and 20 are air-conditioned and 20 equipped with TVs. The mattresses are a bit worn but still comfortable. The tiny bathrooms contain a basket of body care products but no hair dryers.

Hotel do Pozzi. Corte do Pozzi, San Marco 2373, 30124 Venezia. ☎ **041-520-7855.** Fax 041-522-9413. E-mail: hotel.dopozzi@flashnet.it. 35 units. MINIBAR TV TEL. 330,000L ($165) double. Rates include breakfast. AE, DC, MC, V. Vaporetto: Santa Maria del Giglio.

A short stroll from the Grand Canal and Piazza San Marco, this small place feels more like a country tavern than a hotel. Its original structure is 200 years old, opening onto a paved courtyard with potted greenery. The sitting and dining rooms are furnished with antiques (and near-antiques) intermixed with utilitarian modern decor. The guest rooms range from small to medium, with half opening onto the street, half onto a view of an inner garden where breakfast is served in summer. Some have Venetian styling with antique reproductions; others are in a more contemporary and more sterile vein. A major refurbishing has given a fresh touch to the bathrooms. Laundry and baby-sitting are available.

Hotel La Fenice et des Artistes. Campiello de la Fenice, San Marco 1936, 30124 Venezia. ☎ **041-523-2333.** Fax 041-520-3721. E-mail: fenice@fenicehotels.it. 69 units. TV TEL. 240,000–360,000L ($120–$180) double; 420,000–480,000L ($210–$240) suite. Rates include breakfast. AE, DC, MC, V. Vaporetto: San Marco.

This hotel offers widely varying accommodations in two connected buildings, each at least 100 years old. One is rather romantic, though a bit timeworn, with an impressive staircase leading to the ornate rooms (one even has its own small garden and terraces). Your satin-lined room may have an inlaid desk and a wardrobe painted in the Venetian manner to match a baroque bed frame. The main building, site of the reception desk, is the more desirable, furnished in a more typically Venetian style, with nicely padded walls and art reproductions, gilt mirrors, Murano chandeliers, and spacious old bathrooms (ask for a hair dryer at the front desk). All but about three rooms are air-conditioned.

Hotel Montecarlo. Calle dei Specchieri, San Marco 463, 30124 Venezia. ☎ **041-520-7144.** Fax 041-520-7789. www.doge.it. E-mail: mocarl@doge.it. 48 units. A/C TV TEL. 200,000–600,000L ($100–$300) double. Rates include buffet breakfast. AE, CB, DC, MC, V. Vaporetto: San Marco.

A 2-minute walk from Piazza San Marco, this hotel opened some years ago in a 17th-century building but was recently renovated to include modern bathrooms. The upper halls are lined with paintings by Venetian artists. The guest rooms are nicely proportioned and decorated with Venetian-style furniture (plus firm mattresses) and Venetian-glass chandeliers. They range from small to medium, though some are quite dark, the curse of many Venetian hotels. The bathrooms come with hair dryers. The Antico Pignolo restaurant serves lunch and dinner and features both Venetian and international dishes.

INEXPENSIVE

Hotel ai do Mori. Calle Larga San Marco, San Marco 658, 30124 Venezia. ☎ **041-520-4817.** Fax 041-520-5328. www.hotelaidomori.com. E-mail: reception@hotelaidomori.com. 11 units, 7 with private bathroom. A/C TV TEL. 150,000L ($75) double without bathroom, 160,000–200,000L ($80–$100) double with bathroom. MC, V. Vaporetto: San Marco.

This 1450s town house lies about 10 paces from tourist central. You'll have to balance your need for space with your love of views (and your ability to climb stairs, since there's no elevator): The lower-level rooms are larger but don't have views; the third- and fourth-floor rooms are cramped but have sweeping views over the basilica's domes. The building is frequently upgraded by owner Antonella Bernardi. The furniture in the guest rooms is simple and modern, and most of the street noise is muffled by double-paned windows. The tiled bathrooms have hair dryers. The dozens of cafes in the neighborhood make up for the fact that no meals are served.

CASTELLO/RIVA DEGLI SCHIAVONI

Several of the hotels in this section are also very close to Piazza San Marco.

VERY EXPENSIVE

✪ **Danieli Royal Excelsior.** Riva degli Schiavoni, Castello 4196, 30122 Venezia. ☎ **800/325-3535** in the U.S. and Canada, or 041-522-6480. Fax 041-520-0208. www.ittsheraton.com. 238 units. A/C MINIBAR TV TEL. 750,000–1,050,000L ($375–$525) double; 1,100,000–5,060,000L ($550–$2,530) suite. AE, CB, DC, MC, V. Vaporetto: San Zaccaria.

The Danieli was built as a grand showcase by Doge Dandolo in the 14th century and in 1822 was transformed into a "hotel for kings." In a spectacular Grand Canal position, it has sheltered not only kings but also princes, cardinals, ambassadors, and such literary figures as George Sand and Charles Dickens. You enter into a four-story stairwell, with Venetian arches and balustrades. The atmosphere is luxurious; even the balconies opening off the main lounge are illuminated by stained-glass skylights. The guest rooms range widely in price, dimension, decor, and vistas (those opening onto the lagoon cost a lot more). Alfred de Musset and Ms. Sand made love in room no. 10, the most requested accommodation. You're housed in one of three buildings: a modern structure (least desirable), a 19th-century building, and the 14th-century Venetian-Gothic Palazzo Dandolo (most desirable). On the downside, the palazzo rooms, though the most romantic, are the smallest. The beds are sumptuous, with luxury mattresses and fine linen, and the grand bathrooms come with hair dryers.

Dining/Diversions: From the rooftop Terrazza Danieli, you have a perfect view of the canals and "crowns" of Venice. There's also an intimate cocktail lounge and a bar offering piano music.

Amenities: Room service, baby-sitting, laundry/valet, hotel launch to the Lido in summer.

✪ **Londra Palace.** Riva degli Schiavoni, Castello 4171, 30122 Venezia. ☎ **041-520-0533.** Fax 041-522-5032. www.hotelondra.it. E-mail: info@hotelondra.it. 53 units. A/C MINIBAR TV TEL. 614,000–748,000L ($307–$374) double; 940,000–1,045,000L ($470–$522.50) junior suite. Rates include breakfast. AE, DC, MC, V. Vaporetto: San Zaccaria.

The Londra is a gabled manor on the lagoon, a few yards from Piazza San Marco. The hotel's most famous guest was arguably Tchaikovsky, who wrote his Fourth Symphony in room no. 108 in December 1877; he also composed several other works here. The cozy reading room is reminiscent of an English club, boasting leaded windows and paneled walls with framed blowups of some of Tchaikovsky's sheet music. The guest rooms are luxurious, often with lacquered Venetian furniture. Romantics ask for one of the two Regency-style attic rooms with beamed ceilings. The courtyard rooms are quieter and cheaper, opening onto rooftop views instead of the Grand Canal. The best units are those on the fifth floor, with beamed ceilings and private terraces. The bathrooms often have whirlpool tubs and come with deluxe toiletries and robes.

Dining/Diversions: The hotel has a popular piano bar and an excellent restaurant, Do Leoni (see "Dining," below).

Amenities: Room service, baby-sitting, laundry/valet, conference hall.

EXPENSIVE

Hotel Bisanzio. Calle della Pietà, Riva degli Schiavoni 3651, 30122 Venezia. ☎ **041-520-3100.** Fax 041-520-4114. www.bisanzio.com. E-mail: email@bisanzio.com. 47 units.

A/C MINIBAR TV TEL. 390,000–490,000L ($195–$245) double. Rates include breakfast. AE, DC, MC, V. Vaporetto: San Zaccaria.

A few steps from St. Mark's Square, this hotel in the former home of sculptor Alessandro Vittoria offers good service. It has an elevator and terraces, plus a little bar and a mooring for gondolas and motorboats. The guest rooms are generally quiet, each in a Venetian antique style; beds have quality mattresses. The most requested rooms are the eight opening onto private balconies. The bathrooms are well kept, with hair dryers. The lounge opens onto a traditional courtyard, and amenities include 24-hour room service, baby-sitting, and laundry.

Hotel Savoia & Jolanda. Riva degli Schiavoni, Castello 4187, 30122 Venezia. ☎ **041-520-6644.** Fax 041-520-7494. www.elmoro.com/savoia&jolanda. E-mail: savoia.ve.sa@iol.it. 75 units. MINIBAR TV TEL. 390,000–450,000L ($195–$225) double; 550,000–600,000L ($275–$300) suite. Rates include buffet breakfast. AE, DC, MC, V. Vaporetto: San Zaccaria.

The Savoia & Jolanda occupies a prize position on Venice's main street, with a lagoon as its front yard. Although its exterior reflects old Venice, the interior is somewhat spiritless; the staff, however, makes life comfortable. Most of the modern guest rooms have a view of the boats and the Lido; they contain desks and armchairs. An addition holds 20 units with air-conditioning, phones, minibars, and TVs. All the rooms were last renovated in 1998 and 1999, and new mattresses and linens were added. Some units are large enough to contain three or four beds. The bathrooms come with hair dryers. The Principessa restaurant is open daily for lunch and dinner, serving specialties like spaghetti Bragozo with mussels and clams.

MODERATE

Hotel Campiello. Campiello del Vin, Castello 4647, 30122 Venezia. ☎ **041-520-5764.** Fax 041-520-5798. www.hcampiello.it. E-mail: campiello@hcampiello.it. 16 units. A/C TV TEL. 240,000–300,000L ($120–$150) double. Rates include breakfast. AE, DC, MC, V. Closed Jan. Vaporetto: San Zaccaria.

This pink-fronted Venetian town house dates from the 1400s, but today you'll find cost-conscious Venetian-style accommodations that were last renovated in the mid-1990s. This two-star hotel is better than its rating implies because of a spectacular location nearly adjacent to the more expensive hotels and because of such Renaissance touches as marble mosaic floors and carefully polished hardwoods. Elderly or infirm guests can opt for the only room with a separate entrance, a ground-floor hideaway that fortunately has been flooded by high tides only once during the previous century. The cozy guest rooms range from small to medium, offering firm mattresses. The bathrooms are well kept and contain hair dryers. Breakfast is the only meal served.

✪ **La Residenza.** Campo Bandiera e Moro, Castello 3608, 30122 Venezia. ☎ **041-528-5315.** Fax 041-523-8859. 16 units. A/C MINIBAR TV TEL. 250,000L ($125) double. Rates include breakfast. AE, MC, V. Vaporetto: Arsenale.

La Residenza, in a 14th-century building that looks a lot like a miniature Doge's Palace, is on a residential square where children play soccer and older people feed the pigeons. After gaining access (press the button outside), you'll pass through a stone vestibule lined with ancient Roman columns before ringing another bell at the bottom of a flight of stairs. First an iron gate and then a door will open into an enormous salon filled with antiques, 300-year-old paintings, and some of the most marvelously preserved walls in Venice. The guest rooms are far less opulent, with contemporary pieces and good beds, plus small tidy bathrooms. The choice rooms are usually booked far in advance, especially for Carnevale.

Inexpensive

Albergo Al Piave. Ruga Giuffa, Castello 4838–4840, 30122 Venezia. ☎ **041-528-5174.** Fax 041-523-8512. www.elmoro.com/alpiave. E-mail: hotel.alpiave@iol.it. 15 units. A/C. 200,000–260,000L ($100–$130) double; 340,000–420,000L ($170–$210) suite for 3. Rates include continental breakfast. AE, DC, MC, V. Vaporetto: San Zaccaria.

For Venice, this centrally located hotel is a real bargain, and the Puppin family welcomes you with style. The hotel is rated only one star, but its level of comfort is excellent, and its decor and ambience are inviting. Even some guests who could afford to pay more select the Piave for its cozy warmth. The small guest rooms come with good beds and mattresses and tiny tiled bathrooms. A visit here is relaxed and enjoyable, but very down-to-earth.

Doni Pensione. Calle de Vin, Castello 4656, 30122 Venezia. ☎ **041-522-4267.** Fax 041-522-4267. 13 units, 3 with bathroom. 130,000L ($65) double without bathroom, 170,000L ($85) double with bathroom. Rates include breakfast. No credit cards. Vaporetto: San Zaccaria.

The Doni sits about a 3-minute walk from St. Mark's. Most of its very basic guest rooms overlook either a little canal, where four or five gondolas are usually tied up, or a garden with a tall fig tree. Simplicity and cleanliness prevail, especially in the down-to-earth rooms. The beds, often brass, are a little worn but still comfortable, and the plumbing is antiquated but still working fine.

Near the Ponte di Rialto

Moderate

Hotel Marconi. Riva del Vin, San Polo 729, 30125 Venezia. ☎ **041-522-2068.** Fax 041-522-9700. www.hotelmarconi.it. E-mail: info@hotelmarconi.it. 26 units. A/C MINIBAR TV TEL. 200,000–450,000L ($100–$225) double. Rates include breakfast. AE, DC, MC, V. Vaporetto: Rialto.

The Marconi, less than 50 feet from the Rialto Bridge, was built in 1500 when Venice was at the height of its supremacy. The drawing-room furnishings would be appropriate for visiting archbishops, and the Maschietto family operates everything efficiently. Only four of the lovely old guest rooms open onto the Grand Canal, and these are the most eagerly sought. The rooms vary from small to medium, each with a comfortable bed. The tiled bathrooms are small. Meals are usually taken in a room with Gothic chairs, but in fair weather the sidewalk tables facing the Grand Canal are preferred by many.

Hotel Rialto. Riva del Ferro, San Marco 5149, 30124 Venezia. ☎ **041-520-9166.** Fax 041-523-8958. www.rialtohotel.com. E-mail: info@rialtohotel.com. 77 units. A/C MINIBAR TV TEL. 280,000–490,000L ($140–$245) double; 500,000–650,000L ($250–$325) junior suite. Rates include buffet breakfast. AE, CB, DC, MC, V. Vaporetto: Rialto.

The Rialto opens right onto the Grand Canal at the foot of the Ponte di Rialto, the famous bridge flanked with shops. Its guest rooms combine modern or Venetian furniture with ornate Venetian ceilings and wall decorations. The hotel has been considerably upgraded to second class, and private bathrooms have been installed. The most desirable and expensive doubles overlook the canal. The tiled bathrooms are well cared for. The dining room and its adjacent bar are open daily April to October. Additional amenities include concierge, room service, newspaper delivery on request.

✪ **Locanda Sturion.** Calle del Sturion, San Polo 679, 30125 Venezia. ☎ **041-523-6243.** Fax 041-522-8378. www.locandasturion.com. E-mail: info@locandasturion.com. 11 units. A/C MINIBAR TV TEL. 230,000–340,000L ($115–$170) double; 350,000–500,000L ($175–$250) triple. Rates include continental breakfast. AE, MC, V. Vaporetto: Rialto.

In the early 1200s, the Venetian doges commissioned this site where foreign merchants could stay for the night. After long stints as a private residence, the Sturion continues to cater to visitors. A private entrance leads up four steep flights of marble steps, past apartments, to a labyrinth of cozy, clean, but not overly large guest rooms. Most have views over the terra-cotta rooftops of this congested neighborhood; two open onto Grand Canal views. The tiled bathrooms have hair dryers. The intimate breakfast room is a honey—almost like a parlor, with red brocaded walls, a Venetian chandelier, and a trio of big windows overlooking the canal.

IN CANNAREGIO

EXPENSIVE TO MODERATE

Hotel Giorgione. Campo SS. Apostoli, Cannaregio 4587, 30131 Venezia. ☎ **041-522-5810.** Fax 041-523-9092. www.hotelgiorgione.com. E-mail: giorgione@hotelgiorgione.com. 68 units. A/C MINIBAR TV TEL. 310,000–550,000L ($155–$275) double; 350,000–580,000L ($175–$290) suite. Rates include buffet breakfast. AE, DC, MC, V. Vaporetto: Ca' d'Oro.

Here's a modern hotel with traditional Venetian decor. The lounges and public rooms boast fine furnishings and decorative accessories, and the comfortable and stylish guest rooms are designed to coddle guests. Each accommodation comes with an excellent bed. The tiled bathrooms are well equipped, with hair dryers. The hotel also has a typical Venetian garden. It's rated second class by the government, but the Giorgione maintains higher standards than many first-class places. Breakfast is the only meal served, but many trattorie lie nearby. Additional amenities include concierge, room service, laundry.

Locanda ai Santi Apostoli. Strada Nuova, Cannaregio 4391, 30131 Venezia. ☎ **041-521-2612.** Fax 041-521-2611. 11 units. A/C MINIBAR TV TEL. 330,000–450,000L ($165–$225) double, 520,000L ($260) double with Grand Canal view; 720,000L ($360) suite. Rates include breakfast. AE, DC, MC, V. Vaporetto: Ca d'Oro.

If your dot-com stock didn't hit it big and you can't afford the Gritti, but you still fantasize about living in a palazzo overlooking the Grand Canal, near the Rialto, here's a chance. The inn knows the advantage of its location, however, and doesn't come that cheap, but it's a lot less expensive than the palaces nearby. The hotel is on the top floor of a 15th-century building, and the guest rooms, though simple, are roomy and decorated in pastels, often containing antiques. Naturally, the two rooms opening onto the canal are the most requested. The mattresses are fairly new, and the bathrooms are small but tidy. This is one of three 14th- or 15th-century Venetian palaces still owned by the family that built it. Breakfast is the only meal served.

Hotel Abbazia. Calle Priuli ai Cavaletti, Cannaregio 68, 30121 Venezia. ☎ **041-717-333.** Fax 041-717-949. www.venezialberghi.com. E-mail: abbazia@iol.it. 39 units. A/C MINIBAR TV TEL. 150,000–380,000L ($75–$190) double. Rates include buffet breakfast. AE, DC, MC, V. Vaporetto: Ferrovia.

The benefit of staying here is there's no need to transfer onto any vaporetto—the hotel is accessible entirely by bridge and street from the rail station, a 10-minute walk away. It was built in 1889 as a monastery for barefooted Carmelite monks, who established a verdant garden in what's now the courtyard; it's planted with subtropical plants that seem to thrive almost miraculously thanks to the way they're sheltered from the cold Adriatic winds. There's no restaurant and no bar, though drinks can be carried to your spot in the lobby if you request them. You'll find a highly accommodating staff and comfortable but very plain guest rooms. Twenty-five overlook the courtyard, ensuring quiet in an otherwise noisy neighborhood. The tiled bathrooms are small, each with a hair dryer.

Inexpensive

Hotel Geremia. Campo San Geremia, Cannaregio 290A, 30121 Venezia. ☎ **041-716-245.** Fax 041-524-2342. 20 units, 14 with bathroom. TV TEL. 160,000L ($80) double without bathroom, 240,000L ($120) double with bathroom. Rates include breakfast. Discounts of 20% in winter. AE, MC, V. Vaporetto: Ferrovia.

For years, the small Geremia survived as a one-star hotel that many guests considered worthy of two-star status. In 1997 the government raised it to two stars, justifying an increase in rates. Located in a modernized early 1900s setting, this hotel is a 5-minute walk from the rail station. Inside, you'll find well-maintained pale-green guest rooms (none with water views but all with safes). They're often small, but each comes with a good bed and a small bathroom with a hair dryer. There's no elevator, but no one can deny that the price is appealing.

In Santa Croce

Moderate

Hotel San Cassiano Ca' Favretto. Calle della Rosa, Santa Croce 2232, 30135 Venezia. ☎ **041-524-1768.** Fax 041-721-033. www.sancassiano.it. E-mail: info@sancassiano.it. 35 units. A/C MINIBAR TV TEL. 200,000–450,000L ($100–$225) double. Rates include breakfast. AE, DC, MC, V. Vaporetto: San Stae.

The hotel's gondola pier and dining room porch afford views of the lacy Ca' d'Oro, perhaps Venice's most beautiful building. The hotel is a 14th-century palace (it contained the studio of 19th-century painter Giacomo Favretto), and the owner has worked closely to preserve the original details, like a 20-foot beamed ceiling in the entrance. Fifteen of the conservatively decorated guest rooms overlook one of two canals, and many are filled with antiques or high-quality reproductions. Generally the housekeeping is excellent, and the beds have good mattresses. The bathrooms are small but exceedingly well maintained. The hotel has added an American bar with a terrace overlooking the canal.

In San Polo

Moderate

Hotel Carpaccio. San Tomà, San Polo 2765, 30125 Venezia. ☎ **041-523-5946.** Fax 041-524-2134. 17 units. MINIBAR TV TEL. 320,000–360,000L ($160–$180) double. Rates include breakfast. MC, V. Closed mid-Nov to Feb. Vaporetto: San Tomà.

Don't be put off by the winding alleys leading to the wrought-iron entrance of this hotel—this building was meant to be approached by gondola. Once inside, you'll realize that your location in the heart of the oldest part of the city justifies the confusing arrival. This used to be the Palazzo Barbarigo della Terrazza, and part of it is still reserved for private apartments. The guest rooms, small to medium, are filled with serviceable furniture and comfortable mattresses. Most of the bathrooms were added to rooms not really designed to have bathrooms and so tend to be cramped. The salon is decorated with gracious pieces, marble floors, and an arched window overlooking the Grand Canal. Breakfast is the only meal served.

In Dorsoduro

Expensive

American Hotel. Campo San Vio, Accademia 628, 30123 Venezia. ☎ **041-520-4733.** Fax 041-520-4048. www.hotelamerican.com. E-mail: hotameri@tin.it. 29 units. A/C MINIBAR TV TEL. 400,000–440,000L ($200–$220) double. Rates include buffet breakfast. AE, MC, V. Vaporetto: Accademia.

On a small waterway, the American (there's nothing American about it) lies in an ocher building across the Grand Canal from the most heavily touristed areas. The modest lobby is filled with murals, warm colors, and antiques. The guest rooms are comfortably furnished in a Venetian style, but they vary in size; some of the smaller ones are a bit cramped. Many rooms with their own private terrace face the canal. The small blue-tiled bathrooms come with hair dryers. On the second floor is a beautiful terrace where guests can relax over drinks. The staff is attentive and helpful.

MODERATE

Hotel La Calcina. Zattere al Gesuati, Dorsoduro 780, 30123 Venezia. ☎ **041-520-6466.** Fax 041-522-7045. E-mail: la.calcina@libero.it. 29 units. A/C TEL. 180,000–280,000L ($90–$140) double. Rates include buffet breakfast. AE, DC, MC, V. Vaporetto: Zattere.

Recently renovated (and not a moment too soon), La Calcina lies in a secluded and less-trampled district that used to be the English enclave before the area developed a broader base of tourism. John Ruskin, who wrote *The Stones of Venice,* stayed here in 1877, and he charted the ground for his latter-day compatriots. This pensione is absolutely spotless, and the furnishings are well chosen but hardly elaborate. The guest rooms are cozy and comfortable, each with a decent mattress on a comfortable bed. The tiled bathrooms have hair dryers.

✪ **Pensione Accademia.** Fondamenta Bollani, Dorsoduro 1058, 30123 Venezia. ☎ **041-523-7846.** Fax 041-523-9152. E-mail: pensione.accademia@flashnet.it. 27 units. A/C TV TEL. 270,000–400,000L ($135–$200) double. Rates include breakfast. AE, DC, MC, V. Vaporetto: Accademia.

The Accademia is the most patrician of the pensioni, in a villa whose garden extends into an angle created by the junction of two canals. The interior features Gothic-style paneling, Venetian chandeliers, and Victorian-era furniture, and the upstairs sitting room is flanked by two large windows. This place has long been a favorite of the *Room with a View* crowd of Brits and scholars; it's often booked months in advance. The guest rooms are airy and bright, decorated in part with 19th-century furniture. The bathrooms are medium-sized; only some have hair dryers.

INEXPENSIVE

Hotel Galleria. Dorsoduro 878A (at the foot of the Accademia Bridge), 30123 Venezia. ☎ **041-52-32-489.** Fax 041-520-41-72. www.hotelgalleria.it. E-mail: galleria@tin.it. 10 units, 8 with bathroom. 155,000–165,000L ($77.50–$82.50) double without bathroom, 190,000–230,000L ($95–$115) double with bathroom. Rates include continental breakfast. AE, DC, MC, V. Vaporetto: Accademia.

If you've dreamed of opening your windows to find the Grand Canal before you, step through this 17th-century palazzo's leaded-glass doors. But reserve way in advance—these are the cheapest rooms on the canal and the most charming, thanks to new owners Luciano Benedetti and Stefano Franceschini. Six guest rooms varying in size overlook the canal, and the others have partial views that include the Accademia Bridge over an open-air bar/cafe, a location that can be annoying to anyone hoping to sleep before the bar closes. The bathrooms are small but were redone in 1998.

The owners also run the **Locanda Leone Bianco,** in a converted 13th-century palazzo on the Rio degli Apostoli, Cannaregio 5629, across the Grand Canal from the Rialto Market (☎ and fax **041-523-35-72;** www.leonbianco.it). The Leone Bianco has 10 spacious rooms, all with private bathroom, and 3 overlooking the Grand Canal northeast of the Rialto Bridge (200,000 to 250,000L/$100 to $125 double).

✪ **Locanda Montin.** Fondamenta di Borgo, Dorsoduro 1147, 31000 Venezia. ☎ **041-522-7151.** Fax 041-520-0255. 10 units, 5 with bathroom. TEL. 155,000L ($77.50) double without bathroom, 200,000L ($100) double with bathroom. AE, DC, MC, V. Vaporetto: Accademia.

The Montin is an old-fashioned Venetian inn whose adjoining restaurant is one of the area's most loved. It's listed as a fourth-class hotel, but the guest rooms are considerably larger and better than that rating would suggest. They're cozy and quaint, with mattresses that have seen wear but still have comfort left. Only a few units have private bathrooms, and these are very cramped. Most guests have to share the small corridor bathrooms, which are barely adequate in number, especially if the house is full. The inn is a bit difficult to locate (it's marked by only a small carriage lamp etched with the name) but is worth the search.

ON ISOLA DELLA GIUDECCA

VERY EXPENSIVE

✪ **Hotel Cipriani.** Isola della Giudecca 10, 30133 Venezia. ☎ **800/992-5055** in the U.S., or 041-520-7744. Fax 041-520-7745. www.orient-expresshotels.com. E-mail: info@hotelcipriani.it. 110 units. A/C MINIBAR TV TEL. 1,450,000–2,500,000L ($725–$1,250) double; from 2,850,000L ($1,425) suite. Rates include breakfast. AE, DC, MC, V. Closed Nov–Mar. Vaporetto: Zitelle.

With its isolated location, impeccable service, and exorbitant prices, the Cipriani is in a class by itself. Set in a 16th-century cloister on Giudecca, this pleasure palace was opened in 1958 by the late Giuseppe Cipriani, the founder of Harry's Bar and the one real-life character in Hemingway's Venetian novel. The guest rooms range in design from tasteful contemporary to grand antique, but all have splendid views and are sumptuous. Each has a private safe. We prefer the corner rooms, the most spacious and most elaborately decorated. The bathrooms are large, with phones, plush towels, hair dryers, robes, and deluxe toiletries. The Cipriani, incidentally, is the only hotel on Giudecca, which otherwise is calm and quiet. Service is the best in Venice, with two employees for every room.

Dining: Lunch is served in the bar, Il Gabbiano, either indoors or on terraces overlooking the water. More formal meals are served at night in the restaurant.

Amenities: A private launch service ferries guests, at any hour, to/from the hotel's own pier near Piazza San Marco. Room service, baby-sitting, laundry/valet; Olympic-size pool with filtered saltwater, tennis courts, sauna, fitness center.

ON THE LIDO

VERY EXPENSIVE

✪ **Excelsior Palace.** Lungomare Marconi 41, 30126 Venezia Lido. ☎ **800/325-3535** in the U.S. and Canada, or 041-526-0201. Fax 041-526-7276. www.starwood.com. E-mail: res_excelsior@sheraton.com. 197 units. A/C MINIBAR TV TEL. 837,000–1,073,000L ($418.50–$536.50) double; from 2,300,000L ($1,150) suite. Rates include breakfast. AE, DC, MC, V. Parking 35,000L ($17.50). Closed Nov–Mar 15. Vaporetto: Lido, then bus A, B, or C.

When the Excelsior was built, it was the world's biggest resort hotel and its presence helped make the Lido fashionable. Today it offers the most luxury on the Lido, though it doesn't have the antique character of the Hotel des Bains (see below). Its guest rooms range in style and amenities from cozy singles to grand suites, all with walk-in closets and private safes. The good-sized bathrooms are as you'd expect, boasting deluxe toiletries, hair dryers, and robes. Most of the social life takes place around the angular pool or on the flowered terraces leading up to the cabanas on the sandy beach.

Dining/Diversions: The hotel features one of the most elegant dining rooms of the Adriatic, the Tropicana. The Blue Bar has piano music and views of the beach.

Amenities: 24-hour room service, baby-sitting, laundry/valet, six tennis courts, pool, private pier with boat rental. A private launch makes hourly runs to the Gritti and the Danieli on the Grand Canal.

✪ **Hotel des Bains.** Lungomare Marconi 17, 30126 Lido di Venezia. ☎ **800/325-3535** in the U.S. and Canada, or 041-526-5921. Fax 041-526-0113. www.starwood.com. E-mail: res_desbains@sheraton.com. 191 units. A/C MINIBAR TV TEL. 695,000–975,000L ($347.50–$487.50) double; from 1,450,000L ($725) suite. Rates include breakfast. AE, DC, MC, V. Closed Nov–Mar. Vaporetto: Lido, then bus A, B, or C.

This hotel was built in the grand era of European resort hotels, but its supremacy on the Lido was long ago lost to the Excelsior (above). It has its own wooded park and beach with individual cabanas. Thomas Mann stayed here several times before making it the setting for his *Death in Venice,* and later it was used as a set for the film. The renovated interior exudes the flavor of the leisurely life of the belle epoque. The guest rooms are fairly large, each elegantly furnished with rich fabrics, Oriental rugs, antiques, paneled walls, and beds with deluxe mattresses. The bathrooms have dual basins, hair dryers, and robes.

Dining: Guests can dine in a large veranda room cooled by Adriatic sea breezes. The food is first-rate and the service superior.

Amenities: Room service, baby-sitting, laundry/valet, two tennis courts, outdoor heated pool, beauty salon. A motorboat shuttles back and forth between Venice and the Lido. Many resort-type services are available at the Golf Club Alberoni (tennis courts, large pool, private pier).

EXPENSIVE

✪ **Hotel Quattro Fontane.** Via Quattro Fontane 16, 30126 Lido di Venezia. ☎ **041-526-0227.** Fax 041-526-0726. www.quattrofontane.com. E-mail: quafonve@tin.it. 58 units. A/C MINIBAR TV TEL. 450,000–550,000L ($225–$275) double. Rates include buffet breakfast. AE, DC, MC, V. Closed Nov–Apr 4. Vaporetto: Lido, then bus A, B, or C.

In its price bracket, the Quattro Fontane is one of the most charming hotels on the Lido. The trouble is, a lot of people know that, so it's likely to be booked. This former summer home of a 19th-century Venetian family is most popular with the British, who seem to appreciate the homey atmosphere, the garden, the helpful staff, and the rooms with superior amenities, not to mention the good food served at tables set under shade trees. Many of the guest rooms are furnished with antiques, and all have tile or terrazzo floors and excellent beds. The refurbished tiled bathrooms come with hair dryers.

Dining: The dining room is open April to October. There's a bar adjacent to the restaurant.

You Oughta Be in Pictures

The ✪ **Venice International Film Festival** is second only to Cannes for sheer glamour. It brings together stars, directors, producers, and filmmakers from all over the world during the first week or so of September. Films are shown more or less constantly between 9am and 3am in various areas of the Palazzo del Cinema on the Lido. Although a good number of the seats are reserved for international jury members, the public can attend virtually whenever they want, pending available seats. Better still, there's great people-watching all over the city. For information, contact the **Venice Film Festival,** c/o the La Biennale office, Ca' Giustinian, Calle del Ridotto 1364A, 30124 Venezia. Call ☎ **041-521-8838** for details on getting tickets, or check out www.labiennale.com.

Amenities: Concierge, room service, laundry/dry cleaning, newspaper delivery on request, twice-daily maid service. The hotel maintains changing booths and about a dozen private cabanas on the beach, a short walk away. There's also a tennis court.

MODERATE

Hotel Belvedere. Piazzale Santa Maria Elisabetta 4, 30126 Lido di Venezia. ☎ **041-526-0115.** Fax 041-526-1486. E-mail: hbelve@tin.it. 30 units. A/C TV TEL. 240,000–340,000L ($120–$170) double. Rates include breakfast. AE, DC, MC, V. Vaporetto: Lido.

The modernized Belvedere has been run by the same family since 1857, and its restaurant is justifiably popular (see "Dining," later in this chapter). Right across from the vaporetto stop, the hotel is open all year, which is unusual for the Lido, and offers simply furnished guest rooms ranging from small to medium, each with a good bed and small tiled bathroom. There's parking in its garden. As an added courtesy, the Belvedere offers guests free entrance to the Casino Municipale and, in summer, guests can use the hotel's cabanas on the Lido.

Hotel Helvetia. Gran Viale 4, 30126 Lido di Venezia. ☎ **041-526-0105.** Fax 041-526-8903. www.hotelhelvetia.com. E-mail: hotelhelvetia@hotelhelvetia.com. 57 units. TV TEL. 200,000–360,000L ($100–$180) double. Rates include breakfast. AE, DC, MC, V. Closed Nov–Mar. Vaporetto: Lido.

The Helvetia is a russet-colored 19th-century building with stone detailing on a side street near the lagoon side of the island, an easy walk from the vaporetto stop. The quieter guest rooms face away from the street, and rooms in the older wing have belle epoque high ceilings and attractively comfortable furniture. The newer wing is more streamlined and has a more conservative style. Twenty-six of the accommodations have recently been rejuvenated. Breakfast is served, weather permitting, in a flagstone-covered wall garden behind the hotel. Baby-sitting, laundry, and 24-hour room service are available.

4 Dining

Even though Venice doesn't grow much of its own produce, it's surrounded by a rich agricultural district and plentiful vineyards, and specializes in fresh seafood. Venice's restaurants are among the most expensive in Italy, but we've found some wonderful moderately priced trattorie.

NEAR PIAZZA SAN MARCO

VERY EXPENSIVE

Do Forni. Calle dei Specchieri, San Marco 468. ☎ **041-523-2148.** Reservations recommended. Main courses 90,000–120,000L ($45–$60). AE, DC, MC, V. Daily noon–3pm and 7pm–midnight. Vaporetto: San Marco. VENETIAN.

Centuries ago, this was where bread was baked for monasteries, but today it's the busiest restaurant in Venice, even when the rest of the city slumbers under a wintertime Adriatic fog. It's divided into two sections, separated by a narrow alley. The locals prefer the front part, which is decorated in Orient Express style. The larger section in back is like a country tavern, with ceiling beams and original paintings (don't expect country tavern prices, though—the seafood can really make your bill skyrocket). The English menu (with at least 80 dishes, prepared by 14 cooks) is entitled "food for the gods" and lists specialties like spider crab in its own shell, risotto primavera, linguine with rabbit, and sea bass in parchment.

✪ **Harry's Bar.** Calle Vallaresso, San Marco 1323. ☎ **041-528-5777.** Reservations required. Main courses 80,000–95,000L ($40–$47.50). AE, DC, MC, V. Apr–Oct, daily 10:30am–1am; Nov–Mar, daily 10:30am–11pm. Vaporetto: San Marco. VENETIAN.

Harry's Bar serves the best food in Venice, though your tab will be painful. Harry, by the way, is an Italian named Arrigo, son of the late Commendatore Cipriani. Like his father, Arrigo is an entrepreneur extraordinaire known for his fine cuisine. His bar is a big draw for martini-thirsty Americans, but Hemingway and Hotchner always ordered Bloody Marys in their day. The most famous drink, which was originally concocted here, is the Bellini (prosecco and white-peach juice), wonderful when created properly, though we've had a watered-down horror here in the off-season (a real disappointment at 18,000L/$11). You can have your choice of dining in the bar downstairs or the room with a view upstairs. We recommend the Venetian fish soup, followed by the scampi Thermidor with rice pilaf or the seafood ravioli. The food is relatively simple but absolutely fresh.

EXPENSIVE

✪ **Antico Martini.** Campo San Fantin, San Marco 1983. ☎ **041-522-4121.** Reservations required. Main courses 36,000–59,000L ($18–$29.50); fixed-price menus 78,000–98,000L ($39–$49) 4-course, 78,000–132,000L ($39–$66) 6-course. AE, DC, MC, V. Wed 7–11:30pm; Thurs–Mon noon–2:30pm and 7–11:30pm. Vaporetto: San Marco or Santa Maria del Giglio. VENETIAN/INTERNATIONAL.

Antico Martini elevates Venetian cuisine to its highest level (though we still give Harry's a slight edge over it). Elaborate chandeliers glitter and gilt-framed oil paintings adorn the paneled walls. The courtyard is splendid in summer. An excellent beginning is the *risotto di frutti di mare* (fruits of the sea) in a creamy Venetian style with plenty of fresh seafood. For a main dish, try the *fegato alla veneziana,* tender liver fried with onions and served with polenta, a yellow cornmeal mush. The chefs are better at regional dishes than at international ones. The restaurant has one of the city's best wine lists, featuring more than 350 choices. The yellow Tocai is an interesting local wine and especially good with fish dishes.

La Caravella. In the Hotel Saturnia International, Calle Larga XXII Marzo, San Marco 2397. ☎ **041-520-8901.** Reservations required. Main courses 44,000–80,000L ($22–$40); fixed-price lunch 95,000L ($47.50). AE, DC, MC, V. Daily noon–3pm and 7pm–midnight. Vaporetto: San Marco. VENETIAN/INTERNATIONAL.

La Caravella has an overblown nautical atmosphere and a leather-bound menu that may make you think you're in a tourist trap. But you're not. The restaurant contains four dining rooms and a courtyard that's open in summer. The decor is rustically elegant, with frescoed ceilings, flowers, and wrought-iron lighting fixtures. You might begin with an antipasti *misto de pesce* (fish) with olive oil and lemon juice or prawns with avocado. Star specialties are *granceola* (Adriatic sea crab on carpaccio) and chateaubriand for two. The best item to order, however, is one of the poached fish, such as bass, priced according to weight and served with a tempting sauce. The ice cream in champagne is a soothing finish.

Quadri. Piazza San Marco, San Marco 120–124. ☎ **041-528-9299.** Reservations required. Main courses 45,000–79,000L ($22.50–$39.50). AE, DC, MC, V. Tues–Sun noon–2:30pm and 7–10:30pm; July–Aug, Tues–Sun 7–10:30pm. Vaporetto: San Marco. INTERNATIONAL.

One of Europe's most famous restaurants, the Quadri is even better known as a cafe (see "Venice After Dark"); its elegant premises open onto Piazza San Marco, where a full orchestra often adds to the magic. Many diners come just for the view and are

Venice Dining

Ai Tre Spiedi **33**
Al Covo **36**
Al Graspo de Uva **30**
Al Mascaron **25**
Antico Martini **13**
Da Ivo **17**
Do Forni **22**
Do Leoni **35**
Fiaschetteria Toscana **4**
Gelateria Paolin **8**
Harry's Bar **19**
Il Milion **31**
La Caravella **15**
La Furatola **6**
Le Chat Qui Rit **23**
Linea d'Ombra **7**
Locanda Montin **7**
Nuova Rivetta **24**
Osteria alle Botteghe **9**
Osteria da Fiore **2**
Pasticceria Marchini **11**
Poste Vechie **3**
Quadri **21**
Restaurant da Bruno **26**
Ristorante al Mondo Novo **34**
Ristorante à la Vecia Cavana **37**
Ristorante Corte Sconta **27**
Ristorante da Raffaele **14**
Ristorante Noemi **20**
Rosticceria San Bartolomeo **29**
Sempione **28**
Taverna la Fenice **12**
Tiziano Bar **32**
Trattoria alla Madonna **5**
Trattoria Antica Besseta **1**
Trattoria da Fiore **10**
Trattoria La Colomba **18**
Vini da Arturo **16**

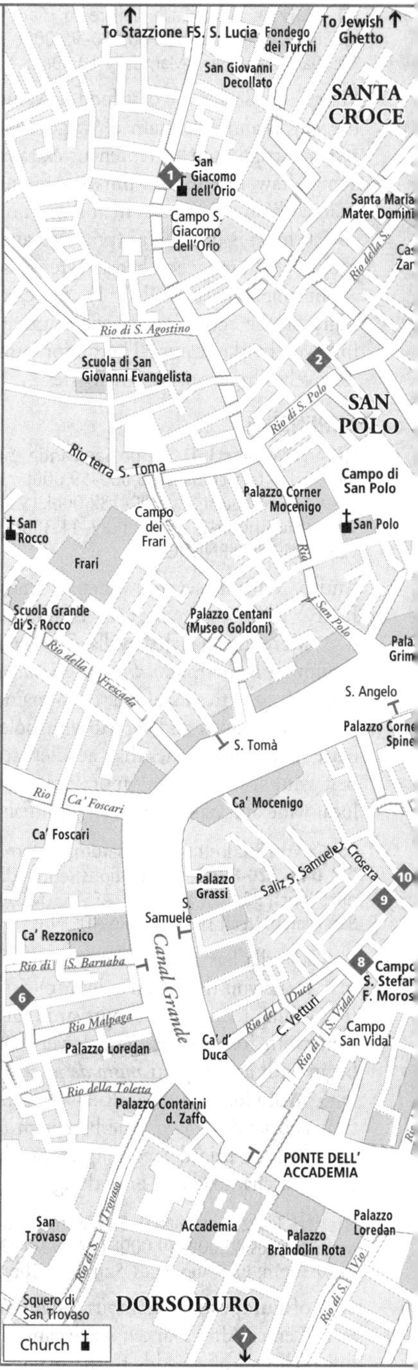

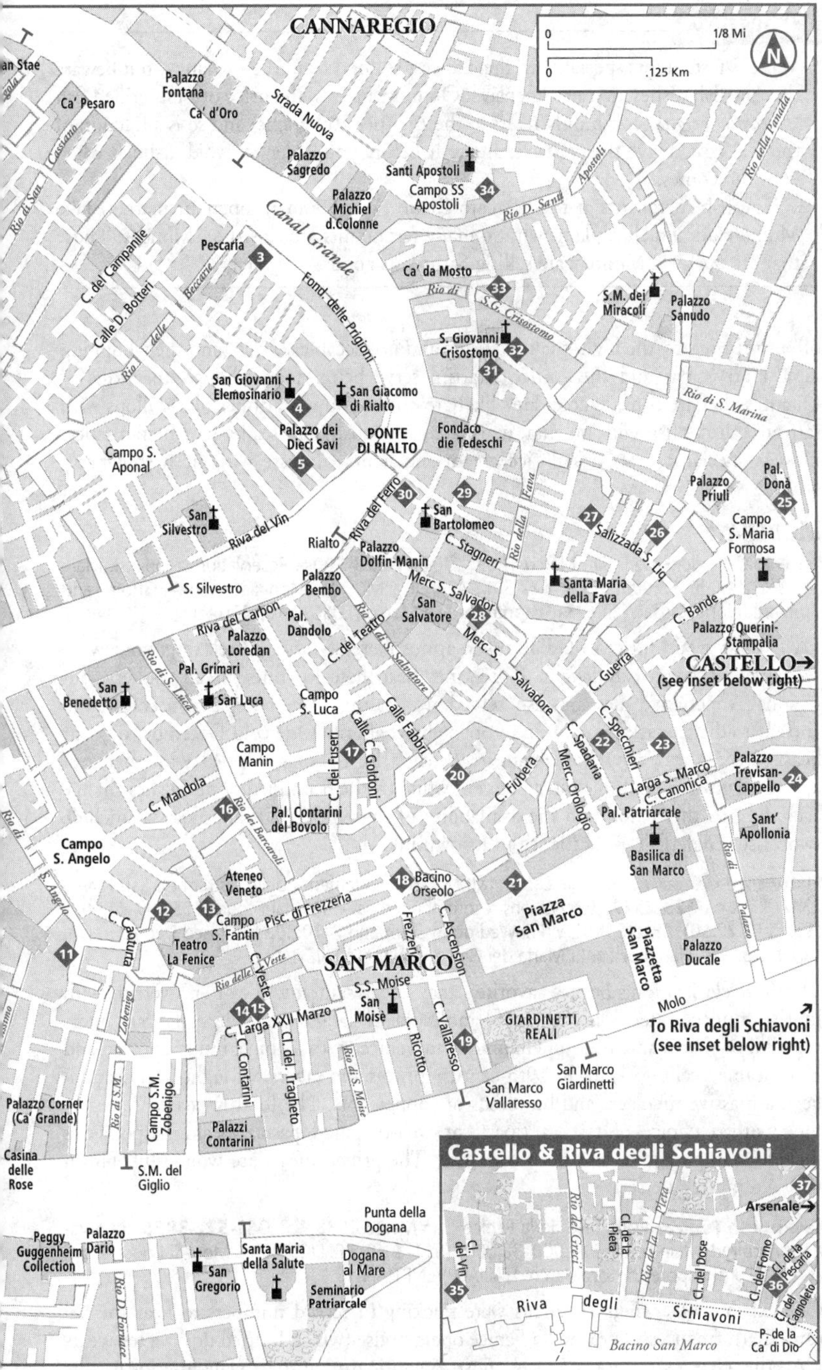
CANNAREGIO
0
1/8 Mi
0
.125 Km
N
San Stae
Palazzo Fontana
Ca' Pesaro
Ca' d'Oro
Strada Nuova
Rio di San Cassiano
Palazzo Sagredo
Santi Apostoli
Campo SS Apostoli
Apostoli
Rio della Panada
Rio D. Santi
Palazzo Michiel d.Colonne
Canal Grande
Pescaria
C. del Campanile
Calle D. Botteri
Rio delle Beccarie
Fond. delle Prigioni
Ca' da Mosto
Rio di S.G. Crisostomo
S.M. dei Miracoli
Palazzo Sanudo
S. Giovanni Crisostomo
San Giovanni Elemosinario
San Giacomo di Rialto
Rio di S. Marina
Palazzo dei Dieci Savi
PONTE DI RIALTO
Fondaco die Tedeschi
Campo S. Aponal
Riva del Ferro
San Bartolomeo
Palazzo Priuli
Pal. Donà
San Silvestro
Riva del Vin
Rialto
Palazzo Dolfin-Manin
C. Stagneri
Rio della Fava
Salizzada S. Liq
Campo S. Maria Formosa
S. Silvestro
Palazzo Bembo
Merc S. Salvador
Santa Maria della Fava
San Salvatore
Riva del Carbon
Pal. Dandolo
Rio di S. Salvatore
C. Bande
Palazzo Querini-Stampalia
Palazzo Loredan
C. del Teatro
Merc. S. Salvadore
CASTELLO→
(see inset below right)
Rio di S. Luca
Pal. Grimari
C. Guerra
San Benedetto
San Luca
Campo S. Luca
Calle Fabbri
C. Specchieri
Campo Manin
C. dei Fuseri
Calle C. Goldoni
C. Spadaria
Palazzo Trevisan-Cappello
C. Fiubera
Merc. Orologio
C. Larga S. Marco
C. Canonica
C. Mandola
Rio dei Barcaroli
Pal. Contarini del Bovolo
Pal. Patriarcale
Sant' Apollonia
Rio di S. Angelo
Campo S. Angelo
Basilica di San Marco
Ateneo Veneto
Bacino Orseolo
Rio di Palazzo
Piazza San Marco
Campo S. Fantin
Pisc. di Frezzeria
C. Caotorta
Frezzeria
C. Ascensione
Piazzetta San Marco
Teatro La Fenice
Palazzo Ducale
SAN MARCO
Rio delle Veste
C. Veste
S.S. Moise
San Moisè
Rio Zobenigo
Molo
C. Larga XXII Marzo
C. Ricotto
C. Vallaresso
GIARDINETTI REALI
↗ To Riva degli Schiavoni
(see inset below right)
C. Contarini
Cl. del Tragheto
Rio di S. Moise
Rio di S.M.
Campo S.M. Zobenigo
San Marco Giardinetti
San Marco Vallaresso
Palazzo Corner (Ca' Grande)
Palazzi Contarini
Casina delle Rose
S.M. del Giglio
Punta della Dogana
Peggy Guggenheim Collection
Palazzo Dario
Santa Maria della Salute
San Gregorio
Dogana al Mare
Seminario Patriarcale
Rio D. Fornace
Castello & Riva degli Schiavoni
Cl. del Vin
Rio del Greci
Cl. de la Pietà
Rio de la Pietà
Cl. del Dose
Cl. del Forno
Cl. de la Pescaria
Cl. del Cagnoleto
Arsenale→
Riva degli Schiavoni
P. de la Ca' di Dio
Bacino San Marco
3
4
5
11
12
13
14
15
16
17
18
19
20
21
22
23
24
25
26
27
28
29
30
31
32
33
34
35
36
37

Fish Tips

Venice's restaurants specialize in the choicest seafood from the Adriatic—but beware that the fish dishes are *very* expensive. On most menus, the price of fresh grilled fish (*pesce alla griglia*) commonly refers to the *etto* (per 100 grams) and so is a fraction of the real cost. Have the waiter estimate it before you order to avoid a shock when your bill comes.

The fish merchants at the Mercato Rialto (Venice's main open-air market) take Monday off, which explains why so many restaurants are closed on Monday. Those that are open on Monday are selling Saturday's goods—beware!

often surprised by the high-quality cuisine and impeccable service (and the whopping tab). Harry's Bar and the Antico Martini serve better food, though the skills of Quadri's chef are considerable. He's likely to tempt you with dishes like scallops with saffron, salt codfish with polenta, marinated swordfish, and sea bass with crab sauce. Dessert specialties are "baked" ice cream and lemon mousse with fresh strawberry sauce.

MODERATE

Da Ivo. Calle dei Fuseri, San Marco 1809. ☎ **041-528-5004.** Reservations required. Main courses 44,000–55,000L ($22–$27.50). AE, DC, MC, V. Mon–Sat noon–2:30pm and 7pm–midnight. Closed Jan 6–31. Vaporetto: San Marco. TUSCAN/VENETIAN.

Da Ivo has a faithful crowd. The rustic atmosphere is cozy and relaxing, your well-set table bathed in candlelight. Florentines head here for fine Tuscan cookery, but regional Venetian dishes are also served. In season, game, prepared according to ancient traditions, is cooked over an open charcoal grill. One cold December day our hearts were warmed by homemade *tagliatelle* (flat noodles) topped with slivers of *tartufi bianchi,* the unforgettable pungent white truffle from Piedmont. Dishes change according to the season and the availability of ingredients but are likely to include swordfish, anglerfish, or cuttlefish in its own ink.

Ristorante da Raffaele. Calle Larga XXII Marzo (Fondamenta delle Ostreghe), San Marco 2347. ☎ **041-523-2317.** Reservations recommended Sat–Sun. Main courses 25,000–45,000L ($12.50–$22.50). AE, DC, MC, V. Fri–Wed noon–3pm and 7–10:30pm. Closed Dec 10 to Jan. Vaporetto: San Marco or Santa Maria del Giglio. ITALIAN/VENETIAN.

The Raffaele has long been a favorite canal-side restaurant. It's often overrun with tourists, but the veteran kitchen staff handles the onslaught well. The restaurant offers the kind of charm and atmosphere unique to Venice, with its huge inner sanctum and high-beamed ceiling, 17th- to 19th-century pistols and sabers, wrought-iron chandeliers, a massive fireplace, and hundreds of copper pots. The food is excellent, beginning with a choice of tasty antipasti or well-prepared pastas. Seafood specialties include scampi, squid, and deep-fried fish. The grilled meats are wonderful. Finish with a tempting dessert.

Taverna la Fenice. Campiello de la Fenice, San Marco 1938. ☎ **041-522-3856.** Reservations required. Main courses 22,000–38,000L ($11–$19). AE, DC, MC, V. Mon–Sat noon–3pm and 7–11pm. Vaporetto: San Marco. ITALIAN/VENETIAN.

Opened in 1907, when Venetians were flocking in record numbers to hear the bel canto performances in nearby La Fenice opera house (which burned down a few years ago), this taverna is one of Venice's most romantic dining spots. The interior is suitably elegant, but the preferred spot in fine weather is outdoors beneath a canopy. The service is smooth and efficient. The most appetizing beginning is the selection of seafood antipasti. The fish is fresh from the Mediterranean. You might enjoy the *risotto con scampi e arugula, tagliatelle* (flat noodles) with cream sauce and exotic mushrooms, John Dory fillets with butter and lemon, turbot roasted with potatoes and tomato sauce, scampi with tomatoes and rice, or *carpaccio alla Fenice.*

Trattoria La Colomba. Piscina Frezzeria, San Marco 1665. ☎ **041-522-1175.** Reservations recommended. Main courses 35,000–65,000L ($17.50–$32.50). AE, DC, MC, V. Daily noon–3pm and 7–11pm. Closed Wed Nov–Apr. Vaporetto: San Marco or Rialto. VENETIAN/INTERNATIONAL.

This is one of Venice's most distinctive trattorie, its history going back at least a century. Modern paintings adorn the walls; they change periodically and are usually for sale. Menu items are likely to include at least five daily specials based on Venice's time-honored cuisine, as well as *risotto di funghi del Montello* (risotto with mushrooms from the local hills of Montello) and *baccalà alla vicentina* (milk-simmered dry cod seasoned with onions, anchovies, and cinnamon and served with polenta). The fruits and vegetables used are for the most part grown on the lagoon islands.

Vini da Arturo. Calle degli Assassini, San Marco 3656. ☎ **041-528-6974.** Reservations recommended. Main courses 30,000–45,000L ($15–$22.50). No credit cards. Mon–Sat noon–2:30pm and 7–10:30pm. Closed Aug. Vaporetto: San Marco or Rialto. VENETIAN.

Vini da Arturo attracts many devoted regulars to its seven tables, including an artsy crowd. You get delectable local cooking, not just the standard clichés (and not seafood, which may be unique for a Venetian restaurant). Instead of ordering plain pasta, try the tantalizing *spaghetti alla Gorgonzola.* The beef is also good, especially when prepared with a cream sauce flavored with mustard and pepper. The salads are made with fresh ingredients, often in unusual combinations; particularly interesting is the pappardelle radicchio.

INEXPENSIVE

Le Chat Qui Rit. Calle Frezzeria, San Marco 1131. ☎ **041-522-9086.** Main courses 10,000–18,000L ($5–$9); pizzas 9,000–14,000L ($4.50–$7). No credit cards. Nov–Mar, Sun–Fri 11am–9:30pm; Apr–Oct, daily 11am–9:30pm. Vaporetto: San Marco. VENETIAN/PIZZA.

This self-service cafeteria/pizzeria offers food prepared "just like mamma made." It's very popular because of its low prices. Dishes might include cuttlefish simmered in stock and served on a bed of yellow polenta, or various fried fish. You can also order a steak grilled very simply, flavored with oil, salt, and pepper or a little garlic and herbs. Main-dish platters are served rather quickly after you order them.

Osteria alle Botteghe. Calle delle Botteghe, San Marco 3454. ☎ **041-522-8181.** Main courses 12,000–25,000L ($6–$12.50). AE, DC, MC, V. Mon–Sat 11am–4pm and 7–10pm. Vaporetto: Accademia or Sant'Angelo. VENETIAN/ITALIAN.

Once you've located the bigger-than-life Campo Santo Stefano, you'll find this osteria a great choice for a light snack or an elaborate meal. Stand-up hors d'oeuvres *(cichetti)* and fresh sandwiches can be enjoyed at the bar or the window-side counter; more serious diners can choose from pasta dishes or *tavola calda* (a buffet of prepared dishes like eggplant parmigiana, lasagna, and fresh cooked vegetables in season, reheated when you order) and repair to tables in the back. Vegetarians will be happy with the vegetable lasagna. Classic dishes include a tender Venetian liver with polenta.

Ristorante Noemi. Calle dei Fabbri, San Marco 912. ☎ **041-522-5238.** Reservations recommended. Main courses 26,000–45,000L ($13–$22.50). AE, DC, MC, V. Tues–Sun 11:30am–midnight. Closed Dec 15–Jan 15. Vaporetto: San Marco. VENETIAN.

The decor of this simple place includes a multicolored marble floor in abstract patterns and swag curtains covering big glass windows. The foundations date from the 14th

Something Sweet

If you're in the mood for some tasty gelato, head to the **Gelateria Paolin,** Campo Stefano Morosini (☎ **041-522-5576**), which offers 20 flavors. It has stood on the corner of this busy square since the 1930s, making it Venice's oldest ice-cream parlor. You can order your ice cream to go or eat it at one of the sidewalk tables (it costs more if you eat it at a table). April to October, it's open daily 8am to midnight; November to March, hours are daily 8am to 8:30pm.

One of the city's finest pastry shops is the **Pasticceria Marchini,** Ponte San Maurizio, San Marco 2769 (☎ **041-522-9109**), whose cakes, muffins, and pastries are the stuff of childhood memories for many locals. The high-calorie output of the busy kitchens is displayed behind glass cases and sold by the piece for eating at the bar (there are few tables) or by the kilogram for take-out. The pastries include traditional versions of *torte del Doge,* made from almonds and pine nuts; *zaleti,* made from a mix of cornmeal and eggs; and *bigna,* akin to zabaglione, concocted from chocolate and cream. It's open Wednesday to Monday 8:30am to 8:30pm.

century, and the restaurant opened in 1927, named after the matriarch of the family that continues to own it. Specialties, many bordering on *nuova cucina,* include thin black spaghetti with cuttlefish in its own sauce, salmon crepes with cheese, and fillet of sole Casanova, with a velouté of white wine, shrimp, and mushrooms. For dessert, try the special lemon sorbet, made with sparkling wine and fresh mint.

Sempione. Ponte Beretteri, San Marco 578. ☎ **041-522-6022.** Reservations recommended. Main courses 30,000–60,000L ($15–$30). AE, DC, MC, V. Daily 11:30am–3pm and 6:30–10pm. Closed Thurs Nov–Dec. Vaporetto: Rialto. VENETIAN.

The Sempione has done an admirable job of feeding locals and visitors for almost 90 years. Set adjacent to a canal in a 15th-century building near Piazza San Marco, it contains three dining rooms done in a soothingly traditional style, a well-trained staff, and a kitchen focusing on traditional cuisine. Examples are grilled fish, spaghetti with crabmeat, risotto with fish, fish soup, and delectable Venetian calves' liver that hasn't been significantly changed since the restaurant was founded. Try for a table by the window so you can watch the gondolas glide by.

Trattoria da Fiore. Calle delle Botteghe, San Marco 3561. ☎ **041-523-5310.** Reservations suggested. Pasta dishes 9,000–20,000L ($4.50–$10); main courses 20,000–30,000L ($10–$15). AE, DC, V. Wed–Mon noon–3pm and 7–10pm. Vaporetto: Accademia. VENETIAN/ITALIAN.

Don't confuse this trattoria with the well-known and very expensive Osteria da Fiore. You might not eat better here, but it'll seem that way when your bill arrives. Start with the house specialty, *penne alla Fiore* (prepared with olive oil, garlic, and seven in-season vegetables), and you may be happy to call it a night. Or skip right to another popular specialty, *fritto misto,* comprising more than a dozen varieties of fresh fish and seafood. The *zuppa di pesce,* a delicious bouillabaisselike soup, is stocked with mussels, crab, clams, shrimp, and chunks of fresh tuna. This is a great place for an afternoon snack or light lunch at the Bar Fiore next door (10:30am to 10:30pm).

CASTELLO

INEXPENSIVE

Al Mascaron. Calle Lunga Santa Maria Formosa, Castello 5225. ☎ **041-522-5995.** Reservations recommended. Main courses 25,000–32,000L ($12.50–$16). No credit cards. Mon–Sat noon–3pm and 7:30–11pm. Vaporetto: Rialto or San Marco. VENETIAN.

Crowd into one of the three loud, boisterous dining rooms here, where you'll probably be directed to sit next to a stranger at a long trestle table. The waiters will come by and slam down copious portions of fresh-cooked local specialties: deep-fried calamari, spaghetti with lobster, monkfish in a salt crust, pastas, savory risottos, and Venetian-style calves' liver (which locals prefer rather pink), plus the best seafood of the day made into salads. There's also a convivial bar, where locals drop in to spread the gossip of the day, play cards, and order vino and snacks.

Nuova Rivetta. Campo San Filippo, Castello 4625. ☎ **041-528-7302.** Reservations required. Main courses 18,000–32,000L ($9–$16). AE, MC, V. Tues–Sun 10am–10pm. Closed July 23–Aug 20. Vaporetto: San Zaccaria. SEAFOOD.

Nuova Rivetta is an old-fashioned trattoria where you get good food at a good price. The most popular dish is *frittura di pesce,* a mixed fish fry that includes squid or various other "sea creatures" from the day's market. Other specialties are gnocchi stuffed with spider crab, pasticcio of fish (a main course), and spaghetti flavored with squid ink. The most typical wine is sparkling prosecco, whose bouquet is refreshing and fruity with a slightly sharp flavor; for centuries it has been one of the most celebrated wines of the Veneto.

Restaurant da Bruno. Calle del Paradiso, Castello 5731. ☎ **041-522-1480.** Main courses 17,000–25,000L ($8.50–$12.50); fixed-price menu 25,000L ($12.50). AE, DC, MC, V. Daily noon–3pm and 7–11pm. Vaporetto: San Marco or Rialto. VENETIAN.

On a narrow street about halfway between the Rialto Bridge and Piazza San Marco, this "country taverna" grills its meats on an open-hearth fire. You get your antipasti at the counter and watch your prosciutto being prepared—paper-thin slices of spicy ham wrapped around breadsticks (*grissini*). In season, Bruno does some of Venice's finest game dishes; if featured, try its *capriolo* (roebuck) or its *fagiano* (pheasant). A typical Venetian dish prepared well here is *zuppa di pesce* (fish soup). Other specialties are beef fillet with pepper sauce, scampi and calamari, veal scaloppini with wild mushrooms, and squid with polenta.

On or Near Riva degli Schiavoni

Expensive

Do Leoni. In the Londra Palace, Riva degli Schiavoni, Castello 4171. ☎ **041-520-0533.** Reservations required. Main courses 30,000–60,000L ($15–$30); 3-course lunch (without drinks) 45,000L ($22.50). Guests of the Londra Palace receive 20% off (excludes fixed-price menu). AE, DC, MC, V. Restaurant, daily noon–3pm and 7:30–11pm; bar, daily 10am–1am. Vaporetto: San Zaccaria. VENETIAN/INTERNATIONAL.

For years, this restaurant was known by the French version of its name, Les Deux Lions. In the elegant Londra Palace, it offers a panoramic view of a 19th-century equestrian statue ringed with heroic women taming (you guessed it) lions. The restaurant is filled with scarlet and gold, a motif of lions patterned into the carpeting, and reproductions of English furniture. Lunches are brief buffet-style affairs, where diners serve themselves from a large choice of hot and cold Italian and international food. The appealing candlelit dinners are more formal, emphasizing Venetian cuisine. The chef's undeniable skill is reflected in such dishes as chilled fish terrine, baked salmon in champagne sauce, and baby rooster with green-pepper sauce. If the weather permits, you can dine out on the piazza overlooking the lions and their masters.

Moderate

✪ **Al Covo.** Campiello della Pescaria, Castello 3968. ☎ **041-522-3812.** Reservations recommended for dinner. Main courses 40,000L ($20); fixed-price lunch 54,000L ($27). No credit cards. Fri–Tues 12:45–2pm and 7:30–10pm. Vaporetto: Arsenale. VENETIAN/SEAFOOD.

Al Covo has a special charm, due to its atmospheric setting, sophisticated service, and the fine cooking of Cesare Benelli and his Texas-born wife, Diane. What's their preferred dish? They respond, "That's like asking us, 'Which of your children do you prefer?' since we strongly attach ourselves to the development of each dish." Look for a reinvention of a medieval version of fish soup; potato gnocchi flavored with go (local whitefish); seafood ravioli; linguine blended with zucchini and fresh peas; and delicious *fritto misto* with scampi, squid, a bewildering array of fish, and deep-fried vegetables like zucchini flowers. Al Covo prides itself on not having any freezers, guaranteeing that all food is fresh every day. Note that this place is near Piazza San Marco, not near Rialto, as you might think when you see a square on your map with a similar name.

Near the Arsenale

Moderate

Ristorante Corte Sconta. Calle del Pestrin, Castello 3886. ☎ **041-522-7024.** Reservations required. Main courses 25,000–40,000L ($12.50–$20); fixed-price menus 80,000–100,000L ($40–$50). AE, DC, V. Tues–Sat 12:30–2:30pm and 7:30–9:30pm. Closed Jan 7–Feb 7 and July 15–Aug 15. Vaporetto: Arsenale. SEAFOOD.

The Corte Sconta is behind a narrow storefront you'd ignore if you didn't know about this place. This modest restaurant boasts a multicolored marble floor, plain wooden tables, and not much of an attempt at decoration. It has become well known, however, as a gathering place for artists, writers, and filmmakers. As the depiction of the satyr chasing the mermaid above the entrance implies, it's a fish restaurant, serving a variety of grilled creatures (much of the "catch" is largely unknown in North America). The fresh fish is flawlessly fresh; the gamberi, for example, is placed live on the grill. A great start is marinated salmon with arugula and pomegranate seeds in olive oil. If you don't like fish, a tender beef fillet is available. The big bar is popular with locals.

NEAR THE PONTE DI RIALTO

Expensive

Fiaschetteria Toscana. Campo San Giovanni Crisostomo, Cannaregio 5719. ☎ **041-528-5281.** Reservation required. Main courses 18,000–38,000L ($9–$19). AE, DC, MC, V. Wed–Sun 12:30–2:30pm and 7:30–10:30pm; Mon 12:30–2:30pm. Vaporetto: Rialto. VENETIAN.

There may be some rough points in the service at this hip restaurant (the staff is frantic), but lots of local foodies come here to celebrate special occasions or to soak in the see-and-be-seen ambience. The dining rooms are on two levels, the upstairs of which is somewhat more claustrophobic. In the evening, the downstairs is especially appealing with its romantic candlelit ambience. Menu items include *frittura della Serenissima* (mixed platter of fried seafood with vegetables), veal scallops with lemon-marsala sauce and mushrooms, ravioli stuffed with whitefish and herbs, and several kinds of Tuscan-style beefsteak.

Ristorante à la Vecia Cavana. Rio Terà SS. Apostoli, Cannaregio 4624. ☎ **041-528-7106.** Main courses 40,000–60,000L ($20–$30); fixed-price menu 50,000L ($25). AE, DC, MC, V. Tues–Sun noon–3pm and 6:30–10:30pm. Vaporetto: Ca' d'Oro. SEAFOOD.

This restaurant is off the tourist circuit and well worth the trek through the winding streets. A *cavana* is a place where gondolas are parked, a sort of liquid garage, and the site of this restaurant was such a place in the Middle Ages. When you enter, you'll be greeted by brick arches, stone columns, terra-cotta floors, framed modern paintings, and a photo of 19th-century fishermen relaxing after a day's work. The menu specializes in seafood, like a mixed grill from the Adriatic, fried scampi, fresh sole, squid, three types of risotto (each with seafood), and a spicy *zuppa di pesce* (fish soup).

Antipasti di pesce Cavana is an assortment of just about every sea creature. The food is authentic and seems prepared for the Venetian palate—not necessarily for the visitor's.

MODERATE

✪ **"Al Graspo de Uva."** Calle Bombaseri, San Marco 5094. ☎ **041-520-0150.** Reservations required. Main courses 26,000–40,000L ($13–$20). AE, DC, MC, V. Tues–Sun noon–3pm and 8–11pm. Closed Aug 5–20. Vaporetto: Rialto. SEAFOOD/VENETIAN.

"The Bunch of Grapes" is a great place for a special meal. Decorated in old taverna style, it offers several air-conditioned dining rooms. One has a beamed ceiling, hung with garlic and copper bric-a-brac. Among Venice's best fish restaurants, it's hosted biggies like Liz Taylor, Jeanne Moreau, and Giorgio de Chirico. You can help yourself to all the hors d'oeuvres you want (the menu tells you it's "self-service mammoth"). Next try the *gran fritto dell'Adriatico,* a mixed treat of deep-fried fish. The desserts are also good, especially the peach Melba.

Il Milion. Corte Prima al Milion, Cannaregio 5841. ☎ **041-522-9302.** Reservations recommended. Main courses 20,000–32,000L ($10–$16). No credit cards. Thurs–Tues noon–2pm and 6:30–11pm. Closed Aug. Vaporetto: Rialto. VENETIAN.

With a tradition extending back more than 300 years and a location near the rear of San Giovanni Crisostomo, this restaurant is named after the book written by Marco Polo, *Il Milion,* describing his travels. In fact, it occupies a town house once owned by members of the explorer's family. The bar, incidentally, is a favorite with some of the gondoliers. The menu items read like a who's who of well-recognized Venetian platters, each fresh and well prepared. Examples are veal kidneys, calves' liver with fried onions, grilled sardines, spaghetti with clams, risotto with squid ink, and fritto misto of fried fish. The staff is charming and friendly.

Poste Vechie. Pescheria Rialto, San Polo 1608. ☎ **041-721-822.** Reservations recommended. Main courses 21,000–45,000L ($10.50–$22.50). AE, DC, MC, V. Wed–Mon noon–3:30pm and 7–10:30pm. Vaporetto: Rialto. SEAFOOD.

This charming restaurant is near the Rialto fish market and connected to the rest of the city by a small privately owned bridge. It opened in the early 1500s as a post office, and the kitchen used to serve food to fortify the mail carriers. Today it's the oldest restaurant in Venice, with a pair of intimate rooms (both graced with paneling, murals, and 16th-century mantelpieces) and a courtyard. Menu items include super-fresh fish from the nearby markets; a salad of shellfish and exotic mushrooms; tagliolini flavored with squid ink, crabmeat, and fish sauce; and the pièce de résistance, *seppie* (cuttlefish) *à la veneziana* with polenta. If you don't like fish, calves' liver or veal shank with ham and cheese are also well prepared. The desserts come rolling to your table on a trolley and are usually delicious.

Ristorante al Mondo Novo. Salizzada di San Lio, Castello 5409. ☎ **041-520-0698.** Reservation recommended. Main courses 23,000–35,000L ($11.50–$17.50). AE, DC, MC, V. Daily 11:30am–11pm. Vaporetto: Rialto or San Marco. VENETIAN/SEAFOOD.

In a Renaissance building, with a dining room outfitted in a regional style, this restaurant offers professional service and a kindly staff. Plus, it stays open later than many of its nearby competitors. Menu items include a selection of seafood, prepared as *frittura misto dell'Adriatico* or charcoal grilled. Other items are *maccheroni alla verdura* (with fresh vegetables and greens), an antipasti of fresh fish, and beef fillets with pepper sauce and rissole potatoes. Locals who frequent the place always order the fresh fish, since the owner is a wholesaler in the Rialto fish market.

Rosticceria San Bartolomeo. Calle della Bissa, San Marco 5424. ☎ **041-522-3569.** Main courses 20,000–45,000L ($10–$22.50). AE, DC, MC, V. Tues–Sun 9am–9pm (Easter–Nov 14 and for Carnevale open daily). Vaporetto: Rialto. VENETIAN/ITALIAN.

This *rosticceria* is Venice's most popular fast-food place and has long been a blessing for cost-conscious travelers. Downstairs is a *tavola calda* where you can eat standing up, but upstairs is a restaurant with waiter service. Typical dishes are *baccalà alla vicentina* (codfish simmered in herbs and milk), deep-fried mozzarella (which the Italians call *in carrozza*), and *seppie con polenta* (squid in its own ink sauce, served with polenta). Everything is accompanied with typical Veneto wine.

✪ **Trattoria alla Madonna.** Calle della Madonna, San Polo 594. ☎ **041-522-3824.** Reservations recommended but not always accepted. Main courses 20,000–40,000L ($10–$20). AE, MC, V. Thurs–Tues noon–3pm and 7:15–10pm. Closed Dec 24–Jan and Aug 4–17. Vaporetto: Rialto. VENETIAN.

No, this place has nothing to do with *that* Madonna. It opened in 1954 in a 300-year-old building and is one of Venice's most characteristic trattorie, specializing in traditional Venetian recipes and grilled fresh fish. A good beginning might be the *antipasto frutti di mare* (fruits of the sea). Pastas, polentas, risottos, meats (including *fegato alla veneziana,* liver with onions), and many kinds of irreproachably fresh fish are widely available. Many creatures of the sea are displayed in a refrigerated case near the entrance.

Inexpensive

✪ **Ai Tre Spiedi.** Salizzada San Cazian, Cannaregio 5906. ☎ **041-520-8035.** Main courses 16,000–28,000L ($8–$14). MC, V. Tues–Sat noon–2:30pm and 7–9:30pm, Sun 12:30–3:30pm. Vaporetto: Rialto. VENETIAN.

Venetians bring their visiting friends here to make a good impression without breaking the bank and then swear them to secrecy. Rarely will you find such a pleasant setting and such an appetizing meal as you will in this casually elegant trattoria with exposed beam ceilings. There's reasonably priced fresh fish plus selections to keep meat-eaters happy as well. If you order à la carte, ask the English-speaking waiters to estimate the cost of your fish entree, since it'll typically appear priced by the *etto* (100 grams).

Tiziano Bar. Salizzada San Crisostomo, Cannaregio 5747, in front of the Sanctuary. ☎ **041-523-5544.** Main courses 10,000–15,000L ($5–$7.50). No credit cards. Daily 7:30am–10:30pm. Vaporetto: Rialto. SANDWICHES/PASTA/PIZZA.

The Tiziano Bar is a *tavola calda* (hot table). There's no waiter service; you eat standing at a counter or sitting on one of the high stools. The place is known in Venice for selling pizza by the yard. From noon to 3pm, it serves hot pastas such as rigatoni and cannelloni. But throughout the day you can order sandwiches or perhaps a plate of mozzarella.

In Santa Croce

Moderate

Trattoria Antica Besseta. Campo SS. de Ca' Zusto, Santa Croce 1395. ☎ **041-721-687.** Reservations required. Main courses 30,000–35,000L ($15–$17.50). AE, MC, V. Thurs–Mon noon–2:30pm and 7–10:30pm. Vaporetto: Rive di Biasio. VENETIAN.

If you manage to find this place (go with a good map), you'll be rewarded with true Venetian cuisine at its most unpretentious. Head for Campo San Giacomo dell'Orio; then negotiate your way across infrequently visited piazzas and winding alleys. Push through saloon doors into a bar area filled with modern art. The dining room is hung with paintings and illuminated with wagon-wheel chandeliers. Nereo Volpe and his wife, Mariuccia, and one of their sons are the guiding force, the chefs, the buyers, and even the "talking menus." The food depends on what looked good in the market that morning, so the menu could include roast chicken, fried scampi, fritto misto, spaghetti in sardine sauce, various roasts, and a selection from the day's catch. The Volpe family produces two kinds of their own wine, a Pinot Blanc and a Cabernet.

IN SAN POLO

EXPENSIVE

✪ **Osteria da Fiore.** Calle del Scaleter, San Polo 2202. ☎ **041-721-308.** Reservations required. Main courses 36,000–48,000L ($18–$24). AE, DC, MC, V. Tues–Sat 12:30–2:30pm and 8–10:30pm. Closed 3 weeks in Aug and Dec 25–Jan 14. Vaporetto: San Tomà. SEAFOOD.

The breath of the Adriatic seems to blow through this place, though how the wind finds this little restaurant tucked away in a labyrinth is a mystery. An imaginative fare is served, depending on the availability of fresh fish and produce. If you have a love of maritime foods, you'll find everything from scampi (a sweet Adriatic prawn, cooked in as many ways as there are chefs) to granzeola, a type of spider crab. In days gone by, we've sampled fried calamari (cuttlefish), risotto with scampi, tagliata with rosemary, masenette (tiny green crabs you eat shell and all), and canoce (mantis shrimp). For your wine, we suggest prosecco, with a distinctive golden-yellow color and a bouquet that's refreshing and fruity. The proprietors extend a hearty welcome to match their fare.

IN DORSODURO

MODERATE

La Furatola. Calle Lunga San Barnaba, Dorsoduro 2870A. ☎ **041-520-8594.** Reservations required. Main courses 26,000–45,000L ($13–$22.50). AE, DC, MC, V. Fri–Sun 12:30–2:30pm and 7:30–10:30pm; Mon 7:30–10:30pm. Closed Aug and Jan. Vaporetto: Ca' Rezzonico. SEAFOOD.

La Furatola is very much a neighborhood hangout, but it has captured the imagination of local foodies. It occupies a 300-year-old building, along a narrow flagstone-paved street that you'll need a good map and a lot of patience to find. Perhaps you'll have lunch here after a visit to San Rocco, a short distance away. In the simple dining room, the specialty is fish brought to your table in a wicker basket so you can judge its size and freshness by its bright eyes and red gills. A display of seafood antipasti is set out near the entrance. A standout is the baby octopus boiled and eaten with a drop of red-wine vinegar. Eel comes with a medley of mixed fried fish, including baby cuttlefish, prawns, and squid rings.

Linea d'Ombra. Fondamente delle Zattere, Dorsoduro 19. ☎ **041-528-5259.** Reservations not necessary. Main courses 28,000–50,000L ($14–$25). AE, DC, DISC, MC, V. Thurs–Tues noon–3:30pm; Thurs–Sat 8pm–1am. Vaporetto: Salute. VENETIAN.

This popular bar/pub that spills onto a panoramic terrace during fine weather doubles as an informal trattoria featuring traditional recipes. You can order dishes like Venetian-style risotto with octopus and squid ink; Venetian-style calves' liver; a wide selection of fish; piquant grilled scampi; and *bigoli in salsa.* A lot of famous Venetian painters come here, among them Emilio Vedova, Roberto Ferruzzi, and Renato Borsato.

In 1998 a scene from the film *Everyone Says I Love You* with Julia Roberts and Woody Allen was filmed on the terrace, and both the interior and the terrace were included in *I Dreamed of Africa,* starring Kim Basinger.

Locanda Montin. Fondamenta di Borgo, Dorsoduro 1147. ☎ **041-522-7151.** Reservations recommended. Main courses 20,000–36,000L ($10–$18). AE, DC, MC, V. Thurs–Tues 12:30–2:30pm; Thurs–Mon 7:30–9:30pm. Closed 10 days in mid-Aug and 20 days in Jan. Vaporetto: Accademia. INTERNATIONAL/ITALIAN.

The Montin opened after World War II, and has hosted Ezra Pound, Jackson Pollock, Mark Rothko, and the artist friends of the late Peggy Guggenheim. It's owned and run by the Carretins, who have covered the walls with paintings donated by or bought from their many friends and guests. The arbor-covered garden courtyard is filled with regulars, many of whom allow their favorite waiter to select most of the items for their meal. The frequently changing menu includes a variety of salads, grilled meats, and fish caught in the Adriatic. Desserts might include *semifreddo di fragoline,* a tempting chilled liqueur-soaked cake, capped with whipped cream and wild strawberries.

ON ISOLA DELLA GUIDECCA

VERY EXPENSIVE

✪ **Ristorante Cipriani.** In the Hotel Cipriani, Isola della Giudecca 10. ☎ **041-520-7744.** Reservations required. Main courses 30,000–70,000L ($15–$35). AE, DC, MC, V. Daily 12:30–3pm and 8–10:30pm. Closed Nov–Mar. Vaporetto: Zitelle. ITALIAN.

The grandest of the hotel restaurants, the Cipriani offers a sublime but relatively simple cuisine, with the freshest of ingredients used by one of the best-trained staffs along the Adriatic. This isn't the place to bring the kids—in fact, children under 6 aren't allowed (a baby-sitter can be arranged). You can dine in the formal room with Murano chandeliers and Fortuny curtains when the weather is nippy or on the extensive terrace overlooking the lagoon. Freshly made pasta is a specialty, and it's among the finest we've ever sampled. Try the *taglierini verdi* with noodles and ham au gratin. Chef's specialties include mixed fried scampi and squid with tender vegetables and sautéed veal fillets with spring artichokes. Come here in October for the last Bellinis of the white peach season and the first white truffles of the season served in champagne risotto.

EXPENSIVE

Harry's Dolci. Fondamenta San Biago 773, Isola della Giudecca. ☎ **041-520-8337.** Reservations recommended, especially Sat–Sun. Main courses 30,000–50,000L ($15–$25); fixed-price menus 77,000–85,000L ($38.50–$42.50). AE, MC, V. Wed–Mon noon–3pm and 7–10:30pm. Closed Nov–Mar 30. Vaporetto: Santa Eufemia. INTERNATIONAL/ITALIAN.

The people at the famed Harry's Bar (see above) have established their latest enclave far from the maddening crowds of Piazza San Marco on this little-visited island. From the quayside windows of this chic place, you can watch seagoing vessels, from yachts to lagoon barges. White napery and uniformed waiters grace a modern room, where no one minds if you order only coffee and ice cream or perhaps a selection from the large pastry menu (the zabaglione cake is divine). Popular items are carpaccio Cipriani, chicken salad, club sandwiches, gnocchi, and house-style cannelloni. The dishes are deliberately kept simple, but each is well prepared.

ON THE LIDO

MODERATE

Favorita. Via Francesco Duodo 33, Lido di Venezia. ☎ **041-526-1626.** Main courses 23,000–60,000L ($11.50–$30). AE, DC, MC, V. Tues–Sun 12:30–2:30pm and 7:30–10:30pm. Vaporetto: Lido di Venezia. SEAFOOD.

Occupying two rustic dining rooms and a garden, Favorita has thrived here since the 1920s, operated by the Pradel family, now in their third generation of ownership.

Their years of experience contribute to flavorful, impeccably prepared seafood and shellfish, many of them grilled. Try the *trenette* (spaghettilike pasta) with baby squid and eggplant; potato-based gnocchi with crabs from the Venetian lagoon; and grilled versions of virtually every fish in the Adriatic, including eel, sea bass, turbot, and sole.

Ristorante Belvedere. Piazzale Santa Maria Elisabetta 4, Lido di Venezia. ☎ **041-526-0115.** Reservations recommended. Main courses 15,000–35,000L ($7.50–$17.50); fixed-price menu 30,000L ($15). AE, DC, MC, V. Tues–Sun noon–2:30pm and 7–9:30pm. Closed Nov 4 to Easter. Vaporetto: Lido. VENETIAN.

Outside the big hotels, the best food on the Lido is served at the Belvedere, across from the vaporetto stop. It attracts a lot of locals, who come here knowing they can get some of the best fish along the Adriatic. Tables are placed outside, and there's a glass-enclosed portion for windy days. The main dining room is attractive, with cane-backed bentwood chairs and big windows. In back, reached through a separate entrance, is a busy cafe. Main dishes include the chef's special sea bass, grilled dorade (or sole), and fried scampi. You might begin with the special fish antipasti or *spaghetti en papillote* (cooked in parchment).

5 Seeing the Sights

Venice appears to have been created specifically to entertain its legions of callers. Ever since the body of St. Mark was smuggled out of Alexandria and entombed in the basilica, the city has been host to a never-ending stream of visitors, famous, infamous, and otherwise. Venice has perpetually captured the imagination of poets and artists. Wordsworth, Byron, and Shelley addressed poems to the city, and it has been written about or used as a setting by many contemporary writers.

In the pages ahead, we'll explore the city's great art and architecture. But, unlike Florence, Venice would reward its guests with treasures even if they never ducked inside a museum or church. Take some time just to stroll and let yourself get lost in this gorgeous city.

ST. MARK'S SQUARE (PIAZZA SAN MARCO)

✪ **Piazza San Marco** was the heart of Venice in the heyday of its glory as a seafaring republic. If you have only one day for Venice, you need not leave the square, as some of the city's major attractions, like St. Mark's Basilica and the Doge's Palace, are centered here or nearby.

The traffic-free square, frequented by visitors and pigeons and sometimes even by Venetians, is a source of bewilderment and interest. If you rise at dawn, you can almost have the piazza to yourself, and as you watch the sun come up, the sheen of gold mosaics glistens with a mystical beauty. At around 9am, the overstuffed pigeons are fed by the city (if you're caught under the whir, you'll think you're witnessing a remake of Hitchcock's *The Birds*). At midafternoon the tourists reign supreme, and it's not surprising in July to witness a scuffle over a camera angle. At sunset, when the two Moors in the Clock Tower strike the end of another day, lonely sailors begin a usually frustrated search for those hot spots that characterized the Venice of yore. Deeper into the evening, the strollers parade by or stop for an espresso at the Caffè Florian and sip while listening to the orchestra play.

Thanks to Napoléon, the square was unified architecturally. The emperor added the Fabbrica Nuova facing the basilica, thus bridging the Old and New Procuratie on either side. Flanked with medieval-looking palaces, Sansovino's Library, elegant shops, and colonnades, the square is now finished—unlike Piazza della Signoria in Florence.

If Piazza San Marco is Europe's drawing room, then the piazza's satellite, **Piazzetta San Marco,** is Europe's antechamber. Hedged in by the Doge's Palace, Sansovino's Library, and a side of St. Mark's, the tiny square faces the Grand Canal. Two tall granite columns grace the square. One is surmounted by a winged lion, representing St. Mark. The other is topped by a statue of a man taming a dragon, supposedly the dethroned patron saint Theodore. Both columns came from the East in the 12th century.

During Venice's heyday, dozens of victims either lost their heads or were strung up here, many of them first being subjected to torture that would've made the Marquis de Sade flinch. One, for example, had his teeth hammered in, his eyes gouged out, and his hands cut off before being strung up. Venetian justice became notorious throughout Europe. If you stand with your back to the canal, looking toward the south facade of St. Mark's, you'll see the so-called *Virgin and Child of the Poor Baker,* a mosaic honoring Pietro Fasiol (also Faziol), a young man unjustly sentenced to death on a charge of murder.

To the left of the entrance to the Doge's Palace are four porphyry figures, whom, for want of a better description, the Venetians called "Moors." These puce-colored fellows are huddled close together, as if afraid. Considering the decapitations and tortures that have occurred on the piazzetta, it's no wonder.

✪ **St. Mark's Basilica (Basilica di San Marco).** Piazza San Marco. ☎ **041-522-5205.** Basilica free; treasury 4,000L ($2); presbytery 3,000L ($1.50); Marciano Museum 3,000L ($1.50). Basilica and presbytery Apr–Sept, Mon–Sat 9:30am–5:30pm, Sun 2–5:30pm; Oct–Mar, Mon–Sat 10am–4:30pm, Sun 2–4:30pm. Treasury Mon–Sat 9:30am–5pm, Sun 2–5pm. Marciano Museum Apr–Sept, Mon–Sat 10am–5:30pm, Sun 2–4:30pm; Oct–Mar, Mon–Sat 10am–4:45pm, Sun 2–4:30pm. Vaporetto: San Marco.

Dominating Piazza San Marco is the Church of Gold (*Chiesa d'Oro*), one of the world's greatest and most richly embellished churches, its cavernous candlelit interior gilded with mosaics added over some 7 centuries. In fact, it looks as if it had been moved intact from Istanbul. The basilica is a conglomeration of styles, though it's particularly indebted to Byzantium. Like Venice, St. Mark's is adorned with booty from every corner of the city's once far-flung mercantile empire: capitals from Sicily, columns from Alexandria, porphyry from Syria, and sculpture from old Constantinople.

The basilica is capped by a dome that, like a spider plant, sends off shoots, in this case a quartet of smaller-scale bulbed cupolas. Spanning the facade is a loggia, surmounted by replicas of the four famous St. Mark's horses, the *Triumphal Quadriga.* The facade's rich marble slabs and mosaics depict scenes from the lives of Christ and St. Mark. One of the mosaics re-creates the entry of the evangelist's body into Venice—according to legend, St. Mark's body, hidden in a pork barrel, was smuggled out of Alexandria in A.D.. 828 and shipped to Venice. The evangelist dethroned Theodore, the Greek saint who up until then had been the patron of the city that had outgrown him.

In the **atrium** are six cupolas with mosaics illustrating scenes from the Old Testament, including the story of the Tower of Babel. The interior of the basilica, once the private chapel and pantheon of the doges, is a stunning wonderland of marbles,

A St. Mark's Warning

A dress code for men and women prohibiting shorts, bare arms and shoulders, and skirts above the knee is strictly enforced at all times in the basilica. You *will* be turned away. In addition, you must remain silent and cannot take photographs.

Basilica di San Marco

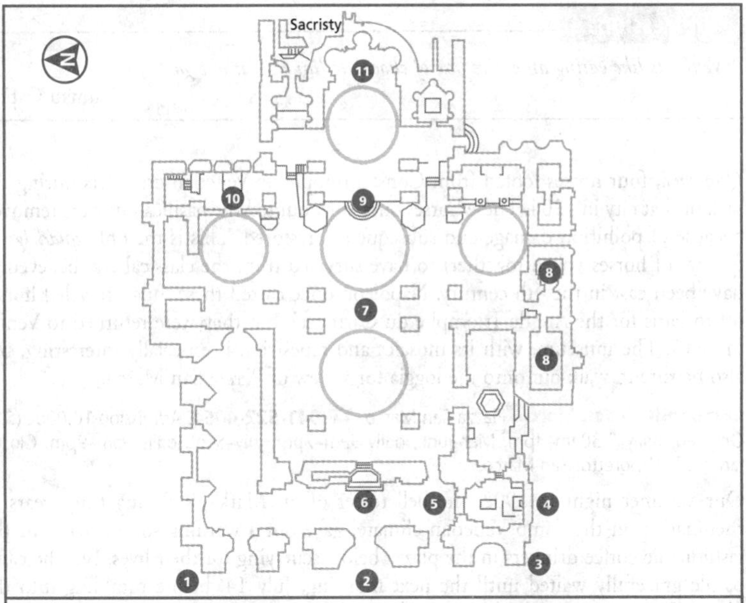

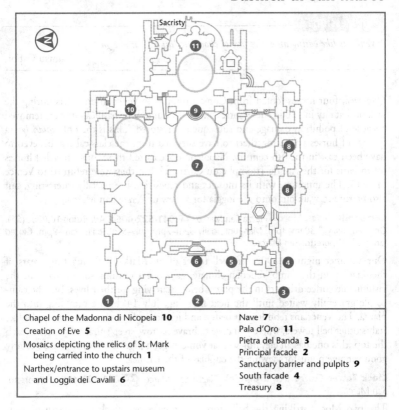

Chapel of the Madonna di Nicopeia **10**
Creation of Eve **5**
Mosaics depicting the relics of St. Mark being carried into the church **1**
Narthex/entrance to upstairs museum and Loggia dei Cavalli **6**
Nave **7**
Pala d'Oro **11**
Pietra del Banda **3**
Principal facade **2**
Sanctuary barrier and pulpits **9**
South facade **4**
Treasury **8**

alabaster, porphyry, and pillars. You'll walk in awe across the undulating multicolored ocean floor, patterned with mosaics.

To the right is the **baptistry,** dominated by the Sansovino-inspired baptismal font, upon which John the Baptist is ready to pour water. If you look back at the aperture over the entry, you can see a mosaic of the dance of Salome in front of Herod and his court. Salome, wearing a star-studded russet-red dress and three white fox tails, is dancing under a platter holding John the Baptist's head. Her glassy face is that of a Madonna, not an enchantress.

After touring the baptistry, proceed up the right nave to the doorway to the oft-looted **treasury** ***(tesoro)***. Here you'll find the inevitable skulls and bones of some ecclesiastical authorities under glass, plus goblets, chalices, and Gothic candelabra. The entrance to the **presbytery** is nearby. In it, on the high altar, the alleged sarcophagus of St. Mark rests under a green marble blanket and is held by four Corinthian alabaster columns. Behind the altar is the rarest treasure at St. Mark's: the Byzantine-style **Pala d'Oro,** a golden altar screen measuring 10 feet by 4 feet. It's set with 300 emeralds, 300 sapphires, 400 garnets, 100 amethysts, and 1,300 pearls, plus rubies and topazes accompanying 157 enameled rondels and panels. Second in importance is the 10th-century ***Madonna di Nicopeia,*** a bejeweled icon taken from Constantinople and exhibited in its own chapel to the left of the high altar.

On leaving the basilica, head up the stairs in the atrium to the **Marciano Museum** and the **Loggia dei Cavalli.** The star of the museum is the world-famous *Triumphal*

Impressions

Venice is like eating an entire box of chocolate liqueurs at one go.

—Truman Capote

Quadriga, four horses looted from Constantinople by Venetian crusaders during the sack of that city in 1204. These horses once surmounted the basilica but were removed because of pollution damage and subsequently restored. This is the only *quadriga* (a quartet of horses yoked together) to have survived from the classical era, believed to have been cast in the 4th century. Napoléon once carted these much-traveled horses off to Paris for the Arc de Triomphe du Carrousel, but they were returned to Venice in 1815. The museum, with its mosaics and tapestries, is especially interesting, but also be sure to walk out onto the loggia for a view of Piazza San Marco.

Campanile di San Marco. Piazza San Marco. ☎ **041-522-4064.** Admission 10,000L ($5). Oct–Feb, daily 9:30am–4pm, Mar–June, daily 9am–7pm, July–Sept, daily 9am–9pm. Closed Jan 7–31. Vaporetto: San Marco.

One summer night in 1902, the bell tower of St. Mark's, suffering from years of rheumatism in the damp Venetian climate, gave out a warning sound that sent the fashionable coffee drinkers in the piazza below scurrying for their lives. But the campanile gracefully waited until the next morning, July 14, before tumbling into the piazza. The Venetians rebuilt their belfry, and it's now safe to climb to the top. Unlike Italy's other bell towers, where you have to brave narrow, steep spiral staircases to reach the top, this one has an elevator so that you can get a pigeon's view. It's a particularly good vantage point for viewing the cupolas of the basilica.

Clock Tower (Torre dell'Orologio). Piazza San Marco. ☎ **041-522-4951.** Vaporetto: San Marco.

The two Moors striking the bell atop this Renaissance clock tower, soaring over the Old Procuratie, are one of the most characteristic Venetian scenes. The clock under the winged lion not only tells the time but also is a boon to the astrologer: It matches the signs of the zodiac with the position of the sun. If the movement of the Moors striking the hour seems slow in today's fast-paced world, remember how many centuries the poor wretches have been at their task without time off. The "Moors" originally represented two European shepherds, but after having been reproduced in bronze, they've grown darker with the passing of time. As a consequence, they came to be called Moors by the Venetians.

The base of the tower has always been a favorite *punto di incontro* for Venetians ("meet me at the tower") and is the entrance to the ancient **Mercerie** (from the word for merchandise), the principal souklike retail street of both high-end boutiques and trinket shops that zigzags its way to the Rialto Bridge.

The clock tower was closed for years, despite original plans to reopen it in time for the 500-year anniversary of its construction in 1996. The clock mechanism has been getting a cleaning up by Piaget, the sponsor of its elaborate renovation. Although it didn't make a revised timetable (to ring in the Jubilee Year 2000), it should be open by the time you arrive in Venice, and visits to the top will resume upon the tower's reopening. The cost of admission was tentatively slated to be 5,000L ($2.50); hours were planned to be daily from 9:45am to 4pm.

✪ **Ducal Palace & Bridge of Sighs (Palazzo Ducale & Ponte dei Sospiri).** Piazzetta San Marco. ☎ **041-522-4951.** Admission 18,000L ($9). Mar–Oct, daily 9am–5:30pm (to 3:30pm Nov–Feb). Vaporetto: San Marco.

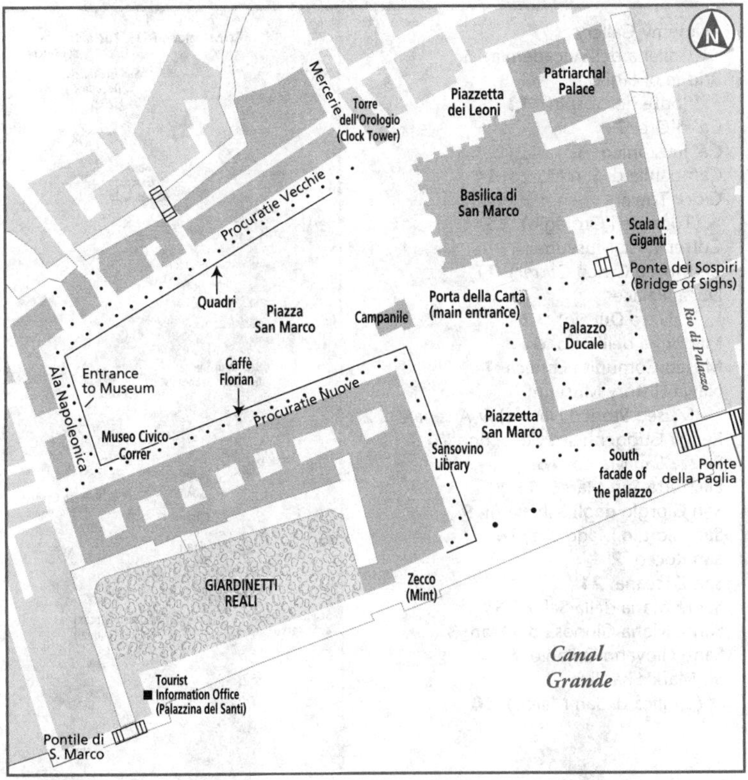

You enter the Palace of the Doges through the magnificent 15th-century **Porta della Carta** at the piazzetta. This Venetian Gothic palazzo gleams in the tremulous light somewhat like a frosty birthday cake in pinkish-red marble and white Istrian stone. Italy's grandest civic structure, it dates to 1309, though a 1577 fire destroyed much of the original building. That fire made ashes of many of the palace's masterpieces and almost spelled doom for the building itself, as the new architectural fervor of the post-Renaissance was in the air. However, sanity prevailed. Many of the greatest Venetian painters of the 16th century contributed to the restored palace, replacing the canvases or frescoes of the old masters.

If you enter from the piazzetta, past the four porphyry Moors, you'll be in the splendid Renaissance courtyard, one of the most recent additions to a palace that has benefited from the work of many architects with widely varying tastes. To get to the upper loggia, you can take the **Giants' Stairway (Scala dei Giganti),** so called because of the two Sansovino statues of mythological figures.

If you want to understand something of this magnificent palace, the fascinating history of the 1,000-year-old Maritime Republic, and the intrigue of the government that ruled it, search out the infrared **audioguide** at the entrance, costing 7,000L ($4.10). Unless you can tag along with an English-language tour group, you may otherwise miss out on the importance of much of what you're seeing.

After climbing the Sansovino stairway, you'll enter some get-acquainted rooms. Proceed to the **Sala di Anti-Collegio,** housing the palace's greatest works, notably

Venice Attractions

Academy Gallery
(Galleria dell'Accademia) **5**
Bridge of Sighs
(Ponte dei Sospiri) **11**
Ca' d'Oro **7**
Ca' Rezzonico **4**
Campanile di San Marco **14**
Clock Tower
(Torre dell'Orologio) **15**
Correr Civic Museum
(Museo Civico Correr) **17**
Ducal Palace
(Palazzo Ducale) **12**
Madonna dell'Orto **6**
Museo Comunitá Ebraica **1**
Naval History Museum
(Museo Storico Navale) & Arsenale **22**
Peggy Guggenheim Collection **20**
Piazza San Marco **16**
Piazzetta San Marco **13**
San Giorgio degli Schiavoni **9**
San Giorgio Maggiore **18**
San Rocco **2**
San Zaccaria **21**
Santa Maria della Salute **19**
Santa Maria Gloriosa dei Frari **3**
Santi Giovanni e Paolo **8**
St. Mark's Basilica
(Basilica di San Marco) **10**

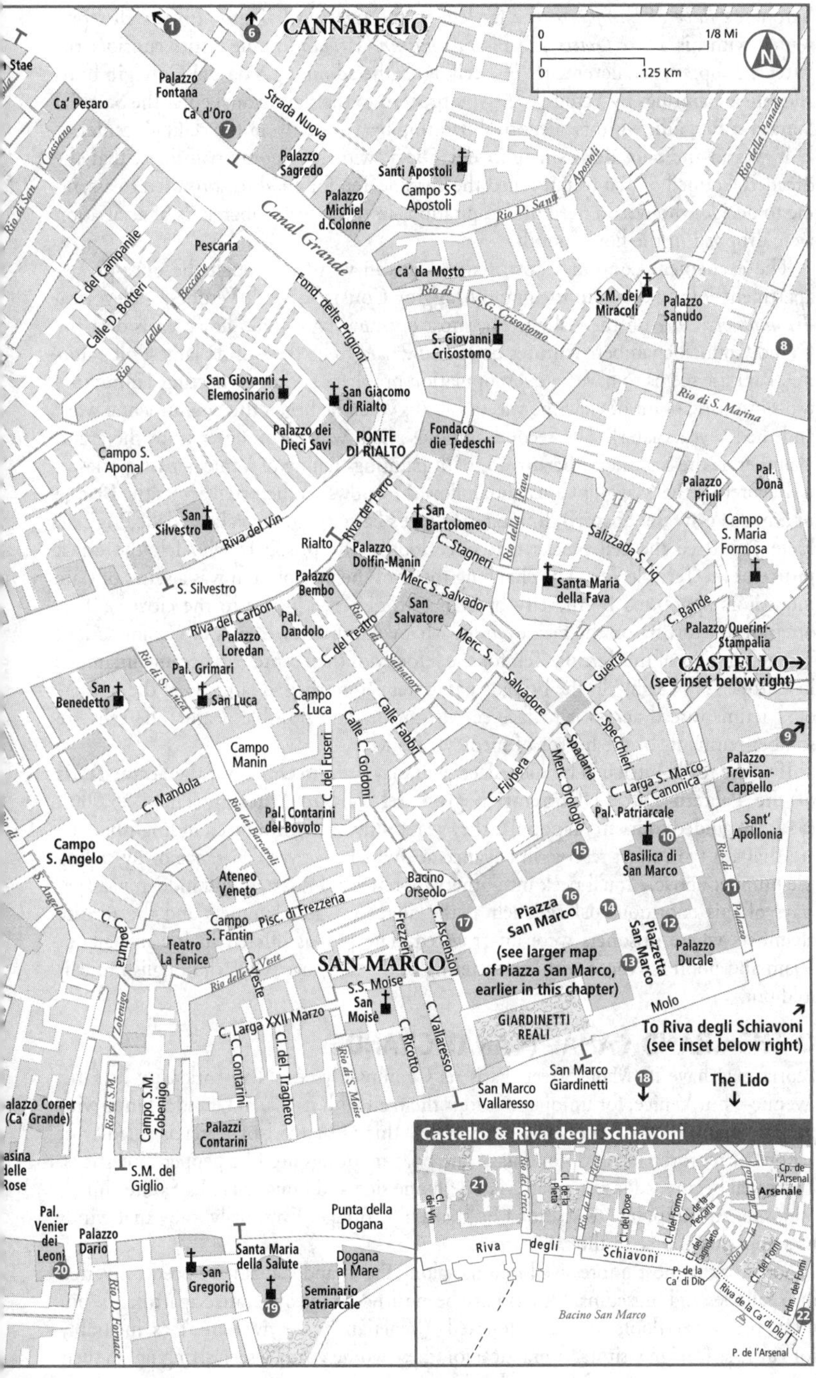

CANNAREGIO
0 1/8 Mi
0 .125 Km
N
Stae
Palazzo Fontana
Ca' Pesaro
Ca' d'Oro
Strada Nuova
Palazzo Sagredo
Santi Apostoli
Campo SS Apostoli
Palazzo Michiel d.Colonne
Canal Grande
Rio D. Santi Apostoli
Rio della Panada
Rio di San Cassiano
Pescaria
C. del Campanile
Calle D. Botteri
Rio delle Beccarie
Fond. delle Prigioni
Ca' da Mosto
Rio di S.G. Crisostomo
S.M. dei Miracoli
Palazzo Sanudo
S. Giovanni Crisostomo
San Giovanni Elemosinario
San Giacomo di Rialto
Rio di S. Marina
Palazzo dei Dieci Savi
PONTE DI RIALTO
Fondaco die Tedeschi
Campo S. Aponal
Pal. Donà
Palazzo Priuli
Rio della Fava
San Bartolomeo
Riva del Ferro
San Silvestro
Riva del Vin
Rialto
Palazzo Dolfin-Manin
C. Stagneri
Salizzada S. Liq
Campo S. Maria Formosa
S. Silvestro
Palazzo Bembo
Merc S. Salvador
Santa Maria della Fava
Riva del Carbon
Pal. Dandolo
San Salvatore
C. Bande
Palazzo Loredan
Rio di S. Salvatore
Merc. S. Salvadore
Palazzo Querini-Stampalia
C. del Teatro
CASTELLO→
(see inset below right)
Rio di S. Luca
Pal. Grimari
San Benedetto
San Luca
Campo S. Luca
Calle Fabbri
C. Guerra
C. Specchieri
C. Spadaria
Calle C. Goldoni
C. dei Fuseri
Campo Manin
C. Fiubera
Merc. Orologio
C. Larga S. Marco
C. Canonica
Palazzo Trevisan-Cappello
C. Mandola
Rio dei Barcaroli
Pal. Contarini del Bovolo
Pal. Patriarcale
Sant' Apollonia
Campo S. Angelo
Basilica di San Marco
Rio di Palazzo
Ateneo Veneto
Bacino Orseolo
Rio di S. Angelo
Pisc. di Frezzeria
Piazza San Marco
Piazzetta San Marco
C. Caotorta
Campo S. Fantin
Frezzeria
C. Ascensione
Teatro La Fenice
(see larger map of Piazza San Marco, earlier in this chapter)
Palazzo Ducale
SAN MARCO
Rio delle Veste
C. Veste
S.S. Moise
San Moisè
Molo
Rio Zobenigo
C. Larga XXII Marzo
C. Vallaresso
GIARDINETTI REALI
To Riva degli Schiavoni (see inset below right)
C. Contarini
Cl. del Traghetto
C. Ricotto
Rio di S. Moise
San Marco Giardinetti
The Lido
Rio di S.M.
Campo S.M. Zobenigo
San Marco Vallaresso
alazzo Corner (Ca' Grande)
Palazzi Contarini
asina delle Rose
S.M. del Giglio
Castello & Riva degli Schiavoni
Cl. del Vin
Rio dei Greci
Cl. de la Pietà
Rio de la Pietà
Cl. del Dose
Cl. del Forno
Cl. de la Pescaria
Cp. de l'Arsenal
Arsenale
Cl. del Cagnoletto
Cl. del Forni
Fdm. del Forni
Riva degli Schiavoni
P. de la Ca' di Dio
Riva de la Ca' di Dio
Bacino San Marco
P. de l'Arsenal
Pal. Venier dei Leoni
Palazzo Dario
Punta della Dogana
Santa Maria della Salute
San Gregorio
Dogana al Mare
Seminario Patriarcale
Rio D. Fornace

Veronese's *Rape of Europa,* to the far left on the right wall. Tintoretto is well represented with his *Three Graces* and his *Bacchus and Ariadne.* Some critics consider the latter his supreme achievement. The ceiling in the adjoining **Sala del Collegio** bears allegorical paintings by Veronese. As you proceed to the right, you'll enter the **Sala del Senato o Pregadi,** with its allegorical painting by Tintoretto in the ceiling's center.

It was in the **Sala del Consiglio dei Dieci,** with its gloomy paintings, that the dreaded Council of Ten (often called the Terrible Ten for good reason) used to assemble to decide who was in need of decapitation. In the antechamber, bills of accusation were dropped in the lion's mouth.

The excitement continues downstairs. You can wander through the once-private apartments of the doges to the grand **Maggior Consiglio,** with Veronese's allegorical *Triumph of Venice* on the ceiling. The most outstanding feature, however, is over the Grand Council chamber: Tintoretto's *Paradise,* said to be the world's largest oil painting. Paradise seems to have an overpopulation problem, perhaps reflecting Tintoretto's too-optimistic point of view (he was in his 70s when he began this monumental work and died 6 years later). The second grandiose hall, which you enter from the grand chamber, is the **Sala dello Scrutinio,** with paintings telling of Venice's past glories.

Reentering the Maggior Consiglio, follow the arrows on their trail across the **Bridge of Sighs (Ponte dei Sospiri),** linking the Doge's Palace with the Palazzo delle Prigioni. Here you'll see the cell blocks that once lodged the prisoners who felt the quick justice of the Terrible Ten. The changing roster of the Terrible Ten was a series of state inquisitors appointed by the city of Venice to dispense justice to the citizens. This often meant torture on the rack even for what could be viewed as a minor infraction. The reputation of the Terrible Ten for the ferocity of their sentences became infamous in Europe. The "sighs" in the bridge's name stem from the sad laments of the numerous victims forced across it to face certain torture and possible death. The cells are somber remnants of the horror of medieval justice.

If you're really intrigued by the palace, you may want to check out the **Secret Trails of the Palazzo Ducale (Itinerari Segreti del Palazzo Ducale).** These 25,000L ($12.50) guided tours are so popular they've recently been introduced in English, daily at 10:30am (you must reserve in advance at the ticket-buyers' entrance or by calling the number above). You'll peek into otherwise restricted quarters and hidden passageways of this enormous palace, such as the doge's private chambers and the torture chambers where prisoners were interrogated. The tour is offered in Italian daily at 10am and noon for those with a smattering of the language when the English tour is sold out.

✪ THE GRAND CANAL (CANAL GRANDE)

Peoria may have its Main Street, Paris its Champs-Elysées, New York City its Fifth Avenue—but Venice, for uniqueness, tops them all with its Canal Grande. Lined with palazzi (many in the Venetian Gothic style), this great road of water is filled with vaporetti, motorboats, and gondolas. The boat moorings are like peppermint sticks. The canal begins at Piazzetta San Marco on one side and Longhena's La Salute church opposite. At midpoint it's spanned by the Rialto Bridge. Eventually, the canal winds its serpentine course to the rail station.

Some of the most impressive buildings along the Grand Canal have been converted into galleries and museums. Others have been turned into cooperative apartments, but often the lower floors are now deserted. (Venetian housewives aren't as incurably romantic as foreign visitors. A practical lot, these women can be seen stringing up their laundry to dry in front of thousands of tourists.)

The Five Major Landmarks

Time and again, you'll think you know where you're going, only to wind up on a dead-end street or at the side of a canal with no bridge to get to the other side. Just remind yourself that Venice's complexity is an integral part of its charm, and getting lost is part of the fun.

Fortunately, around the city are yellow signs whose arrows direct you toward one of five major landmarks: **Ferrovia** (the train station), **Piazzale Roma,** the **Rialto** (Bridge), (Piazza) **San Marco,** and the **Accademia** (Bridge). You'll often find these signs grouped together, their arrows pointing off in different directions.

The best way to see the Grand Canal is to board vaporetto no. 1 (push and shove until you secure a seat at the front of the vessel). Settle yourself in, make sure you have your long-distance viewing glasses, and prepare yourself for a view that can thrill even the most experienced world traveler.

MUSEUMS & GALLERIES

Venice is a city of art. Decorating its palazzi and adorning its canvases were artists like Giovanni Bellini, Carpaccio, Titian, Giorgione, Lotto, Tintoretto, Veronese, Tiepolo, Guardi, Canaletto, and Longhi, to name just the important ones. You'll even come across some modern surprises, such as those in the Guggenheim Collection.

✪ **Academy Gallery (Galleria dell'Accademia).** Campo della Carità, Dorsoduro. ☎ **041-522-2247.** Admission 12,000L ($6). Mar–Oct, Tues–Fri 9am–9pm, Sat 9am–11pm, Sun 9am–8pm; Nov–Feb, Tues–Sat 9am–6:30pm, Sun 9am–1:30pm. Vaporetto: Accademia.

The pomp and circumstance, the glory that was Venice, lives on in this remarkable collection of paintings spanning the 13th to the 18th century. The hallmark of the Venetian school is color and more color. From Giorgione to Veronese, from Titian to Tintoretto, with a Carpaccio cycle thrown in, the Accademia has samples of its most famous sons—often their best work. Here we've highlighted only some of the most-renowned masterpieces for the first-timer in a rush.

You'll first see works by such 14th-century artists as Paolo and Lorenzo Veneziano, who bridged the gap from Byzantine art to Gothic (see the latter's *Annunciation*). Next, you'll view Giovanni Bellini's *Madonna and Saint* (poor Sebastian, not another arrow) and Carpaccio's fascinating yet gruesome work of mass crucifixion. As you move on, head for the painting on the easel by the window, attributed to the great Venetian artist Giorgione. On this canvas he depicted the Madonna and Child, along with the mystic St. Catherine of Siena and John the Baptist (a neat trick for Catherine, who seems to have perfected transmigration to join the cast of characters).

Two of the most important works with secular themes are Mantegna's armored *St. George,* with the slain dragon at his feet, and Hans Memling's 15th-century portrait of a young man. A most unusual *Madonna and Child* is by Cosmé Tura, the master of Ferrara, who could always be counted on to give a new twist to an old subject.

The Madonnas and bambini of Giovanni Bellini, an expert in harmonious color blending, are the focus of another room. None but the major artists could stand the test of a salon filled with the same subject, but under Bellini's brush each Virgin achieves her individual spirituality. Giorgione's *Tempest,* displayed here, is the single most famous painting at the Accademia. It depicts a baby suckling from the breast of its mother, while a man with a staff looks on. What might've emerged as a simple pastoral scene by a lesser artist comes forth as rare and exceptional beauty. Summer lightning pierces the sky, but the tempest seems to be in the background, far away from the foreground figures, who are menaced without knowing it.

You can see the masterpiece of Lorenzo Lotto, a melancholy portrait of a young man, before coming to a room dominated by Paolo Veronese's *The Banquet in the House of Levi.* This is really a "Last Supper" but was considered a sacrilege in its day, so Veronese was forced to change its name and pretend it was a secular work. (Impish Veronese caught the hot fire of the Inquisition by including dogs, a cat, midgets, Huns, and drunken revelers in the mammoth canvas.) Four large paintings by Tintoretto, noted for their swirling action and powerful drama, depict scenes from the life of St. Mark. Finally, painted in his declining years (some have suggested in his 99th year, before he died from the plague) is Titian's majestic *Pietà.*

After an unimpressive long walk, search out Canaletto's *Porticato.* Yet another room is heightened by Gentile Bellini's stunning portrait of St. Mark's Square, back in the days (1496) when the houses glistened with gold in the sun. All the works in this salon are intriguing, especially the re-creation of the Ponte de Rialto and a covered wood bridge by Carpaccio.

Also displayed is the cycle of narrative paintings that Vittore Carpaccio did of St. Ursula for the Scuola of Santa Orsola. The most famous is no. 578, showing Ursula asleep on her elongated bed, with a dog nestled on the floor nearby, as the angels come for a visitation. Finally, on the way out, look for Titian's *Presentation of the Virgin,* a fitting farewell to this galaxy of great Venetian art.

Correr Civic Museum (Museo Civico Correr). In the Procuratie Nuove, Piazza San Marco. ☎ **041-522-5625.** Admission (including admission to Ducal Palace above) 18,000L ($9). Mar–Oct daily 9am–7pm (to 5pm Nov–Feb). Vaporetto: San Marco.

This museum traces the development of Venetian painting from the 14th to the 16th century. On the second floor are the red-and-maroon robes once worn by the doges, plus some fabulous street lanterns and an illustrated copy of *Marco Polo in Tartaria.* You can see Cosmà Tura's *Pietà,* a miniature of renown from the genius in the Ferrara School. This is one of his more gruesome works, depicting a bony, gnarled Christ sprawled on the lap of the Madonna. Farther on, search out Schiavone's *Madonna and Child* (no. 545), our candidate for ugliest bambino ever depicted on canvas (no wonder his mother looks askance).

One of the most important rooms boasts three masterpieces: a *Pietà* by Antonello da Messina, a *Crucifixion* by Flemish Hugo van der Goes, and a *Madonna and Child* by Dieric Bouts, who depicted the baby suckling at his mother's breast in a sensual manner. The star attraction of the Correr is the **Bellini salon,** which includes works by founding padre Jacopo and his son, Gentile. But the real master of the household was the other son, Giovanni, the major painter of the 15th-century Venetian school (look for his *Crucifixion* and compare it with his father's treatment of the same subject). A small but celebrated portrait of St. Anthony of Padua by Alvise Vivarini is here, plus works by Bartolomeo Montagna. The most important work is Vittore

A Note on Museum Hours

As throughout Italy, visiting hours in Venice's museums are often subject to major variations. Many visitors who have budgeted only 2 or 3 days for Venice often express disappointment when, for some unknown reason, a major attraction closes abruptly. When you arrive, check with the tourist office for a list of the latest open hours.

Carpaccio's *Two Venetian Ladies,* though their true gender is a subject of much debate. In Venice they're popularly known as "The Courtesans." A lesser work, *St. Peter,* depicting the saint with the daggers piercing him, hangs in the same room.

The entrance is under the arcades of Ala Napoleonica at the western end of the square.

✪ **Ca' d'Oro.** Cannaregio 3931–3932. ☎ **041-523-8790.** Admission 6,000L ($3). Daily 9am–1:30pm. Closed Jan 1, May 1, and Dec 25. Vaporetto: Ca' d'Oro.

The only problem with the use of this building as an art museum is the fact that the Ca' d'Oro is so opulent, its architecture and decor compete with the works. It was built in the early 1400s, and its name translates as "House of Gold," though the gilding that once covered its facade eroded away long ago, leaving softly textured pink and white stone carved into lacy Gothic patterns. Historians compare its majesty to that of the Ducal Palace. The building was meticulously restored in the early 20th century by philanthropist Baron Franchetti, who attached it to a smaller nearby palazzo (Ca' Duodo), today part of the Ca' d'Oro complex. The interconnected buildings contain the baron's valuable private collection of paintings, sculpture, and furniture, all donated to the Italian government during World War I.

You enter into a stunning courtyard, 50 yards from the vaporetto stop. The courtyard has a multicolored patterned marble floor and is filled with statuary. Proceed upstairs to the lavishly appointed palazzo. One of the gallery's major paintings is Titian's voluptuous *Venus.* She coyly covers one breast, but what about the other?

In a special niche reserved for the masterpiece of the Franchetti collection is Andrea Mantegna's icy-cold *St. Sebastian,* the central figure of which is riddled with what must be a record number of arrows. You'll also find works by Carpaccio. If you walk onto the loggia, you'll have one of the grandest views of the Grand Canal, a panorama that inspired even Lord Byron—when he could take his eyes off the ladies.

For a delightful break, step out onto the palazzo's loggia, overlooking the Grand Canal, for a view up and down the aquatic waterway and across to the Pescheria, a timeless vignette of an unchanged city.

Ca' Rezzonico. Fondamenta Rezzonico, Dorsoduro 3136. ☎ **041-241-0100.** Admission 14,000L ($7). Oct–Apr, Sat–Thurs 10am–4pm, May–Sept, daily 10am–5pm. Vaporetto: Ca' Rezzonico.

This 17th- and 18th-century palace along the Grand Canal is where Robert Browning set up his bachelor headquarters and eventually died in 1889. Pope Clement XIII also stayed here. It's a virtual treasure house, known for its baroque paintings and furniture. First you enter the **Grand Ballroom** with its allegorical ceiling, and then you proceed through lavishly embellished rooms with Venetian chandeliers, brocaded walls, portraits of patricians, tapestries, gilded furnishings, and touches of chinoiserie. At the end of the first walk is the **Throne Room,** with its allegorical ceilings by Giovanni Battista Tiepolo.

On the first floor you can walk out onto a **balcony** for a view of the Grand Canal as the aristocratic tenants of the 18th century saw it. Another group of rooms follows, including the library. In these salons, look for a bizarre collection of paintings: One, for example, depicts half-clothed women beating up a defenseless naked man (one Amazon is about to stick a pitchfork into his neck, another to crown him with a violin). In the adjoining room, another woman is hammering a spike through a man's skull.

Upstairs is a survey of 18th-century Venetian art. As you enter the main room from downstairs, head for the **first salon** on your right (facing the canal), which contains the best works, paintings from the brush of Pietro Longhi. His most famous work, *The Lady and the Hairdresser,* is the first canvas to the right on the entrance wall. Others depict the life of the idle Venetian rich. On the rest of the floor are bedchambers, a chapel, and salons, some with badly damaged frescoes, including a romp of satyrs.

✪ **Peggy Guggenheim Collection (Collezione Peggy Guggenheim).** In the Palazzo Venier dei Leoni, Calle Venier dei Leoni, Dorsoduro 701. ☎ **041-520-6288.** Admission 12,000L ($6) adults, 8,000L ($4) students/children. Free for children under 9. Wed–Mon 11am–6pm. Vaporetto: Accademia.

This is one of the most comprehensive and brilliant modern-art collections in the Western world and reveals both the foresight and the critical judgment of its founder. The collection is housed in an unfinished palazzo, the former Venetian home of Peggy Guggenheim, who died in 1979. In the tradition of her family, Peggy Guggenheim was a lifelong patron of contemporary painters and sculptors. In the 1940s, she founded the avant-garde Art of This Century Gallery in New York, impressing critics not only with the high quality of the artists she sponsored but also with her methods of displaying them.

As her private collection increased, she decided to find a larger showcase and selected Venice. While the Solomon R. Guggenheim Museum was going up in New York City according to Frank Lloyd Wright's specifications, she was creating her own gallery here. You can wander through and enjoy art in an informal and relaxed way.

Max Ernst was one of Peggy Guggenheim's early favorites (she even married him), as was Jackson Pollock (she provided a farmhouse where he could develop his technique). Displayed here are works not only by Pollock and Ernst but also by Picasso (see his 1911 cubist *The Poet*), Duchamp, Chagall, Mondrian, Brancusi, Delvaux, and Dalí, plus a garden of modern sculpture with Giacometti works (some of which he struggled to complete while resisting the amorous intentions of Marlene Dietrich). Temporary modern-art shows may be presented during winter. Since Peggy Guggenheim's death, the collection has been administered by the Solomon R. Guggenheim Foundation, which also operates New York's Guggenheim Museum. In the new wing are a museum shop and a cafe, overlooking the sculpture garden.

Naval History Museum (Museo Storico Navale) & Arsenale. Campo San Biasio, Castello 2148. ☎ **041-520-0276.** Admission 3,500L ($1.75). Mon–Sat 9am–1:30pm. Closed holidays. Vaporetto: Arsenale.

The Naval History Museum is filled with cannons, ships' models, and fragments of old vessels dating to the days when Venice was supreme in the Adriatic. The prize exhibit is a gilded model of the *Bucintoro,* the great ship of the doge that surely would've made Cleopatra's barge look like an oil tanker. In addition, you'll find models of historic and modern fighting ships, local fishing and rowing craft, and a collection of 24 Chinese junks, as well as a number of maritime *ex voto* from churches of Naples.

If you walk along the canal as it branches off from the museum, you'll arrive at the Ships' Pavilion, where historic vessels are displayed (about 270 yards from the museum and before the wooden bridge). Proceeding along the canal, you'll soon reach the Arsenale, Campo dell'Arsenale, guarded by stone lions, Neptune with a trident, and other assorted ferocities. You'll spot it readily enough because of its two towers flanking the canal. In its day, the Arsenale turned out galley after galley at speeds usually associated with wartime production.

CHURCHES & GUILD HOUSES

Much of the great art of Venice lies in its **churches** and ***scuole*** (guild houses or fraternities). Most of the guild members were drawn from the rising bourgeoisie. The guilds were said to fulfill both the material and the spiritual needs of their (male) members, who often engaged in charitable works in honor of the saint for whom their scuola was named. Many of Venice's greatest artists, including Tintoretto, were commissioned to decorate these guild houses. Some created masterpieces you can still see today. Narrative canvases that depicted the lives of the saints were called *teleri.*

✪ **San Rocco.** Campo San Rocco, San Polo. ☎ **041-523-4864.** Admission 9,000L ($4.50) adults, 6,000L ($3) children. Mar 28–Nov 2, daily 9am–5:30pm; Nov 3–30 and Mar 1–27, daily 10am–4pm; Dec–Feb, Mon–Fri 10am–1pm, Sat–Sun 10am–4pm. Closed Easter and Dec 25–Jan 1. Vaporetto: San Tomà. Ticket office closes 30 minutes before last entrance.

Of all Venice's scuole, none is as richly embellished as this, filled with epic canvases by Tintoretto. Born Jacopo Robusti in 1518, he became known for paintings of mystical spirituality and phantasmagoric light effects. By a clever trick, he won the competition to decorate this darkly illuminated early–16th-century building. He began painting in 1564, and the work stretched on until his powers as an artist waned; he died in 1594. The paintings sweep across the upper and lower halls, mesmerizing you with a kind of passion play. In the grand hallway, they depict New Testament scenes, devoted largely to episodes in the life of Mary (the ***Flight into Egypt*** is among the best). In the top gallery are works illustrating scenes from the Old and New Testaments, the most renowned being those devoted to the life of Christ. In a separate room is Tintoretto's masterpiece: his mammoth ***Crucifixion.*** In it he showed his dramatic scope and sense of grandeur as an artist, creating a deeply felt scene that fills you with the horror of systematic execution, thus transcending its original subject matter. (Movie trivia: Watch Woody Allen try to pick up Julia Roberts in *Everyone Says I Love You* while she studies the Tintorettos in San Rocco—if you can get past the idea of the lovely Ms. Roberts as an art historian.)

San Giorgio degli Schiavoni. Calle dei Furiani, Castello. ☎ **041-522-8828.** Admission 5,000L ($2.50). Nov–Mar, Tues–Sat 10am–12:30pm and 3–6pm, Sun 10am–12:30pm; Apr–Oct, Tues–Sat 9:30am–12:30pm and 3:30–6:30pm, Sun 9:30am–12:30pm. Vaporetto: San Zaccaria. Last entrance 20 minutes before closing.

At the St. Antonino Bridge (Fondamenta dei Furlani) is the second important guild house to visit. Between 1502 and 1509, Vittore Carpaccio painted a pictorial cycle here of exceptional merit and interest. His works of ✪ **St. George and the Dragon** are our favorite art in all Venice and certainly the most delightful. For example, in one frame St. George charges the dragon on a field littered with half-eaten bodies and skulls. Gruesome? Not at all. Any moment you expect the director to call "Cut!" The pictures relating to St. Jerome are appealing but don't compete with St. George and his ferocious dragon.

Santa Maria Gloriosa dei Frari. Campo dei Frari, San Polo. ☎ **041-522-2637.** Admission 3,000L ($1.50); free Sun. Mon–Sat 9–6pm; Sun 1–6pm. Vaporetto: San Tomà.

Known simply as the Frari, this Venetian Gothic church is only a short walk from the San Rocco and is filled with great art. The best work is Titian's ***Assumption*** over the main altar—a masterpiece of soaring beauty depicting the ascension of the Madonna on a cloud puffed up by floating cherubs. In her robe, but especially in the robe of one of the gaping saints below, "Titian red" dazzles as never before.

On the first altar to the right as you enter is Titian's second major work here: ***Madonna Enthroned,*** painted for the Pesaro family in 1526. Although lacking the power and drama of the ***Assumption,*** it nevertheless is brilliant in its use of color and light effects. But Titian surely would turn redder than his Madonna's robes if he could see the latter-day neoclassical tomb built for him on the opposite wall. The kindest word for it: large.

Facing the tomb is a memorial to Canova, the Italian sculptor who led the revival of classicism. To return to more enduring art, head to the sacristy for a 1488 Giovanni Bellini triptych on wood; the Madonna is cool and serene, one of Bellini's finest portraits of the Virgin. Also, see the almost primitive-looking wood carving by Donatello of St. John the Baptist.

Madonna dell'Orto. Campo dell'Orto, Cannaregio 3512. ☎ **041-719-933.** Admission 3,000L ($1.50). Mon–Sat 10am–5pm; Sun 1–6pm. Vaporetto: Madonna dell'Orto.

At this church, a good reason to walk to this remote northern district, you can pay your final respects to Tintoretto. The brick structure with a Gothic front is famed not only because of its paintings by that artist but also because the great master is buried in the chapel to the right of the main altar. At the high altar are his *Last Judgment* (on the right) and *Sacrifice of the Golden Calf* (left), monumental paintings curving at the top like a Gothic arch. Over the doorway to the right of the altar is Tintoretto's superb portrayal of the presentation of Mary as a little girl at the temple. The composition is unusual in that Mary isn't the focal point; rather, a pointing woman bystander dominates the scene.

The first chapel to the right of the main altar contains a masterly work by Cima de Conegliano, showing the presentation of a sacrificial lamb to the saints (the plasticity of St. John's body evokes Michelangelo). In the first chapel on the left, as you enter, notice the large photo of Giovanni Bellini's *Madonna and Child.* The original, which was noteworthy for its depiction of the eyes and mouths of the mother and child, was stolen as part of a 1994 theft, and pending the possibility of its hoped-for return, the photograph was installed in its place. Two other pictures in the apse are *The Presentation of the Cross to St. Peter* and *The Beheading of St. Christopher.*

San Zaccaria. Campo San Zaccaria, Castello. ☎ **041-522-1257.** Admission 3,000L ($1.50) to museum; church free. Mon–Sat 10am–noon; daily 4–6pm. Vaporetto: San Zaccaria.

Behind St. Mark's is this Gothic church with a Renaissance facade, filled with works of art, notably Giovanni Bellini's restored *Madonna Enthroned,* painted with saints (second altar to the left). Many have found this to be one of Bellini's finest Madonnas, and it does have beautifully subdued coloring, though it appears rather static. Many worthwhile works lie in the main body of the church, but for a view of even more of them, apply to the sacristan for entrance to the church's museum, housed in an area once reserved exclusively for nuns. Here you'll find works by Tintoretto, Titian, Il Vecchio, Anthony van Dyck, and Bassano. The paintings aren't labeled, but the sacristan will point out the names of the artists. In the Sisters' Choir are five armchairs in which the Venetian doges of yore sat. And if you save the best for last, you can see the faded frescoes of Andrea del Castagno in the shrine honoring San Tarasio.

San Giorgio Maggiore. Isola San Giorgio Maggiore, across from Piazzetta San Marco. ☎ **041-522-7827.** Free admission. Apr–Oct, daily 9:30am–12:30pm and 2:30–6pm; Nov–Mar, daily 10am–12:30pm and 2:30–4:30pm. Closed for Mass on Sun and feast days 10:45am–noon. Vaporetto: Take the Giudecca-bound vaporetto on Riva degli Schiavoni and get off at the first stop, right in the courtyard of the church.

This church, on the little island of San Giorgio Maggiore, was designed by the great Renaissance architect Palladio—perhaps as a consolation prize since he wasn't chosen to rebuild the burned-out Doge's Palace. The logical rhythm of the Vicenza architect is played here on a grand scale. But inside it's almost too stark, as Palladio wasn't much on gilded adornment. The chief art hangs on the main altar: two epic paintings by Tintoretto, the *Fall of Manna* to the left and the far more successful *Last Supper* to the right. It's interesting to compare Tintoretto's *Cena* with that of Veronese at the

Accademia. Afterward you may want to take the elevator (for 3,000L/$1.50 to the top of the belfry for a view of the greenery of the island itself, the lagoon, and the Doge's Palace across the way. It's unforgettable.

Santa Maria della Salute. Campo della Salute, Dorsoduro. ☎ **041-523-7951.** Free admission (but offering is expected); sacristy 3,000L ($1.50). Mar–Nov, daily 9am–noon and 3–6pm (to 5:30pm Dec–Feb). Vaporetto: Salute.

Like the proud landmark it is, La Salute, the pinnacle of the baroque movement in Venice, stands at the mouth of the Grand Canal overlooking Piazzetta San Marco and opening onto Campo della Salute. One of Venice's most historic churches, it was built by Longhena in the 17th century (work began in 1631) as an offering to the Virgin for delivering the city from the plague. Longhena, almost unknown when he got the commission, dedicated half a century to working on this church and died 5 years before the long-lasting job was completed. Surmounted by a great cupola, the octagonal basilica makes for an interesting visit: It houses a small art gallery in its sacristy (tip the custodian), which includes a marriage feast of Cana by Tintoretto, allegorical paintings on the ceiling by Titian, a mounted St. Mark, and poor St. Sebastian with his inevitable arrow.

Santi Giovanni e Paolo. Campo SS. Giovanni e Paolo, Castello 6363. ☎ **041-523-5913.** Free admission. Daily 9am–12:30pm and 3–7:15pm. Vaporetto: Rialto or Fondamenta Nuove.

This great Gothic church (aka Zanipolo) houses the tombs of many doges. It was built during the 13th and 14th centuries and contains works by many of the most noted Venetian painters. As you enter (right aisle), you'll find a retable by Giovanni Bellini (which includes a St. Sebastian filled with arrows). In the Rosary Chapel are Veronese ceilings depicting New Testament scenes, including *The Assumption of the Madonna.* To the right of the church is one of the world's best-known equestrian statues, that of Bartolomeo Colleoni, sculpted in the 15th century by Andrea del Verrochio. The bronze has long been acclaimed as his masterpiece, though it was completed by another artist. The horse is far more beautiful than the armored military hero, who looks as if he had just stumbled on a three-headed crocodile.

To the left of the pantheon is the **Scuola di San Marco,** with a stunning Renaissance facade (it's now run as a civic hospital). The church requests that Sunday visits be of a religious nature, rather than for sightseeing.

THE LIDO

The white sands of the Lido have drawn artists and literary types for centuries, and today they still draw a bikini-clad crowd that includes the occasional celeb. The Lido is a resort area complete with deluxe hotels, a casino, and stratospheric prices.

The Lido is past its heyday. A chic crowd still checks into the Excelsior Palace and the Hotel des Bains, but the beach strip is overrun with tourists and opens onto polluted waters. (For swimming, guests use their hotel pools, though they still stroll along the Lido sands and enjoy the views.)

Even if you aren't planning to stay in this area, you should still come over and explore for an afternoon. There's no denying the appeal of a beach so close to one of the world's most romantic cities. The strips of beachfront in front of the big hotels on the Lido are technically considered private, and the public is discouraged from using the facilities. But since you can use the beachfront on either side of their property, no one seems to really care about shooing nonguests away.

If you don't want to tread on the beachfront property of the rarefied hotels (which have huts lining the beach like those of some tropical paradise), you can try the **Lungomare G. d'Annunzio (Public Bathing Beach)** at the end of the Gran Viale

(Piazzale Ettore Sorger), a long stroll from the vaporetto stop. You can book cabins (*camerini*) and enjoy the sand. Rates change seasonally.

To reach the Lido, take vaporetto no. 1, 6, 52, or 82 (the ride takes about 15 minutes). The boat departs from a landing stage near the Doge's Palace.

THE GHETTO

The Ghetto of Venice, called the ✪ **Ghetto Nuovo,** was instituted in 1516 by the Venetian Republic in the Cannaregio district. It's considered to be the first ghetto in the world and also the best kept. The word *geto* comes from the Venetian dialect and means "foundry" (originally there were two iron foundries here where metals were fused). At one time, Venetian Jews were confined to a walled area and obliged to wear red or yellow marks sewn onto their clothing and distinctive-looking hats. The walls that once enclosed and confined the Ghetto were torn down long ago, but much remains of the past.

There are five synagogues in Venice, each built during the 16th century and each representing a radically different aesthetic and cultural difference among the groups of Jews who built them. The oldest is the **German Synagogue** (**Sinagoghe Grande Tedesca**), restored after the end of World War II with funds from Germany. Others are the **Spanish Synagogue** (**Sinagoghe Spagnola**), the oldest continuously functioning synagogue in Europe, the **Italian Synagogue** (**Sinagoghe Italiana**), the **Levantine-Oriental Synagogue** (**Sinagoghe Levantina,** aka the **Turkish Synagogue**), and the **Canton Synagogue** (**Sinagoghe del Canton**).

The best way to visit the synagogues is to take one of the guided tours departing from the **Museo Comunità Ebraica,** Campo di Ghetto Nuovo 2902B (☎ **041-715-359**). It contains a small but worthy collection of artifacts pertaining to the Jewish community of Venice and costs 7,000L ($3.50) adults. From June to September, the museum is open Sunday to Friday 10am to 7pm (October to May to 5pm). However, the museum is by no means the focal point of your experience: More worthwhile are the **walking tours** that begin and end here, costing 20,000L ($10), with free entrance to the museum. The 50-minute tours incorporate a brisk commentary and a stroll through the neighborhood, including visits to the interiors of three of the five synagogues (the ones you visit depend on various factors). From June to September, the tours depart hourly Sunday to Friday 10:30am to 5:30pm (October to May to 3:30pm).

ORGANIZED TOURS

Tours through the streets and canals of Venice are distinctly different from tours through other cities of Italy because of the complete absence of traffic. You can always wander at will through the labyrinth of streets, but many visitors opt for a guided tour to at least familiarize themselves with the city's geography.

American Express, Calle San Moisè, San Marco 1471 (☎ **041-520-0844**), which operates from a historic building a few steps from St. Mark's Square, offers an array of guided city tours. It's open for tours and travel arrangements Monday to Friday 9am to 5:30pm and Saturday 9am to 12:30pm. Call ahead to ask about the current schedule and to make reservations. The offerings include a daily 2-hour guided tour of the city for 40,000L ($20), an Evening Serenade Tour that's accompanied by the sound of singing musicians in gondolas for 55,000L ($27.50), and a tour of the islands of the Venetian lagoon for 30,000L ($15).

If you'd like more-personalized neighborhood tours, contact the **Venice Travel Advisory Service,** 22 Riverside Dr., New York, NY 10023 (☎ and fax **212/873-1964**). Born in New York, Samantha Durell is a professional photographer who has lived and worked in Venice for more than 10 years. She conducts private walking tours, assists with advance-planning services, and is an expert in making wedding arrangements for those who want to get married or renew their vows in Venice. Her expertise also includes advice on how to find out-of-the-way trattorie where you can enjoy typical Venetian cuisine. In addition, she has a wealth of details about shopping, sightseeing, art, history, dining, and entertainment. Morning and afternoon tours, for a maximum of four people, last about 5 hours and are $250 for two people, $50 for each additional adult, and $25 for each child.

6 Shopping

Venetian glass and lace are known throughout the world. However, selecting quality products in either craft requires a shrewd eye, because there's much that's tawdry and shoddily crafted. Some of the glassware hawked isn't worth the cost of shipping it home. Yet other pieces represent some of the world's finest artistic and ornamental glass. Murano is the island famous for its handmade glass. However, you can find little glass-animal souvenirs in shops all over Venice.

For lace, head out to Burano, where the last of a long line of women put in painstaking hours to produce some of the finest lace in the world.

SHOPPING STROLLS

All the main shopping streets, even the side streets, are touristy and overrun. The greatest concentration of shops is around **Piazza San Marco** and the **Rialto Bridge.** Prices are much higher at San Marco, but the quality of merchandise is also higher. There are two major shopping strolls in Venice.

First, from **Piazza San Marco** you can stroll toward spacious **Campo Morosini.** You just follow one shop-lined street all the way to its end (though the name will change several times). You begin at Salizzada San Moisè, which becomes Via 22 Marzo, and then Calle delle Ostreghe, before it opens onto Campo Santa Maria Zobenigo. The street then narrows and changes to Calle Zaguri before widening once more into Campo San Maurizio, finally becoming Calle Piovan before reaching Campo Morosini. The only deviation from this tour is a detour down Calle Vallaressa, between San Moisè and the Grand Canal, which is one of the major shopping arteries with some of the biggest designer names in the business.

The other great shopping stroll wanders from Piazza San Marco to the Rialto in a succession of streets collectively known as the **Mercerie.** It's virtually impossible to get lost because each street name is preceded by the word *merceria,* like Merceria dell'Orologio, which begins near the clock tower in Piazza San Marco. Many commercial places, mainly shops, line the Mercerie before it reaches the Rialto, which then explodes into one vast shopping emporium.

SHOPPING A TO Z

ANTIQUES **Antichita Santomanco,** Frezzeria, San Marco 1504 (☎ **041-523-6643**), is for the well-heeled serious collector. It deals in antique furniture, jewels, silver, prints, and old Murano glass. Of course, the merchandise is ever-changing, but you're likely to pick up some little heirloom item in the midst of the clutter. Many of the items date from the Venetian heyday of the 1600s.

BOOKS The most centrally located bookstore is the **Libreria Sansovino,** Bacino Orseolo, San Marco 84 (☎ **041-522-2623**), to the north of Piazza San Marco. It carries both hard- and softcover books in English. Near the American Express office is the **Libreria San Giorgio,** Calle Larga XXII Marzo, San Marco 2087 (☎ **041-523-8451**), one of whose specialties is books on Venetian art.

BRASS Founded in 1913, ✪ **Valese Fonditore,** Calle Fiubera, San Marco 793 (☎ **041-522-7282**), serves as a showcase for one of the most famous of the several foundries with headquarters in Venice. Many of the brass copies of 18th-century chandeliers produced by this company grace fine homes in the United States, becoming valuable family heirlooms. Some of the most appealing objects are the 50 or 60 replicas of the brass seahorses that grace the sides of many of the gondolas. A pair of medium-sized ones, each about 11 inches tall, begins at 350,000L ($175).

CARNEVALE MASKS Venetian masks, considered collectors' items, originated during Carnevale, which takes place the week before the beginning of Lent. In the old days there was a good reason to wear masks during the riotous Carnevale—they helped wives and husbands be unfaithful to one another and priests break their vows of chastity. Things got so out of hand that Carnevale was banned in the late 18th century. But it came back, and the masks went on again.

You can find shops selling masks practically on every corner. As with glass and lace, however, quality varies. Many masks are great artistic expressions, while others are shoddy and cheap. The most sought-after mask is the *Portafortuna* (luck bringer), with its long nose and birdlike visage. *Orientale* masks evoke the heyday of the Serene Republic and its trade with the Far East. The *Bauta* was worn by men to assert their macho qualities, and the *Neutra* blends the facial characteristics of both sexes. The list of masks and their origins seem endless.

The best place to buy Carnevale masks is the **Laboratorio Artigiano Maschere,** Barbaria delle Tole, Castello 6657 (☎ **041-522-3110**), which sells handcrafted masks in papier-mâché or leather. This well-established store has a particularly good selection, including masks depicting characters of the Commedia dell'Arte. The shop also sells a variety of other handcrafted papier-mâché items, like picture and mirror frames, pots, consoles, and boxes in the shape of pets.

Also good is **Mondonovo,** Rio Terrà Canal, Dorsoduro 3063 (☎ **041-528-7344**), where talented artisans labor to produce copies of both traditional and more modern masks, each of which is one-of-a-kind and richly nuanced with references to Venetian lore and traditions. Prices range from 30,000L ($15) for a fairly basic model to 3,000,000L ($1,500) for something you might display on a wall as a piece of sculpture.

DOLLS The studio/shop **Bambole di Frilly,** Fondamenta dell'Osmarin, Castello 4974 (☎ **041-521-2579**), offers dolls with meticulously painted porcelain faces (they call it a "biscuit") and hand-tailored costumes, including dressy pinafores. Prices begin at 30,000L ($15) and can go as high as 1,500,000L ($750), but even the reasonably priced dolls are made with the same painstaking care.

FABRICS Select outlets in Venice sell some of the greatest fabrics in the world. **Norelene,** Calle della Chiesa, Dorsoduro 727 (☎ **041-523-7605**), sells lustrous hand-printed silks, velvets, and cottons, plus wall hangings and clothing.

Venetia Studium is at two outlets: Calle Larga XXII Marco, San Marco 2403 (☎ **041-522-9281**), and a newer shop at Mercerie, San Marco 723 (☎ **041-522-9859**). For years, Lino Lando worked to crack the secret of fabled designer Mariano Fortuny's plissé (finely pleated silk). Eventually he found the secret. The result can now be yours in his selection of silk accessories, scarves, Delphos gowns, and even silk lamps.

Gaggio Rich, San Marco, San Stefano 3451–3441 (☎ **041-522-8574**), offers unique items, the most stunning of which are velvets and artistic fabrics with filigree, all inspired by the deep colors and designs of Fortuny. The fabrics are very Venetian and very decadent. You can purchase these fabrics by the meter, or they can be fashioned into clothing, shawls, cushions, or whatever.

Yet another Fortuny-inspired outlet is **Vittorio Trois,** Campo San Maurizio, San Marco 2666 (☎ **041-522-2905**). Trois was selected to receive a priceless legacy. The great Mariano Fortuny revealed his exquisite printing techniques to a friend of Trois, the late Contessa Gozzi, and she passed them on to Trois, who made a business of them. Today you can buy the same Fortuny patterns that stunned your grandparents on their visit to Venice decades ago. The radiant designs look like brocade and are sold by the yard.

FASHION The **Belvest Boutique,** Calle Vallaresso, San Marco 1305, near Harry's Bar (☎ **041-528-7933**), is one of Venice's finest boutiques, specializing in clothing for women and men, handmade and ready-to-wear. Fabric from some of the world's leading cloth makers is used in the designs. Linked with Vogini, the famous purveyor of leatherwork, the boutique is a bastion of top-quality craftsmanship and high-fashion style.

In need of some new threads for the film festival? Then **La Bottega di Nino,** Mercerie dell'Orologio, San Marco 223 (☎ **041-522-5608**), is the place for elegant cutting-edge male attire as stylish as anything you'll find in Milan. It features the work of many European designers, even some from England, but shines brightest in its Italian names, such as Nino Cerruti and Zenia. The prices are also better for Italian wear.

La Fenice, Calle Larga XXII Marzo, San Marco 2255 (☎ **041-523-1273**), is a large outlet for a stylish assortment of designers from throughout Europe. The most visible of several members of a city-wide chain, it sells women's clothing from designers like Moschino, Thierry Mügler, German Rena Lang, and the well-received Turkish-born designer Osbek.

By accident we stumbled on **Caberlotto,** San Salvador, San Marco 5114 (☎ **041-522-9242**), with a stunning collection of classic apparel for both women and men, all in jewel-like colors. Head here to see the rich collection of Loro Piana shawls, cashmere sweaters, scarves, and other apparel.

GIFTS The **Bac Art Studio,** San Vio, Dorsoduro 62 (☎ **041-522-8171**), sells paper goods, but it's mainly a graphics gallery, noted for its selection of engravings, posters, and lithographs of Venice at Carnevale time. Items for the most part are reasonably priced, and it's clear that a great deal of care has gone into the choice of merchandise.

Head to **Osvaldo Böhm,** Salizzada San Moisé, San Marco 1349–1350 (☎ **041-522-2255**), for that just right, and light, souvenir of Venice. It has a rich collection of photographic archives specializing in Venetian art, as well as original engravings and maps, lithographs, watercolors, and Venetian masks. You can also see modern serigraphs by local artists and some fine handcrafted bronzes.

In one showroom, **Veneziartigiana,** Calle Larga, San Marco 412–413 (☎ **041-523-5032**), assembles the artisanal production of at least 11 local craftspeople, whose creations are in silver, glass, ceramics, wood, and copper. Look for well-executed dolls, Carnevale masks, picture frames, and posters, any of which would make a well-received gift for relatives or friends back home.

GLASS Venice is crammed with glass shops: It's estimated there are at least 1,000 in San Marco alone. Unless you go to a top-quality dealer, you'll find most stores sell both shoddy and high-quality glassware, and only the most trained eye can often tell the difference. A lot of "Venetian glass" isn't from Venice at all but from the Czech Republic. (Of course, the Czech Republic has some of the finest glassmakers in Europe, so that may not be bad either.) Buying glass boils down to this: If you like an item, buy it. It may not be high quality, but then high quality can cost thousands.

If you're looking for an heirloom, stick to the major houses. One of the oldest (founded in 1866) and largest purveyors of traditional Venetian glass is ✪ **Pauly & Co.,** Ponte Consorzi, San Marco 4392 (☎ **041-520-9899**), with more than two dozen showrooms. Part of the premises is devoted to something akin to a museum, where past successes (now antiques) are displayed. Antique items are only rarely offered for sale, but they can be copied and shipped anywhere, and chandeliers can be electrified to match your standards. They begin at about 2,000,000L ($1,000) but can spiral to as much as 1,000,000,000L ($500,000) if you're a Saudi emir who's designing an entire throne room around them.

The art glass sold by ✪ **Venini,** Piazzetta Leoncini, San Marco 314 (☎ **041-522-4045**), has caught the attention of collectors from all over the world. Many of their pieces, including anything-but-ordinary lamps, bottles, and vases, are works of art representing the best of Venetian craftsmanship. Its best-known glass has a distinctive swirl pattern in several colors, called a venature. This shop is known for the refined quality of its glass, some of which appears almost transparent. Much of it is very fragile, but they learned long ago how to ship it anywhere safely. To visit the furnace, call ☎ **041-739-955.**

Harking back to the days when glass beads were used for trade in Venetian colonies, **Anticlea,** Campo San Provolo, Castello 4719 (☎ **041-528-6949**), offers scores of antique and reproduction glass beads, strung or unstrung, in many sizes, shapes, and colors.

L'Isola, Campo San Moisè, San Marco 1468 (☎ **041-523-1973**), is the shop of Carlo Moretti, one of the world's best-known contemporary artisans working in glass. You'll find all his signature designs in decanters, glasses, vases, bowls, and paperweights.

The **Galleria Marina Barovier,** Salizzada San Samuele, San Marco 3216 (☎ **041-522-6102**), sells some of the most creative modern glass sculptures in Italy. Since it was opened in the early 1980s by its founder, Marina Barovier, in the suburb of Mestre, it has grown until it's now viewed as one of the most glamorous art galleries in the world of glassmaking. Especially sought after are sculptures by master glassmakers Luco Tagliapietra and American artist Dale Chihuly, whose chandeliers represent amusing and/or dramatic departures from traditional Venetian forms. Don't despair if you're on a budget; some simple items begin as low as 25,000L ($12.50). Anything sold can be shipped.

At **Vetri d'Arte,** Piazza San Marco 140 (☎ **041-520-0205**), you can find moderately priced glass jewelry for souvenirs and gifts, as well as a selection of pricier crystal jewelry and porcelain bowls.

Luco Tagliapietra, one of the masters of Venetian glassblowing, has his works distributed by **Domus Vetri d'Arte,** Fondamenta Vetrai 82, Murano (☎ **041-739-215**). This artisan, with his cutting-edge sense of design, began blowing glass at age 12 and by age 21 was recognized as a master—some even called him a genius in glass. Unlike some Venetian glassmakers, inspired by ancient Greece and Rome, Tagliapietra roams the world for inspiration, finding it even in some Native American cultures.

JEWELRY Since 1846, ✪ **Missiaglia,** Piazza San Marco, San Marco 125 (☎ **041-522-4464**), has been the supplier to savvy shoppers from around the world seeking the best jewelry. Go here for a special classic piece, such as handcrafted jewelry with a Venetian twist—everything from a gold gondolier oar pin to a diamond-studded fan brooch with an ebony Carnevale mask. Their specialty is colored precious and semiprecious gemstones set in white or yellow gold.

For antique jewelry, there's no shop finer than **Codognato,** Calle Ascensione, San Marco 1295 (☎ **041-522-5042**). Some of the great heirloom jewelry of Europe is sent here when estates are settled.

LACE Most lace vendors center around Piazza San Marco. Although the price of handmade Venetian lace is high, it's still reasonable considering the painstaking work that goes into the real thing. However, much of the lace is shoddy, and a lot of it isn't lace handmade in Venice but machine-made lace done in who-knows-what-country. The lace shops are like the glassware outlets, selling the whole gamut from the shoddy to the exquisite.

For serious purchases, ✪ **Jesurum,** Mercerie del Capitello, San Marco 4857 (☎ **041-520-6177**), is tops. You'll find Venetian handmade or machine-made lace and embroidery on table, bed, and bath linens as well as hand-printed swimsuits. Prices are high, but quality and originality are guaranteed and special orders accepted. The exclusive linens created here are expensive, but the inventory is large enough to accommodate many budgets. Staff members insist that everything sold is made in or around Venice in traditional patterns.

LEATHER **Marforio,** Campo San Salvador, San Marco 5033 (☎ **041-522-5734**), was founded in 1875 and is Italy's oldest and largest leather-goods retail outlet, run by the same family for five generations. It's known for the quality of its leather products, and there's an enormous assortment of famous European labels, including Valentino, Armani, Ferré, and Cardin, among others.

Bottega Veneta, Calle Vallaresso, San Marco 1337 (☎ **041-520-2816**), is primarily known for its woven leather bags. They're sold elsewhere, but the prices are said to be less at the company's flagship outlet in Venice. The shop also sells women's shoes, suitcases, wallets, belts, and high-fashion accessories.

Furla, Mercerie del Capitello, San Marco 4954 (☎ **041-523-0611**), is a specialist in women's leather bags but sells belts and gloves as well. Many of the bags are stamped with molds, creating alligator- and lizardlike textures. You'll also find costume jewelry, silk scarves, briefcases, and wallets.

Every kind of leather work is offered at **Vogini,** Ascensione, San Marco 1291, 1292, and 1301, near Harry's Bar (☎ **041-522-2573**), especially women's handbags, which are exclusive models. There's also a large assortment of handbags in petit-point embroideries and in crocodile, plus an assortment of men's and women's shoes. Brand names include Armani, Mosquino, and Versace, plus products designed and manufactured by Vogini itself.

MARKETS If you're looking for some bargain-basement buys, head to one of the little shops lining the **Rialto Bridge.** The shops there branch out to encompass fruit and vegetable markets as well. The Rialto isn't the Ponte Vecchio in Florence, but for what it offers it isn't bad, particularly if your lire are running short. You'll find a wide assortment of merchandise, from angora sweaters to leather gloves. The quality is likely to vary widely, so plunge in with your eyes open.

PAPER Florence is still the major center in Italy for artistic paper, especially marbleized paper. However, craftspeople in Venice still make marble paper by hand, sheet by sheet. The technique offers unlimited decorative possibilities and the widest range of possible colors (craftspeople are called "color alchemists"). Each sheet of handmade marbleized paper is one of a kind.

Il Papiro, Calle del Piovan, San Marco 2764 (☎ **041-522-3055**), carries absolutely gorgeous stationery, plus photo albums, address books, picture frames, diaries, and boxes covered in artfully printed paper.

Stylish **Piazzesi,** Campiello della Feltrina, San Marco 2511 (☎ **041-522-1202**), claims to be Italy's oldest purveyor of writing paper (opened 1900). Some of its elegant lines of stationery require as many as 13 artisans to produce. Most of the production is hand-blocked, marbleized, stenciled, and/or accented with dyes that are blown onto each of the sheets with a breath-operated tube. If you want impressive paper for your social thank-you notes or wedding invitations, Piazzesi will undoubtedly have it in stock. Also look for papier-mâché masks and Commedia dell'Arte–style statues representing age-old professions like architects, carpenters, doctors, glassmakers, church officials, and notaries. Seeking something more modern? Consider any of the whimsically decorated containers for CDs and computer disks.

WOOD SCULPTURES A unique outlet in Venice is **Livio de Marchi,** San Samuele, San Marco 3157 (☎ **041-528-5694**). De Marchi and his staff can take almost any item, from cowboy boots to a Vespa to a woman's handbag, and sculpt it in wood in hyperreal detail. Even if you don't buy anything, just stop in to take a look at these stunning items sculpted from wood.

7 Venice After Dark

For such a fabled city, Venice's nightlife is pretty meager. Who wants to hit the nightclubs when strolling the city at night is more interesting than any spectacle staged inside? Ducking into a cafe or bar for a brief interlude, however, is a good way to break up your evening walk. Although Venice offers gambling and a few other diversions, it is pretty much an early-to-bed town. Most restaurants close at midnight.

The best guide to what's happening is **"Un Ospite di Venezia,"** a free pamphlet (part in English, part in Italian) distributed by the tourist office every 15 days. It lists any music and opera or theatrical presentations, along with art exhibits and local special events.

At least 10 of Venice's historic churches host **concerts,** with a constantly changing schedule. These include the Chiesa di Vivaldi, the Chiesa della Pietà, and the Chiesa Santa Maria Formosa. Many concerts are free; others charge an admission that rarely exceeds 25,000L ($12.50). For information about what's on, call ☎ **041-520-8722.**

THE PERFORMING ARTS

In January 1996, a dramatic fire left the fabled **Teatro de La Fenice** at Campo San Fantin, the city's main venue for performing arts, a blackened shell and a smoldering ruin. Opera lovers around the world, including Luciano Pavarotti, mourned its loss. The Italian government has pledged $12.5 million for its reconstruction, but restoration efforts have proceeded at the proverbial snail's pace. Who can predict when it will be done? (City officials now say it'll be late 2001, but 2002 seems more likely.) However, the theater's neoclassical facade survived the blaze and is the subject of sightseeing interest today.

Despite the tragic loss of La Fenice, cultural events have continued in a temporary theater built as a short-term substitute. Designed in the form of a big circus-style tent, within walking distance of Piazzale Roma, is the **Teatro Temporaneo de La Fenice** (aka **PalaFenice**), Isola Tronchetto (☎ **041-520-5422**). For a list of other cultural performances in Venice, contact either the tourist office or City Hall, the **Municipio Comunale di Venezia,** at ☎ **041-274-8200.**

The **Teatro Goldoni,** Calle Goldoni, near Campo San Luca, San Marco 4650B (☎ **041-520-7583**), honors Carlo Goldoni (1707–93), the most prolific and one of the best Italian playwrights. The theater presents a changing repertoire of productions, often plays in Italian, but musical presentations as well. The box office is open Monday to Saturday 10am to 1pm and 4:30 to 7pm, and tickets are 25,000 to 50,000L ($25).

CAFES

All of the cafes on Piazza San Marco offer a simply magical setting, several with full orchestras playing in the background. But you'll pay shockingly high prices (plus a hefty music charge) to enjoy a drink or a snack while you soak in this setting. Prepare yourself for it, and splurge on a beer, a cappuccino, or an ice cream anyway. It'll be the most memorable $15 or $20 (that's per person) you'll drop on your trip.

Venice's most famous spot is ✪ **Caffè Florian,** Piazza San Marco, San Marco 56–59 (☎ **041-528-5338**), built in 1720 and elaborately decorated with plush red banquettes, elaborate murals under glass, and art nouveau lighting. The Florian has hosted everyone from Casanova to Lord Byron and Goethe. Light lunch is served noon to 3pm, costing 25,000L ($12.50) and up, and an English tea 3 to 6pm, when you can select from a choice of pastries, ice creams, and cakes. It's open Thursday to Tuesday 9:30am to midnight. Closed the first week in December and the first week in January.

Previously recommended as a restaurant, ✪ **Quadri,** Piazza San Marco, San Marco 120–124 (☎ **041-522-2105**), stands on the opposite side of the square from Florian's and is as elegantly decorated in antique style. It should be, as it was founded in 1638. Wagner used to drop in for a drink when he was working on *Tristan und Isolde.* The bar was a favorite with the Austrians during their long-ago occupation. April to October, it's open daily 9am to midnight; off-season hours are Tuesday to Sunday 9am to midnight (closed the first week of December and the first week of January). The restaurant on the second floor is open the same hours as the café.

The 18th-century **Gran Caffè Lavena,** Piazza San Marco, San Marco 133–134 (☎ **041-522-4070**), is a popular but intimate cafe under the piazza's arcades. During his stay in Venice, Richard Wagner was a frequent customer; he composed some of his greatest operas here. It has one of the most beautifully ornate glass chandeliers in town. The best tables are near the plate-glass window in front, though there's plenty of room at the stand-up bar as well. It's open daily 9:30am to 12:30am (closed for a few days in January and in November and on Thursday in winter).

Although **Caffè Chioggia,** Piazza San Marco, San Marco 11 (☎ **041-528-5011**), isn't the only cafe whose entrance opens onto the piazza, it's the only one with a view of the Venetian lagoon (off to one side). Starting around 10am and continuing, with reasonable breaks, until 1:30am, music here might begin with the kind of piano music you'd expect in a bar and end with a jazz trio. Don't expect a full-fledged restaurant, as the only food served is light platters and sandwiches. Drinks include whiskey with soda, beer, and endless cups of coffee.

The hippest cafe in Venice today is funky little ✪ **Cip's,** on Isola della Guidecca (☎ **041-520-7744**), run by the owners of Harry's Bar and the Cipriani hotel. Pronounced *chips* (as in potato), this cafe with its summer terrace frames one of the grandest views of Piazza San Marco. If you arrive between May and August, ask for a Bellini, made from prosecco and white-peach purée, or perhaps a *sgroppino,* a slushy mix of lemon gelato and vodka whisked over ice. You can also order the best bitter chocolate gelato in Venice here. Cip's also serves terrific international and Venetian dishes. To reach the place, you'll have to take a vaporetto to Zittelle.

BARS & PUBS

Want more in the way of nightlife? All right, but be warned: The Venetian bar owners may sock it to you when they present the bill.

The single most famous of all the watering holes of Ernest Hemingway is ✪ **Harry's Bar,** Calle Vallaresso, San Marco 1323 (☎ **041-528-5777**). Harry's is known for inventing its own drinks and exporting them around the world, and it's said that carpaccio, the delicate raw-beef dish, was invented here. Fans say that Harry's makes the best Bellini in the world, though many old-time visitors still prefer a vodka martini. (Even Hemingway ordered a Bellini here once, though later he called it a drink for sissies, suggesting it might be ideal for Fitzgerald.) Harry's Bar is now found around the world, but this is the original (the others are unauthorized knockoffs). Celebrities frequent the place during the various film and art festivals. April to October, Harry's is open daily 10:30am to 1am (to 11pm in winter).

Bar ai Speci, in the Hotel Panada, Calle dei Specchieri, San Marco 646 (☎ **041-520-9088**), is a charming corner bar only a short walk from St. Mark's. Its richly grained paneling is offset by dozens of antique mirrors whose glittering surfaces reflect the rows of champagne and scotch bottles and the clustered groups of Biedermeier chairs. It's open Tuesday to Sunday 4:30pm to midnight.

The **Bar Ducale,** Calle delle Ostreghe, San Marco 2354 (☎ **041-521-0002**), occupies a tiny corner of a building near a bridge over a narrow canal. Customers stand at the zinc bar facing the carved 19th-century Gothic-reproduction shelves. Mimosas are the specialty, but tasty sandwiches are also offered. It's ideal for an early evening cocktail as you stroll about. Bar Ducale is open daily 9am to 9pm.

For the best Americano (sweet vermouth, bitters, and soda), head for **Bonifacio,** Calle degli Albanesi, Castello (☎ **041-522-7507**), a bar off the beaten track. This refreshing drink was said to have been invented in Venice. The Americanos here also cost far less than at the bars closer to the San Marco area.

A stone's throw from the Rialto Bridge, **Devil's Forest,** Calle Stagneri, San Marco 5185 (☎ **041-520-0623**), is an authentic Irish pub where you'll find a comfortable balance between the English- and Italian-speaking worlds. A comforting roster of beers and ales is on tap (Guinness, Harp, Kilkenny, and a line of German beers), and platters of food go for about 8,000 to 15,000L ($7.50). It's open daily 10am to 1am.

Five minutes from the Rialto Bridge, **Fiddler's Elbow,** Corte dei Pali, Cannaregio 3847 (☎ **041-523-9930**), is called "the Irish pub" by the Venetians and is run by the same people who operate the equally popular Fiddler's Elbow in Florence and Rome. It has the only satellite TV in Venice with all channels: Sky, American, sports, music, whatever. In summer, there's live outdoor music. It's open daily 5pm to 12:30am.

Do Leoni is in the Londra Palace hotel, Riva degli Schiavoni, Castello 4171 (☎ **041-520-0533**). The interior is a rich blend of scarlet-and-gold carpeting with a lion motif, English pub-style furniture, and Louis XVI–style chairs. While sipping your cocktail, you'll enjoy a view of a 19th-century bronze statue, the lagoon, and the foot traffic along the Grand Canal. A piano player entertains Monday to Saturday. Do Leoni is open daily noon to 3pm and 7:30 to 11pm (bar 10am to 1am).

Venice's oldest pastry shop, **Guanotto,** Ponte del Lovo, San Marco 4819 (☎ **041-520-8439**), is a gelateria/pasticceria/bar. It's said to have virtually invented the spritzer, a combination of soda water, bitters, and white wine. Its drinks and cocktails are renowned, though enjoying a cappuccino here can take the chill off a rainy day. Guanotto is open Monday to Saturday 7:30am to 9:30pm and Sunday 10am to 8pm.

WINE BARS

The historic **Cantina do Spade,** Calle do Spade, San Polo 860 (☎ **041-521-0574**), beneath an arcade near the main fish-and-fruit market, dates from 1475 and was once frequented by Casanova. The place is completely rustic and bare-bones, but regulars come to order *chicchetti,* the equivalent of Spanish tapas. There's no menu, but the kitchen will occasionally turn out typical Venetian fare. Many diners prefer to order one of the 250 sandwiches. Venetians delight in the 220 types of wine; glasses begin at 3,000L ($1.50). Cantina do Spade is open daily 9am to 3pm and 5pm to midnight.

Mascareta, Calle Lunga Santa Maria Formosa, Castello 5183 (☎ **041-523-0744**), opened in 1995 as a showcase for the rich assortment of Italian wines. Especially prevalent are reds and whites from the Veneto, Sicily, Pulia, and Tuscany, beginning at 2,000L ($1.15) per glass. There's only room for about 20 people at the cramped tables in this antique building. No hot food is served, but if you're hungry, you can order simple platters of cold food, from 12,000 to 18,000L ($6 to $9). It's open Monday to Saturday 6:30pm to 1am (closed mid-December to mid-January).

At **Vino Vino,** Calle del Caffettier, San Marco 2007A (☎ **041-523-7027**), you can choose from more than 250 Italian and imported wines. This place is loved by everyone from snobs to young people to almost-broke tourists. It offers wines by the bottle or glass, including Italian grappas. Popular Venetian dishes are served, including pastas, beans, baccalà (codfish), and polenta. The two rooms are always jammed like a vaporetto in rush hour, and there's take-out service if you can't find a place. Main courses are priced around 15,000L ($7.50). It's open Wednesday to Monday 10:30am to midnight.

DINING & DANCING

Near the Accademia, **Il Piccolo Mondo,** Calle Contarini Corfu, Dorsoduro 1056A (☎ **041-520-0371**), is open during the day but comes alive with dance music at night. The crowd is often young. It's open daily 10pm to 4am, but the action actually doesn't begin until after midnight. Cover, including the first drink, is 15,000L ($7.50) Thursday and Friday and 20,000L ($10) Saturday.

The **Martini Scala Club,** Campo San Fantin, San Marco 1980 (☎ **041-522-4121**), is an elegant restaurant with a piano bar. You can enjoy its food and wine until 2am—it's the only kitchen that stays open late. Dishes include smoked goose breast with grapefruit and arugula, fresh salmon with black butter and olives, or gnocchi with butter and sage. The piano bar gets going after 10pm. It's possible to order drinks without having food. The restaurant is open Thursday to Monday noon to 2:30pm and 7 to 11:30pm, Wednesday 7 to 11:30pm. Main courses begin at 36,000L ($18); a fixed-price dinner is 80,000L ($40) for four courses. The bar, which offers a piano bar and food, is open daily 10pm to 3am (closed July and August).

Early every evening except Wednesday, **Paradiso Perduto,** Fondamenta della Misericordia, Cannaregio 2540 (☎ **041-720-581**), functions as a likable tavern, serving well-prepared platters of seafood. If you're interested in dining (the *frittura mista* of fish with polenta is wonderful), main courses are 14,000 to 20,000L ($10) and served Thursday to Tuesday 7 to 11pm, Sunday noon to 3pm. But the place's real heart and soul emerge after 11pm, when a mix of soft recorded music and live piano music creates a backdrop for animated dialogues between the neighborhood crowd and visitors. The chitchat continues until at least 2am.

GAY CLUBS

There are no gay bars in Venice, but you'll find some in nearby **Padua,** a lovely old city about 35 minutes from Venice by train (see chapter 9). However, Venice does have a local division of a government-affiliated agency, **ArciGay ArciLesbica,** Campo San Giacomo dell'Orio, Santa Croce 1507 (☎ **041-721-197**). It serves as a kind of home base for the gay community, with info on gay-friendly accommodations and such. The best hours to call (it's hard to find) are Wednesday, Thursday, and Saturday 6 to 10pm.

CASINOS

Venice is home to two casinos. The larger and busier of the two, the Casino Municipale, lies beside the flat, sandy expanses of the Lido; it's almost deserted in winter and mobbed in summer. As cold winds descend on Venice from the Alps in winter, the action moves back to the center of town, to a cozier venue known as the Vendramin-Calergi Palace.

Regardless of where you might happen to drop your lire, know in advance that a jacket (but not a tie) is requested for men, and basketball sneakers and/or shorts are forbidden. Both casinos contain slot machines, but more interesting are the roulette wheels, where minimum bets are 10,000L ($5) and maximum wagers 360,000L ($180).

If you want to risk your luck and your lire, take a vaporetto ride on the Casino Express, which leaves from stops at the rail station, Piazzale Roma, and Piazzetta San Marco and delivers you to the landing dock of the **Casino Municipale,** Lungomare G. Marconi 4, Lido (☎ **041-529-7111**). The Italian government wisely forbids its nationals to cross the threshold unless they work here, so bring your passport. The building itself is foreboding, looking as if it had been inspired by Mussolini-era architects. Don't worry—the mood changes once you step inside. You can try your luck at blackjack, roulette, baccarat, or whatever. You can also dine, drink at the bar, or enjoy a floor show. Admission is 18,000L ($9), and it's open July to September, daily 3pm to 2:30am.

October to June, the casino action is at the 15th-century **Vendramin-Calergi Palace,** Strada Nuova, Cannaregio 2040 (☎ **041-529-7111**). Incidentally, in 1883 Wagner died in this house, which opens onto the Grand Canal. Admission is 10,000L ($5), and it's open daily 3pm to 2:30am. Only slot machines are maintained during summer, at the same hours.

8 The Lagoon Islands of Murano, Burano & Torcello

MURANO

For centuries, glassblowers on the island of Murano have turned out those fantastic chandeliers Victorian ladies used to prize so highly. They also produce heavily ornamented glasses so ruby-red or so indigo-blue you can't tell if you're drinking blackberry juice or pure grain alcohol. Happily, the glassblowers are still plying their trade, though increasing competition (notably from Sweden) has compelled a greater degree of sophistication in design.

Murano remains the chief expedition from Venice, but it's not the most beautiful nearby island. (Burano and Torcello are far more attractive.)

You can combine a tour of Murano with a trip along the lagoon. To reach Murano, take **vaporetto no. 12 or 13** at Riva degli Schiavoni, a short walk from Piazzetta San Marco. The boat docks at the landing platform at Murano where the first furnace awaits conveniently. It's best to go Monday to Friday 10am to noon if you want to see some glassblowing action.

TOURING THE GLASS FACTORIES & OTHER SIGHTS

As you stroll through Murano, you'll find that the factory owners are only too glad to let you come in and see their age-old crafts. While browsing through the showrooms, you'll need stiff resistance to keep the salespeople at bay. Bargaining is expected. Don't—repeat *don't*—pay the marked price on any item. That's merely the figure at which to open negotiations.

A Special Glass Museum

For a really special museum, call for an appointment to visit the **Barovier & Toso Museum,** Palazzo Contarini, Fondamenta Vetrai 28, Murano (☎ **041-739-049**). Here Angelo Barovier displays rare glass from his private collection acquired over half a century. The museum is open (providing you call first) during foundry hours Monday to Friday 9:30am to noon and 2:30 to 5pm.

However, the prices of made-on-the-spot souvenirs aren't negotiable. For example, you may want to buy a horse streaked with blue. The artisan takes a piece of incandescent glass, huffs, puffs, rolls it, shapes it, snips it, and behold—he has shaped a horse. The showrooms of Murano also contain a fine assortment of Venetian crystal beads, available in every hue. You may find some of the best work to be the experiments of apprentices.

While on the island, you can visit the Renaissance palazzo housing the **Museo Vetrario di Murano,** Fondamenta Giustinian 8 (☎ **041-739-586**), which contains a spectacular collection of Venetian glass. From April to October, it's open Monday, Tuesday, and Thursday to Saturday from 10am to 5pm (to 4pm November to March). Admission is 8,000L ($4).

If you're looking for something different, head to **San Pietro Martire,** Fondamente Vetrai (☎ **041-739-704**), which dates from the 1300s but was rebuilt in 1511 and is richly decorated with paintings by Tintoretto and Veronese. Its proud possession is a *Madonna and Child Enthroned* by Giovanni Bellini, plus two superb altarpieces by the same master. The church lies right before the junction with Murano's Grand Canal, about 250 yards from the vaporetto landing stage. It's open daily 9am to noon and 3 to 6pm; closed for Mass on Sunday morning.

Even more notable is **Santa Maria e Donato,** Campo San Donato (☎ **041-739-056**), open daily 9am to noon and 4 to 6pm with time variations for Sunday Mass. Dating from the 7th century but reconstructed in the 1100s, this building is a stellar example of Venetian Byzantine style, despite its 19th-century restoration. The interior is known for its mosaic floor (a parade of peacocks and eagles, as well as other creatures) and a 15th-century ship's-keel ceiling. Over the apse is an outstanding mosaic of the Virgin against a gold background from the early 1200s.

DINING

Ai Vetrai. Fondamenta Manin 29. ☎ **041-739-293.** Reservations recommended. Main courses 17,000–35,000L ($8.50–$17.50). AE, DC, MC, V. Daily 9am–7pm. Closed Jan. Vaporetto: 42 or 61. VENETIAN.

Ai Vetrai entertains and nourishes its guests in a large room not far from the Canale dei Vetrai. If you're looking for fish prepared in the local style, with arguably the widest selection on Murano, this is it. Most varieties of crustaceans and gilled creatures are available on the spot. However, if you phone ahead and order food for a large party, as the Venetians sometimes do, the owners will prepare what they call "a noble fish." You might begin with spaghetti in green clam sauce and follow with *griglia misto di pesce,* a dish that combines all the seafood of the Adriatic or other types of grilled or baked fish accented with vegetables.

BURANO

Burano became world famous as a center of lace making, a craft that reached its pinnacle in the 18th century. The visitor who can spare a morning to visit this island will be rewarded with a charming fishing village far removed in spirit from the grandeur of Venice but only half an hour away by ferry. **Boats** leave from Fondamente Nuove, overlooking the Venetian graveyard (which is well worth the trip all on its own). To reach Fondamente Nuove, take **vaporetto no. 12 or 52** from Riva degli Schiavoni.

EXPLORING THE ISLAND

Once at Burano, you'll discover that the houses of the islanders come in varied colors: sienna, robin's egg or cobalt blue, barn red, butterscotch, grass green.

Check out the **Scuola di Merletti di Burano,** "Museo del Merletto," San Martino Destra 183 (☎ **041-730-034**), in the center of the village at Piazza Baldassare Galuppi. From November to March, the museum is open Wednesday to Monday 10am to 4pm (to 5pm April to October). Admission is 5,000L ($2.50). The Burano School of Lace was founded in 1872 as part of a movement aimed at restoring the age-old craft that had earlier declined, giving way to such lace-making centers as Chantilly and Bruges. On the second floor you can see the lace makers, mostly young women, at their painstaking work and can purchase hand-embroidered or handmade lace items.

After visiting the lace school, walk across the square to the **Duomo** and its leaning **campanile** (inside, look for the *Crucifixion* by Tiepolo). See it while you can, because the bell tower is leaning so precariously it looks as if it may topple at any moment.

DINING

Ostaria ai Pescatori. Piazza Baldassare Galuppi 371. ☎ **041-730-650.** Reservations recommended. Main courses 24,000–35,000L ($12–$17.50). Thurs–Tues noon–3pm and 6–9:30pm. Closed Jan. Vaporetto: Line 12 or 52. SEAFOOD.

This restaurant opened 200 years ago in a building that was antique even then. Today, Paolo Torcellan and his wife are the gracious owners, serving a cuisine prepared with gusto by his stalwart mother, Iolanda, in her 70s. The place has gained a reputation as the preserver of a type of simple restaurant unique to Burano. Patrons often take the vaporetto from other sections of Venice (the restaurant lies close to the boat landing) to eat at the plain wooden tables set up indoors or on the small square in front. Specialties feature all the staples of the Venetian seaside diet, like fish soup, *risotto di pesce,* pasta seafarer style, tagliolini in squid ink, and a wide range of crustaceans, plus grilled, fried, and baked fish. Dishes prepared with local game are also available, but you must request them well in advance. Your meal might include a bottle of fruity wine from the region.

TORCELLO

Of all the islands of the lagoon, Torcello, the so-called Mother of Venice, offers the most charm. If Burano is behind the times, Torcello is positively antediluvian. You can stroll across a grassy meadow, traverse an ancient stone bridge, and step back into that time when the Venetians first fled from invading barbarians to create a city of Neptune in the lagoon.

To reach Torcello, take **vaporetto no. 12** from Fondamenta Nuova on Murano. The trip takes about 45 minutes.

Warning: If you go to Torcello on your own, don't listen to the gondoliers who hover at the ferry quay. They'll tell you that the cathedral and the locanda are miles away. Actually, they're both reached after a leisurely 12- to 15-minute stroll along the canal.

EXPLORING THE ISLAND

Torcello has two major attractions: a church with Byzantine mosaics good enough to make Empress Theodora at Ravenna turn as purple with envy as her robe, and a locanda (inn) that converts day-trippers into inebriated angels of praise. First the spiritual nourishment, then the alcoholic sustenance.

Cattedrale di Torcello, also called **Santa Maria Assunta Isola di Torcello** (☎ **041-730-084**), was founded in A.D. 639 and subsequently rebuilt. It stands in a lonely grassy meadow beside an 11th-century campanile. The stars here are its Byzantine mosaics. Clutching her child, the weeping Madonna in the apse is a magnificent sight, and on the opposite wall is a powerful *Last Judgment.* Byzantine artisans, it seems, were at their best in portraying hell and damnation. In their *Inferno,* they've re-created a virtual human stew with the fires stirred by wicked demons. Reptiles slide in and out of the skulls of cannibalized sinners. The church is open daily: April to October 10am to 12:30pm and 2:30 to 6pm (to 5pm November to March). Admission is 2,000L ($1).

DINING

Locanda Cipriani. Piazza San Fosca 29, Torcello. ☎ **041-730-150.** Reservations recommended. Main courses 30,000–45,000L ($15–$22.50). AE, DC, MC, V. Wed–Mon noon–3pm; Fri–Sat 7–10pm. Closed Jan 15–Feb 15. Vaporetto: Line 12 and 14. VENETIAN.

This place is operated by the same folks behind the Hotel Cipriani and Harry's Bar (actually by the very cosmopolitan Bonifacio Brass, nephew of Harry Cipriani). This artfully simple locanda is deliberately rustic, light-years removed from the family's grander venues. Menu items are uncompromisingly classic, with deep roots in family tradition. A good example is *filleto di San Pietro alla Carlina* (fillet of John Dory in the style of Carla, a late and much-revered matriarch, who made the dish for decades using tomatoes and capers). Also look for carpaccio Cipriani, *risotto alla Torcellano* (with fresh vegetables and herbs from the family's garden), fish soup, *tagliolini verdi gratinati,* and a traditional roster of veal, liver, fish, and beef dishes.

9 The Veneto & the Dolomites

Venice doesn't have a monopoly on art or architectural treasures. Of the cities of interest that you can easily reach from Venice, in the area known as the Veneto, three tower above the rest: Verona, home of the eternal lovers Romeo and Juliet; Padua, the city of Mantegna, with frescoes by Giotto; and Vicenza, the city of Palladio, with streets of Renaissance palazzi and hills studded with villas. If time remains, you can also explore the Riviera del Brenta, with its Venetian palazzi and such historic old cities as Treviso and Bassano del Grappa. The miracle of these cities is that, even though Venice dominated them for centuries, the Serene Republic didn't completely siphon off their creative drive.

If you have even more time, you can venture farther afield to the limestone **Dolomites (Dolomiti),** one of Europe's greatest natural attractions. Some of these peaks in the northeastern Italian Alps soar to 10,500 feet. The Dolomiti are a year-round destination, with two high seasons: midsummer, when the hiking is great, and winter, when the skiers slide in. At times, the Dolomiti form fantastic shapes, combining to create a primordial landscape, with mountain chains resembling the teeth of a giant dragon. Clefts descend precipitously along jagged rocky walls, and at other points a vast flat tableland, spared nature's fury, emerges.

The provinces of Trent and Bolzano (Bozen in German) form the **Trentino–Alto Adige** region, full of German-speaking visitors who flock to the spas located in its pristine alpine lakes and mountains. Many of its waters (some of which are radioactive) are said to have curative powers. The Alto Adige province around Bolzano was until 1919 known as South Tyrol and was part of Austria. And even though today it belongs to Italy, it's still very much Tyrolean in character, both in its language (German) and in its dress. Today, the Trentino–Alto Adige region functions with a great deal of autonomy from the national government.

Readers with an extra day or so to spare may first want to postpone their Dolomite adventure for a detour to **Trieste,** the unofficial capital of **Friuli–Venezia Giulia.** It was Venice's main rival in the Adriatic from the 9th to the 15th century. Even though Trieste doesn't boast Venice's charm, it is still one of Italy's most interesting ports, with Hapsburg monuments at its core and the world's largest accessible cave on its outskirts.

1 The Riviera del Brenta

The **Brenta Canal,** running from Fusina to Padua, functioned as a mainland extension of Venice during the Renaissance, when wealthy merchants began using the area as a retreat from the city's summer heat. Dubbed the Riviera del Brenta, the 10½-mile (17km) stretch along the banks of the canal from Malcontenta to Stra is renowned for its gracious villas, 44 of which are still visible.

The region's primary architect was **Andrea di Pietro,** known as **Palladio** (1508–80), who designed 19 of the villas. Inspired by ancient Roman architecture, Palladio's singular design—square, perfectly proportioned, functionally elegant—became the standard by which villas were judged. His designs are familiar to Americans as the basis for most state capitals and for Jefferson's Monticello, and to the British as the most common design for country estates. The importance of villa life to the Venetians was such that it gained immortality in *The Merchant of Venice,* in which Portia's home is a villa at Belmont along the Brenta.

ESSENTIALS

GETTING THERE Consider an all-day guided excursion by **boat** along the Brenta Canal as far as Padua, including many of the most important Renaissance monuments en route. **American Express (☎ 041-520-0844)** will sell you tickets for the Burchiello Excursion Boat. March to October, trips depart from the piers at Piazza San Marco every Tuesday, Thursday, and Saturday at 9am for a ride that includes a running bilingual commentary from an on-board host. The price is 125,000L ($62.50) per person, plus 50,000L ($25) for an optional lunch in historic Oriago. You get glimpses of the elegant villas that seem to cling to the shorelines, guided visits through the evocative villas at Malcontenta and Oriago, and a somewhat rushed tour through the most spectacular sights of Padua after the boat docks. At 6:10pm, you board a bus for transit back to Venice.

You can tour the Brenta Riviera by means of **buses** leaving from Venice headed for Padua. The buses, operated by the local **ACTV** line (**☎ 041-528-7886**), depart from the Venetian company's ticket office in Piazzale Roma Monday to Saturday every 15 to 30 minutes starting at 6:10am. A one-way ticket to Villa Foscari is 1,500L (75¢) and a one-way fare to the Villa Pisano 5,000L ($2.50).

If you have a **car,** note that all villas open to the public are on the north bank of the canal directly along Rte. S11 headed west out of Venice toward Padua. The road follows the canal, offering you a chance to glimpse the other villas, situated on both banks. At the APT in Venice, you can pick up the visitor's guide "Riviera del Brenta Venezia," offering background info on the villas and a map of their locations between Malcontenta and Stra.

The most luxurious way to tour the villas is by **personal guide.** Rates depend on where you want to go and how much you want to take in during a day. A list of guides along with their fixed fees is available from the principal **APT tourist office** at San Marco 71/F, off Piazza San Marco in Venice (**☎ 041-529-8711**). You can also contact the **Guides Association** in Venice at Calle San Antonio, Castello 5448A (**☎ 041-520-9038**).

VISITOR INFORMATION Contact the **APT tourist office** of Riviera del Brenta, Via Don Minzoni 26, 30034 Mira Porte, Venezia (**☎ 041-424-973**). April to September, it's open Tuesday to Saturday 8:30am to 1:30pm and 2 to 4pm; October to March, hours are Thursday 3 to 5pm, Friday and Saturday 10am to 2pm.

The Veneto & the Dolomites

Mittewald
Drau
Millstatter See
Weissensee
Liesing
Gail
Forni Avoltri
S. Stefano di Cad.
Sappada
Paluzza
Pontebba
Vigo
Forni di Sopra
Ampezzo
Dogna
Tolmezzo
Villa Santina
Resiutta
Stolvizza
M. Pramaggiore
A23
Venzone
Bohinjsko Jazero
S. Francesco
Gemona d. Friuli
Chievolis
Claut
Mecuno
Kobarid
Tarcento
Maniago
Pinzano
Cividale d. Friuli
Spilimbergo
Udine
Kanal
Avrano
S. Martino di C.
Digliano
Paparotti
S. Giorgio
Fontanafredda
Tagliamento
Pordenone
S13
Pozzuolo
Manzano
Nova Gorica
A23
Gorizia
Casarsa
Flambro
Palmanova
Brugnera
Villalta
Torsa
Cervignano di Friuli
Annone
Oderzo
Marano
Ausa-corno
Monfalcone
Aquileia
A4
Portogruaro
Grignano
Ponte di Piave
Ceggia
Trieste
Lignano Sabbiadoro
Grado
Livenza
Brussa
Golfo di Trieste
S. Dona di Piave
Bibione
Caposile
Caorle
Lido di Jesolo
Golfo di Venezia

TOURING THE VILLAS

The villa closest to Venice that's open for tours is the **Villa Foscari (Villa La Malcontenta)**, Via dei Turisti 9, Malcontenta (☎ **041-520-3966**), on Rte. S11 about 2½ miles (4km) west of where the canal empties into the Venetian Lagoon. It was constructed by Palladio for the Foscari family in 1560. A Foscari wife was exiled here for some alleged misdeed she did to her husband, and the unhappiness surrounding the incident gave the name Malcontenta (unhappy one) to the villa and its village. It's open Tuesday and Saturday 9am to noon, with a 12,000L ($6) admission; you can call Monday to Friday and make reservations to see it on other days.

In Stra, 20 miles (32km) west of Venice on Rte. S11, stands the **Villa Pisani (Villa Nazionale;** ☎ **049-502-074)**. Built in 1720 as a palatial retreat for Doge Alvise Pisani, it became the Italian home of Napoléon and later served as the initial meeting site of Mussolini and Hitler. Given this historical context, it's no surprise that the villa is the largest and grandest. A reflecting pool out front gives added dimension, and a small army of statues stands guard over the premises. The highlights of a visit are the magnificent Giambattista Tiepolo frescoes, painted on the ballroom ceiling to depict the *Glory of the Pisani Family*, in which family members are surrounded by hovering angels and saints. From October to March, the villa is open daily 9am to 4pm and from April to September 9am to 6pm. Admission is 10,000L ($5) for both the park and museum but only 5,000L ($2.50) to explore just the park.

There are other villas you can visit along the Riviera, each with a stately private home whose owners appreciate and fiercely protect the unique nature of their property. Although each welcomes the occasional appropriately respectful visitor, call in advance before you drop in. These structures don't follow the gracefully symmetrical rhythms of Palladio: Each appears to be a larger version of the palazzi lining Venice's Grand Canal.

They include the **Villa Sagredo,** Via Sagredo (☎ **049-503-174;** after hours, 041-412-967), half a mile northwest of the hamlet of Vigonovo. In a suitably gnarled garden, it was built on ancient Roman foundations, and the form it has today dates from around 1700, the result of frequent rebuildings. You must reserve in advance, and they prefer scheduled visits Tuesday to Friday 5 to 10pm or Saturday and Sunday 2 to around 8pm. A restaurant and a bar serve simple food and drink. Admission is free.

Also appealing, but without any public facilities, is the private home of **Dr. Bruno Bellemo,** Villa Gradenigo, Riviera San Pietro 75 in Oriago (☎ **049-876-0233**). Adjacent to the pier where boats from Venice and Padua are moored, it's a pure 16th-century adaptation of a Venetian palazzo whose interior is noted for a series of frescoes

Wine Tasting

Important vineyards in the Veneto include **Azienda Vinicola Fratelli Fabiano,** Via Verona 6, 37060 Sona, near Verona (☎ **045-608-1111**), and **Fratelli Bolla,** Piazza Cittadella 3, 37122 Verona (☎ **045-809-0911**). Smaller, but well respected because of recent improvements to its vintages, is **Nino Franco** (known for its sparkling prosecco), in the hamlet of Valdobbiadene, Via Garibaldi 177, 31049 Treviso (☎ **0423/972-051**). For information on these and the dozens of other producers in the Veneto, contact the **Azienda di Promozione Turistica,** Via Leoncino 61, 37121 Verona (☎ **045-592-828**). If you plan to tour around the countryside and do a little wine tasting and vineyard touring, it's best to call ahead and make an appointment and get detailed directions. See also "The Wine Roads from Treviso" box under "Treviso" later in this chapter.

executed by the brothers of Veronese, Paolo and Benedetto Caliari. Look for a small but verdant garden around it. Visitors and art students, if it's convenient for the owners, are welcomed inside, usually for free or a donation of 10,000L ($5), but only Tuesday to Friday 9am to noon and 2:30 to 6pm or Saturday and Sunday 10am to 6pm. Unless you're traveling with a group, it's best to call ahead.

ACCOMMODATIONS

Dolo, 15 minutes by car from Venice or Padua, is at the midpoint of the Brenta Canal. It contains several villas from the 17th and 18th centuries, most of which are still inhabited. **Mira** is 10 minutes from Venice and 20 minutes from Padua at the most scenic bend of the Brenta; it's no wonder that several villas lie in the area.

Villa Ducale. Riviera Martiri della Libertà 75, 30031 Dolo. ☎ **041-560-8020.** Fax 041-560-8004. www.villaducale.it. E-mail: info@villaducale.it. 11 units. A/C MINIBAR TV TEL. 220,000–280,000L ($110–$140) double; 300,000L ($150) suite. Rates include breakfast. AE, DC, MC, V. Free parking in lot.

This villa, built in 1884 by Count Giulio Rocca, has been turned into a hotel. Restored to its original grandeur, it's graced with Murano glass chandeliers, elaborate frescoes, luxurious fabrics, and antique furnishings. The beautifully furnished guest rooms overlook the statue-filled grounds and come with safe-deposit boxes, trouser presses, and firm mattresses. The baths have hair dryers. Le Colonne restaurant specializes in Venetian seafood.

Villa Margherita. Via Nazionale 416–417, 30030 Mira, Venezia. ☎ **041-426-5800.** Fax 041-426-5838. www.charminghotels.it or www.romantikhotels.com. 19 units. A/C MINIBAR TV TEL. 345,000–440,000L ($172.50–$220) double. Rates include buffet breakfast. AE, DC, MC, V.

This 17th-century villa is on a particularly scenic bend of the Brenta. It features marble columns and fireplaces, marble and terra-cotta floors, frescoes and stucco work, a sunny breakfast room, and guest rooms that blend individualized traditional elegance with modern comfort. The rooms come in various shapes and sizes, each containing quality mattresses and first-rate linen. The tiled bathrooms are well equipped and have adequate shelf space. An immense park opens up behind the villa.

Dining/Diversions: The restaurant serves the freshest Venetian seafood as well as a large selection of fine wines and champagnes.

Amenities: Room service, laundry/dry cleaning, newspaper delivery, baby-sitting, bike rental, nature trails, and access to a nearby health club and 18-hole golf course.

DINING

Trattoria Nalin. Via Nuovissimo 29, Mira. ☎ **041-420-083.** Reservations recommended. Main courses 20,000–30,000L ($10–$15). AE, DC, MC, V. Tues–Sun noon–2:30pm; Tues–Sat 7:30–10pm. Closed Aug and Dec 26–Jan 6. VENETIAN/SEAFOOD.

Most of the Riviera del Brenta's restaurants focus on seafood, and this one is no exception. In a century-old building, the restaurant has flourished as a family-run enterprise since the 1960s. It's adjacent to the canal near the town center, and you'll probably gravitate to the terrace, where potted shrubs and flowers bloom in summer. The specialties vary with whatever happens to be in season but are likely to include *tagliatelle con salsa di calamaretti* (with squid sauce), *spaghetti al nero* (with octopus ink), crabs from the Venetian lagoon, and variations on polenta and risotto.

2 Padua

25 miles (40km) W of Venice, 50 miles (81km) E of Verona, 145 miles (233km) E of Milan

Padua (Padova) no longer looks as it did when Richard Burton's Petruchio tamed Elizabeth Taylor's Katerina in the Zeffirelli adaptation of *The Taming of the Shrew.* However, it remains a major art center of the Veneto.

Many visitors stay in more affordable Padua and commute to high-priced Venice. Of course, Padua doesn't have the beauty of Venice and suffers from high-rises and urban blight, but its inner core has a wealth of attractions. Its university, Italy's second oldest, adds life and vibrancy, even though such visitors and professors as Dante and Galileo haven't been seen here in a while.

ESSENTIALS

GETTING THERE The **train** is best if you're coming from Venice, Milan, or Bologna. Trains depart for/arrive from Venice once every 30 minutes (trip time: 30 minutes), costing 4,500L ($2.25) one way. Trains to/from Milan run every hour (trip time: 2¹/₂ hours) for 20,000L ($10) one way. For information and schedules, call ☎ **049-875-1800** or 1478-88-088 toll-free in Italy. Padua's main rail terminus is at Piazza Stazione, north of the historic core and outside the 16th-century walls. A bus will connect you to the center.

Buses from Venice arrive every 30 minutes (trip time: 45 minutes), costing 5,200L ($2.60) one-way. There are also connections from Vicenza every 30 minutes (trip time: 30 minutes) at 5,100L ($2.55) one way. Padua's bus station is at Via Trieste 42 (☎ **049-820-6844**), near Piazza Boschetti, 5 minutes from the rail station.

If you have a **car,** take A4 west from Venice.

VISITOR INFORMATION The **tourist office** is at Riviera Mugnai 8 (☎ **049-876-7911**). April to October, it's open Monday to Saturday 9am to 7pm and Sunday 9am to noon; November to March, hours are Monday to Saturday 9:15am to 5:45pm and Sunday 9am to noon..

SEEING THE SIGHTS

A university that grew to fame throughout Europe was founded here as early as 1222. The **University of Padua** has remained one of the great centers for learning in Italy. The physics department counts Galileo among its past professors, and Petrarch lectured here. Today its buildings are scattered around the city. The historic main building is called **Il Bo,** after an inn on the site that used an ox as its sign. The chief entrance is on Via Otto Febbraio. Of particular interest is an anatomy theater, which dates from 1594 and was the first of its kind in Europe. For 5,000L ($2.50), you can join a guided tour of the university. On Tuesday, Thursday, and Saturday tours depart at 9, 10, and 11am; Monday, Wednesday, and Friday at 3, 4, and 5pm.

For information, contact the **Associazione Guide di Padova** at ☎ **049-820-9711.**

If you're on a tight schedule, concentrate on the Cappella degli Scrovegni (Giotto frescoes) and the Basilica di Sant'Antonio.

A **combination ticket** valid for admission to all of Padua's museums costs 15,000L ($7.50). It is available at the tourist office or any of the city's museums.

✪ **Chapel of the Scrovegni (Cappella degli Scrovegni).** Piazza Eremitani, off Corso Garibaldi. ☎ **049-820-4550.** Admission 15,000L ($7.50) (including entry to Civil Museums, Palace of Law). Feb–Oct daily 9am–7pm (to 6pm Nov–Jan). Bus: 3, 8, 12, or 18.

This modest chapel is the best reason for visiting Padua, for it contains remarkably preserved **Giotto frescoes.** Sometime around 1305 and 1306, Giotto did a cycle of more than 35 frescoes here, which, along with those at Assisi (see chapter 6), form the basis of his claim to fame. Like an illustrated storybook, the frescoes unfold biblical scenes. The third bottom panel (lower level on the right) depicts Judas kissing a most skeptical Christ and is the most reproduced panel. On the entrance wall is Giotto's *Last Judgment,* in which hell wins out for sheer fascination. The master's representation of the *Vices and Virtues* is bizarre; it reveals the depth of his imagination in personifying nebulous evil and elusive good. One of the most dramatic panels depicts the raising of Lazarus from the dead—a masterfully balanced scene, rhythmically ingenious for its day. The swathed and cadaverous Lazarus, however, looks indecisive as to whether or not he'll rejoin the living.

Civic Museum (Museo Civico di Padova). Piazza Eremitani 8. ☎ **049-820-4550.** Admission included with entry to Cappella degli Scrovegni and to Palace of Law. Apr–Oct Tues–Sun 9am–7pm (to 6pm Nov–Mar). Bus: 3, 8, 12, or 18.

This picture gallery is filled with minor works by major Venetian artists, some dating from the 14th century. Look for a wooden Crucifix by Giotto and two miniatures by Giorgione. Other works are Giovanni Bellini's *Portrait of a Young Man* and Jacopo Bellini's miniature *Descent into Limbo,* with its childlike devils. The 15th-century Arras tapestry is also on display. Other works are Veronese's *Martyrdom of St. Primo and St. Feliciano,* plus Tintoretto's *Supper in Simone's House* and *Crucifixion,* probably the finest single painting in the gallery.

Chiesa degli Eremitani. Piazza Eremitani 9. ☎ **049-875-6410.** Free admission (donations accepted). Mon–Sat 8am–12:30pm and 4–6pm; Sun and religious holidays 9:30am–noon and 4–6pm. Bus: 3, 8, 12, or 18.

One of Padua's tragedies occurred when this church was bombed on March 11, 1944. Before that, it housed one of the greatest treasures in Italy, the **Ovetari Chapel (Cappella Ovetari),** with the first significant cycle of frescoes by Andrea Mantegna (1431–1506). The church was rebuilt, but, alas, you can't resurrect 15th-century frescoes. To the right of the main altar are the fragments left after the bombing. The most interesting fresco saved is a panel depicting the dragging of St. Christopher's body through the streets. Note also the *Assumption of the Virgin.* Like Leonardo, the artist had a keen eye for architectural detail.

✪ **Basilica di Sant'Antonio.** Piazza del Santo 11. ☎ **049-824-2811.** Free admission. Daily 7:30am–7pm. Bus: 8, 12, 18, 22, M, or T.

This basilica was built in the 13th century and dedicated to St. Anthony of Padua, who's interred within. It's a synthesis of styles, with mainly Romanesque and Gothic features. Campaniles and minarets combine to give it an Eastern appearance. Inside, the church is richly frescoed and decorated, filled with pilgrims devoutly touching the saint's **marble tomb.** One of the more unusual relics is in the treasury: the 7-centuries-old, still-uncorrupted tongue of St. Anthony.

The great art treasurers are the **Donatello bronzes** at the main altar, with a realistic Crucifix towering over the rest. Seek out as well the **Donatello relief** depicting the removal of Christ from the cross (at the back of the high altar), a unified composition expressing in simple lines and with an unromantic approach the tragedy of Christ and the sadness of the mourners.

Among his other innovations, Donatello restored the lost art of the **equestrian statue** with the well-known example in front of the basilica. Although the man it honors (Gattamelata) is of little interest to art lovers, the 1453 statue is of prime importance. The large horse is realistic, as Donatello was a master of detail. He cleverly directs the eye to the commanding face of the Venetian military hero, nicknamed "Spotted Cat." Gattamelata was a dead ringer for the late Laurence Olivier.

Palace of Law (Palazzo della Ragione). Via VIII Febbraio, between Piazza delle Erbe and Piazza dell Frutta. ☎ **049-820-5006.** Admission included with entry to Cappella degli Scrovegni and to the Civil Museum. Tues–Sun 9am–7pm. Bus: 8 or A.

This palazzo, dating from the early 13th century, is among the most remarkable buildings of northern Italy. It sits in the marketplace, ringed with loggias and with a roof shaped like the hull of a sailing vessel. Climb the steps and enter the grandiose **Salone,** a 270-foot assembly hall containing a gigantic 15th-century wooden horse. The walls are richly frescoed with symbolic paintings that replaced the frescoes by Giotto and his assistants that were destroyed by fire in 1420.

SHOPPING

Padua is an elegant town with a rich university life, a solid industrial base, and an economy too diversified to rely exclusively on tourism. Therefore, you'll find a wide roster of upscale consumer goods and luxury items and less emphasis on souvenirs and handcrafts. For insights into the good life *alla Padovese,* trek through the neighborhood around the landmark **Piazza Insurrezione,** especially the **Galleria Borghese,** a conglomeration of shops off Via San Fermo.

Droves of shoppers head to the **Prato delle Valle** on the third Sunday of every month, when more than 200 antiques and collectibles vendors set up shop for the day. The square, one of the largest in all Europe, also hosts a smaller **weekly market** on Saturday. Shoes from nearby Brenta factories are the prevalent product, but the range of goods offered remains eclectic.

The outdoor markets (Monday through Saturday) in the twin **Piazza delle Erbe** (for fresh produce) and **Piazza della Frutta** (dry goods), flanking the enormous Palazzo della Ragione, are some of Italy's best.

ACCOMMODATIONS

✪ **Albergo Leon Bianco.** Piazzetta Pedrocchi 12, 35122 Padova. ☎ **049-875-0814.** Fax 049-875-6184. E-mail: leonbianco@toscanelli.com. 22 units. A/C MINIBAR TV TEL. From 169,000L ($84.50) double. Breakfast 15,000L ($7.50). AE, MC, V. Parking 27,000L ($13.50). Bus: 18.

This is Padua's most old-fashioned and historic hotel, built "sometime after 1850." At the time, this "White Lion" was much larger, but during the 20th century it was whittled away to only 22 rooms. It has bright (sometimes jarring) colors, an odd-looking modern entrance set into a massive arch, and a cafe/breakfast area on the panoramic rooftop (during warm weather, it blossoms with an exotic collection of geraniums). The guest rooms range from small to medium, each fitted with a quality mattress and crisp linen. The tiled bathrooms are compact (hair dryers are available at the desk). Breakfast is the only meal served, and the staff is much more articulate and charming than at similar hotels in the region.

Hotel Donatello. Piazza del Santo 102–104, 35123 Padova. ☎ **049-875-0634.** Fax 049-875-0829. 53 units. A/C MINIBAR TV TEL. 240,000–255,000L ($120–$127.50) double; 330,000–420,000L ($165–$210) suite. Breakfast 20,000L ($10). AE, DC, MC, V. Closed Dec 15–Jan 15. Parking 28,000L ($14). Bus: 3, 8, or 12.

The Donatello is a renovated hotel with an ideal location near the basilica. Its facade is pierced by an arched arcade, and the chandeliers of its lobby combine with the checkerboard marble floor to create a hospitable ambience. The guest rooms are reasonably comfortable, if unremarkable. Most come with private balconies; the compact tiled bathrooms have hair dryers. The Donatello's terraced restaurant is its most alluring feature.

Hotel Europa. Largo Europa 9, 35137 Padova. ☎ **049-661-200.** Fax 049-661-508. 64 units. A/C MINIBAR TV TEL. 234,000L ($117) double. Rates include breakfast. AE, DC, MC, V. Parking 25,000L ($12.50).

The Europa was built in the 1960s and looks its age, but it's still a good buy. The compact and serviceable guest rooms have simple built-in furnishings and open onto small balconies. The tiled bathrooms come with hair dryers. The public rooms are enhanced by cubist murals, free-form ceramic plaques, and furniture placed in conversational groupings. The American bar is popular, and the Zaramella Restaurant features a good Paduan cuisine, with an emphasis on seafood.

Hotel Plaza. Corso Milano 40, 35139 Padova. ☎ **049-656-822.** Fax 049-661-117. www.plazapadova.it. E-mail: direzione@plazapadova.it. 142 units. A/C MINIBAR TV TEL. 310,000L ($155) double; 380,000–500,000L ($190–$250) suite. Rates include buffet breakfast. AE, DC, MC, V. Parking 25,000L ($12.50). Bus: 5, 7, or 10.

The Plaza is Padua's leading inn, a business hotel with brown ceramic tiles and concrete-trimmed square windows. The entrance is under a modern concrete arcade leading into a contemporary lobby. The guest rooms are comfortable and well decorated, though a bit sterile. Nonetheless, each comes with a good mattress and a tiled bathroom. The bar, which you reach through a stairwell and an upper balcony dotted with modern paintings, is a relaxing place for a drink. The restaurant serves a Venetian and international cuisine and is open Monday to Saturday 7:30 to 10:30pm.

Majestic Hotel Toscanelli. Piazzetta dell'Arco 2, 35122 Padova. ☎ **049-663-244.** Fax 049-876-0025. www.toscanelli.com. E-mail: majestic@toscanelli.com. 32 units. 270,000L ($135) double; from 350,000L ($175) suite. Rates include buffet breakfast. AE, CB, DC, DISC, MC, V. Parking 27,000L ($13.50). Bus: 8.

This four-star pink hotel has wrought-iron balconies and stone-edged French windows on its facade. A Renaissance well and dozens of potted shrubs are in front. The breakfast room is surrounded by a garden of green plants, and the lobby has white marble floors, Oriental rugs, an upper balcony, and a mix of old and new furniture. The guest rooms have elegant cherrywood furniture crafted by Tuscan artisans, along with mahogany and white-marble touches. The beds are among the most comfortable in town, and each bathroom comes with a hair dryer. On-site is a good budget pizzeria that offers freshly made pastas in addition to pies.

DINING

✪ **Caffè Pedrocchi**, Piazzetta Pedrocchi 15 (☎ **049-876-2576**), off Piazza Cavour, is a neoclassical landmark, hailed as Europe's most elegant coffeehouse when it opened in 1831 under Antonio Pedrocchi. Its green, white, and red rooms reflect the national colors. On sunny days, you might want to sit on one of the two stone porches; in winter, you'll have plenty to distract you inside. The sprawling bathtub-shaped travertine bar has a brass top and brass lion's feet, and the velvet banquettes have maroon upholstery, red-veined marble tables, and Egyptian Revival chairs. There's also a more conservatively decorated English-style pub, whose entrance is under a covered arcade a few steps away. Coffee is 1,500L (75¢) at the stand-up bar or 3,000L ($1.50) at a table. It's open Tuesday to Sunday 9:30am to 12:30pm and 3:30 to 8pm.

✪ **Antico Brolo.** Corso Milano 22. ☎ **049-66-45-55.** Reservations recommended. Main courses 24,000–40,000L ($12–$20). AE, DC, MC, V. Tues–Sun 12:30–2:30pm and 7:30–10:30pm. Closed 2nd and 3rd weeks of Aug. Bus: 5, 7, or 10. ITALIAN.

Across from the ornate *Teatro de Padova* (Civic Theater), this is the city's best restaurant. Even though the 16th-century dining room evokes the Renaissance, many patrons prefer a table in the garden, where candlelit tables are set on a terrace. The cuisine follows the tenets of most of Italy, with special emphasis on seasonal ingredients and the traditions of the Veneto and Emilia-Romagna. Especially delicious are the made-on-the-premises *graganelli* (similar to the tubular shape of penne) with garlic sauce, onion soup baked in a crust, chateaubriand with balsamic vinegar, and grilled fish. The perfect dessert is *zuppa inglese,* a cream-enriched equivalent to zabaglione.

Osteria Speroni. Via Speroni 36. ☎ **049-875-3370.** Reservations recommended. Main courses 18,000–35,000L ($9–$17.50). AE, V. Mon–Sat 12:30–2:30pm and 8–10:30pm. Closed Aug 1–25. Bus: 8, 12, 18, 22, M, or T. SEAFOOD.

This affordable fish restaurant occupies a 16th-century building a 3-minute walk from the cathedral. You'll dine in one of the three antique-looking rooms, each with exposed stone. Don't expect a lot of meat on the menu. The best way to begin is with antipasti from the buffet table, where you'll find fried calamari, marinated octopus, garlic-marinated shrimp, and a wide assortment of fried or marinated vegetables. A special pasta is *spaghetti alla busara,* with shrimp, tomatoes, and lots of garlic. Also look for sea bass roasted in a salt crust.

PADUA AFTER DARK

You can hang out with students in town at any of the crowded cafes along **Via Cavour** or walk over to the wine and beer dives around **Piazza delle Frutte** to find out where most of the college crowd is being cool. But other than a quiet stroll through the town's historic core, there's little happening in the city.

For dancing in Padua, try **Disco-Bar Limbo,** Via San Fermo 44 (☎ **049-656-882**), where electronic games alternate with recorded and (occasionally) live music. However, the most popular discos lie outside the city along the road between Padua and the spa town of Abano Terme, where the music is louder and the lights are dimmer. An example is **King's Club,** in Abano Terme, 10 miles (16km) from Padua (☎ **049-667-895**). En route, about 2 miles (3km) west of Padua, are **Disco Extra Extra,** Via Ciamician 5 (☎ **049-620-044**), and its neighbor **Disco P1,** Viale Giusti (☎ **049-860-1633**).

The leading gay bar is **Flexo,** Via Nicola Tommaseo 96 (☎ **049-807-4707**), open Wednesday to Sunday 9:30pm to at least 2am. The first Saturday of every month is leather night. The leading gay disco (mainly for men) is **Black & White,** Viale Navigazione Interna 38A (☎ **049-776-414**), open Thursday to Sunday 10pm to dawn. Entrance is 25,000L ($12.50), including the first drink.

3 Palladio's Vicenza

126 miles (203km) E of Milan, 42 miles (68km) W of Venice, 32 miles (52km) NE of Verona

In the 16th century, Vicenza was transformed into a virtual laboratory for the architectural experiments of Andrea di Pietro, known as **Palladio** (1508–80). One of the greatest architects of the High Renaissance, he was inspired by the classical art and architecture of ancient Greece and Rome. Palladio peppered the city with palazzi and basilicas and the surrounding hills with villas for patrician families.

The architect was particularly important to England and America. In the 18th century, Robert Adam was inspired by him, as is reflected by many country homes in England. Then, through the influence of Adam and others even earlier, the spirit of Palladio was brought to America (examples are Jefferson's Monticello and plantation homes in the antebellum South). Palladio even lent his name to this architectural style,

Palladianism, which is identified by regularity of form, imposing size, and an adherence to lines established in the ancient world. Visitors arrive in Vicenza today principally to see the works left by Palladio, and it's for this reason the city was designated a UNESCO World Heritage Site in 1994.

Vicenza isn't entirely living off its former glory. Dubbed the Venice of Terra Firma, Vicenza is ringed with light industry on its outskirts, its citizens earning one of the highest average incomes in the country. Federico Faggin, inventor of the silicon chip, was born here, and many local computer component industries are prospering. Gold manufacturing is another traditional and rich industry.

ESSENTIALS

GETTING THERE Most visitors arrive from Venice via the **train** (trip time: 1 hour), costing 5,900L ($2.95) one way. Trains also arrive frequently from Padua (trip time: 25 minutes), charging 3,900L ($1.95) one-way. There are also frequent connections from Milan (trip time: 2½ hours), at 16,000L ($8) one way. For information and schedules, call ☎ **1478-88-088** toll-free in Italy. Vicenza's rail station lies at Piazza Stazione (Campo Marzio), at the southern edge of Viale Roma.

If you have a **car** and are in Venice, take A4 west toward Verona, bypassing Padua.

VISITOR INFORMATION The **tourist office** is at Piazza Matteotti 12 (☎ **0444/320-854**), open Monday to Saturday 9am to 1pm and 2:30 to 6pm, Sunday 9am to 1pm.

EXPLORING THE WORLD OF PALLADIO

Basilica Palladiana & Torre Bissara. Piazza dei Signori. Free Admission. Tues–Sat 9:30am–noon and 2:30–3pm; Sun, Apr–Sept 9am–12:30pm and 2–7pm; Oct–Mar 9:30am–12:30pm.

This basilica was partially designed by Palladio. The loggias rise on two levels, the lower tier with Doric pillars, the upper with Ionic. In its heyday, this building was much frequented by the Vicentino aristocrats, who lavishly spent their gold on villas in the neighboring hills. They met here in a kind of social fraternity, perhaps to talk about the excessive sums being spent on Palladio-designed or -inspired projects. The original basilica was done in the Gothic style and served as the *Palazzo della Ragione* (Hall of Justice). The roof collapsed following a 1945 bombing but has been subsequently rebuilt. Although there aren't any treasures inside, two or three times a year art exhibits are held here.

Beside the basilica is the 13th-century **Torre Bissara,** soaring almost 270 feet. Across from the basilica is the **Loggia del Capitanio (Captain of the Guard),** designed by Palladio in his waning years.

✪ **Olympic Theater (Teatro Olimpico).** Piazza Matteotti. ☎ **0444/222-800.** Admission 12,000L ($6), including entry to the Civic Museum and the Archaeological Museum. Sept–July 3 Tues–Sun 9am–5pm; July 4– Aug Tues–Sun 10am–7pm.

Palladio's masterpiece and last work—ideal for performances of classical plays—is one of the world's greatest theaters still in use. It was completed in 1585, 5 years after Palladio's death, by Vincenzo Scamozzi, and the curtain went up on the Vicenza premiere of Sophocles's *Oedipus Rex.* The arena seating area, in the shape of a half moon, is encircled by Corinthian columns and balustrades. The simple proscenium abuts the arena. What's ordinarily the curtain in a conventional theater is here a permanent facade, U-shaped, with a large central arch and a pair of smaller ones flanking it. The permanent stage set represents the ancient streets of Thebes, combining architectural detail with trompe l'oeil. Above the arches (to the left and right) are rows of additional classic statuary on pedestals and in niches. Over the area is a dome, with trompe l'oeil clouds and sky, giving the illusion of an outdoor Roman amphitheater.

Civic Museum (Museo Civico). In the Palazzo Chiericati, Piazza Matteotti 37–39. ☎ **0444/321-348.** Admission 12,000L ($6) including entry to the Olympic Theater and the Archaeological Museum. Sept–July 4 Tues–Sun 9am–5pm; July 5–Aug Tues–Sun 10am–7pm.

This museum is housed in one of the most outstanding buildings by Palladio. Begun in the mid–16th century, it wasn't finished until the late 17th, during the baroque period. Visitors come chiefly to view its excellent collection of Venetian paintings on the second floor. Works by lesser-known artists (Paolo Veneziano, Bartolomeo Montagna, and Jacopo Bassano) hang alongside paintings by giants like Tintoretto *(Miracle of St. Augustine)*, Veronese *(The Cherub of the Balustrade)*, and Tiepolo *(Time and Truth)*.

Santa Corona. Via Santa Corona. ☎ **0444/323-644.** Free admission. Daily 8:30am–noon and 2:30–6:30pm.

This much-altered Gothic church was founded in the mid–13th century. Visit it to see Giovanni Bellini's *Baptism of Christ* (fifth altar on the left). In the left transept, a short distance away, is another of Vicenza's well-known artworks, this one by Veronese, depicting the three Wise Men paying tribute to the Christ child. The high altar with its intricate marble work is also worth a look. A visit to Santa Corona is more rewarding than a trek to the Duomo, which is only of passing interest.

✪ **Villa Rotonda.** Via della Rotonda 25. ☎ **0444/321-793.** Admission 12,000L ($6) to interior; 6,000L ($3) to grounds. Interior, Wed 10am–noon and 3–6pm; grounds, Tues–Sun 10am–noon and 3–6pm. Closed Nov 5–Mar 14.

This is Palladio's most famous villa, featuring his trademark design inspired by the Roman temples. The interior lacks the grand decor of many lesser-known villas, but the exterior is the focus anyway, having inspired Christopher Wren's English country estates, Jefferson's Monticello, and the work of a slew of lesser-known architects designing U.S. state capitols and Southern antebellum homes. The building was begun by Palladio in 1567, though he didn't live to see it finished. The final work was carried out by Scamozzi between Palladio's death in 1580 and 1592 and is now listed as a UNESCO World Heritage site. If you aren't here during the limited open hours, you can still view it clearly from the road.

Villa Valmarana "Ai Nani." Via San Bastiano 8. ☎ **0444/543-976.** Admission 10,000L ($5). Mar–Apr Tues–Sat 2:30–5:30pm; May–Sept Tues–Sat 3–6pm; Oct–Nov Tues–Sat 2–5pm. Closed Dec–Feb.

The most magnificent thing about this 17th-century villa, built by Palladio disciple Mattoni, is the series of frescoes by Giambattista Tiepolo that, taken together, create an elaborate mythological world. In the garden, you'll find miniature statues, which are the *nani* (dwarves) referred to in its name. Winter tours, available by appointment, require a group of 10 or more.

ACCOMMODATIONS

Hotel Campo Marzio. Viale Roma 27, 36100 Vicenza. ☎ **0444/545-700.** Fax 0444/320-495. www.hotelcampomarzio.com. E-mail: hcm@tradenet.it. 35 units. A/C MINIBAR TV TEL. 240,000–380,000L ($120–$190) double. Rates include buffet breakfast. AE, DC, MC, V. Parking 25,000L ($12.50).

This contemporary hotel is ideally situated in a peaceful part of the historic center, adjacent to a park. The guest rooms have undergone a complete renovation, and the

La Città del Palladio

His name was Andrea di Pietro, but his friends called him Palladio. In time, he become the most prominent architect of the Italian High Renaissance, living and working in his beloved Vicenza. This city remains, despite the destruction of 14 of his buildings during World War II air raids (luckily, they were photographed and documented before their demise), a living museum of his architectural achievements. In time, Vicenza became known as La Città del Palladio. Palladio was actually born in Padua in 1508, where he was apprenticed to a stone carver but fled in 1523 to Vicenza, where he lived for most of his life, dying here in 1580.

In his youth, Palladio journeyed to Rome to study the architecture of the Roman Vitruvius, who had a profound influence on him. Returning to Vicenza, Palladio perfected the "Palladian style," with its use of pilasters and a composite structure on a gigantic scale. The "attic" in his design was often surmounted by statues. One critic of European architecture wrote, "The noble design, the perfect proportions, the rhythm, and the logically vertical order invites devotion." Palladio's treatise on architecture, published in four volumes, is required reading for aspiring architects.

By no means was Palladio a genius, in the way the Florentine Brunelleschi was. No daring innovator, Palladio was more like an academician who went by the rules. Although all his buildings are harmonious, there are no surprises in them. One of his most acclaimed buildings is the **Villa Rotonda** in Vicenza, a cube with a center circular hall crowned by a dome. On each external side is a pillared rectangular portico. The classic features, though dry and masquerading as a temple, captured the public's imagination. This same type of villa soon reappeared all over England and America.

The main street of Vicenza, **Corso Andrea Palladio,** honors its most famous hometown boy, who spent much of his life building villas for the wealthy. The street is a textbook illustration of the great architect's work (or that of his pupils), and a walk along the Corso is one of the most memorable in Italy.

sunny lobby has a conservatively comfortable decor that extends into the rooms. The tiled bathrooms are small. A cozy restaurant offers regional dining Monday to Friday.

Hotel Continental. Viale G. G. Trissino 89, 36100 Vicenza. ☎ **0444/505-478.** Fax 0444/513-319. 55 units. A/C MINIBAR TV TEL. 250,000L ($125) double. Rates include breakfast. AE, DC, MC, V.

The Continental is among the best choices for an overnight stop. It has been renovated in a modern style and offers comfortable rooms ranging from small to medium. Each comes with a fine mattress and a small tiled bathroom. The hotel has a good restaurant; however, there's no meal service on Saturday or Sunday or in August or around Christmas. There's a solarium on the premises.

Hotel Cristina. Corso San Felice e Fortunato 32, 36100 Vicenza. ☎ **0444/323-751.** Fax 0444/543-656. E-mail: hotel.cristina@keycomm.it. 34 units. A/C MINIBAR TV TEL. 225,000L ($112.50) double. Rates include buffet breakfast. AE, DC, MC, V. Parking 15,000L ($7.50).

The Cristina is a cozy place near the city center, with an inside courtyard where you can park. The recently refurbished decor consists of lots of marble, parquet flooring, and exposed paneling, coupled with comfortable furniture in the public rooms. The high-ceilinged guest rooms are also well furnished, though some are small. The mattresses were recently renewed, and some rooms are suitable for the disabled. The tiled bathrooms are compact. Breakfast is the only meal served.

✪ **Jolly Hotel Europa.** Strada Padana Verso Verona 11, 36100 Vicenza. ☎ **800/221-2626** in the U.S., or 0444/564-111. Fax 0444/564-382. 127 units. A/C MINIBAR TV TEL. 350,000–400,000L ($175–$200) double. Rates include buffet breakfast. AE, DC, MC, V. Free parking. Bus: 1 or 14.

Outside of town, the Jolly is the area's finest hotel. It's a somewhat sterile but well-run place flying the flags of many nations and geared to the business traveler, since it lies in the Exhibition Center with easy access to the autostrada; however, it can also serve vacationers. The guest rooms are done in a jazzy Italian style and are medium-sized, each with a quality mattress, and a small safe. The marble or tile baths come with hair dryers (some with Jacuzzis). Some rooms are set aside for nonsmokers. Le Ville restaurant offers international dishes and regional food of the Veneto.

DINING

Antica Trattoria Tre Visi. Corso Palladio 25. ☎ **0444/324-868.** Reservations required. Main courses 20,000–35,000L ($10–$17.50). AE, DC, MC, V. Tues–Sun 12:30–2:30pm; Tues–Sat 7:30–10:30pm. Closed July. VICENTINO/INTERNATIONAL.

This restaurant opened as a simple tavern in the early 1600s. After many variations, it was named "The Three Faces" more than a century ago after the rulers of Austria, Hungary, and Bavaria, whose political influence was powerful in the Veneto. The decor is rustic, with a fireplace, ceramic wall decorations, baskets of fresh fruit, tavern chairs, and an open kitchen. Along with the good selection of regional wines, you can enjoy dishes like *baccalà* (salt codfish) *alla vicentina, zuppa di fagioli* (bean soup), and spaghetti with duck sauce. Another specialty is *capretto alla gambalaro* (kid marinated for 4 days in wine, vinegar, and spices, then roasted). The best-known dessert is the traditional *pincha alla vicentina,* made with yellow flour, raisins, and figs.

✪ **Cinzia e Valerio.** Piazzetta Porta Padova 65–67. ☎ **0444/505-213.** Reservations recommended. Main courses 18,000–35,000L ($9–$17.50). AE, DC, MC, V. Tues–Sun noon–2:30pm; Tues–Sat 7:30–9:30pm. Closed Aug 4–25 and Dec 26–Jan 1. SEAFOOD.

This is Vicenza's best and most elegant restaurant, where you'll be greeted by a polite staff and masses of seasonal flowers. The house fish specialties are time-tested recipes from the Adriatic coast. Your meal might begin with mollusks and shellfish arranged into an elegant platter. Other dishes are risotto flavored with squid, a collection of crab and lobster that might surprise you by its size and weight, and an endless procession of fish cooked any way you prefer.

Ristorante Grandcaffè Garibaldi. Piazza dei Signori 2. ☎ **0444/542-455.** Main courses 20,000–35,000L ($10–$17.50). MC, V. Restaurant daily 12:30–3pm and 7:30–11:30pm. Cafe Thurs–Tues 7:30am–midnight. VICENTINO/ITALIAN/MEDITERRANEAN.

The most impressive cafe/restaurant in the town center has a design worthy of the city of Palladio, with a wide terrace and an ornate ceiling, marble tables, and a long glass case of sandwiches from which you can make a selection before you sit down (the waitress will bring them to your table). In the cafe, *panini* (sandwiches) cost 5,000 to 8,000L ($4) and a cappuccino 3,500L ($1.75). Prices are slightly lower if you stand at the bar. There's also an upstairs restaurant with trays of antipasti and fresh fruit set up on a central table. The menu's array of familiar Italian specialties is among the best in town.

VICENZA AFTER DARK

In Vicenza, you can enjoy music presented in settings of architectural splendor. The outdoor **Teatro Olimpico** hosts cultural events from April to late September. Look for a changing program of classical Greek tragedy (*Oedipus Rex* is an enduring favorite), Shakespearean plays (sometimes translated into Italian), chamber music concerts, and dance recitals. You can pick up schedules and buy tickets either at the gate or from the series' administrative headquarters near Vicenza's basilica at **Viarte,** Contra San Marco 33 (☎ **0444/540-072**). Tickets are 20,000 to 40,000L ($10 to $20), though in rare instances some nosebleed seats go for 15,000L ($7.50).

More esoteric, and with a shorter season, is a series of concerts scheduled in June, the **Concerti in Villa.** Every year, it includes chamber music performed in or near often privately owned villas in the city's outskirts. Look for orchestras set up on loggias or under formal pediments and audiences sitting on chairs in gardens or inside. Note that these depend on the whims of both local musicians and villa owners. Contact the tourist office (see "Essentials," above) for details.

4 Verona

71 miles (114km) W of Venice, 312 miles (502km) NW of Rome, 50 miles (81km) W of Padua

Verona was the setting for the most famous love story in the English language, Shakespeare's *Romeo and Juliet.* A long-forgotten editor of an old volume of the Bard's plays once wrote: "Verona, so rich in the associations of real history, has even a greater charm for those who would live in the poetry of the past." It's not known if a Romeo or a Juliet ever existed, but the remains of Verona's recorded past are much in evidence today. Its Roman antiquities are unequaled north of Rome.

In its medieval golden age under the despotic Scaligeri princes, Verona reached the pinnacle of its influence and prestige, developing into a town that, even today, is among the great cities of Italy. The best-known member of the ruling Della Scala family, Cangrande I, was a patron of Dante. His sway over Verona has often been compared to that of Lorenzo the Magnificent over Florence.

Verona stands in contrast to Venice, even though both are tourist towns. Despite the day-trippers, most of the people walking the streets of Verona are actually residents and not visitors. For a city that hit its peak in the 1st century A.D., Verona is doing admirably well. However, stick to the inner core and not the newer sections, which are blighted by industry and tacky urban development.

ESSENTIALS

GETTING THERE A total of 37 **trains** a day make the 2-hour run between Venice and Verona, at 10,500L ($5.25) one way. If you're in the west (say, at Milan), there are even more connections, some 40 trains a day, taking 2 hours to reach Verona at 12,100L ($6.05) one way. Six daily trains arrive from Rome; it's a 6-hour trip costing 18,000L ($9) on a regular train, or a 4½-hour trip costing 70,000L ($35) on a *rapido.* Rail arrivals are at Verona's **Stazione Porta Nuova,** Piazza XXV Aprile (☎ **045-590-688**), south of the centrally located Arena and Piazza Brà; call ☎ **1478-88-088** toll-free in Italy for information. At least six bus lines service the area, taking you frequently into the core.

If you have a **car** and are in Venice, take A4 west to the signposted cutoff for Verona, marked Verona Sud. If you're reaching Verona from the south or north, take A22 and get off at the exit marked Verona Nord.

VISITOR INFORMATION The **main tourist office** is at Piazza Erbe (☎ **045-800-0065**). Hours are Tuesday to Sunday 10am to 7pm. There's **another information office** at the rail station, Piazzale XXV Aprile (☎ **045-800-0861**). In summer, it's open daily 8am to 7:30pm; off-season hours are Monday to Saturday 9am to 6pm.

SPECIAL EVENTS Opera festivals on a scale more human and accessible than those in cities like Milan are presented in Verona annually between July and August. The setting is the ancient ✪ **Arena di Verona,** a site that's grand enough to accommodate as many elephants as might be needed for a performance of *Aïda.* Schedules vary every year, so for more information and tickets call ☎ **045-800-51-51.** Prices of tickets vary with view lines and whatever is being staged but usually are 25,000 to 40,000L ($12.50 to $20).

For tickets and information on the opera or ballet in Verona, **Edwards & Edwards** has a U.S. office (1270 Ave. of the Americas, Suite 2414, New York, NY 10020) from which you can buy tickets before you go, or call ☎ **800/223-6108** or 914/328-2150 (fax 914/328-2752). A personal visit isn't necessary, and they can mail vouchers or fax a confirmation to allow you to pick up the tickets half an hour before curtain call.

The **Teatro Romano** is known for its Shakespeare Festival from June through August. In recent years, it has included a week of English-language performances by the Royal Shakespeare Company. Festival performances begin in late May and June with jazz concerts. In July and August, there are also a number of ballets (such as Prokofiev's *Romeo and Juliet*) and modern dance performances. Check for a current schedule at ☎ **045-80-77-111** or with the tourist office.

EXPLORING THE CITY

Verona lies along the Adige River. The city is most often visited on a quick half-day excursion but deserves more time—it's meant for wandering and contemplation. If you're rushed, head first to the old city. In addition to the sights listed below, there are other attractions that might merit a visit.

Opening onto **Piazza dei Signori,** the handsomest in Verona, is the **Palazzo del Governo,** where Cangrande extended the shelter of his hearth and home to the fleeing Florentine Dante Alighieri. A marble statue of the "divine poet" stands in the center of the square, with an expression as cold as a Dolomite icicle, but unintimidated pigeons perch on his pious head. Facing Dante's back is the late-15th-century **Loggia del Consiglio,** frescoed and surmounted by five statues. Five arches lead into Piazza dei Signori.

The **Arche Scaligere** are outdoor tombs surrounded by wrought-iron gates that form a kind of open-air pantheon of the Scaligeri princes. One tomb, that of Cangrande della Scala, rests directly over the door of the 12th-century **Santa Maria Antica.** The mausoleum contains many Romanesque features and is crowned by a copy of an equestrian statue (the original is now at the Castelvecchio). The tomb nearest the door is that of Mastino II; the one behind it, and the most lavish of all, is that of Cansignorio.

Piazza delle Erbe (Square of the Herbs) is a lively square, flanked by palaces, that was formerly the Roman city's forum. Today, it's the fruit-and-vegetable market, milling with Veronese shoppers and vendors. In the center is a fountain dating from the 14th century and a Roman statue dubbed *The Virgin of Verona.* The pillar at one end of the square, crowned by a chimera, symbolizes the many years Verona was dominated by Venice. Important buildings include the early-14th-century **House of Merchants (Casa di Mercanti);** the **Torre Gardello,** built by one of the Della Scala

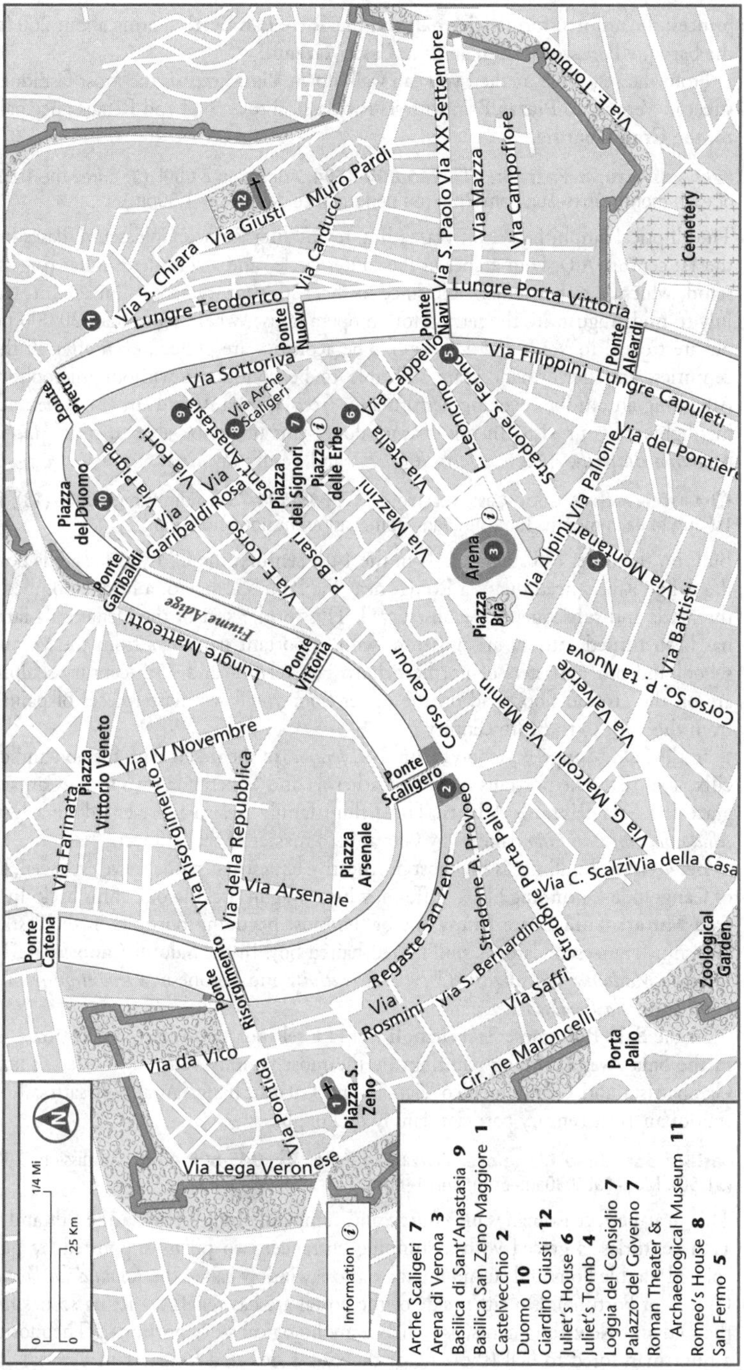
Arche Scaligeri 7
Arena di Verona 3
Basilica di Sant'Anastasia 9
Basilica San Zeno Maggiore 1
Castelvecchio 2
Duomo 10
Giardino Giusti 12
Juliet's House 6
Juliet's Tomb 4
Loggia del Consiglio 7
Palazzo del Governo 7
Roman Theater & Archaeological Museum 11
Romeo's House 8
San Fermo 5
Information
0 1/4 Mi
0 .25 Km
N
Fiume Adige
Ponte Pietra
Ponte Nuovo
Ponte Navi
Ponte Aleardi
Ponte Garibaldi
Ponte Vittoria
Ponte Scaligero
Ponte Catena
Ponte Risorgimento
Piazza del Duomo
Piazza dei Signori
Piazza delle Erbe
Piazza Brà
Arena
Piazza Vittorio Veneto
Piazza Arsenale
Piazza S. Zeno
Porta Palio
Cemetery
Zoological Garden
Lungre Teodorico
Via S. Chiara
Via Giusti
Muro Pardi
Via Carducci
Via S. Paolo
Via XX Settembre
Via Mazza
Via Campofiore
Via E. Torbido
Lungre Porta Vittoria
Via Filippini
Lungre Capuleti
Via del Pontiere
Via Sottoriva
Via Arche Scaligeri
Via Cappello
L. Leoncino
Stradone S. Fermo
Via Pallone
Via Forti
Via Pigna
Via Sant'Anastasia
Via Rosa
Via Garibaldi
Via Stella
Via Mazzini
Corso P. Bosari
Via E. Corso
Via Alpini
Via Montanari
Via Battisti
Corso Cavour
Lungre Matteotti
Via Manin
Corso So. P. ta Nuova
Via Valverde
Via G. Marconi
Via IV Novembre
Via Risorgimento
Via della Repubblica
Via Arsenale
Via Farinata
Regaste San Zeno
Stradone A. Provoeo
Stradone Porta Palio
Via C. Scalzi
Via della Casa
Via Rosmini
Via S. Bernardino
Via Saffi
Cir. ne Maroncelli
Via da Vico
Via Pontida
Via Lega Veronese

princes; the restored former **city hall** and the **Torre Lamberti,** soaring about 260 feet; the baroque **Palazzo Maffei;** and the **Casa Mazzanti.**

From the vegetable market, you can walk down **Via Mazzini,** the most fashionable street in Verona, to **Piazza Brà,** with its neoclassical town hall and Renaissance palazzo, the **Gran Guardia.**

Arena di Verona. Piazza Brà. ☎ **045-800-3204.** Admission 6,000L ($3); free the 1st Sun of each month. Tues–Sun 9am–7pm (on performance days, 9am–1:30pm).

The elliptical amphitheater on Piazza Brà, resembling Rome's Colosseum, dates from the 1st century A.D. Four arches of the "outer circle" and a complete "inner ring" still stand, which is rather remarkable since in the 12th century an earthquake hit. Mid-July to mid-August, it's the setting for an opera house, where more than 20,000 people are treated to Verdi and Mascagni. The acoustics are perfect, even after all these centuries, and performances are still able to be conducted without microphones. Attending an outdoor evening performance (see "Verona After Dark") can be one of highlights of your visit. In one season alone, you might be able to hear *Macbeth, Madama Butterfly, Aïda, Carmen, Rigoletto,* and Verdi's *Requiem.*

✪ **Castelvecchio.** Corso Castelvecchio 2. ☎ **045-594-734.** Admission 6,000L ($3); free 1st Sun of each month. Tues–Sun 9am–7pm. Last admission at 6:30pm.

Built on the order of Cangrande II in the 14th century, the Old Castle stands beside the Adige River (head out Via Roma) near the Ponte Scaligero, a bridge bombed by the Nazis and subsequently reconstructed. This former seat of the Della Scala family has been turned into an art museum, with important paintings from the Veronese school and other masters of northern Italy. Fourteenth- and 15th-century sculpture are on the ground floor, and on the upper floor you'll see masterpieces of painting from the 15th to the 18th century.

In the **Sala Monga** is Jacopo Bellini's *St. Jerome,* in the desert with his lion and crucifix. Two sisterlike portraits of Saint Catherina and Veneranda by Vittore Carpaccio grace the **Sala Rizzardi Allegri.** The Bellini family is also represented by a lyrical *Madonna con Bambino* painted by Giovanni, a master of that subject.

Between the buildings is the most provocative equestrian statue we've ever seen, that of Cangrande I, grinning like a buffoon, with a dragon sticking out of his back. In the **Sala Murari dalla Corte Brà** is one of the most beguiling portraits in the castle—Giovanni Francesco Caroto's smiling red-haired boy. In the **Sala di Canossa** are Tintoretto's *Madonna Nursing the Child* and *Nativity* and Veronese's *Deposition from the Cross* and *Pala Bevilacqua Lazise.*

In the **Sala Bolognese Trevenzuoli** is a rare self-portrait of Bernardo Strozzi, and in the **Sala Avena,** among paintings by the most famous Venetian masters, such as Gianbattista and Giandomenico Tiepolo and Guardi, hangs an almost satirical portrait of an 18th-century patrician family by Longhi.

Basilica San Zeno Maggiore. Piazza San Zeno. ☎ **045-800-4325.** Admission 3,000L ($1.50). Mon–Sat 9:30am–6pm; Sun 1–6pm.

This near-perfect Romanesque church and campanile built between the 9th and the 12th centuries is graced with a stunning entrance: two pillars supported by puce-colored marble lions and surmounted by a rose window called the *Ruota della Fortuna* (Wheel of Fortune). On either side of the portal are bas-reliefs depicting scenes from the Old and New Testaments, as well as a mythological story portraying Theodoric as a huntsman lured to hell (the king of the Goths defeated Odoacer in Verona). The panels on the bronze doors, nearly 50 in all, are a remarkable achievement of medieval art, sculpted perhaps in the 12th century. They reflect a naive handling of their subject (see John the Baptist's head resting on a platter). The artists express themselves with such candor they achieve the power of a child's storybook. The interior, somber and severe, contains a major Renaissance work at the main altar: a triptych by Andrea Mantegna, showing an enthroned Madonna and Child with saints. Although not remarkable in its characterization, it reveals the artist's genius for perspective.

Basilica di Sant'Anastasia. Piazza Sant'Anastasia. ☎ **045-800-4325.** Admission 3,000L ($1.50). Mar–Oct Mon–Sat 9:30am–6:30pm, Sun 1–6pm; Nov–Mar daily 10am–4pm.

Verona's largest church was built from 1290 to 1481. Its facade isn't complete, yet nevertheless it's the finest representation of Gothic design in the city. Many artists in the 15th and 16th centuries decorated the interior, but few of the works are worthy of being singled out. The exception is the **Pellegrini Chapel (Cappella Pellegrini),** with terra-cotta reliefs by the Tuscan artist Michele, and the **Giusti Chapel (Cappella Giusti),** with a fresco by Pisanello representing St. George preparing to face his inevitable dragon. The patterned floor is especially impressive. As you enter, look for two *gobbi* (hunchbacks) supporting holy water fonts. The church also has a beautiful **campanile** from the 1300s that's richly decorated with sculpture and frescoes.

Duomo. Piazza del Duomo. ☎ **045-595-627.** Admission 3,000L ($1.50). Mar–Oct Mon–Fri 9:30am–6pm, Sat to 4pm; off-season Mon–Sat 9:30am–1pm and 2–6pm.

Verona's cathedral is less interesting than San Zeno Maggiore but still merits a visit. It was begun in the 12th century but not completed until the 17th. A blend of Romanesque and Gothic, its facade contains (lower level) 12th-century sculptured reliefs by Nicolaus depicting scenes of Roland and Oliver, two of the legendary dozen knights attending Charlemagne. In the left aisle (first chapel) is Titian's ***Assumption,*** the stellar work of the Duomo. The other major work is the **rood screen** in front of the presbytery, with Ionic pillars, designed by Samicheli.

San Fermo. Stradone San Fermo. ☎ **045-800-7287.** Admission 3,000L ($1.50). Mon–Sat 9:30am–6pm, Sun 1–6pm.

This 11th-century Romanesque church forms the foundation of the 14th-century Gothic building surmounting it. Through time, it has been used by both the Benedictines and the Franciscans. The interior is unusual, with a single nave and a splendid roof constructed of wood and exquisitely paneled. The most important work inside is Pisanello's frescoed ***Annunciation,*** to the left of the main entrance (at the Brenzoni tomb). Delicate and graceful, the work reveals the artist's keen eye for architectural detail and his bizarre animals.

✪ **Roman Theater (Teatro Romano) & Archaeological Museum (Museo Archeologico).** Rigaste Redentore 2. ☎ **045-800-0360.** Admission 6,000L ($3); free the first Sun of each month. Tues–Sun 9am–6:30pm.

The Teatro Romano, built in the 1st century A.D., now stands in ruins at the foot of St. Peter's Hill. For nearly a quarter of a century, a Shakespearean festival has been staged here in July and August; of course, a unique theater-going experience is to see *Romeo and Juliet* or *Two Gentlemen of Verona* in this setting. The theater is across the Adige River (take the Ponte di Pietra). After seeing the remains of the theater, you can take a rickety elevator to the 10th-century Santi Siro e Libera church towering over it. In the cloister of St. Jerome is the Archaeological Museum, with interesting mosaics and Etruscan bronzes.

Giardino Giusti. Via Giardino Giusti 2. ☎ **045-803-4029.** Admission 8,000L ($4). Apr–Sept daily 9am–8pm (to 7pm off-season).

One of Italy's oldest and most famous gardens, the Giardino Giusti was created at the end of the 14th century. These well-manicured Italian gardens, studded with cypress trees, form one of the most relaxing and coolest spots in Verona for strolls. You can climb up to the "monster balcony" for an incomparable view of the city.

The layout was given to the gardens by Agostino Giusti. All its 16th-century characteristics—the grottoes, statues, fountains, box-enclosed flower garden, and maze—have remained intact. In addition to the flower displays, you can admire statues by Lorenzo Muttoni and Alessandro Vittoria, Roman remains, and the great cypress mentioned by Goethe. The gardens, with their adjacent 16th-century palazzo, form one of Italy's most interesting urban complexes. The maze of myrtle hedges faithfully reproduces the 1786 plan of the architect Trezza. Its complicated pattern and small size make it one of the most unusual in Europe. The gardens lie near the Roman Theater, only a few minutes' walk from the heart of the city.

✪ **Juliet's Tomb (Tomba di Giulietta).** Via del Pontiere 5. ☎ **045-800-0361.** Admission 5,000L ($2.50); free the 1st Sun of each month. Tues–Sun 9am–6:30pm.

The so-called Juliet's tomb is sheltered in a Franciscan monastery, which you enter on Via Luigi da Porto, off Via del Pontiere. "A grave? O, no, a lantern .... For here lies Juliet, and her beauty makes this vault a feasting presence full of light." Don't you believe it! Still, the cloisters, near the Adige River, are graceful. Adjoining the tomb is a museum of frescoes, dedicated to G. B. Cavalcaselle.

✪ **Juliet's House (Casa di Giulietta).** Via Cappello 23. ☎ **045-803-4303.** Admission 6,000L ($3). Tues–Sun 9am–7pm.

"Juliet's house" is a small home with a balcony and a courtyard. There's no evidence any family named Capulet lived here, but it was acquired by the city in 1905 and turned into this contrived sight. So powerful is the legend of Juliet that millions flock to this house, not seeming to care whether Juliet lived here or not. Tradition calls for visitors to rub the right breast of a bronze statue of Juliet that's now brightly polished by millions of hands. With a little bit of imagination, it's not difficult to hear Romeo say: "But, soft! What light through yonder window breaks? It is the east, and Juliet is the sun!"

If you're wondering where Juliet's heartthrob lived, check out the so-called **Romeo's House (Casi di Romeo),** Via Arche Scaligeri 2, said to have been the home of the Montecchi family, the model for Shakespeare's Montagues. It's been turned into a very good, atmospheric, and affordable restaurant called the **Osteria dal Duca** (☎ **045-59-44-74**).

SHOPPING

The byword for shopping in Verona is *elegance,* and shops feature the fashions being touted in Milan and Rome. Don't look for touristy products or rustic crafts and souvenirs, but rather for more upscale versions of all-Italian fashion and accessories. A worthwhile shop for men is **Class Uomo,** Via San Rocchetto 13B (☎ **045-595-775**). Every Veronese knows the allure for both genders of **Armani,** Via Cappello 25 (☎ **045-594-727**).

You'll find a dense concentration of vendors selling antiques or old bric-a-brac in the streets around **Sant'Anastasia** or head to **Piazza delle Erbe** for a more or less constant roster of merchants in flea market–style kiosks selling the dusty, and often junkier, collectibles of yesteryear, along with aromatic herbs, fruits, and vegetables.

ACCOMMODATIONS

Hotel rooms tend to be scarce during the County Fair in March and the opera and theater season in July and August.

Very Expensive

✪ **Due Torri Hotel Baglioni.** Piazza Sant'Anastasia 4, 37121 Verona. ☎ **045-595-044.** Fax 045-800-4130. www.baglionihotel.com. E-mail: duetorri.verona@baglionihotel.com. 90 units. A/C MINIBAR TV TEL. 570,000–750,000L ($285–$375) double; from 1,000,000L ($500) suite. Rates include breakfast. AE, DC, MC, V. Parking 50,000L ($25).

This began as the 1400s home of the Scaligeri dynasty. During the 18th and 19th centuries, it hosted VIPs like Mozart, Goethe, and Tsar Alexander I. In the 1950s, legendary hotelier Enrico Wallner transformed the palace into a hotel with a stunning collection of antiques. The hotel was bought in 1990 by the upscale Cogeta Palace chain, who richly restored the entire hotel over 4 years. Many antiques remain in the public areas and guest rooms—a range of Directoire, Empire, Louis XVIII, and Biedermeier. Most rooms are generous in size, with deluxe mattresses; the Portuguese marble bathrooms come with deluxe toiletries.

Dining/Diversions: One of Verona's most distinguished restaurants, the Ristorante All'Aquila serves typical local and light cuisine (see "Dining," below). There's also an elegant bar.

Amenities: 24-hour room service, in-room massage, baby-sitting, laundry/valet.

✪ **Hotel Gabbia d'Oro.** Corso Porta Borsari 4A, 37100 Verona. ☎ **045-800-3060.** Fax 045-590-293. 27 units. A/C MINIBAR TV TEL. 400,000–600,000L ($200–$300) double; 890,000–1,400,000L ($445–$700) suite. Rates include breakfast except June 25–Sept 30. AE, DC, MC, V. Parking 50,000L ($25).

This hotel in an 18th-century palazzo opened in 1990, the first hotel in years to give the Baglioni serious competition. It has a more romantic atmosphere than its older and more fabled rival. Small and discreet, it contains many of the building's original grandiose frescoes, its beamed ceiling, and (in the cozy bar area) much of the carved paneling. The interior courtyard contains potted plants, flowering shrubs, and tables devoted to drinking and dining in clement weather. The guest rooms boast framed engravings, antique furniture, and (in some cases) narrow balconies with wrought-iron detailing overlooking the street or the courtyard. The bathrooms are in marble or tile, with deluxe toiletries and fluffy towels. Meals are served for special occasions or on request.

Amenities: Concierge, room service, laundry/dry cleaning, newspaper delivery on request, in-room massage, twice-daily maid service, baby-sitting, and secretarial services.

Expensive

Hotel Accademia. Via Scala 12, 37121 Verona. ☎ **045-596-222.** Fax 045-800-8440. www.accademiavr.it. E-mail: accademia@accademiavr.it. 98 units. A/C MINIBAR TV TEL. 340,000–410,000L ($170–$205) double; 480,000–600,000L ($240–$300) suite. Rates include buffet breakfast. AE, DC, MC, V. Parking 25,000L ($12.50).

This is one of Verona's few older hotels that was custom built rather than being transformed from a monastery or palazzo. Dating from the late 1800s, it contains Oriental carpets, a medieval tapestry, and a pair of grandiose marble columns flanking the polished stone stairwell leading to the three floors of rooms. The high-ceilinged guest rooms are conservatively traditional and contain excellent furnishings, especially quality mattresses and fine linen. The bathrooms are in tile or marble.

Dining/Diversions: There's a paneled modern bar and a restaurant (the Accademia) that operate under a separate management. Guests receive a 10% discount on meals.

Amenities: Concierge, room service, baby-sitting, laundry/dry cleaning.

Moderate

Colomba d'Oro. Via C. Cattaneo 10, 37121 Verona. ☎ **045-595-300.** Fax 045-594-974. 51 units. A/C MINIBAR TV TEL. 280,000–330,000L ($140–$165) double; 330,000–400,000L ($165–$200) suite. Rates include buffet breakfast. AE, DC, MC, V. Parking 27,000L ($13.50).

The Colomba d'Oro was built as a villa in the 1600s and later transformed into a monastery. During the 18th and 19th centuries, it served as an inn for travelers and employees of the postal service and eventually grew into this large hotel. The building is efficiently organized and has an atmosphere somewhere between semitraditional and contemporary. The guest rooms, medium-sized, are nicely furnished with matching fabrics and comfortable furniture (including first-rate mattresses). Some bathrooms are clad in marble; all come with heated towel racks and hair dryers. Breakfast is the only meal served.

Hotel de' Capuleti. Via del Pontiere 26, 37122 Verona. ☎ **045-800-0154.** Fax 045-803-2970. E-mail: capuleti@easy1.easynet.it. 42 units. A/C MINIBAR TV TEL. 270,000L ($135) double. Rates include breakfast. AE, DC, MC, V. Closed Dec 22–Jan 10.

The Capuleti is an attractively pristine place, conveniently a few steps from Juliet's (supposed) tomb and the chapel where she's said to have married Romeo. The reception area has stone floors and leather couches, along with a tastefully renovated decor that's reflected upstairs in the comfortable guest rooms. Most rooms are small and standardized, but each has a good mattress. The tiled bathrooms are tiny.

Inexpensive

Hotel Aurora. Piazzetta XIV Novembre 2 (off Piazza Erbe), 37121 Verona. ☎ **045-594-717.** Fax 045-801-0860. 19 units. A/C TV TEL. 160,000–210,000L ($80–$105) double. Rates include breakfast. AE, MC, V. Parking free on street; 20,000L ($10) in public lot (a 10-min. walk).

The foundations of this tall and narrow hotel were already at least 400 years old when the building was constructed in the 1500s. In 1994 its owners completed a radical renovation that improved all the hidden systems (structural beams, electricity, plumbing) but retained hints of the building's antique origins. The Aurora is set behind a sienna-colored facade on a square that's transformed every morning, at around 7:30am, into Verona's busiest emporium of fruits and vegetables. Views from all but a few of the simply furnished guest rooms encompass a full or partial look at the activity in the square. The rooms are small but the beds comfortable, having recently been fitted with new mattresses. The bathrooms are cramped. The hotel's bar is open 24 hours.

Hotel Giulietta e Romeo. Vicolo Tre Marchetti 3, 37121 Verona. ☎ **045-800-3554.** Fax 045-801-0862. E-mail: info@giulettacromeo.com. 30 units. A/C MINIBAR TV TEL. 180,000–280,000L ($90–$140) double. Rates include breakfast. AE, DC, MC, V. Parking 30,000L ($15).

This place makes a slightly saccharine use of Shakespeare's great love story as its theme. Most of the rooms in this once-stately palazzo look out over the Roman arena. In honor of the maiden Juliet, the hotel maintains at least one marble balcony that might be appropriate in a modern-day revival of the great play. The guest rooms are tastefully modernized, not overly large, and have burnished hardwoods, comfortable furnishings (like firm mattresses), and lighting you can actually read by, plus marble-sheathed bathrooms. The service is cordial, and the location is central, though on a quiet side street.

Hotel Torcolo. Vicolo Listone 3, 37121 Verona. ☎ **045-800-7512.** Fax 045-800-4058. 19 units. A/C MINIBAR TV TEL. 175,000L ($87.50) double. Breakfast 30,000L ($15). AE, MC, V. Parking 20,000–25,000L ($10–$12.50) in nearby public lot.

The setting is modest but, thanks to the devoted efforts of its trio of hardworking owners (Silvia Pomari and her colleagues, Marina and Diana), it's spotless. You'll find the Torcolo near the Roman arena and Piazza Brà, in a building erected around 1825. Some guest rooms are furnished with antiques. Since each room has a different artistic style (Liberty, Italian, English, and the like), you'd better call in advance to reserve the one you'd like best. Each comes with a firm mattress, plus a small bath. The staff speaks English.

DINING

EXPENSIVE

✪ **Arche.** Via Arche Scaligere 6. ☎ **045-800-7415.** Reservations required. Main courses 30,000–45,000L ($15–$22.50); fixed-price menus 85,000–100,000L ($42.50–$50). AE, DC, MC, V. Mon 7:30–9:30pm; Tues–Sat 12:30–2:30pm and 7:30–9:30pm. Closed Jan. ITALIAN.

This classic restaurant is acclaimed by some as the finest in Verona. We give that honor to Il Desco (see below), but Arche is a close runner-up. It was founded in 1879 by the great-grandfather of owner Giancarlo Gioco, and the seafood dishes are based on recipes passed down from generation to generation, including some discovered in ancient cookbooks. Giancarlo and his wife, Paola, insist on market-fresh fish, with sole, sea bass with porcini mushrooms, and scampi among the favorites. Baked "sea scorpion" with black olives and the ravioli stuffed with sea bass and served with clam sauce are the finest specialties. The furnishings in this 1420s building are Liberty style, enhanced by candlelight and fresh flowers.

✪ **Ristorante Il Desco.** Via Dietro San Sebastiano 7. ☎ **045-595-358.** Reservations recommended. Main courses 30,000–45,000L ($15–$22.50); tasting menu 150,000L ($75). AE, DC, MC, V. Mon–Sat 12:30–2pm and 7:30–10pm. Closed Jan 1–7 and Dec 25–26. ITALIAN.

The tops in Verona, Il Desco is a handsome restaurant occupying a renovated palazzo that's one of the city's civic prides. The menu steers closer to the philosophy of cuisine moderne than anything in town. The freshest ingredients are used in the specialties: shrimp purée, potato pie with mushrooms and black truffles, calamari salad with shallots, tortellini with sea bass, risotto with radicchio and truffles, and tagliolini with fresh mint, lemon, and oranges. The wine cellar is superb, and the sommelier will help if you're unfamiliar with regional vintages.

Ristorante Re Teodorico. Piazzale di Castel San Pietro 1. ☎ **045-834-9990.** Reservations required. Main courses 35,000–40,000L ($17.50–$20). AE, DC, MC, V. Thurs–Tues noon–3pm and 7–10pm. Closed Jan. REGIONAL/INTERNATIONAL.

Ristorante Re Teodorico is perched high on a hill at the edge of town, with a panoramic view of Verona and the Adige. From its entrance, you descend a cypress-lined road to the ledge-hanging restaurant suggestive of a lavish villa. Tables are set out on a wide flagstone terrace edged with classical columns and an arbor of red, pink, and yellow flowering vines. Specialties are homemade pasta, always delectable; swordfish with tomatoes, capers, and fresh basil; and chateaubriand with béarnaise sauce. The dessert specialty is crêpes suzette.

MODERATE

Ristorante All'Aquila. In the Due Torri Hotel Baglioni, Piazza Sant'Anastasia 4. ☎ **045-595-044.** Reservations recommended. Main courses 28,000–36,000L ($14–$18). AE, DC, MC, V. Daily 12:30–2:30pm and 7:30–10pm. ITALIAN/INTERNATIONAL.

Verona's most appealing upscale restaurant, boasting an art nouveau decor, has an impeccably trained staff headed by Sr. Mattia, who trained at Claridge's in London.

The menu is almost completely rewritten every 6 months but is likely to include smoked horsemeat with arugula and shaved parmigiano, marinated trout with citrus sauce, and tartare of fish with fresh cucumber. Pastas include ravioli with a medley of soft cheeses, spinach, and watercress sauce and subtly flavored tagliatelle with cream, herb, and egg-yolk sauce. A main course could include braised arugula and eggplant and perch fillets with sage. And desserts choices might be tiramisu and ricotta mousse. The list of mostly Italian wine is comprehensive.

Ristorante 12 Apostoli. Vicolo Corticella San Marco 3. ☎ **045-596-999.** Reservations recommended. Main courses 28,000–35,000L ($14–$17.50). AE, DC, MC, V. Tues–Sun 12:30–2:30pm; Tues–Sat 7:30–10pm. Closed June 15–July 5. ITALIAN.

Operated by the two Gioco brothers, this is Verona's oldest restaurant, in business for 250 years. It's a festive place, steeped in tradition, with frescoed walls and two dining rooms separated by brick arches. Giorgio, the artist of the kitchen, changes his menu daily, while Franco directs the dining room. For a main course, consider Giorgio's salmon baked in a pastry shell (the fish is marinated the day before, seasoned with garlic, and stuffed with scallops) or chicken stuffed with shredded vegetables and cooked in four layers of paper. To begin, we recommend the tempting *antipasti alla Scaligera.* For dessert, try the homemade cake.

INEXPENSIVE

VeronAntica. Via Sottoriva 10. ☎ **045-800-4124.** Reservations recommended. Main courses 15,000–28,000L ($7.50–$14). AE, DC, MC, V. Sept–June, Wed–Mon noon–2:30pm and 7–10:45pm; July–Aug, daily noon–10:45pm. INTERNATIONAL.

The VeronAntica is a distinguished local restaurant on the ground floor of a town house a short block from the river, across from a cobblestone arcade similar to the ones used in Zeffirelli's *Romeo and Juliet.* This place attracts locals, not just tourists. It's made even more romantic at night by a hanging lantern that dimly illuminates the street. The chef knows how to prepare all the classics as well as some innovative ones. Try *bretelline* (tagliatelle made with rice flour) with rughetta salad and asparagus, or select salmon in papillote with fresh mussels, seafood, and tomatoes. From June to September, you can dine on an open-air terrace.

VERONA AFTER DARK

The grande dame of local cafe society is the **Antico Caffè Sante** in the beautiful Piazza dei Signori (☎ **045-59-52-49**). Inside Verona's oldest cafe, the setting is rather formal, and meals are pricey; so you may want to instead snag an outdoor table, where you can soak in the million-dollar view of one of Verona's loveliest ancient squares.

Oenophiles will think they've died and gone to heaven when they discover the unmatched 80,000-bottle selection at ✪ **Bottega del Vino,** Via Scudo di Francia 3 (off Via Mazzini; ☎ **045-80-04-535**). This atmospheric bottega first opened in 1890, and the old-timers who spend hours in animated conversation seem to have been here ever since. The atmosphere and conviviality are reason enough to come by for a tipple at the well-known bar, where five dozen wines are available by the glass. Regulars, journalists, and local merchants often fill the few wooden tables at mealtimes, ordering simple and affordable but excellent dishes, such as homemade risottos.

Put on your dancing shoes and head for **Disco Berfis Club,** Via Lussemburgo (☎ **045-508-024**), or **Bar/Disco Tribu,** Via Calderara 17 (☎ **045-566-470**), where the rhythms echo what's being broadcast in New York and Milan. More closely linked to Verona's historic core is **Bar Campidoglio,** Piazza Tira Bosco (☎ **045-594-448**), which is more subdued and more evocative of the Italy of long ago.

Gays and lesbians can call **Circolo Pink,** Via Scriminari 7 (☎ **045-801-2854**), to get details on gay cultural activities, parties, or newly opened bars. You can call the hot line only Monday or Thursday 9 to 11pm and Saturday 6 to 9pm.

5 Treviso

19 miles (31km) N of Venice

Treviso is known to culinary fans for the cherries grown in its environs and the creation of tiramisu ("pick me up"), a delicious blend of ladyfingers, mascarpone cheese, eggs, cocoa, liqueur, and espresso. Art aficionados know Treviso for its many works by Tomaso da Modena.

ESSENTIALS

GETTING THERE There are four **trains** per hour from Venice, a trip of 30 minutes costing 3,000L ($1.50) one way, and hourly trains from Udine, a trip of 1½ hours for 10,000L ($5) one way. Treviso's station (☎ **1478-88-088** toll-free in Italy) is at Piazza Duca d'Aosta on the southern end of town.

The station at Lungosile Mattei 21 receives **buses** on the La Marca bus line (☎ **0422-577-311**) from Bassano del Grappa nine times daily, a trip of 1 hour costing 5,800L ($2.90) one way; from Padua, buses arrive every 30 minutes, a trip of 1 hour, 10 minutes costing 5,800L ($2.90) one way. The ACT line (☎ **0422-541-821**) runs two buses an hour from Venice, a 30-minute trip for 4,800L ($2.40).

If you have a **car** and are in Venice, take A11 through Mestre, a distance of 6 miles (10km); head northeast on A4 for 3 miles; then take Rte. S13 for 10 miles (16km) north to Treviso.

VISITOR INFORMATION The **tourist office** is on Piazza Monte Pietà (☎ **0422-547-632**). April to September, it's open Monday to Friday 9am to noon and 3 to 6pm, Saturday 8:30am to noon. October to March, hours are Monday to Tuesday 9am to 1pm, Wednesday to Saturday 9am to 1pm and 3 to 6pm.

SEEING THE SIGHTS

The huge Romanesque-Gothic **San Nicolò,** Via San Nicolà (☎ **0422-32-47**), boasts some important treasures, including its ornate vaulted ceiling with 14th-century frescoes by Tomaso da Modena on its columns. Even more impressive is the **Dominican Chapter (Capitolo dei Dominicani)** of the **Episcopal Seminary (Seminario Vescovile),** next door to the church. Here Modena captured in 40 portraits the diverse personalities of a series of Dominican monks seated at their desks. There's no admission fee, and both buildings are open daily 8am to 6:30pm.

No longer a church, **Santa Caterina,** Piazzetta Mario Botter, houses the frescoes comprising Modena's depiction of the Christian legend of the Ursula Cycle, with its 11,000 virgins all accounted for. At press time, a restoration program is nearing completion, so it should be open again by the time you arrive. Call the **Civic Museum (Museo Civico),** B. Cavour 24 (☎ **0422-658-442**), for hours or an appointment. The museum houses the strange *Il Castragatti* (The Cat Fixer) by Sebastiano Florigero, a *Crucifixion* by Bassano, and the fresco *San Antonio Abate* by Pordenone. Hours are Tuesday to Saturday 9am to 12:30pm and 2:30 to 5pm, Sunday 9am to noon. Admission is 4,000L ($2).

You can visit the **Duomo,** Piazza del Duomo at Via Canoniche 2 (☎ **0422-545-720**), Monday to Saturday 8am to noon and 3:30 to 7pm, Sunday 7:30am to 1pm and 3:30 to 8pm. It contains more frescoes by Pordenone as well as an *Annunciation* by Titian. The crypt is open after 10:30am.

The Wine Roads from Treviso

The gently rolling foothills of the Dolomites around Treviso are known for producing fine wines. For a view of the ancient vines, take a drive along the two highways known as the **Strade dei Vini del Piave** in honor of the nearby Piave River. Both begin at the medieval town of **Conegliano,** where the tourist office is at XX Settembre 61 (☎ **0438-21-230**), open Tuesday to Friday 9am to 1pm and 3 to 6pm, Saturday 9am to 1pm. **Altamarca** (☎ **0423-972-655**), a small tour group, provides English-speaking tours of the vineyards between Conegliano and Valdobbiadene. Call for tour times and admission prices.

You won't find route numbers associated with either of these wine roads, but each is clearly signposted en route, beginning in central Conegliano. The less interesting is the **Strada del Vino Rosso (Red Wine Road),** running through 25 miles (40km) of humid flatlands southeast of Conegliano. Significant points en route include the scenic hamlets of Oderzo, Motta, and Ponte di Piave.

Much more scenic and evocative is the **Strada del Vino Bianco (White Wine Road),** or, more specifically, the **Strada del Prosecco,** meandering through the foothills of the Dolomites for about 24 miles (39km) northwest of Conegliano, ending at Valdobbiadene. It passes through particularly prestigious regions famous for their sparkling prosecco, a quality white meant to be drunk young, with the characteristic taste and smell of ripe apples, wisteria, and acacia honey. The most charming of the many hamlets you'll encounter (blink an eye and you'll miss them) are San Pietro di Feletto, Follina, and Pieve di Soligno. Each is awash with family-run cantinas, kiosks, and roadside stands, all selling the fermented

A stroll through **Piazza dei Signori** offers views of several interesting Romanesque buildings, like the municipal **bell tower,** the **Palazzo Trecento,** and the nearby **Loggia dei Cavalieri** on Via Martiri della Libertà.

SHOPPING

The city is known for its production of wrought iron and copper utensils, and the best places to find these goods are **Prior,** Via Palestro 12 (☎ **0422-545-886**) and **Morandin,** Via Palestro 50 (☎ **0422-543-651**).

The cherries grown in the surrounding area ripen in June. At that time, you can buy them at all local markets, especially the **open-air market** on Tuesday and Saturday morning sprawling across Via Pescheria. Otherwise, one of the best selections of this fruit is found at **Pam** supermarket, Piazza Borso 12 (☎ **0422-583-913**). If you'd like to sample both the famous tiramisu or desserts made from fresh Treviso cherries, go to the cafe **Nascimben,** Via XX Settembre 3 (☎ **0422-512-91**).

ACCOMMODATIONS

Ca' del' Galletto. Via Santa Bona Vecchia 30, 31100 Treviso. ☎ **0422-432-550.** Fax 0422-432-510. www.sevenonline.it/cadelgalletto. E-mail: cadelgalletto@sevenonline.it. 58 units. A/C MINIBAR TV TEL. 220,000–300,000L ($110–$150) double; 350,000L ($175) junior suite. Rates include buffet breakfast. AE, DC, MC, V. Free parking. Bus: 5.

This thoroughly modern hotel offers comfortable soundproof guest rooms with safe-deposit boxes and trouser presses. Deluxe rooms also include Jacuzzis. The bathrooms are small but tidily organized, with hair dryers. An enclosed garden allows fruits of the local harvest and offering platters of prosciutto, local cheese, and crusty bread.

The two best hotels for establishing a base here are in Conegliano. The three-star **Canon d'Oro,** Via XX Settembre 129, 31015 Conegliano (☎ and fax **0438-34-246**), occupies a 15th-century building near the rail station and charges 150,000L ($75) double. The four-star **Hotel Città di Conegliano,** Via Parrilla 1 (☎ **0438-21-445;** fax 0438-410-950), is the best in town, an elegant landmark with unusual frescoes on the facade and doubles for 145,000 to 150,000L ($72.50 to $75).

If you're looking for a bite to eat in Conegliano, try our favorite restaurant, **Tre Panoce,** Via Vecchia Trevigiano 50 (☎ **0438-60-071**). Occupying a 16th-century stone building, it charges around 50,000L ($25) for full meals that include a celebration of whatever is in season (wine not included). Your pasta may be flavored with radicchio, fresh mushrooms, wild herbs, or local cheese. Tre Panoce is in the hills above Conegliano, half a mile from the town center. It's open Tuesday to Sunday noon to 2:30pm and Tuesday to Saturday 8 to 10pm (closed August). The most formal restaurant in town is **Al Salisà,** Via XX Settembre 2 (☎ **0438-24-288**), occupying a stone building with 12th-century foundations. The excellent menu includes roasted veal with wild herbs, sea bass with seasonal vegetables and basil-flavored white-wine sauce, and fettuccine with wild duck. Expect to spend 50,000L ($25) and up for a full meal. It's open Thursday to Tuesday noon to 3pm and Thursday to Monday 7:30 to 10:30pm.

you outdoor privacy in the city. The lobby bar is open 24 hours, and the Ristorante Albertini next door serves rich Venetian seafood and other traditional specialties.

✪ **Hotel Al Fogher.** Viale della Repubblica 10, 31100 Treviso. ☎ **800/528-1234** in the U.S., or 0422-432-950. Fax 0422-430-391. www.bestwestern.com. 55 units. A/C TV TEL. 270,000L ($135) double; 320,000L ($160) suite. Rates include breakfast. AE, DC, MC, V.

We especially recommend this business favorite of wine merchants, just north of the medieval fortifications of Treviso. The decor contrasts antique statuary with modern art prints and marble with glass bricks. The guest rooms are outfitted in an internationally modern style, with firm mattresses. The tiled bathrooms are compact.

The top floor has a panoramic terrace where guests congregate for views over the countryside, and the basement restaurant serves seasonal Venetian dishes made from the freshest ingredients (it's popular, so reservations are suggested). The wine list is substantial. The restaurant is closed in August and the first week of January.

Nearby Accommodations

✪ **Villa Condulmer.** Via Zermanese 1, 31020 Zerman di Mogliano Veneto. ☎ **041-457-100.** Fax 041-457-134. www.tsi.it/condulmer. 42 units. A/C MINIBAR TEL. 340,000L ($170) double; 360,000L ($180) junior suite; 400,000L ($200) apt. Rates include breakfast. AE, DC, MC, V. Drive 7 miles (11km) south on S13 to Zerman, just outside Mogliano Veneto.

The finest place to stay is outside Treviso, where Giuseppe Verdi fled in 1853 after the Venetian debut of *La Traviata* was met with catcalls. This house was built in 1743 by the Condulmer family, whose wealth and power can be traced to 14th-century ancestor Pope Eugene IV. It passed from the family's hands in the early 19th century, when frescoes by Moretti Laresi were added. You'll find elaborate stuccowork, marble floors, crystal chandeliers, Oriental carpets, period furnishings, and large guest rooms in the main house as well as in two annexes with lofts. Each room is sumptuous, with a luxury mattress and a bathroom with ample space.

Dining/Diversions: There's also a piano bar and a restaurant, which grows its own produce to supplement the market's fresh fish and game.
Amenities: The back garden houses a private chapel, and beyond it stretches a park with a small lake, hillocks, ruins, a pool, a 27-hole golf course, a tennis court, and riding grounds.

DINING

Beccherie. Piazza Ancilotto 10. ☎ **0422-56-601.** Reservations recommended. Main courses 20,000–35,000L ($10–$17.50). AE, DC, MC, V. Tues–Sun 12:30–2pm; Tues–Sat 7:30–10pm. Closed July 15–31. VENETIAN.

Despite its parking lot, this stone-sided building still evokes the era of its construction (1830). The cuisine and the flavorings of the dishes vary with the seasons and include such midwinter game dishes as *faraona in salsa peverada* (guinea hen in peppery sauce) and a spring/summer favorite, *pasticcio di melanzane* (eggplant casserole). In between, look for enduring traditions like fried crabs from the Venetian lagoon served with herb-flavored polenta, salt cod Vicenza style, osso bucco, fiery hot pastas, roasted chicken, or pasta e fagioli with radicchio.

El Toulà da Alfredo. Via Collalto 26. ☎ **0422-540-275.** Reservations required Fri–Sat. Main courses 18,000–40,000L ($9–$20). AE, DC, MC, V. Tues–Sat noon–2:30pm and 7:30–11pm; Sun noon–2:30pm. Closed 10 days in Aug. INTERNATIONAL/VENETIAN.

This is the restaurant that launched what's now a nine-member chain known throughout Italy for its food and service. It offers regional dishes whose inspiration varies with the seasonality of ingredients and the chef's intelligent takes on local traditions. In one of the two art nouveau dining rooms, you can order superb versions of risotto with baby peas, pappardelle with baby asparagus tips and herbs, Venetian-style calves' liver, veal kidneys in mustard sauce, *risotto con funghi* (rice with mushrooms), and blinis with caviar. The lengthy dessert roster includes light, sweet sorbets, often made from local fruit. The service is impeccable.

6 Bassano del Grappa

23 miles (37km) N of Venice

At the foot of Mount Grappa in the Valsugana Valley, this hideaway along the Brenta River draws Italian vacationers because of its proximity to the mountains and its panoramic views. Bassano is best known for its liquor, grappa, a brandy usually made from grape pomace left in a winepress, but it's is also known for pottery, porcini mushrooms, white asparagus, and radicchio.

ESSENTIALS

GETTING THERE There's direct **train** service from Trent eight times a day, a 2-hour journey costing 8,300L ($5) one way. There are also trains requiring a change at Castelfranco from Padua and Venice. From Padua, the ride is a 1-hour trip arriving 12 times daily for 10,100L ($5.05); from Venice, 16 trains arrive daily, taking 1 hour, 20 minutes for 5,900L ($2.95). Contact the train station (☎ **0424-525-034**) for information and schedules.

There are many more **buses** to Bassano than trains. The FTV bus line (☎ **0424-30-850**) offers service hourly from Vicenza (trip time: 1 hour) for 5,300L ($2.65) one way. **CO.APT** (☎ **0424-820-68-11**) arrives from Padua every 30 minutes, the trip taking 1 hour and costing 6,000L ($3).

If you have a **car** and are in Asolo, take Rte. 248 for 7 miles (11km) west.

VISITOR INFORMATION The **tourist office** is at Largo Corona d'Italia 35, off Via Jacopo del Ponte (☎ **0424-524-351**); it hands out the *Bassano News,* a monthly information/accommodation guide with a town map. The office is open Monday to Friday 9am to 12:30pm and 2 to 5pm, Saturday 9am to 12:30pm.

EXPLORING THE TOWN

The village is lovely and the liquor strong, but there aren't a lot of specific sights. Bassono's best-known landmark is the **Ponte dei Alpini,** a covered wooden bridge over the Brenta, which has been replaced numerous times because of flooding, but each version is faithful to the original 1209 design.

Housing numerous paintings by Basano, the **Civic Museum (Museo Civico),** in Piazza Garibaldi at Via Museo 12 (☎ **0424-522-235**), also has works by Canova, Tiepolo, and others. It's open Tuesday to Saturday 9am to 6pm, with an admission of 7,000L ($3.50). That ticket will also admit you to the **Palazzo Sturm,** Via Schiavonetti (☎ **0424-524-933**), home of the Ceramics Museum, featuring 4 centuries of finely crafted regional pottery. April to October, hours are Tuesday to Saturday 9am to 12:30pm and 3:30 to 6:30pm, Sunday 3:30 to 6:30pm. June to September, the museum keeps the same hours but is open also Sunday 10am to 12:30pm. Admissions for Palazzo Sturm is 5,000L ($2.50).

If you don't get sick from overindulging on grappa, you may want to pick some up to take home. The best-known distillery is the 18th-century **Nardini,** Via Madonna Monte Berico 4 (☎ **0424-567-040**), next to the Ponte degli Alpini, where juniper, pear, peach, and plum versions supplement the grape standard. Other grappa shops are **Poli,** Via Gamba (☎ **0424-524-426**), and **Bassanina,** Via Angarano (☎ **0424-502-140**). Because you're in the heart of grappa country, you can also find good smaller labels like Folco Portinari, Maschio, Jacopo de Poli, Rino Dal Tosco, Da Ponte, and Carpene Malvolti.

ACCOMMODATIONS

Al Castello. Piazza Terraglio 19, 36061 Bassano del Grappa. ☎ and fax **0424-228-665.** 11 units. A/C TV TEL. 140,000L ($70) double. Breakfast 10,000L ($5). AE, MC, V. Free parking.

Opened in the heart of town by the Cattapan family more than 25 years ago, this is a simple hotel outfitted to provide you with a comfortable stay at a bargain rate. This antique town house has been renovated but retains a classical style. The guest rooms are small to medium in size, each fitted with a firm mattress, and the tiled bathrooms are a bit cramped. There's no restaurant, but you can relax over coffee or a drink at a cafe/bar with a sidewalk terrace.

Bonotto Hotel Belvedere. Piazzale Generale Giardino 14, 36061 Bassano del Grappa. ☎ **0424-529-845.** Fax 0424-529-849. www.bonotto.it. E-mail: info@bonotto.it. 87 units. A/C MINIBAR TV TEL. 160,000–290,000L ($80–$145) double; junior suite 320,000–400,000L ($160–$200). Rates include breakfast. AE, DC, MC, V. Parking 20,000–25,000L ($10–$12.50).

The first inn in the village, the Belvedere opened in the 15th century as a place to rest and change horses before traveling on to Venice. The third-floor rooms attest to the hotel's age, with rustic exposed beams. All the guest rooms incorporate classical, Venetian, and Bassanese styles. The hotel recently added five superior doubles and

Off the Beaten Path to a Human Chess Game

Four and a half miles (7km) west of Bassano del Grappa on Rte. 248, **Marostica** hosts the **Game of Life,** a reminder of how far relations between the sexes have actually progressed. The second week of September in even-numbered years, the town square in front of the Castello da Basso is used as a chessboard, and costumed townspeople become its pieces in order to re-create the medieval practice of playing *scacchi* to claim the hand of the kingdom's most beautiful woman (the loser got a homelier maiden). For more information, contact the **Associazione Pro Marostica,** Piazza Castello 1 (☎ **0424-72-127**). While you're here, you might want to indulge in the wonderful cherries that are the town's other claim to fame.

---

renovated 14 others. The tiled bathrooms are well maintained and beautifully kept. The public rooms are luxurious, with Oriental rugs and tapestries, fresh flowers, and curvaceous wooden furniture covered with rich fabrics. The lounge houses a baby grand piano, a fireplace, and a wooden ivy-covered balcony. The chandeliered Del Buon Ricordo specializes in *baccalà alla vicentina,* and you get to take your plate, illustrated with a drawing of the Bassano bridge, home as a souvenir. The restaurant is shared with the Bonotto Hotel Palladio, 500 yards away, whose gym facilities are open to Belvedere guests.

Bonotto Hotel Palladio. Via Gramsci 2, 36061 Bassano del Grappa. ☎ **0424-523-777.** Fax 0424-524-050. www.bonotto.it. E-mail: palladiohotel@bonotto.it. 66 units. A/C MINIBAR TV TEL. 150,000– 300,000L ($75–$150). Rates include breakfast. AE, DC, MC, V. Parking 20,000L ($10).

This is the Belvedere's sibling (they're 500 yards apart and share a restaurant, a gym, and parking facilities), but you'd never guess they were related. This hotel's facade is modern with cut stone and stepped glass panels. The interior is contemporary as well, and the lobby boasts a curved wood-and-brass counter and modern recessed lighting. They do have common interior elements though, mainly in the form of mottled marble floors and Oriental rugs. The guest rooms are modern and streamlined, small to medium in size, with firm mattresses. The bathrooms are small but tidy. Step over to the Belvedere to partake in meals at Del Buon Ricordo. Three golf courses are within a 10- to 20-mile (16km–32km) drive.

Villa Palma. Via Chemin Palma 30, 36065 Mussolente. ☎ **0424-577-407.** Fax 0424-87-687. 21 units. A/C MINIBAR TV TEL. 315,000L ($157.50) double. Rates include buffet breakfast. AE, DC, MC, V. Free parking.

Just 3 miles (5km) from Bassano, this 18th-century villa was opened as a hotel in 1991 after renovations that preserved features like its beamed and vaulted brick ceilings. The guest rooms are individualized by mixing antiques, carpets, and tapestries to create a comfortable yet elegant atmosphere. Most rooms are fairly spacious, and all have excellent mattresses and fine linen. Some bathrooms have sauna showers or Jacuzzis. La Loggia restaurant is closed on Monday and for 2 weeks in August and 1 week following New Year's, but at other times it creates wonderful regional meals.

DINING

Al Sole. Via Jacopo Vittorelli 41. ☎ **0424-523-206.** Reservations recommended. Main courses 20,000–30,000L ($10–$15). AE, DC, MC, V. Tues–Sun noon–3pm and 7:30–10pm. Closed 20 days in July. VENETIAN.

Gian-Franco Chiurato's successful restaurant occupies this cavernous early-19th-century palazzo, where both dining rooms are decorated with local ceramics. The cuisine is rooted in the Veneto's traditions and celebrates two annual crops: In springtime, look for the region's distinctive white asparagus blended into pastas and risottos, used as a garnish for main courses, and often featured as a refreshing course on its own. In autumn and winter, look for similar variations on mushrooms, especially porcini, which are absolutely addictive with game birds and venison. The rest of the year, expect polenta with codfish, puff pastry layered with local cheeses and mushrooms, homemade bigoli pasta drenched with duck meat and mushrooms, and baked lamb with herbed polenta.

✪ **Birreria Ottone.** Via Matteoti 48–50. ☎ **0424-522-206.** Reservations recommended Fri–Sat. Main courses 15,000–32,000L ($7.50–$16). AE, DC, MC, V. Wed–Mon 10am–3:15pm; Wed–Sun 7pm–midnight. AUSTRIAN/ITALIAN/VENETO.

Occupying a 13th-century building across from City Hall, this is the most appealing beer hall in the region. Thanks to generous portions and copious amounts of beer, the site is preferred by extended families and groups of friends, some of whom actually dine. Look for two dining rooms encircled with chiseled stone, marble accents, and ceramic tiles and food items that include goulash, Wiener schnitzel, frankfurters, roasted lamb, and Venetian-style calves' liver. In spring, look for savory local asparagus.

7 Trieste

72 miles (116km) NE of Venice, 414 miles (667km) NE of Rome, 253 miles (407km) E of Milan

Remote Trieste, a shimmering city with many neoclassical buildings, is perched on the half-moon Gulf of Trieste, which opens into the Adriatic. Trieste has had a long history, with many changes of ownership. The Hapsburg emperor Charles VI declared it a free port in 1719, but by the 20th century it was an ocean outlet for the Austro-Hungarian Empire. After World War I and a secret deal among the Allies, Trieste was ceded to Italy. In 1943 Trieste again fell to foreign troops—this time the Nazis, who were ousted by Tito's Yugoslav army in 1945. In 1954, after much hassle, the American and British troops withdrew as the Italians marched in, with the stipulation that the much-disputed Trieste would be maintained as a free port. Today that status continues. Politics, as always, dominates the agenda here. There's racial tension, and many Italian Fascists and anti-Slav parties are centered in Trieste.

Trieste has known many glamorous literary associations, particularly in the pre–World War II years. As a stop on the Orient Express, it became a famed destination. Dame Agatha Christie came this way, as did Graham Greene. James Joyce, eloping with Nora Barnacle, arrived in 1904. Out of money, Joyce got a job teaching at the Berlitz School and lived in Trieste for nearly 10 years. He wrote *A Portrait of the Artist as a Young Man* here and may have begun his masterpiece *Ulysses* here as well. Poet Rainer Maria Rilke also lived in the area. Author Richard Burton, known for his *Arabian Nights* translations, lived in Trieste from 1871 until he died about 20 years later.

Trieste, squashed between Slovenia and the Adriatic, has been more vulnerable to conditions following the collapse of Yugoslavia than any other city in Italy. Civil war and turmoil have halted the flow of thousands who used to cross the border to buy merchandise—mainly jeans and household appliances. The port has also suffered from crises in the shipbuilding and steel industries. Trieste remains Italy's insurance capital, and one-fourth of its population of 150,000 residents is retired (it has the highest per capita pensioner population in Italy).

ESSENTIALS

GETTING THERE Trieste is serviced by an **airport** at **Ronchi dei Legionari** (☎ **0481/773-224**), 21½ miles (35km) northwest of the city. Daily flights on Alitalia connect it with Linate airport in Milan (trip time: 50 minutes), Franz Josef Strauss airport in Munich (1 hour, 10 minutes), and Leonardo da Vinci airport in Rome (1 hour, 10 minutes).

Trieste lies on a direct **rail** link from Venice. Trip time to Venice is 2½ hours, and a one-way ticket is 14,000L ($7). The station is on Piazza della Libertà (☎ **040-418-207,** or 1478-88-088 toll-free in Italy), northwest of the historic center. It's better to fly, drive, or take the train to Trieste. Once here, you'll find a network of **local buses** servicing the region from Corso Cavour (☎ **040-336-0300**).

If you have a **car** and are coming from Venice, continue northeast along A4 until reaching the end of the line at Trieste.

VISITOR INFORMATION The **tourist office** is at Via San Nicolò 20 (☎ **040-679-611**), open Monday to Friday 9am to 7pm and Saturday 8:30am to 1pm. A **second office** is in Stazione Centrale (☎ **040-420-182**), open Monday to Saturday 9am to 7pm and Sunday 10am to 1pm and 4 to 7pm.

EXPLORING THE CITY

The heart of Trieste is the neoclassic ✪ **Piazza dell'Unità d'Italia,** Italy's largest square that fronts the sea. Opening onto the square is the town hall with a clock tower, the Palace of the Government, and the main office of the Lloyd Triestino ship line. Flanking it are numerous cafes and restaurants, popular at night with locals who sip an aperitif, then promenade along the seafront esplanade.

After visiting the main square, you may want to view Trieste from an even better vantage point. Head up the hill for another cluster of attractions—you can take an antiquated **tram** leaving from Piazza Oberdan and get off at Obelisco. At the **belvedere,** the city of the Adriatic will spread out before you.

Cathedral of St. Just (Cattedrale di San Giusto). Piazza Cattedrale, Colle Capitolino. ☎ **040-302-874.** Free admission. Daily 8:30am–noon and 4–7pm.

Dedicated to the patron saint of Trieste, who was martyred in A.D. 303, this basilica was consecrated in 1330, incorporating a pair of churches that had been separate until then. The front is Romanesque style, enhanced by a rose window. Inside, the nave is flanked by two pairs of aisles. To the left of the main altar are the best of the Byzantine mosaics in Trieste (note especially the blue-robed Madonna and Child). The main altar and the chapel to the right contain less interesting mosaics. To the left of the basilica entrance is a campanile from the 14th century, which you can scale for a view of Trieste and its bay. At its base are preserved the remains of a Roman temple from the 1st century. You may prefer to take a taxi up to the cathedral and then walk a leisurely 15 minutes back down. From the basilica you can also stroll to the nearby San Giusto Castle (see below).

St. Just Castle (Castello di San Giusto). Piazza Cattedrale 3. ☎ **040-309-362.** Castle 3,000L ($1.50); museum 3,000L ($1.50). Castle, daily 9am–sunset; museum, Tues–Sun 9am–1pm.

Constructed in the 15th century by the Venetians on the site of a Roman fort, this fortress maintained a sharp eye on the bay, watching for unfriendly visitors arriving by sea. From its bastions, panoramic views of Trieste unfold. Inside is a museum with a collection of arms and armor. The castle's open-air theater hosts a film festival in July and August.

Trieste

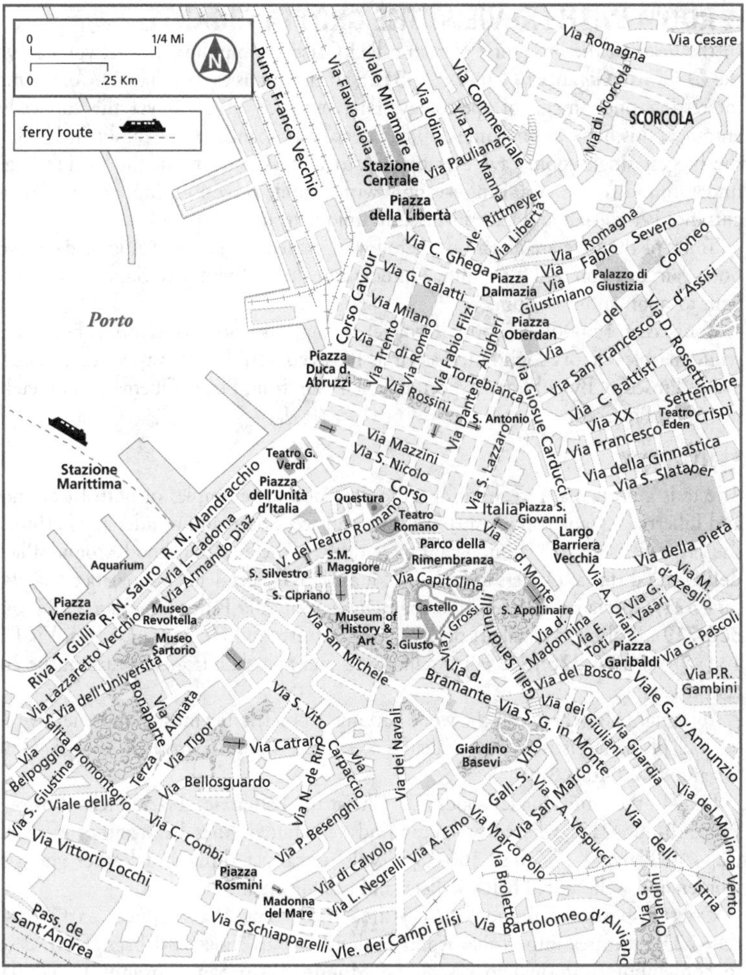

✪ **Miramare Castle (Castello di Miramare).** Viale Miramare, Grignano (4 1/2 miles (8km) northwest of town). ☎ **040-224-143.** Admission 8,000L ($4). Apr–Sept daily 9am–6pm; Oct–Mar daily 9am–4pm. Bus: 36.

Overlooking the Bay of Grignano, this castle was built by Archduke Maximilian, the brother of Franz Josef, the Hapsburg emperor of Austria. Maximilian, who married Princess Charlotte of Belgium, was the commander of the Austrian navy in 1854. In an ill-conceived move, he and "Carlotta" sailed to Mexico in 1864, where he became the emperor in an unfortunate, brief reign. He was shot in 1867 in Querétaro, Mexico. His wife lived until 1927 in a château outside Brussels, driven insane by the Mexican episode. On the ground floor, you can visit Maximilian's bedroom (built like a ship's cabin) and Charlotte's, as well as an impressive receiving room and more parlors, including a chinoiserie salon.

Enveloping the castle are magnificently designed grounds (the **Parco di Miramare**), ideal for pleasant strolls. In July and August, a **sound-and-light presentation** in the park depicts Maximilian's tragedy in Mexico. Tickets begin at 15,000L ($7.50).

A ROOM WITH NO VIEW: THE GROTTA GIGANTE

In the heart of the limestone plateau called Carso surrounding Trieste, you can visit the ✪ **Grotta Gigante** (☎ **040-327-312**), an enormous cavern that's one of the most interesting phenomena of speleology. First explored in 1840 via the top ceiling entrance, this huge room, some 380 feet deep, was opened to the public in 1908. It's the biggest single-room cave ever opened to visitors and one of the world's largest underground rooms. You can visit only with a guide on a 40-minute tour. Near the entrance is the Man and Caves Museum, unique in Italy.

Tours of the cave are given on the following schedule: July and August daily every hour 9am to noon and 2 to 5pm; September to June, Tuesday to Sunday every hour 9am to noon and 2 to 5pm.

Tours cost 15,000L ($7.50). If you're driving, take Strada del Friuli beyond the white marble Victory Lighthouse as far as Prosecco. On the freeway, you can take the exit at Prosecco. By public transport, take the tram from Piazza Oberdan and then bus no. 45 to Prosecco.

SHOPPING

Trieste is a great place to shop for antiques. Look for examples of both Biedermeier and Liberty (Italian art nouveau) furniture and accessories and wander at will through the city's densest collection of antiques dealers, the neighborhood around **Piazza dell'Unità d'Italia.** Dealers to look out for are **Davia,** Via dell'Annunziata 6 (☎ **040-304-321**), specializing in antique engravings; **Jésu,** Via Felice Venezian 9 (☎ **040-300-719**), dealing in small art objects and furniture; and **Dr. Fulvio Rosso,** Via Diaz 13 (☎ **040-306-226**), specializing in crystal and porcelain from the turn of the 20th century.

You might also check out the wood carvings from Trieste's most comprehensive collection of half-Austrian, half-Italian accessories, **Paolo Hrovatin,** Borgo Grotte Gigante (☎ **040-327-077**).

Fine leather and suede goods fill **Christine Pellettrie,** Piazza della Borso 15 (☎ **040-366-212**), where women can find well-crafted shoes, bags, and pants. **Fendi,** Capo di Piazza 1 (☎ **040-366-464**), sells upscale clothing and leather goods for women and well-crafted belts, wallets, and ties for men.

Offering both casual and formal attire, **Max Mara,** Via Carducci 23 (☎ **040-636-723**), features impeccable women's designs, plus shoes and bags. From classic to contemporary, formal to casual, **Le Monde,** Passo San Giovanni 1 (☎ **040-636-343**), offers clothing for men and women. A waterfront shop, **Spangher,** Riva Gulli 8 (☎ **040-305-158**), sells trendy sportswear and an Italianized version of Abercrombie & Fitch.

The 130-year-old **La Bomboniera,** Via XXX Ottobre 3 (☎ **040-632-752**), is a candy store as beautifully wrapped as the chocolates it sells, with etched glass, carved walnut shelves, and an elaborate glass chandelier. Besides fine chocolates, it offers traditional sweets and pastries of the region, as well as a few Austro-Hungarian specialties.

ACCOMMODATIONS

✪ **Grand Hotel Duchi d'Aosta.** Piazza Unità d'Italia 2, 34124 Trieste. ☎ **040-760-0011.** Fax 040-366-092. 55 units. A/C MINIBAR TV TEL. 365,000L ($182.50) double; from 620,000L ($310) suite. Rates include breakfast. AE, DC, MC, V. Parking 37,000L ($18.50).

This glamorous hotel began about 200 years ago as a restaurant for the dock workers who toiled nearby. In 1873 one of the most beautiful facades in Trieste—a white neoclassical shell with delicate carving, arched windows, and a stone crown of heroic sculptures—was erected over the existing building. The design is very much that of an 18th-century palace, enhanced by views over the fountains and lamps of the square and the sea beyond it, while the Victorian public rooms give it a 19th-century ambience. The interior was practically rebuilt in the 1970s, and each guest room boasts a well-stocked minibar, antiqued walls, and tasteful furniture (including the town's most sumptuous beds). The tiled bathrooms are well equipped, with hair dryers.

Dining: The Ristorante Harry's Grill is so good we've reviewed it under "Dining."

Amenities: Concierge, room service, twice-daily maid service, laundry/dry cleaning.

Hotel al Teatro. Capo di Piazza G. Bartoli 1, 34124 Trieste. ☎ **040-366-220.** Fax 040-366-560. 45 units, 35 with bathroom. TEL. 145,000L ($72.50) double without bathroom, 170,000L ($85) double with bathroom. Rates include breakfast. AE, MC, V.

The theatrical mask carved into the stone arch above the entrance is an appropriate symbol of this hotel, a favorite with many of Trieste's visiting opera stars. It's a few steps from the seaside panorama of Piazza dell'Unità d'Italia and about a 10-minute walk from the station. The slightly old-fashioned guest rooms have parquet floors, lots of space, and comfortable but minimal furniture (with decent mattresses). The hotel was built in 1830 as a home and served as British army headquarters following World War II.

Novo Hotel Impero. Via Sant'Anastasio 1, 34132 Trieste. ☎ **040-364-242.** Fax 040-365-023. 50 units. TV TEL. 240,000L ($120) double; 340,000L ($170) suite. Rates include breakfast. AE, DC, MC, V. Parking 20,000L ($10).

This restored member of Fenice hotels occupies a neoclassical building in front of the rail station and still retains much of the original glamour of its facade. Next to the historical center and the business area, it offers tastefully, though sparsely, furnished guest rooms, each with a good mattress and completely modernized bathroom.

DINING

Ai Due Triestini. Via Cadorna 10. ☎ **040-303-759.** Main courses 16,000–25,000L ($8–$12.50). No credit cards. Mon–Sat noon–3pm. Closed Sept. AUSTRIAN/INTERNATIONAL/TRIESTINO.

For one of the best lunch bargains in Trieste, we suggest this little trattoria behind Piazza dell'Unità d'Italia. Run by a husband-and-wife team, it covers its tablecloths with plastic and doesn't bother to print a menu. Some of the cooking is heavily influenced by neighboring Austria. Try *spezzatino,* chunks of beef in a goulash ragout, with fresh peas and potatoes. The Hungarian goulash is quite good, as is a rich strudel in the tradition of Budapest. Fresh fish, calamari, and octopus lend an Italian flavor.

Al Bragozzo. Riva Nazario Sauro 22. ☎ **040-303-001.** Reservations recommended. Main courses 16,000–45,000L ($8–$22.50). AE, DC, MC, V. Tues–Sat 11am–3pm and 7–10pm. Closed June 22–July 10 and Dec 25–Jan 10. SEAFOOD.

This is the best-known restaurant at the port. If you're a steak lover, you've come to the wrong place—only fish and pasta are served. The simply yet creatively prepared meals pay homage to the sea and its heritage by combining the elements of Italian cuisine and the riches of the Mediterranean. Specialties include *spaghetti alla Giorgio* (with tomatoes and herbs), ravioli stuffed with herbs, monkfish braised with artichokes and cooked with white wine, spaghetti with lobster, and many preparations of salmon and shrimp. If you visit in summer, you can dine at the outdoor tables sheltered by a canopy.

Al Granzo. Piazza Venezia 7. ☎ **040-306-788.** Reservations recommended. Main courses 20,000–35,000L ($10–$17.50); fixed-price menu 45,000–80,000L ($22.50–$40). AE, DC, MC, V. Thurs–Tues 12:30–3pm; Mon–Tues and Thurs–Sat 7:30–10:30pm. SEAFOOD.

This restaurant was opened in 1923 by the ancestors of the three brothers who run it today. It's one of Trieste's leading seafood restaurants, serving flavorful versions of that curious mix of Italian, Austrian, and Yugoslav cuisines known as Triestino. Menu items include *brodetto,* a traditional bouillabaisse spiced with saffron and other herbs; vermicelli with black mussels; and risotto with seafood. Fresh fish are displayed on crushed ice in a wagon, and there's an impressive selection of fresh *contorni* (vegetables, sold individually). A suitable wine would be a local Tocai Friulano, aromatic and somewhat tart. Dessert might be homemade strudel.

Antica Trattoria Suban. Via Comici 2, at San Giovanni. ☎ **040-54-368.** Reservations recommended. Main courses 20,000–35,000L ($10–$17.50). AE, DC, MC, V. Wed–Sun 12:30–2:30pm; Wed–Mon 7:30–10pm. Closed 15 days in Aug. ITALIAN/CENTRAL EUROPEAN.

This tavern is 2$^{1}/_{2}$ miles (4km) north of Trieste in the district of San Giovanni, on a spacious terrace opening onto a hill view. The landscape contains glimpses of the Industrial Age, but the brick and stone walls, the terrace, and the country feeling are still intact. The restaurant is run by descendants of the founding family, and the cuisine is both hearty and delicate, drawing its inspiration from northeastern Italian, Slavic, Hungarian, and Germanic traditions. Dishes include a flavorful risotto with herbs, beef with garlic sauce, a perfectly prepared chicken Kiev, veal croquettes with parmigiano and egg yolks, crepes stuffed with basil and roasted veal, and haunch of veal with roasted potatoes. The chef's handling of grilled meats is adept, and the rich pastries, such as the honey strudel, are worth the calories.

Ristorante Harry's Grill. In the Grand Hotel Duchi d'Aosta, Piazza dell'Unità d'Italia 2. ☎ **040-365-646.** Reservations required. Main courses 30,000–40,000L ($15–$20); Sun brunch 50,000L ($25). AE, DC, MC, V. Daily 12:15–3pm and 7:15–10:30pm. INTERNATIONAL.

In Trieste's most upscale hotel, this restaurant manages to be both elegant and relaxed, where you can have an American-style martini followed by a simple plate of pasta or a full meal. The big lace-covered curtains complement the paneling, the polished brass, and the blue Murano chandeliers. In summer, tables are set up in the traffic-free piazza. The outdoor terrace, sheltered by a canopy, has a separate area for bar patrons. The Mediterranean-inspired cuisine is good but not great and includes fresh shrimp with oil and lemon, pasta and risotto dishes, boiled salmon in sauce, calves' liver with onions, bigoli (fat spaghetti) with duck meat, and beef fillet with red-wine sauce. The adjoining bar (not related to Italy's other famed Harry's Bars) is one of the most popular rendezvous spots in town.

TRIESTE AFTER DARK

Trieste's most impressive theater, the **Teatro Verdi,** Corso Cavour (☎ **040 672-2111**), has been compared to a blend of the Vienna State Opera and Milan's La Scala. Built in 1801 and massively renovated in the mid-1990s, it presents classical concerts and operas throughout the year. Tickets range from 25,000 to 120,000L ($12.50 to $60).

The town's loveliest cafe, almost adjacent to the above-mentioned theater, is the **Caffè Tommaseo,** Riva III Novembre 3 (☎ **040-366-765**).

If you're interested in dancing the night away, the neighborhood around Piazza dell'Unità d'Italia offers the town's most animated disco, **Mandracchio,** Passo di Piazza (☎ **040-366-292**), which is rivaled by **Disco Machiavelli,** Viale Miramare 285

(☎ **040-44-104**), a crowded see-and-be-seen dance hall whose only drawback is its location 4 miles (6km) north of Piazza dell'Unità d'Italia. Catering to a more mature crowd is **Bar Jamin,** a woodsy-looking hideaway in the Il Giulia Shopping Center, Via Giulia 75 (☎ **040-569-306**).

8 Cortina d'Ampezzo: Gateway to the Dolomites

100 miles (161km) N of Venice, 82 miles (132km) E of Bolzano, 255 miles (411km) NE of Milan

This chic resort town is your best center for exploring the snowy Dolomiti. Its reputation as a tourist mecca dates from before World War I, but its recent growth has been phenomenal, spurred by the 1956 Olympics held here. Cortina d'Ampezzo draws throngs of nature lovers in summer and both Olympic-caliber and neophyte skiers in winter. (So expect high hotel prices in July and August as well as in the 3 months of winter.)

Cortina is in the middle of a valley ringed by enough Dolomite peaks to cause Hannibal's elephants to throw up their trunks and flee in horror. Regardless of which road you choose for a drive, you'll find the scenery rewarding. And Cortina sets an excellent table, inspired by the cuisine of both Venice and Tyrol.

ESSENTIALS

GETTING THERE Frequent **trains** run between Venice and Calalzo di Cadore (trip time: 2½ hours), 19 miles (31km) south of Cortina. You proceed the rest of the way by bus. For information about schedules, call ☎ **01478-88-088** in Calalzo. About 14 to 16 **buses** a day connect Calalzo di Cadore with Cortina. Buses arrive at the Cortina bus station on Viale Marconi (☎ **0436-27-41**).

If you have a **car,** take A27 from Venice to Pian de Vedoia, continuing north along S51 all the way to Cortina d'Ampezzo.

VISITOR INFORMATION The **tourist office** is at Piazzetta San Francesco 8 (☎ **0436-32-31**), open Monday to Friday 9am to 12:30pm and 4 to 7pm, Saturday 10am to 12:30pm and 4 to 7pm, and Sunday 10am to 12:30pm.

EXPLORING THE PEAKS OF THE DOLOMITES

One of the main attractions in Cortina is to take a **cable car** "halfway to the stars," as the expression goes. On one of them, at least, you'll be just a yodel away from the pearly gates: the **Freccia nel Cielo** ("Arrow of the Sky"). July 12 to September 28 and December 20 to mid-April beginning at 9am, cars depart from the base behind Cortina's Olympic Stadium every 20 minutes (call ☎ **0436-50-52** for departures the rest of the year). A round-trip is 30,000L ($15) in winter and 45,000L ($22.50) in summer. An ascent to the summit of the cable-car run requires two changes en route and an uphill ride through three separate cable-car segments. The first station is Col Druscie at 5,752 feet, the second Ra Valles at 8,027 feet, and the top Tofana di Mezzo at 10,543 feet. At Tofana on a clear day, you can see as far as Venice.

Part of the Alps, the snowy peaks of the **Dolomiti** stretch along Italy's northwestern tier, following the line of the Austrian border between the valleys of the Adige and Brenta Rivers.

Although the highest peak is the Marmolada (a few feet shy of 11,000 feet above sea level), the range contains 18 peaks in Italian territory that rise above 10,000 feet. Escaping from the often intense heat of other parts of the country, Italians travel here to breathe the Dolomiti's cool mountain air and to ski and play in resorts like Cortina.

The mix of limestone and porphyry, combined with the angle of the sun, contributes to the peaks' dramatic coloration. Most pronounced in the morning and at dusk, their colors range from soft pinks to brooding russets. When the sun shines directly overhead, the hues fade to a homogenized dull gray. Fortunately for tourists, trekkers, and skiers, the climate isn't as bone-chilling as it is in the alpine regions of western Italy and in the Alps of the Tyrol, farther north.

Throughout the Dolomiti, networks of **hiking trails** are clearly marked with signs, and local tourist offices (as well as most hotel staffs) can help you choose a good hike that suits your time and ability level. Maps of hiking trails are broadly distributed, and any tourist office can refer you to the nearest branch of the Associazione Guide Alpine. If you decide to ramble across the Dolomiti, you'll need stout shoes, warm clothing, and a waterproof jacket (storms erupt quickly at these altitudes). Rustically charming *refugi* (mountain huts) offer the opportunity for an overnight stay or just a rest. (While you're hiking, please refrain from picking the wildflowers because many of them, including the Austrian national flower, the edelweiss, are endangered species. Picking flowers or destroying vegetation is punishable by stiff fines.)

SKIING & OTHER OUTDOOR PURSUITS

DOWNHILL SKIING The **Faloria-Cristallo area** surrounding Cortina is known for its 18½ miles (30km) of slopes and 10 miles (16km) of fresh-snow runs. At 4,014 feet above sea level, Cortina's altitude isn't particularly forbidding (at least compared with that of other European ski resorts); and though snowfall is usually abundant from late December to early March, a holiday in November or April might leave you stranded without adequate snow. Die-hard Cortina enthusiasts usually compensate for that, at least during the tail end of the season, by remaining only at the surrounding slopes' higher altitudes (there's lots of skiability at 9,000 feet) and traversing lower-altitude snowfields by cable car.

As Italy's premier ski resort, Cortina boasts more than 50 cable cars and lifts spread out across the valley of the Boite River. The surrounding mountains contain about two dozen restaurants, about 90 miles (145km) of clearly designated ski trails, and a virtually unlimited number of off-piste trails for cross-country enthusiasts. Cortina boasts plenty of sunshine, a relative lack of crowds, and an array of slopes that will suit intermediate, advanced intermediate, and novice skiers alike. During winter, ski lifts are open daily 9am to between 4 and 5pm, depending on the time of sunset.

Cortina boasts eight distinct ski areas, each with its own challenges and charms. Regrettably, because they sprawl rather disjointedly across the terrain, they're not always easy to interconnect. The most appealing of the ski areas are the **Tofana-Promedes, Forcella Rossa,** and **Faloria-Tondi** complexes. The **Pocol, Mietres,** and **Socepres** areas are specifically for novices, the **Cinque Torre** is valuable for intermediates, and the outlying **Falzarego** is a long, dramatic, and sometimes terrifying downhill jaunt not recommended for anyone except a very competent skier.

Despite the availability of dozens of cable cars originating outside the town center along the valley floor, Cortina's most dramatic cable cars are the **Freccia nel Cielo** ("Arrow to the Sky"), the region's longest and most panoramic (see above), and the **Funivia Faloria** (Faloria chairlift), which begins 200 yards east of town, adjacent to the Olympic Ice Stadium. Both of these cable cars are patronized even by visitors who'd never dream of skiing. A single round-trip ticket on either is 45,000L ($22.50), though if you plan on spending time in Cortina it's almost always more economical to buy a ski pass (see below).

Ski passes are issued for from 1 to 21 days. They can include access to just the lifts around Cortina (about 50) or to all the ski lifts in the Dolomiti (around 464). By far the better value is the more comprehensive pass. This Dolomiti Super Ski Pass allows you unlimited access to a vast network of chairlifts and gondolas stretching over Cortina and the mountains flanking at least 10 other resorts. The single-day pass is 60,000L ($36), but the daily cost goes down as you increase the days of the pass. For example, a 7-day pass is 320,000L ($160) (45,000L/$22.50 per day) and a 21-day pass 730,000L ($365) (35,000L/$17.50 per day). The Cortina-only pass sells for about 10% less, but few people opt for it. Children under 8 ski for free.

Included in any pass is free transport on any of Cortina's bright yellow ski buses that run the length of the valley in season, connecting the many cable cars. Depending on snowfall, the two ski lifts mentioned above, as well as most of the other lifts in Cortina, are closed from around April 20 to July 15 and September 15 to around December 1. For information, call ☎ **0436-862-171.**

CROSS-COUNTRY SKIING The trails start about 2 miles (3km) north of town. Some, but not all, run parallel to the region's roads and highways. For information about their location, instruction, and rental of equipment, contact the **Scuola Italiana Sci Fondo Cortina** in Fiames at ☎ **0436-867-088.**

FISHING If you opt to fish in the cold, clear waters of the River Boite, you should first arrange with the tourist office for a permit, costing 10,000L ($5) per day. Many visitors, however, prefer to fish in any of the three lakes around Cortina, the best stocked of which is the Lago di Aial. For fishing in any of the lakes, you won't be charged for a permit until you actually catch something—lake access roads leading from Cortina have checkpoints with the Italian equivalent of a park ranger, who charges you a small fee based on the size and weight of your catch. For information on fishing in Cortina and the surrounding region, contact the tourist office at ☎ **0436-32-31.**

ICE SKATING In winter, two rinks operate in the **Stadio Olimpico del Ghiaccio,** Via dello Stadio (☎ **0436-26-61**). One of the two remains frozen throughout summer, but the other is converted to a concrete surface suitable for in-line skating. Regardless of the season, you'll pay 15,000L ($7.50), with skates rented for an additional fee.

ACCOMMODATIONS

The tourist office has a list of all the private homes that take in paying guests. It's a good opportunity to live with a Dolomite family in comfort and informality. However, the office won't personally book you into a private home. Even though there are nearly 4,700 hotel beds available, it's best to reserve ahead, especially in August and December 20 to January 7.

✪ **Hotel Ancora.** Corso Italia 62, 32043 Cortina d'Ampezzo. ☎ **0436-32-61.** Fax 0436-32-65. www.sunrise.it/cortina/alberghi/ancora. E-mail: hancora@sunrise.it. 56 units. MINIBAR TV TEL. Summer 360,000–620,000L ($180–$310) double; 460,000–820,000L ($230–$410) suite. Winter 370,000–560,000L ($185–$280) double; 470,000–760,000L ($235–$380) suite. Rates include half-board. AE, DC, MC, V. Closed after Easter to June and Sept 15–Dec 20. Valet parking 45,000L ($22.50).

This "Romantik Hotel" (one of a chain of hotels known for their nostalgic architecture) is the domain of the empress of the Dolomiti, Flavia Bertozzi, who gathered its antique sculptures and objets d'art during her trips throughout Italy. The Ancora attracts sporting guests from all over the world, hosts modern art exhibits and classical concerts, and boasts terraces with outdoor tables and umbrellas (the town center for sipping and gossiping). Garlanded wooden balconies encircle the five floors. Most guest rooms open onto these sunny porches, and all are well furnished, comfortable, and especially pleasant, many with sitting areas. Each bathroom comes with a hair dryer; the suites boast Jacuzzis.

Dining/Diversions: The cuisine served in the dining room is excellent; you may want to dine here even if you're not a guest. Signora Bertozzi demands that the chefs keep topping themselves—if they don't quite succeed, they continue to maintain their culinary standards and continue to delight. The cuisine is creatively prepared and exquisitely presented. The Petite Fleur is a chic piano bar.

Amenities: Concierge, room service, laundry, newspaper delivery, in-room massage, baby-sitting, twice-daily maid service, secretarial services, game rooms, nearby sauna and jogging track, golf arrangements nearby, business center, tennis courts nearby, sundeck.

Hotel Corona. Via Val di Sotto 10, 32040 Cortina d'Ampezzo. ☎ **0436-32-51.** Fax 0436-867-339. www.sunrise.it/cortina/alberghi/corona. E-mail: hcorona@sunrise.it. 44 units. TV TEL. 280,000–400,000L ($140–$200) double. Rates include half-board. AE, MC, V. Closed Apr 2–July and Sept–Dec 3.

Since 1935, the Corona has been one of Cortina's leading hotels. For anyone interested in modern Italian art, a stop here is an event—the walls are hung with dozens of works. Many of the most important artists of Italy (and a few from France) from 1948 to 1963 are represented by paintings, sculptures, and ceramic bas-reliefs acquired by manager Luciano Rimoldi. The guest rooms are cozy, with varnished pine and local artifacts and first-rate mattresses. The tiled bathrooms are compact, each with a hair dryer. Rimoldi is also a ski instructor (he once coached Princess Grace in her downhill technique) and was head of the Italian ice-hockey team during the 1988 Winter Olympics, at which one of his former pupils, Alberto Tomba, began his Olympic domination of Alpine events. The hotel prefers guests to take the half-board meal plan (breakfast and dinner).

Hotel Dolomiti. Via Roma 118, 32043 Cortina d'Ampezzo. ☎ **0436-861-400.** Fax 0436-862-140. 42 units. TV TEL. 130,000–220,000L ($65–$110) double. Rates include breakfast. AE, DC, MC, V. Parking 15,000L ($7.50).

This hotel offers many amenities, though it's a sterile choice after the other atmospheric places we list. But it's a good bet if you're watching your lire or arrive in Cortina off-season, when virtually everything else is closed. Its convenient location on the main road just outside the center of town, coupled with its comfortable, no-nonsense format, has gained it increasing favor with visitors. The guest rooms are predictably furnished and fairly quiet, and the management is helpful. The restaurant serves good food, featuring regional specialties.

✪ **Hotel Menardi.** Via Majon 112, 32043 Cortina d'Ampezzo. ☎ **0436-24-00.** Fax 0436-86-2183. www.sunrise.it/cortina/alberghi/menardi. E-mail: hmenardi@sunrise.it. 51 units. TV TEL. 230,000–350,000L ($115–$175) double. Rates include breakfast. AE, MC, V. Closed Apr 10–May and Sept 20–Dec 19. Parking 15,000L ($7.50).

This eye-catcher in the upper part of Cortina looks like a great country inn, with wooden balconies and shutters. Its rear windows open onto a flowery meadow and a view of the Dolomite crags. The inn is 100 years old and run by the Menardi family, who still know how to speak the old Dolomite tongue, Ladino. The guest rooms are decorated in the Tyrolean fashion, each with its own distinct personality. The tiled bathrooms are small. Considering what you get—the quality of the facilities, the reception, and the food—we'd rate this as one of the best values here.

✪ **Miramonti Majestic Grand Hotel.** Via Peziè 105, 32043 Cortina d'Ampezzo. ☎ **0436-42-01.** Fax 0436-867-019. 105 units. MINIBAR TV TEL. 440,000–1,100,000L

($220–$550) double; 1,200,000–2,220,000L ($600–$1,110) suite. Rates include half-board. AE, DC, MC, V. Closed Apr–June and Sept–Nov. Parking 30,000L ($15) in garage, free outside. Hotel shuttle to/from town center every 30 min.

Built in 1893, this hotel, one of the grandest in the Dolomiti, is a short distance from the center of town. It consists of two ocher-colored buildings with alpine hipped roofs and dignified facades. The rustic interior is filled with warm colors, lots of exposed timbers, and the most elegant crowd in Cortina. The well-furnished guest rooms look like those of a private home, complete with matching accessories, built-in closets, and all the modern amenities, with luxury mattresses. The bathrooms contain hair dryers and deluxe toiletries.

Dining/Diversions: In an opulent setting, the hotel serves a refined cuisine, with regional and international specialties. Many owners of winter villas come here for special occasions. There's always a roaring fire in the cozy bar on winter nights.

Amenities: Concierge, room service, laundry/dry cleaning, baby-sitting, car-rental desk; sports facility with indoor pool, exercise and massage equipment, sauna, hydrotherapy, and physical therapy. Other sports facilities for winter and summer exercises are nearby, including golf and tennis.

DINING

Da Beppe Sello. Via Ronco 68. ☎ **0436-32-36.** Reservations recommended. Main courses 25,000–40,000L ($12.50–$20). AE, DC, MC, V. High season daily 12:30–2pm and 7:30–10pm; low season Wed–Sun 12:30–2pm and 7:30–10pm. Closed Mar 20–May 20 and Sept 20–Nov 20. ALPINE/INTERNATIONAL/ITALIAN.

This down-to-earth and reasonably priced restaurant is located in a Tyrolean-style hotel at the edge of the village. Named after the double nicknames of the hotel's founder, Joseph (Beppe) Menardi (Sello), and run by his multilingual niece, Elisa, it's a bastion of superb regional cuisine. Menu items include venison fillet with pears, polenta, and *marmellata di mirtilli* (marmalade made from an Alpine berry like a huckleberry or blueberry); pappardelle with rabbit sauce; tagliolini with porcini mushrooms; roast chicken with bay leaves; and fillet steak flavored with bacon. You get to keep your plate as a souvenir.

El Toulà. Località Ronco 123. ☎ **0436-33-39.** Reservations required. Main courses 32,000–45,000L ($16–$22.50). AE, DC, MC, V. Tues–Sun 12:30–2:30pm and 8–11pm. Closed Easter to late July and Sept–Christmas. ITALIAN/VENETIAN.

Located 2 miles (3km) east of Cortina toward Pocol, this was the first El Toulà, now a chain of 11 restaurants throughout Italy and the world. It's a wood-framed structure with picture windows and a terrace. You get excellently prepared dishes, like grilled squab with an expertly seasoned sauce and veal braised with white truffle sauce. Try the frittata of sea crabs "Saracen" style, *pasta e fagioli* (pasta and beans) Veneto style, pasticcio of eggplant, or Venetian-style calves' liver.

✪ **Ristorante Tivoli.** Località Lacedel. ☎ **0436-866-400.** Reservations required. Main courses 25,000–36,000L ($12.50–$18). AE, DC, MC, V. High season daily 12:30–2:30pm and 7:30–10pm; off-season closed Mon. Closed May–June and Oct–Nov. ALPINE.

The low-slung Alpine chalet whose rear seems almost buried in the slope of the hillside is Cortina's best restaurant and one of the area's finest. About a mile from the resort's center, Tivoli is beside the road leading to the hamlet of Pocol. It derives its excellence from the hardworking efforts of the gracious Calderoni family, who use only the freshest ingredients. Try the stuffed rabbit in onion sauce, wild duck with honey and orange, veal fillet with basil and pine nuts, or salmon flavored with saffron. The pastas are made fresh daily. For dessert, you might try an aspic of exotic fruit.

CORTINA AFTER DARK

In true European alpine resort style, Cortina's bar and disco scene does a roaring business in winter, virtually closes down in spring and autumn, and reopens rather half-heartedly in midsummer. Most clubs lie off or along the pedestrian-only Corso Italia, and by the time you read this, the nightlife landscape will probably feature two or three newcomers. Here are a few of the longtime favorites.

Area, Via Ronco (☎ **0436-867-393**), keeps up-to-date with the latest nightlife trends of Rome, Milan, and London. You enter a bar on the street level but go down to the basement to dance. A rocking competitor popular mostly with Europeans is the **Bilbo Club,** Galleria Nuovo Centro 7 (☎ **0436-55-99**), whose interior is dark, woodsy, and just battered enough that no one minds if you spill your beer. More dancing is available in the cellar of the **Hyppo Dance Hall,** Largo Poste (☎ **0436-23-33**). All ages will feel comfortable at **Limbo,** Corso Italia 97 (☎ **0436-860-026**), whose restaurant is open later than anything else in town (until 3am).

Less frenetic is **Enoteca Cortina,** Via del Mercato 5 (☎ **0436-862-040**), a relaxed wine bar with a carefully polished interior that might remind you of an English pub. Locals happily mingle with skiers in winter and mountain climbers in summer. An equivalent kind of calm is available at the **Piano Bar** in the lobby of the Splendid Hotel Venezia, Corso Italia 209 (☎ **0436-/55-27**), with soothing music during midwinter and midsummer from dusk until midnight.

THE GREAT DOLOMITE ROAD

Stretching from Cortina d'Ampezzo in the east to Bolzano in the west, the ✪ **Great Dolomite Road (Grande Stada delle Dolomiti)** follows a circuitous route of about 68 miles (109km) and ranks among the grandest scenic drives in all Europe. The first panoramic pass you'll cross is **Falzarego,** about 11 miles (18km) from Cortina and 6,900 feet above sea level. The next great pass is **Pordoi,** at about 7,350 feet above sea level, the loftiest point. (You can get out of your car and ride a cable car, the Funiculare Porta Vescovo, between the roadside parking lot and the mountain's summit. At both ends, you'll find alpine-style restaurants, hotels, and cafes. Cable cars depart at 30-minute intervals throughout daylight hours. For fares and more information, contact the tourist office in Cortina.) In spring, edelweiss grows in the surrounding fields; in winter, virtually everything except the surface of the road is blanketed in snow. After crossing the pass, you'll descend to the little resort of **Canazei,** then much later pass by sea-blue Carezza Lake.

9 Trent

36 miles (58km) S of Bolzano, 144 miles (232km) NE of Milan, 63 miles (101km) N of Verona

A northern Italian city that basks in its former glory, the medieval Trent (Trento) on the left bank of the Adige is famous as the host of the Council of Trent (1545–63). Beset with difficulties, such as the rising tide of "heretics," the Ecumenical Council convened at Trent, leading to the Counter-Reformation. Trent lies on the main rail line from the Brenner Pass, and many visitors like to stop off here before journeying farther south into Italy.

Although it has an Alpine setting, Trent still has a definite Italian flavor. As capitals of provinces go, Trent is rather sleepy and provincial. It hasn't been overly commercialized and is still richly imbued with a lot of architectural charm, with a small array of attractions. Nonetheless, it makes a good refueling stop for those exploring this history-rich part of Italy.

ESSENTIALS

GETTING THERE Trent enjoys excellent **rail** connections. It lies on the rail line for Bologna, Verona, the Brenner Pass, and Munich; and trains pass through day and night. The trip from Milan takes 2¾ hours and from Rome 7 hours. Trains also connect Trent with Bolzano once every hour. Seven trains per day make the 3½-hour run from Venice. For rail information and schedules, call ☎ **1478-88-088** toll-free in Italy.

Both the train and the bus stations lie between the Adige River and the public gardens of Trent. The heart of town is to the east of the Adige. From the station, turn on Via Pozzo, which becomes Via Orfane and Via Cavour before reaching the city's heartbeat, Piazza del Duomo.

If you have a **car,** Trent lies on A22, south of Bolzano and north of Verona.

VISITOR INFORMATION The **tourist office** is on Via Alfieri 4 (☎ **0461-983-880**), open Monday to Saturday 9am to 1pm (to 6pm Sunday).

EXPLORING THE CITY

Trent is loaded with old-fashioned charm and alpine flair. For a quick glimpse of the old town, head for **Piazza del Duomo,** dominated by the **Cattedrale di San Vergilio.** Built in the Romanesque style and much restored over the years, it dates from the 12th century. A medieval crypt under the altar holds a certain fascination, and the ruins of a 6th-century Christian basilica were recently discovered beneath the church. You're entitled to visit these remains by paying your admission to the **Diocese Museum (Museum Diocesano),** facing the cathedral (☎ **0461-234-419**), with its religious artifacts on display relating to the Council of Trent, which met in the Duomo from 1545 to 1563. The museum is open Tuesday, Thursday, and Saturday 10am to noon and 4 to 7pm, costing 6,000L ($3). The Duomo is open daily 8:30am to noon and 2:30 to 8pm. In the center of the square is a mid-18th-century **Fountain of Neptune (Fontana di Nettuno).**

The ruling prince-bishops of Trent, who held sway until they were toppled by the French in the early 19th century, resided at the medieval **Castello del Buonconsiglio** (☎ **0461-233-770**), reached from Via Bernardo Clesio 3. The **Historical Museum (Museo Storico),** at the castle (☎ **0461-230-482**), contains mementos related to the period of national unification between 1796 and 1948. The museum and castle are open Tuesday to Sunday: September 27 to June 24, 9am to noon and 2 to 5pm; June 25 to September 26, 10am to 6pm. Admission is 10,000L ($5).

Wine Tasting

The two most important wine-producing regions of northwestern Italy are the Alto Adige (also known as the Bolzano or Sudtirol region) and Trento. The loftier of the two, the Alto Adige, grows an Italian version of the gewürztraminers (a fruity white) that would more often be found in Germany, Austria, and Alsace. Venerable wine growers include **Alois Lageder** (founded in 1855), Tenuta Loüwengang, Vicolo dei Conti, in the hamlet of Magré (☎ **0471/817-256**), and **Schloss Turmhof,** Entiklar, Kurtatsch, 39040 (☎ **0471/880-122**). The Trentino area, a short distance to the south, is one of the leading producers of Chardonnay and sparkling wines fermented by using methods developed centuries ago. A winery worth a visit is **Cavit Cantina Viticoltori,** Via del Ponte 31, 38100 Trento (☎ **0461-922-055**). If you plan to tour around the countryside and do a little wine tasting and vineyard touring, it's best to call ahead for an appointment and get detailed directions.

Trent makes a good base for exploring **Monte Bondone,** a sports resort about 22 miles (35km) from the city center; **Paganella,** slightly more than 12 miles (19km) from Trent (the summit is nearly 7,000 feet high); and the **Brenta Dolomiti.** The last excursion, which will require at least a day for a good look, will reward you with some of the finest mountain scenery in Italy. En route from Trent, you'll pass by **Lake Tobli-no** and then travel a winding road past jagged boulders. A 10-minute detour from the main road at the turnoff to the Genova valley offers untamed scenery. Take the detour at least to the thunderous **Nardis waterfall.** A good stopover point is the little resort of **Madonna di Campiglio.**

If you don't have time to drive around, you'll get a breezy view over Trent and a heart-thumping aerial ride, as well, by taking the **cable car** from Ponte di San Lorenzo near the train station up to Sardagna, a village on one of the mountainsides that enclose the city. You may want to pack sandwiches and enjoy an alpine picnic on one of the grassy meadows nearby. The cable car (☎ **0461-910-332**) runs daily, every 30 minutes from 7am to 6:30pm and the fare is 1,500L (75¢) round-trip.

SHOPPING

The most memorable food-and-wine shop in town is the **Enoteca del Corso,** Corso 3 Novembre 54 (☎ **0461-916-424**), with wines from the region and everywhere else in Italy, as well as the salamis, olives, cheeses, and other salty tidbits that go well with them. Another outlet for the reds and whites produced through the Trentino and the rest of Italy as well is the **Enoteca Lunelli,** Largo Carducci 12 (☎ **0461-982-496**).

If you're looking for handcrafts, ceramics, woodcarvings, and metal work, head for the largest store of its type in town, **Artigianato Trentino,** Via Manchi 62 (☎ **0461-234-892**).

ACCOMMODATIONS

Albergo Accademia. Vicolo Colico 6, 38100 Trento. ☎ **0461-233-600.** Fax 0461-230-174. 43 units. A/C MINIBAR TV TEL. 260,000L ($130) double; from 350,000L ($175) suite. Rates include breakfast. AE, DC, MC, V. Closed Dec 24–Jan 6. Parking 20,000L ($10).

This Alpine inn behind the Renaissance Santa Maria Maggiore is made up of three buildings that have been joined to create an attractive hotel. One of the structures is believed to be of 11th- or 12th-century origin, based on a brick wall similar to the city walls found during renovation work. According to legend, the older part of the Accademia housed church leaders who attended the Council of Trent in the 16th century. The guest rooms are done in light natural wood, and a suite at the top of the house has a terrace with a view of the town and mountains. The rooms are comfortable and cozy, each with a good mattress and a compact bathroom. The alpine influence is carried over to the bar and the restaurant (closed Monday).

Hotel Buonconsiglio. Via Romagnosi 14–16, 38100 Trento. ☎ **0461-272-888.** Fax 0461-272-889. E-mail: hotelhb@tin.it. 46 units. MINIBAR TV TEL. 210,000L ($105) double; 300,000L ($150) suite. Rates include breakfast. AE, DC, MC, V. Parking 15,000L ($7.50).

Built shortly after World War II and massively renovated in the 1990s, this is an immaculate hotel with pleasant rooms and an English-speaking staff. It's on a busy street near the rail station and has a slight edge over the Accademia (see above). In the lobby is a collection of abstract modern paintings. Each guest room has a personal safe, a good mattress, and soundproofing against traffic noise; some are air-conditioned.

DINING

It's almost a requirement to stroll down Trent's Renaissance streets with a gelato from **Torre-Verde-Gelateria Zanella** on Via Suffragio 6 (☎ **0461-232-039**). Many flavors are made from fresh local fruits in season.

Orso Grigio. Via degli Orti 19. ☎ **0461-984-400.** Reservations recommended. Main courses 18,000–30,000L ($9–$15). AE, DC, MC, V. Mon–Sat 12:30–2:30pm and 7:30–10pm. ITALIAN/TRENTINE.

This elegant restaurant lies about 30 yards from Piazza Fiera, in a building whose origins may go back to the 1500s. When you see the immaculate table linen, well-cared-for plants, and subdued lighting, you'll know something is going right. The menus are seasonally adjusted to take advantage of the finest fresh produce. Rufioli (a green tortellini) and *squazzet con polenta* (Trentine-style fried tripe) are two regional specialties. Finish with chocolate mousse. The wines of the province are a special feature here.

✪ **Restaurant Chiesa.** Via San Marco 64. ☎ **0461-238-766.** Reservations recommended. Main courses 16,000–28,000L ($8–$14); fixed-price "apple menu" 80,000L ($40). AE, DC, MC, V. Mon–Sat noon–2:30pm and 7–10pm. TRENTINE.

Restaurant Chiesa offers the largest array of dishes we've ever seen made with apples. Owners Allesandro and Alberto recognized that Eve's favorite fruit, which grows more abundantly around Trent than practically anywhere else, was the base of dozens of traditional recipes. Specialties include risotto with apple, liver pâté with apple, perch fillet with apple, and a range of other well-prepared specialties (a few of which, believe it or not, don't contain apples).

TRENT AFTER DARK

Trent is an early-to-bed/early-to-rise kind of town. Your most appealing option might be an after-dark stroll around **Piazza del Duomo,** where three bars offer conviviality.

Still in the town center but farther afield, you might be attracted to **Bar Picaro,** Via San Giovanni 36 (☎ **0461-230-145**), where live loud music attracts the under-30 crowd. More soothing is the hideaway piano bar in the previously recommended **La Cantinotta,** Via San Marco 24 (☎ **0461-238-527**). Every night from 10pm to around 4am, you'll find a singer, usually an Italian who speaks and sings good amounts of English, will perform stylish songs, including any you might request.

If you want to dance, head for the village of Pergine, 6 miles (10km) east of Trent, to the region's most popular disco, **Paradisi,** Via al Lago (☎ **0461-532-694**). There are at least two bars; one side of the place is devoted to amusing versions of such old-fashioned dances as the waltz and jitterbug, the other to disco.

10 Milan, Lombardy & the Lake District

Among the most progressive of all the Italians, the Lombards have charted an industrial empire unequaled in Italy. Often, the dream of the underfed and jobless in the south is to go to Milano for the high wages and the good life, though thousands end up finding neither. Lombardy isn't all manufacturing, however. Milan is filled to the brim with important attractions, and nearby are old Lombard art cities like Bergamo, Cremona, and Mantua.

Conquerors from barbarians to Napoléon have marched across the plains of Lombardy, and even Mussolini came to his end here. He and his mistress (both already dead) were strung up in a Milan square as war-weary residents vented their rage.

The **Lake District,** with its flower-bedecked promenades, lemon trees, villas, parks and gardens, and crystal-blue waters, is an old-fashioned resort area, with some grand old hotels. The lakes themselves—notably Garda, Como, and Maggiore—form one of the most enchanting splashes of scenery in northern Italy. They've attracted poets and writers, everybody from Goethe to d'Annunzio. But after World War II, the Italian lakes seemed to be largely the domain of matronly English and German types. In our more recent swings through the district, however, we've seen a new, younger crowd, particularly at resorts like Limone on Lake Garda. Even if your time is limited, you'll want to have at least a look at Lake Garda.

1 Milan

355 miles (572km) NW of Rome, 87 miles 140km) NE of Turin, 88 miles (142km) N of Genoa

Southern Italians, perhaps resentful of the north's hard-earned prosperity, sometimes declare the Milanese are like the nearby no-nonsense Swiss. With two million inhabitants, Milan (Milano) is Italy's most dynamic city. Milan is Italy's window on Europe, its most sophisticated and high-tech city, devoid of the dusty history that sometimes paralyzes modern developments in Rome and Florence or the watery rot that seems to pervade Venice.

Part of the work ethic that has catapulted Milan into the 21st century may stem from the Teutonic origins of the Lombards (originally from northwestern Germany), who occupied Milan and intermarried with its population after the collapse of the Roman Empire. In the

Lombardy & the Lake District

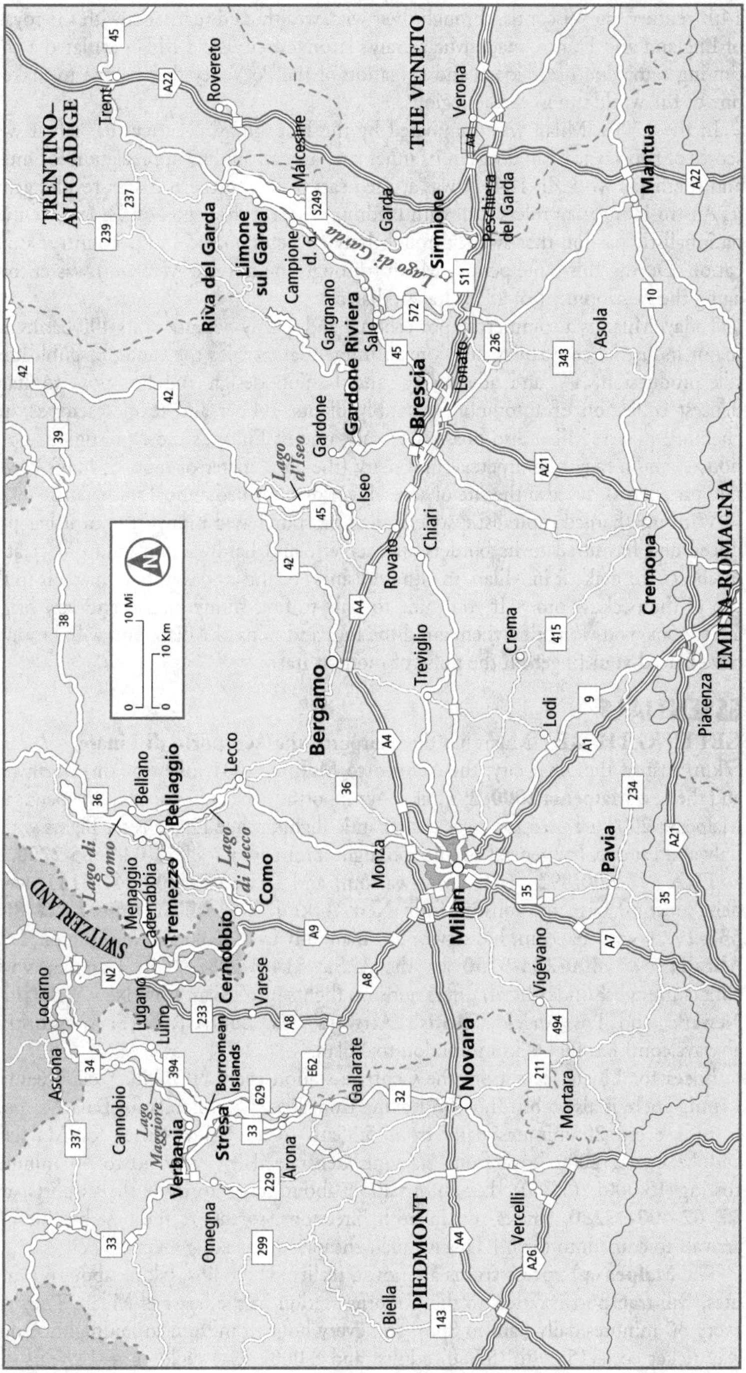

14th century, the Viscontis, through their wits, wealth, and marriages with the royalty of England and France, made Milan Italy's strongest city. And Milan initiated a continuing campaign of drainage and irrigation of the Po Valley that helped to make it one of the world's most fertile regions.

In the 1700s, Milan was dominated by the Hapsburgs, a legacy that left it with scores of neoclassical buildings in its inner core and an abiding appreciation for music and (perhaps) work. In 1848 it was at the heart of the northern Italian revolt against its Austro-Hungarian rulers and, with Piedmont, was at the center of the 19th-century nationalistic passion that swept through Italy and culminated in the country's unification. During this same period, Milan (through the novelist Manzoni) was encouraging the development of a Pan-Italian dialect.

Today, Milan is a commercial powerhouse and, partly because of its 400 banks and major industrial companies, Italy's most influential city. It's the center of publishing, silk production, TV and advertising, and fashion design and lies close to Italy's densest collection of automobile-assembly plants, rubber and textile factories, and chemical plants. Milan also boasts La Scala, one of Europe's most prestigious opera houses, and a major commercial university (the alma mater of most of Italy's corporate presidents). It's also the site of several world-renowned annual trade fairs.

With unashamed capitalistic style, Milan has purchased more art than it has produced and has lured to its borders an energetic and hardworking group of creative intellects. To make it in Milan, in either business or the arts, is to have made it to the top of the pecking order. If you came to Italy to find sunny piazzas and lazy bright afternoons, you won't find them amid the fogs and rains of Milan. You will, however, have placed your finger on the pulse of modern Italy.

ESSENTIALS

GETTING THERE Milan has three airports: the **Aeroporto di Linate,** 4½ miles (7km) east of the inner city; the **Aeroporto Malpensa,** 31 miles (50km) northwest; and the new **Malpensa 2000,** 2½ miles (4km) north of the old Malpensa. Malpensa and Malpensa 2000 are used for most transatlantic flights, while Linate is for flights within Italy and Europe. For general airport and flight information, call ☎ **02-7485-2200.**

TWA (☎ **800/892-4141;** www.twa.com) and **Delta** (☎ **800/241-4141;** www.delta-air.com) both fly nonstop from New York's JFK to Milan. **United** (☎ **800/538-2929;** www.ual.com) has service to Milan only from Dulles in Washington, D.C. **Alitalia** (☎ **800/223-5730** in the U.S., 514/842-8241 in Canada; www.alitalia.it/english/index.html) offers nonstop flights into Milan from New York (JFK), Newark, and Los Angeles. **British Airways** (☎ **800/AIRWAYS;** www.british-airways.com) has flights from London to Milan.

Buses for Linate leave from the Centrale station every 30 minutes daily 6am to 11pm. There is also a bus (no. 73) leaving from Piazza San Babila for Linate airport. It runs every 20 minutes daily from 5:35am to 12:30am. **Buses** for Malpensa and Malpensa 2000 leave from Stazione Centrale daily every 30 to 45 minutes, costing 15,000L ($7.50). For information about buses to/from the airports, call ☎ **02-400-99280.** (Buses run in both directions, so they're the best bet for new arrivals to come into town.) This is much cheaper than taking a taxi.

The **Malpensa Express trains** are now a reality. The trains, taking about 45 minutes, will transport travelers to the Cadorna station in the heart of Milan. They run every 30 minutes daily 5am to 8pm, and every hour from 9pm to midnight. A one-way ticket costs 15,000L ($7.50) adults, and 8,000L ($4) children 4–12 years old. Alitalia passengers ride the Malpensa Express for free.

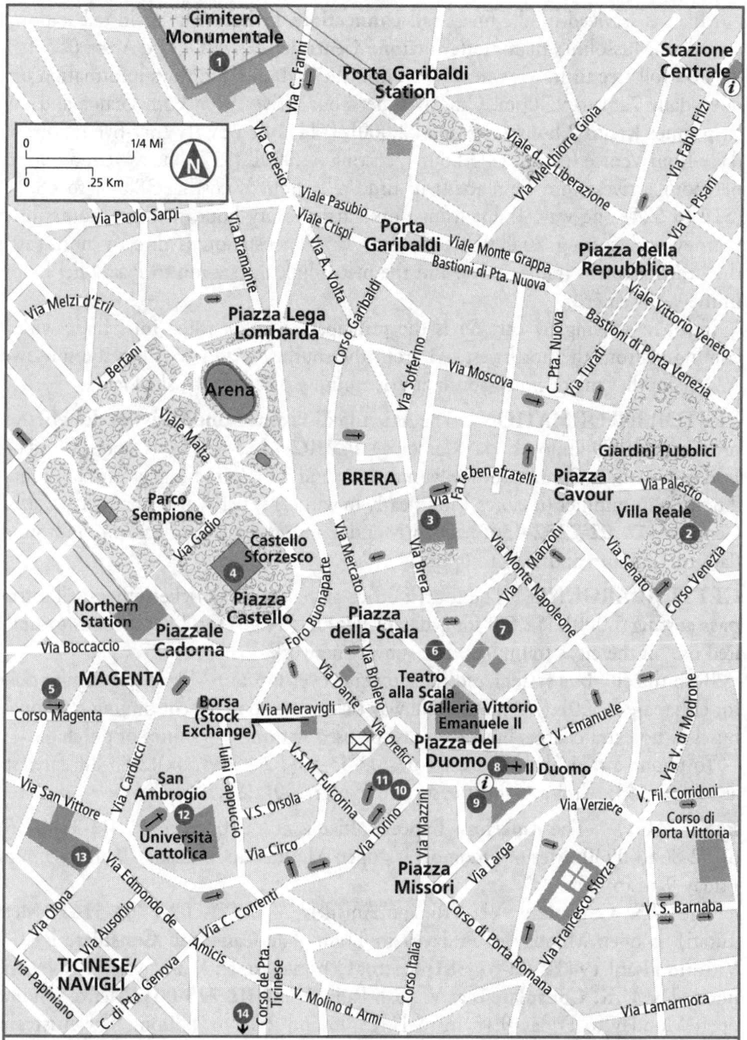

- Ambrosiana Library & Picture Gallery **11**
- Basilica di San Ambrogio & Basilica Museum **12**
- Basilica di Sant'Eustorgio **14**
- Brera Picture Gallery **3**
- Civic Gallery of Modern Art **2**
- Duomo Museum & Civic Museum of Contemporary Art **9**
- Il Duomo & Baptistry **8**
- La Scala & La Scala Museum **6**
- Leonardo da Vinci National Museum of Science & Technology **13**
- Monumental Cemetery **1**
- Museo Poldi-Pezzoli **7**
- Museum of Ancient Art **4**
- Santa Maria delle Grazie *(The Last Supper)* **5**
- Santa Sitiro **10**

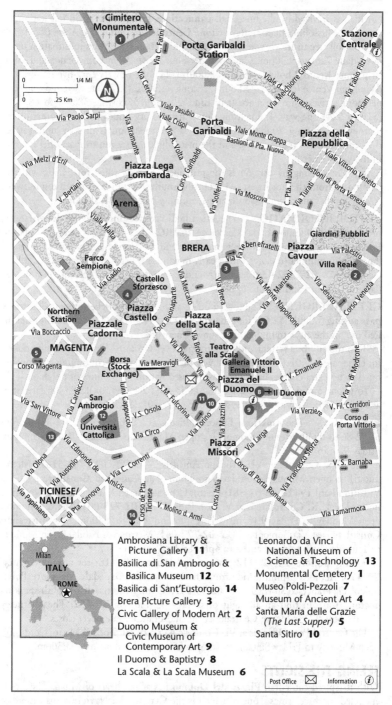

Post Office ✉ Information ⓘ

Milan is serviced by the finest **rail connections** in Italy. The main rail station for arrivals is Mussolini's mammoth **Stazione Centrale,** Piazza Duca d'Aosta (☎ **1478-88-088** toll-free in Italy), where you'll find the National Railways information office open daily 7am to 9:30pm. One train per hour arrives from both Genoa and Turin (trip time: 1½ to 2 hours), costing 22,000L ($11) one way. Twenty-five trains arrive daily from Venice (trip time: 3 hours), costing 34,000L ($17) one way; and one train per hour arrives from Florence (trip time: 2½ hours), costing 38,000 to 48,000L ($19 to $24) one way. Trains from Rome arrive every hour, taking 5 hours for the journey and costing 70,000L ($35) one way. The station is directly northeast of the heart of town; trams, buses, and the metro link the station to Piazza del Duomo in the very center.

If you're arriving by **car,** A4 is the principal east-west route for Milan, with A8 coming in from the northwest, A1 from the southeast, and A7 from the southwest. A22 is another major north-south artery, running just east of Lake Garda.

VISITOR INFORMATION The **Azienda di Promozione Turistica del Milanese,** on Piazza del Duomo at Via Marconi 1 (☎ **02-7252-4301**), is open Monday to Friday 8:30am to 8pm, Saturday 9am to 1pm and 2 to 7pm, Sunday 9am to 1pm and 2 to 6pm in summer (it closes 1 hour early in winter). There's also a branch at Stazione Centrale (☎ **02-7252-4360**), open Monday to Saturday 8am to 7pm and Sunday 9am to 12:30pm and 1:30 to 6pm.

GETTING AROUND The tourist office and all subway ticket offices sell a **travel pass** costing 5,000L ($2.50) for 1 day or 9,000L ($4.50) for 2 days, good for unlimited use on the city's tram, bus, and subway network.

Both the city **bus** system and the **subway** cover most of Milan, and regular tickets for either are 1,500L (75¢). Some subway tickets are good for continuing trips on city buses at no extra charge, but they must be used within 75 minutes of purchase.

To phone a **taxi,** dial ☎ **02-67-67,** 02-53-53, 02-85-85, or 02-83-88; fares start at 6,000L ($3), with a nighttime surcharge of 5,000L ($2.50).

FAST FACTS The **American Express** office is at Via Brera 3 (☎ **02-7200-3693** or 02-8646-0930; Metro: Duomo); it's open Monday to Thursday 9am to 5:30pm, Friday 9am to 5pm.

The **U.S. Consulate,** Via Prìncipe Amedeo 2-10 (☎ **02-2903-5141;** Metro: Turati), is open Monday to Friday 9 to 11am. The **Canadian Consulate** is at Via Vittorio Pisani 19 (☎ **02-67-581;** Metro: Centrale), open Monday to Friday 9am to noon. The **U.K. Consulate** is at Via San Paolo 7 (☎ **02-723-001;** Metro: Duomo), open Monday to Friday 9:15am to 12:15pm and 2:30 to 4:30pm. The **Australian Consulate** is at Via Borgogna 2 (☎ **02-777-041;** Metro: San Babila), open Monday to Thursday 9am to noon and 2 to 4pm, Friday 9am to noon.

For the **police,** call ☎ **112;** for an **ambulance,** ☎ **118;** for any **emergency,** ☎ **113.** About a 5-minute ride from the Duomo, the **Ospedale Maggiore Policlinico,** Via Francesco Sforza 35 (☎ **02-55-031;** Metro: Crocetta), has English-speaking doctors. You can find an all-night **pharmacy** by phoning ☎ **192.** The pharmacy (☎ **02-669-0735;** Metro: Centrale) at the Stazione Centrale never closes.

The **Central Post Office** is at Via Cordusio 4 (☎ **02-805-6812;** Metro: Cordusio), open Monday to Friday 8:30am to 7:15pm and Saturday 8:30am to 3:30pm.

SEEING THE SIGHTS

With its spired cathedral, **Piazza del Duomo** lies at the heart of Milan. The city is encircled by three "rings," one of which is the **Cerchia dei Navigli,** a road more or less following the outline of the former medieval walls. The road runs along what was formerly a series of canals—hence the name "Navigli." The second ring, known both as **Bastioni** and **Viali,** follows the outline of the Spanish Walls from the 16th century. It's now a tram route (no. 29 or 30). A much more recent ring is the **Circonvallazione Esterna,** connecting with the main roads coming into Milan.

If you're traveling within the relatively small Cerchia dei Navigli, you can do so on foot. We don't recommend that you attempt to drive in this circle unless you're heading for a garage. All the major attractions, including Leonardo's *Last Supper,* La Scala, and the Duomo, lie in this ring.

One of Milan's most important streets, **Via Manzoni,** begins near the Teatro alla Scala and will take you to **Piazza Cavour,** a key point for the traffic arteries. The **Arch of Porta Nuova,** a remnant of the medieval walls, marks the entrance to Via Manzoni. To the northwest of Piazza Cavour is the **Giardini Pubblici,** and to the northwest of these gardens is **Piazza della Repubblica.** From this square, Via Vittorio Pisani leads into **Piazza Duca d'Aosta,** site of the cavernous Stazione Centrale.

At Piazza Cavour, you can head west on Via Fatebenefratelli into the **Brera** district, whose major attraction is the Pinacoteca di Brera. This district in recent years has become a major center in Milan for offbeat shopping and after-dark diversions.

For an excellent **city overview,** hop aboard **tram no. 20,** distinguished by CIAO MILANO emblazoned on its sides, for a tour with commentary in English and five other languages. The $1^3/_4$-hour tours run daily at 11am, 1pm, and 3pm and start at Piazza Castello; the cost is 30,000L ($15). For more information, call **STAB,** ☎ **02-805-5323.**

THE TOP ATTRACTIONS

Despite its modern architecture and industry, Milan is still a city of great art. The serious art lover should give it at least 2 days. If your schedule is frantic, see the Duomo; the Brera Picture Gallery; and one of the most important galleries of northern Italy, the Ambrosiana Library and Picture Gallery.

✪ **Il Duomo & Baptistry.** Piazza del Duomo. ☎ **02-8646-3456.** Cathedral free; roof via stairs 6,000L ($3), roof via elevator 9,000L ($4.50); crypt free; baptistry 3,000L ($1.50). Cathedral daily 6:45am–6:50pm. Roof daily 9am–5:30pm. Crypt daily 9am–noon and 2:30–6pm. Baptistry Tues–Sun 10am–noon and 3–5pm. Metro: Duomo.

Milan's impressive lacy Gothic cathedral, 479 feet long and 284 feet wide at the transepts, ranks with St. Peter's in Rome and the cathedral at Seville, Spain, as among the world's largest. It was begun in 1386 and has seen numerous architects and builders (even Milan's conqueror, Napoléon, added his ideas to the facade). This imposing structure of marble is the grandest and most flamboyant example of the Gothic style in Italy.

Built in the shape of a Latin cross, the Duomo is divided by soaring pillars into five naves. The overall effect is like a marble-floored Grand Central Terminal (that is, in space), with far greater dramatic intensity. In the **crypt** rests the tomb of San Carlo Borromeo, the cardinal of Milan. To experience the Duomo at its most majestic, you must ascend to the **roof,** on which you can walk through a forest of pinnacles, turrets, and marble statuary. Alfred, Lord Tennyson, rhapsodized about the panorama of the Alps as seen from this roof. A gilded Madonna towers over the tallest spire.

If you're interested in antiquity, you may want to explore the **Baptistry (Battistero Paleocristiano),** which you enter through the cathedral. This is a subterranean ruin going back to the 4th century and lying beneath the cathedral's piazza. It's believed this is the site where Ambrose, the first bishop and the patron saint of the city, baptized Augustine.

Duomo Museum (Museo del Duomo) & Civic Museum of Contemporary Art (Museo Civico d'Arte Contemporaneau). In the Palazzo Reale, Piazza del Duomo 12 and 14. ☎ **02-860-358** (Duomo Museum), or 02-62-08-39-14 (Contemporary Art Museum). Duomo Museum 12,000L ($6). Contemporary Art Museum free admission. Duomo Museum Tues–Sun 9:30am–12:30pm and 3–6pm. Contemporary Art Museum Tues–Sat 9am–5:30pm. Metro: Duomo.

Housed in the *Palazzo Reale* (Royal Palace), the **Duomo Museum** is like a picture story- book of the cathedral's 6 centuries of history. It has exhibits of statues and decorative sculptures, some from the 14th century. There are also antique art objects, stained-glass windows (some from the 15th century), and ecclesiastical vestments, many as old as the 16th century.

The palazzo also houses the **Civic Museum of Contemporary Art.** Contemporary as interpreted by this museum could mean anything painted in the 20th century, even a work executed in 1900. You're often greeted with some of the best modern art exhibits in Italy, typically the works of artists who are either world class or the more daring of the avant-garde. However, permanent works include those by Picasso, De Chirico, and Modigliani. There's also a fine collection of Italian Futurist art.

✪ **Ambrosiana Library & Pictury Gallery (Biblioteca-Pinacoteca Ambrosiana).** Piazza Pio XI 2. ☎ **02-806-92210.** Admission 12,000L ($6). Tues–Sun 10am–5:30pm. Metro: Duomo or Cordusio.

Near the Duomo, the Ambrosiana Library and Picture Gallery were founded in the early 17th century by Cardinal Federico Borromeo. On the second floor, the **Picture Gallery** contains a remarkable collection of art, mostly from the 15th to the 17th century. Most notable are a *Madonna and Angels* by Botticelli; works by Brueghel (which have impressive detail and are among the best pieces); paintings by Lombard artists, including Bramantino's *Presepe,* in earthy primitive colors; a curious miniature *St. Jerome with Crucifix* by Andrea Solario; and works by Bernardino Luini. The museum owns a large sketch by Raphael on which he labored before painting *The School of Athens* for the Vatican. The most celebrated treasures are the productions of Leonardo da Vinci's *Codice Atlantico.* (In Milan, the master had as a patron the powerful Ludovico Sforza, known as "the Moor.") After seeing the sketches (in facsimile), you can only agree with Leonardo's evaluation of himself as a genius without peer. Attributed to him is a portrait of a musician, believed to have been Franchino Gaffurio. The **Library** contains many medieval manuscripts, which are shown for scientific examination only.

✪ **Santa Maria delle Grazie & *The Last Supper*.** Piazza Santa Maria delle Grazie (off Corso Magenta). ☎ **02-498-7588.** Church free; *The Last Supper* 14,000L ($7). Reservations required for *The Last Supper.* Church Mon–Sat 7:30am–noon and 3–7pm, Sun 3:30–6:30pm; *The Last Supper* Tues–Sat 9am–6:15pm, Sun 9am–7:15pm. Metro: Cadorna or Conciliazione.

This Gothic church was erected by the Dominicans in the mid–15th century, and a number of its more outstanding features, such as the cupola, were designed by the great Bramante. But visitors from all over the world flock here to gaze on a mural in the convent next door. In what was once a refectory, the incomparable Leonardo da Vinci adorned one wall with ***The Last Supper.***

Commissioned by Ludovico the Moor, the 28-by-15-foot mural was finished about 1497; it began to disintegrate almost immediately and was totally repainted in the 1700s and the 1800s. Its gradual erosion makes for one of the most intriguing stories in art. In 1943, it narrowly escaped being bombed, but the bomb demolished the roof; astonishingly, the painting was exposed to the elements for 3 years before a new roof was built. The current restoration has been controversial, drawing fire from some art critics (as has the Sistine Chapel restoration). The chief restorer of *The Last Supper,*

Pinin Brambilla Barcilon, said the Sistine Chapel was a "simple window wash" compared with the Leonardo.

It has been suggested that all that's really left of the original *Last Supper* is a "few isolated streaks of fading color"—that everything else is the application and color of artists and restorers who followed. What remains, however, is Leonardo's "outline," and even it is suffering badly. As an Italian newspaper writer put it: "If you want to see *Il Cenacolo,* don't walk—run!" A painting of grandeur, the composition portrays Christ at the moment he announces to his shocked apostles that one of them will betray him. Vasari called the portrait of Judas "a study in perfidy and wickedness."

Only 25 viewers are admitted at a time (be prepared to wait in line), and you're required to pass through antechambers to remove pollutants from your body. After viewing the painting, for 15 minutes only, you must walk through two additional filtration chambers as you exit.

✪ **Brera Picture Gallery (Pinacoteca di Brera).** Via Brera 28. ☎ **02-722-63229.** Admission 10,000L ($5). Tues–Sat 9am–5pm; Sun 9am–12:15pm. Metro: Cairoli, Lanza, or Montenapoleone.

This is one of Italy's finest galleries, boasting an exceptional collection of works by both Lombard and Venetian masters. Like a Roman emperor, Canova's nude Napoléon, a toga draped over his shoulder, stands in the courtyard (fittingly, a similar statue ended up in the Duke of Wellington's house in London).

Among the notable pieces, the *Pietà* by Lorenzo Lotto is a work of great beauty, as is Gentile Bellini's *St. Mark Preaching in Alexandria* (it was finished by his brother, Giovanni). Seek out Andrea Mantegna's *Virgin and the Cherubs,* from the Venetian school. Three of the most important prizes are Mantegna's *Dead Christ,* Giovanni Bellini's *La Pietà,* and Carpaccio's *St. Stephen Debating.*

Other paintings include Titian's *St. Jerome,* as well as such Lombard art as Bernardino Luini's *Virgin of the Rose Bush* and Andrea Solario's *Portrait of a Gentleman.* One of the greatest panels is Piero della Francesca's *Virgin and Child Enthroned with Saints*

Get Thee to a Renaissance Monastery

The ✪ **Certosa (Charter House) of Pavia,** Via Monumento 4 (☎ **0382/925-613**), marks the pinnacle of the Renaissance statement in Lombardy. The Carthusian monastery is 19 miles (31km) south of Milan and 5 miles (8km) north of Pavia. It was founded in 1396 but not completed until years afterward and is one of the most harmonious structures in Italy. The facade, studded with medallions and adorned with colored marble and sculptures, was designed in part by Amadeo, who worked on it in the late 15th century. Inside, much of its rich decoration is achieved by frescoes reminiscent of an illustrated storybook. You'll find works by Perugino *(The Everlasting Father)* and Bernardino Luini *(Madonna and Child).* Gian Galeazzo Visconti, the founder of the Certosa, is buried in the south transept.

Through an elegantly decorated portal you enter the cloister, noted for its exceptional terra-cotta decorations and continuous chain of elaborate "cells," attached villas with their own private gardens and loggia. Admission is free, but donations are requested. It's open Tuesday to Sunday 9 to 11:30am and 2:30 to 7:30pm.

Buses run between Milan and Pavia daily every hour 5am to 10pm, taking 50 minutes and costing 5,000L ($2.50) one way. Trains leave Milan bound for Pavia once every hour, costing 3,800L ($1.90) one way. Motorists can take Rte. 35 south from Milan or A7 to Binasco and continue on Rte. 35 to Pavia and its Certosa.

and Angels and the *Kneeling Duke of Urbino in Armor.* Another work to seek out is the *Christ* by Bramante. One wing, devoted to modern art, offers works by such artists as Boccioni, Carrà, and Morandi. One of our favorite paintings in the gallery is Raphael's *Wedding of the Madonna,* with a dancelike quality. The moving *Last Supper at Emmaus* is by Caravaggio.

OTHER ATTRACTIONS

✪ **Museo Poldi-Pezzoli.** Via Manzoni 12. ☎ **02-794-889.** Admission 10,000L ($5). Tues–Sun 10am–6pm. Closed Jan 1, Easter, May 1, Aug 15, Nov 1, Dec 8, and Apr 25. Metro: Duomo or Montenapoleone.

This fabulous museum is done in great taste and rich with antique furnishings, tapestries, frescoes, and Lombard wood carvings. It also displays a remarkable collection of paintings by many of the old masters of northern and central Italy, like Andrea Mantegna's *Madonna and Child,* Giovanni Bellini's *Cristo Morto,* and Filippo Lippi's *Madonna, Angels, and Saints* (superb composition). One portrait that enjoys the same fame in Milan that the *Mona Lisa* does worldwide is Antonio Pollaiolo's *Portrait of a Lady,* a work of haunting originality. One buyer from Paris's garment district says he comes here on every trip to Milan, regardless of how rushed he is, just to gaze in wonder at this stunning portrait. One room is devoted to Flemish artists, and there's a collection of ceramics and also one of clocks and watches. The museum grew out of a private collection donated to the city in 1881.

Museum of Ancient Art (Museo d'Arte Antica). In the Castello Sforzesco, Piazza Castello. ☎ **02-7600-2378.** Free admission. Daily 9am–5:45pm. Metro: Cairoli.

The Castle Sforzesco is an ancient fortress rebuilt by Francesco Sforza, who launched another governing dynasty. It's believed that both Bramante and Leonardo contributed architectural ideas to the fortress. Following extensive World War II bombings, it was painstakingly restored and continues its activity as a Museum of Ancient Art. On the ground floor are sculptures from the 4th century A.D., medieval art mostly from Lombardy, and armor. The most outstanding exhibit, however, is Michelangelo's *Rondanini Pietà,* on which he was working the week he died. In the rooms upstairs, besides a good collection of ceramics, antiques, and bronzes, is the important picture gallery, rich in paintings from the 14th to the 18th century. Included are works by Lorenzo Veneziano, Mantegna, Lippi, Bellini, Crivelli, Foppa, Bergognone, Cesare da Sesto, Lotto, Tintoretto, Cerano, Procaccini, Morazzone, Guardi, and Tiepolo.

Leonardo da Vinci National Museum of Science & Technology (Museo Nazionale della Scienza e della Tecnica Leonardo da Vinci). Via San Vittore 21. ☎ **02-485-551.** Admission 12,000L ($6) adults. Tues–Fri 9:30am–5pm; Sat–Sun 9:30am–6:30pm. Metro: San Ambrogio. Bus: 50, 54, 58, or 94.

If you're a fan of Leonardo da Vinci, you'll want to visit this vast museum complex where you could practically spend a week. For the average visitor, the most interesting section is the Leonardo da Vinci Gallery, displaying copies and models from the Renaissance genius. There's a reconstructed convent pharmacy, a monastic cell, and collections of antique carriages and even sewing machines. You'll also see exhibits relating to astronomy, telecommunications, watchmaking, goldsmithery, motion pictures, and the subjects of classic physics.

Civic Gallery of Modern Art (Galleria Civica d'Arte Moderna). In the Villa Reale (Villa Comunale), Via Palestro 16. ☎ **02-7600-2819.** Free admission. Daily 9am–6pm. Metro: Palestro.

Housed in one of the historic core's most prestigious palaces, this is Milan's most important collection of late-19th-century and early-20th-century art, mostly from

1850 to 1918. The palace was built from 1790 to 1793 by noted architect Leopold Pollack and served as the Milanese home of both Napoléon and Eugène de Beauharnais (son of Josephine from her first marriage). This is also the site of many weddings, whose participants appreciate the building's sense of history and its ornate decor. The exhibit space is divided into three collections (the Carlo Grassi, the Vismara, and the Marino Marini), all showing the development of Impressionism and modernism as defined by Italian, and especially Lombard, painters. Major emphasis is given to Marino Marini, a 20th-century sculptor whose artworks (more than 200) were donated to the museum in 1973. Other artists whose works are displayed are Picasso, Matisse, Rouault, Renoir, Modigliani, Corot, Millet, Manet, Cézanne, Bonnard, and Gauguin.

Basilica di Sant'Eustorgio. Piazza Sant'Eustorgio 1. ☎ **02-5810-1583.** Basilica free; chapel 5,000L ($2.50). Daily 8:30am–noon and 3–6:30pm. Metro: Genova.

The bell tower of this 4th-century basilica dates from the 13th century; it was built in the romantic style by patrician Milanese families. It has the first tower clock in the world, made in 1305. Originally this was the tomb of the Three Kings (4th century A.D.). Inside, its greatest treasure is the **Portinari Chapel (Cappella Portinari),** designed by the Florentine Michelozzo in Renaissance style. The chapel is frescoed and contains a bas-relief of angels at the base of the cupola. In the center is an intricately carved tomb containing the remains of St. Peter Martyr, supported by 13th-century marble statuary by Balduccio of Pisa. The basement has a Roman crypt.

Basilica di San Ambrogio & San Ambrogio Basilica Museum (Museo della Basilica di San Ambrogio). Piazza San Ambrogio 15. ☎ **02-8645-0895.** Basilica free; museum 3,000L ($1.50). Basilica Mon–Sat 9:30am–noon and 2:30–6:30pm; museum Wed–Sat 10am–noon and 3–5pm. Sun 3–5pm. Closed Aug. Metro: San Ambrogio.

This church was first built by St. Ambrose in the later years of the 4th century A.D., but the present structure was built in the 12th century in the Romanesque style. The remains of St. Ambrose rest in the crypt. The church, entered after passing through a quadrangle, is rather stark and severe, in the style of its day. The atrium is its most distinguishing feature. In the apse are interesting mosaics from the 12th century. The Lombard tower at the side dates from 1128, and the facade, with its two tiers of arches, is impressive. In the church is the **Museo della Basilica di San Ambrogio,** containing some frescoes, 15th-century wood paneling, silver and gold objects originally for the altar, paintings, sculpture, and Flemish tapestries.

Monumental Cemetery (Cimitero Monumentale). Piazzale Cimitero Monumentale 1. ☎ **02-659-9938.** Free admission. Tues–Sun 8:30am–5:15pm. Metro: Garibaldi. Tram: 3, 4, 11, 12, 14, 29, 30, or 33.

This cemetery has catered for more than 100 years to the whims of Milan's elite. The only requirements for burial here are that you're dead and that when you were alive you were able to buy your way into a plot. Some families have paid up to 200,000,000L ($120,000) just for the privilege of burying their dead here. The graves are marked not only with brass plates or granite markers but also with Greek temples, elaborate obelisks, or such original works as an abbreviated version of Trajan's Column.

This outdoor museum has become such an attraction that a superintendent has compiled an illustrated guidebook—a sort of "Who Was Who." Among the cemetery's outstanding sights is a sculpted version of *The Last Supper.* Several fine examples of art nouveau sculpture dot the hillside, and there's a tasteful example of Liberty-style (Italy's version of art nouveau) architecture in a tiny chapel designed to hold the remains of Arturo Toscanini's son, who died in 1906. Among the notables buried here are Toscanini himself and novelist Alessandro Manzoni. In the Memorial Chapel is the tomb of Salvatore Quasimodo, who won the 1959 Nobel prize in literature. Here also rest the ashes of Ermann Einstein, father of the scientist. In the Palanti Chapel is a monument commemorating the 800 Milanese citizens slain in Nazi concentration camps. (A model of this monument is displayed in New York's Museum of Modern Art.) The cemetery is a few blocks east of Stazione Porta Garibaldi, in the urban congestion of Milan, 2 miles (3km) north of Il Duomo.

La Scala Museum (Museo Teatrale alla Scala). In the Teatro alla Scala, Piazza della Scala. ☎ **02-805-3418.** Admission 6,000L ($3). May–Oct, daily 9am–12:30pm and 2–5:30pm; Nov–Apr, Mon–Sat 9am–12:30pm and 2–5:30pm. Metro: Duomo.

Opera lovers will want to visit this museum, opened in 1913. It contains a rich collection of historical mementos and records of the heady world of opera. Among them are busts and portraits of such artists as Beethoven, Chopin, Donizetti, Verdi, and Puccini. Two halls are devoted to Verdi, including such objects as scores written in Verdi's own hand and the spinet on which he learned to play. Rossini's eyeglasses and his pianoforte tuning key are in a case, and there are many other such treasures, including a death-cast of Chopin's left hand. A small gallery honors Toscanini, with his batons, medals, and pince-nez. One of the greatest thrills for those who aren't in town during opera season or who can't get tickets will be the view from the third floor: You can look down on the theater's ornate auditorium with its velvet draperies.

✪ SHOPPING

Milan is one of Europe's top shopping cities, with an incredible concentration of sophisticated, high-style boutiques—and that's only fitting, since Milan is the dynamo of the Italian fashion industry. The shops say it all—Dolce & Gabbana, Ferré, Krizia, Moschino, Prada, Armani, and Versace have all catapulted to international stardom from design studios based here.

Most shops are closed all day Sunday and Monday (though some open on Monday afternoon). Some stores open at 9am, unless they're very chic, and then they're not likely to open until 10:30am. They remain open, for the most part, until 1pm, reopening again between 3:30 and 7:30pm.

The best time for the savvy shopper to visit Milan is for the **January sales,** when saldi ("sale") signs appear in the windows. Sales usually begin in mid-January and in some cases extend all the way through February. Prices in some emporiums are cut by as much as 50% (but don't count on it). Of course, items offered for sale are most often last season's merchandise, but you can get some good buys. Items bought on sale can't be returned.

SHOPPING AREAS

THE GOLDEN TRIANGLE One well-heeled shopper from Florida recently spent the better part of her vacation in Italy shopping for what she called "the most unbelievable variety of shoes, clothes, and accessories in the world." A walk on the fashion subculture's focal point, **Via Montenapoleone,** heart of the **"Golden Triangle,"** will quickly confirm that impression. It's one of Italy's three great shopping streets. But expect high prices, and service based on the salesperson's impression of how much money you plan to spend.

CORSO BUENOS AIRES Bargain hunters leave the Golden Triangle and head for a mile-long stretch of **Corso Buenos Aires,** where you can find style at more affordable prices. What to look for? Virtually everything. Saturday is the worst time to go because of overcrowding. Most self-guided shopping tours begin at **Piazza Oberdan,** the square closest to the heart of Milan. Clothing abounds on Corso Buenos Aires, especially casual wear. But you'll find a vast array of merchandise, from scuba-diving equipment to soft luggage. Some shops hawk rip-offs of designer merchandise, especially clothing.

BRERA DISTRICT You'll find more bargains in the **Brera,** the name given to a sprawling shopping district around the Brera Museum. This area is far more attractive than Corso Buenos Aires and has often been compared to New York's Greenwich Village because of its cafes, shops, antiques stores, and art students. Skip the main street, **Via Brera,** and concentrate on the side streets, especially **Via Solferino, Via Madonnina,** and **Via Fiori Chiari.** To get here, start by the La Scala opera house and continue to walk along Via Verdi, which becomes Via Brera. Running off from Via Brera to the left is the pedestrian-only Via Fiori Chiari, good for bric-a-brac and even some fine art deco and art nouveau pieces. Via Fiori Chiari will lead to another traffic-free street, Via Madonnina, which has some excellent clothing and leather-goods buys. Via Madonnina connects with busy Corso Garibaldi. This will take you to Via Solferino, the third-best shopping street. In addition to traditional clothing and styling, a lot of eye-catching but eccentric modern clothing is sold here.

The best time to visit the Brera area is for the **Mercantone dell'Antiquariato,** which takes place on the third Saturday of each month (it's especially hectic at Christmas time) along Via Brera in the shadow of La Scala. Artists and designers, along with antiques dealers and bric-a-brac peddlers, turn out in droves.

SHOPPING A TO Z

BOOKS There are bigger and flashier bookstores in Milan, but the **American Bookstore,** Via Camperio 16 (☎ **02-878-920;** Metro: Cairoli), will probably have that paperback novel you're looking for or the scholarly volume of Milanese artwork you should've reviewed before your trip. It stocks only English-language books and periodicals. Milan has one gay bookstore, the **Libreria Babele,** Via Sammartini (☎ **02-669-2986;** Metro: Centrale).

A DEPARTMENT STORE & A MALL **La Rinascente,** Piazza del Duomo (☎ **02-88-521;** Metro: Duomo), bills itself with accuracy as Italy's largest fashion department store. In addition to clothing, the basement carries a wide variety of giftware, including handwork from all regions of Italy. There's a ground-floor information desk, and on the seventh floor are a bank, a travel agency, a hairdresser, an Estée Lauder Skincare Center, a coffee bar, and the Brunch and Bistro restaurants.

One of Milan's most famous landmarks, the huge ✪ **Galleria Vittorio Emanuele II,** Corso Vittorio Emanuelle II, is reminiscent of a rail station, and the architectural details are impressive, with vaulted glass ceilings merging in a huge central dome, decorative window and door casings, elaborate bas-reliefs, huge arched frescoes, wrought-iron globe lamps, and a decorative tile floor. You can browse in shops that include a Prada boutique and a Rizzoli bookstore or grab a coffee from one of the bistros or restaurants (see the Savini review under "Dining," below) and relax while people-watching. It's worth a stop even if shopping isn't your top priority.

FASHION In the Brera district, **Accademia,** Via Solferino 11 (☎ **02-659-5961;** Metro: Moscova), is the store for men's and women's outdoor clothing, carrying a variety of classical and casual styles. This is also where to go to for men who need clothes in hard-to-find dimensions because Accademia offers a "made-to-measure" service; however, it takes more than a month (alterations take 4 to 5 extra days).

Also in the Brera, **Drogheria Solferino,** Via Solferino, at the corner of Via Pontaccio (☎ **02-878-740;** Metro: Moscova), is an affordable store, stocking a wide range of clothing. Look especially for the line of knitwear and the cotton or silk blouses. You can find rather elegant men's and women's ready-to-wear clothing and shoes.

Despite its name, **Il Drug Store,** Corso Buenos Aires 28 (☎ **02-2951-5592;** Metro: Lima), sells affordable but trendy clothing for the young and the young at heart. There's an interesting selection of sweaters both embroidered and ornamented. Knits and dresses with that young look are always sold, but there's a fast turnover.

After searching the shops in Milan's fabled Golden Triangle, you may decide you can't afford anything. Don't despair. There's always **Il Salvagente,** 16 Via Fratelli Bronzetti (☎ **02-7611-0328;** Tram: 12; Bus: 60 or 73), for the fashion-conscious shopper without an unlimited wallet. On the second floor is the selection of men's clothing; the women's wear, including sweaters, clothes, shoes, and belts, is on the main floor. Here you'll find Versace gowns at cut-rate prices. Of course, it'll be last year's style or something that didn't sell, but who'll ever know?

Another place for affordable stylish clothes is **Primavera,** Via Torino 47 (☎ **02-874-565;** Metro: Duomo).

Darsena, Corso Buenos Aires 16 (☎ **02-2952-1535;** Metro: Lima), which has far better prices than competitors in the Golden Triangle, carries high-quality men's clothing that's both casual and elegant. Most items are the store brand, but they also sell items with names like Armani, Valentino, and Trussardi.

Ermenegildo Zenga, Via Pietro Verri 3 (☎ **02-7600-6437;** Metro: Montenapoleone), offers a complete range of menswear, beginning with the Sartorial line of suits, jackets, trousers, and accessories. The "soft line" is dedicated to a younger customer, and the sportswear collection and yachting line allow you to wander the globe with the right apparel. The shop also offers a "made-to-measure" service with a selection of 300 fabrics per season. They can make an outfit in about 4 weeks, then ship it to any destination.

Giorgio Armani, Via San Andrea 9 (☎ **02-7600-3234;** Metro: Montenapoleone), houses the style we've come to expect in a large showroom vaguely reminiscent of an upscale aircraft hangar. Armani's trademark look incorporates unstructured clothing draped loosely over firm bodies—elegant upholstery for elegant people.

At **Mila Schön,** Via Montenapoleone 2 (☎ **02-781-190;** Metro: Montenapoleone), the sophisticated look is casually chic, hip, and expensive. If you're male and relatively muscular, you'll look terrific. Mila's women's line is on the ground floor. Even the somewhat flippant accessories are stratospherically expensive.

Gianfranco Ferré, Via della Spiga 11–13 (☎ **02-7600-0385;** Metro: Montenapoleone), is the only outlet in Milan for the famous designer whose fashions are worn by some of the world's most elegant women. The range is wide, from soft knitwear to sensual evening dresses, along with refined leather accessories. Next door to the women's shop is an outlet for the designer's men's clothing. It's closed in August.

✪ **Prada,** Via della Spiga 1 (☎ **02-7600-2019;** Metro: Montenapoleone), has the best leather goods and other stylish accessories in Milan for women; it's a fashion industry phenomenon. The black nylon backpack is the most popular item. (Now Prada has another store in Galleria Vittorio Emanuele.)

GIFTS In the tiny **G. Lorenzi,** Via Montenapoleone 9 (☎ **02-7602-2848;** Metro: Montenapoleone), you'll find everything you were looking for in the way of small gifts—and a lot of stuff you've never seen before. Many are one-of-a-kind items.

✪ **JEWELRY** At ✪ **Mario Buccellati,** Via Montenapoleone 4 (☎ **02-7600-2153;** Metro: Montenapoleone), you'll find Italy's best-known and most expensive silver and jewels. The designs of the cast-silver bowls, tureens, and christening cups are nothing short of rhapsodic.

In the Brera district, ✪ **Meru,** Via Solferino 3 (☎ **02-8646-0700;** Metro: Moscova), sells avant-garde jewelry to beautiful young European film stars and anyone else who can afford it. Many of the pieces are set into enameled backgrounds and often include unusual types of gemstones like rose quartz, coral, and amber. Leather-and-gold combinations are also used. All pieces are made by Meru craftspeople. It's closed July 30 to September 10.

LACE **Jesurum,** Via Verri 4 (☎ **02-7601-5045;** Metro: Montenapoleone), is the Milanese outlet of a Venice-based lace company that has been famous since 1870. On a very short street where none of the buildings has an obvious street number, it sells all-lace or lace-edged tablecloths, doilies, and lots of great wedding gifts. It also sells lace blouses and even a swimsuit, plus lace by the meter.

LEATHER GOODS & SHOES The prices on the merchandise at **Alfonso Garlando,** Via Madonnina 2 (☎ **02-8646-3733;** Metro: Cairoli), range up to the very expensive, but the shop's size and its lack of concern for a stylish showroom guarantee a reasonable choice at a reasonable price. It sells shoes for men and women but not children.

At ✪ **Beltrami,** Via Montenapoleone 10 (☎ **02-7600-2975;** Metro: Montenapoleone), the prices are chillingly high, but the leather goods for men and women are among the best you'll find in the world. The showroom is glamorous and the merchandise chic. Beltrami has another shop at Piazza San Babila 4A (☎ **02-7600-0546;** Metro: San Babila).

The factory outlet **Calzaturificio di Parabiago,** Corso Buenos Aires 52 (☎ **02-2940-6851;** Metro: Lima), carries classic and casual shoes for men and women. The prices vary from relatively inexpensive to expensive. But most of the merchandise is sold at discount prices along this "street of bargains." Parabiago is one of the major shoe-manufacturing areas of the country.

Gucci, Via Montenapoleone 5 (☎ **02-7601-3050;** Metro: Montenapoleone), is the Milanese headquarters for the most famous leather-goods distributor in Italy. Its shoes, luggage, and wallets for men and women, handbags, and leather accessories usually have the colors of the Italian flag (olive and crimson) stitched in the form of a more-or-less discreet ribbon across the front.

At ✪ **Salvatore Ferragamo,** Via Montenapoleone 3 (☎ **02-7600-6660;** Metro: Montenapoleone), the label is instantly recognizable and the quality high. Rigidly controlled by an extended second generation of the original founders, it's still a leader in style and allure. The store contains inventories of shoes, luggage, and accessories for women and men. Also for sale are Ferragamo leather jackets, pants, and a small selection of clothing.

Sebastian, Via Roeino 13 (☎ **02-86666-91;** Metro: Montenapoleone), sells excellent shoes for men and women from a ready-made stockpile of more than 150 fashionable models, which Sebastian makes in its own factories. For almost the same price (if you don't mind waiting 2 months or more), you can order custom-made shoes, shipped anywhere (they're usually available only in women's styles). This place is a boon for those with wide, narrow, large, or small feet.

LINENS You'll find some great buys (as much as 50% off) in linens at the company headquarters of **Frette,** Via Montenapoleone 21 (☎ **02-7600-3791;** Metro: Montenapoleone). Frette is one of the finest names in Italian linens, so this is an exceptional deal, especially if you're looking for damask tablecloths in the vibrant colors of Italy, everything from apple green to sunflower yellow.

If you've got the time and are a dedicated shopper, you can head for the **Spaccio Frette** shop at 45 Via Vittorio Veneto in Concorezzo (☎ **039/604-93-90**), in the northeastern outskirts. Remainders from hotel and restaurant orders are sold at even greater discounts than at the main headquarters.

PAPER & STATIONERY In the Brera district, **I Giorni di Carta,** Corso Garibaldi 81 (☎ **02-655-2514;** Metro: Moscova), is one of the city's most unusual outlets for stationery, with dozens of colors, textures, and weights. Much of the inventory is made from recycled paper. It also sells briefcases, pens and ink, notebooks, lamps, dishes, dolls, and ornamental paperweights.

Papier, 4 Via San Maurilio (☎ **02-865-221;** Metro: Missori), is the premier address for stationery, including "extreme paper" (plasticized and plaited paper given a metallic sheen evoking fabric). Banana-leaf pages from Thailand and Nepal are sold, even hairy coconut sheets resembling the real thing. History buffs can order the parchment paper.

PERFUME In the Brera district, **Profumo,** Via Brera 6 (☎ **02-7202-3334;** Metro: Duomo), sells some of Italy's most exotic perfumes for women, plus cologne and after-shave lotions for men.

PORCELAIN & CRYSTAL Since 1735, **Richard Ginori,** Corso Buenos Aires 1 (☎ **02-2951-6611;** Metro: Lima), has manufactured and sold porcelain in many price ranges. A household word in Italy, Ginori sells ovenproof porcelain in both modern and traditional themes, as well as crystal and silverware that they either make themselves or inventory from other manufacturers, such as Baccarat and Wedgwood.

PRINTS & ENGRAVINGS **Raimondi di Pettinaroli,** Corso Venezia 6 (☎ **02-7600-2412;** Metro: San Babila), is the finest shop in Milan for antique prints and engravings, plus reprints of old engravings made from the original copper plates. Of particular interest are the engravings of Italian cityscapes during the 19th century, many of them treasures that'll be worth framing after you return home.

ACCOMMODATIONS

In Milan, you'll find some deluxe hotels and an abundance of first- and second-class hotels, most of which are big on comfort but short on romance. In the third- and fourth-class bracket and on the *pensione* (boardinghouse) level are dozens of choices, though the budget hotels in Milan are not nearly as nice as those in Italy's other major cities. If you can afford it, spend more on your hotel in Milan and opt for budget accommodations in Rome, Florence, and Venice, which have clean, comfortable, and often architecturally interesting third- and fourth-class hotels and pensioni.

VERY EXPENSIVE

✪ **Four Seasons Hotel Milano.** Via Gesú 8, 20121 Milano. ☎ **02-77-088.** Fax 02-7708-5000. www.fourseasons.com. 98 units. A/C MINIBAR TV TEL. 900,000–1,100,000L ($450–$550) double; from 1,150,000L ($575) suite. AE, DC, MC, V. Parking 80,000L ($40). Metro: Montenapoleone or San Babila.

Milan's most exciting five-star hotel opened in 1993 on a side street opening onto Via Montenapoleone's upscale boutiques. The building was first a 15th-century monastery, then the residence of the Hapsburg-appointed governor of northern Italy in the 1850s, and later the site of luxury apartments. The medieval facade, many of the frescoes and columns, and the original monastic details were incorporated into a modern edifice accented with bronze, stone floors, glass, pearwood cabinetry, Murano chandeliers, and acres of Fortuny fabrics. The guest rooms are cool, conservative, and spacious, with a sense of understated luxury and first-class mattresses. The state-of-the-art bathrooms offer lavish vanities, deep European soaking tubs, bidets, robes, hair dryers, and fine toiletries.

Dining: The hotel lounge contains the architectural renderings for stage sets used at the nearby La Scala. Il Teatro serves dinner daily 8pm to midnight (see "Dining," below). Less formal, La Veranda serves meals daily 11am to 11pm.

Amenities: Concierge, 24-hour room service, same-day valet/laundry, high-tech fitness center/spa, business center.

Hotel Excelsior Gallia. Piazza Duca d'Aosta 9, 20124 Milano. ☎ **800/225-5843** in the U.S., or 02-678-51. Fax 02-6671-3239. www.excelsiorgallia.it. 237 units. A/C MINIBAR TV TEL. 600,000–700,000L ($300–$350) double; from 1,000,000L ($500) suite. AE, DC, MC, V. Parking 20,000–40,000L ($10–$20). Metro: Stazione Centrale. Tram: 33 or 59.

This Liberty-style monument was built by the Gallia family in 1933. It's a prominent hotel, once one of Italy's tops—but today it's more of an upscale rail station hotel. The 1994 renovations combined some of the smaller rooms into larger and more comfortable accommodations. The guest rooms are in two categories: modern and comfortable in the newer wing and graciously old-fashioned in the original core. All are soundproofed, with firm mattresses and marble bathrooms with phones, hair dryers, and radios.

Dining/Diversions: The noted Gallia's serves haute Lombard and international dishes. The Baboon Bar is stylish, and a piano player sometimes performs in the lobby.

Amenities: Room service, laundry/valet, baby-sitting, business center, fitness club/massage center, gym, whirlpool, sauna.

Hotel Prìncipe di Savoia. Piazza della Repubblica 17, 20124 Milano. ☎ **800/325-3535** in the U.S., or 02-623-01. Fax 02-653-799. www.luxurycollection.com. 399 units. A/C MINIBAR TV TEL. 780,000–1,450,000L ($390–$725) double; from 1,485,000L ($742.50) suite. Breakfast 65,000L ($32.50). AE, DC, MC, V. Parking 35,000–75,000L ($17.50–$37.50). Metro: Repubblica.

The Prìncipe was built in 1927 to fill the need for a luxurious hotel near Stazione Centrale, then was completely restored in 1991. It offers solid comfort amid crystal, detailed plasterwork, fine carpets, and polished marble. The guest rooms are spacious, decorated in a 19th-century Lombard style. All contain leather chairs and other stylish furniture, plus first-rate mattresses and safes. The front rooms face the hysterical traffic of Piazza della Repubblica, but the ones in back are more tranquil, opening onto the Alps. The marble bathrooms are extravagant, with robes, deluxe toiletries, scales, and hair dryers.

Dining/Diversions: There's a spacious bar area, Il Giardino d'Inverno, off the main lobby. The hotel has a notable restaurant, Galleria, serving both regional and international dishes. It also offers the popular Doney cafe (see "Dining," below). That breakfast charge is scandalous, though.

Amenities: Room service, baby-sitting, laundry/valet, sauna, health club, solarium, indoor pool, limited facilities for travelers with disabilities.

Sheraton Diana Majestic Hotel. Viale Piave 42, 20129 Milano. ☎ **800/325-3535** in the U.S. and Canada, or 02-205-81. Fax 02-205-820-58. www.ittsheraton.com. 99 units. A/C MINIBAR TV TEL. 620,000–650,000L ($310–$325) double; from 1,100,000L ($550) suite. Breakfast 34,000–50,000L ($17–$25). Free parking. Metro: Porta Venezia.

Opened in 1908, the Diana Majestic has been brought back to its original splendor with the completion of a $10 million renovation. In restoring the public areas, particular attention was paid to the stucco and decorative details, as well as to the original wooden floors. The 1925 French art deco style incorporated during that era is prevalent in the new carpeting and upholstery, leather armchairs, and authentically reproduced furniture. The guest rooms and suites are decorated in classical imperial style, with maximum comfort. All include direct-line phones with personalized voice messaging, computer and fax modems, safe-deposit boxes, and individually controlled air-conditioning. A number overlook the inside garden. The marble bathrooms are beautiful, with hair dryers.

Dining/Diversions: Il Milanese restaurant has its own access from Viale Piave and overlooks the inner garden. The menu offers a choice of gourmet specialties from both traditional Milanese and Mediterranean cuisines. The garden offers outdoor dining featuring barbecued specialties during summer. Before or after dining, guests can relax in an area between Il Milanese and a semicircular glass hall where the new bar is located. Ideal for a lighter lunch, Il Glicine offers a selection of pizzas, pasta salads, and desserts and a choice of wines by the glass.

Amenities: Concierge, room service, laundry/valet, business center, fitness center.

The Westin Palace. Piazza della Repubblica 20, 20124 Milano. ☎ **800/325-3535** in the U.S., 167/780-525 toll-free in Italy, or 02-63-361. Fax 02-654-485. www.luxurycollection.com. 216 units. A/C MINIBAR TV TEL. 710,000–800,000L ($355–$400) double; from 1,300,000L ($650) suite. Breakfast 45,000L ($22.50). AE, DC, MC, V. Parking 60,000–85,000L ($30–$42.50). Metro: Repubblica.

The Palace stands aloof on a hill near the rail station, with a formal car entrance and a facade boasting tiers of balconies. Though primarily a business hotel, the Palace welcomes tourists and occasional entertainers. The guest rooms are furnished with pastel upholstery and reproductions of Italian antiques as well as luxury mattresses. The deluxe bathrooms come with hair dryers, robes, scales, and heated towel racks.

Dining/Diversions: The hotel bar attracts an international crowd, and the Grill Casanova is acclaimed as one of the finest in Milan, offering both regional and international dishes.

Amenities: Room service, baby-sitting, laundry/valet, fitness center.

EXPENSIVE

Hotel Galles Milano. Via Ozanam 1 (Corso Buenos Aires), Milano 20129. ☎ **800/528-1234** in the U.S., or 02-204-841. Fax 02-204-8422. www.galles.it. E-mail: reception@galles.it. 120 units. A/C MINIBAR TV TEL. 250,000–600,000L ($125–$300) double; from 700,000L ($350) suite. Rates include continental breakfast. AE, DC, MC, V. Parking 40,000L ($20). Metro: Lima.

The Galles was built in 1901, and in 1990 Italian investors financed an elegant rehabilitation, producing a hotel favored by businesspeople, conventioneers, and visitors looking for unpretentious lodgings. The interior lacks the art nouveau glamour of many of its competitors, but this doesn't seem to bother many people. The guest rooms come in a variety of shapes and sizes, each with comfortable furnishings. The rooftop La Terrazza restaurant has additional seating on a canopy-covered terrace, plus a cocktail bar. In spring and summer there's a roof garden with a solarium and Jacuzzi.

MODERATE TO INEXPENSIVE

✪ **Antica Locanda dei Mercanti.** Via San Tommaso 6, 20123 Milano. ☎ **02-805-4080.** Fax 02-805-4090. www.locanda.it. E-mail: locanda@locanda.it. 14 units. 210,000–350,000L ($105–$175) double. Breakfast 15,000L ($7.50). Parking 35,000L ($17.50). AE, MC, V. Tram: 1, 14, or 24. Metro: Cairoli, Cordusio, or Duomo.

The building containing this reasonably priced but sophisticated hotel was built in the late 1800s by a merchant. In 1996 a former model, Paola Ora, gutted the second floor and installed a streamlined hotel, custom designing each room and naming each after a Milanese mercantile family. The furnishings are upholstered in top-echelon Milanese fabrics and the bathrooms sheathed in marble. Some rooms have canopied beds, each with a quality mattress. Terraced rooms have air-conditioning, the others ceiling fans. Don't be startled by the severe-looking monumental entrance or the businesslike appearance of three of the building's four floors, most of which are occupied by crafts studios for the jewelry industry. Breakfast (in bed) is the only meal served. The neighborhood was described in Alessandro Manzoni's 19th-century classic, *I Promessi Sposi* (The Promised Spouse).

✪ **Antica Locanda Solferino.** Via Castelfidardo 2, 20121 Milano. ☎ **02-657-0129.** Fax 02-657-1361. 11 units. TV TEL. 210,000–260,000L ($105–$130) double. Rates include breakfast. AE, DC, MC, V. Parking 25,000–30,000L ($12.50–$15) nearby. Metro: Moscova or Repubblica.

When this hotel opened in 1976, the neighborhood was a depressed backwater. Today it's an avant-garde community of actors, writers, and poets, and this inn deserves some of the credit. It got off to a great start soon after opening when editors from *GQ* stayed here while working on a fashion feature. Since then, celebrities have either stayed in the old-fashioned rooms or dined in the ground-floor restaurant (see "Dining," below). Each guest room is unique, reflecting the 19th-century floor plan of the building. The furnishings include Daumier engravings and art nouveau or late-19th-century bourgeois pieces, as well as excellent beds with firm mattresses. Since the hotel is small and often fully booked, reserve as far in advance as possible.

Casa Svizzera. Via San Raffaele 3, 20121 Milano. ☎ **02-869-2246.** Fax 02-7200-4690. 45 units. A/C MINIBAR TV TEL. 310,000L ($155) double. Rates include breakfast. AE, DC, MC, V. Parking 50,000L ($25). Metro: Duomo.

Casa Svizzera, right off Piazza del Duomo, is one of the most serviceable hotels in the city. The homelike guest rooms have air-conditioning that can be independently regulated, as well as paneled double windows and soundproofing to keep out the noise. Most are medium in size, each with an excellent mattress and well-equipped bathroom.

Hotel Gran Duca di York. Via Moneta 1A (Piazza Cordusio), 20123 Milano. ☎ **02-874-863.** Fax 02-869-0344. 33 units. TV TEL. 250,000L ($125) double; 300,000L ($150) triple. Rates include breakfast. AE, MC, V. Parking 35,000–40,000L ($17.50–$20). Closed Aug. Metro: Cordusio or Duomo.

When it was built by the Catholic Church in the 1890s, this Liberty-style palace housed dozens of priests from the Duomo. Among them was the cardinal of Milan, who later became Pope Pius XI. Today anyone can rent one of the pleasantly furnished and well-kept rooms, ranging from small to medium in size, each with a fine mattress and a bathroom sheathed in patterned tiles. Behind the ocher-and-stone facade, you'll find a bar in an alcove of the severely elegant lobby, where a suit of armor and leather-covered armchairs contribute to the restrained tone.

Hotel Manzoni. Via Santo Spirito 20, 20121 Milano. ☎ **02-7600-5700.** Fax 02-784-212. 52 units. TV TEL. 280,000L ($140) double. Rates include breakfast. AE, DC, MC, V. Parking 25,000–60,000L ($12.50–$30). Metro: Montenapoleone or San Babila.

The Manzoni, built around 1910 and renovated frequently since, charges reasonable prices considering its location near the most-fashionable shopping streets. Each of its rather small guest rooms contains color-coordinated comfortable furniture and carpeting as well as fine mattresses; many have TVs. The tiled bathrooms are also small. A brass-trimmed winding staircase leads from the lobby into a bar and TV lounge. The English-speaking staff is cooperative.

Hotel Star. Via dei Bossi 5, 20121 Milano. ☎ **02-801-501.** Fax 02-861-787. www.starhotel.it. E-mail: information@starhotel.it or reservation@starhotel.it. 30 units. A/C MINIBAR TV TEL. 265,000–280,000L ($132.50–$140) double. Rates include buffet breakfast. AE, MC, V. Parking 35,000–40,000L ($17.50–$20). Closed Aug and Christmas. Metro: Cordusio or Duomo.

The Ceretti family welcomes guests to its well-run little hotel a few blocks from La Scala and the Duomo. The lobby has been brightened, and the guest rooms are pleasant but still a bit dour. They range from small to medium, each containing a comfortable bed. Amenities like hair dryers have been installed in the bathrooms (about 15 rooms have a personal sauna and hydromassage tub), and double-glass windows cut down on street noise. The breakfast includes jams, pâté, yogurts, cheese, eggs, ham, and fruit salad, along with cereal, croissants, and various teas, juices, and coffee.

Hotel Valganna. Via Varè 32, 20158 Milano. ☎ **02-3931-0089.** Fax 02-3931-2566. www.traveleurope.it. E-mail: hotel.valganna@traveleurope.it. 40 units. A/C MINIBAR TV TEL. 150,000–305,000L ($75–$152.50) double. Rates include buffet breakfast. AE, CB, DC, DISC, MC, V. Parking 15,000L ($7.50). Bus: 82 or 92. Metro: Bovisa.

This tasteful, modern hotel offers amenities like satellite TVs and piped music in each renovated room. Some, however, are a bit cramped. All the accommodations come with excellent beds and well-equipped bathrooms. The grand buffet is served in the breakfast lounge, and later in the day a refined bar welcomes you. For sunbathing, there's a spacious terrace, and the reception staff is happy to assist you with transportation tickets to get to the nearby lakes of Como and Maggiore.

DINING

VERY EXPENSIVE

A Santa Lucia. Via San Pietro all'Orto 3. ☎ **02-7602-3155.** Reservations recommended. Main courses 55,000–60,000L ($27.50–$30). MC, V. Tues–Sun noon–3pm and 7:30pm–1am. Closed Aug. Metro: San Babila. MEDITERRANEAN/SEAFOOD.

A Santa Lucia pulls out hook, line, and sinker to lure you with some of the best fish dinners in Milan. A festive place, it's decked out with photographs of pleased celebs, who attest to the skill of its kitchen. You can order such specialties as a savory fish soup, a meal in itself; fried baby squid; or good-tasting sole. *Spaghetti alla vongole* evokes the tang of the sea with its succulent clam sauce. Pizza also reigns supreme: Try either the calzone of Naples or the *pizza alla napoletana.*

✪ **Giannino.** Via Amatore Sciesa 8. ☎ **02-5519-5582.** Reservations required. Main courses 60,000–80,000L ($30–$40); fixed-price menus 110,000–130,000L ($55–$65). AE, DC, MC, V. Tues–Sat 12:30–3pm and 7:30pm–midnight; Mon 7:30pm–midnight. Closed 2 weeks in Aug. Metro: San Babila. Bus: 73. MILANESE/SEAFOOD.

Giannino enchants its loyal patrons and wins new fans every year. It's one of the top restaurants in all Lombardy and has been since 1899. You have a choice of several attractive rooms, and eyes rivet on the tempting offerings of the *specialità gastronomiche milanesi.* The choice is excellent, including such dishes as breaded veal cutlet and risotto simmered in broth and coated with parmigiano. We have special affection for the *tagliolini con scampi al verde* (fresh homemade noodles with prawn tails in herb sauce). Also superb are the cold fish and seafood salad and the beautifully seasoned *orata al cartoccio* (fish baked in a paper bag with shrimp butter and fresh herbs).

EXPENSIVE

Al Chico. Via Sirtori 24. ☎ **02-2953-0280.** Reservations recommended. Main courses 35,000–40,000L ($17.50–$20). AE, DC, MC, V. Mon–Sat noon–3pm and 7–11pm. Closed 10 days in Aug. Metro: Porta Venezia. TUSCAN/ITALIAN.

Al Chico, a good neighborhood place specializing in such fare as onion soup and fondue bourguignonne, opened in the 1970s in a renovated century-old building. Tuscan specialties like Florentine beefsteak are also featured, and the chef is rightly proud of his pappardelle with porcini mushrooms, *branzini* (sea bass) cooked in salt crust, and spaghetti with mushrooms and spring onions. The place is usually crowded, but it's worth the wait. The service is good, and the ingredients are fresh and well selected. There is a stock of good house wines from Tuscany, including Chianti Classico. In summer you can eat on the veranda.

Bistro Duomo. Via San Raffaele 2. ☎ **02-877-120.** Reservations required. Main courses 35,000–42,000L ($17.50–$21); fixed-price menus 60,000–80,000L ($30–$40). AE, MC, V. Mon 7–10:15pm; Tues–Sat noon–2:30pm and 7–10:15pm. Closed 2 weeks in Aug (dates vary). Metro: Duomo. LOMBARD/ITALIAN.

Duomo was created by Gualtiero Marchesi, once hailed by *Time* as among the world's 10 top chefs. He's moved on to a newer, very expensive restaurant, but left behind this terraced bistro as a token of love for Milan. It boasts one of the city's best views of the cathedral, for it's on the top floor of the Rinascente Center, across from the Duomo. For your antipasti, consider such delights as steamed vegetables with hazelnut oil and toasted almonds, salmon carpaccio with soy sauce, or swordfish salad with fennel and oranges. The potato soup with leeks and black truffles might also get you going. The chefs prepare superb fish dishes, and a meat specialty is a perfectly rendered osso buco.

Doney. In the Prìncipe di Savoia Hotel, Piazza della Repubblica 17. ☎ **02-62-30.** Reservations recommended. Main courses 38,000–48,000L ($19–$24); fixed-price dinner 100,000L ($50); afternoon tea 25,000–35,000L ($12.50–$17.50). AE, DC, MC, V. Daily 12:30–3pm and 7–11pm (afternoon tea 4–7pm). Metro: Repubblica. Tram: 1, 4, 11, 29, or 30. LIGHT INTERNATIONAL/AFTERNOON TEA/LOMBARD/VEGETARIAN.

Its burnished paneling, plush upholstery, and soaring frescoed ceiling are some of the high points of one of Milan's most recent (and most expensive) hotel restorations. Doney borrowed its name from a historic cafe in Rome and much of its decorative allure from the Liberty style. Its menu features elegant but simple preparations of salads (lobster, artichokes, and pears), sandwiches (smoked salmon on brown bread), and steaks. During teatime you can select from nine kinds of tea and pastries and finger sandwiches from a trolley. At any hour, the place is a popular meeting point.

Il Teatro. In the Four Seasons Hotel Milano, Via Gesù 8. ☎ **02-7708-1435.** Reservations recommended. Main courses 36,000–48,000L ($18–$24); fixed-price menus 95,000–150,000L ($47.50–$75). AE, DC, MC, V. Mon–Sat 7:30–11:45pm. Metro: Montenapoleone or San Babila. MEDITERRANEAN.

This is the culinary showcase of the shopping district's most glamorous hotel, often hosting big names in the fashion business. It's located in a 1400s Milanese palazzo. The patio overlooks a garden, and the dining room is sheathed in burnished paneling and rich leather under a ceiling of tented champagne silk. The menu changes at least four times a year but may include a tantalizing *involtini* of eggplant with ricotta and mint, crispy crayfish with a puree of tomatoes, and red mullet fillet with essence of tomato and black truffles. Everything tastes as fresh as the day it was picked, harvested, or caught. Dessert might be a *mille-feuille croquante* layered with walnuts, chocolate mousse, and raspberries.

✪ **Savini.** In the Galleria Vittorio Emanuele II. ☎ **02-7200-3433.** Reservations required. Main courses 42,000–110,000L ($21–$55). AE, DC, MC, V. Mon–Sat noon–2pm and 7:30–11pm. Closed Dec 24–Jan 2 and Aug 10–25. Metro: Duomo. LOMBARD/INTERNATIONAL.

Savini provides a heavenly introduction to the cookery of Lombardy and has attracted everybody from Puccini to Pavarotti. Perched in the great glass-enclosed arcade opposite the Duomo, the restaurant draws both out-of-towners and discriminating locals to its terrace and its old-world dining room with crystal chandeliers. Many of the most memorable dishes are unassuming, like the *cotoletta alla milanese,* tender veal coated with egg batter and bread crumbs, then fried a rich brown. The pièce de résistance, most often ordered before the main course, is *risotto alla milanese*—rice simmered in a veal broth and dressed with whatever the artiste in the kitchen selects. The restaurant is excellently stocked with wine (the staff will gladly assist you).

Take a Gelato Break

You can find organic gelato at the **Gelateria Ecologica,** Corso di Porta Ticinese 40 (☎ **02-5810-1872;** Metro: Sant'Ambrogio or Missori), in the Ticinese/Navigli neighborhood. It's so popular, there's no need for a sign out front. Strollers in the atmospheric Brera neighborhood sooner or later stumble on the **Gelateria Toldo,** Via Ponte Vetero 11 (☎ **02-8646-0863;** Metro: Cordusio or Lanza), where the gelato is wonderfully creamy and many of the sorbetto selections are so fruity and fresh they seem healthy.

Passerini, Via Hugo 4 (☎ **02-8646-4995;** Metro: Cordusio), is more than the typical stand-up counter. This elegant ice-cream parlor a few blocks west of the Duomo upholds its 80-year tradition gallantly, serving several dozen variations of the creamy concoctions, including a *cioccolato gianduia* (chocolate hazelnut topped with whipped cream) that brings chocolate lovers back time and again.

St. Andrews. Via Sant'Andrea 23. ☎ **02-798-236.** Reservations required. Main courses 35,000–50,000L ($17.50–$25). AE, DC, MC, V. Mon–Sat noon–4pm and 7pm–2am. Closed Aug. Metro: Montenapoleone or San Babila. LOMBARD/INTERNATIONAL.

This restaurant has boasted one of the finest kitchens in Lombardy for many years. The menu includes an unusual appetizer of steak tartare mixed with caviar and seasonings, John Dory in salt crust, and rack of lamb Provençal style. The dessert specialty is a *tartatelli,* pastry with honey-and-strawberry sauce. At lunch the place seems like a private club and is apt to be filled with businesspeople. The armchairs are covered in black leather, the paneling is dark wood, and the lighting is discreet. The formally attired waiters give superb service.

Taverna del Gran Sasso. Piazza Principessa Clotilde 10. ☎ **02-659-7578.** Reservations not required. All-you-can-eat meal 75,000L ($37.50); all-you-can-eat fish meal on request (call in advance) 85,000 lire ($42.50). AE, MC, V. Mon–Fri noon–2pm and 7–11:30pm; Sat 7:30–10:30pm. Closed Jan 1 and Aug. Metro: Repubblica. ABRUZZI.

This tavern is filled with lots of sentimental baubles, its walls crowded ceiling to floor with copper molds, ears of corn, strings of pepper and garlic, and cart wheels. A tall open hearth burns with a charcoal fire, and a Sicilian cart is laden with baskets of bread, dried figs, nuts, and kegs of wine. As you enter, you'll find a mellowed wooden keg of wine with a brass faucet (you're supposed to help yourself, using glass mugs). The cuisine features a number of specialties from the Abruzzi, like *maccheroni alla chitarra,* a distinctively shaped macaroni with savory meat sauce. Meals are an all-you-can-eat feast.

MODERATE

Al Porto. Piazzale Generale Cantore. ☎ **02-832-1481.** Reservations required several days in advance. Main courses 28,000–45,000L ($14–$22.50). AE, DC, MC, V. Mon 7:30–10:30pm; Tues–Sat 12:30–2:30pm and 7:30–10:30pm. Closed Dec 24–Jan 3 and Aug. Metro: Porta Genova or Sant'Agostino. SEAFOOD.

Opened in 1907, Al Porto is among the most popular seafood restaurants in Milan, with a lovely glassed-in garden room. Menu items include *orata* (dorado) with pink peppercorns and *branzini* (sea bass) with white Lugurian wine and olives. Many diners come just for the *risotto ai frutti di mare,* with an assortment of "sea creatures." You might begin with a warm antipasto, follow with a risotto, and then order the traditional *fritto misto* (almost anything that swims is likely to turn up on the plate), though some find this far too much food. Everything tastes better with a Friuli wine.

Boeucc Antico Ristorante. Piazza Belgioioso 2. ☎ **02-7602-0224.** Reservations required. Main courses 30,000–45,000L ($15–$22.50). AE. Mon–Fri 12:40–2:30pm; Sun–Fri 7:40–10:30pm. Closed Aug, Easter, and Christmas. Metro: Duomo, Montenapoleone, or San Babila. INTERNATIONAL/MILANESE.

This restaurant, opened in 1696, is a trio of rooms in a severely elegant old palace, within walking distance of the Duomo and the major shopping streets. Throughout you'll find soaring stone columns and modern art. In summer, guests gravitate to a terrace for open-air dining. You might enjoy spaghetti in clam sauce, a salad of shrimp with arugula and artichokes, or grilled liver, veal, or beef with aromatic herbs. In season, sautéed zucchini flowers accompany some dishes.

La Banque. Via Bassano Porrone 6. ☎ **02-8699-6565.** Reservations required. Main courses 25,000–38,000L ($12.50–$19). AE, DC, MC, V. Mon–Sat 6pm–3am. Metro: Cordusio or Duomo. REGIONAL/ITALIAN.

In an early 1900s building, Le Banque gets its name from its former role as a bank and is one of Milan's hottest restaurants. The chef often takes regional dishes and modernizes them, adding his own touch. The *risotto alla Milanese,* for example, comes in an updated version as a rice timbale with saffron-flavored sauce. Most of the dishes are cooked fast and simply in the best virgin olive oil. Perfectly cooked lobster appears on a bed of barley, and a delicious Lomellina salami is served in mustard sauce. One of the finest pasta dishes is made with clams and fresh zucchini. A superb main course is tender Nebraska beef fillet marinated in balsamic vinegar. Diners have free access to the cellar disco.

✪ **Peck's Restaurant.** Via Victor Hugo 4. ☎ **02-876-774.** Reservations required. Main courses 32,000–48,000L ($16–$24). AE, DC, MC, V. Mon–Sat 12:15–2:30pm and 7:15–10:30pm. Closed 10 days in Jan and July 1–21. Metro: Duomo. MILANESE/ITALIAN.

Peck's is owned by the famous delicatessen, viewed as the Milanese equivalent of Fauchon's in Paris. It was opened by Francesco Peck, who came to Milan from Prague in the 19th century. His small restaurant went on to become a food empire. In an environment filled with shimmering marble and modern Italian paintings, an alert staff serves an elegant cuisine. The fresh specialties include a classic version of *risotto milanese,* rack of lamb with fresh rosemary, *ravioli alla fonduata,* and *lombo di vitello* (veal) with artichokes, followed by chocolate meringue for dessert. Its cured meats are said to be the richest in Italy. There's also a less-expensive Peck's (see below).

10 Corso Como Café. Corso Como 10. ☎ **02-2901-3581.** Reservations recommended. Main courses 25,000–35,000L ($12.50–$17.50). AE, DC, MC, V. Daily 11am–midnight. Metro: Moscova. ITALIAN/INTERNATIONAL.

In the Brera, the hottest cafe in the Milanese fashion world is the domain of Carla Sozzani, part of her stylish bazaar at 10 Corso Como, which also includes an art gallery, a music room, a boutique, and a bookstore. It pushes the envelope of chic yet isn't unduly expensive. The minimalist decor of cast iron, stained glass, and steel is Milanese modern at its best. Oh, yes, the food. Of course, everyone likes to stay fashionably thin around here, so expect a selection of Mediterranean sushi or sashimi and beautifully flavored Italian fresh vegetables and fish tempura. The pastas have distinctive and original flavors, including one with toasted pine nuts and fresh marjoram. This trendsetter of a place also offers a wide selection of tea from all over the world. On Saturday and Sunday, an American-style brunch is served till 2pm.

✪ **Trattoria Bagutta.** Via Bagutta 14. ☎ **02-7600-2767.** Reservations required. Main courses 25,000–38,000L ($12.50–$19). AE, DC, MC, V. Mon–Sat 12:30–2:30pm and 7:30–10:30pm. Closed Dec 24 and Jan 6. Metro: San Babila. INTERNATIONAL.

Patronized by artists, this restaurant is Milan's most celebrated trattoria. Dating from 1927, the Bagutta is known for the caricatures (framed and frescoed) covering its walls. Of the many bustling dining rooms, the rear one with its picture windows is most enticing. The food draws from the kitchens of Lombardy, Tuscany, and Bologna for inspiration. On offer are assorted antipasti, and main-dish specialties include fried squid and scampi, *lingua e puré* (tongue with mashed potatoes), linguine with shrimp in tomato-cream sauce, and *scaloppine alla Bagutta.*

INEXPENSIVE

Al Tempio d'Oro. Via delle Leghe 23. ☎ **02-2614-5709.** Main courses 12,000–20,000L ($6–$10). No credit cards. Mon–Sat 8pm–2am. Closed 2 weeks in mid-Aug. Metro: Pasteur. ITALIAN/INTERNATIONAL.

This restaurant, near the central rail station, offers inexpensive and well-prepared meals. The chef is justifiably proud of his fish soup, Spanish paella, and North African couscous. The crowd scattered among the ceiling columns is relaxed, and they contribute to an atmosphere somewhat like that of a beer hall. No one will mind if you stop by just for a drink.

La Magolfa. Via Magolfa 15. ☎ **02-832-1696.** Reservations not needed. Pastas 8,000–12,000L ($4–$6); pizza 7,000–15,000L ($3.50–$7.50). AE, DC, MC, V. Thurs–Tues noon–3pm and 7pm–2am. Metro: Porta Genova. LOMBARD/INTERNATIONAL.

La Magolfa, one of the city's dining bargains, offers a great value in pizzas and pastas. The building is a country farmhouse whose origins date from the 1500s, though the restaurant opened only in 1960. It's likely to be crowded with young people, as is every other restaurant in Milan that offers such value. If you don't mind its location away from the center of town, in Zona Ticinese in the southern part of the city, you'll be treated to some hearty food and gargantuan helpings. A general air of conviviality reigns, and there's music of local origin nightly.

✪ **Peck.** Via Victor Hugo 4. ☎ **02-802-3161.** Reservations not needed. Main courses 20,000–30,000L ($10–$15). AE, DC, MC, V. Mon–Sat 7:30am–9pm. Closed 10 days in Jan and July 1–21. Metro: Duomo. MILANESE/LOMBARD.

Peck offers one of the best values in Milan—food served in a glamorous cafeteria associated with the most famous delicatessen in Italy (the higher-priced restaurant in the basement is listed above). Only a short walk from the Duomo, Peck has a stand-up bar and well-stocked display cases of specialties fresh from their treasure trove of produce. Armed with a plastic tray, you can sample such temptations as artichoke-and-parmigiano salad, marinated carpaccio, slabs of tender veal in herb sauce, risotto marinara, and selections from a carving table laden with a juicy display of roast meats.

ON THE OUTSKIRTS

✪ **Antica Osteria del Ponte.** Piazza G. Negri 9, Cassinetta di Lugagnano. ☎ **02-942-0034.** Reservations required. Main courses 25,000–45,000L ($12.50–$22.50); fixed-price menu 170,000L ($85). AE, DC, MC, V. Tues–Sat 12:30–2:30pm and 7:30–10:30pm. Closed Aug and Dec 25–Jan 12. ITALIAN.

One of our favorite restaurants in the area is not in Milan but 18 miles (29km) outside (see directions below). A country inn since the 18th century, this hosteria was taken over 20 years ago by Mr. and Mrs. Ezio Santin, who turned it into one of Lombardy's most acclaimed restaurants. Mr. Santin studied under one of France's greatest chefs, Roger Vergé, and has devised a menu reflecting both lessons learned in France and his own inventive touches. The Santin son, Maurizio, is the creative pastry chef. On our most recent rounds, we were thrilled by the shrimp marinated with olive oil and lemon sauce and served with caviar and a touch of vanilla. The risotto with fresh young artichoke hearts, anchovies, and parmigiano was among the finest versions of this dish we've ever found. For a regal taste treat, try the baked goose stuffed with foie gras.

From the center of Milan, take the SS Vigevanese until you reach Abiategrasso; then cross the bridge over the Naviglio Canal. At the first traffic light, turn right and follow the directions to Novara/Magenta. Go straight for 2 miles (3km) until you come to an intersection with a signpost marking the way to Cassinetta di Lugagnano. Turn left and follow this sign to the restaurant.

MILAN AFTER DARK

As in Rome, many of the top nightclubs in Milan shut down for the summer, when the cabaret talent and the bartenders pack their bags and head for the hills or the seashore. However, Milan is a big city, and there are always plenty of after-dark diversions. This sprawling metropolis is also one of Europe's cultural centers.

THE PERFORMING ARTS The most complete list of cultural events appears in the large Milan newspaper, the left-wing ***La Repubblica.*** Try for a Thursday edition, which usually has the most complete listings.

If you have only a night for Milan and are here between mid-December and July, try to attend a performance at the world-famous ✪ **Teatro alla Scala,** Piazza della Scala (☎ **02-7200-3744;** Metro: Duomo). If you're visiting in summer, check with the box office about special performances. Built to the designs of Giuseppe Piermarini, it was inaugurated with *Europa Riconosciuta* by Antonio Sallieri, a friend and rival of Mozart, and won instant praise for its marvelous acoustics. The neoclassic opera house was restored after World War II bomb damage. The greatest opera stars appear here, and the Milanese first-night audience is the hardest to please in the world.

Tickets are extremely hard to come by and are sold out weeks in advance, costing 35,000 to 300,000L ($17.50 to $150). However, you do stand a chance of getting gallery tickets (though they're nosebleed seats). The box office is open Tuesday to Sunday noon to 3pm. If you're a serious opera fan and don't want to take your chances at the last minute, you can get tickets to La Scala before leaving home by contacting a Milanese tour operator called **Agencia Sertur** (☎ **02-7602-4314**), which usually packages tickets to La Scala with hotel overnights for out-of-towners. Otherwise, you can check schedules and purchase tickets on the Web at www.lascala.milano.it, or phone for tickets by calling ☎ **02-7200-3339.** These range in price from 20,000 to 150,000L ($10 to $75), depending on the location of the seats and the performance, although tickets to some opening-night performances can go as high as 250,000L ($125) each. The opera house is closed in midsummer, parts of July and all of August. The new season begins every year on December 7, although the program for the upcoming season is announced the previous September.

Opera lovers will also want to visit the **Museo Teatrale alla Scala** in the same building (see "Seeing the Sights," above).

The **Conservatorio,** Via del Conservatorio 12 (☎ **02-762-1101** or 02-7600-1755; Metro: San Babila), in the San Babila neighborhood, features the finest in classical music. Year-round, a cultured Milanese audience enjoys high-quality programs of widely varied classical concerts. Tickets are 25,000 to 50,000L ($12.50 to $25).

The **Piccolo Teatro,** Via Rivoli 2, near Via Dante (☎ **02-7233-3222;** Metro: Cordusio), hosts a wide variety of Italian-language performances. Its director, Giorgio Strehler, is acclaimed as one of the most avant-garde and talented in the world. The theater lies between the Duomo and the Castle of the Sforzas. It's sometimes hard to obtain seats. Performances are Tuesday to Sunday at 8:30pm (closed August). Tickets are 50,000 to 65,000L ($25 to $32.50).

LIVE-MUSIC CLUBS The **Ca'Bianca Club,** Via Lodovico il Moro 117 (☎ **02-8912-5777;** Metro: Bisceglie), offers live music and dancing on Wednesday night, from folk music to cabaret to Dixieland jazz. This is a private club, but no one at the door will prevent nonmembers from entering. The show, whatever it may be, begins at 10:30pm (closed Sundays and closed in August). Cover is 30,000L ($15) for the show and the first drink, or 90,000 to 100,000L ($45 to $50) for dinner.

Capolinea, Via Lodovico il Moro 119 (☎ **02-8912-2024;** Metro: Bisceglie), is one of the most appealing jazz clubs in town, with a roster of jazz acts of every imaginable ilk. Music is performed 10:30pm to 1 or 1:30am. The first drink is 15,000L ($7.50) and the others are 7,000 to 14,000L ($3.50 to $7). There's also a restaurant serving affordable meals.

At **Le Scimmie,** Via Ascanio Sforza 49 (☎ **02-8940-2874;** Bus: 59), bands play everything from funk to blues to creative jazz to an appreciative audience that shows up every night except Tuesday. Doors open around 8pm, and music is presented 10pm to around 1am.

Rolling Stone, Corso XXII Marzo 32 (☎ **02-733-172;** Tram: 4 or 20), features head-banging rock bands. It's open every night, usually 10:30pm to 4am, but don't even consider showing up until at least midnight. Closed in July and August. Cover for men on Friday and Saturday is 20,000L ($10) and other days 15,000L ($7.50). Cover for women is 15,000L ($7.50).

CAFES The decor of the **Berlin Cafe,** Via Gian Giacomo Mora 9 (☎ **02-839-2605;** Tram: 15, 19, or 24), emulates a cafe in turn-of-the-century Berlin; the ambience is enhanced with etched glass and marble-topped tables. It's a great spot for coffee or a drink, though we've had gruff service here. A variety of simple snack food is available, primarily during the day, though the cafe is open till 2am.

Boasting a chic crowd of garment-district workers and shoppers, **Cafe Cova,** Via Montenapoleone 8 (☎ **02-7600-0578;** Metro: Montenapoleone), has been around since 1817, serving pralines, chocolates, brioches, and sandwiches. The more elegant sandwiches contain smoked salmon and truffles. Sip your espresso from fragile gold-rimmed cups at one of the small tables in an elegant inner room or while standing at the prominent bar. The cafe is open Monday to Saturday 8am to 8:30pm; closed in August.

Opened in 1910, the **Pasticceria Taveggia,** Via Visconti di Modrone 2 (☎ **02-7602-1257;** Metro: San Babila), is one of Milan's most historic cafes. Behind ornate glass doors set into the 19th-century facade, Taveggia makes the best cappuccino and espresso in town. To match this quality, a variety of brioches, pastries, candies, and tortes is offered. You can enjoy them while standing at the bar or seated in the Victorian tearoom. Taveggia is open Tuesday to Sunday 7:30am to 8:30pm; closed in August.

BARS & PUBS Decorated a bit like a 19th-century bohemian parlor, **Al Teatro,** Corso Garibaldi 16 (☎ **02-864-222;** Metro: Garibaldi or Moscova), is a popular bar across from the Teatro Fossati. It opens for morning coffee Tuesday to Sunday at 2pm and closes (after several changes of ambience) at 8am. Most of the time the crowd seems perfectly happy to drink, gossip, and flirt. In addition to coffee and drinks, it serves toasts and tortes. In fine weather, tables are set out on Corso Garibaldi.

Bar Giamaica, Via Brera 32 (☎ **02-876-723;** Metro: Duomo), is loud and bustling and seats its customers with a no-nonsense kind of gruff humor. The personalities who work here haven't changed in years. If you want only a drink, you'll have lots of company among the office workers who jostle around the tiny tables, often standing because of the lack of room. It's open as a restaurant Monday to Saturday noon to 2:30pm and 7:30 to 10pm, serving affordable meals. The bar opens at 9am Monday to Saturday and remains open until around 2am; closed 1 week in mid-August.

Despite its name, the **Grand Hotel Pub,** Via Ascanio Sforza 75 (☎ **02-8951-1586;** Bus: 59), doesn't rent rooms or even pretend to be grand. Instead, it's a large animated restaurant/pub with frequent live music or cabaret. In summer, the crowds can move quickly from the smoky interior into a sheltered garden. Thursday and Friday, entertainment is live jazz and rock music, perhaps cabaret. Most visitors come here only for a drink, but if you're hungry you can get a moderately priced meal here. The place is open Tuesday to Sunday 8pm to 2am. Entrance is usually free.

DANCE CLUBS & NIGHTCLUBS **Killer Plastic,** Viale Umbria 120 (☎ **02-733-996;** Bus: 92), is a favorite disco. Thursday is gay night, welcoming gay men (and some lesbians) onto the high-tech dance floors, and Saturday is crammed with the cream of the city's *alta moda* crowd. Other nights, it's fun, high-energy, and exhibitionistic. Doors usually open Thursday to Sunday 10:30pm to around 3am or later, depending on the crowd. The cover is 20,000L ($10) but rises to 25,000L ($12.50) on Saturday.

Usually packed with a good-looking crowd, **Rock Hollywood,** Corso Como 15 (☎ **02-659-8996;** Metro: Garibaldi or Moscova), is small and has a sound system that's so good you might get swept up in the fun of it all. It's open Tuesday to Sunday 10:30pm to at least 3am with a 25,000 to 30,000L ($15) cover that includes the first drink.

Club Astoria, Piazza Santa Maria Beltrade 2 (☎ **02-8646-3710;** Metro: Duomo), is especially popular among the expense-account crowd. When there's a floor show, drinks might cost around 50,000L ($25), taking the place of a cover; otherwise, they begin at 30,000L ($15). The Astoria is open Monday to Saturday 10:30pm to 4am.

Coquetel, Via Vetere 14 (☎ **02-836-0688;** Bus: 59), is loud and wild and celebrates the American-style party-colored cocktail with a whimsy that could only be all Italian. The action around here, coupled with babble from dozens of regulars, ain't exactly sedate, and you might just get swept away by the energy. It's open Monday to Saturday 8pm to 2am.

Facsimile, Via Tallone 11 (☎ **02-738-0635;** Bus: 54), is a popular bar/birreria where Milanese rockers can commune with their favorite video stars in living color. There are outdoor tables for stargazing. The bar is open Tuesday to Sunday 9am to 1am. There's no cover but a one-drink minimum.

GAY & LESBIAN CLUBS **Nuova Idea International,** Via de Castillia 30 (☎ **02-6900-7859;** Metro: Garibaldi), is the largest, oldest, most active, and most fun gay disco in Italy, very much tied to Milan's urban bustle. It prides itself on mimicking the large all-gay discos of northern Europe and draws a patronage of young and not-so-young men, many of whom are film or theater actors. There's a large video screen and occasional live entertainment. It's open Thursday to Sunday 10pm to 2:30am. Cover is 15,000L ($7.50) on Thursday, Friday, and Sunday and 25,000L ($12.50) on Saturday, including the first drink.

Up two flights of stairs, **Sottomarino Giallo,** Via Donatello 2 (☎ **02-2940-1047;** Metro: Loreto), is a women-only disco open Wednesday to Friday 10pm to 2:30am.

2 Bergamo

31 miles (50km) NE of Milan, 373 miles (601km) NW of Rome

Known for its defenses and wealth since the Middle Ages, Bergamo is one of the most characteristic Lombard hill towns. Many of the town's stone fortifications were built on Roman foundations by the medieval Venetians, who looked on Bergamo as one of the gems of their trading network during several centuries of occupation. Set on a hilltop between the Seriana and the Brembana valleys, Bergamo lies in the alpine foothills.

The Upper Town, 900 feet above sea level, is buttressed by, and terraced on, the original Venetian fortifications. About half a mile downhill is the Lower Town (usually identified by residents simply as "Bergamo"), with many 19th-century and early-20th-century buildings lining its wide streets. This modern metropolis and industrial center contains the bus and rail stations, most of the hotels, and the town's commercial and administrative center.

ESSENTIALS

GETTING THERE **Trains** arrive from Milan once every hour, depositing passengers in the center of the Lower Town. The trip takes an hour, costing 9,000L ($4.50) one way. For information about rail connections in Bergamo, call ☎ **1478-88-088** toll-free in Italy. The **bus station** in Bergamo is across from the train station. For information or schedules, call ☎ **035-248-150.** Buses arrive from Milan once every 30 minutes, costing 8,000L ($4) one way.

If you have a **car** and are coming from Milan, head east on A4.

VISITOR INFORMATION The **tourist office** is on Piazzale Marconi, Vicolo Aquila Nera 2 (☎ **035-242-226**), open daily 9am to 12:30pm and 2 to 5:30pm.

EXPLORING THE UPPER TOWN (CITTÀ ALTA)

The higher you climb, the more rewarding the view will be. The ✪ **Upper Town (Città Alta)** is replete with narrow circuitous streets, old squares, splendid monuments, and imposing and austere medieval architecture that prompted d'Annunzio to call it "a city of muteness." To reach the Upper Town, take bus no. 1 or 3 and then walk for 10 minutes up Viale Vittorio Emanuele.

The heart of the Upper Town is **Piazza Vecchia,** which has witnessed most of the town's upheavals and a parade of conquerors ranging from Attila to the Nazis. On the square is the Palazzo della Ragione (town hall), an 18th-century fountain, and the Palazzo Nuovo of Scamozzi (town library).

A vaulted arcade connects Piazza Vecchia with **Piazza del Duomo.** Opening onto the latter is the cathedral of Bergamo, which has a baroque overlay.

Basilica di Santa Maria Maggiore & Baptistry. Piazza del Duomo. Free admission. Mon–Sat 8am–noon and 3–6pm; Sun 9am–12:45pm and 3–6pm.

Built in the Romanesque style, the church was founded in the 12th century but much later was given a baroque interior and a disturbingly busy ceiling. Displayed are exquisite Flemish and Tuscan tapestries incorporating such themes as the Annunciation and the Crucifixion. The choir, designed by Lotto, dates from the 16th century. In front of the main altar is a series of inlaid panels depicting themes like Noah's Ark and David and Goliath.

Facing the cathedral is the baptistry, dating from Giovanni da Campione's design in the mid–14th century, but it was rebuilt at the end of the 19th century.

✪ **Colleoni Chapel (Cappella Colleoni).** Piazza del Duomo. Free admission. Mar–Oct Tues–Sun 9am–noon and 2–6:30pm; off-season Tues–Sun 9am–noon and 2:30–4:30pm.

Also opening onto Piazza del Duomo is this Renaissance chapel honoring the inflated ego of the Venetian military hero Bartolomeo Colleoni, with an inlaid marble facade reminiscent of Florence. It was designed by Giovanni Antonio Amadeo, who's chiefly known for his creation of the Certosa in Pavia. For the condottiere, Amadeo built an elaborate tomb, surmounted by a gilded equestrian statue. (Colleoni, who was once the ruler of the town and under whose watch the town fell to the Republic of Venice, which he then served, was also the subject of one of the world's most famous equestrian statues, now standing on a square in Venice.) The tomb sculpted for his daughter, Medea, is much less elaborate. Giovanni Battista Tiepolo painted most of the frescoes on the ceiling.

EXPLORING THE LOWER TOWN (CITTÀ BASSA)

✪ **Carrara Academy Gallery (Galleria dell'Accademia Carrara).** Piazza Giacomo Carrara 82A. ☎ **035-399-640.** Admission 5,000L ($2.50). Wed–Mon 9:30am–12:30pm and 2:30–5:30pm.

Filled with a wide-ranging collection of the works of homegrown artists, as well as Venetian and Tuscan masters, the academy draws art lovers from all over the world. The most important works are on the top floor—head here first if your time is limited. The Botticelli portrait of Giuliano de' Medici is well known, and one room contains three versions of Giovanni Bellini's favorite subject, the *Madonna and Child.* It's interesting to compare his work with that of his brother-in-law, Andrea Mantegna, whose *Madonna and Child* is also displayed, as is Vittore Carpaccio's *Nativity of Maria,* seemingly inspired by Flemish painters.

Farther along, you encounter a most original treatment of the old theme of the Madonna and Child, this one by Cosmà Tura of Ferrara. Also displayed are three tables of a predella by Lotto and his *Holy Family with St. Catherine* (wonderful composition) and Raphael's *St. Sebastian.* The entire wall space of another room is taken up with paintings by Moroni (1523–78), a local artist who seemingly did portraits of everybody who could afford it. In the salons to follow, foreign masters, like Rubens, van der Meer, and Jan Brueghel, are represented, along with Guardi's architectural renderings of Venice and Longhi's continuing parade of Venetian high society.

ACCOMMODATIONS

Hotel Agnello d'Oro. Via Gombito 22, 24100 Bergamo. ☎ **035-249-883.** Fax 035-235-612. 20 units. TV TEL. 155,000L ($77.50) double. AE, DC, V. Bus: 1, then funicular.

The Agnello d'Oro is an intimate 17th-century country inn in the heart of the Città Alta. It's an atmospheric background for good food or an adequate room, all refurbished in 1995. When you enter the cozy reception lounge, ring an old bell to bring the owner away from the kitchen. The guest rooms come in different shapes and sizes, though most are quite small; each has a fine mattress on a comfortable bed, either a double or twin. The bathrooms are small, too. In the restaurant, you dine at wooden tables and sit on carved ladderback chairs. Among the à la carte offerings are three worthy regional specialties: Try *casoncelli alla bergamasca* (a succulent ravioli dish), *quaglie farcite* (stuffed quail with polenta), and tagliatelle with vegetables and pizzoccheri cheese. The room becomes a tavern lounge between meals and is closed Sunday night and Monday.

Hotel Cappello d'Oro. Viale Papa Giovanni XXIII 12, 24100 Bergamo. ☎ **035-232-503.** Fax 035-242-946. www.hotelcappellodoro.it. E-mail: cappello@hotelcappellodoro.it. 120 units. A/C MINIBAR TV TEL. 250,000L ($125) double. Rates include breakfast. AE, DC, MC, V. Parking 30,000L ($15).

The Cappello d'Oro is a renovated 150-year-old corner building on a busy street in the center of the Città Bassa. The 19th-century facade has been stuccoed, and the public rooms and guest rooms are functional, high-ceilinged, and clean. The rooms are adequately but rather plainly furnished, with firm mattresses. The tiled bathrooms are compact. If you need a parking space, reserve it along with your room.

Hotel Excelsior San Marco. Piazza della Repubblica 6, 24122 Bergamo. ☎ **035-366-111.** Fax 035-223-201. www.hotelsanmarco.com. E-mail: info@hotelsanmarco.com. 158 units. A/C MINIBAR TV TEL. 330,000L ($165) double; 480,000L ($240) suite. Rates include breakfast. AE, DC, MC, V. Parking 35,000L ($17.50) indoors, 20,000L ($10) outdoors.

This four-decade-old place at the edge of a city park is about midway between the Città Alta and Città Bassa, both of which might be visible from the balcony of your room. The lobby contains a small bar, reddish stone accents, and low-slung leather chairs. The most prominent theme of the ceiling frescoes is the lion of St. Mark. The guest rooms are attractively furnished and comfortable, most medium size to spacious, and all with quality mattresses. The modernized bathrooms come with hair dryers. The hotel has both a sauna and a fitness room. The restaurant La Colonna serves regional and international specialties.

DINING

✪ **Ristorante da Vittorio.** Viale Papa Giovanni XXIII 23. ☎ **035-218-060.** Reservations required. Main courses 22,000–50,000L ($11–$25); fixed-price dinner 70,000–170,000L ($35–$85). AE, DC, MC, V. Thurs–Tues noon–3pm and 7:30–10:30pm. Closed 3 weeks in Aug. REGIONAL/INTERNATIONAL.

This restaurant on the Città Bassa's main boulevard serves a cuisine almost better than anything else found in Milan. The menu offers more than a dozen risottos, more than 20 pastas, and around 30 meat dishes, as well as just about every kind of fish that swims in Italy's waters. Examples are grilled "fantasy of the sea" with fresh seasonal vegetables, goose breast with a tapenade of black olives, and tartare of salmon with avocado. The service is efficient, directed by members of the Cerea family, who by now are among the best-known citizens of Bergamo.

BERGAMO AFTER DARK

The opera season lasts from September to November, with a drama being staged from then until April at the **Teatro Donizetti,** Piazza Cavour (☎ **035-416-0611**). A program of free events, **Viva La Tua Città,** is staged every summer. The tourist office (under "Essentials," above) will provide a pamphlet.

If visiting a *birreria* (beer hall) is what you want, head for **Via Gombito** in the Città Alta. It's lined with places to drink. One of the most popular joints is **Papageno Pub,** Via Colleoni (☎ **035-236-624**), which makes the best sandwiches and bruschetta in town. In the Città Bassa, **Capolinea,** Via Giacomo Quarenghi 29 (☎ **035-320-981**), has an active bar up front, always packed with a young crowd.

3 Mantua

25 miles (40km) S of Verona, 95 miles (153km) SE of Milan, 291 miles (469km) NW of Rome, 90 miles (145km) SW of Venice

Mantua (Mantova) had a flowering of art and architecture under the Gonzaga dynasty who held sway over the city for nearly 4 centuries. Originally an Etruscan settlement and then a Roman colony, it has known many conquerors, including the French and the Austrians in the 18th and 19th centuries. Virgil, the great Latin poet, has remained its most famous son (he was born outside the city in a place called Andes). Verdi set *Rigoletto* here, Romeo (Shakespeare's creation, that is) took refuge here, and writer Aldous Huxley called Mantua "the most romantic city in the world."

Mantua is an imposing and at times even austere city. It's very much a city of the past and is within easy reach of a number of cities in northern Italy. The historic center is traffic-free.

ESSENTIALS

GETTING THERE Mantua has excellent **train** connections, lying on direct lines to Milan, Cremona, Modena, and Verona. Nine trains a day arrive from Milan, taking 2¼ hours and costing 15,000L ($7.50) one way. From Cremona, trains arrive every hour (trip time: 1 hour), costing 6,800L ($3.40) one way. The train station is on Piazza Don Leoni (☎ **1478-88-088**). Take bus no. 3 from outside the station to get to the center of town.

Most visitors arrive by train, but Mantua has good **bus** connections with Brescia; 17 buses a day make a 1¾-hour journey at a cost of 9,500L ($4.75) one way. The bus station is on Piazza Mondadori (☎ **0376-327-237**).

If you have a **car** and are in Cremona, continue east along Rte. 10.

VISITOR INFORMATION The **tourist office** is at Piazza Andrea Mantegna 6 (☎ **0376-328-253**), open Monday to Saturday 8:30am to 12:30pm and 3 to 6pm, Sunday 9:30am to 12:30pm.

EXPLORING THE TOWN

The best shopping is at the **open-air market** that operates only on Thursday morning at Piazza delle Erbe and Piazza Sordello. Here you can find a little bit of everything, from cheap clothing (often designer rip-offs) to bric-a-brac. The place is like an outdoor traveling department store.

✪ **Museo di Palazzo Ducale.** Piazza Sordello 40. ☎ **0376-320-283.** Admission 12,000L ($6). Mon–Sat 9am–7pm; Sun 9am–1pm and 2–8pm. Last admission 1 hour before closing.

The ducal apartments of the Gonzagas, with more than 500 rooms and 15 courtyards, are the most remarkable in Italy—certainly when judged from the standpoint of size. Like Rome, the compound wasn't built in a day, or even in a century. The earlier buildings, erected to the specifications of the Bonacolsi family, date from the 13th century. The 14th and early 15th centuries saw the rise of the **Castle of St. George (Castello di San Giorgio),** designed by Bartolino da Novara. The Gonzagas also added the **Palatine Basilica of Santa Barbara (Basilica Palatina di Santa Barbara)** by Bertani.

Over the years, the historic monument of Renaissance splendor has lost many of the art treasures collected by Isabella d'Este during the 15th and 16th centuries in her efforts to turn Mantua into *La Città dell'Arte*. Her descendants, the Gonzagas, sold the most precious objects to Charles I of England in 1628, and 2 years later most of the remaining rich collection was looted during the sack of Mantua. Even Napoléon did his bit by carting off some of the objects still there.

What remains of the painting collection is still superb, including works by Tintoretto and Sustermans and a "cut-up" Rubens. The display of classical statuary is impressive, gathered mostly from the various Gonzaga villas at the time of Maria Theresa of Austria. Among the more inspired sights are the **Zodiac Room (Sala dello Zodiaco);** the **Hall of Mirrors (Salone degli Specchi),** with a vaulted ceiling from the beginning of the 17th century; the **River Chamber (Sala del Fume);** the **Apartment of Paradise (Appartamento del Paradiso);** the **Apartment of Troia**

(Appartamento di Troia), with frescoes by Giulio Romano; and a scale reproduction of the **Holy Staircase (Scala Santa)** in Rome. The most interesting and best-known room in the castle is the **Bridal Chamber (Camera degli Sposi),** frescoed by Andrea Mantegna. Winged cherubs appear over a balcony at the top of the ceiling. Look for a curious dwarf and a mauve-hatted portrait of Christian I of Denmark. There are many paintings by Domenico Fetti, along with a splendid series of nine tapestries woven in Brussels and based on cartoons by Raphael. A cycle of frescoes on the age of chivalry by Pisanello has recently been discovered. A guardian takes visitors on a tour to point out the many highlights.

Basilica di Sant'Andrea & Campanile. Piazza Mantegna. ☎ **0376-328-504.** Free admission. Mon–Sat 8am–noon; daily 3–6pm.

Built to the specifications of Leon Battista Alberti, this church opens onto Piazza Mantegna, just off Piazza delle Erbe, where you'll find fruit vendors. The actual work was carried out by a pupil of Alberti's, Luca Fancelli. However, before Alberti died in 1472, it's said that, architecturally speaking, he knew he had "buried the Middle Ages." The church wasn't completed until 1782, when Juvara crowned it with a dome.

As you enter, check out the first chapel to your left, which contains the tomb of the great Mantegna (the paintings are by his son, except for the *Holy Family* by the old master himself). The sacristan will light it for you. In the crypt, you'll encounter a representation of one of the more fanciful legends in the history of church relics: St. Andrew's claim to possess the blood of Christ, "the gift" of St. Longinus, the Roman soldier who's said to have pierced His side. Beside the basilica is a 1414 **campanile** (bell tower).

Palazzo Te. Viale Te 13. ☎ **0376-323-266.** Admission 12,000L ($6). Tues–Sun 9am–6pm; Mon 1–6pm. Last admission 30 minutes before closing. Closed Jan 1, May 1, Dec 25.

This Renaissance palace is known for its frescoes by Giulio Romano and his pupils. Fun-loving Federigo II, one of the Gonzagas, had it built as a place where he could slip away to see his mistress, Isabella Boschetto. The name, Te, is said to have been derived from the word *tejeto,* which in the local dialect means "a cut to let the waters flow out." This was once marshland drained by the Gonzagas for their horse farm.

The frescoes in the various rooms, dedicated to everything from horses to Psyche, rely on mythology for subject matter. The **Room of the Giants (Sala dei Giganti),** the best known, has a scene depicting heaven venting its rage on the giants who had moved threateningly against it. Federico's motto was, "What the lizards lack is that which tortures me," an obscure reference to the reptile's cold blood as opposed to his hot blood. The **Cupid and Psyche Room (Sala di Amore e Psiche)** forever immortalizes the tempestuous love affair of these swingers; it's decorated with erotic frescoes on the theme of the marriage of Cupid and Psyche, two other "hot bloods."

ACCOMMODATIONS

✪ **Albergo San Lorenzo.** Piazza Concordia 14, 46100 Mantova. ☎ **0376-220-500.** Fax 0376-327-194. www.hotelsanlorenzo.it. E-mail: hotel@sanlorenzo.it. 33 units. A/C MINIBAR TV TEL. 320,000L ($160) double; 400,000L ($200) junior suite. Rates include buffet breakfast. AE, DC, MC, V. Parking 30,000L ($15).

Your best bet is this four-star hotel in the historic center. The building is ancient but received a 1996 renovation in which restorers paid great attention to the architectural details and the furnishings, most of which are antique. The great service makes you feel right at home. The guest rooms are furnished with dark woods (antique reproductions), gilded mirrors, and good mattresses; the air-conditioning is individually adjustable (a godsend in steamy Mantua), and the tiled bathrooms come with hair dryers. Breakfast is the only meal served, but the hotel offers a panoramic terrace with a view.

Hotel Dante. Via Corrado 54, 46100 Mantova. ☎ **0376-326-425.** Fax 0376-221-141. 40 units. A/C MINIBAR TV TEL. 175,000L ($87.50) double. Breakfast 15,000L ($7.50). AE, DC, MC, V. Parking 20,000L ($10) inside, free outside.

This boxy modern hotel is your best bet on a budget. On a narrow street in the busy commercial center, it has a recessed entrance area and a marble-accented interior, parts of which look out over a flagstone-covered courtyard. Some of the simply furnished but clean guest rooms have air-conditioning and minibars. The bathrooms are a bit cramped.

Mantegna Hotel. Via Fabio Filzi 10B, 46100 Mantova. ☎ **0376-328-019.** Fax 0376-368-564. 38 units. A/C TV TEL. 180,000L ($90) double; 230,000L ($115) suite. Breakfast 15,000L ($7.50). AE, DC, DISC, MC, V. Closed Dec 24–Jan 6. Free parking.

The Mantegna is in a commercial section, a few blocks from one of the entrances to the old city. The lobby is accented with gray and red marble slabs, along with enlargements of details of paintings by Mantegna. About half the guest rooms look out over a sunny rear courtyard, though the rooms facing the street are fairly quiet. They're small to medium in size, each with a quality mattress and a small bathroom. The hotel is a good value for the rates charged.

Rechigi Hotel. Via P. F. Calvi 30, 46100 Mantova. ☎ **0376-320-781.** Fax 0376-220-291. 52 units. A/C TV TEL. 250,000–300,000L ($125–$150) double; 310,000L ($155) suite. Breakfast 30,000L ($15). AE, DC, MC, V. Parking 30,000L ($15).

Near the center of the old city stands the Rechigi, rivaled only by the San Lorenzo. It's a cozy nest but short on style. The lobby is warmly decorated with modern paintings and contains an alcove bar. The owners maintain the property well and have decorated the guest rooms in good taste. Most rooms are medium in size, and all were renovated in 1996, with new mattresses added. The bathrooms are compact and tiled. Breakfast is the only meal served.

DINING

The local specialty is **donkey stew** *(stracotto di asino).* Legend claims you'll never be a man until you've sampled it.

Il Cigno Trattoria dei Martini. Piazza Carlo d'Arco 1. ☎ **0376-327-101.** Reservations recommended. Main courses 25,000–35,000L ($12.50–$17.50). AE, DC, MC, V. Wed–Sun 12:30–1:45pm and 7:40–10pm. Closed Jan 7–14 and Aug. MANTOVANO.

This trattoria overlooks a cobblestone square in the old part of Mantua. The exterior is a faded ocher, with wrought-iron cross-hatched window bars within sight of the easy parking on the piazza outside. After passing through a large entrance hall studded with frescoes, you'll come to the bustling dining rooms. The menu offers both freshwater and saltwater fish and dishes like *agnoli* (a form of pasta) in a light sauce or risotto. *Bollito misto* (a medley of boiled meats) is served with various sauces, including one made of mustard. One excellent pasta, *tortelli di zucca,* is stuffed with pumpkin.

✪ **L'Aquila Nigra (The Black Eagle).** Vicolo Bonacolsi 4. ☎ **0376-327-180.** Reservations recommended. Main courses 25,000–30,000L ($12.50–$15). AE, DC, MC, V. Tues–Sat, noon–2pm and 8–10pm (also Sun noon–2pm Apr–May and Sept–Oct). Closed Jan 1–15 and Aug. MANTOVANO/ITALIAN.

This restaurant is in a Renaissance mansion on a narrow passageway by the Bonacolsi Palace. The foundations were laid in the 1200s, but the restaurant dates from 1984. In the elegant rooms, you can choose from such dishes as pike from the Mincio River, served with *salsa verde* (green sauce) and polenta, as well as other regional specialties. You also might order *gnocchi alle ortiche* (potato dumplings tinged with pureed nettles), eel marinated in vinegar (one of the most distinctive specialties of Mantua), or *tortelli di zucca* (with a pumpkin base).

Ristorante Pavesi. Piazza delle Erbe 13. ☎ **0376-323-627.** Reservations recommended. Main courses 15,000–28,000L ($7.50–$14). AE, DC, MC, V. Fri–Wed 12:30–2:30pm and 7:30–10:30pm. Closed Nov 19–27 and Feb–Mar 7. MANTOVANO/ITALIAN.

The Pavesi has the advantage of being located under an ancient arcade on Mantua's most beautiful square. The walls partially date from the 1200s, though the restaurant goes back only before World War II. It's an intimate family-run place with hundreds of antique copper pots hanging from the single-barrel vault of the plaster ceiling; tables spill out into the square in summer. The antipasti table is loaded with delicacies, and specialties include *agnolotti* (a form of tortellini) with meat, cheese, sage, and butter, as well as *risotto alla mantovana* (with pesto). Also try the roast fillet of veal (deboned and rolled) and a blend of *fagioli* (white beans) with onions.

MANTUA AFTER DARK

The major cultural venue is the **Teatro Sociale di Mantova,** Piazza Cavallotti (☎ **0376-323-860**), lying off Corso Vittorio Emanuele. Operas are staged in October, followed by a season of Italian dramas and classical music concerts December to May. Tickets cost from 35,000 to 100,000L ($17.50 to $50). In lieu of any other major entertainment, locals depend on **festivals,** with **chamber music series** in April and May. The tourist office (under "Essentials," above) has details.

If you're just looking for a place to drink and meet some companions, head for **Leoncino Rosso,** Via Giustiziati 33 (☎ **0376-323-277**), behind Piazza Erbe. This osteria opened in 1750 and hasn't changed some of its recipes (such as tortellini with nuts or pumpkin) since then. It's closed August and 2 weeks in January. The best selection of beer in town is at **Oblo,** Via Arrivabene 50 (☎ **0376-360-676**), which also has a good offering of reasonably priced wine, such as the fizzy red Lambrusco.

4 Lake Garda

The easternmost of the northern Italian lakes, **Lake Garda** is also the largest, 32 miles (52km) long and 11½ miles (19km) at its widest. Sheltered by mountains, its scenery, especially the part on the western shore that reaches from Limone to Salo, has been compared to that of the Mediterranean; you'll see olive, orange, and lemon trees and even palms. The almost-transparent lake is ringed with four art cities: Trent to the northeast, Brescia to the west, Mantua to the south, and Verona to the east.

The lake's eastern side is more rugged and less developed, but the resort-studded western strip is far more glamorous to the first-timer. On the western side, a circuitous road skirts the lake through one molelike tunnel after another. You can park your car at several secluded belvederes for a panoramic lakeside view. In spring the scenery is splashed with color, everything from wild poppies to oleander. Garda is well served by buses, or you can traverse the lake on steamers or motorboats. The lake, once a mandatory stop on the Grand Tour, has attracted everyone from the Romans to Mussolini.

LAKE GARDA ESSENTIALS

GETTING THERE Eight **buses** a day make the 1-hour trip from Trent to Riva del Garde, costing 6,000L ($3) one way. For information and schedules, call the **Autostazione on Viale Trento** in Riva at ☎ **1478-880-88.** The nearest **train** station is at Roverto, a 20-minute ride from Riva. Frequent buses make the 20-minute trip from the train station to Riva, costing 3,700L ($1.85) one way.

If you have a **car** and are coming from Milan or Brescia, A4 east runs to the southwestern corner of the lake. From Mantua, take A22 north to A4 west. From Verona and points east, take A4 west.

GETTING AROUND For getting around Lake Garda, you'll need a **car.** Most drivers take the road along the western shore, S572, north to Riva di Garda. For a less-congested drive, try heading back down the lake along its eastern shore on the Gardesana Orientale (S249). S11 runs along the south shore.

The twisting roads following the shores of Lake Garda would be enough to rattle even the most experienced driver. Couple the turns, dimly lit tunnels, and emotional local drivers with convoys of tour buses and trucks that rarely stay in their lane and you have one of the more frightening drives in Italy. Use your horn around blind curves and be warned that Sunday is especially risky, since everyone on the lake and from the nearby cities seems to take to the roads after a long lunch with lots of heady wine.

Both **ferries** and **hydrofoils** operate on the lake from Easter to September. For schedules and information, contact **Navigazione Lago di Garda** at ☎ **030-914-951** (its main office in Desenzano) or 0464-55-26-25 (its Riva del Garda branch). Ferries connect Riva's harbor, Porto San Nicolà, with the major lakeside towns, such as Gardone (trip time: 2½ hours), costing 10,000L ($5) one way; Sirmione (trip time: 4 hours), 13,000L ($6.50) one way; and Desenzano (trip time: 4 hours, 20 minutes), 16,000L ($8) one way.

These ferries provide the best opportunity for leisurely admiring the shorelines and the lake's beauty and are also the most affordable way to see the lake. Following the same routes, at more or less the same times, are a battalion of hydrofoils, which cut the travel time to each of the above destinations in half. Transit on any of them requires a supplement of 1,800 to 5,000L ($2.50), depending on the distance you intend to travel. If you want to admire the lake from a waterside vantage, a well-recommended mode of attack is traveling in one direction via conventional ferry and returning to Riva del Garda by hydrofoil. Early November to late February, there's no transportation offered in/out of Riva del Garda's port, or anywhere else along the lake's northern tier, and only very limited transportation options are available from Desenzano, in the south.

RIVE DEL GARDA

Some 195 feet above sea level, **Riva del Garda** is the lake's oldest and most traditional resort. It consists of both an expanding new district and an old town, the latter centered at **Piazza III Novembre.**

ESSENTIALS

GETTING THERE Riva del Garda is linked to the Brenner-Modena motorway (Rovereto Sud/Garda Nord exit) and to the railway (Rovereto station) and is near Verona's airport.

VISITOR INFORMATION Go to the **Palazzo dei Congressi,** Giardini di Porta Orientale 8 (☎ **0464-554-444**). Mid-September to Easter, it's open Monday to Friday 9am to noon and 2 to 7pm; Easter to mid-September, hours are Monday to Saturday 9am to noon and 2 to 7pm; mid-June to mid-September, it's also open Sunday 10am to noon and 4 to 6:30pm.

What to See & Do

Situated on the northern banks of the lake, between the Benacense plains and towering mountains, Riva offers the advantages of the Riviera and the Dolomites. Its climate is classically Mediterranean—mild in winter and moderate in summer. Vast areas of rich vegetation combine with the deep blue of the lake. Many people come for the healthy air and climate; others for business conferences, meetings, and fairs. Riva is popular with tour groups from Germany and England.

Riva is the windsurfing capital of Italy. Windsurfing schools offer lessons and also rent equipment. The best one is **Nautic Club Riva,** Viale Rovereto 132 (☎ **0464-552-453**), closed November to Easter. It has full rentals, including life jackets, wet suits, and boards, for 60,000L ($30) per day. If you'd like to explore the lake by bike, go to **Girelli Mountain Bike,** Viale Damiano Chiesa 15–17 (☎ **0464-554-719**), where rentals are 30,000L ($15) per day.

Most of the town's shopping consists of unremarkable souvenirs, but a large **open-air market,** the best on Lake Garda, comes to town on the second and fourth Wednesdays of every month. It mainly sprawls along Viale Dante, Via Prati, and Via Pilati. You can buy virtually anything, from alpine handcrafts to busts of Mussolini. While shopping, drop in at the **Pasticceria Copat di Fabio Marzari,** Viale Dante 37 (☎ **0464-551-885**), for delectable pastries.

On the harbor, at Piazza III Novembre, you'll see the town's highest building, a 13th-century watchtower, the **Tower of Apponale (Torre d'Apponale).** It isn't open for visits, but the angelic-looking trumpeter adorning its pinnacle has been adopted as the symbol of the town itself. There's also a severe-looking castle, **La Rocca,** Piazza Battisti 3 (☎ **0464-57-38-69**). Built in 1124 and owned at various times by both the ruling Scaligeri princes of Verona and the Viennese Hapsburgs (who used it as a prison), La Rocca has been turned into a **Civic Museum (Museo Civico La Rocca),** which you might visit on a rainy day to see its exhibits of local artworks and attractions reflecting local traditions. Admission is 8,000L ($4). From January to June and September to December, it's open Tuesday to Sunday 9:30am to 12:30pm, July and August 4 to 10pm.

Accommodations

✪ **Hotel du Lac et du Parc.** Viale Rovereto 44, 38066 Riva del Garda. ☎ **0464-551-500.** Fax 0464-555-200. www.garna.com/dulac. E-mail: info@hoteldulac-riva.it. 170 units (33 bungalows). A/C MINIBAR TV TEL. 230,000–530,000L ($115–$265) double; 560,000–720,000L ($280–$360) suite; 240,000–450,000L ($120–$225) bungalow for 4. Rates include breakfast. AE, CB, DC, MC, V. Closed Oct 20–Mar 20. Free parking.

This deluxe Spanish-style hotel, the best in town, is set back from the busy road behind a shrub-filled parking lot. The interior of the main building is freshly decorated, with arched windows and lots of comfort. The well-trained staff speaks many languages and seems genuinely concerned with everyone's well-being. The guest rooms are well furnished (54 are air-conditioned) and come in various shapes and sizes, each with a quality mattress. Each bathroom is well organized, with a hair dryer.

Dining: There's a huge dining room and an attractive bar, plus two more informal restaurants, each serving international and regional specialties.

Amenities: Concierge, room service, baby-sitting, laundry/dry cleaning, garden with two pools, lakeside beach, two tennis courts, sauna, fitness room, beauty salon.

Hotel Sole. Piazza III Novembre 35, 38066 Riva del Garda. ☎ **0464-552-686.** Fax 0464-552-811. www.hotelsole.net. E-mail: info@hotelsole.net. 52 units. MINIBAR TV TEL. 130,000–150,000L ($65–$75) double; 180,000–210,000L ($90–$105) suite. Rates include breakfast. AE, DC, MC, V. Closed Jan 8–Mar 20 and Nov–Dec 27. Parking 15,000L ($7.50).

The medium-priced Sole, an overgrown villa with arched windows and colonnades, had farsighted founders who snared the best position on the waterfront. The hotel has amenities worthy of a first-class rating. The character and the quality of the guest rooms vary considerably according to their position (most have lake views). Some are almost suites, with living-room areas; the smaller ones are less desirable. Nevertheless, all have quality mattresses and bathrooms with hair dryers. You can dine in the formal interior room or on the flagstone lakeside terrace. There's a sauna and a solarium.

Hotel Venezia. Viale Rovereto 62, 38066 Riva del Garda. ☎ **0464-552-216.** Fax 0464-556-031. www.rivadelgarda.com/venezia. E-mail: venezia@rivadelgarda.com. 24 units. TV TEL. 166,000–210,000L ($83–$105) double. Rates include breakfast. MC, V. Closed Nov–Easter.

This one of the most attractive budget hotels in town. The main section of the Venezia's angular modern building is raised on stilts above a private parking lot set back from the lakefront promenade. The complex is surrounded by trees on a quiet street bordered with flowers and private homes. The reception area is at the top of a flight of red marble steps. There's a private pool surrounded by palmettos, and a clean and sunny dining room with Victorian reproduction chairs. The guest rooms are pleasantly furnished and well maintained.

DINING

Ristorante San Marco. Viale Roma 20. ☎ **0464-554-477.** Reservations recommended. Main courses 20,000–35,000L ($10–$17.50). AE, DC, MC, V. Tues–Sun noon–2:30pm and 7–10pm. Closed Feb. ITALIAN/SEAFOOD.

Set back from the lake on one of the main shopping streets of the resort, San Marco was built in the 19th century as a hotel and converted into a restaurant in 1979. The superb food is classically Italian and the service excellent. You might begin with pasta, such as spaghetti with clams or tortellini with prosciutto. They serve many good fish dishes, including sole and grilled scampi. Among the meat selections, try the tournedos opera or veal cutlet bolognese. During summer, you may dine in the garden.

RIVA AFTER DARK

Begin your evening with a drink at the **Pub al Gallo,** Via San Rocca 11 (☎ **0464-551-177**), which stays open until 3am. The best disco is **Discoteca Tiffany,** Giardini di Porta Orientale (☎ **0464-552-512**), open only Thursday to Sunday. You can also shake it at **Après Club,** Via Monte d'Oro 14 (☎ **0464-552-187**), open most of the year Wednesday to Sunday 9pm to 2:30am (though the owners will often cut hours to just Friday and Saturday in spring and autumn).

LIMONE SUL GARDA

Limone sul Garda lies 6 miles (10km) south of Riva on the western shore of Lake Garda and is one of the liveliest resorts on the lake.

Limone snuggles close to the water at the bottom of a narrow, steep road, so its shopkeepers, faced with no building room, dug right into the rock. There are 2½ miles (4km) of beach from which you can bathe, sail, or surf. The only way to get about is on foot, but at Limone you can enjoy tennis, soccer, and other sports, as well as discos that seem to come and go every year.

If you're bypassing Limone, you may still want to make a detour south of the village to the turnoff to **Tignale,** in the hills. You can climb a modern highway to the town for a sweeping vista of Garda, one of the most scenic spots on the entire lake.

A **tourist office** is operated at Via Comboni 15 (☎ **0365-954-070**), open Monday to Saturday 9am to 12:30pm and 2:30 to 6pm.

Accommodations & Dining

Hotel Capo Reamol. Via IV Novembre 92, 25010 Limone sul Garda. ☎ **0365-954-040.** Fax 0365-954-262. E-mail: hcreamol@anthesi.com. 58 units. MINIBAR TV TEL. 240,000–360,000L ($120–$180) double; 300,000–420,000L ($150–$210) suite. Rates include half-board. AE, CB, DC, MC, V. Closed Nov–Easter.

You won't even get a glimpse of this 1960s hotel from the main highway because it nestles on a series of terraces well below road level. Pull into a roadside area indicated at 1¼ miles (2km) north of Limone; then follow the driveway down a steep narrow hill.

The guest rooms are well furnished and freshly decorated, ranging from medium size to spacious; all are fitted with good mattresses. The bathrooms are tidily kept. The bar, restaurant, and sports facilities are on the lowest level. You can swim in the lake or the pool and rent Windsurfers and take a windsurfing class on the graveled beach. The restaurant serves an Italian cuisine and many fine Italian wines, with live music on weekends. The new spa/fitness facility may remind you of the spas of France but on a lesser scale.

Hotel Le Palme. Via Porto 36, 25020 Limone sul Garda. ☎ **0365-954-681.** Fax 0365-954-120. www.lepalme.com. E-mail: lepalme@limone.com. 28 units. TV TEL. 140,000–230,000L ($70–$115) double. Rates include buffet breakfast. MC, V. Closed Nov–Easter.

Opening directly onto Lake Garda, this Venetian-style villa with period furniture stands in the shade of palm trees 2 centuries old. It offers well-furnished guest rooms, each individually decorated and with a compact tiled bathroom. The second floor has a comfortable reading room with a TV and the third floor a wide terrace. The ground floor contains a large dining room with decorative sculpture, opening onto a wide terrace where in fair weather you can order meals and drinks. The cuisine, backed up by a good wine list, is excellent (it's best to make reservations).

GARDONE RIVIERA

On Lake Garda's western shore 60 miles (97km) east of Milan, **Gardone Riviera** is well equipped with a number of good hotels and sporting facilities. Its lakeside promenade attracts a wide range of predominantly European tourists for most of the year. When it used to be chic for patrician Italian families to spend their holidays by the lake, many of the more prosperous families built elaborate villas not only in Gardone Riviera but also in neighboring Fasano (some have been converted to receive guests). The town also has the major attraction along the lake, d'Annunzio's Villa Vittoriale.

Essentials

GETTING THERE The resort lies 26 miles (42km) south of Riva on the west coast. During the day, buses from Brescia arrive every 30 minutes, the trip taking 1 hour and costing 5,000L ($2.50) one way. Two buses make the 3-hour trip from Milan, costing 15,000L ($7.50) one way. For schedule information, call ☎ **0365-21-061.**

VISITOR INFORMATION The **tourist office** is at Corso della Repubblica 35 (☎ **0365-20-347**), open Wednesday to Saturday and Monday 9am to 12:30pm and 3 to 6pm.

What to See & Do

There are many scenic hiking trails and walking paths through the area; the staff at your hotel or the tourist office can help you choose a route that fits your available time and ability level. One easy day hike with charming scenery starts from the edge of the lake, near the town center, and goes 3 miles up a gentle hill to the north, taking you to the village of **San Michele**. There you'll find a cluster of ancient houses and a village church, with views over the surrounding landscapes.

Wine Tasting

This region produces everything from dry still reds to sparkling whites with a champagnelike zest. **Guido Berlucchi,** Piazza Duranti 4, Borgonato di Cortefranca, 25040 Brescia (☎ **030-984-451**), one of Italy's largest wineries, is especially willing to receive visitors. If you'd like to drive around the countryside to taste wine and tour a vineyard, call them to make an appointment and get detailed directions.

Closer to the town center is **Rimbalcello,** on the via Zanardelli (☎ **0365-21-069**), site of a half-dozen tennis courts that anyone can use for around 20,000L ($10) an hour. Within the same compound, you'll find access to a free beach, a disco that rocks and rolls after dark beginning around 9:30pm, and a restaurant.

If you want to get out on the lake, you can rent motorboats or sailboats at **Nautica Benaco,** along the lakefront of the nearby village of Manerba del Garda (☎ **0365-654074**), 9 miles from Gardone.

✪ **Villa Vittoriale.** Via Vittoriale 12. ☎ **0365-20-130.** Admission 10,000L ($6) to grounds only, 20,000L ($10) to grounds and villa. Summer daily 9am–5pm; winter Tues–Sun 9am–1pm and 2–5pm. Head out Via Roma, connecting with Via Colli.

This villa was the home of Gabriele d'Annunzio (1863–1938), the poet and military adventurer, another Italian who believed in la dolce vita, even when he couldn't afford it. Most of the celebrated events in d'Annunzio's life occurred before 1925, including his love affair with Eleonora Duse and his bravura takeover as a self-styled commander of a territory being ceded to Yugoslavia. In the later years of his life, until he died in the winter before World War II, he lived the grand life at his private estate on Garda.

The furnishings and decor passed for avant-garde in their day but now evoke the Radio City Music Hall of the 1930s. D'Annunzio's death mask is of morbid interest, and his bed with a "Big Brother" eye adds a curious touch of Orwell's *1984* (over the poet's bed is a faun casting a nasty sneer). The marble bust of Duse ("the veiled witness" of his work) seems sadly out of place, but the manuscripts and old uniforms perpetuate the legend. In July and August, d'Annunzio plays are presented at the amphitheater on the premises. Villa Vittoriale is a bizarre monument to a hero of yesteryear.

ACCOMMODATIONS

You can also rent a luxury room at the **Villa Fiordaliso,** where Mussolini once trysted with his lover, Claretta (see "Dining," below).

Bellevue Hotel. Via Zanardelli 81, 25083 Gardone Riviera. ☎ **0365-290-088.** Fax 0365-290-080. www.hotelbellevuegardone.com. E-mail: hbellevue@tin.it. 30 units. TV TEL. 170,000L ($85) double. Rates include breakfast. V. Closed Oct 10–Apr. Free parking.

This villa, perched above the main road, has many terraces surrounded by trees and flowers, and an unforgettable view. You can stay here even on a budget, enjoying the advantages of lakeside villa life complete with a pool. The guest rooms come in a variety of shapes and sizes, each with a good mattress. The bathrooms are small for the most part. The lounges are comfortable, and the dining room affords a view through the arched windows and offers excellent meals (no skimpy helpings here). In fair weather you can dine in a large garden.

✪ **Grand Hotel.** Via Zanardelli 84, 25083 Gardone Riviera. ☎ **0365-20-261.** Fax 0365-22-695. www.grangardone.it. E-mail: ghg@grangardone.it. 180 units. A/C MINIBAR TV TEL. Apr and Oct 260,000L ($130) double; 340,000L ($170) junior suite. May–June and Sept 300,000L ($150) double; 380,000L ($190) junior suite. July–Aug 350,000L ($175) double;

430,000L ($215) junior suite. Rates include buffet breakfast. Half-board 40,000L ($20) per person. AE, DC, MC, V. Closed mid-Oct to end of Mar. Parking 20,000L ($10).

When it was built in 1881, this was the most fashionable hotel on the lake and one of the biggest resorts in Europe. Famous guests have included Winston Churchill, Gabriele d'Annunzio, and Somerset Maugham. It's only a rumor that Vladimir Nabokov was inspired to write *Lolita* after spotting a young girl here. The main salon's sculpted ceilings, parquet floors, and comfortable chairs make it an ideal spot for reading or watching the lake. The guest rooms for the most part are spacious and traditionally furnished, always inviting. Each comes with a quality mattress. All the bathrooms come with hair dryers and deluxe toiletries.

Dining/Diversions: The piano bar has the appropriate romantic atmosphere to put you in the mood for the refined cuisine served in the old-world dining room, with its menu of international and regional dishes. In summer, there's dining on the lakeside terrace.

Amenities: Concierge, room service, laundry/dry cleaning, twice-daily maid service, baby-sitting, in-room massage, series of garden terraces, private beach, pool. The staff can arrange horse riding in the hills, tennis at courts within a 5-minute walk, and golf within a radius of 8 miles (13km).

Nearby Accommodations

Fasano del Garda is a satellite resort of Gardone Riviera, 1¼ miles (2km) to the north. Many prefer it to Gardone.

✪ **Hotel Villa del Sogno.** Via Zanardelli 107, Fasano d. Garda, 25083 Gardone Riviera. ☎ **0365-290-181.** Fax 0365-290-230. www.gsnet.it/sogno. E-mail: sogno@gsnet.it. 38 units. MINIBAR TV TEL. 320,000–550,000L ($160–$275) double; 570,000–800,000L ($285–$400) suite. Rates include breakfast. AE, DC, MC, V. Closed Oct 20–Apr 1. Free parking.

This 1920s re-creation of a Renaissance villa offers sweeping views of the lake and spacious old-fashioned guest rooms (nine are air-conditioned). The rooms come in various shapes and sizes and all are elegantly comfortable, with quality mattresses. The bathrooms are also well equipped, each with a hair dryer and deluxe toiletries. This "Villa of the Dream" is far superior to anything in the area, having long ago surpassed the Grand (see above). The baronial stairway of the interior, as well as many of the ceilings and architectural details, were crafted from wood.

Dining: The hotel serves the finest food among the area's hotel dining rooms, offering international and regional specialties. There are two formal restaurants, though many guests prefer to dine on the lake-view terrace, where in summer both a buffet breakfast and a romantic evening dinner are served.

Amenities: Concierge, laundry/dry cleaning, room service, private beach, pool.

DINING

Most visitors take their meals at their hotels. However, there are some good independent choices.

Ristorante La Stalla. Via dei Colli Strada per Il Vittoriale. ☎ **0365-21-038.** Reservations recommended. Main courses 16,000–32,000L ($8–$16); fixed-price menu 35,000L ($17.50). AE, DC, MC, V. Wed–Mon 12:30–2:30pm and 7:30–9:30pm. Closed Jan 8–20. INTERNATIONAL.

This charming restaurant, set in a garden ringed with cypresses on a hill above the lake, is frequented by local families. It occupies a handcrafted stone building with a brick-columned porch, outdoor tables, and an indoor room loaded with rustic artifacts and tables. To get here, follow the signs toward Il Vittoriale (the building was commissioned by d'Annunzio as a horse stable) to a quiet residential street. Depending on the shopping that day, the specialties might include a selection of freshly prepared antipasti, risotto with cuttlefish, or crepes fondue. Polenta is served with Gorgonzola and walnuts, or you may prefer beef fillet in beer sauce. Sunday afternoon can be crowded.

✪ **Villa Fiordaliso.** Via Zanardelli 150, 25083 Gardone Riviera. ☎ **0365-20-158.** www.relaischateaux.fr/fiordaliso. E-mail: fiordaliso@relaischateau.fr. Reservations required. Main courses 35,000–80,000L ($17.50–$40); fixed-price menus 95,000–145,000L ($47.50–$72.50). AE, DC, MC, V. Wed–Sun 12:30–2pm and 7:30–10pm; Tues 7:30–10:30pm. ITALIAN.

This deluxe restaurant is a Liberty-style villa from 1924 with gardens stretching down to the lake. Not only is it the most scenic and beautiful on Lake Garda, but also it serves the finest cuisine. This is personalized by the chef and likely to include a terrine of eel and salmon in herb-and-onion sauce, a timbale of rice and shellfish with curry, and several fish and meats grilled over a fire. Other specialties are ravioli with Bergoss (a salty regional cheese), sardines from a nearby lake baked in an herb crust, and scampi in a sauce of tomatoes and wild onions. This little bastion of fine food has impeccable service to match.

Today this famous villa is owned by Rosa Tosetti, who runs it beautifully and also offers guest rooms in a setting of cypresses, pine trees, and olive trees, near a private beach. Each room is exquisitely furnished and comes with a tiled bath. It was here that poet Gabriele D'Annunzio used to gaze out through the villa's stained-glass windows. It was also here that Mussolini and his lover, Claretta, trysted in the 1940s, and the hotel's one suite is named after her. The six standard rooms are 300,000 to 600,000L ($150 to $300), with Claretta's suite at 800,000L ($400).

SIRMIONE

Perched at the tip of a narrowing strip on the southern end of Lake Garda, **Sirmione** juts out 2½ miles (4km) into the lake. Noted for its thermal baths (used to treat deafness), the town is a major resort, just north of the autostrada connecting Milan and Verona, that blooms in spring and wilts in late autumn.

ESSENTIALS

GETTING THERE Sirmione lies 3½ miles (6km) from the A4 exit and 5 miles (8km) from Desanzano. Buses run from Brescia and from Verona to Sirmione every hour (trip time from either, depending on traffic: 1 hour). A one-way ticket from Brescia is 5,400L ($2.70) and from Verona 4,600L ($2.30). There's no rail service. The nearest train terminal is at Desenzano, on the Venice–Milan rail line. From here, there's frequent bus service to Sirmione; the bus trip takes 30 minutes, costing 2,100L ($1.05) one way.

VISITOR INFORMATION The **tourist office** is at Viale Marconi 2 (☎ **030-916-245**). April to October, it's open daily 9am to 12:30pm and 3 to 6pm; November to March, hours are Monday to Friday 9am to 12:30pm and 3 to 6pm, Saturday 9am to 12:30pm.

WHAT TO SEE & DO

Known for its beaches (which are invariably overcrowded in summer), Sirmione is Garda's major lakeside resort. The best beach is **Lido delle Bionde,** which you reach by taking Via Dante near the castle. Here vendors will rent you a chaise longue with an umbrella for 15,000L ($7.50). If you're feeling more athletic, other vendors will hook you up with a **pedal boat** at 20,000L ($10) per hour or a **kayak** at 15,000L ($7.50) per hour.

If you'd like to go biking in the area, head for **Bar Chocolat,** Via Verona 47 (☎ **030-990-5297**), with rentals at 6,000L ($3) per hour.

The resort is filled with souvenir shops, many hawking cheaply made trinkets aimed at the day-tripper. However, the best buys are on Friday 8am to 1pm when an **outdoor market** blossoms in Piazza Montebaldo. Vendors bring their wares here not only from nearby lake villages but also from towns and villages to the south.

The resort was a favorite of Giosuè Carducci, the Italian poet who won the Nobel Prize for literature in 1906. In Roman days it was frequented by another poet, the hedonistic Catullus, who died in 54 B.C. Today the **Grotte di Catullo,** on Via Catullo (☎ **030-916-157**), is the chief sight, an unbeatable combination of Roman ruins and a panoramic lake view. You can wander through the remains of this once-great villa Tuesday to Sunday: April to September 8:30am to 7pm and October to March 9am to 4pm. Admission is 8,000L ($4).

At the entrance to the town stands the moated 13th-century **Castello Scaligera,** Piazza Castello (☎ **030-916-468**), which once belonged to the powerful Scaligeri princes of Verona. You can climb to the top and walk the ramparts April to September daily 9am to 6pm and October to March Tuesday to Sunday 9am to 1pm. Admission is 8,000L ($4).

ACCOMMODATIONS

During the peak summer season, you have to have a hotel reservation to bring a car into this crowded town. However, there's a large parking area at the town entrance. Accommodations are plentiful.

Flaminia Hotel. Piazza Flaminia 8, 25019 Sirmione. ☎ **030-916-078.** Fax 030-916-193. 85 units. A/C TV TEL. 185,000–220,000L ($92.50–$110) double. Rates include breakfast. V. Free parking.

This is one of the best little hotels in Sirmione, recently renovated with a number of modern facilities and amenities. It's right on the lakefront, with a terrace extending into the water. The guest rooms are made attractive by French doors opening onto private balconies. The rooms come in different shapes and sizes, and each is fitted with a good mattress and a tiled bathroom. The lounges are furnished in a functional modern style. Breakfast is the only meal served.

Grand Hotel Terme. Viale Marconi 1, 25019 Sirmione. ☎ **030-916-261.** Fax 030-916-568. www.termedisirmione.com. E-mail: ght@termedisirmione.com. 58 units. A/C MINIBAR TV TEL. Mar–May and Oct–Nov 300,000–500,000L ($150–$250) double, 820,000L ($410) suite; June–Sept 360,000–580,000L ($180–$290) double, 890,000L ($445) suite. Rates include breakfast. AE, DC, MC, V. Closed Nov–Easter.

This rambling hotel at the entrance of the old town is on the lake next to the Scaligeri Castle. After Villa Cortine (see below), it's the second choice, known especially for its lake-bordering garden. The wide marble halls and stairs lead to well-furnished balconied guest rooms ranging from medium in size to spacious, each coming with a luxurious mattress. The tiled bathrooms have hair dryers and deluxe toiletries.

Dining: The traditional Italian cuisine served in the indoor/outdoor dining room is excellent, with such offerings as prosciutto and melon, risotto with snails, fettuccine with fresh porcini, and a wide choice of salads and fruits.

Amenities: Concierge, room service, laundry/dry cleaning, solarium, gym, pool, Jacuzzi, sauna, car-rental desk. Beauty and therapeutic treatments are also available.

Olivi. Via San Pietro 5, 25019 Sirmione. ☎ **030-990-5365.** Fax 030-916-472. www.gardalake.it/hotel-olivi. E-mail: hotel-olivi@gardalake.it. 58 units. A/C TV TEL. 210,000–320,000L ($105–$160) double. Rates include breakfast. Half-board 40,000L ($20) extra per person. AE, MC, V. Closed Dec–Jan.

This hotel has an excellent location on the rise of a hill in a grove of olive trees at the edge of town. The all-glass walls of the major rooms never let you forget you're in a garden spot. Even the streamlined guest rooms have walls of glass leading onto open balconies. The tiled bathrooms, though a bit small, still have adequate shelf space. The hotel serves typically Italian meals. Sometimes live music is featured—even country music when the hotel stages a barbecue. There's an outdoor pool, a solarium, and laundry and room service.

✪ **Villa Cortine Palace Hotel.** Via Grotte 12, 25019 Sirmione. ☎ **030-990-5890.** Fax 030-916-390. www.hotelvillacortine.com. E-mail: info@hotelvillacortine.com. 54 units. A/C TV TEL. 520,000L ($260) double with breakfast, 800,000L ($400) double with half-board; 830,000L ($415) suite with breakfast, 1,300,000L ($650) suite with half-board. Half-board compulsory June 18–Sept 19. AE, DC, MC, V. Closed end of Oct to Easter.

This first-class choice, whose original building dates from 1905, is set apart from the town, surrounded by sumptuous gardens. For serenity, atmosphere, professional service, and even good food, there's nothing to equal it in Sirmione. Today all but a handful of its guest rooms are in the new wing, and the bar and reception area are located in the older building. Some rooms offer minibars. Most rooms are medium to spacious, each with a quality mattress and an excellent bathroom containing deluxe toiletries. The formal drawing room boasts much gilt and marble—it's positively palatial.

Dining/Diversions: There's an informal restaurant and a more formal dining room serving Italian and international cuisine, with an excellent selection of wines. There's also an elegant cocktail bar. At lunch, the hotel often offers a barbecue, mainly with fresh fish from the lake.

Amenities: Concierge, room service, laundry/dry cleaning, baby-sitting, pool, clay tennis court, private beach.

Dining

La Rucola. Vicolo Strentelle 5. ☎ **030-916-326.** Reservations recommended. Main courses 25,000–30,000L ($12.50–$15); fixed-price menu 90,000L ($45). AE, MC, V. Fri–Wed 12:30–2:30pm and 7:30–10:30pm. Closed Jan–Feb 8. ITALIAN.

This restaurant lies on a small alley a few steps from the main gate leading into Sirmione. The building looks like a vine-laden, sienna-colored country house and was a stable 150 years ago. Full meals could include fresh salmon, langoustines, mixed grilled fish, and a more limited meat selection. Meats, such as Florentine beefsteak, are most often grilled or flambéed. More innovative items include *gnocchetti di riso* with baby squid and squid ink, and turbot fillet with potatoes and zabaglione of spinach. A good pasta dish is spaghetti with clams. Many of the desserts are made for two, including crêpes Suzette and banana flambé.

Ristorante Grifone da Luciano. Via delle Bisse 5. ☎ **030-916-097.** Main courses 15,000–25,000L ($7.50–$12.50). AE, DC, MC, V. Thurs–Tues noon–2:30pm and 7–10:30pm. Closed Nov–Mar 15. INTERNATIONAL.

One of the most attractive restaurants in town is separated from the castle by a row of shrubbery, a low stone wall, and a moat. From your seat on the flagstone terrace, you'll have a view of the crashing waves and the plants ringing the dining area. The main building is an old stone house surrounded by olive trees, but many diners gravitate toward the low glass-and-metal extension. The staff is charming and fun, and the chef talented. The food includes many varieties of fish and many standard Italian dishes, such as *gnocchetti dragoncella* (with tomatoes and aromatic herbs), risotto with shellfish, Venetian-style calves' livers with onions, beef fillet flambéed with whisky, and beef cutlets *(costello di Manzo).*

✪ **Vecchia Lugana.** Piazzale Vecchia Lugana 1, Lugana di Sirmione. ☎ **030-919-012.** Reservations recommended. Main courses 18,000–30,000L ($9–$15). AE, DC, MC, V. Wed–Sun 12:30–2pm and 7:30–10:30pm. Closed Jan to mid-Feb. LOMBARD/ITALIAN.

The grandest eating along Lake Garda is found here at the base of the peninsula outside town. Vecchia Lugana not only serves some of the best cuisine along the lake but also surfaces near the top of the best restaurants in Italy. The guiding light is Pierantonio Ambrosi, who uses only the freshest ingredients prepared with great care. He claims the important thing is to offer a genuine cuisine in an informal setting. He also cares more about the food's substance and quality than about its artistic arrangement. Every day his staff prepares several kinds of fresh pasta, from tagliatelle to *orecchiette*—count on it being served with a savory sauce. The chefs are known for their fresh fish, grilled to perfection with a touch of olive oil, lemon sauce, and freshly chopped herbs. The perch fillet with fresh artichokes is a delight. For dessert, try one of the pretty fresh fruit tarts.

5 Lake Como

More than 30 miles (48km) north of Milan, romantic and lovely Lake Como is a shimmering deep blue, spanning 2½ miles (4km) at its widest point. With its flower-filled gardens, villas built for the wealthy of the 17th and 18th centuries, and mild climate, it's among the most scenic spots in Italy.

The scenery around Lake Como has been fabled since the days when residents of the flat, sometimes steamy, fields of nearby Lombardy sought refuge from heat waves. The best way to admire the lake's many faces is by taking a boat tour, pulling into selected ports of call en route for a meal, an espresso, a stroll, or some shopping or swimming.

LAKE COMO ESSENTIALS

GETTING THERE **Trains** arrive daily at Como from Milan every hour. The trip takes 40 minutes, and a one-way fare is 9,200L ($4.60). The main station, **Stazione San Giovanni,** Piazzale San Gottardo (☎ **1478-880-88**), lies at the end of Viale Gallio, a 15-minute walk from the center (Piazza Cavour). If you have a **car,** the city of Como is 25 miles (40km) north of Milan and is reached via A9. Once at the Como, a small road (S583) leads to the popular resort of Bellagio.

GETTING AROUND Bus service is offered by **SPT,** Piazza Matteotti (☎ **031-304-744**), to the most important centers on the lake. A one-way fare to the most popular resort at Bellagio is 4,300L ($2.15). Travel time depends on the traffic.

COMO

At the southern tip of the lake, 25 miles (40km) north of Milan, Como is known for its silk industry. Most visitors pass through here to take a boat ride on the lake (see above).

Because Como is also an industrial city, we don't recommend staying overnight here (head to one of the more attractive resorts along the lake, like Bellagio). But train passengers who don't plan to rent a car may prefer Como (the city, that is) for convenience.

For centuries, the destiny of the town has been linked to that of Milan. Como is still called the world capital of silk, the silk makers of the city joining communal hands with the fashion designers of Milan. Como has been making silk since Marco Polo first returned with silkworms from China (since the end of World War II, Como has left the cultivating of silk to the Chinese and just imported the thread to weave into fabrics). Designers like Giorgio Armani and Bill Blass come here to discuss the patterns they want with silk manufacturers.

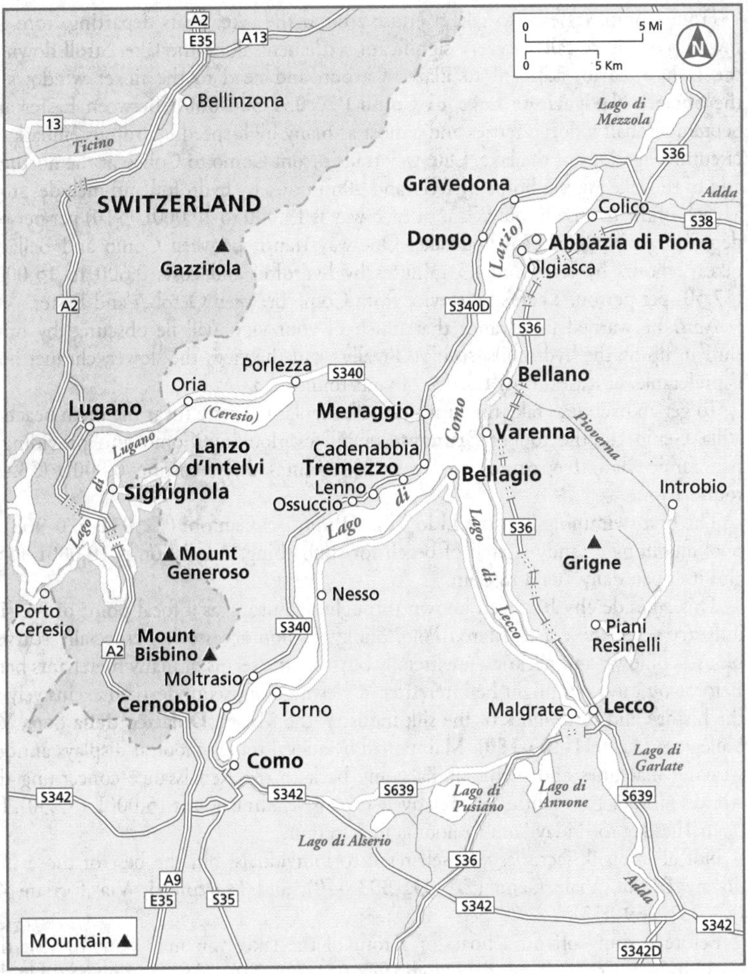

Essentials

GETTING THERE See "Lake Como Essentials," above.

VISITOR INFORMATION The **tourist office** is at Piazza Cavour 17 (☎ **031-269-712**), open Monday to Saturday 9am to 12:30pm and 2:30 to 6pm.

SPECIAL EVENTS The most fun is in July, when **Jazz & Co.** stages five concerts at Piazza San Federale. The tourist office will supply details.

What to See & Do

The heart of Como is **Piazza Cavour** with its hotels, cafes, and steamers departing for lakeside resorts. Immediately to the west, the **Public Gardens (Giardini Pubblici)** make for a pleasant stroll, especially if you're heading for the **Tempio Voltiano,** Viale Marconi (☎ **031-574-705**), honoring native son Alessandro Volta, the physicist and pioneer of electricity. The temple contains memorabilia of his life and experiments. It's open Tuesday to Sunday: April to September 10am to noon and 3 to 6pm, October to March 10am to noon and 2 to 4pm. Admission is 5,000L ($2.50).

From Como, it's easy to take a cruise around the lake; boats departing from the town's piers make calls at every significant settlement along the lake. Stroll down to the **Lungo Lario,** adjacent to Piazza Cavour, and head to the ticket windows of the **Società Navigazione Lago di Como** (☎ **031-304-060**). Between Easter and September, half a dozen ferries and almost as many high-speed hydrofoils embark for circumnavigations of the lake. One-way transit from Como to Colico at the northern end of the lake takes 4 hours by ferry and 90 minutes by hydrofoil and includes stops at each of the towns en route. Transit each way is 13,000 to 20,000L ($10) per person, depending on which boat you take. One-way transit between Como and Bellagio takes 2 hours by ferry and 45 minutes by hydrofoil and costs 9,600 to 15,000L ($7.50) per person. There's no service from Como between October and Easter.

Note: Be warned in advance that much of your view will be obscured by mists thrown up by the hydrofoils, so if you really want the view, the slower, cheaper boat is preferable, at least during one leg of your round-trip.

To get an overview, take the funicular at Lungolario Trieste (near the main beach at Villa Genio) to the top of **Brunante,** a hill overlooking Como and providing a panoramic view. Departures are every 30 minutes daily, costing 6,800L ($3.40) round-trip.

The best swimming is at the **Lido Villa Olmo,** Via Cantoni (☎ **031-570-968**), a pool adjoining a sandy stretch of beach for sunbathing. Admission is 10,000L ($5), and it's open daily 10am to 6pm.

This lakeside city has been known throughout Europe as a focal point of the silk industry since the era of Marco Polo. Slinky fashion accessories, especially scarves, blouses, pillows, and neckties, are literally bursting the seams of many merchants here. Before you buy, you might be interested in viewing a museum devoted exclusively to the history and techniques of the silk industry, the **Museo Didatico della Sete,** Via Vallegio 3 (☎ **031-303-180**). Maintained by a local trade school, it displays antique weaving machines and memorabilia going back to the Renaissance concerning the world's most elegant fabric. The relatively expensive admission is 15,000L ($7.50). It's open Tuesday to Friday 9am to noon and 3 to 6pm.

Not all the silk factories will sell retail to individuals, but the best of those that do are **Binda,** Viale Geno (☎ **031-303-440**), and **Martinetti,** Via Torriani 41 (☎ **031-269-053**).

Before rushing off on a boat for a tour of the lake, you may want to visit the **Cattedrale di Como,** Piazza del Duomo (☎ **031-265-244**). Construction began in the 14th century in the Lombard Gothic style and continued on through the Renaissance until the 1700s. The exterior, frankly, is more interesting than the interior. Dating from 1487, the exterior is lavishly decorated with statues, including those of Pliny the Elder (A.D. 23–79) and the Younger (A.D. 62–113), who one writer once called "the beautiful people of ancient Rome." Inside, look for the 16th-century tapestries depicting scenes from the Bible. The cathedral is open Monday to Saturday 7am to noon and 3 to 6:30pm.

On the other side of the Duomo lie the colorfully striped **Brolette** (town hall) and, adjoining it, the **Torre del Comune.** Both are from the 13th century.

If time remains, head down the main street, **Via Vittorio Emanuele,** where, two blocks south of the cathedral, rises the five-sided **San Fedele,** a 12th-century church standing on Piazza San Fedele. It's known for its unusual pentagonal apse and a doorway carved with "fatted" figures from the Middle Ages. Farther along, you come to the **Garibaldi National Unity Civic Museum (Museo Civico del Risorgimento Garibaldi),** Piazza Medaglie d'Oro Comasche (☎ **031-271-343**), the virtual "attic" of Como, displaying artifacts collected by the city from prehistoric times through

World War II. The museum is open Tuesday to Sunday 9:30am to 12:30pm and Tuesday to Saturday 2 to 5pm. Admission is 5,000L ($2.50).

The art museum of Como is of passing interest: The small **Pinacoteca Palazzo Volpi,** Via Diaz 84 (☎ **031-269-869**), has several old and wonderful paintings from the Middle Ages, most of which were taken from the monastery of Santa Margherita del Broletto. Two of the museum's best paintings are anonymous: that of St. Sebastian riddled with arrows (though appearing quite resigned to the whole thing) and a moving *Youth and Death.* The museum is open Monday to Saturday 9:30am to 12:30pm and 2 to 5pm, Sunday 10am to 1pm. Admission is 5,000L ($2.50).

After the museum, continue down Via Giovio until you come to the **Porta Vittoria,** a gate from 1192 with five tiers of arches. A short walk away, passing through a dreary commercial area leads you to Como's most interesting church, the 11th-century **Sant'Abbondio,** a Romanesque gem. From Porta Vittoria, take Viale Cattaneo to Viale Roosevelt, turning left onto Via Sant'Abbondio on which the church stands. Because of its age, it was massively restored in the 19th century. Heavily frescoed, the church has five aisles.

ACCOMMODATIONS

Hotel Barchetta Excelsior. Piazza Cavour 1, 22100 Como. ☎ **031-3221.** Fax 031-302-622. www.hotelbarchetta.com. E-mail: info2@hotelbarchetta.com. 84 units. A/C MINIBAR TV TEL. 290,000–370,000L ($145–$185) double; 390,000–420,000L ($195–$210) suite. Rates include buffet breakfast. AE, DC, MC, V. Parking 30,000L ($15).

This first-class hotel is at the edge of the main square in the commercial section of town. Major additions have been made to the 1957 structure, including the alteration of its restaurant and an upgrading of the guest rooms, which are comfortably furnished, most with balconies overlooking the square and the lake. All accommodations are soundproof and have radios, and most have lake views. Some are set aside for nonsmokers. The bathrooms come with hair dryers and fluffy towels, and a few are fitted with Jacuzzis. There's a parking lot behind the hotel, plus a covered garage about 50 yards away.

Hotel Metropole & Suisse. Piazza Cavour 19, 22100 Como. ☎ **-031-269-444.** Fax 031-300-808. www.hotelmetropolesuisse.com. E-mail: suisse@galactica.it. 71 units. A/C MINIBAR TV TEL. 180,000–280,000L ($90–$140) double; 270,000–320,000L ($135–$160) suite. AE, DC, MC, V. Parking 25,000L ($12.50).

This hotel offers good value. Near the cathedral and the major square that fronts the lake, it's composed of three lower floors dating from around 1700, with upper floors added about 60 years ago. A photo of the Swiss creator of the hotel with his staff in 1892 hangs behind the reception desk. The guest rooms come in various shapes and sizes, rich with character for the most part. All are comfortable, with quality mattresses. The bathrooms have hair dryers and plush towels. A parking garage and the city marina are nearby. The popular Ristorante Imbarcadero, under separate management (see below), fills most of the ground floor.

DINING

Ristorante Imbarcadero. In the Hotel Metropole & Suisse, Piazza Cavour 20. ☎ **031-270-166.** Reservations recommended. Main courses 24,000–35,000L ($12–$17.50); fixed-price menu 50,000L ($25). AE, DC, MC, V. Daily 12:30–3:30pm and 7:30–10pm. Closed Dec 26–Jan 10. INTERNATIONAL/LOMBARD.

Opened more than a decade ago in a 300-year-old building near the edge of the lake, this restaurant is filled with a pleasing blend of carved Victorian chairs, panoramic windows, and potted palms. The summer terrace set up on the square is ringed with shrubbery and illuminated with evening candlelight. First-class ingredients are deftly handled by the kitchen. The chef makes his own tagliatelle, or you may want to order spaghetti with garlic, oil, and red pepper. The fish dishes are excellent, especially slices of sea bass with braised leek and aromatic vinegar and sage-flavored Como lake whitefish. Try the breaded veal cutlet Milanese style or breast of pheasant flavored with port and shallots. Desserts might include a parfait of almonds, hazelnuts, and apple sorbet flavored with Calvados.

CERNOBBIO

Cernobbio, 3 miles (5km) northwest of Como and 33 miles (53km) north of Milan, is a small, chic resort frequented by wealthy Europeans, who come largely to check into its famous deluxe hotel, the 16th-century Villa d'Este. But its idyllic setting on the lake is available to everyone, as there are a number of more affordable hotels as well.

The **tourist office** is at Via Regina 33B (☎ **031-510-198**), open Monday to Saturday 9:30am to 12:30pm and 2:30 to 5:30pm; closed January.

ACCOMMODATIONS & DINING

✪ **Grand Hotel Villa d'Este.** Via Regina 40, 22012 Cernobbio. ☎ **031-34-81.** Fax 031-348-844. www.villadeste.it. E-mail: info@villadeste.it. 164 units. A/C MINIBAR TV TEL. 726,000–1,045,000L ($363–$522.50) double; from 1,162,000L ($581) suite. Rates include breakfast. Spa packages available. AE, DC, MC, V. Closed Nov 15–Mar 1. Free parking.

One of Italy's most legendary hotels, the Villa d'Este was built in 1568 as a lakeside home/pleasure pavilion for Cardinal Tolomeo Gallio. One of the most famous Renaissance-era hotels in the world, designed in the neoclassical style by Pellegrino Pellegrini di Valsolda, it passed from owner to illustrious owner for 300 years until it was transformed into a hotel in 1873.

The hotel remains a kingdom unto itself, a splendid palace surrounded by 10 acres of some of the finest hotel gardens in Italy. The interior lives up to the enthralling beauty of the grounds. The silken wall coverings of the Salon Napoleone were embroidered especially for the emperor's visit; the Canova Room is centered around a statue of Venus by Canova himself; and the Grand Ballroom is suitable for the most festive banquets. The frescoed ceilings, impeccable antiques, and attentive service create one of the world's most envied hotels. Each guest room has an individual decor and a roster of famous former occupants. Some 34 of the hotel's 166 accommodations are in the Queen's Pavilion, an elegant annex built in 1856. The large bathrooms are beautifully appointed, with deluxe toiletries and hair dryers.

Dining/Diversions: The hotel contains two restaurants, both of culinary merit serving formal à la carte dinners. The cooking is sublime. Lunches are less expensive, especially in summer, when light buffets are set on long tables within view of the gardens. Throughout the year there's always at least a live pianist on most nights, and in midsummer a small orchestra plays dance music three evenings a week. There is another, less formal restaurant called Il Grill that's open for dinner only (closed Monday); the Enoteca, with a wide selection of wines and light snacks; and a disco that's open Thursday to Sunday.

Amenities: Spa center, room service, baby-sitting, laundry/valet, hairdresser, massage, pool floating atop Lake Como, access to the world-class golf course at nearby Montofano, red-clay tennis courts, gym, sauna, Turkish bath, squash court, waterskiing, and other sports.

BELLAGIO

Sitting on a promontory at the point where Lake Como forks, 48 miles (77km) north of Milan and 18 miles (29km) northeast of Como, Bellagio is often called "the prettiest town in Europe." A sleepy veil hangs over the arcaded streets and little shops. Bellagio is rich in memories, having attracted fashionable and even royal visitors, such as Leopold I of Belgium, who used to own the 18th-century Villa Giulia. Still going strong, though no longer the aristocratic address it once was, Bellagio is a 45-minute drive north of Como.

The **tourist office** is at Piazza della Chiesa 14 (☎ **031-950-204**). April to October, it's open daily 9am to noon and 3 to 5pm; November to March, hours are Monday and Wednesday to Saturday 8:30am to noon and 3 to 6pm.

WHAT TO SEE & DO

To reach many of the places in Bellagio, you must climb streets that are really stairways. Its lakeside promenade blossoms with flowering shrubbery. From the town, you can take tours of Lake Como and enjoy sports like rowing and tennis or just lounge at the **Bellagio Lido** (the beach).

Bellagio's most important attraction is the garden of the **Villa Melzi Museum and Chapel,** Lungolario Marconi (☎ **031-950-318**). The villa was built in 1808 for Duca Francesco Melzi d'Eril, vice-president of the Italian republic founded by Napoléon. Franz Liszt and Stendhal are among the illustrious guests who've stayed here. The park has many well-known sculptures, and if you're here in spring you can enjoy the azaleas. Today it's the property of Conte Gallarti Scotti, who opens it March 22 to October, daily 9am to 6pm. The museum contains a not very distinguished collection of Egyptian sculptures. Admission is 5,000L ($2.50).

If time allows, try to explore the gardens of the **Villa Serbelloni,** Piazza della Chiesa (☎ **031-950-204**), the Bellagio Study and Conference Center of the Rockefeller Foundation (not to be confused with the Grand Hotel Villa Serbelloni by the waterside in the village). The landlord here used to be Pliny the Younger. The villa isn't open to the public, but you can visit the park on 1½-hour guided tours starting at 11am and 4pm. Tours are conducted mid-April to mid-October, Tuesday to Sunday, at a cost of 6,000L ($3); the proceeds go to local charities.

From Como, car ferries sail back and forth across the lake to **Cadenabbia** on the western shore, another lakeside resort, with hotels and villas. Directly south of Cadenabbia on the run to Tremezzo, the **Villa Carlotta** (☎ **0344-40-405**) is the most-visited attraction of Lake Como, and with good reason. In a serene setting, the villa is graced with gardens of exotic flowers and blossoming shrubbery, especially rhododendrons and azaleas. Its beauty is tame, cultivated, much like a fairy tale that recaptures the halcyon life available only to the very rich of the 19th century. Dating from 1847, the estate was named after a Prussian princess, Carlotta, who married the duke of Sachsen-Meiningen. Inside are a number of art treasures, like Canova's *Cupid and Psyche,* and neoclassical statues by Bertel Thorvaldsen, a Danish sculptor who died in 1844. There are also neoclassical paintings, furniture, and a stone-and-bronze table ornament that belonged to Viceroy Eugene Beauharnais. It's open daily: March and October 9 to 11:30am and 2 to 4:30pm; April to September 9am to 6pm. Admission is 12,000L ($6).

You may spend a lot of your time just sunbathing and enjoying that glorious lakeside scenery. Most of the lakefront hotels have their own swimming **beaches.** (The swimmable lakefront section that's maintained by the Grand Hotel Villa Serbelloni, open only to hotel residents, is especially well-maintained.) Otherwise, you can walk 10 minutes north of the town center to swim in the lake at the free public facilities at **La Punta.** Anyone can rent either of the two **tennis courts,** for around 20,000L ($10) an hour, at the Grand Hotel Villa Serbelloni, and anyone can visit that hotel's **fitness center** for a fee of around 30,000L ($15).

If you're interested in a **boat tour,** in a motorized craft suitable for up to six passengers, **Ezio Giradone** (☎ **031-950-201**) will take your group for rides on the lake, priced at around 200,000L ($100) per hour.

Shoppers gravitate to the clusters of **boutiques** along the Salita Serbelloni and the Salita Mella, in the town center. And although there's not a lot of raucous nightlife in this quiet town, you can always hang out in a couple of **bars: La Divina Commedia,** on Salita Mella, and **Le Streghe,** on Salita Plinio (☎ **031-951-680** for both bars); both sometimes have live music.

ACCOMMODATIONS & DINING

✪ **Grand Hotel Villa Serbelloni.** Via Roma 1, 22021 Bellagio. ☎ **031-950-216.** Fax 031-951-529. www.villaserbelloni.com. E-mail: inforequest@villaserbelloni.it. 83 units. A/C MINIBAR TV TEL. 515,000–790,000L ($257.50–$395) double; 990,000–1,250,000L ($495–$625) suite. Rates include breakfast. AE, DC, MC, V. Closed Nov 1–Mar 27. Parking 35,000L ($17.50).

This lavish old hotel, surpassed only by the Villa d'Este, is grand indeed. It stands proud at the edge of town against a backdrop of hills, surrounded by beautiful gardens. The public rooms rekindle the spirit of the baroque: a drawing room with a painted ceiling, marble columns, a glittering chandelier, and gilt furnishings and a mirrored neoclassical dining room. The guest rooms are wide-ranging, from elaborate suites with recessed tile bathrooms, baroque furnishings, and lake-view balconies to more chaste quarters. The most desirable rooms open onto the lake. The tiled bathrooms are well appointed, with hair dryers. You can sunbathe on the waterside terrace or doze under a willow tree.

Dining: The great Royal Dining Room offers a high standard of Italian and international cooking. In summer guests prefer a table on the lakeside terrace.

Amenities: Concierge, room service, laundry/dry cleaning, in-room massage, twice-daily maid service, baby-sitting, secretarial services, children's center, business center. The fitness and beauty center offers four programs ranging from 2 to 6 days (prices are 600,000 to 2,450,000L/$300 to $1,225, which includes meals and treatments but not the hotel room); health and fitness center, outdoor heated pool, lakeside beach, Jacuzzi, sauna, jogging track, golf course nearby.

Hotel du Lac. Piazza Mazzini 32, 22021 Bellagio. ☎ **031-950-320.** Fax 031-951-624. 49 units. A/C MINIBAR TV TEL. 250,000–300,000L ($125–$150) double. Rates include breakfast. MC, V. Closed Nov–Mar 25. Parking 20,000L ($10).

The Hotel du Lac was built 150 years ago, when the lake waters came up to the front door. Landfill has since created Piazza Mazzini, and today there's a generous terraced expanse of flagstones in front with cafe tables and an arched arcade. The guest rooms are comfortably furnished, containing such amenities as satellite TVs, firm mattresses, and hair dryers. On the second floor is a glassed-in terrace restaurant, and you can bask in the sun or relax in the shade on the rooftop garden, opening onto panoramic views of the lake.

✪ **Hotel Florence.** Piazza Mazzini 45, 22021 Bellagio. ☎ **031-950-342.** Fax 031-951-722. www.bellagio.co.nz. E-mail: hotfloize@tim.it. 36 units. TV TEL. 260,000–320,000L ($130–$160) double; 360,000–380,000L ($180–$190) suite. Rates include breakfast. AE, CB, DC, DISC. Closed Oct 25–Apr 1.

The entrance to this green-shuttered villa is under a vaulted arcade near the ferry landing. Wisteria climbs over the iron balustrades of the lake-view terraces, and the entrance hall's vaulted ceilings are supported by massive timbers and granite Doric columns. The main section was built around 1720, though most of what you see today was added around 1880. For 150 years, the Florence has been run by the Ketzlar family, and you'll probably be welcomed by the charming Roberta Ketzlar, her brother

Ronald, and their mother, Friedl. The guest rooms are scattered amid spacious sitting and dining areas and often have high ceilings, antiques, and lake views. All have excellent mattresses and tiled bathrooms. In the 1990s, the hotel was vastly improved, with the addition of a gourmet restaurant and the America Bar, which becomes a kind of jazz club on Sunday evening.

TREMEZZO

Reached by frequent ferries from Bellagio, Tremezzo, 48 miles (77km) north of Milan and 18 miles (29km) north of Como, is another popular west-shore resort that opens onto a panoramic view of Lake Como. Around the town is a district known as Tremezzina, with luxuriant vegetation like citrus trees, palms, cypresses, and magnolias. Since Tremezzo lies in the middle of the western bank of Como, it's easy to use it as a base for taking scenic drives either to the north of the lake or else all the way south to the city of Como. From here, it's also easy to visit Villa Carlotta (see the section on Bellagio, above), but note that accommodations in Tremezzo are much more limited than those in Bellagio.

The **tourist office** is at Via Regina 3 (☎ **0344-40-493**). May to October, it's open Monday to Wednesday and Friday to Saturday 9am to noon and 3:30 to 6:30pm.

ACCOMMODATIONS

Grand Hotel Tremezzo Palace. Via Regina 8, 22019 Tremezzo. ☎ **0344-42-491.** Fax 0344-40-201. E-mail: info@grandhoteltremezzo.com. 101 units. MINIBAR TV TEL. 252,000–546,000L ($126–$273) double; 550,000–895,000L ($275–$447.50) suite. Rates include breakfast. AE, CB, DC, MC, V. Closed Nov 15–Feb. Parking 30,000L ($15) in a garage, free outside.

Built in 1910 on a terrace several feet above the lakeside road, this hotel is one of the region's best examples of the Italian Liberty style. In 1990 most of it was discreetly modernized, and the guest rooms on two of the hotel's four floors received air-conditioning. (Many guests still reject the air-conditioning in favor of the lakefront breezes.) The high-ceilinged rooms are comfortable, traditionally furnished, and priced according to views of the lake (most expensive, often with balconies) or the rear park and garden. The bathrooms are neatly arranged, with hair dryers.

Dining/Diversions: There are three restaurants and an outdoor dining terrace (closed during inclement weather). All serve regional and international cuisines. On a platform beside the lake is the Club l'Escale, a bar popular with residents of surrounding communities.

Amenities: Room service, baby-sitting, laundry/valet, very large park, two pools, tennis court, lido beside the lake, jogging track, billiard room, heliport, conference facilities.

Hotel Bazzoni & du Lac. Via Regina 26, 22019 Tremezzo. ☎ **0344-40-403.** Fax 0344-41-651. 126 units. MINIBAR TEL. 175,000–200,000L ($87.50–$100) double. Rates include breakfast. AE, DC, MC, V. Closed Oct 10–Apr 24. Ferry from Ballagio or hydrofoil from Como.

There was an older hotel on this spot during Napoléon's era, bombed by the British 5 days after the official end of World War II. Today the reconstructed hotel is a collection of glass-and-concrete walls, with prominent balconies. It's one of the best choices in a resort town filled with hotels of grander format but much less desirable rooms. They were renovated early in 1999, with new mattresses, private safes, and redone bathrooms that now contain hair dryers. The main restaurant has a baronial but unused fireplace, contemporary frescoes of the boats on the lake, and scattered carvings. The pleasantly furnished sitting rooms include antique architectural elements from older buildings. A summer restaurant near the entrance is constructed like a small island of glass walls.

Nearby Accommodations

✪ **Grand Hotel Victoria.** Via Lungolago Castelli 7–11, 22017 Menaggio. ☎ **0344-32-003.** Fax 0344-32-992. . E-mail: hotelvictoria@palacehotel.it. 53 units. A/C MINIBAR TV TEL. 330,000–390,000L ($165–$195) double; from 500,000L ($250) junior suite. Rates include breakfast. Half-board 60,000L ($30) per person. AE, DC, MC, V. Free parking.

This is one of the best hotels on the lake, built in 1806. It's been renovated over the years, but lovely old touches remain, like the ornate plasterwork of the ceiling vaults. The modern furniture and amenities in the guest rooms include bathroom tiles designed by Valentino. The rooms are generally spacious, each with a quality mattress. The bathrooms come with hair dryers. The beach in front of the hotel is one of the best spots on Lake Como for windsurfing, especially between 3 and 7pm.

Dining/Diversions: Guests enjoy drinks on the outdoor terrace near the stone columns of the tree-shaded portico or in the antique-filled public rooms. The restaurant serves well-prepared food under art nouveau chandeliers and an embellished ceiling showing the fruits of an Italian harvest and mythical beasts.

Amenities: Room service, baby-sitting, laundry/valet, pool, beach, tennis court, private boats.

DINING

Al Veluu. Via Rogaro 11, Rogaro di Tremezzo. ☎ **0344-40-510.** Reservations recommended. Main courses 20,000–35,000L ($10–$17.50). AE, MC, V. Wed–Mon noon–2pm and 7:30–10pm. Closed Nov–Mar 1. LOMBARD/INTERNATIONAL.

Al Veluu, 1 mile north of the resort in the hills, is an excellent regional restaurant with plenty of relaxed charm and personalized attention from owner Carlo Antonini and his son, Luca. The terrace tables offer a panoramic sweep of the lake, and the rustic dining room with its fireplace and big windows is a welcome refuge in inclement weather. Most of the produce comes freshly picked from the garden; even the butter is homemade, and the best cheeses come from a local farmer. The menu is based on the flavorful cuisine of northern Italy. Examples are *missoltini* (dried fish from the lake, marinated, and grilled with olive oil and vinegar), *penne al Veluu* (with spicy tomato sauce), *risotto al Veluu* (with champagne sauce and fresh green peppers), and an unusual lamb pâté.

6 Lake Maggiore

The waters of Lake Maggiore wash up on the banks of Piedmont and Lombardy in Italy, but its more austere northern basin (Locarno, for example) lies in the mountainous region of Switzerland. It stretches more than 40 miles (64km) and is 6$^1/_2$ miles (10km) at its widest. A wealth of natural beauty awaits you: mellowed lakeside villas, dozens of lush gardens, sparkling waters, and panoramic views. A veil of mist seems to hover at times, especially in early spring and late autumn.

Maggiore is a most rewarding lake to visit from Milan, especially because of the Borromean Islands in its center (most easily reached from Stresa). If you have time, drive around the entire basin; on a more limited schedule, you may find the resort-studded western shore the most scenic.

LAKE MAGGIORE ESSENTIALS

GETTING THERE The major resort of the lake, Stresa, is just 1 hour by **train** from Milan on the Milan–Domodossola line. Service is every hour, costing 7,200 to

15,000L ($3.60–$7.50) one way, depending on the train. For information and schedules, call ☎ **1478-880-88.**

If you have a **car** and are in Milan, take a 51-mile (82km) drive northwest along A8 (staying on E62 out of Gallarate until it joins SS33 up the western shore of the lake) to Stresa.

GETTING AROUND S33 goes up the west side of the lake to Verbania, where it becomes S34 on its way to the Swiss town of Locarno, about 25 miles (40km) away. If you want to drive around the lake, you'll have to clear Swiss Customs before passing through such famed resorts as Ascona and eventually Locarno. From Locarno you can head south again along the eastern, less touristy shore, which becomes SS493 on the Italy side. At Luino, you can cut off on SS233, then A8 to return to Milan, or continue along the lake shore (the road becomes SS629) to the southern point again, where you can get E62 back toward Milan.

Cruising Lake Maggiore with modern **boats** and fast **hydrofoils** is great fun. There's a frequent ferry service for cars and passengers between Intra (Verbania) and Laveno. Boats leave from Piazza Marconi along Corso Umberto I in Stresa. For boat schedules, contact the **Navigazione Sul Lago Maggiore,** Viale F. Baracca 1 (☎ **0322-46-651**), in the lakeside town of Arona.

STRESA

On the western shore, 407 miles (655km) northwest of Rome and 51 miles (82km) northwest of Milan, **Stresa** has skyrocketed from a simple village of fisherfolk to a first-class international resort. Its vantage on the lake is almost unparalleled, and its accommodations level is superior to that of other Maggiore resorts in Italy. The scene of sporting activities and an international **Festival of Musical Weeks** (beginning in July), it swings into action in April, stays hopping all summer, then quiets down at the end of October. For information call Settimane Musicali (☎ **0323-310-95**).

The **tourist office** is at Via Principe Tommaso 70–72 (☎ **0323-30-150**). April to September, hours are Monday to Saturday 8:30am to 12:30pm and 3 to 6:15pm and Sunday 9am to noon; October to March, hours are Monday to Saturday 8:30am to 12:30pm and Monday to Friday 3 to 6:15pm.

Near the resort of Pallanza, north of Stresa, the **Botanical Gardens (Giardini Botanici) at Villa Taranto,** Via Vittorio Veneto 111, Verbania-Pallanza (☎ **0323-556-667**), spread over more than 50 acres of the Castagnola Promontory jutting out into Lake Maggiore. In this dramatic setting between the mountains and the lake, more than 20,000 species of plants from all over the world thrive in a cultivated institution begun in 1931 by a Scotsman, Capt. Neil McEacharn. Plants range from rhododendrons and azaleas to specimens from such faraway places as Louisiana. Seasonal exhibits include fields of Dutch tulips (80,000 of them), Japanese magnolias, giant water lilies, cotton plants, and rare varieties of hydrangeas. The formal gardens are carefully laid out with ornamental fountains, statues, and reflection pools. Among the more ambitious creations is the elaborate irrigation system that pumps water from the lake to all parts of the gardens and the Terrace Gardens, complete with waterfalls and pool.

March 28 to October 31, the gardens are open daily 8:30am to 6:30pm. To arrange an hour-long guided tour (groups only), contact the **Palazzo dei Congressi di Stresa** (☎ **0323-30-389**). You may also take a round-trip **boat ride** from Stresa, docking at the Villa Taranto pier adjoining the entrance to the gardens. You pay an admission of 14,000L ($7).

ACCOMMODATIONS

Albergo Ariston. Corso Italia 60, 28049 Stresa. ☎ and fax **0323-31-195.** 11 units. 150,000L ($75) double. Rates include breakfast. Half-board 90,000L ($45) per person. AE, DC, MC, V. Closed Dec–Apr 1. Free parking.

Here's a good bargain. The hotel is listed as third class, but its comfort is superior. The small guest rooms are well kept and attractively furnished, each with a good mattress. Nonguests can stop in for a meal, ordering lunch or dinner on the terrace, which has a panoramic view of the lake and gardens. Your hosts are the Balconi family.

✪ **Grand Hotel des Iles Borromées.** Corso Umberto I 67, 28838 Stresa. ☎ **0323-938-938.** Fax 0323-938-32405. www.stresa.net/hotel/stresa.htm. E-mail: borromees@stresa.net. 175 units. A/C MINIBAR TV TEL. 450,000–570,000L ($225–$285) double; 920,000–2,000,000L ($460–$1,000) suite. Rates include breakfast. AE, DC, MC, V. Free parking.

On the edge of the lake in a flowering garden, this is by far Stresa's leading resort hotel. You can see the Borromean Islands from many rooms, which are furnished in an Italian/French Empire style, including rich ormolu, burnished hardwoods, plush carpets, and pastel colors. The bathrooms look as if every quarry in Italy were scoured for matched marble. The hotel opened in 1863, attracting titled notables and guests like J. P. Morgan. Hemingway sent the hero of *A Farewell to Arms* here to escape World War I. The elegant public rooms, with two-tone ornate plasterwork and crystal chandeliers, once hosted a top-level meeting among the heads of state of Italy, Great Britain, and France in an attempt to stave off World War II.

The hotel also operates a 27-room Residenza in a separate building, where the prices are 20% lower and the rooms decorated in a modern style, with air-conditioning, TVs, and minibars.

Dining: The restaurant serves specialties of Lombardy and Piedmont. Special dishes include fillet of perch with sage and tenderloin cooked on a black stone.

Amenities: Room service, laundry, baby-sitting, medically supervised health/exercise program, fitness room, two outdoor pools, tennis court, sauna.

Hotel Astoria. Corso Umberto I 31, 28038 Stresa. ☎ **0323-32-566.** Fax 0323-933-785. www.stresa.net/hotel/astoria. E-mail: h.astoria@interbusiness.it. 99 units. A/C MINIBAR TV TEL. 200,000–300,000L ($100–$150) double; 370,000L ($185) suite. Rates include breakfast. AE, DC, MC, V. Closed late Oct–Mar 27. Free parking.

A 5-minute walk from the rail station or the center of Stresa, this hotel fronting the lake was partially rebuilt in 1993, giving an even more modern gloss to an already contemporary hotel. Each room has a triangular balcony jutting out for the view. The rooms are streamlined and spacious, each with a firm mattress and a tiled bathroom. The public lounges have walls of glass opening toward the lake view and the garden. The portion of the dining room favored by most guests is the open-air front terrace, where under shelter you dine on good Italian and international cuisine. There's also a heated pool, Turkish bath, small gym, roof garden, and Jacuzzi.

Hotel Moderno. Via Cavour 33, 28838 Stresa. ☎ **0323-933-773.** Fax 0323-933-775. www.hms.it. E-mail: moderno@hms.it. 52 units. TV TEL. 210,000L ($105) double. Rates include breakfast. AE, DC, MC, V. Closed Nov–Mar. Parking 18,000L ($9).

A block from the lake and boat-landing stage, the Moderno lies in the center of Stresa. It dates from the turn of the 20th century, but subsequent modernization, most recently in 1989, has rendered the building's original lines unrecognizable. The small guest rooms have a personalized decor and good beds. The Moderno has three restaurants, unusual for such a small hotel.

Regina Palace. Corso Umberto I 33, 28049 Stresa. ☎ **0323-933-777.** Fax 0323-933-776. www.stresa.net/hotel/regina. E-mail: h.regina@stresa.net. 166 units. MINIBAR TV TEL. 440,000L ($220) double; from 700,000L ($350) suite. Rates include breakfast. AE, DC, MC, V. Closed Oct–Easter. Parking 25,000L ($12.50) in garage, free outside.

The Regina was built in 1908 in a boomerang shape whose central curve faces the lakefront. Inside, the art deco columns of illuminated glass are topped with gilded Corinthian capitals, and a wide marble stairwell is flanked with carved oak lions. The guest roster has included George Bernard Shaw, Ernest Hemingway, Umberto I of Italy, and Princess Margaret. Lately, about half the guests are American, many with the tour groups that stream through town. The rooms are equipped with all the modern comforts, and many have views of the Borromean Islands. The tiled bathrooms contain hair dryers. Facilities include a pool, tennis and squash courts, a Jacuzzi, saunas, a health club, and a Turkish bath. The hotel also has two dining rooms, one reserved only for guests; the other is the Charleston.

DINING

Ristorante Pescatore. Vicolo del Poncivo 1. ☎ **0323-31-986.** Main courses 26,000–32,000L ($13–$16). MC, V. Fri–Wed noon–3pm and 6–10pm. SPANISH/ITALIAN SEAFOOD.

One of the smallest (only 30 seats) restaurants in Stresa occupies a single dining room in a simple building in the historic core. An additional trio of tables extend into a garden. The focus is on seafood that's fresh, generously portioned, and sometimes prepared in the national style of Spain, since the owners and some of the staff are from the province of Galicia. Look for a succulent *zarzuela de pescada* (fish stew) and a *paella* you'd imagine came from Valencia, redolent with shellfish, saffron-flavored rice, fish, chicken, and sausage. More authentically Italian are *zuppe di pesce* (fish soup) or any of a medley of grilled or braised fish, most of which were hauled out of the sea only a few hours before you eat them. Favorite garnishes are garlic-and-wine sauce, lemon and oil, or a garlicky green sauce with pesto.

Taverna del Pappagallo. Via Principessa Margherita 46. ☎ **0323-30-411.** Reservations recommended. Main courses 18,000–25,000L ($9–$12.50); pizzas 8,000–20,000L ($4–$10). No credit cards. Thurs–Mon 11:30am–2:30pm and 6:30–10:30pm. ITALIAN/PIZZA.

This formal little garden restaurant and tavern is operated by the Ghiringhelli brothers, who turn out some of the least expensive meals in Stresa. Specialties include gnocchi, many types of scaloppine, *scalamino allo spiedoe fagioli* (grilled sausage with beans), and *saltimbocca alla romana* (a veal-and-prosciutto dish). At night, pizza is king (try the pizza Regina). The service has a personal touch.

THE BORROMEAN ISLANDS

In the middle of Lake Maggiore lie the **Borromean Islands,** a chain of tiny islands that were turned into sites of lavish villas and gardens by the Borromeo clan. Boats leave from Stresa about every 30 minutes in summer, and the trip takes 3 hours. The **navigation offices** at Stresa's center port (☎ **0323-30-393**) are open daily 7am to 7pm. The best deal is to buy an excursion ticket for 18,000L ($9) entitling you to go back and forth to all three islands during the day.

Dominating the **Isola Bella (Beautiful Island)** is the major sight: the 17th-century **Borromeo Palazzo** (☎ **0323-30-556**). From the front, the figurines in the garden seem straight off the top of a wedding cake. Napoléon slept here. On conducted tours, you're shown through the airy palace, whose views are remarkable. A special feature is the six grotto rooms, built piece by piece like a mosaic. In addition, there's a collection of quite good tapestries, with gory, cannibalistic animal scenes. Outside, the white peacocks in the garden enchant year after year. March 27 to October 24, the palace and its grounds are open daily 9am to noon and 1:30 to 5:30pm. Admission is 14,000L ($7).

The largest of the chain, the **Isola Madre (Mother Island)** is visited chiefly for its **Botanical Garden (Orto Botanico).** You wander through a setting ripe with pomegranates, camellias, wisteria, rhododendrons, bougainvillea, hibiscus, hydrangea, magnolias, and even a cypress tree from the Himalayas. You can also visit the 17th-century **palace** (☎ **0323-31-261**), which contains a rich collection of 17th- and 18th-century furnishings. Of particular interest is a collection of 19th-century French and German dolls belonging to Countess Borromeo and the livery of the House of Borromeo. The unique 18th-century marionette theater, complete with scripts, stage scenery, and devices for sound, light, and other special effects, is on display. Peacocks, pheasants, and other birds live and roam freely on the grounds. March 27 to October 24, the palace is open daily 9am to 12:30pm and 1:30 to 5:30pm. Admission to the palace and grounds is 14,000L ($7).

The **Isola del Pescatori (Fisher's Island)** doesn't have major sights or lavish villas, but in many ways it's the most colorful. Less a stage setting than its two neighbors, it's inhabited by fisherfolk who live in cottages that haven't been converted to souvenir shops. It's a lovely place for a stroll.

Piedmont & Valle d'Aosta

11

Towering snowcapped alpine peaks; oleander, poplar, and birch trees; sky-blue lakes; river valleys and flowering meadows; the chamois and the wild boar; medieval castles; Roman ruins and folklore; the taste of vermouth on home ground; Fiats and fashion—northwestern Italy is a fascinating area to explore.

The Piedmont (*Piemonte*) is largely agricultural, though its capital, Turin, is one of Italy's front-ranking industrial cities (with more mechanics per square foot than any other location in Europe). The influence of France is strongly felt, both in the dialect and in the kitchen.

The Valle d'Aosta (really a series of valleys) traditionally has been associated with Piedmont, but in 1948 it was given wide-ranging autonomy. Most of the residents in this least-populated district of Italy speak French. Closing in Valle d'Aosta to the north on the French and Swiss frontiers are the tallest mountains in Europe, including Mont Blanc (15,780 ft.), the Matterhorn (14,690 ft.), and Monte Rosa (15,200 ft.). The road tunnels of Great St. Bernard and Mont Blanc (opened in 1965) connect France and Italy.

1 Turin

140 miles (225km) SW of Milan, 108 miles (174km) NW of Genoa, 414 miles (667km) NW of Rome

In Turin (Torino), the capital of Piedmont, the Italian Risorgimento (unification movement) was born. While the United States was fighting its Civil War, Turin became the first capital of a unified Italy, a position it later lost to Florence. Turin was once the capital of Sardinia. Much of the city's history is associated with the House of Savoy, a dynasty that reigned for 9 centuries, even presiding over the kingdom of Italy when Vittorio Emanuele II was proclaimed king in 1861. The family ruled, at times in name only, until the monarchy was abolished in 1946.

In spite of extensive bombings, Turin found renewed prosperity after World War II, largely because of the Fiat manufacturers based here (it has been called the Detroit of Italy). Many buildings were destroyed, but much of its 17th- and 18th-century look remains. Located on the Po River, Turin is well laid out, with wide streets, historic squares, churches, and parks. For years it has had a reputation as the least-visited and least-known of Italy's major cities, but it's become an increasingly dynamic center for industry and the arts.

Turin's biggest draw, the **Cattedrale di San Giovanni,** home to the **Shroud of Turin,** was damaged by fire in 1997. The Chapel of the Holy Shroud, where the silver reliquary that protects the controversial Christian symbol is usually on display, and the west wing of the neighboring Royal Palace sustained most of the damage. Luckily, the shroud had been moved into the cathedral itself because the dome of its chapel was being renovated.

Turin is one of Italy's richest cities, with some million Turinese, many of whom are immigrants who came here to get a piece of the pie. This "Car Capital of Italy" (also now home to high-tech and aerospace industries) is surrounded by some hideous suburbs that are ever-growing, but its Crocietta district is home to some of the most aristocratic residences in Italy and its inner core is one of grace and harmony. One of Italy's most feared and powerful men, Gianni Agnelli, lives in Turin. The city was also once the home of Antonio Gramsci, who staged "occupations" of the Fiat factory and later helped found the Italian Communist Party before dying in a Fascist prison. On a cultural note, Turin is the center of modern Italian writing; it was here that such major authors as Primo Levi, Cesare Pavese, and Italo Calvino were first published. Major exhibitions and shows are being booked all the time.

Note that Turin has been named as the host city for the **Olympic Winter Games** in the year 2006. Details of the upcoming event can be learned on the Web at www.torino2006.it. Turin itself will host the opening and closing ceremonies, the Olympic Village, and the press operations, as well as some of the events. Other events, such as downhill skiing, will be held in small towns just outside Turin.

ESSENTIALS

GETTING THERE Alitalia flies into the **Caselle International Airport (Aeroporto Internazionale di Caselle;** ☎ **011-567-6361** for flight information or 041/567-8124 for tourism info), about 9 miles (14km) north of Turin. It receives direct scheduled flights from 22 cities (7 domestic and 15 from major European centers); it's used by 13 scheduled carriers operating regular flights. Its Air Passenger Terminal is one of Europe's most technologically advanced structures, covering a total area of more than 43,000 square yards and handling up to three million passengers a year.

Turin is a major **rail** terminus, with arrivals at **Stazione di Porta Nuova,** Corso Vittorio Emanuele (☎ **011-561-3333**), or **Stazione Centrale,** Corso Vittorio Emanuele II (☎ **1478-880-88**), in the heart of the city. It takes 1¼ hours to reach Turin by train from Milan, but anywhere from 9 to 11 hours to reach Turin from Rome, depending on the connection. The one-way fare from Milan is 18,000L ($9) and from Rome 55,000L ($27.50).

If you have a **car** and are coming from France via the Mont Blanc Tunnel, you can pick up the autostrada at Aosta. You can also reach Turin by autostrada from both the French and the Italian Rivieras, and there's an easy link from Milan.

VISITOR INFORMATION Go to the office of **APT,** Piazza Castello 161 (☎ **011-535-901**), open daily 8:30am to 7:30pm. There's another office at the Porta Nuova train station (☎ **011-531-327**), open the same hours.

SPECIAL EVENTS Turin stages two major cultural fests every year: the **Giarni d'Estate festival** in July, with programs devoted to dance, music, and theater; and the monthlong **Settembre Musica** in September, with dozens of classical music performances at various parts of the city. For details about these festivals, contact the **Assesorato per la Cultura,** Via San Francisco do Paolo 3 (☎ **011-442-4715**).

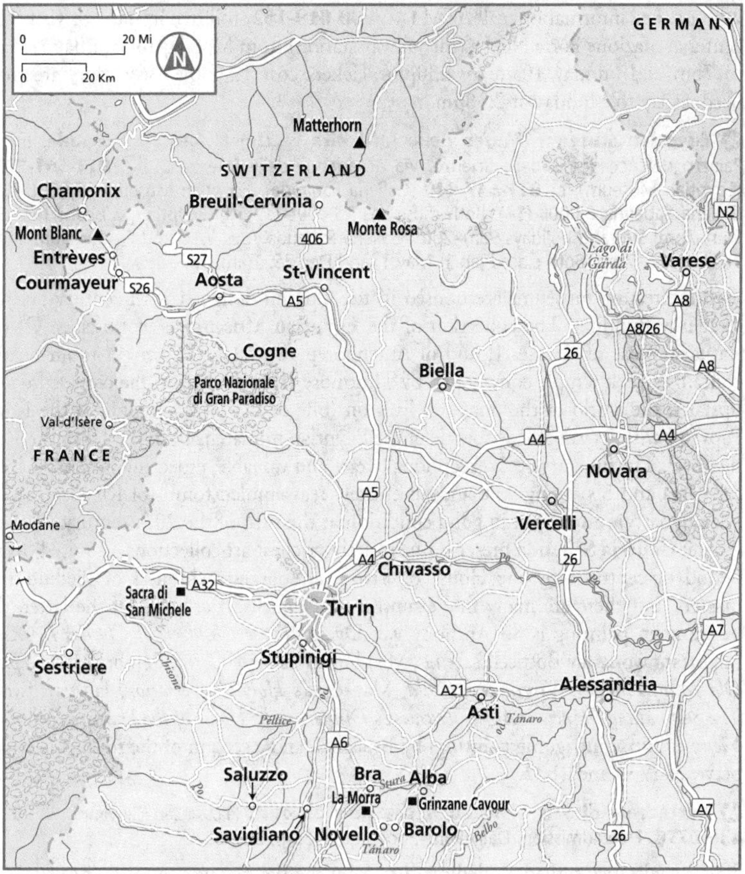

EXPLORING THE CITY

Stazione di Porta Nuova is in the very center of town. The Po River, which runs through Turin, lies to the east of the station. One of the main arteries running through Turin is **Corso Vittorio Emanuele II,** directly north of the station. Turin is also a city of fashion, and you may want to walk along the major shopping street, **Via Roma,** which begins north of the station, leading eventually to two squares that join each other, **Piazza Castello** and **Piazza Reale.** In the middle of Via Roma is **Piazza San Carlo,** the heartbeat of Turin.

Begin your explorations at ✪ **Piazza San Carlo.** Though it was heavily bombed during World War II, it's still the loveliest and most unified square in the city. It was designed by Carlo di Castellamonte in the 17th century and covers about $3^1/_2$ acres. The two churches are those of **Santa Cristina** and **San Carlo.** Some of the most prestigious figures in Italy once sat on this square, sipping coffee and plotting the unification of Italy.

ATM, the Public Transportation Company of Turin, offers a **"Touristbus"** that brings visitors around the city with a guide. Tours depart from Piazza Castello and last

2 hours. For information, call ATM (☎ **800-019-152,** toll free in Italy) or visit their center at Stazione Porta Nuova (the railway station) from Monday to Saturday 7:15am to 7pm and Sunday 10am to 4:30pm. Tickets cost 12,000L ($6); tours are from Wednesday to Monday at 2:30pm.

✪ **Egyptian Museum (Museo delle Antichità Egizie) & Galleria Sabauda.** In the Palazzo dell'Accademia delle Scienze, Via Accademia delle Scienze 6. ☎ **011-561-7776** (Egyptian Museum), or **011-547-440** (Galleria Sabauda). Egyptian Museum 12,000L ($6). Galleria Sabauda 8,000L ($4). Both museums 15,000L ($7.50). Egyptian Museum Tues–Sat 9am–7pm; Sun and holidays 9am–2pm. Galleria Sabauda Tues–Wed and Fri–Sun 9am–2pm; Thurs 10am–7pm. Both closed Jan 1, May 1, and Dec 25. Tram: 18.

Two interesting museums are housed in the Guarini-designed 17th-century Science Academy Building. The collection of the **Egyptian Museum** is world-class. Of the statuary, those of Ramses II and of Amenhotep II are best known. A room nearby contains a rock temple consecrated by Thutmose III in Nubia. In the crowded wings upstairs, the world of the pharaohs lives on (one of the prized exhibits is the Royal Papyrus, with its valuable chronicle of the Egyptian monarchs from the 1st to the 17th dynasty). The funerary art is exceptionally rare and valuable, especially the chapel built for Maia and his young wife and an entirely reassembled tomb (of Kha and Merit, 18th dynasty), discovered in good condition at the turn of the 20th century.

The **Galleria Sabauda** presents one of Italy's richest art collections, acquired over a period of centuries by the House of Savoy. The largest exhibit is of Piedmontese masters, but there are many fine examples of Flemish art as well. Of the latter, the best-known painting is Sir Anthony van Dyck's *Three Children of Charles I.* Other important works are Botticelli's *Venus,* Memling's *Passion of Christ,* Rembrandt's *Sleeping Old Man,* Duccio's *Virgin and Child,* Mantegna's *Holy Conversation,* Jan van Eyck's *The Stigmata of Francis of Assisi,* Veronese's *Dinner in the House of the Pharisee,* Bellotto's *Views of Turin,* intriguing paintings by Brueghel, and a section of the royal collections between 1730 and 1832.

✪ **Cattedrale di San Giovanni & the Holy Shroud.** Piazza San Giovanni. ☎ **011-436-0790.** Free admission. Daily 9am–noon and 3–5pm. Bus: 63.

This Renaissance cathedral, dedicated to John the Baptist, was swept by fire on April 12, 1997, with major damage sustained by Guarini's **Chapel of the Holy Shroud (Cappella della Santissima Sindone),** the usual resting place of the contested Christian relic. Fortunately, the shroud itself was undamaged. The shroud made world headlines in 1998 when it was put on public display for the first time in 20 years. At its unveiling for only the fourth time in this century, on the occasion of the cathedral's 500th anniversary, some three million pilgrims traveled to Turin to see it. Most visitors to the cathedral must content themselves with a series of dramatically backlit photos of the relic near the entrance. The chapel is somberly clad in black marble, but as if to suggest that better things await in the heavens, it ascends to an airy, light-flooded, six-tiered dome, one of the masterpieces of Italian baroque architecture.

The shroud is rarely on view. It's usually tucked away at the **Holy Shroud Museum (Museo della Santissima Sindone),** Via San Domenico 28 (☎ **011-436-5832**), a small, dusty library/research center near the cathedral that's open only to scholars and church officials.

Royal Palace (Palazzo Reale). Piazza Castello. ☎ **011-436-1455.** Admission 8,000L ($4). Tues–Sun 9am–7pm. Bus: 63.

The palace the Savoys called home was begun in 1645. The halls, the columned ballroom by Palagi, the tea salon, and the Queen's Chapel are richly baroque in style. The original architect was Amedeo de Castellamonte, but numerous builders supplied

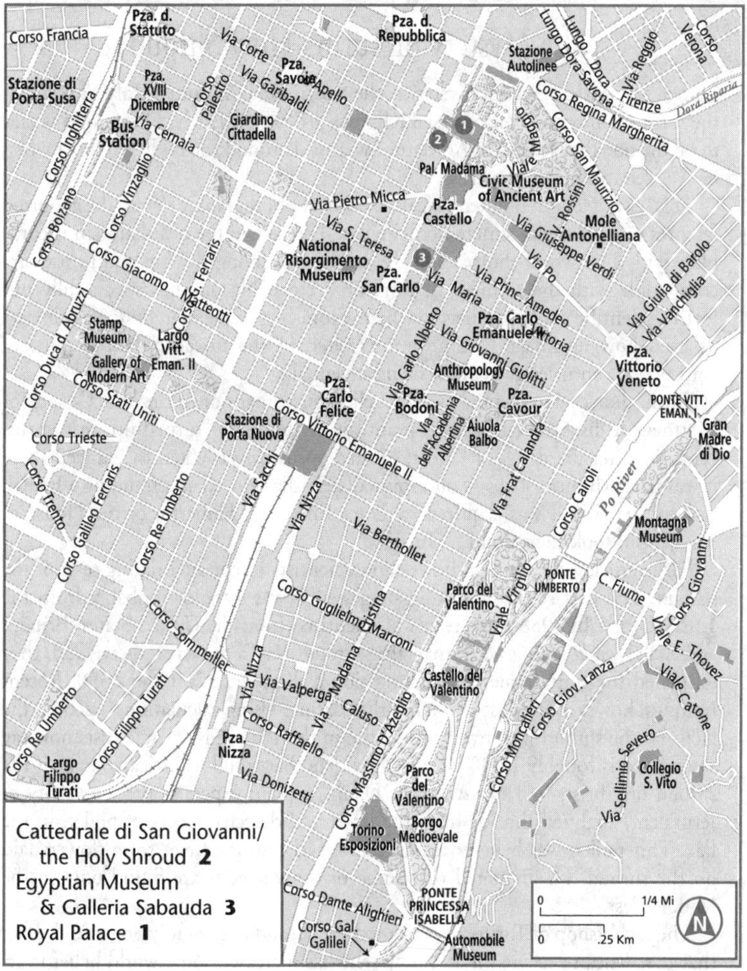

ideas and effort before the palazzo was completed. As in nearly all ducal residences of that period, the most bizarre room is the one bedecked with flowering chinoiserie.

The Throne Room is of interest, as is the tapestry-draped Banqueting Hall. Le Nôtre, the famous Frenchman, mapped out the gardens, which may also be visited along with the Royal Armory (*Armeria Reale*), containing a large collection of arms and armor and many military mementos. Guided tours are offered every 20 minutes.

The west wing of the palace was damaged when fire spread through the chapel of the neighboring cathedral on April 12, 1997. Restoration of this wing could take years.

SHOPPING

The most adventurous shopping is at the **Gran Balôn,** an old-fashioned flea market set up every second Sunday in Piazza della Repubblica. Some of the merchandise peddled here is from the homes of various immigrants.

Some of the best-known drinks in the world are produced in Torino. For the best sampling, head for **Paissa,** Piazza San Carlo 196 (☎ **011-562-8364**), where among

The Mystery of Turin's Holy Shroud

One of the world's greatest mysteries, the **Santissima Sindone (Holy Shroud)** is the most famous and controversial religious artifact on Earth. The shroud is said to be the one that Joseph of Arimathea wrapped around the body of Christ when he was removed from the cross.

This 4-yard length of linen reveals, in almost photographic detail, the agonized features of a man who suffered crucifixion. The face of the bearded man is complete with a crown of thorns, and the marks of a thonged whip and bruises are compatible with the torment of carrying a cross. No one has successfully put forth a scientific explanation as to why the imprints of the man on the cloth exist or even how its image became impregnated in the threads. Photography, of course, was centuries away from being invented.

Turin didn't always possess this relic. First mentioned in the Gospel of Matthew, it disappeared in history until it mysteriously "turned up" in Cyprus, centuries after the death of Christ. From Cyprus, it was taken to France, where it was first exhibited in 1354 and immediately denounced as a fraud by a French bishop. In 1578 it was acquired by Duca Emanuele Filiberto, of the House of Savoy, who took the shroud to Turin.

For centuries, the church didn't allow scientists to conduct dating tests of the shroud. The first scientific testing suggested it was a fraud, probably from the 12th century. In 1988 three teams of scientists (from the United States, Britain, and Italy) each announced that the shroud was a clever forgery, and they estimated the time frame of its fabrication as between 1260 and 1390. Recent findings, however, propose a much earlier dating. Using calculations based on the fact that the shroud was involved in a fire in the 16th century, scientists now say the shroud is roughly 1,800 years old—a date that could realistically make it the shroud of Christ. In 1997 Avinoam Danin, a plant expert at the University of Jerusalem, analyzed threads from the linen and detected traces of pollen in the flax. This pollen was believed to have dropped into the linen from flowers laid on the shroud. Danin stated that some of those species are found only in the Middle East.

The archbishop of Turin has presented the shroud to the Holy See, and the fact that the Vatican accepted it as a holy relic has increased some world belief in its validity. However, the Vatican has refrained from pronouncing it "the true shroud." The shroud remains encased in a silver casket. Only two keys can unlock the casket, one held by the archbishop of Turin and the other by the Palatine cardinals, church seniors who are based permanently in the Vatican. The key unlocks only the casket—not the mystery of the shroud.

the wine and food items available, you'll find the best deals on Cinzano and Martini & Rossi vermouths.

ACCOMMODATIONS

Like Milan, Turin is an industrial city first and a tourist center second. Most of its hotels were built after 1945 with an eye toward modern comfort but not necessarily style.

EXPENSIVE

✪ **Jolly Hotel Principi di Piemonte.** Via Gobetti 15, 10123 Torino. ☎ **800/221-2626** or 800/247-1277 in the U.S., or 011-562-9693. Fax 011-562-0270. www.jollyhotels.it. E-mail: principidipiemonte@jollyhotels.it. 107 units. A/C MINIBAR TV TEL. 390,000–450,000L ($195–$225) double; from 750,000L ($375) suite. Rates include breakfast. AE, DC, MC, V. Parking 35,000L ($17.50). Bus: 9.

A favorite of Fiat executives, this 10-story hotel is in the city center, near the rail station. It dates from 1939, but some of Italy's finest architects and designers were involved in its wholesale revamping. The public rooms are grand, with bas-relief ceilings, gold wall panels, silk draperies, Louis XVI–style chairs, and baroque marble sideboards. The guest rooms, medium size to spacious, are traditionally furnished and perfectly maintained, containing fine draperies and spreads, upholstered chairs, generous storage space, and quality mattresses. The bathrooms have deluxe toiletries and hair dryers.

Dining/Diversions: There are both formal and informal dining rooms serving Piedmontese food, as well as a fashionable drinking lounge.

Amenities: Concierge, room service, laundry/dry cleaning, baby-sitting, secretarial services, access to nearby health club.

✪ **Villa Sassi.** Via Traforo del Pino 47, 10132 Torino. ☎ **011-898-0556.** Fax 011-898-0095. www.villasassi.com. E-mail: info@villassi.com. 17 units. A/C MINIBAR TV TEL. 420,000L ($210) double; 520,000L ($260) junior suite. Rates include breakfast. AE, DC, MC, V. Closed Aug. Bus: 61. Tram: 15.

For tranquillity, head to this 17th-century–style estate 4 miles (6km) east of the town center, surrounded by park grounds. The impressive original architectural details are still intact, like the entrance hall's wooden staircase. The drawing room features an overscale mural and life-sized baroque figures holding bronze torchiers, and the intimate drinking salon has red-velvet walls, a bronze chandelier, and low, cushioned seating. Each guest room has been individually decorated with antiques and reproductions, plus a quality mattress and a perfectly kept bathroom with a hair dryer. The manager sees that the hotel is run in a personal way.

Dining: See "Dining," below, for a recommendation of El Toulà–Villa Sassi.

Amenities: Concierge, room service, laundry, secretarial services.

MODERATE TO INEXPENSIVE

Hotel Due Mondi. Via Saluzzo 3, 10125 Torino. ☎ **011-650-5084.** Fax 011-669-9383. www.hotelduemondi.it. E-mail: duemondi@hotelduemondi.it. 43 units. TV TEL. 200,000–240,000L ($100–$120) double. Buffet breakfast 20,000L ($10). AE, DC, MC, V. Closed Aug 10–20. Bus: 52. Tram: 1 or 9.

Located off Corso Vittorio Emanuele and within walking distance of Stazione di Porta Nuova, this little hotel is near the top for those seeking old-fashioned yet affordable grace. Everything is smartly outfitted, often in dark patterns and woods. The guest rooms are medium in size, and about 30 are air-conditioned. The best are those on the third and fourth floors because they have been recently renewed. The bathrooms are well equipped, with a little private sauna in each. Breakfast is the only meal served, but there are many restaurants nearby. Amenities include a concierge, room service, laundry/dry cleaning, and secretarial services.

Hotel Genio. Corso Vittorio Emanuele II 47, 10125 Torino. ☎ **011-650-5771.** Fax 011-650-8264. www.hotelres.it. E-mail: hotel.genio@torino.hotelres.it. 109 units. A/C MINIBAR TV TEL. 250,000–320,000L ($125–$160) double. Rates include breakfast. AE, CB, DC, MC, V. Parking 20,000L ($10). Bus: 9 or 18. Tram: 52, 67, or 68.

Built at the end of the 19th century, this four-story hotel in the center of town was renovated into a streamlined modern format in 1990. Its accommodations contain a comfortable blend of contemporary and early-20th-century furniture and have double-paned windows for soundproofing. They're small but reasonably comfortable, each with a firm mattress and a compact tiled bathroom.

Hotel Piemontese. Via Berthollet 21, 10125 Torino. ☎ **011-669-8101.** Fax 011-669-0571. www.hotelres.it. E-mail: hotel.piemontese@hotelres.it. 40 units. A/C MINIBAR TV TEL. 180,000–200,000L ($90–$100) double; 220,000–260,000L ($110–$130) suite. Rates include breakfast. AE, DC, MC, V. Parking 15,000L ($7.50). Tram: 1, 9, or 18.

The Piemontese is in a 19th-century building near Stazione Centrale, its facade covered with iron balconies and ornate stone trim. The restructured interior is well maintained. The guest rooms range from small to medium, and half of them were renovated in 1998. All are somewhat functionally furnished but equipped with all the standard comforts, such as first-rate mattresses. The small tiled bathrooms have hair dryers. Breakfast, taken in a sunny room, is the only meal served, but nearby restaurants are willing to offer ample fixed-price menus to guests. Laundry and 24-hour room service are available. Guests have access to a nearby sports center with a pool.

DINING

EXPENSIVE

Del Cambio. Piazza Carignano 2. ☎ **011-543-760.** Reservations required. Main courses 32,000–40,000L ($16–$20); fixed-price menu 110,000L ($55). AE, MC, V. Mon–Sat 12:30–2:30pm and 8–10:30pm. Bus: 18. PIEDMONTESE/MEDITERRANEAN.

At Del Cambio you dine in a setting of white-and-gilt walls, crystal chandeliers, and gilt mirrors. Opened in 1757, it's the oldest restaurant in Turin. Statesman Camillo Cavour was a loyal patron, and his regular corner is immortalized with a bronze medallion. The chef has received many culinary honors, and white truffles are featured in many of his specialties. The assorted fresh antipasti are excellent; the best pasta dish is the regional *agnolotti piemontesi.* Among the main dishes, the agnolotti with truffles and the beef braised in Barolo wine deserve special praise. Some trademark specialties derive from old recipes of the southwestern Alps: artichokes stewed with bone marrow and truffles; *girello aromatizzato alla piemontese* (flank steak marinated in sugar, salt, and aromatic herbs, sliced paper-thin and served with parmigiano and vegetables); and *tonno di coniglio à la maniére antica* (rabbit).

✪ **El Toulà–Villa Sassi.** In the Villa Sassi, Via Traforo del Pino 47. ☎ **011-898-0556.** Reservations recommended. Main courses 28,000–40,000L ($14–$20); fixed-price menu 100,000L ($50). AE, DC, MC, V. Mon–Sat noon–2pm and 8–10:30pm. Closed Aug, Dec 24, and Jan 6. Bus: 61. Tram: 15. PIEDMONTESE/INTERNATIONAL.

This 17th-century villa is on the rise of a hill 4 miles (6km) east of the town center. The stylish antique-decorated place has seen the addition of a modern dining room with glass walls (most tables have excellent garden views). Some of the food comes from the villa's own farm—not only the vegetables, fruit, and butter but also the beef.

Wine Tasting

Reds with rich and complex flavors make up most of the wine output of this rugged high-altitude region near Italy's border with France. One of the most interesting vineyards is headquartered in a 15th-century abbey near the hamlet of Alba, south of Turin: **Antiche Cantine dell'Annunziata,** Abbazia dell'Annunziata, La Morra, 12064 Cuneo (☎ **0173/50-185**). If you'd like to drive through the countryside for a little wine tasting and a vineyard tour, call to make an appointment and get detailed directions.

For an appetizer, try the frogs' legs cooked with broth-simmered rice or the *fonduta* (a Piedmont fondue with Fontina cheese and white truffles). If it's featured, try the prized specialty: *camoscio in salmi*—chamois (a goatlike antelope) in a sauce of olive oil, anchovies, and garlic, laced with wine and served with polenta. Other menu items worth noting are agnolotti with a sauce of roasted veal and fresh tomatoes, *nodino di vitello* (roasted veal fillet) with rosemary and sage, and braised sturgeon slices with orange-pepper-cinnamon sauce.

✪ **La Prima Smarrita.** Corso Unione Sovietica 244. ☎ **011-317-9657.** Reservations required. Main courses 26,000–45,000L ($13–$22.50). AE, CB, DC, MC, V. Daily 12:30–3:30pm and 8:30pm–midnight. Bus: 63. Tram: 4. PIEDMONTESE/MEDITERRANEAN.

Hailed as the best restaurant in hard-to-please Turin, La Prima Smarrita lies a short walk from the city center. The owner, Mr. Grossi, is proud of his vast selection of Italian and international wines and his fine Piedmontese fare and innovative Mediterranean dishes. Even a simple fish salad with cherry tomatoes and fresh basil is made with flair. Only the best of regional beef goes into the beef fillet with mushroom-laced cream sauce. Among the pasta dishes, try *tortelli di borraigine* (fresh pasta stuffed with borage, with a savory tomato sauce). You might follow with a main course of sea bass cooked with diced potatoes, green olives, and fresh young artichokes. All the desserts are made fresh daily: Count yourself lucky if the chef has prepared his hazelnut chocolate mousse.

MODERATE TO INEXPENSIVE

Caffè Torino. Piazza San Carlo 204. ☎ **011-545-118.** Main courses 18,000–30,000L ($9–$15). AE, DC, MC, V. Daily 7am–1am. Bus: 9, 12, 58, or 63. ITALIAN.

Opened in 1903, this famous coffeehouse is the best re-creation in Turin of the days of Vittorio Emanuele. It's set on one of the most elegant squares in northern Italy and decorated with faded frescoes, brass and marble inlays, and a somewhat battered 19th-century formality. Don't be surprised if the staff has all kinds of rules about where and when you can be seated. There's a stand-up bar near the entrance, a rather formal dining room off to the side, and a cafe area with tiny tables and unhurried service.

Da Mauro. Via Maria Vittoria 21. ☎ **011-817-0604.** Reservations not accepted. Main courses 15,000–20,000L ($7.50–$10). No credit cards. Tues–Sun noon–2:30pm and 7:30–10pm. Closed July. Tram: 13. ITALIAN/TUSCAN.

Within walking distance of Piazza San Carlo, this place, the best of the town's affordable trattorie, is generally packed. The food is conventional but does have character; the chef borrows freely from most of the gastronomic centers of Italy, though the cuisine is mainly Tuscan. An excellent pasta specialty is the cannelloni. Most main dishes consist of well-prepared fish, veal, and poultry. The desserts are consistently enjoyable.

✪ **Ristorante C'Era una Volta.** Corso Vittorio Emanuele II 41. ☎ **011-655-498.** Reservations recommended. Main courses 18,000–24,000L ($9–$12). Fixed-price menu 50,000L ($25). AE, CB, DC, MC, V. Mon–Sat 8–midnight. Closed Aug. Bus: 52, 67, or 68. Tram: 9 or 18. PIEDMONTESE.

Near the Porta Nuova train station, this restaurant is entered from the busy street through carved doors; you take an elevator one floor above ground level. Because it adheres to classic Piedmontese cuisine, it's a good introduction to the food of the Italian alpine regions. The decor is in the typical style, with hanging copper pots and thick walls of stippled plaster. Fixed-price meals feature an aperitif, a choice of seven or eight antipasti, and two first and two main courses, with vegetables, dessert, and coffee. The fare includes polenta, crepes, rabbit, and guinea fowl. Piedmont's most typical dish served here is *bagna caoda,* raw vegetables dipped into a sauce made with garlic, anchovies, and olive oil.

TURIN AFTER DARK

Turin is the cultural center of northwestern Italy, a major stopover for concert artists performing between Genoa and Milan. The daily newspaper of Piedmont, ***La Stampa,*** lists complete details of current cultural events.

Classical music concerts are presented at the **Auditorium della RAI,** Via Rossini 15 (☎ **011-88-00**), throughout the year, though mainly in winter. Turin is also home to one of the country's leading opera houses, the **Teatro Regio,** Piazza Castello 215 (☎ **011-88-151**). Concerts and leading ballets are also presented here. The box office (☎ **011-881-5241** or 011-881-5242) is open Tuesday to Friday 10:30am to 6pm and Saturday 10:30am to 4pm (closed in August).

Opera and other classical productions are presented in summer outside the gardens of the **Palazzo Reale.** The last remaining government-subsidized (RAI) orchestra performs at Via Nizza 294. The **orchestra hall** (☎ **011-664-4111**) is part of the extensive Lingotto exhibition/conference center that grew out of Fiat's first large-scale automobile assembly plant. Ticket prices vary for each performance.

The city's other nightlife is like a smaller version of Milan. **Alcatraz,** Manzani Po (☎ **011-836-900**), is hypermodern, with an avant-garde design and the latest dance mixes. Its main rival is **Discoteca Atlantide,** Via Monginevro 10 (☎ **011-936-7783**), and the somewhat corny **Lo Scoppiato,** Via Villarbasse 26 (☎ **011-338-567**), where karaoke contests with local wannabes might either intrigue or repel you. Another karaoke club is **Luca's,** Via Fredour 26 (☎ **011-776-4604**), where sports talk and karaoke contests bring out the exhibitionism of cinematic hopefuls. **Ziegfild Follies,** Via Pomba 7 (☎ **011-812-7395**), offers disco music, restaurant service, and a bar where you might strike up a fun conversation. The more punkish **Exit,** Via Barge 4C (☎ **011-434-8233**), is a pub with live music from north Italian punk bands, techno artists, and rock bands.

Turin has several elegant cafes where you can pass the time sipping coffee, enjoying a cocktail, or simply people-watching. Among the landmarks are **Caffè San Carlo,** Piazza San Carlo 156 (☎ **011-515-317**), which serves until 1am under a huge chandelier of Murano glass in a glittering setting of gilt, mirrors, and marble.

2 Aosta

114 miles (184km) NW of Milan, 78 miles (126km) N of Turin, 463 miles (745km) NW of Rome

Founded by the Emperor Augustus, Aosta has lost much of its quaintness today. It's called the "Rome of the Alps," but that's just tourist propaganda. Aostanas number about 40,000 now and live in the shadow of the peaks of Mont Blanc and San Bernardo. The economy is increasingly dependent on tourism.

Lying as it does on a major artery, Aosta makes for an important stop, either for overnighting or as a base for exploring Valle d'Aosta or taking the cable car to the Conca di Pila, the mountain that towers over the town.

ESSENTIALS

GETTING THERE Thirteen **trains** per day run directly from Turin to Aosta (trip time: 2 hours), costing 12,000L ($6) one way. From Milan, the trip takes 4½ hours and costs 18,000L ($9) one way; you must change trains at Chivasso. For information and schedules, call ☎ **0165-262-057** or 1478-880-88 toll-free in Italy. The train station is at Piazza Manzetti, only a 5-minute stroll over to the Piazza Chanoux, the very core of Aosta.

If you have a **car** and are coming from Turin, continue north along A5, which comes to an end just east of Aosta.

VISITOR INFORMATION The **tourist office** is at Piazza Chanoux 8 (☎ **0165-236-627**), open Monday to Saturday 9am to 1pm and 3 to 8pm, Sunday 9am to 1pm.

EXPLORING AOSTA

The town's Roman ruins include the **Arch of Augustus,** built in 24 B.C., the date of the Roman founding of the town. Via Sant'Anselmo, part of the old city from the Middle Ages, leads to the arch. Even more impressive are the ruins of a **Roman theater,** reached by the Porta Pretoria, a major gateway built of huge blocks dating from the 1st century B.C. The ruins are open year-round Monday to Friday 9am to 7pm; entrance is free. A **Roman forum** is today a small park with a crypt, lying off Piazza San Giovanni near the cathedral.

The town is also enriched by its medieval relics. The Gothic **Collegiata dei Santi Pietro e Orso,** directly off Via Sant'Anselmo (☎ **0165-262-026**), was founded in the 12th century and is characterized by its landmark Romanesque steeple. You can explore the crypt, but the cloisters, with capitals of some three dozen pillars depicting biblical scenes, are more interesting. The church is open Monday to Saturday 9am to 7pm and Sunday 3 to 6pm.

A SIDE TRIP TO A GREAT NATIONAL PARK

Aosta is a good base for exploring the ✪ **Great Paradise National Park (Parco Nazionale di Gran Paradiso),** five lake-filled valleys that in 1865 were a royal hunting ground of Vittorio Emanuele II. Even back then, long before the term *endangered species* was common, he awarded that distinction to the ibex, a nearly extinct species of mountain goat. In 1919 Vittorio Emanuele III gave the property to the Italian state, which established a national park in 1922. The park encompasses some 1,400 square miles of forest, pastureland, and alpine meadows, filled with not only ibex but also the chamois and other animals that roam wild.

The main gateway to the park is **Cogne,** a popular resort. The best time to visit is in June, when the wildflowers are at their most spectacular. You can get a sampling of this rare alpine fauna by visiting the **Paradise Alpine Garden (Giardino Alpino Paradiso),** near the village of Valnontey, a mile south of Cogne. It's open June 10 to September 10, daily 9:30am to 12:30pm and 2:30 to 6:30pm, charging an admission of 3,000L ($1.50); free for children under 10. For information about the park, visit the **park headquarters** at Via Umberto I, Noasca (☎ **0124/901-070**). Cogne lies about 18 miles (29km) south of Aosta and is reached along S35 and S507.

SHOPPING

Valle d'Aosta is known for its wood carvings and wrought-iron work. For a sampling, head for the permanent craft exhibits in the arcades of **Piazza Chanoux,** the center of Aosta. You're not expected to pay the first price quoted, so test your bargaining skill. The market here swells during the last 2 days in January, when dozens of artisans from all around the Italian Alps appear en masse to sell their handcrafts, mostly carved wood and stonework. Count yourself lucky if you pick up some handmade lace from neighboring Cogne. It's highly valued for its workmanship.

Valdostan handcrafts can be found at **IVAT,** Via Xavier de Maistre 1 (☎ **0165-41-462**), where sculpture, bas-relief, and wrought iron are offered. The shop owners can also provide you with a list of local furniture makers. Antique furniture and

Reserving Winery Tours

You may want to visit one of the region's outstanding wineries. To call for an appointment, refer to the Piedmont section under "The Best Wine-Growing Regions," in chapter 1.

paintings are the domain of **Bessone,** Via Edouard Aubert 53 (☎ **0165-40-853**), while **New Gallery,** Via Sant'Anselmo 115 (☎ **0165-40-929**), features a more diverse selection of antiques.

ACCOMMODATIONS

Hotel Le Pageot. Via Giorgio Carrel 31, 11100 Aosta. ☎ **0165-32-433.** Fax 0165-33-217. 18 units. TV TEL. 130,000L ($65) double. Breakfast 15,000L ($7.50). AE, DC, MC, V. Parking 20,000L ($10).

Built in 1985, this hotel is one of the best values in town. It has a modern angular facade of brown brick with big windows and floors crafted from carefully polished slabs of mountain granite. The guest rooms are clean and functional but not a lot more, though they offer reasonable comfort. The bathrooms are small. The well-lit public areas include a breakfast room and a TV room (but no restaurant).

Hotel Roma. Via Torino 7, 11100 Aosta. ☎ **0165-41-000.** Fax 0165-32-404. 38 units. TV TEL. 120,000–135,000L ($60–$67.50) double. Breakfast 15,000L ($7.50). AE, DC, MC, V. Parking 10,000L ($5).

Silvio Lepri and Graziella Nicoli are the owners of this hotel on a peaceful alley in a cubist-style white stucco building; it's surrounded by the balconies and windows of what appear to be private apartments. The small guest rooms are modern, simple, and well maintained, with touches of varnished pine, excellent mattresses, and modern tiled bathrooms. The entrance is at the top of an exterior concrete stairwell. The public rooms include a warmly paneled bar area, big windows, and a homelike decor filled with bright colors and rustic accessories.

Hotel Valle d'Aosta. Corso Ivrea 146, 11100 Aosta. ☎ **0165-41-845.** Fax 0165-236-660. 104 units. MINIBAR TV TEL. 170,000–230,000L ($85–$115) double. Rates include breakfast. AE, DC, MC, V. Closed Dec 1–27. Free garage parking.

This modern hotel with its zigzag concrete facade is one of Aosta's leading choices. Located on a busy road leading from the old town to the entrance of the autostrada, it's a prominent stop for motorists using the Great St. Bernard and Mont Blanc tunnels into Italy. The sunny lobby has beige stone floors, deep leather chairs, and an oversized bar. All guest rooms have double windows and views angled toward the mountains. Each is medium in size with standard (not spectacular) comfort and a small bathroom. The Ristorante Le Foyer is reviewed under "Dining," below. The hotel also offers room service, baby-sitting, and laundry.

DINING

Ristorante Le Foyer. In the Hotel Valle d'Aosta, Corso Ivrea 146. ☎ **0165-32-136.** Reservations recommended. Main courses 20,000–30,000L ($10–$15). AE, DC, MC, V. Wed–Mon 12:15–1:50pm; Wed–Sun 7:30–9:30pm. Closed Jan 8–25 and July 5–20. VALDOSTAN/INTERNATIONAL.

This restaurant sits beside a traffic artery on the outskirts of town. The full Valdostan meals are both flavorful and affordable. In a wood-paneled dining room illuminated by a wall of oversized windows, you can dine on specialties like salmon trout, beef tagliata with balsamic vinegar, vegetable flan with fondue, or fresh noodles with smoked salmon and asparagus. There's also a good selection of French and Italian wines.

Ristorante Piemonte. Via Porta Pretoria 13. ☎ **0165-40-111.** Reservations recommended. Main courses 22,000–38,000L ($11–$19); fixed-price menus 30,000–65,000L ($15–$32.50). MC, V. Sat–Thurs noon–3pm and 7–10pm. Closed Feb. VALDOSTAN/INTERNATIONAL.

On a relatively traffic-free street, this is a charming, unpretentious trattoria with all the authenticity its 250-year-old premises deserve. Its known for its savory versions of age-old mountain recipes. Surrounded by vaulted ceilings and terra-cotta floors, you can order at least four set menus, all featuring either truffles or mushrooms, when they're in season. Other tried-and-true favorites are heaping platters of charcuterie, cannelloni in the style of the chef, several versions of fondue, risotto with roasted pork, and an array of desserts that could include fresh strawberries from local suppliers. Especially interesting is roast chamois prepared with a Barolo sauce.

Vecchia Aosta. Piazza Porta Pretoria 4. ☎ **0165-361-186.** Reservations recommended. Main courses 19,000–32,000L ($9.50–$16). AE, DC, MC, V. Thurs–Tues noon–3pm and 7:30–10pm. Closed Nov 15–30. VALDOSTAN/INTERNATIONAL.

The most unusual restaurant in Aosta lies in the narrow niche between the inner and outer Roman walls of the Porta Pretoria. It's in an old structure that, though modernized, still bears evidence of the superb building techniques of the Romans, whose chiseled stones are sometimes visible between patches of modern wood and plaster. Full meals are served on at least two levels in a labyrinth of nooks and isolated crannies and may include homemade ravioli, beef fillet with mushrooms, pepperoni flan, eggs with cheese fondue and truffles, roasted duck with tomatoes and orange sauce, and a cheese-laden version of Valdostan fondue.

AOSTA AFTER DARK

You won't lack for diversions in this alpine capital. The town's leading disco is **La Compagnia dei Motori,** Piazza Arco d'Augusto (☎ **0165-363-484**), where a partially metallic interior includes a network of dance floors and bars; it's the trendy disco-of-the-minute. The **Sweet Rock Café,** Via Piccolo St. Bernardo 18 (☎ **0165-553-251**), caters to a 25-to-45 crowd, featuring rock and jazz with live music on Mondays.

3 Courmayeur & Entrèves: Skiing & Alpine Beauty

COURMAYEUR

Courmayeur, a 22-mile (35km) drive northwest of Aosta, is Italy's best all-around ski resort, with two "high seasons," attracting skiers in winter and other active types who come to play in the mountain scenery in summer. Its popularity was given a considerable boost with the opening of the Mont Blanc road tunnel (☎ **04-50-53-06-15** in France), feeding traffic from France into Italy (estimated trip time: 20 minutes). By the time of your visit, this vital link between France and Italy might be up and running again, though it was closed by a tragic fire in spring 1999 (as of this writing, it appeared that the repair might be finished by December 2000).

With Europe's highest mountain in the background, Courmayeur sits snugly in a valley. Directly to the north of the resort is the alpine village of Entrèves, sprinkled with a number of chalets (some of which take in paying guests).

ESSENTIALS

GETTING THERE First, you'll take a **train to Aosta.** From there, you can take any of 11 **buses** leaving daily for Courmayeur from the bus terminal, Piazza Narbonne (☎ **0165-841-305**), adjacent to the train station. There's a bus every hour, costing

4,800L ($2.90) each way or 8,500L ($4.25) round-trip. Transit time is 1 hour. Departures are daily, beginning in the early morning, with the last departure from Aosta scheduled for 10:15pm.

If you're **driving,** continue west from Aosta on Route 26 heading toward Monte Bianco.

VISITOR INFORMATION The **tourist office** for Courmayeur is on Piazzale Monte Bianco (☎ **0165-842-060**), open Monday to Friday 9am to 12:30pm and 3 to 6:30pm, Saturday to Sunday 9am to 7pm.

Fun On & Off the Slopes

The **ski season** begins in mid-December and lasts until some time in April, depending on snow conditions in the area. The skiing, although good, has little to attract experts, who head instead for Chamonix across Mont Blanc in France; Courmayeur is more for beginners and intermediates. **Lift tickets** in Courmayeur cost 54,000L ($27) for one day, and 100,000L ($50) for two days. For **snow reports** in and around Courmayeur, call ☎ **0165-843-566.**

Near Courmayeur, you can take one of the most unusual **cable cars** in Europe across Mont Blanc all the way to Chamonix, France. It's a ride across glaciers that's altogether frightening and thrilling. Departures on the **Funivie Monte Bianco** are from La Palud, near Entrèves. The three-stage cable car heads for the intermediate stations, Pavillon and Rifugio Torino, before reaching its peak at Punta Helbronner at 11,254 feet. At the latter, you'll be on the doorstep of the glacier and the celebrated 11½-mile (19km) Vallée Blanche ski run to Chamonix, France, usually opened at the beginning of February every year. The round-trip price for the cable car ride is 50,000L ($25). Departures are every 20 minutes, and service is daily 8:30am to 12:40pm and 2 to 4pm. At the top is a bar, a snack bar, and a terrace for sunbathing. Bookings are possible at **Esercizio Funivie,** Frazione La Palude 22 (☎ **0165-89-925**).

Other than riding the cable cars, the nonskier can take long walks in the area (the tourist office will provide suggestions), go shopping, or go for country drives. Many nonskiing visitors come just for the bracing mountain air and the panoramic views. The shopping is excellent, especially on **Via Roma,** and many of the most prestigious retailers in Milan or Rome maintain branches here.

In **summer** the scenery is gorgeous, with towering Mont Blanc in the distance. Some 32 miles southeast of Courmayeur is the **Parco Nazionale del Gran Paradise,** once the private domain of King Vittorio Emanuele II (1820–78). Presented to the nation at the end of World War I in 1918, it is one of the most unspoiled wilderness areas remaining in Italy. It's at its most glorious in spring when the wildflowers burst into bloom. The park is ideal for hikes and daylong excursions.

Accommodations

Courmayeur has a number of attractive hotels, many of which are open seasonally. Always reserve ahead in high season, either summer or winter.

Expensive

Grand Hotel Royal e Golf. Via Roma 87, 11013 Courmayeur. ☎ **0165-846-787.** Fax 0165-842-093. www.hotelroyalegolf.com. 94 units. MINIBAR TV TEL. 450,000–780,000L ($225–$390) double; 670,000–1,100,000L ($335–$550) suite. Rates include half-board. AE, DC, MC, V. Parking 20,000L ($10) inside, free outside.

Built in 1950, this hotel is in a dramatic location above the heart of the resort between the most fashionable pedestrian walkway and a heated outdoor pool. It is a top choice, exceeded only by the more tranquil and elegant Pavillon (see below). Much of its angular facade is covered with rocks, so it fits in neatly with the mountainous landscape. The guest rooms are generally medium-sized, with built-in furnishings and streamlined bathrooms. Rooms on the fifth floor contain private balconies. The rooms most requested are those with southern exposure with a great view of Mont Blanc; those on the north side open onto a valley.

Dining/Diversions: A large, comfortable lounge is flanked by a bar and a dais that features a pianist nightly in season. There's a formal dining room called La Grill dell'Hotel Royal e Golf, plus a more casual restaurant.

Amenities: Room service, baby-sitting, laundry/valet, hydromassage, pool, sauna, Jacuzzi, solarium, Turkish bath.

Hotel Pavillon. Strada Regionale 62, 11013 Courmayeur. ☎ **0165-846-120.** Fax 0165-846-122. www.valdigne.com/courmayeur/pavillon. E-mail: pavillon@courmayeur.valdigne.com. 50 units. MINIBAR TV TEL. 360,000–560,000L ($180–$280) double; 500,000–800,000L ($250–$400) suite. Rates include half-board. AE, DC, MC, V. Closed May–June 15 and Oct–Dec 2. Valet parking 15,000L ($7.50).

This is easily the swankiest hotel at the resort, despite its small size. Built in 1965, renovated in 1990, and designed like a chalet, the hotel is a 4-minute walk south of Courmayeur's inner-city pedestrian zone. The guest rooms, entered through leather-covered doors, feature built-in furniture and a conservative decor; all but two have private balconies. Accommodations range from medium-sized to spacious, each with a firm mattress. The bathrooms come with toiletries and hair dryers. The hotel is only a short walk from the funicular that goes to Plan Checrouit.

Dining/Diversions: The half-board requirement is no hardship, as the hotel serves market-fresh ingredients deftly prepared by a skilled kitchen staff in its Grill Le Bistroquet (winter only) or its regular year-round restaurant. Skiers and others are also fond of gathering at its chic rendezvous, the American Bar.

Amenities: Concierge, room service, laundry/dry cleaning, twice-daily maid service, baby-sitting, secretarial services, hydrotherapy facilities, solarium, covered pool.

Moderate

Hotel del Viale. Viale Monte Bianco 74, 11013 Courmayeur. ☎ **0165-846-712.** Fax 0165-844-513. www.valdigne.com/courmayeur/viale. E-mail: viale@courmayeur.valdigne.com. 23 units. MINIBAR TV TEL. 250,000–450,000L ($125–$225) double. Rates include half-board. AE, DC, MC, V. Closed May and Nov. Parking 20,000L ($9) inside, free outside.

This old-style mountain chalet at the edge of town is a good place to enjoy the indoor/outdoor life. There's a front terrace with tables set under trees in fair weather, and the rooms inside are cozy and pleasant in the chillier months. The guest rooms, though small, have an alpine charm, each with an especially good mattress and an efficient little tiled bathroom. In winter, guests can gather in the taproom to enjoy après-ski life, drinking at pine tables and warming their feet before the open fire.

✪ **Palace Bron.** Località Plan Gorret 41, 11013 Courmayeur. ☎ **0165-846-742.** Fax 0165-844-015. 27 units. TV TEL. 280,000–380,000L ($136–$190) double. Rates include breakfast. AE, DC, MC, V. Closed Easter–July 1 and mid-Sept to Dec 8.

About 1¼ miles (2km) from the heart of the resort, this tranquil oasis is one of the plushest hotels in town. The white-walled chalet is the most noteworthy building on the pine-studded hill. You're made to feel like a member of a baronial household. The guest rooms are handsomely furnished and well maintained, ranging from medium to spacious, with deluxe tiled bathrooms. Winter visitors appreciate its proximity to the many ski lifts. Walking from the chalet to the center of town is a good way to exercise after your formal dinner selected from the kitchen's filling international cuisine. The hotel's piano bar is especially lively in winter. Also offered are room service, baby-sitting, laundry, and valet.

Inexpensive

Hotel Bouton d'Or. Strada Traforo del Monte Bianco 10 (off Piazzale Monte Bianco), 11013 Courmayeur. ☎ **0165-846-729.** Fax 0165-842-152. www.hotelboutondor.com. E-mail: info@hotelboutondor.com. 35 units. TV TEL. 160,000–200,000L ($80–$100) double. 180,000–260,000L ($90–$130) apt for 3; 200,000–320,000L ($100–$160) apt for 4. AE, DC, MC, V. Rates include breakfast. Closed June and Nov. Free parking.

Named after the buttercups that cover the surrounding hills in summer, this hotel is owned by the Casale family, who built it in 1970 and renovated it in 1990. French windows lead from the guest rooms onto small balconies. The rooms are a bit cramped, but you'll find reasonable comfort for the price. The hotel is about 100 yards (toward the Mont Blanc tunnel) from the most popular restaurant in Courmayeur, Le Vieux Pommier (see below), which is owned by the same family. The hotel also has a garage, sauna, solarium, and garden.

Hotel Courmayeur. Via Roma 158, 11013 Courmayeur. ☎ **0165-846-732.** Fax 0165-845-125. www.hotelcourmayeur.com. E-mail: info@hotelcourmayeur.com. 26 units. TV TEL. 150,000–220,000L ($90–$132) double. Rates include half-board. AE, DC, MC, V. Closed Sept–Nov and May. Free parking.

The Hotel Courmayeur, in the center of the resort, was built so that most of its rooms would have unobstructed views of the mountains. It's a small, unpretentious hotel with immaculate rooms and low prices. A number of the guest rooms, furnished in the mountain chalet style, also have wooden balconies. Even nonguests can dine on regional food in the hotel restaurant.

DINING

✪ **Cadran Solaire.** Via Roma 122. ☎ **0165-844-609.** Reservations required. Main courses 25,000–40,000L ($12.50–$20). AE, MC, V. Wed–Sun 12:30–2pm and 7:30–11pm. Closed May and Oct. VALDOSTAN.

In the center of town is Courmayeur's most interesting restaurant, named after the sundial *(cadran solaire)* embellishing the upper floor of its chalet facade and owned by Leo Garin, whose La Maison de Filippo (see Entrèves, below) is Valle d'Aosta's most popular restaurant. Try to come for a before-dinner drink in the vaulted bar; in the 16th century, its massive stones were crafted into long spans by using techniques the Romans perfected. The rustically elegant dining room has a stone fireplace, a beamed ceiling, and wide plank floors. Specialties change with the season but are likely to include warm goat cheese blended with a salad, noodles with seasonal vegetables, baked cheese-and-spinach casserole, and duck breast with plums. The desserts are sumptuous.

Leone Rosso. Via Roma 71. ☎ **0165-846-726.** Reservations recommended. Main courses 20,000–40,000L ($10–$20). AE, MC, V. Daily noon–2pm and 7–10pm. Closed May–June and Oct. VALDOSTAN.

Leone Rosso is in a stone- and timber-fronted house in a slightly isolated courtyard, a few paces from the busy pedestrian traffic of Via Roma. It serves well-prepared Valdostan specialties, such as fondues, a thick and steaming regional version of minestrone, *tagliatelle* (flat noodles) with mushrooms and *en papillote* (in parchment), and a selection of creamy desserts. Some meats you grill yourself at your table. This place isn't to be confused with the Red Lion pub.

Le Vieux Pommier. Piazzale Monte Bianco 25. ☎ **0165-842-281.** Reservations recommended. Main courses 26,000–30,000L ($13–$15). AE, DC, MC, V. Tues–Sun noon–2pm and 7–9:30pm. Closed Oct and 10–15 days in May. VALDOSTAN/INTERNATIONAL.

The hacked-up trunk of the "old apple tree" that was cut down to build this place was re-erected inside and serves as the focal point of the restaurant, which is located on the main square. The exposed stone, the copper-covered bar, and the thick pine tables arranged in an octagon create a charming atmosphere. Today Alessandro Casale, the son of the founder, directs the kitchen, assisted by his wife, Lydia. Your meal might consist of three kinds of dried alpine beef, followed by noodles in ham-studded cream sauce or an arrangement of three pastas or four fondues, including a regional variety with Fontina, milk, and egg yolks. Then it's on to chicken supreme *en papillote* (in parchment) or four or five unusual meat dishes cooked mountain style, right at your table.

Courmayeur After Dark

Not to be confused with a less desirable bar of the same name at the end of the same street, the **American Bar,** Via Roma 43 (☎ **0165-846-707**), is one of the most popular bars on the après-ski circuit. It's rowdy and sometimes outrageous but most often a lot of fun. Most guests end up in one of the two rooms, beside either an open fireplace or a long crowded bar. The place is open all day every day, till 1:30am in ski season; it's sometimes closed on Tuesday other times of year. The **Café della Posta,** Via Roma 51 (☎ **0165-842-272**), the oldest cafe in Courmayeur, is as sedate as its neighbor, the American Bar, is unruly. Many guests prefer to remain in the warmly decorated bar area, never venturing into the large salon with its glowing fireplace. The place changes its stripes throughout the day, opening as a morning cafe at 8:30am.

Entrèves

Even older than Courmayeur, Entrèves is an ancient community that's small and compact, really a mountain village of wood houses. Many visitors prefer its alpine charm to the more bustling resort of Courmayeur; they ski the slopes at Courmayeur and enjoy its shopping, dining, and nightlife but retreat here to stay in a quieter, less congested setting. It's reached by a steep and narrow road. Many gourmets visit just to enjoy the regional fare for which the village is known.

Just outside Entrèves on the main highway lies the **Val Veny cable car,** which skiers take in winter to reach the Courmayeur lift system.

Entrèves is 2 miles (3km) north of Courmayeur (signposted off Rte. 26). Buses from the center of Courmayeur run daily to Entrèves. For more information, contact Courmayeur's tourist office (see above).

Accommodations

✪ **La Grange.** Strada La Brenva 1, 11013 Courmayeur-Entrèves. ☎ **0165-869-733.** Fax 0165-869-744. www.lagrange-it.com. E-mail:lagrange@courmayeurvaldigne.com. 23 units. MINIBAR TV TEL. 200,000L ($100) double; from 410,000L ($205) suite. Rates include breakfast. AE, DC, MC, V. Free parking. Closed May–June and Oct–Nov.

This will be one of the first buildings you'll see as you enter this rustic alpine village. A few foundation stones date from the 1300s, when the hotel was a barn. What you'll see today is a stone building whose balconies and gables are outlined against the steep hillside into which it's constructed. The Berthod family transformed a dilapidated property into a rustic and comfortable hotel in 1979. It's enthusiastically managed by Bruna Berthod Perri and her nephew, Stefano Pellin. The unusual decor includes a collection of antique tools and a series of thick timbers, stucco, and exposed stone walls. The guest rooms are imbued with a cozy alpine charm, each with a soft mattress and a tiled bathroom. There's a piano in the bar, plus an exercise room and sauna. A rich breakfast is the only meal served.

DINING

La Brenva. La Palud 12, Frazione Entrèves di Courmayeur, 11013 Courmayeur-Entrèves. ☎ **0165-869-780.** Fax 0165-869-726. Reservations required. Main courses 25,000–40,000L ($12.50–$20); fixed-price menus 40,000–65,000L ($20–$32.50). AE, MC, V. Tues–Sun 12:30–2pm and 7:30–10:30pm. Closed May and Oct. VALDOSTAN/FRENCH.

Many skiers make a special trip to Entrèves just for a drink at the old-fashioned bar of this hotel/restaurant. The copper espresso machine topped by a brass eagle and many of the other decorative accessories are at least a century old. The core of the building was constructed in 1884 as a hunting lodge for Vittorio Emanuele. In 1897 it became a hotel, and in 1980 the owners enlarged it with the addition of extra rooms and a larger eating area. The restaurant consists of exposed stone walls, wide flooring planks, hunting trophies, copper pots, and straw-bottomed chairs. Fires burn in winter, and many diners prefer an aperitif in the unusual salon, within view of the well-chosen paintings. On any given day the menu could include prosciutto, fonduta for two, carbonada with polenta, scaloppini with fresh mushrooms, Valle d'Aostan beefsteak, and zabaglione for dessert.

Each of the 12 simple and comfortable guest rooms has a bathroom, TV, phone, and lots of peace and quiet. Many have covered loggias. With breakfast included, they rent for 100,000 to 150,000L ($50 to $75) per person. The inn takes a vacation in either May or June.

La Maison de Filippo. Frazione Entrèves di Courmayeur. ☎ **0165-869-797.** Reservations required. Fixed-price menus 55,000–70,000L ($27.50–$35). MC, V. Wed–Mon 12:30–2:30pm and 7:30–10:30pm. Closed May 16–June and Nov–Dec 20. VALDOSTAN.

This colorful tavern, the creation of Leo Garin, is for those who enjoy a festive atmosphere and bountiful regional food. The three-story open hallway seems like a rustic barn, with an open, worn wooden staircase leading to the various dining nooks. The outdoor summer beer garden has a full view of Mont Blanc. You pass by casks of nuts, baskets of fresh fruits, bowls of salad, fruit tarts, and loaves of fresh-baked bread. Mr. Garin features local specialties on an all-you-can-eat basis, earning the place the nickname "Chalet of Gluttony." A typical meal might begin with a selection of antipasti, followed by a 2-foot-long platter of about 60 varieties of sausage. Next comes a parade of pasta dishes. For a main course, you can pick everything from fondue to *camoscio* (chamois meat) to trout with almond-butter sauce.

12 Genoa & the Italian Riviera

For years the retreat of the wintering wealthy, the Italian Riviera now enjoys a broad base of tourism. It's popular even in winter, though not for swimming (the average January temperature hovers around 50°F). The protection provided by the Ligurian Apennines looming in the background makes for balmy weather. Genoa, dividing the Riviera in two, is the capital of Liguria. It's a big bustling port that has charm for those willing to take the time to seek out its treasures.

The winding coastline of the Rivieras, particularly the one stretching from the French border to San Remo, is especially familiar to moviegoers as the background for countless flicks about sports-car racing, jewel thieves, and spies. Over the years, Italy's northwestern coast has seen the famous and the infamous, especially literary figures: Percy Shelley (who drowned offshore), Gabriele d'Annunzio, Lord Byron, Katherine Mansfield, George Sand, and D. H. Lawrence.

The Mediterranean landscape is dotted with pines, olives, citrus trees, and cypresses. The western Riviera—the **Riviera di Ponente (Setting Sun),** from the border to Genoa—is sometimes known as the Riviera of Flowers (*Riviera dei Fiori*) because of its profusion of blossoms. Starting at the French border, Ventimiglia is the gateway city to Italy. Along the way you'll encounter the first big resort, Bardighera, followed by San Remo, the major center of tourism. On the eastern Riviera—the **Riviera di Levante (Rising Sun)**—are three dramatically situated small resorts: Rapallo, Santa Margherita, and Portofino (the favorite of the yachting set).

The Ligurians are famous for ceramics, lace, silver and gold filigree, marble, velvet, olive wood, and macramé, and all the towns and villages of the region hold outdoor markets either in the main square or on the waterfront. Haggling is a way of life, so good deals do exist, but English speakers be warned that prices may not fall as low as they would if you were negotiating in the local dialect.

1 San Remo

10 miles (16km) E of the French border, 85 miles (137km) SW of Genoa, 397 miles (639km) NW of Rome

San Remo has been known as a resort ever since Emperor Frederick William wintered in a villa here. In time, Empress Maria Alexandrova, wife of Czar Alexander II, showed up, trailed by a Russian colony that included Tchaikovsky, who composed the Fourth Symphony here during a stay in 1878. Alfred Nobel, the father of dynamite and the founder of the famous prizes in Stockholm, died here in 1896.

The flower-filled resort is today something of a mini-Vegas by the sea, complete with a casino, race track, 18-hole golf course, and the deluxe Royal Hotel. Its climate is the mildest on the western Riviera, and the town offers mile after mile of well-maintained beaches.

ESSENTIALS

GETTING THERE San Remo lies on the coast between Ventimiglia and Imperia, 6 miles (10km) from each, and it's a major stop for many **trains.** A train leaves Genoa heading for the French border once per hour, stopping in San Remo. Rome is 8 hours by train from San Remo. For train information and schedules, call ☎ **1478-88-088** toll-free in Italy.

If you have a **car,** A10, running east-west along the Riviera, is the fastest way to reach San Remo from either the French border or Genoa.

VISITOR INFORMATION The **tourist office** is on Corso Nuvoloni 1 (☎ **0184-571-571**), open Monday to Saturday 8am to 7pm and Sunday 9am to 1pm.

SAFETY The harbor, particularly after dark, isn't for the squeamish. If you go wandering, don't go alone and don't carry valuables. Genoa is rougher than Barcelona, more comparable to Marseille. A woman is likely to lose her purse not only in the harbor area but also on any side street running downhill if she doesn't take precautions.

WHAT TO SEE & DO

Even if you're just passing through San Remo, you might want to visit **La Città Vecchia** (also known as **La Pigna**), the old city atop the hill. Far removed in spirit from the burgeoning sterile-looking town down near the water, old San Remo blithely ignores the present, and its tiny houses on narrow, steep lanes capture the past. In the new town, the palm-flanked **Corso dell'Imperatrice** (aka the **Passeggiata dell'Imperatrice**) attracts promenaders; at one end of the passeggiata stands the Russian Orthodox **San Basilio,** boasting onion-shaped domes. For a scenic view, drive to the top of **San Romolo** and **Monte Bignone** (4,265 ft.).

October to June daily 6 to 8am, you can visit the most famous flower market in Italy, the **Mercato dei Fiori,** held in the market hall between Corso Garibaldi and Piazza Colombo. You'll see some 20,000 tons of roses, mimosa, and carnations, which are grown in the balmy climate of the Riviera in winter before shipment to all parts of Europe.

Outside of town, you can visit **Bussana Vecchia (Old Bussana),** 5 miles (8km) west of San Remo (it's signposted). Too well inhabited to really be considered a ghost town, Bussana Vecchia is, however, a rather unofficial town. A substantial 1887 earthquake killed thousands of its residents and destroyed many buildings. The survivors, too frightened to stay, started a new Bussana $1^1/_4$ miles (2km) closer to the sea. The original town, with several buildings still standing, has gradually been taken over by artist-squatters who've revamped interior spaces (but not exteriors—no reason to draw that much attention to themselves) and hooked up water, electricity, and phones. They live off their art, so haggling can get you a good deal on a painting.

The pebbly **beach** below the Passeggiata dell'Imperatrice is where many visitors spend their days. Beach huts offer showers, snack bars, beach chairs, lounges, and umbrellas. Expect to spend at least 10,000L ($5) for a basic lounge and up to 25,000L ($12.50) for a more elaborate sun-bed arrangement with an umbrella.

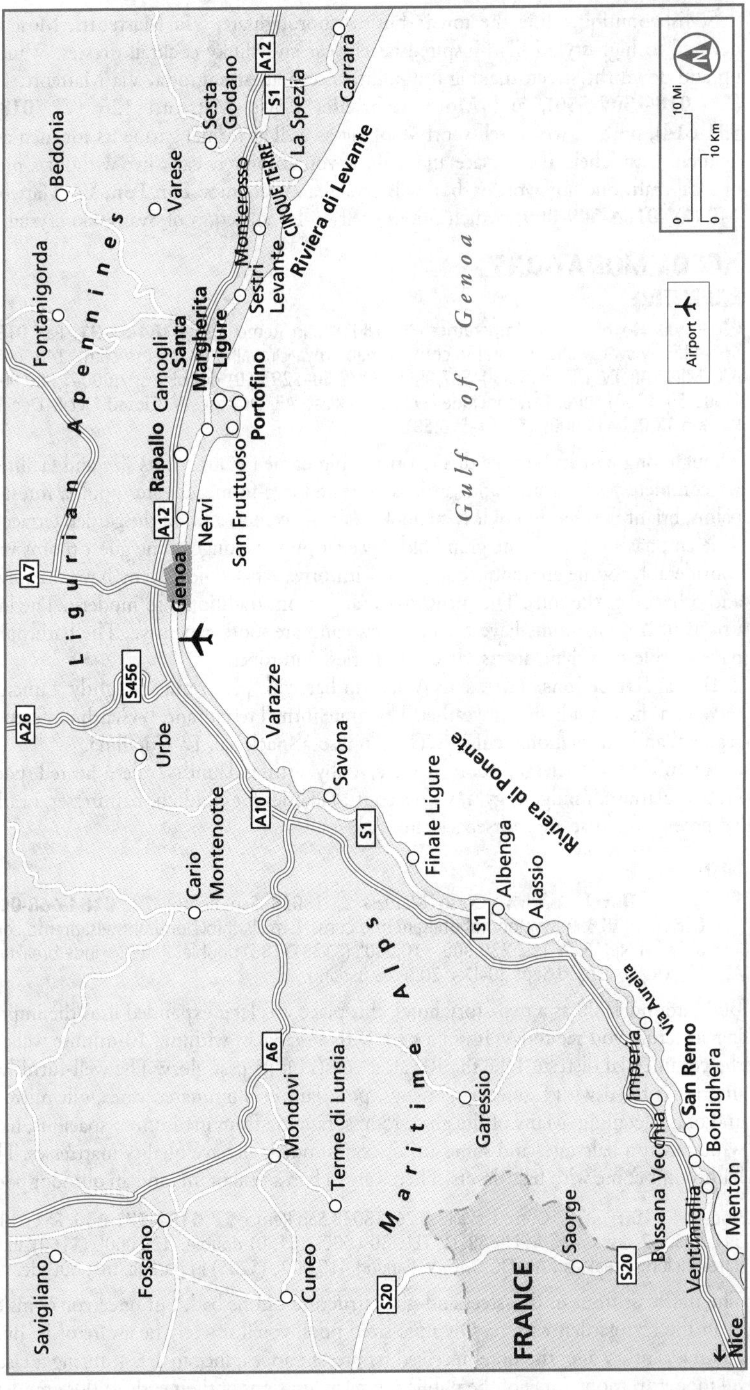
Savigliano
Fossano
Cuneo
Mondovi
Terme di Lunsia
Garessio
Maritime Alps
FRANCE
Saorge
Nice
Menton
Ventimiglia
Bordighera
Bussana Vecchia
San Remo
Imperia
Via Aurelia
Alassio
Albenga
Finale Ligure
Riviera di Ponente
Cario
Montenotte
Savona
Varazze
Urbe
Ligurian Apennines
Genoa
Nervi
San Fruttuoso
Rapallo
Camogli
Portofino
Santa
Margherita
Ligure
Fontanigorda
Sestri
Levante
Monterosso
Levante
CINQUE TERRE
Riviera di Levante
Varese
Bedonia
Sesta
Godano
La Spezia
Carrara
Gulf of Genoa
A26
S456
A7
A12
A10
S1
A6
S20
Airport
0
10 Mi
10 Km
N

Stylish boutiques line the town's busiest thoroughfare, **Via Matteotti.** Most are devoted to high-style Milan-inspired beachwear and slinky cocktail dresses. Wander up and down the street, making it a point to stop at **Annamoda,** Via Matteotti 141 (☎ **0184-505-550**), and **Moro Gabrielle,** Corso Matteotti 126 (☎ **0184-531-614**), both of which sell sporty-looking as well as formal garments for men and women, with labels like Versace and YSL. If you absolutely can't live without a piece of local craft, one noteworthy shop sells crystal and ceramics: **Pon Pon,** Via Matteotti 140 (☎ **0184-509-069**), which prides itself on its collection of Svarowski crystal.

ACCOMMODATIONS

EXPENSIVE

✪ **Royal Hotel.** Corso Imperatrice 80, 18038 San Remo. ☎ **0184-53-91.** Fax 0184-661-445. www.royalhotelsanremo.com. E-mail: royal@royalhotelsanremo.com. 140 units. A/C MINIBAR TV TEL. 345,000–587,000L ($172.50–$293.50) double; 607,000–1,080,000L ($303.50–$540) suite. Rates include buffet breakfast. AE, DC, MC, V. Closed Oct 8–Dec 19. Parking 17,000–33,000L ($8.50–$16.50).

Though long past its heyday, this resort is a big name because of its size and facilities. It's complete with terraces and gardens, a heated free-form saltwater pool, a forest of palms, bright flowers, and hideaway nooks. Activity centers around the garden terrace—little emphasis is put on the grand old dowager public lounges. The guest rooms vary considerably: Some are tennis-court size with private balconies, many have sea views, and others face the hills. The furnishings range from traditional to modern. The luxurious fifth-floor rooms have the best views and are more expensive. The bathrooms have marble tubs, hair dryers, deluxe toiletries, and robes.

Dining/Diversions: There's an American bar with piano music nightly. Lunch is served on the veranda in fair weather. The more formal restaurant, Il Giardino, features regional and international cuisine. There is also a snack bar, La Corallina.

Amenities: Concierge, room service, baby-sitting, laundry/valet, heated pool, sauna, solarium, minigolf, gym, tennis court, facilities for children, hairdresser, nearby 18-hole golf course and horseback riding.

MODERATE

✪ **Grand Hotel Londra.** Corso Matuzia 2, 18038 San Remo. ☎ **0184-668-000.** Fax 0184-668-073. www.londrahotelsanremo.com. E-mail: info@londrahotelsanremo.com. 130 units. MINIBAR TV TEL. 230,000–310,000L ($138–$186) double. Rates include breakfast. AE, DC, MC, V. Closed Sept 30–Dec 20. Free parking.

Built around 1900 as a two-story hotel, this place was later expanded into the imposing structure you see today. It's in a park with a sea view, within a 10-minute walk of the commercial district. Like the Royal, it coasts on its past glory. The well-furnished interior is filled with framed engravings, porcelain in illuminated cases, gilt mirrors, and brass detailing. Many of the guest rooms, ranging from medium to spacious, have wrought-iron balconies and some are air-conditioned; all have quality mattresses. The bathrooms come with hair dryers. There's also a bar, a restaurant, and an outdoor pool.

Hotel Méditerranée. Corso Cavallotti 76, 18038 San Remo. ☎ **0184-571-000.** Fax 0184-541-106. 62 units. A/C MINIBAR TV TEL. 300,000L ($150) double; 320,000L ($160) suite. Rates include breakfast. AE, DC, MC, V. Parking 410,000L ($205) in garage, free outside.

The traffic in front of this steel-and-glass structure can be bad, but once you're inside or in the rear garden with its Olympic-sized pool, you'll scarcely be aware of it. Built about a century ago, the hotel received its present appearance in 1974 during a tasteful modernization. Some of the public rooms retain signs of their early 1900s grandeur and are filled with potted plants, polished floors, and modern sculptures. The guest rooms are contemporary and well furnished, each with a firm mattress, and the bathrooms are tidily kept. The restaurant serves regional and international cuisine, and in summer lunch is served in the garden near the pool.

Hotel Miramare Continental Palace. Corso Matuzia 9, 18038 San Remo. ☎ **0184-667-601.** Fax 0184-667-655. 59 units. TV TEL. 230,000–340,000L ($115–$170) double; 430,000–600,000L ($215–$300) suite. Rates include breakfast. AE, DC, MC, V. Free parking.

A curved drive leads past palmettos to this traditional building set behind semitropical gardens bordering a busy street. A private underpass gives direct access to the beach. After passing through the well-appointed public rooms, you'll discover a garden with a 300-year-old magnolia, sculptures, and plenty of verdant hideaways. The guest rooms are clean and comfortable, ranging from small to medium; some are in a neighboring annex with garden views. The tiled bathrooms are compact. The hotel's good restaurant specializes in Ligurian seafood, and meals are served outside in summer. A covered saltwater pool is in one of the outbuildings, and there's also a sauna, solarium, and gym.

Suite Hotel Nyala. Strada Solaro 134, 18038 San Remo. ☎ **0184-667-668.** Fax 0184-666-059. www.nyalahotel.com. E-mail: reservations@nyalahotel.com. 80 units. A/C MINIBAR TV TEL. 280,000–340,000L ($140–$170) double; 430,000L ($215) suite. Rates include breakfast. AE, DC, MC, V. Free parking.

Built in 1984 and doubled in size in 1993, this comfortable hotel lies in what was a century ago the English-style park of a since-demolished villa. Although it's in a residential neighborhood with some impressive antique villas, this is San Remo's most modern hotel. The accommodations are divided among three buildings interconnected with corridors. Most guest rooms have a view over the sea and a sun-filled terrace; about half are junior suites, with a separate sitting area and larger balconies. Mainly medium in size, the rooms are nicely done, with firm mattresses. The tiled bathrooms contain hair dryers. On the premises are a dining room, a palm-fringed outdoor pool, and a bar.

INEXPENSIVE

Hotel Belsoggiorno Juana. Corso Matuzia 41, 18038 San Remo. ☎ **0184-667-631.** Fax 0184-667-471. 43 units. TEL. 125,000–250,000L ($62.50–$125) double. Rates include breakfast. Half-board 90,000–110,000L ($45–$55) per person. DC, MC, V. Parking 15,000L ($7.50) in garage, free outside.

This centrally located hotel is near the Corso dell'Imperatrice, the main seaside walkway, and the beaches. Attractively furnished and inviting, it contains a large reception area, plenty of living rooms for lounging, and TV rooms. The guest rooms are contemporary and functional, not very stylish. Nonetheless, they're quite comfortable, though the bathrooms are small. This hotel also provides a pleasant garden in which to sit and enjoy the sun and plants. Because the food is good, you may prefer to order the fixed-price menu if you're not staying on half-board.

Hotel Eletto. Corso Matteotti 44, 18038 San Remo. ☎ **0184-531-548.** Fax 0184-531-506. 29 units. TV TEL. 150,000L ($75) double. Half-board 130,000L ($65) per person. AE, MC, V. Free parking.

This hotel, on the main artery of town, has a 19th-century facade with cast-iron balconies and ornate detailing. The rear is set in a small garden with perhaps San Remo's biggest tree casting shade over the flower beds. This pleasant stop has public rooms filled with carved panels, old mirrors, and antique furniture, and guest rooms that are old-fashioned and comfortable. Each comes with a worn but still comfortable mattress, plus a small tiled bathroom. The sunny dining room serves inexpensive meals, and the hotel provides a cabana on the beach.

Hotel Mariluce. Corso Matuzia 3, 16038 San Remo. ☎ **0184-667-805.** Fax 0184-667-655. 23 units, 18 with bathroom. 100,000L ($50) double without bathroom, 120,000L ($60) double with bathroom. DC, MC, V. Closed Nov–Dec 20.

As you walk along the promenade away from the center, you'll note a flowering garden enclosed on one side by the walls of a Polish church; one wall is emblazoned with a gilded coat-of-arms. Behind the garden is the building that until 1945 was a refugee center that Poles throughout Europe used for finding friends and relatives. Today it's a reasonably priced hotel, a bargain for San Remo, offering sunny public rooms and simply furnished small guest rooms with cramped tiled bathrooms. No breakfast is served. A passage under the street leads from the garden to the beach.

DINING

EXPENSIVE

✪ **Paolo e Barbara.** Via Roma 47. ☎ **0184-531-653.** Reservations recommended. Main courses 48,000–75,000L ($24–$37.50); fixed-price lunch (with wine) 80,000L ($40); tasting menu (without wine) 150,000L ($75). AE, DC, MC, V. Fri–Tues 12:30–2pm and Thurs–Tues 8–10pm. LIGURIAN/ITALIAN.

Named after the husband-and-wife team who owns it (the Masieris), this restaurant near the casino has caught the imagination of San Remo. It specializes in traditional regional recipes plus a handful of innovative dishes. Meals tend to be drawn-out affairs, so allow adequate time. Depending on the season, the menu may feature a tartare of raw marinated mackerel with garlic mousse and potato, tomato, and basil-flavored garnish; *trenette* (a regional pasta) with fresh pesto; or grilled crayfish on onion purée with fresh herbs, olive oil, and pine nuts. The specialty is an antipasto called *cappon magro,* a mix of steamed fish and vegetables covered with a sauce made of parsley, anchovies, olives, and capers.

MODERATE

✪ **Da Giannino.** Lungomare Trento e Trieste 23. ☎ **0184-504-014.** Reservations required. Main courses 30,000–50,000L ($15–$25); fixed-price menus 80,000–130,000L ($40–$65). AE, DC, MC, V. Tues–Sat 12:30–2:30pm and 7:30–10pm; Sun 12:30–2:30pm. LIGURIAN/SEAFOOD.

This restaurant is still acclaimed as San Remo's finest restaurant, though Paolo e Barbara is closing in fast. In a conservatively elegant setting, you can enjoy such specialties as warm seafood antipasti, a flavorful risotto laced with cheese and a pungently aromatic green sauce, and a selection of main courses that changes with the availability of ingredients. An exotic selection is marinated cuttlefish gratinée. The wine list features many of the better vintages of both France and Italy.

Il Bagatto. Via Matteotti 145. ☎ **0184-531-925.** Reservations required. Main courses 26,000–38,000L ($13–$19). MC, V. Mon–Sat noon–3pm and 7:30–10pm. Closed July. LIGURIAN/SEAFOOD.

Il Bagatto provides good meals in the 16th-century home of an Italian duke, with dark beams and provincial chairs. It's in the shopping district, about two blocks from the sea. Our most recent dinner began with a choice of creamy lasagna and savory hors d'oeuvres. Especially pleasing are the scaloppine with artichokes and asparagus and the mixed grill of Mediterranean fish. All orders are accompanied by potatoes and a choice of vegetables, then followed by crème caramel. Diners can select from many kinds of Ligurian fish, including sea bass fillet in a sauce of fresh peppers and *gallinella,* the quintessential white-flesh Ligurian fish, roasted with potatoes and olives.

La Lanterna. Via Molo di Ponente al Porto 16. ☎ **0184-506-855.** Reservations required Sat–Sun. Main courses 20,000–40,000L ($10–$20); fixed-price menu 45,000–60,000L ($22.50–$30). AE, DC, MC, V. Fri–Wed 12:30–2:30pm and 7:30–10pm. Closed Dec–Jan. SEAFOOD.

Many locals recommend La Lanterna, a nautical place near the harbor. Opened around 1917, it's one of the few restaurants that has survived in San Remo from the heady days of its Edwardian grandeur. The crowd can get very fashionable, especially in summer, when outdoor tables are set within view of the harbor. Meals might include an excellent fish soup *(brodetto di pesce con crostini),* a Ligurian fish fry, or a meat dish like scaloppini in marsala sauce. Sea bass and red snapper are available, and your selection might be served grilled or perhaps fried with olive oil, herbs, and lemon, or even baked with artichokes, olives, and white-wine sauce.

SAN REMO AFTER DARK

Most nightlife revolves around the **San Remo Casino,** Corso Inglesi 18 (☎ **0184-5951**), in the center of town. For decades, visitors have dined in high style in the restaurant, reserved tables at the roof garden's cabaret, or tested their luck at the gaming tables. Like a white-walled palace, the pristine-looking casino stands at the top of a steep flight of stone steps above the main artery of town.

Today you can attend a variety of shows, fashion parades, concerts, and theatrical presentations staged throughout the year. The entrance fee is 15,000L ($7.50) for the American gaming rooms, open Sunday to Friday 4:45pm to 3am and Saturday 4:45pm to 4am. The European gaming rooms are open daily 2:30pm to 3am. Presentation of a passport is required, and a jacket and tie are requested for men. For the slot machines section, open Sunday to Friday 10am to 3am and Saturday 2:30pm to 3:30am, entrance is free and there's no dress code. The casino restaurant is open nightly 7pm to 1:30am, charging 60,000 to 100,000L ($30 to $50) per person for dinner. Its orchestra plays everything from waltzes to rock. The roof-garden cabaret is open June to September on Friday and Saturday, with shows beginning at 10:30pm. If you visit for drinks only (not dinner), the cost is 35,000L ($17.50) per drink.

You should also check out your hotel's bar or the bar in one of the grand palaces (especially the Royal, see above), whose bars are always open to well-dressed nonguests. You can always strike out for the cafes along **Via Matteotti,** which serve drinks until late at night.

2 Genoa

88 miles (142km) SW of Milan, 311 miles (501km) NW of Rome, 120 miles (193km) NE of Nice

It was altogether fitting that "Genova the Proud" (Repubblica Superba) gave birth to Christopher Columbus. Its link with the sea dates back to ancient times. However, Columbus did his hometown a disservice. By blazing the trail to the New World, he dealt a devastating blow to Mediterranean ports in general, because the balance of trade shifted to newly developing centers on the Atlantic.

Even so, Genoa (Genova) today is Italy's premier port and ranks with Marseilles in European importance. In its heyday (the 13th century), its empire, extending from colonies on the Barbary Coast to citadels on the Euphrates, rivaled that of Venice. Apart from Columbus, its most famous son was Andrea Doria (yes, the ill-fated ocean liner was named after him), who wrested his city from the yoke of French domination in the early 16th century.

With a population of some 820,000, Genoa is the capital of Liguria and one of the richest cities in Italy. Though shipping remains its major business, other industries have become highly developed in recent years, including insurance, communications, banking, and electronics.

ESSENTIALS

GETTING THERE Alitalia and other carriers fly into the **Aeroporto Internazionale di Genova Cristoforo Colombo,** 4 miles (6km) west of the city center in Sestri Ponente (call ☎ **010-601-51** for flight information).

Genoa has good **rail** connections with the rest of Italy; it lies only 1½ hours from Milan, 3 hours from Florence, and 1½ hours from the French border. Genoa has two major rail stations, **Stazione Prìncipe** and **Stazione Brignole.** Chances are you'll arrive at the Prìncipe, Piazza Acquaverde, nearest to the harbor and the old part of the city. The Brignole, on Piazza Verde, lies in the heart of the modern city. Both trains and municipally operated buses run between the two stations. For train information, call ☎ **1478-88-088** toll-free in Italy.

If you have a **car,** Genoa is right along the main autostrada (A10) that begins at the French border and continues along the Ligurian coastline.

There's a 22-hour **ferry** service to Genoa originating in Palermo (Sicily), costing from 110,000L ($55) per person. Ferries also leave Porto Torres (Sardinia) for Genoa, costing from 100,000L ($50). For information, the number to call in Genoa is the Stazione Marittima at ☎ **010-256-682.**

VISITOR INFORMATION The **Azienda di Promozione Turistica** is on Via al Porto Antico (☎ **010-248-711**), open daily 9am to 6:30pm. You'll also find **information booths** dispensing tourist literature at the rail stations and the airport. The rail station office at Prìncipe (☎ **010-246-2633**) is open Monday to Saturday 8am to 8pm and Sunday 9am to noon; the airport office (☎ **010-601-15-247**) is open Monday to Saturday 8am to 8pm.

FAST FACTS **Currency exchange** is available at **Basso,** Via Gramsci 245 (☎ **010-26-10-67**), open Monday to Friday 8am to 6pm and Saturday and Sunday 8am to 1pm. There are also exchange offices in both the Brignole and the Prìncipe rail stations, open daily 7am to 10pm.

For assistance in a medical, police, or fire emergency, dial ☎ **113** at any time, from any phone in Genoa. For automobile trouble, call **ACI,** Soccorso Stradale at ☎ **116.**

The city's largest hospital, **Ospedale San Martino,** Viale Benedetto XV 10 (☎ **010-55-51**), maintains a roster of emergency services and can link you with an appropriate specialist.

At least one of Genoa's pharmacies remains open 24 hours, based on a revolving schedule that changes from week to week. One of the largest of the city's pharmacies is **Pescetto,** Via Baldi 31R (☎ **010-246-2696**), across from the Prìncipe rail station.

To call a **taxi,** dial ☎ **010-59-66.**

SEEING THE SIGHTS

Like a half moon, the port encircles the Gulf of Genoa. Its hills slope down to the water, so walking is an up- and downhill affair. The center of the city's maritime life, the harbor makes for an interesting stroll, particularly in the part of the old town bordering the water. Sailors from many lands search for adventure and women in the little bars and cabarets occupying the back alleys. Often the streets are merely medieval lanes, with foreboding buildings closing in.

Genoa

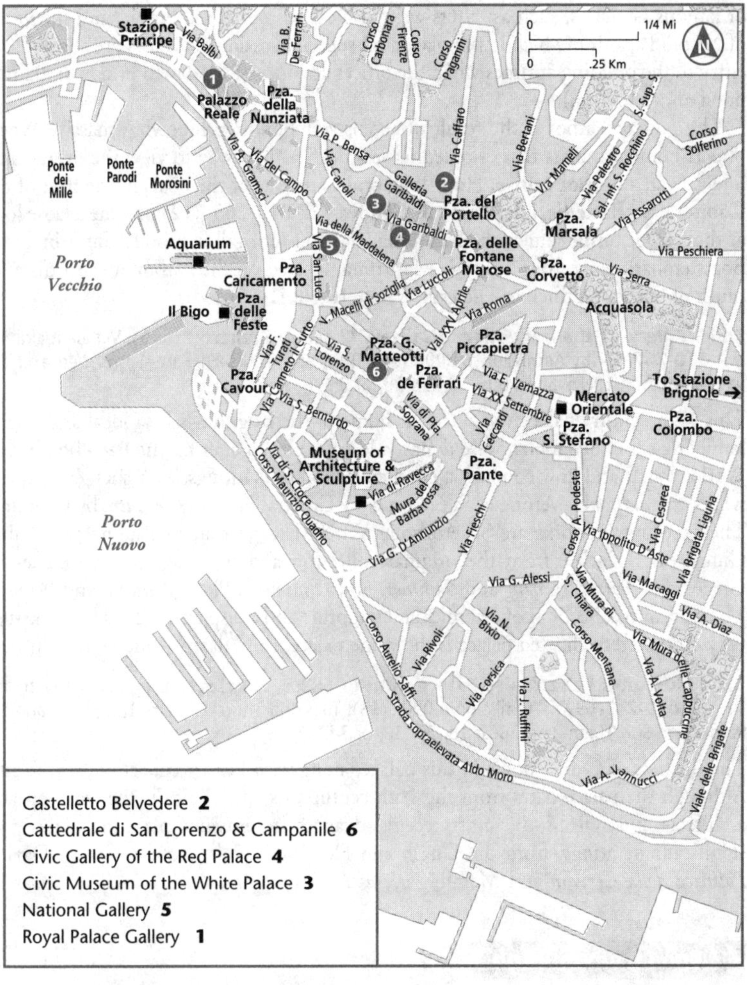

Most of the section of interest lies between the two rail stations, **Stazione Prìncipe,** on the western fringe of the town near the port, and **Stazione Brignole,** to the northeast, opening onto Piazza Verdi. A major artery is **Via XX Settembre,** running between Piazza Ferrari in the west and Piazza della Vittoria in the east. **Via Balbi** is another major artery, beginning east of Stazione Prìncipe, off Piazza Acquaverde. Via Balbi ends at Piazza Nunziata.

From here, a short walk along Via Cairola leads to the most important street in Genoa, ✪ **Via Garibaldi,** the street of patricians, on which noble Genovese families erected splendid palazzi in late Renaissance times. The guiding hand behind the general appearance and most of the architecture was Alessi, who grew to fame in the 16th century (he studied under Michelangelo). Aside from the art collections housed in the **Palazzo Bianco** and **Palazzo Rosso** (see below), the street contains a wealth of treasures. The **Palazzo Podesta,** no. 7, hides a beautiful fountain in its courtyard, and the **Palazzo Turisi,** no. 9, now housing the municipal offices, proudly displays artifacts of famous Genoans, such as letters written by Christopher Columbus and the violin of Nicolò Paganini (which is still played on special occasions); visitors are allowed free entry to the building at times when the offices are open (Monday to Friday 8:30am to noon and 1 to 4pm).

The present harbor is the result of extensive rebuilding, following massive World War II bombardments that crippled its seaside. The best way to view the overall skyline is from a **harbor cruise.** Hour-long cruises on one of the boats in the fleet of the **Cooperativa Battellieri dei Porto di Genova** (☎ **010-265-712**) provide a close look at the harbor bustle and at the **Lanterna,** the 360-foot-tall lighthouse built in 1544. Boats embark daily from Stazione Marittima, located on the harbor, a short distance south of Stazione Prìncipe. The cruises cost 10,000L ($5).

Civic Gallery of the Red Palace (Galleria Civica di Palazzo Rosso). Via Garibaldi 18. ☎ **010-247-6368.** Admission 6,000L ($3). Tues and Thurs–Fri 9am–1pm; Wed and Sat 9am–7pm; Sun 10am–6pm. Bus: 18, 20, 30, or 34.

This 17th-century palace was once the home of the Brignole-Sale, a local aristocratic family that founded a Genovese dynasty. It was restored after having been bombed in World War II and now contains a good collection of paintings, with such exceptional works as *Giuditta* by Veronese, *St. Sebastian* by Guido Reni, and *Cleopatra* by Guercino. The best-known works are Sir Anthony Van Dyck's portrait of Pauline and Anton Giulio Brignole-Sale from the original collection and the magnificent frescoes by Gregorio de Ferrari (*Spring* and *Summer*) and Domenico Piola (*Autumn* and *Winter*). There are also collections of ceramics and sculpture and a display of gilded baroque statuary. Across from this red palace is the white palace, the Palazzo Bianco (see below).

Civic Museum of the White Palace (Museo Civico di Palazzo Bianco). Via Garibaldi 11. ☎ **010-247-6377.** Admission 6,000L ($3). Tues and Thurs–Fri 9am–1pm; Wed and Sat 9am–7pm; Sun 10am–6pm. Bus: 18, 20, 30, or 34.

The duchess of Gallier donated this palace, along with her art collection, to the city. Although the palace dates from the 16th century, its appearance is the work of later architects and reflects the most recent advances in museum planning. The most significant paintings, from the Dutch and Flemish schools, include Gerard David's *Polittico della Cervara* and Memling's *Jesus Blessing the Faithful,* as well as works by

Genoa from on High

From Piazza Portello (at the eastern end of Via Garibaldi), a funicular climbs to the **Castelletto belvedere,** which offers stunning views and refreshing breezes. It costs 600L (30¢) each way and runs daily 6:40am to midnight.

A similar climb is via the **Granarolo funicular,** leaving from Piazza del Prìncipe, behind the rail station of the same name, and ascending 1,000 feet to Porto Granarolo, one of the gates in the city's 17th-century walls; there's a parklike belvedere in front. It costs 1,500L (75¢) each way and operates every 15 minutes daily 6am to 11:45pm.

An elevator costing 5,000L ($2.50) lifts you to the top of **Il Brigo,** the mastlike tower that is Genoa's new landmark, built to commemorate the 1992 Columbus quincentennial; the observation platform provides an eagle's-eye view of one of Europe's busiest ports. March to August, it operates Tuesday to Saturday 11am to 1pm and 3 to 6pm, Sunday 11am to 1pm and 2:30 to 6:30pm; September to February, hours are Tuesday to Friday 11am to 1pm and 2:30 to 4pm, Sunday 11am to 1pm and 2:30 to 5pm.

Sir Anthony Van Dyck and Peter Paul Rubens. A wide-ranging survey of European and local artists is presented, with paintings by Caravaggio, Zurbarán, and Murillo and works by Bernardo Strozzi (a whole room) and Alessandro Magnasco (an excellent painting of a scene in a Genovese garden).

National Gallery (Galleria Nazionale). In the Palazzo Spinola, Piazza della Pellicceria 1. ☎ **010-247-7061.** Admission 8,000L ($4). Mon 9am–1pm; Tues–Sat 9am–7pm; Sun 2–7pm. Bus: 18, 20, 30, or 34.

This gallery houses a major painting collection. Its notable works include Joos van Cleve's *Madonna in Prayer,* Antonello da Messina's *Ecce Homo,* and Giovanni Pisano's *Guistizia.* The gallery is also known for its decorative arts collection (furniture, silver, and ceramics, among other items). The palace itself was designed for the Grimaldi family in the 16th century as a private residence, though the Spinolas took it over eventually.

Royal Palace Gallery (Galleria di Palazzo Reale). Via Baldi 10. ☎ **010-271-0201.** Admission 8,000L ($4). Sun–Tues 9am–1:45pm; Wed–Sat 9am–6:30pm. Bus: 18, 19, or 20.

A 5-minute walk from Stazione Prìncipe, the Royal Palace was started about 1650, and work continued until the early 18th century. It was built for the Balbi family, was sold to the Durazzos, and became one of the royal palaces of the Savoias in 1824. King Charles Albert modified many of the rooms around 1840. As in all Genovese palazzi, some of these subsequent alterations marred the original designs. Its gallery is filled with paintings and sculpture, works by Van Dyck, Tintoretto, G. F. Romanelli, and L. Giordano. Frescoes and antiques from the 17th to the 19th century are displayed. Seek out, in particular, the **Hall of Mirrors** and the **Throne Room.**

✪ **Cattedrale di San Lorenzo & Campanile.** Piazza San Lorenzo, Via Tommaso Reggio 17. ☎ **010-311-269.** Admission 12,000L ($6). Mon–Sat 9am–noon and 3–6pm. Bus: 42.

Genoa is noted for its medieval churches, and this one towers over them all. A British shell fired during World War II almost spelled its doom, but miraculously the explosion never went off. The cathedral is distinguished by its bands of black-and-white marble adorning the facade in the Pisan style. In its present form, it dates from the 13th century, though it was erected on the foundation of a much earlier structure. Alessi designed the dome, and the *campanile* (bell tower) dates from the 16th century. The **Chapel of John the Baptist (Cappella di San Giovanni),** with interesting Renaissance sculpture, is said to contain the remains of the saint for whom it's named. Off the nave and in the vaults, the cathedral **treasury** contains a trove of artifacts acquired during Genoa's heyday as a mercantile empire. Some of the claims are a bit hard to believe, however (a crystal dish reputed to have been used for dinner service at the Last Supper and a blue chalcedony platter on which the head of John the Baptist was placed for its delivery to Salome). Other treasures include an 11th-century arm reliquary of St. Anne and a jewel-studded Byzantine Zaccaria Cross.

SHOPPING

Shopping in Genoa includes a good selection of apparel, antiques, jewelry, and foodstuff. Classic but contemporary **Berti,** Via XII Ottobre 94R (☎ **010-540-026**), carries a line of Burberry items, as well as British-inspired creations by designers like Valentino and Pedroni. Elegant **Pescetto,** Via Scurreria 8 Rosso (☎ **010-247-3433**), offers men's and women's designer outfits and fragrances, plus accessories like leather bags and wallets.

On a street overrun with goldsmiths, the reputable **Code-villa,** Via Orefici 53R (☎ **010-247-2567**), fashions jewelry and small objects out of gold, silver, and a wide variety of precious and semiprecious stones.

In the historic center of town, the **Dallai Libreria Antiquaria,** Piazza de Marini 11R (☎ **010-247-2338**), handles first editions and rare books and prints from the 18th and 19th centuries.

Pecchiolo, Via Pisa 13 (☎ **010-362-5082**), sells upscale dinner- and cookware of ceramic, crystal, and silver.

If you'd rather have a one-stop shopping excursion, **La Rinascente,** Via Vernazza 1 (☎ **010-586-995**), and **Coin,** Via XII Ottobre 4 (☎ **010-543126**), are the two biggest department stores in town.

ACCOMMODATIONS

Generally, hotels in Genoa are second-rate, but some good finds await those who search diligently.

Warning: Some of the cheap hotels and pensions in and around the waterfront are to be avoided. Our recommendations, however, are suitable even for women traveling alone.

EXPENSIVE TO MODERATE

Bristol Palace. Via XX Settembre 35, 16121 Genova. ☎ **010-592-541.** Fax 010-561-756. www.hotelbristolpalace.com. E-mail: info@hotelbristolpalace.com. 133 units. A/C MINIBAR TV TEL. 190,000–490,000L ($95–$245) double; 500,000–750,000L ($250–$375) suite. Rates include breakfast. AE, DC, MC, V. Parking 30,000L ($15). Bus: 17, 18, 19, 20, 37, or 44.

The late-19th-century Bristol boasts a number of features that'll make your stay in Genoa special, even though it's in the grimy heart of the old town. Its obscure entrance behind colonnades is misleading; the public rooms are decorated nicely with traditional pieces, though both the fabrics and the furnishings are beginning to show their age. The larger of the guest rooms have an old-fashioned elegance, often with chandeliers, Queen Anne desks, and padded headboards. All the rooms contain at least one antique and often several, plus first-rate mattresses. The bathrooms are generally large, with hair dryers and heated racks; some come with whirlpool tubs. The hotel's stairway is one of the most stunning in Genoa.

Dining/Diversions: The English bar is a favorite rendezvous point, and the small but elegant Caffè de Bristol offers daily lunches and dinners.

Amenities: Concierge, room service, laundry/dry cleaning, baby-sitting.

City Hotel. Via San Sebastiano 6, 16123 Genova. ☎ **010-5545.** Fax 010-586-301. www.bestwestern.com. E-mail: city.ge@bestwestern.it. 64 units. A/C MINIBAR TV TEL. 420,000L ($210) double; 700,000L ($350) suite. Rates include breakfast. AE, DC, MC, V. Parking 40,000L ($20). Bus: 17 or 18.

A good solid choice, the City occupies a starkly angular stucco-and-travertine building, surrounded by crumbling town houses. The convenient location, near Piazza Corvetto and Via Garibaldi, is one of the best features. Other pluses are a welcoming staff, a comfortable wood-and-granite lobby, and guest rooms with parquet floors, specially designed furniture, and up-to-date amenities. The tiled bathrooms are compact.

Dining/Diversions: The cocktail bar serves snacks, and the first-class restaurant offers many regional specialties. A short list of cold and hot foods is served room service–style during the day and early evening.

Amenities: Concierge, room service, laundry/dry cleaning, twice-daily maid service.

Columbus Sea Hotel. Via Milano 63, 16126 Genova. ☎ **010-265-051.** Fax 010-255-226. www.columbussea.com. E-mail: columbussea@mclink.it. 80 units. A/C MINIBAR TV TEL. 220,000–390,000L ($110–$195) double; from 430,000L ($215) junior suite. Rates include buffet breakfast. AE, CB, DC, DISC, MC, V. Free parking. Bus: 1, 3, 7, 8, 18, 19, 20, 30, or 34.

One of the best moderately priced hotels in town, the Columbus Sea looks out at the new cruise-ship terminal. It's warmer and more inviting inside than its cold boxy exterior suggests, with guest rooms that are spacious for the most part, in muted colors with Oriental carpeting; four are suitable for travelers with disabilities. Each accommodation comes with an excellent mattress and a compact tiled bathroom. The public rooms are more gracious, with a certain flair. A popular rendezvous is Il Mandraccio, the hotel's American bar. La Lanterna serves excellent Ligurian specialties and treats you to a panoramic view of the harbor and city. The hotel offers many of the amenities of far more expensive hotels, like a concierge, room service, laundry/dry cleaning, secretarial services, a courtesy car, and baby-sitting on request.

Hotel Savoia Majestic. Via Arsenale di Terra 5, 16126 Genova. ☎ **010-261-641.** Fax 010-261-883. 120 units. A/C MINIBAR TV TEL. 300,000–350,000L ($150–$175) double; from 420,000L ($210) suite. Rates include breakfast. AE, DC, MC, V. Valet parking 30,000L ($15). Bus: 19, 20, 35, 37, or 41.

Situated across from Piazza Prìncipe, the 1887 Savoia still contains some of its original accessories, though its heyday has long since passed. The decor of the high-ceilinged guest rooms ranges from modern to conservatively old-fashioned. Try for a room on the sixth floor for the best harbor views. Some of the bathrooms are unusually large, with pink marble surfaces, while others are extremely cramped. Because the rooms vary so widely from good to bad, your experience will depend entirely on where you're stashed for the night. The lobby and reception area are shared with the Hotel Londra & Continentale (same phone as above), where doubles are 220,000L ($110).

Dining: The restaurant is so routine you'll want to seek better fare at one of the nearby trattorie.

Amenities: Concierge, room service, laundry/dry cleaning, newspaper delivery, twice-daily maid service, baby-sitting, secretarial services, courtesy car.

Jolly Hotel Plaza. Via Martin Piaggio 11, 16122 Genova. ☎ **800/221-2626** in the U.S., 800/237-0319 in Canada, or 010-831-61. Fax 010-839-1850. www.jollyhotels.it. E-mail: genova @jollyhotels.it. 147 units. A/C MINIBAR TV TEL. 360,000–400,000L ($180–$200) double; 900,000L ($450) suite. Rates include breakfast. AE, DC, MC, V. Parking 36,000L ($18) nearby. Bus: 18, 34, or 37.

A four-star member of the Jolly chain, this hotel is newer than its modified classic facade would suggest. Near Piazza Corvetto, it was built in 1950 to replace an older hotel destroyed during a World War II air raid. In 1992 the hotel was renovated and enlarged, linking two former hotels, the Baglioni Eliseo and the Plaza. The rooms in the old Eliseo are generally more spacious than those in the Plaza (and better decorated). Elegant touches include mother-of-pearl inlay in the doors and marble bathrooms. Special rooms are set aside for nonsmokers or travelers with disabilities. The bathrooms are small, but each comes with a hair dryer.

Dining: On the premises are an American-style bar and a grill room, La Villetta di Negro. When business is slow, the management sometimes opts not to open the restaurant on weekends.

Amenities: Concierge, room service, laundry/dry cleaning.

INEXPENSIVE

✪ **Albergo Viale Sauli.** Viale Sauli 5, 16121 Genova. ☎ **010-561-397.** Fax 010-590-092. www.eurhotels.com. E-mail: htl.sauli@mclink.it. 56 units. A/C MINIBAR TV TEL. 190,000L ($95) double. Rates include breakfast. AE, CB, DC, MC, V. Parking 25,000L ($12.50) nearby. Bus: 33 or 37.

This hotel is on the second floor of a modern concrete office building, just off a busy shopping street. It's scattered over three floors, each reachable by elevator from the lobby. The high-ceilinged public rooms include a bar, a breakfast room, and a reception area. Enore Sceresini is the opera-loving owner, and his guests usually include businesspeople who appreciate cleanliness and comfort. Each guest room has a firm mattress, marble floors, and a spacious bathroom.

Hotel Agnello d'Oro. Vico delle Monachette 6, 16126 Genova. ☎ **010-246-2084.** Fax 010-246-2327. 38 units. TV TEL. 150,000L ($75) double. Breakfast 15,000L ($7.50). AE, DC, MC, V. Bus: 18, 19, 20, 30, 32, or 41.

When the Doria family owned this structure and everything around it in the 1600s, they carved their family crest on the walls near the top of the alley. The symbol was a golden lamb, and you can still see one at the point where the narrow street joins the busy boulevard leading to Stazione Prìncipe. The hotel, named after the animal on the crest, is a 17th-century building that includes vaulted ceilings and paneling in the lobby. About half the guest rooms are in a newer wing, but if you want the oldest ones, ask for room no. 6, 7, or 8. Each comes with a firm mattress and a compact tiled bathroom. Today the hotel is maintained by a family who has installed a small bar and restaurant off the lobby.

Hotel Astoria. Piazza Brignole 4, 16122 Genova. ☎ **010-873-316.** Fax 010-831-7326. 69 units. TV TEL. 170,000–250,000L ($85–$125) double. Rates include breakfast. AE, DC, MC, V. Parking 25,000L ($12.50). Bus: 18.

Built in the 1920s but opened as a hotel only in 1978, this place has lots of polished paneling, wrought-iron accents, beige marble floors, and a baronial carved fireplace. The guest rooms are comfortably furnished and well maintained. In 1998 the entire hotel was renewed, with all the mattresses replaced. The hotel sits on an uninspiring square that contains a filling station, and its view encompasses a traffic hub and many square blocks of apartment buildings. There's a bar but no restaurant.

Hotel Vittoria Orlandi. Via Baldi 33–45, 16126 Genova. ☎ **010-261-923.** Fax 010-246-2656. www.gattei.it/vittoria. 47 units. A/C MINIBAR TV TEL. 120,000–150,000L ($60–$75) double. Breakfast 15,000L ($7.50). AE, DC, MC, V. Bus: 35, 37, or 41.

Since this hotel is built on one of the hillsides for which Genoa is famous, its entrance is under a tunnel opening at a point about a block from Stazione Prìncipe. An elevator will take you up to the reception area. The guest rooms are standardized and fairly basic, each medium-sized, and the beds, either twins or doubles, are fitted with fine mattresses. The bathrooms are small. Many rooms have balconies, and about half are air-conditioned and contain minibars. Best of all, the hotel is quiet because of the way it's sheltered from the boulevards by other buildings.

DINING

✪ **Da Giacomo.** Corso Italia 1R. ☎ **010-362-9647.** Reservations recommended. Main courses 25,000–45,000L ($12.50–$22.50); fixed-price menus 75,000–120,000L ($37.50–$60). DC, V. Thurs–Tues 12:30–2:30pm and 7:30–11pm. Closed 1 week in Aug. Bus: 18. LIGURIAN.

Many food critics regard Da Giacomo as the premier restaurant of Genoa (though we give a slight edge to the Gran Gotto, below). The service is excellent, as is the modern dining room, graced with plants. Ligurian cooking is dominated by the sea, and the menu begins with superb seafood antipasti, some of which is raw, carved with the exquisite care you find in Tokyo. Meat, fish, and poultry dishes are prepared with unusual flair. Pesto sauce accompanies many dishes, especially the pasta. (During the Crusades, it was reported that the Genovese contingent could always be identified by the aroma of pesto surrounding them.) Guests can choose from some of the finest regional wines in Italy, and the desserts are made fresh daily. There's also a piano bar where you can dance.

Focaccia & Farinata on the Run

Fast food is a Genoese specialty, and any number of storefronts disburse *focaccia,* the heavenly Ligurian flat bread often stuffed with cheese and topped with herbs, olives, onions, and other vegetables. Two favorites are **La Focacceria di Teobaldo,** Via Balbi 115R (☎ **010-246-2294**), and **Il Fornaio di Sattanino,** Via Fiasella 18R (☎ **010-580-972**).

Another Genovese favorite is *farinata,* a cross between a ravioli and a crepe made from chickpea flour and stuffed with spinach and ricotta, lightly fried, and often topped with walnut-cream sauce. Locals say this delicious concoction gets no better than at the two outlets of **Antica Sciamada** (☎ **010-280-843**), Via Ravecca 19R and Via San Giorgio 14R.

✪ **Gran Gotto.** Viale Brigate Bisagno 69R. ☎ **010-583-644.** Reservations recommended. Main courses 30,000–40,000L ($15–$20). AE, MC, V. Daily 12:30–2:30pm and 7:30–10:30pm. Closed Aug 12–31. Bus: 31. SEAFOOD.

Our pick for Genoa's top restaurant opened in 1937 and has been in the same family since. The emphasis is on seafood, but the meat and pasta dishes aren't neglected. The most typical offering is *trenette al pesto,* paper-thin noodles served with pesto. The delicately simmered risotto is also tempting. The main dishes are reasonably priced and of high standard, including the mixed fish fry, French baby squid, and *rognone al cognac* (tender calves' kidneys cooked and delicately flavored in cognac). The *zuppa di pesce* (fish soup) has made many a luncheon for many a gourmet.

Ristorante Saint Cyr. Piazza Marsala 4. ☎ **010-886-897.** Reservations required. Main courses 30,000–35,000L ($15–$17.50). AE, DC, MC, V. Mon–Fri noon–3pm and 8–11pm; Sat 8–11pm. Closed Dec 23–Jan 7 and 2 weeks in Aug. Bus: 33, 34, or 36. LIGURIAN/PIEDMONTESE.

Our favorite time to come to this restaurant is at night, when some of the most discriminating palates in Genoa might be seen enjoying dishes adapted from regional recipes. Menu items change daily, though recent offerings featured rice with truffles and cheese, a timbale of fresh spinach, a charlotte of fish, and a variety of braised meats, each delicately seasoned. Specialties include *scamone* (a certain cut of beef) cooked in Barolo wine and *ravioli al sugo di carne* (with a sauce made from meat juices). At lunch, the patrons are likely to be businesspeople discussing shipping contracts.

Ristorante Zeffirino. Via XX Settembre 20. ☎ **010-591-990.** Reservations recommended. Main courses 30,000–60,000L ($18–$36); fixed-price menus 70,000–90,000L ($35–$45). AE, DC, MC, V. Daily noon–midnight. Bus: 17, 18, 19, 20, 37, or 44. LIGURIAN.

Located in a cul-de-sac just off one of the busiest boulevards, this place has hosted everyone from Frank Sinatra and Luciano Pavarotti to Pope John Paul II and Liza Minnelli. At least 14 members of the Zeffirino family prepare the best pasta in the city, using recipes collected from all over Italy. These include lesser-known varieties like quadrucci, pettinati, and cappelletti, as well as the more familiar tagliatelle and lasagna. Next, you can select from a vast array of meat and fish, along with 1,000 kinds of wine. Ligurian specialties, including *risotto alla pescatore* and beef stew with artichokes, are featured. Try a wide array of shellfish, either baked or steamed, served with seasonal vegetables.

GENOA AFTER DARK

Warning: Keep your wits about you after dark in Genoa, especially in the labyrinthine alleys of the medieval core. The neighborhoods around the bus station and Piazza Matteotti are especially dubious; they're a center for the drug trade and prostitution.

You'll find enough discos to keep you fully occupied every night. The best of them is **Caffè Nessundorma,** Via Porta d'Arci 74 (☎ **010-561-773**), where live music, beginning at 10:30pm, usually segues into recorded music, often from the 1970s and 1980s; it's part singles bar and part hip cafe. Somewhat more elegant is **Mako,** Corso Italia 28R (☎ **010-367-652**), which has a piano bar, a disco, and a restaurant. Two other centrally located contenders for the bar/disco trade are **Vanilla,** Via Brigata Salerno 4R (☎ **010-399-0872**), and **Eccentrica,** Via Ceccardi 24 (☎ **010-570-2809**), which are neither as vanilla nor as eccentric as their names imply.

Looking for a simple pint of beer, some pub grub, and a dose of English humor? Head for the **Britannia Pub,** Vicolo della Cassana, near Piazza de Ferrari (☎ **010-247-4532**), where groups of friends fill a woodsy-looking setting.

The most popular gay spot is **La Cage,** Via Sampierdarena 167R (☎ **010-645-4555**), attracting mainly males 21 to 40. There's no cover, and it's open Tuesday to Saturday 10pm to 3:30am.

3 Rapallo

296 miles (477km) NW of Rome, 17 miles (27km) SE of Genoa, 100 miles (161km) S of Milan

Known for years to the chic crowd that lives in the villas on the hillside, Rapallo occupies a remarkable site overlooking the Gulf of Tigullio. In summer the crowded heart of Rapallo takes on a carnival air, as hordes of sunbathers occupy the rocky sands along the beach. In the area is an 18-hole golf course, as well as an indoor pool, a riding club, and a modern harbor.

You can also take a cable car or a bus to the **Montallegro Sanctuary** (**Santuario di Montallegro**). Inside this 16th-century church are some interesting frescoes and a curious Byzantine icon of the Virgin that allegedly flew here on its own from Dalmatia. The views over the sea and valleys are the main reason to come up here, though, and they're even more breathtaking from the summit of **Monte Rosa,** a short uphill hike away. There are many opportunities for summer **boat trips,** not only to Portofino but also to the Cinque Terre.

Rapallo's long history is often likened to Genoa's. It became part of the Repubblica Superba in 1229, but Rapallo had existed long before that. Its **cathedral** dates from the 6th century when it was founded by the bishops of Milan. Walls once enclosed the medieval town, but now only the **Saline Gate** remains. Rapallo has also been the scene of many an international meeting, the most notable of which was the 1917 conference of wartime allies.

Today Rapallo is a bit past its heyday, though it was once known as one of Europe's most fashionable resorts, numbering among its residents Ezra Pound and D. H. Lawrence. Other artists, poets, and writers have been drawn to its natural beauty, which has been marred in part by an uncontrolled building boom brought on by tourism. At the innermost corner of the Gulf of Tiguillio, Rapallo is still the most famous resort on the Riviera di Levante, a position it owes to its year-round mild climate.

ESSENTIALS

GETTING THERE Three **trains** from Genoa stop here each hour 4:30am to midnight, costing 2,800L ($1.40) one way. A train also links Rapallo with Santa Margherita every 30 minutes, costing 1,500L (75¢) one way. For more information, dial ☎ **1478-880-88** toll-free in Italy. From Santa Margherita, a **bus** operated by Tigullio runs every 20 to 25 minutes to Rapallo, costing 1,400L (85¢) one way and taking half an hour. The bus information office is at Piazza Vittorio Veneto in Santa Margherita (☎ **0185-288-834**).

If you have a **car** and are coming from Genoa, go southeast along A12.

VISITOR INFORMATION The **tourist office** is at Via Diaz 9 (☎ **0185-230-346**), open daily 9:30am to 12:30pm and 2:30 to 5:30pm, Sunday 9am to 12:30pm.

ACCOMMODATIONS

Grand Hotel Bristol. Via Aurelia Orientale 369, 16035 Rapallo. ☎ **0185-273-313.** Fax 0185-55-800. www.tigullio.net/bristol. E-mail: info.bristol@tigulio.net. 91 units. A/C MINIBAR TV TEL. 300,000–400,000L ($150–$200) double; from 850,000L ($425) suite. Rates include breakfast. AE, MC, V. Parking 25,000L ($12.50) in garage, free outdoors.

This hotel, one of the Riviera's grand old buildings, is still a viable choice despite falling standards. Built in 1908, it was reopened in 1984 and the pink-and-white facade was spruced up but basically left unchanged. The interior, however, was gutted. Some guest rooms have private terraces, and all contain electronic window blinds, lots of mirrors, and oversized beds with firm mattresses. The bathrooms are large, with hair dryers. The inviting waters of a pool are visible from many rooms, and the kitchens are about the most modern anywhere.

Dining/Diversions: The hotel has several restaurants, including a rooftop restaurant that's often closed when it's too hot. If business is slow, only one restaurant might be open.

Amenities: Room service, baby-sitting, laundry/valet, hairdresser, beautician, massage salon, free-form pool, conference rooms.

Hotel Eurotel. Via Aurelia di Ponente 22, 16035 Rapallo. ☎ **0185-60-981.** Fax 0185-50-635. www.tigullio.net/eurotel. E-mail: hoteleurotel@tigullio.net. 65 units. A/C MINIBAR TV TEL. 240,000–270,000L ($120–$135) double. Rates include buffet breakfast. AE, CB, DC, MC, V. Parking 25,000L ($12.50) in garage, free outdoors.

With seven floors, this vivid sienna-colored structure is one of the tallest hotels in town, set above the port at the top of a winding road where you'll have to negotiate the oncoming traffic with care. (Many of the units, though, are privately owned condos.) All the guest rooms contain built-in cabinets, arched loggias with views over the gulf of Rapallo, and beds that fold, Murphy-style, into the walls. The tiled bathrooms, though a bit small, are neatly organized.

Dining/Diversions: A bar and a second-floor panoramic restaurant, Antica Aurelia, are on the premises.

Amenities: Concierge, room service, laundry/dry cleaning, massage, baby-sitting, small rectangular pool.

Hotel Giulio Cesare. Corso Colombo 52, 16035 Rapallo. ☎ **0185-50-685.** Fax 0185-60-896. 33 units. A/C TV TEL. 200,000L ($100) double with breakfast; 150,000L ($75) per person double with half-board. AE, MC, V. Closed Nov 6–Dec 20. Parking 15,000L ($7.50).

This modernized villa, on the coast road about 90 feet from the sea, is a bargain. When the genial owner skillfully renovated it, he kept expenses down to keep room rates lower. The guest rooms are furnished with tasteful reproductions and good mattresses, featuring views of the Gulf of Tigullio (most have balconies). Ask for the top-floor rooms if you want a better view and more quiet. Twenty-five rooms are air-conditioned. The meals are prepared with fine ingredients (the fresh fish dishes are superb).

Hotel Miramare. Lungomare Vittorio Veneto 27, 16035 Rapallo. ☎ **0185-230-261.** Fax 0185-273-570. 28 units. MINIBAR TV TEL. 150,000–200,000L ($75–$100) double; 200,000–250,000L ($100–$125) suite. Half-board 120,000–160,000L ($60–$80) per person. AE, DC, MC, V. Closed Nov. Parking 25,000L ($12.50).

On the water near a stone gazebo is this 1929 re-creation of a Renaissance villa, with exterior frescoes that have faded in the salt air. The gardens in front have been replaced by a glass extension that contains a contemporary restaurant (see "Dining," below). The accommodations are clean and simple, comfortable, and high-ceilinged; many have iron balconies that stretch toward the harbor.

DINING

Ristorante da Monique. Lungomare Vittorio Veneto 6. ☎ **0185-50-541.** Reservations recommended. Main courses 15,000–30,000L ($7.50–$15). AE, DC, MC, V. Wed–Mon noon–2:30pm and 7:30–10pm. Closed Jan 7–Feb 10. SEAFOOD.

This is one of the most popular seafood restaurants along the harbor, especially in summer, featuring a nautical decor and big windows overlooking the boats in the marina. As you'd expect, fish is the specialty, including seafood salad, fish soup, risotto with shrimp, spaghetti with clams or mussels, grilled fish, and both tagliatelle and scampi "Monique." Some of these dishes may not always hit the mark, but you'll rarely go wrong ordering the grilled fish.

Ristorante Elite. Via Milite Ignoto 19. ☎ **0185-50-551.** Reservations recommended. Main courses 20,000–40,000L ($12–$24); *menù turistico* 40,000L ($20); tasting menu 55,000L ($27.50). AE, MC, V. Fri–Wed noon–2:30pm and 7:30–10pm. Closed Nov. SEAFOOD.

This restaurant is set back from the water on a busy commercial street in the center of town. Mainly fish is served; the offering depends on the catch of the day. Your dinner might consist of mussels marinara, minestrone Genovese style, risotto marinara, *trenette al pesto,* scampi, *zuppa di pesce,* turbot, or a mixed fish fry. A limited selection of standard meat dishes is available, too. At the peak of the midsummer invasion, the restaurant is likely to be open every day.

Ristorante Miramare. In the Hotel Miramare, Lungomare Vittorio Veneto 27. ☎ **0185-230-261.** Reservations recommended. Main courses 18,000–35,000L ($9–$17.50); fixed-price menu 45,000L ($22.50). AE, DC, MC, V. Daily 12:30–2pm and 7:30–9:30pm. SEAFOOD/LIGURIAN.

This restaurant serves well-prepared unpretentious food in a modern dining room overlooking the sea. Your dinner might include fried calamari, spaghetti with clams, sea bass or turbot baked with potatoes and artichokes, veal in marsala sauce, or flavorful versions of fish soup.

4 Santa Margherita Ligure

19 miles (31km) E of Genoa, 3 miles (5km) S of Portofino, 296 miles (477km) NW of Rome

Like Rapallo, Santa Margherita Ligure occupies a beautiful position on the Gulf of Tigullio. Its attractive palm-fringed harbor is usually thronged with fun seekers, and the resort offers the widest range of accommodations in all price levels on the eastern Riviera. It has a festive appearance, with a promenade, flower beds, and palms swaying in the wind. As is typical of the Riviera, its beach combines pebbles and sand. Santa Margherita Ligure is linked to Portofino by a narrow road. The climate is mild, even in winter, when many elderly guests visit the resort.

The town dates from A.D. 262. The official name of Santa Margherita Ligure was given to the town by Vittorio Emanuele II in 1863. Before that it had many other names, including Porto Napoleone, an 1812 designation from Napoléon.

Landlubbers congregate in the cafes that spill out into the town's two seaside squares, **Piazza Martiri della Liberta** and **Piazza Vittorio Veneto.** Santa Margherita's one landmark of note is its namesake **Basilica di Santa Margherita,** just off the seafront on Piazza Caprera (☎ **0185-286-555**). The interior is richly embellished, with Italian and Flemish paintings, along with relics of the saint for whom the town was named. Admission is free, and it's open daily 8am to 5pm.

ESSENTIALS

GETTING THERE Three **trains** per hour arrive from Genoa daily 4:30am to midnight, costing 2,800L ($1.40) one way. The train station in Santa Margherita is at Piazza Federico Raoul Nobili. For more information, call ☎ **1478-88-088** toll-free in Italy. **Buses** run frequently between Portofino and Santa Margherita Ligure daily, costing 1,700L (85¢) one way. You can also catch a bus in Rapallo to Santa Margherita; during the day one leaves every 20 to 25 minutes. For information, call ☎ **010-231-108.** If you have a **car,** take Route 227 southeast from Genoa.

VISITOR INFORMATION The **tourist office** is at Via 25 Aprile 24 (☎ **0185-287-485**), open Monday to Saturday 9am to 12:30pm and 2:30 to 5:30pm, Sunday 9am to 12:30pm.

ACCOMMODATIONS

EXPENSIVE

✪ **Grand Hotel Miramare.** Via Milite Ignoto 30, 16038 Santa Margherita Ligure. ☎ **800/223-6800** in the U.S., or 0185-287-013. Fax 0185-284-651. www.grandhotelmiramare.it. E-mail: miramare@pn.inet.it. 90 units. A/C MINIBAR TV TEL. 390,000–500,000L ($195–$250) double; from 730,000L ($365) suite. Rates include breakfast. AE, CB, DC, MC, V. Parking 30,000–35,000L ($15–$17.50).

The top hotel in town, this 1929 palace has kept up with the times better than has the Imperiale. Its 1904 core was the home of Giacomo Costa, who transformed it into a hotel that attracted celebrities like Laurence Olivier and Vivien Leigh. It was on the terrace here in 1933 that Marconi succeeded in transmitting telegraph and telephone signals a distance of more than 90 miles (145km). Separated from a stony beach by a busy boulevard, it's a 3-minute walk from the center of town. The guest rooms are classically furnished, with elegant beds and deluxe mattresses, and many of the bathrooms are spacious (all are packed with amenities, from hair dryers to plush towels). Even some of the standard rooms have large terraces with sea views. The curved outdoor pool adjoins a raised sun terrace dotted with parasols and iron tables.

Dining: The hotel restaurant has many Victorian touches, including fragile chairs and blue-and-white porcelain set into the plaster walls.

Amenities: Room service, baby-sitting, laundry/valet, heated saltwater outdoor pool, private beach, Miramare Skywater School.

Imperiale Palace Hotel. Via Pagana 19, 16038 Santa Margherita Ligure. ☎ **0185-288-991.** Fax 0185-284-223. www.hotelimperiale.com. E-mail: info@hotelimperiale.com. 97 units. A/C MINIBAR TV TEL. 430,000–630,000L ($215–$315) double; 730,000–1,100,000L ($365–$550) suite. Rates include breakfast. AE, DC, MC, V. Free parking. Closed Nov–Mar.

The Imperiale looks like a gilded palace. Though still regal, it's fading a bit, and the Miramare (see above) has overtaken it. It's built against a hillside at the edge of the resort, surrounded by semitropical gardens. The public rooms live up to the hotel's name, with vaulted ceilings, satin-covered antiques, ornate mirrors, and inlaid marble floors. The guest rooms vary widely, from royal suites to simple singles away from the sea. Many have elaborate ceilings, balconies, brass beds, chandeliers, and antique furniture, but others are rather sparse. The large tiled or marble bathrooms come with hair dryers, heated racks of plush towels, and robes.

Dining/Diversions: The formal dining room, Novecento, serves Ligurian and international meals, and there's a two-decker open-air restaurant. Most inviting is a music room, with a grand piano and satin chairs, for teatime. In summer, live music is presented on the terrace.

Amenities: Room service, laundry/valet, festive recreation center with oval flagstone pool, extended stone wharf, cabanas.

MODERATE

Hotel Continental. Via Pagana 8, 16038 Santa Margherita Ligure. ☎ **0185-286-512.** Fax 0185-284-463. www.hotel-continental.it. E-mail: continental@hotel-continental.it. 76 units. MINIBAR TV TEL. 230,000–285,000L ($115–$142.50) double. Rates include breakfast. AE, DC, MC, V. Parking 15,000–25,000L ($7.50–$12.50).

The Continental is the only hotel directly on the water, and the high-ceilinged public rooms give a glimpse of the gardens leading down to a private beach. In fair weather, it operates a snack bar here. The guest rooms are filled with comfortable if somewhat faded furnishings and often have French windows opening onto wrought-iron balconies; the small- to medium-sized bathrooms come with hair dryers. Try for a top-floor room in the main building (the annex contains lackluster lodgings). The view from the restaurant encompasses the curved harbor in the center of town, a few miles away. Since the early 1900s, the Ciana family has managed this property and also the Regina Elena, Metropole, and Laurin.

Hotel Regina Elena. Lungomare Milite Ignoto 44, 16038 Santa Margherita Ligure. ☎ **0185-287-003.** Fax 0185-284-473. www.reginaelena.it. E-mail: h.regina.elena@reginaelena.it. 107 units. A/C MINIBAR TV TEL. 268,000–318,000L ($134–$159) double, including breakfast; 334,000–414,000L ($167–$207) double with half-board. AE, CB, DC, MC, V. Free parking.

This pastel-painted hotel is along the scenic thoroughfare leading to Portofino. The guest rooms are modern and of medium size, most opening onto a balcony with a sea view. An annex in the garden contains additional, but not as desirable, units. The hotel was built in 1908 and many turn-of-the-century details remain, including a marble staircase. It's operated by the Ciana family, which has been receiving guests for almost 100 years. They also operate the Continental, Metropole, and Laurin. The dining room is a 12-sided glass-walled structure serving excellent cuisine. The hotel offers room service, baby-sitting, and laundry/valet. There's also a conference center and a roof garden pool with a Jacuzzi.

Park Hotel Suisse. Via Favale 31, 16038 Santa Margherita Ligure. ☎ **0185-289-571.** Fax 0185-281-469. E-mail: parkhotelsuisse@liero.it. 85 units. TV TEL. 170,000–400,000L ($85–$200) double; 230,000–500,000L ($115–$250) suite. Rates include continental breakfast. No credit cards.

Set in a garden above the town center, the Suisse features a panoramic view of the sea and harbor. It has seven floors, all modern in design, with occasional deep private balconies that are like alfresco living rooms. On the lower terrace is a free-form saltwater pool surrounded by semitropical vegetation. A water slide, diving boards, and a cafe with parasol tables all make for fun in the sun. The medium-sized guest rooms that open onto the rear gardens, without sea view, cost slightly less. You have to cross a small street to reach the water.

INEXPENSIVE

Albergo Conte Verde. Via Zara 1, 16038 Santa Margherita Ligure. ☎ **0185-287-139.** Fax 0185-284-211. E-mail: cverde@zeus.newnetworks.it. 35 units, 26 with bathroom. TEL. 80,000–140,000L ($40–$70) double without bathroom, 100,000–200,000L ($50–$100) double with bathroom. Rates include buffet breakfast. AE, DC, MC, V. Closed Jan–Feb. Parking 25,000L ($12.50).

This place offers one of the warmest welcomes in town. Only two blocks from the sea, this third-class hotel has been revamped, and its guest rooms are simple but adequate, ranging from small to medium (the more spacious units also have minibars, TVs, and terraces). All have first-rate mattresses and small tiled bathrooms. The front terrace has swing gliders and the lounge has period furnishings, including rockers. All is consistent with the villa exterior of shuttered windows, flower boxes, and a small front garden and lawn where tables are set out for refreshments.

Hotel Jolanda. Via Luisito Costa 6, 16038 Santa Margherita Ligure. ☎ **0185-287-513.** Fax 0185-284-763. www.hoteljolanda.it. E-mail: manager@hoteljolanda.it. 40 units. A/C MINIBAR TV TEL. 155,000–210,000L ($75.50–$105) double with breakfast; 110,000–140,000L ($55–$70) per person with half-board. AE, DC, MC, V. Parking 20,000L ($10).

Since the 1940s, the Pastine family has been welcoming visitors to its little hotel, a short walk from the sea on a peaceful little street. A patio serves as a kind of open-air living room. The guest rooms are comfortably furnished, ranging from small to medium, each with a good mattress. The bathrooms are small but well organized. Guests often gather in the bar before proceeding to the restaurant, where an excellent Ligurian cuisine is served.

DINING

Ristorante il Faro. Via Maragliano 24A. ☎ **0185-286-867.** Reservations recommended. Main courses 15,000–30,000L ($7.50–$15); fixed-price menu 45,000L ($22.50). AE, DC, MC, V. Wed–Mon noon–2:30pm and 7:30–10pm. Closed Nov. REGIONAL/ITALIAN.

The distinguished culinary background of the Fabbro family is reflected here in one of the town's best restaurants. Roberto Fabbro sets a great table and feeds you well. The atmosphere is comfortable and cozy, and on any night 50 diners can be fed well. High-quality meats and fresh fish dishes are served with flair and style. Try the *gamberi alla Santa Margherita,* sweet-tasting grilled shrimp in light olive oil, lemon, and mint sauce. The sautéed fish from the Mediterranean is the way to go, each dish served with fresh vegetables cooked al dente for the most part. The pastas are some of the resort's best, especially that Ligurian favorite, trenette with pesto sauce made from only the freshest and most aromatic basil.

Trattoria Baicin. Via Algeria 9. ☎ **0185-286-763.** Reservations not necessary. Main courses 18,000–30,000L ($9–$15); fixed-price menu 30,000L ($15). AE, DC, MC, V. Tues–Sun noon–3pm and 7–10:30pm. Closed Nov 1–Dec 15. LIGURIAN.

The husband-and-wife owners, Piero and Carmela, make everything fresh daily, from fish soup to gnocchi, and still manage to find time to greet diners at the door. You can get a glimpse of the sea if you choose to sit at one of the tables out front, and the owners/cooks are most happy preparing fish, which they buy fresh every morning; the sole, simply grilled, is especially good, and the *fritto misto di pesce* constitutes a memorable feast. You must begin your meal with one of the pastas made that morning, especially if *trofie alla genovese* (gnocchi, potatoes, fresh vegetables, and pesto) is available.

Trattoria Cesarina. Via Mameli 2C. ☎ **0185-286-059.** Reservations recommended, especially in midsummer. Main courses 16,000–35,000L ($8–$17.50). AE, DC, MC, V. Wed–Mon 12:30–2:30pm and 7:30–10pm. Closed Jan. SEAFOOD.

This is the best of the trattorie, beneath the arcade of a short but monumental street running into Piazza Fratelli Bandiere. In an atmosphere of bentwood chairs and discreet lighting, you can enjoy a variety of Ligurian dishes. Specialties include meat, vegetables, and seafood antipasti, along with such classic Italian dishes as taglierini with seafood and pappardelle in a fragrant sausage sauce, plus seasonal fish like red snapper or dorado, best when grilled.

SANTA MARGHERITA LIGURE AFTER DARK

Nightlife here seems geared to sipping wine or cocktails on terraces with sea views, flirting with sunburned strangers, and flip-flopping along the town's sandy beachfront promenades. But if you want to put on your dancing shoes, head for either of the town's most appealing discos, **Covo di Nord Est,** Via Rossetti 1 (☎ **0185-286-558**), or **Disco Carillon,** Localitá Paraggi (☎ **0185-286-721**). Both cater to dance and music lovers ages 20 to 40.

Looking for a completely unpretentious place to shoot some pool? Head for the **Old Inn Bar,** Piazza Mazzini 40 (☎ **0185-286-041**), where you can play pool for 8,000L ($4) per person per hour, drink bottled beers, and generally hang out with a crowd of young locals.

5 Portofino

22 miles (35km) SE of Genoa, 106 miles (171km) S of Milan, 301 miles (485km) NW of Rome

Portofino is about 4 miles (6km) south of Santa Margherita Ligure, along one of the most beautiful coastal roads in all Italy. Favored by the yachting set, the resort is in an idyllic location on a harbor, where the water reflects all the pastel-washed little houses running along it. In the 1930s, it enjoyed a reputation with artists; over the next few decades, the town became known as a celebrity hideout. Lots of famous names could be seen arriving by yacht, lounging poolside at the luxury hotels, and vacationing in private villas in the hills, including Rex Harrison and Elizabeth Taylor. The Splendido Hotel alone has hosted such illustrious guests as the Duke and Duchess of Windsor, Ernest Hemingway, Greta Garbo, Ingrid Bergman, Aristotle Onassis, Clark Gable, and John Wayne. Portofino may not have such star power today, but some rich and powerful people still occupy those private villas, coexisting right alongside all the tourists who pour in by the busloads during the day.

The thing to do in Portofino: Take a walk, preferably before sunset, leading toward the tip of the peninsula. When you come to the entrance of an old castle (where a German baron once lived), step inside the walls to enjoy a lush garden and the views of the town and harbor below; it's open daily 10am to 6pm (to 5pm October to April), and admission is 3,000L ($1.50). Continuing on, you'll pass old private villas, towering trees, and much vegetation before you reach the lighthouse (*faro*). Allow an hour at least. When you return to the main piazza, proceed to one of the two little drinking bars, on the left side of the harbor, that rise and fall in popularity.

Before beginning that walk to the lighthouse, however, you can climb the steps from the port leading to the little parish church of **San Giorgio,** built on the site of a sanctuary that Roman soldiers dedicated to the Persian god Mithras. From here you'll get a panoramic view of the port and bay.

In summer you can also take **boat rides** around the coast to such points as San Fruttuoso. Or set out for a long hike on the paths crossing the Monte Portofino Promontory to the **Abbazia di San Fruttuoso,** about a 2-hour walk from Portofino. The tourist office provides maps.

ESSENTIALS

GETTING THERE Take the **train** first to Santa Margherita Ligure (above); then continue the rest of the way by bus. Tigullio **buses** leave Santa Margherita Ligure once every 30 minutes bound for Portofino, costing 2,500L ($1.25) one way, and you can buy tickets aboard the bus. Call ☎ **0185-288-8334** for information and schedules. If you have a **car** and are in Santa Margherita, continue south along the only road, hugging the promontory, until you reach Portofino. In summer, traffic is likely to be heavy.

VISITOR INFORMATION The **tourist office** is at Via Roma 35 (☎ **0185-269-024**). It's open daily: summer 9:30am to 1pm and 1:30 to 6:30pm; off-season 9:30am to 12:30pm and 2:30 to 5:30pm.

ACCOMMODATIONS

Portofino just doesn't have enough hotels. In July and August, you may be forced to book a room in nearby Santa Margherita Ligure or Rapallo.

✪ **Albergo Nazionale.** Via Roma 8, 16034 Portofino. ☎ **0185-269-575.** Fax 0185-269-138. www.nazionaleportofino.com. E-mail: hotel.nazionale.portofino@newnetworks.it. 13 units. A/C MINIBAR TV TEL. 375,000L ($187.50) double; 470,000–570,000L ($235–$285) suite. Breakfast 25,000L ($12.50). MC, V. Parking 35,000L ($17.50) nearby. Closed Nov 20–Mar 20.

At stage center right on the harbor, this old villa is modest yet well laid out and was restored and renovated in the mid–1980s. The suites are tastefully decorated, and the little lounge has a brick fireplace, a coved ceiling, antique furnishings, and good reproductions. Most of the guest rooms, furnished in a mix of styles (hand-painted Venetian in some rooms), open onto a view of the harbor. The tiled bathrooms are small but tidy, with hair dryers.

✪ **Albergo Splendido.** Viale Baratta 13, 16034 Portofino. ☎ **800/237-1236** in the U.S., or 0185-267-801. Fax 0185-267-806. www.orient-expresshotels.com. E-mail: reservations@splendido.net. 69 units. A/C MINIBAR TV TEL. 1,330,000–1,550,000L ($665–$775) double; from 2,600,000L ($1,300) suite. Rates include half-board. AE, CB, DC, DISC, MC, V. Closed Jan 3–Mar 25. Parking 35,000L ($17.50).

This Relais & Châteaux property, reached by a steep and winding road from the port, provides a luxury base for those who moor their yachts in the harbor or have closed down their Palm Beach residences for the summer and can afford its outrageous prices. The four-story structure was built as a monastery during the Middle Ages, but pirates attacked so frequently that the monks abandoned it. Later it became a family summer home. The building opened as a hotel in 1901 and has attracted the likes of Winston Churchill. There are several levels of public rooms and terraces to maximize the views over the sea, which you'll also enjoy from the guest rooms. Each room is furnished in a personal way, with no two alike; all have private safes, VCRs, bedside controls, and luxury mattresses. The bathrooms are the finest at the resort, clad in marble or tile, each with heated racks, robes, and hair dryers. Some of the superior rooms are also equipped with whirlpool tubs.

Dining: The dining room is divided by arches and furnished with Biedermeier chairs, flowers, and a fine old tapestry. The restaurant terrace enjoys a beautiful view and serves traditional Ligurian and international specialties.

Amenities: Room service, baby-sitting, laundry/valet, massage, hotel speedboat, heated saltwater pool, beauty center, solarium, sauna.

Hotel Eden. Vico Dritto 18, 16034 Portofino. ☎ **0185-269-091.** Fax 0185-269-047. E-mail: eden@ifree.it. 9 units. A/C TV TEL. 250,000–380,000L ($125–$190) double. Rates include breakfast. AE, CB, DC, MC, V. Closed Dec 1–20. Public parking 30,000L ($15).

Just 150 feet from the harbor in the heart of the village and set in a garden (hence its name), this hotel is a budget holdout in an otherwise high-fashion resort. Though it doesn't have a harbor view, there's a winning vista from the front veranda, where breakfast is served. The guest rooms are small and very simply furnished, though each has a comfortable bed and a bathroom with a hair dryer. The hotel is run by Mr. Ferruccio, and life here is decidedly casual.

DINING

Da U'Batti. Vico Nuovo 17. ☎ **0185-269-379.** Reservations recommended. Main courses 45,000–50,000L ($22.50–$25); fixed-price menu 120,000L ($60). AE, DC, MC, V. Tues–Sun noon–3pm and 8–11pm. Closed Dec–Jan. SEAFOOD.

Informal and colorful, this place is on a narrow cobblestone-covered piazza a few steps above the port. A pair of barnacle-encrusted anchors hanging above the arched entrance hint at the seafaring specialties that have become the restaurant's trademark. Owner/sommelier Giancarlo Foppiano serves delectable dishes, which might include a soup of "hen clams," rice with shrimp or crayfish, or fish alla Battista. There is a good selection of grappa, as well as French and Italian wines.

Delfino. Piazza Martiri dell' Olivetta 41. ☎ **0185-269-081.** Reservations recommended Sat. Main courses 40,000–60,000L ($20–$30). AE, DC, MC, V. Apr–Oct, daily noon–3pm and 7–11pm; Nov–Mar, Tues–Sun noon–2:30pm and 7–10:30pm. SEAFOOD.

Opened in the 1800s on the village square that fronts the harbor, Delfino is Portofino's most fashionable dining spot (along with Il Pitosforo, below). It's both nautically rustic and informally chic and offers virtually the same type of food as Il Pitosforo, including *lasagne al pesto.* The fish dishes are the best bets: *zuppa di pesce* (a soup made of freshly caught fish with a secret spice blend) and risotto with shrimp, sole, squid, and other sea creatures. The chef also prides himself on his sage-seasoned *vitello all'uccelletto,* roast veal with a gamey taste. Try to get a table near the front so you can enjoy (or at least be amused by) the parade of visitors and villagers.

Il Pitosforo. Molo Umberto I 9. ☎ **0185-269-020.** Reservations required. Main courses 50,000–70,000L ($25–$35). AE, DC, MC, V. Wed–Sun 7:30–11pm. Closed end of Nov–Feb and for lunch Apr–Oct. LIGURIAN/ITALIAN.

You have to climb some steps to reach this place, which draws raves when the meal is served and often wails when the tab is presented. While not blessed with an especially distinguished decor, its position right on the harbor gives it all the natural charm it needs. *Zuppa di pesce* is a delectable Ligurian fish soup, or you may prefer the bouillabaisse. The pastas are especially tasty and include *lasagne al pesto,* wide noodles prepared in typical Genovese sauce. Fish dishes feature mussels *alla marinara* and *paella valenciana* for two, and saffron-flavored rice studded with seafood and chicken. Some meat and fish dishes are grilled over hot stones; others over charcoal.

Ristorante da Puny. Piazza Martiri dell'Olivetta. ☎ **0185-269-037.** Reservations required. Main courses 28,000–45,000L ($14–$22.50). No credit cards. Fri–Wed noon–3pm and 7–11pm. Closed Dec 15–Feb 20. SEAFOOD.

Da Puny is set up on the stone square that opens onto the harbor. Because of its location, it's practically in the living room of Portofino, within sight of the evening activities of the oh-so-chic and oh-so-tan yachting set. Green-painted tables are set under trees at night on a slate-covered outdoor terrace. The menu includes *pappardelle* Portofino, antipasto of the house, spaghetti with clams, baked fish with potatoes and olives, fried zucchini flowers, and an array of freshly caught fish.

PORTOFINO AFTER DARK

La Gritta American Bar, Calata Marconi 20 (☎ **0185-269-126**), vies for business with its rival a few storefronts away (below). The crowd is often an interesting mix of celebrities, tourists, and U.S. Navy personnel—this is a legendary watering hole from way back. It's open in summer daily 9pm to 3am (in winter, Friday to Wednesday).

Scafandro American Bar, Calata Marconi 10 (☎ **0185-269-105**), is one of the village's chic bars, a place that has attracted a slew of yachting guests. The three-quarter-round banquettes inside contribute to the general feeling of well-being. If some international celebrity doesn't happen to come in while you're here, you can always study one of the series of unusual nautical engravings adorning the walls. June to September, it's open daily 10am to 3am (Wednesday to Monday the rest of the year).

6 The Cinque Terre

Monterosso: 56 miles (8km) E of Genoa, 6 miles (10km) W of La Spezia

Among olive and chestnut groves on steep, rocky terrain overlooking the gulf of Genoa, the communities of Corniglia, Manarola, Riomaggiore, and Vernazza offer a glimpse into another time. These rural villages, inaccessible by car, are an agricultural belt where garden and vineyard exist side by side. Together with their "city cousin" Monterosso, they're known as the *Cinque Terre* (five lands). The northernmost town, Monterosso, is the tourist hub of the region, with traffic, crowds, and the only notable glimpse of contemporary urban life here.

The area is best known for its culinary delights, culled from forest, field, and sea. Here the land yields an incredible variety of edible mushrooms; and oregano, borage, rosemary, and sage grow abundantly. The pine nuts essential to pesto are easily collected from the forests, as are chestnuts for making flour and olives for the oil that is the base of all dishes. Garlic and leeks flavor sautéed dishes, and beets turn up unexpectedly in ravioli and other dishes. Fishing boats add their rich hauls of anchovies, mussels, squid, octopus, and shellfish; and to wash it all down, vineyards produce Sciacchetra, a DOC wine, rarer than many other Italian varieties because of the low 25% yield characteristic of the Vermentino, Bosco, and Albarola grapes from which it's derived.

Most visitors explore the villages by excursion boat. To avoid these crowds and really get to know the region, you may want to hike along the renowned walking paths that meander scenically for miles across the hills and through the forests.

ESSENTIALS

GETTING THERE Hourly **trains** run from Genoa to La Spezia, a trip of $1^1/_2$ hours, where you must backtrack by rail to any of the five towns you wish to visit. Once in the Cinque Terre, local trains, which run frequently between the five stops, offer daily unlimited travel at a cost of 5,000L ($3). Don't expect views, however. The entire ride is within tunnels. For more information, dial ☎ **1478-88-088** toll-free in Italy.

If you have a **car** and are coming from Genoa, take A12 and exit at Monterosso—the only town of the five you can actually approach by car. A gigantic parking lot accommodates visitors, who then travel between the towns by rail, boat, or foot. The **Navigazione Golfo del Porto** (☎ **01871/967-676**) plies the waters between Monterosso and Manarola or Riomaggiore five times daily, whereas Motobarca Vernazza runs hourly to Vernazza.

VISITOR INFORMATION The **APT office** for the five villages is in Monterosso, Via Fegina 38 (☎ **0187-817-506**). April to October, it's open Monday to Saturday 10am to noon and 5 to 7:30pm, Sunday 10am to noon.

EXPLORING THE COAST

There are 14 **walking trails** laid out for exploring the wilds of the area; they're also a viable way to go from town to town. The APT office (see above) offers a brochure, "Footpaths Along the Cinque Terre and the Eastern Riviera," which defines and maps out routes ranging as far north as Deiva Marina and as far south as Portovenere but suggests several within the boundaries of the Cinque Terre as well. Each hike takes from 20 minutes to 5 hours. For example, it's a mere 20-minute stroll between Monterosso and Vernazzi but a 2-hour strenuous climb between Manarola and Riomaggiore. Some trails turn inland, emphasizing the hills and forests of the region. The longest and most scenic, highlighting both coast and forest, is the *Sentieri Azzurri* ("azure path along the coast"), running from Monterosso, starting near the town hall, to Riomaggiore, ending along Via dell'Amore. En route, you pass through Vernazza, Corniglia, and Manarola. Many routes are steep and some include hazards like frequent landslides. In case you run into trouble, the **local emergency phone number** is ☎ **115.**

The only sandy **beach** in the Cinque Terre is the crowded strand in **Monterosso,** where you can rent a beach chair from a vendor for about 2,500L ($1.25). **Guvano Beach** is an isolated pebbly strand that stretches just north of Corniglia and is popular with nudists. You can clamber down to it from the Vernazza–Corniglia path, but the drop is steep and treacherous. A weird alternative route takes you through an unused train tunnel, entered from a point near the north end of Corniglia's train station; you must ring the bell at the gated entrance and wait for a custodian to arrive to unburden you of 5,000L ($2.50), which is good for passage through the dimly lit mile-long gallery that emerges onto the beach at the far end. There's a long rocky beach to the south of **Corniglia,** easily accessible by some quick downhill scrambles from the Corniglia–Manrola path. **Riomaggiore** has a tiny crescent-shaped beach reached by a series of stone steps on the south side of the harbor.

ACCOMMODATIONS

IN MONTEROSSO

Hotel Baia. Via Fegina 88, 19016 Monterosso. ☎ **0187-817-512.** Fax 0187-818-322. 29 units. TV TEL. 210,000L ($105) double. Rates include breakfast. MC, V. Closed Nov–Feb.

Opened in 1911, this hotel features a private beach and pleasant guest rooms where the whitewashed furniture lends an illusion of size and space. Each comes with a good bed and small tiled bathroom. The restaurant serves regional seafood specialties, and patio dining is available overlooking the beach. What the hotel doesn't offer is air-conditioning or shuttle service, but the train station is only 110 yards away.

Hotel Pasquale. Via Fegina 4, 19016 Monterosso. ☎ **0187-817-477.** Fax 0187-817-056. www.pasini.com. E-mail: pasquale@pasini.com. 15 units. A/C TV TEL. 190,000L ($95) double. Rates include breakfast. MC, V.

This small hotel sits right by the beach, offering both intimacy and privacy since its small number of guest rooms are spread out across four floors. It's modern and has been decorated in the manner of a private Genovan home. The bar/restaurant is reminiscent of an Italian coffee shop, with gleaming marble floors, glass cases, dark wood wainscoting, window frames, and a service counter accented with a brass rail and foot guard.

✪ **Hotel Porto Roca.** Via Corone 1, 19016 Monterosso. ☎ **0187-817-502.** Fax 0187-817-692. www.portoroca.it. E-mail: portoroca@cinqueterre.it 43 units. A/C MINIBAR TV TEL. 280,000–390,000L ($140–$195) double. Rates include breakfast. AE, MC, V. Closed Nov–Mar.

You give up direct beach access to stay here, but it's a small price to pay for accommodations as gracious as these. The hotel is set on a cliff offering panoramic views of the village and harbor, and every corner is filled with antiques, knickknacks, and art. The guest rooms range from medium to spacious, each with a quality mattress and a tidy bathroom. The terrace is alive with lush greenery and an assortment of blossoming white flowers that complement the blue of the bay. The restaurant serves local seafood, and its large dining room offers privacy through the placement of columns and Liberty-style glass screens. In the bar, furniture clusters create cozy pockets for chatting. Its fanciful fireplace adds warmth on cool days.

In Manarola

Hotel Marina Piccola. Via Discovolo 16, 19010 Manarola. ☎ **0187-920-103.** Fax 0187-920-966. 10 units. TEL. 135,000L ($67.50) per person double. Rates include half-board. AE, DC, MC, V. Closed Nov.

With 10 rooms spread across five floors, this former home is a hotel as vertical as the town that houses it. There's a rustic charm to the small guest rooms, which feature wrought-iron beds with good mattresses. The tiled bathrooms are small. There's no bar, but the restaurant, as simply decorated as the hotel, offers a great view of the harbor. The cuisine is typical of the region (see "Dining," below).

In Riomaggiore

Villa Argentina. Via de Gaspari 170, 19017 Riomaggiore. ☎ and fax **0187-920-213.** E-mail: villaargentina@libero.it. 15 units. TV. 180,000L ($90) double, including breakfast; 125,000–135,000L ($62.50–$67.50) per person with half-board. No credit cards. Closed Nov.

This hotel's greatest asset is its quiet country setting just outside town. If you don't feel like walking, an efficient shuttle service will transport you into the village. There's no air-conditioning, but each room has a ceiling fan. The guest rooms are small and basic but the mattresses firm. The bathrooms are very cramped. There's a small restaurant and a bar on the premises. Although the Argentina is a no-frills choice, the price is certainly right.

Dining

In Monterosso

Il Gigante. Via IV Novembre 9. ☎ **0187-817-401.** Reservations recommended on holidays. Main courses 18,000–30,000L ($9–$15). AE, DC, MC, V. Daily noon–3pm and 6:30–10pm. Closed some Mon. LIGURIAN.

This trattoria is one of the best places to introduce yourself to Liguria's flavorful cuisine, and there's no better introduction than *zuppa di pesce.* Actually the fish soup is enough for a main course, but locals are rarely satisfied with just soup. Another pleasing first course is *minestrone alla genovese,* a bean-and-vegetable soup flavored with pesto. Waiters cite the daily specials, none more delectable than risotto made with freshly plucked shellfish. To go truly Ligurian, opt for the spaghetti with octopus sauce. The mixed grill is another savory offering. Although the restaurant in theory is open daily, watch for erratic closings on Monday.

In Manarola

Aristide. Via Discovolo 290. ☎ **0187-920-000.** Reservations recommended. Main courses 18,000–30,000L ($9–$15); fixed-price menu 75,000L ($37.50). AE, MC, V. Apr–Sept daily noon–2:30pm and 7–10pm; off-season Tues–Sun noon–2:30pm and 7–10pm. LIGURIAN.

This comfortable old trattoria showcases the simplicity of the region's cuisine, combining a few key ingredients in tasty combinations. The weekday fixed-price menu includes wine with the meal, and the weekend version also features antipasto and coffee. House specialties include *lasagne al pesto, penne all'aragosta,* and *zuppa di pesce,* one of the most savory kettles of fish in the "five lands." Traditional recipes have never been forgotten and are always part of the menu.

Marina Piccola. Via Discovolo 16. ☎ **0187-920-103.** Reservations recommended. Main courses 18,000–30,000L ($9–$15). AE, DC, MC, V. Wed–Mon noon–3pm and 7–10pm. LIGURIAN.

This simple restaurant is next to the inn of the same name (see "Accommodations," above). Gruff but well-meaning, it's devoid of any pretensions. For a Ligurian palate tantalizer, try *cozze ripiene,* mussels cooked in white wine and served with butter sauce. Squid in its own ink tastes best when combined with homemade spaghetti. Fresh sardines are a local crowd pleaser, and another homemade pasta, trenette, comes flavored with some of the best-tasting pesto on the coast. Grilled fish is the invariable favorite for a main dish—always fresh and perfectly prepared, though seasoned simply, as is the Ligurian style.

IN VERNAZZA

Il Gambero Rosso. Piazza Marconi 7. ☎ **0187-812-265.** Reservations recommended Sat–Sun. Main courses 20,000–38,000L ($10–$19); fixed-price menus 60,000–95,000L ($30–$47.50). AE, DC, MC, V. Tues–Sun 12:30–3pm and 7:30–10:30pm. Closed mid-Dec to Mar 1. LIGURIAN.

Opened 108 years ago, this restaurant is high up on a rocky cliff overlooking the sea. Ask for a table on the terrace to make the most of this setting. The food is typically Ligurian, with house specialties like ravioli stuffed with fresh fish. The wonderful porcini mushrooms that are harvested in the area figure into some dishes. Many of the recipes were passed by word of mouth from mother to daughter, and a lot of the flavoring is based on the use of herbs and other ingredients that grow in the hills. The pesto is made with the best olive oil and mixed with basil, grated cheese, pine nuts, and fresh marjoram.

Taverna del Capitano. Piazza Marconi 21, in the Locanda Barbara. ☎ **0187-812-201.** Reservations recommended. Main courses 15,000–30,000L ($7.50–$15). AE, DC, MC, V. Thurs–Tues 7:30am–3pm and 7–10pm. Closed Dec–Jan. LIGURIAN.

This tavern is on the top floor of a two-story hotel whose street level contains the Locanda Barbara, under separate management. It's one of the best eateries in all the Cinque Terre, seating 60 in three informal and nautically rustic dining rooms. Its most popular dishes are grilled prawns, grilled beef fillet, potato-based gnocchi, pasta with pesto sauce, and linguine flavored with crabmeat.

13 Campania

Campania is in many ways Italy's most memorable and beautiful region. It forms a fertile crescent around the bays of Naples and Sorrento and stretches inland into a landscape of limestone rocks dotted with patches of fertile soil. The geological oddities of Campania include a smoldering and dangerous volcano (already famous for having destroyed Pompeii and Herculaneum), sulfurous springs that belch steam and smelly gases, and lakes that ancient myths refer to as the gateway to Hades. Its seaside highway is the most beautiful, and probably the most treacherous, in the world, combining danger at every hairpin turn with some of Italy's most reckless drivers. Despite such dark images, Campania is a most captivating region, sought out by native Italians and visitors alike for its combination of earth, sea, and sky. Coupled with this are Europe's densest collection of ancient ruins, each celebrated by classical scholars as among the very best of its kind.

It was off the shores of Campania that Ulysses ordered his crew to tie him to the mast of his ship, ears unstopped, so he alone would hear the songs of the sirens without throwing himself overboard to sample their pleasures. The ancient Romans dubbed the land "Campania Felix" and constructed hundreds of private villas there. In some ways, the beauty of Campania contributed to the decay of the Roman Empire, as emperors, their senators, and their courtiers spent more and more time pursuing its pleasures and abandoning the cares of Rome's administrative problems. Even today, seafront land here is so desirable that hoteliers have poured their life savings into buildings that are sometimes bizarrely cantilevered above rock-studded cliffs. Despite their numbers, these hotels tend to be profitably overbooked in summer.

Although residents of Campania sometimes stridently praise its cuisine, it's not the most renowned in Italy. The region's produce, however, is superb, its wine is heady, and its pizzas are memorable.

Today Campania typifies the conditions that northern Italians label "the problem of the south." Although the inequities are the most pronounced in **Naples,** the entire region, outside the resorts along the coast, has a lower standard of living and education and higher crime rates, plus less-developed standards of health care, than the more affluent north.

When the English say "see Naples and die," they mean the city and the bay, with majestic Vesuvius in the background. When the Germans use the expression, they mean the **Amalfi Drive.** Indeed, several motorists do die each year on the dangerous coastal road, which is too narrow to accommodate the heavy stream of summer traffic, especially the large tour buses that almost sideswipe one another as they try to pass. When driving along the coast, you sometimes find it difficult to concentrate on the road because of the view. The drive, remarked André Gide, "is so beautiful that nothing more beautiful can be seen on this earth." Those of you who've driven Highway 1 along the California coast will have some idea of what to expect on this gorgeous drive (but toss in terrible traffic and aggressive drivers and make the scenery even more spectacular).

Sorrento and **Amalfi** are in the vanguard, with the widest range of facilities; **Positano** has more snob appeal and is popular with artists; **Ravello** is still the choice of the discriminating few (such as Gore Vidal) who desire relative seclusion. To cap off an Amalfi adventure, you can take a boat from Sorrento to Capri, one of the most beautiful islands in the world.

The gorgeous island of **Capri** was known to emperors before international travelers discovered it. But the popularity of the resort-studded Amalfi Coast is a more recent phenomenon. It was discovered by German officers during World War II, then later by American and English servicemen (Positano was a British rest camp in the last months of the war). When the war was over, many of these servicemen returned, often bringing their families. The fishing villages in time became major tourism centers, with hotels and restaurants in all price ranges.

In addition to the stunning scenery and the lovely seaside towns, there are some world-class sightseeing attractions as well—the haunting ruins of **Pompeii** and the Greek temples of the ancient city of **Paestum** are among the highlights of all Italy.

1 Naples

136 miles (219km) SE of Rome, 162 miles (263km) W of Bari

Naples (Napoli) is Italy's most controversial city: You'll either love it or hate it. Is it paradiso or the inferno? It's louder, more intense, more unnerving, but perhaps ultimately more satisfying than almost anywhere else in Italy.

To foreigners unfamiliar with the complexities of the multifarious "Italys" and their regional types, the Neapolitan is still the quintessence of the country and easy to caricature ("O Sole Mio," "Mamma Mia," bel canto). If Sophia Loren (a native who moved elsewhere) evokes the Italian woman for you, you'll find more of her look-alikes here than in any other city. Naples also gave the world Enrico Caruso.

In recent years, Naples has made world headlines for its cultural renaissance and its fight against crime. Despite Mafia-directed crime, political corruption, prostitution, street hoodlums, chaotic traffic, and pervasive unemployment, the longtime mayor of Naples, Antonio Bassolino, has chosen culture as a weapon to clean up the city's image. Since taking office in December 1993, the former Communist party official has made cultural revaluation his top priority. And it seems to be working.

Bassolino received a national government grant of $30 million to make Naples look safer and more presentable and has been aided by a group of concerned citizens who since 1984 have collected funds for the upkeep of the city's treasures and monuments. The first civic move was to restore and reopen scores of neglected museums and palaces in dilapidated neighborhoods. Muggers, prostitutes, and cars were driven from many historic plazas, especially Piazza del Plebiscito, and from around the San Carlo opera house and Royal Palace areas. All this activity seemed to spark a minor renaissance among the city's musicians, writers, moviemakers, artists, and playwrights. The Neapolitan art scene has been given a shot in the arm.

The Amalfi Coast

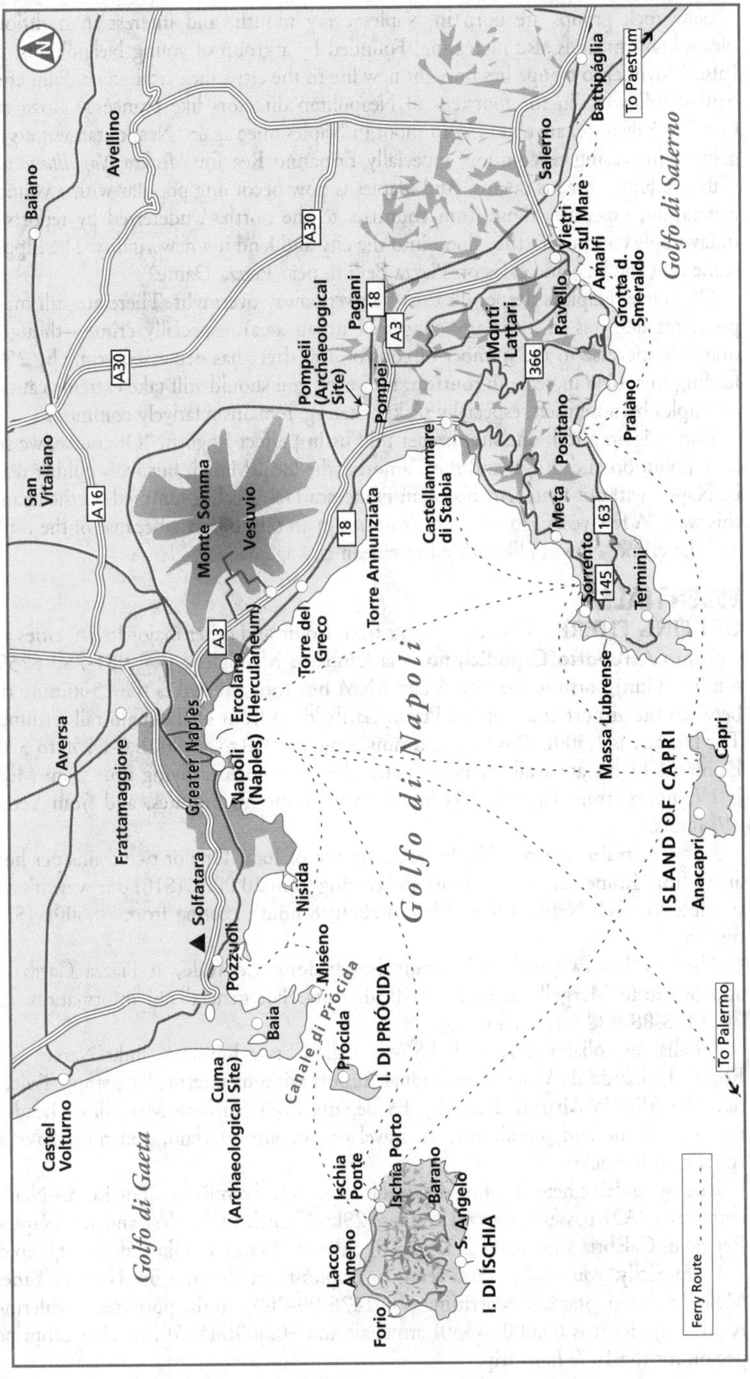

New rock groups are born in Naples every month, and interest in traditional Neapolitan music is also increasing. Founded by a group of young Neapolitans, the Falso Movimento troupe has brought new life to the city's theatrical scene. Film companies, following in the footsteps of Neapolitan directors like Francesco Rossi and Gabriele Salvatore, are choosing to shoot in Naples once again. Neapolitan writers are gaining increasing recognition, especially Ermanno Rea for *Mistero Napolitano* and Gabriele Frasca for his poems. And Naples is now becoming popular with a younger generation, especially those from countries to the north. Undeterred by reports of unfavorable conditions, they flood into the city and lend it a new vitality. The hippest scene is at the bars and cafes on Piazza Bellini, near Piazza Dante.

Of course, Naples's deeper ills can't be swept away overnight. There are still major problems here (as in most any congested urban area), especially crime—though a dramatic increase in the number of cops on the street has decreased crime by 25%, leading to a 40% increase in tourism. However, you should still take extreme caution in Naples because theft, especially pickpocketing, remains relatively common.

Naples is on a roll, one shopkeeper told us in perfect English. "Of course, we still have pollution and drugs, and the Camorra [the local Mafia], but we wouldn't really be Naples without that." Art historian Francesca Del Vecchio summed up the change this way: "A few years ago we couldn't sit out in an outdoor cafe because of the traffic and the crime. Now it's like a Mediterranean city again."

ESSENTIALS

GETTING THERE Domestic flights from Rome and other major Italian cities put you into **Aeroporto Capodichino,** Via Umberto Maddalena (☎ **081-789-6259**), 4 miles (6km) north of the city. A city **ANM bus** (no. 14) makes the 15-minute run between the airport and Naples's Piazza Garibaldi in front of the main rail terminus. The bus fare is 1,500L (75¢)—a **taxi** runs about 35,000 to 40,000L ($17.50 to $20). Domestic flights are available on Alitalia, Alisarda, and Ati. Flying time from Milan is 1½ hours, from Palermo 1¼ hours, from Rome 50 minutes, and from Venice 1¼ hours.

Frequent **trains** connect Naples with the rest of Italy. One or two trains per hour arrive from Rome, taking 2½ hours and costing from 20,000L ($10) one way. It's also possible to reach Naples from Milan in about 8 hours, costing from 70,000L ($35) one way.

The city has two main rail terminals: **Stazione Centrale,** at Piazza Garibaldi, and **Stazione Mergellina,** at Piazza Piedigrotta. For general rail information, call ☎ **1478-88-088** toll-free in Italy.

Alitalia, in collaboration with FS, the Italian State Railways, links Naples with Rome's Leonardo da Vinci International Airport without intermediate stops. Twice a day, the **Alitalia Airport Train by FS** departs from Stazione Mergellina, heading north to Rome and the airport. To travel on the airport train, you must have an Alitalia airline ticket.

It's easy to **drive** here, heading down the autostrada from Rome. The Rome–Naples autostrada (A2) passes Caserta 18 miles (29km) north of Naples, and the Naples–Reggio di Calabria autostrada (A3) runs by Salerno, 33 miles (53km) north of Naples.

From Sicily, you can go on a **ferry** to Naples from Palermo on **Tirrenia Lines,** Molo Angionio, Stazione Marritima (☎ **1478-99-000**), in the port area of Palermo. A one-way ticket is 60,000L ($30) armchair and 90,000L ($45) first-class cabin per person for the 10½-hour trip.

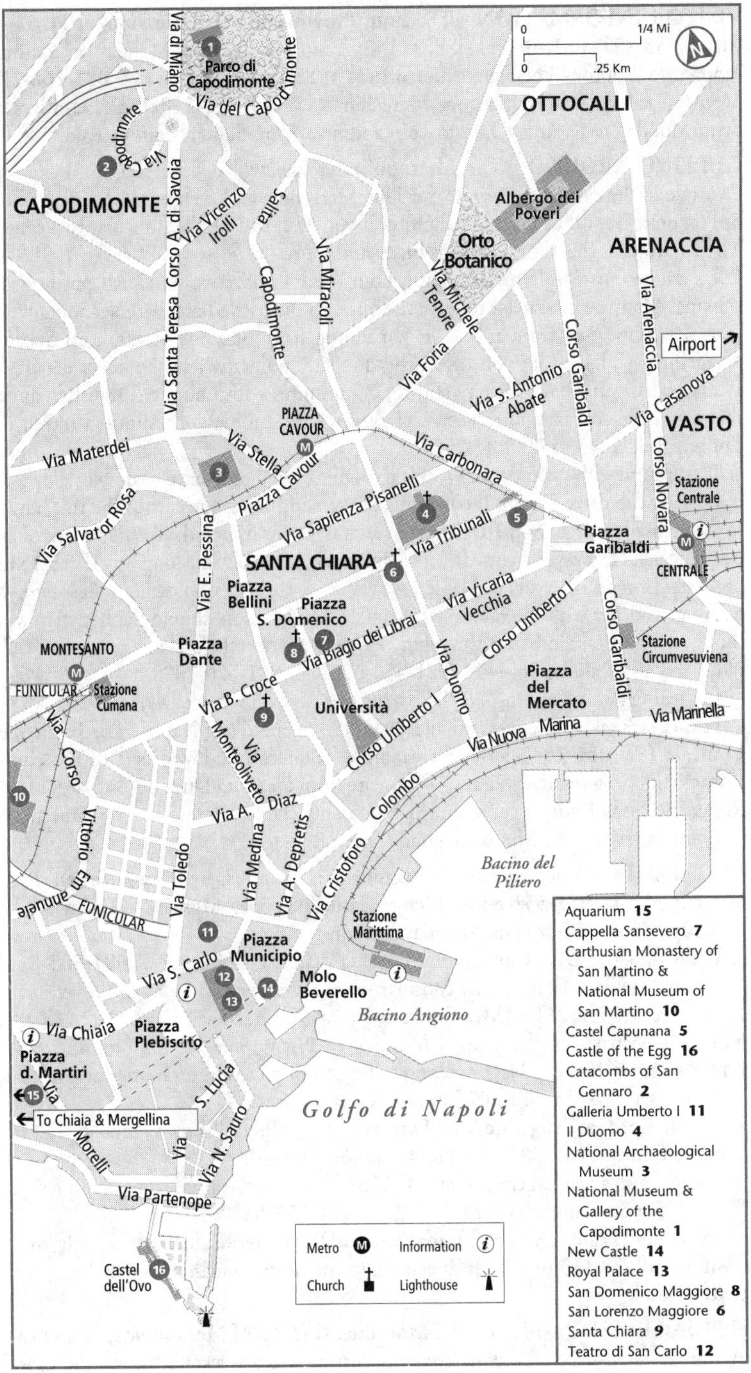
0 1/4 Mi
0 .25 Km
N
Parco di Capodimonte
Via di Miano
Via del Capodimonte
Via Capodimonte
CAPODIMONTE
Corso A. di Savoia
Via Vicenzo Irolli
Salita Capodimonte
Via Miracoli
OTTOCALLI
Albergo dei Poveri
Orto Botanico
Via Michele Tenore
ARENACCIA
Via Arenaccia
Airport
Via Santa Teresa
Via Foria
Via S. Antonio Abate
Corso Garibaldi
Via Casanova
VASTO
PIAZZA CAVOUR
Via Materdei
Via Stella
Piazza Cavour
Via Carbonara
Corso Novara
Stazione Centrale
Via Salvator Rosa
Via Sapienza Pisanelli
Via Tribunali
Piazza Garibaldi
CENTRALE
Via E. Pessina
SANTA CHIARA
Piazza Bellini
Piazza S. Domenico
Via Vicaria Vecchia
Corso Umberto I
Stazione Circumvesuviena
MONTESANTO
Piazza Dante
Via Biagio dei Librai
Via Duomo
Piazza del Mercato
FUNICULAR
Stazione Cumana
Via B. Croce
Università
Via Marinella
Via Corso
Via Monteoliveto
Via Nuova Marina
Via A. Diaz
Colombo
Vittorio Emanuele
Via Toledo
Via Medina
Via A. Depretis
Via Cristoforo
Bacino del Piliero
FUNICULAR
Stazione Marittima
Piazza Municipio
Via S. Carlo
Molo Beverello
Bacino Angiono
Via Chiaia
Piazza Plebiscito
Piazza d. Martiri
Via Morelli
S. Lucia
To Chiaia & Mergellina
Golfo di Napoli
Via
Via N. Sauro
Via Partenope
Castel dell'Ovo
Metro
Information
Church
Lighthouse
Aquarium 15
Cappella Sansevero 7
Carthusian Monastery of San Martino & National Museum of San Martino 10
Castel Capunana 5
Castle of the Egg 16
Catacombs of San Gennaro 2
Galleria Umberto I 11
Il Duomo 4
National Archaeological Museum 3
National Museum & Gallery of the Capodimonte 1
New Castle 14
Royal Palace 13
San Domenico Maggiore 8
San Lorenzo Maggiore 6
Santa Chiara 9
Teatro di San Carlo 12

VISITOR INFORMATION The **Ente Provinciale per il Turismo,** at Piazza dei Martiri 58 (☎ **081-405-311;** Bus: 152; Tram: 1), is open Monday to Saturday 8:30am to 3:30pm. There are **other offices** at Stazione Centrale (☎ **081-268-779;** Metro: Garibaldi) and at Stazione Mergellina (☎ **081-761-2102**). These offices are open Monday to Saturday 9am to 1pm and 3 to 7pm, Sunday 9am to 1pm.

GETTING AROUND The **Metropolitana** line will deliver you from Stazione Centrale in the east all the way to Stazione Mergellina and even beyond to the suburb of Pozzuoli. Get off at Piazza Piedigrotta if you wish to take the funicular to Vómero. The Metro uses the same tickets as buses and trams.

It's dangerous to ride **buses** at rush hours—never have we seen such pushing and shoving. Many people prefer to leave the buses to the battle-hardened Neapolitans and take the subway or **tram** no. 1 or 4, running from Stazione Centrale to Stazione Mergellina. (It'll also let you off at the quayside points where the boats depart for Ischia and Capri.) For a ticket valid for 75 minutes with unlimited transfers during that time, the cost is 1,500L (75¢). However, for a full day of unlimited travel, you can buy a ticket for 5,000L ($2.50)

If you survive the **taxi** driver's reckless driving, you'll only have to do battle over the bill. Many cab drivers claim the meter is broken and assess the cost of the ride, always to your disadvantage. Some legitimate surcharges are imposed, like night drives and extra luggage. However, many drivers deliberately take you "the long way there" to run up costs. In repeated visits to Naples, we've never yet been quoted an honest fare. We no longer bother with the meter; we estimate what the fare should be, negotiate with the driver, and take off into the night. If you want to take a chance, you can call a radio taxi at ☎ **081-556-4444,** 081-556-0202, or 081-570-7070.

Regarding getting around Naples by **car,** we have one word: *Don't.*

Funiculars take passengers up and down the steep hills of Naples. The **Funicolare Centrale** (☎ **081-7632-507**), for example, connects the lower part of the city to Vómero. Departures, daily 7am to 10pm, are from Piazzetta Duca d'Aosta, just off Via Roma. Be careful not to get stranded by missing the last car back. The same tickets valid for buses and the Metro are good for the funicular.

FAST FACTS American Express business is handled by **Every Tours,** Piazza Municipo 5 (☎ **081-551-8564;** Metro: Garibaldi), open Monday to Friday 9:30am to 1:30pm and 3:30 to 7pm, Saturday 9:30am to 1pm.

You'll find the **U.S. Consulate** on Piazza della Repubblica (☎ **081-583-8111;** Metro: Margellina; Tram: 1). Its consular services are open Monday to Friday 8am to 1pm and 2 to 5pm. The **U.K. Consulate** is at Via Francesco Crispi 122 (☎ **081-663-511;** Metro: Amedeo), open Monday to Friday 8am to 1:30pm. Citizens of **Canada, Australia,** and **New Zealand** will need to go to the embassies or consulates in Rome (see "Fast Facts: Rome" in chapter 3).

If you need a drugstore, try **Farmacia Helvethia,** Piazza Garibaldi 11, near Stazione Centrale (☎ **081-554-8894;** Metro: Garibaldi).

If you have an emergency, dial ☎ **113.** To reach the police or carabinieri, call ☎ **112.** For an ambulance, call ☎ **113** or **081-752-8282.**

For medical care, try the **Guarda Medica Permanente,** located in each area of town, or call ☎ **113** or ask for directions to the nearest Guarda Medica Permanente at your hotel.

SPECIAL EVENTS **Maggio dei Monumenti (May of Monuments)** is sponsored by the Council of Naples, with events occurring every weekend during the month. Each year the theme is slightly different. One of the most interesting parts of this event is a series of guided walks through the historic district, even through the city's underground passages. May is also the month for a variety of exhibits and fairs. Chamber music recitals, concerts, operettas, performances of classic Neapolitan songs, and even soccer matches and horse races add to the celebration. If you're in Naples in May, consult the tourist office for a full program of events, some of which are free.

SEEING THE SIGHTS

If you arrive by train at Stazione Centrale, in front of **Piazza Garibaldi,** you'll want to escape from that horror by taking one of Naples's major arteries, **Corso Umberto,** in the direction of the Santa Lucia district. Along the water, many boats, such as those heading for Capri and Ischia, leave from **Porto Beverello** (not within walking distance—take a taxi).

Many people confine their visit to the bayside **Santa Lucia** area and perhaps venture into another section to see an important museum. Most of the major hotels lie along **Via Partenope,** which looks out not only to the Gulf of Naples but also to the Castel dell'Ovo. To the west is the **Mergellina** district, site of many restaurants and dozens of apartment houses. The far western section of the city is known as **Posillipo.**

One of the most important squares is **Piazza del Plebiscito,** north of Santa Lucia. The Palazzo Reale opens onto this square. A satellite is **Piazza Trento e Trieste,** with its Teatro San Carlo and entrance to the famed Galleria Umberto I. To the east is the third most important square, **Piazza Municipio.** From Piazza Trento e Trieste, you encounter the main shopping street, **Via Toledo/Via Roma,** on which you can walk as far as Piazza Dante. From that square, take Via Enrico Pessina to the most important museum, located on **Piazza Museo Nazionale.**

THE TOP MUSEUMS

✪ **National Archaeological Museum (Museo Archeologico Nazionale).** Piazza Museo Nazionale 18–19. ☎ **081-292-823.** Admission 12,000L ($6). Mon and Wed–Sat 9am–2pm; Sun 9am–9pm. Metro: Piazza Cavour.

With its Roman and Greek sculpture, this museum contains one of Europe's most valuable archaeological collections—particularly notable are the select Farnese acquisitions and the mosaics and sculpture excavated at Pompeii and Herculaneum. The building dates from the 16th century and was turned into a museum 2 centuries later by Charles and Ferdinand IV of Bourbon.

The nude statues of Armodio and Aristogitone are the most outstanding in one ground-floor room. A famous bas-relief (from a 5th-century B.C. original) in a nearby salon depicts Orpheus and Eurydice with Mercury. The spear-bearing nude *Doryphorus,* copied from a work by Polyclitus the Elder and excavated at Pompeii, enlivens another room. Also see the gigantic but weary *Farnese Hercules,* a statue of remarkable boldness that was discovered in Rome's Baths of Caracalla and is a copy of an original by Lysippus, the 4th-century B.C. Greek sculptor for Alexander the Great. On a more delicate pedestal is the decapitated but exquisite *Venus* (Aphrodite). The *Psyche of Capua* shows why Aphrodite was jealous. And the *Group of the Farnese Bull* presents a pageant of violence from the days of antiquity; the statue, which is one of the most frequently reproduced, was likewise discovered at the Baths of Caracalla and

A Museum Note

Reconfirm any museum hours before going there. Opening hours have been known to change from month to month, depending on how little money is in the city treasury. Even when the opening hours are actually posted, they seem more ornamental than reliable.

is a copy of a 2nd- or a 3rd-century B.C. Hellenistic statue. The marble group depicts a scene in the legend of Amphion and Zethus, who tied Dirce, wife of Lycus of Thebes, to the horns of a rampaging bull.

The mezzanine galleries are devoted to mosaics excavated from Pompeii and Herculaneum. These include scenes of cockfights, dragon-tailed satyrs, an aquarium, and *Alexander Fighting the Persians,* the finest of all. On the top floor are some of the celebrated bronzes dug out of the Pompeii volcanic mud and the Herculaneum lava. Of particular interest is a Hellenistic portrait of Berenice, a comically drunken satyr, a statue of a sleeping satyr, and Mercury on a rock.

✪ **National Museum & Gallery of the Capodimonte (Museo e Gallerie Nazionali di Capodimonte).** In the Palazzo Capodimonte, Parco di Capodimonte (off Amedeo di Savoia), Via Milano 2. ☎ **081-744-1307.** Admission 14,000L ($7). Tues–Sat 10am–7pm; Sun 9am–8pm. Bus: 22 or 23.

This museum and gallery, of Italy's finest, are housed in the 18th-century Capodimonte Palace, built in the time of Charles III and set in a park. Seven Flemish tapestries, made according to the designs of Bernaert van Orley, show grand-scale scenes from the Battle of Pavia (1525), in which the forces of François I of France, more than 25,000 strong, lost to those of Charles V. Bernaert, who lived in a pre-*Guernica* day, obviously considered war not a horror but a romantic ballet.

One of the picture gallery's greatest possessions is Simone Martini's *Coronation,* depicting the brother of Robert of Anjou being crowned king of Naples by the bishop of Toulouse. You'll want to linger over the great Masaccio's *Crucifixion,* a bold expression of grief. The most important room is literally filled with the works of Renaissance masters, notably an *Adoration of the Child* by Luca Signorelli, a *Madonna and Child* by Perugino, a panel by Raphael, a *Madonna and Child with Angels* by Botticelli, and—the most beautiful—Fillipino Lippi's *Annunciation and Saints.*

Look for Andrea Mantegna's *St. Eufemia* and portrait of Francesco Gonzaga, his brother-in-law Giovanni Bellini's *Transfiguration,* and Lotto's *Portrait of Bernardo de Rossi* and *Madonna and Child with St. Peter.* In one room is Raphael's *Holy Family and St. John* and a copy of his celebrated portrait of Pope Leo X. Two choice sketches are Raphael's *Moses* and Michelangelo's *Three Soldiers.* Displayed farther on are the Titians, with Danae taking the spotlight from Pope Paul III.

Another room is devoted to Flemish art: Pieter Brueghel's *Blind Men* is outstanding and his *Misanthrope* devilishly powerful. Other foreign works include Joos van Cleve's *Adoration of the Magi.* You can climb the stairs for a panoramic view of Naples and the bay, a finer landscape than any you'll see inside.

The State Apartments downstairs deserve inspection. Room after room is devoted to gilded mermaids, Venetian sedan chairs, ivory carvings, a porcelain chinoiserie salon, tapestries, the Farnese armory, and a large glass and china collection.

Carthusian Monastery of San Martino (Certosa di San Martino) & National Museum of San Martino (Museo Nazionale di San Martino). Largo San Martino 5 (in the Vómero district). ☎ **081-578-1769.** Admission 9,000L ($4.50). Tues–Sun 9am–2pm. Funicular: Centrale from Via Toledo.

Magnificently situated on the grounds of the Castel Sant'Elmo, this museum was founded in the 14th century as a Carthusian monastery but fell into decay until the 17th century, when it was reconstructed by architects in the Neapolitan baroque style. The marble-clad **church** has a ceiling painting of the *Ascension* by Lanfranco in the nave, along with 12 *Prophets* by Giuseppe Ribera, who also did the *Institution of the Eucharist* on the left wall of the choir (Lanfranco painted the *Crucifixion* and Guido

Impressions

The museum is full, as you know, of lovely Greek bronzes. The only bother is that they all walk about the town at night.

—Oscar Wilde, letter to Ernest Dowson (October 11, 1897)

Reni the *Nativity* at the choir's back wall). In the church treasury is Luca Giordano's ceiling fresco of the *Triumph of Judith* (1704) and Ribera's masterful *Descent from the Cross.*

Now a **museum** for the city of Naples, the church displays two stately carriages, historic documents, ships' replicas, china and porcelain, silver, Campagna paintings of the 18th and 19th centuries, military costumes and armor, and a lavishly adorned crib by Cuciniello. The vast collection of *presepi* (Neapolitan Christmas creches) includes a cast of thousands of peasants and holy figures that have come out of the workshops of Naples's greatest craftsmen over the past 4 centuries. (At press time a few of the rooms were closed, but they should be opened again by the time you arrive.) A balcony opens onto a panoramic view of Naples and the bay, as well as Vesuvius and Capri. Many people come here just to drink in the view. The colonnaded cloisters have curious skull sculptures on the inner balustrade.

Next to the monastery is the star-shaped **Castel Sant'Elmo** (☎ **081-578-4030**), built by the Angevins in a strategic position above the city from 1329 to 1343. It was enlarged in the 16th century and today offers a magnificent 360° panorama of Naples and its bay after a walk through the echoey medieval stone halls now used for conferences and exhibits. Admission is 4,000L ($2).

More Attractions

Royal Palace (Palazzo Reale). Piazza del Plebiscito 1. ☎ **081-580-8216.** Admission 8,000L ($4). Thurs–Fri and Sun–Tues 9am–2pm; Sat 9am–7pm. Bus: 106 or 150.

This palace was designed by Domenico Fontana in the 17th century, and the eight statues on the facade are of Neapolitan kings. Located in the heart of the city, the square on which the palace stands is one of Naples's most architecturally interesting, with a long colonnade and a church, San Francesco di Paolo, that evokes the style of the Pantheon in Rome. Inside the Palazzo Reale you can visit the royal apartments, adorned in the baroque style with colored marble floors, paintings, tapestries, frescoes, antiques, and porcelain. Charles de Bourbon, son of Philip IV of Spain, became king of Naples in 1734. A great patron of the arts, he installed a library here, one of the finest in the south, with more than 1,250,000 volumes.

New Castle (Castel Nuovo). Piazza del Municipo. ☎ **081-795-2003.** Admission 10,000L ($5). Mon–Sat 9am–7pm. Tram: 1 or 4. Bus: R2.

The New Castle, housing municipal offices, was built in the late 13th century on orders from Charles I, king of Naples, as a royal residence for the House of Anjou. It was badly ruined and virtually reconstructed in the mid–15th century by the House of Aragón. The castle is distinguished by a trio of imposing round battle towers at its front, and between two of the towers, guarding the entrance, is a triumphal arch designed by Francesco Laurana to commemorate the 1442 expulsion of the Angevins by the forces of Alphonso I. It's a masterpiece of the Renaissance. The Palatine Chapel in the center is from the 14th century, and the city commission of Naples meets in the Barons' Hall, designed by Segreta of Catalonia. You'll find some frescoes and sculptures (of minor interest) from the 14th and 15th centuries in the castle.

Castle of the Egg (Castel dell'Ovo). Porto Santa Lucia (follow Via Console along the seafront from Piazza del Plebiscito to Porto Santa Lucia; Castel dell'Ovo is at the end of the promontory). ☎ **081-764-5688.** Free admission. Mon–Sat 9am–3pm. Tram: 1 or 4.

This 2,000-year-old fortress overlooks the Gulf of Naples. The site was important centuries before the birth of Christ and was fortified by early settlers. In time, a major stronghold to guard the bay was erected and duly celebrated by Virgil. It's said that Virgil built it on an enchanted egg of mystical powers submerged on the floor of the ocean. Legend has it that if the egg breaks, Naples will collapse.

Actually, most of the fortress was constructed by Frederick II and later expanded by the Angevins. Though there's little to see here today, the Castel dell'Ovo is one of the most historic spots in Naples, perhaps the site of the original Greek settlement of Parthenope. In time it became the villa of Lucullus, the Roman general and philosopher. By the 5th century, the villa had become the home in exile for the last of the western Roman emperors, Romulus Augustulus. The Goths found him too young and stupid to be much of a threat to their ambitions and pensioned him off here. You can still see columns of Lucullus's villa in the dungeons. The view from here is panoramic. It's not open to the public except for special exhibits.

✪ **Santa Chiara.** Via Santa Chiara 49. ☎ **081-552-6209.** Free admission. Mon–Sat 8:30am–12:30pm and 3:30–6pm; Sun 8:30am–12:30pm. Metro: Montesanto.

On a palazzo-flanked street, this church was built on orders from Robert the Wise, king of Naples, in the early 14th century. It became the church for the House of Anjou. Though World War II bombers heavily blasted it, it has been restored somewhat to its original look, a Gothic style favored by the Provençal architects. The light-filled interior is lined with chapels, each of which contains some leftover bit of sculpture or fresco from the medieval church, but the best three pieces line the wall behind the High Altar. In the center is the towering multilevel tomb of Robert the Wise d'Angio, sculpted by Giovanni and Pacio Bertini in 1343. To its right is Tino di Camaino's tomb of Charles, duke of Calabria; and on the left is the 1399 monument to Mary of Durazza. In the choir behind the altar are more salvaged medieval remnants of frescoes and statuary, including bits of a Giotto *Crucifixion.*

You have to exit the church and walk down its left flank to enter one of Naples's top sights—and the most relaxing retreat from the bustle of the city—the 14th-century **Cloisters of the Order of the Clares (Chiostri dell'Ordine di Santa Chiara).** In 1742 Domenico Antonio Vaccaro took the courtyard of these flowering cloisters and lined the four paths to its center with arbors that are supported by columns, each of which is plated with colorfully painted majolica tiles; interspersed among the columns are tiled benches. In the **museum** rooms off the cloisters are a scattering of Roman and medieval remains.

On the piazza outside is one of Naples's several baroque spires, the **Guglia dell'Immacolata,** a tall pile of statues and reliefs sculpted in 1750.

Il Duomo. Via del Duomo 147. ☎ **081-449-097.** Free admission. Daily 9am–7pm. Metro: Piazza Cavour.

The Duomo of Naples may not be as impressive as some in other Italian cities, but it merits a visit nonetheless. Consecrated in 1315, it was Gothic in style, but the centuries have witnessed many changes; the facade, for example, is from the 1800s. A curiosity of the Duomo is that it has access to the 4th-century Basilica of St. Restituta, the earliest Christian basilica erected in Naples. But an even greater treasure is the **Chapel of San Gennaro (Cappella di San Gennaro),** which you enter from the south aisle. The altar is said to contain the blood of St. Gennaro, patron saint of Naples. St. Gennaro may have been a Christian assimilation of Janus, the Roman god.

The church contains two vials of the saint's blood, said to liquefy and boil three times annually (the first Sunday in May, September 19, and December 16).

San Domenico Maggiore. Piazza San Domenico Maggiore 8A. ☎ **081-557-3111.** Free admission. Daily 7:30am–noon and 4:30–7pm. Bus: E1, R1, R3, R4, V10, 24, 42, 105, or 105r.

This massive Gothic edifice was built from 1289 to 1324 and then rebuilt in the Renaissance and early baroque eras. You enter from under the apse end, where you'll see that the body of the church was overhauled in neo-Gothic style in the 1850s. Walk down the left aisle (which is on your right, since you're coming in from the wrong end) to the last chapel, where you'll find Luca Giordano's *Crowning of St. Joseph.* Now turn around to attack the church from the proper direction.

The first chapel on the right aisle is a Renaissance masterpiece of design and sculpture by Tuscans Antonio and Romolo da Settignano. The third chapel on the right contains frescoes from 1309 by Roman master Pietro Cavallini (a contemporary of Giotto). The seventh chapel on the right is the **Crucifixion Chapel (Cappella del Crocifisso),** with some Renaissance tombs and a copy of the 12th-century *Crucifixion* painting that spoke to St. Thomas Aquinas. Next door, the theatrical **Sacristy** has a bright ceiling fresco by Francesco Solimena (1706) and small caskets containing the ashes of Aragonese rulers and important courtiers, lining a high shelf. What acts like a right transept was actually a preexisting church grafted onto this one, the **Chiesa Antica di Sant'Angelo a Morfisa,** today an oversize chapel containing lots of finely carved Renaissance tombs.

On Piazza San Domenico is another of Naples's baroque spires, this one a 1737 confection called the **Guglia di San Domenico** by Domenico Antonio Vaccaro.

✪ **Cappella San Severo.** Via F. de Sanctis 19 (near Piazza San Domenico Maggiore). ☎ **081-551-8470.** Admission 8,000L ($4). Wed–Sun 10am–6pm (to 5pm Nov–June). Bus: E1, R1, R3, R4, V10, 24, 42, 105, or 105r.

If you want the best example of how baroque can be ludicrously over the top, hauntingly beautiful, and technically brilliant all at once, search out the nondescript entrance to one of Italy's most fanciful chapels. This 1590 chapel is a festival of marbles, frescoes, and, above all, sculpture—in relief and in the round, masterfully showing off the technical abilities and storytelling of a few relatively unknown Neapolitan baroque masters. At the center is Giuseppe Sammartino's remarkable alabaster *Veiled Christ* (1753), one the most successful and convincing illusions of soft reality crafted from hard stone, depicting the dead Christ lying on pillows under a transparent veil.

Three wall sculptures stand out as well: Francesco Celebrano's 1762 relief of the *Deposition* behind the altar, Antonio Corradini's allegory of *Modesty* (a marble statue of a woman whose nudity is covered only by a decidedly immodest clinging veil), and Francesco Queirolo's virtuoso allegory of *Disillusion,* represented by a man struggling with a rope net carved entirely of marble.

San Lorenzo Maggiore. Piazza San Gaetano 316. ☎ **081-290-580** or 081-454-948 for *scavi* (ruins). Admission to church free; scavi 5,000 L ($2.50). Church daily 9am–1pm and 4–6:30pm. Scavi Mon–Sat 9am–1:30pm. Bus: E1, 42, 105, or 105r.

The greatest of Naples's layered churches was built in 1265 for Charles I over a 6th-century basilica, which lay over many ancient remains. The interior is pure Gothic, with tall pointed arches and an apse off of which radiate nine chapels. This is where, in 1334, Boccaccio first caught sight of Robert of Anjou's daughter Maria, who became "Fiammetta" in his writings. Aside from some gorgeously baroque chapels of inlaid marbles, the highlight of the interior is Tino da Camaino's **canopy tomb of Catherine of Austria** (1323–25).

Wine Tasting

The wines produced in the harsh, hot landscapes of Campania seem stronger, rougher, and in many cases more powerful than those grown in gentler climes. Among the most famous are the *Lacryma Christi* (Tears of Christ), a white that grows in the volcanic soil near Naples, Herculaneum, and Pompeii; Taurasi, a potent red; and Greco di Tufo, a pungent white laden with the odors of apricots and apples. One of the most frequently visited vineyards is **Mastroberardino,** 75–81 Via Manfredi, Atripalda, 83042 Avellino (☎ **0825/626-123**), which is reached by taking the A16 east from Naples. If you'd like to spend a day outside the city, driving through the countryside and doing a little wine tasting, call them to make an appointment.

San Lorenzo preserves the best and most extensive (still rather paltry) **remains of the ancient Greek and Roman cities** currently open to the public. The church foundations are actually the walls of Neapolis's basilican law courts. In the **cloisters** are excavated bits of the Roman city's treasury and marketplace. In the **crypt** are the rough remains of a Roman-era shop-lined street, a Greek temple, and a medieval building.

Aquarium (Acquario). Inside Villa Comunale, Via Caracciolo 1. ☎ **081-583-3111.** Admission 3,000L ($1.50). Tues–Sat 9am–5pm; Sun 9am–2pm. Tram: 1 or 4.

The Aquarium is in a municipal park, Villa Comunale, between Via Caracciolo and the Riviera di Chiaia. Established by a German naturalist in the 1800s, it's the oldest aquarium in Europe and displays about 200 species of marine plants and fish, all found in the Bay of Naples (they must be a hardy lot).

Catacombe di San Gennaro (St. Januarius). In the Chiesa del Buon Consiglio, Via di Capodimonte 13. ☎ **081-741-1071.** Admission 5,000L ($2.50). Tours daily 9:30, 10:15, 11, and 11:45am. Tram: 1 or 4.

A guide will show you through this two-story underground cemetery, dating from the 2nd century and boasting many interesting frescoes and mosaics. You enter the catacombs on Via di Capodimonte (head down an alley going alongside the Madre del Buon Consiglio Church). These wide tunnels lined with early Christian burial niches grew around the tomb of an important pagan family, but they became a pilgrimage site when the bones of San Gennaro himself were transferred here in the 5th century. Along with several well-preserved 6th-century frescoes, there's a depiction of San Gennaro (A.D. 400s) whose halo sports an alpha and an omega and a cross—symbols normally reserved exclusively for Christ's halo. The tour takes you through the upper level of tunnels, passing through several small early basilicas carved from the *tufa* rock. The cemetery remained active until the 11th century, but most of the bones have since been blessed and reinterred in ossuaries on the lower levels (closed to the public). The catacombs survived the centuries intact, but those precious antique frescoes suffered some damage when these tunnels served as an air raid shelter during World War II.

SHOPPING

The shopping in Naples can't compare to that in Milan, Venice, Florence, and Rome. Nevertheless, there are some good buys for those willing to seek them out. The finest shopping area lies around **Piazza dei Martiri** and along such streets as **Via dei Mille, Via Calabritto,** and **Via Chiaia.** There's more commercial shopping between Piazza Trieste e Trento and Piazza Dante along **Via Toledo/Via Roma.**

Coral is much sought after by collectors. Much of the coral is now sent to Naples from Thailand, but it's still shaped into amazing jewelry at one of the workrooms at

Torre del Greco, on the outskirts of Naples, off the Naples–Pompeii highway. Cameos are also made there.

Modeled on Milan's galleria, the **Galleria Umberto I,** Via San Carlo (see "Naples After Dark" for more), was built as part of Naples's urban renewal scheme following an 1884 cholera epidemic. The massive glass- and iron-frame barrel vaults of its four wings and central dome soar some 187 feet above the inlaid marble flooring (it had to be largely rebuilt after World War II bomb damage). It makes for a pleasant shopping stroll. You'll find a wide range of stores selling typical area products, from fashion to ceramics.

ACCOMMODATIONS

EXPENSIVE

Grand Hotel Parker's. Corso Vittorio Emanuele 135, 80121 Napoli. ☎ **081-761-2474.** Fax 081-663-527. www.bcedit.it/parkershotel.htm. E-mail: ghparker@tin.it. 83 units. A/C MINIBAR TV TEL. 395,000–480,000L ($97.50–$240) double; 900,000L ($450) suite. Rates include breakfast. AE, DC, MC, V. Parking 20,600L–40,000L ($10–$20). Metro: Piazza Amedeo.

Parker's, on a hillside avenue, is one of the finest hotels in town, topped only by the Vesuvio. It was created in 1870, when architects cared about the beauty of their work—neoclassic walls, fluted pilasters, and ornate ceilings. The guest rooms are traditionally furnished, some quite formal; each is in a different style, like Louis XVI, Directoire, Empire, or Charles X. Most guests seek out one of the front rooms where narrow terraces open onto bay views. The bathrooms are clad in part with marble and contain robes and hair dryers.

Dining: The roof-garden restaurant offers fine views along with an international/Mediterranean cuisine.

Amenities: Laundry/valet, baby-sitting, room service, currency exchange, business center.

✪ **Grande Albergo Vesuvio.** Via Partenope 45, 80121 Napoli. ☎ **081-764-0044.** Fax 081-764-4483. www.prestigehotels.it. E-mail: info@prestigehotels.it. 181 units. A/C MINIBAR TV TEL. 530,000L ($265) double; from 800,000L ($400) suite. Rates include buffet breakfast. AE, DC, MC, V. Parking 35,000–40,000L ($17.50–$20). Bus: 104, 120, or 140.

Built in 1882, the Vesuvio was restored about 50 years later and features a marble-and-stucco facade with curved balconies. It's the foremost hotel along the fabled bay; many aristocratic English flocked here, to be followed later by Bogie and Errol Flynn. The 1930s-style guest rooms have lofty ceilings, cove moldings, parquet floors, and large closets. Traditionalists should request second-floor rooms, decorated in a 1700s style. The comfortable beds come with feather pillows and luxury mattresses, and the marble-clad bathrooms are spacious, with hair dryers and deluxe toiletries. You'll also find a scattering of antiques throughout the echoing halls.

Dining/Diversions: The hotel has a first-class restaurant, Caruso, plus a roof garden and a comfortable bar evoking the most stylish decor of the 1950s.

Amenities: Concierge, room service, laundry/dry cleaning, baby-sitting, secretarial services, health club, Jacuzzi, sauna. The tennis court is a 5-minute walk away.

Hotel Excelsior. Via Partenope 48, 80121 Napoli. ☎ **081-764-0111.** Fax 081-764-9743. www.prestigehotels.it. E-mail: info@prestigehotels.it. 62 units. A/C MINIBAR TV TEL. 500,000L ($250) double; 750,000–1,500,000L ($375–$750) suite. Rates include breakfast. AE, CB, DC, MC, V. Parking 35,000L ($17.50). Bus: 140, 152, or C25.

The Excelsior occupies a dramatic position on the waterfront, with views of Santa Lucia and Vesuvius. After a long decline, the hotel has bounced back under Sheraton (which also owns the posh Vesuvio next door) and boasts elegant details like Venetian chandeliers, Doric columns, wall-sized murals, and bronze torchiers. Most of the spacious guest rooms are furnished in the Empire style, with heavy wood furniture, elegant fabrics, paneled walls, brass trim, and safes. Carrara marble cloaks the walls of the bathrooms, which come with deluxe toiletries, phones, and hair dryers.

Dining: Both Neapolitan and international dishes are served at the restaurant La Terrazza, which has a roof garden offering a breathtaking view of Naples's gulf.

Amenities: Concierge, room service, baby-sitting, laundry/valet.

Hotel Miramare. Via Nazario Sauro 24, 80132 Napoli. ☎ **081-764-7589.** Fax 081-764-0775. www.hotelmiramare.com. E-mail: info@hotelmiramare.com. 31 units. A/C MINIBAR TV TEL. Mon–Thurs 390,000–495,000L ($195–$247.50) double; Fri–Sun 330,000–450,000L ($165–$225) double (minimum 2 nights). Rates include buffet breakfast. AE, DC, MC, V. Parking 35,000L ($17.50). Bus: 104, 140, or 150.

In a superb location, seemingly thrust out toward the harbor on a dockside boulevard, the Miramare was originally an aristocratic villa but was transformed into a hotel in 1944 after serving for a short period as the American consulate. Its lobby evokes a little Caribbean hotel with a semitropical look. The guest rooms have been renovated and are pleasantly furnished, with soundproof windows, safes, fax machines, VCRs, comfortable mattresses, and bathrooms with hair dryers.

Dining: Breakfast is the only meal served, although there are many dining spots a short walk from the entrance of the hotel. Guests in summer enjoy drinks on the roof garden or year-round at the American Bar.

Amenities: Concierge, limited room service, baby-sitting, laundry.

Hotel Royal. Via Partenope 38–44, 80121 Napoli. ☎ **081-764-4800.** Fax 081-764-5707. www.hotelroyal.it. E-mail: royalcon@tin.it. 251 units. A/C MINIBAR TV TEL. 300,000-400,000L ($150–$200) double; 650,000L ($325) suite. Rates include breakfast. AE, DC, MC, V. Parking 26,000–35,000L ($13–$17.50). Tram: 1.

The 10-story Royal is in a desirable location on this busy street beside the bay in Santa Lucia. It's a bustling choice that's often filled with tour groups. You enter a greenery-filled vestibule, where the stairs leading to the modern lobby are flanked by a pair of stone lions. Each of the guest rooms has a balcony and aging modern furniture; some offer a water view. The tiled bathrooms are small but have adequate shelf space.

Dining: The restaurant has panoramic views but only mediocre food.

Amenities: A seawater pool with an adjacent flower-dotted sun terrace is on the roof—the pool is vastly preferred over the polluted bay.

Hotel Santa Lucia. Via Partenope 46, 80121 Napoli. ☎ **081-764-0666.** Fax 081-764-8580. www.santalucia.it. E-mail: reservations@santalucia.it. 101 units. A/C MINIBAR TV TEL. 459,000–579,000L ($229.50–$289.50) double; from 649,000L ($324.50) suite. Rates include breakfast. AE, DC, MC, V. Parking 35,000L ($17.50). Bus: C25, 152, or 140.

The Santa Lucia, whose neoclassical facade overlooks a sheltered marina, competes with the nearby Royal and is better maintained. From the windows of about half the rooms, you can watch boats and yachts bobbing at anchor. The interior has undergone extensive renovations and is decorated in Neapolitan style, with terrazzo floors. The guest rooms are large, containing quality mattresses on beds with wrought-iron headboards and ceiling stenciling that lends a classical effect. The tiled bathrooms are equipped with hair dryers, phones, and often party-size whirlpools. The rooms in back are quieter but have no views. The balconied front rooms bring you lots of traffic noise but panoramic views of the Bay of Naples.

Dining/Diversions: There's an American-inspired bar, plus the Restaurant Megaris, serving a superb Mediterranean cuisine.

Amenities: Concierge, room service, baby-sitting.

MODERATE

Hotel Britannique. Corso Vittorio Emanuele 133, 80121 Napoli. ☎ **081-761-4145.** Fax 081-660-457. www.napleshotels.na.it/hotelbritannique. E-mail: britannique@napleshotels.na.it. 100 units. A/C MINIBAR TV TEL. 270,000L ($135) double; 300,000L ($150) junior suite. Rates include breakfast. AE, DC, MC, V. Parking 20,000–25,000L ($10–$12.50). Metro: Piazza Amedeo. Bus: C16 or C28.

Situated on the curve of a wide hillside boulevard, this remake of a former aristocratic villa has seen better days, but its view of the Bay of Naples and even Vesuvius is so compelling that many guests rave about the place. Tropical plants and flowers abound in the garden, but the lobby is a bit seedy. The guest rooms, from small to spacious, have some antiques, but mostly the look is functional, with comfortable mattresses. The plumbing is aging but still humming along. The hotel restaurant specializes in Italian and continental cuisine, and there's also a bar.

✪ **Hotel Majestic.** Largo Vasto a Chiaia 68, 80121 Napoli. ☎ **081-416-500.** Fax 081-410-145. www.majestic.it. 135 units. A/C MINIBAR TV TEL. 300,000L ($150) double; 450,000L ($225) suite. Rates include breakfast. AE, DC, MC, V. Parking 30,000–35,000L ($15–$17.50). Metro: Piazza Amedeo.

The four-star Majestic was built in 1959 and is one of the most up-to-date hotels in a city filled with decaying mansions. A favorite with the conference crowd, it's in the antiques district, so at your doorstep will be dozens of boutiques. The guest rooms range from small to medium, each particularly cozy, with firm mattresses. The bathrooms have adequate shelf space and hair dryers. There's a cozy bar, and the La Giara restaurant serves Neapolitan dishes and international specialties Monday to Saturday. The garage is small, so reserve parking space with your room.

Hotel Paradiso. Via Catullo 11, 80122 Napoli. ☎ **800/528-1234** in the U.S., or 081-761-4161. Fax 081-761-3449. www.bestwestern.it. E-mail: paradiso.na@bestwestern.it. 74 units. A/C MINIBAR TV TEL. 300,000L ($150) double; 500,000L ($250) junior suite. Rates include breakfast. AE, DC, MC, V. Parking 25,000–30,000L ($12.50–$15) nearby.

This hotel might be paradise, but only after you reach it. It's 3½ miles (6km) from the central station, but one irate driver claimed it takes about 3½ hours to get here. Once you arrive, however, your nerves will be soothed by the view, one of the most panoramic of any hotel in Italy. The Bay of Naples unfolds before you, and in the distance Vesuvius looms menacingly. The guest rooms range from medium to spacious, each with a firm mattress, and the bathrooms are tidy. Should you elect not to go out at night, you can patronize the fine hotel restaurant, serving Neapolitan and Italian specialties. From the Paradiso, you can either take taxis to the major attractions or use a funicular that takes you from a hillside site near the hotel to the center of Naples.

INEXPENSIVE

Albergo San Germano. Via Beccadelli 41, 80125 Napoli. ☎ **081-570-5422.** Fax 081-570-1546. 105 units. A/C MINIBAR TV TEL. 220,000L ($110) double. Rates include breakfast. AE, DC, MC, V. Bus: C52. From the autostrada, follow the signs to Tangenziale Napoli; exit 8 miles (13km) later at Agnano Terme. The hotel is on your right less than a mile from the toll booth.

Designed like an Italian version of a Chinese pagoda, this brick-and-concrete hotel is ideal for late-arriving motorists reluctant to negotiate the traffic of Naples. A terraced pool and garden are welcome respites after a day of sightseeing. The guest rooms are clean but simple. All are a bit small but tidily maintained, with good mattresses. Each tiled bath is a bit cramped. There's a lobby bar and a modern restaurant.

Hotel Rex. Via Palepoli 12, 80132 Napoli. ☎ **081-764-9389.** Fax 081-764-9227. 38 units. A/C TV TEL. 190,000L ($95) double. Rates include breakfast. AE, DC, MC, V. Parking 35,000L ($17.50). Bus: 104.

Santa Lucia's most famous budget hotel, the Rex has played host to lire-watchers from around the world since 1938. Some like it and others don't, but proof of its popularity is that its rooms are often fully booked when other hotels have vacancies. The architecture of the building itself is lavishly ornate, but the guest rooms are simple and some are very cramped. All the beds have firm mattresses, and the bathrooms are small. Breakfast is the only meal served.

Hotel Serius. Viale Augusto 74, 80125 Napoli. ☎ **081-239-4844.** Fax 081-239-9251. 69 units. A/C MINIBAR TV TEL. 175,000L ($87.50) double. Rates include breakfast. AE, MC, V. Free parking. Metro: Piazza Leopardi. Tram: 1 or 4.

Built in 1974, this hotel is on a palm-lined street in a calm neighborhood known as Fuorigrotto, a short bus ride north of the center. The paneled split-level lobby contains an intimate bar and several metal sculptures of horses and birds. The guest rooms are simply furnished, with boldly patterned fabrics and painted furniture. They range from small to medium, each with a firm mattress and a tiny bathroom. The dining room is pleasantly contemporary.

DINING

Naples is the home of pizza and spaghetti, and it's great fun to sample the authentic versions. However, if you like subtle cooking and have an aversion to olive oil or garlic, you won't fare as well.

EXPENSIVE

✪ **Giuseppone a Mare.** Via Ferdinando Russo 13. ☎ **081-575-6002.** Reservations required. Main courses 20,000–36,000L ($10–$18). AE, DC, MC, V. Tues–Sun 12:30–3:30pm and 8pm–midnight. Closed Aug 16–31. Bus: 140. SEAFOOD.

At this restaurant, which is known for serving the best and freshest seafood in Campania, you can dine in Neapolitan sunshine on an open-air terrace with a bay view. The only better restaurant is La Cantinella (see below). Diners make their selections from a trolley likely to include everything from crabs to eels. You might precede your fish dinner with some fritters (a batter whipped up with seaweed and fresh squash blossoms). Naturally, the offerings include linguine with clams—the chef adds squid and mussels. Much of the day's catch is deep-fried a golden brown. The pièce de résistance is an octopus casserole. If the oven's going, you can order a pizza. They stock some fine southern Italian wines too, especially from Ischia and Vesuvio.

Il Gallo Nero. Via Torquato Tasso 466. ☎ **081-643-012.** Reservations recommended. Main courses 30,000–45,000L ($15–$22.50); fixed-price menus 75,000L ($37.50) with meat, 85,000L ($42.50) with fish. AE, DC, MC, V. Tues–Sat 7pm–midnight; Sun 12:30–3pm. Closed Aug. Metro: Mergellina. NEAPOLITAN.

Gian Paolo Quagliata, with a capable staff, maintains his hillside villa with its period furniture and accessories. In summer, the enthusiastic crowd is served on an elegant terrace. Many of the dishes are based on 100-year-old recipes, though a few are more recent inventions. You might enjoy the Neapolitan linguine with pesto, rigatoni with fresh vegetables, tagliatelle primavera, or macaroni with peas and artichokes. The fish dishes are usually well prepared—grilled, broiled, or sautéed. The meat dishes include slightly more exotic creations, like prosciutto with orange slices and veal cutlets with artichokes.

✪ **La Cantinella.** Via Cuma 42. ☎ **081-764-8684.** Reservations required. Main courses 22,000–35,000L ($11–$17.50). AE, DC, MC, V. May–Sept daily 12:30–3pm and 7:30pm–midnight (Mon–Sat in Oct–Apr). Closed 1–2 weeks mid-Aug. Bus: 104, 140, or 150. SEAFOOD.

You get the impression of 1920s Chicago as you approach this place, where speakeasy-style doors open after you ring. The restaurant is on a busy street skirting the bay in Santa Lucia. You'll find a well-stocked antipasto table and—get this—a phone on each table. The chefs have a deft way of handling the region's fresh produce and turn out both Neapolitan classics and more imaginative dishes. The menu includes four preparations of risotto (including one with champagne), many kinds of pasta (including penne with vodka and linguine with scampi and seafood), and most of the classic beef and veal dishes of Italy. Best known for its fish, Cantinella serves grilled seafood at its finest.

Moderate to Inexpensive

Giovanni Scaturchio, Piazza San Domenico Maggiore 19 (☎ **081-551-6944**), offers the most caloric pastries in Naples; it's been satisfying and fattening locals since around 1900. Pastries include the entire selection of Neapolitan sweets, cakes, and candies, like brioches soaked in liqueur, *cassate* (pound cake) filled with layered ricotta, Moor's heads, and cheesy ricotta pastries known as *sfogliatelle.* Another specialty is *ministeriale,* a chocolate cake filled with liqueur and chocolate cream. Pastries start at 2,600L ($1.30) if consumed standing up or at 3,600L ($1.80) if enjoyed at a table. The shop is open Wednesday to Monday 7:20am to 8:40pm (closed 2 to 3 weeks in August).

Dante e Beatrice. Piazza Dante 44–45. ☎ **081-549-9438.** Reservations recommended. Main courses 15,000–30,000L ($7.50–$15); fixed-price menus 30,000–50,000L ($15–$25). No credit cards. Thurs–Tues 1:30–4pm and 8–midnight. Closed Aug 15–30. Tram: R1 or R4. NEAPOLITAN.

Gregarious and unpretentious and named after the players in one of the great romantic tragedies of the Middle Ages, Dante e Beatrice opened in 1956 and remains one of the best restaurants in its neighborhood. It specializes in all the staples of the Neapolitan cuisine, serving flavorful portions of lasagna, minestrone, spaghetti with clams, tagliatelle, *pasta e fagioli* (pasta and beans), and grilled fish. Other notable items are *maccheroni* or spaghetti with seafood and "frittata" of spaghetti, with a sauce made of mozzarella, prosciutto, and salami, bound together with tomatoes.

Don Salvatore. Strada Mergellina 4A. ☎ **081-681-817.** Reservations recommended. Main courses 12,000–30,000L ($6–$15). AE, DC, MC, V. May–Oct daily 1–4pm and 8pm–1am; Nov–Apr, Thurs–Tues 1–4pm and 8pm–1am. Metro: Mergellina. SEAFOOD.

This is the creative statement of a serious restaurateur who directs his waterfront place with passion and dedication. Antonio Aversano takes his wine as seriously as his food. The latter is likely to include linguine with shrimp or squid, an array of fish, and a marvelous assortment of fresh Neapolitan vegetables grown in the countryside. The fish, priced according to weight, comes right out of the Bay of Naples (which may, but possibly may not, be a plus). Rice comes flavored in a delicate fish broth, and you can get a reasonably priced bottle from the wine cellar, said to be the finest in Campania. The restaurant is on the seafront near the departure point of hydrofoils for Capri.

La Sacrestia. Via Orazio 116. ☎ **081-761-1051.** Reservations required. Main courses 18,000–60,000L ($9–$30). AE, DC, MC, V. Daily 12:30–4:30pm and 7:30–11pm. July closed Sun. Closed 2 weeks mid-Aug. Funicular: from Mergellina. PASTA/SEAFOOD.

The trompe l'oeil frescoes on the two-story interior and the name La Sacrestia vaguely suggest the ecclesiastical, but that's not the case. Perched near the top of a seemingly endless labyrinth of streets winding up from the port (take a taxi or go by funicular), this bustling place is sometimes called "the greatest show in town." In summer a terrace with its flowering arbor provides a view over the harbor lights. Meals emphasize well-prepared dishes with strong doses of Neapolitan drama. You might try what's said to be the most luxurious macaroni dish in Italy ("Prince of Naples"), made with truffles and mild cheeses. Less ornate selections are a full array of pastas and dishes composed of octopus, squid, and shellfish.

Masaniello. Via Donnalbina 28. ☎ **081-552-8863.** Reservation recommended. Main courses 16,000–30,000L ($8–$15). AE, DC, MC, V. Mon–Sat 12:30–3pm and 8–11:30pm (daily in Dec and May). NEAPOLITAN.

In a former stable, this hard-to-find restaurant is named for the celebrated leader of a people's uprising in 1647. It prints no menus, so the owner or waiter will tell you what's offered. The food is cooked to order after elaborate consultations about the taste of each customer. The cuisine is exquisitely prepared and based on only the freshest of ingredients. If you put yourself into the hands of the owner, be prepared for a bounteous feast. The traditional dishes based on antique recipes include linguine with *lupini di mare* (Neapolitan clams) and pecorino cheese. Another special dish of which the chef is proud is pasta with potatoes; though it sounds like an unlikely combination, it's filled with flavor from the smoked provola cheese and the fresh little tomatoes.

✪ **Pizzaria Brandi.** Salita Santa Anna di Palazzo. ☎ **081-416-928.** Reservations required. Main courses 15,000–28,000L ($7.50–$14); pizza from 8,000L ($4). AE, MC, V. Tues–Sun noon–3pm and 6:30pm–midnight. Bus: 106 or 150. NEAPOLITAN/PIZZA.

The most historic pizzeria in Italy, Brandi was opened by Pietro Colicchio in the 19th century. His successor, Raffaele Esposito, who enjoyed the reputation his hard work had earned, was requested one day to prepare a banquet for Margherita di Savoia, the queen of Italy. So successful was the reception of the pizza made with tomato, basil, olive oil, and mozzarella (the colors of the newly united Italy's flag) that the queen accepted the honor of having the dish named after her. Thus was pizza Margherita born from the kitchens here. Today you can order the pizza that pleased a queen, as well as linguine with scampi, fettuccine "Regina d'Italia," and a full array of seafood dishes. Even Chelsea Clinton gave this place a thumbs-up.

Ristorante La Fazenda. Via Marechiaro 58A. ☎ **081-575-7420.** Reservations required. Main courses 15,000–30,000L ($7.50–$15). AE, MC, V. Tues–Sat 1–4pm and 7:30pm–12:30am; Sun 1–4pm; Mon 7:30pm–12:30am. Closed 15 days in mid-Aug. Bus: 106 or 150. SEAFOOD.

It would be hard to find a more typically Neapolitan restaurant than this place, with its panoramic view that on a clear day can include Capri. The decor is rustic, loaded with agrarian touches and an assortment of Neapolitan families, lovers, and visitors who have made it one of their preferred places. In summer the overflow from the dining room spills onto the terrace. Menu specialties include linguine with scampi, fresh grilled fish, sautéed clams, a mixed Italian grill, savory stews, and many chicken dishes, along with lobster with fresh grilled tomatoes. Look for "Mr. Nappo," allegedly "the largest pizza ever."

Rosolino. Via Nazario Sauro 2–7. ☎ **081-764-9873.** Reservations required. Main courses 15,000–28,000L ($7.50–$14); fixed-price menus 45,000–70,000L ($22.50–$35). AE, DC, MC, V. Mon–Sun 12:30–3:30pm; Mon–Sat 8pm–midnight. Tram: 1 or 4. INTERNATIONAL/ITALIAN/SEAFOOD.

This stylish place isn't defined as a nightclub by its owners but rather as a restaurant with dancing. Set on the waterfront, it's divided into two areas: On Saturday evenings

Dining in the Past

The city's most unusual dining experience is the weekly banquet at **Simposium,** Via Benedetto Croce 38 (☎ **081-551-8510**), Friday and Saturday at 9pm. Reservations are essential. This cultural institution celebrates a different historical era with a fascinating lecture followed by a banquet featuring a cuisine based on recipes from that era. Waiters in period costumes serve the banquets. Perhaps the offering will be called *di fine Settecento* (from the end of the 18th century), accompanied by a live performance of selections from *Don Giovanni.* At the banquet, men sit on one side, women on the other, and wine is served in clay pitchers. Don't expect grand cuisine. The food is almost too simplistic—perhaps a plate of gruel, authentic to the time, with overcooked vegetables and a turnover stuffed with something (you're too polite to ask what). But the music and the setting make this one of Naples's hottest reservations. A dinner for two is about 160,000L ($80), including wine, service chargetip service, and tax.

there's a piano bar near the entrance, where you might have a drink before passing into a much larger dining room. Here you can dine within sight of a bandstand reminiscent of the big band era. In the dining room, live music happens on Friday and Saturday nights, featuring a light guitar in the style of Naples. The food is traditional, not very imaginative but well prepared with fresh vegetables. Dishes include rigatoni with zucchini and meat sauce, pusillo (a locally made pasta), an impressive array of fresh shellfish, and such beef dishes as tournedos and veal scaloppini. Most fresh fish is priced according to weight. There are three wine lists, including one for French wines and champagne.

Umberto. Via Alabardieri 30. ☎ **081-418-555.** Reservations required. Main courses 13,000–30,000L ($6.50–$15). AE, CB, DC, DISC, MC, V. Daily 9:30am–4pm, Tues–Sun 7pm–midnight. Closed Aug. Bus: 1 or 152. NEAPOLITAN.

Off Piazza dei Martiri, Umberto is one of the most atmospheric places to dine; there's even likely to be a dance band playing at dinner. The tasteful dining room has been directed for many a year by the same extended family. The excellent Italian specialties include pizzas, gnocchi with potatoes, grilled meats and fish, savory stews, and a host of pasta dishes.

Vini e Cucina. Corso Vittorio Emanuele 762. ☎ **081-660-302.** Reservations recommended. Main course 28,000L ($14). No credit cards. Mon–Sat 11:30am–3:30pm and 7pm–midnight. Closed Aug 10–28. Metro: Mergellina. NEAPOLITAN.

The best ragout sauce in all Naples is said to be made at this trattoria, which has only 20 tables. You can get a really satisfying meal, but we must warn you—it's almost impossible to get in. Get there early and resign yourself to a wait. The cooking is the best home-style version of Neapolitan cuisine we've been able to find in this tricky city. The spaghetti, along with that fabulous sauce, is served al dente. The restaurant is in front of the Mergellina station.

NAPLES AFTER DARK

A **sunset walk through Santa Lucia** and along the waterfront is one of the lasting pleasures in Naples. Visitors are also fond of riding around town in ***carrozzelle*** (horse-drawn wagons), though fewer of them stay in business each passing year. The limited number that remain tend to line up along the edges of the Piazza Municipio during daylight hours. The cost is usually between 30,000 and 40,000L ($15 to $20) for a ride that lasts between 30 and 40 minutes.

Or you can stroll by the glass-enclosed **Galleria Umberto I,** off Via Roma across from the Teatro San Carlo. The 19th-century gallery is still standing today, though a little the worse for wear. It's a kind of social center for Naples, with lots of shopping and dining possibilities.

Naples's oldest cafe, dating from 1860, is the palatial **Gran Caffè Gambrinus,** Via Chiaia 1, near the Galleria Umberto I (☎ **081-417-582**). Along the vaulted ceiling of an inner room, Empire-style caryatids spread their togas in high relief above frescoes of mythological playmates. The cafe is known for its espresso and cappuccino, as well as pastries and cakes whose variety dazzles the eye. You can also order potato-and-rice croquettes and fried pizzas for a light lunch. Cappuccino goes for 4,000L ($2) at a table. The cafe is open daily 8am to midnight.

OPERA The ✪ **Teatro San Carlo,** Via San Carlo 98, across from the Galleria Umberto (☎ **081-797-2111**), is one of the largest opera houses in Italy, with some of the best acoustics. Built in only 6 months' time for King Charles's birthday in November 1737, it was restored in a gilded neoclassical style. Grand-scale productions are presented on the main stage. December to October, the box office is open Tuesday to Sunday 10am to 1pm and 4:30 to 6:30pm. Tickets are 80,000 to 200,000L ($40 to $100).

BARS & CLUBS On its nightclub/cabaret circuit, Naples offers more sucker joints than any other Mediterranean port. If you're starved for action, you'll find plenty of it—and you're likely to end up paying for it dearly.

Chez Moi, Via del Parco Margherita 13 (☎ **081-407-526**), is one of the city's best-managed nightclubs, strictly refusing entrance to anyone who looks like a trouble-maker. This is appreciated by the designers, government ministers, and visiting socialites who enjoy the place. The crowd tends to be over 25. The place is open Friday and Saturday 10:30pm to 4 or 5am. Occasionally there's a cabaret act or a live pianist at the bar, but more frequently the music is disco. The cover is 25,000L ($12.50).

Madison Street, Via Sgambati 47 (☎ **081-546-6566**), is the largest disco in Naples. The youngish crowd, usually between 18 and 25, mingles and dances and generally has an uninhibited good time. If you tire yourself out on the dance floor, you can watch video movies or videotaped rock concerts on one of several screens. The place is open Tuesday and Thursday to Saturday 10pm to 3am, Sunday 8pm to 2am. The Friday crowd tends to be older and slightly more sedate. The cover ranges from 15,000 to 30,000L ($7.50 to $15) depending on the night.

A leading Naples hot spot is **Piazza di Spagna,** Via Petrarca 101 (☎ **081-575-48-82**), in Vómero. It features dancing Friday to Sunday from September to July; go after 10pm and expect a 15,000 to 20,000L ($7.50 to $10) cover.

The best local jazz is often heard at **Riot,** Via San Biagio 38 (☎ **081-552-32-31**), open Thursday to Tuesday 10:30am to 3am.

If you're mature and want a piano bar ambience, head for **Airone,** Via Petrarca 123 (☎ **081-575-0175**).

Looking for gay action? Head for **Tongue,** Via Mazonik 207 (☎ **081-769-0800**), which has a mixed crowd, a large part of whom are gay, dancing to techno music. It's open only weekends 9pm to 3am, charging a cover of 15,000 to 25,000L ($7.50 to $12.50). There are no all-exclusive lesbian or gay clubs, but **ARCI-Gay/Lesbica** (☎ **081-551-8293**) is a support group that can help you learn about the city's gay scene. They operate during limited hours, usually three evenings a week, 7 to 10pm. Some of the volunteers speak English.

2 The Environs of Naples: The Phlaegrean Fields & Herculaneum

THE PHLAEGREAN FIELDS

One of the bizarre attractions of southern Italy, the **Phlaegrean Fields (Campi Flegrei)** form a backdrop for a day's exploring west of Naples and along its bay. An explosive land of myth and legend, the fiery fields contain the dormant volcano Solfatara, the cave of the Cumaean Sibyl, Virgil's gateway to the "Infernal Regions," the ruins of thermal baths and amphitheaters built by the Romans, deserted colonies left by the Greeks, and lots more.

If you're depending on public transport, the best center for exploring the area is **Pozzuoli,** reached by Metropolitana (subway) from Stazione Centrale in Naples. The fare is 1,500L (75¢). Once in Pozzuoli, you can catch one of the SEPSA buses at any bus stop and be in Baia in 20 minutes. You can also go to Cumae on one of these buses or to Solfatara or Lago d'Averno.

✪ **SOLFATARA** About 7½ miles (12km) west of Naples, near Pozzuoli, is the ancient **Vulcano Solfatara,** Via Solfatara 161 (☎ **081-5262-341**). It hasn't erupted since the final year of the 12th century but has been threatening ever since. It gives off sulfurous gases and releases scalding vapors through cracks in the earth's surface. In fact, Solfatara's activity (or inactivity) has been observed for such a long time that the crater's name is used by *Webster's* dictionary to define any "dormant volcano" emitting vapors.

You can visit the crater daily 8:30am to 1 hour before sunset at a cost of 8,000L ($4). From Naples, take bus no. 152 from Piazza Garibaldi or the Metropolitana from Stazione Centrale. Once you get off at the train station, you can board one of the city buses that go up the hill or you can walk to the crater in about 20 minutes.

POZZUOLI Just 1½ miles (2km) from Solfatara, the port of Pozzuoli opens onto a gulf screened from the Bay of Naples by a promontory. The ruins of the **Anfiteatro Flavio,** Via Nicola Terracciano 75 (☎ **081-526-6007**), built in the last part of the 1st century, testify to past greatness. One of the finest surviving ancient arenas, it's particularly distinguished by its "wings," which, considering their age, are in good condition. You can see the remains where exotic beasts from Africa were caged before being turned loose in the ring to test their jungle skill against a gladiator. The amphitheater is said to have entertained 40,000 spectators at the height of its glory. June to August, you can visit daily 9am to 6pm (to 4pm September to March and to 5pm April and May). Admission is 6,000L ($3).

In another part of town, the **Tempio di Serapide** was really the Macellum (market square), and some of its ruined pillars still project upward. It was erected during the reign of the Flavian emperors. You can reach Pozzuoli by subway from Stazione Centrale in Naples.

BAIA In the days of Imperial Rome, the emperors—everybody from Julius Caesar to Hadrian—came here to frolic in the sun while enjoying the comforts of their luxurious villas and Roman baths. It was here that Emperor Claudius built a grand villa for his first wife, Messalina, who spent her days and nights reveling in debauchery and plotting to have her husband replaced by her lover (for which she was beheaded). And it was here that Claudius was poisoned by his last wife, Agrippina, the controlling mother of Nero. Nero is said to have had Agrippina murdered at nearby Bacoli, with its Pool of Mirabilis—after she had survived his first attempt on her life, a collapsing boat meant to send her to a watery rest. Parts of Baia's illustrious past have been dug out, including both the **Temple of Baiae** and the **Thermal Baths,** among the greatest erected in Italy.

You can explore this archaeological district (☎ **081-868-7592**) daily 9am to 1 hour before sunset. Admission is 6,000L ($3). Ferrovia Cumana trains depart from Stazione Centrale for the 15-minute trip from Naples.

LAGO D'AVERNO About 10 miles (16km) west of Naples, a bit north of Baia, is a lake occupying an extinct volcanic crater. Known to the ancients as the **Gateway to Hades,** it was for centuries shrouded in superstition. Its vapors were said to produce illness and even death, and Lake Averno could well have been the source of the expression "Still waters run deep." Facing the lake are the ruins of what has been known as the **Temple of Apollo** from the 1st century A.D. and what was once thought to be the Cave of the Cumaean Sibyl (see below). According to legend, the Sibyl is said to have ferried Aeneas, son of Aphrodite, across the lake, where he traced a mysterious spring to its source, the River Styx. In the 1st century B.C., Agrippa turned it into a harbor for Roman ships by digging out a canal. Take the Napoli–Torre Gaveta bus from Baia to reach the site.

CUMA Cuma was one of the first outposts of Greek colonization in what's now Italy. Located 12 miles (19km) west of Naples, it's of interest chiefly because it's said to have contained the **Cave of the Cumaean Sibyl.** The cave of the oracle, really a gallery, was dug by the Greeks in the 5th century B.C. and was a sacred spot to them. Beloved by Apollo, the Sibyl is said to have written the *Sibylline Oracles,* a group of books of prophecy bought, according to tradition, by Tarquin the Proud. You may visit not only the caves but also the ruins of temples dedicated to Jupiter and Apollo (later converted into Christian churches), daily 9am to 1 hour before sunset; admission is 8,000L ($4) adults (children under 18 free). On Via Domitiana, to the east of Cuma, you'll pass the **Arco Felice,** an arch about 64 feet high, built by Emperor Domitian in the 1st century A.D. Ferrovia Cumana trains run here, departing from Stazione Centrale in Naples.

✪ HERCULANEUM

The builders of Herculaneum (Ercolano) were still working to repair the damage caused by an A.D. 62 earthquake when Vesuvius erupted on that fateful August day in A.D. 79. Herculaneum, about one-fourth the size of Pompeii, didn't start to come to light again until 1709, when Prince Elbeuf launched the unfortunate fashion of tunneling through it for treasures, more intent on profiting from the sale of objets d'art than in uncovering a dead Roman town.

Subsequent excavations at the site, the **Ufficio Scavi di Ercolano,** Corso Resina, Ercolano (☎ **081-739-0963**), have been slow and sporadic. In fact, Herculaneum, named after Hercules, is not completely dug out today. One of the obstacles has been that the town was buried under lava, much heavier than the ash and pumice stone that piled onto Pompeii. Of course, this formed a greater protection for the buildings buried underneath—many of which were more elaborately constructed than those at Pompeii, since Herculaneum was a seaside resort for patricians. The complication of having the slum of Resina resting over the yet-to-be-excavated district has further impeded progress and urban renewal.

Although all the streets and buildings of Herculaneum hold interest, some ruins merit more attention than others. The **baths (*terme*)** are divided between those at the forum and the **Suburban Baths (Terme Suburbane)** on the outskirts, near the more elegant villas. The municipal baths, which segregated the sexes, are larger, but the ones at the edge of town are more lavishly adorned. The **Palestra** was a kind of sports arena, where games were staged to satisfy the spectacle-hungry denizens.

The typical plan for the average town house was to erect it around an uncovered atrium. In some areas, Herculaneum possessed the forerunner of the modern apartment house. Important private homes to seek out are the **House of the Bicentenary (Casa del Bicentenario), House of the Wooden Cabinet (Casa a Graticcio), House of the Wooden Partition (Casa del Tramezzo di Legno),** and **House of Poseidon (Casa di Poseidon),** as well as the **Amphitheater (Anfiteatro),** the last containing the best-known mosaic discovered in the ruins.

The finest example of how the aristocracy lived is the **Casa dei Cervi,** named the **House of the Stags** because of the sculpture found inside. Guides are fond of showing the males on their tours a statue of a drunken Hercules urinating. Some of the best of the houses are locked and can be seen only by permission.

You can visit the ruins daily 9am to 1 hour before sunset. Admission is 12,000L ($6). To reach the archaeological zone, take the regular train service from Naples on the Circumvesuviana Railway, a 20-minute ride leaving about every half hour from Corso Garibaldi 387, just south of the main train station (you can also catch Circumvesuviana trains underneath the main Stazione Centrale itself; follow the signs). This train will get you to Vesuvius (same stop), Pompeii, and Sorrento. Otherwise, it's a 4½-mile (7km) drive on the autostrada to Salerno (turn off at Ercolano).

3 Pompeii

15 miles (24km) S of Naples, 147 miles (237km) SE of Rome

When Vesuvius erupted in A.D. 79, Pliny the Younger, who later recorded the event, thought the end of the world had come. The ruined Roman city of ✪ **Pompeii (Pompei),** now dug out from the inundation of volcanic ash and pumice stone that rained on it, vividly brings to light the life of 19 centuries ago and has sparked the imagination of the world.

Numerous myths have surrounded Pompeii, one of which is that a completely intact city was rediscovered. Actually the Pompeians (that is, those who escaped) returned to their city when the ashes had cooled and removed some of the most precious treasures from the thriving resort. But they left plenty behind to be uncovered at a later date and carted off to museums throughout Europe and America.

After a long medieval sleep, Pompeii was again brought to life in the late 16th century, quite by accident, by architect Domenico Fontana. However, it was in the mid-18th century that large-scale excavations were launched. Somebody once remarked that Pompeii's second tragedy was its rediscovery, that it really should have been left to slumber for another century or two, when it might have been better excavated and maintained.

ESSENTIALS

GETTING THERE The **Circumvesuviana Railway** departs Naples every half hour from Piazza Garibaldi. However, be sure you get on the train headed toward *Sorrento* and get off at Pompeii/Scavi (*scavi* means "ruins"). If you get on the Pompeii train, you'll end up in the town of Pompeii and have to transfer there to the Sorrento train to get to the ruins. A round-trip costs 3,000L ($1.50); trip time is 45 minutes each way. Circumvesuviana trains leave Sorrento several times during the day for Pompeii, costing 2,500L ($1.25) one way. There's an entrance about 50 yards from the

Herculaneum

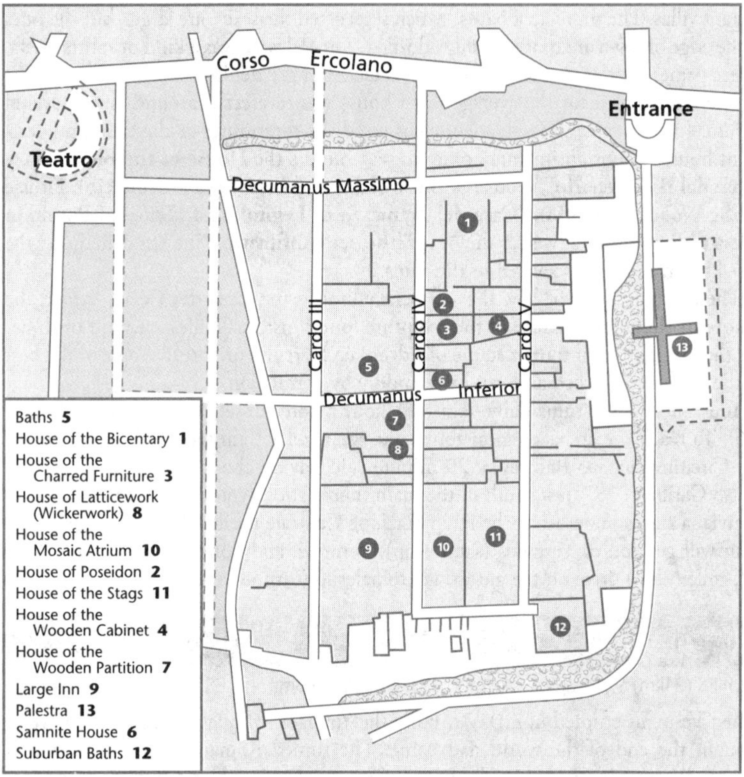

rail station at the Villa dei Misteri. At the rail station in the town of Pompeii, **bus** connections take you to the entrance to the excavations.

To reach Pompeii by **car** from Naples, take the 13½-mile (22km) drive on the autostrada to Salerno. If you're coming from Sorrento, head east on SS145, where you can connect with A3 (marked Napoli). Then take the signposted turnoff for Pompeii.

VISITOR INFORMATION The **tourist office** is at Via Sacra 1 (☎ **081-8575-280**). October to March, it's open Monday to Friday 8am to 3:40pm and Saturday 8am to 2pm; April to September, hours are Monday to Friday 8am to 7pm and Saturday 8am to 2pm. They can fill you in on the **Panatenee Pompeiane,** a festival of the performing arts with a series of classical plays in July and August.

LOGISTICAL TIPS After you pay for your entrance to the ruins, you'll find a **bookstore,** where you can purchase informative guides to the ruins (available in English and complete with detailed photos) that will help you understand what you're seeing. We highly recommend that you purchase one before you set out.

If you're here on a sunny day, wear sunscreen and bring along a bottle of water. There's almost no place in Pompeii to escape the sun's rays, and it can often be dusty.

EXPLORING THE RUINS

Most of the curious visit the ✪ **Ufficio Scavi di Pompei,** Piazza Esedra (☎ **081-861-0744**), the best preserved 2,000-year-old ruins in Europe, on a day trip from

Naples (allow at least 4 hours for even a superficial look at the archaeological site). The ruins are open daily 9am to 4pm. Admission is 12,000L ($6).

The most elegant of the patrician villas is the **House of the Vettii (Casa dei Vettii),** boasting a courtyard, statuary (such as a two-faced Janus), paintings, and a black-and-red Pompeian dining room known for its frescoes of delicate cupids. The house was occupied by two brothers named Vettii, both of whom were wealthy merchants. As you enter the vestibule, you'll see a painting of Priapus resting his gargantuan phallus on a pair of scales. The guard will reveal other erotic fertility drawings and statuary, though most such material has been removed to the Archaeological Museum in Naples. This house is the best example of a villa and garden that's been restored.

The second most important villa, the **House of the Mysteries (Villa dei Misteri),** near the Porto Ercolano, is outside the walls (go along Viale alla Villa dei Misteri). What makes the villa exceptional, aside from its architectural features, are its remarkable frescoes, depicting scenes associated with the sect of Dionysus (Bacchus), one of

Treading Lightly on Mt. Vesuvius

Stand at the bottom of the great market-place of Pompeii, and look up at the silent streets.... over the broken houses with their inmost sanctuaries open to the day, away to Mount Vesuvius, bright and snowy in the peaceful distance; and lose all count of time, and heed of other things, in the strange and melancholy sensation of seeing the Destroyed and the Destroyer making this quiet picture in the sun.

—Charles Dickens, *Pictures from Italy*

A volcano that has struck terror in Campania, the towering, pitch-black **Mt. Vesuvius** looms menacingly over the Bay of Naples. August 24, A.D. 79, is the infamous date when Vesuvius burst forth and buried Pompeii, Herculaneum, and Stabiae under its mass of ash and volcanic mud. What many fail to realize is that Vesuvius has erupted periodically ever since (thousands were killed in 1631): The last major spouting of lava occurred in this century (it blew off the ring of its crater in 1906). The last spectacular eruption was on March 31, 1944. The approach to Vesuvius is dramatic, with the terrain growing foreboding as you near the top. Along the way you'll see villas rising on its slopes and vineyards—the grapes produce an amber-colored wine known as *Lacrimae Christi* (Tears of Christ); the citizens of ancient Pompeii enjoyed wine from here, as excavations have revealed. Closer to the summit, the soil becomes puce colored and an occasional wildflower appears.

Though it may sound like a dubious invitation (Vesuvius, after all, is an active volcano), it's possible to visit the rim of the crater's mouth. As you look down into its smoldering core, you may recall that Spartacus, a century before the eruption that buried Pompeii, hid in the hollow of the crater, which was then covered with vines.

To reach Vesuvius from Naples, take the Circumvesuviana Railway or (summer only) bus service from Piazza Vittoria, which hooks up with bus connections at Pugliano. You get off the train at the Ercolano station, the 10th stop. Six SITA buses per day go from Herculaneum to the crater of Vesuvius, costing 4,500L ($2.25) round-trip. Once at the top, you must be accompanied by a guide, which will cost 5,000L ($2.50).

the cults that flourished in Roman times. Note the Pompeian red in some of the backgrounds. The largest house, called the **House of the Faun (Casa del Fauno)** because of a bronze statue of a dancing faun found there, takes up a city block and has four dining rooms and two spacious peristyle gardens. It sheltered the celebrated *Battle of Alexander the Great* mosaic that's now in a Naples museum.

In the center of town is the **Forum (Foro)**—rather small, it was nonetheless the heart of Pompeian life, known to bakers, merchants, and the aristocrats who lived in the villas. Parts of the Forum were severely damaged in an earthquake 16 years before the eruption of Vesuvius and hadn't been repaired when the final destruction came. Three buildings surrounding the Forum are the **basilica** (the city's largest single structure), the **Temple of Apollo (Tempio di Apollo),** and the **Temple of Jupiter (Tempio di Giove).** The **Stabian Thermae** (baths)—where both men and women lounged in between games of knucklebones—are in good condition, among the finest to come down from antiquity. Here you'll see some skeletons. In the **brothel (Lupanare)** are some erotic paintings (tip the guide to see them).

Other buildings of interest include the **Great Theater (Teatro Grande),** built in the 5th century B.C. During the Hellenistic period from 200 to 150 B.C., it was largely rebuilt, as it was again by the Romans in the 1st century A.D. This open-air theater could hold 5,000 spectators, many of them bloodthirsty as they screamed for death in the battles between wild animals and gladiators. The **House of the Gilded Cupids (Casa degli Amorini Dorati)** was a flamboyant private home, its owner unknown, though he probably lived during the reign of Nero. Obviously he had theatrical flair, attested to by the gilded and glass cupids known as *amorini.* Even though badly ruined, the house still contains a peristyle with one wing raised almost like a stage. The **House of the Tragic Poet (Casa del Poeta Tragico)** gets its name from a mosaic discovered here (later sent to Naples). It depicts a chained watchdog on the doorstep with this warning: Cave Canem ("Beware of the dog").

ACCOMMODATIONS

Accommodations in Pompeii appear to be for earnest archaeologists only, with the two below the only really suitable choices (it's easy to drop in for the day from a base elsewhere, so not many people stay overnight). Some hotels in Pompeii aren't considered safe because of robberies. Protect your valuables and your person, and don't wander the streets at night. Most visitors look at the excavations and then seek better accommodations at either Naples or Sorrento.

Hotel Villa dei Misteri. Via Villa dei Misteri 11, 80045 Pompei-Scavi. ☎ **081-861-3593.** Fax 081-862-2983. www.ptn.pandora.it/hmisteri. E-mail: hmisteri@ptn.pandora.it. 41 units. 90,000L ($45) double. Breakfast 8,000L ($4). DC, MC, V. Free parking. From the Naples rail station Circumvesuviana, take the Sorrento train and get off at the Villa dei Misteri stop.

Located 250 yards from the Scavi Station, this 1930s hotel is suitable for motorists. About 1$^1/_2$ miles (2km) south of the center of town, it features a pool, a little garden, and a place to park your car. The family-style welcome may compensate for a certain lack of amenities. The place could stand a face-lift, but many readers have expressed their fondness for it. The only guest rooms are bare-bones doubles, with mattresses that are a bit thin—but considering the price, you'll find reasonable comfort. A swimming pool is open from the end of May to October, and air conditioning is available on request for 15,000L ($7.50).

Villa Laura. Via della Salle 13, 80045 Pompei. ☎ **081-863-1024.** Fax 081-850-4893. 25 units. A/C MINIBAR TV TEL. 150,000L ($75) double. Rates include breakfast. AE, DC, MC, V. Parking 10,000L ($5).

Pompeii

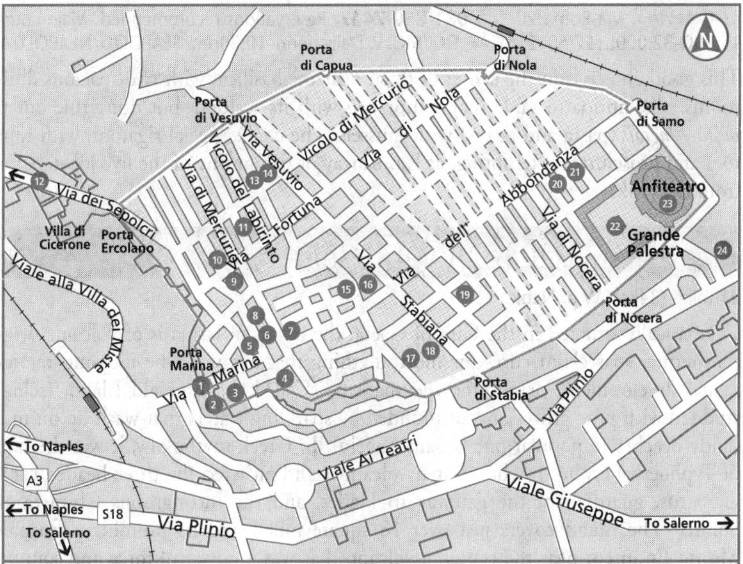

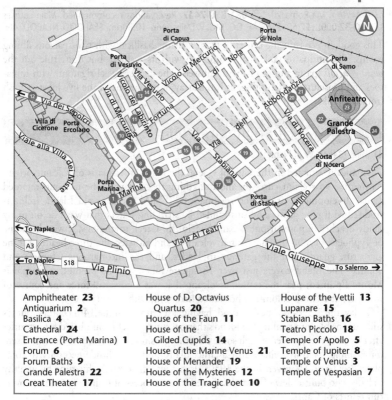

Amphitheater **23**
Antiquarium **2**
Basilica **4**
Cathedral **24**
Entrance (Porta Marina) **1**
Forum **6**
Forum Baths **9**
Grande Palestra **22**
Great Theater **17**
House of D. Octavius Quartus **20**
House of the Faun **11**
House of the Gilded Cupids **14**
House of the Marine Venus **21**
House of Menander **19**
House of the Mysteries **12**
House of the Tragic Poet **10**
House of the Vettii **13**
Lupanare **15**
Stabian Baths **16**
Teatro Piccolo **18**
Temple of Apollo **5**
Temple of Jupiter **8**
Temple of Venus **3**
Temple of Vespasian **7**

The Villa Laura is the best hotel in town, though the competition isn't exactly stiff. On a somewhat hidden street, it escapes a lot of the noise that plagues Pompeii hotels and is mercifully air-conditioned. The guest rooms, rather small, are comfortably but not spectacularly furnished, with small bathrooms. Try for one with a balcony. The breakfasts are a bit dull, but for lunch and dinner you can try one of the restaurants below. The hotel also has a garden and a bar.

DINING

✪ **Il Principe.** Piazza Bartolo Longo. ☎ **081-850-5566.** Reservations required. Main courses 26,000–35,000L ($13–$17.50); fixed-price menu 65,000L ($32.50). AE, DC, DISC, MC, V. Apr–Sept daily 12:30–3pm and 7:30–11:30pm; Oct–Mar Tues–Sun 12:30–3pm and 7:30–11:30pm. CAMPANIAN/MEDITERRANEAN.

Pompeii's leading restaurant, Il Principe is also acclaimed one of the best restaurants in Campania. The decor incorporates the best decorative features of ancient Pompeii, including a scattering of bright frescoes and mosaics. You can dine in its beautiful interior or at a sidewalk table on the town's most important square, with views of the basilica. You might start with carpaccio or a salad of porcini mushrooms, then follow with one of the pastas, perhaps *spaghetti vongole* (with baby clams). You can also order superb fish dishes, like sea bass and turbot; *saltimbocca* (sage-flavored veal with ham); or steak Diane.

Zi Caterina. Via Roma 20. ☎ **081-850-7447.** Reservations recommended. Main courses 15,000–32,000L ($7.50–$16). AE, DC, MC, V. Daily noon–10:30pm. SEAFOOD/NEAPOLITAN.

This good choice is in the center of town near the basilica, with two spacious dining rooms. The antipasto table may tempt you with its seafood, but don't rule out the *pasta e fagioli* (pasta and beans) with mussels. The chef's special rigatoni, with tomatoes and prosciutto, is tempting, as is the array of fish or one of the live lobsters fresh from the tank.

4 The Emerald Island of Ischia

21 miles (34km) W of Naples

Dramatically situated in the Gulf of Gaeta, the island of Ischia is of volcanic origin. Its thermal spas claim cures for most anything that ails you—be it "gout, retarded sexual development, or chronic rheumatism." Called the Emerald Island, Ischia is studded with pine groves and surrounded by sparkling waters that wash up on many sandy beaches (a popular one is Sant'Angelo). In Greek mythology, it was the home of Typhoeus (Typhon), who created volcanoes and fathered the three-headed canine Cerberus, guardian of the gateway to Hades, and the incongruous Chimera and Sphinx. The island covers just over 18 square miles, and its prominent feature is **Monte Epomeo,** near the center, a volcano that was a powerful force and source of worry for the Greek colonists who settled here in the 8th century B.C.

Today, the 2,590-foot peak is dead, having last erupted in the 14th century, but it's still responsible for warming the island's thermal springs. Ischia slumbered for centuries after its early turbulence, though some discerning visitors discovered its charms. Ibsen, for example, lived in a villa near Casamicciola to find the solitude necessary to complete *Peer Gynt.* However, in the 1950s, Ischia was discovered, this time by wealthy Italians who built a slew of first-class hotels in the process of trying to avoid the overrun resorts of Capri.

The island is known for its sandy beaches, health spas (which utilize the hot springs for hydromassage and mud baths), and vineyards producing the red and white Monte Epomeo, the red and white Ischia, and the white Biancolella. The largest community is at **Ischia Porto** on the eastern coast, a circular town seated in the crater of an extinct volcano that functions as the island's main port of call. The most lively town is **Forio** on the western coast, with its many bars along tree-lined streets. The other major communities are **Lacco Ameno** and **Casamicciola Terme,** on the north shore, and **Serrara Fontana** and **Barano d'Ischia,** inland and to the south.

ESSENTIALS

GETTING THERE The easiest way to get to the island is from Naples, from which both **hydrofoils** (passengers only) and **ferries** (passengers with their cars) make frequent runs throughout the year. With departures three to seven times a day, depending on the season, the hydrofoil is the most convenient option, charging 17,000L ($8.50) per person each way. Transit by hydrofoil takes about 40 minutes; transit by ferry takes about 1 hour and 20 minutes but costs only 10,000L ($5) for foot passengers. On the ferry, a medium-sized vehicle, with as many passengers as will fit inside, costs from 70,000L ($35) each way. Hydrofoils depart from Naples's Mergellina Pier, near the Hotel Vesuvio; ferries leave from Molo Beverello, near Piazza Municipio. Two companies maintain both hydrofoils and ferries: **Caremar** (☎ **081-551-3882** in Naples, or 081-991-781 in Ischia) and **Linee Lauro** (☎ **081-552-2838** in Naples, or 081-837-7577 in Ischia). Caremar is somewhat more upscale, with better-maintained ships and a more cooperative staff.

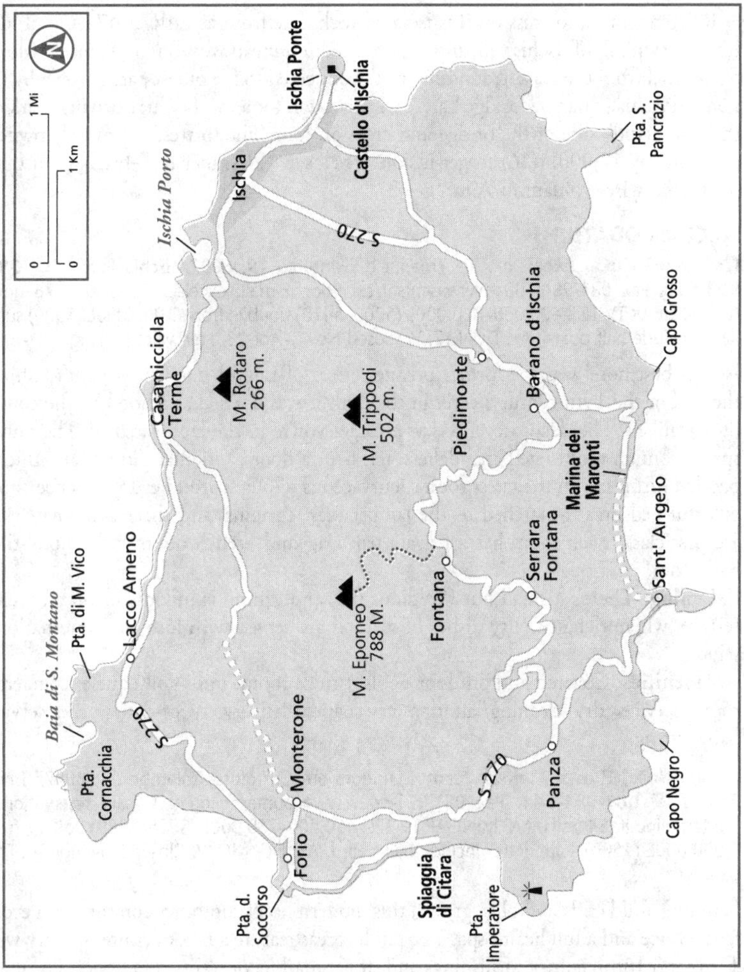

If you don't want to depart from Naples, you can take a **hydrofoil from Sorrento.** These run several times daily, with a fare of 18,000L ($9) one way. Service is provided by **Lines Marittime Partenopee** (☎ **081-99-18-88**).

VISITOR INFORMATION In Porto d'Ischia, **Azienda Autonoma di Soggiorno e Turismo** at Corso Vittoria Colonna 116 (☎ **081-507-4211**) is open Monday to Saturday 9am to noon and 2 to 5pm.

ISCHIA PORTO

This harbor actually emerged from the crater of a long-dead volcano. Most of the population and the largest number of hotels are centered in **Ischia Porto.** The **Castello Aragonese** (☎ **081-992-834**) once guarded the harbor from raids. At the castle lived poet Vittoria Colonna, the confidante of Michelangelo, to whom he wrote celebrated letters.

References to a fortress on this isolated rock date from as early as 474 B.C. Today it's the symbol of Ischia, jutting like a Mediterranean version of France's Mont-St.-Michel from the sea surrounding it. It's connected to the oldest part of town by the Ponte d'Ischia, a narrow bridge barely wide enough for a car. If you're driving, park on the "mainland" side of the bridge and cross on foot. The fortress is privately owned, and you pay 12,000L ($6) to get inside. It's closed November to February, but open daily otherwise, 9:30am to 7pm.

ACCOMMODATIONS

✪ **Grand Hotel Excelsior.** Via Emanuele Gianturco 19, 80077 Ischia Porto. ☎ **081-991-020.** Fax 081-984-100. www.ischia.it/excelsior. E-mail: excelsior@pointel.it. 76 units. A/C MINIBAR TV TEL. 400,000–820,000L ($200–$410) double; from 1,000,000L ($500) suite. Rates include half-board. AE, DC, MC, V. Closed Nov 3–Apr 23. Free valet parking.

Ischia's best hotel was the former private retreat of English nobleman James Nihn at the end of the 19th century; early in the 20th it was opened as a hotel by the counts of Micangeli. The decor never lets you forget you're in the lap of luxury: The public spaces contain multitiered chandeliers, terra-cotta floors, Oriental carpets, and thickly padded furniture. In the guest rooms, curvaceous wrought-iron headboards rise above colorful bedspreads matched to the lampshades, curtains, and sheers; the mattresses are first class. Each room has a private patio beyond French doors and a floral-tiled bathroom.

Dining: There's a small but fastidious bar, and dining is indoors or on a covered terrace, where rich specialty dishes of seafood are served with local and international wines.

Amenities: Covered and outdoor pools, fitness room, mini-golf course, concierge, room service, dry cleaning/laundry, newspaper delivery, twice-daily maid service, baby-sitting.

Grand Hotel Punta Molino Terme. Lungom are Cristoforo Colombo 23, 80077 Ischia Porto. ☎ **081-991-544.** Fax 081-991-562. www.puntamolino.it. E-mail: reservations@puntamolino.it. 84 units. A/C MINIBAR TV TEL. 450,000–760,000L ($225–$380) double; from 1,000,000L ($500) suite. Rates include half-board. AE, DC, MC, V. Closed Nov–Apr 14. Free parking.

Standing amid cliffs and olive groves, this modern hotel combines comfort with excellent service and a full health spa. The public areas feature a mix of contemporary with 17th- and 18th-century furnishings and stone, marble, or terra-cotta floors. The guest rooms are constantly updated and come in a wide variety of shapes and sizes; however, each is fitted with a luxury mattress, elegant fabrics, and reproductions. The tiled bathrooms have hair dryers and robes. Fresh-cut flowers and living plants add life and color, unifying the interior with the lush grounds.

Dining: Candlelit dining in the restaurant offers a wide selection of Italian dishes, such as succulent seafood specialties. Meals taken on the terrace feature regional barbecued specialties. Both offer views of the sea and a lengthy wine list.

Amenities: Indoor and outdoor pools heated by thermal springs, freshwater outdoor pool, sauna, nearby tennis courts, solarium, gym, concierge, room service, dry cleaning/laundry, baby-sitting, secretarial services, courtesy car, car-rental desk.

Hotel Continental Terme. Via M. Mazzella 74, 80077 Ischia Porto. ☎ **081-991-588.** Fax 081-982-929. www.ischia.it/contiterme. E-mail: contiterme@pointel.it. 244 units. A/C MINIBAR TV TEL. 320,000–360,000L ($160–$180) double; from 480,000L ($240) suite. Rates include half-board. AE, DC, MC, V. Closed Nov–Mar. Free valet parking.

The thermal springs at this sprawling complex are among the largest on the island. There are five thermal water pools (three covered), surrounded by the exotic greenery of 32,700 square yards of gardens. The public spaces feature polished marble and terra-cotta floors, contemporary Italian seating, and wicker-and-glass tables, accented by cut flowers and plant life. The guest rooms are luxuriously furnished, set in a diverse collection of town-house villas scattered throughout the grounds. They range from medium to spacious, each with a firm mattress. The bathrooms contain hair dryers.

Dining/Diversions: There's a bar lounge, a poolside bar, and a piano bar that provides evening entertainment. Meals, which you can enjoy in the dining room or on the terrace, feature the island's bountiful seafood offered with a lengthy list of wines.

Amenities: Spa facilities include a gym, thermal pools, advanced physiotherapy equipment, and a full-service beauty salon offering thermal mud treatments. Swimming pool, concierge, room service, laundry/dry cleaning, baby-sitting, twice-daily maid service, secretarial services, boutiques.

Hotel Il Moresco. Via Emanuele Gianturco 16, 80077 Ischia Porto. ☎ **081-981-355.** Fax 081-992-338. www.ischia.it/moresco. E-mail: moresco@pointel.it. 76 units. 420,000–700,000L ($210–$350) double; from 680,000L ($340) suite. Rates include half-board. AE, DC, MC, V. Closed Oct 29–Apr 14. Free parking.

This hotel's spa facilities and health/beauty center are amazingly complete. It sits in a sun-dappled park whose pines and palmettos grow close to its arched loggias. From some angles, the Moorish-inspired exterior looks almost like a cubist fantasy. Inside, the straightforward design re-creates a modern oasis in the southern part of Spain, with matador-red tiles coupled with stark-white walls and Iberian furniture. Each well-furnished guest room has a terrace or a balcony. Most are medium in size and attractively furnished, with a firm mattress. The tiled bathrooms have hair dryers.

Dining/Diversions: The hotel attracts a chic crowd, especially to its piano bar. In the restaurant overlooking the pool, you can dine on a savory Mediterranean cuisine with a scattering of well-prepared international specialties—all served by a highly professional staff.

Amenities: Large spa and fitness center; beauty center, with heated pool in natural cave; and physiotherapy center with indoor thermal pool with whirlpool. Concierge, room service, laundry/dry cleaning, newspaper delivery, twice-daily maid service, baby-sitting, secretarial services.

✪ **Hotel La Villarosa.** Via Giacinto Gigante 5, 80077 Ischia Porto. ☎ **081-991-316.** Fax 081-992-425. 37 units. MINIBAR TV TEL. 270,000–360,000L ($135–$180) double. Rates include half-board. AE, DC, MC, V. Closed Nov–Mar.

This is Ischia's finest pensione, set in a garden of gardenias and banana, eucalyptus, and fig trees. The dining room is in the informal country style, with terra-cotta tiles, lots of French windows, and antique chairs. The meals are a delight, served with a variety of offerings, including the local specialties. And what looks like a carriage house in the garden has been converted into an informal tavern with more antiques. The staff is selected to maintain the personal atmosphere. The bright and airy guest rooms are well kept, conveying a homelike flavor. The bathrooms, though small, have adequate shelf space.

DINING

Ristorante Damiano. Via delle Vigne. ☎ **081-983-032.** Reservations recommended. Main courses 50,000–80,000L ($25–$40). DC, MC, V. Daily 8pm–midnight; Apr–June and Sept–Oct also Sun 1–3pm. Closed Nov–Mar. ISCHIAN.

In a circa-1980 building that was angled for maximum exposure to the coastline, this charming restaurant is about a mile southwest of the ferry terminal. Damiano Caputo infuses his seafood with zest and very fresh ingredients. In the consciously rustic setting that includes long communal tables and fresh flowers, you can select from an array of antipasti; linguine that might be studded with lobster, shrimp, or clams; steamy bowls of minestrone; at least four kinds of seafood salad, including a version with mussels; and grilled fresh fish or lobster. Desserts include tiramisu and wonderful gelati.

LACCO AMENO

Jutting up from the water, a rock named **Il Fungo (The Mushroom)** is the landmark natural sight of **Lacco Ameno.** The spa is the center of the good life (and contains some of the best and most expensive hotels on the island). People come from all over the world either to relax on the beach and be served top-level food or to take the cure. The radioactive waters at Lacco Ameno have led to the development of a modern spa with extensive facilities for thermal cures, everything from underwater jet massages to mud baths.

ACCOMMODATIONS

Hotel La Reginella. Piazza Santa Restituta 1, 80076 Lacco Ameno d'Ischia. ☎ **081-994-300.** Fax 081-980-481. 78 units. A/C MINIBAR TV TEL. 320,000–500,000L ($160–$250) double. Rates include half-board. AE, DC, MC, V. Closed Nov 3–Mar. Free parking.

Set in a lush garden typical of the island's accommodations, this hotel boasts a Mediterranean decor combining printed tile floors with light woods and pastel or floral fabrics. Although aging, the guest rooms are still very comfortable, with wood furnishings and firm mattresses. The bathrooms come with hair dryers and robes.

Dining: You can enjoy fresh seafood dishes and a selection of wines either indoors or out.

Amenities: The spa facilities feature Finnish saunas, outdoor thermal pool, indoor version with underwater jet massage and against-current swimming; use of private beach at nearby Regina Isabella. Solarium, gym, tennis courts, concierge, room service, dry cleaning/laundry, baby-sitting, car-rental desk.

Hotel Regina Isabella e Royal Sporting. Piazza Santa Restituta, 80076 Lacco Ameno d'Ischia. ☎ **081-994-322.** Fax 081-900-190. www.reginaisabella.it. E-mail: info@reginaisabella.it. 133 units. A/C MINIBAR TV TEL. 400,000–1,300,000L ($200–$650) double; from 1,470,000L ($735) suite. Rates include half-board. 3-day minimum stay. AE, DC, MC, V. Free parking.

This resort offers the finest accommodations and service in Lacco Ameno, plus a refined setting that successfully contrasts contemporary furnishings with rococo and less ornate antique styles. In the guest rooms, serene blues and greens are prevalent, and some printed tile floors are offset by earthy brown tiles and woodwork. The rooms range from medium to spacious, with firm mattresses and balconies for the most part. The bathrooms come with hair dryers.

Dining/Diversions: The hotel restaurant features a dining room and a terrace, serving seafood specialties and eclectic wines with a view over the gardens to the sea. You can take a break in the piano bar.

Amenities: Outdoor freshwater pool; indoor thermal pool; private beach with windsurfing and motorboat rental; spa offerings like regimented stretching and walking programs, various types of massages and mud baths, and "cures" for almost anything; concierge; room service; baby-sitting; twice-daily maid service; and secretarial services.

Hotel Terme di Augusto. Viale Campo 128, 80076 Lacco Ameno d'Ischia. ☎ **081-994-944.** Fax 081-980-244. 118 units. A/C MINIBAR TV TEL. 300,000–350,000L ($150–$175) double. Rates include half-board. AE, DC, MC, V. Closed Dec 1–27. Free parking.

This hotel, 50 yards from the shore, provides excellent service in a setting less ostentatious than that of many competing resorts. It combines prominent arched ceilings, patterned tile floors, and floral drapery and upholstery to create light, airy spaces.

Most guest rooms are medium-sized but all are quite comfortable, with first-rate mattresses. The tiled bathrooms come with hair dryers.

Dining: The dining room and terrace restaurant offer local, national, and international cuisine and wines, served with great attention to detail.

Amenities: Freshwater outdoor pool; fully equipped gym with Jacuzzi and sauna; indoor pool with a temperature range up to 96.8°F; thermal beauty center offering mud packs, massage, and treatments; tennis courts; car-rental desk; beauty salon; concierge; room service; dry cleaning/laundry; baby-sitting.

✪ **Hotel Terme San Montano.** Via Monte Vico, 80076 Lacco Ameno d'Ischia. ☎ **081-994-033.** Fax 081-980-242. www.ischiagrandialberghi.it. E-mail: sanmontano@ischiagrandialberghi.it. 77 units. A/C MINIBAR TV TEL. 460,000–620,000L ($230–$310) double. Rates include half-board. AE, DC, MC, V. Closed Nov–Easter. Free parking.

Man Ray was once a faithful guest here, as were opera stars Mario del Monaco and Giuseppi di Stefano. The grounds spread out around the hotel in a luxuriant garden. Aged woods, leather, and brass are combined in the furnishings, and marine lamps shed light on almost every room. The headboards resemble a ship's helm, the windows are translated as portholes, and miniature ships and antiquated diving gear are decoratively scattered about. The guest rooms are medium to spacious, each well cared for, with firm mattresses. Rooms with sea views, of course, are the most requested. The tiled bathrooms come with hair dryers.

Dining/Diversions: The roof restaurant offers a panoramic view of the island, or you can dine indoors in grand comfort. The cuisine is typically Mediterranean, with only the freshest ingredients. The Neapolitan pastry specialties are especially delectable. Every week, evening galas or barbecues with Neapolitan guitar music are presented. After dinner, guests retreat to the piano bar with its soft music.

Amenities: Full gym; solarium; natural sauna; thermal and freshwater pools; spa/beauty center; private beach; massage; mud baths; full range of health-related treatments; tennis, squash, and water skiing lessons; boat and car rental; room service; baby-sitting; secretarial services.

FORIO

A short drive from Lacco Ameno, **Forio** stands on the west coast of Ischia, opening onto the sea near the Bay of Citara. Long a favorite with artists (filmmaker Lucchino Visconti has a villa here), it's now developing a broader base of tourism. Locals produce some of the finest wines on the island. On the way from Lacco Ameno, stop at the **beach of San Francesco,** with its sanctuary. At sunset, many visitors head for a rocky spur on which sits the church of **Santa Maria del Soccorso.** The lucky ones get to witness the famous "green flash" over the Gulf of Gaeta. It appears on occasion immediately after the sun sets.

ACCOMMODATIONS

✪ **Grande Albergo Mezzatorre.** Via Mezzatorre, 80075 Forio d'Ischia. ☎ **081-986-111.** Fax 081-986-015. www.mezzatorre.it. E-mail: info@mezzatorre.it. 58 units. A/C MINIBAR TV TEL. 340,000–780,000L ($170–$390) double; 740,000–980,000L ($370–$490) suite. Rates include half-board. AE, DC, MC, V. Closed Nov–Apr. Free parking.

The best hotel in Forio, this complex is built around a 16th-century villa whose stone tower once guarded against invaders; now it houses the least expensive of the doubles. The five postmodern buildings run a few hundred feet downhill to a waterfront bluff. A casual airiness prevails in the public spaces, which contrast soft lighting with terra-cotta floors. The decor in the guest rooms is contemporary, with wooden furniture and bright upholstered seating. Most rooms are medium-sized, and all come with firm mattresses. The tiled bathrooms are small but still have adequate shelf space.

Dining/Diversions: A delightful Mediterranean cuisine, one of the finest on the island, is served in the hotel dining room. Fresh seafood is the chef's specialty. Many nonguests dine here, including some of the rich island set. You can also enjoy terraces and an elegant bar.

Amenities: Seaside outdoor pool, private dock, thermal baths, health club, Jacuzzi, sauna, tennis courts, concierge, room service, laundry/dry cleaning, baby-sitting, beauty salon.

DINING

La Romantica. Via Marina 46. ☎ **081-997-345.** Reservations recommended. Main courses 15,000–25,000L ($7.50–$12.50). AE, DC, MC, V. Daily noon–3pm and 7pm–midnight. Closed Wed Nov–Mar. NEAPOLITAN/ISCHIAN.

Near the dry-docked fishing vessels of Forio's old port, this is the most appealing non-hotel restaurant. It occupies a Neapolitan-style building whose facade has been enlarged with a jutting wooden extension that has welcomed everyone from Josephine Baker to heart surgeon Christian Barnard. Your meal may include linguine with clams or scampi or a house specialty, "penne 92," garnished with artichoke hearts and shrimp. Swordfish, grilled and served with lemon sauce or with herb-flavored green sauce, is delicious, as are the baked spigola and several risotto and veal dishes. You might prefer, weather permitting, a seat on the outdoor terrace.

SANT'ANGELO

The most charming settlement on Ischia, **Sant'Angelo** juts out on the southernmost tip. The village of fishers is joined to the "mainland" of Ischia by a 300-foot-long lava-and-sand isthmus. Driving into the town is virtually impossible. In summer you may have to park a long way away and walk. Its **beach** is among the best on the island.

ACCOMMODATIONS

Park Hotel Miramare. 80070 Sant'Angelo d'Ischia. ☎ **081-999-219.** Fax 081-999-325. 50 units. MINIBAR TV TEL. 295,000–325,000L ($147.50–$162.50) double. Rates include breakfast. MC, V. Closed Nov–Feb.

Right on the sea, this hotel has no beach to speak of, but there's a concrete terrace with chairs and umbrellas and a stairway that clears the rocky shore, leading into the water. Curved wrought-iron balconies, white wicker, and canopied iron bed frames are reoccurring decorative elements. Since 1923, the same family has welcomed guests to its old-fashioned accommodations with renewed bathrooms. The dining room features the seafood the island is known for, and a snack bar offers an informal option. The hotel's health spa is a short walk away, down a flower-lined path. Among its offerings are massage, 12 thermal pools, mud treatments, a sauna, and designated nudist areas.

5 Sorrento

31 miles (50km) S of Naples, 159 miles (256km) SE of Rome, 31 miles (50km) W of Salerno

Borrowing from Greek mythology, the Romans placed the legendary abode of the sirens (those wicked mermaids who lured seamen to their deaths with their sweet songs) at Sorrento (Surrentum). Ulysses resisted their call by stuffing the ears of his crew with wax and having himself bound to the mast of his ship. Perched on high cliffs overlooking the bays of Naples and Salerno, Sorrento has been sending out its siren call for centuries—luring everybody from Homer to Lord and Lady Astor to busloads of international tourists, who invade every summer.

The streets in summer tend to be as noisy as a carnival. And the traffic is horrendous (no traffic signals in such a bustling city!). The hotels on the "racing strip," **Corso**

Italia, need to pass out earplug kits when they tuck you in for the night, though perhaps you'll have a hotel on a cliff side in Sorrento with a view of the sea (and paths and private elevators to take you down).

ESSENTIALS

GETTING THERE Sorrento is served by frequent express **trains** from Naples (trip time: 1 hour). The high-speed train, called Ferrovia Circumvesuviana, leaves from one floor underground at Stazione Centrale.

If you have a **car** and are in Naples, head south on Rte. 18, cutting west at the junction with Rte. S145.

VISITOR INFORMATION The **tourist office** is at Via de Maio 35 (☎ **081-807-4033**), which winds down to the port where ships headed for Capri and Naples anchor. It's open Monday to Saturday 8:30am to 2:30pm and 3:30 to 6:30pm.

EXPLORING THE CITY

For such a famous resort, Sorrento's **beaches** are limited—most of them are just piers extending into the water. Chaise longues and umbrellas line these decks along the rock-strewn coastline. The best beach is **Punta del Capo,** reached by going along Corso Italia to Via del Capo.

If you'd like to go **hiking,** you can explore the green hills above Sorrento. Many of the trails are marked, and the tourist office will advise.

From Sorrento, the more confident drivers among you can undertake the gorgeous but nerve-racking **Amalfi Drive.** If you want to leave the driving to someone else, you can take a blue SITA bus that runs between Sorrento and Salerno or Amalfi. In Sorrento, bus stations with timetables are outside the rail station and in the central piazza.

Although few visitors come to Sorrento to look at churches and monuments, there are some worth exploring. The **Chiesa di San Francesco,** Via San Francesco (☎ **081-878-1269**), dates from the 14th century. This cloister is a pocket of beauty in overcrowded Sorrento, with delicate arches and a garden dotted with flowering vines. The convent is also an art school offering exhibits, and in July and September jazz and classical music are performed almost nightly in the outdoor atrium. Show time is 9pm, with an admission of 20,000 to 30,000L ($10 to $15). The cloister is otherwise open daily 9am to 6pm, and admission is free.

If time remains, visit the **Museo Correale di Terranova,** Via Correale (☎ **081-878-1846**), north of Piazza Tasso. A former palace, it has displays of ancient statues, antiques, and Italian art. Here's a chance to introduce yourself to *intarsia,* a technique of making objects with paper-thin pieces of patterned wood. Neapolitan bric-a-brac and other curiosities finish off the exhibits. After a visit to the museum, you can stroll through the gardens. April to September, it's open Monday and Wednesday to Saturday 9am to 12:30pm and 5 to 7pm, Sunday 9am to 12:30pm; off-season hours are Monday and Wednesday to Saturday 9 to 11:30am and 3 to 5pm, Sunday 9 to 11:30am. Admission is 8,000L ($4) to the museum and gardens.

Sorrento has better **shopping** than anywhere else along the Amalfi Drive. The city's cobbled alleyways and flower-ringed piazzas encourage strolls, and the best ones for window-shopping are **Piazza Tasso** and **Via San Cesareo,** densely packed with shoppers on weekend afternoons.

Gargiulo & Jannuzzi, Piazza Tasso (☎ **081-878-1041**), is the region's best-known maker of marquetry furniture. Opened in 1863, the shop demonstrates the centuries-old technique in the basement, where an employee will combine multihued pieces of wood veneer to create patterns of arabesques and flowers. The sprawling showrooms

Sorrento

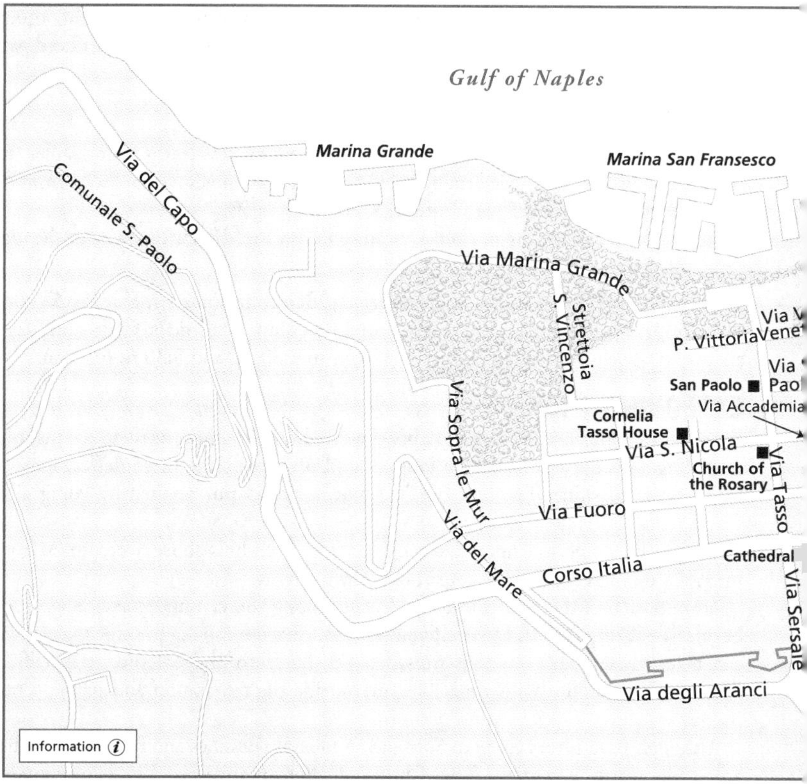

feature an array of card tables, clocks, and partners' desks, each inlaid with patterns of elm wood, rosewood, bird's-eye maple, or mahogany. Upstairs is a collection of embroidered table linens, and the outlet has its own ceramic factory. The pottery can be shipped anywhere.

Embroidery and lace are two of the best bargains in Sorrento, and **Luigia Gargiulo,** Corso Italia 48 (☎ **081-878-1081**), comes recommended for embroidered sheets and tablecloths but also offers children's clothing. In **Cuomo's Lucky Store,** Piazza Antica Mura 2–7 (☎ **081-878-5649**), you'll find a little bit of everything made in the area, including displays of porcelain from the 1700s.

One of the most appealing assortments of cameos, meticulously hand-carved from seashells, is available at the reasonably priced **Ciro Bimonte,** Via Guiliani 61 (☎ **081-807-1880**). And if you're feeling underdressed or underaccessorized, consider checking out **Coin,** Via San Cesareo 39 (☎ **081-807-1747**), or **Max & Co.,** Corso Italia 62 (☎ **081-807-4529**), both selling clothing of all degrees of formality for men, women, and children.

ACCOMMODATIONS

Sorrento has excellent choices in all price ranges.

EXPENSIVE

Grand Hotel Ambasciatori. Via Califano 18, 80067 Sorrento. ☎ **081-878-2025.** Fax 081-807-1021. www.maniellohotels.it. E-mail: ambasciatori@maniellohotels.it. 109 units.

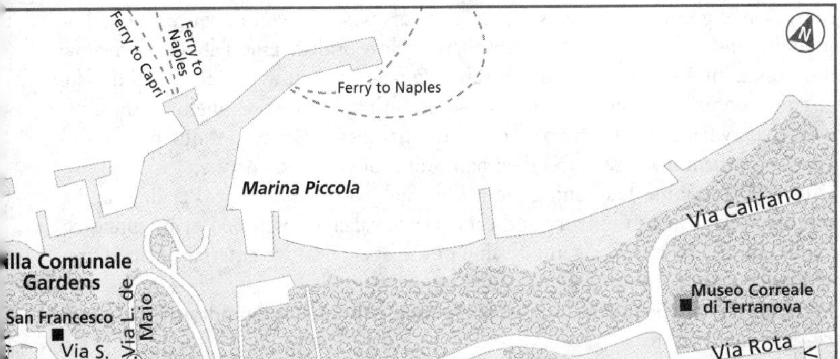

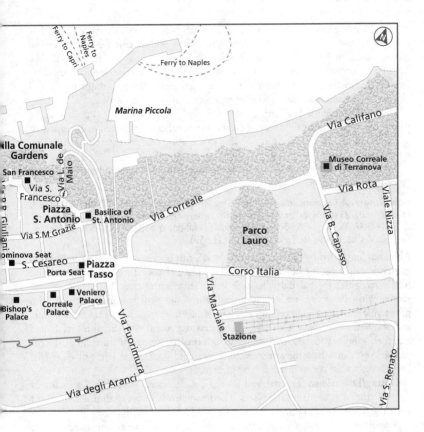

A/C TV TEL. 410,000L ($205) double; 520,000L ($260) suite. Rates include breakfast. AE, DC, MC, V. Free parking.

The heavily buttressed foundation that prevents this cliff-side hotel from plunging into the sea looks like something from a medieval monastery, and it was landscaped to include several rambling gardens along the precipice. A set of steps and a private elevator lead to the wooden deck of a bathing wharf. Inside, a substantial collection of Oriental carpets and armchairs provides plush comfort. The guest rooms come in a variety of shapes and sizes, each containing a firm mattress and a compact tiled bathroom with a hair dryer.

Dining/Diversions: The restaurant serves regional/international fare; there's also a bar and a snack bar by the pool where live Neapolitan songs are presented twice a week.

Amenities: Swimming pool, room service, concierge, laundry/dry cleaning, baby-sitting.

✪ **Grand Hotel Excelsior Vittoria.** Piazza Tasso 34, 80067 Sorrento. ☎ **081-807-1044.** Fax 081-877-1206. www.exvitt.it. E-mail: exvitt@exvitt.it. 107 units. MINIBAR TV TEL. 488,000–694,000L ($244–$347) double; from 1,020,000L ($510) suite. Rates include breakfast. AE, DC, MC, V. Free parking.

This luxury bastion, built between 1834 and 1882 on the edge of a cliff overlooking the Bay of Naples and surrounded by semitropical gardens with lemon and orange trees, combines 19th-century glamour with modern amenities. The terrace theme predominates, especially on the water side, where you can enjoy the cold drinks served at sunset while gazing at Vesuvius. Three elevators will take you down to the harbor to sunbathe and swim. Inside, the atmosphere is old-worldish, especially in the mellow dining room. In 1921 Enrico Caruso stayed in the suite now named for him. The huge guest rooms boast their own drama, some with balconies opening onto the cliff-side drop; they have a wide mix of furnishings that include many antique pieces, and all come with firm mattresses and tiled bathrooms offering hair dryers.

Dining/Diversions: The dining room is formal, with hand-painted ceilings and a panoramic view. You'll sit in ivory-and-cane provincial chairs while enjoying topnotch Sorrento cuisine. In summer you can dine in the open air. Live entertainment is presented twice a week.

Amenities: Large pool, concierge, room service, baby-sitting, laundry/dry cleaning, twice-daily maid service.

Hotel Imperial Tramontano. Via Vittorio Veneto 1, 80067 Sorrento. ☎ **081-878-2588.** Fax 081-807-2344. www.tramontano.com. E-mail: info@tramontano.com. 116 units. A/C MINIBAR TV TEL. 430,000L ($215) double. Half-board 65,000L ($32.50) per person. AE, MC, V. Closed Jan–Feb. Parking 25,000L ($12.50).

Although outclassed by the Vittoria (see above), this pocket of posh in a semitropical garden is still a leading hotel. It was the birthplace of poet Torquato Tasso, yet he'd hardly recognize the palatial villa, as it has been much altered. The spacious guest rooms, with tile floors, are well furnished, and some have balconies opening onto panoramic sea views. High ceilings and gilt-framed mirrors provide a traditional look, and the bathrooms have hair dryers. The drawing room, with English and Italian antiques, modifies its spaciousness by its informal treatment of furnishings. In the garden, you can inhale the sweet-smelling trees and walk down paths of oleanders, hydrangea, acacia, coconut palms, and geraniums.

Dining/Diversions: The bar and lounge are decorated with antiques, many of them Victorian-style mahogany pieces. The restaurant is a worthy choice if you don't want to go out in the evening, serving a flavorful Mediterranean cuisine.

Amenities: Swimming pool, concierge, room service, twice-daily maid service, laundry/dry cleaning, baby-sitting.

MODERATE

Hotel Regina. Via Marina Grande 10, 80067 Sorrento. ☎ **081-878-2722.** Fax 081-878-2721. www.belmare-travel.com. E-mail: info@belmare-travel.com. 36 units. TV TEL. 300,000L ($150) double. Rates include half-board. AE, DC, DISC, MC, V. Closed Nov 15–Jan. Parking 10,000L ($5).

Evenly spaced rows of balconies jut out over the Regina's well-tended garden. On its uppermost floor, a glassed-in dining room and a terrace encompass views of the Mediterranean extending as far as Naples and Vesuvius. The functional rooms have tile floors and private terraces; a dozen open onto views from balconies and are the most requested. Only 10 rooms are air-conditioned. The hotel employs a helpful staff that provides road maps and offer hints about sightseeing. Although small, the inn does provide some amenities found in first-class hotels, like a concierge, room service, baby-sitting, and laundry service.

Villa di Sorrento. Via Fuorimura 4, 80067 Sorrento. ☎ **081-878-1068.** Fax 081-807-2679. 21 units. A/C TV TEL. 230,000L ($138) double. Rates include breakfast. AE, CB, DC, MC, V. Parking 20,000L ($10) nearby.

This is a pleasant villa in the center of town. Architecturally romantic, the Sorrento attracts travelers with its petite wrought-iron balconies, tall shutters, and vines climbing the facade. The comfortably furnished guest rooms have such niceties as bedside tables and lamps and decent mattresses, and some contain terraces. The tiled bathrooms are tiny.

INEXPENSIVE

Hotel Bristol. Via Capo 22, 80067 Sorrento. ☎ **081-878-4522.** Fax 081-807-1910. www.acampora.it/bristol. E-mail: bristol@acampora.it. 135 units. A/C MINIBAR TV TEL. 105,000–280,000L ($52.50–$140) double; 150,000–320,000L ($75–$160) suite. Rates include buffet breakfast. AE, DC, MC, V. Free parking.

The Bristol was built pueblo style on a hillside at the edge of town, and all but 15 rooms have a view of Vesuvius and the Bay of Naples. (Those 15 open onto a brick wall.) The hotel lures with its contemporary decor and spaciousness and with well-appointed public and private rooms. The guest rooms are warm and inviting, with built-in niceties. Most have balconies overlooking the sea, and some contain minibars. The hotel has two panoramic restaurants, a pool, minigolf, an American bar, a solarium, and a Finnish sauna. In summer you can dine on the terrace.

Hotel Désirée. Via del Capo 31B, 80067 Sorrento. ☎ and fax **081-878-1563.** 22 units. TEL. 110,000–150,000L ($55–$75) double. Rates include breakfast. No credit cards. Closed Nov–Dec 15 and Jan 10–Mar 8. Free parking.

The Désirée is half a mile from the town center at the beginning of the Amalfi Drive. This tranquil hotel, directed by the Gargiulo family, is ringed with terraces whose flowered masonry overlooks the Bay of Naples and nearby trees. A few guest rooms have balconies opening onto a view of the sea, but these are generally reserved for guests who book for at least three nights. The rooms range from small to medium, each with a quality mattress and a tiled bathroom. You'll recognize the hotel by its green glass lanterns in front and the awning over the entrance. An elevator leads to the private beach, and there's a solarium.

DINING

EXPENSIVE

✪ **Don Alfonso.** Piazza Sant'Agata 11, Sant'Agata, 6 miles (10km) south of Sorrento. ☎ **081-878-0026.** Reservations recommended. Main courses 45,000–50,000L ($22.50–$25); set-price menus 120,000–160,000L ($60–$80). AE, DC, MC, V. Wed–Sun 12:30–2:30pm and 8–10:30pm. Closed Mon June–Sept, and Jan 10–Feb 25. By car, follow the signs to Sant'Agata; by bus, take the blue-and-white SITA bus marked Sant'Agata from the piazza in front of Sorrento's rail station. SOUTHERN ITALIAN.

One of southern Italy's most highly recommended restaurants, a Relais & Châteaux member, occupies a turn-of-the-century faux-Pompeian building adjacent to Santa Maria delle Grazie, the centerpiece of the hamlet of Sant'Agata, perched more than 1,200 feet above sea level. The chef/co-owner, Alfonso Laccarino, makes it a point to hire as many international assistants as possible, many of whom spend a year here. Alfonso's wife, Livia, directs the dining room and maintains the award-winning wine cellars.

The menu items include lots of organic vegetables and greens from the family's sprawling gardens nearby, adding tremendously to the appeal of a Mediterranean diet of fish and shellfish. The free-range chicken with garlic and home-grown herbs is particularly wonderful, as is the mixed fish fry. Two ongoing favorites are the Neapolitan casseruolla of lobster, squid, clams, mussels, and assorted saltwater fish (for two) and the calamari stuffed with tiny zucchini, sweet pepper, broccoli, and cauliflower and topped with a zabaglione of aged red-wine vinegar.

Don Alfonso also offers three suites, two with kitchens and all with air-conditioning, TVs, and phones. They rent for 230,000L ($115), including breakfast.

Moderate

L'Antica Trattoria. Via P. R. Giuliani 33. ☎ **081-807-1082.** Reservations recommended. Main courses 22,000–44,000L ($11–$22). AE, MC, V. Tues–Sun noon–3:30pm and 6pm–midnight. Closed Jan 10–Feb 10. CAMPANESE/ INTERNATIONAL.

Inside the weather-beaten walls of what was built 300 years ago as a stable, this 200-year-old restaurant, one of the best in Sorrento, is charming. Although all its food is well prepared, the real highlight is its antipasti. You'll find several varieties of fish cooked in a salt crust, which transforms the dish into a sweetly scented firm but flaky delicacy, and a daunting array of pastas from lasagna to ravioli (the best is stuffed with seafood). The house special pasta, *spaghetti alla ferrolese,* is made with fish roe, shrimp, red cabbage, and cream. A particularly delicious specialty is seafood pezzogna, with pulverized cherry tomatoes, olive oil, garlic, parsley, crushed red pepper, and shellfish. The assortment of ice creams is especially tempting.

Inexpensive

La Favorita—O'Parrucchiano. Corso Italia 71. ☎ **081-878-1321.** Main courses 14,000–25,000L ($7–$12.50). MC, V. Daily noon–3:30pm and 7–11:30pm. Closed Wed Nov 15–Mar 15. NEAPOLITAN/SORRENTINE.

This is a good choice on the busiest street in town. The building is like an old tavern, with an arched ceiling in the main dining room. On the terrace you can dine in a garden of trees, rubber plants, and statuary. Among the à la carte dishes, classic Italian fare is offered, like ravioli *Caprese* (filled with fresh cheese and covered with tomato sauce), cannelloni, a mixed fish fry from the Bay of Naples, and veal cutlet Milanese. The chef will also prepare a pizza for you.

SORRENTO AFTER DARK

At the **Taverna dell' 800,** Via dell'Accademia 29 (☎ **081-878-5970**), owner Tony Herculano dispenses flavorful home-style macaroni (pink-tinged, it combines tomatoes with ham, cream, and bacon) and good cheer. From 9pm to midnight, the music of a guitar and a piano duet enlivens a cozy bar with flickering candles and a cross-cultural polyglot of languages. There's no cover charge, and the food is cheap. The joint is open Tuesday to Sunday 8am to 4:30am and does lots of business throughout the day as a cafe and pub.

For a dose of Neapolitan-style folklore, head for the **Circolo de Forestière,** Via Luigi de Maio 35 (☎ **081-877-3012**), a bar/cafe whose views extend out over a flowering terrace and the wide blue bay. Music from the live pianist is interrupted only for episodes of folkloric dancing and cheerful music from a troupe of players.

The town's central square, **Piazza Tasso,** is the site of two worthwhile nightclubs. The one that presents folkloric music is **Fauno** (☎ **081-878-1021**), where you can slug down a beer or two during the sporadic performances of tarantella. Brief but colorful, they interrupt a program otherwise devoted to recorded dance (usually disco) music. There's usually no cover. At **The Club** (☎ **081-878-4052**), dance music blares out to a youngish crowd from throughout Europe and North America. The cover is 30,000L ($15) and includes the first drink. It's open daily 10pm to 3am (depending on the crowd).

6 Capri

3 miles (5km) off the tip of the Sorrentine peninsula

The island of ✪ **Capri** (pronounced *Cap*-ry, not Ca-*pree*) is one of the loveliest resorts in Italy, a dramatic island soaring upward from the sea, with sweeping views, white-washed homes and villas, fragrant lemon trees, narrow winding lanes, and flower-filled courtyards. It's completely overrun in summer (actually from Easter to the end of

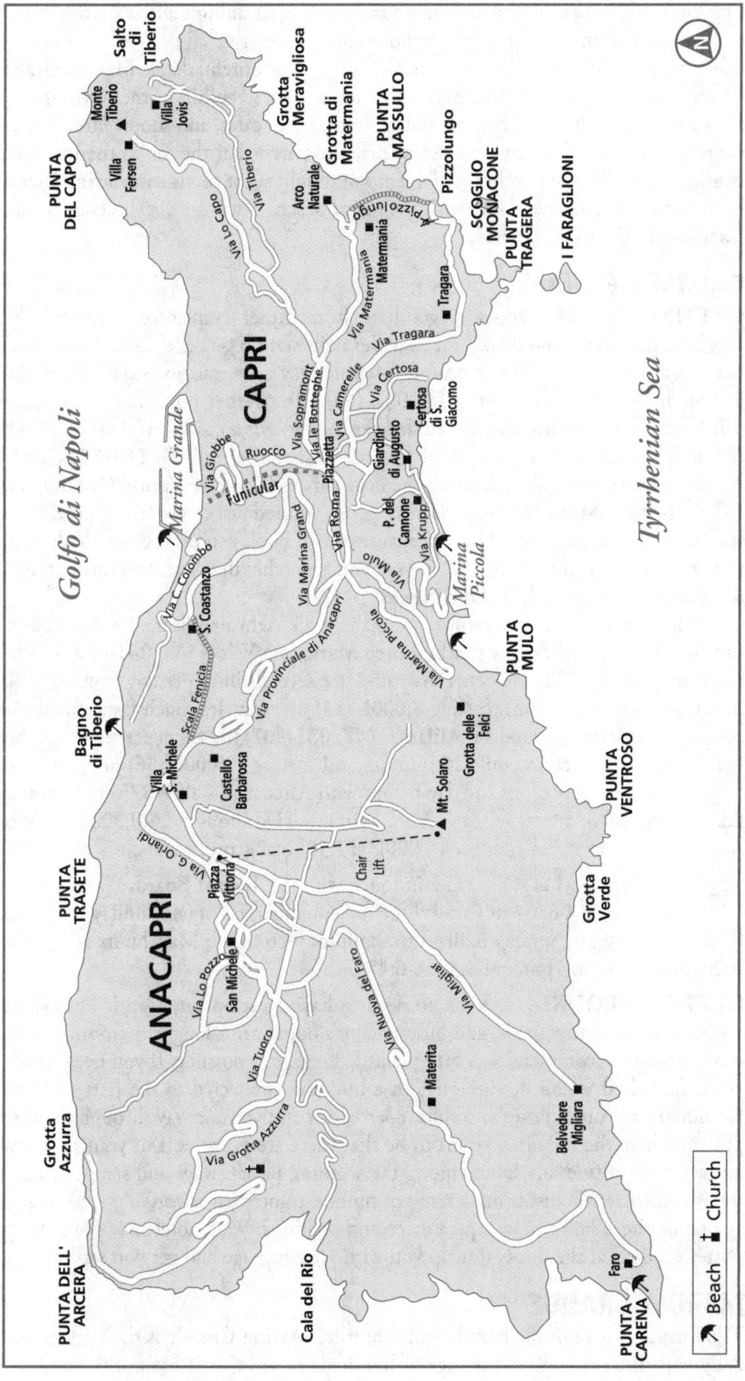
Golfo di Napoli
Tyrrhenian Sea
CAPRI
ANACAPRI
PUNTA DEL CAPO
Monte Tiberio
Salto di Tiberio
Villa Fersen
Villa Jovis
Via Lo Capo
Via Tiberio
Grotta Meravigliosa
Arco Naturale
Grotta di Matermania
PUNTA MASSULLO
Pizzolungo
Via Pizzolungo
Matermania
Via Matermania
SCOGLIO MONACONE
PUNTA TRAGERA
I FARAGLIONI
Tragara
Via Tragara
Via Camerelle
Via Certosa
Certosa di S. Giacomo
Via Sopramont
Via le Botteghe
Piazzetta
Ruocco
Via Giobbe
Marina Grande
Funicular
Via Roma
Giardini di Augusto
P. del Cannone
Via Krupp
Marina Piccola
Via Mulo
Via Marina Grand
Via C. Colombo
S. Coastanzo
Via Provinciale di Anacapri
Via Marina Piccola
PUNTA MULO
Scala Fenicia
Bagno di Tiberio
Villa S. Michele
Castello Barbarossa
Grotta delle Felci
PUNTA VENTROSO
Mt. Solaro
Via G. Orlandi
Piazza Vittoria
Chair Lift
PUNTA TRASETE
Grotta Verde
San Michele
Via Lo Pozzo
Via Migliar
Via Nuova del Faro
Via Tuoro
Materita
Belvedere Migliara
Grotta Azzurra
Via Grotta Azzurra
PUNTA DELL' ARCERA
Cala del Rio
Faro
PUNTA CARENA
Beach
Church

October), as throngs of international tourists and vacationing Italians arrive every day to soak up its romantic atmosphere and gorgeous scenery.

Touring the island is relatively simple. You dock at unremarkable **Marina Grande,** the port area. You can then take the funicular up the steep hill to the town of **Capri** above, where you'll find the major hotels, restaurants, cafes, and shops. From Capri, a short bus ride will deliver you to **Anacapri,** also perched at the top of the island near Monte Solaro. The only other settlement you might want to visit is **Marina Piccola,** on the south side of the island, with the major beach. There are also beaches at **Punta Carnea** and **Bagni di Tiberio.**

CAPRI ESSENTIALS

GETTING THERE You can get here from either Naples or Sorrento. From Naples's Molo Beverello dock (not near the train station—take a taxi), the **hydrofoil** takes just 45 minutes. The hydrofoil (*aliscafo*) leaves several times daily (some stop at Sorrento). A one-way trip is 18,000L ($9). It's cheaper but takes longer (about $1^1/_2$ hours) to go by regularly scheduled **ferry** *(traghetto),* costing 10,000 to 12,000L ($5 to $6) one way. For ferry and hydrofoil schedules, call ☎ **081-551-3882** in Naples. There's no need to check all the dock offices for the best price. **Ontano Tours** (☎ **081-580-0341**) is a central clearing house, located just to the left of the driveway leading into the dock area. This travel agency will book you on the next hydrofoil or ferry out, tell you which line it is, and sell you a voucher that you then carry onto that line's dock office to trade in for a ticket.

If you're coming from Sorrento, go to the dock right off Piazza Tasso, where you can board one of the **ferries** run by **Linee Marittime Veloci** (☎ **081-878-1430**) or **Caremar** (☎ **081-807-3077**). Departures are several times per day from 7am (last departure back at 7:45pm), costing 8,000L ($4) one way. It's much faster to take one of the **hydrofoils** operated by **Alilauro** (☎ **081-807-3024**), departing every hour daily 7am to 4pm, taking only 15 minutes and costing 12,000L ($6) one way.

If you make reservations the day before with **Alicost** (☎ **089-875-092**), you can take a hydrofoil or a ferry to Capri from Positano. Hydrofoils cost 20,000L ($10) one way, while a ferry ticket goes for 15,000L ($7.50) one way.

VISITOR INFORMATION Get in touch with the **Tourist Board,** Piazza Umberto I 19 (☎ **081-837-0686**), at Capri. June to September, it's open Monday to Saturday 8:30am to 8:30pm, Sunday 8:30am to 2:30pm; October to May, hours are Monday to Saturday 9am to 1pm and 3:30 to 6:45pm.

GETTING AROUND There's no need to have a car on tiny Capri. The island is serviced by funiculars, taxis, and buses. Capri's hotels are a long way from the docks, so we strongly recommend you bring as little luggage as possible. If you need a porter, you'll find their union headquarters in a building connected to the jetty at Marina Grande. Here you can cajole, coddle, coerce, or connive your way through the hiring process where the only rule seems to be that there are no rules. But your porter will know where to find any hotel among the winding passageways and steep inclines of the island's arteries. Just bring a sense of humor. (Note that if you've got reservations at one of the island's more upscale accommodations, your hotel may have its own porter on duty at the docks to help you with your luggage and get you settled.)

MARINA GRANDE

The least attractive of the island's communities, **Marina Grande** is the port, bustling daily with the comings and goings of hundreds of visitors. It has a little sand-cum-pebble beach, on which you're likely to see American sailors (on shore leave from Naples) playing ball, occasionally upsetting a Coca-Cola over mamma and bambino.

If you're just spending the day on Capri, you may want to see the island's biggest attraction, the ✪ **Grotta Azzurra (Blue Grotto),** open daily 9am to 1 hour before sunset. In summer, boats leave frequently from the harbor at Marina Grande to transport passengers to the entrance of the grotto for 25,000L ($12.50) round-trip. Once at the grotto, you'll pay 18,000L ($9) for the small rowboat that takes you inside.

The Blue Grotto is one of the best-known natural sights of the region, though the way passengers are hustled in and out of it makes it a tourist trap. It's truly beautiful, however. Known to the ancients, it was later lost to the world until an artist stumbled on it in 1826. Inside the cavern, light refraction (the sun's rays entering from an opening under the water) achieves the dramatic Mediterranean cerulean color. The effect is stunning, as thousands testify yearly.

If you wish, you can take a trip around the entire island, passing not only the Blue Grotto but also the **Baths of Tiberius,** the **Palazzo al Mare** built in the days of the empire, the **Green Grotto** (less known), and the much-photographed rocks called the **Faraglioni.** Motorboats circle the island in about 1½ hours at 30,000L ($15) per person.

Connecting Marina Grande with the town of Capri is a frequently running **funicular** charging 1,500L (75¢) one way. However, the funicular, really a cog railway, doesn't operate off-season (you'll take a bus from Marina Grande to Capri for the same price).

SWIMMING & SUNNING

Though it's a summer resort, Capri doesn't have great sandy beaches, because of its mountainous landscape. There are some spots for swimming, most of which have clubs called *stabilimenti balneari,* which you must pay to visit. Most people relax at their hotel's swimming pools and take in the gorgeous views from there.

The coastline surrounding Capri is punctuated with jagged rocks that allow for very few sandy beaches. You can head for the **Bagni Nettuno,** Via Grotta Azzurra 46 (☎ **081-837-1362**), a short distance from the Blue Grotto in Anacapri. Surrounded by scenic cliff-sides, with an undeniable drama, it charges 15,000L ($7.50) adults and 12,000L ($6) children under 12. The price includes use of a cabana, towels, and deck chairs. Mid-March to mid-November, it's open daily 9am to sunset. From a point nearby, you can actually swim into the narrow, rocky entrance guarding the Blue Grotto, but this is advisable only after 5pm, when the boat services into the grotto have ended for the day, and only during relatively calm seas.

Another possibility for swimming is the **Bagni di Tiberio,** a sandy beach a short walk from the ruins of an ancient Roman villa. To reach it, you have to board a motorboat departing from Marina Grande for the 15-minute ride to the site. Passage costs 8,000L ($4) per person, unless you want to walk 30 minutes north from Marina Grande, through rocky landscapes with flowering plants and vineyards.

Closer to the island's south side is the **Marina Piccola,** a usually overcrowded stretch of sand extending between jagged lava rocks. You can rent a small motorboat here from the **Bagni le Sirene** (☎ **081-837-0221**) for around 70,000L ($35) per hour, depending on its size and amenities.

THE TOWN OF CAPRI

The main town of Capri is the center of most of the hotels, restaurants, and elegant shops—and the milling throngs. The heart of the resort, **Piazza Umberto I,** is like a grand living room, lined with cafes.

One of the most popular walks from the main square is down Via Vittorio Emanuele, past the deluxe Quisisana hotel, to the **Giardini di Augusto,** the choice spot on Capri for views and relaxation. From this park's perch, you can see the legendary **I Faraglioni,** the rocks once inhabited by the "blue lizard." At the top of the park is a belvedere overlooking emerald waters and Marina Piccola. Nearby you can visit the **Certosa,** a Carthusian monastery erected in the 14th century to honor St. James. It's open Tuesday to Sunday 9am to 2pm and charges no admission.

Back at Piazza Umberto I, head up Via Longano, then Via Tiberio, all the way to Monte Tiberio. Here you'll find the **Villa Jovis,** the splendid ruin of the estate from which Tiberius ruled the empire from A.D. 27–37. Actually, the Jovis was one of a dozen villas that the depraved emperor erected on the island. Apparently Tiberius had trouble sleeping, so he wandered from bed to bed, exploring his "nooks of lechery," a young girl one hour, a young boy the next. From the ruins there's a view of both the Bay of Salerno and the Bay of Naples, as well as of the island. You can visit the ruins of the imperial palace daily 9am to 1 hour before sunset for 5,000L ($2.50). For information, call the tourist board at ☎ **081-370-686.**

SHOPPING

A little shop on Capri's luxury shopping street, **Carthusia-Profumi di Capri,** Via Camerelle 10 (☎ **081-837-0368**), specializes in perfume made on the island from local herbs and flowers. Since 1948 this shop has attracted such clients as Elizabeth Taylor (before she started touting her own perfume). The scents are unique, and many women consider Carthusia perfumes collector's items.

Carthusia also has a **Perfume Laboratory,** Via Matteotti 2 (☎ **081-837-0368**), which you can visit daily 9:30am to 6pm. There's another **Carthusia shop** in Anacapri, at Via Capodimonte 26 (☎ **081-837-3668**), next to the Villa Axel Munthe. The shops are closed November to March, but the laboratory remains open year-round.

One of the recent commercial blockbusters invented on Capri is **limoncello,** a liqueur whose recipe was conceived several generations ago by members of the Canali family. It consists of lemon zest (not the juice or pith) mixed with alcohol, sugar, water, and herbs to produce a tart kind of "hyper-lemonade" with a mildly alcoholic lift. It's consumed alone as either an aperitif or a digestive, or mixed with vodka or sparkling wines for a lemony cocktail. In 1989 the Canalis formalized their family recipe, established modern distilleries on Capri and in nearby Sorrento, and hired professionals to promote the product as far away as the United States and Japan. Limoncello is sold at **Limoncello di Capri,** 79 Via Roma (☎ **081-837-5561**) in Capri, or at Via Capodimonte 27 (☎ **081-837-2927**) in Anacapri, often in lovely bottles that make nice, affordable gifts.

Shoppers here also look for deals on sandals, cashmere, and jewelry, the town's big bargains. The cobblers at **Canfora,** Via Camerelle 3 (☎ **081-837-0487**), make all the sandals found in their shop. If you don't find what you need, you can order custom-made footwear. They also sell shoes but don't make those themselves. You can find a good selection of men's cashmere pullovers at **Russo Uomo,** Piazzetta Quisisina 8–10 (☎ **081-838-8208**). But for cashmere pullovers for the whole family, go to **Russo Donna,** Via Vittorio Emanuele 55 (☎ **081-838-8207**). The eight talented jewelers at **La Perla,** Piazza Umberto 10–21 (☎ **081-837-0641**), work exclusively with gold and gems and can design and create anything you want.

ACCOMMODATIONS

Don't even think of coming in summer without a reservation.

This is a ritzy resort; even the lesser accommodations are able to charge high prices. If you're really watching your lire, you may have to visit for the day and return to the mainland for the night.

Very Expensive

✪ **Grand Hotel Quisisana Capri.** Via Camerelle 2, 80073 Capri. ☎ **081-837-0788.** Fax 081-837-6080. www.quisi.com. E-mail: info@quisi.com. 165 units. A/C MINIBAR TV TEL. 420,000–800,000L ($210–$400) double; from 1,000,000L ($500) suite. Rates include breakfast. AE, DC, MC, V. Closed Nov 1 to mid-Mar.

The island's grande dame, this is the favorite of a regular international crowd and a bastion of luxury. The sprawling buildings are painted a distinctive yellow and accented with vines and landscaping. Its guest rooms range from cozy singles to spacious suites—all opening onto wide arcades with a stunning view over the coast. They vary greatly in decor, with traditional and conservatively modern furnishings. Accommodations differ in size, but all have a lovely, airy style, and all come with comfortable beds and tile or marble bathrooms containing robes and hair dryers.

Dining/Diversions: The hotel terrace is where everybody who is anybody goes for cocktails before dinner. The hotel has two restaurants, both under famed chef Gualtiero Marchesi. The Colombaia (lunch only) is proud of its fresh-tasting and attractively displayed fish dishes, as well as its lush fruits and vegetables. The Quisi (dinner only) is alluring with candlelight, serving a creative Mediterranean and local cuisine. The American bar overlooks the pool on the lower terrace.

Amenities: Sauna, Turkish bath/massage facilities, indoor and outdoor pools, beauty salon, health club, tennis courts, room service, baby-sitting, laundry/valet.

La Scalinatella (Little Steps). Via Tragara 8, 80073 Capri. ☎ **081-837-0633.** Fax 081-837-8291. 30 units. A/C MINIBAR TV TEL. 370,000–850,000L ($185–$425) junior suite. Rates include breakfast. AE, MC, V. Closed Nov–Easter.

This delightful hotel is constructed like a private villa above terraces offering a panoramic view. It's an exclusive pair of 200-year-old houses, with a vaguely Moorish design, run by the Morgano family. The ambience is one of unadulterated luxury; all units are junior suites that include a phone beside the bathtub, beds set into alcoves, elaborate wrought-iron accents ringing both the inner stairwell and the ornate balconies, and a sweeping view over the gardens and pool. The spacious bathrooms contain scales and hair dryers. Half the accommodations boast two bathrooms each, one with a whirlpool tub.

Dining/Diversions: The hotel contains a restaurant open only at lunchtime, where a flavorful Mediterranean cuisine is served on a terrace beside the pool.

Amenities: Concierge, room service, laundry/dry cleaning, pool, Jacuzzi, sauna, access to health club and tennis courts nearby.

Expensive

Casa Morgano. Via Tragara 6, 80073 Capri. ☎ **081-837-0158.** Fax 081-837-0681. www.caprionline.com/morgano. E-mail: casamorgano@capri.it. 28 units. A/C MINIBAR TV TEL. 380,000–480,000L ($190–$240) double; 600,000–700,000L ($300–$350) junior suite. Rates include breakfast. AE, DC, MC, V.

One of the newest hotels to open in Capri, the Casa Morgano lies next to La Scalinatella. It houses you in grand comfort in 20 of its rooms, which are spacious and deluxe; eight others are quite small. The best units are nos. 201 to 205 and 301 to 305. Most units contain good-sized sitting areas along with terraces opening onto sea views. The bathrooms comes with hair dryers and a hydromassage bathtub or shower.

Dining/Diversions: Although it's one of the top four hotels of Capri, Casa Morgano serves only breakfast, though many good restaurants are nearby. There is a bar and terrace with a view.

Amenities: Limited room service, concierge, laundry/dry cleaning, baby-sitting.

Hotel Luna. Viale Matteotti 3, 80073 Capri. ☎ **081-837-0433.** Fax 081-837-7459. www.caprionline.com/luna. E-mail: luna@capri.it. 54 units. A/C MINIBAR TV TEL. 380,000–580,000L ($190–$290) double. Rates include breakfast. AE, DC, MC, V. Closed Oct 21–Easter.

This first-class hotel stands on a cliff overlooking the sea and the rocks of Faraglioni. The guest rooms are a mix of contemporary Italian pieces and Victorian decor (with good mattresses), most with recessed terraces overlooking the garden of flowers and semitropical plants. The tiled bathrooms offer private phones and hair dryers.

Dining/Diversions: There's a clubby drinking lounge, and the dining room lures with good cuisine.

Amenities: Pool, access to nearby health club and jogging track, Jacuzzi, concierge, laundry/dry cleaning, newspaper delivery, twice-daily maid service, secretarial services, baby-sitting.

Hotel Punta Tragara. Via Tragara 57, 80073 Capri. ☎ **081-837-0844.** Fax 081-837-7790. www.hoteltragara.com. E-mail: info@hoteltragara.com. 45 units. A/C MINIBAR TV TEL. 380,000–450,000L ($190–$225) double; 590,000–730,000L ($295–$365) suite. Rates include buffet breakfast. AE, DC, MC, V. Closed Nov–Easter.

This former private villa, designed higgledy-piggledy by Le Corbusier, stands above rocky cliffs at the southwest tip of the most desirable panorama on Capri. With mottled carpeting, big windows, substantial furniture, and all the modern comforts, each guest room opens onto a terrace or balcony that's brightened with flowers and vines, plus a sweeping view. Private safes are among the other amenities, as are spacious bathrooms with robes and hair dryers. The hotel is isolated from many other island activities, which is either a drawback or a plus, depending on your point of view.

Dining/Diversions: At the open-air Bussola, you can dine on the veranda by candlelight. It offers a savory Mediterranean cuisine prepared by the chefs with flair and served by friendly, efficient waiters. There's also a nightclub built entirely into the rocks.

Amenities: Pool, Jacuzzi, sundeck, beauty salon, concierge, room service, laundry, newspaper delivery, twice-daily maid service.

Villa Brunella. Via Tragara 24, 80073 Capri. ☎ **081-837-0122.** Fax 081-837-0430. www.caprionline.com/villabrunella. E-mail: villabrunella@capri.it. 20 units. A/C MINIBAR TV TEL. 440,000L ($220) double; 550,000L ($275) suite. Rates include breakfast. AE, CB, DC, MC, V. Closed Nov 6–Mar 20.

A 10-minute walk from many of Capri's largest hotels, the Brunella was built in the late 1940s as a private villa. In 1963 it was transformed into a pleasant hotel by its present owner, Vincenzo Ruggiero, who named it after his hardworking wife. The hotel has been completely renovated, and can hold its own with the other hotels in town. All the double have balconies or flowery terraces with sea views. All the doubles have balconies or terraces and views. The rooms come in various shapes and sizes, each with a firm mattress and a small tiled bathroom. There's also a carefully landscaped pool, a bar, and a cozy restaurant.

Moderate

Hotel La Vega. Via Occhio Marino 10, 80073 Capri. ☎ **081-837-0481.** Fax 081-837-0342. 24 units. A/C MINIBAR TV TEL. 280,000–420,000L ($140–$210) double. Rates include breakfast. AE, DC, MC, V. Closed Nov–Easter.

This hotel began in the 1930s as the private home of the family that continues to run it today. It has a clear sea view and is nestled amid trees against a sunny hillside. The oversized guest rooms have decoratively tiled floors and Jacuzzis, and some beds have wrought-iron headboards; each has a private balcony overlooking the water. Below is a garden of flowering bushes, and on the lower edge is a free-form pool with a grassy border for sunbathing and a bar for refreshments. Breakfast is served on your balcony or on a terrace surrounded by trees and large potted flowers.

Hotel Regina Cristina. Via Serena 20, 80073 Capri. ☎ **081-837-0744.** Fax 081-837-0550. 55 units. A/C MINIBAR TV TEL. 250,000–400,000L ($125–$200) double; 580,000L ($290) suite. Rates include breakfast. AE, DC, MC, V.

The white facade of the Regina Cristina rises four stories above one of the most imaginatively landscaped gardens on Capri. It was built in 1959 and has a sunny design of open spaces, sunken lounges, and cool tiles. Each guest room has its own balcony and is very restful; most have Jacuzzis. Their sizes range from small to medium, but each has a good mattress and a compact tiled bathroom. In general, the prices are high for what you get, but on Capri in July and August you're sometimes lucky to find a room at any price.

Villa Sarah. Via Tiberio 3A, 80073 Capri. ☎ **081-837-7817.** Fax 081-837-7215. www.villasarah.it. E-mail: info@villasarah.it. 20 units. MINIBAR TV TEL. 260,000–300,000L ($130–$150) double. Rates include buffet breakfast. AE, MC, V. Closed late Oct–Mar 19.

The modern Sarah, though far removed from the day-trippers from Naples, is still very central. A steep walk from the main square, it seems part of another world with its Capri garden and good views. All it lacks is a pool. One of the bargains of the island, it's often fully booked, so reserve ahead in summer. The sea is visible only from the upper floors. Some rooms have terraces. Most of the guest rooms are quite small, but each has a firm mattress. The tiled bathrooms are small. Breakfast, the only meal, is sometimes served on the terrace.

Inexpensive

Villa Krupp. Via Matteotti 12, 80073 Capri. ☎ **081-837-7473.** Fax 081-837-6489. 15 units. TEL. 200,000–270,000L ($100–$135) double. Rates include breakfast. MC, V. Closed Nov–Mar 15.

During the early 20th century, Russian revolutionaries Gorky and Lenin called this villa home. Surrounded by shady trees, it offers panoramic views of the sea and the Gardens of Augustus from its terraces. At this family-run place, the front parlor is all glass with views of the seaside and semitropical plants set near Hong Kong chairs, intermixed with painted Venetian-style pieces. Your room may be large, with a fairly good bathroom. Others are a bit small, but each comes with a firm mattress on a comfortable bed. Breakfast is the only meal offered.

DINING

Expensive

Da Paolino. Via Palazzo a Mare 11. ☎ **081-837-6102.** Reservations required. Main courses 26,000–40,000L ($13–$20). AE, DC, MC, V. June–Sept daily 8–11pm. Closed Wed Oct–May. CAPRESE/ITALIAN.

Favored by celebrities, this is a chic restaurant in Capri, the spot where the visiting movie star is likely to turn up. The food is about the most authentic Caprese cuisine served on the island, at least at a major restaurant. Try everything from a Caprese salad to sautéed ravioli stuffed with fresh cacciotta cheese. The rigatoni pasta with sautéed pumpkin flowers is worthy of *Gourmet* magazine. Equally delectable is the penne with eggplant and fresh mozzarella. Just as enchanting as the food is the dining area placed in a lemon grove. The lemon motif pervades the restaurant, ranging from the waiters' vests to the plates placed before you.

Moderate

Ai Faraglioni. Via Camerelle 75. ☎ **081-837-0320.** Reservations required. Main courses 18,000–35,000L ($9–$17.50). AE, DC, MC, V. Daily noon–3pm and 7:30–11:30pm. Closed Nov to mid-Mar. SEAFOOD/CONTINENTAL.

Some locals say the food is secondary to the scene at this popular restaurant, where tables are set out onto the main street in nice weather. Stylish and appealing and occupying a stone-sided building at least 150 years old, it has a kitchen that turns out well-prepared European specialties, usually based on seafood from the surrounding waters. Examples are linguine with lobster, seafood crepes, rice Creole, fisherman's risotto, grilled or baked fish, and a wide assortment of meat dishes, like pappardelle with rabbit. For dessert, try one of the regional pastries mixed with fresh fruit.

✪ **La Capannina.** Via Le Botteghe 12B–14. ☎ **081-837-0732.** Reservations required for dinner. Main courses 22,000–35,000L ($11–$17.50). AE, DC, MC, V. Daily noon–3pm and 7:30–midnight. Closed Jan 9–Mar 19. CAMPANA/ITALIAN.

This restaurant has drawn a host of glamorous people, but they come for its lack of pretentiousness. Part of its charm derives from the American-born wife, Aurelia de Angelis, of the fifth-generation owner, who's always on hand to translate or help with menu selections. The three dining rooms are decorated tavern style, though the main draw in summer is the inner courtyard, with ferns and hanging vines. At a table covered with a colored cloth, you can select from baby shrimp au gratin, *pollo* (chicken) *alla Capannina,* or *scaloppini Capannina.* If featured, a fine opener is Sicilian macaroni. The most savory skillet of goodies is the *zuppa di pesce,* a soup made with fish from the bay. Some of the dishes were obviously inspired by the nouvelle cuisine school. Wine is from vineyards owned by the restaurant.

La Pigna. Via Lo Palazzo 30. ☎ **081-837-0280.** Reservations recommended. Main courses 24,000–36,000L ($12–$18). AE, DC, MC, V. Aug daily noon–3pm and 8pm–2am; July and Sept Tues 8pm–2am, Wed–Mon noon–3pm and 8pm–2am; Apr–June and Oct Wed–Mon noon–3pm and 8pm–2am; Nov–Mar daily noon–3pm. NEAPOLITAN.

La Pigna serves the finest meals for the money on the island. Dining here is like attending a garden party, and this has been true since 1875. It isn't as chic as it once was, but the food is as good as ever. The owner loves flowers almost as much as good food, and the greenhouse ambience includes purple petunias, red geraniums, bougainvillea, and lemon trees. Much of the produce comes from the restaurant's gardens in Anacapri. Try in particular the penne tossed in eggplant sauce, the chicken supreme with mushrooms, or the herb-stuffed rabbit. The dessert specialty is an almond-and-chocolate torte. Another specialty is the homemade liqueurs, one of which is distilled from local lemons. The waiters are courteous and efficient, and the atmosphere is nostalgic, as guitarists stroll by singing sentimental Neapolitan ballads.

Inexpensive

✪ **CasaNova.** Via Le Botteghe 46. ☎ **081-837-7642.** Reservations required at dinner in summer. Main courses 18,000–40,000L ($9–$20). AE, DC, MC, V. Mar–Nov daily noon–3pm and 7–11pm. Closed Dec to mid-Mar. NEAPOLITAN/CAPRESE/SEAFOOD.

Run by the D'Alessio family and only a short walk from Piazza Umberto I, this is one of the finest dining rooms on Capri. Its cellar offers a big choice of Italian wines, with most of the favorites of Campania, and its cooks turn out a savory blend of Neapolitan and Italian specialties. You might begin with cheese-filled ravioli and then go on to veal Sorrento or red snapper "crazy waters" (with baby tomatoes). The seafood is always fresh and well prepared. A tempting buffet of antipasti is at hand. In a small wine cellar, you can enjoy a good selection of Italian and foreign wines with a variety of cheeses. Most meals are inexpensive, but some exotic dishes and specialties that appear infrequently can cause your check to soar. Lunch offers some lighter choices such as simple pizzas and salads.

Da Gemma. Via Madre Serafina 6. ☎ **081-837-0461.** Reservations recommended. Main courses 15,000–28,000L ($7.50–$14). AE, DC, MC, V. Daily noon–3pm and 7pm–midnight. CAPRESE/SEAFOOD.

Da Gemma is reached by passing through a vaulted tunnel beginning at Piazza Umberto I and winding through dark underground passages. The cuisine includes authentic versions of Caprese favorites, with an emphasis on fish, to more modern dishes like pizzas. You might begin with a creamy version of mussel soup, followed by one of many kinds of grilled fish, as well as fillets of veal or chicken prepared with lemon and garlic or with marsala wine. A specialty is a *fritta alla Gemma,* a medley of fried foods that includes fried zucchini blossoms, potato croquettes, fried mozzarella, and a miniature pizza. During warm weather, the site expands from its cramped 14th-century core onto a covered open-air terrace with sweeping views of the Gulf of Naples. (To reach the terrace, you'll have to wander through the same labyrinth of covered passages, then cross the street.)

La Cantinella di Capri. In the Giardini Augusto, Viale Matteotti 8. ☎ **081-837-0616.** Reservations recommended. Main courses 18,000–30,000L ($9–$15). AE, DC, MC, V. Tues–Sun 12:30–3pm and 7:30pm–12:30am. Closed Nov–Mar. NEAPOLITAN/FRENCH.

One of the most scenically located restaurants, this place occupies a circa 1750 villa in a verdant park a short but soothing distance from the town center and a short walk from the Gardens of Augustus. It was acquired in 1996 by the owners of a popular restaurant in Naples, who shuttle between Naples and Capri, thereby catering to as broad-based a crowd as possible. Menu items include lots of pungent sauces and fresh seafood that's sometimes combined into pastas like linguine *Sant Lucia* (with octopus, squid, whitefish, and tomato sauce). Worth the trip here is the superb fish, including the local pezzogna baked in a salt crust to preserve its aromatic flavors. Try the veal scaloppini prepared with lemon and white wine or parmigiana style. The *pasta fagiole* (beans and pasta) is hearty, and such desserts as tiramisu are invariably velvety smooth.

La Cisterna. Via Madre Serafina 5. ☎ **081-837-5620.** Reservations required. Main courses 15,000–24,000L ($7.50–$12). AE, DC, MC, V. Fri–Wed noon–3:30pm and 7pm–midnight. Closed mid-Nov to mid-Mar. SEAFOOD.

This excellent small restaurant is run by brothers Francesco and Salvatore Trama, who extend a warm welcome. Ask what the evening specials are. They might be mama's green lasagna or whatever fish was freshest that afternoon, marinated in wine, garlic, and ginger and broiled. You could also try the lightly breaded and deep-fried baby squid and octopus, a mouth-watering saltimbocca, spaghetti with clams, and a filling *zuppa di pesce* (fish soup). Pizza begins at 6,000L ($3.60). La Cisterna is only a short walk from Piazza Umberto I via a labyrinth of covered "tunnels."

Ristorante al Grottino. Via Longano 27. ☎ **081-837-0584.** Reservations required for dinner. Main courses 18,000–30,000L ($9–$15). AE, MC, V. Daily noon–3pm and 7pm–midnight. Closed Nov–Mar. SEAFOOD/NEAPOLITAN.

Founded in 1937, this was the retreat of the rich and famous during its 1950s heyday. Ted Kennedy, Ginger Rogers, the Gabor sisters, and Princess Soraya of Iran once dined here, and the place is now popular among ordinary folk. To reach it, you walk down a narrow alley branching off from Piazza Umberto I. Bowing to the influence of the nearby Neapolitan cuisine, the chef offers four different dishes of fried mozzarella, any one of which is highly recommended. Try a big plate of the mixed fish fry from the seas of the Campania. The *zuppa di cozze* (mussel soup) is a savory opener, as is the *ravioli alla caprese.* The linguine with scampi is truly wonderful.

Capri After Dark

You'll find some fun nightclubs on the island, all of which you can enter without a cover. Foremost among them is **Number Two,** Via Camerelle 1 (☎ **081-837-7078**), rivaled closely by **New Pentothal,** Via Vittorio Emmanuele 45 (☎ **081-837-6793**). Both cater to all ages and all nationalities, but only between late April and September.

The presence of these high-tech dance clubs doesn't keep the crowds out of the dozens of cafes, bars, and taverns scattered throughout the narrow streets of Capri's historic center. Among the most appealing is **Taverna Guarracino,** Via Castello 7 (☎ **081-837-0514**), a convivial place to enjoy a beer or a glass of wine.

One of the major pastimes in Capri is cafe-sitting at an outdoor table on Piazza Umberto I. Even some permanent residents (and this is a good sign) patronize **Bar Tiberio,** Piazza Umberto I (☎ **081-837-0268**), open daily 7am to 2am (sometimes to 4am). Larger and a little more comfortable than some of its competitors, this cafe has tables both inside and outside that overlook the busy life of the square.

Anacapri

Even farther up in the clouds than Capri is the town of Anacapri, which is more remote, secluded, and idyllic than the main resort—and reached by a daring 4,000L ($2) round-trip bus ride more thrilling than any roller coaster. One visitor remarked that all bus drivers to Anacapri "were either good or dead." At one point in island history, Anacapri and Capri were connected only by the *Scala Fenicia,* the Phoenician Stairs (which have been reconstructed a zillion times).

When you disembark at **Piazza della Victoria,** you'll find a village of charming dimensions.

To continue your ascent to the top, hop aboard a chairlift (Segiovia) to **Monte Solaro,** the loftiest citadel on the island at 1,950 feet. The ride takes about 12 minutes and operates winter, spring, and fall 9:30am to sunset; a round-trip costs 7,500L ($3.75). At the top, the panorama of the Bay of Naples is spread before you.

You can head out on Viale Axel Munthe from Piazza Monumento for a 5-minute walk to the **Villa San Michele,** Capodimonte 34 (☎ **081-837-1401**). This was the home of Axel Munthe, the Swedish author *(The Story of San Michele),* physician, and friend of Gustav V, king of Sweden, who visited him several times on the island. The villa is as Munthe (who died in 1949) furnished it, in a harmonious and tasteful way. From the rubble and ruins of an imperial villa built underneath by Tiberius, Munthe purchased several marbles, which are displayed inside. You can walk through the gardens for another in a series of endless panoramas of the island. Tiberius used to sleep out here alfresco on hot nights. You can visit the villa daily: May to September 9am to 6pm, April and October 9:30am to 5pm, March 9:30am to 4:30pm, and November to February 10:30am to 3:30pm. Admission is 8,000L ($4).

Accommodations

Expensive

Capri Palace. Via Capodimonte 2, 80071 Anacapri. ☎ **081-837-3800.** Fax 081-837-3191. www.capri-palace.com. E-mail: info@capri-palace.com. 80 units. A/C MINIBAR TV TEL. 450,000–700,000L ($225–$350) double; 700,000–850,000L ($350–$425) junior suite. Rates include breakfast. AE, DC, MC, V. Closed Nov 15–Easter, Apr 1.

On the slopes of Monte Solaro, the contemporary, first-class Capri Palace sparkles. Its bold designer obviously loved wide-open spaces and vivid colors. The landscaped gardens with palm trees and plenty of bougainvillea have a large pool, which most guests use as their outdoor living room. Although lacking the intimate charms of La Scalinatella in Capri (see above), it's still a wonderful choice because of its setting and its Capri Beauty Farm, offering spa treatments. Each of the guest rooms is attractively and comfortably furnished, and from some on a clear day you can see smoking Vesuvius. Many beds (mostly twins) are canopied, and all of them contain quality mattresses. The bathrooms are tiled or marbled, each with deluxe toiletries. Each of the four special suites has a private pool and private garden.

Dining: The hotel restaurant, L'Olivo, is known for its fine cuisine with Neapolitan and other Mediterranean specialties, even with some nouvelle cuisine. A snack bar, Il Gazebo, with light lunches is in the pool area.

Amenities: Pool, beauty spa, room service, baby-sitting, laundry/valet.

Moderate

Hotel Bella Vista. Via Orlandi 10, 80071 Anacapri. ☎ **081-837-1821.** Fax 081-837-0957. 14 units. TEL. 175,000–250,000L ($87.50–$125) per person double. Rates include breakfast. AE, MC, V. Closed Nov 1–Easter.

Only a 2-minute walk from the main piazza, this is a modern vacation retreat with a panoramic view and a distinct sense of a family-run regional inn. Lodged into a mountainside, the hotel is decorated with primary colors and has large living and dining rooms and terraces with sea views. The breakfast and lunch terrace has garden furniture and a rattan-roofed sun shelter, and the cozy lounge features an elaborate tile floor and a hooded fireplace. The guest rooms are pleasingly contemporary (a few have a bed mezzanine, a sitting area on the lower level, and a private entrance). The tiled bathrooms are compact. The restaurant is open daily.

Hotel San Michele di Anacapri. Via Orlandi 1–3, 80071 Anacapri. ☎ **081-837-1427.** Fax 081-837-1420. E-mail: smichele@capri.it. 56 units. TV TEL. 200,000–260,000L ($100–$130) double. Rates include breakfast. AE, MC, V. Closed Nov 6–Mar 31.

This well-appointed hotel has spacious cliff-side gardens and unmarred views as well as enough shady or sunny nooks to please everybody. It also has the largest pool on Capri. Guests linger peacefully in its private gardens, where the green trees are softened by splashes of color from hydrangea and geraniums. The view for diners includes the Bay of Naples and Vesuvius. The guest rooms carry out the same theme, with a respect for the past, but also with sufficient examples of today's amenities, like good beds and tiled bathrooms.

Inexpensive

Hotel Loreley. Via Orlandi 16, 80071 Anacapri. ☎ **081-837-1440.** Fax 081-837-1399. E-mail: loreley@mbox.caprinet.it. 16 units. TEL. 130,000–170,000L ($65–$85) double. Rates include breakfast. AE, MC, V. Closed Nov 8–Mar 19.

The Loreley is cozy, with a genial, homey atmosphere. It features an open-air veranda with a bamboo canopy, rattan chairs, and a good view. The guest rooms overlook lemon-bearing trees that have (depending on the season) either scented blossoms or fruit. The rooms are quite large, with unified colors and enough furniture to make a sitting area. Each has a balcony. You approach the hotel through a white iron gate, past a stone wall. It lies off the road toward the sea and is surrounded by fig trees and geraniums.

DINING

La Rondinella. Via Orlandi 295. ☎ **081-837-1223.** Reservations recommended. Main courses 18,000–30,000L ($9–$15). AE, DC, MC, V. Daily noon–3pm and 7pm–midnight. Closed Thurs in winter. SOUTHERN ITALIAN.

Despite the competition from the more formal restaurants in some of Anacapri's hotels, this is the most appealing place, thanks to the likable staff, garden view, and a location adjacent to the Santa Sophia church. The menu items are tried-and-true versions of classics, yet the chefs manage to produce everything in copious amounts and with lots of robust flavors. Look for succulent homemade ravioli stuffed with cheese and tomatoes, a mixed grill of fresh seafood, braised radicchio and/or artichokes, and fillet of veal or chicken slathered with mozzarella, tomatoes, and fresh herbs. For dessert, you might try the sugary version of Sicilian tiramisu.

MARINA PICCOLA

You can reach the little south-shore fishing village and beach of **Marina Piccola** by bus (later you can take a bus back up the steep hill to Capri). The village opens onto emerald-and-cerulean waters, with the Faraglioni rocks of the sirens jutting out at the far end of the bay. Treat yourself to lunch at **La Canzone del Mare,** Via Marina Piccola 93 (☎ **081-837-0104**), daily noon to 4pm. Seafood and Neapolitan cuisines are served. Closed November to Easter.

7 Positano

35 miles (56km) SE of Naples, 10 miles (16km) E of Sorrento, 165 miles (266km) SE of Rome

A Moorish-style hillside village on the southern strip of the Amalfi Drive, Positano opens onto the Tyrrhenian Sea with its legendary (now privately owned) Sirenuse Islands, Homer's siren islands in the *Odyssey,* which form the miniarchipelago of Li Galli (The Cocks). Once, Positano was part of the powerful Republic of the Amalfis, a rival of Venice as a sea power in the 10th century. It's said that the town was "discovered" after World War II when Gen. Mark Clark stationed troops in nearby Salerno. Like many European resorts, it began as a sleeping fishing village that was visited by painters and writers (Paul Klee, Tennessee Williams) and then taken over by visitors in search of bohemia, until a full-scale tourism industry was born.

Today smart boutiques dot the village, and bikinis add vibrant colors to the gray beach, where you're likely to get pebbles in your sand castle. Prices have been rising sharply over the past few years. The 500L-a-night rooms that were popular with sunset-painting artists have gone the way of your baby teeth. The topography of the village, you'll soon discover, is impossibly steep. Wear comfortable walking shoes—no heels!

If you make reservations the day before with **Alicost** (☎ **089-875-092**), you can take a hydrofoil or a ferry to Capri from Positano. Hydrofoils cost 20,000L ($10) one way, while a ferry ticket goes for 15,000L ($7.50) one way.

ESSENTIALS

GETTING THERE SITA **buses** leave from Sorrento frequently throughout the day, more often in summer than winter, for the rather thrilling ride to Positano; a one-way fare is 2,500L ($1.25). For information, call SITA at ☎ **089-871-016.**

If you have a **car,** Positano lies along Route 145, which becomes Route 163 at the approach to the resort.

VISITOR INFORMATION The **tourist office** is at Via del Saracino 4 (☎ **089-875-067**), open Monday to Friday 8:30am to 2pm and Saturday June to September 8:30am to noon.

SHOPPING

In a town famous for beach and casual wear, **La Brezza,** Via del Brigantino 1 (☎ **089-875-811**), on the shore, has the perfect location for selling its swimsuits, beach towels, and summer clothes. Clothing that's a bit more formal, and better suited to a glamorous dinner, is **Nadir,** Via Pasitea 42/46 (☎ **089-875-975**). Another sleek fashion option is **Carro Fashion,** Via Pasitea (☎ **089-875-780**). The shop at the Hotel Le Sirenuse (below), **Emporio Le Sirenuse,** 109 Via Cristoforo Colombo (☎ **089-811-468**), is presided over by Carla Sersale, who has the town's toniest merchandise, everything from ballerina slippers from Porselli (who designs them for Milan's La Scala) to sexy one-piece bathing suits.

If you're in the market for brightly colored, intricately patterned regional pottery, visit **Umberto Carro,** Via Pasitea 98 (☎ **089-811-596**), where the focus is on dishes, cookware, and ceramic tiles. For the best collection of ceramics from the Amalfi town of Vietri sul Mare, head for **Ceramica Assunta,** Via Cristoforo Colombo 97 (☎ **089-875-008**), known for its colorful ceramics with fine artisanal decorations.

In the overcrowded **Cafiero,** 171 Via Cristoforo Colombo (☎ **089-875-838**), you find odd-shaped colored glass bottles and vases. There's nothing like it along the coast.

Cose Antiche, 21 Via Cristoforo Colombo 21 (☎ **089-811-089**), sells Amalfi Coast landscapes painted in the 19th century.

La Myricae, Piazza Mulini 71 (☎ **089-875-882**), has the coast's best selection of antique jewelry, some from the 17th century. There are some excellent buys here in art deco jewelry.

ACCOMMODATIONS

VERY EXPENSIVE

✪ **Hotel Le Sirenuse.** Via Cristoforo Colombo 30, 84017 Positano. ☎ **089-875-066.** Fax 089-811-798. www.sirenuse.it. E-mail: hotel@sirenuse.it. 60 units. A/C MINIBAR TV TEL. 440,000–946,000L ($220–$473) double; from 1,260,000L ($630) suite. Rates include breakfast. AE, CB, DC, MC, V. Parking 30,000L ($15).

La Sirenuse, an old villa a few minutes' walk up from the bay, is owned by the Marchesi Sersale family; it was their home until 1951. The marchesa selects all the furnishings, which include fine carved chests, 19th-century paintings and old prints, a spinet piano, upholstered pieces in bold colors, and a Victorian cabinet. The sophisticated crowd includes numerous artists and writers. The guest rooms, many with Jacuzzis, are varied, and all have terraces overlooking the village. Your room may have an iron bed, high and ornate and painted red, as well as a carved chest and refectory tables. The bathrooms are luxurious, with robes, deluxe toiletries, hair dryers, and whirlpool tubs.

Dining: Meals are well served on one of the three terraces, and the chef caters to the international palate with a regional cuisine. The hotel boasts one of the best dining rooms along the coast (see "Dining," below).

Amenities: Outdoor heated pool, health club, Jacuzzi, sauna, tour desk, concierge, dry cleaning/laundry service, newspaper delivery, in-room massage, twice-daily maid service, baby-sitting.

✪ **Hotel di San Pietro.** Via Laurito 2, 84017 Positano. ☎ **089-875-455.** Fax 089-811-449. www.relaischateaux.fr/sanpietro. E-mail: sanpietro@relaischateaux.fr. 60 units. A/C MINIBAR TV TEL. 660,000–760,000L ($330–$380) double; 900,000–1,250,000L ($450–$625) suite. Rates include breakfast. AE, DC, MC, V. Closed Nov 3–Easter. Free parking.

A mile from Positano toward Amalfi, the San Pietro is signaled only by a miniature 17th-century chapel projecting out on a high cliff. The hotel opened in 1970 and has been renovated virtually every winter since. An elevator takes you down to the cliff ledges of the choicest resort along the coast. The suitelike guest rooms are superglamorous, many with picture windows beside the bathtubs (there's even a huge sunken Roman bath in one suite). Antiques and art objects add glamour. The bathrooms are state of the art, with robes, hair dryers, and deluxe toiletries. Room no. $8^1/_2$ is named for Fellini (a longtime guest) and his movie. Bougainvillea from the terraces reaches into the ceilings of many living rooms. Guests have included Julia Roberts and Sting.

Dining/Diversions: Guests gather at sunset in the piano bar. A dining room cut into the cliff features picture windows and a refined international cuisine. There's also a lovely tiled terrace on which you can sip drinks while enjoying the view.

Amenities: Pool, private beach, tennis court, room service, baby-sitting, laundry/valet.

Expensive

Hotel Poseidon. Via Pasitea 148, 84017 Positano. ☎ **089-811-111.** Fax 089-875-833. www.starnet.it/poseidon. E-mail: poseidon@starnet.it. 52 units. A/C MINIBAR TV TEL. 360,000–450,000L ($180–$225) double; 580,000–760,000L ($290–$380) suite. Rates include breakfast. AE, DC, MC, V. Closed Jan 9–Apr 18. Parking 40,000L ($20).

This hotel was built in 1950 by the Aonzo family as their summer residence. In 1955 it was enlarged and transformed into a hotel, still owned and managed by the Aonzos. It's charming, discreet, and elegant, with antique furniture and objects. In the guest rooms you get luxury and style without the very high rates of San Pietro and Le Sirenuse. The rooms are generously spacious, each with a fine mattress and a bathroom with a hair dryer.

Dining: Along with its terraces and garden, the hotel offers both indoor and outdoor dining; its chefs feature regional and continental cuisine.

Amenities: Freshwater pool; health club with sauna, hydromassage spa, and gym with professional trainer; concierge; room service; laundry/dry cleaning; twice-daily maid service; secretarial services; baby-sitting.

Hotel Villa Franca. Viale Pasitea 318, 84017 Positano. ☎ **089-875-655.** Fax 089-875-735. www.starnet.it/villa_franca. E-mail: hvf@starnet.it. 38 units. A/C MINIBAR TV TEL. 300,000–480,000L ($150–$240) double. Rates include breakfast. AE, DC, MC, V. Parking 26,000–30,000L ($13–$15). Bus: 318.

At the top of Positano, about a 10-minute walk from the center, this hotel is a little gem. It offers brightly decorated guest rooms, ranging from small to medium and containing quality mattresses. The bathrooms are beautifully tiled. The top floor contains somewhat small rooms, but they open onto little balconies with the best views. The finest rooms are the three deluxe corner units; they're more spacious and also have great views of the coast. Ten rooms are in the less inspired annex. The rooftop pool is a mere tiny tub but, still, it's the only spot in town with a 360° view of Positano.

✪ **Palazzo Murat.** Via dei Mulini 23, 84017 Positano. ☎ **089-875-177.** Fax 089-811-419. www.starnet.it/murat. E-mail: hpm@starnet.it. 28 units. A/C MINIBAR TV TEL. 320,000–500,000L ($160–$250) double. Rates include breakfast. AE, DC, MC, V. Closed Jan to 1 week before Easter. Parking 35,000L ($17.50) nearby.

Once this was the retreat of Napoléon's brother-in-law, the king of Naples, who was notorious for confiscating statuary and church art from the former occupants, an order of Benedictine monks. The jasmine and bougainvillea are so profuse in its garden they spill over their enclosing wall onto the arbors of the narrow street. The best (and most expensive) rooms are nos. 1 to 5 in the original building, which boasts high ceilings and antiques; the newer annex has smaller and less atmospheric rooms. All contain first-rate mattresses; only the third-floor rooms have views of the sea. The tiled bathrooms are a bit small but have adequate shelf space. The Ristorante Al Palazzo is one of the town's finest. If the weather permits, skip its dull indoor dining room and head to its courtyard to enjoy wonderfully delicate food like ravioli stuffed with sea bass and shrimp and topped with tomato-and-shrimp sauce.

MODERATE

Albergo L'Ancora. Via Colombo 36, 84017 Positano. ☎ **089-875-318.** Fax 089-811-784. 18 units. MINIBAR TV TEL. 250,000–300,000L ($125–$150) double. Rates include breakfast. AE, DC, MC, V. Closed Nov–Apr 1. Free parking.

This is a hillside villa turned hotel with the atmosphere of a private club. It's fresh and sunny. Each guest room, 11 of them air-conditioned, is like a bird's nest on a cliff, with a private terrace. The main lounge has clusters of club chairs, tile floors, and chandeliers. Most rooms are medium-sized, with firm mattresses and bathrooms. Well-chosen antiques, such as fine inlaid desks, are mixed with contemporary pieces. Only guests can dine on the informal terrace under a vine-covered sun shelter.

Albergo Miramare. Via Trara Genoino 27, 84017 Positano. ☎ **089-875-002.** Fax 089-875-219. 16 units. A/C TEL. 290,000–360,000L ($145–$180) double; 380,000–450,000L ($190–$225) triple. Rates include breakfast. AE, MC, V. Closed Nov–Mar 15. Parking 16,000L ($8).

On a cliff in the town center, the Miramare is for those who like the personal touch only a small inn can provide. Guests stay in one of two tastefully furnished buildings amid citrus trees and flamboyant bougainvillea. Your bed (with a firm mattress) will most likely rest under a vaulted ceiling, and the white walls will be thick. The bathrooms have a sense of whimsy, with pink porcelain clamshells as wash basins (the water rushes from a sea-green ceramic fish with coral-pink gills). Nine rooms have a glass wall in the bathroom, so while soaking in the tub you can enjoy a panoramic sea view. The conversation piece is room 210's glass bathtub (once an aquarium) on a flowery terrace. The beach is a 3-minute walk away down a series of stairs.

Albergo Ristorante Covo dei Saraceni. Via Regina Giovanna 5, 84017 Positano. ☎ **089-875-400.** Fax 089-875-878. www.starnet.it/covo. E-mail: covo@starnet.it. 58 units. A/C MINIBAR TV TEL. 350,000–380,000L ($175–$190) double; 470,000–780,000L ($235–$390) junior suite. Rates include buffet breakfast. AE, DC, MC, V. Closed Jan 8–Mar 31. Parking 30,000L ($15).

You'll find this rambling yellow-ochre building a few steps above the port. The side closest to the water culminates in a rounded tower of rough-hewn stone, inside of which is an appealing restaurant open to the breezes. The guest rooms range from small to medium, all with firm mattresses and cramped tiled bathrooms. On the premises is a saltwater pool and two bars (one next to the pool).

Buca di Bacco. Via Rampa Teglia 8, 84017 Positano. ☎ **089-875-699.** Fax 089-875-731. www.bucadibacco.it. E-mail: bacco@starnet.it. 53 units. A/C MINIBAR TV TEL. 300,000–450,000L ($150–$225) double; 470,000–570,000L ($235–$285) junior suite. Rates include buffet breakfast. AE, DC, MC, V. Closed Oct 31–Mar. Parking 40,000L ($20).

This is one of the best moderately priced hotels, with one of the area's best restaurants (see "Dining," below). The main beach of Positano often draws guests who patronize only its bar. A large terrace opens onto the beach, and you can enjoy a cocktail while still in your swimsuit. The oldest and most expensive part, the Buca Residence, was an old seaside mansion at the dawn of the 19th century. The guest rooms are well furnished, with many facilities, like balconies facing the sea. The finest accommodations are 6 superior rooms with terraces facing on the sea, though there are 36 standard rooms with balconies opening onto sea views. The other rooms don't have sea views. The hotel was renovated in 1999.

INEXPENSIVE

Casa Albertina. Via Tavolozza 3, 84017 Positano. ☎ **089-875-143.** Fax 089-811-540. www.casaalertina.it. E-mail: info@casaalbertina.it. 20 units. A/C MINIBAR TEL. 240,000–300,000L ($120–$150) double with breakfast; 340,000–400,000L ($170–$200) double with half-board. Half-board compulsory Apr–Oct. AE, CB, DC, DISC, MC, V. Parking 30,000–35,000L ($15–$17.50) nearby.

This villa guest house, up a steep and winding road, offers a view of the coast from its perch. The guest rooms are gems, color coordinated in mauve or blue and furnished with well-selected pieces, like gilt mirrors and fruitwood end tables. Each has wide French doors leading out to a private balcony, and a few have Jacuzzis. You can breakfast on the terra-cotta tiled terrace and enjoy lunch and dinner in the good restaurant specializing in fresh, grilled fish. Laundry service and a baby-sitter are available on request, and the hotel has a bar and a solarium.

DINING

EXPENSIVE

Buca di Bacco. Via Rampa Teglia 8. ☎ **089-875-699.** Reservations required. Main courses 35,000–55,000L ($17.50–$27.50). AE, DC, MC, V. Daily 12:30–3:30pm and 8–11pm. Closed Oct 31–Mar. CAMPANIA/ITALIAN.

Right on the beach you'll find one of Positano's top restaurants, opened just days after the end of World War II. Guests often stop for a drink in the bar before heading up to the dining room on a big covered terrace facing the sea. On display are fresh fish, special salads, and fruit, such as luscious black figs and freshly peeled oranges soaked in caramel. An exciting opener is a salad made with fruits of the sea, or you may prefer the *zuppa di cozze* (mussels) in a tangy sauce. Other items not to miss are linguine with lobster and *grillata del Golfo,* a unique mixed fish fry. The pasta dishes are homemade and the meats well prepared with fresh ingredients. Finish with a *limoncello,* the lemon liqueur celebrated along the Amalfi Drive.

✪ **La Cambusa.** Piazza Amerigo Vespucci 4. ☎ **089-875-432.** Reservations recommended. Main courses 30,000–50,000L ($15–$25). AE, DC, MC, V. Daily 12:30–3pm and 8pm–midnight. CAMPANIA/SEAFOOD.

If you like local fish grilled to perfection, head here. The local fishermen save only the finest catch for owner Luigi Russo (you can see them bringing in their catch early in the morning). The food items are prepared with care, and all the cooking is designed to bring out the natural flavor in the fish. Try the linguine with cozze (mussels) or an excellent patelle (limpets), a kind of Mediterranean shellfish. Little Neapolitan tomatoes are used for the sauces, and they not only add extra flavor to the sauce but also enrich most of the fish dishes. For a special treat, ask for the zucchini soufflé flavored with basil and parmigiano.

✪ **Ristorante La Sirenuse.** In the Hotel La Sirenuse, Via Cristoforo Colombo 30. ☎ **089-875-066.** Reservations required. Main courses 30,000–70,000L ($15–$35); set-price menu 110,000L ($55). AE, DC, MC, V. Daily 1–2:30pm and 8–10pm. Closed Jan 6–Mar 15. SOUTHERN ITALIAN.

One of Italy's most stylish hotel restaurants occupies the third floor of the previously recommended La Sirenuse. Waiters will tell you its terrace is "just 80 steps above the level of the sea." Bougainvillea, geraniums, hibiscus, and lemon trees are artfully massed in the terrace corners, and during clement weather the inside dining room closes completely in favor of the alfresco experience. The menu items revolve around what's available at the seafood markets and include linguine le Sirenuse, with lobster, scampi, and crayfish; linguine with artichoke hearts and scampi that's been cooked en papillote; fresh salads and antipasti; and a grilled medley of fish and shellfish prepared for two or more. Expect lots of Mediterranean herbs, mozzarella, and homemade pastries.

Moderate to Inexpensive

Chez Black. Via del Brigantino 19–21. ☎ **089-875-036.** Reservations required in summer. Main courses 18,000–35,000L ($9–$17.50). AE, DC, MC, V. Daily 12:30–3pm and 7:30–11pm. Closed Jan–Feb 7. SEAFOOD.

Chez Black occupies a desirable position near the beach, and in summer it's in the heart of the action. The interior seems like an expensive yacht with varnished ribbing, a glowing sheath of softwood and brass, and semaphore symbols. A stone-edged aquarium holds fresh lobsters, and the racks and racks of local wines give you a vast choice. Seafood is the specialty, as well as a wide selection of pizzas. The best-known dish is the spaghetti with crayfish, but you might be tempted by linguine with fresh pesto, grilled sole, swordfish, or shrimp, plus an array of veal, liver, chicken, and beef dishes. One of the most prized and sought-after dishes is the spicy *zuppe di pesce* (fish soup)—a meal in itself, brimming with succulent finned creatures.

✪ **Da Adolfo.** Via Laurito, Località Laurito. ☎ **089-875-022.** Reservations recommended. Main courses 11,000–25,000L ($5.50–$12.50). No credit cards. Late June to Sept 10am–6pm; July–Aug also Sat 8pm–midnight. SOUTHERN ITALIAN.

Don't even think of coming here via car or taxi because you'd have to descend around 450 rugged stone steps from the highway above. The husband/wife team of Sergio (Italian) and Amanda (Australian) provide a 25-passenger motorboat to take you from Positano's main jetty across the water to the restaurant. (You'll recognize the boat by the large red fish on its side.) During the season when Da Adolfo is open, the boat departs daily every 30 minutes 10am to 1pm and 4pm to whenever the last customer has left the beach, usually sometime between 6:30 and 8pm or even later on Saturdays in July and August (these late-summer Saturday evenings are the only time dinner is served). The shuttle service is free, as is the use of the sands, changing rooms, and freshwater showers maintained by the restaurant. The only things you'll pay for are whatever you eat and drink in the restaurant and the optional rental of a beach chair (7,000L/$3.50) and an umbrella (5,000L/$2.50).

Da Adolfo seems like a beachfront restaurant in Greece, complete with pungent summery food, a casual attitude toward toplessness, an utter lack of pretension, and sun and fun. Menu items focus on the fish, herbs, mozzarella, and zest of the Mediterranean. Especially appealing are the heaping bowl of mussel soup, slices of fresh mozzarella wrapped in lemon leaves, and *scialetti,* pasta with stewed clams and mussels.

Positano After Dark

Music on the Rocks, Spiaggia Grande Via Marina (☎ **089-875-874**), is designed on two levels, one of which contains a quieter piano bar. It's owned by the same man who owns the chic Chez Black (see above).

Similar in its choice of music, crowd, and setting is **L'Africana,** Vettica Maggiore (☎ **089-874-042**), in the nearby resort of Praiano, about 2 miles from Positano. Local fishermen come in during the most frenzied peak of the dancing and dredge a sinkhole at the edge of the dance floor with nets, pulling up a bountiful catch of seafood for the local restaurants. The contrast of new-age music with old-world folklore is as riveting as it is bizarre. Many chic guests from Positano arrive here by boat. Both clubs are open nightly June to August, but only Friday and Saturday in May and September, and they're closed the rest of the year.

8 Amalfi

38 miles (61km) SE of Naples, 11 miles (18km) E of Positano, 21 miles (34km) W of Salerno, 169 miles (272km) SE of Rome

From the 9th to the 11th century, the seafaring Republic of Amalfi rivaled the great maritime powers of Genoa and Venice. Its maritime code, the Tavole Amalfitane, was followed in the Mediterranean for centuries. But raids by Saracens and a flood in the 14th century devastated the city. Amalfi's power and influence weakened, until it rose again in modern times as the major resort on the Amalfi Drive.

From its position at the slope of the steep Lattari hills, it overlooks the Bay of Salerno. The approach to Amalfi is dramatic, whether you come from Positano or from Salerno. Today Amalfi depends on tourist traffic, and the hotels and pensioni are located right in the milling throng of vacationers. The finest and most highly rated accommodations are on the outskirts.

ESSENTIALS

GETTING THERE SITA **buses** run every 2 hours during the day from Sorrento, costing 4,000L ($2) one way. There are also SITA bus connections from Positano, costing 2,000L ($1) one way. Information about schedules is available in Amalfi by calling the bus terminal at the waterfront on Piazza Flavio Gioia (☎ **089-871-009**).

If you have a **car,** from Positano continue east along the Amalfi Drive (S163) with its narrow hairpin turns.

VISITOR INFORMATION The **tourist office** is at Corso delle Repubbliche Marinare 19–21 (☎ **089-871-107**), open Monday to Friday 8:30am to 2pm and 3:30 to 6pm, Saturday 8:30am to noon.

EXPLORING THE TOWN

Amalfi lays some claim to being a beach resort, and narrow public **beaches** flank the harbor. In addition, between rocky sections of the coast, many of the first-class and deluxe hotels have carved out small stretches of sand reserved for their guests. However, better and more expansive beaches are adjacent to the nearby villages of **Minori** and **Maiori,** a short drive along the coast. Those beaches are lined with a handful of cafes, souvenir kiosks, and restaurants that thrive mostly during the summer. You can reach the villages by buses leaving from Amalfi's Piazza Flavio Gioia at 30-minute intervals during the day. Expect to pay 3,000L ($1.50) each way.

The ✪ **Duomo,** Piazza del Duomo (☎ **089-871-059**), evokes Amalfi's rich past. It is named in honor of St. Andrew (Sant'Andrea), whose remains are said to be buried inside the crypt (see below). Reached by climbing steep steps, the cathedral is characterized by its black-and-white facade and mosaics. The one nave and two aisles are all richly baroque. The cathedral dates from the 11th century, though the present structure has been rebuilt. Its bronze doors were made in Constantinople, and its *campanile* (bell tower) is from the 13th century, erected partially in the Romanesque style. The Duomo is open daily 7:30am to 7pm and charges no admission.

You can also visit the **Cloister of Paradise (Chiostro del Paradiso),** to the left of the Duomo, originally a necropolis for members of the Amalfitan "establishment." This graveyard dates from the 1200s and contains broken columns and statues, as well as sarcophagi. The aura is definitely Moorish, with a whitewashed quadrangle of interlaced arches. One of the treasures is fragments of Cosmatesque work, brightly colored geometric mosaics that once formed parts of columns and altars, a specialty of this region. The arches create an evocative setting for concerts, both piano and vocal, held on Friday nights July to September, with tickets at 5,000L ($2.50). The cloister is open daily 9am to 7pm and charges 5,000L ($2.50) admission. You reach the **crypt** from the cloister. Here lie the remains of St. Andrew—that is, everything except his face. The pope donated his face to St. Andrew's in Patras, Greece, but the back half of his head remained here.

A minor attraction, good for that rainy day, is the **Civic Museum (Museo Civico),** Piazza Municipio (☎ **089-871-001**), which displays original manuscripts of the Tavoliere Amalfitane. This was the maritime code that governed the entire Mediterranean until 1570. Some exhibits relate to Flavio Gioia, Amalfi's most famous merchant adventurer. Amalfitani claim he invented the compass in the 12th century. "The sun, the moon, the stars and—Amalfi," locals used to say. What's left from the "attic" of their once great power is preserved here. The museum is free and open Monday to Saturday 9am to 1pm.

For your most **scenic walk** in Amalfi, start at Piazza del Duomo and head up Via Genova. The classic stroll will take you to the **Valley of the Mills (Valle dei Mulini),** so called because of the paper mills along its rocky reaches (the seafaring republic is said to have acquainted Italy with the use of paper). You'll pass by fragrant gardens and scented citrus groves. If the subject interests you, you can learn more details about the industry at the **Museum of Paper (Museo della Carta),** Via Valle dei Mulini (☎ **089-872-615**), filled with antique presses and yellowing manuscripts from yesterday. It's open Tuesday to Thursday and Saturday and Sunday 9am to 1pm. Admission is 3,000L ($1.50).

SHOPPING

The coast has long been known for its **ceramics,** and the area at **Piazza del Duomo** is filled with hawkers peddling "regional" ware (which often means Asian). But the real thing is still made at nearby **Vietri sul Mare,** 8 miles (13km) west of Amalfi. The pottery made in Vietri is distinguished by its florid colors and sunny motifs. Vietri's best outlet is **Ceramica Solimene,** Via Madonna degli Angeli 7 (☎ **089-210-243**), which has been producing quality terra-cotta ceramics for centuries. It's fabled for its production of lead-free surface tiles, dinner and cookware, umbrella holders, and stylish lamps. You might also check out **La Taverna Paradiso,** Via Diego Taiani 1 (☎ **089-212-509**).

In Amalfi itself, look for **Limoncello,** a sweet lemon liqueur that tastes best chilled. It's manufactured in town by the **Luigi Aceto** factories. You can drop by their headquarters on Salita Chiarito 9 to buy a bottle or two (call ☎ **089-873-288** or 089-873-211 for information). The Aceto Group's product is marketed under the

The Eerie Emerald Grotto

Three miles (5km) west of Amalfi is the millennia-old ✪ **Emerald Grotto (Grotta di Smeraldo).** This cavern, known for its light effects, is a chamber of stalactites and stalagmites, some even underwater. You can visit daily 9am to 4pm, provided the seas are calm enough not to bash boats to pieces as they try to land. The SITA bus (traveling toward Amalfi) departs from Piazza Flavio Gioia at 30-minute intervals throughout the day. En route to Sorrento, it stops at the Emerald Grotto. From the coastal road, you descend via an elevator and then take a boat ride traversing this eerie world (5,000L/$2.50). For more information about SITA buses, call ☎ **089-871-009.** However, the best way to go is by boat all the way from Amalfi's docks; it costs 10,000L ($5) round-trip, plus the 5,000L ($2.50) entry fee.

Limoncello Cata label and sold at many outlets around town. A bottle of limoncello costs about 15,000L ($7.50). At **Antichi Sapori d'Amalfi,** Piazza Duomo 39 (☎ **089-872-062**), you get not only limoncello but a full array of local products, like jams, honeys, lemon perfumes, and grappa.

Looking for fancy paper and stationery? You can visit the showroom at **Antonio Cavaliere,** Via Fiume (☎ **089-871-954**). It sells traditional cream-colored, high-fiber paper that seems appropriate for invitations to a royal wedding, as well as versions that amalgamate dried flowers, faintly visible through the surface, into the manufacturing process. The artisan here makes paper completely by hand, using antique methods.

One of Amalfi's best retail outlets is **Criscuolo,** Largo Scario 2 (☎ **089-871-089**). Established by the ancestors of the present owners in 1935 as a site selling only cigarettes and newspapers, it has expanded to specialize in jewelry, including a charming collection of cameos, locally crafted ceramics, and general souvenirs.

At **La Grotta di Mansaniello,** Piazzetta degli Arsenale della Antica Repubblica (☎ **089-871-929**), owner Francesco Mangieri (call him Mao), makes exquisite sculptures from ancient pieces of marble or a stalactite or stalagmite from one of the nearby sea grottoes.

ACCOMMODATIONS

VERY EXPENSIVE

✪ **Hotel Santa Caterina.** Via Nazaionale 9, 84011 Amalfi. ☎ **089-871-012.** Fax 089-871-351. www.starnet.it/santacaterina. E-mail: info@hotelsantacaterina.it. 65 units. A/C MINIBAR TV TEL. 400,000–720,000L ($200–$360) double; 800,000–1,300,000L ($400–$650) suite. Rates include breakfast. Half-board 85,000L ($42.50) per person. AE, DC, MC, V. Parking 30,000L ($15) in garage, free outside.

Perched atop a cliff, Santa Caterina has an elevator that'll take you down to a private beach. Built in 1880, the structure was destroyed by a rockslide on Christmas Eve 1902, prompting a rebuilding on a "safer" site in 1904, though the look today is more from the 1930s. You're housed in the main structure or in one of the small "villas" in the citrus groves. The guest rooms are furnished in good taste, with an eye toward comfort as evidenced by the quality mattresses. Most have private balconies facing the sea (the higher the floor, the better the view along the coast). The furniture respects the tradition of the house, and in every room is an antique piece. The bathrooms are spacious, with luxurious fittings and hair dryers.

Dining/Diversions: The food here is among the best at Amalfi. Many of the vegetables are grown in the hotel's garden, and the fish tastes so fresh we suspect the chef has an agreement with local fishers to bring in the "catch of the day." Once or twice a week there's a special evening buffet accompanied by music.

Amenities: Saltwater pool, room service, baby-sitting, laundry/valet.

EXPENSIVE

Hotel Belvedere. Via Smeraldo, Conca dei Marini, 84011 Amalfi. ☎ **089-831-282.** Fax 089-831-439. www.belvederehotel.it. E-mail: belvedere@belvederehotel.it. 36 units. A/C TV TEL. 320,000–400,000L ($160–$200) double; 400,000–540,000L ($200–$270) suite. Rates include breakfast. AE, DC, MC, V. Closed Oct 20–Apr 20. Free parking.

Lodged below the coastal road outside Amalfi on the drive to Positano, the aptly named Belvedere has one of the best pools in the area. The house originated as a private villa in the 1860s and was transformed by its present owners into a hotel in 1962. The guest rooms have terraces overlooking the water, and some offer air-conditioning. Coming in various shapes, they range from small to medium, each with a firm mattress and a tiled bathroom. Signor Lucibello, who owns the hotel, sees to it that guests are happy, and there's a shuttle bus into Amalfi. You can dine on well-prepared Italian meals either inside (where walls of windows allow for views of the coast) or on the terrace. There's also a cocktail bar.

Hotel Luna Convento. Via Pantaleone Comite 33, 84011 Amalfi. ☎ **089-871-002.** Fax 089-871-333. www.amalficoast.it/hotel/luna. E-mail: luna@amalficoast.it. 45 units. TV TEL. 300,000L ($150) double with breakfast. Rates with half-board (breakfast and dinner) required June–Sept 250,000L ($125) per person. AE, DC, MC, V. Valet parking 25,000L ($12.50) in garage, free outside.

This hotel (the best in Amalfi except for the Santa Caterina, above) boasts a 13th-century cloister said to have been founded by St. Francis of Assisi. Most of the building, however, was rebuilt in 1975. The long corridors, where monks of old (and eventually Wagner and Ibsen) used to tread, are lined with sitting areas used by the very unmonastic guests seeking a tan. The guest rooms have sea views, terraces, and modern furnishings, though many are uninspired in decor. The well-maintained bathrooms have hair dryers.

Dining/Diversions: The rather formal dining room has a coved ceiling, high-backed chairs, arched windows opening toward the water, and good food (Italian and international). The hotel has a nightclub that projects toward the sea, and in summer, dancing is offered in the piano bar.

Amenities: Free-form pool, concierge, room service, laundry/dry cleaning, newspaper delivery, in-room massage, baby-sitting.

MODERATE

Excelsior Grand Hotel. Via Pogerola, 84011 Amalfi. ☎ **089-830-015.** Fax 089-830-255. www.venere.it/amalfi/excelsior. 97 units. TV TEL. 220,000–310,000L ($110–$155) double. Rates include breakfast. AE, DC, MC, V. Free parking.

Two miles (3km) north of Amalfi at Pogerola, the Excelsior is a modern first-class hotel on a high mountain perch. Its structure is unconventional: an octagonal glass tower rising above the central lobby, with exposed mezzanine lounges and an open stairs. All its guest rooms are angled toward the view so you get the first glimmer of dawn and the last rays of sunset. They're individually designed, with lots of space and good reproductions, some antiques, king-size beds with firm mattresses, and tile floors. The private balconies, complete with garden furniture, are the most important feature. The social center is the terrazzo-edged pool with filtered mountain spring water. The dignified dining room serves Italian cuisine with French touches, and at the Bar del Night, musicians play for dancing on weekends. Transportation to/from the private beach is provided by boat and bus for 15,000L ($7.50).

Hotel Marina Riviera. Via Comite 19, 84011 Amalfi. ☎ **089-872-394.** Fax 089-871-024. 29 units. A/C MINIBAR TV TEL. 280,000–340,000L ($140–$170) double. Rates include breakfast. AE, MC, V. Closed Oct 31–Mar. Parking 30,000L ($15).

Just 50 yards from the beach, this hotel offers guest rooms with terraces overlooking the sea. Directly on the coastal road, it rises against the foot of the hills, with side verandas and balconies. Two adjoining public lounges are traditionally furnished, and a small bar provides drinks whenever you want them. The newly refurbished guest rooms are comfortable, with firm mattresses and balconies and bathrooms with hair dryers. There's a gracious dining room, but we suggest you dine alfresco. A restaurant called Eolo is right below the hotel and under the same management.

Hotel Miramalfi. Via Quasimodo 3, 84011 Amalfi. ☎ **089-871-588.** Fax 089-871-287. www.miramalfi.it. E-mail: miramalfi@amalficoast.it. 49 units. A/C MINIBAR TV TEL. 230,000–330,000L ($115–$165) double; 330,000–430,000L ($165–$215) suite. Rates include breakfast. Half-board 160,000–210,000L ($80–$105) extra per person. AE, DC, MC, V. Parking 20,000L ($10).

On the western edge of Amalfi, the Miramalfi lies below the coastal road on its own beach. The guest rooms are wrapped around the curving contour of the coast and have unobstructed sea views. The stone swimming pier (used for sunbathing, diving, and boarding motorboats for waterskiing) is down a winding cliff-side path, past terraces of grapevines. The dining room has glass windows and some semitropical plants; the food is good and served in abundant portions. Breakfast is served on one of the main terraces or your own balcony. Each room is well equipped, with built-in headboards, firm mattresses, cool tile floors, and tiled bathrooms. There's a pool and an elevator to the private beach.

INEXPENSIVE

✪ **Hotel Lidomare.** Largo Duchi Piccolomini 9, 84011 Amalfi. ☎ **089-871-332.** Fax 089-871-394. www.amalficoast.it/hotel/lidomare. E-mail: lidomare@amalficoast.it. 15 units. A/C MINIBAR TV TEL. 130,000–160,000L ($65–$80) double. Rates include breakfast. AE, MC, V. Parking 25,000L ($12.50).

One of the best bargains in Amalfi, this pleasant small hotel is a few steps from the sea in a 13th-century building. The high-ceilinged guest rooms are airy and contain a scattering of modern furniture mixed with Victorian-era antiques; most are air-conditioned. The small tiled bathrooms are neat and cozy. The Camera family extends a warm welcome to their never-ending stream of foreign visitors. Breakfast is the only meal served, but you can order it until 11:30am.

DINING

Instead of ordering dessert at one of the restaurants below, walk over to **Porto Salvo Gelateria** (☎ **089-871-655**), which has the best-tasting gelato along the coast. The wild strawberry *(fragola selvatica)* and candied almond *(mandorle candite)* flavors are to die for.

MODERATE

✪ **Da Gemma.** Via Frà Gerardo Sassi 9. ☎ **089-871-345.** Reservations required. Main courses 22,000–50,000L ($11–$25). AE, DC, MC, V. Thurs–Tues 12:45–2pm and 7:45–10:30pm. Closed Jan. SEAFOOD/MEDITERRANEAN.

Occupying a stone-sided building constructed in 1872 near the cathedral, Da Gemma is one of Amalfi's best restaurants, with a strong emphasis on fresh seafood. It has been directed by members of the Grimaldi family for many generations, a fact that caused a lot of fuss when Princess Caroline of Monaco (whose family name is also Grimaldi, but with a link that's very distant) came to dine. The kitchen sends out platefuls of savory spaghetti, grilled or sautéed fish, casseroles, and an enduring favorite—*zuppa di pesce* (fish soup), a full meal in its own right and prepared only for two. For dessert, order the *crostata* (pie with jam), the best you're ever likely to have; it's made with pine nuts and homemade marmalades of lemon, orange, and tangerine. In summer, the size of the intimate dining room more than doubles because of its expansion onto a terrace.

La Caravella–Amalfi. Via Matteo Camera 12. ☎ **089-871-029.** Reservations required. Main courses 18,000–45,000L ($9–$22.50). AE, DC, MC, V. Daily 12:30–3pm and 7:30–11pm. Closed Nov and Tues in Sept–July. CAMPANIA.

The stone building containing this restaurant was a boatyard and marine warehouse during the 1400s. Today, it's one of the most prominent restaurants in town, with a menu featuring authentic Italian specialties. Examples are spaghetti Caravella with seafood sauce and fresh fish with lemon. An even better option is *scialatielli* (wide noodles) with a ragout of shellfish. Grilled fish is also baked in a salt crust to keep the full flavor inside. *Scaloppini alla Caravella* (veal) is served with a tangy clam sauce, and a healthy portion of *zuppa di pesce* (fish soup) is also ladled out. You can have a platter of the mixed fish fry, with crisp bits of shrimp and squid, followed by a lemon soufflé.

Ristorante Luna Convento. In the Hotel Luna Convento, Via Panteleone Comite 33. ☎ **089-871-002.** Reservations recommended. Main courses 26,000–32,000L ($13–$16). AE, DC, MC, V. Daily noon–2pm and 7:30–9pm. ITALIAN.

If you're unable to reserve a table at dinner, try for lunch at this stylish place; there's likely to be less of a crowd and the sunny view over the town and the sea will be clearer. The restaurant is half indoor/half outdoor and staffed by consummate professionals. The menu items are usually based on seafood and include fresh seafood salad, seafood pastas, baked slices of sea bass or monkfish with herbs and garlic, and *risotto alla pescatore* (fisherman's rice); other choices are chicken, veal, beef, and pork. The antipasti are particularly tantalizing.

If you can't get a reservation even for lunch, perhaps try the restaurant's sibling, the **Ristorante Torre Saracena,** a very short walk away; any staff member will contact it for you. The prices, menu, and hours there are more or less the same as here.

9 Ravello

171 miles (275km) SE of Rome, 41 miles (66km) SE of Naples, 18 miles (29km) W of Salerno

✪ **Ravello** is one of the loveliest resorts along the Amalfi Drive. It's attracted artists, writers, and celebrities for years (Richard Wagner, Greta Garbo, André Gide, and even D. H. Lawrence, who wrote *Lady Chatterley's Lover* here). Ravello's reigning celebrity at the moment is Gore Vidal, who purchased a villa here as a writing retreat. William Styron set his novel *Set This House on Fire* here. Boccaccio dedicated part of the *Decameron* to Ravello, and John Huston used it as a location for his film *Beat the Devil,* with Bogie.

The sleepy village seems to hang 1,100 feet up, between the Tyrrhenian Sea and some celestial orbit. You approach from Amalfi, 4 miles (6km) southwest, by a wickedly curving road cutting through the villa- and vine-draped hills that hem in the Valley of the Dragone.

ESSENTIALS

GETTING THERE **Buses** from Amalfi leave for Ravello from the terminal at the waterfront at Piazza Flavio Gioia (☎ **089-871-016** for schedules and information) almost every hour 7am to 10pm, costing 2,000L ($1) one way.

If you have a **car** and are in Amalfi, take a circuitous mountain road north of the town (the road is signposted to Ravello).

VISITOR INFORMATION The **tourist office** is at Piazza del Duomo 10 (☎ **089-857-096**), open May to September, Monday to Saturday 8am to 8pm (to 7pm October to April).

SPECIAL EVENTS The hilltop town is known for its summer **classical music festivals.** Internationally famed artists sometimes appear. The venues range from the Duomo to the gardens of Villa Rufolo. Tickets, which you can buy at the tourist office, start at 40,000L ($20).

SEEING THE SIGHTS

Although most of your time will be spent sunbathing, relaxing, strolling, and taking in the view, Ravello has a few outstanding sightseeing attractions, too.

✪ **Villa Cimbrone.** Via Santa Chiara 26. ☎ **089-857-459.** Admission 8,000L ($4). Daily 9am–7pm.

One of Ravello's most aristocratic-looking palaces is the Villa Cimbrone. A 10-minute walk uphill from the main square, it's accessible only via a signposted footpath punctuated with steps and stairs.

Built in the 15th century, it was occupied by a wealthy and eccentric Englishman, Lord Grimthorpe, who renovated it to its present status. During his tenure, he entertained such luminaries as Edvard Grieg, Henrik Ibsen, D. H. Lawrence, Virginia Woolf, Graham Greene, Greta Garbo and her then-lover Leopold Stokowski, and Tennessee Williams. Lord Grimthorpe died in London in 1917, but his heirs followed his orders and buried his remains near his replica of the Temple of Bacchus.

When you reach the villa's entrance, ring the bell to summon the attendant. You'll be shown vaulted cloisters, evocative architecture, ruined chapels, and panoramic views over the Bay of Salerno. The view from some of the platforms in the garden is simply stunning. Gore Vidal, a nearby resident, referred to the view as "the most beautiful in the world."

You can also stay at the villa, since it's now a hotel (see "Accommodations," below).

Villa Rufolo. Piazza Vescovado. ☎ **089-857-657.** Admission 5,000L ($2.50). Oct–Mar daily 9am–6pm; Apr–Sept daily 9am–8pm.

The Villa Rufolo was named for the patrician family who founded it in the 11th century. Once the residence of kings and popes, such as Hadrian IV, it's now remembered chiefly for its connection with Richard Wagner. He composed an act of *Parsifal* here in a setting he dubbed the "Garden of Klingsor." He also lived and composed at Palazzo Sasso (see "Accommodations," below). Boccaccio was so moved by the spot he included it as background in one of his tales. The Moorish-influenced architecture evokes Granada's Alhambra, and the large tower was built in what's known as the "Norman-Sicilian" style. You can walk through the flower gardens leading to lookout points over the memorable coastline.

Duomo & Campanile. Piazza Vescovado. Duomo free; museum 3,000L ($1.50). Duomo daily 8am–7pm. Museum Easter–Oct daily 9am–1pm and 3–7pm.

It's unusual for such a small place to have a cathedral, but Ravello boasts one because it was once a major bishopric. The building itself dates from the 11th century, but its bronze doors are the work of Barisano da Trani, crafted in 1179. Its **campanile** (bell tower) was erected in the 13th century. One of its major treasures is the pulpit of the Rufolo family, decorated with intricate mosaics and supported by spiral columns resting on the backs of half a dozen white marble lions. This is the work of Nicoló di Bartolomeo da Foggia in 1272. Another, less intricate, pulpit from 1130 features two large mosaics of Jonah being eaten and regurgitated by a dragonlike green whale. To the left of the altar is the **Chapel of San Pantaleone (Cappella di San Pantaleone),** the patron saint of Ravello to whom the cathedral is dedicated. His "unleakable" blood is preserved in a cracked vessel. The saint was beheaded at Nicomedia on July 27, A.D. 290. When Ravello holds a festival on that day every year, the saint's blood is said to liquefy. A minor museum of religious artifacts is also on site.

SHOPPING

When Hillary Rodham Clinton came to visit and to call on Gore Vidal, she also visited **Camo,** Piazza Duomo 9 (☎ **089-857-461**), where owner Giorgio Filocamo designed a coral brooch for her. He can make one for you, too, or sell you any number of pieces of jewelry in cameos and corals. In the back of the shop he has collected his most treasured pieces, all worthy of a museum.

Brothers Marco and Piero Cantarella are waiting for you at **Ceramu,** Via Roma 66 (☎ **089-858-181**), where they'll sell you intricate mosaics in majolica. They also make garden tables with wrought iron or mosaic-bordered mirrors with wood.

ACCOMMODATIONS

The choice of accommodations at Ravello is limited in number but large on charm. The **Ristorante Garden** (see "Dining," below) also rents rooms.

VERY EXPENSIVE

✪ **Hotel Palumbo/Palumbo Residence.** Via San Giovanni del Toro 16, 84010 Ravello. ☎ **089-857-244.** Fax 089-858-133. www.hotel-palumbo.it. E-mail: palumbo@hotel-palumbo.it. 19 units. A/C MINIBAR TV TEL. Hotel 875,000–975,000L ($437.50–$487.50) double; from 1,180,000L ($590) suite. Residence 590,000–650,000L ($295–$325) double. Rates include half-board. AE, DC, MC, V. Parking 30,000L ($15).

This 12th-century palace has been favored by the famous since composer Richard Wagner persuaded the Swiss owners, the Vuilleumiers, to take in paying guests. If you stay, you'll understand why Humphrey Bogart, Ingrid Bergman, Zsa Zsa Gabor, Tennessee Williams, Richard Chamberlain, and a young John and Jacqueline Kennedy found it ideal. D. H. Lawrence even wrote part of *Lady Chatterley's Lover* while staying here.

The hotel offers gracious living in its drawing rooms full of English and Italian antiques. Most of the snug but elegant guest rooms have their own terraces. The original Hotel Palumbo contains by far the more glamorous accommodations; seven functional rooms are in the annex in the garden, but a few have sea views. The bathrooms are often a delight, with gigantic tubs, dual basins, and hair dryers.

Dining: Meals are served in a 17th-century dining room with baroque accents and a panoramic terrace. The cuisine, the finest in Ravello, shows the influence of the Swiss-Italian ownership. It's worth visiting just for the lemon and chocolate soufflés. The Palumbo also produces its own Episcopio wine, stored in 50,000 casks in a vaulted cellar.

Amenities: Room service, baby-sitting, laundry/valet, solarium overlooking the Gulf of Salerno.

✪ **Palazzo Sasso.** Via San Giovanni del Toro 28, 84010 Ravello. ☎ **089-818-181.** Fax 089-858-900. www.palazzosasso.com. E-mail: info@palazzosasso.com. 43 units. A/C MINIBAR TV TEL. 500,000–800,000L ($250–$400) double; from 1,100,000L ($550) suite. Rates include continental breakfast. AE, DC, MC, V. Free parking.

Built in the 1100s for an aristocratic family, this palace began functioning as a hotel in 1880. Richard Wagner composed parts of *Parsifal* here, and Ingrid Bergman found a snug retreat here with producer Roberto Rossellini back in the days when their affair was causing a scandal. The hotel fell into ruin in 1978, but in 1997 it reopened thanks to a flood of money from new owners (Virgin Airlines Holding Co. and Richard Branson), and it welcomed Plácido Domingo as its first guest. The Sasso is perched 1,000 feet above the coast and evokes a Moorish pavilion. The guest rooms are luxurious, even if not overly large, and the views of the Mediterranean compensate for the lack of space. Ask for room no. 1, 201, 204, or 301 or the grand suite, 304, because they have the most all-encompassing views. The marble bathrooms with brass fixtures come with scales, robes, dual basins, and hair dryers.

Dining: The Rossellini Restaurant (named after Roberto, Ingrid, and Isabella) serves savory Mediterranean cuisine in a chic setting. Expect to spend about 120,000L

($60) per person, without drinks. Antonio Genovese, who honed his culinary skills in London, presides over the dining room and is proud that his cuisine matches the panorama from the terrace, which seats 100. A well-recommended specialty is the platter of prawns, bell peppers, tomatoes, and vegetable mousse.

Amenities: Concierge, room service, baby-sitting, laundry/dry cleaning, twice-daily maid service, jogging track, in-room massage, valet parking, sundeck, hydromassage.

Villa Cimbrone. Via Santa Chiara 26, 84010 Ravello. ☎ **089-857-459.** Fax 089-857-777. www.villacimbrone.it/. E-mail: villacimbrone@amalfinet.it. 20 units. MINIBAR TEL. 380,000–480,000L ($190–$240) double; 600,000L ($300) suite. Rates include breakfast. AE, DC, MC, V. Closed Dec–Mar. From the main square of Ravello, walk uphill along a well-marked footpath for an arduous 10 min.

Here you'll find no restaurant and none of the amenities offered by more modern hotels. In fact, you can't even drive up to its entrance, since there's no road. But despite the inconvenience, few connoisseurs of art and literature would pass up the chance to stay in one of the most historically evocative villas in Ravello (see above). Amid gardens dotted with statuary, ancient ruins, and late-19th-century re-creations of Greek and Roman temples, it contains only a handful of rooms—high-ceilinged and gracefully furnished with antiques and fine fabrics, plus quality mattresses. Most rooms enjoy views over the countryside. The best choices are nos. 10 and 11. The Garbo Suite is the most requested (the mysterious Swede had a tryst here in 1938 with her then-lover Leopold Stokowski before dumping him for others). More recently, Hillary Rodham Clinton slept here. If you arrive by car, park it in the municipal parking lot, a short walk downhill from Ravello's main square and then call the hotel for a porter who, with a rolling cart, will haul your luggage up the winding paths to the villa. Breakfast is the only meal served.

EXPENSIVE

Hotel Caruso Belvedere. Via San Giovanni del Toro 2, 84010 Ravello. ☎ **089-857-111.** Fax 089-857-372. 24 units. TEL. June–Sept and Christmas 350,000–500,000L ($175–$250) double; Jan–May and Oct–Dec 22 280,000–440,000L ($140–$220) double. Rates include half-board (breakfast and dinner). AE, DC, MC, V. Parking 25,000L ($12.50) in garage, free outside.

This spacious cliff-top hotel, built into the remains of an 11th-century palace, is operated by the Caruso family, descended from the great Enrico himself. Some of the most famous people of the 20th century, including Greta Garbo, have stayed here. This property has semitropical gardens and a belvedere that overlooks terraced rows of grapes, used to make the hotel's "Grand Caruso" wine, to the Bay of Salerno. Although antiques appear here and there, many rooms are rather plain, about on the same level as some of the town's economy-minded inns. The best ones have sunrooms for breakfast and open onto terraces. The beds, mainly twins, are comfortable (with good mattresses), and the small tiled bathrooms, usually pink, come with robes and hair dryers.

Dining: The dining room retains its original coved ceiling, plus tile floors. It opens onto a wide terrace where meals are served under a canopy. Naturally, the locally produced wines are touted.

Amenities: Room service, baby-sitting, laundry/valet.

Hotel Rufolo. Via San Francesco 3, 84010 Ravello. ☎ **089-857-133.** Fax 089-857-935. www.hotel-rufolo.it. E-mail: rufolo@amalficoast.it. 32 units. A/C MINIBAR TV TEL. 350,000–400,000L ($175–$200) double; 500,000–700,000L ($250–$350) suite. Rates include breakfast. AE, DC, MC, V. Parking 15,000L ($7.50).

This little gem housed D. H. Lawrence for a long while in 1926. The view from the sun decks is superb, and chairs are placed on a wide terrace and around the pool. Some guest rooms are spacious and others cramped; some have air-conditioning; and the suites have Jacuzzis. The tiled bathrooms are compact. Recently enlarged and modernized, the hotel lies in the center between cloisters of pine trees of the Villa Rufolo, from which the hotel takes its name, and the road leading to the Villa Cimbrone. Mr. Schiavo and his family take good care of their guests. The service is efficient.

Dining/Diversions: The hotel's formal restaurant serves a superb cuisine, with an emphasis on fresh fish. Even if you're not a guest, consider dropping in for dinner. There is also a bar.

Amenities: Concierge, baby-sitting, laundry, room service.

MODERATE

Hotel Giordano e Villa Maria. Via Trinità 14, Via Santa Chiara 2, 84010 Ravello. ☎ **089-857-255.** Fax 089-857-071. www.villamaria.it. E-mail: villamaria@villamaria.it. 48 units. A/C TV TEL. Hotel Giordano 220,000–250,000L ($110–$125) double with breakfast; 300,000–350,000L ($150–$175) double with half-board (compulsory May–Sept). Villa Maria 270,000–340,000L ($135–$170) double with breakfast; 340,000–420,000L ($170–$210) double with half-board (compulsory May–Sept); 640,000–720,000L ($320–$360) suite with breakfast. AE, DC, MC, V. Free parking.

The older, but more obviously modernized, of these two hotels is the Giordano, built in the late 1700s as a private manor house of the family who runs it today. In the 1970s, the owners bought the neighboring 19th-century Villa Maria, and the two operate as quasi-independent hotels with shared facilities. Accommodations in the Villa Maria are more plush than those in the Giordano and usually contain high ceilings and antiques and offer sea views. The Giordano's rooms have garden views and reproductions of traditional furniture. You'll find a large heated pool near the Giordano, two bars, and two restaurants. (Unlike its twin, the Villa Maria's restaurant remains open throughout the winter and has a panoramic view.) The beach is a 15-minute walk along ancient paths (you can also take a public bus from Ravello's central square every hour).

INEXPENSIVE

Albergo Toro. Viale Wagner 3, 84010 Ravello. ☎ and fax **089-857-211.** 9 units. TEL. 185,000L ($92.50) double with breakfast. Half-board 130,000L ($65) extra. DC, MC, V. Closed Nov 6–Mar.

Just off the village square with its cathedral, this real bargain is a charming small villa that has been converted into a hotel. You enter the Toro through a garden. It has semi-monastic architecture, boasting deeply set arches, long colonnades, and a tranquil character. The guest rooms are a bit plain but still offer reasonable comfort. The owner is especially proud of the Mediterranean meals he serves.

Hotel Parsifal. Via G. D'Anna 5, 84010 Ravello. ☎ **089-857-144.** Fax 089-857-972. www.italyone.com/hparsifal. E-mail: hparsifal@tin.it. 19 units. TV TEL. 160,000–210,000L ($80–$105) double with breakfast; 230,000–300,000L ($115–$150) double with half-board. AE, DC, MC, V. Free parking.

This little hotel incorporates part of a convent founded in 1288 by Augustinian monks. The cloister, with stone arches and a tile walk, has a multitude of potted flowers and vines, and the garden spots, especially the one with a circular reflection pool, are the favorites. There are chairs placed for watching the setting sun. Dining is on the terrace, where bougainvillea and wisteria scents mix with that of lemon blossoms. The living rooms have bright and comfortable furnishings, set against pure white walls. The guest rooms, though small, are tasteful, with firm mattresses; a few have terraces.

DINING

Most guests take meals at their hotels. But try to escape the board requirement at least once to sample the goods at the following places.

Cumpa' Cosimo. Via Roma 44–46. ☎ **089-857-156.** Reservations recommended. Main courses 18,000–45,000L ($9–$22.50); fixed-price menu 45,000L ($22.50). AE, DC, MC, V. Daily noon–3pm and 6:30–10pm. CAMPANIA.

You're likely to find here everyone from the electrician down the street to a movie star looking for the best home-cooking in town. Pictures of Jackie O, as she was then known, still decorate the walls, a reminder of a long-ago visit. Gore Vidal, who often dines here, recommends it to his visiting guests. It was opened in 1929 by a patriarch known affectionately as Cumpa' (godfather) Cosimo and his wife, Cumma' (godmother) Chiara. Today their daughter, Netta Bottone, runs the place, turning out well-flavored regional food in generous portions. Menu items include homemade versions of seven pastas, served with your choice of seven sauces. Any of these might be followed by a mixed grill of fish, giant prawns, roasted lamb seasoned with herbs, *zuppe di pesce* (fish soup), *frittura di pesce* (fish fry), veal scaloppini, or beefsteak with garlic and wine sauce. The seasonal availability of vegetables is respected in the restaurant's offerings of artichokes, asparagus, or mushrooms. Certain fish dishes are priced according to weight based on daily market quotations.

Ristorante Garden. Via Boccacio 4, 84010 Ravello. ☎ **089-857-226.** Main courses 18,000–28,000L ($9–$14). AE, DC, MC, V. Apr–Sept daily noon–3pm and 7:30–10pm; Nov–Mar Wed–Mon noon–3pm and 7:30–10pm. CAMPANIA.

This pleasant restaurant's greatest claim to fame was in 1962, when Jacqueline Kennedy came from a villa where she was staying to dine here with the owner of Fiat. Today some of that old glamour is still visible on the verdant terrace, which was designed to cantilever over the cliff below. The Mansi family offers well-prepared meals that might include one of four kinds of spaghetti, cheese crepes, an array of soups, a well-presented antipasto table, brochettes of grilled shrimp, a mixed fish fry, and sole prepared in several ways. One of the local wines will be recommended.

The restaurant also rents 10 well-scrubbed doubles, each with its own phone, bathroom, and terrace with a view, for 120,000 to 150,000L ($60 to $75), including breakfast.

10 Paestum & Its Glorious Greek Temples

25 miles (40km) S of Salerno, 62 miles (100km) SE of Naples, 189 miles (304km) SE of Rome

The ancient city of ✪ **Paestum (Poseidonia)** dates from 600 B.C, founded by colonists from the Greek city of Sybaris, which was located in today's Calabria (the "toe" of Italy's boot). It was abandoned for centuries and fell to ruins. But the remnants of its past, excavated in the mid–18th century, are the finest heritage left from the Greek colonies that settled in Italy. The roses of Paestum, praised by the ancients, bloom two times yearly, splashing the landscape of the city with scarlet, a good foil for the salmon-colored temples that still stand in the archaeological garden.

ESSENTIALS

GETTING THERE Paestum is within easy reach of Salerno, an hour away. Wherever you are in the area, you must go to Salerno to get to Paestum via public transportation. You can catch a southbound **train,** which departs Salerno with a stop at Paestum about every 2 hours. For schedules, call ☎ **1478-880-88** toll-free in Italy.

A one-way fare is 4,700L ($2.35), and the journey takes an hour. The **bus** from Salerno leaves from Piazza Concordia (near the rail station) about every 30 minutes. Call ☎ **089-226-604** for information. A one-way fare is 4,700L ($2.35).

If you have a **car,** from Salerno take S18 south.

VISITOR INFORMATION The **tourist office** is at Via Magna Grecia 151–156 (☎ **0828-811-016**), in the archaeological zone, open Monday to Saturday 8am to 2pm.

EXPLORING THE TEMPLES

The ✪ **basilica** is a Doric temple from the 6th century B.C., Italy's oldest temple from the ruins of the Hellenic world. The basilica is characterized by nine Doric pillars in front and 18 on the sides (they're about 5 feet in diameter). The walls and ceiling long ago gave way to decay. Animals were sacrificed to the gods on the altar.

The ✪ **Temple of Neptune (Tempio di Nettuno)** is the most impressive of the Greek ruins at Paestum. It and the Temple of Haphaistos ("Theseum") in Athens remain the best-preserved Greek temples in the world, both from around 450 to 420 B.C. Six columns in front are crowned by an entablature, and there are 14 columns on each side. The **Temple of Ceres (Tempio di Cerere),** from the 6th century B.C., has 34 columns still standing and a large altar for sacrifices to the gods.

The temple zone is open daily 9am to sunset.

You can visit the **National Archaeological Museum of Paestum (Museo Archeologico Nazionale di Paestum),** Via Magna Grecia 169 (☎ **0828-811-023**), across from the Ceres Temple. It displays the metopes removed from the treasury of the Temple of Hera (Juno) and some of southern Italy's finest tomb paintings from the 4th century B.C. The Diver's Tomb is an extraordinary example of painting from the first half of the 5th century B.C. The museum is open daily 9am to 6:30pm (closed the first and third Monday of every month). Admission is 8,000L ($4), but there is also a cumulative ticket which includes the museum and the archaeological area costing 12,000L ($6).

New discoveries have revealed hundreds of Greek tombs, which have yielded many Greek paintings. Archaeologists have called the finds astonishing. In addition, other excavated tombs were found to contain clay figures in a strongly impressionistic vein.

ACCOMMODATIONS

Strand Hotel Schuhmann. Via Marittima, 84063 Paestum. ☎ **0828-851-151.** Fax 0828-851-183. www.hotelschuhmann.com. E-mail: schuhmann@paestum.it. 53 units. A/C MINIBAR TV TEL. 110,000–170,000L ($55–$85) double, with half-board. AE, DC, MC, V. Free parking.

If you'd like to stay awhile for a serious look at Italy's archaeological past and enjoy the first-class amenities of a beachside resort while you do, try the Strand. Set in a pine grove removed from traffic noises, it has a large terrace with a view of the sea and a subtropical garden that overlooks the Gulf of Salerno and the Amalfi Coast to Capri. Its guest rooms are well furnished and maintained, each with a balcony or terrace and a firm mattress. Guests get use of the beach facilities and deck chairs. The hotel restaurant serves a savory Mediterranean cuisine.

DINING

Nettuno Ristorante. Via Principe di Piemonte, Zona Archeologica. ☎ **0828-811-028.** Reservations recommended. Main courses 18,000–40,000L ($9–$20). AE, DC, MC, V. July–Aug daily noon–3:30pm and 7:30–10pm; Sept–June daily noon–3:30pm. CAMPANESE/SEAFOOD.

Nettuno's only drawback is that throughout most of the year it's open only for lunch. At the edge of Paestum's ruins, it's built from the same beige-colored limestone blocks that were used by the ancient Romans. Its core consists of an ancient tower built in the 2nd century B.C. Seated in the dining room or garden ringed with vines, oleander, and pines, you can order *crespolina,* a savory crepe stuffed with mozzarella and Mediterranean herbs; succulent pastas; a wide selection of fish; and veal, chicken, and beef dishes.

Apulia 14

The district of Apulia encompasses the southeasternmost section of Italy, the heel of the boot. It's the country's gateway to the Orient, and for many travelers it's the gateway to Greece from the port of Brindisi. Apulia is little known but fascinating, embracing some of Italy's most poverty-stricken areas and some of its most interesting sections (like the Trulli District).

The land is rich in archaeological discoveries, and some of its cities were shining sapphires in the crown of Magna Graecia (Greater Greece). The Ionian and Adriatic Seas wash up on its shores, which have seen the arrival of diverse civilizations and of the armies seeking to conquer this access route to Rome. The Goths, Germanic hordes, Byzantines, Spanish, and French sought to possess it. Saracen pirates and Turks came to see what riches they might find.

Apulia offers the beauty of marine grottoes and caverns as well as turquoise seas and sandy beaches. Forests of wind-twisted pines, huge old carob trees, junipers, sage, and rosemary grow near the sea; orchards, vineyards, grain fields, and vegetable gardens grow inland. Flocks of sheep and goats dot the landscape.

In recent years, Apulia has been caught in the eye of the "Albanian Hurricane." Political turmoil and economic upheaval have sent tens of thousands of Albanians to commandeer yachts, ferries, and tugboats and cross the narrow Strait of Otranto into this region. This has adversely affected tourism, leading to massive hotel booking cancellations, presumably because of the fear that the deluge of refugees has made the area undesirable.

Regional officials stress there's nothing to worry about and promise that Apulia is now "more of a bargain than ever." The Albanian presence in most tourist zones is barely noticeable, if at all. Actually, most of the refugees are moved elsewhere or housed in camps away from the mainstream sites. The regional tourist commissioner, Rossana Di Bello, assured us, "Visitors can visit our land and find peace and tranquillity."

1 Foggia: A Base for Exploring the Gargano

60 miles (97km) W of Bari, 108 miles (174km) NE of Naples, 225 miles (362km) SE of Rome

Foggia is the capital of Capitanata, Apulia's northernmost province. A history of tragedy, including a serious earthquake in 1731 and extensive bombing during World War II, has left Foggia with little in the way of attractions, though it's a good base for exploring nearby attractions like Lucera and Troia. You can also use the city as a base for a day's drive around the Gargano Peninsula. A 12th-century cathedral remains; the rest of the city is pleasant but thoroughly modern, with parks and wide boulevards and a decent selection of hotels and restaurants. This is a good place to take care of business—rent a car, exchange money, mail postcards, or whatever, because it's relatively safe, easy to get around, and centrally located.

ESSENTIALS

GETTING THERE Foggia is at the crossroads of the Lecce–Bologne **rail** line and the Bari–Naples run, so it's easy to get here from just about anywhere in Italy. Trains from Naples arrive four times daily; the trip lasts about 3 hours and costs 16,000L ($8) one way. Trains arrive from Bari every hour during the day, taking 1½ hours and costing 10,500L ($5.25) one way. There are also three trains daily from Rome, taking 4 hours and costing 45,000L ($22.50). Trains arrive at Foggia's **Stazione Centrale** in the center of Piazza Vittorio Veneto (☎ **0881-703-111**).

If you have a **car,** follow Rte. 90 from Naples directly to Foggia. From Bari, take A14.

VISITOR INFORMATION The **tourist office** is at Via Senatore Emilio Perrone 17 (☎ **0881-776-864**), open Monday to Friday 8am to 1:30pm and Tuesday also 3:30 to 6:30pm.

GETTING AROUND THE REGION It's much less convenient to travel to Foggia by bus than by train. But once you're here you can ride ATAF and SITA buses to many towns in the area. Tickets and information are provided by the train station (see above). There are hourly buses to Lucera, taking 30 minutes and costing 2,800L ($1.40) each way, and service to Manfredonia on the Gargano Peninsula, taking 45 minutes and costing 4,000L ($2) each way.

SEEING THE SIGHTS

The 12th-century **Cattedrale della Santa Maria Icona Vetere** (☎ **0881-773-482**) lies off Piazza del Lago. The province's largest cathedral, it was constructed in an unusual Norman and Apulian baroque style. Today, after extensive repairs and expansions, the Duomo is an eclectic mix of styles. The present **campanile (bell tower)** was built to replace the one destroyed in the 1731 quake. The crypt was built in the Romanesque style, and some of its "excavation" was compliments of Allied bombers in 1943. The cathedral is open daily 8am to noon and 5 to 8pm; admission is free.

The other notable attraction is the **Civic Museum (Museo Civico),** Piazza Nigri (☎ **0881-726-245**), featuring exhibits on Apulia's archaeology and ethnography. It's housed in the remains of the residence of Frederick II and is open daily 9am to 1pm and also Monday, Tuesday, Thursday and Friday 5 to 7pm. Admission is 2,000L ($1).

ACCOMMODATIONS

Grand Hotel Cicolella. Viale XXIV Maggio 60, 71100 Foggia. ☎ **0881-688-890.** Fax 0881-778-984. 106 units. A/C MINIBAR TV TEL. 280,000L ($140) double; from 300,000L ($150) suite. Breakfast 20,000L ($10). AE, DC, V. Parking 20,000L ($10).

The Cicolella is the town's best hotel. The Victorian-era building has been modernized, with glass and marble dominating. The guest rooms are large and pleasantly decorated, each with a quality mattress and a small tiled bathroom.

Dining: Even if you stay elsewhere, you might opt for a meal in one of the hotel's two well-recommended restaurants, the formal Ristorante Cicolella (inside the hotel)

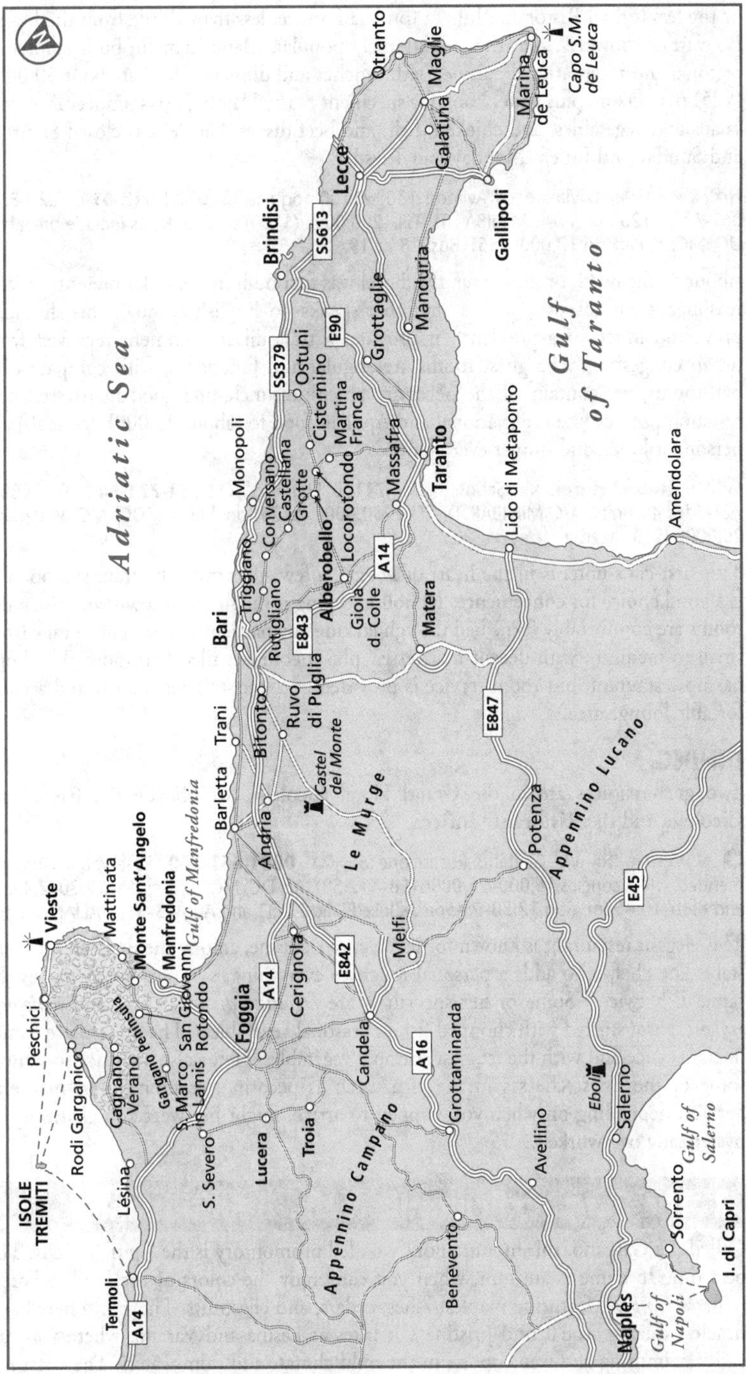
Adriatic Sea
Gulf of Taranto
Gulf of Manfredonia
Gulf of Salerno
Gulf of Napoli
ISOLE TREMITI
Termoli
Lésina
Rodi Garganico
Peschici
Vieste
Mattinata
Monte Sant'Angelo
Manfredonia
San Giovanni Rotondo
Gargano Peninsula
Cagnano Verano
S. Marco in Lamis
S. Severo
Foggia
Lucera
Troia
Barletta
Trani
Andria
Bitonto
Ruvo di Puglia
Castel del Monte
Le Murge
Bari
Rutigliano
Triggiano
Conversano
Monopoli
Castellana Grotte
Alberobello
Locorotondo
Gioia d. Colle
Cisternino
Martina Franca
Ostuni
Brindisi
Grottaglie
Massafra
Taranto
Manduria
Lecce
Gallipoli
Galatina
Maglie
Otranto
Marina de Leuca
Capo S.M. de Leuca
Matera
Lido di Metaponto
Amendolara
Cerignola
Candela
Melfi
Grottaminarda
Potenza
Appennino Lucano
Appennino Campano
Benevento
Avellino
Eboli
Salerno
Sorrento
I. di Capri
Naples
A14
A16
E842
E843
E847
E45
E90
SS379
SS613

or the less formal Ristorante Infiera (on Via Fortore, less than a mile from the hotel). Be warned, however, that they're extremely popular. Menu items in both emphasize regional and international cuisine, with lunches and dinners priced at about 50,000L ($25) per person, plus wine. Look for succulent roasted lamb, pastas, impeccably fresh salads and vegetables, and chicken, fish, and beef dishes. Cicolella is closed Saturday and Sunday and Infiera Monday and Tuesday.

Hotel President. Viale degli Aviatori 130, 71100 Foggia. ☎ **0881-618-010.** Fax 0881-061-7930. 125 units. A/C MINIBAR TV TEL. 200,000L ($100) double. Rates include breakfast. DC, MC, V. Parking 10,000L ($5). Bus: 18 or 19.

About a mile north of the center, this hotel was first built in 1970. Unpretentious and reasonably comfortable, with a staff that speaks no English (though this shouldn't prove too much of a problem), it provides a tranquil environment removed from urban congestion. The guest rooms are angular and functional, with compact tiled bathrooms, yet contain all the necessary amenities, including good mattresses. The restaurant serves fine international and Apulian food for about 45,000L ($22.50) per person, at lunch and dinner every day.

White House Hotel. Via Sabotino 24, 71100 Foggia. ☎ **0881-721-644.** Fax 0881-721-646. 40 units. A/C MINIBAR TV TEL. 250,000L ($125) double. AE, DC, MC, V. Parking 20,000L ($10) nearby.

This first-class hotel is in the heart of Foggia, a few steps from the train station, and is a good choice for convenience. Its housekeeping is the finest in town, and the guest rooms are comfortably furnished though lacking any particular style. They range from small to medium, with decent mattresses, plus a compact tiled bathroom. The hotel has no restaurant, but room service is provided on request. There's a bar and a comfortable lounge area.

DINING

Two great choices are in the Grand Hotel Cicolella (see above): the **Ristorante Cicolella** and the **Ristorante Infiera.**

✪ **Il Ventaglio.** Via Gaetano Postiglione 6E. ☎ **0881-661-500.** Reservations recommended. Main courses 16,000–25,000L ($8–$12.50). AE, DC, MC, V. Tues–Sat 12:30–2:45pm and 8:30–10:45pm; Sun 12:30–2:45pm. Closed Dec 23–31 and Aug 13–31. ITALIAN.

This elegant restaurant is known for its inventive cuisine, among the finest in southern Italy. The chef, who adds a personal touch to everything, says she "never makes the same dish twice." Some of her specialties are *fagottino di pesce* (fish) and *agnolotti ripieni* (pasta stuffed with chopped fish or seasonal vegetables). The orecchiette comes in clam sauce and with the freshest seasonal vegetables. Here's also a chance to sample some of the finest cheeses in the area, such as pecorino, scamorza, and manteca. Service, depending on when you happen to arrive, might be sweet and charming or hysterically overworked.

2 The Gargano Peninsula & the Tremiti Islands

Called the Gargano, this mountainous wooded promontory is the "spur" of Italy. The best time to come is autumn, when you can enjoy the colors of the Umbra Forest (*Foresta Umbra*), featuring maples, ashes, cedars, and chestnuts. The world here has a timeless quality. You'll find pristine salt lakes at Lesina and Varano, where you can enjoy swimming and water sports in the mild climate and calm waters. The coast is a series of cliffs, rocks, caves, islets, and beaches. Vegetable gardens grow inland on a landscape dotted with flocks of sheep and goats. In addition to nature's wild and varied landscape, the promontory is rich in historic interest, boasting monuments that are Byzantine, Romanesque, Norman, and medieval.

It'll take a leisurely 7 hours to drive around the Gargano, staying on Rte. 89. We consider this sometimes difficult route among the most scenic drives in Italy. In ancient times, the peninsula was an island, until the sediment from a river eventually formed a "bridge" linking it to the mainland. Train service into the peninsula is limited to a private spur along the northwestern coast, so for travelers who wish to fully explore the area by bus or car, the gateway will be Manfredonia.

ESSENTIALS

GETTING THERE From Foggia, make a **train** connection to San Severo, 24 miles (39km) north, an hourly trip of 25 minutes costing 3,500L ($2.10), and transfer to the Ferrovia del Gargano (☎ **0882-221-414**), Gargano's private rail, traveling the northwestern edge of the peninsula to Rodi Garganico and a point near Peschici six times daily. You can also take an hourly train to Manfredonia, 27 miles (43km) northeast of Foggia, for 3,750L ($1.90); here buses depart to explore the peninsula. For rail information in Manfredonia, call ☎ **0884-581-015.**

Bus services are provided by the ATAF and SITA lines, which overlap, with hourly buses running from Foggia to Manfredonia, a 45-minute trip costing 4,000L ($2) each way. In Manfredonia, you can make connections seven times daily to Vieste, a 2-hour trip costing 5,000L ($2.50); 16 times daily to Mattinata, a 30-minute trip costing 2,000L ($1); and 17 times daily to Monte Sant'Angelo, a 45-minute trip costing 3,500L ($1.75). Buses also leave from the parking lot of Camping Sports, Via Montesanto 34–40 (☎ **0884-964-015**) in Peschici, following the coastal Rte. 89 to Vieste, a 40-minute trip costing 3,200L ($1.60).

From Vieste, contact **Gargano Viaggi,** Piazza Roma 7 (☎ **0884-708-501**), or **SITA,** Via Montegrappa 9–5 (☎ **0881-773-117**), for participation in a somewhat rushed 4-hour bus tour (summer only) of the peninsula costing 30,000L ($15).

If you have a **car,** you'll note that three roads dissect the peninsula and connect its major sights. Rte. 89 runs an 81-mile (130km) circuit around the coast; Rte. 528 cuts through the heart of the peninsula, starting 5 miles (8km) west of Peschici on the northern coast and running south through the Umbra Forest before ending at Rte. 272 just west of Monte Sant'Angelo; Rte. 272 slices east to west through the southern part of the region, from San Marco in Lamis in the west through San Giovanni Rotondo and over to Monte Sant'Angelo, ending on the coast near Punta Rossa.

VISITOR INFORMATION The **Manfredonia tourist office** is at Corso Manfredi 26 (☎ **0884-581-998**), open Monday to Saturday 9am to 1:30pm. Here you can pick up a map and get advice about touring the Gargano district, including bus and train schedules if you're not driving on your own (important, since in most towns there are no actual bus stations). The **Vieste tourist office** is at Piazza Kennedy 1 (☎ **0884-707-130**), open Monday to Saturday 8:30am to 1pm and 3 to 8pm. It'll give you information about the many excursion possibilities, especially the excellent beaches along the southern shore.

MANFREDONIA

27 miles (43km) NE of Foggia, 74 miles (119km) NW of Bari, 135 miles (217km) NE of Naples

If you approach Gargano from the south, your first stop, perhaps at lunchtime, will be **Manfredonia,** a small port known for its castle. It was named for Manfred, illegitimate son of Frederick II. In the heyday of the Crusades, this was a bustling port, with knights and pilgrims leaving for the Levant. Much later, the town was noted in World War I documents as the place where the first blow of the conflict was launched—the Austrians bombed the rail station in 1915. Manfredonia is on a rail route from Foggia.

After arriving in town, turn right and go along Viale Aldo Moro to Piazza Marconi. Across the square, Corso Manfredi leads to the **Manfredonia Castello,** built for Manfred and later enlarged by the Angevins. Other bastions were constructed in 1607 by the Spanish, who feared an invasion from Turkey. Regrettably, their fortifications didn't do the job, as the Turks arrived in 1620 and destroyed a lot of Manfredonia, leaving only some of its former walls standing. Today the castle is home to the **National Museum of Manfredonia** (**Museo Nazionale di Manfredonia**) ☎ **0884-587-838**, open daily (except the 1st and 4th Monday of each month) 8:30am to 1:30pm and 3:30 to 7:30pm and charging 4,000L ($2) admission. The archaeological remnants and finds include a collection of Stone Age objects from area villages, the most striking of which are the Daunian stelae, stone slabs decorated like human torsos and topped with stone heads, the legacy of the Daunian civilization that settled in the region around the 9th century B.C.

Two miles (3km) outside town is **Santa Maria di Siponto,** a church in a setting of pine woods that once was the site of the ancient city of Siponte, abandoned after being ravaged by an earthquake and a plague. The church, dating from the 11th century, is in the Romanesque style, showing both Tuscan and Arabic influences.

ACCOMMODATIONS

Hotel Gargano. Viale Beccarini 2, 71043 Manfredonia. ☎ and fax **0884-586-021.** 46 units. A/C TV TEL. 180,000L ($90) double. MC, V. Closed Jan. Parking 20,000L ($10).

This is the largest and most appealing hotel in town, a four-star place that's incredibly bargain-priced. The rooms have simple summery furnishings (with decent mattresses), each facing the sea from a private terrace or veranda. The tiled bathrooms are tiny. A seawater pool is close to a dance bar whose recorded music floats over chairs and tables angled for the best panorama of sea and shore. Room service is provided 8am to 10:30pm, and the bar is open 24 hours.

DINING

Il Baracchio. Corso Roma 38. ☎ **0884-583-874.** Reservations recommended. Main courses 12,000–25,000L ($6–$12.50). AE, DC, MC, V. Fri–Wed 12:30–2:30pm and 7:30–10:30pm. APULIAN/SEAFOOD.

Occupying an early 1900s building close to Piazza Municipio, this is the most appealing restaurant in town. It attracts civic and business leaders at lunch and groups of friends at dinner. The great selection of antipasti is mostly seafood and vegetarian. Pasta dishes include spaghetti and orecchiette, prepared in simple versions of tomatoes, pesto, and local cheese; with garlic, olive oil, and fresh broccoli; or more elaborately with seafood, especially octopus. Look for aromatic grilled baby lamb and the chef's special, *zuppetta ai frutti di mare,* the area's most savory shellfish soup.

MONTE SANT'ANGELO

37 miles (60km) NE of Foggia, 84 miles (135km) NW of Bari, 145 miles (233km) NE of Naples

The interior's principal town, Monte Sant'Angelo, 10 miles (16km) north of Manfredonia in the great Umbra Forest, is a good place to start your drive. From here you can venture into a landscape of limes, laurels, towering yews, and such animal life as foxes and gazelles. Narrow passages, streets that are virtually stairways, and little houses washed a gleaming white characterize the town.

The site of Monte Sant'Angelo, standing on a spur, commands panoramic views of the surrounding terrain. Before leaving town, you may want to visit the **Sanctuary of San Michele (Santuario di San Michele),** Via Reale Basilica, built in the Romanesque-Gothic style. The campanile is octagonal, dating from the last years of the 13th century. The sanctuary commemorates the legend of St. Michael, who's said to have left his red cloak after he appeared to some shepherds in a grotto in 490. You can also visit the grotto—to enter from the church, go through some bronze doors, made in Constantinople in the 11th century. Crusaders stopped here to worship before going to the Holy Land. The sanctuary is open daily 7:30am to 12:30pm and 2:30 to 6:30pm, charging no admission.

Opposite the campanile is the **Tomb of Rotharis (Tomba di Rotari).** The tomb is said to hold the bones of the king of the Lombards, Rotharis, although it's a baptistry dating from as early as the 12th century.

Continuing past the sanctuary, you'll find the semirestored ruins of the **Norman Swabian Aragonese Castle (Castello Normanno Aragonese Svevo),** Piazzale Fere, with a second entrance on the Corso Manfredi (☎ **0884-565-444**); it's open daily 8:30am to 1:30pm, charging 4,000L ($2) admission. Its Torre dei Giganti was constructed in 837, though most of the castle dates from later in the Middle Ages. From its ramparts is one of the most sweeping views in the Gargano.

You can also visit the **Tancredi Museum (Museo Tancredi),** Piazza San Francesco d'Assisi (☎ **0884-562-098**), exhibiting artifacts used by local farmers and vintners in their trades. May to September, it's open Monday to Friday 8:30am to 7:30pm, Sunday 10:30am to 12:30pm and 3:30 to 7pm; off-season hours are Monday to Friday 8am to 2pm. Admission is 4,000L ($2).

As you wander about, look for local shops selling **wrought-iron goods,** which are among the finest in Italy. Ironwork has a long tradition here, with sons following in their fathers' footsteps. The locals also make **wooden furniture** and **utensils.** Most shops are located in an area called **Juno,** in the exact center of town.

ACCOMMODATIONS

Hotel Rotary. Via per Pulsano km 1, 71037 Monte Sant'Angelo. ☎ and fax **0884-562-146.** 24 units. TV TEL. 110,000–125,000L ($55–$62.50) double. Rates include breakfast. AE, MC, V. Free parking.

You'll find this 1981 hotel half a mile west of town, amid a sloping terrain with ancient olive groves and almond trees. None of the simple guest rooms are air-conditioned, but because of the hotel's location in relatively high altitudes, ocean breezes usually keep the temperatures comfortable. The rooms range from small to medium, with thin but still acceptable mattresses. The restaurant serves a cuisine based on local culinary traditions.

DINING

Ristorante Medioevo. Via Castello 21. ☎ **0884-565-356.** Reservations recommended. Main courses 30,000–55,000L ($15–$27.50). AE, MC, V. June–Sept daily 12:30–2:30pm and 7:30–11pm; the rest of the year Tues–Sun 12:30–2:30pm and 7:30–11pm. Closed Nov 15–30. CONTADINA.

The Medioevo's dining room takes its name from the weather-beaten but historic neighborhood surrounding it. The cuisine is firmly entrenched in recipes rehearsed by countless generations of *contadine* (peasant women), like *zuppa di pane cotto* (a savory soup made of chicory and fava beans), homemade pasta (especially *orecchiette*), and a wide roster of meat or fish and roasted lamb from rocky nearby meadows. The kitchen is particularly proud of its *orecchiette Medioevo* (ear-shaped pasta with a sauce made from roasted lamb, braised arugula, and fresh tomatoes).

THE TREMITI ISLANDS

7 miles (11km) NW of Gargano

While in the area, consider visiting the jewel-like cluster of the **Isole Tremiti (Tremiti Islands),** northwest of the Gargano Peninsula in the Adriatic. These small limestone islands boast lovely reefs, gin-clear waters, and towering peaks.

June to September, **boats** and **hydrofoils** travel from Vieste, Manfredonia, and Peschici to the Tremiti Islands, and you should make advance reservations in the peak of summer, when the vessels get crowded. In Vieste, contact **Motonave Vieste,** Corso Fazzini 33 on the dock (☎ **0884-707-489**), about boat service, a 1 1/3-hour trip costing 20,000L ($10), or **Adriatica,** Piazza Roma 7 at the Gargano Viaggi office (☎ **0884-708-501**), providing 1-hour hydrofoil service from Vieste for 50,000L ($25) round-trip, as well as a 2-hour trip from Manfredonia for 68,000L ($34) round-trip, leaving from the dock a 3-minute walk south along Piazza Marconi toward Siponto. In Peschici, **Onda Azzurra,** Corso Umberto I 16 (☎ **0884-964-234**), makes daily boat runs to the islands, a trip of just over an hour costing 42,000L ($21) round-trip. Departures from all ports leave at 9:05am daily, with a return at 6pm.

EXPLORING THE TREMITI

By boat or hydrofoil, you'll arrive at the docks of **San Nicola,** the smaller of the two inhabited islands, where you can explore the **castle** from the 15th century (it's not much of a sight, but the view from there is spectacular). You might also want to visit **Santa Maria a Mare,** which grew out of a 9th-century abbey, one of many monasteries that once stood in the Tremiti. The church has been largely rebuilt over the years, retaining only an intricate mosaic floor and early Byzantine cross from its early history. All its treasures were plundered by pirates in 1321.

Between the islands of San Nicola and **San Domino,** the other inhabited island, you can take a shuttle boat running every 15 minutes at 2,000L ($1). San Domino is the largest island of the group, with a rock-strewn shoreline. It's best known for its grottoes—the **Blue Marine Grotto (Grotta del Blu Marino), Salt Grotto (Grotta di Sale),** and **Violet Grotto (Grotta delle Viole),** all stunningly beautiful. The only beaches of the Tremiti are found here, and the **Cala delle Arene,** near the dock, is generally crowded. But you can also make your way to the west and south sides of the island, where the only other approachable beaches (most are at the foot of treacherous cliffs) offer stretches of solitude. As a historical footnote, Charlemagne's quarrelsome Italian father-in-law was exiled on the island, and this is where Augustus banished his daughter, Julia, because of her "excesses" (like sleeping with nearly every man in Rome).

ACCOMMODATIONS & DINING

Hotel Gabbiano. Isola San Domino, 71040 San Nicola di Tremiti. ☎ and fax **0882-463-410.** 40 units. A/C MINIBAR TV TEL. 160,000–230,000L ($80–$115) double with breakfast; 200,000–390,000L ($100–$195) double with half-board. AE, DC, MC, V.

Built in 1973 and renovated in 2000, this is the most appealing hotel on the island. It lies about half a mile from the port, on San Domino's most beautiful stretch of coast, in a palm garden. Most of the ground floor contains the bar, restaurant, solarium, and reception area. The functional-looking guest rooms are a bit cramped and the tiled bathrooms tiny, but you can still sleep well on the firm mattresses. The restaurant is one of the island's most sought-after, with main courses at 20,000 to 30,000L ($10 to $15).

Hotel San Domino. Isola San Domino, 71040 San Nicola di Tremiti. ☎ **0882-463-404.** Fax 0882-463-220. 25 units. TV TEL. 180,000–300,000L ($90–$150) double. Rates include half-board. MC, V.

Less elegant than the Gabbiano (see above), this is a three-star hotel built about a mile from the port. It's within a 5-minute walk from the nearest beach and contains serviceable but simple white guest rooms (with decent mattresses) and cramped tiled bathrooms. There's a restaurant and a bar, but few other amenities.

VIESTE

57 miles (92km) NE of Foggia, 111 miles (179km) NW of Bari, 170 miles (274km) NE of Naples

At Vieste, on the far eastern shore of the Gargano, a legendary monolith stands firmly rooted in the sea. The rock is linked to the woeful tale of Vesta, a beautiful girl supposedly held prisoner on the stone by jealous sirens.

In recent years, the town has blossomed as a summer resort because it offers some of the best beaches in the south. If you're just passing through, take time out to walk through the charming medieval quarter, with its whitewashed houses built on terraces overlooking the sea. Vieste is a good center from which to explore the other excellent sandy beaches along the southern shoreline.

ACCOMMODATIONS

Hotel del Seggio. Piazza del Seggio/Via Veste 7, 71019 Vieste. ☎ **0884-708-123.** Fax 0884-708-727. www.igshei.it/hotelseggio. 30 units. A/C TV TEL. 110,000–160,000L ($55–$80) double. Rates include breakfast. July 31–Aug 21 half-board 140,000L ($70) per person required. AE, DC, MC, V. Free parking.

This is the best affordable hotel, with a historic pedigree more impressive than that of the grander palaces. It occupies a civic monument that between its construction in the 1600s and around 1910 was the city hall. In 1983 it was renovated to become a hotel. The guest rooms come in a wide range of shapes and sizes, each with a comfortable mattress and a small tiled bathroom. One edge of it abuts the seafront; the other, one of the town's main squares.

There's a smallish pool on an outdoor terrace as well as a restaurant, open to nonguests, charging 12,000 to 17,000L ($6 to $8.50) for main courses. On site is a small gym; the hotel also has its own private beach, and umbrellas and deck chairs are available free to guests.

✪ **Pizzomunno Vieste Palace Hotel.** Spiaggia di Pizzomunno, 71019 Vieste. ☎ **0884-708-741.** Fax 0884-707-325. www.pizzomunno.it. E-mail: pizzomunno@viesteonline.it. 210 units. A/C MINIBAR TV TEL. 680,000–940,000L ($340–$470) double; 900,000–1,300,000L ($450–$650) suite. Rates include buffet breakfast. AE, DC, MC, V. Closed late Oct to mid-Mar. Free valet parking.

This five-star hotel is much better than any other contender in Gargano (with correspondingly high prices!) and is proud of its 80% Italian clientele. Its Mediterranean architecture, with five stories growing smaller as they rise, allows lots of private terraces on the fourth and fifth floors. The guest rooms, totally remodeled, are airy and relatively spacious, with big windows and top-grade mattresses. The tiled bathrooms come with thick towels and hair dryers. Within 30 yards is the companion **Hotel La Pineta,** with which it shares the same management. Even the staff is charming.

Dining/Diversions: Ristorante Trabucco is the region's best hotel dining room, serving delectable main courses like roast lamb with fresh herbs, baked or grilled fish, and seafood like sea wolf, lobster, and fresh shrimp. There's also the less formal Il Ristorante sulla Veranda a Mare, serving a regional cuisine, and a pizzeria, Al Pozzo, in a 19th-century house. Bars are found in the hotel disco, at the beach, at poolside, and in the pizzeria.

Amenities: Two pools (one for children), swimming courses, sailing and windsurfing classes, motorboats for waterskiing, sailboats, beach rafts, two tennis courts, archery, fitness trail, basketball court, health club and spa, huge playground for kids, hairdresser, boutique, perfumery, concierge, 24-hour room service, laundry/dry cleaning, newspaper delivery, in-room massage, twice-daily maid service, baby-sitting, secretarial services, courtesy car.

DINING

You can also dine at the wonderful **Ristorante Trabucco** in the Pizzomunno Vieste Palace Hotel (see above).

Al Dragone. Via Duomo 8. ☎ **0884-701-212.** Reservations recommended. Main courses 15,000–28,000L ($7.50–$14). AE, DC, MC, V. Wed–Mon noon–3pm and 7–11pm. Closed Nov to mid-Mar. APULIAN.

Near the cathedral, this is usually the first restaurant anyone mentions when honeymooners are looking for a secluded romantic hideaway. The decor includes flickering candles and raffia-wrapped Chianti bottles, and the cuisine is based on the folkloric traditions of old Apulia. Look for seafood pastas, antipasti buffets, lamb roasted with herbs and potatoes, and flavors lush with garlic, rosemary, and pesto. The owners pride themselves on their comprehensive collection of red and white Apulian wines. An excellent example is Patrilione.

Box 19. Via Santa Maria di Merino 13. ☎ **0884-705-229.** Reservations recommended. Main courses 10,000–24,000L ($5–$12). MC, V. Tues–Sun noon–3pm and 7pm–midnight. APULIAN.

Box 19 makes less of an attempt to capitalize on local folklore than some other competitors and offers a more culturally neutral and relatively sophisticated dining experience. Despite that, the cuisine is Apulian, with an emphasis on fresh fish, tomato-based pastas, roasted lamb with potatoes, and antipasti offerings that might wow you with their pungent fresh fish (especially anchovies and sardines) and marinated vegetables. (The name? This place opened in the early 1980s in a former car-repair shop—its post office box was no. 19.)

3 Alberobello & the Trulli District

45 miles (72km) NW of Brindisi, 37 miles (60km) SE of Bari, 28 miles (45km) N of Taranto

The center of a triangle made up by Bari, Brindisi, and Taranto, the Valley of Itria has long been known for olive cultivation and the beehive-shaped houses dotting its landscape. These curious structures, called ***trulli,*** were built at least as early as the 13th century. Their whitewashed limestone walls and conical fieldstone roofs utilize the materials available in the area in such a way that mortar isn't needed to keep the pieces together. Theories abound as to why they aren't built with mortar, the most popular being that the trulli, considered substandard peasant dwellings, had to be easily dismantled in case of a royal visit. See the box "The Mystery of the Trulli" for more speculation.

The center of the Trulli District, and home to the greatest concentration of trulli, is Alberobello. Here the streets are lined with some 1,000 of the buildings. You may feel as if you've entered into a child's storybook as you walk through the maze of cobbled streets curving through Italy's most fantastic village. The crowds of visitors will quickly relieve you of any such thoughts, however.

Many of the trulli have been converted into souvenir shops where you can buy everything from postcards to miniature models of the dwellings. Be careful though: If you enter you're expected to buy something—and the shop owners will let you know it.

ESSENTIALS

GETTING THERE FSE **trains** leave Bari every hour (every 2 hours on Sunday) heading to Alberobello. The trip takes about 1¾ hours and costs 5,700L ($2.85). To find the trulli, follow Via Mazzini, which turns into Via Garibaldi, until you reach Piazza del Popolo. Turn left on Largo Martellotta, which will take you to the edge of the popular tourist area. If you have a **car,** head south of Bari on S100, then east (signposted) on S172.

VISITOR INFORMATION The **tourist office** in Alberobello is off the central square, Piazza del Popolo, at Piazza Ferdinando IV (☎ **080-432-5171**), open daily 9am to noon and 4 to 7pm.

SEEING THE SIGHTS

The best-known of the trulli is the **trullo sovrano (sovereign trullo)** at Piazza Sacramento in Alberobello. The 50-foot structure, the only true two-story trullo, was built during the 19th century as headquarters for a religious confraternity and carbonari sect. To find it, head down Corso Vittorio Emanuele until you get to the church and then take a right. The trullo sovrano is open daily 10am to 1pm and 3 to 7pm, charging no admission.

On the outskirts of Alberobello, you can also visit the small town of **Castellana,** home to a series of caverns that have been carved out over the centuries by water streaming through the rocky soil. A wide stairway leads you down through a tunnel into a cavern called the **Grave.** From here, a series of paths winds through other underground rooms filled with the strange shapes of stalagmites and stalactites. The culmination of the journey into the earth ends with the majestic **Grotta Bianca,** where alabaster concretions are the result of centuries of Mother Nature's work. You can visit the Grotte di Castellana only on guided tours, usually one per hour until early afternoon at 15,000 to 30,000L ($7.50 to $15); call ☎ **080-496-5511** for a schedule. Be sure to bring a sweater; the average underground temperature is 59°F, even on hot summer days.

Most visitors like to buy the hand-painted clay figurines that abound in every souvenir shop. You can also find a good assortment of fabrics and rugs at reasonable prices. One of the most evocative souvenirs would be a miniature re-creation of the region's legendary trulli. Crafted in the same type of stone that was used by the ancient builders, they're small-scale duplicates of the originals, ranging in size from a simple rendering to a replica of an entire village.

ACCOMMODATIONS

Most people visit the area on a day-long excursion; if you want to stay overnight, know that Alberobello's hotels are limited. You may be able to find individual renovated trulli that are rented to two to eight people for a relatively cheap rate. Call the tourist office for information. Otherwise, the accommodations here are usually more expensive than those in other nearby towns.

Hotel Dei Trulli. Via Cadore 32, 70011 Alberobello. ☎ **080-432-3555.** Fax 080-432-3560. E-mail: htrulli@inmedia.it. 19 units. MINIBAR TV TEL. 190,000L ($95) per person. Rates include half-board. AE, MC, V. Free parking.

Almost a village unto itself, Dei Trulli offers the experience of living in one of the unique beehive-shaped trulli. Each miniapartment may have one, two, or three cones, circular buildings wedged together in Siamese fashion. Most have a bedroom with a good mattress, plus a bathroom, a small sitting room with a fireplace, and a patio. The complex also has a pool and attractively landscaped grounds. In the restaurant, the cuisine is mostly regional; the *pignata* (veal stew) with a glass of red Primotivo wine from Turi makes a good meal.

The Mystery of the Trulli

The architectural mystery of southern Italy, the igloo-shaped trulli are the country's most idiosyncratic homes, built of local limestone without mortar. A hole in the top allows smoke to escape. Southwest of Bari, in an area roughly hemmed in by Gioia del Colle to the west, Ostuni to the south, and the Adriatic coast to the east, these strange whitewashed buildings are roofed with tall spiraling cones of a stone prevalent in the region. Trulli are found nowhere else in the entire country.

The structures look somewhat primitive, giving them an air of being ancient, though most of the existing buildings are less than 2 centuries old. Many are new constructions, since the people of the area are attached to their unique architectural form, using it to house businesses as well as homes. The trulli are of a uniformly small size. If more space is needed, local custom dictates the construction of several connected trulli rather than a single larger one. In fact, only one trullo in the entire area dared expand into a two-story structure (see below).

Some locals call trulli signalmen's houses, and others refer to them as monuments and point out obscure symbols that adorn the most traditional ones. These symbols were copied from the emblems that embellish the few remaining ancient structures. One of the most puzzling things is that, despite the great attachment to the buildings, no one in the region can tell you how the form came into favor in the first place, what the emblems symbolize, or even why they're called by any of the names associated with them.

Only a few scholars have tackled these questions, in the end making halfhearted suggestions that perhaps the trulli are of Saracenic or Greek origin. One

✪ **Hotel Il Melograno.** Contrada Torricella, 70043 Monopoli. ☎ **080-690-9030.** Fax 080-747-908. www.melograno.com. E-mail: melograno@melograno.com. 33 units. A/C MINIBAR TV TEL. 230,000–350,000L ($115–$175) per person double; 470,000–630,000L ($235–$315) per person suite. Rates include breakfast. AE, DC, MC, V. From Alberobello, follow the signs to Monopoli and drive 11 miles (18km) east.

This is the most elegant hotel in Apulia and the only Relais & Châteaux south of Naples. Occupying what was the centerpiece for a large farm and estate during the 16th century and enlarged with a discreet modern wing in the mid-1900s, it sits less than a mile from the hamlet of Monopoli. The creative force behind the place is a hardworking Bari-based antiques dealer, Camillo Gurra. His polite staff spends long hours maintaining the important antiques and paintings in this charming country inn. The guest rooms range from medium to spacious, each with a good mattress, and the bathrooms come with toiletries and adequate shelf space.

Dining: In the main hotel, lunches at about 60,000L ($30) are served beside the pool, and dinners at about 80,000L ($40) are served on a flowering terrace or in a formal dining room. The cuisine is the very finest in the area, both in its preparation (only top chefs are employed) and in its elegant presentation. At the beach club, simple lunches are available.

Amenities: Concierge, room service, twice-daily maid service, laundry/dry cleaning, baby-sitting, pool, shuttle bus (June to September) taking guests at frequent intervals to/from private beach club 3 miles (5km) away.

line of logic points out that limestone, a calcareous rock found in abundant stratification throughout the region, is easily separated into thin layers that can readily be shaped into crude bricks that don't require mortar when relayered. The dome design allows heat to rise, slightly cooling the living space, a significant factor in the region's brutal summer. Given that the area has long been impoverished, perhaps the design is nothing but good old ingenuity, a means of cheaply constructing homes and businesses with the materials at hand—but that still doesn't explain the hieroglyphics.

One suggestion is that the origin of the trulli had to do with outwitting Ferdinand I of Aragón. This king had prohibited the Apulians from building permanent dwellings because he wanted to be able to move the labor force around as he chose. The clever Apulians thus constructed houses that could be dismantled when they spotted the king's agents. Another theory suggests that during Spanish rule a tax was levied on individual homes, except for unfurnished homes, for which the trulli qualified when their roofs were removed.

Other theories link them with similar structures in Mycenae and suggest their origins may be as old as 3000 B.C. Apulia was indeed part of Magna Graecia and so could have come under that influence. Similarities have been noted between the trulli of Apulia and the "sugarloaf" houses of Syria. It's been suggested that this idea, traveling west, influenced builders in southern Italy who initially used the trulli as tombs. It's also been noted that soldiers returning from the Crusades may have brought these architectural curiosities to Alberobello. Got any theories of your own?

DINING

You can also dine at the superb restaurant in the **Hotel Il Melograno** (see above).

✪ **Il Poeta Contadino.** Via Indipendenza 21. ☎ **080-432-1917.** Reservations recommended. Main courses 30,000–34,000L ($15–$17). AE, DC, MC, V. July–Sept daily noon–3pm and 7–11pm; Oct–June Tues–Sun noon–3pm and 7–11pm. ITALIAN/APULIAN.

In the center of Alberobello, beneath the arched and vaulted stone ceilings of what was a barn in the 1700s, this is the region's most elegant restaurant. It's managed by Leonardo Marco and his Canadian-born wife, Carol, who serve sophisticated dishes based mostly on seafood. Their menu changes with the season but is likely to include *involtini* of eggplant, monkfish, and prawns with mussel sauce as well as *pesce alla Leonardo* (sea bass steamed in water, wine, and oil and served with a chilled sauce of cherry tomatoes, chives, olive oil, black olives, and vinegar). The wine list is one of the region's most comprehensive and has won a *Wine Spectator* award.

Trullo d'Oro. Via Cavallotti 27. ☎ **080-432-1820.** Reservations required Sat–Sun. Main courses 30,000–80,000L ($15–$40). AE, CB, DC, DISC, MC, V. Tues–Sun noon–3pm and 8–11pm. Closed Jan 3–Feb 3. ITALIAN/APULIAN.

Housed in several linked trulli, this rustic restaurant is one of the town's best. The cuisine consists mainly of well-prepared local and regional dishes. Specialties are puree of fava beans and chicory leaves, roast lamb with *lampasciuni* (a wild onion), and the chef's special pasta, orecchiette with bitter greens or tomatoes, olive oil, garlic, and arugula. Southern desserts, like ricotta cooked with marmalade, are also served.

4 Lecce

25 miles (40km) SE of Brindisi, 54 miles (87km) E of Taranto, 562 miles (905km) SE of Rome

Often called "the Florence of the South," Lecce lies in the heart of the Salento Peninsula, the "heel" of the Italian boot. The town was founded before the time of the ancient Greeks, but it's best known for the architecture, *barocco leccese* (Lecce baroque), of many of its buildings. Dating from Lecce's heyday in the 16th, 17th, and 18th centuries, these structures are made mostly of fine-grained yellow limestone. Masons delighted in working with the golden material; their efforts turned the city into what one architectural critic called a "gigantic bowl of overripe fruit." Alas, recent restorations have taken away much of the color as workers have whitewashed the buildings.

For centuries, Lecce has been neglected by tourists. Perhaps it's for this reason that many of the baroque-style buildings have remained intact—progress hasn't overrun the city with modern development. Lecce's charm lies in these displays of the lighter baroque (though many buildings are now in dire need of repair).

ESSENTIALS

GETTING THERE Lecce is connected to Brindisi by hourly **train** service on the state-run FS line. For service from points east and south, you'll have to take the FSE line, which isn't known for its speed. Several trains coming from Otranto and Gallipoli enter Lecce each day. The train station is about 1½ miles (2km) from Piazza Sant'Oronzo, in the center of the old quarter. Call ☎ **1478-88-088** toll-free in Italy for schedules and information.

If you have a **car,** take Rte. 613 from Brindisi.

VISITOR INFORMATION The **tourist office** is at Via 25 Luglio (☎ **0832-248-092**), open Monday to Saturday 9am to 1pm (Monday to Friday also 5 to 7pm).

SPECIAL EVENTS July and August bring the **Estate Musicale Leccese,** with nightly music and dance. In July, plays (and sometimes operas) are staged in the city's public gardens. In September, the churches of Lecce are venues for a **festival of baroque music.** The tourist office (see above) will provide complete details.

SEEING THE SIGHTS

Piazza Sant'Oronzo is a good place to begin a stroll through Lecce. The 2nd-century A.D. Roman column, **Colonna Romana,** erected here once stood near its mate in Brindisi and together served to mark the end of the Appian Way. Lightning toppled this column in 1528, and the Brindisians left it lying on the ground until 1661, at which time the citizens of Lecce bought it and set the pillar up in their home town. St. Oronzo, for whom the square is named, now stands atop it guarding the area. At the southern side of the piazza are the remains of a **Roman amphitheater.** Dating from the 1st century B.C., it accommodated 20,000 fans who came to watch bloody fights between gladiators and wild beasts.

North of the piazza, Via Umberto I leads to the **Basilica di Santa Croce** (☎ **0832-261-957**). This ornate display of Leccese baroque architecture took almost 1½ centuries to complete. Architect Gabriele Riccardo began work in the mid–15th century; the final touches weren't added until 1680. The facade bears some similarity to the Spanish Plateresque style and is peopled by guardian angels, grotesque demons, and a variety of flora and fauna. St. Benedict and St. Peter are also depicted. The top part of the facade (the flamboyant part) is the work of Antonio Zimbalo, who was called Zingarello (gypsy). The interior is laid out in a Latin cross plan in a simple Renaissance style. The basilica is open daily 7am to 12:30pm and 4 to 7pm. Admission is free.

Down Via Vittorio Emanuele, the **Duomo,** Piazza del Duomo (☎ **0832-308-557**), stands in a closed square. The building, which has two facades, was reconstructed between 1659 and 1670 by Zingarello. To the left of the duomo, the **campanile** towers 210 feet above the piazza. The cathedral is open daily 7:30am to 12:30pm and 4 to 7pm, and admission is free. On the opposite side of the cathedral is the **Bishop's Palace (Palazzo Vescovile),** where Lecce's archbishop still lives today. Also in the courtyard is a **seminary,** built between 1694 and 1709 by Giuseppe Cino, who was a student of Zimbalo. Its decorations have been compared to those of a wedding cake. A baroque well, extraordinarily detailed with garlands and clusters of flowers and fruit, stands in the seminary's courtyard.

The collection of bronze statuettes, Roman coins, and other artifacts at the **Provincial Museum (Museo Provinciale),** Viale Gallipoli (☎ **0832-247-025**), will keep your interest for a while. It's worth the time to stop by to have a look at the ornately decorated 13th-century gospel cover. Inlaid with enamel of blue, white, and gold, it's a rare treasure. There's also a small picture gallery. It's open Monday to Friday 9am to 1:30pm and 2:30 to 7pm, Saturday and Sunday 9am to 1:30pm. Admission is free.

SHOPPING

The arid landscapes of southern Italy have fostered some of Europe's finest metalworkers. For an example of the town's traditional wrought-iron goods (trivets, ornamental grills, and the like), visit **Salvatore Mancarella,** Via Fanteria 95 (☎ **0832-634-218**). For a different selection of local crafts, including *cartapesta* (papier-mâché), ceramics, and terra-cotta, go to **Mostra dell'Artigianato,** Via Rubichi 21 (☎ **0832-246-758**). And if you're interested in any of the wines and foodstuffs of the region, head for a food emporium that's been here as long as anyone can remember, **Enoteca,** Via Cesare Battisti 23 (☎ **0832-302-832**). Usually, they'll let you taste a glass of whatever wine you're interested in before you buy a bottle.

ACCOMMODATIONS

Lecce's hotels don't offer the baroque architecture for which the town is famous. Most are modern structures built to accommodate large numbers of visitors who care more about seeing the town and surrounding area than spending time in their rooms.

Albergo Delle Palme. Via di Leuca 90, 73100 Lecce. ☎ and fax **0832-347-171.** www.paginegialle.it/dellepalme. E-mail: hdellepalme@tiscalinet.it. 96 units. A/C MINIBAR TV TEL. 160,000–190,000L ($80–$95) double. Rates include breakfast. AE, CB, DC, DISC, MC, V. Free parking.

This is the best hotel of the moderate choices, within easy walking distance of the major monuments. The public rooms, with their overstuffed leather furniture and paneled walls, are warm and inviting. The guest rooms are comfortably decorated with painted iron beds and small sitting areas. The hotel operates a good restaurant, serving both regional and national cuisine.

Hotel Cristal. Via Marinosci 16, 73100 Lecce. ☎ **0832-372-314.** Fax 0832-315-109. 64 units. A/C MINIBAR TV TEL. 180,000L ($90) double. Rates include breakfast. AE, DC, MC, V. Parking 16,000L ($8).

This metal-and-glass high-rise is a good choice for comfort at a reasonable price. The marble lobby/lounge area is severe but not sterile and offers a pleasant place to sit and enjoy a drink. The guest rooms vary in size and are decorated monochromatically in purples, pinks, or blues; a small refrigerator and a safe are standard.

Hotel President. Via Salandra 6, 73100 Lecce. ☎ **0832-311-881.** Fax 0832-372-283. 154 units. A/C MINIBAR TV TEL. 200,000L ($100) double; from 360,000L ($180) suite. Rates include buffet breakfast. AE, DC, MC, V. Parking 20,000L ($10).

Though this hotel is near the historic center of town, it's severely modern. The guest rooms are decorated in the browns and oranges popular in the 1970s, but are large and comfortable. The look is standardized, almost motel-like, but luckily there's good service. Fresh pastries and breads are the highlights of the breakfast buffet, and the restaurant serves good regional and international dishes at lunch and dinner. Amenities include a concierge, room service, laundry/dry cleaning, newspaper delivery, twice-daily maid service, baby-sitting, and a car-rental desk.

DINING

During your stay, be sure to sample some of the specialties of the Salento region, such as a tasty combination of mozzarella and tomato wrapped in a light pastry shell.

I Tre Moschettieri. Via Paisiello, 73100 Lecce. ☎ **0832-308-484.** Reservations recommended. Main courses 15,000–28,000L ($7.50–$14). DC, MC, V. Mon–Sat noon–3pm and 7pm–midnight. ITALIAN/PIZZA/APULIAN.

Although this restaurant has two rooms, most visitors choose to have their meals on the alfresco patio. The tables throughout the restaurant are widely spaced and allow for easy conversation. Offerings from the *cucina rustica* here include a variety of fresh seafood dishes and a vast selection of made-to-order pizzas. Local politicians often frequent this place, where formal service at moderate prices is the rule.

Ristorante Villa G.C. della Monica. Via SS. Giacomo e Fillippo 40. ☎ **0832-458-432.** Reservations recommended. Main courses 12,000–22,000L ($6–$11). AE, DC, MC, V. Wed–Mon 12:30–3pm and 8–10:30pm. Closed Jan. SOUTHERN ITALIAN/INTERNATIONAL.

The charming Valenti family runs this restaurant in one of Lecce's most stately villas, built of chiseled stone between 1550 and 1600. There are four dining rooms (one available only for private parties) and a flower-strewn terrace overlooking a historic neighborhood near Piazza Mazzini. The menu items are steeped in local culinary traditions and emphasize a regional tubular pasta called *strozzapreti* (a bit smaller than penne), usually served with clams, mussels, crabmeat, and squid. Other specialties are well-seasoned fillet steak with black truffles, and fresh fish that seems to taste better when baked in a salt crust to seal in the moisture.

LECCE AFTER DARK

Because of the large student population at the University of Lecce, there's usually something to keep night owls entertained. After nightfall, folks head to the main piazza to join friends for a drink. **Piazzetta del Duca d'Atena** is an especially popular hangout. For a more active night, you may want to head to **Corto Maltese,** Via Giusti 23 (no phone). Wednesday to Monday 9pm to 2am, crowds gather to dance the night away.

A SIDE TRIP TO GALLIPOLI

Twenty-three miles (37km) southwest of Lecce, on the Gulf of Taranto side of the Salento Peninsula, lies **Gallipoli.** This isn't the Gallipoli infamous in history books as the sight of one of the bloodiest battles ever fought; that sad World War I landmark is part of Turkey. The Italian town has a much quieter and less tragic past. Originally named Kallipolis (beautiful city) by the Greeks, the present town still has a distinct Greek look. The medieval quarter, once a small island, is especially inviting to explore, with its twisting lanes and plain whitewashed houses.

It's best to rent a car for this trip; train service to Gallipoli from Lecce is extremely slow and public transportation in the area limited. It's a quick 25-minute drive down to the town from Lecce, perfect for a day trip to the beach.

Seeing the Sights

Many people who come to Gallipoli head straight for the **beaches. Baia Verde,** just south of the town, is especially popular. However, if you take the time to drive down from Lecce, you might as well see what the town has to offer.

One of the most interesting places to visit is the **Civic Museum (Museo Civico),** Via De Pace 108 (☎ **0833-264-224**). There's a little of everything here; it's almost as if the townspeople had cleaned out their closets and made what they found into a museum. The collection covers several centuries and many aspects of life—from unexploded sea mines to clothing from the 18th century. The museum, renovated in 1999, is open in summer daily 9am to 9pm; off-season hours are Monday to Saturday 9am to 1pm and 4 to 6pm.

The Greek **nymphaion,** a fountain elaborately decorated with mythological scenes, can be found in the new town near the bridge. It's the only fountain of this type left in Italy, though there are a few still left in Greece.

The town also has a **cathedral** from the 1400s and a **castle** jutting out into the Ionian sea. The circular fortress has protected the city for centuries; locals fought off Charles of Anjou's men for 7 months here, and troops from England attacked the castle in 1809.

If you drive to Gallipoli, you can continue on to discover the tip of the Salento Peninsula, often called **Finibus Terrae (Land's End).** The Temple of Minerva that was once used by ancient sailors to trace their course has been replaced with the church of Santa Maria di Leuca, though stones and dolmens that stand in the area are reminders of the long-ago civilization.

Also nearby is **Casarano,** the birthplace of Boniface IX, who was pope from 1339 to 1404. The small church of Casaranello is here; early Christian mosaics adorn the walls.

Accommodations

Grand Hotel Costa Brada. Strada Litoranea, 73014 Gallipoli. ☎ **0833-202-551.** Fax 0833-202-555. 80 units. A/C MINIBAR TV TEL. 285,000L ($142.50) double. Rates include breakfast. AE, DC, MC, V.

With two pools, tennis courts, a private beach, and a nightclub, the modern Costa Brada is more resort than hotel. It's located about 4 miles (6km) from Gallipoli down a scenic road. Each attractive guest room boasts a sea-view balcony. Services include a concierge, room service, laundry/dry cleaning, and baby-sitting; amenities include a Jacuzzi, a sauna, Turkish baths, a solarium, a gym, a beauty center, bike rentals, waterskiing facilities, and a heliport. The chefs are expert at preparing international and Apulian cuisine.

Dining

Ristorante Marechiaro. Lungomare Marconi. ☎ **0833-266-143.** Reservations recommended. Main courses 18,000–30,000L ($9–$15). AE, DC, MC, V. Daily noon–4pm and 7pm–midnight. Closed Tues in winter. REGIONAL.

The Marechiaro occupies a circa 1900 villa on a small island connected to the mainland by a bridge. In one of the three dining rooms or on the flowering terrace, you'll enjoy the cuisine of Antonio Giungato. Fish dishes are a staple, with spicy *zuppa di pesce* (fish soup), *risotto alla pescatora* (rice flavored with seafood), and linguine with seafood and creamy white sauce.

5 Taranto

44 miles (71km) W of Brindisi, 62 miles (100km) SE of Bari, 331 miles (533km) SE of Rome

Taranto, known to the ancient Greeks as Taras, is said to have been named for a son of Poseidon who rode into the harbor on a dolphin's back. A less fantastic theory, trumpeted by historians, is that a group of Spartans was sent here in 708 B.C. to found a colony. Taranto was once a major center of Magna Graecia and continued as an important port on the Ionian coast throughout the 4th century B.C.. A long period of rule under Archytas, a Pythagorean mathematician/philosopher, was the high point in the city's history. According to some, Plato himself came to Taranto during this time to muddle through the mysteries of life with the wise and virtuous ruler.

Ten years of war with the Romans in the 3rd century B.C. ended in defeat for Taranto. Although the city lost much of the power and prestige it had been known for, it did survive the Dark Ages and became an important port once more during the time of the Crusades.

Taranto did lend its name to the tarantula, but don't be alarmed; the only spiders here are rather small, harmless brown ones. The dance known today as the *tarantella* also takes its name from this city. (Members of various dancing cults believed individuals who'd been bitten by spiders should dance wildly to rid their bodies of the poison; the inflicted person would sometimes dance for days.) In modern times, the tarantella is characterized by hopping and foot tapping and is one of the most popular folk dances of southern Italy.

Taranto is a modern industrial city that many visitors pass by. The once prosperous old city has begun to crumble and the economy of the town has hit a slump, in part because of the scaling back of naval forces stationed in Taranto. However, the new city, with its wide promenades and expensive shops, still draws crowds. Come here if only to taste some of Italy's best seafood. Taranto's location on a peninsula between two seas, the Mare Piccolo and Mare Grande, is perfect for cultivation of oysters, mussels, and other shellfish.

ESSENTIALS

GETTING THERE Regular service from both Bari and Brindisi is provided by the FS and FSE **train** lines. Trains leave Bari about once an hour for Taranto; the trip takes $1^1/_2$ to 2 hours and costs 8,500L ($4.25). For 5,700L ($2.85), you can take the hour ride from Brindisi; trains leave every 2 hours. Arrivals are on the western outskirts of town, from which you can proceed into the center by bus or taxi. For information and schedules, call ☎ **1478-88-088.**

Three **bus** companies, FSE, SITA, and CTP, provide service to Taranto. From Bari, take the FSE bus, departing every 2 hours. The trip takes from 1 to 2 hours and costs 8,500L ($4.25). The tourist office has schedules. Call ☎ **099-32-4201** for information and schedules.

If you have a **car,** take A14 here from Bari; E90 comes in from Brindisi; and Rte. 7ter makes the trek west from Lecce.

VISITOR INFORMATION The **tourist office** is at Corso Umberto I 119, near Piazza Garibaldi (☎ **099-453-2392**), and is open Monday to Friday 9am to 1pm and 4:30 to 6:30pm, Saturday 9am to noon.

EXPLORING THE CITY

For the best view of the city, walk along the waterfront promenade, the **Lungomare Vittorio Emanuele.** The heart of the old town, the **Città Vecchia,** lies on an island, separating the Mare Piccolo from the Mare Grande. The modern city, the **Città Moderna,** lies to the north of the Lungomare Vittorio Emanuele.

Evidence of Taranto's former glory as an important city in Magna Graecia can be found at the ✪ **Archaeological Museum of Taranto (Museo Archeologico di Taranto),** Corso Umberto 41 (☎ **099-453-2112**), where an assortment of artifacts documenting Pugliese civilization from the Stone Age to modern times is displayed. Most of the items are the results of archaeological digs in the area, especially the excavated necropolis. The museum boasts the world's largest collection of terra-cotta figures, along with a glittering array of Magna Grecian art, such as vases, goldware, marble and bronze sculpture, and mosaics. The designs of many of these works would be considered sophisticated even by today's standards. Admission is 8,000L ($4). The museum is open Monday to Saturday 9am to 2pm.

If the ornate vases at the National Museum enchanted you, you may want to visit **Grottaglie,** a nearby small town that's the ceramics capital of southeast Italy. Modern styles are crafted here, but most shoppers prefer to purchase traditional pieces, such as the giant vases that originally held laundry or the glazed wine bottles that mimic those of the ancient Greeks. You can buy pieces for a standard 50% discount over what you'd pay anywhere else for Grottaglie pottery, which is sold all over Italy. The whole village looks like one great china shop. Plates and vases are stacked on the pavements and even on the rooftops. Just walk along, looking to see what interests you; then bargain, bargain, bargain.

ACCOMMODATIONS

The choices here are limited. Inexpensive accommodations, in fact, may be impossible to find. Many third- or fourth-class hotels, especially around the waterfront, are unsafe. Proceed with caution. Make reservations in advance—the good hotels, though expensive, fill up fast.

Grand Hotel Delfino. Viale Virgilio 66, 74100 Taranto. ☎ **099-732-3232.** Fax 099-730-4654. 204 units. A/C MINIBAR TV TEL. 200,000–270,000L ($100–$135) double; from 300,000L ($150) suite. Rates include breakfast. AE, DC, MC, V. Free parking.

Built in the 1960s and radically renovated in 1994, the Delfino stands on the waterfront, much like a beach club, and is the best place to stay in Taranto. The well-furnished guest rooms are modern and beachy, with tile floors, wooden furniture, and small balconies, plus firm mattresses. The restaurant serves regional cuisine, like excellent fish dishes and Taranto oysters. There's also a cozy country-style drinking lounge and bar. Services include a concierge, room service, laundry/dry cleaning, and babysitting, and there's a pool.

Tracking Down the Sheik of Araby

For years, movie buffs have visited the town of **Castellaneta,** birthplace of Rudolph Valentino, the silent-screen actor known for starring roles in *The Sheik* (1921), *Blood and Sand* (1922), and *Four Horsemen of the Apocalypse* (1921). Valentino was born in 1895 at V. Roma 114; for decades, the town's young men modeled themselves, heavily oiled hair and all, after the star. The town still sells mementos of the matinee idol and souvenir photos. In the town piazza stands a statue of Valentino in full costume as the Sheik of Araby.

Castellaneta is also known for its "cave churches" and views of the Gulf of Taranto and the Basilicata mountains. Set high in a ravine, the village isn't easily accessible except by car. From Taranto, take S7 to the turnoff for Castellaneta.

Hotel Palace. Viale Virgilio 10, 74100 Taranto. ☎ and fax **099-459-4771.** 73 units. A/C MINIBAR TV TEL. 250,000L ($125) double. Rates includes breakfast. AE, DC, MC, V. Parking 15,000L ($7.50).

The Palace is the Delfino's nearest rival, at the eastern end of Lungomare Vittorio Emanuele III, opening onto the Mare Grande. The modern building offers good guest rooms, all with balconies. They range from small to medium, each with a good mattress and a tiled bathroom. A restaurant, bar, and cafe are on the premises. Garage parking is available.

DINING

Taranto is blessed with a bountiful supply of seafood; it's fresh from the water, delicious, and inexpensive. However, avoid anything raw—the locals may like some fish dishes this way, but you don't want to risk spending your vacation in the hospital.

Al Gambero. Vicolo del Ponte 4. ☎ **099-471-1190.** Reservations recommended. Main courses 26,000–30,000L ($13–$15). AE, DC, MC, V. Tues–Sun noon–3pm and 7–10pm. ITALIAN/SEAFOOD.

This restaurant has thrived since 1952 in a modern-looking building near the rail station. It's devoted to the fish dishes for which Taranto is famous, with an emphasis on shellfish, fresh fish, and such signature dishes as pappardelle with herbs and a lobster-flavored cream sauce and risotto with shellfish. You have a choice of enjoying your meal alfresco or in one of the rooms overlooking the harbor and the old city fish market. To start your meal, try the *antipasti frutti di mare,* an assortment of seafood hors d'oeuvres. Main courses include *spaghetti al Gambero;* grilled or braised versions of veal, beef, or pork; and *orecchiette alla Pugliese,* the best-known pasta dish of Apulia.

L'Assassino. Lungomare Vittorio Emanuele III, 29. ☎ **099-459-3447.** Reservations recommended. Main courses 15,000–40,000L ($7.50–$20). AE, DC, MC, V. Sat–Thurs noon–4pm and 9pm–midnight. Closed Christmas and Aug. ITALIAN/INTERNATIONAL.

Described by its owners as "normal but nice," this restaurant is exactly that—nothing too fancy but a pleasant place for a good affordable meal. The dining area offers a panoramic view of the water and a wide range of Italian dishes. Of course, L'Assassino has a variety of fresh fish dishes, including *risotto al frutti di mare* (rice with the "fruits of the sea"). Other specialties are orecchiette and spaghetti marinara. The proprietors, who've run the place for more than 30 years, are friendly and provide good service.

Sicily

15

Sicily is a land unto itself, proudly different from the rest of Italy in its customs and traditions. On the map, the toe of the Italian boot appears poised to kick Sicily away from the mainland, as if it didn't belong to the rest of the country. The largest of the Mediterranean islands, it's separated from Italy by the 2$^1/_2$-mile (4km) Strait of Messina, a dangerously unstable earthquake zone, making the eventual construction of a bridge doubtful.

While the island's economy and its social habits are moving closer to those of Europe and the rest of Italy, its culture is still very much its own. Its vague Arab flavor reminds us that Sicily broke away from the mainland of Africa, not Italy, millions of years ago. Its Greek heritage still lives. Though there are far too many cars in Palermo, and parts of the island are heavily polluted by industrialization, Sicily is still a different country. Life is slower, tradition is respected, and the myths and legends of the past aren't yet forgotten.

Sicily has been inhabited since the Ice Age, and its history is full of natural and political disasters. It has been conquered and occupied over and over: by the Greeks in the 6th to 5th centuries B.C., then the Romans, the Vandals, the Arabs (who created a splendid civilization), the Normans, the Swabians, the fanatically religious House of Aragón, and the Bourbons. When Garibaldi landed at Marsala in 1860, he brought an illusion of freedom, soon dissipated by the patronage system of the Mafia. Besides the invaders, the centuries have brought a series of plagues, volcanic eruptions, earthquakes, and economic hardships to threaten the interwoven culture of Sicily.

This land has a deep archaeological heritage and is full of sensual sights and experiences: vineyards and fragrant citrus groves, horses with plumes and bells pulling gaily painted carts, masses of blooming almond and cherry trees in February, Greek temples, ancient theaters, complex city architecture, and aromatic Marsala wine. In summer the sirocco whirling out of the Libyan deserts dries the fertile fields, crisping the harvest into a sun-blasted palette of browns. Beaches are plentiful around the island, but most are rocky, crowded, or dirty. The best are at Mondello, outside Palermo, and around Taormina in the east. The beaches north of Taormina are better than those south of the resort. Another good beach on the northern coast is Capo San Vito, near Erice.

Like its landscape, Sicily is a hypnotic place of dramatic turbulence, as intense as a play by native son Luigi Pirandello. Luigi Barzini, in

The Italians, wrote: "Sicily is the schoolroom model of Italy for beginners, with every Italian quality and defect magnified, exasperated, and brightly colored . . . Everywhere in Italy, life is more or less slowed down by the exuberant intelligence of the inhabitants: In Sicily it is practically paralyzed by it."

GETTING TO SICILY

BY PLANE Flying time from Rome to Palermo is 1 hour.

Alitalia (☎ **800/223-5730** in the U.S.; toll-free in Italy 1478-656-41 for domestic flights or 1478-656-42 for international; www.alitalia.it/english/index.html) operates at least six flights a day to Palermo from Rome and about half a dozen from Milan (nonstop or with stops in Naples or Rome). From Turin, Venice, Pisa, Genoa, and Bologna, Palermo receives at least one nonstop flight a day and several with a stop at Rome or Naples. Charter flights occasionally land in Trapani, but all other major flights to Sicily land at Catania, with at least one flight a day from Milan, Pisa, Rome, and Turin.

Meridiana (☎ **800/275-5566** in the U.S., 06-478-041 in Rome, or 091-323-141 in Palermo) shares some of its flights and reservation functions with Alitalia. Most of the carrier's Sicilian flights operate between Rome and Palermo and can be booked separately or as part of a transatlantic itinerary through Alitalia. Regardless of how you opt to fly, it's cheaper to have your flight to Palermo written into your ticket when you book your flight from North America. There are two flights a day to/from Milan's Malpensa to Catania and at least one flight a day to/from Rome's Fuimincino.

The quickest and most efficient way to see the major part of Sicily is to fly into Palermo, rent a car, and travel east to Catania, perhaps basing at Taormina instead of in this dull city. You can return the car in Catania. Conversely, you can fly into Catania, perhaps from Rome, and end your itinerary in Palermo, returning the car here before flying back to Rome. The chief advantage of flying in/out of Catania or Palermo is that it literally cuts days off your time, and you avoid the long trip south from Naples to the ferry or hydrofoil link going to Messina on the east coast of Sicily. The time saved can be spent at the beach, enjoying Greek temples, or just absorbing the unique characteristics of the island.

BY TRAIN Trains from all over Europe arrive at the port at Villa San Giovanni, near Reggio di Calabria, and roll onto enormous barges for the 1-hour crossing to Sicily. Passengers remain in their seats during the short voyage across the Strait of Messina, eventually rolling back onto the tracks at Messina, Sicily.

From Rome, the trip to Palermo takes 11 to 13 hours, depending on the speed of the train. A one-way ticket from Rome to Palermo costs 71,000L ($35.50) second class and 120,000L ($60) first, with a per-person supplement of 25,000L ($12.50) for rides on the fastest of the trains. The rail route from Naples takes 9 to 11 hours. From Naples, one-way transit on the slowest of the trains is 58,000L ($29) second class and 95,000L ($47.50) first, with a per-person supplement of 23,000L ($11.50) for access to the faster train. Aboard any of the trains pulling into Palermo, you can rent a couchette for 20,000 to 30,500L ($10 to $15.25) per person, depending on how luxurious it is and the number of persons (between two and six) you share the cabin with.

Many visitors begin their Italian trip in Palermo or Catania and then visit Rome at the end of their tour. For example, you can leave the station at Taormina at 10:30pm at night and arrive in Rome at 8:13am the next morning—a great way to save the cost of a hotel and not waste a day getting to Rome. You're likely to have a great experience traveling the south of Italy by train as well. Of course, it's also possible to take this same trip in reverse—that is, arrive in Rome and take the train to Taormina.

For fares and information, call ☎ **1478-880-88** toll-free in Italy.

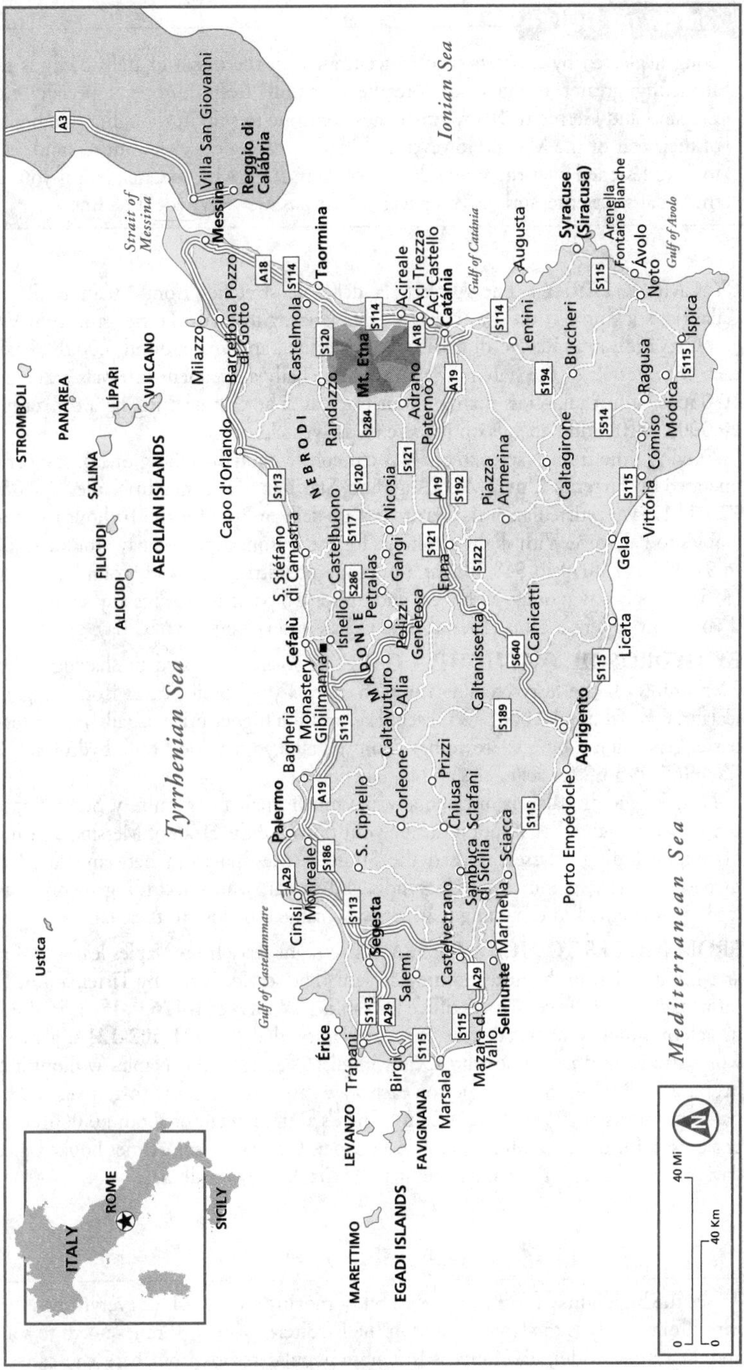
Tyrrhenian Sea
Ionian Sea
Mediterranean Sea
Strait of Messina
Gulf of Castellammare
Gulf of Catània
Gulf of Avolo
AEOLIAN ISLANDS
STROMBOLI
PANAREA
SALINA
LÍPARI
VULCANO
FILICUDI
ALICUDI
Ustica
EGADI ISLANDS
MARETTIMO
LEVANZO
FAVIGNANA
NEBRODI
MADONIE
Mt. Etna
Villa San Giovanni
Reggio di Calàbria
Messina
Taormina
Castelmola
Milazzo
Barcellona Pozzo di Gotto
Capo d'Orlando
S. Stéfano di Camastra
Cefalù
Monastery
Gibilmanna
Isnello
Castelbuono
Petralias
Polizzi Generosa
Gangi
Nicosia
Randazzo
Adrano
Paternò
Acireale
Aci Trezza
Aci Castello
Catània
Augusta
Lentini
Syracuse (Siracusa)
Arenella
Fontane Bianche
Ávolo
Noto
Ispica
Buccheri
Ragusa
Mòdica
Cómiso
Vittòria
Caltagirone
Piazza Armerina
Enna
Caltanissetta
Canicattì
Gela
Licata
Agrigento
Porto Empèdocle
Caltavuturo
Alia
Bagheria
Palermo
Monreale
Cinisi
S. Cipirello
Corleone
Prizzi
Chiusa Sclafani
Sambuca di Sicilia
Sciacca
Marinella
Selinunte
Castelvetrano
Segesta
Salemi
Érice
Trápani
Birgi
Marsala
Mazara d. Vallo
A3
A18
A19
A29
S113
S114
S115
S117
S120
S121
S122
S186
S189
S192
S194
S284
S286
S514
S640
ITALY
ROME
SICILY
0
40 Mi
40 Km

Safety on Sicily

Long neglected by travelers who concentrated on the north of Italy, Sicily is now attracting greater numbers of foreigners, mainly from Europe, especially from England and Germany. Many Americans continue to skip it, though, often because of their fear of the Mafia. However, the Mafia (yes, it does exist, but its hold seems to have lessened over the years) doesn't concern itself with tourists, and if you take the usual safety precautions (keep alert, don't flash jewelry) you'll be fine.

BY CAR & FERRY The Autostrada del Sole stretches from Milan to Reggio Calabria, sticking out on the "big toe," the gateway to Sicily. Ferries run from Villa San Giovanni, near Reggio di Calabria, to Messina, and cost around 5,000L ($2.50) each way. Vessels of the state railway ferry leave daily at frequent intervals 3:20am to 10:05pm, and it takes less than an hour to cross. The cost of bringing a car starts at 20,000L ($10) and depends on the size of the vehicle.

Driving time from Naples to Sicily is cut considerably by taking one of the vessels operated by **Tirrenia Lines,** Molo Angioino, Stazione Marittima, in Naples (☎ **081-720-1111;** www.tirrenia.com). Departures are daily at 8pm for the 10-hour trip from Naples to Palermo. With slight variations for the season, expect to pay around 77,000 to 97,000L ($38.50 to $48.50) for a one-way pedestrian fare and around 150,000L ($75) for one-way passage with a car and up to two passengers, plus any supplements if you want to rent a cabin. Arrival time in Palermo is 7am the next day.

BY HYDROFOIL (WITHOUT A CAR) If you're interested in shaving at least 22 minutes off the ferry crossing time, an *aliscafo* (hydrofoil) leaves from Reggio di Calabria. You'll pay 10,000L ($5) each way, and the higher price usually means fewer passengers—and a bit less crowding. You can't take your vehicle on a hydrofoil. Call ☎ **0965-295-68** for schedules and connections.

Near Reggio di Calabria, incidentally, is a much smaller community, Scilla, famous in Homeric legend. You'll spot it during your transit of the Strait of Messina. Mariners of old, including Ulysses, crossed the Strait of Messina from here and faced the menace of the two monsters, Charybdis and Scylla, who—according to myth and legend—delighted in drowning mariners who came too close to their lairs.

FROM NAPLES TO SICILY BY SEA The night ferry from Naples leaves at 8pm, arriving in Palermo the next morning at 7am. The service is run by Tirrenia S.A. For information, call the company's office in Naples (☎ **081-251-4763**). If you're already in Palermo and want to take the ferry to Naples, dial ☎ **091-602-1214;** alas, you won't always find someone who speaks English. Passage from Naples without a car begins at 120,000L ($60) per person each way. Passage for a car with a driver and one passenger starts at 225,000L ($112.50). There's a supplement of about 60,000L ($30) per person for use of a cabin, double occupancy. Cabins are sometimes booked many days in advance, and there might be space available only on deck.

A Suggested Itinerary

To see the highlights of Sicily requires a bit of moving around, since everything is very spread out (Sicily is the largest island in the Mediterranean, 110 miles north to south and 175 miles wide). Taormina is the most popular resort; from here you can visit Mt. Etna. However, the town is rather isolated in the east, so it's not a good base for seeing the island's other major highlights because of the long distances involved. You may not want to move as many times as we suggest below, but here's one way to link together the region's highlights if you have a car. You can also take this drive in reverse order.

Days 1–2: Arrive in tacky **Messina,** often by car ferry from the mainland. The third-largest city in Sicily (and the setting of Shakespeare's *Much Ado About Nothing*), it doesn't invite lingering. Take A18 down the eastern coast about 30 miles (48km) to ✪ **Taormina.** Set atop Monte Tauro, overlooking the Ionian Sea, this is the most majestic resort on Sicily. Spend the night and then a leisurely day at the beach.

Day 3: A18 continues south to **Catania,** Sicily's second-largest city and a busy seaport, where you might want to have lunch. Continue south from Catania for 36 miles (58km) to Syracuse and stay overnight.

Day 4: Plan on a full day exploring the ruins and monuments of **Syracuse.** In ancient times it was the capital of Magna Graecia (Greater Greece) and was one of the greatest cities on earth. You can spend hours exploring its archaeological zone and attractions like a steep-walled quarry known as the Latomia del Paradiso. Spend another night in Syracuse.

Day 5: South of Syracuse, the autostrada soon ends and Rte. SS115 takes over. It leads to **Noto,** about 12½ miles (20km) from Syracuse, with its Sicilian baroque architecture. Most of the city's monuments are on the main street, Corso Vittorio Emanuele. Back on SS115, proceed to **Ragusa,** encircled by large chemical plants. Hurry on for another 70 miles (113km), passing Gela, until you reach your goal for the night: Agrigento.

Day 6: While based in **Agrigento,** explore the ✪ **Valley of the Temples,** one of the highlights of your tour. See the temples at dawn, when they're hauntingly beautiful, and again at twilight, when floodlights create a spectacle.

Day 7: The route west (SS115) leads to **Sciacca,** 39 miles (63km) from Agrigento. Sciacca is known for its ceramics and its thermal baths. Continue along SS115 for 25 miles (40km) to **Selinunte.** This ancient town, founded in 682 B.C., was one of the most prosperous Greek colonies in Italy. After exploring the incredible ruins, continue on SS115 north to Castelvetrano; then head west for 22 miles (35km) to Marsala. **Marsala** is known for its fortified wine, often compared to sherry. This is where Garibaldi landed with 1,000 men to launch his campaign to liberate Sicily from Bourbon rule. From Marsala, take SS115 north 19 miles (31km) to Trapani and spend the night.

Day 8: In the morning explore **Trapani,** the westernmost Sicilian town. After passing through its dreary suburbs, head for the narrowing promontory to explore the most interesting part of this colorful port. From Trapani continue to **Erice,** 9 miles (14km) northeast. This was ancient Eryx, founded by the Elymnians and mentioned in Virgil's *Aeneid.* With its fortified castles, it owes much of its present look to its Norman conquerors. Take S113 directly out of Erice east for 12 miles (19km) to Segesta. A rival of Selinunte, **Segesta** was founded in the 12th century B.C. It contains one of the world's great Doric temples. From Segesta, follow the autostrada signs (A29) and head east to Palermo for the night.

Days 9–10: In **Palermo,** you'll be busy day and night with the many attractions. You need the ninth day to explore the sights in the environs, including Cefalù and Monreale. Try to work in some time at the beach at Mondello Lido, 7½ miles (12km) east of Palermo.

Sicily is crossed by autostrada, but the system doesn't cover key sectors of the island. For example, there's no autostrada from Catania to Syracuse or along the southern tier.

On the east coast an autostrada connects Messina with Catania, going via Taormina, then cuts west across the central part of the island, heading via Enna before cutting northwest again to the capital of Palermo on the northern coast. From Palermo, there's an autostrada link west to the port of Trapani. If you want to experience more bucolic Sicily off the main highways and if you have time and patience, you can travel the secondary roads of Sicily, though it's unlikely you'll average more than 35 m.p.h.

1 Taormina

33 miles (53km) N of Catania, 33 miles (53km) S of Messina, 155 miles (250km) E of Palermo

✪ **Taormina** was just too good to remain unspoiled. Dating from the 4th century B.C., it hugs the edge of a cliff overlooking the Ionian Sea. The sea, even the railroad track, lies below, connected by bus routes. Looming in the background is Mt. Etna, an active volcano. Noted for its mild climate, Italy's most beautiful town seems to have no other reason to exist than for the thousands upon thousands of visitors who flock here for shopping and eating and enjoying the nearby beaches.

International tourists pack the main street, Corso Umberto I, from April to October. After that, Taormina quiets down considerably. In spite of the hordes who descend in summer, Taormina is still charming, with much of its medieval character intact. It's filled with intimate piazzas and palazzi dating from the 15th to the 19th century. You'll find a restaurant for every day of the week, and countless stores sell everything from fine antiques to cheap souvenirs and trinkets.

You can always escape the throngs during the day by seeking out adventures like climbing Mt. Etna, walking to the Castel Mola, or making a day trip to Syracuse (all described later in this chapter). In summer, of course, you can hang out at the beaches below the town (though Taormina isn't on a beach). At night you can enjoy jazz and disco or just spend some time in a local tavern or restaurant.

A lot of people contributed to putting Taormina on the map. First inhabited by a tribe known as the Siculi, it has known many conquerors, like the Greeks, Carthaginians, Romans, Saracens, French, and Spanish. Its first tourist is said to have been Goethe, who arrived in 1787 and recorded his impressions in his *Journey to Italy.* Other Germans followed, including a red-haired Prussian, Otto Geleng. Arriving at the age of 20 in Taormina, he recorded its beauties in his painted landscapes, which were exhibited in Paris. They caused much excitement—people had to find out for themselves whether Taormina was really that beautiful.

Another German, Wilhelm von Gloeden, arrived to photograph not only the town but also nude boys crowned with laurel wreaths. His pictures sent European high society flocking to Taormina. Von Gloeden's photos, some of which are printed in official tourist literature to this day, form one of the most enduring legends of Taormina. Souvenir shops still sell his pictures, which, though considered scandalous in their day, seem tame, even innocent, by today's standards.

In von Gloeden's footsteps came a host of celebs hoping to see what all the excitement was about: Truman Capote, Tennessee Williams, Marlene Dietrich, Joan Crawford, Rita Hayworth, and Greta Garbo. Always in disguise, sometimes as Harriet Brown, Garbo used Taormina as a vacation retreat from 1950 until her last mysterious arrival in 1979. Many stars, including Garbo, stayed at a villa on the road to Castel Mola owned by Gayelord Hauser, the celebrated dietitian to Hollywood stars of the golden age. In time, another wave of stars arrived, including Elizabeth Taylor and Richard Burton, Cary Grant, and the woman who turned him down, Sophia Loren.

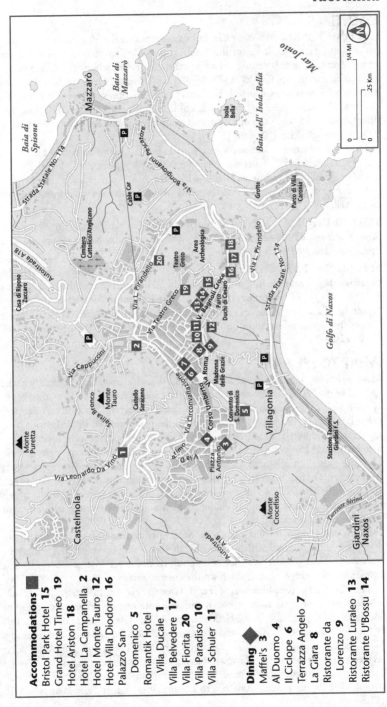

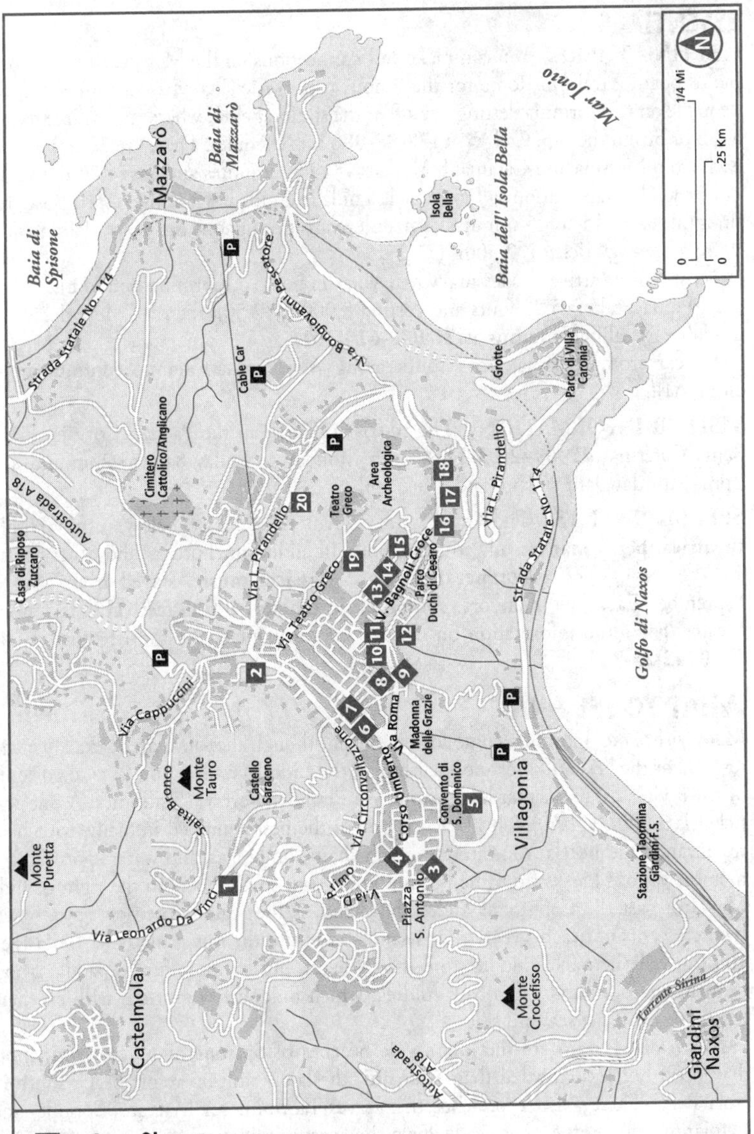
Accommodations
Bristol Park Hotel 15
Grand Hotel Timeo 19
Hotel Ariston 18
Hotel La Campanella 2
Hotel Monte Tauro 12
Hotel Villa Diodoro 16
Palazzo San Domenico 5
Romantik Hotel Villa Ducale 1
Villa Belvedere 17
Villa Fiorita 20
Villa Paradiso 10
Villa Schuler 11
Dining
Maffei's 3
Al Duomo 4
Il Ciclope 6
Terrazza Angelo 7
La Giara 8
Ristorante da Lorenzo 9
Ristorante Luraleo 13
Ristorante U'Bossu 14
Baia di Spisone
Mazzarò
Baia di Mazzarò
Mar Jonio
Isola Bella
Baia dell' Isola Bella
Strada Statale No. 114
Cable Car
Via Bongiovanni Pescatore
Cimitero Cattolico/Anglicano
Autostrada A18
Casa di Riposo Zuccaro
Via L. Pirandello
Teatro Greco
Area Archeologica
Grotte
Parco di Villa Caronia
Via Teatro Greco
V. Bagnoli Croce
Parco Duchi di Cesarò
Golfo di Naxos
Via Cappuccini
Monte Tauro
Salita Bronco
Castello Saraceno
Via Circonvallazione
Via Roma
Corso Umberto
Madonna delle Grazie
Convento di S. Domenico
Villagonia
Monte Puretta
Via Leonardo Da Vinci
Via D. Primo
Piazza S. Antonio
Stazione Taormina Giardini F.S.
Castelmola
Monte Crocefisso
Torrente Sirina
Giardini Naxos
0 1/4 Mi
0 .25 Km
N

ESSENTIALS

GETTING THERE You can make **rail** connections on the Messina line. It's possible to board a train in Rome for the 9-hour trip to Messina where a connection can be made on to Taormina, letting you off at the station below, where it's possible to take a cab or bus to the top. Call ☎ **1478-88-088** for schedules. There are 29 trains a day each from Messina and Catania; both take 45 to 50 minutes and cost 4,700L ($2.35) one way. The train station at Taormina is a mile from the heart of the resort. Buses run up a hill every 15 to 45 minutes (schedules vary throughout the year), daily 9am to 9pm; a one-way ticket is 2,500L ($1.25).

Most visitors arrive in Messina, where you can board a Taormina-bound **bus.** There are 14 a day, taking 1½ hours and costing 5,000L ($2.50) one way. More details are available by calling **Interbus** at ☎ **090-625-301.**

By **car** from Messina, head south along A18. From Catania, continue north along A18.

VISITOR INFORMATION The **tourist office** is in the Palazzo Corvaja, Piazza Santa Caterina (☎ **0942-23-243**), open Monday to Friday 8am to 2pm and 4 to 7pm, Saturday 9am to 1pm and 4 to 7pm.

SPECIAL EVENTS The Greek and Roman theater (see below) offers regular **theatrical performances** July to September. In addition, churches and other venues are the settings for a **summer festival of classical music,** staged from May to September. Each July the resort sponsors an **international film festival** in its amphitheater. For more information on cultural events, contact the tourist office or call ☎ **0942-23-243.**

WHAT TO SEE & DO

Many visitors to Taormina come for the **beach,** though the sands aren't exactly at the resort. For the best and most popular beach, the **Lido Mazzarò,** you have to go south of town via a cable car that leaves from Via Pirandello every 15 minutes. A one-way ticket is 3,000L ($1.50). This beach is one of the best equipped in Sicily, with bars, restaurants, and hotels. You can rent beach chairs, umbrellas, and water-sports equipment at various kiosks from the beginning of April to October. To the right of Lido Mazzarò, past the Capo Sant'Andrea headland, is the region's prettiest cove, where twin crescents of beach sweep from a sand spit out to the miniscule **Isola Bella** islet. You can walk here in a minute from the cable car, but it's more fun to paddle a boat from Mazzarò around Capo Sant'Andrea, which hides a few grottoes with excellent light effects on the seaward side.

North of Mazzarò are the long, wide beaches of **Spisone** and **Letojanni,** more developed but less crowded than **Giardini,** the large built-up resort beach south of Isola Bella. There's also a local bus that leaves Taormina for Mazzarò, Spisone, and Letojanni, and another that heads down the coast to Giardini.

The ✪ **Greek Amphitheater (Teatro Greco),** Via Teatro Greco (☎ **0942-23-220**), is Taormina's most visited monument, offering a view of rare beauty of Mt. Etna and the seacoast. In the Hellenistic period, the Greeks hewed the theater out of the rocky slope of Mt. Tauro, and the Romans remodeled and modified it greatly. What remains today dates from the 2nd century A.D. The conquering Arabs, who seemed intent on devastating the town, slashed away at it in the 10th century. On the premises is an antiquarium containing artifacts from the classical and early Christian periods. The theater is open daily 9am to 2 hours before sunset. Admission is 5,000L ($2.50).

Behind the tourist office, on the other side of Piazza Vittorio Emanuele, is the **Roman Odeon,** a small theater partly covered by the church of Santa Caterina next door. The Romans constructed this theater around A.D. 21, when Taormina was under their rule. Much smaller than the Greek theater and with similar architecture, it was discovered in 1892 by a blacksmith digging in the area. A peristyle (colonnade) was also discovered here, perhaps all that was left of a Greek temple dedicated to Aphrodite. **Santa Caterina** was consecrated to St. Catherine of Alexandria (exact consecration date unknown). It may have been built in the mid-17th century, and the sacristy may have been constructed even earlier. The facade of the sacristy contains two small windows decorated with sea shells, the same motif used on the architrave of its doors. The church's open hours are erratic.

Farther along the main drag, **Corso Umberto I,** you arrive at Piazza del Duomo and the **Duomo (cathedral)** of Taormina. Built around 1400 on the ruins of a church from the Middle Ages, this is a fortress cathedral with a Latin cross plan and a trio of aisles. The nave is held up by half a dozen monolithic columns—three on each side—in pink marble. A fish-scale decoration graces their capitals in honor of the island's maritime tradition. The ceiling of the nave is an attraction, with its wooden beams held up by carved corbels decorated with Arabian scenes. The main portal was reconstructed in 1636, with a large Renaissance-inspired rosette sculpted on it. The cathedral is often open in the early morning or early evening but is likely to be closed during the day. The monsignor apparently opens it when he feels in the mood.

Another thing to do in Taormina is to walk through the **Public Garden (Giardino Pubblico),** Via Bagnoli Croce. The flower-filled garden overlooking the sea is a choice spot for views as well as a place to relax. At a bar in the park you can order drinks. Of course, most visitors come to Taormina not for antiquity or even beautiful gardens, but to shop and go to the beach, as we are about to do (see below).

From Taormina, you may want to set out for the nearby village of **Castel Mola,** 2 miles (3km) northwest. This is one of the most beautiful places in eastern Sicily, and you'll have a great view of Mt. Etna if the day is clear. You might also visit **Castello** on the summit of Mt. Tauro, about 2 miles (3km) northwest of Taormina along the Castel Mola road. If you like walking, you might prefer to hike up to it following a footpath. The summit is at 1,280 feet. Once here, you'll see the ruins of a former acropolis, but most people come for the panoramas.

FARTHER AFIELD TO THE ALCANTARA GORGES

To see some beautiful rapids and waterfalls, head to the **Gole dell'Alcantara** (☎ **0942-98-50-10**), a series of gorges 10½ miles (17km) from Taormina. Uncharacteristically for Sicily, the waters are extremely cold, but quite refreshing in August. During most conditions, it's possible to walk up the river May to September (when the water level is low), though you must check locally for current conditions. From the parking lot, you take an elevator partway down into the scenic abyss and then continue on foot. You're likely to get wet, so take your swimsuit, or you can rent a wet suit for 10,000L ($5). You don't have to bring rubber boots, since locals make a living by renting visitors these boots at the entrance. Allow at least an hour for this trip. October to April, only the entrance is accessible, but the view is always panoramic. It costs 4,000L ($2) to enter the gorge daily 9am to 5pm. If you're driving, head up SS185 for 10½ miles (17km). To get there by bus, take one of the SAIS buses (☎ **0942-625-301**) for the 20-minute trip departing from Taormina at 9:30am and 12:45pm. There's only one bus back, leaving at 2:25pm. The round-trip fare is 9,000L ($4.50). You could also go by taxi from Taormina, but the fare would have to be negotiated with your driver. If you'd like a taxi, call Franco Nunzio at ☎ **0942-510-94.**

Meet Mighty Mt. Etna

Warning: Always get the latest report from the tourist office before setting out for a trip to Mt. Etna, because adventurers have been killed by a surprise "belch" (volcanic explosion).

Looming menacingly over the coast of eastern Sicily, **Mt. Etna** is the highest and largest active volcano in Europe—and we do mean active! The peak changes in size over the years but is currently in the neighborhood of 10,800 feet. Etna has been active in modern times (in 1928 the little village of Mascali was buried under its lava), and eruptions in 1971 and 1992 rekindled Sicilians' fears.

Etna has figured in history and in Greek mythology. Empedocles, the 5th-century B.C. Greek philosopher, is said to have jumped into its crater as a sign he was being delivered directly to Mt. Olympus to take his seat among the gods. It was under Etna that Zeus crushed the multiheaded, viper-riddled dragon Typhoeus, thereby securing domination over Olympus. Hephaestus, the god of fire and blacksmiths, made his headquarters in Etna, aided by the single-eyed Cyclops.

The Greeks warned that whenever Typhoeus tried to break out of his prison, lava erupted and earthquakes cracked the land. That must mean the monster nearly escaped on March 11, 1669, the date of one of the most violent eruptions ever recorded—it destroyed Catania, about 17 miles (27km) away.

For a good view of the ferocious lava-spewing mountain, take one of the trains that circumnavigate the base of the volcano. Board at the **Stazione Borgo,** Via Caronda 350 (☎ **095-932-181**), in Catania, off Viale Leonardo da Vinci. A 5-hour tour from Catania costs 15,000L ($7.50). But if you'd prefer a more

SHOPPING

Shopping is easy in Taormina—just find **Corso Umberto I** and go. The trendy shops here sell everything upscale, from lacy linens and fashionable clothing to antique furniture and jewelry. If you're a little more adventurous, you'll want to veer off the Corso and search out the little shops on the side streets.

Women's fashions are the focus at **Mazzullo,** Corso Umberto I 35 (☎ **0942-23-152**), but it does offer upscale clothing and accessories for both sexes. From curios to furniture, **Giovanni Panarello,** Corso Umberto I 110 (☎ **0942-23-823**), offers one of the best selections of antiques in town. Mixing the new and the old, **Carlo Panarello,** Corso Umberto I 122 (☎ **0942-23-910**), offers Sicilian ceramics (from pots to tables) and also deals in eclectic antique furnishings, paintings, and engravings. A small shop filled with treasures, the **Casa d'Arte Forin,** Corso Umberto I 148 (☎ **0942-23-060**), sells Italian antiques, ranging from furniture to prints, silver, and bronze, with an emphasis on Sicilian and Venetian pieces.

The **Gioielleria Giuseppe Stroscio,** Corso Umberto I 169 (☎ **0942-24-865**), features antique gold jewelry from 1500 to the early 1900s. The jewelers at **Estro,** Corso Umberto I 205 (☎ **0942-24-991**), sell contemporary rings, necklaces, and bracelets. Hand-embroidered lace is the draw at **Galeano** (aka **Concetta**), Corso Umberto I 233 (☎ **0942-625-144**), where bedspreads and tablecloths are meticulously crafted from fine cotton and linen.

structured outing, consider a package tour from Taormina. Contact **CST,** Corso Umberto I 101 (☎ **0942-23-301**), which organizes tours to Etna about twice a week in summer. They cost around 80,000L ($40).

You can also drive here. Etna lies 19 miles (31km) north of Catania and 37 miles (60km) south of Messina. One of the easiest approaches is via E45 south from Messina or Taormina to Acireale. From here you can approach by following the signs west going via the little towns of Aci Sant'Antonio and Viagrande, continuing west until you reach the Nicolosi. Allow about 45 minutes from Acireale to Nicolosi. At Nicolosi, you can book one of the official guides of **Alpine Etna Sud** (☎ **095-791-4755**). From Nicolosi, the road winds its way up to Rifugio Sapienza, the starting point for all expeditions to the crater. At Rifugio Sapienza, you can get on a cable car that takes you toward the summit. The service runs daily 9am to 4pm, costing 18,000L ($9).

From Rifugio Sapienza, it's also possible to hike up to the **Torre del Filosofo (Philosopher's Tower),** at 2,920 meters. The trip there and back takes about 5 hours. At the tower you'll have a panoramic sweep of Etna with its peaks and craters hissing with steam. This is a difficult hike and not for the faint of heart. The climb is along ashy, pebbly terrain, and even once you reach the tower, you have another risky 2-hour hike to the craters. Because the craters can erupt unexpectedly (as they did in the early 1990s, killing 11), all guided tours to the craters have been suspended—if you insist on going all the way, you'll have to do it alone. On the return from the Philosopher's Tower to Rifugio Sapienza, you'll pass Valle de Bove, the original crater of Etna.

ACCOMMODATIONS

The hotels in Taormina are the best in Sicily—in fact, the finest in Italy south of Amalfi. All price levels and accommodations are available, from sumptuous suites to army cots.

If you view Taormina primarily as a beach destination, at least in July and August, then consider staying at Mazzaro, 3 miles (5km) from the center (see below), and trekking up the hill for the shopping, nightlife, and dining. At other times, you may want to lodge in Taormina itself, since it has far more charm and far more attractions than anything down by the sea.

The curse of Taormina hotels in summer is the noise, not only of traffic but of visitors, hundreds of whom view the town as an all-night party. If you're a light sleeper and you've chosen a hotel along Corso Umberto, ask for a room in the rear. You may not get a better view, but at least you might get a good night's sleep.

If you're driving to the top of Taormina to a hotel, call ahead to see what arrangements can be made for your car. Also ask for clear directions, as the narrow one-way streets are bewildering once you get here.

VERY EXPENSIVE

✪ **Grand Hotel Timeo.** Via Teatro Greco 59, 98039 Taormina. ☎ **0942-238-01.** Fax 0942-628-501. www.cormorano.net/framon/timeo. E-mail: timeo@framon-hotels.com. 56 units. A/C MINIBAR TV TEL. 650,000–820,000L ($325–$410) double; from 1,200,000L ($600) suite. Rates include half-board. AE, DC, MC, V. Parking 30,000L ($15).

The San Domenico (see below) has long been Taormina's leading hotel. Not so anymore, since the Timeo has bounced back after a 13-year closing. Hidden in a private park below the Greek amphitheater, it's stylishly decorated with Victorian antiques. The hotel opened in 1873, and "everyone" has stayed here, from King Umberto II, Marconi, and André Gide to Guy de Maupassant, Elizabeth Taylor, and Richard Burton. Now the chic crowd is back. All the guest rooms are spacious and well furnished, with luxury mattresses. The marble bathrooms are large and contain amenities like hair dryers and hydromassage.

Dining/Diversions: Opening onto the most evocative terrace in Taormina, the hotel restaurant, Il Dito e la Luna, offers a refined Sicilian and Mediterranean cuisine. The bar, La Zagara, is the most sophisticated and fashionable on the island.

Amenities: Concierge, room service, shuttle service to beach, baby-sitting, car rental.

✪ **Palazzo San Domenico.** Piazza San Domenico 5, 98039 Taormina. ☎ **0942-23-701.** Fax 0942-625-506. www.cormorano.net/sgas/sandomenico/. E-mail: sandomenico@sgas.com. 110 units. A/C MINIBAR TV TEL. 620,000–780,000L ($310–$390) double; from 1,080,000L ($540) suite. Rates include breakfast. AE, DC, MC, V. Free parking outside; 3 spaces inside 30,000L ($15).

This is one of Europe's great old hotels, converted from a 14th-century Dominican monastery. Past guests have included François Mitterrand and Sir Winston Churchill. In 1997 it was discreetly renovated. Its position is high up from the coast, on different levels surrounded by terraced gardens of almond, orange, and lemon trees. The medieval courtyard is planted with semitropical trees and flowers. The encircling enclosed loggia—the old cloister—is decorated with potted palms and ecclesiastical furnishings. Off the loggia are great refectory halls turned into sumptuous lounges. Though antiques are everywhere, the atmosphere is gracious rather than museumlike. The guest rooms, opening off the cloister, are filled with elaborate carved beds, provincial pieces, Turkish rugs, and Venetian chairs and dressers (some look a bit tired, however). The most desirable rooms are those overlooking the water.

Dining: The cuisine, supervised by a masterful chef and the most refined in Taormina, is a combination of Sicilian and Italian dishes. Dining in the main hall is an event. Meals are served around the pool in summer.

Amenities: Room service, baby-sitting, laundry/valet, pool.

MODERATE

Bristol Park Hotel. Via Bagnoli Croce 92, 98039 Taormina. ☎ **0942-23-006.** Fax 0942-24-519. 52 units. A/C MINIBAR TV TEL. 250,000–300,000L ($125–$150) double; 380,000L ($190) suite. Rates include breakfast. Half-board 40,000L ($20) per person. AE, DC, MC, V. Closed Dec–Feb. Parking 25,000L ($12.50) in garage.

This four-star hotel is one of the town's best in its price range. Constructed high on the cliff side at the edge of Taormina, it offers a panoramic view of the coastline and Mt. Etna from most of its private sun balconies. The plush and ornate interior decor is amusing, with tufted satin. In contrast, the guest rooms (medium to spacious in size) are decorated in traditional style. The bathrooms come with hair dryers. The dining room offers international meals with an occasional Sicilian dish. There's a private beach with free deck chairs and parasols, plus bus service to the beach (June to September), where the hotel maintains a full-service bar. There's also a pool.

Hotel Ariston. Via Bagnoli Croci 168, 98039 Taormina. ☎ **0942-23-838.** Fax 0942-21-137. 176 units. A/C MINIBAR TV TEL. 95,000–160,000L ($47.50–$80) per person with half-board. AE, MC, V. Parking 20,000L ($10) nearby.

This modern hotel rises four stories above a verdant park about 400 yards from the center. It's a favorite with families from Italy and the rest of Europe. The well-maintained guest rooms are airy and comfortable, with firm mattresses; about 36 are in a low-rise garden annex nearby. The tiled bathrooms are small but tidy. On the premises are a pool, a piano bar, and a restaurant with efficient service that offers Sicilian and international specialties. Dinner is served on a poolside terrace in summer.

Hotel Monte Tauro. Via Madonna delle Grazie 3, 98039 Taormina. ☎ **0942-24-402.** Fax 0942-24-403. www.tao.it/hotelmontetauro. E-mail: hotelmontetauro@tao.it. 67 units. A/C MINIBAR TV TEL. 325,000L ($162.50) double; from 385,000L ($192.50) junior suite. Rates include breakfast. AE, DC, MC, V. Closed Jan 15–Mar.

This hotel is built into the side of a scrub-covered hill rising high above the sea. Renovated in the early 1990s, each room has a circular balcony with a sea view, often festooned with flowers. Most rooms are medium in size, each furnished to a high standard, with firm mattresses and tiled bathrooms. The social center is the many-angled pool, whose cantilevered platform is ringed with a poolside bar and dozens of plants.

Hotel Villa Diodoro. Via Bagnoli Croce 75, 98039 Taormina. ☎ **0942-23-312.** Fax 0942-23-391. 102 units. A/C MINIBAR TV TEL. 310,000–350,000L ($155–$175) double. Rates include breakfast. AE, DC, MC, V. Free parking.

This is one of Taormina's better hotels, with tasteful design through and through. The dining room, with tall windows on three sides, faces the sea and Mt. Etna. The outdoor pool is a sunny spot where you can sunbathe, swim, and enjoy the view of mountains, trees, and flowers. The guest rooms are elegant and comfortable, with well-designed furniture and the latest gadgets. Many units are angled toward the sea, with wide-open windows. The compact tiled bathrooms have hair dryers. A shuttle bus makes a half-dozen runs per day (June–Oct) to the beach at nearby Lido Caparena.

Romantik Hotel Villa Ducale. Via Leonardo da Vinci 60, 98039 Taormina. ☎ **0942-281-53.** Fax 0942-287-10. www.hotelvilladucale.it. E-mail: villaducale@tao.it. 15 units. A/C MINIBAR TV TEL. 290,000–400,000L ($145–$200) double; 500,000–650,000L ($250–$325) suite. Rates include breakfast. AE, CB, MC, V. Parking 10,000L ($5).

The Villa Ducale sits on a hillside, a 10-minute uphill walk from the center. Painted depictions of local landscapes are scattered throughout the salons and accommodations. From the tile-floored terrace where afternoon tea and breakfast are served, the view encompasses the bay, Taormina's historic core, and the upward thrust of Mt. Etna. Each guest room has a veranda with a sea view, a handful of antiques, and a firm mattress. The compact tiled bathrooms are well cared for.

✪ **Villa Fiorita.** Via Pirandello 39, 98039 Taormina. ☎ **0942-24-122.** Fax 0942-625-967. 26 units. A/C MINIBAR TV TEL. 200,000L ($100) double; 300,000L ($150) suite. Rates include breakfast. AE, MC, V. Parking 20,000L ($10).

The Villa Fiorita stretches toward the Greek theater from its position beside the road leading to the top of this cliff-hugging town. Its imaginative decor includes a handful of ceramic stoves, which the owner delights in collecting. A well-maintained flower garden with a pool lies alongside an empty but ancient Greek tomb whose stone walls have been classified a national treasure. The guest rooms are arranged in a steplike labyrinth of corridors and stairwells, some of which bend to correspond to the rocky slope on which the hotel was built. Each unit contains a piece of antique furniture, and most have flowery private terraces.

Villa Paradiso. Via Roma 2, 98039 Taormina. ☎ **0942-23-922.** Fax 0942-625-800. 35 units. A/C TV TEL. 220,000–310,000L ($110–$155) double; 310,000–350,000L ($155–$175) junior suite. Rates include breakfast. AE, DC, MC, V. Parking 20,000L ($10).

The creation of Signore Salvatore Martorana, this charming hotel is at one end of the town's main street, near the Greek theater. The living room is furnished in a personal manner, with antiques and reproductions. Each individually decorated guest room, from small to medium, has a balcony; the tiled bathrooms are a bit cramped. Guests spend many hours in the rooftop solarium, the TV room, or the informal bar, which is open 24 hours. Late May to late October, the hotel offers free access to the private Paradise Beach Club 4 miles (6km) east in Letojanni, which has an outdoor pool, a beach, changing rooms, a tennis court, and a Jacuzzi.

Inexpensive

Hotel La Campanella. Via Circonvallazione 3, 98039 Taormina. ☎ **0942-23-381.** Fax 0942-625-248. 12 units. TEL. 120,000L ($60) double. Rates include breakfast. No credit cards.

This hotel is rich in plants, paintings, and hospitality. It sits at the top of a seemingly endless flight of stairs, which begin at a sharp curve of the main road leading into town. You climb past terra-cotta pots and the dangling tendrils of a terraced garden, eventually arriving at the house. The owners maintain clean and uncluttered guest rooms, each containing potted plants and homey touches. The tiled bathrooms are tidy.

✪ **Villa Belvedere.** Via Bagnoli Croci 79, 98039 Taormina. ☎ **0942-23-791.** Fax 0942-625-830. www.villabelvedere.it. E-mail: info@villabelvedere.it. 47 units. TV TEL. 180,000–290,000L ($90–$145) double. Rates include breakfast. MC, V. Closed Nov 15–Dec 15 and Jan 15–Mar 15. Parking 10,000L ($5).

With a friendly reception, professional maintenance, and an old-fashioned style, this hotel near the Giardino Pubblico offers the same view enjoyed by guests at the more expensive first-class hotels nearby. In its garden is a heated pool. Guests congregate on the cliff-side terrace in the rear to enjoy that view of Sicilian skies and the Ionian Sea, plus the cypress-studded hillside and menacing Mt. Etna. The small to medium-sized guest rooms all feature firm mattresses and functional furniture with a touch of class. Most rooms have slivers of balconies from which to enjoy views over the neighboring public gardens to the sea, and top-floor rooms have small terraces from which you can glimpse Mt. Etna (these are also air-conditioned, as are rooms on the back, which have double-paned windows to block noise from the street above). There are two bars, and a snack bar by the pool serves lunch.

Villa Schuler. Piazzetta Bastione, Via Roma, 98039 Taormina. ☎ **0942-23-481.** Fax 0942-23-522. www.tao.it/schuler. E-mail: schuler@tao.it. 26 units. TV TEL. 180,000L ($90) double; 230,000L ($115) junior suite. Rates include breakfast. AE, CB, DC, DISC, MC, V. Parking 18,000L ($9) in garage; free outside.

Filled with the fragrance of bougainvillea and jasmine, this hotel is an ideal retreat for those who like style and comfort on a budget. Family owned and run, it sits high above the Ionian Sea, with views of snow-capped Mt. Etna and the Bay of Naxos. The hotel is only a 2-minute stroll from Corso Umberto I and about a 15-minute walk from the cable car to the beach below. The guest rooms are comfortably furnished, and many have a small balcony or terrace with a view of the sea. The well-maintained bathrooms are neat. Breakfast can be served in your room or taken on a terrace with a panoramic coast view. Facilities and services include a roof terrace solarium, a small library, 24-hour bar and room service, and laundry.

Nearby Accommodations

If you visit Taormina in summer, you may prefer to stay at **Mazzarò,** about 3 miles (5km) away. This is the major beach and has some fine hotels. A bus for Mazzarò leaves from the center of Taormina every 30 minutes daily 8am to 9pm (the return trip schedule is the same). The one-way fare is 1,500L (75¢).

Grande Albergo Capotaormina. Via Nazionale 105, 98039 Mazzaro. ☎ **0942-572-111.** Fax 0942-625-467. www.capotaorminahotel.com. E-mail: prenotazioni@capotaorminahotel.com. 200 units. A/C MINIBAR TV TEL. From 450,000L ($225) double; from 550,000L ($275) suite. Rates include buffet breakfast. AE, CB, DC, MC. V. Closed Oct 30–Mar. Parking 15,000L ($7.50) in garage; free outside.

The Grande Albergo is a world unto itself, atop a rugged cape projecting into the Ionian Sea. It was designed by one of Italy's most famous architects, Minoletti. There are five floors with wide sun terraces, plus a saltwater pool at the edge of the cape. Elevators take you through 150 feet of solid rock to the beach below. The guest rooms are handsome and well proportioned, with deluxe mattresses and wide glass doors opening onto private terraces. The tiled bathrooms are roomy with hair dryers.

Dining/Diversions: The hotel has a simple outdoor cafe. In the more intimate indoor venue, the food is lavishly presented and effectively enhanced by Sicilian wines. There are two bars—one cozy, the other more expansive, with an orchestra for dancing.

Amenities: Concierge, room service, laundry/dry cleaning, solarium, saltwater pool.

✪ **Mazzarò Sea Palace.** Via Nazionale 147, 98030 Mazzarò. ☎ **0942-24-004.** Fax 0942-626-237. www.mazzaroseapalace.tao.it. E-mail: seapalace@tao.it. 87 units. A/C MINIBAR TV TEL. 300,000–500,000L ($150–$250) double; 600,000–860,000L ($300–$430) suite. Rates include half-board. AE, DC, MC, V. Parking 10,000L ($5) nearby.

The Sea Palace, the leading four-star hotel in Mazzarò, opens onto the most beautiful bay in Sicily and has a private beach. Completed in 1962, it has been renovated frequently since, most recently in the mid–1990s. Big windows let in cascades of light and offer views of the coast. The guest rooms are well furnished, filled with wicker and veneer pieces, along with original art, wood or tile floors, and beds with firm mattresses; most have panoramic views. The bathrooms are clad in marble, each with a hair dryer.

Dining/Diversions: The elegant restaurant Bougainvillea opens onto a terrace and offers excellent food and service. The menu, which changes daily, emphasizes seafood and fresh produce. The piano bar is a popular nighttime spot.

Amenities: Concierge, room service, baby-sitting, laundry/dry cleaning, private beach.

Villa Sant'Andrea. Via Nazionale 137, 98030 Taormina Mare. ☎ **0942-23-125.** Fax 0942-24-838. www.cormoran.net/framon/santandrea. E-mail: santandrea@framon-hotels.com. 67 units. A/C MINIBAR TV TEL. 310,000–550,000L ($155–$275) double. Rates include breakfast. AE, DC, MC, V. Parking 25,000L ($12.50).

This hotel lies at the base of the mountain, directly on the sea, and has a private beach. Staying here is like going to a house party at a pretty home. The atmosphere and tasteful refurbishment draw return visits by artists, painters, and other discerning guests. The guest rooms are well maintained and comfortable, though their size and decor vary. Many have sea-facing balconies or terraces. The tiled bathrooms are small but have adequate shelf space. A cable car, just outside the front gates, runs into the heart of Taormina.

Dining/Diversions: Oliviero's, which opens onto delightful views across the bay, serves some of the finest cuisine on the island. The restaurant Sant'Andrea offers international and Sicilian cuisine. A garden terrace is another summer dining venue. A piano bar keeps the evenings lively.

Amenities: Concierge, room service, baby-sitting, laundry/dry cleaning; private beach next to hotel, changing facilities, sports activities such as windsurfing; rentals of sailboats, motorboats, and pedal boats; nearby tennis courts and golf.

DINING

EXPENSIVE

La Giara. Vico la Floresta 1. ☎ **0942-233-60.** Reservations required. Main courses 26,000–38,000L ($13–$19). AE, DC, MC, V. Apr–June and Sept–Oct, Tues–Sun 8:15pm–midnight (Nov–Mar open only Fri–Sat, July–Aug open daily). SICILIAN/ITALIAN.

The food here is full of flavor and is most accomplished, based on the use of fresh ingredients grown in the southern sunshine of Italy. The art deco ambience is also inviting—marble floors and columns shaped from stone quarried in the fields outside Syracuse. The pastas are worthy of meals unto themselves, and we're especially fond of the ricotta-stuffed cannelloni served with zucchini cream au gratin, the tagliolini with savory lemon-and-shrimp sauce, and the ravioli stuffed with pesto-flavored eggplant and covered with tomato sauce. The fresh fish of the day is grilled to perfection, and meats are cooked equally well.

Maffei's. Via San Domenico de Guzman 1. ☎ **0942-240-55.** Reservations required. Main courses 35,000–40,000L ($17.50–$20). AE, DC, MC, V. Daily noon–3pm and 7pm–midnight. Closed Jan 10 to mid-Feb. SICILIAN/SEAFOOD.

Maffei's is very small, with only 10 tables, but serves the best fish in Taormina. Every day the chef selects the freshest fish at the market, and you can tell him how you'd like it prepared. We often select the house specialty, swordfish *alla messinese,* braised with tomato sauce, black olives, and capers. The *fritto misto* (a mixed fish fry with calamari, shrimp, swordfish, and sea bream) is superbly light, since it's prepared with a good-quality virgin olive oil. Among the desserts are velvety lemon mousse and crêpes flambé stuffed with vanilla cream.

MODERATE

Al Duomo. Vico Ebrei 11. ☎ **0942-625-656.** Reservations required. Main courses 18,000–25,000L ($9–$12.50). AE, DC, MC, V. Nov–May Thurs–Tues noon–2:30pm and 7–11pm; June–Oct daily noon–2:30pm and 7–11pm. SICILIAN/MESSINESE.

Known for its outside terrace dining, this restaurant uses the freshest local produce and regional ingredients. It's an attractive place, with brickwork tiles and inlaid marble tables. The romantic terrace provides a view of the square and the cathedral. Try such *piatti tipici* as fave puree or stewed lamb with potatoes, pecorino cheese, and red Sicilian wine. You might start with stockfish salad, fried cheese, and broad beans, before going on to one of the homemade pastas with an array of succulent sauces. The fried calamari is sautéed in extra-virgin olive oil and not overcooked. Another marvelous dish is rissolé of fresh anchovies. For dessert, taste a typical almond cake or a Sicilian cassata.

Il Ciclope. Corso Umberto I 203. ☎ **0942-23-263.** Main courses 18,000–30,000L ($9–$15). AE, DC, MC, V. Thurs–Tues noon–3pm and 6:30–10pm. Closed Jan 10–Feb 10 and Wed Oct–May. SICILIAN/ITALIAN.

This is one of the best of Taormina's low-priced trattorie. Set back from the main street, it opens onto the pint-sized Piazzetta Salvatore Leone. In summer, try for an outside table if you'd like both your food and yourself inspected by the passing parade. The meals are fairly simple but the ingredients fresh and the dishes well prepared. Try the fish soup or Sicilian squid. If those don't interest you, go for entrecôte Ciclope or grilled shrimp. Most diners begin with a selection from the *antipasti di mare,* a savory assortment of seafood hors d'oeuvres.

Ristorante da Lorenzo. Via Roma, near Via Michele Amari. ☎ **0942-23-480.** Reservations required. Main courses 16,000–30,000L ($8–$15). AE, DC, MC, V. Thurs–Tues noon–3pm and 6:30–11pm. Closed Nov 15–Dec 15. SICILIAN/ITALIAN.

This is a bright restaurant on a quiet street near the landmark Palazzo San Domenico, in front of the town hall. The restaurant has a terrace shaded by an 850-year-old tree—the botanical pride of the town—and oil paintings decorating its white walls. Your meal might include a fresh selection of antipasti, spaghetti with sea urchins, scaloppini mozzarella, grilled swordfish, or fillet of beef with Gorgonzola.

INEXPENSIVE

Ristorante Luraleo. Via Bagnoli Croce 27. ☎ **0942-24-279.** Reservations recommended. Main courses 15,000–26,000L ($7.50–$13). DC, MC, V. Summer daily noon–3pm and 7–11pm; winter closed Wed. SICILIAN/INTERNATIONAL.

Luraleo offers excellent value for an attractive price. Many diners prefer the flowery terrace, where pastel tablecloths are shaded by a vine-covered arbor. If you prefer to dine indoors, there's a rustic dining room with tile accents, flowers, evening candlelight, racks of wine bottles, and a rich antipasto table. The grilled fish is a good choice, as are pastas (like homemade macaroni with tomato, eggplant, and basil), regional dishes, and herb-flavored steak. Risotto with salmon and pistachio nuts is a specialty.

Ristorante U'Bossu. Via Bagnoli Croce 50. ☎ **0942-23-311.** Reservations recommended. Main courses 10,000–18,000L ($5–$9); fixed-price menu 30,000L ($15). V. Tues–Sun noon–3pm and 6pm–midnight. Closed Jan 10–May 10. SICILIAN/MEDITERRANEAN.

Vines twine around the facade of this small restaurant in a quiet part of town. Amid fresh flowers, wagon-wheel chandeliers, prominently displayed wine bottles, and burnished wooden panels, you can enjoy a meal pungent with the aromas of an herb garden. Start with the complimentary *bruschetta* (grilled bread with oil and garlic or tomato). Specialties include *pasta con la sarde* (with fish) and *involtini di pesce spada* (swordfish stew), and there's a groaning antipasti table. The restaurant is decorated with a folkloric scene from *Cavalleria Rusticana,* and the chef has paid homage to the famed opera by naming his best pasta dish *maccheroni alla Turiddu,* after the principal character (it contains tuna, olives, capers, onions, wild herbs, tomatoes, and fennel). For dessert, nothing can top the zabaglione with fresh strawberries.

Terrazza Angelo. Corso Umberto I 38. ☎ **0942-24-411.** Reservations recommended. Main courses 16,000–23,000L ($8–$11.50). AE, DC, V. Daily noon–3pm and 7pm–midnight. Closed Nov. SICILIAN/PIZZA.

For years, this old-fashioned rustic place was famous as Giova Rosy, one of the best restaurants in town. Under new management and a new name, it's now receiving mixed reviews. It serves a variety of local specialties, like linguine and risotto dishes. Seafood offerings include spiedini with shrimp and lobster dosed with a generous shot of cognac, tagliolini with seafood, and swordfish cooked *in cartoccio* (in a paper bag). When we were last there the cuisine was uneven, but we hope it will have improved by the time of your visit.

NEARBY DINING

Ristorante Angelo a Mare–Il Delfino. Via Nazionale. ☎ **0942-23-004.** Reservations recommended. Main courses 20,000–45,000L ($10–$22.50). AE, DC, MC, V. Daily noon–3pm and 7pm–midnight. Closed Nov–Mar. MEDITERRANEAN/ITALIAN.

This late–19th-century structure is in Mazzarò, about 3 miles (5km) from Taormina and a 2-minute walk from the cable car station. From the flower-filled terrace, there's a view over the bay. The decor and the menu items are inspired by the sea and carefully supervised by the chef/owner. Mussels *delphio* (cooked with garlic, parsley, olive oil, and lemons) and house-style steak (with fresh tomatoes, onions, garlic, capers, and parsley) are specialties. Other good choices are *involtini* of fish, cannelloni, *risotto marinara* (fisherman's rice), and anchovies roasted with basil.

TAORMINA AFTER DARK

Begin your evening at the **Caffè Wunderbar,** Piazza IX Aprile 7, Corso Umberto I (☎ **0942-625-302**), a popular spot that was once a favorite watering hole of Tennessee Williams. Beneath a vine-covered arbor, the outdoor section is perched as close to the edge of the cliff as safety allows. We prefer one of the Victorian armchairs beneath chandeliers in the elegant interior. There's a well-stocked bar, as well as a piano bar. It's open daily 8:30am to 2:30am; closed Tuesday from November to February.

The entire town is geared to having fun, and you'll find a good many bars and clubs. **Bella Blu,** Guardiola Vecchia (☎ **0942-24-239**), caters to a high-energy European crowd. At the **Club Septimo,** Via San Pancrazio 50 (☎ **0942-625-522**), a sweeping view of the town and sea is framed with reproductions of ancient Roman columns, and the interior has all the strobe and ultraviolet lights you might want. More elegant than either of these is **La Jarra,** Via La Floresta 1, off Corso Umberto I (☎ **0942-23-360**), the only one of the three that's open year-round. A bar with recorded music and occasional dancing is **Le Perroquet,** Piazza San Domenico de Guzman, at Via Roma (☎ **0942-24-462**), which draws a more gay crowd than any of the others here.

A younger, wilder crowd tends to head for the places down by the water. Here the hottest action is at **Tout Va**, Via Pirandello 70 (☎ **0942-238-24**), an open-air club that offers panoramic views and action late into the night.

Taormina also has a cultural side. See "Special Events," under "Essentials," at the beginning of this section for details on its regular summer festivals.

EN ROUTE TO SYRACUSE: A STOP AT BAROQUE CATANIA

Ranking in growth next to Palermo, **Catania** is a suitable base if you're planning a jaunt up Mt. Etna. It lies 32 miles (52km) south of Taormina and 37 miles (60km) north of Syracuse. Largely industrial (with sulfur factories), the important port opens onto the Ionian Sea. In 1693 an earthquake virtually leveled the city, and Etna has rained lava on it on many occasions—so its history is fraught with natural disasters.

Somehow Catania has learned to live with Etna, but the volcano's presence is felt everywhere. For example, in certain parts of the city you'll find hardened remains of lava flows, all a sickly purple color. Grottoes in weird shapes, almost fantasylike, line the shores, and boulderlike islands rise from the water.

Catania's present look, earning for it the title of the "baroque city," stems from just after the 1693 earthquake, when the Camastra duke, with several architects and artists, decided to rebuild the city in the baroque style. This reconstruction took the whole 18th century. The most famous artists involved were Alonzo Di Benedetto, Antonino and Francesco Battaglia, Giovanni Vaccarini, and Stefano Ittar. Fragments of solidified black lava were used (first by the Romans and then until the end of the 19th century) in the construction of walls. This lava, and the way it was positioned into the masonry, gave added strength to the walls.

Splitting the city is **Via Etnea,** flanked with 18th-century palazzi. The locals are fond of strolling through the **Bellini Garden (Giardini Bellini),** named to honor Vicenzo Bellini, the young (dead at 32) composer of operas like *Norma* and *La Sonnambula,* who was born in Catania in 1801. If interested, you can see the home where he lived until he was 16, now the **Bellini Museum (Museo Belliniano),** Piazza San Francesco 3 (☎ **095-7150-535**). Consisting of five rooms, the museum is organized to trace the composer's musical evolution from cradle to grave. At the entrance, note the painting *Apoteosi di'Bellini* (*Bellini's Apotheosis*) by Michele Rapisardi. Among the relics on display are Bellini's funeral mask, a small bust, and a Girolamo Bozza portrait (*Il Ritratto*). Of particular interest are the several musical manuscripts autographed by Bellini. Admission is free. Summer hours are daily 9am to 12:30pm and winter hours Monday to Saturday 9am to 1pm.

Built in the late 11th century, Catania's **Duomo,** Piazza del Duomo (no phone), honors St. Agatha, the city's patroness. It was rebuilt after the 1693 earthquake, and its most outstanding feature is the curving baroque facade, a Vaccarini masterpiece. The chapel to the right as you enter contains the sarcophagus of Costanza, wife of Frederick III of Aragón, who died in 1363. The southern chapel honors St. Agatha. An elaborate Spanish doorway leads into the reliquary and treasury. Note also the carved choir stalls, illustrating scenes from the life of St. Agatha. Admission is free, and the cathedral is open daily 8am to 12:30pm and 3:30 to 6pm.

Most rushed visitors today pass through only on their way to or from Catania's airport, which in Sicily is second in importance only to Palermo's. Flights on Alitalia, including those from Rome, arrive at **Aeroporto Fontanarossa** (☎ **095-730-6266**), 3 miles (5km) south of the city center. From here, you can take the Alibus (or a taxi) into the Catania train station, where you'll find nine trains per day leaving for Taormina, costing 4,700L ($2.35) one way.

ACCOMMODATIONS

✪ **Villa Paradiso dell'Etna.** Via per Viagrande 37, 95030 San Giovanni La Punta. ☎ **095-751-2409.** Fax 095-741-3861. www.cormorano.net/paradisoetna. E-mail: hotelvilla@paradisoetna.it. 34 units. 360,000L ($180) double; 510,000L ($255) suite. AE, DC, MC, V. From Catania, take A18 and exit at Catania Nord; then follow the signs for San Giovanni la Punta.

If you need to stay near the Fontanarossa airport, you may want to spend the night here. This elegant hotel lies on the slopes of Etna, surrounded by gardens and a pool 7 miles (11km) from Catania. It was opened in 1927 by Cosmo Mollica Alagona and is now restored to its former glory. The villa offers the finest rooms in the district, all with Sicilian antiques and views of the volcano. The hotel restaurant, La Pigna, serves Sicilian fare along with traditional Italian and international dishes.

DINING

Trattoria La Paglia. Via Pardo 23. ☎ **095-346-838.** Reservations not needed. Meals from 20,000L ($10). No credit cards. Mon–Sat 12:30–2:30pm and 8–11pm. SICILIAN.

Our favorite restaurant in town is located in the lively fish market. Just ask for Maria and follow her advice. For an opening, request her *la triaca pasta,* pasta in a fresh bean sauce. For a main course, try any of the fish. If you dare not like Maria's offerings of the day, she'll let you step out in the market and buy a fish you do like, and then she'll cook it to your specifications.

2 Syracuse & Ortygia Island

35 miles (56km) SE of Catania

Of all the Greek cities of antiquity that flourished on the coast of Sicily, Syracuse (Siracusa) was the most important, a formidable competitor of Athens. In its heyday, it dared take on Carthage, even Rome. At one time its wealth and size were unmatched by any other city in Europe.

Colonists from Corinth founded Syracuse on the Ionian Sea in about 735 B.C. Much of its history was linked to despots, beginning in 485 with Gelon, the tyrant of Gela, who subdued the Carthaginians at Himera. Syracuse came under attack from

Athens in 415, but the main Athenian fleet was destroyed and the soldiers on the mainland captured. They were herded into the Latomia di Cappuccini at Piazza Cappuccini, a stone quarry. The "jail," from which there was no escape, was particularly horrid—the defeated soldiers weren't given food and were packed together like cattle and allowed to die slowly.

Dionysius I was one of the greatest despots, reigning over the city during its greatest glory, in the 4th century B.C., when it extended its influence as a sea power. But in A.D. 212 the city fell to the Romans under Marcellus, who sacked its riches and art. In that attack, Syracuse lost its most famous son, the Greek physicist/mathematician Archimedes, who was slain in his study by a Roman soldier.

Though Syracuse will be one of the highlights of your trip to Sicily, it has been in a millennia-long decline. Today it's a blend of often unattractive modern development (with supermarkets and high-rises sprouting along speedways) and the ruins of its former glory, a splendor that led Livy to proclaim it "the most beautiful and noble of Greek cities."

A lot of what you'll want to see is on the island of Ortygia, which is filled with not only ancient ruins but also small craft shops and dozens of boutiques. From the mainland, Corso Umberto leads to the Ponte Nuova, which leads to the island. Parking is a serious problem on Ortygia, so if you're driving, park in one of the garages near the bridge, then walk over and explore the island on foot. Allow at least 2 hours to explore, plus another hour to shop along the narrow streets. What you'll also want to do is sit for half an hour or so on Piazza del Duomo, off Via Cavour. This is one of the most elegant squares in Sicily.

The ancient sights are a good half hour's walk back inland from Ortygia, going past a fairly forgettable shopping strip, so you may want to take a cab (they're easily found at all the sights). If you don't see a cab, you can call ☎ **0931-697-35** or 0931-697-22 and one will be sent for you. You'll find buses on Ortygia at Piazza Pancali/Largo XXV Luglio. The harbor front is lined with a collection of 18th- and 19th-century town houses.

Syracuse is a cauldron in summer. You can do as the locals do and head for the sea. The finest **beach** is about 12 miles (19km) away at **Fontane Bianche;** bus nos. 21 and 22 leave from the Syracuse post office, Piazza delle Poste 15. If you're driving, Fontane Bianche lies to the south of the city (it's signposted); take SS115 to reach it. The same buses will take you to **Lido Arenella,** only 5 miles (8km) away but not as good.

ESSENTIALS

GETTING THERE From other major cities in Sicily, Syracuse is best reached by **train.** It's 1½ hours from Catania, 2 hours from Taormina, and 5 hours from Palermo. Usually you must transfer in Catania. For information, call ☎ **1478-88-088.** Trains arrive in Syracuse at the station on Via Francesco Crispi, centrally located midway between the archaeological park and Ortygia.

From Catania, 12 SAIS **buses** daily make the 1¼-hour trip to Syracuse. The one-way fare is 6,500L ($3.25). Phone **SAIS** (☎ **0931-66-710** in Syracuse or 095-536-168 in Catania) for information and schedules.

Read Before You Go

Before your trip, you might want to read Mary Renault's novel *The Mask of Apollo,* set in Syracuse in the 5th century B.C. As one critic put it, "It brings the stones to life."

By **car** from Taormina, continue south along A18 and then E45, past Catania. Although trip time would depend on traffic, allow at least 1½ hours.

VISITOR INFORMATION The **tourist office** is at San Sebastiano 45 (☎ **0931-67-710**), and there's a branch office at the entrance to the archaeological park. Both are open Monday to Saturday 9am to 2pm and 3:30 to 6:30pm.

SPECIAL EVENTS Some of the most memorable cultural events in Sicily are presented in May and June of even-numbered years, when actors from the Instituto Nazionale del Dramma Antico present a repertoire of **classical plays** by Aeschylus, Euripides, and their contemporaries. The setting is the ancient Greek theater (Teatro Greco) in the archaeological park, beneath the open sky. Tickets are 25,000 to 90,000L ($12.50 to $45). For information, schedules, and tickets, write or call **INDA,** Corso G. Matteotti 29, 96100 Siracusa (☎ **0931-674-15** or 1478-822-11 from Italy only).

SEEING THE ANCIENT SIGHTS

✪ **Archaeological Zone (Zona Archeologica).** Via Augusto (off intersection of Corso Gelone and Viale Teocrito). ☎ **0931-66-206.** Admission 8,000L ($4). Apr–Oct daily 9am–6pm; Nov–Mar daily 9am–3pm.

Syracuse's archaeological park contains the town's most important attractions, all on the mainland at the western edge of town, to the immediate north of Stazione Centrale where the trains pull in from other parts of Sicily, including Messina and Taormina. The entrance to the park is down Via Augusto.

On the Temenite Hill, the ✪ **Greek Theater (Teatro Greco)** was one of the great theaters of the classical period. Hewn from rock during the reign of Hieron I in the 5th century B.C., the ancient seats have been largely eaten away by time. You can, however, still stand on the remnants of the stone stage where plays by Euripedes were mounted. The theater was much restored in the time of Hieron II in the 3rd century B.C. In the spring of even-numbered years (and in Segesta in the summer of odd-numbered years), the Italian Institute of Ancient Drama presents classical plays by Euripedes, Aeschylus, and Sophocles. (In other words, the show hasn't changed much in 2,000 years!)

Outside the entrance to the Greek Theater is the most famous of the ancient quarries, the **Paradise Quarry (Latomia del Paradiso),** one of four or five from which stones were hauled to erect the great monuments of Syracuse in its glory days. Upon seeing the cave in the wall, Caravaggio is reputed to have dubbed it the "Ear of Dionysius," because of its unusual shape. But what an ear—it's nearly 200 feet long. You can enter the inner chamber of the grotto, where the tearing of paper sounds like a gunshot. Although dismissed by some scholars as fanciful, the story goes that the despot Dionysius used to force prisoners into the "ear" at night, where he was able to hear every word they said. Nearby is the **Grotta dei Cordari,** where ropemakers plied their craft.

The ✪ **Roman Amphitheater (Anfiteatro Romano)** was created at the time of Augustus. It ranks among the top five amphitheaters left by the Romans in Italy. Like the Greek theater, part of it was carved from rock. Unlike the Greek theater and its classical plays, the Roman amphitheater tended toward gutsier fare. Gladiators (prisoners of war and "exotic" blacks from Africa) faced each other with tridents and daggers, or naked slaves were whipped into the center of a battle to the death between wild beasts. Either way, the victim lost: If his opponent, man or beast, didn't do him in, the crowd would often scream for the ringmaster to slit his throat. The amphitheater is near the entrance to the park, but you can also view it in its entirety from a belvedere on the road.

✪ **Paolo Orsi Regional Archaeological Museum (Museo Archeologico Regionale Paolo Orsi).** In the gardens of the Villa Landolina in Akradina, Viale Teocrito 66. ☎ **0931-464-022.** Admission 8,000L ($4). Tues–Sat 9am–1pm and 3:30–6:30pm; Mon 3:30–6:30pm.

One of the most important archaeological museums in southern Italy surveys the Greek, Roman, and early Christian epochs in sculpture and in fragments of archaeological remains. The museum also has a rich coin collection. The best known of the several excellent statues here is the headless *Venus Anadyomene* (rising from the sea), from the Hellenistic period in the 2nd century B.C. One of the earliest works is of an earth mother suckling two babes, from the 6th century B.C. The pre-Greek vases have great style and elegance.

✪ **Catacombs of St. John (Catacombe di San Giovanni).** Piazza San Giovanni, at end of Viale San Giovanni. ☎ **0931-67-955.** Admission 5,000L ($2.50). Mar 15–Nov 14 daily 9am–6pm; Nov 15–Mar 14 daily 9am–1pm and 3–6pm.

These honeycombed tunnels of empty coffins evoke the catacombs along the Appian Way in Rome. You enter the world below from the Chiesa di San Giovanni, established in the 3rd century A.D. (the present building is much more recent). Included in the early Christian burial grounds is the crypt of St. Marcianus, which lies under what was reportedly the first cathedral erected in Sicily. The catacombs lie on the mainland, immediately to the east of the archaeological zone.

Warning: Make sure you exit in plenty of time before closing. Two readers who entered the catacombs after 5pm were accidentally locked in and managed to escape only after a harrowing ordeal of wandering around in the dark.

EXPLORING ORTYGIA ISLAND

Ortygia, inhabited for many thousands of years, is also called the *Città Vecchia* (old city). It contains the town's Duomo, many rows of houses spanning 500 years of building styles, most of the city's medieval and baroque monuments, and some of the most charming vistas in Sicily. In Greek mythology, it's said to have been ruled by Calypso, daughter of Atlas, the sea nymph who detained Ulysses (Odysseus) for 7 years. The island, reached by crossing the Ponte Nuova, is about a mile long and half again as wide.

Heading out the Foro Italico, you'll come to the **Fonte Arethusa,** also famous in mythology. The river god Alpheius, son of Oceanus, is said to have fallen in love with the sea nymph Arethusa. The nymph turned into this spring or fountain, but Alpheius became a river and "mingled" with his love. According to legend, the spring ran red when bulls were sacrificed at Olympus.

At Piazza del Duomo is the **Duomo,** which was built over the ruins of the Temple of Minerva and employs the same Doric columns; 26 of the originals are still in place. The temple was erected after Gelon the Tyrant defeated the Carthaginians at Himera in the 5th century B.C. The Christians converted it into a basilica in the 7th century A.D. In 1693 an earthquake caused the facade to collapse, and in the 18th century the cathedral was rebuilt in the baroque style by Palermo architect Andrea Palma. It's open daily 8am to noon and 4 to 7pm. Admission is free.

The irregular **Piazza del Duomo** is especially majestic when the facade of the cathedral is dramatically caught by the setting sun or when floodlit after nightfall. Acclaimed as one of the most beautiful squares in Italy, it's filled with other fine baroque buildings. They include the striking **Palazzo Beneventano del Bosco,** with its lovely courtyard. Opposite it is the **Palazzo del Senato,** with an inner courtyard displaying a senator's carriage from the 1700s. At the far end of the square stands **Santa Lucia,** though it hardly competes with the Duomo.

The other important landmark square is **Piazza Archimede,** with its baroque fountain festooned with dancing jets of water and sea nymphs. This square lies directly northeast of Piazza del Duomo, forming the monumental heart of Ortygia. It, not the cathedral square, is the main square of the old city. On this piazza, original Gothic windows grace the 15th-century **Palazzo Lanzo.** As you wander around Ortygia, you'll find that Piazza Archimede is a great place from which to orient yourself. Wander the narrow streets wherever your feet will take you. When you get lost, you can always ask for directions back to Piazza Archimede.

The **Palazzo Bellomo,** Via Capodieci 14, off Foro Vittorio Emanuele II, dates from the 13th century, with many alterations, and is today the home of the **Galleria Regionale** (☎ **0931-69-617**). The palace is fascinating, with its many arches, doors, and stairs, and it also has a fine collection of paintings. The most notable is *Annunciation* by Antonello da Messina (1474). There's also a noteworthy collection of antiques and porcelain. It's open Monday to Saturday 9am to 1:30pm and Sunday 9am to 12:30pm. Admission is 8,000L ($4).

ACCOMMODATIONS

The best place to stay here is on Ortygia at either the Grand Hotel or the Domus Mariae (see below). The island has far more character and charm than "mainland" Syracuse. On the downside, both these hotels might be full, especially during summer. In that case, we've included some backup choices.

EXPENSIVE

✪ **Grand Hotel.** Viale Mazzini 12, 96100 Siracusa. ☎ **0931-464-600.** Fax 0931-464-611. 58 units. A/C MINIBAR TV TEL. 350,000L ($175) double; 450,000–550,000L ($225–$275) suite. Rates include buffet breakfast. AE, DC, MC, V. Free parking.

On Ortygia, this is the grandest place to stay in the entire area. It's a first-class hotel in a tranquil location; a private beach is a short shuttle bus ride away from the main premises. In the early part of the 20th century, it was the most fashionable place in southeastern Sicily, known for its balls and as a gathering point for wealthy Sicilian families and their visitors. Today, the guest rooms are spacious and luxuriously furnished (with top mattresses), opening onto panoramic sea views. They come with all the amenities, like radios and electronic safes, plus state-of-the-art bathrooms with hair dryers. Some rooms are for travelers with disabilities.

Dining/Diversions: The hotel also has a fashionable bar, plus a roof garden restaurant. The chefs offer a superb cuisine of regional Sicilian specialties and international dishes.

MODERATE

Domus Mariae. Via Vittorio Veneto 76, 96100 Siracusa. ☎ **0931-248-54.** Fax 0931-248-58. www.sistemia.it/domusmariae. E-mail: domusmariae@sistema.it. 16 units. A/C MINIBAR TV TEL. 230,000–240,000L ($115–$120) double. Rates include buffet breakfast. AE, DC, MC, V. Free parking outside.

On Ortygia, this is a less plush but correspondingly less expensive option than the Grand (see above). It's delightful in its own way, a three-star hotel with a tasteful decor. Directly on the seafront, it opens onto a view of Mt. Etna. Each of its guest rooms is fairly spacious, with a firm mattress and a small tiled bathroom. The excellent restaurant specializes in typical Sicilian dishes. Other facilities include a bar and a solarium.

Holiday Inn. Viale Teracati 30–32, 96100 Siracusa. ☎ **0931-463-232.** Fax 0931-67-115. 87 units. A/C MINIBAR TV TEL. 240,000–300,000L ($120–$150) double. Rates include buffet breakfast. AE, DC, MC, V. Free parking.

A short drive inland from the Città Vecchia, this branch of a hotel chain is designed for easy access and convenience to motorists. Each monochromatic guest room is functionally furnished but well kept, with a comfortable mattress and a small tiled bathroom. The restaurant attracts locals, who consider the generous portions, unpretentious service, and flavorful specialties worth the trip. Menu items include pastas, stuffed veal, American-style tournedos, salads, and a changing array of fresh fish.

Jolly Hotel. Corso Gelone 45, 96100 Siracusa. ☎ **800/221-2626** in the U.S., 800/237-0319 in Canada, or 0931-461-1111. Fax 0931-461-126. www.jollyhotels.it. 100 units. A/C MINIBAR TV TEL. 235,000–280,000L ($117.50–$140) double. Rates include breakfast. AE, DC, MC, V. Parking 20,000L ($10).

A major stop for tour groups, the six-story Jolly is part of the chain that's the Holiday Inn of Italy. You get no surprises, just tropical-style modern rooms that are a bit worn. Each is your basic motel room, with good beds and a small tiled bathroom. At least the view of Mt. Etna and the sea is panoramic. The hotel restaurant is better than the hotel, offering a standard lunch or dinner of Sicilian or international cuisine. The location is on a dull but busy shopping street, about a 20-minute walk from Ortygia.

INEXPENSIVE

Hotel Bellavista. Via Diodoro Siculo 4, 96100 Siracusa. ☎ **0931-411-355.** Fax 0931-37-927. www.sistemia.it/bellavista. E-mail: bellavista@sistemia.it. 47 units, 42 with bathroom. TV TEL. 100,000L ($50) double without bathroom, 160,000L ($80) double with bathroom. Rates include breakfast. AE, MC, V. Free parking.

Family owned and run, this hotel lies in the commercial center, close to the archaeological zone. There's an annex in the garden for overflow. The spacious main lounge has leather chairs and semitropical plants. The guest rooms are informal and comfortable, often furnished with traditional pieces. Most feature a sea-view balcony. The restaurant serves Sicilian cuisine for hotel guests and groups only.

Hotel Panorama. Via Necropoli Grotticelle 33, 96100 Siracusa. ☎ **0931-412-188.** Fax 0931-412-527. 51 units. A/C TV TEL. 160,000L ($80) double. Rates include continental breakfast. AE, MC, V. Free parking.

Near the entrance to the city, on a rise of Temenite Hill, this bandbox-modern hotel sits on a busy street about 5 minutes from the archaeological park. It's not a motel, but it does provide parking. The small guest rooms are pleasant and up-to-date, with comfortable but utilitarian furniture, including firm mattresses, plus small tiled bathrooms. The dining room serves breakfast only.

DINING

MODERATE

Arlecchino. Via dei Tolomei 5. ☎ **0931-66-386.** Reservations recommended. Main courses 18,000–30,000L ($9–$15). AE, DC, MC, V. Tues–Sun 12:30–3pm and 7:30pm–midnight. Closed Sun Apr–Sept. SEAFOOD/PIZZA.

This restaurant occupies the street level of a 250-year-old palace in the heart of the Città Vecchia, a short walk from the cathedral. Despite its understated decor and inexperienced staff, it serves a memorable cuisine. Many specialties emerge from the fragrant kitchen, including a wide array of homemade pastas, a cheese-laden crespelline of the house, pasta with sardines, spiedini with shrimp, and a selection of pungent beef, fish, and veal dishes. There's also a pizzeria on site.

Gambero Rosso. Via Eritrea 2. ☎ **0931-68-546.** Reservations recommended. Main courses 18,000–32,000L ($9–$16). AE, MC, V. Fri–Wed noon–3:30pm and 7:30–11pm. SICILIAN/MEDITERRANEAN/SEAFOOD.

Near the bridge to the Città Vecchia, this restaurant is in an old tavern, where you can sample the best of Sicilian dishes. Two reliable choices are *zuppa di pesce* (fish soup) and *zuppa di cozze* (a plate brimming with fresh mussels in a tasty marinade). The Sicilian cannelloni are good too. The meat dishes feature a number of choices from the kitchens of Lazio, Tuscany, and Emilia-Romagna. The dining room extends from the restaurant onto a terrace dotted with potted flowers and shrubs that faces the port. Getting a table shouldn't be a worry—the restaurant can seat 120.

✪ **Ristorante Jonico-a Rutta e Ciauli.** Riviera Dionisio il Grande 194. ☎ **0931-65-540.** Reservations recommended. Main courses 18,000–35,000L ($9–$17.50); pizza 8,000–18,000L ($4–$9). AE, MC, V. Wed–Mon noon–3pm and 7–10:30pm. SICILIAN.

This is one of the best restaurants for the typical cuisine and local wines of Sicily. It's right on the sea, with a panoramic view, about 100 yards from Piazzale dei Cappuccini. The decor is pure Liberty (art nouveau) style.

The antipasti array is dazzling, and the homemade pasta dishes are superb—try *pasta rusticana* with eggplant, cheese, ham, and herbs (ask one of the English-speaking waiters to explain the many variations) or spaghetti with fresh tuna and herbs. One of the most interesting fish dishes we recently sampled was *spada a pizzaiola* (swordfish in a savory garlic-flavored sauce). Meat specialties include *bistecca siciliana* (tender beef with pulverized tomatoes, eggplant, onions, white wine, and local cheese); sliced veal with eggplant, tomatoes, onions, and slices of local cheese; and delicious fish stew. The dessert specialty is *cassatine siciliane* (mocha-chocolate ice cream capped with sprinkles of coffee-flavored chocolate, all floating in a lake of English custard). There's also a roof garden with a pizzeria serving typical Sicilian pizza.

Ristorante Rossini. Via Savoia 6. ☎ **0931-24-317.** Reservations recommended. Main courses 20,000–30,000L ($10–$15). AE, DC, MC, V. Wed–Mon noon–2pm and 7–10pm. Closed Dec 25. MEDITERRANEAN.

The Rossini is a homelike enclave of regional gastronomy, offering meals to 50 fortunate diners a night. Pasqualino Guidice is one of the most respected chefs in Sicily; he's become rather famous after conducting many international cooking demonstrations throughout the Americas. The restaurant offers an amply stocked buffet table of antipasti, including fish mousse garnished with shrimp, shellfish risotto with roasted peppers and tomato purée, *pesce alla matelote* (roasted fish with a sauce of capers, tomatoes, olives, herbs, and white wine), and an age-old Sicilian recipe for *pesce alla stimpirata* (with olive oil, garlic, mint, and vinegar). Twice-roasted swordfish is also a specialty.

✪ **Trattoria Archimede.** Via Gemellaro 8. ☎ **0931-697-01.** Reservations not necessary. Main courses 16,000–30,000L ($8–$15). AE, DC, MC, V. Mon–Sat 12:30–3pm and 7:30–11pm. Closed 3 weeks in July. SEAFOOD.

Settle into one of the three large, slightly formal dining rooms here, and prepare to enjoy some of the best-tasting cuisine in Syracuse. This trattoria is an excellent choice for those who wish to dine on historic Ortygia. The menu changes constantly, depending on the market, but you'll always find the freshest of Mediterranean fish, grilled or baked to perfection. The owner, Mr. Zammitti, will also prepare fresh pasta dishes (the best is with shellfish) and good-tasting soups. Sometimes ricci or sea urchin is used to flavor the pasta. For dessert, the specialty is a *cassata,* sweetened ricotta flavored with candied pumpkin and enveloped in alternating squares of sponge cake and green-colored almond paste. Candied cherries are often added. The staff is most welcoming and attentive.

SYRACUSE AFTER DARK

The region's best disco is **Fontana Bianca,** Viale Dei Lidi (☎ **0931-790-611**), 11 miles (18km) southwest of the town center and open June to September. It contains a walled garden, a pool that at night seems mostly ornamental, and a crowd that's older than you'll find at the student hangouts closer to the town center. Another option is the **Discotecca Malibu,** Via Elorina (☎ **0931-721-888**), about 3½ miles (6km) southwest of town on SS115, where a younger crowd dances all night at a seaside pavilion that evokes its California namesake.

On a small street near Via Maestanza in Syracuse, **La Nottola,** Via Gargallo 61 (☎ **0931-60-009**), is a stylish jazz club/piano bar/disco that attracts a well-dressed crowd. If you should happen to arrive in midsummer, head for the **Sporting Club Terrauzza** (☎ **0931-714-505**), centerpiece of the village of Terrauzza, about 6 miles (10km) southwest of Syracuse, where whoever happens to be vacationing on the local beaches shows up to mingle with local 20-somethings.

A SIDE TRIP TO BAROQUE NOTO

From Syracuse, head southwest on A18 for 19 miles (31km) to reach **Noto,** set amid olive groves and almond trees on a plateau overlooking the Asinaro Valley. Noto dates from the 9th century and knew a Greek, a Roman, a Byzantine, an Arab, a Norman, an Aragonese, and even a Spanish culture before 1692, when an earthquake destroyed it. Many Sicilian artists and artisans have worked to rebuild the town into a baroque gem with uniform buildings of soft limestone. It was constructed somewhat like a stage set, with curvaceous and curvilinear accents and potbellied wrought-iron balconies on the facades.

To get your bearings, stop first at the **tourist office** at Piazza XIV Maggio, Villetta Ercole, in front of San Domenico church (☎ **0931-573-779**), to pick up a map and some tips about exploring the town on foot. May to September, office hours are daily 9am to 1pm and 3:30 to 6:30pm; October to March, hours are Monday to Saturday 8am to 2pm and 3:30 to 6:30pm.

Mercifully, traffic has been diverted away from Noto's heart, to protect its fragile buildings, on which restoration began in 1987—and not a moment too soon. (The project was scheduled to be finished in 2000, but as of press time, it was still proceeding along at a snail's pace. There are no hours or admissions set for the buildings and monuments mentioned below.) Your best approach is through the monumental **Royal Gate (Porta Reale),** crowned by three symbols—a dog, a swan, and a tower, representing the town's former allegiance to the Bourbon monarchy. From here, take **Corso Vittorio Emanuele** going through the **old patricians' quarter.** The rich-looking, honey colored buildings along this street are some of the most captivating on the island. This street will take you to the three most important piazzas.

You arrive first at **Piazza Immacolata,** dominated by the baroque facade of **San Francesco all'Immacolata,** which still contains notable artworks rescued from a Franciscan church in the old town. Notable works include a painted wooden *Madonna and Child* (1564), believed to be the work of Antonio Monachello. The church is open daily 7:30am to noon and 4 to 7:30pm; admission is free. Immediately to the left stands the **St. Salvador Monastery (Monastero del Santissimo Salvatore),** characterized by an elegant tower, its windows adorned with wrought-iron balconies. When it reopens, it will contain a minor collection of religious art and artifacts.

The next square is **Piazza Municipio,** the most majestic of the trio. It's dominated by the **Palazzo Ducezio,** a graceful town hall with curvilinear elements enclosed by a classical portico, the work of architect Vincenzo Sinatra (no relation to Ol' Blue Eyes).

The upper section of this palace was added as late as the 1950s. Its most beautiful room is the Louis XI–style Hall of Representation (*Salone di Rappresentanza*), decorated with gold and stucco. On the vault is a Mazza fresco representing the mythological figure of Ducezio founding Neas (the ancient name of Noto).

On one side of the square, a broad flight of steps leads to the **Duomo,** flanked by two lovely horseshoe-shaped hedges. The cathedral was inspired by models of Borromini's churches in Rome and was completed in 1776. In 1996 the dome collapsed, destroying a large section of the nave, and it's still under repair. The date of completion for the extensive renovations is uncertain. On the far side of the cathedral is the **Palazzo Villadorata,** graced with a classic facade. Its six extravagant balconies are supported by sculpted buttresses of galloping horses, griffins, and grotesque bald and bearded figures with chubby-cheeked cherubs at their bellies. The palazzo is divided into 90 rooms, the most beautiful being the Yellow Hall (*Salone Giallo*), the Green Hall (*Salone Verde*), and the Red Hall (*Salone Rosso*), with their precious frescoed domes from the 18th century. The charming Feasts Hall (*Salone delle Feste*) is dominated by a fresco representing mythological scenes. In one of its aisles, the palazzo contains a *pinacoteca* (picture gallery) with antique manuscripts, rare books, and portraits of noble families.

The final square is **Piazza XVI Maggio,** dominated by the convex facade of its **Chiesa di San Domenico,** with two tiers of columns separated by a high cornice. The interior is filled with polychrome marble altars and is open daily 8am to noon and 2 to 5pm. Directly in front of the church is a public garden, the **Villetta d'Ercole,** named for its 18th-century fountain honoring Hercules.

Right off Corso Vittorio Emanuele is one of Noto's most fascinating streets, **Via Nicolaci,** lined with magnificent baroque buildings.

Noto in summer also is known for some fine **beaches** nearby; the best are 3½ miles (6km) away at **Noto Marina.** You can catch a bus at the Giardini Pubblici in Noto. The one-way fare is 1,500L (75¢).

While wandering the streets, you'll find nothing finer on a hot day than one of the highly praised cones from **Corrado Costanza,** Via Silvio Spaventa 7–9 (☎ **0931-835-243**), open Tuesday to Sunday 10am to noon and 4 to 9pm. It enjoys local renown for its gelato, the best in the area. The gelatos come in various flavors and are often made with fresh fruit.

If you don't have a car, you can reach Noto by AST or SAIS **buses** leaving from Syracuse. The ride takes only 40 minutes. On Monday to Saturday there are 11 buses per day, and on Sunday there are 3. A one-way ticket is 4,000L ($2). Noto is also reached by **train** from Syracuse (nine per day), taking 30 minutes and costing 3,200L ($1.60) one way. The train station is 20 minutes uphill from the town.

3 Agrigento & the Valley of the Temples

80 miles (129km) S of Palermo, 109 miles (175km) SE of Trapani, 135 miles (217km) W of Syracuse

Agrigento, with its amazing Valley of the Temples, is one of the most memorable and evocative sights of the ancient world. Greek colonists from Gela (Caltanissetta) called this area Akragas when they established a beachhead in the 6th century B.C. In time, the settlement grew to become one of the most prosperous cities in Magna Graecia. A great deal of that growth is attributed to the despot Phalaris, who ruled from 571 to 555 B.C. and is said to have roasted his victims inside a brass bull. He eventually met the same fate.

Empedocles (ca. 490–430 B.C.), the Greek philosopher and politician (also considered by some the founder of medicine in Italy), was the most famous son of Akragas. He formulated the theory that matter consists of four elements (earth, fire, water, and air), modified by the agents love and strife. In modern times the town produced playwright Luigi Pirandello (1867–1936), who won the Nobel Prize for literature in 1934.

Like nearby Selinunte, the city was attacked by war-waging Carthaginians, beginning in 406 B.C. In the 3rd century B.C., the city changed hands between the Carthaginians and the Romans until it finally succumbed to Roman domination by 210 B.C. It was then known as Agrigentium.

The modern part of Agrigento (in 1927 the name was changed from Girgenti to Agrigento) occupies a hill, and the narrow casbahlike streets show the influence of the conquering Saracens. Heavy Allied bombing during World War II necessitated much rebuilding. The result is for the most part uninspired and not helped by all the cement factories in the area.

Below the town stretch the long reaches of the ✪ **Valley of the Temples (Valle dei Templi),** containing some of the greatest Greek ruins in the world. See "Wandering Among the Ruins," below.

Visit Agrigento for its past, not for the modern incarnation. It's been a long time since Pindar called it "man's finest city." However, once you've been awed by the ruined temples, you can visit the *centro storico,* with its tourist boutiques hawking postcards and T-shirts, and enjoy people-watching at a cafe along Via Atenea. When it gets too hot (as it so often does), flee to a beach at nearby San Leone.

ESSENTIALS

GETTING THERE The **train** trip from Palermo takes 1½ hours and costs 12,100L ($6.05) each way. There are 10 trains daily. The main rail station, **Stazione Centrale,** Piazza Marconi (☎ **1478-88-088**), is downhill from Piazzale Aldo Moro and Piazza Vittorio Emanuele. From Syracuse by rail, you must first take 1 of 9 daily trains to Ragusa, a 2½-hour trip costing 11,000L ($5.50) each way. Three trains a day make the 3½-hour trip from Ragusa to Agrigento, costing 15,500L ($7.75) each way.

Omnia, Via Ragazzi del 99, 10 (☎ **0922-596-490**), runs four **buses** per day from Palermo to Argigento. The trip takes 2½ hours and costs 12,100L ($6.05) one way. **SAIS** buses, Via Favara Vecchia (☎ **0922-595-260**), make the 2½-hour trip from Catania several times a day. The one-way fare is 17,000L ($8.50).

By **car** from Syracuse, take SS115 through Gela. From Palermo, cut southeast along S121, which becomes S188 and S189 before it finally reaches Agrigento and the Mediterranean. Allow about 2½ hours for this jaunt.

VISITOR INFORMATION The **tourist office** is at Via Cesare Battisti 15 (☎ **0922-20-454**) or at Via Empedocle 73 (☎ **0922-20-391**). Both are open Monday to Friday 8:30am to 1pm and 4 to 7pm, Saturday 9am to 1pm.

SPECIAL EVENTS The **Settimana Pirandelliana** is a weeklong festival of plays, operas, and ballets staged in Piazza Kaos at the end of July and August. The tourist office or Piccolo Teatro Pirandelliano (☎ **0922-235-61**) can supply details; tickets cost 15,000 to 30,000L ($7.50 to $15).

WANDERING AMONG THE RUINS

Many writers are fond of suggesting that the Greek ruins in the **Valle dei Templi** be viewed at dawn or sunset, when their mysterious aura is indeed heightened. Regrettably, you can't get very close at those times. Instead, search them out under the cobalt-blue Sicilian sky. The backdrop is idyllic, especially in spring, when the striking almond trees blossom into pink.

Board a bus or climb into your car to investigate. Riding out the Strada Panoramica, you'll first approach (on your left) the ✪ **Temple of Juno (Tempio di Giunone),** erected sometime in the mid–5th century B.C., at the peak of a construction boom honoring the deities. Many of its Doric columns have been restored. As you climb the blocks, note the remains of a cistern as well as a sacrificial altar in front. The temple affords good views of the entire valley.

The ✪ **Temple of Concord (Tempio della Concordia),** which you'll come to next, ranks along with the Temple of Hephaestos (the Theseion) in Athens as the best-preserved Greek temple in the world. With 13 columns on its side, 6 in front and 6 in back, the temple was built in the peripheral hexastyle. You'll see the clearest example in Sicily of what an inner temple was like. In the late 6th century A.D., the pagan structure was transformed into a Christian church, which may have saved it for posterity, though today it has been stripped down to its classical purity.

The **Temple of Hercules (Tempio di Ercole)** is the oldest, dating from the 6th century B.C. Badly ruined (only eight pillars are standing), it once ranked in size with the Temple of Zeus. At one time the temple sheltered a celebrated statue of Hercules. The infamous Gaius Verres, the Roman magistrate who became an especially bad governor of Sicily, attempted to steal the image as part of his temple-looting tear on the island. Astonishingly, you can still see signs of black searing from fires set by long-ago Carthaginian invaders.

The ✪ **Temple of Jove or Zeus (Tempio di Giove)** was the largest in the valley, similar in some respects to the Temple of Apollo at Selinunte, until it was ruined by an earthquake. It even impressed Goethe. In front of the structure was a large altar. The giant on the ground was one of several *telamones* (atlases) used to support the edifice. Carthaginian slave labor built what was then the largest Greek temple in the world, and one of the most remarkable.

The so-called **Temple of Castor and Pollux (Tempio di Dioscuri),** with four Doric columns intact, is composed of fragments from different buildings. At various times it has been designated as a temple honoring Castor and Pollux, the twin sons of Leda and deities of seafarers; Demeter (Ceres), the goddess of marriage and of the fertile earth; or Persephone, the daughter of Zeus who became the symbol of spring. Note that on some maps this temple is called Tempio di Castore e Polluce.

The temples can usually be visited daily 9am until 1 hour before sunset. City **bus** nos. 8, 9, 10, and 11 run to the valley from the train station in Agrigento.

MORE ATTRACTIONS

The **Regional Archaeological Museum (Museo Regionale Archeologico),** near San Nicola, on Contrada San Nicola at the outskirts of town on the way to the Valle dei Templi (☎ **0922-401-565**), is open daily 8am to 1pm. Admission is 8,000L ($4). Its single most important exhibit is a head of the god Telamon from the Tempio di Giove. The collection of Greek vases is also impressive. Many of the artifacts on display were dug up when Agrigento was excavated. Take bus no. 8, 9, 10, or 11.

Pirandello's House (Casa di Pirandello), Contrada Caos, Frazione Caos (☎ **0922-511-102**), is the former home of the 1934 Nobel Prize winner, known worldwide for his plays *Six Characters in Search of an Author* and *Enrico IV.* He died 2 years after winning the prize and its attendant world acclaim. Although Agrigentans back then might not have liked his portrayal of Italy, all is forgiven now, and Pirandello is the local boy who made good. In fact, the Teatro Luigi Pirandello at Piazza Municipio bears his name. His "casa natale" is now a museum devoted to memorabilia pertaining to the playwright's life, including his study and the murals he painted. His tomb lies under his favorite pine tree ("One night in June I dropped down like a firefly beneath a huge pine tree in the garden.") The tomb lies a few hundred yards from the house and grounds, which are open daily 9am to 7pm; admission is 4,000L ($2). The birthplace lies outside of town in the village of Caos (catch bus no. 11 from Piazza Marconi), just west of the temple zone.

ACCOMMODATIONS

Hotel Tre Torri. Strada Statale 115, Viale Canatello, Villaggio Mosè, 92100 Agrigento. ☎ **0922-606-733.** Fax 0922-607-839. www.mediatel.it/public/tre-torri. E-mail: hotel3t@mediatel.it. 118 units. A/C TV TEL. 180,000L ($90) double. Rates include breakfast. AE, MC, V. Free parking.

Though it's near an unattractive commercial district 4½ miles (7km) south of Agrigento, this is among the area's best hotels. Behind a mock-medieval facade of white stucco, chiseled stone blocks, false crenellations, and crisscrossed iron balconies, the Tre Torri is a favorite with Italian business travelers. The small guest rooms are comfortable, with modern furnishings, including firm mattresses. The tiled bathrooms are compact. A pool in the terraced garden is visible from the restaurant, and there's also an indoor pool, a sauna, and a fitness center. The hotel contains a bar, sometimes with live piano music, and a disco.

Hotel Villa Athena. Via dei Templi 33, 92100 Agrigento. ☎ **0922-596-288.** Fax 0922-402-180. 40 units. A/C TV TEL. 350,000L ($175) double. Rates include breakfast. AE, DC, MC, V. Free parking.

This 18th-century former private villa rises from the landscape in the Valley of the Temples, less than 2 miles (3km) from town. It's the best place to stay, even though it's worn and overpriced. In summer you need to reserve at least a month in advance. The guest rooms are modern, with Italian styling, decent mattresses, and tiled bathrooms with aging but still functioning plumbing. Ask for a room with a view of the temple: The perfect choice would be no. 205, which frames a panorama of the Temple of Concord.

During the day, guests sit in the paved courtyard, enjoying a drink and the fresh breezes. At night you have a view of the floodlit temples. There's a pool in a setting of gardenia bushes and flowers. The dining room is in a separate building, serving both regional specialties and international dishes. Even if you're not staying here, try to walk through the garden at night for an amazing view of the lit temple. You can also park here during the day and take a 10-minute walk along a trail to the temples, and then come back for lunch.

DINING

Le Caprice. Strada Panoramica dei Templi 51. ☎ **0922-26-469.** Reservations required. Main courses 20,000–35,000L ($10–$17.50). AE, DC, MC. V. Sat–Thurs 12:30–3pm and 7:30–11pm. Closed July 1–15. SEAFOOD/SICILIAN.

Loyal customers return here for special celebrations and everyday fun. Le Caprice is the only restaurant of any consequence in Agrigento; the rest are simple trattorie. Specialties of the house include an antipasto buffet, a mixed fry of fish from the gulf, and rolled pieces of veal in a flavorful sauce. The chef takes justifiable pride in his stuffed swordfish. One German visitor came here seven nights in a row and ordered the dish each time.

Trattoria del Vigneto. Via Cavalleri Magazzeni 11. ☎ **0922-414-319.** Main courses 14,000–25,000L ($7–$12.50). V. Wed–Mon noon–2:30pm and 7pm–midnight. Closed Nov. SICILIAN.

This is a simple place to go for a Sicilian meal after a visit to the nearby Valley of the Temples. You might try homemade pasta flavored with sardines, pine nuts, and balsamic vinegar; *pasta alla Norma,* with eggplant, ricotta, tomatoes, and fresh basil; or *bistecca vignolo* (steak garnished with prosciutto, mozzarella, and tomatoes). The welcome is sincere and the food perfectly acceptable and often quite flavorful.

4 Selinunte

76 miles (122km) SW of Palermo, 70 miles (113km) W of Agrigento, 55 miles (89km) SE of Trapani

Guy de Maupassant called the splendid jumble of ✪ **ruins at Selinunte** "an immense heap of fallen columns, now aligned and placed side by side on the ground like dead soldiers, now having fallen in a chaotic manner." Regardless of what shape they're in, the only reason to visit Selinunte is for its ruins, not for the tacky modern towns (Mazara del Vallo and Castelvetrano) that have grown up around it.

One of the superb colonies of ancient Greece, Selinunte traces its history to the 7th century B.C., when immigrants from Megara Hyblaea (Syracuse) set out to build a new colony. They succeeded, erecting a city of power and prestige adorned with many temples. But that was calling attention to a good thing. Much of Selinunte's history involves seemingly endless conflicts with the Elymi people of Segesta (see below). Siding with Selinunte's rival, Hannibal virtually leveled the city in 409 B.C. The city never recovered its former glory and ultimately fell into decay.

GETTING THERE

From Palermo, Trapani, or Marsala, you can make **rail** connections to Castelvetrano. Once at Castelvetrano, you must board a bus for Selinunte. Call ☎ **091-616-1806** in Palermo for rail information; the trip takes 2 hours and costs 11,500L ($5.75) each way.

From Agrigento, take one of the four daily **buses** to Castelvetrano, a 2¼-hour trip that costs 10,000L ($5) one way. Buses (about five per day) depart for Selinunte from in front of the rail terminal at Castelvetrano. The one-way fare is 2,500L ($1.25) for the 20-minute trip. For information, call ☎ **091-617-5411.**

Selinunte is on the southern coast of Sicily and is best explored by **car,** because public transportation is awkward. From Agrigento, take Rte. 115 northwest into Castelvetrano; then follow the signposted secondary road marked SELINUNTE, which leads south to the sea. Allow at least 2 hours to drive here from either Palermo or Agrigento.

EXPLORING THE ARCHAEOLOGICAL GARDEN

Selinunte's temples lie in scattered ruins, the honey-colored stone littering the ground as if an earthquake had struck (as one did in ancient times). Some columns and fragments of temples are still standing, with great columns pointing to the sky. From 9am to dusk daily, you can walk through the monument zone. Parts of it have been partially excavated and reconstructed, as much as is possible with the bits and fragments remaining. Admission is 4,000L ($2).

The temples, in varying states of preservation, are designated by letters. They're dedicated to such mythological figures as Apollo and Hera (Juno); most date from the 6th and 5th centuries B.C. Near the entrance, the Doric **Temple E** contains fragments of an inner temple. Standing on its ruins before the sun goes down, you can look across the water that washes up on the shores of Africa, from which the Carthaginian fleet emerged to destroy the city. **Temple G,** in scattered ruins north of Temple E, was one of the largest erected in Sicily and was also built in the Doric style. The ruins of the less impressive **Temple F** lie between Temples E and G. Not much remains of Temple F, and little is known about what it was.

After viewing Temples G, F, and E, all near the parking lot at the entrance, you can get in your car and drive along the Strada dei Templi west to the Acropoli. You can also walk here in about 20 minutes. The site of the western temples was the **Acropoli,** which was enclosed within defensive walls and built from the 6th to the 5th century B.C.

The most impressive site here is **Temple C.** In 1925, 14 of the 17 columns of Temple C were re-erected. This is the earliest surviving temple at ancient Selinus, having been built in the 6th century B.C. and probably dedicated to Hercules or Apollo. The pediment, ornamented with a clay Gorgon's head, lies broken on the ground. Temple C towers over the other ruins and gives you a better impression of what all the temples might have looked like at one time.

Also here is **Temple A,** which, like the others, remains in scattered ruins. The streets of the Acropoli were laid out by Hippodamus of Miletus along classical lines, with a trio of principal arteries bisected at right angles by a grid of less important streets. The Acropoli was the site of the town's most important public and religious buildings, and it was also the residence of the town's aristocrats. If you look down below, you can see the site of the town's harbor, now overgrown. After all this earthquake damage, you can only imagine the full glory of this place in its golden era.

The Carthaginian Hannibal treated Selinunte with ferocity. His battle for the city led to the death of 16,000 Selinuntini and the taking of some 5,000 prisoners. The latter begged him for freedom and for their temples to be spared. After receiving payment, he enslaved or killed them and looted the temples and pulled down their walls.

ACCOMMODATIONS & DINING NEARBY

The site of the ruins contains no hotels, restaurants, or watering holes of note. Most visitors come to visit the temples on a daytrip while they're based elsewhere. But there are a handful of accommodations in the seafront village of Marinella, about a mile east of Selinunte. To reach Marinella, you'll travel along a narrow country road.

Hotel Alceste. Via Alceste 21, 91022 Marinella di Selinunte. ☎ **0924-46-184.** Fax 0924-46-143. 26 units. A/C MINIBAR TV TEL. 140,000–150,000L ($70–$75) double. AE, DC, MC, V.

This hotel, occasionally closed for periods in winter, is about a 15-minute walk from the ruins. The recently renovated small guest rooms have new furniture, including firm mattresses; the tiled bathrooms are cramped. Most visitors, however, stop only for a meal in the plant-filled courtyard. They enjoy a regional Sicilian dinner; the price of a meal starts at 25,000L ($12.50). In summer, there's musical entertainment, dancing, cabaret, and theater in the garden.

5 Segesta

24 miles (39km) SW of Palermo, 91 miles (147km) NW of Agrigento

There's only one reason to come to Segesta: to see a single amazing temple in a lonely field. For some visitors, that's reason enough, because it's one of the best-preserved ancient temples in all Italy. Usually Segesta is included as part of a day trip from Palermo, which takes about an hour. It can also be included as a 30-minute stop en route to Erice.

Segesta was the ancient city of the Elymi, a people of mysterious origin who are linked by some to the Trojans. As the major city in western Sicily, it was brought into a series of conflicts with the rival power nearby, Selinus (Selinunte). From the 6th to the 5th century B.C., there were near-constant hostilities. The Athenians came from the east to aid the Segestans in 415 B.C., but the expedition ended in disaster, eventually forcing the city to turn for help to Hannibal of Carthage.

Twice in the 4th century B.C., Segesta was besieged and conquered, once by Dionysius and again by Agathocles (a particularly brutal victor who tortured, mutilated, or made slaves of most of the citizenry). Segesta in time turned on its old but dubious ally, Carthage. Like all Greek cities of Sicily, it ultimately fell to the Romans.

ESSENTIALS

GETTING THERE One **train** a day runs between Palermo and Segesta. It departs at the inconvenient hour of 6:42am, returning to Palermo at 1pm. The ride takes about 30 minutes each way and costs 9,000L ($4.50).

There's **bus** service between Palermo and the ancient theater, but it's scheduled only in conjunction with the presentation of plays. As many as half a dozen buses leave from Palermo's Piazza Politeama, beginning around 2 hours before the scheduled beginning of any performance. For information, contact either the tourist office in Palermo or **Noema Viaggi,** Via di Marzo 13 (☎ **091-625-4221**). A round-trip ticket is 9,000L ($4.50).

By **car,** drive west from Palermo along A29, branching onto A29dir past Alcamo. From Selinunte, head to Castelvetrano to connect to A29 headed north, branching onto A29dir.

VISITOR INFORMATION Consult the **tourist office** in Palermo (see below).

EXPLORING ANCIENT RUINS & ATTENDING CLASSICAL PLAYS

Visit Segesta for its remarkable ✪ **Doric temple** from the 5th century B.C. Although never completed, it's in an excellent state of preservation (the entablature still remains). The temple was far enough away from the ancient town to have escaped being leveled during the "scorched earth" days of the Vandals and Arabs.

From its position on a lonely hill, the Doric temple commands a majestic setting. Although you can scale the hill on foot, you're likely to encounter boys trying to hustle you for a donkey ride (we advise against it—some of these poor animals have saddle sores and seem to be in pain when ridden). From mid-July until the first of August in odd-numbered years, **classical plays** are performed at the temple. (In the spring of even-numbered years, equivalent performances take place at the ancient theater at Syracuse.) Ask at the tourist information office in Trapani for details. Travel agents in Trapani sell tickets for 15,000 to 30,000L ($7.50 to $15).

In another spot on Mount Barbaro, a **theater,** built in the Greek style into the rise of the hill, has been excavated. It was erected in the 3rd century B.C.

There's a cafe in the parking area leading to the temple; otherwise, Segesta is bereft of dining or accommodation selections.

6 Palermo

145 miles (233km) W of Messina, 448 miles (721km) S of Naples, 580 miles (934km) S of Rome

As you arrive in Palermo, you start spotting blond, blue-eyed *bambini* all over the place. Don't be surprised. If fair-haired children don't fit your concept of what a Sicilian should look like, remember that the Normans landed here in 1060, 6 years before William the Conqueror put in at Hastings, and launched a campaign to wrest control of the island from the Arabs. Today you can see elements of both cultures, notably in Palermo's architecture—a unique style, Norman-Arabic.

The city is Sicily's largest port, its capital, and the meeting place of a regional parliament granted numerous autonomous powers in postwar Italy. Against a backdrop of the citrus-studded Conca d'Oro plain and Monte Pellegrino, it's a city of wide boulevards, old neighborhoods in the legendary Sicilian style (laundry flapping against the wind, smudge-faced kids playing in the street), town houses, architecturally harmonious squares, baroque palaces, and modern buildings (many erected after Allied bombings in 1943). It also has the worst traffic jams in Sicily.

Palermo was founded by the Phoenicians, but it has known many conquerors. Some (Frederick II) established courts of great splendor; others (the Angevins) brought decay.

Today the city of 900,000 is *la brutta e la bella* (the ugly and the beautiful). Overcrowded, decaying in parts, and with unemployment and poverty rampant, it's nevertheless a historically significant showcase of artistic treasures. It has the dubious reputation of being the home turf of the Mafia, sheltering some of the world's most powerful dons (none of whom looks like Marlon Brando).

As you make your way through the city—occasionally seeing an armor-plated Alfa Romeo pass by—avoid Vespa-riding bag snatchers and some of the most nimble-fingered pickpockets in the world, and you should have a fine time.

ESSENTIALS

GETTING THERE If you **fly** from Rome or Naples, you'll land at **Falcone e Borsellino—Punta Raisi** (☎ **1478-656-41** for domestic flights, 1478-656-42 for international), 19 miles (31km) west of Palermo. It's cheaper to catch a local airport **bus** from the airport to Piazza Castelnuovo; the fare is 7,500L ($3.75). For the same trip a **taxi** is likely to charge at least 70,000L ($35)—and more if the driver thinks he can get away with it. It's also possible to rent a **car** at the airport (all the major firms are represented) and drive into Palermo. Allow 20 to 30 minutes, or longer if traffic is bad, to get to the center of town from the airport.

For information about traveling by **train,** see "Getting to Sicily," at the beginning of this chapter. After a 3½-hour ride from Messina across the north coast, you arrive at Palermo's station at **Piazza Giulio Cesare** (☎ **091-616-1806**), which lies on the east side of town and is linked to the center by buses and taxis.

Palermo has **bus** connections with other major cities, operated by **SAIS,** Via Balsamo 16 (☎ **091-616-6028**). Some 23 buses a day make the 2½-hour trip from Catania; the one-way cost is 20,000L ($10). One bus a day (except Sunday) arrives from Syracuse; the trip lasts 4 hours and costs 18,000L ($9) one way. The bus terminal is near the rail station.

After you arrive by **car** from mainland Italy at Messina, head west on A20, which becomes Rte. 113, then A20 again, and finally A19 before its final approach to Palermo.

VISITOR INFORMATION There are **tourist offices** at strategic points, including the **Palermo airport** (☎ **091-591-698**). Hours are Monday to Friday 8am to midnight, Saturday and Sunday 8am to 8pm. The principal office is the **Azienda Autonoma Turismo,** Piazza Castelnuovo 34 (☎ **091-583-847**), open Monday to Friday 8:30am to 2pm and 2:30 to 6pm, Saturday 8:30am to 2pm.

SAFETY Be especially alert. Palermo is home to some of the most skilled pickpockets on the continent. Keep your gems locked away (in other words, don't flaunt any sign of wealth). Women who carry handbags are especially vulnerable to purse snatchers on Vespas (wear the strap over one shoulder and across your chest with the purse hanging on the wall side of the sidewalk). Don't leave valuables in your car. In fact, we almost want to say don't leave your car alone, even knowing how impossible that is unless you put it in a garage (highly recommended). Police squads operate mobile centers throughout the town to help combat street crime.

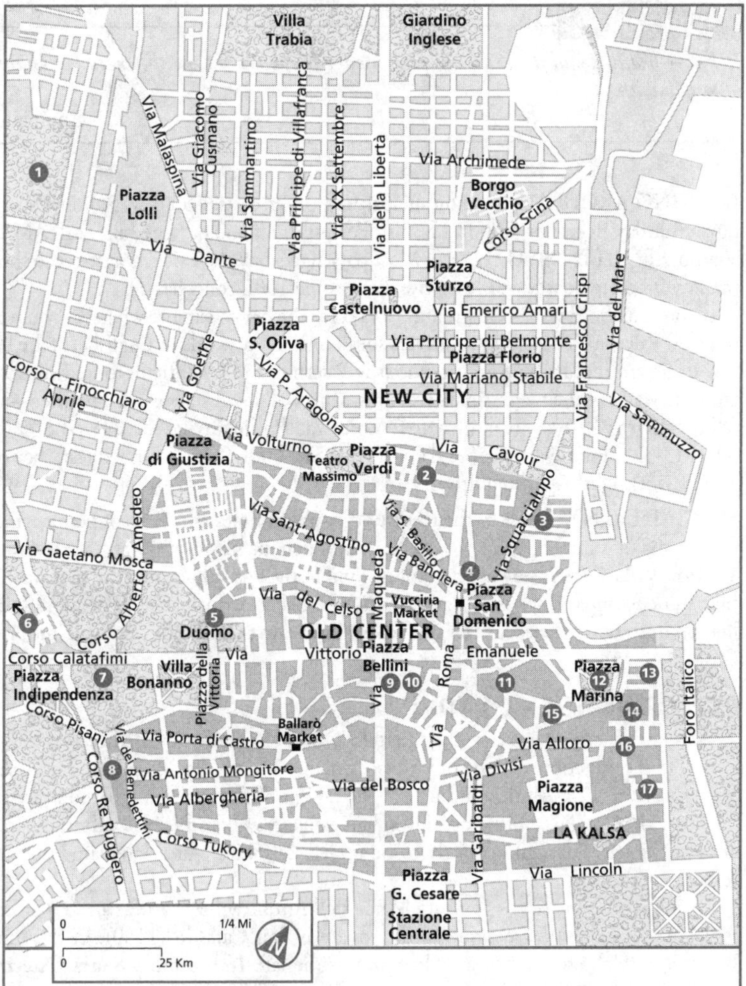

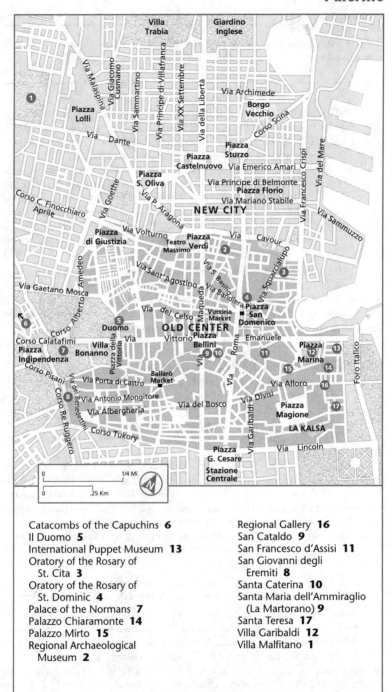

Catacombs of the Capuchins **6**
Il Duomo **5**
International Puppet Museum **13**
Oratory of the Rosary of St. Cita **3**
Oratory of the Rosary of St. Dominic **4**
Palace of the Normans **7**
Palazzo Chiaramonte **14**
Palazzo Mirto **15**
Regional Archaeological Museum **2**
Regional Gallery **16**
San Cataldo **9**
San Francesco d'Assisi **11**
San Giovanni degli Eremiti **8**
Santa Caterina **10**
Santa Maria dell'Ammiraglio (La Martorano) **9**
Santa Teresa **17**
Villa Garibaldi **12**
Villa Malfitano **1**

Impressions

I have heard it said that Sicilians can't use the telephone because they need both hands to talk with.

—Anonymous

GETTING AROUND One municipal **bus** ticket costs 1,500L (75¢), or you can buy a full-day ticket for 5,000L ($2.50). For information and schedules, call **AMAT,** Via Borrelli 16 (☎ **091-321-333**). Most passengers buy their tickets at tobacco shops (*tabacchi*) before boarding. Otherwise, keep some 100L coins handy.

If you can afford it, consider renting a **taxi** for the day to explore whatever you want to see in Palermo. Though most drivers speak only a few words of English, it's the best way to get around. Parking is horrendous in Palermo, and it's difficult to find your way around. Many of the major sights are not within walking distance of each other—just tell the driver where to go and where to wait. Call **Radio Taxi** at ☎ **091-512-727** or 091-513-311. From 9am to 5pm daily, it costs 500,000L ($250). On request, they can provide an English-speaking driver.

SPECIAL EVENTS Ask at the tourist office about times and dates of performances for the major summer event, a festival at an open-air seaside theater, the **Teatro di Verdura Villa Castelnuovo.** The month-long festival usually begins the first week of July and encompasses classical music, jazz, and ballet performances. For more information or to buy tickets, contact the **Teatro Politeama Garibaldi** (see "Palermo After Dark," below).

EXPLORING THE OLD TOWN

The "four corners" of the city, the **Quattro Canti di Città,** is in the heart of the old town, at the junction of Corso Vittorio Emanuele and Via Maqueda. The ruling Spanish of the 17th century influenced the design of this grandiose baroque square, replete with fountains and statues. From here you can walk to **Piazza Bellini,** the most attractive square, though it's likely to be under scaffolding for a long time during a renovation project.

Opening onto the square is **Santa Maria dell'Ammiraglio (La Martorana)** erected in 1143 (see below). Also fronting the square is **San Cataldo** (1160), in the Arab-Byzantine style (also see below). Here, too, is the late-16th-century **Santa Caterina,** attached to a vast Dominican monastery constructed in 1310. The church contains interesting 18th-century multicolored marble ornamentation.

Adjoining the square is **Piazza Pretoria,** dominated by a fountain designed in Florence in 1554 for a villa but acquired by Palermo about 20 years later. A short walk will take you to **Piazza di Cattedrale** and the Duomo.

Il Duomo. Piazza di Cattedrale, Corso Vittorio Emanuele. ☎ **091-334-376.** Free admission (donation appreciated). Apr–Oct daily 7am–7pm; Nov–Mar daily 7am–noon and 4–6pm.

East meets West in this curious spectacle of a cathedral. It was built in the 12th century on the foundation of an earlier basilica that had been converted into a mosque by the Arabs. The impressive Gothic "porch" on the southern front was built in the 15th century. But the cupola, added in the late 18th century, detracts from the overall appearance, and the interior was revamped at the same time, resulting in a glaring incongruity in styles. The pantheon of royal tombs includes that of the Holy Roman Emperor Frederick II, in red porphyry under a canopy of marble.

Santa Maria dell'Ammiraglio (La Martorana). Piazza Bellini 3. ☎ **091-616-1692.** Free admission (donation appreciated). Mon–Sat 9:30am–1pm and 3:30–7pm.

This church, named for Eloisa Martorana, who in 1194 founded a nearby Benedictine convent, is worth a visit for its glorious Byzantine mosaics. In 1143 the church was founded at the request of George of Antioch, an admiral in the fleet of Roger II. Today this Norman church is concealed behind a baroque facade. You enter through a portico-cum-bell tower that, though constructed free standing, was connected to the church in the 1500s. The first two bays of the church were added in the 1500s and frescoed in the 1600s. The mosaics are stunning, created along strict Byzantine lines. Two panels evoke George of Antioch at the feet of the Madonna and Roger II receiving the crown from Christ. Other subjects depict a trio of Archangels (Gabriel, Raphael, and Michael) and in the register below, eight prophets.

✪ **Palace of the Normans (Palazzo dei Normanni).** Piazza del Parlamento. ☎ **091-705-4317.** Free palace tours. Chapel Mon–Sat 9am–noon; Mon–Fri 3–5pm; Sun 9–10am and noon–1pm.

This palace contains one of the greatest art treasures in Sicily, the **Palatine Chapel (Cappella Palatina).** Erected at Roger II's command in the 1130s, it's the finest example of the Arabic-Norman style. The effect of the lushly colored mosaics is awe-inspiring. Dating from 1160, the mosaics in the nave are evocative of those at Monreale's Duomo (see above). If you don't have time to pay a visit to Monreale, you'll have seen the essence of this brilliant type here. Almond-eyed biblical characters from the Byzantine world create a panorama of epic pageantry, illustrating such Gospel scenes as the Nativity. The effect is enhanced by inlaid marble and mosaics as well as by pillars made of granite shipped from the East. For a look at still more mosaics, this time in a more secular vein depicting scenes of the hunt, head upstairs to the **Hall of Roger II (Sala di Ruggero II),** the seat of the Sicilian Parliament, where security is likely to be tight.

Oratory of the Rosary of St. Dominic (Oratorio del Rosario di San Domenico). Via dei Bambinai. Free admission. Mon 3–6pm; Tues–Fri 9am–1pm and 3–5:30pm; Sat 9–1am.

Palermo's most splendid oratory is a gem of stucco decoration by Giacomo Serpotta (1652–1732), what could be called a romp of cherubs. He excelled in the use of marble and polychrome, but it was in stucco that he earned his greatest fame. He worked on this oratory, his masterpiece, from 1714 to 1717. Serpotta depicted the *Joyful Mysteries of the Rosary,* on the left and rear walls, though some of these are the work of Pietro Novelli. Themes throughout the oratory are wide ranging, depicting a *Flagellation* to an *Allegories of the Virtues.* Serpotta also depicted scenes from the *Apocalypse of St. John.* Particularly graphic is a depiction of a writhing Devil falling from Heaven. At the high altar is a masterpiece by Anthony Van Dyck, *Madonna of the Rosary* (1628). Illustrating the *Coronation of the Virgin,* the ceiling was frescoed by Pietro Novelli.

Oratory of the Rosary of St. Cita (Oratorio del Rosario di Santa Cita). Via Valverde 3. ☎ **091-332-779.** Free admission (donation appreciated). Mon–Fri 3–5pm.

You enter the oratory through the Chiesa di Santa Zita. It was the crowning achievement of Giacomo Serpotta, who worked on it between 1686 and 1718. Cherubs and angels romp with abandon, a delight as they climb onto the window frames or spread garlands of flowers in their pathway; they can also be seen sleeping, eating, and just hugging their knees as if in deep thought. The *Battle of Lepanto* bas-relief is meant to symbolize the horrors of war, and other panels depict such scenes as *The Mystery of the Rosary.* The oratory is a virtual gallery of art—everything from scenes of the flagellation

Men of Honor

In Sicily, they don't call it "the Mafia" (from the Arabic *mu'afah* or "protection"). They call it *Cosa Nostra,* literally "our thing," but more accurately, "this thing we have." Its origins are debated, but the world's most famed criminal organization seemed to grow out of the convergence of local agricultural overseers working for absentee Bourbon landowners—hired thugs, from the peasant workers' point of view.

Members of the Sicilian Mafia (or "Men of Honor," as they like to be called) traditionally operated as a network of regional bosses who controlled individual towns by setting up puppet regimes of thoroughly corrupt officials. It was a sort of devil's bargain with the national Christian Democrat party, which controlled Italy's government from World War II until 1993 and, despite its law-and-order rhetoric, tacitly left the Cosa Nostra alone as long as the bosses got out the party vote.

Men of honor trafficked in illegal goods, of course, but until the 1960s and 1970s their income was derived mainly from funneling state money into their own pockets and from running low-level protection rackets and ensuring that public contracts were granted to fellow *mafiosi* (all reasons why Sicily has experienced grotesque unchecked industrialization and modern growth at the expense of its heritage and the good of its communities). But the younger generation of Mafia underbosses got into the highly lucrative heroin and cocaine trades in the 1970s, transforming the Sicilian Mafia into a major world player on the international drug-trafficking circuit—and raking in the dough. This ignited a clandestine

to Jesus in the Garden at Gethsemane. At the high altar is Carlo Maratta's *Virgin of the Rosary* (1690). Allegorical figures protect eight windows along the side walls.

Regional Archaeological Museum (Museo Archeologico Regionale). Via Bara Olivella 24. ☎ **091-611-6807.** Admission 8,000L ($4). Daily 9am–1:30pm; Tues, Wed, and Fri 3–6:30pm.

Occupying a former residence for Philippine friars, this is one of the greatest archaeological collections in southern Italy, where the competition's stiff. Many works displayed were excavated at Selinunte, once one of the major towns in Magna Graecia. See, in particular, the Sala di Selinunte, displaying the celebrated metopes that adorned the classical temples, as well as slabs of bas-relief. The gallery also owns important sculpture from the Temple of Himera. The collection of bronzes is exceptional, including the athlete and the stag discovered in the ruins of Pompeii (a Roman copy of a Greek original) and a bronze ram from Syracuse, from the 3rd century B.C. Among the Greek sculpture is *The Pouring Satyr,* excavated at Pompeii (a Roman copy of a Greek original by Praxiteles).

Regional Gallery (Galleria Regionale della Sicilia). Via Alloro 4, Palazzo Abatellis. ☎ **091-616-4317.** Admission 8,000L ($4). Mon–Sat 9am–1pm; Thurs–Sat 3–7:30pm; Sun 9am–12:30pm.

The Gothic-Renaissance Palazzo Abatellis houses the Regional Gallery, which shows the evolution of art in Sicily from the 13th to the 18th century. On the ground floor is the most famous work, the 15th-century fresco *Triumph of Death,* in all its gory magnificence. A horseback-riding skeleton, representing Death, tramples his victims. Worthy of mention are three majolica plates, valuable specimens of *Loza dorada*

Mafia war that, throughout the late 1970s and 1980s, generated lurid headlines of bloody Mafia hits. The new generation was wiping out the old—and turning the balance of power in their favor.

This situation gave rise to the first Mafia turncoats, disgruntled ex-bosses and rank-and-file stoolies who opened up and told their stories, first to police prefect Gen. Alberto Dalla Chiesa (assassinated in 1982), and later to crusading magistrates Giovanni Falcone (slaughtered on May 23, 1992) and Paolo Borsellino (murdered on July 19, 1992), who staged the "maxitrials" of mafiosi that sent hundreds to jail. The magistrates' 1992 murders, in particular, drew public attention to the dishonorable methods that defined the new Mafia—and perhaps for the first time engendered true shame regarding these actions.

On a broad and culturally important scale, it is these young mafiosi, without a moral center or check on their powers, who have driven many Sicilians to at least secretly break the unwritten code of *omertà,* which translates as "homage" but means "silence," when faced with harboring or even tolerating a man of honor. The Mafia still controls much of Palermo, the small towns south of it, and the provincial capitals of Catania, Trapani, and Agrigento. Throughout the rest of Sicily, though, its power has been slipping. The heroin trade is a far cry from construction schemes and protection money, and the Mafia is swiftly outliving its usefulness and its welcome.

—Reid Bramblett

manufactured in the workshops of Manises, and the *Giara* produced in the workshops of Malaga at the end of the 13th century.

Francesco Laurana's slanty-eyed *Eleonora d'Aragona* is worth seeking out, as are seven grotesque D'Roleries painted on wood. On the second floor, *L'Annunziata* by Antonello da Messina, a portrait of the Madonna executed with depth and originality, is one of the most celebrated paintings in Italy. The 13th room contains a very good series of Flemish paintings from the 15th and 16th centuries; the best is the *Trittico Malvagna* by Jean Gossaert (known as Mabuse).

International Puppet Museum (Museo Internazionale delle Marionette). Via Butera 1. ☎ **091-328-060.** Admission 5,000L ($2.50). Mon–Fri 9am–1pm and 4–7pm; Sat 9am–1pm.

This is one of Europe's great puppet museums. *Pupi,* as Sicilian puppets are called, have long been considered among the finest versions of the art of the marionette. The puppets are based on characters from the French *chansons de geste.* In the first room is the museum's collection of Sicilian puppets, many presented on stage and operated with strings. The most outstanding artisan here is Gaspara Canino, who achieved fame with his theater puppets in the 1800s. In other rooms of the museum you can see results of the marionette art in other countries, including the English Punch and Judy.

San Cataldo. Piazza Bellini 3. Free admission. Mon–Fri 9am–4pm; Sat 8am–1pm; Sun 9am–1pm.

In the Norman heyday of the island in the 12th century, this church was the headquarters of the Knights of the Holy Sepulchre. Today it evokes a Moorish style of architecture, with its perforated window screens and crenellated walls. The bulbous red domes here are often likened by Italians to a eunuch's hat, depicted in many paintings. The interior is rather severe, divided into a trio of aisles. Many of the columns were taken from buildings even older than this Norman edifice. Three domes crown the nave, and the floor is in polychrome marble.

San Giovanni degli Eremiti. Via dei Benedettini 3. ☎ **091-651-5019.** Admission 4,000L ($2). Mon–Sat 9am–1pm and 3–6:30pm; Sun 9am–1pm.

In an atmosphere appropriate for the recluse it honors, St. John of the Hermits (now deconsecrated), with its twin-columned cloister, is one of the most idyllic spots in Palermo. A medieval veil hangs heavy in the gardens, with their citrus blossoms and flowers, especially on a hot summer day as you wander around in the cloister. Built on the order of Roger II in 1132, the church exhibits its Arabic influence, surmounted by pinkish cupolas, while showing the Norman style as well.

Villa Malfitano. Via Dante 167. ☎ **091-681-6133.** Admission 5,000L ($2.50). Mon–Sat 9am–12:30pm.

One of Palermo's great villas, built in the Liberty style, lies within a spectacular garden. The villa was built in 1886 by Joseph Whitaker, grandson of the famous English gentleman and wine merchant, Ingham, who moved to Sicily in 1806 and made a fortune producing Marsala wine. Whitaker arranged to have trees shipped to Palermo from all over the world, and he planted them around his villa. These included such rare species as Dragon's Blood, an enormous banyan tree that is the only example found in Europe. High society in Palermo flocked here for lavish parties, and royalty from Great Britain visited. The villa today is lavishly furnished, with antiques and artifacts from all over the world. The *Sala d'Estate* (Summer Room) is particularly stunning, with trompe l'oeil frescoes covering both the walls and the ceiling.

✪ **Catacombs of the Capuchins (Catacombe dei Cappuccini).** Piazza Cappuccini 1. ☎ **091-212-117.** Admission 2,000L ($1). Tours daily 9am–noon and 3–5pm; closed holidays.

This bizarre site is on the outskirts of the city. The fresco you might have seen in the Regional Gallery, the *Triumph of Death,* dims in comparison with the real thing. These catacombs contained a preservative that helped to mummify the dead. Sicilians (from nobles to maids) were buried here in the 19th century, and it was the custom on Sunday to visit Uncle Luigi and see how he was holding together. If he fell apart, he was wired together or wrapped in burlap sacking. In 1920 the last person was laid to rest here, a little girl almost lifelike in death. Many 19th-century Sicilians are in fine shape, considering—with eyes, hair, and even clothing fairly intact. Some of the expressions on the faces of the skeletons take the fun out of Halloween—this is not a great place to take the kids.

EXPLORING LA KALSA

Although it's a bit dangerous at night, crumbling La Kalsa is the most interesting neighborhood in Palermo (it's relatively safe during the day). Located in the southwestern sector of the old city, it was built by the Arabs as a walled seaside residence for their chief ministers. It's bounded by the port and Via Garibaldi and Via Paternostro to the east and west and by Corso Vittorio Emanuele and Via Lincoln to the north and south; one of its main thoroughfares is **Via Butero**. Later, much of the Arabs' fine work was destroyed when the Spanish viceroys took over, adding their own architectural interpretations. One of the neighborhood's most dramatic churches (though not necessarily the oldest) is the fancifully baroque **Santa Teresa,** Piazza Kalsa (☎ **091-617-1658**).

La Kalsa is one of Europe's least restored, most authentically battered historic neighborhoods. To reach it, begin at the Quattro Canti di Città and walk eastward along **Corso Vittorio Emanuele,** which locals usually refer to simply as "Il Corso." Cross over bustling Via Roma; then turn right onto Via Paternostro until you reach the 13th-century **San Francesco d'Assisi,** on Piazza San Francesco d'Assisi (☎ **091-616-2819**). Visit the church if for no other reason than to see its magnificent Cappella Mastrotonio, carved in 1468. Don't count on the church's being open, however.

From Piazza San Francesco d'Assisi, follow Via Merlo to the **Palazzo Mirto,** Via Merlo 2 (☎ **091-616-4751**), to see how nobility lived in the days when this was an upmarket neighborhood. The palace, a splendid example of a princely residence of the early 20th century, contains its original 18th- and 19th-century furnishings. It's open Monday to Friday 9am to 1pm and 3 to 7pm, Saturday and Sunday 9am to 12:30pm. Admission is 4,000L ($2).

Via Merlo leads into the landmark **Piazza Marina,** one of the most evocative parts of Palermo. The port of La Cala was here, but it silted up in the 1100s. Reminiscent of the American Deep South, a garden is found at the **Villa Garibaldi** in the center of the square. The square is dominated by the **Palazzo Chiaramonte** on the southeast corner, dating from the early 14th century. Renaissance churches occupy the other three corners of this historic square.

SHOPPING

For a touch of local color, join Palermoans for a visit to the **Vucciria,** their main market for meat and fresh vegetables, located off Via Roma in the rear of San Domenico—this is one of Europe's great casbahlike markets. You'll find mountains of food, from fish to meat and vegetables. The array of wild fennel, long-stemmed artichokes, and blood oranges, as well as giant octopus and squid, will astound you. As an offbeat adventure, try dining at **Shangai,** Vicolo Mezzani 34 (☎ **091-589-702**), which cooks virtually anything sold in the market. You can sample several fish specialties, including eel, by ordering the mixed fish fry. The market is open Monday to Saturday 8am to 4pm; Shangai stays open to 11pm. You can also sample the wares offered at various food stalls, including chickpea-flour fritters or deep-fried meat- or cheese-filled pockets of dough *(calzoni)*. To go really local, ask for *guasteddi*—a fresh bun stuffed with narrow strips of calf's spleen and ricotta, dished up with a fiery hot sauce. Everything shuts down on Sunday.

Two shops in one, **Battaglia,** Via Ruggero Settimo 74 (☎ **091-580-224**), sells women's wear. Within it, Hermès offers upscale men's and women's apparel, including ready-to-wear and high-fashion collections. There's also a limited selection of casual and sports shoes, as well as leather accessories, but this shop is really about clothing.

If it comes in linen, **Frette,** Via Ruggero Settimo 12 (☎ **091-585-166**) and Via G. Sciutti 85 (☎ **091-343-288**), sells it. The shop offers sheets, tablecloths, towels, bedspreads, pajamas, nightgowns, curtains, and tapestries. Call for an appointment at **Miroslava Tasic,** Largo Cavalieri di Malta 2 (☎ **091-588-126**), if you're interested in buying handmade sheets, curtains, towels, tablecloths, or upholstery fabrics in fine cottons, silks, and linens, adorned with embroidery or lace trim.

For jewelry in silver or gold, plain or inlaid with the gems of your choice, check out **Ma Gi,** Via Ruggero Settimo 45 (☎ **091-611-1513**). It also carries dishes and cutlery in silver. If you can afford it, they can make it.

For sterling and Sheffield silver pieces from various eras, **Fecarotta,** Via Principe di Belmonte 103B (☎ **091-331-518**), is a market leader. It also sells English and Italian antique furniture and paintings, as well as English silver, antique jewelry, and Sheffield silver plates.

You'll find traditional fruit-filled tarts as well as *cassata siciliana* (tarts with ricotta-based filling) at **Fratelli Magri,** Via Isidoro Carini 42 (☎ **091-584-788**). The shop also makes other types of sweets, and in the summer offers gelato, but come here for the authentic high-calorie pastries.

A carnivore's fantasy, **Mangia Charcuterie,** Via Principe di Belmonte 104D (☎ **091-587-651**), stocks all the meats and meat products produced in Sicily. It's a baffling array of sausages, pâtés, mortadellas, and every possible kind of sausage, as well as a worthy selection of meats and sausages imported from Austria. You can carry these products away for a picnic or arrange to have items shipped.

A celebration of local and national confections, **I Peccatucci di Mamma Andrea,** Via Principe di Scordia 67 (☎ **091-334-835**), tempts newcomers with the bounty of Sicily's traditional fattening desserts. Named after a legendary matriarch whose reputation as a pastry maker was almost celestial (at least in her family), the shop sells desserts that are very, very sweet and very, very Italian. Examples are pralines, *torrone, panetoni,* segments of fruit dripping with Sicilian honey, marzipan, and an age-old specialty known as *ghirlande di croccantini* (a hazelnut torte). Get ready for sugar shock and lots of local color.

One of the most comprehensive bookstores in Palermo is the **Libreria Flaccovio,** Via Ruggero Settimo 37 (☎ **091-589-442**). Most of the inventory is in Italian, with good numbers of art books that celebrate the historic legacies of Sicily; a few volumes (but more than any other outfit in Palermo) are in English.

Four generations have handcrafted tortoiseshell picture frames at **Meli,** Via Dante 294 (☎ **091-682-4213**), where you can also find a selection of stylish prints, etchings, and engravings from the 16th to the 19th century.

One of the best-established emporiums for Sicilian versions of majolica-style stoneware is **De Simone,** which has been making the stuff in a family-run setup since at least the 1920s. There's a shop at Via Gaetano Daita 13B (☎ **091-584-876**), and both a shop and a factory (which can be visited) at Via Principe de Scalea 698 (☎ **091-671-1005**). The shops are open Monday to Saturday, but the factory can be visited only Monday to Friday 8am to 5pm. No reservations are necessary.

Sicilian potters have artfully merged influences from the Arab and Christian worlds in their brightly painted trademark stoneware. **Laboratorio Italiano,** Via Principe di Villafranca 42 (☎ **091-320-282**), sells artfully crafted dinner plates, coffee cups, garden ornaments, jardinieres, and chandeliers, any of which can be insured and shipped to wherever you specify. There's also a factory on the premises, which you can tour without an appointment.

ACCOMMODATIONS

Generally you'll find a poor lot of hostelries, with only a few fine choices. Hunt and pick carefully.

EXPENSIVE

Hotel Centrale Palace. Corso Vittorio Emanuele 327 (at Via Maqueda), 99134 Palermo. ☎ **091-336-666.** Fax 091-334-881. www.bestwestern.com. E-mail: cphotel@tin.it. 63 units. A/C MINIBAR TV TEL. 330,000L ($165) double; 435,000L ($217.50) junior suite. Rates include buffet breakfast. AE, DC, MC, V. Parking 20,000L ($10).

One of the city's most appealing hotels occupies what was an opulent home in the 1600s. About a century ago, it became a hotel and in the early 1990s was renovated into a plush favorite of business travelers. You'll find flowers in the public rooms, a congenial staff, and enough comforts to make you appreciate the amenities of the modern age. The guest rooms come in a variety of shapes and sizes, each with a quality mattress and a tiled bathroom.

Dining/Diversions: Guests gather in the bar before heading for the formal dining room, where the chef specializes in Sicilian and international dishes.

Amenities: Concierge, room service, laundry/dry cleaning, twice-daily maid service, baby-sitting, valet parking.

✪ **Villa Igiea Grand Hotel.** Salita Belmonte 43, 90142 Palermo. ☎ **091-543-744.** Fax 091-547-654. 117 units. A/C MINIBAR TV TEL. 400,000L ($200) double; 820,000L ($410) suite. Rates include breakfast. AE, DC, MC, V. Free parking.

The Villa Igiea was built in the early 1900s as one of Sicily's aristocratic estates, and today it's the third-best luxury hotel on the island (behind the Grand and San Domenico in Taormina). Set in gardens on the sea, the place is lovely if you're going to spend time here sunning and relaxing. But if you're looking for a base for seeing the city, note that town is a 15-minute taxi ride away. Built of the same buff-colored stone as that used by the Greek colonists during the Punic Wars, it resembles a medieval Sicilian fortress whose chiseled walls boast crenellated battlements and watchtowers. A circular temple, buttressed with modern scaffolding, still stands in the garden. Everywhere are clusters of antiques. The guest rooms vary from sumptuous suites with terraces to smaller, less glamorous rooms. Many are a bit worn and faded, though each comes with a luxury mattress. The bathrooms have aging but still functional plumbing. The hotel is reached by passing through an industrial port area north of Palermo.

Dining/Diversions: The hotel's bar is baronial, with a soaring stone vault. You dine on Sicilian and classic Italian meals in a glittering room with paneled walls, ornate ceilings, and chandeliers.

Amenities: Room service, baby-sitting, laundry/valet, terrace overlooking the water, pool, tennis court.

MODERATE

Grande Albergo Sole. Corso Vittorio Emanuele 291, 90133 Palermo. ☎ **091-581-811.** Fax 091-611-0182. www.market.thecity.it/albergosolegb. 150 units. A/C TV TEL. 200,000–210,000L ($100–$105) double. Rates include breakfast. AE, DC, MC, V. Parking 15,000L ($7.50).

This pleasant second-class hotel is in the busy historic center. A 1960s remake of a century-old building, it has a helpful staff and simple guest rooms with modern furniture, often reproductions of Sicilian 19th-century pieces, plus decent mattresses. The small tiled bathrooms have adequate shelf space. There's a lounge, a bar, a restaurant, and a roof garden terrace for sunbathing.

Jolly Hotel del Foro Italico. Via Foro Italico 22, 90133 Palermo. ☎ **800/221-2626** in the U.S., 800/237-0319 in Canada, or 091-616-5090. Fax 091-616-1441. 235 units. A/C MINIBAR TV TEL. 220,000–270,000L ($110–$135) double; 300,000L ($150) suite. Rates include breakfast. Half-board 45,000L ($22.50) per person. AE, DC, MC, V. Parking 20,000L ($10).

Situated off a busy boulevard facing the gulf, this 1960s chain hotel is one of the best in town. The well-organized but small guest rooms contain lots of built-in pieces and comfortable beds. The tiled bathrooms are a bit too small. Try for the quieter rooms on the upper floors (affording at least a glimpse of the Mediterranean) or at the rear. The Jolly also has a garden, a pool, a restaurant that serves Sicilian and Italian food, and an American bar.

President Hotel. Via Francesco Crispi 230, 90139 Palermo. ☎ **091-580-733.** Fax 091-611-1588. 130 units. A/C TV TEL. 235,000L ($117.50) double. Rates include breakfast. AE, DC, MC, V. Parking 15,000L ($7.50).

Rising eight concrete-and-glass stories above the harbor front, this is one of the better and more up-to-date moderately priced hotels in town. You pass beneath the soaring arcade before entering the informal stone-trimmed lobby. One of the most appealing coffee shop/bars in town lies at the top of a short flight of stairs next to the reception area. There's a restaurant on the top floor, plus a guarded parking garage in the basement. The small guest rooms are comfortably furnished though short on style, yet each comes with a firm mattress.

INEXPENSIVE

Albergo Cavour. Via Alessandro Manzoni 11, 90133 Palermo. ☎ and fax **091-616-2759.** 10 units, 4 with bathroom. 55,000L ($27.50) double without bathroom 65,000–70,000L ($32.50–$35) double with bathroom. No credit cards. Parking 10,000L ($5).

The Albergo Cavour is on the fifth floor of a 1930s building conveniently located 150 yards from the central station. The small guest rooms are functional and unpretentious; the manager sees to it that they're well kept and decently furnished, with comfortable mattresses and tiny bathrooms. No meals are served, but many cafes are nearby.

Hotel Sausele. Via Vincenzo Errante 12, 90127 Palermo. ☎ **091-616-1308.** Fax 091-616-7525. www.hotelsausele.it. E-mail: htlsausele@tin.it. 36 units. TEL. 150,000L ($75) double. Rates include breakfast. AE, DC, MC, V. Parking 15,000L ($7.50).

This hotel near the rail station is the best in a run-down area. Owned and managed efficiently by Swiss-born Signora Sausele, it's a modest but pleasant hotel, with small guest rooms just adequate for a good night's rest. The mattresses are a bit worn but still comfortable and the tiled bathrooms a bit cramped. Five of the rooms open onto private balconies. The hotel has an elevator, garage, bar, and TV room. The lounges are air-conditioned.

DINING

MODERATE

Friends' Bar. Via Filippo Brunelleschi 138, Borgo Nuovo. ☎ **091-201-401.** Reservations essential. Main courses 21,000–35,000L ($10.50–$17.50). AE, DC, V. Tues–Sun 12:30–3pm and 8–11pm. Closed 3 weeks in Aug. SICILIAN.

About 6 miles (10km) north of Palermo, this is one of the finest restaurants in the region. Named after the four friends *(amici)* who opened it in the 1970s, it features an air-conditioned dining room and a gazebo-like indoor/outdoor structure that rises from a lush garden. A meal here is a sought-after event for many Sicilians, and a reservation (especially for the garden) may be hard to get. The antipasti, rich with marinated vegetables and grilled fish, are loaded onto a buffet table, and the pastas tend to be strong, aromatic, and laced with flavors like anchovies, fresh basil, and sardines. Grilled swordfish, calamari, and octopus are always worthwhile, and the house wine is redolent with the flavors and sunshine of southern Italy.

La Scuderia. Viale del Fante 9. ☎ **091-520-323.** Reservations recommended. Main courses 24,000–40,000L ($12–$20). AE, DC, MC, V. Mon–Sat 12:30–3pm and 8:30pm–midnight; Sun 12:30–3pm. Closed 2 weeks in Aug. INTERNATIONAL/ITALIAN.

Dedicated professionals direct this restaurant surrounded by trees at the foot of Monte Pellegrino, 3 miles (5km) north of the city center. In summer it has one of the prettiest flowery terraces in town, sought after by everyone from lovers to extended families to vacationing glamour queens. The imaginative cuisine includes a mixed grill of fresh vegetables with a healthy dose of a Sicilian cheese called *caciocavallo,* stuffed turkey cutlet, beef and veal dishes, *involtini* of eggplant or veal, risotto with seafood, and *maccheroni Nettuno* (studded with swordfish, sliced eggplant, and tomato sauce).

INEXPENSIVE

Al Vicolo. Cortile Scimecaz (off Piazza San Francesco Saverio). ☎ **091-651-2464.** Reservations recommended. Main courses 15,000–28,000L ($7.50–$14). No credit cards. Mon–Sat 12:30–3pm and 8–11:30pm. Closed Aug 10–25. SICILIAN.

This is one of the city's most characteristic trattorie, deserving more acclaim than it receives. For antipasti, try *panelle* (chickpea or garbanzo fritters), *arancini* (rice croquettes), or sardines à *beccafico* (stuffed and flavored with laurel). You'll have a choice of many of Sicily's most typical dishes, like pasta mixed with sardines and wild fennel. Any pasta labeled *"alla Norma"* comes with vine-ripened tomatoes and eggplant. The local fish is fresh and abundant, and local meats, including lamb and kid, are always offered. You can accompany the meal (Sicilians say "irrigate") with a selection of regional wines.

Capricci di Sicilia. Via Istituto Pignatelli 6 (off Piazza Sturzo). ☎ **091-327-777.** Reservations recommended. Main courses 15,000–22,000L ($7.50–$11). AE, DC, MC, V. Sept–July daily 1–3:30pm and 8pm–midnight; Aug daily 8pm–midnight. SICILIAN.

Great care goes into the cuisine, both in the preparation of it and in the shopping for fresh ingredients. Some of the dishes are based on recipes so old you'll think the chef is trying to re-create Palermo's baroque past. To go really local, order *polpette* (fishballs of fresh sardines). Pasta is often flavored with sardines and broccoli, and the spaghetti is succulent when made with sea urchins. The swordfish roulade is always dependable, as are any number of other dishes prepared to bring out maximum flavor. In warm weather, meals can be served in a small garden.

PALERMO AFTER DARK

We always like to begin our evening by heading to the century-old **Caffè Mazzara,** Via Generale Magliocco 15 (☎ **091-321-443**). You can sample Sicilian ice cream (among the best in the world), order the richest coffee in the country, or sip a heady Sicilian wine. Besides an espresso bar and pastry shop on the street level, the premises contain a piano bar and pub, plus a well-recommended restaurant. If you can't find a place to eat in Palermo on a Sunday, when virtually everything is shut, Mazzara is a good bet. It's open Sunday to Friday 7:30am to 11pm and Saturday 7:30am to midnight. Signature treats include *cannoli* and *gelati.*

Palermo's most popular dance clubs lie in the city's commercial center. **Il Cherchio,** Viale Strasburgo 312 (☎ **091-688-5421**), and **Grant's Club,** Via Principe di Paternò 80 (☎ **091-346-772**), are open only Friday and Saturday 10:30pm to at least 3am, depending on the crowd. Both charge 15,000 to 25,000L ($7.50 to $12.50), including one drink.

If you're looking for relief from Palermo's oppressive heat, consider a short trek north of the city to Mondello, where you'll find an attractive piano bar in the **Mondello Palace Hotel,** Via Principe di Scalea 12 (☎ **091-450-001**).

Palermo is also a cultural center of some note. The opera and ballet seasons last from January to June. The principal venue is the **Teatro Politeama Garibaldi,** Piazza Ruggero Settimo (☎ **091-605-3315**). Tickets cost 30,000 to 50,000L ($15 to $25). The box office, across from the tourist office, is open Tuesday to Saturday 10am to 1pm and 5 to 7pm.

The city is known also for its puppet performances, the best of which are staged by the **Compagnia Bradamante di Anna Cuticchio,** Via Lombardia 25 (☎ **091-625-9223**). Tickets cost 20,000 to 30,000L ($10 to $15); the box office opens 1 hour before show time.

SIDE TRIPS FROM PALERMO:
MONREALE

The town of Monreale is 6 miles (10km) from Palermo, up Monte Caputo and on the edge of the Conca d'Oro plain. If you don't have a car, you can reach it by taking **bus** no. 389 from Piazza Indipendenza in Palermo.

The Normans under William II founded a Benedictine monastery at Monreale in the 1170s. Eventually a great cathedral was built near the monastery's ruins. Like the Alhambra in Granada, Spain, the ✪ **Chiostro del Duomo di Monreale,** Piazza Guglielmo il Buono (☎ **091-640-4403**), has a relatively drab facade, giving little indication of the riches inside. The interior is virtually covered with shimmering mosaics illustrating scenes from the Bible. The artwork provides a distinctly original interpretation of the old, rigid Byzantine form of decoration. The mosaics have an Eastern look despite the Western-style robed Christ reigning over his kingdom. The ceiling is ornate, even gaudy. On the north and west facades are two bronze doors depicting biblical stories in relief. The **cloisters** are also of interest. Built in 1166, they consist of twin mosaic columns, and every other pair bears an original design (the lava inlay was hauled from Mt. Etna). Admission to the cathedral is free; if you visit the cloisters, there's a charge of 3,000L ($1.50). The cathedral is open daily 8:30am to noon and 3:30 to 6pm. July to September, the cloister is open Monday to Saturday 9am to 1pm; Monday, Wednesday, and Friday 3 to 6pm; and Sunday 9am to 12:30pm. In the off-season ask at the cathedral, because hours vary.

You can also visit the **treasury** and the **terraces;** each charges 2,000L ($1) for admission. They're open daily 8:30am to 12:30pm and 3 to 6pm. The terraces are actually the rooftop of the church, from which you'll be rewarded with a view of the cloisters.

Sampling the Local Vino

Sicily's hot climate and volcanic soil nurture many vineyards, many of which produce just simple table wines. Of the better vintages, the best-known wine is **Marsala,** a sweet dessert wine produced in both amber and ruby tones. One top producer is **Regaleali,** Contrada Regaleali, 93010 Vallelunga, Pratameno Caltanisetta (☎ **0921-542-522**), a historic enterprise near Palermo run by the Tasca d'Almerita family. This winery is also known for its sauvignon-based Nozze d'Oro and such full-bodied reds as Rosso del Conte (whose bouquet has been referred to by connoisseurs as "huge").

Two other names that evoke years of wine-making traditions, thanks to their skill at producing Cerasuolo di Vittoria and Moscato di Pantelleria, are **Cantine Torrevecchia di Favuzza Giuseppe,** Via Ariosto 10A, 90144 Palermo (☎ **0932/989-400**), and **Corvo Duca di Salaparuta,** a 19th-century winery in the hills above Palermo. For information, contact the **Casa Vinicola Duca di Salaparuta,** Via Nazionale, SS113, Casteldaccia, 90014 Palermo (☎ **091-953-988**).

If you'd like to tour the countryside and visit any of these wineries, call ahead to make appointments and get detailed directions.

Before or after your visit to Monreale, drop in at **Bar Italia,** Via Benedetto d'Acquisto 1 (☎ **091-640-2421**), open Wednesday to Monday from 4am to midnight, closing only for 10 days every year in June. It's difficult to find someone here who speaks English, but you can make your wishes known nevertheless. Near the Duomo, the bar serves plain cookies that are filled with flavor and freshness. If you go early in the morning, order one of the freshly baked croissants and a cup of cappuccino, Monreale's best.

For a meal, try **La Botte,** Contrada Lenzitti 20 (☎ **091-414-051**), 12 miles (19km) north of Palermo, beside SS186 and uphill from the center of Monreale. Begin with the savory antipasto offerings (marinated tuna, grilled sardines or anchovies, marinated red peppers). Specialties are *gnocchi alla barra* (stuffed with local cheeses and herbs); *delizia tre naccia* (fettuccine with ricotta, mozzarella, eggplant, tomatoes, and Sicilian herbs); and veal layered with cheese, salami, basil, and herbs. Reservations are recommended. It's open Friday to Sunday noon to 2pm and 8 to 11pm (closed June 20–Aug 30); and American Express, Diners Club, MasterCard, and Visa are accepted.

MONDELLO LIDO

When the summer sun burns hot, and when old men on the square seek a place in the shade and *bambini* tire of their toys, it's beach weather. For Palermo residents, that means **Mondello,** 7½ miles (12km) east. Before this beachfront town started attracting the wealthy class of Palermo, it was a fishing village (and still is), and you can see rainbow-colored fishing boats bobbing in the harbor. A good sandy beach stretches for about a mile and a half, and it's filled to capacity on a July or August day. Some women traveling alone find Mondello more inviting and less intimidating than Palermo. In summer an express **bus** (no. 6, "Beallo") leaves for Mondello from the central train station in Palermo.

CEFALÙ

For another day's excursion, we recommend a trek 50 miles (81km) east from Palermo to the fishing village of **Cefalù**, tucked onto every inch of a spit of land underneath an awesome crag called the Rocca. The village is known for its Romanesque cathedral, an outstanding achievement of Arab-Norman architecture (see below). Its beaches, its medley of architectural styles, and its narrow streets were captured in the Oscar-winning *Cinema Paradiso.* You can tour the town in half a day and spend the rest of the time enjoying life on the beach, especially in summer.

From Palermo, 18 **trains** make the 1-hour trip daily, costing 5,700L ($2.85) one way. For information and schedules, call ☎ **1478-88-088. SPISA,** Via Umberto I, 28 (☎ **0921-424-301**), runs **buses** between Palermo and Cefalù, costing 8,000L ($4) one way for the 1½-hour trip. **Motorists** can follow Rte. 113 east from Palermo to Cefalù. Driving time is about 1½ hours. You'll have to park at the top of the Rocca, then join lines of visitors walking up and down the narrow steep streets near the water. You'll pass a lot of forgettable shops. In the past few years it seems that half the denizens of Cefalù have become trinket peddlers and souvenir hawkers.

You'll find the **tourist office** at Corso Ruggero 77 (☎ **0921-421-050**), open Monday to Saturday 8am to 2pm and Monday to Friday 4 to 7pm.

Make a beeline to Cefalù's Duomo first thing in the morning so you can avoid the coach-bus hordes. Resembling a military fortress, the ✪ **Duomo,** Piazza del Duomo, off Corso Ruggero (☎ **0921-922-021**), was built by Roger II to fulfill a vow he'd made when faced with a possible shipwreck. Construction began in 1131, and in time two square towers rose, curiously placed between the sea and a rocky promontory. The architectural line of the cathedral boasts a severe elegance that has earned it a position in many art-history books. The interior, which took a century to complete, overwhelms you with 16 Byzantine and Roman columns supporting towering capitals. The graceful horseshoe arches are one of the island's best examples of the Saracen influence on Norman architecture. The celebrated mosaic of Christ the Pantocrator, one of only three on Sicily, in the dome of the cathedral apse is alone worth the trip. The nearby mosaic of the Virgin with angels and the Apostles is a well-preserved work from 1148. In the transept is a marble statue of the Madonna. Roger's plan to have a tomb placed in the Duomo was derailed by the authorities at Palermo's cathedral, where he rests today. Admission is free, and the church is open daily 8am to noon and 3:30 to 6:30pm.

Before leaving town, try to visit the **Museo Mandralisca,** Via Mandralisca 13 (☎ **0921-421-547**), opposite the cathedral. It has an outstanding art collection, including the 1470 portrait of an unknown by Antonello da Messina. Some art critics have journeyed all the way from Rome just to stare at this handsome work, and it's often featured on Sicilian tourist brochures. Admission is 3,000L ($1.50), and it's open daily 9:30am to 12:30pm and 3:30 to 7pm.

If you're feeling hungry, try the rustic seaside trattoria **Al Gabbiano,** Lungomare G. Giardina 17 (☎ **0921-421-495**). Fresh fish is the item to order, from a list of nearly unpronounceable sea creatures. You might begin with *zuppa di cozze,* a luscious mussel soup. The vegetables and pastas are good too, especially *pennette alla Norma* (with eggplant). If you speak a little Italian, it helps. Reservations are recommended Saturday and Sunday. It's open Thursday to Tuesday noon to 3pm and 7pm to midnight (closed mid-Dec to mid-Jan); and American Express, Diners Club, MasterCard, and Visa are accepted.

7 The Aeolian Islands

Lipari: 18½ miles (30km) N of Milazzo; Stromboli: 50 miles (81km) N of Milazzo; Vulcano: 12½ miles (20km) N of Milazzo

The Aeolian Islands (*Isole Eolie o Lipari*) have been inhabited for more than 3,000 years, in spite of volcanic activity that even now causes the earth to issue forth sulfuric belches, streams of molten lava, and hissing clouds of steam. Ancient Greek sailors believed these seven windswept islands were the home of Aeolus, god of the winds. He supposedly lived in a cave on Vulcano, keeping the winds of the world in a bag to be opened only with great caution.

Today, visitors seek out the limited accommodations at **Lipari** (14 square miles), the largest and most developed island; **Stromboli** (5 square miles), the most distant and volcanically active; and **Vulcano** (8 square miles), the closest island to the Sicilian mainland, with its brooding, potentially volatile cone and therapeutic mud baths. The other islands (**Salina, Filicudi, Alicudi,** and **Panarea**) offer only bare-bones facilities and are visited mainly by day-trippers.

Despite the volcanoes, the area attracts tourists (mainly Germans and Italians) with crystalline waters that have great snorkeling, scuba, and spearfishing, and photogenic beaches composed of hot black sand and rocky outcroppings jutting into the Tyrrhenian Sea. The volcanoes themselves offer hikers the thrill of peering into a bubbling crater.

AEOLIAN ISLANDS ESSENTIALS

GETTING THERE **Ferry** and **hydrofoil** services to Lipari, Stromboli, and Vulcano are available in Milazzo, on the northeastern coast of Sicily 20 miles (32km) west of Messina, through the **Società Siremar,** Via Dei Mille (☎ **090-928-3242**). The **Società SNAV,** Via L. Rizzo 17 (☎ **090-928-4509**), offers hydrofoil service.

Siremar operates two ferry routes, which are cheaper and slower than the hydrofoils. The Milazzo-Vulcano-Lipari-Salina line leaves Milazzo four to six times daily 7am to 6:30pm. It takes 1½ hours to reach Vulcano, and a one-way ticket costs 13,500L ($6.75). Lipari is 2 hours from Milazzo; tickets cost 10,500L ($5.25) one way. To reach Stromboli, take the Milazzo-Panarea-Stromboli line, which departs from Milazzo at 7am Friday to Wednesday, and at 2:30pm on Thursday. The Stromboli trip takes 5 hours and costs 16,500L ($8.25) one way.

There's also hydrofoil service. The Milazzo-Vulcano-Lipari-Salina line reaches Vulcano in 40 minutes; a one-way ticket costs 24,000L ($12). It takes 55 minutes to reach Lipari and costs 19,500L ($9.75) one way. Siremar makes the trip 6 to 12 times daily 7:05am to 7pm; SNAV makes six runs daily 7:30am to 7:30pm. To reach Stromboli, use the Milazzo-Panarea-Stromboli line, which takes 2½ hours and costs 28,700L ($14.35) one way. Siremar trips leave 4 times daily 6:15am to 3pm; SNAV makes runs daily at 6:40am, 7:25am, and 2:20pm.

If you're **driving,** from Messina, take S113 west to Palermo until you come to the turnoff for Milazzo.

VISITOR INFORMATION The **tourist office** in Lipari is at Via Vittorio Emanuele 202 (☎ **090-988-0095**). July and August, it's open daily 8am to 2pm (Monday to Saturday also 4:30 to 10pm); September to June, hours are Monday to Friday 8am to 2pm and 4:30 to 7:30pm, Saturday 8am to 2pm. There's no information center in Stromboli. The **tourist office** in Vulcano, Via Porto di Levante (☎ **090-985-2028**), keeps the same hours as the Lipari office but is open only June to September.

LIPARI

Homer called it "a floating island, a wall of bronze and splendid smooth sheer cliffs." The offspring of seven volcanic eruptions, Lipari is the largest of the Aeolians. Lipari is also the name of the island's only real town. It's the administrative headquarters of the Aeolian Islands (except autonomous Salina). The town sits on a plateau of red volcanic rock on the southeastern shore, framed by two beaches, Marina Lunga, which functions as the harbor, and Marina Corta.

Its dominant feature is a 16th-century **Spanish castle,** within the walls of which lie a 17th-century cathedral featuring a 16th-century Madonna and an 18th-century silver statue of San Bartolomeo. There's also an **archaeological park** where stratified clues about continuous civilizations dating to 1700 B.C. have been uncovered.

Excellent artifacts from the Stone and Bronze ages, as well as relics from Greek and Roman acropolises that once stood here, are housed next door in the former bishop's palace, now the **Museo Archeologico Eoliano**, Via del Castello (☎ **090-988-0174**), one of Sicily's major archaeological museums. It houses one of the world's finest Neolithic collections. The oldest discoveries date from 4200 B.C. Lustrous red ceramics, known as the "Diana style," come from the last Neolithic period, 3000 to 2500 B.C. Other exhibits are reconstructed necropolises from the Middle Bronze Age and a 6th-century A.D. depiction of Greek warships. Some 1,200 pieces of 4th and 3rd century B.C. painted terra-cotta, including stone theatrical masks, are on exhibit. The museum also houses the only Late Bronze Age (8th century B.C.) necropolis found in Sicily. It's open Monday to Saturday 9am to 1pm and 3 to 6pm. Admission is 8,000L ($4).

The most popular **beaches** are at **Canneto,** about a 20-minute walk north of Lipari on the eastern coast, and just north of it, **Spiaggia Bianca** (named for the white sand, an oddity among the region's predominant black sands). At the latter, nudists gather in spite of the hot sun and sharp rocks. To reach the beach from Canneto, take the waterfront road, climb the stairs of Via Marina Garibaldi, and then veer right down a narrow cobbled path for about 325 yards.

Acquacalda (hot water) is the island's northernmost city, but nobody likes to go on its beaches (the black sand is rocky and unpleasant for walking or lying on). The town is also known for its obsidian and pumice quarries. West of Acquacalda at Quattropani, you can make a steep climb to the **Duomo de Chiesa Barca,** where the point of interest isn't the cathedral but the panoramic view from the church grounds. On the west coast, 2½ miles (4km) from Lipari, the island's other great view is available by making another steep climb to the **Quattrocchi Belvedere.**

Eighteen miles (29km) of road circle the island, connecting all its villages and attractions. Buses run by Lipari's **Autobus Urso Guglielmo,** Via Cappuccini (☎ **090-981-1262**), making 10 circuits of the island per day. The trip to Quattropani and Acquacalda on the north coast costs 3,000L ($1.50); closer destinations cost 2,000L ($1).

Agriculturally, Lipari yields capers, prevalent in the local cuisine, and Malvasia grapes, which produce a malmseylike wine too acidic to compare favorably with many other Italian wines. Figs, ginger, rosemary, and wild fennel also manage to grow in the sulfuric soil.

ACCOMMODATIONS

✪ **Hotel Carasco.** Porto delle Genti, 98055 Lipari. ☎ **090-981-1605.** Fax 090-981-1828. www.carasco.it. E-mail: carasco@tin.it. 88 units. TEL. 140,000–320,000L ($70–$160) double with breakfast; 180,000–380,000L ($90–$190) double with half-board. AE, DC, MC, V. Closed Nov–Feb.

This is Lipari's grandest hotel, consisting of two buildings connected by an addition, sitting on a bluff by the sea with a staircase leading down to the rocky coast. The interior contrasts with the bright heat of the outdoors; it has brown terra-cotta floors and dark wood furniture upholstered with fabrics striped in shades of brown. Each well-furnished guest room features a ceiling fan and rustic artifacts, with a quality mattress. Views from the ample private balconies are panoramic. The bathrooms are state of the art, with hair dryers. Just above the sea, a terrace of tables with umbrellas surrounds a large seawater pool. The hotel offers its own limited nightlife, with a full bar and a piano bar. The restaurant serves Aeolian seafood typical of the islands.

Villa Meligunis. Via Marte 7, 98055 Lipari. ☎ **090-981-2426.** Fax 090-988-0149. www.netnet.it/villameligunis. E-mail: villameligunis@netnet.it. 32 units. A/C MINIBAR TV TEL. 290,000–420,000L ($145–$210) double. Rates include half-board. AE, DC, MC, V. Free parking nearby.

This 18th-century villa has been restored to offer refined Aeolian hospitality. Less than 50 yards from the ferry docks, this appealingly contemporary four-star hotel arose from a cluster of 17th-century fishers' cottages at Marina Corta. The guest rooms are rustic but uncluttered, larger than you might expect, usually with views of the harbor and summery furniture. The hotel's name derives from the name ancient Greek colonists originally gave to Lipari, Meligunia.

DINING

E Pulera. Via Diana 51. ☎ **090-981-1158.** Reservations recommended. Main courses 18,000–35,000L ($9–$17.50). AE, DC, MC, V. Daily 7:30pm–2am. Closed June to mid-Oct. SICILIAN/AEOLIAN.

Owned by the same family who owns the Filippino (see below), this restaurant stresses its Aeolian origins more. Artifacts and maps of the islands fashioned from ceramic tiles are scattered about. Some tables occupy a terrace with a view of a flowering lawn where you'll probably want to linger. Specialties include a delightful version of *zuppe di pesce alla pescatora* (fisher's soup), *bocconcini di pesce spada* (swordfish ragout), and risotto with crayfish or squid in its own ink. Other good choices are a rich assortment of seafood antipasti that's usually laden with basil and garlic, *involtini* of eggplant, and herb-laden versions of roasted lamb. Desserts might include Aeolian cassata and ricotta mousse with wild strawberries and almonds.

✪ **Filippino.** Piazza Municipio. ☎ **090-981-1002.** Reservations recommended. Main courses 20,000–50,000L ($10–$25). AE, DC, MC, V. Daily noon–2:30pm and 7:30–10:30pm. Closed Mon Oct–Mar. SICILIAN.

Surprisingly, in such a remote outpost, this is one of the finest restaurants in Italy. It has thrived in the heart of town, near Town Hall, since 1910, when it was opened by the ancestors of the family that runs it today. You'll dine in one of two large rooms or on an outdoor terrace ringed with flowering shrubs and potted flowers. Menu items are based on old-fashioned Sicilian recipes and prepared with flair. Try the *ravioloni* (large ravioli) stuffed with stone bass and served with salsa macaroni with mozzarella, prosciutto, and ricotta baked in the oven. Veal scaloppini is especially tempting when cooked in Malvasia wine, and the array of fresh fish is broad. Culinary masterpieces are the *cupolette di pesce spada* with basil ("little dome" of swordfish) and the eggplant capponata.

La Nassa. Via G. Franza 36. ☎ **090-981-1319.** Reservations recommended. Main courses 14,000–30,000L ($7–$15). AE, MC, V. July–Oct, daily 8:30am–3pm and 6pm–midnight; Apr–June closed Thurs. Closed Nov–Easter.

At this enchanting family-run restaurant, the delectable cuisine of Donna Teresa matches the friendly enthusiasm of her son Bartolo, who has thousands of interesting stories to tell. Food is the most genuine and fresh you can find on the island, prepared respecting both antique traditions and modern taste. After the *sette perle* (seven pearl) appetizer, a combination of fresh fish, sweet shrimp, and spices, you can try the fish roulades, or any kind of fish you like, cooked in every possible way to satisfy your request. If you are more in a meat mood (which is difficult after you've seen the restaurant's boats coming back with delicious, just-caught fish), you can opt for Teresa's sausages seasoned with Aeolian herbs. As a dessert try cookies with Malvasia wine, a sweet red wine typical of this area.

STROMBOLI

The most distant island in the archipelago, **Stromboli** achieved notoriety and became a household word in the United States in 1950 with the release of the Roberto Rossellini *cinema vérité* film starring Ingrid Bergman. The American public was far more interested in the "illicit" affair between Bergman and Rossellini than in the film. Although the affair was tame by today's standards, it temporarily ended Bergman's American film career, and she was denounced on the Senate floor. Movie fans today are more likely to remember Stromboli for the film version of the Jules Verne novel *Journey to the Center of the Earth*, starring James Mason.

The entire surface of Stromboli is the cone of a sluggish but active volcano. Puffs of smoke can be seen during the day. At night on the **Sciara del Fuoco** (Slope of Fire), lava glows red-hot on its way down to meet the sea with a loud hiss and a cloud of steam—a memorable vision that may leave you feeling a little too vulnerable.

In fact, the island can serve as a fantasyland for those who were bitten by Hollywood's 1997 volcano-mania. The main attraction is a steep, difficult climb to the lip of the 3,000-foot **Gran Cratere.** The view of bubbling pools of ooze (which glow with heat at night) is accompanied by rising clouds of steam and a sulfuric stench. The journey is a 3-hour hike best taken in early morning or late afternoon to avoid the worst of the brutal sunshine—and even then it requires plenty of sunscreen and water and a good pair of shoes. You'll be following in the footsteps of the sad characters who sloshed their way to trouble in Malcolm Lowry's *Under the Volcano.* A 1990 ordinance made it illegal to climb the slope without a guide. The island's authorized guide company is **Guide Alpine Autorizzate** (☎ **090-986-211**), which charges 30,000 to 35,000L ($15 to $17.50) per person. It leads groups on the 3-hour trip up the mountain at 6pm, returning at midnight (the trip down takes 2 hours, leaving you an hour at the rim).

In spite of the volcano and its sloped terrain, there are two settlements. **Ginostra** is on the southwestern shore, little more than a cluster of summer homes with only 15 year-round residents. **Stromboli** is on the northeastern shore, a conglomeration of the villages of Ficogrande, San Vincenzo, and Piscita, where the only in-town attraction is the black-sand beach.

ACCOMMODATIONS & DINING

Albergo Ossidiana Stromboli. Via Picone 18, 98050 Stromboli. ☎ **090-986-006.** Fax 090-986-250. E-mail: ossidiana@stromboli.net. 16 units. TV. 150,000–240,000L ($75–$120) double. Rates include breakfast. MC, V.

Danielle and Pierre Cottens Pestalozzi came to Stromboli in 1994 to pursue their passion of volcanology, then took over this little hotel and restored it. The guest rooms are small but comfortable, with good bathrooms, small fridges, and fans. Some open onto a sea view; the others have a view of the volcano. In front of the hotel is a beach. The bar is reserved for hotel guests only, and amenities include a terrace and a solarium. The owners take people to see the volcano, a subject on which they're experts.

La Sirenetta–Park Hotel. Via Marina 33, 98050 Ficogrande, Stromboli. ☎ **090-986-025.** Fax 090-986-124. www.netnet.it/hotel/lasirenetta. E-mail: lasirenetta@netnet.it. 55 units. A/C MINIBAR TV TEL. 200,000–400,000L ($100–$200) double with breakfast; 260,000–500,000L ($130–$250) double with half-board. AE, CB, DC, MC, V. Closed Nov–Mar 22.

This is a well-maintained hotel, with white tile floors and walls offset by contemporary dark wood furniture and trim in the guest rooms. The rooms are medium-sized, each with a quality mattress. The tiled bathrooms are small. Natural wicker furnishings upholstered with blue floral prints grace the public areas. A large pool is on the terrace overlooking the sea. There's also an Italian fashion boutique, plus a full bar and a restaurant featuring Aeolian and Sicilian seafood dishes.

VULCANO

The island closest to the mainland, the ancient Thermessa figured heavily in the mythologies of the region. The still-active **Vulcano della Fossa** was thought to be not only the home of Vulcan but also the gateway to Hades. Thucydides, Siculus, and Aristotle each recorded eruptions. Three dormant craters also exist on the island, but a climb to the rim of the active **Gran Cratere** (Big Crater) draws the most attention.

It hasn't erupted since 1890, but one look inside the sulfur-belching hole makes you understand how it could've inspired the hellish legends surrounding it. The 1,372-foot peak is an easier climb than the one on Stromboli, taking just about an hour—though it's just as hot, and the same precautions prevail. Avoid midday, load up on sunscreen and water, and wear good hiking shoes.

Here the risks of mounting a volcano aren't addressed by legislation, so you can make the climb without a guide. Breathing the sulfuric air at the summit has its risks, though, because the steam is tainted with numerous toxins. To get to the peak from Porto Levante, the main port, follow Via Piano away from the sea for about 220 yards until you see the first of the CRATERE signs and then follow the marked trail.

The **Laghetto di Fanghi,** famous free mud baths that reputedly cure every known ailment, are along Via Provinciale a short way from the port. Be warned that the mud discolors everything from cloth to jewelry, which is one explanation for the prevalent nudity. Within sight, the acquacalda features hot-water jets that act as a natural Jacuzzi. Either can scald you if you step or sit on the vents that release the heat, so take care if you decide to enter.

The island offers one of the few smooth beaches in the entire chain, the **Spiaggia Sabbie Nere** (Black Sands Beach), with dark sand so hot in the midday sun that thongs or wading shoes are suggested if you plan to while away your day along the shore. You can find the beach by following signs posted along Via Ponente.

A knowledge of street names is worthless, really, because there are no signs. Not to worry—the locals who gather at the dock are friendly and experienced at giving directions to tongue-tied foreign visitors, especially because all they ever have to point out are the paths to the crater, the mud baths, and the beach, the island's only attractions.

ACCOMMODATIONS

Hotel Eolian. Località Porto Ponente, 98050 Vulcano. ☎ **090-985-2151.** Fax 090-985-2153. 88 units. A/C TEL. 240,000–340,000L ($120–$170) double with half-board. AE, DC, MC, V. Closed Oct–Apr.

This hotel consists of a series of white-sided stucco bungalows in a garden studded with palms and tropical plants. None has a view of the water (that's reserved for the restaurant and bar), but most guests spend their days beside the sea anyway. The guest rooms are medium-sized, each with a comfortable mattress and a tiled bathroom. The hotel has a TV room, a solarium, and a full bar. The black sands of the beach lie at the end of a steep staircase. The restaurant, emphasizing Aeolian and Sicilian seafood, is open daily for lunch and dinner, serving a set-price menu at 55,000L ($27.50).

DINING

Restaurant Vincencino. Vulcano Porto. ☎ **090-985-2016.** Reservations recommended. Main courses 12,000–25,000L ($6–$12.50). AE, DC, MC, V. Daily noon–3:30pm and 7–9:30pm. SICILIAN.

This is the most appealing of the limited number of restaurants convenient to the ferry port. In a rustic setting, you can order filling portions of local specialties. Good choices include house-style macaroni (with ricotta, eggplant, fresh tomatoes, and herbs), spaghetti *Vincencino* (with crayfish, capers, and tomato sauce), grilled fish, including an *involtini* of swordfish, and seafood salad. October to March, the menu is limited to a simple array of platters served from the bar.

Appendix A: Italy in Depth

As with most countries, there is good and bad news coming out of Italy today. Having survived the Papal Jubilee 2000, Italy is launching itself into the new millennium with both progress and disappointment.

The good news is that the country is more visitor-friendly than ever. A renaissance seems to have swept the country, even transforming Naples, long known for its crime and drugs, into a vital, happening city.

At the closing of the 20th century, workers throughout Italy, but particularly in Rome, were spending months overhauling and restoring hotels, museums, monuments, churches, fountains—you name it. Rome, especially, was under scaffolding for a couple of years, with most projects emerging just in the time for the millennium celebrations. Now the city is looking better than ever, although there's still a lot of cleanup to do on buildings stained black by car exhaust.

Venice, of course, can never be completely restored, even assuming that any country has *that* much money. Nevertheless, throughout Italy museums are better lit, often expanded, and more geared to the modern traveler who doesn't have hours to poke through dusty Etruscan statues or Roman busts. Visitors no longer have to peer at that Caravaggio amid a shroud of shadows. In addition, many museums have opened up bookshops and cafeterias.

Italy has a long way to go yet—will red tape forever hinder the restoration of Venice's burned La Fenice opera house? Will much of the country's greatest treasures still linger in smaller, relatively unvisited towns? Will measures to prevent earthquake damage to priceless frescoes and architecture ever be instituted (a quake struck Assisi's Basilica di San Francesco in 1997)? The present attention to Italy's riches has been unprecedented in its history and is a welcome sign for visitors in the 21st century even as they await further progress.

Predictably, however, the country's politics remain mired in conflict, corruption, turmoil, and scandal. After all, there have been 57 changes of government since World War II alone. Because of its continuing government crisis, with one party always challenging and trying to overthrow the other, Italy may be losing ground with the European Union. In the late 1990s, a brilliant national effort took place to make Italy one of the top three leading members of the European single-currency union. But now popular disillusionment has set in with the cost of euro membership, which came as a great sacrifice to the economy of the country. Polls charting social trends report a "psychological unease" about where internecine political wars are taking Italy into its uncertain future. Yet as a Roman senator has said, "Italy wouldn't be Italy without that."

1 History 101

THE ETRUSCANS

Of all the early inhabitants of Italy, the most significant were the Etruscans. But who were they? No one knows, and the many inscriptions they left behind (mostly on graves) are of no help, since the Etruscan language has never been deciphered by modern scholars. It's thought they arrived on the eastern coast of Umbria several centuries before Rome was built, around 800 B.C. Their religious rites and architecture show an obvious contact with Mesopotamia; the Etruscans may have been refugees from Asia Minor who traveled westward about 1200 to 1000 B.C. Within 2 centuries, they had subjugated Tuscany and Campania and the Villanova tribes who lived there.

While the Etruscans were building temples at Tarquinia and Caere (present-day Cerveteri), the few nervous Latin tribes who remained outside their sway were gravitating to Rome, then little more than a village of sheepherders. As Rome's power grew, however, it increasingly profited from the strategically important Tiber crossing, where the ancient Salt Way (Via Salaria) turned northeastward toward the central Apennines.

From their base at Rome, the Latins remained free of the Etruscans until about 600 B.C. But the Etruscan advance was inexorable, and though the Latin tribes concentrated their forces at Rome for a last stand, they were swept away by the sophisticated Mesopotamian conquerors. The new overlords introduced gold tableware and jewelry, bronze urns and terracotta statuary, and the best of Greek and Asia Minor art and culture. They also made Rome the governmental seat of all Latium. Roma is an Etruscan name, and the kings of Rome had Etruscan names: Numa, Ancus, Tarquinius, and even Romulus.

The Estruscans ruled until the Roman revolt around 510 B.C., and by 250 B.C. the Romans and their Campania allies had vanquished the Etruscans, wiping out their language and religion. However, many of the former rulers' manners and beliefs remained, assimilated into the culture. Even today, certain Etruscan customs

Dateline

- **Bronze Age** Celts, Teutonic tribes, and others from the Mediterranean and Asia Minor inhabit the peninsula.
- **1000 B.C.** Large colonies of Etruscans settle in Tuscany and Campania, quickly subjugating many of the Latin inhabitants of the peninsula.
- **800 B.C.** Rome begins to take shape, evolving from a strategically located shepherds' village into a magnet for Latin tribes fleeing the Etruscans.
- **600 B.C.** Etruscans occupy Rome, designating it the capital of their empire. The city grows rapidly, and a major seaport opens at Ostia.
- **510 B.C.** The Latin tribes, still centered in Rome, revolt against the Etruscans. Alpine Gauls attack from the north, and Greeks living in Sicily destroy the Etruscan navy.
- **250 B.C.** The Romans, allied with the Greeks, Phoenicians, and native Sicilians, defeat the Etruscans. Rome flourishes and begins the accumulation of a vast empire.
- **49 B.C.** Italy (through Rome) controls the entire Mediterranean world.
- **44 B.C.** Julius Caesar is assassinated. His successor, Augustus, transforms Rome from a city of brick into a city of marble.
- **3rd century A.D.** Rome declines under a series of incompetent and corrupt emperors.
- **4th century A.D.** Rome is fragmented politically as

continues

administrative capitals are established in such cities as Milan and Trier, Germany.

- **A.D. 395** The empire splits; Constantine establishes a "New Rome" at Constantinople (Byzantium). The Goths successfully invade Rome's northern provinces.
- **410–55** Rome is sacked by barbarians.
- **475** Rome falls, leaving only the primate of the Catholic Church in control. The pope slowly adopts many of the powers once reserved for the Roman emperor.
- **800** Charlemagne is crowned Holy Roman Emperor by Pope Leo III. Italy dissolves into a series of small warring kingdoms.
- **Late 11th century** The popes function like secular princes with private armies.
- **1065** The Holy Land falls to the Muslim Turks; the Crusades are launched.
- **1303–77** The Papal Schism occurs; the pope and his entourage move from Rome to Avignon, France.
- **1377** The papacy returns to Rome.
- **1443** Brunelleschi's dome caps the Duomo in Florence as the Renaissance bursts into full bloom.
- **1469–92** Lorenzo il Magnifico rules in Florence as the Medici patron of Renaissance artists.
- **1499** *The Last Supper* is completed by Leonardo da Vinci in Milan.
- **1508** Michelangelo begins work on the Vatican's Sistine Chapel.
- **1527** Rome is sacked by Charles V of Spain, who is crowned Holy Roman Emperor the following year.
- **1796–97** Napoléon's series of invasions arouses Italian nationalism.
- **1861** The Kingdom of Italy is established.

continues

and bloodlines are believed to exist in Italy, especially in Tuscany.

The best places to see the legacy left by these mysterious people are in Cerveteri and Tarquinia outside Rome. Especially interesting is the Etruscan necropolis, just 4 miles southeast of Tarquinia, where thousands of tombs have been discovered. To learn more about the Etruscans, visit the Museo Nazionale di Villa Giulla in Rome.

THE ROMAN REPUBLIC

After the Roman Republic was established in 510 B.C., the Romans continued to increase their power by conquering neighboring communities in the highlands and forming alliances with other Latins in the lowlands. They gave to their Latin allies, and then to conquered peoples, partial or complete Roman citizenship, with the obligation of military service. Citizen colonies were set up as settlements of Roman farmers, and many of the famous cities of Italy originated as colonies. These colonies were for the most part fortified and linked to Rome by military roads.

The stern Roman republic was characterized by a belief in the gods, the necessity of learning from the past, the strength of the family, education through reading books and performing public service, and, most importantly, obedience. The all-powerful Senate presided as Rome defeated rival powers one after the other and grew to rule the Mediterranean. The Punic Wars with Carthage in the 3rd century B.C. cleared away a major obstacle, though people said later that Rome's breaking of its treaty with Carthage (which led to that city's total destruction) put a curse on Rome.

No figure was more towering during the republic than Julius Caesar, the charismatic conqueror of Gaul—"the wife of every husband and the husband of every wife." After defeating the last resistance of the Pompeians in 45 B.C., he came to Rome and was made dictator and consul for 10 years. By then he was almost a king. Conspirators led by Marcus Junius Brutus stabbed him to death in the Senate on March 15, 44 B.C. Beware the ides of March.

Marc Antony, a Roman general, assumed control by seizing Caesar's papers and wealth. Intent on expanding the Republic, Antony met with Cleopatra at Tarsus in 41 B.C. She seduced him, and he stayed in Egypt for a year. When

Antony eventually returned to Rome, still smitten with Cleopatra, he made peace with Caesar's willed successor, Octavius, and, through the pacts of Brundisium, soon found himself married to Octavius's sister, Octavia. This marriage, however, didn't prevent him from openly marrying Cleopatra in 36 B.C. The furious Octavius gathered western legions and defeated Antony at the Battle of Actium on September 2, 31 B.C. Cleopatra fled to Egypt, followed by Antony, who committed suicide in disgrace a year later. Cleopatra, unable to seduce his successor and thus retain her rule of Egypt, followed suit with the help of an asp.

THE ROMAN EMPIRE

By 49 B.C., Italy ruled the entire Mediterranean world, either directly or indirectly, since all political, commercial, and cultural pathways led straight to Rome. The potential for wealth and glory to be found in Rome lured many people, draining other Italian communities of human resources. Foreign imports, especially agricultural imports, hurt local farmers and landowners. Municipal governments faltered, and civil wars ensued. Public order was restored by the Caesars (planned by Julius but brought to fruition under Augustus). On the eve of the birth of Christ, Rome was a mighty empire whose generals had brought the Western world under the sway of Roman law and civilization.

Born Gaius Octavius in 63 B.C., Augustus, the first Roman emperor, reigned from 27 B.C. to A.D. 14. His reign, called "the golden age of Rome," led to the Pax Romana, 2 centuries of peace. He had been adopted by, and eventually became the heir of, his great-uncle Julius Caesar. In Rome you can still visit the remains of the Forum of Augustus, built before the birth of Christ, and the Domus Augustana, where the imperial family lived on the Palatine Hill.

The emperors, whose succession started with Augustus's principate after the death of Julius Caesar, brought Rome to new, almost giddy, heights. Augustus transformed the city from brick to marble, much the way Napoléon III transformed Paris many centuries later. But success led to corruption. The emperors wielded autocratic power, and the centuries witnessed a steady decay in the ideals and traditions on which the empire had been founded. The army became a fifth column of barbarian mercenaries, the tax collector became the scourge of the

- **1915–18** Italy enters World War I on the side of the Allies.
- **1922** Fascists march on Rome; Benito Mussolini becomes premier.
- **1929** A concordat between the Vatican and the Italian government is signed, delineating the rights and responsibilities of each party.
- **1935** Italy invades Abyssinia (Ethiopia).
- **1936** Italy signs "Axis" pact with Germany.
- **1940** Italy invades Greece.
- **1943** U.S. Gen. George Patton lands in Sicily and soon controls the island.
- **1945** Mussolini is killed by a mob in Milan; World War II ends.
- **1946** The Republic of Italy is established.
- **1957** The Treaty of Rome, establishing the European Community (EC), is signed by six nations.
- **1960s** The country's economy grows under the EC, but the impoverished south lags behind.
- **1970s** Italy is plagued by left-wing terrorism; former premier Aldo Moro is kidnapped and killed.
- **1980s** Political changes in Eastern Europe induce Italy's strong Communist Party to modify its program and even to change its name; the Socialists head their first post-1945 coalition government.
- **1994** A conservative coalition, led by Silvio Berlusconi, wins general elections.
- **1995** Following the resignation of Berlusconi, treasury minister Lamberto Dini is named prime minister to head the transitional government.
- **1996** Dini steps down as prime minister, and President Scalfaro dissolves both houses of parliament. In

continues

general elections, the center-left coalition known as the Olive Tree sweeps both the Senate and the Chamber of Deputies.

- **1997–98** Twin earthquakes hit Umbria, killing 11 people and destroying precious frescos in Assisi's basilica. Romano Prodi survives a neo-Communist challenge and continues to press for budget cuts in an effort to "join Europe."
- **1999** Italy officially goes under the euro umbrella as the entire country prepares for Papal Jubilee 2000.
- **2000** Italy welcomes Jubilee visitors in the wake of political discontent.

countryside, and for every good emperor (Augustus, Claudius, Trajan, Vespasian, and Hadrian, to name a few) there were three or four debased heads of state (Caligula, Nero, Domitian, Caracalla, and others).

After Augustus died (by poison, perhaps), his widow, Livia—a crafty social climber who had divorced her first husband to marry Augustus—set up her son, Tiberius, as ruler through a series of intrigues and poisonings. A long series of murders ensued, and Tiberius, who ruled during Pontius Pilate's trial and crucifixion of Christ, was eventually murdered in an uprising of landowners. In fact, murder was so common that a short time later Domitian (A.D. 81–96) became so obsessed with the possibility of assassination that he had the walls of his palace covered in mica so he could see behind him at all times. (He was killed anyway.)

Excesses and scandal ruled the day: Caligula (a bit overfond of his sister Drusilla) appointed his horse a lifetime member of the Senate, lavished money on foolish projects, and proclaimed himself a god. Caligula's successor, his uncle Claudius, was deceived and publicly humiliated by one of his wives, the lascivious Messalina (he had her killed for her trouble); he was then poisoned by his final wife, his niece Agrippina, to secure the succession of Nero, her son by a previous marriage. Nero's thanks was later to murder not only his mother but also his wife, Claudius's daughter, and his rival, Claudius's son. The disgraceful Nero was removed as emperor while visiting Greece; he committed suicide with the cry, "What an artist I destroy."

By the 3rd century A.D., corruption had become so prevalent there were 23 emperors in 73 years. How bad were things? So bad that Caracalla, to secure control of the empire, had his brother Geta slashed to pieces while Geta was lying in his mother's arms. Rule of the empire changed hands so frequently that news of the election of a new emperor commonly reached the provinces together with a report of that emperor's assassination.

The 4th-century reforms of Diocletian held the empire together, but at the expense of its inhabitants, who were reduced to tax units. Diocletian reinforced imperial power while paradoxically weakening Roman dominance and prestige by dividing the empire into east and west halves and establishing administrative capitals at outposts like Milan and Trier, Germany. He instituted not only heavy taxes but also a socioeconomic system that made professions hereditary. This edict was so strictly enforced that the son of a silversmith could be tried as a criminal if he attempted to become a sculptor instead.

Constantine became emperor in A.D. 306, and in 330 he made Constantinople (or Byzantium) the new capital of the Empire, moving the administrative functions away from Rome altogether, partly because the menace of possible barbarian attack in the West had increased greatly. Constantine took the best Roman artisans, politicians, and public figures with him, creating a city renowned for its splendor, intrigue, jealousies, and passion. Constantine was the first Christian emperor, allegedly converting after he saw the True Cross in the heavens, accompanied by the legend, "In This Sign Shall You Conquer." He then defeated the pagan Maxentius and his followers in battle.

THE EMPIRE FALLS

The eastern and western sections of the Roman Empire split in 395, leaving Italy without the support it once received from east of the Adriatic. When the Goths moved toward Rome in the early 5th century, citizens in the provinces, who had grown to hate and fear the cruel bureaucracy set up by Diocletian and followed by succeeding emperors, welcomed the invaders. And then the pillage began.

Rome was first sacked by Alaric, king of the Visigoths, in August 410. The populace made no attempt to defend the city (other than trying vainly to buy him off, a tactic that had worked 3 years before); most people simply fled into the hills or headed to their country estates if they were rich. The feeble Western emperor Honorius hid out in Ravenna the entire time.

More than 40 troubled years passed. Then Attila the Hun invaded Italy to besiege Rome. Attila was dissuaded from attacking thanks largely to a peace mission headed by Pope Leo I in 452. Yet relief was short-lived: In 455 Gaiseric the Vandal carried out a 2-week sack that was unparalleled in its pure savagery. The empire of the West lasted for only another 20 years; finally in 476 the sacks and chaos ended the once-mighty city, and Rome was left to the popes, under the nominal auspices of an exarch from Byzantium (Constantinople).

The last would-be Caesars to walk the streets of Rome were both barbarians: The first was Theodoric, who established an Ostrogoth kingdom at Ravenna from 493 to 526; and the second was Totilla, who held the last chariot races in the Circus Maximus in 549. Totilla was engaged in an ongoing battle with Belisarius, the general of the Eastern emperor Justinian, who sought to regain Rome for the Eastern Empire. The city changed hands several times, recovering some of its ancient pride by bravely resisting Totilla's forces, but eventually it was entirely depopulated by the continuing battles.

Christianity, a new religion that created a new society, was probably founded in Rome about a decade after the death of Jesus. Gradually gaining strength despite early persecution, it was finally accepted as the official religion. The best way today to relive the early Christian era is to visit Rome's Appian Way and its Catacombs, along Via Appia Antica, built in 312 B.C. According to Christian tradition, it was here that an escaping Peter encountered the vision of Christ. The Catacombs of St. Callixtus form the first cemetery of the Christian community of Rome.

THE MIDDLE AGES

Thus a ravaged Rome entered the Middle Ages, its once-proud population scattered and unrecognizable in rustic exile. A modest population started life again in the swamps of the Campus Martius, while the seven hills, now without water since the aqueducts were cut, stood abandoned and crumbling.

After the fall of the Western Empire, the pope took on more and more imperial powers, yet there was no political unity. Decades of rule by barbarians and then by Goths were followed by takeovers in different parts of the country by various strong warriors, such as the Lombards. Italy became divided into several spheres of control. In 731 Pope Gregory II renounced Rome's dependence on Constantinople and thus ended the twilight era of the Greek exarch who had nominally ruled Rome.

Papal Rome turned toward Europe, where the papacy found a powerful ally in Charlemagne, a king of the barbarian Franks. In 800 he was crowned emperor by Pope Leo III. The capital he established at Aachen (Aix-la-Chapelle in French) lay deep within territory known to the Romans a half millennium before as the heart of the barbarian world. Although Charlemagne pledged allegiance to the church and looked to Rome and its pope as the final arbiter in most religious and cultural affairs, he launched northwestern Europe on a course toward bitter political opposition to the meddling of the papacy in temporal affairs.

The successor to Charlemagne's empire was a political entity known as the Holy Roman Empire (962–1806). The new empire defined the end of the Dark Ages but ushered in a period of long bloody warfare. The Lombard leaders battled Franks. Magyars from Hungary invaded northeastern Lombardy and were in turn defeated by the increasingly powerful Venetians. Normans gained military control of Sicily in the 11th century, divided it from the rest of Italy, and altered forever the island's racial and ethnic makeup and its architecture. As Italy dissolved into a fragmented collection of city-states, the papacy fell under the power of Rome's feudal landowners. Eventually even the process for choosing popes came into the hands of the increasingly Germanic Holy Roman emperors, though this balance of power would very soon shift.

Rome during the Middle Ages was a quaint rural town. Narrow lanes with overhanging buildings filled many areas, such as the Campus Martius, that had previously been showcases of ancient imperial power. Great basilicas were built and embellished with golden-hued mosaics. The forums, mercantile exchanges, temples, and theaters of the Imperial Era slowly disintegrated and collapsed. The decay of ancient Rome was assisted by periodic earthquakes, centuries of neglect, and, in particular, the growing need for building materials. Rome receded into a dusty provincialism. As the seat of the Roman Catholic church, the state was almost completely controlled by priests, who had an insatiable need for new churches and convents.

By the end of the 11th century, the popes shook off control of the Roman aristocracy, rid themselves of what they considered the excessive influence of the emperors at Aachen, and began an aggressive expansion of church influence and acquisitions. The deliberate organization of the church into a format modeled on the hierarchies of the ancient Roman Empire put it on a collision course with the empire and the other temporal leaders of Europe. The result was an endless series of power struggles.

The southern half of the country took a different road when, in the 11th century, the Normans invaded southern Italy, wresting control from the local strongmen and, in Sicily, from the Muslim Saracens who had occupied the region throughout the Dark Ages. To the south, the Normans introduced feudalism, a repressive social system that discouraged individual economic initiative, and whose legacy accounts for the social and economic differences between north and south that persist to this day.

In the mid–14th century, the Black Death ravaged Europe, killing a third of Italy's population. Despite such setbacks, the northern Italian city-states grew wealthy from Crusade booty, trade with one another and with the Middle East, and banking. These wealthy principalities and pseudorepublics ruled by the merchant elite flexed their muscles in the absence of a strong central authority.

THE RENAISSANCE

The story of Italy from the dawn of the Renaissance in the 15th century to the Age of Enlightenment in the 17th and 18th centuries is as varied and fascinating as that of the rise and fall of the empire. The papacy soon became essentially a feudal state, and the pope was a medieval (later Renaissance) prince engaged in many of the worldly activities that brought criticism on the church in later centuries. The 1065 fall of the Holy Land to the Turks catapulted the papacy into the forefront of world politics, primarily because of the Crusades, many of which the popes directly caused or encouraged (but most of which were judged military and economic disasters). During the 12th and 13th centuries, the bitter rivalries that rocked Europe's secular and spiritual bastions took their toll on the Holy Roman Empire, which grew weaker as city-states, buttressed by mercantile and trade-related prosperity, grew stronger and as France emerged as a potent nation in its own right. Each investiture of a new bishop to any influential post resulted in endless jockeying for power among many factions.

These conflicts reached their most visible impasse in 1303 during the Great Schism, when the papacy was moved to the French city of Avignon. For more than 70 years, until 1377, viciously competing popes (one in Rome, another under the protection of the French kings in Avignon) made simultaneous claims to the legacy of St. Peter, underscoring as never before the degree to which the church was both a victim and a victimizer in the temporal world of European politics.

The seat of the papacy was eventually returned to Rome, where successive popes were every bit as interesting as the Roman emperors they had replaced. The great families (Barberini, Medici, Borgia) enhanced their status and fortunes impressively when one of their sons was elected pope. For a look at life during this tumultuous period, you can visit Rome's Castel Sant'Angelo, which became a papal residence in the 14th century.

Despite the centuries that had passed since the collapse of the Roman Empire, the age of siege wasn't yet over. In 1527 Charles V, king of Spain, carried out the worst sack of Rome ever. To the horror of Pope Clement VII (a Medici), the entire city was brutally pillaged by the man who was to be crowned Holy Roman Emperor the next year.

During the years of the Renaissance, the Reformation, and the Counter-Reformation, Rome underwent major physical changes. The old centers of culture reverted to pastures and fields, and great churches and palaces were built with the stones of ancient Rome. This construction boom, in fact, did far more damage to the temples of the Caesars than any barbarian sack had done. Rare marbles were stripped from the imperial baths and used as altarpieces or sent to lime kilns. So enthusiastic was the papal destruction of Imperial Rome that it's a miracle anything is left.

This era is best remembered because of its art. The great ruling families, especially the Medicis in Florence, the Gonzagas in Mantua, and the Estes in Ferrara, not only reformed law and commerce but also sparked a renaissance in art. Out of this period arose such towering figures as Leonardo da Vinci and Michelangelo. Many visitors come to Italy to view what's left of the art and glory of that era—everything from Michelangelo's Sistine Chapel at the Vatican to his statue of *David* in Florence, from Leonardo's *Last Supper* in Milan to the Duomo in Florence, graced by Brunelleschi's dome.

A UNITED ITALY

The 19th century witnessed the final collapse of the Renaissance city-states, which had existed since the end of the 13th century. These units, eventually coming under the control of a *signore* (lord), were in effect regional states, with mercenary soldiers, civil rights, and assistance for their friendly neighbors. Some had attained formidable power under such *signori* as the Estes in Ferrara, the Medicis in Florence, and the Viscontis and Sforzas in Milan.

Impressions

It is not impossible to govern Italians. It is merely useless.

—Benito Mussolini

During the 17th, 18th, and 19th centuries, turmoil continued through a succession of many European dynasties. Napoléon made a bid for power in Italy beginning in 1796, fueling his war machines with what was considered a relatively easy victory. During the Congress of Vienna (1814–15), which followed Napoléon's defeat, Italy was once again divided among many factions: Austria was given Lombardy and Venetia, and the Papal States were returned to the pope. Some duchies were put back into the hands of their hereditary rulers, and southern Italy and Sicily went to a Bourbon dynasty. One historic move, which eventually contributed to the unification of Italy, was the assignment of the former republic of Genoa to Sardinia (which at the time was governed by the House of Savoy).

Political unrest became a fact of Italian life, at least some of it encouraged by the rapid industrialization of the north and the almost total lack of industrialization in the south. Despite those barriers, in 1861, thanks to the brilliant efforts of patriots Camillo Cavour (1810–61) and Giuseppe Garibaldi (1807–82), the Kingdom of Italy was proclaimed and Victor Emmanuel (Vittorio Emanuele) II of the House of Savoy, king of Sardinia, became the head of the new monarchy.

Garibaldi, the most respected of all Italian heroes, must be singled out for his efforts, which included taking Sicily, then returning to the mainland and marching north to meet Victor Emmanuel II at Teano, and finally declaring a unified Italy (with the important exception of Rome itself). It must have seemed especially sweet to a man whose efforts at unity had caused him to flee the country fearing for his life on four occasions. It's a tribute to the tenacity of this red-bearded hero that he never gave up, even in the early 1850s, when he was forced to wait out one of his exiles as a candlemaker on Staten Island in New York.

Although the hope, promoted by Europe's theocrats and some of its devout Catholics, of attaining one empire ruled by the pope and the church had long ago faded, there was still a fight, followed by generations of hard feelings, when the Papal States—a strategically and historically important principality under the pope's temporal jurisdiction—were confiscated by the new Kingdom of Italy.

The establishment of the kingdom, however, didn't signal a complete unification of Italy, because Rome was still under papal control and Venetia was still held by Austria. This was partially resolved in 1866, when Venetia joined the rest of Italy after the Seven Weeks' War between Austria and Prussia; in 1871 Rome became the capital of the newly formed country. The Vatican, however, didn't yield its territory to the new order, despite guarantees of nonintervention proffered by the government, and relations between the pope and the country of Italy remained rocky.

THE RISE OF IL DUCE & WORLD WAR II

On October 28, 1922, Benito Mussolini, who had started his Fascist Party in 1919, knew the time was ripe for change. He gathered 50,000 supporters for a march on Rome. Inflation was soaring and workers had just called a general strike, so King Victor Emmanuel II, rather than recognizing a state under siege, recognized Mussolini as the new government leader. In 1929, Il Duce defined the divisions between the Italian government and the Vatican by signing a concordat granting political and fiscal autonomy to Vatican City. The agreement also made Roman Catholicism the official state religion—but that designation was removed in 1978 by a revision of the concordat.

During the Spanish Civil War (1936–39), Mussolini's support of Franco's Fascist party, whose members had staged a coup against the democratically elected government of Spain, helped encourage the formation of the "Axis" alliance between Italy and Nazi Germany. Despite having outdated military equipment, Italy added to the general horror of the era by invading Abyssinia (Ethiopia) in 1935. In 1940 Italy invaded Greece through Albania, and in 1942 it sent thousands of Italian troops to assist Hitler in his disastrous campaign along the Russian front. In 1943 Allied forces, under the command of U.S. Gen. George Patton and British Gen. Bernard Montgomery, landed in Sicily and quickly secured the island as they prepared to move north toward Rome.

In the face of likely defeat and humiliation, Mussolini was overthrown by his own cabinet (Grand Council). The Allies made a separate deal with Victor Emmanuel III, who had collaborated with the Fascists during the previous 2 decades and now easily shifted allegiances. A politically divided Italy watched as battalions of fanatical German Nazis released Mussolini from his Italian jail cell to establish the short-lived Republic of Salò, headquartered on the edge of Lake Garda. Mussolini had hoped for a groundswell of popular opinion in favor of Italian Fascism, but events quickly proved this to be nothing more than a futile dream.

In April 1945, with almost a half million Italians rising in a mass demonstration against him and the German war machine, Mussolini was captured by Italian partisans as he fled to Switzerland. Along with his mistress, Claretta Petacci, and several others of his intimates, he was shot and strung upside-down from the roof of a Milan gas station.

THE POSTWAR YEARS

Disaffected with the monarchy and its identification with the fallen Fascist dictatorship, Italy's citizens voted in 1946 for the establishment of a republic. The major political party that emerged following World War II was the Christian Democratic Party, a right-of-center group whose leader, Alcide De Gasperi (1881–1954), served as premier until 1953. The second-largest party was the Communist Party; however, by the mid-1970s it had abandoned its revolutionary program in favor of a democratic form of "Eurocommunism" (in 1991 the Communists even changed their name to the Democratic Party of the Left).

Even though after the war Italy had been stripped of all its overseas colonies, it quickly succeeded in rebuilding its economy, in part because of U.S. aid under the Marshall Plan (1948–52). By the 1960s, as a member of the European Community (founded in Rome in 1957), Italy had become one of the world's leading industrialized nations, prominent in the manufacture of automobiles and office equipment.

But the country continued to be plagued by economic inequities between the prosperous industrialized north and the economically depressed south. It suffered an unprecedented flight of capital (frequently aided by Swiss banks only too willing to accept discreet deposits from wealthy Italians) and an increase in bankruptcies, inflation (almost 20% during much of the 1970s), and unemployment.

During the late 1970s and early 1980s, Italy was rocked by the rise of terrorism, instigated both by neo-Fascists and by left-wing intellectuals from the Socialist-controlled universities of the north.

THE 1990S & INTO THE NEW MILLENNIUM

By the late 19th century, the Mafia had become a kind of shadow government in the south, and to this day it controls a staggering number of politicians, national officials, and even judges, providing one scandal after another. In the early 1990s, the Italians reeled as many leading politicians were accused of wholesale corruption. As a result, a newly formed right-wing group, led by media magnate Silvio Berlusconi, swept to victory in 1994's general elections. Berlusconi became prime minister at the head of a coalition government. However, in December 1994, he resigned as prime minister after the federalist Northern League Party defected from his coalition and he lost his parliamentary majority. Treasury Minister Lamberto Dini, a nonpolitical banker with international financial credentials, was named to replace Berlusconi.

Dini signed on merely as a transitional player in the topsy-turvy political game. His austere measures enacted to balance Italy's budget, including cuts in pensions and health care, weren't popular among the mostly blue-collar workers or the highly influential labor unions. Aware of a predicted defeat in a no-confidence vote, Dini stepped down. His resignation in January 1996 left beleaguered Italians shouting *"Basta!"* (Enough!). This latest reshuffling in Italy's political deck prompted President Oscar Scalfaro to dissolve both houses of parliament.

Once again the Italians were faced with forming a new government. The elections of April 1996 proved a shocker, not only for the defeated politicians but also for the victors. The center-left coalition known as the Olive Tree, led by Romano Prodi, swept both the Senate and the Chamber of Deputies. The Olive Tree, whose roots stem from the old Communist Party, achieved victory by shifting toward the center and focusing its campaign on a strong platform protecting social benefits and supporting Italy's bid to become a solid member of the European Union.

Prodi carried through on his commitment when he announced a stringent budget for 1997 in a bid to be among the first countries to enter the monetary union. That year saw further upheavals in the Prodi government as he continued to push ahead with cuts to the country's generous social-security system. By autumn, though, Prodi was forced to submit his resignation when he lost critical support in Parliament from the Communist Refounding Party, which balked at pension and welfare cuts in the 1998 budget. The party eventually backed off with its demands and Prodi was returned to office, where he pledged to see legislation for a 35-hour workweek passed by 2001.

In September 1997, twin earthquakes (5.7 and 5.6 on the Richter scale), with an epicenter just outside Assisi, struck within hours of each other. Umbria sustained considerable damage, especially in Acciano and Assisi, where 11 people were killed and another 13,000 forced to take refuge in tents. The following 11 days of aftershocks and tremors hindered the recovery effort by the Italian government and relief organizations and poured salt in the wounds of those left wondering what to do. One of the victims of these quakes was the Basilica of St. Francis in Assisi, where vaults collapsed and magnificent frescoes were reduced to dust.

On the political front, Massimo D'Alema became the first former Communist to lead a Western European government in October 1998 when he formed

Italy's 56th postwar government. He replaced departing prime minister Romano Prodi.

As 1999 neared its end, Italy rushed to complete its myriad renovation and restoration projects so that everything would be perfect for the Jubilee. The big financial news of 1999 was Italy's entrance under the euro umbrella. Italy and the United States faced tense relations in spring 1999 when a military jury cleared a marine captain, Richard J. Ashby, of charges brought against him for flying his plane over a ski resort and severing the cables holding a gondola, plunging 20 people to their deaths in the Italian Alps. After a year of painful recriminations on both sides of the Atlantic and a bitter 3-week trial, the verdict came in with stunning finality.

Italy spent all of 2000 welcoming Jubilee Year visitors from around the world, but everything wasn't a celebration. There is popular disillusionment with the costs of euro membership and with the weakness of the euro against the U.S. dollar and the British pound. Media mogul Silvio Berlusconi, in spite of legal proceedings against him citing corruption, blanketed the country with advertising, hoping to reclaim the prime minister's office. In December 1999, under Prime Minister Massimo D'Alema, Italy received its 57th new government since 1945.

2 Italian Architecture at a Glance

For a glossary of common architectural terms you'll encounter, see Appendix B.

THE ETRUSCANS & THE ROMANS

The mysterious Etruscans, whose earliest origins probably lie somewhere in Mesopotamia, brought the first truly impressive architecture to mainland Italy. Although little remains of their architecture, historical writings by the Romans refer to powerful Etruscan **walls, bridges,** and **aqueducts.** As Rome asserted its own identity and overpowered its Etruscan masters, it borrowed heavily from themes already established by Etruscan architects.

Architecture flourished magnificently in Rome, advancing in size and majesty far beyond the examples set by the Etruscans and Greeks. The most important element of these structures was the fine-tuning of the **arch,** which the Romans used with a new logic, rhythm, and ease. Monumental buildings were erected, each an embodiment of the strength, power, and careful organization of the Empire itself. Examples are the **forums** and **baths** scattered across the Mediterranean world, the greatest of which were **Trajan's Forum** and the **Baths of Caracalla,** both in Rome. Equally magnificent were two other Roman buildings: the **Colosseum** and Hadrian's **Pantheon,** a building that later heavily influenced the Palladians during the Renaissance.

Of course, these immense achievements were made possible by two major resources: almost limitless funds pouring in from all regions of the empire and an unending supply of slaves captured during military campaigns abroad.

The use of **concrete** was also a major influence on Roman architecture, as well as on buildings to come. Concrete, which seemingly lasts forever—as evidenced by the giant concrete dome of Rome's Pantheon and the Baths of Caracalla—made vast buildings possible. Insulae (apartment blocks) rose to seven floors or more, something almost unheard of previously. Even though Romans didn't invent the arch or the aqueduct or even concrete, they perfected these building forms, and their methods and styles were to be used throughout Western culture.

THE ROMANESQUE

The art and architecture in the centuries following the collapse of Rome became known as early medieval or Romanesque. In its many variations, it flourished between A.D. 1000 and 1250, though in isolated pockets away from Europe's mainstream it continued for several centuries later.

During the Romanesque period, Italian architects were influenced by the innumerable **Roman ruins**—classical columns, entablatures, vaults, ornamentation, and whole facades were left intact to inspire future generations. Designs at this time were decidedly Italian, as architects emphasized width and horizontal lines. Italian buildings, especially churches, were larger and lower to the ground than Romanesque designs from northern Europe. **Churches** were designed in three parts, with a separate **baptistry** and **campanile.** Initially, the Italian Romanesque examples were based on early Christian **basilicas,** retaining their **colonnaded atriums** and **narthex entrances.** After about 1100, however, the influence of the atrium on overall design declined and the traditional Italian **portico** became more common. **Arcading** (a series of decorative arches, either open or closed with masonry, supported on columns) was commonly used as a facade, and **timber roofs** became the norm instead of stone vaults.

Climate also affected the way in which Italian Romanesque designs differed from Romanesque designs in the rest of Europe. Because snow and heavy rain weren't factors in Italy, architects could design roofs that had a lower pitch than those commonly seen throughout much of Europe. Intensive sunlight and heat also led to the incorporation of **smaller windows** to exclude, rather than trap, some of the light. Because of the sunny climate, facades were brightly decorated with **glass mosaics** and **variegated marble,** which would reflect the light in a dramatic and beautiful way. Northern European designs still depended on the more traditional stone sculptural and statuary facades. Stone wasn't as plentiful in Italy as in other parts of Europe, but the almost unlimited availability of clay in Italy made **brick** a popular material for structural elements.

Italy, a series of city-states as opposed to a unified country like many other European nations, also had regional variations of Romanesque design. In the north, with Milan as its center, the designs were **Lombard Romanesque,** most closely resembling the designs of France and Germany. In central Italy, the **Tuscan** or **Pisan school,** strongly influenced by the Catholic Church, was most closely based on ancient Roman designs. In the south, including Sicily, **Norman Romanesque** was similar to Norman-influenced architecture found in other European nations, but with additional Saracenic, Byzantine, and Greek elements.

Existing examples of Lombard Romanesque date mostly from the 11th and 12th centuries and are most evident in **Milan, Pavia, Verona,** and near the lakes and Alps at **Como, Aosta,** and **Ivrea.** Structures are mainly of brick in shades of red, pink, and brown, some decorated with stone or marble. Because the climate in these areas was cooler than that in the rest of Italy, buildings here tended to share elements of design (such as more steeply pitched roofs and larger windows) with the rest of Europe. **Stone groin** and **rib vaults** were used extensively, as opposed to the timber roofs favored in the rest of Italy. Arcading was the common external decoration, and **wheel-pattern windows** dominated all other designs. Column designs were in line with the rest of Italy (the columns usually resting on the backs of animals), but the decorations were less classical and introduced a wide range of animals, devils, monsters, flowers, and plants. The most distinctive feature of Lombard Romanesque is the design of the tall and slender squared **campanile** (bell tower), separate from the main body of the church. An excellent example is the bell tower of the **Abbey Church** at Pomposa (ca. 1063). Other fine churches are **San Ambrogio** in Milan; the **cathedral groups** (campanile, cathedral, and baptistry) at Cremona, Ferrara, and Parma; the **Duomo** in Modena; **Sant'Abbondio** at Como; **San Zeno** at Verona; and **San Michele** at Pavia.

Tuscan Romanesque extended from northern Tuscany to Naples, with its center around **Florence, Pisa,** and **Lucca.** This style is known for its brilliant **marble facades** in intricate patterns, churches built by **basilican plan** (rectangular, with a semicircular apse at one of the short ends and a narthex at the other), and timber roofs and exterior arcading. Columns, capitals, and decoration reflect classical influences. The single outstanding example of Tuscan Romanesque is the **cathedral group at Pisa** (including the famous leaning bell tower). Other examples in the region are **San Martino** (exterior only) and **San Michele** and **San Frediano** at Lucca, **San Miniato al Monte** in Florence, the cathedrals at **Assisi** and **Spoleto, Santa Maria in Cosmedin** at Rome, and the **Amalfi** and **Salerno cathedrals.**

The Norman Romanesque style of southern Italy, particularly **Apulia** and **Sicily,** is unique. It blends different cultures and illustrates the turbulent history of the area—colonized by the Greeks, absorbed into the Byzantine Empire, held under Mohammedan domination, and conquered by the Normans in the 11th century. The Normans built the cathedrals here using local craftsmen who incorporated intricate **Byzantine mosaics,** richly carved **Greek sculpture,** and **Saracenic** (rounded) **arches** and **vaults.** Romanesque designs in southern Italy also share characteristics with cathedrals built by the Normans in England, including massive stonework, brick walls, little or no abutment, solid square towers, and rounded doorways and windows. Of course, they differ in their above-mentioned flatter roofs and smaller windows. Examples of Norman Romanesque are the cathedral at **Cefalu,** the **Monreale Abbey Church** and the **Cappella Palatina** in Palermo, the **Palazzo Farsetti** and **Palazzo Loredan** in Venice, and the town of **San Gimignano** near Siena.

THE GOTHIC

Following the Romanesque was the Gothic period (1250–1450), with the popes in exile in France and the Sicilo-Norman rule giving way to Angevin culture and shifting from Palermo to Naples. During this time, architecture in Lombardy remained essentially Romanesque; indeed, it has been argued that Italy didn't have a Gothic period of architecture. But it did, with Italian designs differing from those of the rest of Europe, again, in their continuing acknowledgment of Roman culture. What Italy didn't have were the soaring towers and spires, ribbed vaults, slender paneled towers, and quadrangles of similar English designs. What it did have were **timber roofs, brick faced with marble, pointed arches,** and **carved white marble tracery** and **sculpture** (mainly in relief). Ornament and detail remained mainly classical. Towers became less common but when incorporated were still constructed separately.

The best examples of the Gothic in Italy are in **Tuscany,** south toward **Rome,** and in **Venice.** Fine examples of the style include the **Florence, Siena,** and **Orvieto Duomos.** Many of the churches are less interesting and have largely been altered, but there are numerous exceptions, including **Santa Maria della Spina** at Pisa, **Santi Giovanni e Paolo** and **Santa Maria Gloriosa dei Frari** in Venice, **Santa Croce** in Florence, and **San Francesco** in Assisi. Palaces include the **Ca' d'Oro,** fronting the Grand Canal, and the **Doge's Palace** in Venice. Town halls include the **Palazzo Pubblico** in Siena; the

Palazzo Vecchio in Florence; the **Palazzo dei Priori** in Perugia; the **Palazzo dei Priori** in Volterra; the **Palazzo Pubblico** in Montepulciano; the **Palazzo dei Consoli** at Gubbio; the **Palazzo Contarini-Fasan, Palazzo Foscari, Palazzo Franchetti,** and **Palazzo Pisani** in Venice; and the **Palazzo Stefano** in Taormina, Sicily.

THE EARLY RENAISSANCE

The Renaissance began in Italian art in the 14th century but came relatively late to architecture, first being incorporated in 1420. Designs from this period represent the pinnacle of Italian architecture. Scholars and artists began to question not so much the importance of God but the alleged unimportance of man and turned their gaze to the accomplishments, advancements, and innovations of antiquity, with numerous Roman examples all around (appreciation of all things Greek came much later). All of man's experiences—along with nature in human, animal, and landscape forms—were explored in sculpture, relief, mosaic, and stained glass, without a definitive hierarchy topped by God and religion.

Renaissance architectural style included a return to the use of the **barrel vaults** and **domes** favored by the ancient Romans. In about 1425, Renaissance painters discovered the laws of **perspective,** and **Brunelleschi** was the first to incorporate this in architectural form. As a result, building designs showed control and unity of space and achieved breadth and a feeling of light not found in Gothic churches. Architects became fascinated with Roman and Greek designs of the centrally planned church, which came to be seen as the ultimate classical metaphor. The effect was that design became increasingly concerned with proportion and detail.

During this time, artists became the most important members of the community and, owing to their education and creativity, became more versatile. They embraced multiple forms of expression. Thus, the first Renaissance architect of the Florence Duomo was **Giotto,** the painter. Church builder **Alberti** was first a scholar, writer, and mathematician.

Brunelleschi's masterpiece of the era is the **dome of Florence's Duomo,** which overcame the mathematical problem of how to cover an existing 138-foot octagonal span (too great for timber centering) without exterior abutment. Besides being a sculptor, Brunelleschi had studied mathematics and spent time drawing ancient Roman buildings in and around Rome. This experience aroused his interest in using large vaults and domed construction in the manner of the Roman baths. His solution for the cathedral was to build a dome that embodied Gothic principles with medieval-style ribs and one that, because of the limitations he was facing, was taller than a true hemisphere (which, being a classicist, he would have preferred). To retain the shape of the dome and reduce the strain of its weight, he had it built as two domes, one within the other.

Other examples of Brunelleschi's early Renaissance designs around Florence are **San Spirito** and **San Lorenzo** and the unfinished **Santa Maria degli Angeli,** which, when started in 1437, became the first centrally planned work of the Renaissance. Still other examples are **Santa Maria Novella** in Florence, **Sant'Andrea** in Mantua, and the **Ducal Palace** in Urbino. Florentine palazzi include Alberti's **Rucellai, Medici-Riccardi,** and **Pitti.** Lombardy has few examples because, like Germany and England, its Renaissance was more in decoration than in construction.

Perhaps the greatest example of the Renaissance and its marriage of Christian and pagan ideals is the small temple in the courtyard of **San Pietro** in

Montorio, which exhibits superb form and simplicity in its undecorated architectural elements while commemorating a Christian event (the spot where St. Peter was allegedly crucified).

The **Veneto,** under the domination of the Venetian Republic, had always been subjected to different influences because of its close ties with Constantinople, Dalmatia, and the East and its cultural isolation within Italy itself. Here, Renaissance designs continued with semi-Gothic facades, and in Venice itself there was no need or room for arcaded courtyards. Examples of the early Venetian Renaissance are the **Scuola di San Rocco** and **Santa Zaccaria.** After the 1527 collapse of Rome, some artists moved north, and the architecture began to reflect southern Renaissance styles. In Venice, this can be seen in the **Biblioteca Sansoviniana** (Library of St. Mark), **Zecca** (Mint), and **Palazzo Cornaro.** Another example is the **Bevilacqua** in Verona.

PALLADIO & THE HIGH RENAISSANCE

The High Renaissance was dominated by Bramante, Raphael, and Michelangelo, and its inception is symbolized by Milan falling to the French and Bramante moving to Rome at the beginning of the 16th century. After the French exile of the popes, Pope Sixtus IV began restoring Rome to prominence, with the constructione of **St. Peter's Basilica** (see the box below) as the crowning achievement. Other examples are the cloisters at **Sant'Ambrogio,** an exercise in pure classicism, and Michelangelo's **New Sacristy in San Lorenzo** and the **Medici Family Mausoleum,** both in Florence.

Andrea di Pietro (or **Palladio**) became the towering architect of the High Renaissance—his native city of Vicenza outside Venice is still called the **Città del Palladio.** His designs were adopted around the world, especially in England and America, but Vicenza remains the best place to view his villas. Palladio arrived in Vicenza in 1523 and worked there until his death in 1580. He wasn't a daring innovator but an academician following the rules of classical Roman architecture. His roofs are tiled and hipped; on each of the four external sides is a pillared rectangular portico. The effect is like a Roman temple. The so-called attic in his design was usually surmounted by statues. His most acclaimed building remains the **Villa Rotonda** in Vicenza, a cube with a center circular hall topped by a dome.

THE LATE RENAISSANCE & THE BAROQUE

In 1573 **Giacomo da Vignola** undertook a challenge that was to pave the way for the transition to the baroque (1590–1780). He was called on to design Rome's **Il Gesu,** the mother church of the Society of Jesus, in such a way that every person in a large congregation could hear the service. He responded with a design that included a wide, short barrel-vaulted nave and shallow transepts for good acoustics and the illusion of space. There were no aisles or colonnades, only side chapels, which gave the building a sense of spaciousness and dignity. It was then topped by a large dome with fenestrated drums, flooding the church with dramatic light and unity unknown in Gothic or Renaissance churches.

The church inspired late Renaissance architects, already eager to incorporate more of themselves into their designs, to adapt classical influences into a **functional unity** that more readily suited the needs of society. The transition wasn't without criticism, and the term *baroque* actually means "misshapen pearl" from the Spanish or Portuguese—a derogatory name stemming from the accentuated curves that evolved.

Still entirely classical in concept, baroque architecture became freer than Renaissance structures with the use of **curves**—not only in ceiling design but also in whole walls, which might be alternately concave and convex. The **oval** became the favored building plan, as curves symbolized vitality and movement and were further accented by the use of **dramatic lighting** from only one or two sources.

These changes, as exemplified by the requests made of Vignola in designing Il Gesu, stemmed from a movement away from humanism and back toward the Catholic Church, whose Jesuit visionaries were attempting to reintroduce spiritual values more suited to the modern world. Thus the curve, a more sensual form than the Renaissance rectangle, was used with great exuberance, as the church adopted gaiety and pageantry to try to retain followers who had been seduced by the secular nature of the Renaissance.

In addition to St. Peter's Basilica, the finest examples of early baroque works are the **New Cathedral** of Brescia, **San Pietro** in Bologna, and **Santa Susanna** in Rome. The period reached its zenith in such Rome designs as **Sant'Andrea al Quirinale, San Carlo alle Quattro Fontane,** the **Fountain of the Rivers** at Piazza Navona, and the **Triton Fountain** at Piazza Barberini. Other examples are **Santa Maria della Salute** in Venice; the **Sindone Chapel** (home of the shroud), **San Lorenzo,** and the **Basilica di Superga** in Turin; **Santa Maria Egiziaca** in Naples; **Santa Croce** in Lecce; and **Palermo's Duomo** on Sicily.

THE 18TH & 19TH CENTURIES: A PERIOD OF DECLINE

Around 1780, Italy began to lose the place it had held for several centuries as the leader of architectural innovation. Other nations weren't so directly influenced by the Catholic Church, so the eyes and designs of the world turned to the French rococo style, which was freer and more lighthearted and showed an abandonment of order symbolized by its elegant decoration. The rococo style took over as the dominant tradition throughout Europe, and at the same time the Germans, French, and English began to credit the Greeks as originators of the classical style, thus denying the influence of Italy and its Roman heritage.

Perhaps as a result of these snubs of church and history, Italy didn't respond to the rococo movement with the same enthusiasm as the rest of Europe. Italian designs between 1780 and 1920 were for the most part rather lackluster. Rather than responding to the challenge to Italy's role as an architectural innovator, designers began simply to knock off classical models with just a hint of Byzantine decoration or treatment, as evidenced by the facade of **Florence's Duomo.**

In the rest of the world, the Belgian-initiated **art nouveau** movement, known as **Liberty** style in Italy, attempted to challenge the dominance of the rococo, but its popularity was brief. Art nouveau came into vogue in the 1890s and disappeared by 1910. Like the rest of Europe, Italy wasn't much inspired by this outside movement, though Milan's **Galleria Vittorio Emanuele II,** with its glass-and-metal roof and iron sculpture, as well as its **Casa Castiglione,** are good examples of the fleeting art nouveau trend.

THE 20TH CENTURY

Since the beginning of the 20th century, with a few notable exceptions, architecture worldwide has developed a sameness of design and materials that pays little regard to location and culture. In Italy, the marriage of classicism and innovation has given way to large functional squared concrete structures, such as the apartment block for the **Societa Novocomum** in Como, the **Santa Maria Novella** rail station in Florence, and the University of Rome's **Instituto Fisico** (Department of Physics).

The Birth of St. Peter's

One of the greatest of the baroque designs is **Bernini's Piazza San Pietro** in Rome. And behind the piazza rises the Basilica di San Pietro, the stellar achievement of the late High Renaissance and the early baroque. The use of the vast elliptical colonnade symbolized the embracement of the world by the mother church of Christendom—St. Peter's. The western ends are joined to the basilica facade by two long corridors, successfully creating space to accommodate the vast crowds waiting to witness the pope's blessing of the city. The columns stand four deep, 60 feet high, and are surmounted by an excessive procession of saints starting along the facade and proceeding outward along the piazza.

Bramante was only the first in a series of architects to tackle the awesome basilica. Directed by a succession of popes, the construction took over 120 years. Because of the decades upon decades necessary for its construction, St. Peter's is not a towering piece of organized architecture. Therefore, it's almost impossible to discuss it as a harmonious unit. Each piece stands alone, it seems, as exemplified by **Michelangelo's dome.** Even so, the design of the cathedral is truly a feat, its beautiful proportions from one part to another disguising its huge size. In the classical tradition, it makes use of coffered and paneled barreled vaults, plus vast crossing dome and drum designs.

Michelangelo designed and began the construction of the massive dome, guiding its construction from 1547 to 1564. After his death, the work was continued from models, but other architects added their own ideas. The distance you see today, from the top of the lantern over the dome, is 450 feet, a staggering achievement considering the building techniques of the day. The sheer mass of the structure (about five times the area of a football field) is a lasting impression that all visitors carry away. The nave is an enormous barreled vault, coffered and frescoed. No central plan was followed, and little remains of Bramante's original concept, which was that of a dome-topped Greek cross based on Rome's Pantheon. The baroque ornamentation Bernini sumptuously supplied from 1629 onward certainly did not adhere to Bramante's simpler plan.

For a short while, Mussolini attempted to resurrect national pride through the design of **neoclassical structures,** but the result was the construction of pompous buildings like Milan's **Central Rail Station.** Rather than gaining unity through design, the station's architecture is simply made busy by repeating rectangular arches and windows. Facade decorations were seemingly tacked onto the building just to acknowledge that it's indeed classically inspired. In Rome, the **Foro Italico** stands as one of Mussolini's monumental architectural achievements—it's a large complex of sports arenas, with the name "Duce" repeated thousands of times as a design in black-and-white tiles. If Italy produced any great modern architect in the 20th century, it was **Pier Luigi Nervi,** born in 1891 in Milan. He was innovative, creating new buildings in daring styles and shapes best represented by Rome's **Palazzo della Sport,** designed for the 1960 Olympics.

More recently, **steel-and-concrete designs** have attempted to marry sharp angles and curves with mixed results, but some examples that work fairly well are the **Palace of Labor** in Turin, **Sant'Ildefonso** in Milan, and Rome's **Palazzo** della Sport, Flaminio Stadium, and Termini Station. Nevertheless, where giants of architecture once trod, men and women with visions less grand rule modern building in Italy today. Instead of creating great architecture, many Italian architects are trying to preserve what already exists. The best example is **Venice.** Although there are those who claim the city of palaces and gondolas may already be dead, most don't want to give up so easily. There is much talk but little effort to build colossal dikes to protect Venice from the relentless sea. The reason is money—or the lack of it. When money is available, work proceeds to save buildings from imminent collapse, but the task is like a bottomless pit. We view it as trying to rebuild ancient Rome in a single day.

3 Italy's Rich Heritage of Art

The wealth and breadth of Italian art in all its forms is amazing. In fact, Italy boasts so much art that some world masterpieces that would be the focal points of major museums in other parts of the world are tucked away in obscure rooms of rarely visited museums or churches. There's too much of a good thing and not enough room to display the bounty, much less maintain the art and protect it from thieves, earthquakes, and age.

ETRUSCAN & ROMAN ART

Although not much Etruscan architecture remains, **Etruscan art** survives in the form of a handful of **murals** discovered in tombs and the more numerous examples of finely sculptured **sarcophagi,** many of which rest in Italian museums. The Etruscans were surpassed in the area of sepulchral painting only by the Egyptians. These paintings, most often done as true frescoes right into wet plaster, took as their subject the people and items that the deceased would need to live comfortably in the spirit world—servants, horses, chariots, drinking vessels, and so on. In coloration, however, Etruscan art moved away from reality: Horses might have bright blue or green legs or the coats of animals might be brightened with vivid spots or stripes in an effort to create a celebratory setting for the postlife of the deceased, as opposed to a grim memorial for grieving survivors. The features of human figures in these works are strongly Oriental, perhaps giving a clue to the origins of the mysterious Estruscans themselves, and the use of line and the presentation of figures are strongly influenced by Greek art of the same time period, owing largely to the popularity Greek artists enjoyed among wealthy Etruscan patrons. You can visit several of the most frequently seen of these tombs on day trips from Rome. The best collection of sarcophagi is at the **Museo Nazionale di Villa Giulia** in Rome.

As **Rome** asserted its own identity and overpowered its Etruscan masters, it borrowed heavily from themes already established by Etruscan artists and architects. In time, however, the Romans discovered **Greek art,** fell in love with that country's statuary, and looted much of it.

Eventually, as Rome continued to develop its empire, its artisans began to turn out realistic **portrait sculpture,** which differed distinctly from the more

Let There Be Light

Since so much of Italy's art is stuck away in the dark corners of unlighted churches, it's a good idea to carry a pocketful of small coins that you can drop in boxes to turn on the lights in some churches.

idealized forms of Greek sculpture. Rome was preoccupied with sculpted images—in fact, sculptors made "bodies" en masse and later fitted a particular head on the sculpture upon the demand of a Roman citizen. Most Roman painting that survives is in the form of **murals** in the fresco technique, and most of these were uncovered when **Pompeii** and **Herculaneum** were dug up. Basically, Roman art continued the Hellenistic tradition. Rome's greatest artistic expression was in architecture, not in art such as painting.

EARLY CHRISTIAN & BYZANTINE ART

The aesthetic and engineering concepts of the Roman Empire eventually evolved into **early Christian** and **Byzantine art.** More concerned with moral and spiritual values than with the physical beauty of the human form or the celebration of political grandeur, early Christian artists turned to the supernatural and spiritual world for their inspiration. Basilicas and churches were lavishly decorated with **mosaics** and **colored marble.** Paintings depicted the earthly suffering (and heavenly rewards) of **martyrs** and **saints,** with symbols used in the compositions being strictly dictated to the artist by the church. Three-dimensional representation was disallowed, following the Eastern tradition that all illusions of action or reality were taboo. In fact, the only freedom the painter enjoyed was in choosing colors and composing shapes.

ROMANESQUE ART

Supported by monasteries or churches, **Romanesque art,** which flourished between A.D. 1000 and 1200, was almost wholly concerned with **ecclesiastical subjects,** often with the intention of educating the worshipers who studied it. Biblical parables were carved in stone or painted into frescoes and became useful teaching aids for a church eager to spread its message. For the most part, **sculpture** from this period, created only as architectural decoration, remained largely Byzantine, with a flatness that disallowed detail. An exception was the sculpture of the **Lombard region,** which was under the influence of Germanic tribes. Here sculpture regained a bulkiness that had been lost since antiquity. One school of Lombard sculpture, known by the name of its master, **Benedetto Antelami,** is characterized by stiff posturing that, combined with the dominance of raised features, gives the sculpture its characteristic rigid vigor.

Painting at this time was still limited to church frescoes and illustrations of Christian documents.

GOTHIC ART & THE FORERUNNERS OF THE RENAISSANCE

As the appeal of the Romanesque faded, the Gothic style, or late medieval style, greatly altered preconceptions of Italian art and encouraged a vast increase in the number of works produced. The Italians were inspired by 14th-century **French art,** because a weakened papacy had fallen under the influence of the French monarchy. French art at the time had an affected sentiment (the pose was everything), and this gradually made itself known in Italian works.

Before the Renaissance, Italy's greatest sculptor was **Nicola Pisano** (1206–78), whose major work was the pulpit in Pisa's baptistry, a piece classical in form. The Roman inspiration is evident in the relief figures—relaxed in gesture and lacking individuality—around a high hexagonal box supported on seven Corinthian columns, three of which are propped on the backs of marble lions.

Late in the 13th century, **painting** finally began to break away from its role as architectural adornment, and with the arrival of **Cimabue,** the great age of Italian art was about to dawn. Facts about the life of this towering artist aren't well documented, but he worked, mainly in Tuscany, from 1270 to 1300. He painted a number of frescoes for the upper and lower churches of the **Basilica of San Francesco** at Assisi, but they're in bad condition, his colors obscured over the ages. Some are still being restored after twin 1997 earthquakes shook them down. Cimabue, breaking with the rigidity of Byzantine art, revealed the spirit of his subject, expressing emotion in realistic detail as opposed to the church's symbolic terms. This trailblazing artist was the harbinger of the greatest art movement in history: the Italian Renaissance.

He was followed by **Giotto** (1266–1336), a painter from Florence, a city where commerce was valued more than an obscure God shrouded in the Catholic Church's increasingly abstract codes and rituals. Giotto was undoubtedly influenced by the rise of **St. Francis,** who arrived in the city preaching that all things were of God and should be loved and treated as God, with no priestly intercession needed. Another person who influenced Giotto was his friend **Dante,** who had just published his *Divine Comedy* "in the volgare," the language of the people. By writing in the language of the people rather than in Latin, the language of the intellectuals, he was the first great poet to embrace the working man rather than alienate him.

Although Giotto's paintings continued to explore Christian themes and stories, they were figured with people who walked and talked equally with Christ, allowing viewers to equate themselves with the subjects. This was obviously a big step toward the Renaissance, when artists and intellectuals began to strongly question the insignificance of man in the face of God, exploring human feats and accomplishments down through the ages.

THE ITALIAN RENAISSANCE

The Italian Renaissance was born in **Florence** during the 15th century, when members of the powerful Medici family emerged as some of the greatest art patrons in history. The Renaissance began with major artistic events, such as **Ghiberti** defeating **Brunelleschi** in a contest to design bronze doors for the baptistry of Florence's Duomo. (The original doors have been removed to the Duomo Museum for safekeeping and have been replaced by copies.)

Until the Renaissance, most painters had been viewed as nothing more than stone masons, for example. But in the Renaissance, the artist became an inventor, an architect, an intellectual, a discoverer, and chiefly an interpreter of life. Renaissance painting developed mainly in Florence, where it was formal and intellectual, and in **Venice,** where art was designed to create pleasure. **Portraits** began to appear in art—the delight and triumph of the individual personality. Perspective, space composition, and anatomy came into vogue. The plastic and human values in painting were emphasized as never before. An example of this is **Maccio's** *Adam and Eve* in Florence.

The Renaissance gave birth to artists who excelled in both painting and sculpture. Emerging on the scene was **Jacopo della Quercia** (1375–1438), who brought vitality and a robust quality to sculpture, as exemplified by his major work, *Fonte Gaia,* in the Duomo Museum at Siena. His sculpture brought in the new quality of emotion, which would be seen to greater effect later in the works of Michelangelo.

Donatello (1386–1466) emerged as the first great name in Renaissance sculpture, and his *David* became the first important freestanding nude done in Europe since the days of the Romans. His most famous equestrian statue, *Gattamelata,* done in 1444, stands in Padua's Piazza di Sant'Antonio.

Michelangelo Buonarroti (1475–1564) always thought of himself as a sculptor, though his greatness also lies in his skills as an architect and a painter.

His early triumph came with a *Pietà,* begun at the age of only 23 and now in St. Peter's in Rome. Working virtually day and night for 2 years, from 1501 to 1503, Michelangelo created the idealized man, his magnificent *David* (now on display in Florence's Accademia), a statue of titanic power and grace. His other legacies include the Medici tombs, executed between 1521 and 1534 (next door to San Lorenzo in Florence); the figures of *Night* and *Day* are the best known. The restored Sistine Chapel, of course, remains the artist's unquestioned masterpiece, each section depicting a story from Genesis.

The towering Renaissance painter, of course, was **Leonardo da Vinci** (1452–1519), the epitome of a Renaissance man. Naturalist, anatomist, and engineer, he even conceived of the practicability of mechanical flight. His *Mona Lisa* (now in the Louvre in Paris) is the most famous painting in the world, and his wall painting *The Last Supper* (at Santa Maria delle Grazie in Milan) is his most impressive.

The number of great artists in Italy during this period is mind-boggling, considering that entire centuries have gone by since then without the emergence of even one great artist. Chief among the lesser lights was **Raphael** (1483–1520). He died early, but not before creating lasting works of art, including his masterpiece, *Madonna del Granduca,* in Florence's Pitti Palace. He painted frescoes in the apartments of Pope Julius II in the Vatican while Michelangelo was painting (very reluctantly) his immortal Sistine Chapel nearby.

The Venetian school was different from the Florentine. In Venice color was crucial, whereas in Florence it was only a decorative note, since most Renaissance artists there were concerned with formal relationships and space through the laws of perspective.

Jacopo Bellini (ca. 1400–70) was the founder of the most celebrated family of artists from the Venetian school. **Giovanni Bellini** (ca. 1430–1516) was the greatest master of Venetian painting in the 1400s. He created rich, serene landscapes to depict mankind's spiritual harmony with nature.

Giorgione (1477–1510) created works of mystical charm and surpassed the Bellini family in his achievements. He's credited with one of the great steps forward in the history of painting as a fine art, the popularization of **easel painting**—a picture existing for its own sake, the purpose of which was simply to give pleasure to the viewer. His *La Tempesta,* for example, was, like many of his paintings, both brooding and tranquil—a painting of haunting, hypnotic beauty, defying interpretation.

The period known as the **High Renaissance** was said to last for only about 25 years, beginning in the early 16th century. This period in art saw more and more emphasis on rich color and subtle variations in forms. Works of great technical mastery emerged. Despite the subtle differences between the stages of the Renaissance, Italy remained Europe's artistic leader for nearly 200 years.

MANNERISM

The transitional period between the Renaissance and the baroque came to be called **Mannerism.** This transition was the result of great turmoil in Europe at the time, with François I of France and Charles V of Spain battling for domination of the continent. Much of the fighting took place in northern Italy, and in 1527 Spain's hired German warriors stormed Rome, the beginning of 3 years of rape and pillage that ended only when the pope crowned Charles an emperor of the Holy Roman Empire. Not surprisingly, artists reacted to the strife that had become everyday life by overturning many of the principles that had defined the Renaissance. Painting and sculpture were stripped of balance, stability, and naturalism and were replaced with **distortion, restlessness,** and **false rigidity.**

Out of this period emerged such great artists as Verona-born **Paolo Veronese** (1528–88) and the sensitive **Parmigianino** (1503–40). The towering figure of this movement was Jacopo Robusti, known as **Tintoretto** (1518–94), one of the pioneers of Mannerism, a master of the palette with boldness and imagination, although not the colorist that Titian was. From Michelangelo, Tintoretto borrowed large sculptural forms. Tintoretto's innovation was in the use of light to extract the utmost drama from a subject. His life's major work was done for the Scuola di San Rocco in Venice, a work he launched in 1564 and finished 23 years later. There are more paintings in Venice by Tintoretto than by any other artist. One of his final works was the *Last Supper.*

THE BAROQUE & ROCOCO

On the trail of Mannerism, the **baroque movement** swept Italy in the early 1600s and lasted until well into the 1700s. It was a period that attempted to find balance between the spirituality of the Gothic and the secular nature of the Renaissance—a result of the Catholic Counter-Reformation (in response to the Protestant Reformation) and the absolutism that dominated the politics of Europe. Rather than glorifying the universal man, as in the Renaissance, the baroque movement explored **human ceremony,** a result of a rigid code of courtly behavior. Still the pessimism of the Mannerists was slowly lifting as tight control of kingdoms and the certainty of Jesuit principles allowed a feeling of stability to return to the European nations. Religion continued to play a key role in society, but its expression in the arts was tempered by the worldly scars of the very human conflicts that had occurred. Art responded with an exploration of **depth** and the suggested illusion of **distance,** incorporating a strong sense of **light, color,** and **motion.** It was an age of intensity, drama, and power, which not surprisingly led to a flowering of the dramatic arts as well.

Great artists to emerge during this period include **Giovanni Bernini** (1598–1680), who became renowned both as a sculptor and as a painter. But the two painters who best represented the movement were **Annibale Carracci** (1560–1609), who decorated the Roman palace of Cardinal Farnese, and **Michelangelo da Caravaggio** (1573–1610), one of the pioneers of baroque painting. The even more flamboyant **rococo**—with its increasingly dramatic posturing and use of light—grew out of the baroque style. Much of the work from the baroque period, in fact, is a bit heavy-handed, resulting in an art of unbalanced sentimentality.

THE 19TH CENTURY TO THE PRESENT

By the 19th century, the great light had gone out of art in Italy. (The beacon was picked up by France.) **Neoclassicism**—a return to the aesthetic ideals of ancient Greece and Rome, whose ideals of patriotism were resonant in the growing sense of Pan-Italian patriotism—swept through almost every aspect of the Italian arts. The neoclassicist movement was largely the product of the excitement resulting from the discovery of **Pompeii** and **Herculaneum. Antonio Canova** (1757–1822) became the most famous of the neoclassical sculptors. But neoclassicism never attained the grandeur in Italy that it did in France.

The 20th century witnessed the birth of several major Italian artists whose works once again captured the imagination of the world. **Giorgio de Chirico** (1888–1978) and **Amedeo Modigliani** (1884–1920), whose greatest contribution lay in a new concept of portraiture, were only two among many.

Giorgio Morandi (1890–1964), the Bolognese painter of bottles and jugs, also became known around the world. The greatest Italian sculptor of the 20th century was **Medardo Rosso** (1858–1928).

Since then Italy has been a European leader in sophisticated and witty contemporary design of buildings, paintings, fashion, industrial design, and decor. Many modern Italian artists have infused Italian flair into workaday and utilitarian objects, whose quality, humor, and usefulness have become legendary (witness the success of Alessi kitchen gadgets).

4 A Taste of Italy

Italians are among the world's greatest cooks. Just ask any one of them. Despite the unification of Italy, regional tradition still dominates the various kitchens, ranging from Rome to Lombardy, from the Valle d'Aosta to Sicily. The term "Italian cuisine" has little meaning unless it's more clearly defined as Neapolitan, Roman, Sardinian, Sicilian, Venetian, Piedmontese, Tuscan, or whatever. Each region has a flavor and a taste of its own, as well as a detailed repertoire of local dishes.

Food has always been one of life's great pleasures for the Italians. This has been true even from the earliest days: To judge from the lifelike banquet scenes found in Etruscan tombs, the Etruscans loved food and took delight in enjoying it. The Romans became famous for their never-ending banquets and for their love of exotic treats, such as flamingo tongues.

Although culinary styles vary, Italy abounds in trattorie specializing in local dishes—some of which are a delight for carnivores, like the renowned *bistecca alla fiorentina* (cut from flavorful Chianina beef, then charcoal-grilled and served with a fruity olive oil). Other dishes, especially those found at the antipasti buffet, would appeal to every vegetarian's heart: peppers, greens, onions, pastas, beans, tomatoes, and fennel.

Incidentally, except in the south, Italians don't use as much garlic in their food as many foreigners seem to believe. Most Italian dishes, especially those in the north, are butter based. And spaghetti and meatballs isn't an Italian dish, though certain restaurants throughout the country have taken to serving it "for homesick Americans."

See Appendix B for a glossary of menu terms.

CUISINES AROUND THE COUNTRY

Rome is the best place to introduce yourself to Italian cuisine, because it boasts specialty restaurants representing all the culinary centers of the country. Throughout your Roman holiday, you'll encounter such savory viands as *zuppa di pesce* (a soup or stew of various fish, cooked in white wine and flavored with herbs), *cannelloni* (tube-shaped pasta baked with any number of stuffings), *riso col gamberi* (rice with shrimp, peas, and mushrooms, flavored with white wine and garlic), *scampi alla griglia* (grilled prawns, one of the best-tasting, albeit expensive, dishes in the city), *quaglie col risotto e tartufi* (quail

Impressions

In Italy, the pleasure of eating is central to the pleasure of living. When you sit down to dinner with Italians, when you share their food, you are sharing their lives.

—Fred Plotkin, *Italy for the Gourmet Traveler* (1996)

with rice and truffles), *lepre alla cacciatore* (hare flavored with tomato sauce and herbs), *zabaglione* (a creamy dessert made with sugar, egg yolks, and marsala), *gnocchi alla romana* (potato-flour dumplings with a meat sauce, covered with grated cheese), *abbacchio* (baby spring lamb, often roasted over an open fire), *saltimbocca alla romana* (literally "jump-in-your-mouth"—thin slices of veal with sage, ham, and cheese), *fritto alla romana* (a mixed fry likely to include everything from brains to artichokes), *carciofi alla romana* (tender artichokes cooked with herbs like mint and garlic, flavored with white wine), *fettuccine all'uovo* (egg noodles with butter and cheese), *zuppa di cozze* (a hearty bowl of mussels cooked in broth), *fritto di scampi e calamaretti* (baby squid and prawns, fast-fried), *fragoline* (wild strawberries, in this case from the Alban Hills), and *finocchio* (fennel, a celerylike raw vegetable with the flavor of anisette, often eaten as a dessert or in a salad).

From Rome, it's on to **Tuscany,** where you'll encounter the hearty cuisine of the Tuscan hills. The main ingredient for most any meal is the superb local olive oil, adored for its low acidity and lovely flavor. In Italy's south, the olives are gathered only after they've fallen off the trees, but here they're hand-picked off the trees so they won't get bruised (ensuring lower acidity and milder aroma). Typical Tuscan pastas are *papardelle* and *penne* mingled with a variety of sauces, many of which are tomato based. Tuscans are extremely fond of strong cheeses like *gorgonzola, fontina,* and *parmigiano.* Meat and fish are prepared simply and may seem undercooked, though locals would argue that it's better to let the inherent flavor of the ingredients survive the cooking process.

The next major city to visit is **Venice,** where the cookery is typical of the **Venezia** district. It has long ago been called "tasty, straightforward, and homely" by one food critic, and we concur. Two of the most typical dishes are *fegato alla veneziana* (liver and onions) and *risi e bisi* (rice and fresh peas). Seafood figures heavily in the Venetian diet, and grilled fish is often served with the bitter red radicchio, a lettuce that comes from Treviso.

In **Lombardy,** of which **Milan** is the center, the cookery is more refined and flavorful. No dish here is more famous than *cotoletta alla milanese* (cutlets of tender veal, dipped in egg and bread crumbs, and fried in olive oil until they're a golden brown)—the Viennese call it Wiener schnitzel. *Osso buco* is the other great dish of Lombardy; this is cooked with the shin bone of veal in a ragout sauce and served on rice and peas. *Risotto alla milanese* is also a classic—rice that can be dressed in almost any way, depending on the chef's imagination; it's often flavored with saffron and butter, to which chicken giblets have been added, and seemingly always served with heaps of *parmigiano reggiano* cheese. *Polenta,* a cornmeal mush that's "more than mush," is the staff of life in some parts of northeastern Italy and is eaten in lieu of pasta.

The cooking in the **Piedmont,** of which **Turin** is the capital, and the **Aosta Valley** is different from that in the rest of Italy. Its victuals are said to appeal to strong-hearted men returning from a hard day's work in the mountains. You get such dishes as *bagna cauda,* a sauce made with olive oil, garlic, butter, and anchovies in which you dip uncooked fresh vegetables. *Fonduta* is also celebrated: It's made with melted Fontina cheese, butter, milk, egg yolks, and, for an elegant touch, white truffles.

In the **Trentino–Alto Adige** area, whose chief towns are **Bolzano, Merano,** and **Trent,** the cooking is naturally influenced by the traditions of the Austrian and Germanic kitchens. South Tyrol, of course, used to belong to Austria, and here you get such tasty pastries as strudel.

Liguria, whose chief town is **Genoa,** turns to the sea for a great deal of its cuisine, as reflected by its version of bouillabaisse, a *burrida* flavored with spices. But its most famous food item is *pesto,* a sauce made with fresh basil, garlic, cheese, and walnuts, which is used to dress pasta, fish, and many other dishes.

Emilia-Romagna, with such towns as **Modena, Parma, Bologna, Ravenna,** and **Ferrara,** is one of the great gastronomic centers. Rich in produce, its school of cooking produces many notable pastas now common around Italy: *tagliatelle, tortellini,* and *cappelletti* (larger than tortellini and made in the form of "little hats"). Tagliatelle, of course, are long strips of macaroni, and tortellini are little squares of dough stuffed with chopped pork, veal, or whatever. Equally popular is *lasagne,* which by now everybody has heard of. In Bologna it's often made by adding finely shredded spinach to the dough. The best-known sausage of the area is *mortadella,* and equally famous is a *cotoletta alla bolognese* (veal cutlet fried with a slice of ham or bacon). The distinctive and famous cheese *parmigiano reggiano* is a product of Parma and also Reggio Emilia. *Zampone* (stuffed pig's foot) is a specialty of Modena. Parma is also known for its ham, which is fashioned into air-cured *prosciutto di Parma.* Served in wafer-thin slices, it's deliciously sweet and hailed by gourmets as the finest in the world.

Much of the cookery of **Campania** (spaghetti with clam sauce, pizzas, and so forth), with **Naples** as its major city, is already familiar to North Americans because so many Neapolitans moved to the New World and opened restaurants. *Mozzarella,* or buffalo cheese, is the classic cheese of this area. Mixed fish fries, done a golden brown, are a staple of nearly every table.

Sicily has a distinctive cuisine, with good strong flavors and aromatic sauces. A staple of the diet is *maccheroni con le sarde* (spaghetti with pine seeds, fennel, spices, chopped sardines, and olive oil). Fish is good and fresh in Sicily (try swordfish). Among meat dishes, you'll see *involtini siciliani* on the menu (rolled meat with a stuffing of egg, ham, and cheese cooked in bread crumbs). A *caponata* is a special way of cooking eggplant in a flavorful tomato sauce. The desserts and homemade pastries are excellent, including *cannoli,* cylindrical pastry cases stuffed with ricotta and candied fruit (or chocolate). Their ice creams, called *gelati,* are among the best in Italy.

AND SOME VINO TO WASH IT ALL DOWN

Italy is the largest wine-producing country in the world; as far back as 800 B.C. the Etruscans were vintners. It's said that more soil is used in Italy for the cultivation of grapes than for the growing of food. Many Italian farmers produce wine just for their own consumption or for their relatives in "the big city." However, it wasn't until 1965 that laws were enacted to guarantee regular consistency in wine making. Wines regulated by the government are labeled "DOC" *(Denominazione di Origine Controllata).* If you see "DOCG" on a label (the "G" means *garantita*), that means even better quality control.

THE VINEYARDS OF ITALY

Following traditions established by the ancient Greeks, Italy produces more wine than any other nation. More than 4 million acres of soil are cultivated as vineyards, and recently there has been an increased emphasis on recognizing vintages from lesser-known growers who may or may not be designated as working within a zone of controlled origin and name. (It's considered an honor, and usually a source of profit, to own vines within a DOC. Vintners who are presently limited to marketing their products as unpretentious table wines—*vino di tavola*—often expend great efforts lobbying for an elevated status as a DOC.)

Italy's wine producers range from among the most automated and technologically sophisticated in Europe to low-tech, labor-intensive family plots turning out just a few hundred bottles per year. You can sometimes save money by buying direct from a producer (the signs beside the highway of any wine-producing district will advertise VENDITTA DRETTA). Not only will you avoid paying the retailer's markup, but you also might get a glimpse of the vines that produced the vintage you carry home with you.

Useful vocabulary words for such endeavors are *bottiglieria* (a simple wine shop) and *enoteca* (a more upscale shop where many vintages, from several growers, are displayed and sold like magazines in a bookstore). In some cases you can buy a glass of the product before you buy the bottle, and platters of cold cuts and/or cheeses are sometimes available to offset the tang (and alcoholic effects) of the wine.

Regional Wines

Below we've cited only a few popular wines. Rest assured there are hundreds more, and you'll have a great time sampling them to find your own favorites.

Latium: In this major wine-producing region, many of the local wines come from the Castelli Romani, the hill towns around Rome. Horace and Juvenal sang the praises of Latium wines even in imperial times. These wines, experts agree, are best drunk when young, and they're most often white, mellow, and dry (or "demi-sec"). There are seven types, including **Falerno** (straw yellow in color) and **Cecubo** (often served with roast meat). Try also **Colli Albani** (straw yellow with amber tints, served with both fish and meat). The golden yellow wines of **Frascati** are famous, produced in both a demi-sec and a sweet variety, the latter served with dessert.

Tuscany: Tuscan wines rank with some of the finest reds in France. **Chianti** is the best known, and it comes in several varieties. The most highly regarded is **Chianti Classico,** a lively ruby red wine mellow in flavor with a bouquet of violets. A good label is Antinori. A lesser known but remarkably fine Tuscan wine is **Brunello di Montalcino,** a brilliant garnet red served with roasts and game. The ruby red, almost-purple **Vino Nobile di Montepulciano** has a rich, rugged body; it's a noble wine that's aged for 4 years. The area around San Gimignano produces a light, sweet white wine called **Vernaccia.** While you're in Tuscany, order the wonderful dessert wine called **Vin Santo,** which tastes almost like sherry, and is usually accompanied by biscotti that you dunk into your glass.

Emilia-Romagna: The sparkling **Lambrusco** of this region is by now best known by Americans, but this wine can be of widely varying quality. Most of it is a brilliant ruby red. Be more experimental and try such wines as the dark ruby red **Sanglovese** (with a delicate bouquet) and the golden yellow **Albana,** somewhat sweet. **Trebbiano,** generally dry, is best served with fish.

The Veneto: From this rich breadbasket in northeastern Italy come such world-famous wines as **Bardolino** (a light ruby red often served with poultry), **Valpolicella** (produced in "ordinary quality" and "superior dry," best served with meats), and **Soave,** so beloved by W. Somerset Maugham, which has a pale amber yellow color with a light aroma and a velvety flavor. Also try one of the **Cabernets,** either the ruby red **Cabernet di Treviso** (ideal with roasts and game) or the even deeper ruby red **Cabernet Franc,** which has a marked herbal bouquet and is served with roasts.

Trentino–Alto Adige: This area produces wine influenced by Austria. Known for its vineyards, the region has some 20 varieties of wine. The straw yellow, slightly pale green **Riesling** is served with fish, as is the pale green-yellow

Terlano. Santa Maddalena, a cross between garnet and ruby, is served with wild fowl and red meats, and **Traminer,** straw yellow, has a distinctive aroma and is served with fish. A **Pinot Bianco,** straw yellow with greenish glints, has a light bouquet and a noble history and is also served with fish.

Friuli-Venezia Giulia: This area attracts those who enjoy a "brut" wine with a trace of flint. From classic grapes come **Merlot,** deep ruby in color, and several varieties of **Pinot,** including **Pinot Grigio,** whose color ranges from straw yellow to gray-pink (good with fish). Also served with fish, the **Sauvignon** has a straw yellow color and a delicate bouquet.

Lombardy: These wines are justly renowned, and if you don't believe us, would you instead take the advice of Leonardo da Vinci, Pliny, and Virgil? These great men have sung the praise of this wine-rich region bordered by the Alps to the north and the Po River to the south. To go with the tasty, refined cuisine of the Lombard kitchen are such wines as **Frecciarossa** (a pale straw yellow color with a delicate bouquet; order with fish), **Sassella** (bright ruby red; order with game, red meat, and roasts), and the amusingly named **Inferno** (a deep ruby red with a penetrating bouquet; order with meats).

The Piedmont: The finest wines in Italy, mostly red, are said to be produced on the vine-clad slopes of the Piedmont. Of course, **Asti Spumante,** the color of straw with an abundant champagnelike foam, is the prototype of Italian sparkling wines. While traveling through this area of northwestern Italy, you'll want to sample **Barbaresco** (brilliant ruby red with a delicate flavor; order with red meats), **Barolo** (also brilliant ruby red, best when it mellows into a velvety old age), **Cortese** (pale straw yellow with green glints; order with fish), and **Gattinara** (an intense ruby red beauty in youth that changes with age). Piedmont is also the home of **vermouth,** a white wine to which aromatic herbs and spices, among other ingredients, have been added; it's served as an aperitif.

Liguria: This area doesn't have as many wine-producing regions as other parts of Italy yet grows dozens of different grapes. These are made into such wines as **Dolceacqua** (lightish ruby red, served with hearty food) and **Vermentino Ligure** (pale yellow with a good bouquet; often served with fish).

Campania: From the volcanic soil of Vesuvius, the wines of Campania have been extolled for 2,000 years. Homer praised the glory of **Falerno,** straw yellow in color. Neapolitans are fond of ordering a wine known as **Lacrima Christi** ("tears of Christ") to accompany many seafood dishes. It comes in amber, red, and pink. With meat dishes, try the dark mulberry-colored **Gragnano,** which has a faint bouquet of faded violets. The reds and whites of Ischia and Capri are also justly renowned.

Apulia: The heel of the Italian boot, Apulia produces more wine than any other part of Italy. Try **Castel del Monte,** which comes in shades of pink, white, and red. Other wines of the region are the dull red **Aleatico di Puglia,** with a mellow taste so sweet and aromatic it's almost a liqueur; **Barletta,** a highly alcoholic wine made from grapes grown around Troia; the notably pleasant and fragrant **Mistella,** a real fleshy wine usually offered with desserts; the brilliant amber yellow **Moscato della Murge,** aromatic and sweet; **Moscato di Trani,** which is velvety, tasting of bouquet of faded roses; and **Primitivo di Gioia,** a full-bodied acid wine that when dry appears with roasts or when sweet with desserts. One of the region's best wines to drink with fish is **Torre Giulia,** which is dark yellow tending toward amber—a "brut" wine with a distinctive bouquet.

Sicily: The wines of Sicily, called a "paradise of the grape," were extolled by the ancient poets, including Martial. Caesar himself lavished praise on **Mamertine** when it was served at a banquet honoring his third consulship.

Marsala, an amber-yellow wine served with desserts, is the most famous wine of Sicily; it's velvety and fruity and sometimes used in cooking, as in veal marsala. The wines made from grapes grown in the volcanic soil of Etna come in both red and white varieties. Also try the **Corvo Bianco di Casteldaccia** (straw yellow, with a distinctive bouquet) and the **Corvo Rosso di Casteldaccia** (ruby red, almost garnet, full-bodied and fruity).

OTHER DRINKS

Italians drink other libations as well. Their most famous drink is **Campari,** bright red in color and flavored with herbs; it has a quinine bitterness to it. It's customary to serve it with ice cubes and soda.

Limoncello, a bright yellow drink made by infusing pure alcohol with lemon zest, has become Italy's second most popular drink. It has long been a staple in the lemon-producing region along the Amalfi Coast in Capri and Sorrento, and recipes for the sweetly potent concoction have been passed down by families there for generations. About a decade ago, restaurants in Sorrento, Naples, and Rome started making their own versions. Visitors to those restaurants as well as the Sorrento peninsula began singing limoncello's praises and requesting bottles to go. Now it's one of the most up-and-coming liqueurs in the world, thanks to heavy advertising promotions.

Beer, once treated as a libation of little interest, is still far inferior to wines produced domestically, but foreign beers, especially those of Ireland and England, are gaining great popularity with Italian youth, especially in Rome. This popularity is mainly because of atmospheric pubs, which now number more than 300 in Rome alone, where young people will linger over a pint and a conversation. Most pubs are in the Roman center, and many are licensed by Guinness and its Guinness Italia operations. In a city with 5,000 watering holes, 300 pubs may seem like a drop, but since the clientele is young, the wine industry is trying to devise a plan to keep that drop from becoming a steady stream of Italians who prefer grain to grapes.

High-proof **grappa** is made from the "leftovers" after the grapes have been pressed. Many Italians drink this before or after dinner (some put it into their coffee). It's an acquired taste—to an untrained foreign palate, it often seems rough and harsh.

Italy has many **brandies** (according to an agreement with France, Italians aren't supposed to use the word *cognac* in labeling them). A popular one is **Vecchia Romagna.**

Besides limoncello, there are several popular liqueurs to which the Italians are addicted. Try herb-flavored **Strega** or perhaps an **Amaretto** tasting of almonds. One of the best known is **Maraschino,** taking its name from a type of cherry used in its preparation. **Galliano** is also herb flavored, and **Sambuca** (anisette) is made of aniseed and often served with a "fly" (coffee bean) in it. On a hot day, an Italian orders a vermouth, **Cinzano,** with a twist of lemon, ice, and a squirt of soda water.

5 Recommended Reading

GENERAL & HISTORY

Luigi Barzini's ***The Italians*** (Simon & Schuster, 1996) should almost be required reading for anyone contemplating a trip to Italy—even though it was written in 1964, its insights into modern Italy are surprisingly relevant today. The section on Sicily alone is worth the price of the book. William Murray's

The Last Italian: Portrait of a People (Prentice Hall, 1991) is his second volume of essays on the subject of Italy, its people and its civilization. The *New York Times* called it "a lover's keen, observant diary of his affair."

Edward Gibbon's 1776 ***The History of the Decline and Fall of the Roman Empire*** is published in six volumes, but Penguin issues a manageable abridgement. This work has been hailed as one of the greatest histories ever written. No one has ever captured the saga of the glory that was Rome the way Gibbon did.

Florence, Biography of a City (Norton, 1993) is Christopher Hibbert's overview on the city of the Renaissance, written in his extremely accessible prose. Hibbert also wrote the most readable group biography of Florence's famous rulers in ***The House of Medici: Its Rise and Fall*** (Morrow Quill Paperbacks, 1980).

ART & ARCHITECTURE

The Renaissance seems to capture the public's imagination more than any other era, and one of the best accounts is Peter Murray's ***The Architecture of the Italian Renaissance*** (Schocken, 1986). Giorgio Vasari's ***Lives of the Artists*** **Vols. I and II** (Penguin Classics, 1987) is a collection of biographies of the great artists from Cimabue up to Vasari's 16th-century contemporaries. It's an interesting read full of anecdotes and Vasari's theories on art practice. For a more modern art history take, the indispensable tome is Frederick Hartt's ***History of Italian Renaissance Art*** (Abrams, 1994). For an easier and more colorful introduction, get Michael Levey's ***Early Renaissance*** (Penguin, 1967) and ***High Renaissance*** (Penguin, 1975).

Michelangelo, a Biography by George Bull (St. Martin's, 1995) is a well-written scholarly take on the life of the artist penned by a Renaissance expert and one of the most respected translators of Italian classic literature.

FICTION

Many writers have tried to capture the peculiar nature of Italy. Notable works include Italo Calvino's ***The Baron in the Trees,*** Umberto Eco's ***The Name of the Rose,*** E. M. Forster's ***Where Angels Fear to Tread*** and ***A Room with a View,*** Henry James's ***The Aspern Papers,*** Giuseppe di Lampedusa's ***The Leopard,*** Carlo Levi's ***Christ Stopped at Eboli,*** Thomas Mann's ***Death in Venice,*** Susan Sontag's ***The Volcano Lover,*** Irving Stone's ***The Agony and the Ecstasy,*** and Mark Helprin's ***Soldier of the Great War.***

For a truly juicy read about just how depraved those first emperors were, nothing can beat Robert Graves's ***I, Claudius*** and ***Claudius the God.*** They're fabulous, even if you've already seen the BBC miniseries.

TRAVELOGUE

Mark Twain first became nationally famous for his report on a package tour of Europe and Palestine called ***The Innocents Abroad*** (Oxford University Press, 1996), a good quarter of which is about Italy. Henry James's ***Italian Hours*** (Penguin Classics, 1995) pulls together several essays painting vivid pictures of places and moments.

D. H. Lawrence and Italy (Penguin Travel Library, 1985) is a collection of three of the author's books set in Italy, including *Etruscan Places,* published posthumously. ***A Traveller in Italy*** (Dodd, Mead, 1982/Methuen, 1985) is the informed account that H. V. Morton wrote of his trip through the peninsula in the 1930s.

Poet/professor Frances Mayes makes us all jealous with ***Under the Tuscan Sun*** (Chronicle Books, 1996), an account gleaned from her journals and chronicles about buying and renovating a Tuscan dream house outside Cortona with her husband. The two Californians grow grapes, learn traditional recipes, hop in the car to go on a wine-buying spree, visit the unexplored corners of Tuscany, press their first olive oil, and discover the rhythms of the Italian lifestyle. In 2000, Mayes came out with a follow-up volume entitled ***Bella Tuscany: The Sweet Life in Italy.***

Appendix B: Molto Italiano

1 Basic Vocabulary

English	Italian	Pronunciation
Thank you	**Grazie**	*graht*-tzee-yey
You're welcome	**Prego**	*prey*-go
Please	**Per favore**	*pehr* fah-*vohr*-eh
Yes	**Si**	see
No	**No**	noh
Good morning or Good day	**Buongiorno**	bwohn-*djor*-noh
Good evening	**Buona sera**	*Bwohn*-ah *say*-rah
Good night	**Buona notte**	*Bwohn*-ah *noht*-tay
How are you?	**Come sta?**	*koh*-may *stah*
Very well	**Molto bene**	*mohl*-toh *behn*-ney
Goodbye	**Arrivederci**	ahr-ree-vah-*dehr*-chee
Excuse me (to get attention)	**Scusi**	*skoo*-zee
Excuse me (to get past someone)	**Permesso**	pehr-*mehs*-soh
Where is . . .?	**Dovè . . .?**	doh-*vey*
the station	**la stazione**	lah stat-tzee-*oh*-neh
a hotel	**un albergo**	oon ahl-*behr*-goh
a restaurant	**un ristorante**	oon reest-ohr-*ahnt*-eh
the bathroom	**il bagno**	eel *bahn*-nyoh
To the right	**A destra**	ah *dehy*-stra
To the left	**A sinistra**	ah see-*nees*-tra
Straight ahead	**Avanti (or sempre diritto)**	ahv-vahn-tee (*sehm*-pray dee-*reet*-toh)
How much is it?	**Quanto costa?**	*kwan*-toh *coh*-sta?
The check, please	**Il conto, per favore**	eel kon-toh *pehr* fah-*vohr*-eh
When?	**Quando?**	*kwan*-doh
Yesterday	**Ieri**	ee-*yehr*-ree
Today	**Oggi**	*oh*-jee
Tomorrow	**Domani**	doh-*mah*-nee
Breakfast	**Prima colazione**	*pree*-mah coh-laht-tzee-*ohn*-ay
Lunch	**Pranzo**	*prahn*-zoh
Dinner	**Cena**	*chay*-nah

English	Italian	Pronunciation
What time is it?	**Che ore sono?**	kay *or*-ay *soh*-noh
Monday	**Lunedì**	loo-nay-*dee*
Tuesday	**Martedì**	mart-ay-*dee*
Wednesday	**Mercoledì**	mehr-cohl-ay-*dee*
Thursday	**Giovedì**	joh-vay-*dee*
Friday	**Venerdì**	ven-nehr-*dee*
Saturday	**Sabato**	*sah*-bah-toh
Sunday	**Domenica**	doh-*mehn*-nee-kah

NUMBERS

1	**uno** (*oo*-noh)
2	**due** (*doo*-ay)
3	**tre** (tray)
4	**quattro** (*kwah*-troh)
5	**cinque** (*cheen*-kway)
6	**sei** (say)
7	**sette** (*set*-tay)
8	**otto** (*oh*-toh)
9	**nove** (*noh*-vay)
10	**dieci** (dee-*ay*-chee)
11	**undici** (*oon*-dee-chee)
20	**venti** (*vehn*-tee)
21	**ventuno** (vehn-*toon*-oh)
22	**venti due** (*vehn*-tee *doo*-ay)
30	**trenta** (*trayn*-tah)
40	**quaranta** (kwah-*rahn*-tah)
50	**cinquanta** (cheen-*kwan*-tah)
60	**sessanta** (sehs-*sahn*-tah)
70	**settanta** (seht-*tahn*-tah)
80	**ottanta** (oht-*tahn*-tah)
90	**novanta** (noh-*vahnt*-tah)
100	**cento** (*chen*-toh)
1,000	**mille** (*mee*-lay)
5,000	**cinque milla** (*cheen*-kway *mee*-lah)
10,000	**dieci milla** (dee-*ay*-chee *mee*-lah)

2 A Glossary of Architectural Terms

Ambone A pulpit, either serpentine or simple in form, erected in an Italian church.

Apse The half-rounded extension behind the main altar of a church; Christian tradition dictates that it be placed at the eastern end of an Italian church, the side closest to Jerusalem.

Atrium A courtyard, open to the sky, in an ancient Roman house; the term also applies to the courtyard nearest the entranceway of an early Christian church.

Baldacchino (also ciborium) A columned stone canopy, usually placed above the altar of a church; spelled in English, *baldachin* or *baldaquin.*

Baptistry A separate building or a separate area in a church where the rite of baptism is held.

Basilica Any rectangular public building, usually divided into three aisles by rows of columns. In ancient Rome, this architectural form was frequently used for places of public assembly and law courts; later, Roman Christians adapted the form for many of their early churches.

Caldarium The steam room of a Roman bath.

Campanile A bell tower, often detached, of a church.

Capital The top of a column, often carved and usually categorized into one of three orders: Doric, Ionic, or Corinthian.

Castrum A carefully planned Roman military camp, whose rectangular form, straight streets, and systems of fortified gates quickly became standardized throughout the Empire. Modern cities that began as Roman camps and still more or less maintain their original forms include Chester (England), Barcelona (Spain), and such Italian cities as Lucca, Aosta, Como, Brescia, Florence, and Ancona.

Cavea The curved row of seats in a classical theater; the most prevalent shape was that of a semicircle.
Cella The sanctuary, or most sacred interior section, of a Roman pagan temple.
Chancel Section of a church containing the altar.
Cornice The decorative flange defining the uppermost part of a classical or neoclassical facade.
Cortile Courtyard or cloisters ringed with a gallery of arches or lintels set atop columns.
Crypt The main burial place in a church, usually below the choir.
Cupola A dome.
Duomo Cathedral.
Forum The main square and principal gathering place of any Roman town, usually adorned with the city's most important temples and civic buildings.
Grotesques Carved and painted faces, deliberately ugly, used by everyone from the Etruscans to the architects of the Renaissance; they're especially amusing when set into fountains.
Hypogeum Subterranean burial chambers, usually of pre-Christian origins.
Loggia Roofed balcony or gallery.
Lozenge An elongated four-sided figure that, along with stripes, was one of the distinctive signs of the architecture of Pisa.
Narthex The anteroom, or enclosed porch, of a Christian church.
Nave The largest and longest section of a church, usually devoted to sheltering and/or seating worshipers and often divided by aisles.
Palazzo A palace or other important building.
Piano Nobile The main floor of a palazzo (sometimes the second floor).
Pietra Dura Richly ornate assemblage of semiprecious stones mounted on a flat decorative surface, perfected during the 1600s in Florence.
Pieve A parish church.
Portico A porch, usually crafted from wood or stone.
Pulvin A four-sided stone serving as a substitute for the capital of a column, often decoratively carved, sometimes into biblical scenes.
Putti Plaster cherubs whose chubby forms often decorate the interiors of baroque chapels and churches.
Stucco Colored plaster composed of sand, powdered marble, water, and lime, either molded into statuary or applied in a thin concretelike layer to the exterior of a building.
Telamone Structural column carved into a standing male form; female versions are called *caryatids.*
Thermae Roman baths.
Transenna Stone (usually marble) screen separating the altar area from the rest of an early Christian church.
Travertine The stone from which ancient and Renaissance Rome was built; it's known for its hardness, light coloring, and tendency to be pitted or flecked with black.
Tympanum The half-rounded space above the portal of a church, usually showcasing a sculpture within this semicircular area.

3 Italian Menu Terms

Abbacchio Roast haunch or shoulder of lamb baked and served in a casserole and sometimes flavored with anchovies.
Agnolotti A crescent-shaped pasta shell stuffed with a mix of chopped meat, spices, vegetables, and cheese; when prepared in rectangular versions, the same combination of ingredients is identified as **ravioli.**

Amaretti Crunchy, sweet almond-flavored macaroons.
Anguilla alla veneziana Eel cooked in a sauce made from tuna and lemon.
Antipasti Succulent tidbits served at the beginning of a meal (before the pasta), whose ingredients might include slices of cured meats, seafood (especially shellfish), and cooked and seasoned vegetables.
Aragosta Lobster.
Arrosto Roasted meat.
Baccalà Dried and salted codfish.
Bagna cauda Hot and well-seasoned sauce, heavily flavored with anchovies, designed for dipping raw vegetables; literally translated as "hot bath."
Bistecca alla fiorentina Florentine-style steaks, coated before grilling with olive oil, pepper, lemon juice, salt and parsley.
Bocconcini Veal layered with ham and cheese, then fried.
Bollito misto Assorted boiled meats served on a single platter.
Braciola Pork chop.
Bresaola Air-dried spiced beef.
Bruschetta Toasted bread, heavily slathered with olive oil and garlic and often topped with tomatoes.
Bucatini Coarsely textured hollow spaghetti.
Busecca alla Milanese Tripe (beef stomach) flavored with herbs and vegetables.
Cacciucco ali livornese Seafood stew.
Calzone Pizza dough rolled with the chef's choice of sausage, tomatoes, cheese, and so on, and then baked into a kind of savory turnover.
Cannelloni Tubular dough stuffed with meat, cheese, or vegetables and then baked in a creamy white sauce.
Cappellacci alla ferrarese Pasta stuffed with pumpkin.
Cappelletti Small ravioli ("little hats") stuffed with meat or cheese.
Carciofi Artichokes.
Carpaccio Thin slices of raw cured beef, sometimes in a piquant sauce.
Cassatta alla siciliana A richly caloric dessert combining layers of sponge cake, sweetened ricotta cheese, and candied fruit, bound together with chocolate butter cream icing.
Cervello al burro nero Brains in black-butter sauce.
Cima alla genovese Baked fillet of veal rolled into a tube-shaped package containing eggs, mushrooms, and sausage.
Coppa Cured morsels of pork fillet encased in sausage skins, served in slices.
Costoletta alla milanese Veal cutlet dredged in bread crumbs, fried, and sometimes flavored with cheese.
Cozze Mussels.
Fagioli White beans.
Fave Fava beans.
Fegato alla veneziana Thinly sliced calves' liver fried with salt, pepper, and onions.
Foccacia Ideally, concocted from potato-based dough left to rise slowly for several hours, then garnished with tomato sauce, garlic, basil, salt, and pepper and drizzled with olive oil; similar to a deep-dish pizza most popular in the deep south, especially Bari.
Fontina Rich cow's-milk cheese.
Frittata Italian omelette.
Fritto misto A deep-fried medley of whatever small fish, shellfish, and squid are available in the marketplace that day.
Fusilli Spiral-shaped pasta.

Gelato (produzione propria) Ice cream (homemade).

Gnocchi Dumplings usually made from potatoes (*gnocchi alla patate*) or from semolina (*gnocchi alla romana*), often stuffed with combinations of cheese, spinach, vegetables, or whatever combinations strike the chef's fancy.

Gorgonzola One of the most famous blue-veined cheeses of Europe—strong, creamy, and aromatic.

Granita Flavored ice, usually with lemon or coffee.

Insalata di frutti di mare Seafood salad (usually including shrimp and squid) garnished with pickles, lemon, olives, and spices.

Involtini Thinly sliced beef, veal, or pork that is rolled, stuffed, and fried.

Minestrone A rich and savory vegetable soup usually sprinkled with grated parmigiano and studded with noodles.

Mortadella Mild pork sausage, fashioned into large cylinders and served sliced; the original lunchmeat bologna (because its most famous center of production is Bologna).

Mozzarella A nonfermented cheese, made from the fresh milk of a buffalo (or, if unavailable, from a cow), boiled and then kneaded into a rounded ball, served fresh.

Mozzarella con pomodori (also "caprese") Fresh tomatoes with fresh mozzarella, basil, pepper, and olive oil.

Nervetti A northern Italian antipasto made from chewy pieces of calves' foot or shin.

Osso buco Beef or veal knuckle slowly braised until the cartilage is tender and then served with a highly flavored sauce.

Pancetta Herb-flavored pork belly, rolled into a cylinder and sliced—the Italian bacon.

Panettone Sweet yellow-colored bread baked in the form of a brioche.

Panna Heavy cream.

Pansotti Pasta stuffed with greens, herbs, and cheeses, usually served with a walnut sauce.

Pappardelle alle lepre Pasta with rabbit sauce.

Parmigiano Parmesan, a hard and salty yellow cheese usually grated over pastas and soups but also eaten alone; also known as *granna.* The best is *parmigiano reggiano.*

Peperoni Green, yellow, or red sweet peppers (not to be confused with pepperoni).

Pesci al cartoccio Fish baked in a parchment envelope with onions, parsley, and herbs.

Pesto A flavorful green sauce made from basil leaves, cheese, garlic, marjoram, and (if available) pine nuts.

Piccata al marsala Thin escalope of veal braised in a pungent sauce flavored with marsala wine.

Piselli al prosciutto Peas with strips of ham.

Pizza Specific varieties include *capricciosa* (its ingredients can vary widely depending on the chef's culinary vision and the ingredients at hand), *margherita* (with tomato sauce, cheese, fresh basil, and memories of the first queen of Italy, Marguerite di Savoia, in whose honor it was first made by a Neapolitan chef), *napoletana* (with ham, capers, tomatoes, oregano, cheese, and the distinctive taste of anchovies), *quatro stagione* (translated as "four seasons" because of the array of fresh vegetables in it; it also contains ham and bacon), and *siciliana* (with black olives, capers, and cheese).

Pizzaiola A process whereby something (usually a beefsteak) is covered in a tomato-and-oregano sauce.

Polenta Thick porridge or mush made from cornmeal flour.
Polenta de uccelli Assorted small birds roasted on a spit and served with polenta.
Polenta e coniglio Rabbit stew served with polenta.
Polla alla cacciatore Chicken with tomatoes and mushrooms cooked in wine.
Pollo all diavola Highly spiced grilled chicken.
Ragù Meat sauce.
Ricotta A soft bland cheese made from cow's or sheep's milk.
Risotto Italian rice.
Risotto alla milanese Rice with saffron and wine.
Salsa verde "Green sauce," made from capers, anchovies, lemon juice and/or vinegar, and parsley.
Saltimbocca Veal scallop layered with prosciutto and sage; its name literally translates as "jump in your mouth," a reference to its tart and savory flavor.
Salvia Sage.
Scaloppina alla Valdostana Escalope of veal stuffed with cheese and ham.
Scaloppine Thin slices of veal coated in flour and sautéed in butter.
Semifreddo A frozen dessert; usually ice cream with sponge cake.
Seppia Cuttlefish (a kind of squid); its black ink is used for flavoring in certain sauces for pasta and also in risotto dishes.
Sogliola Sole.
Spaghetti A long, round, thin pasta, variously served: *alla bolognese* (with ground meat, mushrooms, peppers, and so on), *alla carbonara* (with bacon, black pepper, and eggs), *al pomodoro* (with tomato sauce), *al sugo/ragù* (with meat sauce), and *alle vongole* (with clam sauce).
Spiedini Pieces of meat grilled on a skewer over an open flame.
Strangolaprete Small nuggets of pasta, usually served with sauce; the name is literally translated as "priest-choker."
Stufato Beef braised in white wine with vegetables.
Tagliatelle Flat egg noodles.
Tiramisu Richly caloric dessert containing layers of triple-cream cheeses and rum-soaked sponge cake.
Tonno Tuna.
Tortelli Pasta dumplings stuffed with ricotta and greens.
Tortellini Rings of dough stuffed with minced and seasoned meat and served either in soups or as a full-fledged pasta covered with sauce.
Trenette Thin noodles served with pesto sauce and potatoes.
Trippe alla fiorentina Beef tripe (stomach).
Vermicelli Very thin spaghetti.
Vitello tonnato Cold sliced veal covered with tuna-fish sauce.
Zabaglione/zabaione Egg yolks whipped into the consistency of a custard, flavored with marsala, and served warm as a dessert.
Zampone Pig's trotter stuffed with spicy seasoned port, boiled and sliced.
Zuccotto A liqueur-soaked sponge cake, molded into a dome and layered with chocolate, nuts, and whipped cream.
Zuppa inglese Sponge cake soaked in custard.

Index

Index

Index

Index

FROMMER'S® COMPLETE TRAVEL GUIDES

Alaska
Amsterdam
Arizona
Atlanta
Australia
Austria
Bahamas
Barcelona, Madrid & Seville
Beijing
Belgium, Holland & Luxembourg
Bermuda
Boston
British Columbia & the Canadian Rockies
Budapest & the Best of Hungary
California
Canada
Cancún, Cozumel & the Yucatán
Cape Cod, Nantucket & Martha's Vineyard
Caribbean
Caribbean Cruises & Ports of Call
Caribbean Ports of Call
Carolinas & Georgia
Chicago
China
Colorado
Costa Rica
Denmark
Denver, Boulder & Colorado Springs
England
Europe
European Cruises & Ports of Call
Florida
France
Germany
Greece
Greek Islands
Hawaii
Hong Kong
Honolulu, Waikiki & Oahu
Ireland
Israel
Italy
Jamaica
Japan
Las Vegas
London
Los Angeles
Maryland & Delaware
Maui
Mexico
Miami & the Keys
Montana & Wyoming
Montréal & Québec City
Munich & the Bavarian Alps
Nashville & Memphis
Nepal
New England
New Mexico
New Orleans
New York City
New Zealand
Nova Scotia, New Brunswick & Prince Edward Island
Oregon
Paris
Philadelphia & the Amish Country
Portugal
Prague & the Best of the Czech Republic
Provence & the Riviera
Puerto Rico
Rome
San Antonio & Austin
San Diego
San Francisco
Santa Fe, Taos & Albuquerque
Scandinavia
Scotland
Seattle & Portland
Singapore & Malaysia
South Africa
Southeast Asia
South Pacific
Spain
Sweden
Switzerland
Thailand
Tokyo
Toronto
Tuscany & Umbria
USA
Utah
Vancouver & Victoria
Vermont, New Hampshire & Maine
Vienna & the Danube Valley
Virgin Islands
Virginia
Walt Disney World & Orlando
Washington, D.C.
Washington State

FROMMER'S® DOLLAR-A-DAY GUIDES

Australia from $50 a Day
California from $60 a Day
Caribbean from $70 a Day
England from $70 a Day
Europe from $60 a Day
Florida from $60 a Day
Hawaii from $70 a Day
Ireland from $60 a Day
Italy from $70 a Day
London from $85 a Day
New York from $80 a Day
Paris from $85 a Day
San Francisco from $60 a Day
Washington, D.C., from $60 a Day

FROMMER'S® PORTABLE GUIDES

Acapulco, Ixtapa & Zihuatanejo
Alaska Cruises & Ports of Call
Bahamas
Baja & Los Cabos
Berlin
California Wine Country
Charleston & Savannah
Chicago
Dublin
Hawaii: The Big Island
Las Vegas
London
Maine Coast
Maui
New Orleans
New York City
Paris
Puerto Vallarta, Manzanillo & Guadalajara
San Diego
San Francisco
Sydney
Tampa & St. Petersburg
Venice
Washington, D.C.

FROMMER'S® NATIONAL PARK GUIDES

Family Vacations in the National Parks
Grand Canyon
National Parks of the American West
Rocky Mountain
Yellowstone & Grand Teton
Yosemite & Sequoia/Kings Canyon
Zion & Bryce Canyon

FROMMER'S® MEMORABLE WALKS

Chicago
London
New York
Paris
San Francisco
Washington, D.C.

FROMMER'S® GREAT OUTDOOR GUIDES

New England
Northern California
Southern California & Baja
Southern New England
Washington & Oregon

FROMMER'S® BORN TO SHOP GUIDES

Born to Shop: China
Born to Shop: France
Born to Shop: Italy
Born to Shop: London
Born to Shop: New York
Born to Shop: Paris

FROMMER'S® IRREVERENT GUIDES

Amsterdam
Boston
Chicago
Las Vegas
London
Los Angeles
Manhattan
New Orleans
Paris
San Francisco
Seattle & Portland
Vancouver
Walt Disney World
Washington, D.C.

FROMMER'S® BEST-LOVED DRIVING TOURS

America
Britain
California
Florida
France
Germany
Ireland
Italy
New England
Scotland
Spain
Western Europe

THE UNOFFICIAL GUIDES®

Bed & Breakfasts in California
Bed & Breakfasts in New England
Bed & Breakfasts in the Northwest
Beyond Disney
Branson, Missouri
California with Kids
Chicago
Cruises
Disneyland
Florida with Kids
Golf Vacations in the Eastern U.S.
The Great Smoky & Blue Ridge Mountains
Inside Disney
Hawaii
Las Vegas
London
Miami & the Keys
Mini Las Vegas
Mini-Mickey
New Orleans
New York City
Paris
Safaris
San Francisco
Skiing in the West
Walt Disney World
Walt Disney World for Grown-ups
Walt Disney World for Kids
Washington, D.C.

SPECIAL-INTEREST TITLES

Frommer's Britain's Best Bed & Breakfasts and Country Inns
Frommer's Britain's Best Bike Rides
The Civil War Trust's Official Guide to the Civil War Discovery Trail
Frommer's Caribbean Hideaways
Frommer's Food Lover's Companion to France
Frommer's Food Lover's Companion to Italy
Frommer's Gay & Lesbian Europe
Frommer's Exploring America by RV
Hanging Out in Europe
Israel Past & Present
Mad Monks' Guide to California
Mad Monks' Guide to New York City
Frommer's The Moon
Frommer's New York City with Kids
The New York Times' Unforgettable Weekends
Places Rated Almanac
Retirement Places Rated
Frommer's Road Atlas Britain
Frommer's Road Atlas Europe
Frommer's Washington, D.C., with Kids
Frommer's What the Airlines Never Tell You